Contemporary Authors®

NEW REVISION SERIES

ISSN 0275-7176

Contemporary Authors®

**A Bio-Bibliographical Guide to
Current Writers in Fiction, General Nonfiction,
Poetry, Journalism, Drama, Motion Pictures,
Television, and Other Fields**

**HAL MAY
JAMES G. LESNIAK**
Editors

NEW REVISION SERIES
volume **28**

Gale Research Inc. • DETROIT, NEW YORK, FORT LAUDERDALE, LONDON

STAFF

Hal May and James G. Lesniak, *Editors, New Revision Series*

Marilyn K. Basel, Sharon Malinowski, Michael E. Mueller, Bryan Ryan,
Kenneth R. Shepherd, Diane Telgen, and Thomas Wiloch, *Associate Editors*

Marian Gonsior, Cheryl Gottler, Kevin S. Hile, Margaret Mazurkiewicz,
Jani Prescott, and Michaela Swart Wilson, *Assistant Editors*

Jean W. Ross, *Interviewer*

John Ashmead, Jr., Melissa J. Gaiownik, Joan Goldsworthy, Anne Janette Johnson,
Steven G. Kellman, Yolanda Astarita Patterson, and Susan Salter, *Contributing Editors*

Hal May, *Senior Editor, Contemporary Authors*

Mary Rose Bonk, *Research Supervisor*

Jane Cousins-Clegg, Alysa I. Hunton, Andrew Guy Malonis, and Norma Sawaya, *Editorial Associates*

Pamela Atsoff, Reginald A. Carlton, Christine Ferran, Shirley Gates, Elizabeth Parker Henry,
Clare Kinsman, Sharon McGilvray, and Tracey Head Turbett, *Editorial Assistants*

Copyright © 1990
Gale Research Inc.
835 Penobscot Bldg.
Detroit, MI 48226-4094

Library of Congress Catalog Card Number 81-640179
ISBN 0-8103-1982-9
ISSN 0275-7176

Computerized photocomposition by
Typographics, Incorporated
Kansas City, Missouri

Contents

Indexing note: All *Contemporary Authors New Revision Series* entries are indexed in the *Contemporary Authors* cumulative index, which is published separately and distributed with even-numbered *Contemporary Authors* original volumes.

Authors and Media People
Featured in This Volume

Brian W. Aldiss (British novelist, critic, and short story writer)—Recognized as one of England's most important novelists and critics, Aldiss has received virtually every major award in the field of science fiction, including a Hugo Award for *Hothouse*, a Nebula Award for *The Saliva Tree*, and a John W. Campbell Memorial Award for *Helliconia Spring*.

Kingsley Amis (British novelist, poet, essayist, and critic)—Amis, although an eclectic man of letters, is considered one of England's foremost comic novelists, comparable to Evelyn Waugh and P. G. Wodehouse in his witty social commentary and command of satirical idioms. Among his novels are *The Old Devils*, which received the Booker-McConnell Prize in 1986, and the Somerset Maugham Award-winning *Lucky Jim*.

Louis Aragon (French poet and novelist who died in 1982)—In his own lifetime Aragon became a monument in the French literary tradition. A leading theorist of the Dada and Surrealist movements, he later joined the Communist party and sought to promote socialist realism in the arts, most notably in his "Le Monde Reel" ("The Real World") series of novels.

Simone de Beauvoir (French philosopher, novelist, and author of nonfiction who died in 1986)—Famous for her lifelong association with Jean-Paul Sartre, Beauvoir achieved independent recognition through her study of women and their social position in *Le Deuxieme sexe*, translated as *The Second Sex*, and through her autobiographical writings, which not only recount her relationship with Sartre but also depict forty years of Parisian intellectual life.

Thomas Berger (American novelist, playwright, and short story writer)—Berger is considered one of the most successful satiric commentators on postwar American life, a novelist whose talent and versatility range well beyond his most famous work, *Little Big Man.* (Entry contains interview.)

Roy Blount, Jr. (American humorist and journalist)—The intricate wordplay, droll asides, and bizarre images displayed in Blount's *Crackers, One Fell Soup,* and numerous magazine articles have earned him popularity, critical acclaim, and comparisons with Mark Twain, H. L. Mencken, and W. C. Fields. (Entry contains interview.)

Daniel J. Boorstin (American historian)—Former Librarian of Congress Boorstin has enjoyed both popular success and professional recognition for his histories, among them the Pulitzer Prize-winning *The Americans: The Democratic Experience.* (Entry contains interview.)

Joseph Campbell (American professor of mythology, literature, and ancient history who died in 1987)—One of the leading authorities on mythology and folklore, Campbell articulated in *The Power of Myth* his belief that all myth stems from a common source in the biology of man and attempts to explain the essential mystery of creation.

Noam Chomsky (American linguist, philosopher, and political activist)— Chomsky, the father of transformational-generative grammar, revolutionized the modern study of linguistics with his 1957 work *Syntactic Structures,* which emphasizes the creativity of language use and suggests that humans possess an innate ability as children to learn the structures of any language.

Arthur C. Clarke (British science and science fiction writer)—Acknowledged as a master of science fiction, Clarke is the author of the classic novels *Childhood's End, The Fountains of Paradise,* and *Rendezvous with Rama,* as well as the screenplay "2001: A Space Odyssey," written with Stanley Kubrick.

Louis-Ferdinand Destouches (French novelist who died in 1961)—Destouches, better known by his pseudonym Celine, is considered a major figure in twentieth-century French fiction. His works, particularly *Journey to the End of the Night, Death on the Installment Plan,* and *Castle to Castle,* are marked by a scabrous, hallucinatory approach.

Robert Duncan (American poet and editor who died in 1988)—A participant in the Black Mountain school of poetry, Duncan was also instrumental in establishing San Francisco as a hub of poetry in America. His *Bending the Bow, Ground Work,* and other collections exhibit a mystical orientation and an imagist technique reminiscent of Ezra Pound.

Stanley Ellin (American novelist and short story writer who died in 1986)—Ellin received numerous awards for excellence in mystery writing, including the prestigious Grand Master Award for lifetime achievement from the Mystery Writers of America. Among his works are *The Specialty of the House and Other Stories* and *Very Old Money.*

Richard Ellmann (American-born biographer and literary critic who died in 1987)—The first American to teach English literature at Oxford University and the foremost authority on James Joyce, Ellmann set the standard for academic biographies in English. His posthumously published *Oscar Wilde* received both the National Book Critics Circle Award and the Pulitzer Prize in 1989.

Maria Irene Fornes (Cuban-born American playwright)—Fornes has been in the forefront of experimental theatre for over twenty years, writing and directing such Obie Award winners as "Promenade," "The Successful Life of 3," and "The Conduct of Life." (Entry contains interview.)

Gabriel Garcia Marquez (Colombian journalist, short story writer, and novelist)—Nobel laureate Garcia Marquez has received worldwide acclaim for *One Hundred Years of Solitude, Chronicle of a Death Foretold, Love in the Time of Cholera,* and other works of fiction blending elements of history, politics, social realism, and fantasy.

Nadine Gordimer (South African-born novelist, essayist, and short story writer)—Gordimer, whose work provides a cultural collage of South Africa without being didactic, has been called the literary voice and conscience of her society. Among her novels are *A Guest of Honour* and *The Conservationist*. (Entry contains interview.)

John Irving (American novelist)—Irving's *The World According to Garp, The Hotel New Hampshire, The Cider House Rules,* and *A Prayer for Owen Meany* have firmly established his reputation as a gifted storyteller with a remarkably fertile imagination.

David Jones (British poet and artist who died in 1974)—Though his long poems *In Parenthesis* and *The Anathemata* are deemed too subtle and learned to attract a popular audience, Jones is regarded as an important and innovative poet who extended and refined the techniques of literary modernism.

Hugh Kenner (Canadian-American literary critic)—Considered America's preeminent expert on modernism in English, Kenner has written the highly respected *The Poetry of Ezra Pound* as well as important works on James Joyce, T. S. Eliot, and Samuel Beckett.

Elmore Leonard (American novelist and screenwriter)—Leonard's best-selling and award-winning mysteries, most notably *LaBrava, Glitz,* and *Freaky Deaky,* have led many reviewers to rank him among the best crime novelists alive. (Entry contains interview.)

Alistair MacLean (British novelist who died in 1987)—MacLean enjoyed enormous popularity on the basis of such adventure novels as *The Guns of Navarone, Ice Station Zebra,* and *Where Eagles Dare.*

Norman Mailer (American novelist, essayist, and author of works combining journalism and fiction)—A prolific and highly controversial figure, Mailer is one of America's most prominent writers. His better-known works include *The Naked and the Dead* and the Pulitzer Prize winners *Armies of the Night* and *The Executioner's Song.*

Bernard Malamud (Jewish-American novelist and short story writer who died in 1986)—Malamud frequently drew on his Jewish heritage to produce renowned portraits of ordinary people struggling to improve their lives. His novel *The Fixer* garnered both a National Book Award and a Pulitzer Prize.

Oliver Sacks (British-born neurologist)—In *Awakenings* and the best-selling *The Man Who Mistook His Wife for a Hat,* Sacks relates case histories that reveal the mind's complexity and its role in maintaining health. (Entry contains interview.)

Arthur M. Schlesinger, Jr. (American historian and statesman)—Known for his association with the Kennedy administration and his outspoken advocacy of liberalism, Schlesinger is perhaps the most controversial of American historians. His book *A Thousand Days: John F. Kennedy in the White House* earned both a Pulitzer Prize and a National Book Award. (Entry contains interview.)

C. P. Snow (British novelist, scientist, and government administrator who died in 1980)—Snow's career as an administrator, scientist, and writer gave him a unique perspective on the widening chasm between science and literature, the "Two Cultures," in modern Western thought. In his famous 1959 Rede lecture *The Two Cultures and the Scientific Revolution,* he warned that this cultural fragmentation, if unabated, would lead to the end of Western civilization. Entries for his wife, Pamela Hansford Johnson, and his brother, Philip Snow, also appear in this volume.

Mickey Spillane (American writer of mystery and detective novels)—Spillane created the private investigator Mike Hammer in the 1947 novel *I, the Jury* and has enjoyed a loyal audience ever since. Over 180 million copies of his books have been sold in more than sixteen languages.

Peter Straub (American novelist)—Straub's bestsellers *Ghost Story, Floating Dragon, The Talisman* (written with Stephen King), and *Koko* are not only spine-tingling thrillers but also imaginative explorations into the roots of the unreal.

A. E. Van Vogt (Canadian-born science fiction writer)—Along with Robert Heinlein, Van Vogt is considered a major writer of science fiction's Golden Age of the 1940s. In such novels as *Slan, The Voyage of the Space Beagle,* and *The World of A,* he originated and explored ideas and themes that have since become important paradigms of the genre.

Preface

The *Contemporary Authors New Revision Series* provides completely updated information on authors listed in earlier volumes of *Contemporary Authors (CA)*. Entries for active individual authors from *any* volume of *CA* may be included in a volume of the *New Revision Series*. The sketches appearing in *New Revision Series* Volume 28, for example, were selected from more than twenty previously published *CA* volumes.

As always, the most recent *Contemporary Authors* cumulative index continues to be the user's guide to the location of an individual author's listing.

Compilation Methods

The editors make every effort to secure information directly from the authors. Copies of all sketches in selected *CA* volumes published several years ago are routinely sent to the listees at their last-known addresses. Authors mark material to be deleted or changed and insert any new personal data, new affiliations, new writings, new work in progress, new sidelights, and new biographical/critical sources. All returns are assessed, more comprehensive research is done, if necessary, and those sketches requiring significant change are completely updated and published in the *New Revision Series*.

If, however, authors fail to reply or are now deceased, biographical dictionaries are checked for new information (a task made easier through the use of Gale's *Biography and Genealogy Master Index* and other Gale biographical indexes), as are bibliographical sources such as *Cumulative Book Index* and *The National Union Catalog*. Using data from such sources, revision editors select and revise nonrespondents' entries that need substantial updating. Sketches not personally reviewed by the biographees are marked with an asterisk (*) to indicate that these listings have been revised from secondary sources believed to be reliable, but they have not been personally reviewed for this edition by the authors sketched.

In addition, reviews and articles in major periodicals, lists of prestigious awards, and, particularly, requests from *CA* users are monitored so that writers on whom new information is in demand can be identified and revised listings prepared promptly.

Format

CA entries provide biographical and bibliographical information in an easy-to-use format. For example, individual paragraphs featuring such rubrics as "Addresses," "Career," and "Awards, Honors" ensure that a reader seeking specific information can quickly focus on the pertinent portion of an entry. In sketch sections headed "Writings," the title of each book, play, and other published or unpublished work appears on a separate line, clearly distinguishing one title from another. This same convenient bibliographical presentation is also featured in the "Biographical/Critical Sources" sections of sketches where individual book and periodical titles are listed on separate lines. *CA* readers can therefore quickly scan these often-lengthy bibliographies to find the titles they need.

Comprehensive Revision

All listings in this volume have been revised and/or augmented in various ways, though the amount and type of change vary with the author. In many instances, sketches are totally rewritten, and the resulting *New Revision Series* entries are often considerably longer than the authors' previous listings. Revised entries include additions of or changes in such information as degrees, mailing addresses, literary agents, career items, career-related and civic activities, memberships, awards, work in progress, and biographical/critical sources. They may also include extensive bibliographical additions and informative new sidelights.

Writers of Special Interest

CA's editors make every effort to include in each *New Revision Series* volume a substantial number of revised entries on active authors and media people of special interest to *CA*'s readers. Since the *New Revision Series* also includes sketches on noteworthy deceased writers, a significant amount of work on the part of *CA*'s editors goes into the revision of entries on important deceased authors. Some of the prominent writers, both living and deceased, whose sketches are contained in this volume are noted in the list on pages vii-viii headed Authors and Media People Featured in This Volume.

Exclusive Interviews

CA provides exclusive, primary information on certain authors in the form of interviews. Prepared specifically for *CA,* the never-before-published conversations presented in the section of the sketch headed "*CA* Interview" give users the opportunity to learn the authors' thoughts, in depth, about their craft. Subjects chosen for interviews are, the editors feel, authors who hold special interest for *CA*'s readers.

Authors and journalists in this volume whose sketches contain exclusive interviews are Thomas Berger, Roy Blount, Jr., Daniel J. Boorstin, Maria Irene Fornes, Nadine Gordimer, Elmore Leonard, William McPherson, Oliver Sacks, Arthur M. Schlesinger, Jr., and James Spada.

Contemporary Authors Autobiography Series

Designed to complement the information in *CA* original and revision volumes, the *Contemporary Authors Autobiography Series* provides autobiographical essays written by important current authors. Each volume contains from twenty to thirty specially commissioned autobiographies and is illustrated with numerous personal photographs supplied by the authors. Common topics of discussion for these authors include their motivations for writing, the people and experiences that shaped their careers, the rewards they derive from their work, and their impressions of the current literary scene.

Autobiographies included in the series can be located through both the *CA* cumulative index and the *Contemporary Authors Autobiography Series* cumulative index, which lists not only personal names but also titles of works, geographical names, subjects, and schools of writing.

Contemporary Authors Bibliographical Series

The *Contemporary Authors Bibliographical Series* is a comprehensive survey of writings by and about the most important authors since World War II in the United States and abroad. Each volume concentrates on a specific genre and nationality and features approximately ten major writers. Series entries, which complement the information in other *CA* volumes, consist of three parts: a primary bibliography that lists works written by the author, a secondary bibliography that lists works about the author, and a bibliographical essay that thoroughly analyzes the merits and deficiencies of major critical and scholarly works.

These bibliographies can be located through both the *CA* cumulative index and the *Contemporary Authors Bibliographical Series* cumulative author index. A cumulative critic index, citing critics discussed in the bibliographical essays, also appears in each *Bibliographical Series* volume.

CA Numbering System

Occasionally questions arise about the *CA* numbering system. Despite numbers like "97-100" and "127," the entire *CA* series consists of only 95 physical volumes with the publication of *CA New Revision Series* Volume 28. The following information notes changes in the numbering system, as well as in cover design, to help users better understand the organization of the entire *CA* series.

CA First Revisions	• 1-4R through 41-44R (11 books) *Cover:* Brown with black and gold trim. There will be no further *First Revisions* because revised entries are now being handled exclusively through the more efficient *New Revision Series* mentioned below.
CA Original Volumes	• 45-48 through 97-100 (14 books) *Cover:* Brown with black and gold trim. • 101 through 127 (27 books) *Cover:* Blue and black with orange bands. The same as previous *CA* original volumes but with a new, simplified numbering system and new cover design.
CA New Revision Series	• *CANR*-1 through *CANR*-28 (28 books) *Cover:* Blue and black with green bands. Includes only sketches requiring extensive change; **sketches are taken from any previously published *CA* volume.**

CA Permanent Series	• *CAP*-1 and *CAP*-2 (2 books) *Cover:* Brown with red and gold trim. There will be no further *Permanent Series* volumes because revised entries are now being handled exclusively through the more efficient *New Revision Series* mentioned above.
CA Autobiography Series	• *CAAS*-1 through *CAAS*-10 (10 books) *Cover:* Blue and black with pink and purple bands. Presents specially commissioned autobiographies by leading contemporary writers to complement the information in *CA* original and revision volumes.
CA Bibliographical Series	• *CABS*-1 through *CABS*-3 (3 books) *Cover:* Blue and black with blue bands. Provides comprehensive bibliographical information on published works by and about major modern authors.

Retaining *CA* Volumes

As new volumes in the series are published, users often ask which *CA* volumes, if any, can be discarded. The Volume Update Chart on page xiii is designed to assist users in keeping their collections as complete as possible. All volumes in the left column of the chart should be retained to have the most complete, up-to-date coverage possible; volumes in the right column can be discarded if the appropriate replacements are held.

Cumulative Index Should Always Be Consulted

The key to locating an individual author's listing is the *CA* cumulative index, which is published separately and distributed with even-numbered original volumes. Since the *CA* cumulative index provides access to *all* entries in the *CA* series, the latest cumulative index should always be consulted to find the specific volume containing a listee's original or most recently revised sketch.

Those authors whose entries appear in the *New Revision Series* are listed in the *CA* cumulative index with the designation **CANR-** in front of the specific volume number. For the convenience of those who do not have *New Revision Series* volumes, the cumulative index also notes the specific earlier volumes of *CA* in which the sketch appeared. Below is a sample index citation for an author whose revised entry appears in a *New Revision Series* volume.

> Clavell, James (duMaresq) 1925- CANR-26
> Earlier sketch in CA 25-28R
> See also CLC 6, 25

For the most recent *CA* information on Clavell, users should refer to Volume 26 of the *New Revision Series,* as designated by "CANR-26"; if that volume is unavailable, refer to *CA* 25-28 First Revision, as indicated by "Earlier sketch in CA 25-28R," for his 1977 listing. (And if *CA* 25-28 First Revision is unavailable, refer to *CA* 25-28, published in 1971, for Clavell's original listing.)

Sketches not eligible for inclusion in a *New Revision Series* volume because the biographee or a revision editor has verified that no significant change is required will, of course, be available in previously published *CA* volumes. Users should always consult the most recent *CA* cumulative index to determine the location of these authors' entries.

For the convenience of *CA* users, the *CA* cumulative index also includes references to all entries in these related Gale literary series: *Authors in the News, Black Writers, Children's Literature Review, Concise Dictionary of American Literary Biography, Contemporary Literary Criticism, Dictionary of Literary Biography, Short Story Criticism, Something About the Author, Something About the Author Autobiography Series, Twentieth-Century Literary Criticism,* and *Yesterday's Authors of Books For Children.*

Acknowledgments

The editors wish to thank Judith S. Baughman and Armida Gilbert for their assistance with copyediting.

Suggestions Are Welcome

The editors welcome comments and suggestions from users on any aspect of the *CA* series. If readers would like to suggest authors whose *CA* entries should appear in future volumes of the *New Revision Series,* they are cordially invited to write: The Editors, *Contemporary Authors New Revision Series,* 835 Penobscot Bldg., Detroit, MI 48226-4094; or, call toll-free at 1-800-347-GALE.

Volume Update Chart

IF YOU HAVE:	YOU MAY DISCARD:
1-4 First Revision (1967)	1 (1962) 2 (1963) 3 (1963) 4 (1963)
5-8 First Revision (1969)	5-6 (1963) 7-8 (1963)
Both 9-12 First Revision (1974) AND *Contemporary Authors Permanent Series*, Volume 1 (1975)	9-10 (1964) 11-12 (1965)
Both 13-16 First Revision (1975) AND *Contemporary Authors Permanent Series*, Volumes 1 and 2 (1975, 1978)	13-14 (1965) 15-16 (1966)
Both 17-20 First Revision (1976) AND *Contemporary Authors Permanent Series*, Volumes 1 and 2 (1975, 1978)	17-18 (1967) 19-20 (1968)
Both 21-24 First Revision (1977) AND *Contemporary Authors Permanent Series*, Volumes 1 and 2 (1975, 1978)	21-22 (1969) 23-24 (1970)
Both 25-28 First Revision (1977) AND *Contemporary Authors Permanent Series*, Volume 2 (1978)	25-28 (1971)
Both 29-32 First Revision (1978) AND *Contemporary Authors Permanent Series*, Volume 2 (1978)	29-32 (1972)
Both 33-36 First Revision (1978) AND *Contemporary Authors Permanent Series*, Volume 2 (1978)	33-36 (1973)
37-40 First Revision (1979)	37-40 (1973)
41-44 First Revision (1979)	41-44 (1974)
45-48 (1974) 49-52 (1975) ↓ ↓ 127 (1989)	NONE: These volumes will not be superseded by corresponding revised volumes. Individual entries from these and all other volumes appearing in the left column of this chart will be revised and included in the *New Revision Series*.
Volumes in the *Contemporary Authors New Revision Series*	NONE: The *New Revision Series* does not replace any single volume of *CA*. All volumes appearing in the left column of this chart must be retained to have information on all authors in the series.

Contemporary Authors

NEW REVISION SERIES

** Indicates that a listing has been revised from secondary sources believed to be reliable
but has not been personally reviewed for this edition by the author sketched.*

ABELLA, Irving (Martin)   1940-

PERSONAL: Born July 2, 1940, in Toronto, Ontario, Canada; son of Louis (a merchant) and Esther (Shiff) Abella; married Rosie Silberman (a judge), December 8, 1968; children: Jacob Julian, Zachary Joshua. *Education:* University of Toronto, B.A., 1963, M.A., 1964, Ph.D., 1969.

ADDRESSES: Home—375 Glengrove, Toronto, Ontario, Canada. *Office*—Glendon College, York University, 4700 Keele St., North York, Ontario, Canada M3J 1P3.

CAREER: York University, North York, Ontario, instructor, 1968-69, assistant professor, 1969-72, associate professor, 1972-74, professor of history in Glendon College, 1974—.

AWARDS, HONORS: Sir John A. Macdonald Prize in Canadian history, and Leon Jolson Award for a book on the Holocaust, National Jewish Book Awards, both 1983, both for *None Is Too Many: Canada and the Jews of Europe, 1933-48.*

WRITINGS:

Nationalism, Communism, and Canadian Labour: The CIO, the Communist Party, and the Canadian Congress of Labour, University of Toronto Press, 1973.
(Editor) *On Strike: Six Key Labour Struggles in Canada, 1919-1949,* James, Lewis, & Samuel, 1974.
The Canadian Labour Movement, 1902-1960, Canadian Historical Society, 1975.
(Editor with David Miller) *The Canadian Worker in the Twentieth Century,* Oxford University Press, 1978.
(With Harold Troper) *None Is Too Many: Canada and the Jews of Europe, 1933-1948,* Lester & Orpen Dennys, 1982, Random House, 1983.

Also contributor to *The Influence of the United States on Canadian Development: Eleven Case Studies,* edited by Richard A. Preston.

SIDELIGHTS: Irving Abella's award-winning history *None Is Too Many: Canada and the Jews of Europe, 1933-1948,* written with Harold Troper, "is a disturbing book, a tragic tale of a flawed society," writes H. Blair Neatby in the *Quill & Quire.* "It shows that Canadian immigration policies were anti-Semitic. What is worse, it shows that most Canadians wanted them that way." The authors detail Canada's immi-gration practices as "arguably the worst," describes David Stafford in *Saturday Night.* "Far from modifying restrictive immigration policies as Nazi terror intensified, Ottawa tightened regulations at each turn." The critic adds that while "Abella and Troper caution against exaggerating the depth and extent of anti-Semitism in Canada in the 1930s and 1940s, and are careful not to present it as the sole explanation . . . the impressive and detailed evidence they marshal points inescapably to the power of anti-Semitism in the consistently negative response to Jewish pleas." J. L. Granatstein also comments on the quality of the authors's research, noting in the *American Historical Review* that "there has not been a book on Canadian history that so carefully and fully exploits the available sources." Although the critic faults the authors for overlooking some complexities of their subject, overall he calls *None Is Too Many* an important work that is "very good."

MEDIA ADAPTATIONS: On Strike: Six Key Labour Struggles in Canada, 1919-1949, was made into a sound recording in 1975 by James Lorimer & Co.

BIOGRAPHICAL/CRITICAL SOURCES:

PERIODICALS

American Historical Review, June, 1984.
Los Angeles Times Book Review, October 30, 1983.
Quill & Quire, December, 1982.
Saturday Night, September, 1982.

*   *   *

AGNELLI, Susanna   1922-

PERSONAL: Born April 24, 1922, in Turin, Italy; daughter of Edoardo (an industrial manager) and Princess Virginia Bourbon del Monte Agnelli; divorced; children: Ilaria, Samaritana, Cristiano, Delfina, Lupo, Priscilla. *Education:* Received general certificate of education from Classical High School. *Politics:* Liberal. *Religion:* Roman Catholic.

ADDRESSES: Home—Santa Liberata, Grosseto, Italy. *Office*—Senato della Repubblica, 00150 Rome, Italy.

CAREER: Volunteer nurse with Italian Red Cross, c. 1940-45; chairman of the board, Edoardo e Virginia Agnelli School for professional nurses, 1945-75; Monte Argentario, Italy, town councillor, 1970-74, mayor, 1974-83; member of Italian senate, 1983—, Undersecretary of State for Foreign Affairs, 1983—. Member of Parliament for Partito Repubblicano Italiano, 1979-84; member of European Parliament, 1979-81; member, World Commission on Environment and Development, 1984-87, Independent Commission on International Humanitarian Issues, 1984-87, International Institute on Aging, International Council of the University for Peace; board member, Foundation of the International Baccalaureate Office.

MEMBER: Soroptimist Club of Grosseto (Italy).

AWARDS, HONORS: Scanno and Bancarella literary prizes, 1975, Premio Speciale Casentino, 1984, all for *Vestivamo alla Marinara;* honorary doctor of laws, Mount Holyoke College, 1984; Premio Acqui Storia, 1986, for *Addio, Addio mio ultimo amore;* Citation for Distinguished Service to the Arts and Humanistic Studies, American Academy in Rome, 1986.

WRITINGS:

Vestivamo alla Marinara, Mondadori, 1975, translation by Agnelli published as *We Always Wore Sailor Suits*, Viking, 1975.
Gente alla deriva (title means "People Drifting"), Rizzoli, 1980.
Ricordati Gualeguaychu (title means "Remember Gualeguaychu"), Mondadori, 1982.
Addio, Addio mio ultimo amore, Mondadori, 1985.

Contributor of articles to magazines and newspapers.

SIDELIGHTS: Granddaughter of the founder of the Fiat automobile company, Susanna Agnelli became active in city politics to soothe her dissatisfaction with local government. In 1974 the people of Monte Argentario elected Agnelli mayor, at which time she found her stature as an influential, wealthy citizen both an enhancement and a hindrance to her career. "On the plus side," she told Alvin Shuster in a *New York Times* interview, "people think I am in a position where I might be able to get more things done. On the minus side, they look at you as a privileged person who is not going to understand their problems." The politician is credited for her work in encouraging Italian women to take a more active role in public life. "People in Italy sort of think that I am going to make women try harder to go into politics," she explained.

Agnelli's book *We Always Wore Sailor Suits* does not chronicle her political career, but does provide a view of a childhood spent in the opulent atmosphere of Mussolini's Italy. It was written to illustrate Agnelli's life as a privileged citizen, not to reveal the scandal and gossip of fascist Italy. Covering her life until her marriage, the memoir includes a portrait of Agnelli's paternal grandfather, who attempted to gain custody of his grandchildren after their father died, and a loving tribute to her mother, who shared a special relationship with the famous writer Malaparte.

Well received by critics, *We Always Wore Sailor Suits* contains "vivid memories of a life worth retelling," comments a *Washington Post Book World* reviewer. According to Joan Dash in the *New York Times Book Review*, it is "an exquisite concoction" with flavor and texture. "Never is this book a glorification of being rich and powerful," observes N. G. Reed in the *Christian Science Monitor*, "nor an apology for mistakes which . . . [Agnelli] may have made. It is a vivid recording of war-ravaged Italy, seen by a young girl whose normal zest for life—punctuated with naughty humor and teenage romance—was interrupted by a universally unforeseeable, and impartially cruel, world event." Alistair Forbes, writing in the

Times Literary Supplement, calls Agnelli "a natural writer" who "handles her material with superb skill and selectivity."

Agnelli once told *CA:* "I am interested in any question related to suffering human beings—wherever they are and whoever they are."

BIOGRAPHICAL/CRITICAL SOURCES:

PERIODICALS

Best Sellers, January, 1976.
Christian Science Monitor, October 22, 1975.
Guardian Weekly, March 28, 1976.
New Statesman, February 27, 1976.
New York Times, August 27, 1975, October 10, 1975.
New York Times Book Review, October 12, 1975, December 7, 1975.
Observer, February 29, 1976.
Times Literary Supplement, December 19, 1975, April 23, 1976.
Washington Post Book World, November 28, 1976.

*　　*　　*

ALDISS, Brian W(ilson) 1925-
(C. C. Shackleton)

PERSONAL: Born August 8, 1925, in East Dereham, Norfolk, England; son of Stanley (an outfitter) and May (Wilson) Aldiss; married second wife, Margaret Christie Manson, December 11, 1965; children: (first marriage) Clive, Caroline Wendy; (second marriage) Timothy Nicholas, Charlotte May. *Education:* Attended Framlingham College.

ADDRESSES: Home—Woodlands, Boars Hill, Oxford OX1 5DL, England. *Agent*—A. P. Watt Ltd., 26/28 Bedford Row, London WC1, England, and Robin Straus, 229 East 79th St., New York, N.Y. 10021 (literary); Frank Hatherly, 35 Fishers Lane, London W4 1RX, England (media).

CAREER: Writer, editor, critic, bookseller. *Oxford Mail*, Oxford, England, literary editor, 1957-69; Penguin Books, Ltd., London, England, editor of science fiction novels, 1961-64; *The Guardian*, London, art correspondent, 1971—. Judge for Booker-McConnell Prize, 1981. *Military service:* British Army, four years, including service with Royal Corps of Signals; attached to Indian Army, 1945-46; received Burma Star.

MEMBER: International Institute for the Study of Time, International Organization for the Fantastic in the Arts (permanent guest), World Science Fiction Society (president, 1982-84), British Science Fiction Association (president, 1960-64), Science Fiction Writers of America, Science Fiction Research Association, Society of Authors (chairman, 1977-78), PEN, Arts Council of Great Britain (literature panelist, 1978-80), Cultural Exchanges Committee (chairman).

AWARDS, HONORS: Observer book award for science fiction, 1956; named most promising new author of the year, 1958, World Science Fiction Convention; Hugo Award for best short fiction, World Science Fiction Convention, 1962, for *Hothouse;* special British Science Fiction Association Award for Britain's most popular science fiction author, 1964; Nebula Award for best novella, Science Fiction Writers of America, 1966, for *The Saliva Tree, and Other Strange Growths;* Ditmar Award for world's best contemporary science fiction author, 1970; British Science Fiction Association Award, 1972, for *The Moment of Eclipse;* Eurocon III Award, 1976, for *Billion Year Spree: The History of Science Fiction;* James Blish

Award for excellence in science fiction criticism, 1977; Ferrara Silver Comet, 1977, for *Science Fiction Art;* Prix Jules Verne, 1977, for *Non-Stop;* Science Fiction Research Association Pilgrim Award, 1978; John W. Campbell Memorial Award for best novel of 1982, British Science Fiction Association Award for best fiction of 1982, and Kur Lasswitz Award, 1984, all for *Helliconia Spring;* first Inter-American Foundation for the Arts distinguished scholarship award, 1986; Eaton Award for best criticism, 1988.

WRITINGS:

NOVELS

The Brightfount Diaries, Faber, 1955.
Non-Stop, Faber, 1958, Pan Books, 1976, published as *Starship,* Criterion, 1959.
Equator, Digit Books, 1958, published as *Vanguard from Alpha,* Ace, 1959.
Bow Down to Nul, Ace, 1960 (published in England as *The Interpreter,* Digit Books, 1961).
The Male Response, Ballantine, 1961.
The Primal Urge, Ballantine, 1961.
Long Afternoon of Earth, Signet, 1962 (published in England as *Hothouse,* Faber, 1962).
The Dark Light Years, Harcourt, 1964.
Greybeard, Harcourt, 1964.
Earthworks, Faber, 1965, Doubleday, 1966.
The Saliva Tree, and Other Strange Growths, Faber, 1966.
An Age, Faber, 1967, published as *Cryptozoic!,* Doubleday, 1968.
Report on Probability A, Faber, 1968, Doubleday, 1969.
A Brian Aldiss Omnibus, Sidgwick & Jackson, 1969.
Barefoot in the Head: A European Fantasia, Faber, 1969, Doubleday, 1970.
The Hand-Reared Boy, McCall, 1970.
A Soldier Erect, Coward, 1971 (published in England as *A Soldier Erect; or, Further Adventures of the Hand-Reared Boy,* Weidenfeld & Nicolson, 1971).
Brian Aldiss Omnibus 2, Sidgwick & Jackson, 1971.
Frankenstein Unbound (also see below), Random House, 1973.
The Eighty-Minute Hour: A Space Opera, Doubleday, 1974.
The Malacia Tapestry, J. Cape, 1976, Harper, 1977.
Brothers of the Head, illustrated by Ian Pollock, Pierrot, 1977.
A Rude Awakening, Weidenfeld & Nicolson, 1978, Random House, 1979.
Enemies of the System: A Tale of Homo Uniformis, Harper, 1978.
Life in the West, Weidenfeld & Nicolson, 1980.
Moreau's Other Island, J. Cape, 1980, published as *An Island Called Moreau,* Simon & Schuster, 1981.
Helliconia Spring, Atheneum, 1982.
Helliconia Summer, Atheneum, 1983.
Helliconia Winter, Atheneum, 1985.
The Year before Yesterday: A Novel in Three Acts, F. Watts, 1987.
Ruins, Century Hutchinson (London), 1987.
Forgotten Life, Gollancz, 1988, Atheneum, 1989.

NONFICTION

Cities and Stones: A Traveller's Yugoslavia, Faber, 1966.
The Shape of Further Things, Doubleday, 1970.
Billion Year Spree: The History of Science Fiction, Doubleday, 1973.
Science Fiction Art, New English Library, 1975.

This World and Nearer Ones: Essays Exploring the Familiar, Weidenfeld & Nicolson, 1979, Kent State University Press, 1981.
Pile: Petals from St. Klaed's Computer, illustrations by Mike Wilks, J. Cape, 1979, Holt, 1980.
The Pale Shadow of Science, Serconia, 1985.
. . . And the Lurid Glare of the Comet, Serconia, 1986.
(With David Wingrove) *Trillion Year Spree: The History of Science Fiction,* Atheneum, 1986.

STORY COLLECTIONS

Space, Time and Nathaniel, Faber, 1957.
The Canopy of Time, Faber, 1959.
No Time Like Tomorrow, Signet, 1959.
Galaxies Like Grains of Sand, Signet, 1960, reprinted with new introduction by Norman Spinrad, Gregg, 1977.
The Airs of Earth, Faber, 1963.
Starswarm, Signet, 1964.
Best Science Fiction Stories of Brian Aldiss, Faber, 1965, revised edition, 1971, published as *Who Can Replace a Man?,* Harcourt, 1966.
Intangibles Inc., and Other Stories: Five Novellas, Faber, 1969.
Neanderthal Planet, Avon, 1969.
(Contributor) *The Inner Landscape,* Allison & Busby, 1969.
The Moment of Eclipse, Faber, 1971, Doubleday, 1972.
The Book of Brian Aldiss, DAW Books, 1972 (published in England as *Comic Inferno,* New English Library, 1973).
Last Orders and Other Stories, J. Cape, 1977.
New Arrivals, Old Encounters, Harper, 1979.
Foreign Bodies, Chapman (Singapore), 1981.
Seasons in Flight, J. Cape, 1984, Atheneum, 1986.
Best SF Stories of Brian W. Aldiss, Gollancz, 1988, Atheneum, 1989.
Science Fiction Blues: The Show That Brian Aldiss Took on the Road, Avernus, 1988.

EDITOR

Penguin Science Fiction, Penguin, 1961.
More Penguin Science Fiction: An Anthology, Penguin, 1962.
Best Fantasy Stories, Faber, 1962.
Science Fiction Horizons, Numbers 1-2, Arno Press, 1964-65.
Yet More Penguin Science Fiction, Penguin, 1964.
Introducing Science Fiction: A Science Fiction Anthology, Faber, 1964.
(With Harry Harrison) *Nebula Award Stories II,* Doubleday, 1967.
(With Harrison) *All About Venus: A Revelation of the Planet Venus in Fact and Fiction,* Dell, 1968 (published in England as *Farewell Fantastic Venus! A History of the Planet Venus in Fact and Fiction,* Macdonald, 1968).
(With Harrison) *The Astounding Analog Reader,* two volumes, Doubleday, 1973.
Penguin Science Fiction Omnibus: An Anthology, Penguin, 1973.
Space Opera: An Anthology of Way-Back-When Futures, Weidenfeld & Nicolson, 1974, Doubleday, 1975.
(With Harrison) *Hell's Cartographers: Some Personal Histories of Science Fiction Writers,* Doubleday, 1975.
Space Odysseys, Weidenfeld & Nicolson, 1975, Doubleday, 1976.
Evil Earths, Weidenfeld & Nicolson, 1975, Avon, 1979.
Galactic Empires, two volumes, Weidenfeld & Nicolson, 1976, St. Martin's, 1977.

(With Harrison) *Decade: The 1940s,* Pan Books, 1977, St. Martin's, 1978.

(With Harrison) *Decade: The 1950s,* Pan Books, 1977, St. Martin's, 1978.

(With Harrison) *Decade: The 1960s,* Macmillan, 1977.

Perilous Planets, Weidenfeld & Nicolson, 1978, Avon, 1980.

The Penguin World Omnibus of Science Fiction, Penguin Books, 1986.

Also co-editor of "SF Master" series, New English Library, 1976-79.

EDITOR WITH HARRY HARRISON; "BEST SCIENCE FICTION" AN-NUALS

Best Science Fiction: 1967, Berkley Publishing, 1968 (published in England as *The Year's Best Science Fiction 1,* Sphere, 1968).

Best Science Fiction: 1968, Putnam, 1969 (published in England as *The Year's Best Science Fiction 2,* Sphere, 1969).

Best Science Fiction: 1969, Putnam, 1970 (published in England as *The Year's Best Science Fiction 3,* Sphere, 1970).

Best Science Fiction: 1970, Putnam, 1971 (published in England as *The Year's Best Science Fiction 4,* Sphere, 1971).

Best Science Fiction: 1971, Putnam, 1972.

Best Science Fiction: 1972, Putnam, 1973.

Best Science Fiction: 1973, Putnam, 1974.

Best Science Fiction: 1974, Putnam, 1975 (published in England as *The Year's Best Science Fiction,* Sphere, 1975).

Best Science Fiction: 1975, Putnam, 1976 (published in England as *The Year's Best Science Fiction,* Sphere, 1976).

OTHER

"Frankenstein Unbound" (radio play based on the novel of the same title), British Broadcasting Corp. (BBC Radio), 1974, abridged version released as a sound recording by Alternate World Recordings, 1976.

Author of articles and reviews under pseudonym C. C. Shackleton.

WORK IN PROGRESS: Bury My Heart at W. H. Smith's, a book on authorship.

SIDELIGHTS: Brian W. Aldiss is a prolific British author who has published criticism, essays, travelogues, short stories, and traditional novels, but who remains best known for his science fiction writing. Since the appearance of his first science fiction novel *Non-Stop* in 1958, Aldiss has garnered virtually every major award in the field, including a Hugo Award for *Hothouse,* a Nebula Award for *The Saliva Tree,* a John Campbell Memorial Award for *Helliconia Spring,* and a James Blish Award for excellence in science fiction criticism. Unlike many of his colleagues, Aldiss approaches science fiction from a humanist point of view, focusing on character and theme rather than gadget-oriented technology. He demands an authorial autonomy that is rare in the field, and he typically discards worn-out formulas in favor of riskier, creative experiments.

As a critic, Aldiss campaigns for the acceptance of science fiction as a legitimate genre. He argues that science fiction is not just a fad, but will remain a permanent fixture in literature. According to Jonathan White in *Publishers Weekly,* Aldiss believes that science fiction has the potential to evolve, while other genres inevitably disappear after running their courses. The author explains to White: "I don't look upon science fiction as a genre at all; rather, it *contains* genres. For a bit it was the space opera that was in vogue. Then the catastrophe novel. For every kind of story that gets used up, another will

always take its place." His comprehensive history of this genre, *Trillion Year Spree: The History of Science Fiction,* written with David Wingrove, testifies to his vision of science fiction as a serious literary endeavor.

Aldiss has himself experimented with different types of science fiction. *An Age,* for example, deals with the theme of time travel, but it is also "an amalgam . . . of detective story, psychological thriller and visionary fantasy," writes a *Times Literary Supplement* reviewer. *The Eighty-Minute Hour,* "joyously resurrects old SF stereotypes," but it does so with "an amused self-consciousness, stylistic flair and dexterity, and a double-edged humor based in the comic multiple meanings of language," declares Richard Mathews in his *Aldiss Unbound: The Science Fiction of Brian W. Aldiss.* Two of the author's books, *Report from Probability A* and *Barefoot in the Head: A European Fantasia,* are experimental works which are meant to challenge the reader intellectually, Aldiss tells White. *Barefoot* describes a war fought with hallucinogenic drugs, while *Report* is "a kind of fantasy *nouveau roman* of voyeurism," as a *Chicago Tribune Book World* reviewer calls it. Aldiss says in a *Contemporary Authors Autobiography Series* entry that *Report* marks his "commitment to bringing art and artistic concerns into SF." Neither novel was accepted with much critical or public enthusiasm upon publication, but both, especially the repeatedly reissued *Report,* have enjoyed some success since then.

After exploring the many features of the genre in over a dozen books, Aldiss felt he had "written himself out of science fiction," relates Mathews. He ventured into what he terms "ordinary fiction" with the novel *The Hand-Reared Boy* and its two sequels, *A Soldier Erect* and *A Rude Awakening.* Mathews argues that the adjective "ordinary," far from having any negative connotation, is "used in its best sense" because the book, which records the "male rites of passage before the [Second World War,] is one with which any man can identify." It is, the reviewer suggests, far from ordinary in its ability to reach its audience. *The Hand-Reared Boy* is the story of Horatio Stubbs's experiences at a private (or, in British usage, public) boarding school for boys in England. Its sequel, *A Soldier Erect,* follows Stubbs into military service. Mathews finds that "these novels are significant in marking [Aldiss's] return to standard fiction devices, without the aid of stylistic inventions or SF gimmicks."

The frankness of Aldiss's approach to this trilogy, which strongly emphasizes Horatio's sexual exploits, has inspired strong reactions from critics, who either find the characters refreshing or vulgar. A *Times Literary Supplement* reviewer notes that *The Hand-Reared Boy* may seem like "an erotic fantasy. Yet it rings true—however surprising to young readers educated at day-schools." And Valentine Cunningham remarks in the *Times Literary Supplement* that "even a taste for the tasteless has a way of sliding into tastefulness" in *A Rude Awakening,* the last Horatio book. She feels that the post-war wisdom Horatio expresses toward the end of the book is the most tasteful part, though she believes Aldiss wades through too many "bodily fluids" before offering anything of literary substance to his text. *New York Times Book Review* critic Martin Levin also has mixed feelings about the Horatio Stubbs trilogy. Reviewing *The Hand-Reared Boy,* Levin believes that the "disarming keynote" of an otherwise sexually preoccupied book is the "spirit of joyful exuberance" with which Horatio recalls his childhood memories. Levin expresses little tolerance for Horatio's "zest for whoring [which] declines only during bouts of dysentary," but he praises Aldiss's portrayal of war in the

China-Burma-India theater. The vividness of this part of the book comes from the author's personal experiences in Asia during the Second World War. "Mr. Aldiss brings to life this long-dead war, with its vanished mystique and its forgiven and forgotten enemies," declares Levin. Balancing out the blunt corporeal language and situations of this trilogy, this aspect of the Horatio novels has helped mitigate criticism of these publicly well-received books.

Aldiss's *Forgotten Life,* published in 1988, contains descriptions of life in wartime Burma and Sumatra which echo those of the Asian war theater in the Horatio books, but any similarities between this and those earlier works end there. *Forgotten Life* deals with the relationships between mature people, rather than with the maturation processes of a single character. It is concerned with three people, explains *Glasgow Herald* contributor Ian Bell: Clement Winter, an Oxford psychoanalyst who is struggling "for an emotional life of his own," his wife Sheila, a successful science fiction/fantasy novelist, who is "living half her life in a fantasy world," and Clement's brother Joseph, who is striving "to form a lasting relationship free from the rejection he endured at his mother's hands." Jonathan Keates claims in an *Observer* review that "the true protagonist here is Joseph," whose tale is told when Clement reads his brother's journals after the latter's death. "Aldiss's skill," continues Keates, "lies in sustaining [Joseph] in a continuing duel with Clement." Contrary to this opinion, *Punch* critic Simon Brett believes that "too great a percentage of the book is devoted to [Joseph]. And the author has created a self-regarding style for Joseph's writings which, while entirely appropriate for the character, does become a little wearing for the reader."

The organization of the book is complex, shifting in viewpoint as it involves the reader in Joseph's journal, Clement's life in north Oxford, the brothers' childhood lives, the present-day relationships between Clement and his brother's mistress, and Sheila and her American editor. *Times Literary Supplement* contributor John Melmoth believes this approach "fails to cohere," making it a "frustrating experience." But Isabel Quigley writes in the London *Financial Times* that even with "all these shifts of viewpoint, method, sympathy, place and time, [the book] makes a whole and achieves a pattern, likeable, solid and satisfying." Sophia Watson, a *Literary Review* critic, similarly remarks that *Forgotten Life* is "a good read," but she does not believe it should be considered a major work of fiction. Ian Bell feels more strongly about the novel's merits, however, asserting that "this is a fine and satisfying novel of a type which Mr. Aldiss, masterly SF writer that he is, should try more often."

Despite praise for his mainstream fiction, the author has concentrated most of his efforts on science fiction. His most ambitious effort in this genre is the much-critiqued Helliconia trilogy, which Gerald Jonas says in the *New York Times Book Review* "truly deserves the label 'epic.'" The novels, *Helliconia Spring, Helliconia Summer,* and *Helliconia Winter,* are set on a world in a binary star system. The 2,592-year orbit of Helliconia's sun Batalix around the larger sun Freyr "subjects Helliconia to a Great Year whose seasons last for centuries," summarizes Colin Greenland in a *Times Literary Supplement* review of *Summer.* The extremity of the weather on the planet dictates to a great extent the rise and fall of civilizations, the relationship between the humans and beast-like "Phagors," and the biology of the planet's inhabitants (including humans).

Helliconia Spring starts at the end of Helliconia's 600-year-long barbaric ice age and follows the story of Yuli and his descendents as they begin to reestablish civilization in the town of Embruddock, which Yuli renames Oldorando. As the town grows, the men vie for power and battle the Phagors, while the women, led by the sorceress Shay Tal, establish an academy of science and discover how their planet behaves in its solar system. Aldiss fills his alien setting with descriptions of bizarre species of flora and fauna, a feature of the novel which *Los Angeles Times* contributor Carolyn See believes is distracting to the story line. In defense of this part of his trilogy, the author told *CA* that these details of life on Helliconia were "brought about by the joy of invention. The uses of strange species and alien planets were densely related; yet there is hardly a plant or animal which does not have its parallel on Earth."

In a review of *Spring,* Greenland also raises the objection that the plot of the novel depends too much on coincidence and is "overburdened with slabs of undigested science." But these are complaints which critics like See believe to be outweighed by the book's strengths. "For use of climate as character, for making the very long view palatable to the reader, for creating an entire universe that pulses and hums and crackles with life, Aldiss deserves full marks," concludes See. Michael Bishop adds that "Aldiss' unflagging narrative energy, his gift for drawing character, . . . and the many overt or subtle hints of larger, more portentous mysteries underlying the Viking-saga surface of his story" make the novel well worthwhile.

In the trilogy's second book, *Helliconia Summer,* the author focuses on a time period of only a few months. The Phagors have been subjugated (at least temporarily) and the story focuses on JandolAnganol, King of Borlien, and the intrigue and politics between his country and neighboring Oldorando. It is a tale which, according to London *Times* critic Nicholas Shakespeare, "smacks less of science fiction than medieval romance," though the plot also follows the society's progress as the priesthood becomes more and more involved in scientific studies. The concluding book of the series, *Helliconia Winter,* "combines the best of the Helliconia volumes—the breadth, scope, and historical sweep of *Spring* with the finely crafted details and narrow focus of *Summer,*" says *Fantasy Review* contributor Michael R. Collins. In a review of *Helliconia Winter,* Greenland writes that the trilogy signifies "fatalism, fundamentality, the brute biology of it all. Everything comes back to nature, which endures." As civilization struggles to survive the oncoming winter, the reader follows the adventures of Luterin Shokerandit as he goes to war, is imprisoned in the Great Wheel of Kharnabar, and survives the "Fat Death," a disease transmitted by ticks which infest the Phagors and cause the victim's body to change drastically. Strangely enough and unknown to the Helliconians, the virus actually has a beneficial side effect which allows humankind to survive the harsh winter.

While all this is taking place, the importance of the space station Avernus (which was also mentioned in the earlier books) is made more apparent to the reader in *Helliconia Winter.* The purpose of the station is to transmit messages back to Earth about every event that occurs on Helliconia's surface. On Earth, viewing "the social and cultural evolution of other worlds has become our children's children's grandiose equivalent of watching *Dallas,*" remarks Michael Bishop. Greenland feels that Aldiss's inclusion of the events on Avernus and Earth do not add to the story of Helliconia. This parallel story seems "like a dissonant dream, almost trivial beside the main drama," says Greenland. In contrast, an *Extrapolation* reviewer holds that the stories of Earth and Helliconia present a unifying theme of hope for humanity which is finally brought together in the last book. "The endless pictures coming from Helliconia [are] an example from which humanity might learn," suggests the article. The review concludes that as the people on Earth achieve a "new consciousness" which provides "humanity with a new unity instead of the old isolation," the highly technological station Avernus, which is also, in turn, a place of isolation for its caretakers, is replaced by higher, empathic communications. Humanity finds peace and understanding at last through the unification of the people of Earth with the Helliconians.

In a *Los Angeles Times* article, Sue Martin expresses her feeling that overall the trilogy is only "semicompelling" because there are "no real twists" in the plot. In response to this remark, Aldiss told *CA* that he considers such criticism to be imperceptive, since he "was not writing a detective novel." Indeed, many critics believe the Helliconia trilogy to be a considerable achievement. "Though science fiction often has this scope," asserts Greenland, "it has never had this grandeur." Gerald Jonas feels these books comprise "a splendid work of imagination that weds grandeur of concept to a mastery of detail and a sense of style unmatched in modern science fiction." Aldiss says in *Publishers Weekly* that the importance of these books to him is that they signify his attempt "to get on my horse again and write a big, solid novel that *no* one could say wasn't SF. And I think I've managed to do that." According to his own definition of science fiction quoted in the *New York Times Book Review*, this means that he has written a work which attempts "to build some sort of philosophical and metaphysical framework around the immense changes of our times brought about by technological development." The trilogy addresses all these aspects by including a scope of time encompassing thousands of years, the description of technology and its effect on Avernus and Earth, and, in *Science Fiction and Fantasy Book Review* contributor Willis E. McNelly's words, the "artistic, intellectual, theological, even teleological sustenance" which Helliconia offers to Earth.

The trilogy is the author's most ambitious effort to give science fiction credibility as a form of serious literature. *Fantasy Review* contributor Michael R. Collings remarks that "only an author such as Aldiss, who has immersed himself in questions of stasis and change, entropy, ecological balance, and definitions of what it is to be human—and has explored their possibilities for almost three decades—could have completed such a vision" as the Helliconia trilogy. Discussing Aldiss's science fiction work in general, critic Robert E. Colbert writes in *Extrapolation* that Aldiss's "concern for the dearth of ordinary human feeling in so much genre science fiction, its lack of warmth and compassion, is clear. And the specific literary benefits of the reintroduction of such concerns are also clear: an art which renders situations, depicts characters, closer to the more immediate human concerns can only benefit artistically." A number of critics believe that for these reasons, Brian Aldiss's contributions to science fiction have done much to improve its respectability. According to Greenland, Aldiss "continues to represent the acceptable face of science fiction to those literati who still cannot bring themselves to acknowledging the genre."

BIOGRAPHICAL/CRITICAL SOURCES:

BOOKS

Aldiss, Margaret, compiler, *Brian W. Aldiss: A Bibliography, 1954-1988*, Borgo, 1989.
Contemporary Authors Autobiography Series, Volume 2, Gale, 1985.
Contemporary Literary Criticism, Gale, Volume 5, 1976, Volume 14, 1980, Volume 40, 1986.
Dictionary of Literary Biography, Volume 14, *British Novelists since 1960*, Gale, 1983.
Griffin, Brian and David Wingrove, *Apertures: A Study of the Writings of Brian W. Aldiss*, Greenwood Press, 1984.
Mathews, Richard, *Aldiss Unbound: The Science Fiction of Brian W. Aldiss*, Borgo, 1977.
Platt, Charles, editor, *Dream Makers: The Uncommon People Who Write Science Fiction*, Berkley Publishing, 1980.

PERIODICALS

Chicago Tribune Book World, January 25, 1981, February 28, 1982.
Extrapolation, winter, 1982, spring, 1986.
Fantasy Review, April, 1985.
Financial Times (London), October 1, 1988.
Foundation, winter, 1985/86.
Glasgow Herald, October 8, 1988.
Listener, March 25, 1971, July 22, 1976.
Literary Review, September, 1988.
London Magazine, March, 1982.
Los Angeles Times, February 12, 1981, February 25, 1982.
Los Angeles Times Book Review, August 18, 1985.
New Statesman, November 2, 1973.
New York Times, February 17, 1981.
New York Times Book Review, April 19, 1970, August 22, 1971, September 12, 1976, February 26, 1984, April 28, 1985.
Observer, September 25, 1988.
Publishers Weekly, April 19, 1985.
Punch, September 30, 1988.
Science Fiction and Fantasy Book Review, June, 1982.
Science Fiction Studies, Volume 1, number 2, 1973.
Spectator, November 10, 1973, May 27, 1978, May 8, 1980, August 22, 1980.
Times (London), December 8, 1983.
Times Literary Supplement, September 21, 1967, January 22, 1970, May 19, 1978, March 7, 1980, December 2, 1983, September 30, 1988.
Washington Post Book World, March 22, 1981, August 28, 1988.

—*Sketch by Kevin S. Hile*

*   *   *

ALDRIDGE, Adele   1934-

PERSONAL: Born August 12, 1934, in Oceanside, N.Y.; daughter of John Henry and Ruth Louise (Ferris) Thompson; divorced; children: Vicki Adele, John Alan. *Education:* Studied at Parson's School of Design, 1954-56, Art Institute of Chicago, 1960, and Silvermine College of Art, 1965-68; Union Graduate School, Ph.D., 1980.

ADDRESSES: Home and office—215 Bridgeway, Sausauto, Calif. 94965.

CAREER: Painter and printmaker. Co-owner of Magic Circle Press.

MEMBER: National Organization for Women (coordinator of Women in Graphics).

WRITINGS:

Notpoems, Mandala Press, limited edition, 1970, Magic Circle Press, 1972, 3rd edition, Artists and Alchemists, 1976.
Changes: A Book of Prints Inspired by the I Ching, Mandala Press, 1972.
(Contributor) Bill Henderson, editor, *The Publish It Yourself Hand Book,* Pushcart Press, 1973.
Once I Was a Square: And Then I Met a Circle, Magic Circle Press, 1974.
I Ching Meditations, Alchemist Atelier, 1974.
(Illustrator) Donna Ippolito, *Erotica: Words,* Artists and Alchemists, 1975.

WORK IN PROGRESS: The remaining sixty-one hexagrams of the *I Ching Meditations* handprinted in an edition of two hundred, with seven prints in each portfolio, a ten-year project.

SIDELIGHTS: "I have come to the book world via the visual," Adele Aldridge writes *CA.* "[I] consider letters in themselves beautiful. Started working with letters in paintings, then went into concrete poetry. Now incorporating my drawings and personal meditations of the *I Ching* into a unified whole. . . . [I am] interested in elevating the role of women in this and all other societies."

*   *   *

ALLARDYCE, Paula
See TORDAY, Ursula

*   *   *

ALLEN, Charles L(ivingstone)   1913-

PERSONAL: Born June 24, 1913, in Newborn, Ga.; son of John Robert and Lula (Franklin) Allen; married Leila Haynes, June 19, 1934; children: Charles Livingstone, John Franklin, Mary Jane (Mrs. Charles W. Miller). *Education:* Wofford College, A.B., 1933; Emory University, B.D., 1937, D.D., 1948; Piedmont College, D.D., 1946.

ADDRESSES: Home—5100 San Felipe, No. 182, Houston, Tex. 77056. *Office*—Transco Tower, P.O. Box 1396, Houston, Tex. 77251.

CAREER: Ordained Methodist minister, 1933; pastor of Methodist churches in Georgia, 1934-48; Grace Church, Atlanta, Ga., pastor, 1948-60; First Methodist Church, Houston, Tex., pastor, 1960-83. Television preacher, 1949—. Member of board of directors of Houston's Methodist Hospital.

MEMBER: Phi Beta Kappa.

AWARDS, HONORS: D.D. from Emory University, 1960; LL.D. from John Brown University, 1964; named minister of the year in America by Religious Heritage of America, 1981.

WRITINGS:

Roads to Radiant Living, Revell, 1951.
In Quest of God's Power, Revell, 1952.
God's Psychiatry: The Twenty-third Psalm, the Ten Commandments, the Lord's Prayer, the Beatitudes, Revell, 1953.
When the Heart Is Hungry: Christ's Parables for Today, Revell, 1955.
The Touch of the Master's Hand, Revell, 1956.
All Things Are Possible through Prayer, Revell, 1958.

When You Lose a Loved One (also see below), Revell, 1959.
The Twenty-third Psalm: An Interpretation, Revell, 1961.
Healing Words, Revell, 1961.
Twelve Ways to Solve Your Problems, Revell, 1961.
The Life of Christ, Revell, 1962.
(With Charles L. Wallis) *When Christmas Came to Bethlehem,* Revell, 1963.
The Lord's Prayer: An Interpretation, Revell, 1963.
Prayer Changes Things, Revell, 1964.
The Ten Commandments: An Interpretation, Revell, 1965.
The Sermon on the Mount, Revell, 1966.
The Beatitudes: An Interpretation, Revell, 1967.
Life More Abundant, Revell, 1968.
The Riches of Prayer, Revell, 1969.
The Charles L. Allen Treasury, Revell, 1970.
The Miracle of Love, Revell, 1972.
(With Mouzon Biggs) *When You Graduate,* Revell, 1972.
The Miracle of Hope, Revell, 1973.
The Miracle of Love, Revell, 1973.
The Miracle of the Holy Spirit, Revell, 1974.
What I Have Lived By: An Autobiography, Revell, 1976.
(With Wallis) *Christmas,* Revell, 1977.
You Are Never Alone, Revell, 1978.
Perfect Peace, Revell, 1979.
(With Mildred Parker) *How To Increase Your Sunday-School Attendance,* Revell, 1979.
(With Helen Steiner Rice) *When You Lose a Loved One* [and] *Life Is Forever,* Revell, 1979.
The Secret of Abundant Living, Revell, 1980.
Victory in the Valleys of Life, Revell, 1981.
(With Rice) *The Prayerful Heart,* Revell, 1982.
Faith, Hope, and Love, Revell, 1982.
Joyful Living in the Fourth Dimension, Revell, 1983.
When a Marriage Ends, Revell, 1986.
Meet the Methodists, Abingdon, 1986.
(Compiler) *Home Fires,* Word Books, 1987.
God's Seven Wonders for You, Revell, 1988.

Also author of *Inspiring Thoughts for Your Marriage, Kenneth Wyatt's Western Art Interpreted by Charles L. Allen, My Lord, My God,* and *The Happy Birthday Book.* Author of column for *Atlanta Constitution,* 1949-60, and *Houston Chronicle,* 1960-82.

*   *   *

ALLEN, Roger M(ichael) A(shley)   1942-

PERSONAL: Born January 24, 1942, in Tavistock, Devon, England; came to the United States in 1968; son of William Ivor (a tobacco company manager) and Doreen Mabel Lily (Chapell) Allen; married Mary D. North (a teacher), November 25, 1972; children: Timothy, Marianna. *Education:* Lincoln College, Oxford, B.A., 1965, M.A., 1968, D.Phil., 1968.

ADDRESSES: Home—6346 Sherwood Rd, Philadelphia, Pa. 19151. *Office*—Department of Oriental Studies, University of Pennsylvania, Philadelphia, Pa. 19104.

CAREER: University of Pennsylvania, Philadelphia, assistant professor, 1968-73, associate professor, 1973-84, professor of Arabic language and literature, 1984—. Visiting lecturer at Oxford University, 1976. Organist and choirmaster at St. Mary's Episcopal Church in Philadelphia, 1974—.

MEMBER: Middle East Studies Association of North America, American Oriental Society, American Association of Teachers of Arabic (president, 1977-78).

AWARDS, HONORS: American Research Center fellow in Egypt, 1970-71, 1975-76; Lindback Foundation Distinguished Teaching Award, 1972.

WRITINGS:

(Translator from the Arabic with Akef Abadir) Nagib Mahfuz, *God's World: An Anthology of Short Stories,* Bibliotheca Islamica, 1973.

(Contributor) Leonard Binder, editor, *The Study of the Middle East: Research and Scholarship in the Humanities and the Social Sciences,* Wiley, 1976.

(Translator from the Arabic) Mahfuz, *Mirrors: A Novel,* Bibliotheca Islamica, 1977.

(Editor and translator from the Arabic) Yusuf Idris, *In the Eye of the Beholder: Tales of Egyptian Life from the Writings of Yusuf Idris,* Bibliotheca Islamica, 1978.

The Arabic Novel: An Historical and Critical Introduction, Syracuse University Press, 1982.

(Translator from the Arabic with Adnan Hayder) Jabra Ibrahim Jabra, *The Ship,* Three Continents, 1985.

(Editor) *Modern Arabic Literature,* Ungar, 1987.

(Translator from the Arabic) Abd al-Rahman Munif, *Endings,* Quartet Books, 1988.

Contributor to scholarly journals, including *Journal of Arabic Literature, Mundus Artium,* and *Muslim World.* Editor of *Edebiyat,* 1976—; Arabic literature editor, *Twentieth Century Encyclopedia of World Literatures,* 1978—; guest editor of *Nimrod,* 1982, and *Translation,* 1983.

WORK IN PROGRESS: Research on computers, Arabic texts, and the nature of Arabic narrative; a set of essays on Nagib Mahfuz, the 1988 Nobel Laureate in Literature.

SIDELIGHTS: In his book *The Arabic Novel* Roger Allen traces the history of the novel in the Arab world from its origins in 1913 to its later stages of development. Allen's account is divided into two periods, the first covering Arabic literature's growth up to 1939, and the second (which he terms "the period of maturity") from 1939 to the present. Among the novels Allen features are Muhammad Husayn Haykal's *Zaynab* (the book that initiated the genre in 1913), al-Tayyib Salih's *Season of Migration to the North,* and 1988 Noble Prize-winner Nagib Mahfuz's *Chatter on the Nile.* Allen reviews the historical and political events surrounding the emergence of each of these novels and shows the significance of such events in the rise of Arabic literature.

Allen's *Modern Arabic Literature* brings together a collection of critical essays on seventy-four modern Arab litterateurs, providing bio-bibliographical information and a critical survey of selected works by each author. "This work," Allen told *CA,* "allows Western readers to assess for the first time the development of modern criticism in the Arab world." With his translation of *Endings* by the Saudi novelist Abd al-Rahman Munif, Allen continues, "English readers are introduced for the first time to a new and thoroughly original voice in modern Arabic fiction, one who invokes the insights of a social scientist and the narrative techniques of a traditional storyteller in his depictions of life in a desert community."

Allen told *CA:* "The combination of two careers, as a professor of Arabic literature and as a professional church musician, is important to the way of life within which I do much of my writing. I regard the introduction of treasures from Arabic literature—whether from the medieval or modern periods—as increasingly important to a Western world which knows terrifyingly little about cultures other than its own. My most recent work on the novel in Arabic is illustrative of this desire to make the literature of the Arab world accessible to a broader Western audience. It is particularly gratifying to me therefore that, through an article in *World Literature Today,* I was able to play a role in nominating Nagib Mahfuz to the Noble Prize committee. That event ensures that my long-term goal will now begin to be achieved."

BIOGRAPHICAL/CRITICAL SOURCES:

PERIODICALS

Times Literary Supplement, September 10, 1982.
World Literature Today, spring, 1983, spring, 1988.

*   *   *

AMBRUS, Gyozo Laszlo   1935-
(Victor G. Ambrus)

PERSONAL: Born August 19, 1935, in Budapest, Hungary; son of Gyozo (a chemical engineer) and Iren (Toth) Ambrus; married Glenys R. Chapman (an illustrator), 1958; children: Mark, Sandor John. *Education:* Received early education in Hungary and attended Hungarian Academy of Fine Art for three years; Royal College of Art, London, England, Diploma A.R.C.A., 1959. *Politics:* Democrat. *Religion:* Roman Catholic.

ADDRESSES: Home—52 Crooksbury Rd., Farnham, Surrey, England.

CAREER: Author, artist, designer, and illustrator of books for children. Lecturer on illustration, West Surrey College of Art, Surrey, England, 1964-80, and other universities. Member of Council for National Academic Awards of Great Britain. Has exhibited work at the Royal Academy, Biennale of Bratislava, in Bologna, Italy, and in Belgium. Works included in permanent collections at University of Southern Mississippi, Library of Congress, and Oxford University Press, London, England.

MEMBER: Royal College of Art (associate member), Royal Society of Arts (fellow), Royal Society of Painters, Etchers, and Engravers (fellow).

AWARDS, HONORS: Kate Greenaway Gold Medal for most distinguished work in illustration of a children's book, Library Association of Great Britain, 1964, for *The Three Poor Tailors,* and 1975, for *Horses in Battle* and *Mishka;* granted diplomas from Royal Engravers and from Royal Society of Arts.

WRITINGS:

SELF-ILLUSTRATED; UNDER NAME VICTOR G. AMBRUS

The Three Poor Tailors, Oxford University Press, 1965, Harcourt, 1966.
Brave Soldier Janosh, Oxford University Press, 1967.
The Little Cockerell, Oxford University Press, 1968.
The Seven Skinny Goats, Oxford University Press, 1969, Harcourt, 1970.
(Reteller) *The Sultan's Bath,* Harcourt, 1972.
Hot Water for Boris, Oxford University Press, 1972.
A Country Wedding, Oxford University Press, 1973.
Horses in Battle, Oxford University Press, 1975.
Mishka, Oxford University Press, 1975.
(Adaptor) Brothers Grimm, *The Valiant Little Tailor,* Oxford University Press, 1980.

Dracula: Everything You Always Wanted to Know but Were Too Afraid to Ask, Oxford University Press, 1981.
(With D. Lindsay) *Under the Double Eagle: Three Centuries of History in Austria and Hungary,* Oxford University Press, 1981.
Blackbeard, Oxford University Press, 1981.
Dracula's Bedtime Storybook: Tales to Keep You Awake at Night, Oxford University Press, 1982.
Felix, Grandma and Mustapha Biscuit, Morrow, 1983.
Son of Dracula, Oxford University Press, 1985.

ILLUSTRATOR; UNDER NAME VICTOR G. AMBRUS

Ian Serraillier, *The Challenge of the Green Knight,* Oxford University Press, 1966.
Helen Kay, *Henri's Hands for Pablo Picasso,* Abelard-Schuman, 1966.
William Cowper, *The Diverting History of John Gilpin,* Abelard-Schuman, 1969.
Robert J. Unstead, *Living in a Crusader Land,* A. & C. Black, 1971.
Bonnie Highsmith, *Kodi's Mare,* Abelard-Schuman, 1973.
Winifred Finlay, *Cap o' Rushes and Other Folk Tales,* Kaye & Ward, 1973.
Alexander Cordell, *The Traitor Within,* Globe Books, 1975.
Helen Griffiths, *Just a Dog,* Holiday House, 1975.
The Story of Britain, A. & C. Black, 1976.
Sir Bernard Miles, *Favorite Tales from Shakespeare,* Hamlyn, 1976.
Miles, adaptor, *Robin Hood,* Rand McNally, 1978.
Unstead, *The Life of Jesus,* Hamlyn, 1981.
James Riordan, *Tales of King Arthur,* Rand McNally, 1982.
Riordan, *Tales from the Arabian Nights,* Rand McNally, 1983.
Riordan, *Peter and the Wolf,* Oxford University Press, 1987.
Riordan, *Myths and Legends,* Hamlyn, 1988.
Riordan, *Pinocchio,* Oxford University Press, 1988.

Illustrator of over one hundred and fifty additional books.

SIDELIGHTS: Gyozo Laszlo Ambrus told *CA:* "Being an illustrator/author, story and pictures always go together when I am working on an idea for a book. And I am never too sure which comes first! I am also something of a split personality. When other authors stick to a certain line of books, I switch between subjects as far apart as the history of the Habsburg Empire and the comic strip frolics of Count Dracula.

"In many ways this is the most enjoyable thing about working on books—you never know what's going to occupy your drawing board next. In my days I have seen dinosaurs, sailing ships, romantic heroines, horses by the dozen, nursery rhyme characters, knights of King Arthur, Father Christmas—come and go in quick succession. Never a dull moment!

"To me the most rewarding experience as an author is to see a well-worn, dog-eared book of mine on the school library shelves—or to have a small child come up and say—'I know you—you are Dracula.'"

AVOCATIONAL INTERESTS: Military history (especially the Napoleonic wars); collecting arms, armor, and antique weapons; travel; old architecture; paintings.

BIOGRAPHICAL/CRITICAL SOURCES:

BOOKS

Something about the Author Autobiography Series, Volume 4, Gale, 1987.

AMBRUS, Victor G.
See AMBRUS, Gyozo Laszlo

*   *   *

AMI, Ben
See ELIAV, Arie L(ova)

*   *   *

AMIS, Kingsley (William)   1922-
(Robert Markham, William Tanner)

PERSONAL: Born April 16, 1922, in London, England; son of William Robert (an office clerk) and Rosa Annie (Lucas) Amis; married Hilary Ann Bardwell, 1948 (divorced, 1965); married Elizabeth Jane Howard (a novelist), 1965 (divorced, 1983); children: (first marriage) Philip Nicol William, Martin Louis, Sally Myfanwy. *Education:* St. John's College, Oxford, B.A. (with first class honors in English), 1947, M.A., 1948.

ADDRESSES: Home—186 Leighton Rd., London NW5, England. *Agent*—Jonathan Clowes Ltd., 22 Prince Albert Rd., London NW1 7ST, England.

CAREER: University College of Swansea, Swansea, Glamorganshire, Wales, lecturer in English, 1949-61; Cambridge University, Peterhouse, Cambridge, England, fellow, 1961-63; full-time writer, 1963—. Visiting fellow in creative writing, Princeton University, 1958-59; visiting professor of English, Vanderbilt University, 1967-68. *Military service:* British Army, Royal Signal Corps, 1942-45; became lieutenant.

MEMBER: Authors' Club (London), Bristol Channel Yacht Club.

AWARDS, HONORS: Somerset Maugham Award, 1955, for *Lucky Jim;* M.A., Cambridge University, 1961; Booker Prize nomination and *Yorkshire Post* Book of the Year Award, both 1974, for *Ending Up;* John W. Campbell Memorial Award, 1977, for *The Alteration;* Commander of the British Empire, 1981; Booker-McConnell Prize for Fiction, from Great Britain's Book Trust, 1986, for *The Old Devils.*

WRITINGS:

Socialism and the Intellectuals, Fabian Society (London), 1957.
(Author of introduction) Oscar Wilde, *Essays and Poems,* Norton, 1959.
New Maps of Hell: A Survey of Science Fiction, Harcourt, 1960, reprinted, Arno, 1975.
My Enemy's Enemy (short stories; also see below), Gollancz, 1962, Harcourt, 1963, Penguin, 1980.
(Under pseudonym William Tanner) *The Book of Bond, or Every Man His Own 007,* Viking, 1965.
The James Bond Dossier, New American Library, 1965.
Lucky Jim's Politics, Conservative Political Centre (London), 1968.
What Became of Jane Austen? and Other Questions (essays), J. Cape, 1970, Harcourt, 1971, published as *What Became of Jane Austen and Other Essays,* Penguin, 1981.
Dear Illusion (short stories; also see below), Covent Garden Press, 1972.
On Drink (also see below), illustrations by Nicolas Bentley, J. Cape, 1972, Harcourt, 1973.
First Aid for ABA Conventioneers (excerpt from *On Drink*), Harcourt, 1973.
Rudyard Kipling and His World, Scribner, 1975.

(Author of introduction) Arthur Hutchings, *Mozart: The Man, the Music*, Schirmer, 1976.

Interesting Things, edited by Michael Swan, Cambridge University Press, 1977.

The Darkwater Hall Mystery (also see below), illustrations by Elspeth Sojka, Tragara Press, 1978.

An Arts Policy?, Centre for Policy Studies, 1979.

Collected Short Stories (includes *My Enemy's Enemy, Dear Illusion,* and *The Darkwater Hall Mystery*), Hutchinson, 1980, Penguin, 1983, revised edition, 1987.

Every Day Drinking, illustrations by Merrily Harper, Hutchinson, 1983.

How's Your Glass? A Quizzical Look at Drinks and Drinking, Wiedenfeld & Nicolson, 1984, edition with cartoons by Michael Heath, Arrow, 1986.

The Amis Anthology, Century Hutchinson, 1988.

NOVELS

Lucky Jim, Doubleday, 1954, Gollancz, 1984, edited and abridged edition by D. K. Swan, illustrations by William Burnard, Longmans, 1963, abridged edition with glossary and notes by R. M. Oldnall, Macmillan, 1967.

That Uncertain Feeling, Gollancz, 1955, Harcourt, 1956, reprinted, Panther Books, 1975.

I Like It Here, Harcourt, 1958, reprinted, Panther Books, 1975, Gollancz, 1984.

Take a Girl Like You, Gollancz, 1960, Harcourt, 1961, reprinted, Penguin, 1976.

One Fat Englishman, Gollancz, 1963, Harcourt, 1964, Penguin, 1980.

(With Robert Conquest) *The Egyptologists*, J. Cape, 1965, Random House, 1966, Panther Books, 1975.

The Anti-Death League, Harcourt, 1966, Gollancz, 1978, Penguin, 1980.

(Under pseudonym Robert Markham) *Colonel Sun: A James Bond Adventure*, Harper, 1968.

I Want It Now, J. Cape, 1968, collected edition, 1976, Harcourt, 1969.

The Green Man, J. Cape, 1969, Harcourt, 1970, Academy Chicago, 1986.

Girl, 20, J. Cape, 1971, Harcourt, 1972.

The Riverside Villas Murder, Harcourt, 1973.

Ending Up, Harcourt, 1974.

The Alteration, J. Cape, 1976, Viking, 1977.

Jake's Thing (also see below), Hutchinson, 1978, Viking, 1979.

Russian Hide-and-Seek: A Melodrama, Hutchinson, 1980, Penguin, 1981.

Stanley and the Women (also see below), Hutchinson, 1984, Summit Books, 1985.

The Old Devils (also see below), Hutchinson, 1986, Summit Books, 1987.

The Crime of the Century, Dent, 1987.

A Kingsley Amis Onmibus (includes *Jake's Thing, The Old Devils,* and *Stanley and the Women*), Hutchinson, 1987.

POETRY

Bright November, Fortune Press, 1947.

A Frame of Mind: Eighteen Poems, School of Art, Reading University, 1953.

Poems, Oxford University Poetry Society, 1954.

Kingsley Amis, Fantasy Press, 1954.

A Case of Samples: Poems, 1946-1956, Gollancz, 1956, Harcourt, 1957.

(With Dom Moraes and Peter Porter) *Penguin Modern Poets 2*, Penguin, 1962.

The Evans Country, Fantasy Press, 1962.

A Look Round the Estate: Poems 1957-1967, J. Cape, 1967, Harcourt, 1968.

Collected Poems: 1944-1979, Hutchinson, 1979, Viking, 1980.

EDITOR

(With James Michie) *Oxford Poetry, 1949*, Basil Blackwell, 1949.

(With Conquest) *Spectrum: A Science Fiction Anthology*, Volume 1, Gollancz, 1961, Harcourt, 1962, Volume 2, Gollancz, 1962, Harcourt, 1963, Volume 3, Gollancz, 1963, Harcourt, 1964, published as *Spectrum III: A Third Science Fiction Anthology*, Berkley Publishing, 1965, Volume 4, Harcourt, 1965, Volume 5, Gollancz, 1966, Harcourt, 1967.

Selected Short Stories of G. K. Chesterton, Faber, 1972.

Tennyson, Penguin, 1973.

The New Oxford Book of English Light Verse, Oxford University Press (New York), 1978 (published in England as *The New Oxford Book of Light Verse*, Oxford University Press, 1978).

Harold's Years: Impressions from the "New Statesman" and the "Spectator," Quartet Books, 1978.

The Faber Popular Reciter, Faber, 1978.

(And author of introduction) *The Golden Age of Science Fiction*, Hutchinson, 1981, Penguin, 1983.

CONTRIBUTOR

Martin Starkey and Roy Macnab, editors, *Oxford Poetry, 1948*, Basil Blackwell, 1948.

(And author of introduction) D. J. Enright, editor, *Poets of the 1950's*, Kenkyusha (Tokyo), 1955.

Winter's Tales 1, St. Martin's, 1955.

Conquest, editor, *New Lines: An Anthology*, Macmillan (London), 1956, St. Martin's, 1957.

Donald Hall and others, editors, *New Poets of England and America*, Meridian, 1957, 2nd edition, 1962.

Paul Engle and Joseph Langland, editors, *Poet's Choice*, Dial, 1962.

Malcolm Brinnan and Bill Read, editors, *The Modern Poets*, McGraw, 1963.

C. B. Cox and A. E. Dyson, editors, *Fight for Education: A Black Paper*, Critical Quarterly Society, 1968.

Penguin Modern Stories 11, Penguin, 1972.

Cox and Dyson, editors, *Black Paper 1975: The Fight for Education*, Dent, 1975.

OTHER

(Compiler with James Cochrane) *The Great British Songbook*, illustrations by Ronald Searle, Pavilion Books, 1986.

Also author of a science fiction radio play, "Something Strange," and of television plays "A Question about Hell," 1964, "The Importance of Being Harry," 1971, "Dr. Watson and the Darkwater Hall Mystery," 1974, and "See What You've Done," 1974. Author of recordings, "Reading His Own Poems," Listen, 1962, and with Thomas Blackburn, "Poems," Jupiter, 1962. Author of column on beverages in *Penthouse*. Contributor to periodicals, including *Spectator, Encounter, New Statesman, Listener, Observer,* and *London Magazine.*

WORK IN PROGRESS: Difficulties with Girls, a novel about newlyweds.

SIDELIGHTS: "I think of myself like a sort of mid- or late-Victorian person," says Kingsley Amis in *Contemporary Literature,* "not in outlook but in the position of writing a bit of poetry (we forget that George Eliot also wrote verse), writing novels, being interested in questions of the day and occasionally writing about them, and being interested in the work of other writers and occasionally writing about that. I'm not exactly an entertainer pure and simple, not exactly an artist pure and simple, certainly not an incisive critic of society, and certainly not a political figure though I'm interested in politics. I think I'm just a combination of some of those things.'' Though an eclectic man of letters, Amis is best known as a prolific novelist who, in the words of Blake Morrison in the *Times Literary Supplement,* has the ''ability to go on surprising us.'' He won critical acclaim in 1954 with the publication of his first novel, *Lucky Jim,* and after producing three other comic works was quickly characterized as a comic novelist writing in the tradition of P. G. Wodehouse and Evelyn Waugh. Since his early works, however, Amis has produced a spate of novels that vary radically in genre and seriousness of theme. He keeps ''experimenting with ways of confounding the reader who hopes for a single focus,'' claims William Hutchings in *Critical Quarterly,* though Clancy Sigal suggests in *National Review* that Amis simply ''has the virtue, rare in England, of refusing to accept an imposed definition of what a Serious Writer ought to write about.''

Amis, who admits in *Contemporary Literature* that he considers poetry a ''higher art'' than prose writing, was publishing poems before novels. ''I would have been a poet entirely if I had had my way,'' Amis told *CA* interviewer Jean W. Ross. A respected poet influenced by Philip Larkin, Amis not only eschews the grandiose subject matter and lofty tones of Romanticism; as editor of several collections of British verse, he encourages his peers to do the same. Because his poems focus on the realities of contemporary life, which he renders with ''innovative technique,'' Amis has a place in British poetry as an important minor poet, Neil Brennan notes in a *Dictionary of Literary Biography* essay.

Clive James, writing in the *New Statesman,* suggests, ''Only the fact that he is so marvellously readable can now stop Kingsley Amis from being placed in the front rank of contemporary poets.'' Yet, it was through his early novels that Amis became widely known and respected as a writer. When *Lucky Jim* first appeared, it attracted unusually wide review attention and led to a Somerset Maugham Award, a successful film, and a paperback sale of over a million copies in America. Edmund Fuller praised it in the *New York Times* as ''written with the cool, detached, sardonic style which is the trademark of the British satirical novelist. *Lucky Jim* is funny in something approaching the Wodehouse vein, but it cuts a bit deeper.'' Other critics also likened it to P. G. Wodehouse's works, and Walter Allen in *The Modern Novel* called it ''the funniest first novel since [Evelyn Waugh's] *Decline and Fall.*'' William Van O'Connor summed up the book's virtues this way in *The New University Wits and the End of Modernism,* ''The characterizations are extremely good, the dialogue is natural, the narrative pacing is excellent, and Jim himself is not only a wonderfully funny character, he is almost archetypical.''

Jim Dixon, the protagonist, is, according to Anthony Burgess in *The Novel Now,* ''the most popular anti-hero of our time.'' Though a junior lecturer at a provincial university, Jim has no desire to be an intellectual, a ''gentleman,'' because of his profound, almost physical, hatred of the social and cultural affectations of university life. This characteristic of Jim's has led several critics to conclude that he is a philistine, and, moreover, that beneath the comic effects, Amis is really attacking culture and is himself a philistine. Brigid Brophy, for

example, writes in *Don't Never Forget: Collected Views and Reviews* that the ''apex of philistinism'' is reached ''when Jim hears a tune by the composer whom either he or Mr. Amis . . . thinks of as 'filthy Mozart.'''

Ralph Caplan, however, claims in Charles Shapiro's *Contemporary British Novelists* that *Lucky Jim* ''never [promises] anything more than unmitigated pleasure and insight, and these it keeps on delivering. The book [is] not promise but fulfillment, a commodity we confront too seldom to know how to behave when it is achieved. This seems to be true particularly when the achievement is comic. Have we forgotten how to take humor straight? Unable to exit laughing, the contemporary reader looks over his shoulder for Something More. The trouble is that by now he knows how to find it.''

Amis himself states in a *Publishers Weekly* interview that to see *Lucky Jim* as a polemic on culture is to misinterpret it: '''This is the great misunderstanding of it. People said I was part of an emergent group of angry young men writing novels of protest. But the idea that Jim was an 'outsider' just won't do. He was an *insider.* This still eludes people, especially Americans.''' As to the charges of philistinism, Amis says to Dale Salwak in *Contemporary Literature:* ''Jim and I have taken a lot of bad mouthing for being philistine, aggressively philistine, and saying, 'Well, as long as I've got me blonde and me pint of beer and me packet of fags and me seat at the cinema, I'm all right.' I don't think either of us would say that. It's nice to have a pretty girl with large breasts rather than some fearful woman who's going to talk to you about Ezra Pound and hasn't got large breasts and probably doesn't wash much. And better to have a pint of beer than to have to talk to your host about the burgundy you're drinking. And better to go to see nonsensical art exhibitions that nobody's really going to enjoy. So it's appealing to common sense if you like, and it's a way of trying to denounce affectation.''

Critics generally see the three novels that followed *Lucky Jim* as variations on this theme of appealing to common sense and denouncing affectation. Discussing *Lucky Jim, That Uncertain Feeling, I Like It Here,* and *Take a Girl Like You* in the *Hudson Review,* James P. Degnan states: ''In the comically outraged voice of his angry young heroes—e.g., Jim Dixon of *Lucky Jim* and John Lewis of *That Uncertain Feeling*—Amis [lampoons] what C. P. Snow . . . labeled the 'traditional culture,' the 'culture of the literary intellectuals,' of the 'gentleman's world.''' James Gindin notes in *Postwar British Fiction* that the similarity of purpose is reflected in a corresponding similarity of technique: ''Each of the [four] novels is distinguished by a thick verbal texture that is essential comic. The novels are full of word play and verbal jokes. . . . All Amis's heroes are mimics: Jim Dixon parodies the accent of Professor Welch, his phony and genteel professor, in *Lucky Jim;* Patrick Standish, in *Take a Girl Like You,* deliberately echoes the Hollywood version of the Southern Negro's accent. John Lewis, the hero of *That Uncertain Feeling,* also mimics accents and satirically characterizes other people by the words and phrases they use.''

The heroes in these four novels are in fact so much alike that Brigid Brophy charges Amis with ''rewriting much the same novel under different titles and with different names for the characters,'' although Walter Allen insists that the ''young man recognizably akin to Lucky Jim, the Amis man as he might be called, . . . has been increasingly explored in depth.'' Consistent with her assessment of Jim Dixon in *Lucky Jim,* Brophy sees the other three Amis heroes also as ''militant philistines,'' a view that is not shared by Caplan, Burgess, or Degnan. Caplan explains that though the Amis hero in these novels is seemingly anti-intellectual, he is nonetheless ''always cerebral,'' and Burgess points out that the hero ''always earns his living by purveying culture as teacher, librarian, journalist, or publisher.'' Representing a commonsensical approach to life, the Amis protagonist, according to Degnan, is an inversion of a major convention of the hero ''as 'sensitive soul,' the convention of the 'alienated' young man of artistic or philosophical pretensions struggling pitifully and hopelessly against an insensitive, middle-class, materialistic world. . . . In place of the sensitive soul as hero, Amis creates in his early novels a hero radically new to serious contemporary fiction: a middle-class hero who is also an intellectual, an intellectual who is unabashedly middle-brow. He is a hero . . . whose chief virtues, as he expresses them, are: 'politeness, friendly interest, ordinary concern and a good natured willingness to be imposed upon. . . .' Suspicious of all pretentiousness, of all heroic posturing, the Amis hero . . . voices all that is best of the 'lower middle class, of the non-gentlemanly' conscience.''

Degnan, however, does believe that Patrick Standish in *Take a Girl Like You* comes dangerously close to ''the kind of anti-hero—e.g., blase, irresponsible, hedonistic—that Amis's first three novels attack,'' and that this weakens the satirical aspect of the novel. Echoing this observation in *The Reaction against Experiment in the English Novel, 1950-1960*, Rubin Rabinovitz detects an uncertainty as to what ''vice and folly'' really are and who possesses them: ''In *Take a Girl Like You* Amis satirizes both Patrick's lechery and Jenny's persistence in preserving her virginity. . . . The satire in *Lucky Jim* is not divided this way: Jim Dixon mocks the hypocrisy of his colleagues in the university and refuses to be subverted by it. [In *Lucky Jim*] the satire is more powerful because the things being satirized are more boldly defined.''

After *Take a Girl Like You*, Amis produced several other ''straight'' novels, as *Time*'s Christopher Porterfield describes them, as well as a James Bond spy thriller, written under the pseudonym of Robert Markham, called *Colonel Sun: A James Bond Adventure;* a work of science fiction, *The Anti-Death League;* and a ghost story, *The Green Man.* When Gildrose Productions, the firm to which the James Bond copyright was sold after Ian Fleming's death, awarded the first non-Fleming sequel to Amis, the literary world received the news with a mixture of apprehension and interest. Earlier, Amis had done an analysis of the nature of Fleming's hero, *The James Bond Dossier*, and he appeared to be a logical successor to Bond's creator. But the reactions to *Colonel Sun* have been mixed. Though Clara Siggins states in *Best Sellers* that Amis has ''produced an exciting narrative with the expertise and verve of Fleming himself,'' S. K. Oberbeck claims in the *Washington Post Book World* that the changes Amis makes ''on Bond's essential character throw the formula askew. . . . In humanizing Bond, in netting him back into the channel of real contemporary events, Amis somehow deprives him of the very ingredients that made his barely believable adventures so rewarding.'' Similarly, David Lodge, discussing the book in *The Novelist at the Crossroads and Other Essays on Fiction and Criticism*, considers *Colonel Sun* ''more realistic'' yet ''duller'' than most of the Fleming novels, because ''the whole enterprise, undertaken, apparently, in a spirit of pious imitation, required Amis to keep in check his natural talent for parody and deflating comic realism.''

Amis's comic spirit, so prominent in his first four novels and muted in *Colonel Sun*, is noticeably absent from *The Anti-*

Death League, which was published two years before the Bond adventure. Bernard Bergonzi comments in *The Situation of the Novel* that in *The Anti-Death League* Amis ''has written a more generalised kind of fiction, with more clearly symbolic implications, than in any of his earlier novels. There is still a trace of sardonic humor, and his ear remains alert to the placing details of individual speech; but Amis has here abandoned the incisive social mimicry, the memorable responses to the specificity of a person's appearance or the look of a room that have previously characterized his fiction.''

The story concerns a British army officer who becomes convinced that a nonhuman force of unlimited malignancy, called God, is responsible for a pattern of seemingly undeserving deaths. Bergonzi views the work as a provocative, anti-theological novel of ideas, and maintains that it ''represents Amis's immersion in the nightmare that flickers at the edges of his earlier fiction.'' He does, however, find one shortcoming in the novel: ''*The Anti-Death League* . . . is intensely concerned with the questions that lead to tragedy—death, cruelty, loss of every kind—while lacking the ontological supports—whether religious or humanistic—that can sustain the tragic view of life.'' A *Times Literary Supplement* reviewer admits that the rebellion against the facts of pain and death ''seems rather juvenile, like kicking God's ankle for doing such things to people,'' but asserts: ''[Amis] takes the argument to more audacious and hopeful lengths. . . . We do care about his creatures; the agents intrigue us and the victims concern us. The handling is vastly less pompous than the theme: oracular, yes, but eloquent and earthly and even moving.''

Porterfield believes *The Green Man* ''undoubtedly will make people mad. Nearly everything about Amis does. One sizable body of readers has never forgiven him for not devoting his career to rewriting other versions of *Lucky Jim*, an understandable complaint considering the skill and savage glee with which that book [skewers] bores, snobs, and all the petty conspiracies of circumstance that can stand in the way of a fellow simply getting on with a job, a girl, a few drinks.'' Described by Amis in the *Paris Review* as a ghost story ''combined with a reasonably serious study of human relations, in this case the problem of selfishness,'' *The Green Man* is, according to Melvin Maddocks in the *Christian Science Monitor*, ''a desperate book'' which marks a clear departure from Amis's earlier novels. Maddocks sees a ''chilling fatalism'' permeating the novel, ''as though everything was predestined—jokes and all.''

Jonathan Yardley, however, claims in the *New Republic* that though ''balleyhooed as a new departure . . . , [*The Green Man*] is strictly old hat. That means it is frequently funny, tedious when the dialogue turns weighty, determinedly suave, [and] a shade too nimble in plot.'' Other critics also see a continuity with Amis's earlier work. Porterfield characterizes the book as ''an Amis novel with ghosts,'' adding, ''its tensions are dissipated at crucial moments by cold dashes of caustic humor. . . . It remains pretty high-grade Amis.'' And Anthony Burgess, who recognizes the philosophical preoccupation with a malign universe in the novel, says in a *Life* review, ''If admirers of *Lucky Jim* are puzzled as to how Amis has, after that uproarious first novel, arrived at that position, perhaps they ought to read *Lucky Jim* again. . . . Amis knows how to chill us as much as he knows how to make us laugh.''

Amis followed *The Green Man* with *Girl, 20,* a comic novel with serious overtones. Like Burgess's assessment of the former, Paul Schleuter views the latter as a harmonious addition to Amis's body of work. He writes in *Saturday Review* that in *Girl, 20* Amis's "talent for creating humorous situations, characters, and dialogue is as fresh as ever.... Amis also has a distinct undercurrent of pathos, darkness, and trauma. The result is not really a 'new' Amis so much as a more mature examination of human foibles and excesses than was the case in his earlier novels." But Amis's next novel, *The Riverside Villas Murder,* "offers no comfort to those who look for consistency in [his] work," according to a *Times Literary Supplement* reviewer.

A departure from Amis's previous works, *The Riverside Villas Murder* is a detective story, though there is some debate among critics whether it is to be read "straight" or as a parody of the genre. Patrick Cosgrave, for example, claims in *Saturday Review/World* that the book is "a straight detective story, with a murder, several puzzles, clues, a great detective, and an eminently satisfying and unexpected villain. So bald a statement is a necessary introduction in order to ensure that nobody will be tempted to pore over *The Riverside Villas Murder* in search of portentousness, significance, ambiguity, or any of the more tiresome characteristics too often found in the work of a straight novelist who has turned aside from the main road of his work into the byways of such subgenres as crime and adventure. More, the book is straight detection because Amis intended it to be such: It is written out of a great love of the detective form and deliberately set in a period—the Thirties—when that form was ... most popular." The *Times Literary Supplement* reviewer, however, considers the book "something more and less than a period detective story. Mr. Amis is not one to take any convention too seriously, and on one plane he is simply having fun." Patricia Coyne, writing in the *National Review,* and *Time*'s T. E. Kalem express similar opinions. Coyne describes the story as "a boy discovers sex against a murder-mystery backdrop," and Kalem concludes that by making a fourteen-year-old boy the hero of the novel, "Amis cleverly combines, in mild parody, two ultra-British literary forms—the mystery thriller with the boyhood adventure yarn."

Some critics consider the plot of *The Riverside Villas Murder* weak, but the characterization and style particularly strong. Angus Wilson writes in the *New York Times Book Review* that the "mechanism of the murder, who did it and how, is at once creaky, obvious, and entirely improbable" yet he believes that the book contains "an almost perfect creation of the character of a young adolescent boy." Moreover, Wilson lauds Amis's prose as "probably the most pleasant to read of any good writers of English today. I know no other writer who can forgo all ornament without either aridity or pseudo-simplicity.... Each sentence, each paragraph, each chapter is organized to do its job, and the whole is therefore always satisfactory within its limits." Coyne, who also maintains that the mystery is not engaging enough, finds the characterization and the style of the highest quality: "[Amis's] may be the best secondary characters—most notably, his old men—since Dickens. And equally satisfying is his style, the often complex sentences falling clear and true with that deceptive ease that marks the master craftsman."

John Vaizey states in *Listener* that stylistic grace is one feature Amis "connoisseurs" expect, and they will find it in *Ending Up.* "There is no writer now alive, other than Anthony Powell," asserts Vaizey, "who writes such classically pure English which is at the same time accurately and exactly idiomatic. This is a very rare gift that Mr. Amis has cultivated, so that there is nothing he cannot say economically and precisely if he wants to." What surprises Vaizey, among others,

about *Ending Up* is "the quite extraordinary degree of compassion that Mr. Amis shows toward his characters and that they show towards each other.... Each person has a ghastly problem, derived from the fact of being old, and nobody—except the spinster—really feels deeply about anybody else. Nevertheless, they do not only put up, on the whole, with each other; for the most part, they make a go of it, which of course, most people do. It is a kind of celebration of ordinariness."

Ironically, other critics see a lack of compassion in Amis's treatment of his five protagonists—all over seventy years old—who suffer from a variety of diseases. Roger Sale argues in the *Hudson Review* that the "characters exist only so Amis can wound them, and when he tires of the fun he just kills them off with casual carelessness." In the *National Review,* Charles Nicol compares reading *Ending Up* to "watching a clock run down. When there is nothing more to be exploited from the interactions of his five old people, Amis squeezes out a final drop of humor by killing them all off [almost simultaneously]." And *Time*'s Timothy Foote writes: "Somewhere before a surprise ending with more deaths than Act V of *Hamlet,* it becomes evident that Author Amis is enjoying his caricatured geriatricks in some way that might be appropriate to Goneril and Regan in *King Lear* but is simply hateful in Tuppenny-happenny Cottage."

Vaizey admits that *Ending Up* has a "brooding sense of disaster, or evil, even," one that reminds him of *The Green Man;* but he nevertheless maintains that there "seems to be added a new depth of human feeling." Matthew Hodgart reaches a similar conclusion in the *New York Review of Books:* "[Ending Up] describes the futility and meaninglessness of life as it must sooner or later appear to many old people. Despite his continual joking, and sometimes apparently callous indifference, Amis has written a very moving study of the pain of old age."

Almost as if to befuddle readers searching for consistency in his work, Amis followed his detective story *The Riverside Villas Murder* and straight novel *Ending Up* with *The Alteration,* which *Time*'s Paul Gray says "flits quirkily between satire, science fiction, boy's adventure, and travelogue. The result is what *Nineteen Eighty-Four* might have been like if Lewis Carroll had written it: not a classic, certainly, but an oddity well worth an evening's attention." According to Bruce Cook in *Saturday Review, The Alteration* belongs to a rare subgenre of science fiction: "the so-called counterfeit- or alternative-world novel." Though set in the twentieth century (1976), the book has as its premise that the Protestant Reformation never occurred and, as a result, that the world is essentially Catholic. The plot centers on the discovery of a brilliant boy soprano, the Church's plans to preserve his gift by "altering" his anatomy through castration, and the debate on the justice of this decision.

Thomas R. Edwards notes in the *New York Review of Books* that though "Amis isn't famous for his compassion," in *The Alteration* he "affectingly catches and respects a child's puzzlement about the threatened loss of something he knows about only from descriptions." John Carey insists in the *New Statesman* that the book "has almost nothing expectable about it, except that it is a study of tyranny." What Carey refers to is the destructive power of the pontifical hierarchy to emasculate life and art, which he sees as the theme of the novel. Bruce Cook shares this interpretation. Calling *The Alteration* "the most overtly and specifically theological of all [Amis's] books," Cook argues: "Fundamentally, *The Alteration* is another of

Kingsley Amis's angry screeds against the Catholic faith and the Catholic idea of God. And it is not just what Amis sees as the life-hating, sex-hating aspect of High Christianity—something that made possible such monstrous phenomena as the castrati—that concerns him here [but] . . . Christianity itself. At the end of *The Anti-Death League,* his oddest and most extreme book and in some ways his best, Amis allows some talk of reconciliation, of forgiving God the wrongs He has done humanity. But there is none of that in *The Alteration.* It is an almost bitter book by a man grown angry in middle age.''

W. Hutchings, however, does not regard the novel as an attack on Catholicism. Despite sharing Cook's conviction that Amis's concern in his works since *The Anti-Death League* has been increasingly metaphysical, even theological, Hutchings maintains that the novel presents Amis with a way of making sense of a world "both absurd and threatening. Death, which dominates much of his fiction (for example, *The Anti-Death League, The Green Man,* and *Ending Up*), may be meaningless, but it cannot be viewed dispassionately. If death is horrible and God, should he exist, is either cruel or teasing, life has all the more to be lived for its present values. If we don't want it now, we'll never get it. . . . It is here that *The Alteration* represents a fascinating new step in Amis's career. If art is to have any value in such a world, then it must be part of the reason for wanting it now. The structure of the novel and its use of a musically talented main character bring a consciousness of the importance of art directly into its presentation of some problems of life.''

From *The Alteration* to *Jake's Thing,* Amis again made the transition from science fiction to "comic diatribe," according to V. S. Pritchett in the *New York Review of Books.* Pritchett considers *Jake's Thing* "a very funny book, less for its action or its talk than its prose. . . . Mr. Amis is a master of laconic mimicry and of the vernacular drift." A reviewer writes in *Choice* that this is "the Amis of *Lucky Jim,* an older and wiser comic writer who is making a serious statement about the human condition.''

The story focuses on Jake Richardson, a sixty-year-old reader in Early Mediterranean History at Oxford who in the past has been to bed with well over a hundred women but now suffers from a loss of libido. Referred to sex therapist Dr. Proinsias (Celtic, pronounced "Francis") Rosenberg, Jake, says *Nation*'s Amy Wilentz, "is caught up in the supermarket of contemporary life. The novel is filled with encounter groups, free love, women's liberation, and such electronic contrivances as the 'nocturnal mensurator,' which measures the level of a man's arousal as he sleeps." Christopher Lehmann-Haupt of the *New York Times* notes that Amis "makes the most of all the comic possibilities here. Just imagine sensible, civilized Jake coming home from Dr. Rosenberg's office with . . . assignments to study 'pictorial pornographic material' and to 'write out a sexual fantasy in not less than six hundred words.' Consider Jake struggling to find seventy-three more words, or contemplating the nudes in *Mezzanine* magazine, which 'had an exotic appearance, like the inside of a giraffe's ear or a tropical fruit not much prized by the locals.''

But for all the hilarity, there is an undercurrent of seriousness running through the novel. "It comes bubbling up," writes Lehmann-Haupt, "when Jake finally grows fed up with Dr. Rosenberg and his experiments." Wilentz argues that the novel expresses "outrage at, and defeat at the hands of, modernity, whose graceless intrusion on one's privacy is embodied in Dr.

Rosenberg's constantly repeated question, 'I take it you've no objection to exposing your genitals in public?''' Malcolm Bradbury shares this interpretation, writing in the *New Statesman:* "Amis, watching [history's] collectivising, behaviourist, depersonalizing progress, would like nice things to win and certain sense to prevail. Indeed, a humanist common sense—along with attention to farts—is to his world view roughly what post-Heideggerian existentialism is to Jean-Paul Sartre's.''

John Updike, however, offers another interpretation. Reviewing the book in the *New Yorker,* he calls the satire "more horrifying than biting, more pathetic than amusing." Updike claims that the book does not demonstrate that Dr. Rosenberg, in peddling the ideas and techniques of sex therapy, is a charlatan, "though Jake comes to believe so, and the English reader might be disposed to expect so. To an American, conditioned to tolerance of all sorts of craziness on behalf of the soul, the exercises of group therapy seem at least a gallant attack upon virtually intractable forms of human loneliness and mental misery." Updike views *Jake's Thing* as a portrait of a man infuriated by the times in which he lives. As such, he concludes it is "satisfyingly ambiguous, relentless, and full. Jake has more complaints than the similarly indisposed Alexander Portnoy [in *Portnoy's Complaint* by Philip Roth]. . . . He suffers from moments of seeing 'the world in its true light, as a place where nothing had ever been any good and nothing of significance done.' He is in a rage. Yet he is also dutiful, loyal in his fashion, and beset; we accept him as a good fellow, an honest godless citizen of the late twentieth century, trying hard to cope with the heretical possibility that sex isn't everything.''

After the problems of libido in *Jake's Thing,* writes Blake Morrison in the *Times Literary Supplement, Russian Hide-and-Seek* "signals the return of the young, uncomplicated, highly sexed Amis male; . . . the more important connection, however, is with Amis's earlier novel, *The Alteration.*'' Another example of the "alternative world" novel, *Russian Hide-and-Seek* depicts an England, fifty years hence, that has been overrun by the Soviet Union; oddly enough, though, the Soviets have abandoned Marxism and returned to the style of Russia under the czars. Paul Binding describes the book in the *New Statesman* as "at once a pastiche of certain aspects of nineteenth-century Russian fiction and an exercise in cloak-and-dagger adventure. The two genres unite to form a work far more ambitious than those earlier *jeux*—a fictional expression of the author's obsessive conviction that, whatever its avatar, Russian culture is beastly, thriving on conscious exploitation, enamoured of brutality.''

Binding considers the indictment of Russian culture only moderately successful, citing as a weakness Amis's characterizations: "For the most part he has accorded his twenty-first-century Russians only the outward rituals and attitudes—and indeed attitudinisings—of their ancestors. . . . If Amis believes that [the ideologies and social structure of the Soviet Union] now contain the germinating seeds of reversion, then—even in a fictional parable—evidence should be given." Morrison admits *Russian Hide-and-Seek* "is not all it might be" but maintains it is a novel "of interest and subtlety." He believes that along with *The Alteration, Russian Hide-and-Seek* confirms in Amis's body of work "a development away from the provincial, lower-middle class comic novels of the 1950s and the metropolitan, upper-middle, satirical ones of the 1960s and early 1970s towards an interest in serious politico-historical fiction (*The Anti-Death League* was an early forerunner).''

Amis placed himself at the center of political controversy with his next novel, *Stanley and the Women*. Published first and well-received in England, the book was rejected by publishing houses in the United States twice because of objections to its main character's misogyny, say some sources. "When rumors that one of Britain's most prominent and popular postwar novelists was being censored Stateside by a feminist cabal hit print [in early 1985], the literary flap echoed on both sides of the Atlantic for weeks," reports *Time*'s Paul Gray. After the book found an American publisher a critical debate ensued, with some reviewers condemning its uniformly negative depiction of women, and others defending the book's value nonetheless.

In a *Washington Post Book World* review, Jonathan Yardley charges, "Amis has stacked the deck against women, reducing them to caricatures who reinforce the damning judgments made by Stanley and his chums." Though Yardley feels that "much else in the novel is exceedingly well done," he also feels that its "cranky mysogynism" is too prominent to be ignored. Indeed, Stanley casts himself as the victim of a gang of female villains: a self-centered ex-wife; a current wife who stabs herself and accuses Stanley's emotionally unstable son; and a psychiatrist who deliberately mishandles the son's case and blames Stanley for the son's schizophrenia. On the other hand, "The men in the novel hardly fare any better," remarks Kakutani of the *New York Times*. In her view, shared by Susan Fromberg Schaeffer in the *New York Times Book Review*, *Stanley and the Women* proves Amis to be "not just a misogynist, but a misanthrope as well. Practically every character in the novel is either an idiot or a scheming hypocrite." Amis, who observes that British women take less offense from the book, claims it is not anti-female; *Time* presents his statement that "All comedy, . . . all humor is unfair. . . . There is a beady-eyed view of women in the book, certainly. . . . But a novel is not a report or a biographical statement or a confession. If it is a good novel, it dramatizes thoughts that some people, somewhere, have had."

Viewing the book from this perspective, some critics find it laudable. *Spectator* contributor Harriet Waugh argues, "It does have to be admitted . . . that Mr. Amis's portrayal of Stanley's wives as female monsters is funny and convincing. Most readers will recognise aspects of them in women they know. . . . [Amis] has written a true account of the intolerableness of women in relation to men." Such a tract, she feels, is comparable in many respects to novels by women that show women "downtrodden" by men. Writes Gray, "Amis has excelled at rattling preconceptions ever since the appearance of his classically comic first novel, *Lucky Jim*. . . . Is this novel unfair to women? Probably. Is the question worth asking? No. . . . The females in the world of this book all commit 'offences . . .', at least in the eyes of Stanley, who is . . . nobody's idea of a deep thinker." In the *Times Literary Supplement*, J. K. L. Walker concludes, "*Stanley and the Women* reveals Kingsley Amis in the full flood of his talent and should survive its ritual burning in William IV Street unscathed."

The author's next novel, *The Old Devils*, "manifests little of the female bashing that made the satiric *Stanley and the Women* (1985) so scandalous. In fact, dissatisfied wives are given some tart remarks to make about their variously unsatisfactory husbands. . . . Even so, these concessions never denature Amis's characteristic bite," writes Gray. In a London *Times* review, Victoria Glendinning concurs, "This is vintage Kingsley Amis, 50 percent alcohol, with splashes of savagery about getting old, and about the state of the sex-war in marriages of thirty or more years' standing." Reviewers most admire the book's

major female character; Amis gives her a relationship with her daughter "so close, candid and trusting that the most ardent feminist must applaud," notes Champlin in the *Los Angeles Times Book Review*. Her husband, Alun, an aggressive womanizer, draws the most disfavor. In what Gray feels is the author's "wisest and most humane work," both sexes enjoy their best and worst moments. "This is one of Amis's strengths as a novelist, not noticeably to the fore in recent work but making a welcome return here: 'bad' characters are allowed their victories and 'good' characters their defeats. Yet Amis comes down against Alun in a firmly 'moral' conclusion," comments Morrison in the *Times Literary Supplement*.

Alun's funeral near the close of the book is balanced with "the reconciliation of two of the feuding older generation, and the marriage of two of the younger," such that the ending has "an almost Shakespearean symmetry," relates Morrison. But the mood, he warns, is not exactly one of celebration. He explains that the character Amis seems to most approve "belongs in that tradition of the Amis hero who would like to believe but can't," whose "disappointed scepticism" keeps him from seeing a romantic encouragement behind a pleasant scene. "Finally," reflects Bryan Appleyard in the London *Times*, "it is this sense of an empty, somewhat vacuous age which seems to come close to the heart of all [Amis's] work. His novels are no-nonsense, well-made, good-humored products. They are about the struggle to get by in the gutter and their heroes seldom roll over to gaze at the stars. Like Larkin he is awestruck by the *idea* of religion but he cannot subscribe. Instead, his novels are happily committed to the obliteration of cant without thought of what to put in its place."

For *The Old Devils*, Amis received the Booker-McConnell Prize for Fiction, the most prestigious book award in England. Among critics who feel the prize was well-deserved is Champlin, who refers to "its sheer storytelling expertise, and its qualities of wit, humanity, and observation." In the *New York Times Book Review*, William H. Pritchard recognizes *The Old Devils* as Amis's "most ambitious and one of his longest books, . . . neither a sendup nor an exercise in some established genre. It sets forth, with full realistic detail, a large cast of characters at least six of whom are rendered in depth. . . . 'The Old Devils' is also Mr. Amis's most inclusive novel, encompassing kinds of feeling and tone that move from sardonic gloom to lyric tenderness." Also to the author's credit, says Pritchard, "one is constantly surprised by something extra, a twist or seeming afterthought signifying an originality of mind that is inseparable from the novelist's originality of language." Adds Champlin, "For long-term admirers of the Amis of 'Lucky Jim' and after, 'The Old Devils' is welcome evidence that the master remains masterful, able now to conjoin the mischievous with the mellow. As always, he is an insightful guide through the terrain where what is said is not meant and what is felt is not said, but where much of life is lived."

Critics prize *The Old Devils* for revealing yet another facet of a versatile author. Offers Yardley in the *Washington Post Book World*, "His prose is as tart as ever, which is of course good news, but the softening effect of his feelings for his old devils is even more welcome. More than in any of his previous novels, Kingsley Amis has allowed himself to show a bit of heart; it becomes him." Suggests Morrison, "Words at once true and kind do not come easily to a writer so much of whose energy is taken up in iconoclasm, but *The Old Devils*, like Larkin's similarly undeceived 'The Old Fools', manages at best to be not untrue and not unkind, and not unattracted to the emblem of a man and woman facing uncertainty together hand in hand—all of which helps make this the most affecting of Amis's novels for some time.''

Amis's versatility, particularly apparent in his attempts at genre fiction, makes categorizing him as a novelist difficult. Though some critics share Morrison's perception of an increasing seriousness in his work, others continue to see him primarily as a comic novelist with some serious overtones. Hutchings, a member of the former group, suggests one reason for the conflict: ''A disturbing co-existence of [farce and seriousness] is often to be found in an Amis novel.'' Hutchings points out that this quality of alternating the farcical with the serious has even led some critics to claim that Amis belongs to a line of English novelists exemplified by Henry Fielding: ''Tom Jones, like many of Amis's heroes, finally gets the girl in a triumph of goodheartedness over hypocrisy and meanness.'' But he argues that despite the similarity, ''we are really in a different mode of writing with Amis: What has he to substitute for Fielding's exact relation to past values and literary norms in his use of picaresque and mock-epic? Amis's points of reference are uncompromisingly modern: hence the ghost story of *The Green Man* or (loosely) the science fiction of *The Alteration.*''

Amis continues to elude categorization partly because he actively fights it. ''He loves to bait his readers,'' observes Frederick Busch in a *Chicago Tribune Book World* review of *Stanley and the Women*. More importantly, Amis loves to explore his own capabilities as a novelist. ''I agree with Kipling,'' he explains in a *Publishers Weekly* interview, that ''as soon as you find you can do something, try something you can't. As a professional writer one should range as widely as possible.'' Reflecting on efforts to categorize him and on his excursions into new areas of fiction, Amis muses in *Contemporary Literature:* ''So I'm a funny writer, am I? [*Ending Up*], you'll have to admit, is quite serious. Oh, so I'm primarily a comic writer with some serious overtones and undertones? Try that with *The Anti-Death League* and see how that fits. So I'm a writer about society, twentieth-century man and our problems? Try that one on *The Green Man*. Except for one satirical portrait, that of the clergyman, it is about something quite different. So there is a lot of sex? Try that on [*Ending Up*], in which sexual things [are] referred to, but they've all taken place in the past because of the five central characters the youngest is seventy-one. So you dislike the youth of today, Mr. Amis, as in *Girl, 20?* Try that on [*Ending Up*] where all the young people are sympathetic and all the old people are unsympathetic. This can be silly, but I think it helps to prevent one from repeating oneself, and [Robert] Graves [said] the most dreadful thing in the world is that you're writing a book and you suddenly realize you're writing a book you've written before. Awful. I haven't quite done that yet, but it's certainly something to guard against.''

For *CA* interview with this author, see earlier entry in *CANR-8*.

MEDIA ADAPTATIONS: British Lion filmed *Lucky Jim* in 1957 and *That Uncertain Feeling*, renamed ''Only Two Can Play'' and starring Peter Sellers, in 1961. Columbia produced *Take a Girl Like You* in 1971.

AVOCATIONAL INTERESTS: Music (jazz, Mozart), thrillers, television, science fiction.

BIOGRAPHICAL/CRITICAL SOURCES:

BOOKS

Allen, Walter, *The Modern Novel*, Dutton, 1984.

Allsop, Kenneth, *The Angry Decade*, P. Owen, 1958.
Authors in the News, Volume 2, Gale, 1976.
Bergonzi, Bernard, *The Situation of the Novel*, University of Pittsburgh Press, 1970.
Brophy, Brigid, *Don't Never Forget: Collected Views and Reviews*, Holt, 1967.
Burgess, Anthony, *The Novel Now: A Guide to Contemporary Fiction*, Norton, 1967.
Contemporary Literary Criticism, Gale, Volume 1, 1973, Volume 2, 1974, Volume 3, 1975, Volume 5, 1976, Volume 8, 1978, Volume 13, 1980, Volume 40, 1987, Volume 44, 1988.
Dictionary of Literary Biography, Gale, Volume 15: *British Novelists, 1930-1959*, 1983, Volume 27: *Poets of Great Britain and Ireland, 1945-1960*, 1984.
Dictionary of Literary Biography Yearbook, 1986, Gale, 1987.
Feldman, Gene and Max Gartenberg, editors, *The Beat Generation and the Angry Young Men*, Citadel, 1958.
Gardner, Philip, *Kingsley Amis*, Twayne, 1981.
Gindin, James, *Postwar British Fiction*, University of California Press, 1962.
Gooden, Philip, *Makers of Modern Culture*, Facts on File, 1981.
Johnson, William, compiler, *Focus on the Science Fiction Film*, Prentice-Hall, 1972.
Karl, Frederick R., *The Contemporary English Novel*, Farrar, Straus, 1962.
Lodge, David, *Language of Fiction*, Columbia Unviersity Press, 1966.
Lodge, David, *The Novelist at the Crossroads and Other Essays on Fiction and Criticism*, Cornell University Press, 1971.
Nemerov, Howard, *Poetry and Fiction: Essays*, Rutgers University Press, 1963.
Rabinovitz, Rubin, *The Reaction against Experiment in the English Novel, 1950-1960*, Columbia University Press, 1967.
Shapiro, Charles, editor, *Contemporary British Novelists*, Southern Illinois University Press, 1963.
Wilson, Edmund, *The Bit between My Teeth: A Literary Chronicle of 1950-1965*, Farrar, Straus, 1965.

PERIODICALS

America, May 7, 1977.
Atlantic, April, 1956, April, 1958, July, 1965, June, 1968, June, 1970, February, 1977, November, 1985.
Best Sellers, May 15, 1968, April 4, 1969.
Books and Bookmen, December, 1965, July, 1968, January, 1969, September, 1969, October, 1978.
Bookseller, November 11, 1970.
British Book News, June, 1981.
Chicago Tribune Book World, October 13, 1985.
Choice, November, 1979.
Christian Science Monitor, January 16, 1958, September 24, 1970, September 11, 1985, March 10, 1987.
Commonweal, March 21, 1958.
Contemporary Literature, winter, 1975.
Critical Quarterly, summer, 1977.
Critique, spring-summer, 1966, Volume IX, number 1, 1968, summer, 1977.
Encounter, November, 1974, January, 1979, September/October, 1984.
Essays in Criticism, January, 1980.
Hudson Review, summer, 1972, winter, 1973-74, winter, 1974-75, winter, 1980-81.

Library Journal, July, 1970.

Life, May 3, 1968, March 14, 1969, August 28, 1970.

Listener, November 9, 1967, January 11, 1968, November 26, 1970, May 30, 1974, October 7, 1976, May 22, 1980, October 23, 1980, May 24, 1984, October 16, 1986.

London Magazine, January, 1968, August, 1968, October, 1968, January, 1970, January, 1981, October, 1986.

London Review of Books, June 7-June 20, 1984, September 18, 1986, December 4, 1986, April 2, 1987.

London Sunday Times, September 28, 1986.

Los Angeles Times, September 25, 1985.

Los Angeles Times Book Review, May 4, 1980, April 26, 1987.

Manchester Guardian, February 2, 1954, August 23, 1955, November 30, 1956.

Nation, January 30, 1954, August 20, 1955, April 28, 1969, May 5, 1969, October 5, 1970, April 7, 1979.

National Observer, September 15, 1969, June 29, 1977.

National Review, June 18, 1968, June 3, 1969, August 25, 1970, October 27, 1973, February 1, 1974, March 14, 1975, October 27, 1983, February 22, 1985, May 8, 1987.

New Leader, September 21, 1970, December 6, 1976.

New Republic, March 24, 1958, September 19, 1970, October 12, 1974, May 28, 1977, November 26, 1977, February 25, 1985, May 30, 1987.

New Statesman, January 30, 1954, August 20, 1955, January 18, 1958, September 24, 1960, November 28, 1963, July 7, 1967, December 1, 1967, October 11, 1968, November 21, 1975, October 8, 1976, September 15, 1978, April 13, 1979, May 23, 1980, December 5, 1980, September 19, 1986.

Newsweek, March 2, 1964, May 8, 1967, May 6, 1968, September 14, 1970, September 30, 1974, January 17, 1977, February 4, 1985.

New Yorker, March 6, 1954, March 24, 1958, April 26, 1969, September 13, 1969, October 21, 1974, March 14, 1977, August 20, 1979, April 27, 1987.

New York Review of Books, October 6, 1966, August 1, 1968, March 9, 1972, March 20, 1975, April 15, 1976, March 3, 1977, May 17, 1979, March 26, 1987.

New York Times, January 31, 1954, February 26, 1956, February 23, 1958, April 25, 1967, April 25, 1968, March 12, 1969, August 17, 1970, January 6, 1972, May 11, 1979, September 14, 1985, October 8, 1985, November 8, 1986, February 25, 1987.

New York Times Book Review, April 28, 1963, July 25, 1965, April 28, 1968, May 19, 1968, March 23, 1969, August 23, 1970, November 11, 1973, October 20, 1974, April 18, 1976, January 30, 1977, May 13, 1979, January 13, 1985, June 13, 1985, September 22, 1985, March 22, 1987.

Observer, October 10, 1976, December 12, 1976, February 12, 1978, July 23, 1978.

Observer Review, November 12, 1967, October 6, 1968.

Paris Review, winter, 1975.

Poetry, spring, 1968, July, 1969.

Publishers Weekly, October 28, 1974.

Punch, April 24, 1968, August 28, 1968, October 12, 1968, October 22, 1969, November 18, 1970, October 4, 1978.

Saturday Review, February 20, 1954, May 7, 1955, February 25, 1956, July 27, 1957, March 8, 1958, April 6, 1963, April 5, 1969, February 5, 1977, May/June, 1985.

Saturday Review/World, May 8, 1973.

Spectator, January 29, 1954, September 2, 1955, January 17, 1958, September 23, 1960, October 11, 1969, October

9, 1976, June 2, 1984, September 13, 1986, November 29, 1986, December 6, 1986.

Time, May 27, 1957, August 31, 1970, September 10, 1973, September 30, 1974, January 3, 1977, June 12, 1978, September 20, 1985, September 30, 1985, March 9, 1987.

Times (London), May 15, 1980, December 31, 1980, May 17, 1984, May 24, 1984, December 15, 1984, September 4, 1986, September 11, 1986, October 23, 1986, December 12, 1987, March 26, 1988.

Times Literary Supplement, February 12, 1954, September 16, 1955, January 17, 1958, September 21, 1962, November 23, 1967, March 28, 1968, September 24, 1971, April 6, 1973, October 8, 1976, September 22, 1978, May 16, 1980, October 24, 1980, November 27, 1981, May 25, 1984, September 12, 1986, December 26, 1986.

Tribune Books (Chicago), March 8, 1987.

Vanity Fair, May, 1987.

Village Voice, October 25, 1973.

Washington Post, September 10, 1973.

Washington Post Book World, May 5, 1968, August 8, 1968, October 20, 1968, September 1, 1985, March 1, 1987.

Wilson Library Bulletin, May, 1958, May, 1965.

World, May 8, 1973.

World Literature Today, summer, 1977, winter, 1977.

Yale Review, autumn, 1969, summer, 1975.*

—*Sketch by Marilyn K. Basel*

*   *   *

AMRAM, David (Werner III)   1930-

PERSONAL: Born November 17, 1930, in Philadelphia, Pa.; son of Philip Werner (a lawyer and writer) and Emilie (Weyl) Amram; married Lora Lee Ecobelli, January 7, 1979; children: Alana Asha. *Education:* Attended Oberlin Conservatory of Music, 1948-49; George Washington University, B.A., 1952; Manhattan School of Music, graduate study, 1955-56; studied composition with Vittorio Giannini, and french horn with Gunther Schuller.

ADDRESSES: Home—461 Sixth Ave., New York, N.Y. 10011. *Office*—c/o Barna Ostertag, 501 Fifth Ave., Room 1410, New York, N.Y. 10017.

CAREER: Composer, conductor, musician. Worked at various odd jobs prior to stage assignments, including truck driver, gym teacher, and short order cook. Musician, National Symphony Orchestra, 1951-52, United States Information Agency, and Hotel des Etats Unis, Paris, France; played with various jazz groups, including those of Charlie Mingus, Sonny Rollins, Oscar Pettiford; played with his own group, Amram-Barrow Jazz Quartet, 1955. Musical director, New York Shakespeare Festival, New York City, 1956-68, and Phoenix Theatre, 1958. Guest composer in residence, Marlboro Music Festival, Ver., 1961; first composer in residence, New York Philharmonic Orchestra, New York City, 1966-67, and at city schools of Birmingham, Ala., 1972; first composer/conductor in residence, All-State High School Orchestra, Saratoga Springs, New York, 1970. Conductor for World Council of Churches in Kenya, Africa, 1975. Conductor of own work on "Sound Stage," PBS-TV, 1978. Cultural ambassador for the State Department in ten countries, including Brazil, May, 1969, Central America, 1977, and the Middle East, 1978. *Military service:* U.S. Army, horn player in Seventh Army Symphony Orchestra, 1952-54.

MEMBER: American Federation of Musicians.

AWARDS, HONORS: Obie Award, *Village Voice,* 1959, for compositions for Phoenix Theatre and New York Shakespeare Festival; Doctor of Laws, Moravian College, 1979.

WRITINGS:

Vibrations: The Adventures and Musician Times of David Amram (autobiography), Macmillan, 1968.

COMPOSITIONS

"The Passion of Joseph D." (incidental music for play of the same title), first produced on Broadway at Ethel Barrymore Theatre, February 11, 1964.
Two Anthems for Mixed Voices A Cappella (choral work), C.F. Peters, 1964.
Three Songs for Marlboro, Horn and Violincello (chamber music), C. F. Peters, 1964.
Shir L'Erev Shabat: Friday Evening Service for Tenor Solo, SATB, and Organ (first performed in New York at Town Hall by Beaux Arts Quartet with George Shirley, February 20, 1962), C.F. Peters, 1965.
(With others) "A Year in Our Land" (cantata), first performed in New York City at Town Hall by Interracial Chorus and Orchestra, May 13, 1965.
(With Langston Hughes) "Let Us Remember" (cantata), first performed at San Francisco Bay Opera House, November, 1965.
(With Arnold Weinstein) "The Final Ingredient" (opera), first networked by American Broadcasting Companies (ABC-TV) for "Directions '65," April 11, 1965.
"Twelfth Night" (opera), first produced in Lake George, N.Y., at Lake George Opera Festival, August 1, 1968.
"Three Songs for America" (voice and orchestra), first performed on National Educational Television, April 27, 1969.

Author of jazz poetry and music for jazz poetry reading with Jack Kerouac at Brata Art Gallery, New York, N.Y. Also composer of choral works *By the River of Babylon, The American Bell, Let Us Remember, Five Shakespearean Songs, The Trail of Beauty, Kaddish, May the Words of the Lord, Yigdal, Rejoice in the Lord,* and *Thou Shalt Love the Lord, Thy God,* and others, all published by C.F. Peters; Composer of symphonies, chamber music, incidental music for theater, and film and television scores.

SIDELIGHTS: Praised by musical critics and musicians of various genres, David Amram has been called by *Saturday Review* contributor Victor Chaplin "a composer who may write the great American opera and already has created some of the best incidental theatre music of our time." Amram's autobiography, *Vibrations: The Adventures and Musician Times of David Amram,* has likewise received critical praise. Thomas Lask states in the *New York Times* that "the great quality of his book is zest. He relishes everything. He is always moving forward to meet life. He is the least introspective of men; he never apologizes for his existence; he never tries to explain it away; he enjoys it. His responses are infectious."

AVOCATIONAL INTERESTS: Kayaking, sailing, skiing, running track, playing jazz, learning languages.

BIOGRAPHICAL/CRITICAL SOURCES:

BOOKS

Amram, David, *Vibrations: The Adventures and Musician Times of David Amram,* Macmillan, 1968.

PERIODICALS

Life, August 11, 1967.

Nation, December 9, 1968.
New York Times, October 15, 1968, February 20, 1969.
Saturday Review, November 2, 1968, November 16, 1968.
Washington Post, October 18, 1968, November 2, 1968.

*   *   *

ANDERSON, J(ohn) K(inloch)   1924-
   (John K. Anderson)

PERSONAL: Born January 3, 1924, in Multan, Pakistan; son of Sir James Drummond and Jean (MacPherson) Anderson; married Esperance Batham, August 10, 1954; children: Elizabeth, John, Katherine. *Education:* Oxford University, B.A., 1949, M.A., 1958. *Politics:* Conservative. *Religion:* Church of England.

ADDRESSES: Home—1020 Middlefield Rd., Berkeley, Calif. 94709. *Office*—Department of Classics, University of California, Berkeley, Calif. 94720.

CAREER: University of Otago, Dunedin, New Zealand, lecturer in classics, 1953-58; University of California, Berkeley, assistant professor, 1958-60, associate professor of classical archaeology, 1960—. Participated in excavations in Corinth, Greece, with American School of Archaeology, 1945, and in Greece and Turkey with British School of Archaeology, 1949-52. *Military service:* British Army, 1942-46; became lieutenant.

MEMBER: Archaeological Institute of America (former president, San Francisco branch), Society of Hellenic Studies (London).

AWARDS, HONORS: Guggenheim fellowship, 1966-67; Society of Antiquaries (London) fellow, 1976.

WRITINGS:

Greek Vases in the Otago Museum, Otago Museum, 1955.
Ancient Greek Horsemanship, University of California Press, 1961.
Military Theory and Practice in the Age of Xenophon, University of California Press, 1971.
Xenophon, Scribner, 1974.
(Editor) H. R. W. Smith, *Funerary Symbolism in Apulian Vase-Painting,* University of California Press, 1976.
(Under name John K. Anderson) *Horses and Riding* (juvenile), Bellerophon Books, 1979.
(Under name John K. Anderson) *Tales of Great Dragons,* Bellerophon Books, 1980.
(Under name John K. Anderson) *Alexander the Great,* Bellerophon Books, 1981.
Hunting in the Ancient World, University of California Press, 1985.
(Editor) J. Fontenrose, *Didyma,* University of California Press, 1988.

Contributor of articles and reviews to scholarly journals.

SIDELIGHTS: J. K. Anderson, author of *Hunting in the Ancient World,* is a professor of classical archaeology and himself an experienced hunter. Peter Green in the *Times Literary Supplement* praises Anderson's profile of "ancient venery" for its "lavish quotations from ancient sources and crisply authoritative glossing of technical problems." Green continues: "Anderson brings to his task a cool eye as well as a most elegant style: both seat and hands, you might say, are eminently reliable."

BIOGRAPHICAL/CRITICAL SOURCES:

PERIODICALS

Times Literary Supplement, April 25, 1986.

* * *

ANDERSON, John K.
See ANDERSON, J(ohn) K(inloch)

* * *

ANDERSON, Madelyn Klein

PERSONAL: Born in New York, N.Y.; daughter of Max W. and Fannie (Siegel) Klein; married Douglas Ray Anderson (deceased); children: Justin Lee. *Education:* Hunter College (now Hunter College of the City University of New York), B.A., 1951; New York University, certificate in occupational therapy, 1958; Pratt Institute, M.L.S., 1974.

ADDRESSES: Home—80 North Moore St., New York, N.Y. 10013. *Agent*—Paul Reynolds, Inc., 12 East 41st St., New York, N.Y., 10017.

CAREER: Beth Israel Hospital, New York City, director of occupational therapy, 1959-63; New York Infirmary, New York City, director of occupational therapy, 1968-72; Julian Messner, Inc., New York City, senior editor, 1974-83; free-lance editor, 1983—. *Military service:* U.S. Army, Women's Medical Specialist Corps, 1954-55; became lieutenant.

MEMBER: PEN, Beta Phi Mu.

WRITINGS:

Iceberg Alley, Messner, 1976.
Sea Raids and Rescues: The United States Coast Guard, McKay, 1979.
Counting on You: The U.S. Census, Vanguard Press, 1980.
Oil in Troubled Waters: Cleaning up Oil Spills, Vanguard Press, 1983.
Greenland: Island at the Top of the World, Dodd, 1983.
The New Zoos, F. Watts, 1986.
Environmental Disease, F. Watts, 1987.
Siberia, Dodd, 1988.
Arthritis, F. Watts, 1989.
Poe, F. Watts, in press.

SIDELIGHTS: Madelyn Klein Anderson comments that the death of her husband in Vietnam "led to a drastic career change which in turn led to the development of my writing. I had travelled extensively as a military wife, but my most exciting trip was in connection with *Iceberg Alley,* when I travelled on a Coast Guard C130 to Newfoundland and Greenland. Travel and collecting rare books and antiques keeps me busy—and broke—in between books."

BIOGRAPHICAL/CRITICAL SOURCES:

PERIODICALS

Washington Post Book World, March 13, 1988.

* * *

ANTHONY, Geraldine C(ecilia) 1919-

PERSONAL: Born October 5, 1919, in Brooklyn, N.Y.; daughter of William (a pharmacist) and Agnes (Murphy) Anthony. *Education:* Attended Boston College, 1945-47; Mount St. Vincent University, B.A., 1951; St. John's University, New York, N.Y., M.A., 1956, Ph.D., 1963; post-doctoral study at Exeter College, Oxford, University of Minnesota, and Columbia University.

ADDRESSES: Home—51 Marlwood Dr., Wedgewood Park, Halifax, Nova Scotia, Canada B3M 3H4. *Office*—Department of English, Mount St. Vincent University, 166 Bedford Highway, Halifax, Nova Scotia, Canada B3M 2J6.

CAREER: Member of Roman Catholic women's congregation, the Sisters of Charity, 1939—; junior high school teacher at Roman Catholic schools in Dorchester, Mass., 1942-48, Lowell, Mass., 1948-51, and Bellmore, N.Y., 1951-62; high school teacher of English in Halifax, Nova Scotia, 1963-65; Mount St. Vincent University, Halifax, assistant professor, 1965-71, associate professor, 1971-77, professor of English, 1977-87, professor emeritus, 1987—, director of summer school, 1966-68, chairman of department, 1983-86. Visiting professor at Hofstra University, summers, 1970-74. Coordinator of annual Mount St. Vincent University/Oxford University summer school, 1985—.

MEMBER: Modern Language Association of America, Association for Canadian Theatre History (member of executive board), Association of Canadian and Quebecois Literature, Association of Canadian University Teachers of English, Delta Kappa Gamma (founding member of Nova Scotia chapter).

AWARDS, HONORS: Wall Street Journal fellow at University of Minnesota, 1965; Canada Council grants, 1975, 1976, 1977, and 1978, for research to complete *Gwen Pharis Ringwood;* British High Council grant, 1983.

WRITINGS:

John Coulter, G. K. Hall, 1976.
(Editor) *Profiles in Canadian Drama,* three volumes, Gage, 1977.
Stage Voices, Doubleday, 1978.
Gwen Pharis Ringwood, G. K. Hall, 1981.
(Contributor) *Canadian Biographical Dictionary,* University of British Columbia Press, 1982.
"Nunc et Semper: A Call to Radical Sisterhood" (multi-media documentary play), first produced in Halifax, Nova Scotia, July 3, 1988.

Also author of *This Is Barbara's Life,* 1956. Author of children's plays. Contributor to *Dictionary of Literary Biography* and *Canadian Book Review Annual.* Contributor to periodicals, including *Atlantis, Canadian Drama, Canadian Theatre Review, Canadian Library Journal, Cithara, World Literature, Canadian Children's Literature, Canadian Review of American Studies, Prairie Forum, Theatre History in Canada, Great Plains Quarterly,* and *Canadian Literature.* Member of editorial board of *Canadian Drama/L'Art Dramatique Canadien.*

WORK IN PROGRESS: A book on historical and political Canadian drama; a biography of notable Sister of Charity, Sister Irene Farmer.

SIDELIGHTS: Geraldine C. Anthony told *CA* her interest in theatre "stemmed from my childhood in New York and my father's keen interest in the Broadway musicals. He stimulated me to a love of theatre that has become a passion, transferred from American to Canadian drama when I moved to Canada in 1963 and discovered that very little had been done in the way of dramatic literary criticism. Today many Canadian scholars are devoting more and more time to research in this field. I am happy to have been one of the first.''

Anthony continued: ''Thirty years ago, I had the temerity to write a few children's plays and had them produced in St. Barnabas School in New York in the 1950's. Until recently, the only other creative theatre venture was a slide projection show with voice-over on the life of the Sister of Charity, plus a book on the same topic: *This Is Barbara's Life*. In 1988, at the request of the Congregation, I wrote a multi-media documentary on the three hundred year history of the Sisters of Charity from its foundation in France in the seventeenth century by St. Vincent de Paul, to its American foundation by St. Elizabeth Ann Seton in the early nineteenth century, to its Halifax branch in 1849, and finally to the extraordinary changes in today's religious life after Vatican II in 1968. The present status of Roman Catholic religious congregations of women is highlighted in this play, 'Nunc et Semper: A Call to Radical Sisterhood.'

''Present day supporters of the feminist movement might see in this play all the desirable elements of the feminist cause, such as independence, a flexible life style, financial support for higher education in professional fields, colleague support in the strength and dedicated love of fellow religious, concentrated work for the poor and destitute in North America and in Third World countries. Again, theatre provides the means for a graphic portrayal of contemporary life—this time in the lives of nuns moving rapidly into the twenty-first century, newly dedicated to solidarity with the economically poor. I am glad that my academic life centered on theatre. It has made all the difference in my own life in contact with the theatre people whom I am proud to call my friends.''

*　　*　　*

ANTHONY, Piers 1934-
(Robert Piers, a joint pseudonym)

PERSONAL: Name originally Piers Anthony Dillingham Jacob; born August 6, 1934, in Oxford, England; came to United States, 1940, naturalized, 1958; son of Alfred Bennis and Norma (Sherlock) Jacob; married Carol Marble (a computer programmer), June 23, 1956; children: Penelope Carolyn, Cheryl. *Education:* Goddard College, B.A., 1956; University of South Florida, teaching certificate, 1964. *Politics:* Independent. *Religion:* ''No preference.''

ADDRESSES: Office—c/o Press Relations, Ace Books, Berkley Publishing Corp., 200 Madison Ave., New York, N.Y. 10016.

CAREER: Electronic Communications, Inc., St. Petersburg, Fla., technical writer, 1959-62; free-lance writer, 1962-63; Admiral Farragut Academy, St. Petersburg, teacher of English, 1965-66; free-lance writer, 1966—. *Military service:* U.S. Army, 1957-59.

AWARDS, HONORS: Nebula Award nomination, Science Fiction Writers of America, 1966, for short story ''The Message''; Nebula Award nomination, 1967, and Hugo Award nomination, World Science Fiction Convention, 1968, both for *Chthon;* science fiction award, Pyramid Books/*Magazine of Fantasy and Science Fiction*/Kent Productions, 1967, and Hugo Award nomination, 1968, both for *Sos the Rope;* Hugo Award nomination, 1969, for novella ''Getting through University,'' and 1970, for *Macroscope* and for best fan writer; Nebula Award nomination, 1970, for short story ''The Bridge,''

and 1972, for novelette ''In the Barn''; British Fantasy Award, 1977, and Hugo Award nomination, 1978, both for *A Spell for Chameleon.*

WRITINGS:

Chthon (science fiction), Ballantine, 1967, reprinted, Berkley Publishing, 1982.
(With Robert E. Margroff) *The Ring*, Ace Books, 1968.
Macroscope (science fiction), Avon, 1969, reprinted, Gregg Press, 1985.
(With Margroff) *The E.S.P. Worm*, Paperback Library, 1970, reprinted, Tor Books, 1986.
Prostho Plus (science fiction), Gollancz, 1971, Bantam, 1973.
Race against Time (juvenile), Hawthorne, 1973.
Rings of Ice (science fiction), Avon, 1974.
Triple Detente (science fiction), DAW Books, 1974.
Phthor (sequel to *Chthon;* science fiction), Berkley Publishing, 1975.
(With Robert Coulson) *But What of Earth?* (science fiction), Laser (Toronto), 1976.
Steppe (science fiction), Millington, 1976, Tor Books, 1985.
Hasan (fantasy), Borgo Press, 1977.
(With Frances Hall) *The Pretender* (science fiction), Borgo Press, 1979.
God of Tarot (first section of *Tarot;* also see below), Jove, 1979.
Vision of Tarot (second section of *Tarot;* also see below), Berkley Publishing, 1980.
Faith of Tarot (third section of *Tarot;* also see below), Berkley Publishing, 1980.
Mute (science fiction), Avon, 1981.
Anthonology (short stories), Tor Books, 1985.
Ghost (science fiction), Tor Books, 1986.
Shade of the Tree, St. Martin's, 1986.
(With Margroff) *Dragon's Gold*, Tor Books, 1987.
Tarot (contains *God of Tarot*, *Vision of Tarot*, and *Faith of Tarot*), Ace Books, 1987.
Bio of an Ogre (autobiography), Ace Books, 1988.
(With Margroff) *Serpent's Silver*, Tor Books, 1988.
Balook, Underwood-Miller, 1989.
(With Robert Kornwise) *Through the Ice*, Underwood-Miller, 1990.

''APPRENTICE ADEPT'' SERIES; SCIENCE FICTION/FANTASY NOVELS

Split Infinity (also see below), Del Rey, 1980.
Blue Adept (also see below), Del Rey, 1981.
Juxtaposition (also see below), Del Rey, 1982.
Out of Phaze, Ace Books, 1987.
Robot Adept, Ace Books, 1988.
Unicorn Point, Ace Books, 1989.
Phase Doubt, Ace Books, in press.

''BATTLE CIRCLE'' SERIES; SCIENCE FICTION NOVELS

Sos the Rope (also see below), Pyramid, 1968.
Var the Stick (also see below), Faber, 1972, Bantam, 1973.
Neq the Sword (also see below), Corgi, 1975.

''BIO OF A SPACE TYRANT'' SERIES; SCIENCE FICTION NOVELS

Refugee, Avon, 1983.
Mercenary, Avon, 1984.
Politician, Avon, 1985.
Executive, Avon, 1985.
Statesman, Avon, 1986.

"CLUSTER" SERIES; SCIENCE FANTASY NOVELS

Cluster, Avon, 1977 (published in England as *Vicinity Cluster*, Panther, 1979).
Chaining the Lady, Avon, 1978.
Kirlian Quest, Avon, 1978.
Thousandstar, Avon, 1980.
Viscous Circle, Avon, 1982.

"INCARNATIONS OF IMMORTALITY" SERIES; FANTASY NOVELS

On a Pale Horse, Del Rey, 1983.
Bearing an Hourglass, Del Rey, 1984.
With a Tangled Skein, Del Rey, 1985.
Wielding a Red Sword, Del Rey, 1987.
Being a Green Mother, Del Rey, 1987.
For Love of Evil, Morrow, 1988.
And Eternity, Morrow, in press.

"JASON STRIKER" SERIES; WITH ROBERTO FUENTES; MARTIAL ARTS NOVELS

Kiai!, Berkley Publishing, 1974.
Mistress of Death, Berkley Publishing, 1974.
The Bamboo Bloodbath, Berkley Publishing, 1975.
Ninja's Revenge, Berkley Publishing, 1975.
Amazon Slaughter, Berkley Publishing, 1976.

"MAGIC OF XANTH" SERIES; FANTASY NOVELS

A Spell for Chameleon (also see below), Del Rey, 1977.
The Source of Magic (also see below), Del Rey, 1979.
Castle Roogna (also see below), Del Rey, 1979.
Centaur Aisle, Del Rey, 1981.
Ogre, Ogre, Del Rey, 1982.
Night Mare, Del Rey, 1983.
Dragon on a Pedestal, Del Rey, 1983.
Crewel Lye: A Caustic Yarn, Del Rey, 1985.
Golem in the Gears, Del Rey, 1986.
Vale of the Vole, Avon, 1987.
Heaven Cent, Avon, 1988.
Man from Mundania, Avon, in press.

"OMNIVORE" SERIES; SCIENCE FICTION NOVELS

Omnivore, Ballantine, 1968.
Orn, Avon, 1971.
Ox, Avon, 1976.

OTHER

(Contributor) Anthony Cheetham, editor, *Science against Man*, Avon, 1970.
(Contributor) Harry Harrison, editor, *Nova One: An Anthology of Original Science Fiction*, Delacorte Press, 1970.
(Contributor) Harlan Ellison, editor, *Again, Dangerous Visions*, Doubleday, 1972.
(Contributor) David Gerrold, editor, *Generation*, Dell, 1972.
Battle Circle (omnibus volume; includes *Sos the Rope*, *Var the Stick*, and *Neq the Sword*), Avon, 1978.
(Contributor) Victoria Schochet and John Silbersack, editors, *The Berkley Showcase*, Berkley Publishing, 1981.
The Magic of Xanth (omnibus volume; includes *A Spell for Chameleon*, *The Source of Magic*, and *Castle Roogna*), Doubleday, 1981.
Double Exposure (omnibus volume; includes *Split Infinity*, *Blue Adept*, and *Juxtaposition*), Doubleday, 1982.
(Editor with Barry Malzberg and Martin Greenberg) *Uncollected Stars* (short stories), Avon, 1986.

Also contributor, with Robert Margroff, under joint pseudonym Robert Piers, of a short story to *Adam Bedside Reader*.

Also contributor of short stories to science fiction periodicals, including *Analog, Fantastic, Worlds of If, Worlds of Tomorrow, Amazing, Magazine of Fantasy and Science Fiction*, and *Pandora*.

WORK IN PROGRESS: Firefly, a horror story; *Tatham Mound*, a historical novel; *The Illustrated Encyclopedia of Xanth*, with Jody Lynn Nye.

SIDELIGHTS: "Piers Anthony," states Michael R. Collings in his study *Piers Anthony*, ". . . has become one of the most prolific and controversial writers in the genre" of fantasy/science fiction. An author whose "early fiction earned him a name as a solid writer with flashes of brilliance," Anthony "survived a blackballing by publishers" to emerge in the 1980s as a highly successful novelist with a broad readership and a large output, according to Daryl Lane, Bill Vernon, and David Carson in their introduction to Anthony's interview in *The Sound of Wonder: Interviews from "The Science Fiction Radio Show," Volume 2*. His works, including the highly popular "Magic of Xanth," "Apprentice Adept," and "Bio of a Space Tyrant" series, are often enjoyed by people who do not ordinarily read science fiction or fantasy, and his novels have appeared on bestseller lists.

The author suggests, in an interview with Charles Platt published in *Dream Makers Volume II: The Uncommon Men and Women Who Write Science Fiction*, that his light fantasy is popular because his readers are "tired when they come home, they don't want to read *War and Peace*, they just want to relax and be entertained." Yet Anthony's popularity does not detract from the quality of his work. Baird Searles and his fellow editors state in *A Reader's Guide to Science Fiction*, "Piers Anthony is one of those authors who can perform magic with the ordinary; he manages to take what at first glance seems to be a fairly pedestrian plot and make of it something rather special." "He is highly imaginative, but at the same time self-consistent; much of what is said about one novel is applicable to others. He is a careful craftsman in his plotting and in creating an array of truly alien characters," declares Collings. "Anthony is a craftsman," conclude the editors of *A Reader's Guide to Science Fiction*, "and, like a skilled furniture builder who can make a chair much more than a place to sit, makes a book more than words to read. Don't be misled by plot summary of any of his works; even if it sounds like you may have read it before by another author, Anthony will give you something extra." "That something," according to Collings, "is frequently an irrepressible sense of fun, of excitement, and of energy."

Anthony's first published novel, the Nebula and Hugo Award nominee *Chthon*, and its sequel *Phthor* share characteristic structures and themes with the rest of his fiction. In these books, declares Collings, Anthony "weaves a complex tapestry of myth and legend drawn from classical antiquity; from Norseland; from the Christian Eden and Paradise Lost; from Dante's Purgatory; from the modern mythologies of psychoanalysis and psychology; from literature; and from folk tales of magicians and dragons." *Chthon* relates the adventures of Aton Five, a prisoner sentenced to dwell inside a hellish planet. Eventually he establishes contact with the planet itself—Chthon, an intelligent mineral entity—and comes to terms with it. *Phthor* tells of Aton's son, Arlo, who brings the conflict between the collected mineral and organic intelligences to a destructive conclusion. Both books showcase Anthony's representative themes and devices, says Collings: control and order in civilization, the unity of life, punning and wordplay, and fertility or sterility. "The novels are complex, convoluted, inverted—and powerful," states Collings. "In incorporating the multiple strands of technique and theme and intertwining them with pre-existent strands of mythology, Anthony has himself created an enduring and a moving myth."

Other novels also explore themes relevant to science fiction and fantasy. *Dictionary of Literary Biography* contributors Stephen Bucchleugh and Beverly Rush note, "In Anthony's best fiction, questions of man's place in the ecology of the natural universe blend with considerations of the individual's role in providing satisfactory and humane answers." This is especially evident in the "Omnivore" books, where "Anthony assesses the human race, finds it lacking in certain essential areas, and then devises a structure by which it might be guided in its progress," says Collings. *Omnivore* itself is "an overt plea for respect for all life—human and animal," he continues. The "Battle Circle" trilogy takes place in a post-nuclear war America, and underlines the need for order in a civilization. *Macroscope*, Anthony's Hugo Award-nominated novel, presents the effects of a machine that shows how unimportant humanity is in comparison to the rest of the universe, and "in doing so, it becomes an allegory on the fate of the individual diminished and possibly destroyed by mass society," declare Bucchleugh and Rush. On a less galactic level, the *Tarot* novel—originally published in three volumes as *God of Tarot*, *Vision of Tarot*, and *Faith of Tarot*—takes as its theme "questions of individual belief," according to Bucchleugh and Rush. "Much of the quest here is an internal one as Brother Paul of the secular Holy Order of Vision is sent to the planet Tarot to investigate the strange animations which may represent manifestations of the deity," they continue. "Paul's journey is both inward and outward as he finds companions in his quest, confronts temptations, fails and recovers, and finally faces his own personal hell."

Characterized by a light-hearted approach and the extensive use of puns, Anthony's "Xanth" fantasy novels are perhaps his most popular work. Xanth is a magic peninsula, sometimes resembling Florida, that makes occasional contacts with the outside world, known as Mundania. Populated with a variety of curious creatures—shoe-trees that grow shoes and chocolate-chip cookie bushes, for instance, as well as dragons, ogres, centaurs and nymphs—the country provides a rich background for Anthony's questing characters. *Fantasy Review* contributor Richard Mathews calls the Xanth series "one of the happiest things to happen to fantasy in a very long time." He maintains that *Dragon on a Pedestal*, the seventh Xanth novel, "exudes energy, humor and delightful invention." "This, like all the Xanth tales, is episodic in structure, and rich in classic mythic reference," he continues. "Anthony is assembling, bit by bit, his own *Arabian Nights*." Mathews concludes by stating his belief that "the entire Xanth series ranks with the best of American and classic fantasy literature." Bob Collins, also writing for *Fantasy Review*, echoes Mathews's assessment, comparing Xanth to L. Frank Baum's land of Oz.

Other reviewers are not so enthusiastic. They find too much sexist humor and too great a reliance on puns in the "Xanth" novels. Baird Searles and his fellow editors in the *Reader's Guide to Fantasy*, for instance, consider the Xanth novels "a wee bit cute in their humor," and suggest that they "may tend to irritate some feminists." "The punning, more subdued in earlier books, goes wild here from the title onward," asserts *Science Fiction Review* contributor Philip M. Cohen, writing about the fourth Xanth novel, *Centaur Aisle*. He concludes: "You must be prepared to suspend disbelief—by the neck,

until dead—and maturity as well; the ideal audience of this book is probably fourteen-year-olds. If you do, it's fun." Paul McGuire, also of *Science Fiction Review*, says of *Crewel Lye: A Caustic Yarn*, "At times the writing can be relentlessly cute, and it takes the plot a long time to get started. On the other hand, there is a fair amount of genuine wit in addition to the endless puns, the bumbling lout who is the hero does grow on one, a peculiar logic underlies the silliness of Xanth, and Anthony is a storyteller." When ordinary fantasy fare palls, he declares, "Xanth at the very least is something different inside, and a quite pleasant read."

Anthony states in his *Sound of Wonder* interview that he conceived the "Apprentice Adept" series to challenge two mutually exclusive audiences: science fiction readers who don't like fantasy and fantasy readers who won't read science fiction. "I thought the 'fantasy as pollution' people would be angry and so would the other side," he remarks. "I don't think I received a single negative comment on it; everybody seemed to like it, and they wanted more." Indeed, many critics support Anthony's assessment. "Aliens and unicorns in the same novel!" exclaims a reviewer for the *Science Fiction Chronicle*, writing about *Out of Phaze*. "It's easily the most interesting of Anthony's recent novels." *Science Fiction and Fantasy Book Review*'s Richard W. Miller declares, "In fact, Anthony shows nice growth in his treatment of women in this series; they are not so stereotyped as, say, in the Xanth series." "What Anthony has done here (also in the Xanth series, but better in this [series])," Miller continues, "is to argue effectively for the basic human need for magic. Even the dedicated SF fan is likely to find that the magical (yet natural) world of Phaze has more appeal than its parallel/adjacent scientific (and ecologically controlled) analog, Proton."

The "Bio of a Space Tyrant" and "Incarnations of Immortality" series introduce what Roland Green of *Booklist* calls "Anthony's new 'serious' phase." Although the "Incarnations" volumes are fantasy and the "Bio" sequence is space opera, Anthony uses the forms as vehicles for social commentary. For instance, the "Incarnations of Immortality" feature Death, Time, Space, War, and Nature as protagonists, involved in a conflict against Satan. Mary S. Weinkauf of *Fantasy Review* calls *On a Pale Horse*, the first volume of the "Incarnations" series, "allegorical fantasy set in a future not much different from ours except in the use of magical stones and flying carpets." The "Bio of a Space Tyrant" series is "based on the Vietnamese boat people, really," Anthony tells Platt. It chronicles the rise of a space refugee to power on Jupiter, exploring problems of contemporary America in a science fictional setting. By the end of the third novel in the sequence, says Collings in *Fantasy Review*, Anthony "has explored capital punishment, warfare as political tool, US/Soviet relations, rights for the aged, bilingual education and flaws in the current electoral system."

Anthony tells the interviewers in *The Sound of Wonder*: "I'd like to think I'm on Earth for some purpose other than just to feed my face. I want to do something and try to leave the universe a better place than it was when I came into it. If there is anything in my power I can do to improve things, then I want to do it. I try to do this through the ability that I have as a writer, so I want to write, in the guise of fiction, material that people will read and become better persons for or get ideas that they wouldn't ordinarily have. . . . I want to do something so that when I die, I can look back and say I've done something useful in the world."

BIOGRAPHICAL/CRITICAL SOURCES:

BOOKS

Anthony, Piers, *Bio of an Ogre,* Ace Books, 1988.

Collings, Michael R., *Piers Anthony,* Starmont House, 1983.

Contemporary Literary Criticism, Volume 35, Gale, 1985.

Dictionary of Literary Biography, Volume 8: *Twentieth-Century American Science Fiction Writers,* Gale, 1981.

Lane, Daryl, William Vernon, and David Carson, *The Sound of Wonder: Interviews from "The Science Fiction Radio Show," Volume 2,* Oryx Press, 1985.

Platt, Charles, *Dream Makers Volume II: The Uncommon Men and Women Who Write Science Fiction,* Berkley Publishing, 1983.

Searles, Baird, Beth Meacham, and Michael Franklin, *A Reader's Guide to Fantasy,* Avon, 1982.

Searles, Baird, Martin Last, Beth Meacham, and Michael Franklin, *A Reader's Guide to Science Fiction,* Avon, 1979.

PERIODICALS

Analog Science Fact/Science Fiction, March 30, 1981.

Booklist, June 1, 1979, July, 1984.

Books and Bookmen, July, 1969, December, 1969, April, 1970.

Fantasy Review, March, 1984, April, 1984, June, 1984, August, 1984, October, 1984, April, 1985, October, 1985, November, 1985, December, 1985, January, 1986, March, 1986, April, 1986, May, 1986, September, 1986, October, 1986, November, 1986, December, 1986, March, 1987, July, 1987.

Los Angeles Times Book Review, August 17, 1980, December 11, 1983, January 1, 1984, March 3, 1985.

Magazine of Fantasy and Science Fiction, July, 1986.

New York Times Book Review, April 20, 1986.

Observer, January 10, 1971.

Punch, April 4, 1984.

Science Fiction and Fantasy Book Review, March, 1982, July, 1982, October, 1983.

Science Fiction Chronicle, July, 1985, January, 1986, July, 1986, August, 1986, October, 1986, December, 1986, November, 1987.

Science Fiction Review, November, 1977, November, 1979, August, 1982, November, 1983, February, 1985, May, 1985, November, 1985, May, 1986, August, 1986.

Science Fiction Studies, Volume 2, 1975.

Times (London), May 14, 1983.

Times Literary Supplement, May 22, 1969, February 11, 1972, July 5, 1974.*

—*Sketch by Kenneth R. Shepherd*

*   *   *

ANVIC, Frank
See SHERMAN, Jory (Tecumseh)

*   *   *

ARAGON, Louis   1897-1982
(Albert de Routisie, Arnaud de Saint Roman, Francois La Colere, Francois Lacolere)

PERSONAL: Original name Louis Andrieux; born October 3, 1897, in Neuilly, France; died December 24, 1982, in Paris, France; son of Louis Andrieux (an innkeeper) and Marguerite Toucas; married Elsa Triolet Kagan (a writer), February 28,

1939 (died June 16, 1970). *Education:* Studied medicine at the University of Paris, 1916-17. *Politics:* Communist.

CAREER: Poet and novelist. Member of staff of French Communist Party newspapers, *L'Humanite* and *Commune,* in early 1930s; *Ce Soir* (French Communist Party daily newspaper), Paris, France, co-director, 1937-39; editor of clandestine periodical *La Drome en armes* during World War II; Editeurs Francais Reunis (publishing house), Paris, founder and managing director, beginning 1944; *Ce Soir,* Paris, editor, 1947-53; *Les Lettres Francaises* (weekly literary and political review), Paris, staff member, 1949-53, director, 1953-72. Member of central committee of French Communist Party; member of Lenin Peace Prize committee; member of advisory board of *Europe* (monthly literary review), beginning 1958; member of Academie Concourt, 1967-68. *Wartime service:* Medical auxiliary with the French Army in early World War I; entered combat with 355th Infantry Regiment in 1917; awarded Croix de Guerre; during World War II, served as auxiliary doctor with French Army until the fall of Dunkirk; fought remainder of war as a member of the French Resistance; awarded Croix de Guerre and Medaille Militaire.

MEMBER: International Association of Writers for the Defense of Culture (founder, 1935; secretary of French division), Association of Combatant Writers (vice-president, 1945-60), French National Committee of Authors, American Academy of Arts and Letters (honorary member).

AWARDS, HONORS: Prix Renaudot, 1936, for *Les Beaux Quartiers;* Lenin Peace Prize, 1957, for poem "Ode to Stalin"; Ph.D., University of Prague, 1963, and University of Moscow, 1965; Order of the October Revolution, 1972; Chevalier de la Legion d'Honneur, 1981.

WRITINGS:

POEMS

Feu de joie (also see below; title means "Bonfire"), Au Sans-Pareil (Paris), 1920.

Le Mouvement perpetuel (also see below; title means "Perpetual Motion"), Nouvelle Revue Francaise (Paris), 1925.

La Grande Gaite (title means "High Spirits"), with drawings by Yves Tanguy, Gallimard (Paris), 1929.

Persecute persecuteur, Editions Surrealistes (Paris), 1931.

The Red Front, translation by E. E. Cummings, Contempo Publishers, 1933.

Hourra l'Oural (title means "Hurrah, the Urals"), Denoel et Steele (Paris), 1934.

Le Creve-Coeur (title means "Heartbreak"), Gallimard, 1941, [New York], 1942, new edition, Gallimard, 1946, reprinted, 1980.

Cantique a Elsa (title means "Canticle to Elsa"), Editions de la Revue Fontaine (Algiers), 1941.

Broceliande (also see below), Editions de la Baconniere (Neuchatel, Switzerland), 1942.

Les Yeux d'Elsa (also see below; title means "Elsa's Eyes"), Cahiers du Rhone (Neuchatel), 1942, Pantheon, 1944, new edition with critical essays, P. Seghers (Paris), 1945, reprinted, 1966.

(Under pseudonym Francois La Colere) *Le Musee Grevin* (also see below; title means "The Grevin Museum"), Editions de Minuit (Paris), 1943.

France, ecoute (title means "France, Listen"), Editions de la Revue Fontaine, 1944.

En Etrange pays dans mon pays lui-meme (also see below; contains *Broceliande* and *En Francais dans le texte*), P. Seghers, 1945.

(Under pseudonym Francois Lacolere) *Neuf Chansons interdites, 1942-1944* (title means "Nine Banned Songs"), Bibliotheque Francaise (Paris), 1945.

La Diane francaise (also see below; title means "The French Diana"), P. Seghers, 1945, reprinted, 1960.

Le Musee Grevin, Les Poissons noirs et quelques poems inedits (title means "The Grevin Museum, The Black Fishes and Some Unpublished Poems"), Editions de Minuit, 1946.

Le Nouveau Creve-Coeur (title means "The New Heartbreak"), Gallimard, 1948.

Les Yeux et la memoire (title means "Eyes and Memory"), Gallimard, 1954.

Mes Caravanes, et autres poemes (1948-1954) (title means "My Caravans, and Other Poems"), P. Seghers, 1954.

Le Roman inacheve (autobiographical poem; title means "The Unfinished Romance"), Gallimard, 1956, new edition, 1978.

Elsa, Gallimard, 1959.

Poesies: Anthologie, 1917-1960, Le Club de Meilleur Livre (Paris), 1960.

Les Poetes (autobiographical poem; title means "The Poets"), Gallimard, 1960, revised editions, 1969 and 1976.

Le Fou d'Elsa (title means "Elsa's Madman"), Gallimard, 1963.

Il ne m'est Paris que d'Elsa (anthology; title means "There Is Only Elsa's Paris for Me"), Laffont (Paris), 1964, new edition with photographs, 1968.

Le Voyage de Hollande, P. Seghers, 1964, 5th edition published as *Le Voyage de Hollande et autres poemes*, 1965.

Elegie a Pablo Neruda (title means "Elegy to Pablo Neruda"), Gallimard, 1966.

Les Chambres; poeme du temps qui ne passe pas, Editeurs Francais Reunis, 1969.

L'Oeuvre poetique, 15 volumes, Livre Club Diderot, 1974-81.

Mes Voyages avec un poeme unedit d'Aragon, with illustrations by Fernand Leger, Bibliographique Artes, 1976.

Les Adieux et autres poemes, Temps Actuels, 1981.

Choix de poemes, Temps Actuels, 1983.

"LE MONDE REEL" (title means "The Real World") SERIES

Les Cloches de Bale, Denoel et Steele, 1934, reprinted, Gallimard, 1969, translation by Haakon M. Chevalier published as *The Bells of Basel*, Harcourt, 1936.

Les Beaux Quartiers, Denoel et Steele, 1936, reprinted, Gallimard, 1972, translation by Chevalier published as *Residential Quarter*, Harcourt, 1938.

Les Voyageurs de l'imperiale, Gallimard, 1942, translation by Hannah Josephson published as *The Century Was Young*, Duell, Sloane and Pearce, 1941 (published in England as *Passengers of Destiny*, Pilot Press, 1947), definitive French edition, Gallimard, 1947, reprinted, 1972.

Aurelien, Gallimard, 1944, reprinted, 1966, translation by Eithne Wilkins published under same title, Duell, Sloane and Pearce, 1947.

Les Communistes, six volumes, Bibliotheque Francaise, 1949-51, reprinted, Le Livre de Poche, 1967-68.

NOVELS

Anicet; ou, Le panorama (title means "Anicet; or, The Panorama"), Nouvelle Revue Francaise, 1921, reprinted, Gallimard, 1972.

Les Aventures de Telemaque, Gallimard, 1922, new edition, 1966, translation by Renee Hubert and Judd Hubert published as *The Adventures of Telemachus*, University of Nebraska Press, 1988.

Le Paysan de Paris, Gallimard, 1926, reprinted, 1972, translation by Frederick Brown published as *Nightwalker*, Prentice-Hall, 1970, translation by Simon Watson Taylor published as *Paris Peasant*, Cape, 1971.

La Semaine sainte, Gallimard, 1958, translation by Chevalier published as *Holy Week*, Putnam, 1961.

La Mise a mort (also see below; title means "The Moment of Truth"), Gallimard, 1965.

Blanche ou l'oubli, Gallimard, 1967, published with afterword by author, 1972.

(Under pseudonym Albert de Routisie) *Irene*, L'Or du Temps (Paris), 1968.

Henri Matisse; Roman, two volumes, Gallimard, 1971, translation by Jean Stewart published as *Henri Matisse, a Novel*, Harcourt, 1972.

Theatre/Roman (also see below), Gallimard, 1974.

Aragon; ou, Les Metamorphoses (excerpts from *La Mise a mort* and *Theatre/Roman*), Gallimard, 1977.

STORY COLLECTIONS

Servitude et grandeur des Francais; Scenes des annees terribles (seven stories; title means "Servitude and Greatness of the French; Scenes from the Terrible Years"), Bibliotheque Francaise, 1945.

(Under pseudonym Arnaud de Saint Roman) *Trois Contes* (title means "Three Tales"), Burrup, Mathieson, 1945.

Shakespeare, translation by Bernard Frechtman, with illustrations by Pablo Picasso, Abrams, 1966.

Le Mentir-vrai, Gallimard, 1981.

COLLECTIONS

Le Libertinage (also see below; includes the play "L'Armoire a glace un beau soir" and essays), Nouvelle Revue Francaise, 1924, translation published as *Libertine*, Riverrun Press, 1987.

Aragon, Poet of the French Resistance (includes translations of wartime poetry and prose and critical essays on Aragon), edited by Josephson and Malcolm Cowley, Duell, Sloane and Pearce, 1945 (published in England as *Aragon, Poet of Resurgent France*, Pilot Press, 1946).

Aragon, une etude (selections from his writings), edited and with a critical essay by Claude Roy, P. Seghers, 1945.

L'Un ne va pas sans l'autre: Un perpetuel printemps, suivi de Paroles a Saint-Denis (poetry and a speech), privately printed, 1959.

La Diane francaise, suivi de En etrange pays dans mon pays lui-meme, Seghers, 1962.

Ouevres romanesques croisees d'Elsa Triolet et Aragon (complete works of Aragon and his wife, Elsa Triolet), forty-two volumes, Laffont, 1964-74.

Aragon (selected works), edited and with an introduction by Georges Sadoul, P. Seghers, 1967.

Les Yeux d'Elsa, suivi de La Diane francaise, illustrations by Cecile Picoux, P. Seghers, 1968.

Le Mouvement perpetuel; procede de Feu de joie et suivie de Ecritures automatiques (includes *Le Mouvement perpetuel* and *Feu de joie*), Gallimard, 1970.

NONFICTION

Traite du style (literary criticism and surrealist manifesto), Nouvelle Revue Francaise, 1928.

Le Peinture au defi (essays), Editions Surrealistes, 1930.
Pour un realisme socialiste (lectures), Denoel et Steele, 1935.
(With others) *Authors Take Sides on the Spanish War*, Left Review (London), 1937.
En Francais dans le texte (essay), Ides et Calendes (Paris), 1943.
Le Crime contre l'esprit (les martyrs) par le temoin des martyrs, Editions de Minuit, 1944.
Apologie de luxe (art criticism), Skira (Geneva), 1946.
L'Enseigne de Gersaint (essays), Ides et Calendes, 1946.
L'Homme communiste (title means "The Communist Man"), Gallimard, Volume I, 1946, Volume II, 1953.
Chroniques du bel canto (essays and lectures), Skira, 1947.
La Culture et les hommes (essays), Editions Sociales (Paris), 1947.
Hugo, poete realiste (literary criticism), Editions Sociales, 1952.
L'Exemple de Courbet (art criticism), Cercle d'Art (Paris), 1952.
Le Neveu de M. Duval, suivi d'un lettre d'icelui a l'auteur de ce livre (title means "The Nephew of M. Duval, Followed by a Letter from Him to the Author of This Book"), Editeurs Francais Reunis, 1953.
Journal d'une poesie nationale (critical anthology), Ecrivains Reunis (Lyons), 1954.
La Lumiere de Stendhal (essays and lectures), Denoel, 1954.
Litteratures sovietiques (essays and lectures), Denoel, 1955.
J'abats mon jeu (essays), Editeurs Francais Reunis, 1959.
(With Maurice Thorez) *Il faut appeler les choses par leur nom* [and] *Problemes de notre epoque* (addresses), Parti Communiste Francaise, 1959.
(With Andre Maurois) *Histoire parallele* (historical study of the United States and the Soviet Union), four volumes, Presses de la Cite (Paris), 1962, new edition published in five volumes as *Les Deux Geants; Histoire des Etats-Unis et de l'U.R.S.S., de 1917 a nos jours*, Editions du Pont Royal (Paris), 1962-64, translation of Volumes I and II by Patrick O'Brian published as *A History of the USSR from Lenin to Khrushchev*, two volumes, McKay, 1964, Volumes I and II also published in three volumes as *Histoire de l'U.R.S.S., 1917 a 1960*, Union Generale d'Editions (Paris), 1972.
Les Collages (art criticism), Hermann (Paris), 1965.
(With others) *Dictionnaire abrege du surrealisme*, new edition (Aragon not associated with earlier editions), Corti (Paris), 1969.
Je n'ai jamais appris a ecrire ou Les Incipit, Skira, 1969.
(With others) *La Superletteratura e A. Rimbaud*, L. Lucarini (Rome), 1975.
Paris des poetes, F. Nathan, 1977.
(With others) *Les Poetes de la Revue Fontaine*, Cherche Midi, 1978.
(With others) *Essais de critique genetique*, Flammarion, 1979.
Chroniques de la pluie et du beau temps, Temps Actuels, 1979.
Essai de bibliographie, Grant & Cutler, Volume 1: *Oeuvres, 1918-59*, 1979, Volume 2: *Oeuvres, 1960-77*, 1980.
Ecrits sur l'art moderne, Flammarion, 1981.
Reflexions sur Rimbaud, Editions de Musee-Bibliotheque Arthur Rimbaud, 1983.

AUTHOR OF PREFACE OR INTRODUCTION

Exposition de collages, Jose Corti, 1930.
(Under pseudonym Francois La Colere) Jean Cassou, *33 Sonnets composes au secret*, Editions de la Baconniere, 1946.

Gilbert Debrise, *Cimetieres sans tombeaux*, Bibliotheque Francaise, 1946.
Andre Fougerson, *Dessins*, Les 13 Epis (Paris), 1947.
Pablo Picasso, *Sculptures et dessins* (exhibition catalog), Maison de la Pensee Francaise (Paris), 1952.
(And of reviews) IUrii IAnovski, *Les Cavaliers*, Gallimard, 1957.
Fernand Leger, *Contrastes: 13 Aquarelles*, Au Vent d'Arles (Paris), 1959.
Marc Chagall: Recent Paintings, 1966-68 (exhibition catalog), Pierre Matisse Gallery (New York), 1968.

OTHER

Les Plaisirs de la capitale, [Berlin], 1923.
"Au pied du mur" (play), first produced in 1924.
(Translator) Lewis Carroll, *La Chasse au snark, une agonie en huit crises*, Hours Press, 1929.
Le Temoin des martyrs, printed clandestinely in Paris, 1942.
(Under pseudonym Arnaud de Saint Roman) *Les Bons Voisins*, Editions de Minuit, 1942.
Matisse-en-France, Martin Fabiani, 1943.
Saint-Pol-Roux, ou l'espoir, P. Seghers, 1945.
(Contributor) Gabriel Peri, *Toward Singing Tomorrows*, International Publishers, 1946.
(Translator and author of preface) *Cinq Sonnets de Petrarque*, A la Fontaine de Vaucluse, 1947.
(Contributor) *Henri Matisse: Retrospective Exhibition of Paintings, Drawings and Sculpture*, Philadelphia Museum of Art, 1948.
La Lumiere et la paix, Lettres Francaises, 1950.
(Editor and author of commentary) *Avez-vous lu Victor Hugo?*, Editeurs Francais Reunis, 1952.
La Vraie Liberte de la culture, reduire notre train de mort pour accroitre notre train de vie, Lettres Francaises, 1952.
Les Egmont d'aujourd'hui s'appellent Andre Stil, Lettres Francaises, 1952.
(Editor and author of preface) *Introduction aux litteratures sovietiques: Contes et nouvelles*, Gallimard, 1956.
(With Jean Cocteau) *Entretiens sur le Musee de Dresde*, Cercle d'Art, 1957, translation by Francis Scarfe published as *Conversations on the Dresden Gallery*, Holmes & Meier, 1982.
(Translator and author of preface) Tchinghiz Aitmatov, *Djamilia*, Editeurs Francais Reunis, 1959.
(Editor and author of critical essays) *Elsa Triolet, choisie par Aragon*, Gallimard, 1960.
Entretiens avec Francis Cremieux (ten radio interviews), Gallimard, 1964.
(Contributor) Michael Benedikt and George E. Wellwarth, editors, *Modern French Theatre*, Dutton, 1964.
(Contributor) Roger H. Guerrand, *L'Art nouveau en Europe*, Plon (Paris), 1965.
Aragon parle avec Dominique Arban, P. Seghers, 1968.
Fernand Sequin recontre Louis Aragon, Editions de l'Homme (Montreal), 1969.
(Contributor) Robert G. Marshall and Frederic C. St. Aubyn, editors, *Trois Pieces surrealists*, Appleton, 1969.
(Editor with Andre Breton) *La Revolution surrealiste: Collection complete de la revue (Nos. 1 a 12; 1er decembre 1924 au 15 decembre 1929)*, J. Place, 1975.
(Contributor) Daniel Wallard, *Aragon: Un portrait*, Editions Cercle d'Art, 1979.
La Defense de l'infini et Les Aventures de Jean-Foutre la Bite, Gallimard, 1987.

Co-editor, *Litterature,* 1918-20; co-editor, *La Revolution surrealiste,* 1924-29.

SIDELIGHTS: Louis Aragon's long career was marked by two distinct, even contradictory phases. He began as one of the leading theorists of the avant-garde art movements of Dada and Surrealism, calling for uninhibited freedom for the creative imagination. In the early 1930s, however, he joined the French Communist Party, rising to become a member of the party's Central Committee. For the next half century Aragon was a doctrinaire loyalist who promoted the idea of socialist realism in the arts and carefully followed the party line. This unlikely odyssey, and the drastic changes it entailed, caused Aragon to be labeled an opportunist or political hack by some observers, while his political allies praised his writings. He was best known to the French public as the "Poet of the Resistance," the poet whose stirring patriotic works inspired the nation's fight against the Nazi occupation forces of World War II. His largely nonpolitical novels *Paris Peasant (Le Paysan de Paris)* and *Holy Week (La Semaine sainte)* won critical praise as well. Because of those works, his place in twentieth-century French literature is secure. As a writer for the *New York Times* observed, "Aragon was among France's foremost men of letters in this century." Upon his death in 1982, French President Francois Mitterand announced that "France is grief-stricken by the death of one of its greatest writers. . . . I bow before his memory."

The illegitimate son of a Parisian innkeeper, Aragon spoke little of his childhood or family, usually beginning his life story with his student days at the University of Paris just before the First World War. It was while studying medicine with hopes of becoming a doctor that Aragon first met fellow student Andre Breton. The two young men shared an interest in literature, particularly the experimental works of French poet Guillaume Apollinaire. After serving in the French army as a medical auxiliary and soldier, for which he was awarded a Croix de Guerre, Aragon found himself in 1918 back in Paris. Returning to school seemed pointless after the horrors he had experienced in the war. As a *National Review* writer noted, Aragon "was traumatized emotionally by his experiences." He and Breton decided to devote their time to writing. Following the lead of Tristan Tzara and other artists of the time, he and Breton called for an artistic rebellion against the society that had caused such a devastating and senseless war. As part of their rebellion, the two writers, along with poet Philippe Soupault, founded the ironically-titled magazine *Litterature.*

Litterature quickly became one of the voices for Dada, a radically anti-art movement begun during the war in Zurich, Switzerland, by Tzara, Hugo Ball, and other artists. Dada was a movement of nihilistic rebellion which attacked reason, the rational mind, the established social order, and all other "causes" of the First World War. It called for the abolition of museums, opposed all art theories and schools, and promoted the unrestricted expression of the creative impulse. As Sarane Alexandrian wrote in *Surrealist Art,* "Dada was a detonation of anger which showed itself in insults and buffoonery." Dadaists experimented with sound poems, simultaneous poems, and randomly assembled writings and artwork. They gave public shows wearing grotesque costumes, shouting derision at the audience, and performing senseless, mysterious acts, all accompanied by a cacophony of whistles, horns, gunshots, and drumbeats. Along with Francis Picabia and a small group of other writers and artists, Aragon and Breton were among the most active Dadaists in Paris.

But by 1922, Breton had grown dissatisfied with the essential pointlessness of Dada as a movement. He wanted a more serious artistic enterprise which retained many of Dada's concerns but explored them in a somber and systematic manner. Dada had revealed the limitations of rational thought; Breton now wished to explore what lay beyond those limitations. Heavily influenced by the ideas of Sigmund Freud, Breton called for an art which would liberate man's unconscious desires and integrate them with ordinary waking life to create a super-reality, or surreality. At the "Congress of Paris," organized in 1922 by Breton, the Paris Dadaists and other avant-garde artists met to discuss this new direction. Out of this meeting was born the art movement Surrealism. Aragon was a founding member of the new group.

The early surrealists experimented with a host of methods and techniques meant to free the unconscious, and Aragon played a prominent role in the research. Chance occurrences, dream analysis, the Tarot deck, the ouija board, group hypnosis sessions, psychoanalysis, and automatic writing were all employed. Automatic writing in particular, Alexandrian wrote, "was intended to lay bare the 'mental matter' which is common to all men, and to separate it from thought, which is only one of its manifestations." The startling and spontaneous nature of such writing, which was done while the writer actively suppressed his control and allowed the sentences to form themselves, especially impressed the surrealists, who incorporated the technique into much of their written work.

Another experiment conducted at this time was the deliberate provoking of unaccustomed sensations that went beyond the rational thinking process or usual emotions. Objects of beauty were thought to be able to spur such overwhelming reactions. Roger Cardinal and Robert Stuart Short stated in *Surrealism: Permanent Revelation:* "To witness beauty as Surrealism sees it is to undergo a kind of psychic disorientation, a disturbance that affects both mind and senses." This intense, surreal moment was defined and described by Aragon and Breton. "At times," Cardinal and Short wrote, "Aragon felt this vertigo, this sense of the pavements of everyday opening up beneath his feet to reveal what he called 'magical precipices'—moments in which normality is shaken by something *other,* moments which can suggest panic, but which Aragon as a surrealist welcomes wholeheartedly."

The surrealists believed that certain locations around Paris, because of their striking, mysterious nature, were also able to provoke these intense moments. A passageway at the Paris Opera, the Tower of Saint-Jacques, and the Pon des Suicides at the Buttes-Chaumont were among the sites credited by the surrealists with special evocative powers. Aragon was especially attuned to finding such places. Years later, when speaking to Andre Parinaud in *Entretiens, 1913-1952,* Breton recalled Aragon's ability: "I can still remember him as an extraordinary walking companion. . . . No one was more skilled than Aragon in detecting the unusual in all of its forms; no one else could have been led to such intoxicating reveries about the hidden life of the city."

Aragon used two of these sites in his surrealistic novel *Paris Peasant,* published in 1926. Several critics praised this book in the highest of terms. "The prose of *Le Paysan de Paris,*" Cardinal and Short stated, "has the freshness and conviction of a masterpiece." Lucile F. Becker, writing in her *Louis Aragon,* called the book "one of the masterpieces of French twentieth-century literature." Discussing Aragon's use of two of the surrealists' evocative sites, Cardinal and Short stated that the novel "contains a cryptic discussion of *la mythologie moderne* and *le merveilleux,* exemplified by evocations of two 'elective places' for the urban surrealist, the Passage de l'Opera and the Buttes-Chaumont park. In these innocuous corners of Paris Aragon intuits an immanent surreality almost bordering on the mystical: 'I began to discover the face of the infinite behind the concrete forms which escorted me as I walked along the pathways of this earth.'" M. Adereth, writing in *Commitment in Modern French Literature: A Brief Study of 'Litterature Engagee' in the Works of Peguy, Aragon, and Sartre,* found that unlike other surrealistic prose, Aragon's novel was based on the real world. "Surrealists," Adereth noted, "tended to despise prose and the novel and to condemn descriptions of real places as incompatible with automatic writing.... [But *Paris Peasant* is] based, not on an imaginary city, but on the Paris which [Aragon] loved so much.... He revealed many unknown aspects of the capital, and although his style is in the best surrealist manner—lyrical, poetic and spontaneous—the source of his inspiration is thoroughly realistic."

In 1926 Aragon and Breton led a small group of surrealists into the French Communist Party where, they hoped, the surrealist aesthetic would be adopted and the surrealist vision of a life in which the conscious and unconscious minds are integrated could be realized. A year later they left the party, angered and disillusioned by the group's pedestrian conception of the arts and hostility to surrealist ideas. For their part, the communists found the surrealists to be nothing but bohemian artists not seriously committed to the revolution. Breton and other surrealists became supporters of exiled Russian communist leader Leon Trotsky instead, creating an independent radical position in which psychic and political liberation were compatible.

But Aragon rejoined the Communist Party in 1930 and made a visit to the Soviet Union that same year to attend a writers conference. The visit changed his life. "Like other foreign intellectuals before and after him," a writer for the London *Times* explained, "he was overwhelmed by his first direct experience of the 'homeland of socialism.'" Aragon agreed to renounce surrealism, admit his previous mistakes, and become a model communist. He explained publicly that his involvement with the surrealists had been a youthful error. For the next five decades Aragon was to hold true to his communist commitment. Speaking of this political conversion in his *The History of Surrealism,* Maurice Nadeau reported: "Aragon merely followed the current that with increasing power swept the advanced intellectuals of every nation toward the USSR, at a time when this adherence no longer occasioned any disadvantage for those who adopted it, quite the contrary. The surrealists did not choose to regard Aragon's move as a development, but as a palinode, 'a betrayal' which they were to censure him for bitterly down through the years." As late as 1966, the surrealists, in a book entitled *Aragon au defi* or "Aragon Challenged," were still attacking him as an opportunist who had sold out his ideals.

Aragon's loyalty to the Communist Party and the Soviet Union withstood onslaughts that led less committed members to defect. During the Soviet Union's purge trials of the 1930s, in which thousands of Soviet dictator Joseph Stalin's political rivals were executed, Aragon served as Communist Party apologist for the action. He was a supporter, too, of the Soviet-Nazi friendship pact and of the two countries' subsequent invasion of Poland in 1939 which triggered the Second World War. In 1956, when the Soviets first publicly admitted some of the crimes of the late Stalin, Aragon claimed to be "over-

whelmed" by the revelations. And yet the following year he wrote the poem "Ode to Stalin," which won him the Soviet Union's Lenin Peace Prize. When, in 1968, the French Communist Party broke with the Soviets over the Russian invasion of Czechoslovakia, Aragon also criticized the attack in his periodical *Les Lettres Francaises.* The Soviet government responded by banning the magazine in Eastern Europe and canceling party-approved subscriptions. The magazine was forced out of business. Aragon learned his lesson. When the Soviets invaded Afghanistan in 1980, Aragon supported the move.

From the early 1930s until the end of his life, Aragon's writings were usually of a political nature and displayed little if any of his earlier surrealist style. His "Real World" series of historical novels were examples of socialist realism, a school which calls for a realistic depiction of the class struggle in literature and the arts. His six-volume novel *The Communists* told of the French Communist Party's heroic role in the Resistance movement of World War II. Aragon also wrote and edited several of the official publications of the French Communist Party and served on the party's Central Committee, the ruling council of the organization. David Gascoyne, writing in the *Times Literary Supplement,* reported that Aragon's apartment was even "opposite the Soviet Embassy."

Aragon's first overtly political work was a long poem entitled *The Red Front,* published in French in the early 1930s. A searing, provocative poem, *The Red Front* "brought down the wrath of the authorities upon [Aragon's] head," Philip Rahv commented in the *Nation,* "as their police minds would not put down to poetic license his open advocacy of the shooting of prominent politicians." Another of his early political works was *Hourra l'Oural,* which means "Hurrah, the Urals," a hymn of praise for the Soviet government.

With the "Real World" series of novels published during the 1930s and 1940s, Aragon turned to the history of the late nineteenth and early twentieth century for inspiration, transforming his vision of the period into effective political commentary. The first of these novels is *The Bells of Basel* (*Les Cloches de Bale*), set in France before the First World War and focusing on three women of the time. Each woman comes from a different social class, and so their careers illustrate the range of possibilities afforded by French society. Two of the women are fictional creations but the third, Clara Zetkin, is based on a real communist organizer of the early twentieth century. This novel, Rahv noted, "is built around the lives of three women, who become the focus of [Aragon's] insights into the society that produced them."

Aragon later admitted that he had learned how to write novels by writing *The Bells of Basel,* and some of the faults of an apprentice novel mar the work. As Frederick Brown commented in the *Southern Review,* in Aragon's novels his characters "*are* players, actors who, as the novel progresses, become increasingly aware that it and their roles must end in favor of History.... Aragon reveals this scheme most crudely in the first novel of *The Real World—The Bells of Basel.*" Malcolm Cowley, reviewing the novel for the *New Republic,* was "disappointed" to realize that Aragon was "a writer whose personality as revealed in his books is more brilliant and coherent than the books themselves."

More successful as fiction was the second novel in the "Real World" series, *Residential Quarter* (*Les Beaux Quartiers*). The story revolves around a young man who becomes involved in strike-breaking activity at a French automobile manufacturing plant but eventually joins the strikers. "In this novel,"

Cowley wrote, "there are types of writing that Aragon does supremely well—for example, satire of the middle class in its own language, lyrical apostrophes to Paris and its workers, outright melodrama. . . . *Residential Quarter* is an absorbing and brilliant novel."

In *The Century Was Young* (*Les Voyageurs de l'imperiale*), Aragon wrote of France at the turn of the century and of the attitudes which led the nation into the First World War. The book argues against an aloofness to political matters and instead calls for political involvement. R. E. Roberts of the *Saturday Review of Literature* described the novel as "a pitiless portrayal of human stupidity, human corruption, human vanity, and of that astounding toughness which, in itself quite unmoral, may breed a strange nobility." Although he believed the book "doesn't quite add up," Clifton Fadiman of the *New Yorker* called Aragon potentially "one of the most important of contemporary French novelists. He is very intelligent and conscientious, with deep social sympathies, a wide culture, and great lingual dexterity." Roberts was "reminded of Dickens and Dostoievsky. . . . There is in [*The Century Was Young*] the same warm humanity, the same refusal to despise the most despicable, and the same note of warning to the smug and self-satisfied of the world."

Aurelien, the fourth of the "Real World" novels, was written during the Second World War and published just after the war's end. Because it tells a love story, Aragon was criticized by his political allies who felt it a frivolous work. As Adereth noted, "a number of Aragon's friends, including some narrow-minded Soviet critics, were shocked at the thought that he had found nothing better to do in those [war] years."

Yet, much of Aragon's work during the Second World War concerned love. He wrote a series of love poems to his wife, Elsa Triolet, which were published as *Cantique a Elsa* and *Les Yeux d'Elsa*. Gascoyne noted that after first meeting Elsa in 1928, Aragon "became an adoringly one-woman man, mythologizing his companion in a number of poetic works, and using her name as a symbol of the new revolutionary woman." As late as the 1960s Aragon was still publishing poetry collections inspired by her. His patriotic war poems revealed another kind of love, his love for France. These poems, first published pseudonymously because Aragon was working underground for the French Resistance, are still among his most praised works. As Becker claimed, Aragon's poems of the 1940s about Elsa and patriotism "are among the finest written in the French language."

Many of these poems were collected in *Aragon: Poet of the French Resistance*, a book of his poems and prose from the war. Writing in the *Weekly Book Review*, Karl Shapiro called the collection "in many respects the most extraordinary example of poetic creativity to emerge from the struggle. With its thrilling lyricism, its inspired translations, and its fine emotionality, it forms a collection which is simultaneously a tribute to Aragon and an Aragon triumph." Reviewing the book for the *New York Times*, Donald Stauffer claimed that "Aragon represents such a miracle—brilliance and hope born out of war, defeat, despair."

The last of Aragon's "Real World" novels, the six-volume *The Communists*, was published in the late 1940s and early 1950s. Meant as a fictionalized account of the French Communist Party's role in the Resistance of the Second World War, the novel was never completed. The six published volumes cover only the early history of the war; poor sales forced Aragon to abandon the project. Although Claude Roy, writing in his *Aragon*, found the novel "never a *simplistic* book" and Aragon "marvelously accurate and attentive," most critics felt that the book's political intent devalued its literary worth. Nadeau remarked in *The French Novel since the War:* "As the spokesman in France of the theory of 'socialist realism,' Aragon was obliged to set a good example. He undertook to recount in a series of novels the struggles, anxieties and victories of his political friends. However, in his [*The Communists*] . . . historical truth is so mishandled, the characters are so vague and improbable, even the writing itself so foreign to the author, that he did not persevere in his self-imposed task." "The fictional chronicle [Aragon] writes," Germaine Bree and Margaret Otis Guiton state in *An Age of Fiction: The French Novel from Gide to Camus*, "is shamelessly partial and its fictional value almost nil."

Because he had long written politically oriented fiction for a limited audience, by the 1950s Aragon was little noticed outside his political circle. "Even in France," Becker reported, "very little critical material has appeared on Aragon other than in the Communist press, which hailed all of his work indiscriminately." With the appearance of *Holy Week* in 1958, however, Aragon reached a wider critical audience. The story of French king Louis XVIII's escape from Napoleon in the nineteenth century, *Holy Week* is far less politically motivated than are other of Aragon's novels. Despite the fact that, as Leon S. Roudiez observed in the *Saturday Review*, "a philosophy of history, a social ethic, and a political ideology inform [the novel's] entire structure . . . its Marxist flavor is rarely obtrusive." Becker noted that "critics who had ignored or discounted Aragon's previous work because of his political sympathies praised what they termed his return to objectivity."

Holy Week is an exception to the usually strident propaganda tone of Aragon's later work. During the 1960s and 1970s, he published collections of political speeches he had delivered before the French Communist Party, essays on political topics, and several works on Soviet history and literature. One of these, *A History of the USSR from Lenin to Khrushchev*, was described by Harry Schwartz of the *Saturday Review* as "Soviet history as seen through the eyes of a Khrushchev supporter who obediently follows the Khrushchev line." The novel *La Mise a mort*, in which Aragon "condemns his blind acceptance of Soviet propaganda in the thirties," as Adereth reports, nonetheless ends with Aragon's continued support of communism, "despite the monstrous distortions which it suffered," as Adereth commented. Speaking of Aragon's work as director of the periodical *Les Lettres Francaises*, Francois Bondy of the *New Republic* wrote that he "combined a campaign to seduce the younger 'uncommitted' writers with a most aggressive and fanatical defense of the cult of Stalinism. . ., to a degree unparalleled by any other known writer, justifying the most obviously monstrous political trials, insulting the victims of these proceedings, and slandering those who protested against them."

Critical evaluations of Aragon's career are often colored by his political activities and by the fact that he wrote prolifically, producing much work of an ephemeral nature. A writer for the London *Times* said at the time of his death that Aragon "was a writer of undoubted distinction but curiously uneven achievement." J. W. Kneller of the *French Review* found that "the case of Louis Aragon is one of the most controversial in contemporary French letters. Aside from political matters, he has been a source of disagreement among critics on purely literary grounds. Some consider him one of the most gifted writers of his generation. Others call him an elegant failure.''

Because of this continuing controversy, Aragon's stature as a writer is still largely in dispute. Most critics do credit him, however, with several notable works of lasting interest, including *Paris Peasant, Holy Week,* and his poems of the Second World War. A *New York Times* writer commented at the time of his death that ''even those who disagreed with his politics admired his talents as a poet and as a novelist.'' A *National Review* writer called him ''a great twentieth century poet'' and ''one of the relatively few genuine heroes of the Resistance.'' Looking back over Aragon's long and controversial career, Gascoyne believed that ''in the end the renown of Louis Aragon will be that of a poet, novelist and critic who tried his best to give Communist writing in France a human face.''

BIOGRAPHICAL/CRITICAL SOURCES:

BOOKS

Adereth, M., *Commitment in Modern French Literature: A Brief Study of "Litterature Engagee" in the Works of Peguy, Aragon, and Sartre,* Gollancz, 1967.
Alexandrian, Sarane, *Surrealist Art,* Praeger, 1970.
Aragon au defi, Le Terrain Vague, 1966.
Balakian, Anna, *Surrealism: The Road to the Absolute,* Dutton, 1970.
Becker, Lucille E., *Louis Aragon,* Twayne, 1971.
Bree, Germaine, and Margaret Otis Guiton, *An Age of Fiction: The French Novel from Gide to Camus,* Rutgers University Press, 1957.
Breton, Andre, *Entretiens, 1913-1952,* Gallimard, 1952.
Burnsham, Stanley, editor, *The Poem Itself,* Holt, 1960.
Cardinal, Roger, and Robert Stuart Short, *Surrealism: Permanent Revelation,* Studio Vista/Dutton, 1970.
Caute, David, *Communism and the French Intellectuals, 1914-60,* Andre Deutsch, 1964.
Contemporary Literary Criticism, Gale, Volume 3, 1975, Volume 22, 1982.
Dictionary of Literary Biography, Volume 72: *French Novelists, 1930-1960,* Gale, 1988.
Juin, Hubert, *Aragon,* Gallimard, 1960.
Lecherbonnier, Bernard, *Aragon,* Bordas, 1971.
Lindsay, Jack, *Meetings with Poets,* Ungar, 1969.
Nadeau, Maurice, *The History of Surrealism,* Macmillan, 1965.
Nadeau, Maurice, *The French Novel since the War,* Methuen, 1967.
Raymond, Marcel, *From Baudelaire to Surrealism,* Methuen, 1970.
Roy, Claude, *Aragon,* P. Seghers, 1951.
Savage, Catherine, *Malraux, Sartre, and Aragon as Political Novelists,* University of Florida Press, 1965.
Tetel, Marcel, editor, *Symbolism and Modern Literature: Studies in Honor of Wallace Fowlie,* Duke University Press, 1978.

PERIODICALS

Comparative Drama, spring, 1977.
French Review, December 1952, May, 1965.
Mainstream, January, 1962.
Nation, September 26, 1936.
New Republic, October 7, 1936, November 23, 1938, December 25, 1961, December 16, 1972.
New Yorker, November 1, 1941.
New York Times, December 16, 1945.
Saturday Review, October 7, 1961, August 8, 1964.

Saturday Review of Literature, December 24, 1938, November 15, 1941.
Southern Review, spring, 1967.
Spectator, October 13, 1961.
Times (London), January 4, 1983.
Times Literary Supplement, January 23, 1961.
Transformation, Number 3, 1945.
Weekly Book Review, December 16, 1945.
Yale French Studies, fall-winter, 1948.
Yale Review, September, 1945.

OBITUARIES:

PERIODICALS

AB Bookman's Weekly, February 14, 1983.
National Review, January 21, 1983.
Newsweek, January 10, 1983.
New York Times, December 25, 1982.
Time, January 10, 1983.
Times (London), January 4, 1983.
Washington Post, December 25, 1982.*

—*Sketch by Thomas Wiloch*

*   *   *

ARNOLD, Guy   1932-

PERSONAL: Born May 6, 1932, in Birkenhead, England; son of George Croft and Margaret Arnold. *Education:* Oxford University, M.A. (with honors), 1955. *Politics:* Radical. *Religion:* Agnostic.

ADDRESSES: Home—163 Seymour Pl., London W.1, England. *Agent*—Michael Shaw, Curtis Brown Ltd., 162-168 Regent St., London W1R 5TB, England.

CAREER: Free-lance writer, lecturer, and traveler, 1955-58, 1960-61; teacher of English in Newmarket, Ontario, 1958-60; Ryerson Institute, Toronto, Ontario, lecturer in political geography, 1961-63; Government of Northern Rhodesia, consultant in youth services, 1963-64; Overseas Development Institute, London, England, researcher, 1965-66; writer and lecturer, 1966—. Director, Africa Bureau (London), 1968-72. *Military service:* British Army, 1951-52; became lieutenant.

WRITINGS:

Longhouse and Jungle, Chatto & Windus, 1959.
Towards Peace and a Multiracial Commonwealth, Chapman & Hall, 1964.
Economic Co-operation in the Commonwealth, Pergamon, 1967.
Kenyatta and the Politics of Kenya, Dent, 1974.
The Last Bunker, Quartet, 1976.
(With Ruth Weiss) *Strategic Highways of Africa,* Friedman, 1977.
Modern Nigeria, Longman, 1977.
Britain's Oil, Hamish Hamilton, 1978.
Aid in Africa, Kogan Page, 1979.
Held Fast for England, Hamish Hamilton, 1980.
The Unions, Hamish Hamilton, 1981.
Modern Kenya, Longman, 1981.
Aid and the Third World, Robert Royce, 1985.
Third World Handbook, Cassell, 1989.
The Black Forest to the Black Sea (travel), Cassell, 1989.
Britain since 1945, Cassell, 1989.

Contributor to journals.

WORK IN PROGRESS: An Illustrated Atlas of the Commonwealth; British Brainwashing.

SIDELIGHTS: Guy Arnold led a scientific expedition to the interior of Borneo, 1955-56, collected folklore in Guiana among the Wapisiana Indiana, and assisted in the establishment of the Canadian University Service Overseas.

*   *   *

ARTHUR, Tiffany
    See PELTON, Robert W(ayne)

*   *   *

ASHLOCK, Robert B.   1930-

PERSONAL: Born September 17, 1930, in Indianapolis, Ind., son of Hobert Dean (an engineer) and Juanita (Kinzer) Ashlock; married Julia Ann Bronnenberg, December 23, 1951; children: Joli Ann, Alan Dean. *Education:* Attended Ball State University, 1948-51, and Wheaton College, Wheaton, Ill., 1955; Butler University, B.S., 1957, M.S., 1959; Indiana University, Ed.D., 1965. *Religion:* Presbyterian.

ADDRESSES: Home—1005 Ft. Stephenson Ter., Lookout Mountain, Ga. 30750. *Office*—Department of Education, Covenant College, Lookout Mountain, Ga. 30750.

CAREER: Elementary school teacher and principal in Noblesville, Ind., 1957-64; University of Maryland, College Park, assistant professor, 1965-68, associate professor, 1968-73, professor of education, 1973-80, director of Arithmetic Center, 1972-80; Reformed Theological Seminary, Jackson, Miss., professor of education, 1980-87; Belhaven College, Jackson, professor of education, 1985-88; Covenant College, Lookout Mountain, Ga., professor of education, 1988—.

MEMBER: National Education Association (life member), National Council of Teachers of Mathematics, Research Council for Diagnostic and Prescriptive Mathematics (president, 1979-81; secretary, 1987-89), School Science and Mathematics Association, Textbook Authors Association.

WRITINGS:

(Editor with Wayne Herman) *Current Research in Elementary School Mathematics*, Macmillan, 1970.
Error Patterns in Computation: A Semi-Programmed Approach, C. E. Merrill, 1972, 5th edition, 1990.
(With James Humphrey) *Teaching Elementary School Mathematics through Motor Learning*, C. C Thomas, 1976.
(With Martin L. Johnson, Wilmer L. Jones, and John W. Wilson) *Guiding Each Child's Learning of Mathematics*, C. E. Merrill, 1983.
(With Jon Engelhardt and James Wiebe) *Helping Children Understand and Use Numerals*, Allyn & Bacon, 1984.

Contributor of about thirty articles and reviews to education journals.

SIDELIGHTS: Robert B. Ashlock told *CA:* "Most of my writings are concerned with helping children understand and enjoy success using arithmetic to solve problems. I want them to perceive computation as a written record of observations in physical reality, something that makes sense. I also want the operations of arithmetic to make sense to children so they will know when to use them."

*   *   *

ASHMEAD, John, Jr.   1917-

PERSONAL: Born August 22, 1917, in New York, N.Y.; son of John (in advertising) and Mildred (Hinkel) Ashmead; married Ann Harnwell, October 15, 1949 (divorced, 1972); children: John III, Graham Gaylord, Gaylord Harnwell, Louisa Harnwell, Theodora Wheeley. *Education:* Attended Loomis Institute, 1930-34; Harvard University, B.A. (magna cum laude), 1938, M.A., 1939, Ph.D., 1950.

ADDRESSES: Home—10 Railroad Ave., Apt. 2B, Haverford, Pa. 19041.

CAREER: Haverford College, Haverford, Pa., instructor, 1947-49, assistant professor, 1949-60, associate professor, 1961-67, professor of English, 1968-88, head of department, 1973-75. Lecturer in English, Bryn Mawr College, 1949; lecturer, Athens College, Athens, Greece, 1956-57. Fulbright lecturer, Osaka University of Foreign Studies, Japan, 1955-56, National Chengchi University and Taiwan Normal University, Taipei, Taiwan, 1960-61, and Banaras Hindu University, Varanasi, India, 1964-65. Lecturer at other universities in the Far East and in India. Writer in residence, Temple University Conference Workshop on Creative Communication, 1967. Director, National Endowment for the Humanities film project, 1973-75; member, National Board of Consultants on Humanities, National Endowment for the Humanities, 1974—. *Military service:* U.S. Navy, 1942-46; became lieutenant; served in Pacific theater and in Japanese occupation.

MEMBER: Modern Language Association (chairman of Conference Group on Oriental-Western Literary Relations), School and College Conference on English (vice-chairman), Association for Asian Studies, Authors League of America, Authors Guild, American Studies Association, Phi Beta Kappa.

AWARDS, HONORS: American Council of Learned Societies grant, 1955, for research on Lafcadio Hearn; grants from American Institute of Indian Studies and Asia Society, both 1965, both for research on modern Indian fiction; Ford Foundation research grant, and Haverford College grant, both 1970, both for work on film; Distinguished Lecturer award, National Council of Teachers of English, 1972; Wemyss Foundation grant, 1974; Mellon Foundation grant and Haverford College grant, both 1979-80, both with John Davison for teaching and research on Anglo-American lyrics; Haverford College grant, 1984, for research into computer analysis and generation of poetry.

WRITINGS:

(Editor) *The Reeds* (translations from Japanese fiction and poetry), Osaka University of Foreign Studies, 1956.
The Mountain and the Feather (fiction), Houghton, 1961.
English 12 (rhetoric), Ginn, 1967.
The Idea of Japan, Eighteen Fifty-three to Eighteen Ninety-five: Japan as Described by American and Other Travellers from the West, edited by Stephen Orgel, Garland, 1987.

CONTRIBUTOR

The Teaching of English Overseas, Methuen, 1963.
American Studies in Transition, University of Pennsylvania Press, 1964.
On Teaching English to Speakers of Other Languages, National Council of Teachers of English, 1965.
The Humanity of English, National Council of Teachers of English, 1972.
Richard Kostelanetz, editor, *American Writing Today*, United States International Communication Agency, 1982.

Jean Barth Toll and Michael J. Schwager, editors, *Montgomery County: The Second Hundred Years,* Montgomery County Federation of Historical Societies, 1983.

OTHER

Contributor of short stories, book reviews, and articles to magazines, including *Atlantic Monthly, Harper's,* and *Virginia Quarterly Review.* Associate editor, *Literature East and West,* 1968-70; editorial consultant, *PMLA,* 1969.

WORK IN PROGRESS: The Songs of Robert Burns, with John Davison, three volumes, for University of Pennsylvania Press; *Who Sleeps on Brambles,* a novel; computer programs for critical analysis of literature, and for the generation of free verse, haiku, limericks, and the Shakespearean sonnet.

SIDELIGHTS: John Ashmead told *CA:* "My major interest is always in the uses of language, whether in rhetoric, fiction, poetry, or film. Thanks to the Pacific War in which I served as a Japanese language officer, I have a special interest in Japanese-American cultural relations."*

*   *   *

ASHTON, Sharon
   See VAN SLYKE, Helen (Lenore)

*   *   *

ASKEW, Jack
   See HIVNOR, Robert

*   *   *

ASTIN, Alexander W(illiam) 1932-

PERSONAL: Born May 30, 1932, in Washington, D.C.; son of Allen Varley (director of National Bureau of Standards) and Margaret L. (Mackenzie) Astin; married Helen Stavridou (a professor of education), February 11, 1956; children: John Alexander, Paul Allen. *Education:* Gettysburg College, A.B. (music), 1953; University of Maryland, M.A., 1954, Ph.D., 1957. *Politics:* Independent. *Religion:* None.

ADDRESSES: Home—2681 Cordelia Rd., Los Angeles, Calif. 90049. *Office*—Department of Education, 201 Moore Hall, University of California, 405 Hilgard Ave., Los Angeles, Calif. 90024.

CAREER: U.S. Veterans Administration, Washington, D.C., counseling psychologist in Perry Point, Md., 1954-57, assistant chief of psychology research unit at Veterans Administration Hospital in Baltimore, Md., 1959-60; National Merit Scholarship Corp., Evanston, Ill., 1960-65, began as research associate, became director of research; American Council on Education, Washington, D.C., director of research, 1965-73; University of California, Los Angeles, professor of education, 1973—; Higher Education Research Institute, Los Angeles, president, 1974-83. Trustee, Gettysburg College, 1983-86, Eckerd College, 1986—, St. Xavier College, Chicago, and Marjorie Webster Junior College, Washington, D.C. Consultant to U.S. Surgeon General's Advisory Committee on Smoking and Health. *Military service:* U.S. Public Health Service, 1957-59; served as department chief of psychology research, USPHS Hospital in Lexington, Ky.; became lieutenant commander.

MEMBER: American Psychological Association (fellow), American Educational Research Association, Psychometric Society, American Association for the Advancement of Science (fellow), American Association for Higher Education (director), Center for Advanced Study of Behavioral Science (fellow), American Personnel and Guidance Association, American College Personnel Association (senior scholar), Phi Sigma Kappa.

AWARDS, HONORS: Award for outstanding research, American Personnel and Guidance Association, 1965, for studies of college characteristics and college effects; Institute for Advanced Study in the Behavioral Sciences fellow, 1967-68; award for distinguished contribution to research and literature, National Association of Student Personnel Administrators, 1976; Outstanding Contribution to Knowledge Award, American College Personnel Association, 1978; Litt.D., Gettysburg College, 1981; LL.D., Alderson-Broaddus College, 1982, Whitman College, 1986; E. F. Lindquist Award, American Educational Research Association/American College Testing Program, 1983, for outstanding research dealing with college student growth and development; Distinguished Alumnus, Phi Sigma Kappa Fraternity, 1984; "Most admired for creative, insightful thinking," *Change* magazine poll, 1985; Excellence in Education Award, National Association of College Admissions Counselors, 1985; Outstanding Service award, Council of Independent Colleges, 1986; Outstanding Research award, Association for the Study of Higher Education, 1987; L.H.D., Chapman College, 1987; Doctor of Pedagogy, Rhode Island College, 1987.

WRITINGS:

Who Goes Where to College?, Science Research Associates, 1965.
(Contributor) C. W. Taylor, editor, *Widening Horizons in Creativity,* Wiley, 1965.
The College Environment, American Council on Education, 1968.
(With Robert J. Panos) *The Educational and Vocational Development of College Students,* American Council on Education, 1969.
Predicting Academic Performance in College, Free Press, 1971.
(With C. B. T. Lee) *The Invisible Colleges,* McGraw, 1972.
(With wife, Helen S. Astin) *Open Admissions at City University of New York,* Prentice-Hall, 1974.
Preventing Students from Dropping Out: A Longitudinal, Multi-Institutional Study of College Dropouts, Jossey-Bass, 1975.
(With others) *The Power of Protest: A National Study of Student and Faculty Disruptions with Implications for the Future,* Jossey-Bass, 1975.
Academic Gamesmanship: Student-Oriented Change in Higher Education, Praeger, 1976.
Four Critical Years: Effects of College on Beliefs, Attitudes, and Knowledge, Jossey-Bass, 1977.
Maximizing Leadership Effectiveness, Jossey-Bass, 1981.
Minorities in American Higher Education: Recent Trends, Current Prospects, and Recommendations, Jossey-Bass, 1982.
Achieving Educational Excellence: A Critical Assessment of Priorities and Practices in Higher Education, Jossey-Bass, 1985.

Contributor of over two hundred articles to more than forty professional journals.

*   *   *

ASTIN, Helen S(tavridou) 1932-

PERSONAL: Born February 6, 1932, in Serras, Greece; naturalized U.S. citizen; daughter of Pericles and Soteria (Boukouvala) Stavrides; married Alexander W. Astin (a professor of education), February 11, 1956; children: John Alexander, Paul Allen. *Education:* Pedagogical Academy, Salonika, Greece, diploma in elementary education, 1951; Adelphi University, B.A., 1953; Ohio University, M.S., 1954; University of Maryland, Ph.D., 1957.

ADDRESSES: Home—2681 Cordelia Rd., Los Angeles, Calif. 90049. *Office*—Department of Education, 201 Moore Hall, University of California, 405 Hilgard Ave., Los Angeles, Calif. 90024.

CAREER: University of Maryland, College Park, assistant in department of psychology and counseling center, 1954-57; U.S. Public Health Service Hospital, Lexington, Ky., clinical psychologist, 1957-59; University of Maryland Medical School, instructor in pediatrics, 1960; National College of Education, Evanston, Ill., instructor in psychology, 1961-65; Gallaudet College, Washington, D.C., associate professor of psychology, 1965; National Academy of Sciences, Commission of Human Resources and Advanced Education, Washington, D.C., research associate in communicaton, human resources and advanced education, 1965-67; Stanford University, Institute for the Study of Human Problems, Stanford, Calif., research associate and lecturer, 1967-68; Bureau of Social Science Research, Washington, D.C., research associate, 1968-70; University Research Corp., Washington, D.C., director of research, 1970-73; University of California, Los Angeles, professor of higher education, 1973—. Trustee of Hampshire College.

MEMBER: American Psychological Association (fellow), American Educational Resource Association, American Association for Higher Education.

AWARDS, HONORS: Outstanding contribution to research and literature award, National Association of School Personnel Administration, 1976.

WRITINGS:

The Woman Doctorate in America: Origins, Career, and Family, Russell Sage, 1969.
(With J. K. Folger and A. E. Bayer) *Human Resources and Higher Education,* Russell Sage, 1969.
(With others) *Themes and Events of Campus Unrest in Twenty-Two Colleges and Universities,* Bureau of Social Science Research, 1969.
Educational Progress of Disadvantaged Students, Human Service Press, 1970.
Personal and Environmental Factors in Career Decisions of Young Women, U.S. Office of Education, Bureau of Research, 1970.
(With others) *Higher Education and the Disadvantaged Student,* Behaviorial Publications, 1972.
(With Nancy Suniewick and Susan Dweck) *Women: A Bibliography on Their Education and Careers,* Behavioral Publications, 1974.
(With husband, Alexander W. Astin) *Open Admissions at City University of New York,* Prentice-Hall, 1974.
(Editor) Allison Parelman and Anne Fisher, *Sex Roles: A Research Bibliography,* National Institute of Mental Health, 1975.
Some Action of Her Own, Lexington Books, 1976.
(With Michele Harway) *Sex Discrimination in Career Guidance and Education,* Praeger, 1977.
(With Harway and Jeanne M. Suhr) *A Selected Annotated Bibliography on Counseling Women,* American Psychological Association, 1977.

(Editor with Werner Z. Hirsch) *The Higher Education of Women: Essays in Honor of Rosemary Park,* Praeger, 1978.

Also author, with others, of *The Power of Protest,* for Jossey-Bass. Author of several studies, reports, and booklets on educational and women's problems. Contributor to psychology and education journals. Member of editorial boards, *Journal of Vocational Behavior, Journal of Counseling Psychology, Signs,* and *Psychology of Women Quarterly.**

*   *   *

ATKINSON, Hugh C(raig)   1933-1986

PERSONAL: Born November 27, 1933, in Chicago, Ill.; died October 24, 1986, in Urbana, Ill.; buried in Champaign, Ill.; son of Craig and Margaret (Ritchey) Atkinson; married Mary Nugent, January 12, 1957; children: George, Mary Susan, Ann. *Education:* Attended St. Benedict's College, Atchison, Kan., 1951-53; University of Chicago, B.A., 1957, M.S.L.S., 1959; U.S. National Archives, certificate in archival administration, 1958.

ADDRESSES: Home—904 Sunnycrest Dr., Urbana, Ill. 61801. *Office*—University of Illinois Library, Urbana, Ill. 61801.

CAREER: Lawrence Scudder & Co. (certified public accountants), Chicago, Ill., junior accountant, 1951-56; University of Chicago Library, Chicago, Ill., assistant in rare books section, 1957-58; Pennsylvania Military College, Chester, reader's services librarian, 1958-61; State University of New York at Buffalo, head of library reference department, 1961-64, assistant director of technical services libraries, 1964-67, acting assistant director of health sciences libraries, 1966-67; Ohio State University, Columbus, assistant professor, 1967-69, associate professor, 1969-74, professor of library administration, 1974-76, assistant director of public services libraries, 1967-71, director of libraries, 1971-76; University of Illinois at Urbana-Champaign, director of libraries, 1976-86, professor of library administration, 1976-86. Visiting lecturer, School of Library Science, State University of New York at Geneseo, 1970. Institutional representative of Center for Research Libraries, 1971-86; member of advisory committee of Ohio Project for Research in Information Science, 1972, 1973; Ohio College Library Center, chairman of committee on direct borrowing, 1973-76, trustee, 1978-86, chairman of auditing committee, 1978-79, member of nominating committee, 1985-86; trustee, Interuniversity Communication Council, 1976-79.

MEMBER: International Federation of Documentalists, American Library Association (member of council, 1970-75), American Society for Information Science, Association of Research Libraries (member of board of directors, 1982-86; member of government relations committee, 1986), American Association of University Professors, Committee on Institutional Cooperation, Ohio Library Association, Illinois Library Association, Franklin County Library Association, University of Chicago Graduate Library School Alumni Association (president, 1974-75).

AWARDS, HONORS: United Office of Education grant, 1968-70.

WRITINGS:

(Editor with Joseph Katz and Richard A. Ploch) *Twenty-One Letters from Hart Crane to George Bryan,* Ohio State University Libraries, 1968.
(Compiler) William White, editor, *The Merrill Checklist of Theodore Dreiser,* C. E. Merrill, 1969.

(Editor with White) *Theodore Dreiser: A Checklist*, Kent State University Press, 1971.
(Contributing editor and compiler) White, editor, *The Bowker Annual of Library and Book Trade Information*, 16th-23rd editions, 1971-78.
(Contributor) Melvin J. Voigt, editor, *Advances in Librarianship*, Academic Press, 1974.
(Contributor) Peter Spyers-Duran and Daniel Gore, editors, *Management Problems in Serials Work: Proceedings of the Florida Atlantic University Conference*, Greenwood Press, 1974.
(Contributor) Spyers-Duran and John F. Harvey, editors, *Austerity Management in Academic Libraries*, Scarecrow, 1984.

Author of text for "Automated Circulation Systems" (seven cassette tapes), recorded at the Information Science and Automation Division, Los Angeles Institute, 1977. Contributor to *Library Journal*, *Library Trends*, *Protean*, and library conference journals. Member of the editorial board of the *Journal of Library Administration*.

BIOGRAPHICAL/CRITICAL SOURCES:

PERIODICALS

Today's Education, January, 1973.

OBITUARIES:

PERIODICALS

American Libraries, December, 1986.
Chicago Sun Times, October 28, 1986.
Chicago Tribune, October 29, 1986.*

*   *   *

AURELIO, John R.   1937-

PERSONAL: Born September 19, 1937, in New York, N.Y.; son of John and Anna (Santospirito) Aurelio. *Education:* St. Bonaventure University, B.A., 1959; Fordham University, M.S.W., 1962; received degree from Christ the King Seminary, 1966.

ADDRESSES: Home—St. John the Evangelist Rectory, 2315 Seneca St., Buffalo, N.Y. 14210. *Office*—St. John the Evangelist Church, Buffalo, N.Y. 14210.

CAREER: Ordained Roman Catholic priest, 1966; pastor of Roman Catholic churches in Hinsdale, N.Y., 1966, and Albion, N.Y., 1967; teacher at Roman Catholic high school in Dunkirk, N.Y., 1968; affiliated with West Seneca Developmental Center, West Seneca, N.Y., 1968; currently pastor of St. John the Evangelist Church, Buffalo, N.Y. Social worker for Catholic Charities of Buffalo, 1960—; program director of Buffalo's Cuban refugee program, summer, 1961; director of social work department at Buffalo's Sisters of Charity Hospital, summer, 1962; social worker with unwed mothers at Our Lady of Victory Infant Home, 1966-70. Member of U.S. Catholic Conference Committee on the Handicapped; chairman of New York State Catholic Advisory Council on the Handicapped; member of Erie County Child Protection Advisory Committee, Center for Handicapped Children, and Buffalo Mayor's Advisory Council on the Handicapped.

MEMBER: Academy of Certified Social Workers, National Apostolate for the Mentally Retarded, American Association on Mental Deficiency, New York State Hospital Chaplains Association, Association for Retarded Children of Western New York.

AWARDS, HONORS: Humanitarian award from Buffalo Port Council of American Federation of Labor/Congress of Industrial Organizations, 1973; named man of the year by Erie County chapter of Association for Retarded Children, 1973; service to mankind award from Buffalo and Western New York chapter of Sertoma, 1974; outstanding citizen award from *Buffalo Evening News*, 1976; community service citation from D'Youville College, 1978; Bishop McNulty Youth Award from Catholic Youth Organization of Buffalo, 1978; humanitarian award from Region X of American Association of Mental Deficiency, 1978; award from Buffalo Holy Name Society, 1978.

WRITINGS:

Story Sunday: Christian Fairy Tales for All Ages, Paulist Press, 1978.
The Beggar's Christmas, Paulist Press, 1979.
The Boy Who Stole the Christmas Star, Crossroad Publishing, 1981.
(Contributor) *Visions of Wonder: An Anthology of Christian Fantasy* (anthology), edited by Boyer and Zahorski, Avon, 1981.
Gather Round, Paulist Press, 1982.
Mosquitoes in Paradise, Crossroad Publishing, 1985.
Once Upon a Christmas Time, Paulist Press, 1986.
(Contributor) *Storytelling: Imagination and Faith* (anthology), edited by William J. Bausch, Twenty-Third Publications, 1986.
Fables for God's People, Crossroad Publishing, 1988.
The Garden of Life, Crossroad Publishing, 1989.

Work represented in numerous anthologies.

WORK IN PROGRESS: Family Stew: Fables for the Entire Family; Skipping Stones: Reflections on the Old Testament.

SIDELIGHTS: John R. Aurelio wrote *CA*, "Life is a mystery to be lived, a puzzle to be solved, and a story to be enjoyed."

*   *   *

AZAR, Edward E(lias)   1938-

PERSONAL: Born March 2, 1938, in Beshamoon, Lebanon. *Education:* American University of Beirut, B.A., 1960; University of the Pacific, M.A., 1965; Stanford University, Ph.D., 1969.

ADDRESSES: Home—4800 College Ave., College Park, Md. 20740.

CAREER: Arabian American Oil Co., Saudi Arabia, translator and affiliated with government relations department, 1960-64; San Francisco State University, San Francisco, Calif., part-time lecturer, 1967-68; Michigan State University, East Lansing, assistant professor of political science, 1968-71; University of North Carolina at Chapel Hill, associate professor, 1971-76, professor of political science, beginning 1976.

MEMBER: International Studies Association, International Political Science Association, Peace Science Society (president of Southern branch, 1971-72), Consortium on Peace Research, Teaching and Development.

WRITINGS:

Probe for Peace: Small State Hostilities, Burgess, 1973.
(Editor with Joseph Ben-Dak) *Theory and Practice of Events Research*, Gordon & Breach, 1974.

The Codebook of the Conflict and Peace Data Bank, Center for International Development, University of Maryland, 1982.

(With others) *The Emergence of a New Lebanon: Fantasy or Reality?,* Praeger, 1984.

United States: Arab Cooperation, University of Maryland, 1985.

(With John W. Burton) *International Conflict Resolution: Theory and Practice,* L. Rienner, 1986.

(With Chung-In Moon) *National Security in the Third World,* Elgar, 1988.

Contributor of articles to numerous periodicals, including *International Studies Quarterly, Journal of Conflict Resolution, Peace Research Reviews, International Interactions,* and *Middle East Focus.* Guest editor, *Journal of Conflict Resolution,* 1972; editor, *Review of Peace Science,* 1973, and *International Interactions,* beginning 1974.

WORK IN PROGRESS: A book about protracted social conflict in the Third World.

B

BABITZ, Eve 1943-

PERSONAL: Born May 13, 1943, in Hollywood, Calif.; daughter of Sol (a musician) and Mae (an artist; maiden name, LaViolette) Babitz. *Education:* Attended high school in Hollywood, Calif.

ADDRESSES: Agent—Erica Spellman, International Creative Management, 40 West 57th St., New York, N.Y. 10019.

CAREER: Office manager, *East Village Other,* 1966; office manager, *Ramparts,* 1967; free-lance illustrator and designer of covers for record albums, 1967-72; writer, 1967—.

WRITINGS:

Eve's Hollywood, Seymour Lawrence, 1974.
(Editor) *Los Angeles Manifesto* (stories), privately printed, 1976.
Slow Days, Fast Company: The World, the Flesh, and L.A. Tales (stories), Knopf, 1977.
Sex and Rage (novel), Knopf, 1979.
Fiorucci, the Book, Harlin Quist, 1980.
L.A. Woman (novel), Linden Press, 1982.

Contributor of stories to magazines, including *Cosmopolitan, Rolling Stone, Saturday Evening Post,* and *Vogue.*

WORK IN PROGRESS: Screenplays.

SIDELIGHTS: Regarding Eve Babitz's 1977 collection of stories about Southern California, *Slow Days, Fast Company: The World, the Flesh, and L.A. Tales,* Julia Whedon wrote in the *New York Times Book Review:* "The author's sensibility presides and prevails throughout, threading together restaurants and landscape, friendship and fornication, diets and death, as if they were all set out *en buffet.* . . . Her enthusiastic prose style. . . . has the bright, nutty, incisive quality of good gossip." A reviewer for *Time* added that while Babitz's "style is often derivative of Tom Wolfe and Joan Didion . . . [she] has the one indispensable quality for her kind of work: true glitz." Babitz's 1982 novel *L.A. Woman,* "is a portrait of Sophie Lubin, a self-absorbed, uneducated, uninteresting and not very intelligent young lady who likes Los Angeles a lot," wrote P. J. O'Rourke in the *New York Times Book Review.* James Kaufmann, in the *Los Angeles Times Book Review,* described the novel as "more a collection of vignettes stitched together like a crazy quilt and possessed of . . . enigmatic logic." Kaufmann praised Babitz's prose as being "calculated, breathy, glib and precocious," adding that "her eclectic approach to plotting gives the novel hyperkinesis."

Babitz once wrote: "I became a writer when I felt I was too old to design rock'n'roll album covers any more. As I could no longer drink Southern Comfort till three o'clock A.M. with nineteen-year-old bass players from Mississippi, I felt that my days in rock'n'roll were numbered. I knew I'd be a writer eventually, and I decided to write stories about Los Angeles that weren't depressing. And I did."

BIOGRAPHICAL/CRITICAL SOURCES:

PERIODICALS

Atlantic, April, 1974.
Los Angeles Times, May 1, 1977, February 8, 1980.
Los Angeles Times Book Review, May 30, 1982.
Ms., May, 1975, February, 1980, June, 1982.
New Yorker, November 12, 1979, May 10, 1982.
New York Times, July 15, 1977.
New York Times Book Review, June 19, 1977, December 2, 1979, May 2, 1982.
Saturday Review, May, 1982.
Time, July 4, 1977.
Village Voice, June 27, 1977, October 15, 1979.*

*   *   *

BABITZ, Sol 1911-1982

PERSONAL: Born October 11, 1911, in Brooklyn, N.Y.; died February 18, 1982; son of Abraham (a union organizer) and Luba (Pogorelsky) Babitz; married Mae LaViolette (an artist), 1942; children: Eve, Miriam. *Education:* Attended Berlin Hochschule fuer Musik, 1930-31, Paris Ecole Normale, 1931, and University of Southern California, 1951.

ADDRESSES: Home and office—1955 North Wilton Pl., Hollywood, Calif. 90068.

CAREER: Los Angeles Philharmonic Orchestra, Los Angeles, Calif., first violinist, 1933-37; studio violinist in Hollywood, Calif., 1933-61; Early Music Laboratory, Hollywood, founding director, beginning 1948. Fulbright lecturer in Germany, 1961-63. Editor of string parts for Igor Stravinsky scores, beginning 1942.

MEMBER: American Musicological Society (honorary president, 1952-57).

AWARDS, HONORS: Ford Foundation grant, 1961-62; American Council of Learned Societies award, 1967.

WRITINGS:

Problems of Rhythm in Baroque Music, Early Music Laboratory, 1967.
Modern Errors in Mozart Performance: With Additions and Corrections as of May 1969, Including Remarks on Beethoven Performance, Early Music Laboratory, 1970.
The Great Baroque Hoax: A Guide to Baroque Performance for Musicians and Connoisseurs, Early Music Laboratory, 1970, 2nd edition issued with phonodisc, "The Future of Baroque Music," 1970.
On Using Early Keyboard Fingering, Early Music Laboratory, 1971.
(Translator) Guiseppe Tartini, *Treatise on Ornaments of Music,* Early Music Laboratory, 1971.
(Editor and compiler) *J. S. Bach's Six Violin Solos,* Early Music Laboratory, 1972.

Also author of numerous articles on musicology, published by Early Music Laboratory. Editor of violin department, *International Musician,* 1941-61.

The Sol Babitz Archive of Music was dedicated to the University of California, Los Angeles, Music Library on February 18, 1983.

BIOGRAPHICAL/CRITICAL SOURCES:

PERIODICALS

Fine Line (University of California, Los Angeles), spring, 1983.*

[Death date provided by wife, Mae Babitz]

*   *   *

BAHADUR, K(rishna) P(rakash)   1924-

PERSONAL: Born February 21, 1924, in Allahabad, British India (now India); son of Iqbal (in government service) and Chameli Bahadur; married Premlata Saran, May 4, 1946; children: Arti (daughter), Ajaj (son), Sanjay (son; deceased), Sandhya (daughter; deceased). *Education:* Allahabad University, B.A., 1943, M.A., 1945.

ADDRESSES: Home—1 Lal Bahadur Shastri Rd., Windsor Place, Lucknow, Uttar Pradesh, India 226001.

CAREER: Government of India, Indian Administrative Service, magistrate in Jhansi, 1946-48, sub-divisional magistrate in Barabanki, 1948-52, deputy custodian of evacuee property in Lucknow, 1952-57, assistant land reforms commissioner, board of revenue, Lucknow, 1957-59, additional district magistrate in Allahabad, 1959-60, deputy secretary of Uttar Pradesh government, 1960-64, district magistrate in Pilibhit, 1964-67, district magistrate and administrator of municipal board in Bulandshahr, 1967-70, district magistrate in Muzaffarnagar, 1970-73, joint secretary of Uttar Pradesh government, 1973-75, special secretary, 1975-76, commissioner and secretary of twenty point programme for social and youth welfare and national integration, 1976-77, administrator of municipal corporation, Varanasi, 1977-78, inspector-general of Uttar Pradesh prisons, 1978-81, chairman of vigilance commission, 1981-82. Managing director of Majhola Sugar Factory, 1964-67.

Chairman of L. H. Ayurvedic College, 1964-67; administrator of Lakhaoti College, 1967-70.

AWARDS, HONORS: Rotary Club Special Public Services Certificate for meritorious public service and good administration as district magistrate, 1969-70; Vidya Visharada from Arogya Asraman (Madras), 1970, for *Poems of Love and Wisdom;* Vidyaratnakar from Akhila Bharatiya Shri Pandit Parishad Varanasi, 1979.

WRITINGS:

The Story of Rama (juvenile), Indian Press (Allahabad), 1961.
Love in the East, Jaico Publishing (Bombay), 1971.
Stories for Children, two volumes, Sterling Publishers (New Delhi), 1971.
Folk Tales of Uttar Pradesh, Sterling Publishers, 1972.
Ramacharitmanasa: A Study in Perspective, Ess Ess Publications (New Delhi), 1976.
Son of Wisdom (verse), Rajhans Publishers, 1976.
Five Windows to God, Somayia, 1977.
Population Crisis in India, National Publishers (Calcutta), 1977.
Caste, Tribes, and Cultures of India, nine volumes, Ess Ess Publications, 1977-85.
A History of Indian Civilization, six volumes, Ess Ess Publications, 1979-83.
The Seen and the Unseen, Anuj Publications (Lucknow), 1980.
A Humourist's Hoo's Hoo, Sterling Publishers, 1980.
Eve in the East, Jaico Publishing, 1985.
A History of the Freedom Movement in India, four volumes, Ess Ess Publications, 1986-88.

FICTION IN ENGLISH

The Wiles of Women, Hind Pocket Books (Shahdara), 1973.
The Case of the Poisoned Cat, Sterling Publishers, 1974.
Murder in the Delhi Mail, Sterling Publishers, 1976.

FICTION IN HINDI

Apradhi Kaun (title means "Who Is the Killer"), Ajai Publications (New Delhi), 1969.
Sone Ki Chori (title means "Gold Thief"), Vijay Pocket Books, 1971.
Husn Aur Hire (title means "Youth and Diamonds"), Arvind Pocket Books, 1972.
Hatyara Kaun (title means "Who Is the Murderer"; collection of detective stories), Anurag Prakashan (Varanasi), 1978.

"WISDOM OF INDIA" SERIES

The Wisdom of Yoga: A Study of Pantanjali's Yoga Sutra, Sterling Publishers, 1977.
The Wisdom of Saankhya, Sterling Publishers, 1978.
The Wisdom of Nyaaya, Sterling Publishers, 1978.
The Wisdom of Vaisheshika, Sterling Publishers, 1979.
The Wisdom of Meemaansaa, two volumes, Sterling Publishers, 1983.
The Wisdom of Vedaanta, Sterling Publishers, 1983.
The Upanishads, Sterling Publishers, in press.

EDITOR

A. Bingley, *Caste, Tribes, and Culture of Rajputs,* Ess Ess Publications, 1978.
(And author of introduction) A. Bingley, *History, Caste, and Culture of Jats and Gujars,* 2nd revised edition, Ess Ess Publications, 1978.

TRANSLATOR

The Burning Bush (verse translation of the Gita), Indian Press, 1961, published as *The Gita,* Anuj Publications, 1980.
Poems of Love and Wisdom (selections from the Satsais of Behari), Jaico Publishing, 1970.
The Rasikapriya of Keshavadasa, Motilal Banarsidass (New Delhi), 1972.
Five Verse Upanishads, New Light Publishers (New Delhi), 1972.
Selections from Ramachandrika of Keshavadasa, Motilal Banarsidass, 1976.
Rangilal Pandit, *The Parrot and the Starling,* Motilal Banarsidass, 1977.
Love Poems of Ghananand, Motilal Banarsidass, 1977.
One Hundred Rural Songs of India, Motilal Banarsidass, 1978.
Bangla Love Poems, Dreamland Publication (Varanasi), 1978.
The Satasai of Bahari (verse translation), Penguin (India), in press.

OTHER

Also author of *The Silver Lining,* Vishv Vijay Publishers; contributor to *Major World Writers,* St. James, 1984.

WORK IN PROGRESS: The Definitive Gita, for Penguin (India).

SIDELIGHTS: K. P. Bahadur told *CA:* ''Curiously enough though I have written very little verse, it was with verse that I started in 1958—a small poem 'The Wink of Brahma,' a prize winner in an all-India poetry competition organised by *The Caravan,* a weekly magazine. After that I tried my hand at verse in my UNESCO translations [published by Motilal Banarsidass], but it was hard finding a publisher (though in the end I got one). I was reminded of 'Silly Bananas' who, on the advice of an editor, underwent the suffering he lacked to become a poet, only to be told by him 'Forget it, poetry doesn't sell.'

''I began writing because I found it a fascinating hobby. It made me think I had created something, however humble. Recently I rediscovered in it a spiritual elixir. When in just two years I suddenly lost two grown-up children, it was writing *alone* which gave me strength. I wrote desperately in those years, not to create, but to forget.

''When I write I take a blank exercise book, and I plunge into it with the determination of a man who, bent on learning to swim, would jump into a river. It is only the first lines which seem difficult. Once a few pages are filled up, I am through. My love is philosophy, because in writing about that I not only write; I also learn. It is things unseen that have intrigued men most of all. Even if one can't know them, one can come nearer them in philosophy. I recall for instance a verse from Tulsidasa's *Ramacharitmanasa:* 'In a dream a beggar may become a king, a king a beggar,/ On waking neither the one gains nor the other loses anything:/ Such is this delusive living.'

''Unfortunately sex has begun to dominate life and letters; people have little time and many tensions. And so serious books gather dust on library shelves. Still the worthwhile author must, I believe, be content in finding 'fit audience, though few.' It is better I think to die a poor author who is remembered, than a rich one who is forgotten.

''I consider writing twenty percent inspiration and eighty percent hard work (some of it pure drudgery, like making the index and typing, if one does it himself). The author has to be a persistent guy. Before he gets into print he must be pre-pared to collect quite a few polite rejection slips. But just as somewhere there is a life companion waiting for every eligible bachelor, so for every worthwhile author there is a publisher waiting. The greatest reward of writing, however, is not in seeing oneself in print but acquiring soul purity. All creative writing elevates the soul. When one produces a truly noble work he may be doing a good turn to one who reads it, but he profits most himself.''

BIOGRAPHICAL/CRITICAL SOURCES:

PERIODICALS

Aaj Ki Kheti (New Delhi), August, 1972.
Books Abroad, January, 1974.
Hindustan Times Weekly, June 3, 1979.
Times (India), February 18, 1979.

*   *   *

BAKER, William Howard
    See McNEILLY, Wilfred (Glassford)

*   *   *

BALDUCCI, Ernesto   1922-

PERSONAL: Born August 6, 1922, in St. Fiora, Grosseto, Italy. *Education:* Attended University of Florence.

ADDRESSES: Home—Badia Fiesolana, San Domenico di Fiesole, Florence, Italy.

CAREER: Roman Catholic priest.

WRITINGS:

Papa Giovanni, Vallecchi, 1964, translation by Dorothy White published as *John, ''The Transitional Pope,''* McGraw, 1965.
La Chiesa come Eucaristia, Queriniana, 1970.
I servi inutili, Cittadella, 1970.
Diario dell'esodo, Vallecchi, 1971.
La fede dalla fede, Cittadella, 1975.
Fede e scelta politica, Mandadori, 1977.
Le ragioni della speranza, Coines, 1977.
Il mandorlo e il fuoco, Borla, Volume 1, 1979, Volume 2, 1980, Volume 3, 1981.
Cittadini del mondo, Principato, 1981.
Il terzo millennio, Bompiani, 1981.
La pace, realismo di un'utopia, Principato, 1983.
Storia del pensiero umano, three volumes, Edizioni Cremonese, 1986.
L'uomo planetario, Edizioni Camunia, 1986.
Il cerchio che si chiude, Edizioni Marzitti, 1987.
Giorgio La Pira, Edizioni Cultura, 1987.
Gandhi, Edizioni Cultura, 1988.

*   *   *

BALLINGER, W. A.
    See McNEILLY, Wilfred (Glassford)

*   *   *

BALSIGER, Dave
    See BALSIGER, David (Wayne)

BALSIGER, David (Wayne)   1945-
    (Dave Balsiger; David Penn, David Wayne)

PERSONAL: Born December 14, 1945, in Monroe, Wis.; son of Leon C. (a real estate broker) and Dorothy May (a sales clerk; maiden name, Meythaler) Balsiger; married Janie Frances Lewis (an office administrator), September 26, 1969 (divorced, 1982; remarried, 1988); married Robyne Lynn Betzsold (a high school teacher) July 10, 1982 (divorced, 1987); children: (first marriage) Lisa Atalie, Lori Faith; (second marriage) Jennifer Ann. *Education:* Attended Pepperdine University, 1964-66, Cypress Junior College, 1966, Chapman College World Campus Afloat, 1967-68, and International College in Copenhagen, 1968; National University, B.A., 1977. *Religion:* Protestant.

ADDRESSES: Office—P.O. Box 10428, Costa Mesa, Calif. 92627.

CAREER: Bank of America, teller in Los Angeles, Santa Ana, and El Toro, Calif., 1964-66; *Anaheim Bulletin,* Anaheim, Calif., chief photographer and feature writer, 1968-69; *Money Doctor* (consumer magazine), Anaheim, publisher and editor, 1969-70; Walt Neill Associates (advertising and public relations agency), Anaheim, office manager, 1969-70; World Evangelism, San Diego, Calif., media director, 1970-72; Master Media (marketing agency), owner and manager, San Diego, 1972; Logos International (book publishers), Plainfield, N.J., director of marketing and news editor, 1972-74; Donald S. Smith Associates (advertising agency), Anaheim, vice-president, 1974-76, 1982-84; Schick Sunn Classic Productions, Inc., Los Angeles, director of research development, 1976-78; Balsiger Enterprises (publishing firm), Costa Mesa, Calif., owner, 1978—; Writeway Professional Literary Associates (literary agency), Costa Mesa, president, 1984—; Biblical News Service (specialty publisher), publisher and editor, 1984—.

Researcher and technical advisor for various films and television programs, including "Operation Thanks," in which he also appeared, 1965, "In Search of Noah's Ark," 1976, "The Life and Times of Grizzly Adams," 1976-77, "The Lincoln Conspiracy," 1977, "The Bermuda Triangle," 1977, "Beyond and Back," 1977, "The Last of the Mohicans," 1977, and "The Incredible Rocky Mountain Race," 1977. Visiting professor, National University, 1978-79. Assistant press agent for Ronald Reagan for Governor campaign, 1966; associate member of Orange County and San Diego World Affairs Councils, 1969-70; manager of James E. Johnson's campaign for U.S. Senate, 1974; member of California Republican Assembly, 1975-78, 1981—; Republican candidate for U.S. Congress, 1978. Has appeared as guest on such television programs as "Face the Nation," "Good Morning, America," "The Today Show," and "Nightline." Member of board of directors of Chapman College World Campus Afloat, 1967, and Chrisma Ministries, 1969-73. Member of board of directors, Christian Public Policy Council.

MEMBER: International Church Relief Fund (member of board), National Citizens Action Network (NCAN; formerly Restore a More Benevolent Order Coalition [RAMBOC]; founder and president), National University Presidents Associates, National University Alumni Association, National Writers Club, California Alliance, Religion in Media Association, Christian Public Policy Council (member of board of directors), Anatole Fellowship (executive committee member), Coalition on Revival (steering committee member).

AWARDS, HONORS: Leadership citation from alumni board of Pepperdine University, 1965; Vietnam appreciation citation, American Soldiers in Vietnam, 1966; named "Writer of the Month" by *California Writer,* 1967; L.H.D., Lincoln Memorial University, 1977, for "outstanding Lincoln research"; received Key to the City of Costa Mesa, Calif., 1977, for outstanding community service; named to Literary Hall of Fame, 1977; George Washington Honor Medals, Freedoms Foundation, 1978, for *The Lincoln Conspiracy,* and 1979, for *Beyond Defeat;* Top Silver Angel Trophy Awards, National Religion in Media Association, 1979, for *Beyond Defeat,* 1980, for *Presidential Biblical Scorecard,* 1986, for *Candidates Biblical Scorecard,* and 1987, for *Family Protection Scorecard: Special Edition on South Africa,* which also won the Grand Winner Mercury Award for Public Affairs, and Gold Mercury Award for Public Affairs magazine, National Media Conference Competition, 1987.

WRITINGS:

(Under name Dave Balsiger; with Mike Warnke and Les Jones) *The Satan-Seller* (biography about Warnke), Logos International, 1972.

The Back Side of Satan (documentary), Creation House, 1973.

(Under name Dave Balsiger; with Don Musgraves) *One More Time* (personal narratives), Bethany Fellowship, 1974.

Noah's Ark: I Touched It, Logos International, 1974.

(Under name Dave Balsiger; with Randy Bullock) *It's Good to Know* (biography about Bullock), Mott Media, 1975.

(Under name Dave Balsiger; with Charles E. Sellier, Jr.) *In Search of Noah's Ark,* Schick Sunn Classic Books, 1976.

(With Sellier) *The Lincoln Conspiracy,* Schick Sunn Classic Books, 1977.

(With James E. Johnson) *Beyond Defeat* (biography about Johnson), introduction by Charles W. Colson, Doubleday, 1978.

(Under name Dave Balsiger; with Marvin Ford and Don Tanner) *On the Other Side* (biography about Ford), Logos International, 1978.

Presidential Biblical Scorecard, Biblical News Service, 1980, new edition, 1984.

Candidates Biblical Scorecard, Biblical News Service, 1986.

(Editor and author of introduction) *Family Protection Scorecard: Special Edition on South Africa,* Biblical News Service, 1987.

(Editor and author of introduction) *Family Protection Scorecard: Special Edition on AIDS,* Biblical News Service, 1987.

"MINI GUIDE BOOK" SERIES

Local Area Maps: Orange County, Disneyland, Knott's Berry Farm, Beaches, Greater Los Angeles Airports, and Southern California, Balsiger's Mini Guide Books, 1979.

Greater Los Angeles Airports: Los Angeles, John Wayne, Burbank, Ontario, Palm Springs, and Long Beach Airports, Balsiger's Mini Guide Books, 1979.

Fun, Food, and Lodging near O. C. Airport, Lion Country, and in Newport Beach, Balsiger's Mini Guide Books, 1979.

Southern California Amusement Attractions, Balsiger's Mini Guide Books, 1979.

Fun and Food around Disneyland and Knott's Berry Farm, Balsiger's Mini Guide Books, 1979.

Lodging near Disneyland and Knott's Berry Farm: Includes Campgrounds, RV Parks, Youth Hostels, Home Stays,

Maps, and Information Hotlines, Balsiger's Mini Guide Books, 1979.
Unique Restaurants of Orange County, Balsiger's Mini Guide Books, 1979.
42 Miles of Fun: The Orange County Beach Scene, Balsiger's Mini Guide Books, 1979.

OTHER

Midnight Alarm (special edition tabloid), C.C.T.V. Publications, 1985.

Also author with Barbara Lowe of screenplay "Mistah Abe," 1982. Foreign feature correspondent for regional magazines and southern California newspapers, covering nearly sixty countries abroad. Contributor of articles and photographs, sometimes under pseudonyms David Penn and David Wayne, to magazines, including *Christian Bookseller, National Courier, National Star, Your Church, California Farmer,* and *Time.* News editor of *Logos Journal,* 1972-73. Frequent "Debate Page" columnist for *USA Today.*

WORK IN PROGRESS: Mistah Abe, a nonfictional account of life with the Lincolns from 1850 to 1860 as told by their house servant, based on Balsiger's screenplay of the same title.

SIDELIGHTS: A trained private investigator, David Balsiger spearheaded investigative efforts that resulted in a Grand Jury probe of the Orange County, California, Tax Assessor's Office in 1974. The Grand Jury eventually issued criminal indictments and convictions against a congressman, local officials, and an officer of a large business conglomerate. In 1978 Balsiger ran as a Republican candidate for the 38th California Congressional District, losing by 979 votes. Balsiger was also active in a coalition that opposed the Soviet Union's participation in the 1984 Summer Olympic Games.

MEDIA ADAPTATIONS: Sunn Classic Pictures filmed "In Search of Noah's Ark" in 1976 and "The Lincoln Conspiracy" in 1977, both of which were based on Balsiger's books of the same title, and were featured on NBC-TV's "Movie of the Week."

AVOCATIONAL INTERESTS: Hiking, camping, and ocean fishing.

BIOGRAPHICAL/CRITICAL SOURCES:

PERIODICALS

California Writer, November, 1967.
Los Angeles Times, October 9, 1977.
Monroe Evening Times, May 30, 1975.
Orange County Register, August 2, 1987, August 25, 1987, September 1,1987.
Register (Santa Ana, Calif.), April 27, 1984.
Salt Lake Tribune, September 18, 1977.
San Clemente Sun Post, April 10, 1978.
Washington Post, May 9, 1984.

*   *   *

BANGLEY, Bernard K. 1935-

PERSONAL: Born November 27, 1935, in Suffolk, Va.; son of James H. (a fire chief) and Ethel (a secretary; maiden name, Modlin) Bangley; married Anna Hollowell (a water colorist), February 1, 1958; children: David, Diane, Jennifer. *Education:* Hampden-Sydney College, B.A., 1959; Union Theological Seminary, Richmond, Va., M.Div., 1962.

ADDRESSES: Office—Quaker Memorial Presbyterian Church, P.O. Box 4056, Lynchburg, Va. 24502.

CAREER: Ordained Presbyterian minister, 1962; pastor of Presbyterian churches in Ararat, Va., 1962-66, and Rockbridge Baths, Va., 1967-77; First Presbyterian Church, Lynchburg, Va., associate pastor, 1977-80; Pine Shores Presbyterian Church, Sarasota, Fla., pastor, 1981-84; Quaker Memorial Presbyterian Church, Lynchburg, pastor, 1984—. Lecturer in psychology at Virginia Military Institute, 1971-73.

AWARDS, HONORS: Grants from Virginia Foundation for the Humanities and Public Policy.

WRITINGS:

(Editor and translator) *Growing in His Image,* Harold Shaw, 1983.
Bible Basic: Bible Games for Personal Computers, Harper, 1983.
Spiritual Treasure, Paulist Press, 1985.
Forgiving Yourself, Harold Shaw, 1986.

FILMS

"Descent" (clay animation), Atlantis Films, 1973.
"What Mean These Stones?," Virginia Foundation for the Humanities and Public Policy, 1976.
"Portrait of a Farmer," Virginia Foundation for the Humanities and Public Policy, 1977.
"Echoes from the Garden" (biography), Virginia Foundation for the Humanities and Public Policy, 1979.

OTHER

Also composer of music, including "Requiem," performed in Lexington, Va., winter, 1977. Contributor to magazines.

SIDELIGHTS: "Writing is in my blood," Bernard K. Bangley told *CA.* "I have honestly enjoyed the steady discipline of writing imposed by the ministry. I have also been grateful for a lifetime of reading in fields that range widely."

BIOGRAPHICAL/CRITICAL SOURCES:

PERIODICALS

Hampden-Sydney Record, winter, 1973.
Roanoke Times, July 15, 1973.

*   *   *

BARRANGER, M(illy) S(later) 1937-

PERSONAL: Born February 12, 1937, in Birmingham, Ala.; daughter of Clem C. (an engineer) and Mildred (Hilliard) Slater; married Garic Kenneth Barranger (an attorney), August 26, 1961; children: Heather D. *Education:* Alabama College (now University of Montevallo), B.A., 1958; Tulane University, M.A., 1959, Ph.D., 1964.

ADDRESSES: Home—10 Branbury Lane, Chapel Hill, N.C. 27514. *Office*—Dramatic Art Department, University of North Carolina, CB# 3230, Graham Memorial, Chapel Hill, N.C. 27599.

CAREER: Louisiana State University in New Orleans (now University of New Orleans), special lecturer in English, 1964-69; Tulane University, New Orleans, La., assistant professor, 1969-73, associate professor of theatre and speech, 1973-82, chairman of department, 1971-82; Visiting Young Professor of Humanities, University of Tennessee, 1981-82; University of North Carolina at Chapel Hill, professor of dramatic art and chairman of department, 1982—. Executive director of Tulane Center Stage Theatre, 1973-78; executive producer of Playmakers Repertory Company, 1982—. Scholar-in-residence, Yale Drama School, 1982. Member of board of directors, Paul Green Foundation and Institute of Outdoor Drama.

MEMBER: American Theatre Association (vice-president of administration, 1975-77; president, 1978-79), Association for Theatre in Higher Education, American Theatre Association College of Fellows, National Theatre Conference (president, 1988, 1989), League of Professional Theatre Women (member of New York branch), Ibsen Society of America, Southeastern Theatre Conference.

AWARDS, HONORS: New Orleans Bicentennial Award for Achievement in the Arts, 1976; Southwest Theatre Conference Award for Professional Achievement, 1978; President's Award for Outstanding Achievement in the Performing Arts, University of Montevallo, 1979.

WRITINGS:

(Editor with Daniel Dodson) *Generations: A Thematic Introduction to Drama*, Harcourt, 1971.
(Contributor) *Dictionary of Church History*, Westminster, 1971.
Theatre: A Way of Seeing, Wadsworth, 1980.
Theatre: Past and Present, Wadsworth, 1984.
(Co-editor) *Notable Women in the American Theatre*, CIS Press, 1989.
Understanding Plays, Allyn & Bacon, 1989.

Contributor of articles to *College Language Association Journal, Modern Drama, Theatre Journal, Theatre News, Southern Quarterly, Southern Theatre, New Orleans Review*, and *Quarterly Journal of Speech*.

AVOCATIONAL INTERESTS: Music, films, travel.

*   *   *

BATES, Robert H(inrichs) 1942-

PERSONAL: Born December 5, 1942, in Brooklyn, N.Y.; son of David H. (a physician) and Lucy (Thomas) Bates; married Margaret Rouse (a college administrator), June 6, 1964; children: Elizabeth. *Education:* Haverford College, B.A. (summa cum laude), 1964; Massachusetts Institute of Technology, Ph.D., 1969.

ADDRESSES: Office—Room 214, Perkins Library, Department of Political Science, Duke University, Durham, N.C. 27706.

CAREER: California Institute of Technology, Pasadena, assistant professor, 1969-76, associate professor, 1976-79, professor of social studies, 1981-84; Duke University, Durham, N.C., Henry R. Luce Professor, 1985—.

MEMBER: American Political Science Association, African Studies Association, Phi Beta Kappa.

AWARDS, HONORS: Recipient of fellowships from Woodrow Wilson National Fellowship Foundation, 1964-65, Center for International Studies at Massachusetts Institute of Technology, 1969, Social Science Research Council, 1969-70 and 1983, National Institutes of Health, 1971-73, National Science Foundation, 1977-79 and 1983-84, Guggenheim Foundation, 1985, and Center for Advanced Studies in the Behavioral Sciences, 1986.

WRITINGS:

Unions, Parties, and Political Development, Yale University Press, 1971.
Patterns of Uneven Development, Graduate School of International Studies, University of Denver, 1974.
Rural Responses to Industrialization, Yale University Press, 1976.
(With Michael Lofchie) *Agricultural Development in Africa*, Praeger, 1980.
Markets and States in Tropical Africa: The Political Basis of Agricultural Policies, University of California Press, 1981.
Essays on the Political Economy of Rural Africa, Cambridge University Press, 1983.
Toward a Political Economy of Development, University of California Press, 1988.
Beyond the Miracle of the Market, Cambridge University Press, 1989.

Also contributor of chapters to books. Contributor to political science and African studies journals.

WORK IN PROGRESS: Research on peasant politics, rural development, and agricultural development.

BIOGRAPHICAL/CRITICAL SOURCES:

PERIODICALS

Times Literary Supplement, February 26, 1982.

*   *   *

BAXTER, Angus 1912-

PERSONAL: Born June 8, 1912, in Bristol, England; immigrated to Canada, 1953; son of William (a company director) and Joyce (Cantle) Baxter; married Nan Pearson, June 19, 1943; children: Susan Baxter Barcsay. *Education:* University of Bristol, B.A., 1933.

ADDRESSES: Home—5 Katherine St., Lakefield, Ontario, Canada K0L 2H0.

CAREER: Writer and genealogist. Seccombe House, Ltd., Toronto, Ontario, vice president of publishing and marketing, 1953-71. Gives lectures; appears on television and radio shows. *Military service:* British Army, 1939-46; became lieutenant colonel; received Order of the Red Cross of Belgium.

MEMBER: Ontario Genealogical Society, Society of Genealogists.

AWARDS, HONORS: In Search of Your European Roots: A Complete Guide to Tracing Your Ancestors in Every Country in Europe was chosen one of the four best reference books published in 1986 by the American Library Association.

WRITINGS:

In Search of Your Roots, Macmillan, 1978, revised edition, 1984.
In Search of Your British and Irish Roots: A Complete Guide to Tracing Your English, Welsh, Scottish, and Irish Ancestors, Morrow, 1982, revised edition 1988.
Tracing Your Origins, Methuen, 1983.
In Search of Your European Roots: A Complete Guide to Tracing Your Ancestors in Every Country in Europe, Macmillan, 1984.
In Search of Your German Roots: A Complete Guide to Tracing Your Ancestors in the Germanic Areas of Europe, Genealogical Publishing Co., 1987, revised edition, 1988.

Angus Baxter's Dos and Don'ts for Ancestor-Hunters, Genealogical Publishing Co., 1987.
In Search of Your Canadian Roots, Macmillan, 1989.

WORK IN PROGRESS: A fictionalized historical family chronicle based on research into the lives of the author's family and his wife's family.

SIDELIGHTS: Angus Baxter's books offer tips on tracing one's ancestry and relate, often humorously, both his successes and failures in tracing his own family heritage. Baxter told *CA:* ''I am enthusiastic about ancestor-hunting and have been ever since I stumbled around in 1950 when I started to trace my forebears. Now I can look back over seven centuries of detailed knowledge about the Baxters and their houses and farms in a remote valley in the Lake District of England. One of my ancestors founded a free grammar school in 1703 with the proviso that 'the Latin and Greek tongues be taught.' This led to a local saying: 'Nowadays in Swindale they plow the fields in Latin and shear the sheep in Greek.' Another ancestral discovery that amused me was the fact that my grandfather was known as 'Whisky Willie.' I have one thing in common with him and it is not his first name!

''I receive at least one letter a day from somewhere in the world asking for help and advice in solving a difficult genealogical problem. I always reply, although I've been heard to say, 'I wish they would pay the return postage.' On the other hand, I get much pleasure from later letters of thanks that tell of distant ancestors and long-lost cousins found as the result of my advice.

''Ancestor-hunting is fun. As you go back, open your heart and mind to the past—don't be content with names and dates and births and deaths—find out what they did, how they lived, what part they played in the life of their town or village. These are the leaves for the bare branches of the family tree.''

AVOCATIONAL INTERESTS: Travel (Greece, Nepal, Malaysia, Sri Lanka, Australia, New Zealand, Tahiti, South Africa, and some eighty other countries).

*   *   *

BAXTER, Glen   1944-

PERSONAL: Born March 4, 1944, in Leeds, England; son of Charles (a welder) and Florence B. (Wood) Baxter; married Carole Suzanne Turner (a teacher), February 3, 1970; children: Zoe, Harry. *Education:* Leeds College of Art, diploma, 1965. *Politics:* ''None.'' *Religion:* ''None.''

ADDRESSES: Home—London, England. *Agent*—Wylie Aitken & Stone, 250 West 57th St., Suite 2106, New York, N.Y. 10107.

CAREER: Victoria & Albert Museum, London, England, teacher, 1968-74; writer and artist. Part-time lecturer at Royal College of Art, Canterbury, England, and in Norwich, England. Art exhibited in galleries in London, Amsterdam, Venice, San Francisco, Sydney, Bruges, Antwerp, Brussels, Paris, and New York City, and Les Sables d'Olonne, France.

WRITINGS:

SELF-ILLUSTRATED

The Works, Wyrd Press, 1977.
Atlas, DeHarmonie, 1979, Knopf, 1983.
The Impending Gleam, J. Cape, 1981, Knopf, 1982.

Glen Baxter, His Life: The Years of Struggle, Thames & Hudson, 1983, Knopf, 1984.
Jodhpurs in the Quantocks, J. Cape, 1986.

OTHER

(Illustrator) William and Brendan Kennedy, *Charlie Malarkey and the Belly-Button Machine*, Atlantic Monthly Press, 1986.

Drawings have been published as postcards by Bug House Productions. Contributor to periodicals, including *London* magazine.

WORK IN PROGRESS: Drawings and stories in collaboration with American poets Clark Coolidge and Larry Fagin; illustrations for ''Elk Hunting in Sweden'' by Sir George Washington Baxter, and ''America and Japan Must Work Together,'' by William Joseph Baxter.

SIDELIGHTS: While also an artist, the multi-talented Glen Baxter is best known in America for his humorous illustrations, drawn in the pen and ink style of early twentieth-century children's fiction. The pictures bear zany, inappropriate captions which highlight the bizarre activities of characters such as a young man in a turn-of-the century Boy Scout uniform fleeing in terror from ''Another slim volume of English Poetry!'' or of ''The Halitosis Kid,'' a cowboy whose major weapon is his bad breath. According to a *Publishers Weekly* contributor, Baxter's work is what you would get ''if you crossed Edward Gorey's mock-serious macabre cartoons with Monty Python's off-the-wall humor.'' And Michael Heath of *Punch* feels Baxter is ''rather like Max Ernst with laughs.''

In *Atlas,* Baxter often adds strange appendages to his characters, including nose cones and tails, yet the characters involved behave as if their situations were perfectly normal. ''Whatever seems recognizable is only a foxy ruse to trapdoor our equilibrium,'' warns David Meltzer in the *American Book Review.* He continues that the cartoons are ''all drawn with proper adoration and captioned with cuckoo paraphrases of all that's awesome and winsome in vanished prose styles of the pulp era of the 1930's and 40's.'' *Books and Bookmen* contributor John Walsh, however, finds that ''somehow Baxter's accompanying captions seem too often to occupy a world excessively far from that of the pictured image, and the resulting dislocation seems rather less than hilarious.'' But most reviewers enjoy Baxter's work, including a reviewer for the *New York Times Book Review*, who describes the cartoons as ''deadpan drawings . . . at once beguiling and entertaining.'' And a critic in the *Times Literary Supplement* concludes that Baxter ''applies techniques of fusing the familiar with the absurd and the improbable, but also a memorably fresh eye and ear, to the task of giving new, surprising and hilarious life to verbal and visual cliches.''

Among the highlights of the cartoon collection *The Impending Gleam* are grown men feuding over the use of wimples and cowboys debating the merits of abstract art. ''The result is like a catalogue of the world seen through an agreeably demented prism, as though the horizontal hold had just got integrated with a Portuguese-English phrase book for enthusiasts of amateur dramatics,'' describes *Listener* contributor Stephen Bayley. ''Familiar characters from the folklore of the storybook crowd into an ark of the absurd: Robin Hood admires a laminate finish television set, adventitiously deposited in Sherwood Forest.'' And a *Newsweek* contributor calls Baxter's work ''cartoons that look innocent until they explode like little bombs of madcap incongruity.''

In *Glen Baxter, His Life: The Years of Struggle,* the artist has drawn his autobiography and presented it in his usual farcical manner. Victor Neuburg states in *British Book News* that Baxter's creation "is really a very funny world, and the drawings that depict it are superbly done. . . . It is also a rather sinister world. The laughter is real enough, and long-lasting, but at the same time it has overtones that are far from comforting." *Voice Literary Supplement* contributor Eliot Fremont-Smith, however, not only believes that the autobiography should be taken seriously, but that it brings out a new side of the cartoonist: "Suffice it to say that we are in the hands not only of a master adventurist and romancer, but of an acutely self-plumbing intellect as well. The clarifications tumble forth one upon the other—from the exact nature of young Baxter's sister's household chores to how father Baxter, momentarily in arrears, economized in restaurants; from what the local constable intended to show the lad in his bedroom to how the youth, during school initiation rites, contrived to convey *by bicycle* the great Blackherst Anvil all the way back from Dredgehampton. Inspiring, stirring stuff, and clever, too—though with an edge of melancholy." Fremont-Smith cites one revealing comment from *Glen Baxter:* "Throughout childhood, the constant spectre of family ruin dogged our every movement. We were lectured on the importance of clean underwear, especially when crossing busy roads. There seemed to be some mysterious connection between personal hygiene and traffic flow."

Baxter once told *CA:* "My interest in the works of Ron Padgett, Larry Fagin, Bill Zavatsky, and Clark Coolidge first brought me to America, and especially to New York City. It was here that I gave my first public reading of my work at St. Mark's Church in 1974 and that the Gotham Book Mart Gallery first showed my drawings and watercolors, also in 1974.

"My inspiration for my work can be blamed partly on reading Roger Shattuck's *The Banquet Years* when I was at college. Much earlier influences were Ludwig Wittgenstein, Randolph Scott, and Gabby Hayes."

BIOGRAPHICAL/CRITICAL SOURCES:

BOOKS

Baxter, Glen, *Glen Baxter, His Life: The Years of Struggle,* Thames & Hudson, 1983, Knopf, 1984.

PERIODICALS

American Book Review, July, 1983.
Books and Bookmen, October, 1982.
British Book News, February, 1984.
Listener, November 26, 1981.
Los Angeles Times Book Review, March 11, 1984.
Newsweek, July 19, 1982.
New York Times, February 19, 1988.
New York Times Book Review, May 16, 1982.
Publishers Weekly, December 23, 1983.
Punch, October 28, 1981.
Times Literary Supplement, November 6, 1981.
Village Voice, June 1, 1982.
Voice Literary Supplement, February, 1984.
Washington Times, March 17, 1988.

OTHER

"The South Bank Show" (thirty-minute television program), London Weekend Television, 1984.

BEARDSLEY, John 1952-

PERSONAL: Born October 28, 1952, in New York, N.Y. *Education:* Harvard University, A.B., 1974.

ADDRESSES: Office—Corcoran Gallery of Art, 17th St. at New York Ave., Washington, D.C. 20006.

CAREER: Hirshhorn Museum, Washington, D.C., member of curatorial staff, 1974-78; free-lance art critic and curator, 1978-80; National Endowment for the Arts, Washington, D.C., writer, 1980-81; Corcoran Gallery of Art, Washington, D.C., adjunct curator, 1981—.

WRITINGS:

Probing the Earth: Contemporary Land Projects, Smithsonian Institution Press, 1977.
Art in Public Places, Partners for Livable Places, 1981.
(With Jane Livingston) *Black Folk Art in America: 1930-1980* (museum catalogue), Corcoran Gallery of Art and University Press of Mississippi, 1982.
Earthworks and Beyond: Contemporary Art in the Landscape, Abbeville Press, 1984, 2nd edition, 1989.
A Landscape for Modern Sculpture: The Storm King Art Center, Abbeville Press, 1985.
Hispanic Art in the United States: Thirty Contemporary Painters and Sculptors, Abbeville Press, 1987.

SIDELIGHTS: In his *Voice Literary Supplement* review of *Black Folk Art in America: 1930-1980,* critic Jeff Weinstein notes that museum catalogues are becoming a valuable source of art information, offering "reproductions and art criticism unavailable elsewhere." Weinstein continues, "Such is the case with *Black Folk Art in America,*" observing also that while it is "at first merely a gorgeous selection of works by a few familiar and many just discovered artists, it becomes, as the text unfolds the pictures, a messenger bearing a new definition of contemporary folk art."

BIOGRAPHICAL/CRITICAL SOURCES:

PERIODICALS

Voice Literary Supplement, May, 1982.

*   *   *

BEAUVOIR, Simone (Lucie Ernestine Marie Bertrand) de 1908-1986

PERSONAL: Born January 9, 1908, in Paris, France; died August 14, 1986, of a respiratory ailment in Paris, France; daughter of Georges Bertrand (an advocate to the Court of Appeal, Paris) and Francoise (Brasseur) de Beauvoir; children: (adopted) Sylvie Le Bon. *Education:* Sorbonne, University of Paris, licencie es lettres and agrege des lettres (philosophy), 1929. *Religion:* Atheist.

ADDRESSES: Home—1 bis rue Schoelcher, 75014 Paris, France.

CAREER: Philosopher, novelist, autobiographer, nonfiction writer, essayist, editor, lecturer, and political activist. Instructor in philosophy at Lycee Montgrand, Marseilles, France, 1931-33, at Lycee Jeanne d'Arc, Rouen, France, 1933-37, at Lycee Moliere and Lycee Camille-See, both Paris, France, 1938-43. Founder and editor, with Jean-Paul Sartre, of *Les Temps modernes,* beginning 1945.

MEMBER: International War Crimes Tribunal, Ligue du Droit des Femmes (president), Choisir.

AWARDS, HONORS: Prix Goncourt, 1954, for *Les Mandarins;* Jerusalem Prize, 1975; Austrian State Prize, 1978; Sonning Prize for European Culture, 1983; L.L.D. from Cambridge University.

WRITINGS:

L'Invitee (novel), Gallimard, 1943, reprinted, 1977, translation by Yvonne Moyse and Roger Senhouse published as *She Came to Stay,* Secker & Warburg, 1949, World Publishing, 1954, reprinted, Flamingo, 1984.

Pyrrhus et Cineas (philosophy; also see below), Gallimard, 1944.

Les Bouches inutiles (play in two acts; first performed in Paris), Gallimard, 1945, translation published as *Who Shall Die,* River Press, l983.

Le Sang des autres (novel), Gallimard, 1946, reprinted, 1982, translation by Moyse and Senhouse published as *The Blood of Others,* Knopf, 1948, reprinted, Pantheon, 1984.

Tous les hommes sont mortel (novel), Gallimard, 1946, reprinted, 1974, translation by Leonard M. Friedman published as *All Men Are Mortal,* World Publishing, 1955.

Pour une morale de l'ambiguite (philosophy; also see below), Gallimard, 1947, reprinted, 1963, translation by Bernard Frechtman published as *The Ethics of Ambiguity,* Philosophical Library, 1948, reprinted, Citadel, 1975.

Pour une morale de l'ambiguite [and] *Pyrrhus et Cineas,* Schoenhof's Foreign Books, 1948.

L'Existentialisme et la sagesse des nations (philosophy; title means "Existentialism and the Wisdom of the Ages"), Nagel, 1948.

L'Amerique au jour le jour (diary), P. Morihien, 1948, translation by Patrick Dudley published as *America Day by Day,* Duckworth, 1952, Grove, 1953.

Le Deuxieme Sexe, two volumes, Gallimard, 1949, translation by H. M. Parshley published as *The Second Sex,* Knopf, 1953, reprinted, Random House, 1974 (Volume 1 published in England as *A History of Sex,* New English Library, 1961, published as *Nature of the Second Sex,* 1963), reprinted, Random House, 1974.

The Marquis de Sade (essay; translation of *Faut-il bruler Sade?;* also see below; originally published in *Les Temps modernes*), translation by Annette Michelson Grove, 1953 (published in England as *Must We Burn de Sade?,* Nevill, 1953, reprinted, New English Library, 1972).

Les Mandarins (novel), Gallimard, 1954, reprint published in two volumes, French and European, 1972, translation by Friedman published as *The Mandarins,* World Publishing, 1956, reprinted, Flamingo, 1984.

Privileges (essays; includes *Faut-il bruler Sade?*), Gallimard, 1955.

La Longue Marche: Essai sur la Chine, Gallimard, 1957, translation by Austryn Wainhouse published as *The Long March,* World Publishing, 1958.

Memoires d'une jeune fille rangee (autobiography), Gallimard, 1958, reprinted, 1972, translation by James Kirkup published as *Memoirs of a Dutiful Daughter,* World Publishing, 1959, reprinted, Penguin, 1984.

Brigitte Bardot and the Lolita Syndrome, translated by Frechtman, Reynal, 1960, published with foreword by George Amberg, Arno, 1972.

La Force de l'age (autobiography), Gallimard, 1960, reprinted, 1976, translation by Peter Green published as *The Prime of Life,* World Publishing, 1962.

(With Gisele Halimi) *Djamila Boupacha,* Gallimard, 1962, translation by Green published under same title, Macmillan, 1962.

La Force des choses (autobiography), Gallimard, 1963, reprinted, 1977, translation by Richard Howard published as *The Force of Circumstance,* Putnam, 1965.

Une Mort tres douce (autobiography), Gallimard, 1964, reprinted with English introduction and notes by Ray Davison, Methuen Educational, 1986, translation by Patrick O'Brian published as *A Very Easy Death,* Putnam, 1966, reprinted, Pantheon, 1985.

(Author of introduction) Charles Perrault, *Bluebeard and Other Fairy Tales of Charles Perrault,* Macmillan, 1964.

(Author of preface) Violette Leduc, *La Batarde,* Gallimard, 1964.

(Author of preface) Jean-Francois Steiner, *Treblinka,* Simon & Schuster, 1967.

Les Belles Images (novel), Gallimard, 1966, translation by O'Brian published under same title, Putnam, 1968, reprinted with introduction and notes by Blandine Stefanson, Heinemann Educational, 1980.

La Femme rompue (three novellas), Gallimard, 1967, translation by O'Brian published as *The Woman Destroyed,* Putnam, 1969, reprinted, Pantheon, 1987.

La Vieillesse (nonfiction), Gallimard, 1970, translation by O'Brian published as *The Coming of Age,* Putnam, 1972 (published in England as *Old Age,* Weidenfeld & Nicolson, 1972).

Tout compte fait (autobiography), Gallimard, 1972, translation by O'Brian published as *All Said and Done,* Putnam, 1974.

Quand prime le spirituel (short stories), Gallimard, l979, translation by O'Brian published as *When Things of the Spirit Come First: Five Early Tales,* Pantheon, 1982.

Le Ceremonie des adieux: Suivi de entretiens avec Jean-Paul Sartre (reminiscences), Gallimard, 1981, translation published as *Adieux: A Farewell to Sartre,* Pantheon, 1984.

(Contributor with Jean-Paul Sartre; also editor) *Lettres au Castor et a quelques autres,* Gallimard, 1983, Volume I: *1926-1939,* Volume II: *1940-1963.*

SIDELIGHTS: At Simone de Beauvoir's funeral on April 19, 1986, flowers from all over the world filled the corner of the Montparnasse cemetery where she was laid to rest next to Jean-Paul Sartre (1905-1980). Banners and cards from the American-based Simone de Beauvoir Society, women's studies groups, women's health centers and centers for battered women, diverse political organizations, and publishing houses attested to the number of lives that the author had touched during her seventy-eight years. Five thousand people, many of them recognizable figures from the political, literary, and film worlds, made their way along the boulevard du Montparnasse past her birthplace, past the cafes where she, Sartre, and their friends had discussed their ideas and written some of their manuscripts, to the cemetery.

Beauvoir was a perceptive witness to the twentieth century, a witness whose works span the period from her early childhood days before World War I to the world of the 1980s. Born in Paris in 1908, in the fourteenth "arrondissement" or district where she continued to live throughout most of her life, Beauvoir was raised by a devoutly Catholic mother from Verdun and an agnostic father, a lawyer who enjoyed participating in amateur theatrical productions. The contrast between the beliefs of the beautiful, timid, provincial Francoise de Beauvoir and those of the debonair Parisian Georges de Beauvoir led the young Simone to assess situations independently, unbiased by the solid parental front presented by the more traditional families of many of her classmates. As family finances dwindled during World War I, Beauvoir observed the uninspiring household chores that fell upon her mother and decided that she herself would never become either a housewife or a mother. She had found such pleasure in teaching her younger sister Helene everything she herself was learning at school that she decided to pursue a teaching career when she grew up.

Beauvoir and her best friend Zaza "Mabille" (Beauvoir often assigned fictional names to friends and family members described in her autobiographical writings) sometimes discussed the relative merits of bringing nine children into the world, as Zaza's mother had done, and of creating books, an infinitely more worthwhile enterprise, the young Beauvoir believed. As the girls matured, Beauvoir observed the degree to which Zaza's mother used her daughter's affection and commitment to Christian obedience to manipulate Zaza's choice of career and mate. When Zaza, tormented by her parents' refusal to grant her permission to marry Maurice Merleau-Ponty, the "Jean Pradelle" of the memoirs, died at twenty-one, Beauvoir felt that her friend had been assassinated by bourgeois morality. Many of Beauvoir's early fictional writings attempted to deal on paper with the emotions stirred by her recollection of the "Mabille" family and of Zaza's death. Only many years later did she learn that Merleau-Ponty, who became a well-known philosopher and writer and remained a close friend of Beauvoir's and Sartre's, was unacceptable to the "Mabilles" because he was an illegitimate child.

Despite her warm memories of going as a little girl to early morning mass with her mother and of drinking hot chocolate on their return, Beauvoir gradually pulled away from the traditional values with which Francoise de Beauvoir hoped to imbue her. She and her sister began to rebel, for example, against the restrictions of the Cours Adeline Desir, the private Catholic school to which they were being sent. Weighing the pleasures of this world against the sacrifices entailed in a belief in an afterlife, the fifteen-year-old Beauvoir opted to concentrate on her life here on earth. Her loss of faith erected a serious barrier to communication with her mother.

Beauvoir was convinced during several years of her adolescence that she was in love with her cousin Jacques Champigneulles ("Jacques Laiguillon" in her memoirs), who introduced her to books by such French authors as Andre Gide, Alain-Fournier, Henry de Montherlant, Jean Cocteau, Paul Claudel, and Paul Valery; these books scandalized Beauvoir's mother, who had carefully pinned together pages of volumes in their home library that she did not want her daughters to read. Jacques Champigneulles, however, seemed unwilling to make a commitment either to Beauvoir or to anything else, and the Beauvoir sisters were totally disillusioned when this bright bohemian opted to marry the wealthy and generously dowried sister of one of his friends.

Because family finances did not allow Georges de Beauvoir to provide dowries, his daughters became unlikely marriage prospects for young middle-class men, and both Simone and Helene were delighted to have this excuse for continuing their studies and pursuing careers. Even as a young girl, Beauvoir had a passion for capturing her life on paper. In the first volume of her autobiography, *Memoires d'une jeune fille rangee* (*Memoirs of a Dutiful Daughter*), she looked back with amusement at her determination, recorded in her adolescent diary, to "tell all"; yet her memoirs, her fiction, her essays, her interviews, and her prefaces do indeed record events, attitudes, customs, and ideas that help define approximately seven decades of the twentieth century.

It was through Rene Maheu, a Sorbonne classmate called "Andre Herbaud" in the memoirs, that Beauvoir first met Jean-Paul Sartre in a study group for which she was to review the works and ideas of German philosopher Gottfried Wilhelm von Leibniz. In Sartre, Beauvoir found the partner of whom she had dreamed as an adolescent. As she remarked in *Memoirs of a Dutiful Daughter*, "Sartre corresponded exactly to the ideal I had set for myself when I was fifteen: he was a soulmate in whom I found, heated to the point of incandescence, all of my passions. With him, I could always share everything." And so she did, for fifty-one years, from the time they became acquainted at the Sorbonne in 1929 until his death on April 15, 1980.

Together Sartre and Beauvoir analyzed their relationship, deciding that they enjoyed an indestructible essential love but that they must leave themselves open to "contingent loves" as well, to expand their range of experience. Although marriage would have enabled them to receive a double teaching assignment instead of being sent off to opposite ends of the country, they were intent upon escaping the obligations that such a "bourgeois" institution would entail. That neither had a particular desire for children was an added reason to avoid marriage. A daring and unconventional arrangement during the early 1930s, their relationship raised consternation in conservative members of Beauvoir's family.

Except for a brief period during World War II, Beauvoir and Sartre never lived together but spent their days writing in their separate quarters and then came together during the evenings to discuss their ideas and to read and criticize one another's manuscripts. As both became well-known figures in the literary world, they found it increasingly difficult to maintain their privacy; as *La Force des choses* (*The Force of Circumstance*) records, they had to alter their routine and avoid certain cafes during the years after the war in order to protect themselves from the prying eyes of the public.

Sartre's autobiography, *Les Mots* (*The Words*), published in 1963, dealt only with the early years of his life. Beauvoir's autobiographical writings provide a much more complete and intimate account of the adult Sartre. In several volumes of reminiscences, Beauvoir described their mutual reluctance to leave their youth behind and become part of the adult world, their struggles to set aside adequate time for writing, the acceptance of their works for publication, their travels, their friendships, their gradually increasing commitment to political involvement; her final autobiographical volume, *Le Ceremonie des adieux: Suivi de entretiens avec Jean-Paul Sartre* (*Adieux: A Farewell to Sartre*), recreates her anguish in witnessing the physical and mental decline of a lifelong companion who had been one of the most brilliant philosophers of the twentieth century.

For Beauvoir, writing was not only a way of preserving life on paper but also a form of catharsis, a means of working out her own problems through fiction. Her early short stories, written between 1935 and 1937 and originally rejected by two publishers, were brought out by Gallimard in 1979. The tales in *Quand prime le spirituel* (*When Things of the Spirit Come First: Five Early Tales*) captured Beauvoir's infatuation with Jacques, the tragedy of Zaza's death, the young philosophy teacher's ambivalence about the impact her ideas and her lifestyle might have on her impressionable lycee students in Marseille and Rouen, and her sense of excitement as she saw the world opening up before her. Beauvoir identified strongly with her central character Marguerite who, in the final paragraphs of the book, perceives the world as a shiny new penny ready for her to pick up and do with as she wishes. Terry Keefe's *Simone de Beauvoir: A Study of Her Writings* provides a detailed discussion of each of the five stories that make up this collection.

Experimenting with nontraditional relationships, Sartre and Beauvoir had formed a trio with Beauvoir's lycee student Olga Kosakiewicz in 1933. The anguish experienced by Beauvoir as a result of this intimate three-way sharing of lives led to the writing of her first published work, *L'Invitee* (*She Came to Stay*). In this novel, the author relived the hothouse atmosphere generated by the trio, and she chose to destroy the judgmental young intruder, the fictional Xaviere, on paper, but to dedicate her novel to Olga. The real life situation resolved itself less dramatically after Olga became interested in Jacques-Laurent Bost, a former student of Sartre's, and broke away from the trio; the four principals remained lifelong friends, however. In her 1986 study, *Simone de Beauvior,* Judith Okely suggests that *She Came to Stay* reflects not only the Beauvoir-Sartre-Olga trio but also the young Simone's rivalry with her mother for her father's affections.

With World War II Beauvoir's attention shifted from the concerns and crises of her personal life to a broader spectrum of philosophical, moral, and political issues. In the short essay *Pyrrhus et Cineas,* written during a three-week period in 1943, she launched an inquiry into the value of human activity, examining questions of freedom, communication, and the role of the other in the light of the existentialist ideas presented in Sartre's *L'Etre et le neant: Essai d'ontologie phenomenologique* (*Being and Nothingness: Essay on Phenomenological Ontology*). In his 1975 monograph, *Simone de Beauvoir,* Robert Cottrell discusses *Pyrrhus et Cineas* as "a popularization of existentialist thought."

Beauvoir's second novel, *Le Sang des autres* (*The Blood of Others*), focused on the dilemma of dealing with the consequences of one's acts. The liberal Jean Blomart, shaken by the accidental death of a young friend he inspired to participate in a political demonstration, struggles throughout much of the narrative to avoid doing anything that may inadvertently harm another human being, his "search for a saintly purity," as Carol Ascher labels it in *Simone de Beauvoir: A Life of Freedom.* The female protagonist, Helene Bertrand, intent on protecting her own happiness in a world turned upside down by war and the German Occupation, is shaken out of her inertia by the cries of a Jewish mother whose small daughter is being wrenched away from her by the Gestapo. Helene seeks an active and ultimately fatal involvement in terrorist Resistance activities orchestrated by Jean Blomart, who has decided finally that violence is perhaps the only rational response to Hitler's insanity. Infused with the euphoria of Resistance camaraderie, the novel highlights a question that is also central to Sartre's play *Les Mains sales* (*Dirty Hands*)—the relationship between intellectuals and violence.

Moral and ethical issues continued to dominate Beauvoir's works in the 1940s. Caught up in the success of Sartre's play *Les Mouches* (*The Flies*) during the Occupation, she decided that she too would like to write for the theatre. *Les Bouches inutiles* (*Who Shall Die?*), based on a historical incident which took place in the fourteenth century, reprises the main theme of *The Blood of Others,* examining the consequences of a young man's determination to remain pure and blameless by not taking part in the decisions of the town council. The play also protests the assumption that ablebodied young men are the only truly useful citizens in a besieged community. Beauvoir frankly related in her memoirs dramatist Jean Genet's criticism of her theatrical sense, confessing that he sat beside her shaking his head disapprovingly throughout the entire opening night performance. She never again attempted to write for the theatre, although Keefe notes the dramatic potential of her plot and the "spare and sharp" quality of the dialogue in Act I.

One of the most difficult aspects of the war years for Beauvoir and her friends was the often senseless deaths of their contemporaries. In *Simone de Beauvoir: Encounters with Death,* Elaine Marks focuses on the preoccupation with death premeating the writer's works and on what Marks labels her evasions of confrontation with death. For Beauvoir, death was an outrage, a scandal, and in 1943, she began to write a third novel, *Tous les hommes sont mortel* (*All Men Are Mortal*), for which she created a hero who has become immortal and who therefore meanders from his thirteenth-century birthplace in Italy on through to the twentieth century. Because Raymond Fosca's alternating attempts to seize political power and to establish peace on earth all result in disappointment and frustration, the reader concludes that immortality would be a curse rather than a blessing, that life's value is derived from sharing experiences with one's contemporaries and from a willingness to take the risks implicit in human mortality. According to *The Force of Circumstance,* this novel was Beauvoir's attempt to deal with her own feelings and anxieties about death. Konrad Bieber, in his 1979 study *Simone de Beauvoir,* senses the presence of "the philosopher behind the novelist" throughout the book yet also notes "long moments of drama, of genuine poignancy, that bring to the fore all that is human."

As Beauvoir's works and Sartre's became better known, the label "existentialist" was regularly attached to them. At first Beauvoir resisted the use of the term, but she and Sartre gradually adopted it and began to try to explain existentialist philosophy to the public. In *Pour une morale de l'ambiguite* (*The Ethics of Ambiguity*), published in 1947, Beauvoir defined existentialism as a philosophy of ambiguity, one which emphasized the tension between living in the present and acting with an eye to one's mortality; she also attempted to answer critics who had accused existentialists of wallowing in absurdity and despair. In the four essays published the following year as *L'Existentialisme et la sagesse des nations* ("Existentialism and the Wisdom of the Ages") Beauvoir argued for the importance of a philosophical approach to modern life. Here she defended existentialism against accusations of frivolity and gratuitousness and explained that existentialists considered man neither naturally good nor naturally bad: "He is nothing at first; it is up to him to make himself good or bad depending upon whether he assumes his freedom or denies it." Emphasizing the fact that man can be "the sole and sovereign master of his destiny," Beauvoir insisted that existentialist philosophy was essentially optimistic; in *Simone de Beauvoir and the Limits of Commitment,* however, Anne Whitmarsh sees the author's existentialism as "a stern ethical system."

With the end of the war came the opportunity to travel again. Beauvoir spent four months in the United States in 1947, lecturing on college campuses throughout the country about the moral problems facing writers in postwar Europe. She recorded her impressions through journal entries dating from January 25 to May l9, 1947, in *L'Amerique au jour le jour* (*America Day by Day*) dedicated to black author Richard Wright and his wife Ellen. Her perceptive eye took in a great variety of detail but saw everything through a lens whose focus was influenced by certain preconceived notions. Keefe finds the value of the book in the record it presents of Beauvoir's "excitement and disappointment at a historical moment when many Europeans knew little about America and were eager to expose themselves to its impact, for better or worse." Consistently critical of capitalist traditions and values, *America Day by Day* can be paired with Beauvoir's account of her 1955 trip to China, *La Longue Marche: Essai sur la Chine* (*The Long March*), in which she euphorically accepts everything in communist China. While praising Beauvoir's ability to evoke settings and glimpses of life in China, Keefe sees *The Long March* as "first and foremost a long, extremely serious attempt to explain the situation of China in 1955-56 and justify the direction in which the new regime [was] guiding the country."

Ready after the war to begin her purely autobiographical works, Beauvoir realized that she first needed to understand the extent to which being born female had influenced the pattern of her life. She therefore spent hours at the Biblotheque Nationale (National Library) in Paris seeking documentation for each section of the book that was to become the battle cry of feminism in the latter half of the twentieth century. When *Le Deuxieme Sexe* (*The Second Sex*) appeared in 1949, reactions ranged from the horrified gasps of conservative readers to the impassioned gratitude of millions of women who had never before encountered such a frank discussion of their condition. The opening statement of the section on childhood, "One is not born a woman, one becomes one," has become familiar throughout the world, and the book advises women to pursue meaningful careers and to avoid the status of "relative beings" implied, in its author's view, by marriage and motherhood. Donald L. Hatcher's 1984 study, *Understanding "The Second Sex,"* provides valuable information about the philosophical framework of what is undoubtedly Beauvoir's best-known work.

Before turning to her memoirs, Beauvoir wrote the novel that won her the prestigious Goncourt Prize. *Les Mandarins* (*The Mandarins*) presents the euphoria of Liberation Day in Paris and the subsequent disillusionment of French intellectuals who had been temporarily convinced that the future was theirs to fashion as they saw fit, but who found themselves gradually dividing into factions as the glow of Resistance companionship and of victory over the Nazis dimmed. Beauvoir always denied that *The Mandarins* was a *roman a clef,* with Robert Dubreuilh, Henri Perron, and Anne Dubreuilh representing Sartre, Albert Camus, and herself; nonetheless, echoes of the developing rift between Sartre and Camus, of the discussions of staff members of *Les Temps modernes* (the leftist review founded by Sartre, Beauvoir, and their associates), and of the concern of French intellectuals over the revelation of the existence of Soviet work camps are clearly audible throughout the novel. Moreover, Lewis Brogan is certainly a fictionalized portrait of Chicago author Nelson Algren, who became one of Beauvoir's "contingent loves" during her 1947 trip to the States and to whom the novel is dedicated. Whether or not the work is a *roman a clef,* it is generally regarded, in Ascher's words, as Beauvoir's "richest, most complex, and most beautifully wrought novel."

The first volume of Beauvoir's autobiography appeared in 1958. In *Memoirs of a Dutiful Daughter,* the author chronicled the warmth and affection of the early years of her life, her growing rebellion against bourgeois tradition, her sense of emancipation when she moved from the family apartment on the rue de Rennes to a rented room at her grandmother's. Highlighted in these pages are her close association with her sister—"I felt sorry for only children," she declared, her relationship with Zaza, her infatuation with Jacques. Jean-Paul Sartre appears only in the concluding pages of this volume. In *Simone de Beauvoir on Woman,* Jean Leighton focuses on the portrait of Zaza in *Memoirs of a Dutiful Daughter,* finding that she "epitomizes . . . traditional feminine qualities. Next to Simone de Beauvoir she is the most vivid person in the book."

Beauvoir dedicated the second volume of her autobiography, *La Force de l'age* (*The Prime of Life*), to Sartre. The first half of the narrative tells the story of their lives from 1929 to 1939, recounting the exhilarating sense of freedom they experienced as they pooled their money to travel throughout France and to London, Italy, Germany, and Greece. Here the memoir looks back on the experiment of the trio, on the illness which put Beauvoir in a clinic for several weeks, on her insistence upon living in the present and trying to ignore the menacing news filtering through from Hilter's Germany. The second half of the book begins in 1939, as the German occupation of France was about to begin, and ends with Liberation Day in Paris in August 1944. These pages provide one of the most vivid accounts of life in France during World War II, as the reader witnesses the lines of people waiting for gas masks, the sirens and descents into metro stations during air raids, and the struggle to find enough food to survive. These were the years when leftist intellectuals remained in close contact with one another, when Albert Camus, actress Maria Casares, writers Michel Leiris and Raymond Queneau, theatrical director Charles Dullin, and artist Pablo Picasso joined Beauvoir, Sartre, Olga, and Bost in "fiestas" that provided occasional nights of relaxation amidst the bombings and the anticipation of the Allied landing. The emotions of Liberation Day were unforgettable for Beauvoir, who asserted: "No matter what happened afterward, nothing would take those moments away from me; nothing has taken them away; they shine in my past with a brilliance that has never been tarnished."

What did become tarnished, however, were Beauvoir's hopes of participating in the creation of a brave new world, preferably one in which socialism would solve the problems of society. The third volume of autobiography, *The Force of Circumstance,* begins with the Liberation and covers the period from 1944 to early 1963. Despite the success of her many books that were published during those years, despite her extensive travels and increasing political involvement, *The Force of Circumstance* was written with a heavy heart because of the anguish associated with the Algerian war. These were also the years during which Beauvoir began to reflect upon aging and death, began to realize that there were certain activities in which she was engaging for perhaps the last time. The final sentence in the memoir's epilogue has been widely discussed: "I can still see . . . the promises with which I filled my heart when I contemplated that gold mine at my feet, a whole life ahead of me. They have been fulfilled. However, looking back in amazement at that gullible adolescent I once was, I am stupefied to realize to what extent I have been cheated." She felt cheated because the goals she had set for herself did not lead to the sense of fulfillment that she had anticipated; she felt cheated too because all human activity, no matter how successful, leads uncompromisingly to the same impasse, the death of the individual. For Konrad Bieber, *The Force of Circumstance* is "a remarkable monument to the crucial years of the cold war. . . . A whole era, with its ups and downs, its hopes and disillusionments, is seen through the temperament of a highly gifted writer."

Nineteen sixty-three was a time of personal crisis for Beauvoir both because of her vision of the state of the modern world and because of the death of her mother. Deeply affected by watching her mother valiantly struggle against cancer, Beauvoir shared with her readers the anxiety of knowing more about her mother's condition than she could reveal to her, the dilemma of how far to authorize heroic medical measures, the pain of helplessly watching a life ebb away. In the moving pages of *Une Mort tres douce* (*A Very Easy Death*), a slender volume dedicated to her sister, the author recaptured the warmth of her childhood relationship with her mother and reactivated her admiration for this woman who had always "lived against herself" yet could still appreciate a ray of sunlight or the song of the birds in the tree outside her hospital window. Looking back at her interaction with her mother, Beauvoir realized the full impact of Francoise de Beauvoir's unhappy childhood, of the unfortunate social restraints that kept her mother from finding a satisfying outlet for the energy and vitality which she had passed on to her daughters but which she had never been able to use appropriately herself. Sartre considered *A Very Easy Death* Beauvoir's best work; Marks, who has commented on its "excruciating lucidity," calls the book the only one of the author's writings "in which the hectic rhythm which she projects on the world is abruptly interrupted and the interruption prolonged."

Tout compte fait (*All Said and Done*), dedicated to Sylvie Le Bon whom Beauvoir later adopted, covers the decade following the publication of *The Force of Circumstance*. Here Beauvoir abandons the chronological treatment of events employed in the earlier volumes of memoirs; instead she devotes one section to speculation about what might have happened *if* she had been born into a different family, she had not met Sartre at the Sorbonne, or had married her cousin Jacques, for example; other sections explore her dreams and provide accounts of her trips to places such as Japan, the U.S.S.R., Israel, and Egypt. After expressing a sense of satisfaction about her ability to communicate the tone of her life to her readers, she leaves it to them to draw whatever conclusions they wish from this partical volume of her autobiography.

Adieux: A Farewell to Sartre, a companion piece to *A Very Easy Death,* records Beauvoir's efforts to cope with the anguish of watching age and illness take their toll on her companion of fifty years. It is dedicated to "those who have loved Sartre, who love him and who will love him." Beauvoir's subsequent publication of Sartre's *Lettres au Castor et a quelques autres* further attempts to share the quality of their relationship with her readers. "Castor" was a nickname invented by her Sorbonne classmate Rene Maheu, who noted the similarity between the name Beauvoir and the English word "beaver" (*castor* in French) and who considered it an appropriate appellation for the hard-working Beauvoir. The two volumes of Sartre's letters cover a period from 1926 to 1963 and include quite detailed references to his involvements with other women. Some feminist criticism has seen *Adieux,* with its rather graphic account of Sartre's mental and physical decline, as Beauvoir's revenge on her partner for the pain inflicted upon her by his numerous "contingent" affairs. In an essay appearing in *Philosophy and Literature,* Hazel Barnes disagrees, considering these passages "both factual reporting and a tribute" and noting "the profound respect which Sartre and Beauvoir had for each other, something deeper than the obvious affection, companionship and commonality of values, more bedrock than love."

During the mid-1960s Beauvoir had also returned to fiction with a novel, *Les Belles Images.* Dedicated to Claude Lanzmann, one of the younger staff writers for *Les Temps modernes*

and a "contingent love" of Beauvoir's from 1952 to 1958, *Les Belles Images* describes a milieu quite alien to Beauvoir, that of the mid-century technocrats. The novel centers on a bright, attractive career woman, comfortably married and the mother of two daughters, who suddenly finds herself caught between two generations as she attempts to help her estranged mother cope with the loss of her wealthy lover and to answer the probing questions of her own ten-year-old daughter about poverty and misery. As she gradually develops sensitivity she has been taught by her mother to restrain, Laurence despairs of ever changing anything in her own life, yet vows in the concluding lines of the novel that she will raise her daughters to express their feelings, to allow themselves to be moved by the plight of undernourished children in Third World countries, of factory workers shackled to uninspiring jobs. Laurence is an incarnation of the contemporary superwoman who attempts to juggle her commitments to her career, her husband, her children, her aging parents, even her lover, until she eventually falls apart under the strain of such responsibilities.

The three stories in the 1967 collection *La Femme rompue* (*The Woman Destroyed*) reflect the degree to which Beauvoir had been listening to the women who wrote and spoke to her about the problems of their more traditional lives. One of the stories, "Age of Discretion," focuses on a recently retired woman professor, author of several books, for whom life seems to lose all meaning when her son abandons academia for a more lucrative business job and when critics suggest that her latest book merely repeats ideas presented in earlier ones. "Monologue" takes the reader through a New Year's Eve of neurotic ranting by the twice-divorced Murielle, whose possessiveness has driven her sixteen-year-old daughter to suicide and who wants to force her son and her second husband to live with her once again so that she will regain her social status as a wife and mother. The title story highlights the plight of the middle-aged Monique, who abandoned her medical studies in order to marry and have children and who suddenly discovers that her husband is having an affair with a younger and more independent woman. In each case the protagonist has allowed herself to be relegated to the status of a "relative being" dependent upon others for her sense of identity. According to Mary Evans in *Simone de Beauvoir: A Feminist Mandarin,* the setting of both *Les Belles Images* and *The Woman Destroyed* is "the culture in which people become objects, but the objects least able to manipulate their fate are women."

In the late 1960s Beauvoir turned her attention to an important study of old age, a companion piece to *The Second Sex.* She gave her book, published in 1970, the straightforward title *La Vieillesse* ("Old Age"), but the title was euphemistically translated as *The Coming of Age* in the United States. The work focuses upon the generally deplorable existence of most elderly people, and along with a film entitled "Promenades au pays de la vieillesse" ("Wandering through the Pathways of Old Age"), in which Beauvoir appeared, this book defines one of the as yet unresolved dilemmas of the late twentieth century. Bieber sees in *The Coming of Age* an example of Beauvoir's "boundless empathy" and of her understanding of human frailty; Ascher, in contrast, finds it "shocking for its lack of feeling for the special plight of old women" and asserts that for the author the universal is male, at least among the elderly.

Several critics have taken Beauvoir to task for her apparently negative presentation of women and their values. Leighton sees the women of Beauvoir's fiction as "finely etched portraits of various types of femininity [that] personify in a compelling way the pessimistic and anti-feminine bias of *The Second Sex.*" Ascher's personal letter to Beauvoir in the middle of her *Simone de Beauvoir: A Life of Freedom* speaks of "my resistance to accepting your grim view of women's condition." For Evans there is an assumption in Beauvoir's works that "traditionally male activities (the exercise of rationality, independent action, and so on) are in some sense superior, and are instances almost of a higher form of civilization than those concerns—such as child care and the maintenance of daily life—that have traditionally been the preserve of women." Whitmarsh is critical of the author's confining her political commitment to the ethical and the literary rather than extending her activities to the practical aspects of everyday politics. Okely finds that many of Beauvoir's generalizations are based on her limited experience in a small Parisian intellectual circle and do not apply as readily to cultures that are neither western, white, nor middle class.

A substantial number of interviews granted by Beauvoir gave her the opportunity to clarify many of her ideas and to answer her critics. Speaking with Francis Jeanson in an interview published as *Simone de Beauvoir ou l'entreprise de vivre,* she elaborated on her childhood, on her relationship with both her parents, on her conviction that being a woman had never hindered her progress toward the goals she had set for herself. At that particular time (the mid-1960s), she defined feminism as a way of living individually and of fighting collectively and strongly opposed any tendency to consider men as the enemy. Literature, in her opinion, should serve to make people more transparent to one another. She acknowledged a puritanical strain in herself caused by her early upbringing and spoke with Jeanson about what she labeled her "schizophrenia," a determination to throw herself wholeheartedly into any project she undertook and an accompanying unwillingness to deviate from her original plan even when intervening circumstances made it no longer practical.

Betty Friedan's *It Changed My Life* contains a dialogue with Beauvoir, to whom Friedan looked for answers to the questions raised by the American feminist groups that were forming in the 1970s. In her introduction to this dialogue, Friedan acknowledges her debt to Beauvoir: "I had learned my own existentialism from her. It was *The Second Sex* that introduced me to that approach to reality and political responsibility that . . . led me to whatever original analysis of women's existence I have been able to contribute." When they spoke, however, she and Beauvoir disagreed completely about the viability of motherhood for women seeking their independence and about the possibility of providing salaries for housewives in order to enhance their self-image. In *It Changed My Life,* Friedan expressed disappointment over what she saw in Beauvoir as detachment from the lives of real women, and concluded: "I wish her well. She started me out on a road on which I'll keep moving. . . . There are no gods, no goddesses. . . . We need and can trust no other authority than our own personal truth."

Six interviews taped by Alice Schwarzer between 1972 and 1982 and published in English as *After "The Second Sex": Conversations with Simone de Beauvoir,* provide further insight into the evolution of Beauvoir's ideas. Here she traced the development of her own commitment to feminism, noting her gradual realization that Marxism and socialism did little to encourage equality for women. She spoke about becoming actively involved in the women's movement from the time of its inception in France in 1970, of campaigning to make contraception and abortion available for all women, of urging women to pursue careers in order to achieve economic auton-

omy and to think carefully before becoming "trapped" in marriage and maternity. In 1976 she defined her position as follows: "I am not militant in the strict sense of the word. I'm not thirty years old, I'm sixty-seven, and I'm an intellectual who uses words as weapons—but I'm ready to listen and to help the M.L.F. [Women's Liberation Movement in France]."

In 1980 she warned that although there were token women in the French Academy, in graduate programs, and in visible positions in the business and political world, one should not assume the battle for equality had been won and women had only themselves to blame for not succeeding. Asked about the widespread influence her ideas and her works had had throughout the world, she remarked to Schwarzer, ". . . one never sees oneself as an idol. I am Simone de Beauvoir for others, not for myself."

Who was Simone de Beauvoir for others? The newspaper and magazine articles that appeared after her death provide a variety of answers to that question. For many women, she was the person who led the way, who opened up horizons and suggested possibilities of breaking out of the mold society had previously forged for them. The caption on the front page of *Le Nouvel Observateur,* taken from an article by philosophy professor Elisabeth Badinter, proclaimed, "Women, you owe her everything!" According to American feminist Kate Millett, quoted in London's *Observer,* "She had opened a door for us. All of us . . . women everywhere, their lives touched and illumined ever after." In the *New York Times* Gloria Steinem remarked that "More than any other single human being, she's responsible for the current international women's movement," and Betty Friedan labeled her "an authentic heroine in the history of womanhood." Despite her determination never to have children of her own, she became the "symbolic mother" of several generations of women. Josyane Savigneau declared in *Le Monde* that women in responsible positions today are "the descendants of this woman without children . . . who, obstinately, for more than sixty years . . . affirmed that there was nothing wrong with being born a woman." The members of the Simone de Beauvoir Audio-Visual Center in Paris paid tribute to the author as they proclaimed on the same page of *Le Monde,* "We are all orphans now."

Most appraisals of Beauvoir's writings focused on *The Second Sex,* called by Philip Wylie in the *New York Times* "one of the few great books of our era." However, Bertrand Poirot-Delpech, who noted in *Le Monde* that Beauvoir was "a much less minor novelist than one might think," described *The Mandarins* as one of the best sources of documentation on the committed intellectuals of the cold war period. Millett pronounced "The Woman Destroyed" "a literary masterpiece" and Beauvoir's books on aging and death great social documents. Michel Contat, writing for *Le Monde,* saw the 1946 novel *All Men Are Mortal* as Beauvoir's most powerful philosophical work, "the most daring, the most scandalous and the most strangely passionate interrogation launched by this great rationalist intellectual against the human condition."

Many newspapers emphasized the relationship between Beauvoir and Sartre. Georges Suffert, writing for *Figaro,* saw the author as "a woman like any other: she tried to live a love story." For Bernard Pascuito of *France-Dimanche,* Beauvoir was "a great lady who dedicated her life to literature but also to the love of a man." Robin Smyth contended in the *Observer* that the Beauvoir-Sartre alliance "will be remembered as one of the great relationships of the century." A *Paris-Match* reporter considered Sartre's almost daily letters to Beauvoir the most meaningful tribute anyone could pay her.

Still other French newspapers highlighted Beauvoir's intelligence and underlined the fact that at twenty-one she was the youngest student ever to receive the "agregation" degree in philosophy. Friends emphasized, however, that her keen mind was accompanied by sincere concern for other people. Jean Cathala noted in *Le Monde* that "her remarkable intelligence was inseparable from her remarkable hearts; Millett cited her "endless generosity and patience" in giving of herself and her time to others; singer Juliette Greco recalled in *Le Monde* Beauvoir's "generosity, human tenderness and . . . ability to listen."

Equally praised in the press was Beauvoir's tireless commitment to causes in which she believed. Contacted by *Le Monde* for his reaction to the author's death, Jack Lang, former Minister of Culture under Francois Mitterrand, described Beauvoir as "a generous human being who never hesitated to defend the cause of the oppressed." The League for the Rights of Women, which Beauvoir was instrumental in organizing, noted in *Le Monde* the degree to which she helped numerous causes by putting her literary talents to practical use. Claudine Serre recorded in *Le Monde Aujourd'hui* that to the last days of her life, Beauvoir remained "a free woman opposed to servitude, and nothing ever appeased her anger. . . . Her commitment . . . did not diminish with age."

MEDIA ADAPTATIONS: The Mandarins was adapted for film by Twentieth Century-Fox in 1969; *The Blood of Others* was adapted for film by Home Box Office starring Jodie Foster in 1984.

BIOGRAPHICAL/CRITICAL SOURCES:

BOOKS

Ascher, Carol, *Simone de Beauvoir: A Life of Freedom*, Beacon Press, 1981.

Beavoir, Simone de, *Pour une morale de l'ambiquite*, Gallimard, 1947, reprinted, 1963, translation by Bernard Frechtman published as *The Ethics of Ambiguity*, Philosophical Library, 1948, reprinted, Citadel, 1975.

Beauvoir, Simone de, *L'Existentialisme et la sagesse des nations* (philosophy; title means "Existentialism and the Wisdom of the Ages"), Nagel, 1948.

Beauvoir, Simone de, *L'Amerique au jour le jour* (diary), P. Morihien, 1948, translation by Patrick Dudley published as *America Day by Day*, Duckworth, 1952, Grove, 1953.

Beauvoir, Simone de, *Le Deuxieme Sexe*, two volumes, Gallimard, 1949, translation by H. M. Parshley published as *The Second Sex*, Knopf, 1953, reprinted, Random House, 1974 (Volume 1 published in England as *A History of Sex*, New English Library, 1961, published as *Nature of the Second Sex*, 1963).

Beauvoir, Simone de, *Memoires d'une jeune fille rangee* (autobiography), Gallimard, 1958, reprinted, 1972, translation by James Kirkup published as *Memoirs of a Dutiful Daughter*, World Publishing, 1959, reprinted, Penguin, 1984.

Beauvoir, Simone de, *La Force de l'age* (autobiography), Gallimard, 1960, reprinted, 1976, translation by Peter Green published as *The Prime of Life*, World Publishing, 1962.

Beauvoir, Simone de, *La Force des choses* (autobiography), Gallimard, 1963, reprinted, 1977, translation by Richard Howard published as *The Force of Circumstance*, Putnam, 1965.

Beauvoir, Simone de, *Une Mort tres douce* (autobiography), Gallimard, 1964, reprinted with English introduction and notes by Ray Davison, Methuen Educational, 1986, translation by Patrick O'Brian published as *A Very Easy Death*, Putnam, 1966, reprinted, Pantheon, 1985.

Beauvoir, Simone de, *Tout compte fait* (autobiography), Gallimard, 1972, translation by O'Brian published as *All Said and Done*, Putnam, 1974.

Beauvoir, Simone de, *Quand prime le spirituel* (short stories), Gallimard, 1979, translation by O'Brian published as *When Things of the Spirit Come First: Five Early Tales*, Pantheon, 1982.

Beauvoir, Simone de, *Le Ceremonie des adieus: Suivi de entretiens avec Jean-Paul Sartre* (reminiscences), Gallimard, 1981, translation published as *Adieux: A Farewell to Sartre*, Pantheon, 1984.

Bieber, Konrad, *Simone de Beauvoir*, Twayne, 1979.

Bree, Germaine, *Women Writers in France: Variations on a Theme*, Rutgers University Press, 1973.

Brombert, Victor, *The Intellectual Hero*, Lippincott, 1961.

Brophy, Brigid, *Don't Never Forget: Collected Views and Reviews*, Holt, 1966.

Contemporary Literary Criticism, Gale, Volume 1, 1973, Volume 2, 1974, Volume 4, 1975, Volume 8, 1978, Volume 14, 1980, Volume 31, 1985, Volume 44, 1987, Volume 50, 1988.

Cottrell, Robert D., *Simone de Beauvior*, Ungar, 1975.

Dayan, Josee and Malka Ribowska, *Simone de Beauvoir, un film*, Gallimard, 1979.

Dictionary of Literary Biography Yearbook: 1986, Gale, 1987.

Evans, Mary, *Simone de Beauvoir: A Feminist Mandarin*, Tavistock, 1985.

Francis, Claude and Fernande Gontier, *Les Ecrits de Simone de Beauvoir*, Gallimard, 1979.

Francis, Claude and Fernande Gontier, *Simone de Beauvoir: A Life . . . A Love Story*, Librairie Academique Perrin, 1985.

Friedan, Betty, *It Changed My Life*, Random House, 1976.

Hatcher, Donald L., *Understanding "The Second Sex,"* P. Lang, 1984.

Jeanson, Francis, *Simone de Beauvoir ou l'entreprise de vivre*, Editions du Seuil, 1966.

Keefe, Terry, *Simone de Beauvoir: A Study of Her Writings*, Barnes, 1983.

Leighton, Jean, *Simone de Beauvoir on Woman*, Associated University Presses, 1975.

Madsen, Axel, *Hearts and Minds: The Common Journey of Simone de Beauvoir and Jean-Paul Sartre*, Morrow, 1977.

Marks, Elaine, *Simone de Beauvior: Encounters with Death*, Rutgers University Press, 1973.

Nedeau, Maurice, *The French Novelist since the War*, Methuen, 1967.

Okely, Judith, *Simone de Beauvoir*, Pantheon, 1986.

Sartre, Jean-Paul, *Les Mots*, Gallimard, 1963, translation by Bernard Fechtman published as *The Words*, Braziller, 1964.

Schwarzer, Alice, *After "The Second Sex": Conversations with Simone de Beauvoir*, Pantheon Books, 1984.

Whitmarsh, Anne, *Simone de Beauvoir and the Limits of Commitment*, Cambridge University Press, 1981.

Zephir, Jacques J., *Le Neo-Feminisme de Simone de Beauvoir*, Editions Denoel/Gonthier, 1982.

PERIODICALS

Antioch Review, Volume 31, number 4, 1971-72.

Atlantic, June, 1958.

Canadian Forum, October, 1965.
Catholic Forum, October, 1965.
Catholic World, August, 1958.
Chicago Tribune Book World, March 20, 1983.
Commentary, August, 1965, August, 1972.
Contemporary French Civilization, spring, 1984.
Dalhousie Review, autumn, 1970.
Feminist Studies, summer, 1979.
Fontaine, October, 1945.
Forum for Modern Languages Studies, April, 1975.
France-Dimanche, April 27, 1986.
French Review, April, 1979.
Globe & Mail (Toronto), April 19, 1986.
Hecate, Volume 7, number 2, 1981.
Journal de la Ligue des Droits de l'Homme, Number 33, 1984.
La Vie en rose, March 16, 1984.
Le Monde, March 20, 1948, April 16, 1986.
Le Nouvel Observateur, April 18-24, 1986.
L'Express, November 7, 1963.
Los Angeles Times, April 25, 1984.
MOSAIC: A Journal for the Comparative Study of Literature and Ideas, spring, 1975.
Nation, June 8, 1958, June 27, 1959, June 14, 1975.
New Statesman, June 6, 1959, January 5, 1968.
Newsweek, June 8, 1959, February 9, 1970.
New Yorker, February 22, 1947.
New York Review of Books, July 20, 1972.
New York Times, June 2, 1974, May 6, 1984, April 15, 1986.
New York Times Book Review, May 18, 1958, June 7, 1959, March 3, 1968, February 23, 1969, July 21, 1974, November 7, 1982.
Paris-Match, April 25, 1986.
Paris Review, spring/summer, 1965.
Philosophy and Literature, Volume 9, number 1, 1985.
Saturday Review, May 22, 1956.
Signs, Volume 5, number 2, 1979.
Time, March 20, 1966, May 22, 1972.
Times (London), January 21, 1982, August 12, 1982, May 11, 1984.
Times Literary Supplement, June 5, 1959, May 5, 1966, March 30, 1967, April 4, 1980, December 25, 1981, January 21, 1983.
Washington Post Book World, August 18, 1974, May 20, 1984.

OBITUARIES:

PERIODICALS

Chicago Tribune, April 15, 1986.
Detroit Free Press, April 15, 1986.
Figaro, April 20, 1986.
Le Monde aujourd'hui, April 20-21, 1986.
Los Angeles Times, April 15, 1986.
Newsweek, April 28, 1986.
Observer, April 20, 1986.
Publishers Weekly, May 2, 1986.
Time, April 28, 1986.
Times (London), April 15, 1986.
USA Today, April 15, 1986.
Village Voice, May 27, 1986.
Washington Post, April 15, 1986.*

—*Sidelights by Yolanda Astarita Patterson*

*   *   *

BECKETT, Kenneth A(lbert) 1929-
   (Keith Bower)

PERSONAL: Born January 12, 1929, in Brighton, England;
son of Albert Henry (a tax inspector) and Gladys (a secretary; maiden name, Bower) Beckett; married Gillian Tuck (a writer and editor), August 1, 1973; children: Keith Christopher. *Education:* Royal Horticultural Society School of Horticulture, diploma, 1953.

ADDRESSES: Home and office—Bramley Cottage, Stanhoe, King's Lynn, Norfolk PE31 8QF, England.

CAREER: Brighton Parks Department, apprentice, 1943-47, improver, 1949-51; St. Louis Botanic Garden, St. Louis, Mo., horticulturist, 1954; John Innes Research Institute, Bayfordbury, England, technical assistant, 1955-63; Glasgow Botanic Garden, Glasgow, Scotland, assistant curator, 1963-65; *Gardeners' Chronicle,* London, England, technical editor, 1965-69; free-lance writer, 1969—. *Military service:* British Army, 1947-49.

MEMBER: International Dendrological Society, Royal Horticultural Society (committee member), Botanical Society of the British Isles, British Pteridological Society, Hardy Plant Society, Hebe Society, European Bamboo Society, Alpine Garden Society.

AWARDS, HONORS: Veitch Memorial Medal, Royal Horticultural Society, 1987, for advancement of the science and practice of horticulture.

WRITINGS:

(With Tom Stobart) *Reader's Digest Pocket Guide to Herbs* (booklet), Reader's Digest Association (London), 1971.
(Editor) *The Gardener's Bedside Book,* Arco, 1973.
The Love of Trees, Octopus, 1975.
(With wife, Gillian Beckett, and Roy Hay) *Dictionary of House Plants,* Rainbird, 1975.
(With G. Beckett) *Illustrated Encyclopaedia of Indoor Plants,* Doubleday, 1976.
Illustrated Dictionary of Botany, Tribune Books, 1977.
Green Fingers Encyclopaedia, Orbis, 1978.
Amateur Greenhouse Gardening, Ward, Lock, 1979.
(With G. Beckett) *Planting Native Trees and Shrubs,* Jarrold, 1979.
(Editor and contributor) *The Love of Gardening,* Cassell, 1980.
The Complete Book of Evergreen Trees, Shrubs, and Plants, Van Nostrand, 1981.
Growing Hardy Perennials, Biblio Distribution, 1981.
(Editor with G. Beckett) J. Rhia and R. Subik, *The Illustrated Encyclopedia of Cacti and Other Succulents,* Octopus, 1981.
Growing under Glass, Simon & Schuster, 1982.
(With David Carr and David Stevens) *The Contained Garden: A Complete Illustrated Guide to Growing Plants, Flowers, Fruits, and Vegetables Outdoors in Pots,* Viking, 1983.
Climbing Plants, Croom Helm, 1983.
The R. H. S. Encyclopedia of House Plants, Century Hutchinson, 1987.

BOOKLETS

Let's Grow Chrysanthemums, Charles Letts, 1976.
. . . Dahlias, Charles Letts, 1976.
. . . Handy Bulbs, Charles Letts, 1976.
. . . House Plants, Charles Letts, 1976.
. . . Gladioli, Charles Letts, 1976.
. . . Lilies, Charles Letts, 1976.
. . . Sweet Peas, Charles Letts, 1976.
. . . Roses, Charles Letts, 1976.

. . . Plants in Window Boxes, Charles Letts, 1976.

"THE GARDEN LIBRARY" SERIES

Herbs, Ballantine, 1984.
Annuals and Biannuals, Ballantine, 1984.
Roses, Ballantine, 1984.
Flowering House Plants, Ballantine, 1984.

"AURA GARDEN HANDBOOKS" SERIES

Alpines, Marshall Cavendish, 1985.
Conifers, Marshall Cavendish, 1985.
Fuchsias, Marshall Cavendish, 1985.
Colourful Shrubs, Marshall Cavendish, 1985.
Lawns, Marshall Cavendish, 1985.

OTHER

Contributor of horticulture articles to magazines, sometimes under pseudonym Keith Bower. Former editor, *News Bulletin* of the Botanical Society of the British Isles and *Bulletin* of the Hardy Plant Society.

WORK IN PROGRESS: Editing a massive encyclopaedia of alpine and rock plants, for the Alpine Garden Society.

SIDELIGHTS: Kenneth A. Beckett told *CA:* "I began writing articles on plants in 1955 because I wanted to share my enthusiasm with fellow gardeners. It was never my intention to write books, but as soon as I became a free-lance writer and consultant I was asked by the Reader's Digest Association to act as a technical adviser during the compilation of their (now best selling) book, *Encyclopaedia of Garden Plants and Flowers.* This opened my eyes to the possibilities of book authorship and when Octopus Books Ltd. asked me to write a general book on trees I was keen to have a go. *The Love of Trees* was my first book. It was not horticultural and gave me the opportunity to concentrate on the plants and their homelands, a particular interest of mine.

"Over the years I have been asked more and more to write and edit encyclopaedic gardening books. This certainly puts my knowledge to the test and gives quite a lot of satisfaction, though the work can be very repetitive, tedious and mentally tiring. The books I have enjoyed writing most of all concentrate on the plants in detail and are on subjects of my own choice, for example, *Climbing Plants* and *The Complete Book of Evergreen Trees, Shrubs, and Plants.* But though of my own choosing, the books were commissioned and given a word number total to work to. The latter book was one of a series of eighty so-called "complete" guides and so I was landed with an impossible title for a book which could not be complete with just 60,000 words. Such titles are an embarrassment to author and publisher alike!

"To earn a living writing gardening books and articles, one has to do what the publisher asks, no more and no less. It would be a real luxury to sit down and write a series of books on the plants and places seen on my travels about the world, but no publisher is interested and one has to admit that such a project would never be financially viable in our monetarist society!"

Beckett participated in a plant-hunting expedition to Chile in 1971 and 1972 and has also visited New Zealand, Australia, Hawaii, Tahiti, Easter Island, Japan, and five countries of Europe.

BIOGRAPHICAL/CRITICAL SOURCES:

PERIODICALS

Globe and Mail (Toronto), May 19, 1984.
Los Angeles Times Book Review, August 5, 1984, August 12, 1984, September 27, 1987.

*   *   *

BECKHAM, Stephen Dow   1941-

PERSONAL: Born August 31, 1941, in Coos Bay, Ore.; son of Ernest Dow (a teacher, logger, and salesman) and Anna M. (Adamson) Beckham (a teacher); married Patricia Joan Cox (a music teacher), August, 1967; children: Andrew Dow, Ann-Marie C. *Education:* University of Oregon, B.A., 1964; University of California, Los Angeles, M.A., 1966, Ph.D., 1969. *Politics:* Democrat. *Religion:* Baptist.

ADDRESSES: Home—1389 Southwest Hood View Lane, Lake Oswego, Ore. 97034. *Office*—Department of History, Lewis and Clark College, Portland, Ore. 97219.

CAREER: Long Beach State College (now California State University, Long Beach), Long Beach, Calif., lecturer in history, 1968-69; Linfield College, McMinnville, Ore., assistant professor, 1969-72, associate professor, 1972-76; Lewis and Clark College, Portland, Ore., associate professor, 1977-81, professor of history, 1981—. Consultant to Coos, Lower Umpqua, and Siuslaw Indian Tribes, 1972-85, Small Tribal Organization of Western Washington, 1973, 1980—, Chinook Indian Tribe, 1978—, Cow Creek Band of Umpqua Tribe of Indians, 1979—, and to Cowlitz Indian Tribe, 1978—. Member of board of advisers, National Trust for Historic Preservation, 1977-83; member of Oregon advisory committee on historic preservation, 1977-84; board member, John and LaRee Caughey Foundation, Los Angeles, 1984—, and Native American Arts Council, Portland Art Museum, 1988—. Expert witness in federal courts in Oregon and Washington in a number of cases concerning Indian tribes.

MEMBER: American Historical Association, Organization of American Historians, Western History Association.

AWARDS, HONORS: Grant from National Endowment for the Humanities, 1972; faculty enrichment grant, Canadian government, 1986; Oregon Preservationist of the Year award, 1986; national award for contributions in American history, Daughters of the American Revolution, 1986.

WRITINGS:

Requiem for a People: The Rogue Indians and the Frontiersmen, University of Oklahoma Press, 1971.
The Simpsons of Shore Acres, Arago Books, 1971.
Lonely Outpost: The Army's Fort Umpqua, Oregon Historical Society, 1971.
Coos Bay: The Pioneer Period, 1851-1890, Arago Books, 1973.
(Editor and author of introduction) *Tall Tales from Rogue River: The Yarns of Hathaway Jones,* Indiana University Press, 1974.
(Contributor) William Loy and Allan Stuart, editors, *Historical Atlas of Oregon,* University of Oregon Press, 1976.
The Indians of Western Oregon: This Land Was Theirs, Arago Books, 1977.
Identifying and Assessing Historical Cultural Resources, Forest Service, U.S. Department of Agriculture, 1978.
(With Rick Minor and Kathryn Anne Toepel) *Cultural Resource Overview of the BLM Lake District, South-Central*

Oregon: Archaelology, Ethnography, History, Department of Anthropology, University of Oregon, 1980.
(With Minor and Toepel) *Cultural Resource Overview of BLM Lands in Northwestern Oregon: Archaeology, Ethnography, History,* Department of Anthropology, University of Oregon, 1980.
(With Minor and Toepel) *Prehistory and History of BLM Lands in West-Central Oregon: A Cultural Resource Overview,* Department of Anthropology, University of Oregon, 1981.
(With Minor and Toepel) *Native American Religious Practices in the Coastal Zone of Oregon,* Department of Anthropology, University of Oregon, 1984.
(Co-editor with Harriet Duncan Munnick) *Catholic Church Records of the Pacific Northwest,* Volume 6: *Grand Ronde Indian Reservation, 1860-1898,* Binford & Mort, 1987.

Also author of *Land of the Umpqua: A History of Douglas County, Oregon,* 1986, and of televison series "This Land Was Theirs: The Indians of the Oregon Coast," produced by Columbia Broadcasting System and Oregon Educational Broadcasting Co., 1971-72. Author or co-author of seventy-one cultural resource consultant studies in Pacific Northwest archaeology, ethnohistory, and history for federal and state agencies, 1974—, including Army Corps of Engineers, Forest Service, Bureau of Land Management, Bureau of Reclamation, U.S. Coast Guard, and the Oregon State Historic Preservation Office. Author or co-author of petitions for federal acknowledgement by the Bureau of Indian Affairs for the Chinook Indian Tribe and the Cowlitz Indian Tribe, 1981—. Contributor to *Handbook of the American Indian,* edited by William Sturtevant. Contributor to professional journals.

SIDELIGHTS: Stephen Dow Beckham told *CA:* "As a teacher I have always felt that I should ask of myself what I ask of my students. I believe that my role in the classroom is, in part, to set an example as well as to display enthusiasm and commitment to the subjects I teach. I believe in getting into history: researching it, reflecting on it, and, if need be, putting on my boots and hiking to where it happened. To teach and write about the past requires the expenditure of time and energy and the marshalling of multiple resources and approaches to bring it alive. Knowledge of the past helps us understand who we are, where we have been, and where we ought to be. It is a mirror to human accomplishment, aspiration, and frailty. My life's work has been concerned with linking past to present through teaching, researching, and writing. It is an enterprise I much enjoy."

*   *   *

BECKMAN, Patti
   See BOECKMAN, Patti

*   *   *

BEER, Edith Lynn   1930-
   (Edith Lynn Hornik, Edith Lynn Hornik-Beer)

PERSONAL: Born November 4, 1930, in Zurich, Switzerland; naturalized U.S. citizen; daughter of Simon (a tobacco manufacturer) and Rosa (Bruell) Beer; married Josef Bernard Hornik (a machine tool engineer), February 9, 1958 (divorced, 1979); children: Robert Bernard, Abigail. *Education:* Simmons College, B.S., 1953; University of Lausanne, graduate study, 1954.

ADDRESSES: Home—865 First Ave., 6D, New York, N.Y. 10017.

CAREER: Free-lance writer. Lecturer on literature and creative writing; appeared on television and radio programs.

MEMBER: Authors Guild, Authors League of America, American Society of Journalists and Authors, National Writers Union.

WRITINGS:

(Under name Edith Lynn Hornik) *You and Your Alcoholic Parent,* Association Press, 1974.
(Under name Edith Lynn Hornik) *The Drinking Woman,* Association Press, 1977.
(Under name Edith Lynn Beer) *Monarch's Dictionary of Investment Terms,* Monarch, 1983.
(Under name Edith Lynn Hornik-Beer) *A Teenager's Guide to Living with an Alcoholic Parent,* Hazelden, 1984.

Also author of weekly column, "The Young World" in *Scarsdale Inquirer, Riverdale Press,* and *Patent Trader,* 1964-67. Contributor to magazines and newspapers in the United States and abroad, including *New York Times, Young Miss, Ingenue, McCall's, Town and Country, Newsday, Annabelle* (Switzerland), *Neue Zuercher Zeitung,* and *Berlin Tagesblatt.*

WORK IN PROGRESS: "My autobiography."

SIDELIGHTS: Edith Lynn Beer wrote *CA:* "My beginnings were interesting and painful. I was born in the city of Zurich in Switzerland shortly before Germany welcomed Hitler's Nazi idealogy. Even though Switzerland is a neutral country some of its citizens were attracted to the politics across its borders.... When I finally started school I felt that my teacher did not like me. He kept pulling my hair, throwing in disgust my exercise book down the center aisle of the classroom and yelling at me. I thought I must be extremely stupid. In front of our classroom window was a large chestnut tree. I repaid my teacher by ignoring him and studying this large tree and the many different kinds of birds which settled on its branches....

"Shortly after our exams our parents decided to take us to the United States. Hitler's army had marched into Poland. France and England were ready to enter the war. On my last day in Switzerland my mother told me to tell my teacher that I was taking my school books with me to the United States. Instead of wishing me well my teacher said, 'Hah, you're Jewish and you're afraid.' It dawned on me only then that that was why he might have been pulling my hair so unnecessarily....

"Within a two year period, until my parents decided where to settle, I attended four different schools in the New York City area. I was happy because no one pulled my hair or threw my copy books down the aisle.... One day my mother came to our public school to ask our teacher how I was doing. 'Wonderful,' the teacher informed her. My parents discussed this verdict. They disagreed with my teacher. They felt my education had been neglected. They took me to a very small local private school, Woodmere Academy, and asked them to test me. The academy agreed with my parents. I did not even know multiplication or division. I was by now supposed to be going into fifth grade. [The academy] informed my parents that they would admit me to the academy as an experiment.... The teachers at the academy with the utmost patience showed me that I could catch up. They never permitted me to neglect my work and praised me whenever I did well.... My history teacher, Mr. Carter, recognized my love for books and.... gave me back my courage to express my independent thoughts, something the Swiss schools had beaten out of me....

"By the time I went to college, I knew that I wanted to be a writer. I now kept notebooks of my thoughts, feelings and observations. The year I started college, the Second World War was over and my parents moved back to Switzerland. I was determined not to move back to a country where women could not vote. Simmons College promised me a scholarship if my parents would cease to pay my tuition.

"My first article was published under a pseudonym in Switzerland shortly after I graduated college. My policy was to write whatever I thought was worth writing about. When my children were born I went into labor with a yellow pad next to me. By the time my second child was born I had my own weekly newspaper column and writing seemed to me as natural as having children. . . . When I had my own newspaper column, 'The Young World,' I noted how the children who were on drugs kept saying, '[Drugs are] better than the martinis at home.' My first book, *You and Your Alcoholic Parent*, was born from those statements.

"My children are now grown. I am for the moment alone. Something new has come into my life: poetry. It comes to me in unexpected moments. I write them into my notebooks among my thoughts and observations. I frequently turn down offers to write articles, for I feel the mature years in life are a gift and I want to use them wisely. I am now writing my autobiography, not because of my life, but because of what I observed before the war and after the war in both Europe and the United States. It should be told and retold in the manner my old history teacher and Latin teacher had encouraged me to do: prudently."

*   *   *

BEETON, Max
See REDDING, Robert Hull

*   *   *

BELFIGLIO, Valentine J(ohn)   1934-

PERSONAL: Surname is pronounced Bell-*feel*-yo; born May 8, 1934, in Troy, N.Y.; son of Edmond L. (a pharmacist) and Mildred (Sherwood) Belfiglio; married Jane M. Searles, May 27, 1957 (divorced October, 1969); children: Valentine E. *Education:* Union University, B.S., 1956; University of Oklahoma, M.A., 1967, Ph.D., 1970. *Politics:* Republican. *Religion:* Roman Catholic.

ADDRESSES: Home—704 Camilla Lane, Garland, Tex. 75040. *Office*—Department of History and Government, Texas Woman's University, Denton, Tex. 76204.

CAREER: Hospital unit training officer in U.S. Air Force, 1959-67, retired as a captain; University of Oklahoma, Norman, instructor in political science, 1967-70; Texas Woman's University, Denton, assistant professor, 1970-77, associate professor, 1977-87, professor of history and government, 1987—.

MEMBER: International Studies Association, American Political Science Association, Mensa.

WRITINGS:

The Essentials of American Foreign Policy, Kendall-Hunt, 1971.
The United States and World Peace, McCutchan, 1971.
American Foreign Policy, University Press of America, 1979, 2nd edition, 1983.

The Italian Experience in Texas, Eakin (Austin, Tex.), 1983.
The Best of Italian Cooking, Eakin, 1985.
Alliances, Ginn Custom, 1986.
Go for Orbit, Eakin, 1987.

Contributor to newspapers and professional publications, including *International Studies, International Problems, Strategic Digest, Rocky Mountain Social Science Journal, Asian Survey,* and *Asian Studies.*

WORK IN PROGRESS: The preparation of biographical sketches of prominent Italo-Texans for the revised version of *The Handbook of Texas,* for Texas State Historical Society.

SIDELIGHTS: Valentine J. Belfiglio told *CA:* "The broad masses of the people can be moved to immediate action by the power of the spoken word. But the power of the written word is more long-lasting and can inspire the opinion-shaping elite of society to act, centuries after the Angel of Death has embraced the author."

AVOCATIONAL INTERESTS: Gourmet cooking, bridge, golf, sailing, travel (Europe and the Orient).

*   *   *

BELL, Madison (Smartt)   1957-

PERSONAL: Born August 1, 1957, in Nashville, Tenn.; son of Henry Denmark (an attorney) and Allen (a farmer; maiden name, Wigginton) Bell; married Elizabeth Spires (a poet), June 15, 1985. *Education:* Princeton University, B.A. (summa cum laude), 1979; Hollins College, M.A., 1981.

ADDRESSES: Office—Department of English, Goucher College, Towson, Md. 21204.

CAREER: Security guard at Unique Clothing Warehouse (boutique), 1979; production assistant for Gomes-Lowe Associates (commercial production house), 1979; sound man for Radiotelevisione Italiana (Italian national network), 1979; Franklin Library (publishing firm), New York City, picture research assistant, 1980, writer of reader's guides, 1980-83; Berkley Publishing Corp., New York City, manuscript reader and copy writer, 1981-83; Goucher College, assistant professor of English, 1984-86, 1988-89. Visiting writer, Poetry Center, 92nd Street Y, New York City, 1984-86, Iowa Writers' Workshop, 1987-88, and Johns Hopkins Writing Seminars, 1989. Director of 185 Corporation (media arts organization), 1979-84.

MEMBER: PEN American Center, Authors Guild, Poets and Writers, Phi Beta Kappa.

AWARDS, HONORS: Ward Mathis Prize, 1977, for short story "Triptych," Class of 1870 Junior Prize, 1978, Francis LeMoyne Page Award, 1978, for fiction writing, and Class of 1859 Prize, 1979, all from Princeton University; Andrew James Purdy Fiction Award from Hollins College.

WRITINGS:

The Washington Square Ensemble (novel), Viking, 1983.
Waiting for the End of the World (novel), Ticknor & Fields, 1985.
History of the Owen Graduate School of Management (nonfiction), Vanderbilt University, 1985.
Straight Cut (novel), Ticknor & Fields, 1986.
Zero db (short fiction), Ticknor & Fields, 1987.
The Year of Silence (novel), Ticknor & Fields, 1987.
Soldier's Joy (novel), Ticknor & Fields, 1989.
Barking Man (short stories), Ticknor & Fields, 1990.

Contributor of short fiction to periodicals and anthologies, including *Best American Short Stories, The New Writers of the South, New Stories from the South, Atlantic, Harper's, Hudson Review,* and *North American Review.* Contributor of reviews and essays to *Harper's, New York Times Book Review, Village Voice,* and *Los Angeles Times Book Review.*

WORK IN PROGRESS: Doctor Sleep, a novel "about an American hypnotist living in London and trying to execute certain empowering rituals devised by the Hermetic philosopher-magician Giordano Bruno in the 16th century."

SIDELIGHTS: Madison Bell told *CA:* "After six years of a professional (that's to say published) writer, my reasons for writing fiction remain much the same as they ever were. The pleasure of the activity continues to outweigh its difficulties, and I still believe that writing or reading fiction is the best thought experiment that can be conducted on human life, the penultimate test of ideas in action.

"After four or five years of teaching writing here and there, often to extremely talented students, I am beginning to have the extraordinary pleasure of seeing some of my former students publish their first books. And I have come to believe that the apprentice writers who succeed are the most stubborn, the most intransigent—the ones who won't believe what anybody else tells them unless they also discover it on their own."

BIOGRAPHICAL/CRITICAL SOURCES:

PERIODICALS

Harper's, August, 1986.
Los Angeles Times, September 16, 1985, September 15, 1986, February 20, 1987, November 3, 1987.
Los Angeles Times Book Review, February 27, 1983.
New York Times Book Review, February 20, 1983, August 18, 1985, October 12, 1986, February 15, 1987, November 15, 1987, December 27, 1987.
Times (London), November 14, 1985, November 19, 1987.
Times Literary Supplement, August 26, 1983, November 22, 1985, November 6, 1987.
Tribune Books (Chicago), November 22, 1987.
Washington Post, October 25, 1986.
Washington Post Book World, February 16, 1983, September 1, 1985, October 26, 1986, February 1, 1987, November 22, 1987.

*   *   *

BERGER, Thomas (Louis) 1924-

PERSONAL: Born July 20, 1924, in Cincinnati, Ohio; son of Thomas Charles and Mildred (Bubbe) Berger; married Jeanne Redpath (an artist), June 12, 1950. *Education:* University of Cincinnati, B.A. (honors), 1948; Columbia University, graduate study, 1950-51.

ADDRESSES: Agent—Don Congdon Associates, 156 Fifth Ave., New York, N.Y. 10010.

CAREER: Novelist, short story writer, playwright. Librarian, Rand School of Social Science, 1948-51; staff member, *New York Times Index,* 1951-52; associate editor, *Popular Science Monthly,* 1952-53; film critic, *Esquire,* 1972-73; writer-in-residence, University of Kansas, 1974; Distinguished Visiting Professor, Southampton College, 1975-76; lecturer, Yale University, 1981, 1982; Regents' lecturer, University of California, Davis, 1982. *Military service:* U.S. Army, 1943-46.

MEMBER: Authors Guild, Authors League of America.

AWARDS, HONORS: Dial fellowship, 1962; Western Heritage Award, and Richard and Hinda Rosenthal Award, National Institute of Arts and Letters, both 1965, for *Little Big Man;* Ohioana Book Award, 1982, for *Reinhart's Women;* Pulitzer Prize nomination, 1984, for *The Feud;* Litt.D., Long Island University, 1986; honorary member, Phi Alpha Theta.

WRITINGS:

NOVELS

Crazy in Berlin, Scribner, 1958, Delacorte, 1982.
Reinhart in Love, Scribner, 1962, Delacorte, 1982.
Little Big Man, Dial, 1964, Delacorte, 1979.
Killing Time, Dial, 1967.
Vital Parts, Baron, 1970, Delacorte, 1982.
Regiment of Women, Simon & Schuster, 1973.
Sneaky People, Simon & Schuster, 1975.
Who Is Teddy Villanova?, Delacorte, 1977.
Arthur Rex, Delacorte, 1978.
Neighbors, Delacorte, 1980.
Reinhart's Women, Delacorte, 1981.
The Feud, Delacorte, 1983.
Nowhere, Delacorte, 1985.
Being Invisible, Little, Brown, 1987.
The Houseguest, Little, Brown, 1988.
Changing the Past, Little, Brown, 1989.

OTHER

"Other People" (play) first produced at Berkshire Theatre Festival, 1970.
Granted Wishes (short stories), Lord John Press, 1984.

Also author of "The Burglars," a play published in *New Letters,* fall, 1988. Contributor to numerous magazines, including short stories in *Gentleman's Quarterly, American Review, Penthouse, Playboy, Saturday Evening Post,* and *Harper's.*

SIDELIGHTS: "Thomas Berger belongs, with Mark Twain and [H. L.] Mencken and Philip Roth, among our first-rate literary wiseguys," writes John Romano in the *New York Times Book Review.* "Savvy and skeptical, equipped with a natural eloquence and a knack for parody, he has been expertly flinging mud at the more solemn and self-important national myths for more than 20 years." Other critics agree with this assessment of Berger's talent, rating him as one of the leading American satiric novelists. Brom Weber of *Saturday Review* writes that Berger is "one of the most successful satiric observers of the ebb and flow of American life after World War II. His prolificacy promises a continued development of the tragicomic mode of vision." Writing in the *National Review,* Guy Davenport calls Berger "the best satirist in the United States, the most learned scientist of the vulgar, the futile, and the lost, and the most accurate mimic in the trade." In a later *National Review* piece, Davenport elaborates his praise, calling Berger "a comedian whose understanding of humanity is devilishly well informed and splendidly impartial. Nothing is exempt from the splash of his laughter. The result is an amazing universality."

Berger, who often says he writes to celebrate the creative possibilities of language, works with a variety of traditional kinds of fiction. His aim is not to produce parody, satire, or to diagnose social ills, though critics recognize all these features in most of his novels. Critics have especially emphasized the comic social commentary in the books; and in at least two of his novels—*Killing Time* and *Sneaky People*—Berger makes serious comments on modern society. But Berger's forte is the kind of mock-heroism found in his best-known novel, *Little Big Man*. Some critics state that the movie version produced in 1970, which was a box-office success, did not do justice to the novel. Michael Harris opines in the *Washington Post Book World* that "*Little Big Man*, unfortunately obscured by the movie, is nothing less than a masterpiece. American history itself provided Berger with his types—a set of buckskin-fringed waxworks bedizened with legend—and in blowing the myths up to ridiculous proportions he paradoxically succeeded in reclaiming history." Gerald Green, writing in *Proletarian Writers of the Thirties*, believes that "the glory of *Little Big Man* lies in the way Berger imposes his comic view of life on a deadly accurate portrait of the Old West. . . . It is the truest kind of humor, a humor that derives from real situations and real people. Who can resist Berger's Cheyennes who refer to themselves haughtily as 'The Human Beings?' Or his description of the way an Indian camp smells? Or the Indians' disdain for time, schedules, anything contiguous—a trait which causes them to hate the railroad?"

Although *Little Big Man* was not an immediate success when it was first published in 1964, "its reputation has spread and solidified since then," according to R. V. Cassill of the *New York Times Book Review*. "Now a great many people understand that it was one of the very best novels of the decade and the best novel ever written about the American West. On the strength of this prodigious work alone, the author's reputation can rest secure." *Atlantic*'s David Denby believes the book to be "probably as close as sophisticated men can come to a genuine folk version of the Old West. Its central character, Jack Crabb, is not so much a hero as an Everyman—an essentially passive recorder of vivid experience. American history happens to him, runs over him, and fails to break him. . . . Crabb himself is decent, competent, hopeful, and neither outstandingly courageous or weak; life is sordid, absurd, and as Crabb always survives, surprisingly persistent in its ability to make him suffer. . . . Crabb just wants to survive."

Another Berger character who is, more than anything else, a survivor is Carlo Reinhart, protagonist of *Crazy in Berlin*, *Reinhard in Love*, *Vital Parts*, and *Reinhart's Women*. Jib Fowles comments in *New Leader* that both "Reinhart and Crabb were people that Berger obviously liked having around. . . . Reinhart was neither a comedian nor a scapegoat, but he was never far from things comic or painful. . . . Like most of us, Reinhart could not qualify as a hero or anti-hero; he got through, and Berger set it all down in wry and superbly-told accounts." Unlike Crabb, Reinhart lives in the twentieth century and the four books in which he appears take him from his youthful days in World War II (*Crazy in Berlin*) to his middle years in the late 1970s (*Reinhart's Women*). A *Newsweek* reviewer notes that "Berger loves Carlo Reinhart, and he makes us love him, and he does this without resorting to tricks. . . . Reinhart is an unlikely hero: fat, 'bloated with emptiness,' scorned by women and animals, looked through as though he were polluted air, in debt, a voyeur, 'redundant in the logistics of life,' he nonetheless is a splendid man. He is novel, quick to forgive and hope."

The reviewers' opinions on the effectiveness of the Reinhart series and of the individual books differ. Writing in the *National Review*, Davenport believes that the Reinhart saga "stands well against all contenders as the definitive comic portrait of our time." Cassill expresses both the quality and the problems of the series in the *New York Times Book Review*: "There are so very many fine things in all the Reinhart novels and such a heroic unfolding conception that one hates to mention the

difficulties of taking them in. Yet, trying to gather Reinhart whole into the mind is like trying to embrace a whale and finding not only that the stretch is terrific but that somehow it isn't quite the same whale when your hands feel their way to the other side of it. . . . Yet, the whole ambiguous carcass is so imposing and looms so enticingly amid the deep waters of the recent past that there is really no choice for the serious reader except to go after it with Ahab's passions. The great thing is that Reinhart and his story are not just Mr. Berger's private whale. They are compounded of our mysterious blessings and curses as well."

Who Is Teddy Villanova? is Berger's exploitation of what the *New York Times*'s John Leonard calls "the pulp detective story, in which, of course, nothing is as it seems and nothing ever makes any sense. The story, moreover, is populated entirely by people who talk like books, usually, but not always, 19th-century books by such Englishmen as Thomas Babington Macaulay and John Ruskin." Writing in the *New York Times Book Review*, Leonard Michaels comments on Berger's style, comparing it to that of S. J. Perelman—"educated, complicated, graceful, silly, destructive in spirit, and brilliant—and it is also something like Mad Comics—densely, sensuously detailed, unpredictable, packed with gags. Beyond all this, it makes an impression of scholarship—that is, Berger seems really to know what he jokes about. This includes not only Hammett and Chandler, but also Racine, Goethe, Ruskin, Elias Canetti, New York and the way its residents behave. . . . His whole novel . . . is like a huge verbal mirror. Its reflections are similar to what we see in much contemporary literature—hilarious and serious at once."

Having exposed the humor of American life from the Old West in *Little Big Man* to the twentieth century in the Reinhart series, Berger turns in *Arthur Rex* to a parody of ancient myth and literature. The *New Republic*'s Garrett Epps calls the book "a massive retelling of the Camelot legend" and says that *Arthur Rex* "may be Berger's most ambitious book, at least in size and literary scale." Commenting in the *New York Times Book Review* on Berger's method in the retelling of this morality tale, John Romano explains that he paints his mythical landscapes "in his droll, relentlessly straight-faced prose, so as to empty them of romance, and let the brutal/crummy facts stare out. His pages swarm with bawdy puns and slapstick and bookish in-jokes; but even at his most absurd, his intrinsic tone is that of a hard-nosed realist who won't let the myths distort his essentially grouchy idea of the way things are."

In *Neighbors*, his tenth novel, Berger returns to the present suburban neighborhood and, according to the *New York Times*'s Christopher Lehmann-Haupt, "parodies all the rituals of neighborliness—the competitiveness, the bonhommie, the striving for civility in the face of what seems to be barbarism—and compresses into a single day a lifetime of over-the-back-fence strife." Paul Gray of *Time* calls *Neighbors* "a tour de force, [Berger's] most successfully sustained comic narrative since *Little Big Man*. . . . Like the best black humor of the 1960s, *Neighbors* offers a version of reality skewed just enough to give paranoia a good name." Berger agrees with Gray's assessment; in a *New York Times Book Review* interview, he told Richard Schickel: "As my tenth novel, begun at the close of my twentieth year as a published novelist, it is appropriately a bizarre celebration of whatever gift I have, the strangest of all my narratives. . . . A poor devil named Earl Keese is tormented by the newcomers in the house next door—who, however, may be essentially better sorts than he. The morality of this work, like that of all my other volumes, will be in doubt until the end of the narrative—and perhaps to the end of eternity, now that I think about it.''

Berger said that in *Neighbors* he is paying homage to ''[Franz] Kafka, who has always been one of my masters. It was Kafka who taught me that at any moment banality might turn sinister, for existence was not meant to be unfailingly genial.'' Several reviewers note the debt to Kafka. As Frederick Busch explains in the *Chicago Tribune Book World*, ''Kafka has made it clear to us that a middle-class household can breed nightmares *that become true.''* Writing in the *Washington Post,* Joseph McLellan comments that ''Berger's debt to Kafka is evident in the slippery way the book's realities keep shifting, the constant confrontation with uncertainty.... There is also a trace of Kafka in the way identities tend to dissolve and shift, and in the constant recurrence of absurdity as a basic plot ingredient. In his exploration of these elements, Berger takes an honorable place in the lineage not only of Kafka but of [master novelists James] Joyce and [Vladimir] Nabokov.''

Writing in the *New York Times Book Review,* Thomas Edwards believes that *Neighbors* ''raises yet again the embarrassing question of why Thomas Berger isn't more generally recognized as one of the masters of contemporary American fiction.'' Isa Kapp writes in the *New Republic:* ''It is a mystery of literary criticism, that Thomas Berger, one of the most ambitious, versatile, and entertaining of contemporary novelists, is hardly ever mentioned in the company of America's major writers. He is a wit, a fine caricaturist, and his prose crackles with Rabelaisian vitality.'' Edwards postulates, ''No doubt the trouble has something to do with obtuse notions that funny writing can't really be serious, that major talents devote themselves to 'big' subjects and elaborate fictional techniques, that Mr. Berger is too eclectic and unpredictable to be important.... But *Neighbors* proves once again that Thomas Berger is one of our most intelligent, witty and independent-minded writers, that he knows, mistrusts and loves the texture of American life and culture as deeply as any novelist alive, and that our failure to read and discuss him is a national disgrace.''

In *The Feud,* reports *New York Times Book Review* contributor Anne Tyler, ''a gigantic sprawl of disasters [is] triggered by the smallest of events.'' The owner of a hardware store sees a fire hazard in a customer's unlit cigar; discussion over this perceived threat ends when Reverton, the owner's cousin, forces the customer to apologize at gunpoint. The gun, it turns out, is harmless, but the series of revenges that follow are not; businesses, lives and futures are destroyed before the novel's end. Berger makes the story comic as well as sad; thus, the usual conventions of the feud novel gain new life from Berger, say reviewers. ''What makes Thomas Berger's version so fresh is the innocent bewilderment of most of the people involved,'' Tyler notes. Garrett Epps, writing in the *Washington Post Book World,* concurs: ''In presenting this pageant of ignorance, rage, and deceit, Berger is harsh but never cruel. In all their variety, his novels have consistently presented a serious view of humanity as a race utterly spoiled by something that looks a lot like Original Sin. This merciless vision frees Berger somehow to love even his less prepossessing creations.''

Critics found *The Feud* remarkable for a number of reasons. As Epps sees it, Berger ''taps into'' the hidden fire of human hostility ''and turns it into something cleansing and safe. That he makes it look easy only adds to the achievement.'' *New York Times* reviewer Lehmann-Haupt offers, ''For all its slapstick comedy and manic plot machinery, what 'The Feud' rather surprisingly adds up to is an ugly portrait of middle America

in the 1930's. I can't quite figure out how Mr. Berger has achieved such a realistic mood using such anti-realistic techniques.'' With similar admiration, *Chicago Tribune Book World* contributor Howard Frank Mosher remarks, ''Berger has once again written a novel that spoofs a literary tradition while simultaneously becoming its best contemporary example.''

Critical assessments of *Nowhere* and *Being Invisible* generally rate them both as limited successes in comparison to Berger's other novels. A cross between a spy-thriller and an updated *Gulliver's Travels, Nowhere* allows Berger to joke about private eyes while examining human nature, remarks David W. Madden in the *San Francisco Review of Books.* Lehmann-Haupt of the *New York Times* finds it a courageous attempt ''to poke fun at every excess of the world from the cold war to racial prejudice,'' a text troubled by the same kinds of excesses it ridicules. More important to Madden is Berger's ''ability of consistently exploring new fictional possibilities'' while at the same time returning to characters and themes seen in his earlier novels.

''There is a certain type of scene that no writer does better than Mr. Berger: the depiction of the instant when the most routine social encounter becomes—suddenly and without provocation or warning—pure hell; the simplest exchange of banalities turns sour, then surly, then rancorous, then violent,'' and accordingly, *Being Invisible* has its ''moments of random brutality,'' writes Francine Prose in the *New York Times Book Review.* The fact that Fred Wagner, the non-hero of *Being Invisible,* can disappear at will gives his story some ''marvelous ironies,'' including Fred's distaste ''for the voyeurism, the petty crime, the guilty, secret delights'' available to him when he vanishes, Prose relates. In this ''fantasy of the white male as victim,'' as it is described by *Los Angeles Times* reviewer Carolyn See, Fred is ''outnumbered by jerks— pushy, stupid, self-satisfied,'' notes Prose. Fred's blandness beside them becomes a problem for Berger, say reviewers. Fred does not rise beyond ''the strictly mundane; no fabulistic soarings are permitted him, no flights, no dizzying privy perspectives on the great world,'' explains *Times Literary Supplement* reviewer John Clute. However, he points out, ''If *Being Invisible* was meant to give modest pleasure and then disappear, it may then be reckoned a success, even in the hour of its passing.''

Though *Being Invisible* lacks some of the depth of character achieved in other novels, Fred's world—''one in which total strangers will humiliate you for the fun of it,'' or kill you for a piece of cheap jewelry—is familiar to Berger fans, Prose adds. Balancing her dissatisfaction with Berger's cartoon-like characters and the disparaging view of female behavior presented in the book, Prose applauds Berger for providing another thought-provoking view of the contemporary world: ''As our Government works to persuade us that life is good, that everything is all right, it's an enormous *relief* to hear Mr. Berger's voice sneering, shrill, combative, insisting that life isn't all right or likely to be, that strangers will just as soon kill you as give you the time of day. It is a sign of the times that we feel such affection for Thomas Berger's dogged, cranky courage, and for the denizens of his unwelcoming and chaotic corner of the fictional world.''

Many critics feel, as does MacDonald Harris of the *Washington Post Book World,* that Berger excels when observing a quarrel ''from the sidelines'' in *Neighbors* and *The Feud.* ''In *The Houseguest,''* says Harris, Berger ''takes up the Quarrel again, and treats it in a way that is more complicated, more subtle, and more odd than anything in his previous work.'' The antagonist, in this case, is a charming visitor who gradually takes control of a well-to-do family's household. At first, his hosts, the Graves family, do not resist, because he serves them as handyman and gourmet cook. But after the outsider steals from them and tricks their daughter into having sex with him, they decide to kill him. He not only survives their violent attacks, but wins a place in the Graves household by providing the amenities which they have grown to expect.

Harris finds *The Houseguest* the most interesting of Berger's novels ''because it seems to suggest something more subtle going on under the surface,'' perhaps an allegorical significance that points to relations between the privileged and underprivileged in America. Since neither class under Berger's gaze behaves admirably, it is clear that ''Berger will not take sides,'' Art Seidenbaum relates in the *Los Angeles Times Book Review*. Seidenbaum calls this a weakness, but other critics find it consistent with the view of humanity expressed in Berger's other books. In *The Houseguest*, says Harris, Berger remains ''ready to strain our credence with . . . the loutish realism of his events. His humor is Rabelaisian: larger than life, improbable and always on the edge of vulgarity; his penchant for stripping off the dirty underwear of life is unrelenting.''

MEDIA ADAPTATIONS: The movie version of *Little Big Man*, starring Dustin Hoffman, was released in 1970; the movie version of *The Neighbors*, starring John Belushi, was a Universal Studios release in 1981.

CA INTERVIEW

CA interviewed Thomas Berger by mail in August, 1988.

CA: From comments you've made previously on the subject, it would appear that your writing is above all a long and happy love affair with words. Language, you've said, is for you ''a morality and a politics and a religion.'' When did this fascination with language begin, if one can know such a thing, and how has it been nurtured?

BERGER: My interest in the written language began very early. I could spell a good many words, using alphabet blocks and then my own hand-printing, long before I first went to school. Both my mother and father were great readers, and the former was an obsessive diary-keeper (to the degree that on a vacation, while everyone else was in the water, she would remain indoors at a desk, writing furiously in her journal) and is still, at ninety-one and with impaired vision, a prolific correspondent, posting me weekly a ten- or twelve-page letter written with unflagging energy.

CA: Were you sure early on that you wanted to write?

BERGER: Yes, though for many years I wasn't sure just what I wanted to write. Not till after returning from World War II, in my early twenties, did I think of writing fiction, and more years went by before I tried to do it. I was almost thirty before my efforts could be called sustained.

CA: You introduced Carlo Reinhart, your first main character and the subject of four books to date, in Crazy in Berlin, *which was set in Europe just after World War II but not published until 1958. Did Reinhart go through a difficult process of development before you began to put him down on paper?*

BERGER: I served with an Army medical unit, with the first American Occupation troops in Berlin, arriving in that devastated city only a few weeks after the collapse of the Third Reich. When Hitler came to power, I was nine years old, in a little Ohio town (population 5,000). When he invaded Poland I was fifteen, mowing lawns and delivering a weekly newspaper. Yet at twenty-one, here I stood in the ruins of his chancellery on what was left of the Wilhelmstrasse—where, relentless tourist that I was, I furnished myself with a supply of embossed letterheads and used them for no nobler purpose than to write infantile notes to old Ohio pals (''Please come for the weekend. Bring your own beer. I've got the pretzels. Your buddy, Adolf.'') I recognized that I was at last having an experience that I might write about, but as can be seen from the quality of the persiflage in the bogus Hitler letter, I was still some years away from acquiring an adequate voice. Not until 1954 did I really begin *Crazy in Berlin,* and when I did, it was with, as hero, an inanimate dummy greatly resembling myself. For two and a half years I tried without success to breathe life into this stiff. Finally I sent him up in smoke and started all over again with somebody who, though possessing my old serial number and having shared some of my upbringing, was not me but rather a kind of son of mine. The novel as published was written in about a year and a half, making four for the project.

CA: After Reinhart in Love *and* Vital Parts, Carlo Reinhart *emerged with dignity and hope in* Reinhart's Women. *Does Reinhart have special meaning for you among your cast of characters?*

BERGER: It might be unusual to have a son as old as oneself, but I love the old fellow and am always interested in what he does—which since *Crazy* has not in any way reflected my own history.

CA: In those last two questions I was avoiding the words hero and protagonist. Do you have any particular feelings about the words, their use or misuse in fiction generally, and how they apply or don't apply to your characters?

BERGER: Either is quite okay by me. Are you implying that these are offensive words in some quarters? I wonder why. But then I have read hardly any criticism since leaving Columbia Graduate School in 1951.

CA: Are there any of your characters with whom you feel some special identity?

BERGER: I usually feel a special sympathy for, rapport with, the more highly charged, possessed, or demented personae, like Reverton, in *The Feud*, who without ever emerging from his fantasy becomes a hero in fact; or the wicked, blustering knights who are invariably humiliated by Arthur's modest paragons of virtue; or Ramona, in *Neighbors*, with her wonderfully vulgar verve. In life these are just the tiresome people I can't stand. But that's art for you.

CA: Writing about Little Big Man *in the* Nation, *Frederick Turner commented on your use of generally neglected material in researching the book. Would you talk about that research and how it led you to the voice of your narrator, Jack Crabb?*

BERGER: If memory serves, I read sixty or seventy books as preparation for writing *Little Big Man*, but never did I do any research that could be called systematic, and the notes I took were not copious. I read only that which fascinated me sufficiently to nourish my imagination. A Western scholar some years ago published a learned essay on the fidelity of the text of *Little Big Man* to history, which pleased me greatly, but during the composition of the narrative I had the illusion that I was not retelling an old story but rather living a new one. As to Jack Crabb's voice, it was based on that of the character named Kit Carson, a grizzled old Munchausen of the West who entertains the barflies with his tales ("Did I ever tell you how I herded cattle on a bicycle?"), in William Saroyan's play, "The Time of Your Life."

CA: I learned from the same Nation *essay that you'd read "German literature back to the Middle Ages" as preparation for* Crazy in Berlin. *Is research a part of the writing process that you especially enjoy, as it would seem from the two instances Turner gave?*

BERGER: I went back even further, reading, for example, Tacitus's *Germania.* But as with the later *Little Big Man,* I did none of this as dogged scholarship. I was fascinated with the subject of Germany, about which, though I am partly of German descent, I knew little at the outset. I am not attracted to research as such, which is why I have rarely undertaken any kind of journalism. My gift, such as it is, is predominantly concerned with fancy, not fact.

CA: When you decided to take on the Arthurian legend in the book that became Arthur Rex, *did you anticipate any particular problems or set yourself deliberate challenges in rendering your own version of the old familiar tales?*

BERGER: I began the earliest version many years before writing the novel that was published, and got nowhere with it, for I had undertaken to invent new episodes rather than retell the classic stories in my own way. The tradition is too glorious to defy. Goethe said to someone who criticized Sophocles, "If you must do that, do it on your knees." So with contributing to the Arthurian legends by the likes of me. Failure to submit in this case is trivial vanity, not pride. Having done so with respect to substance, I felt I had a license as to style—so long as I went no further than a parody of courtliness: I could not have endured knights who spoke droll Brooklynese or Cajun or Ohio-rube, any more than I can bear Shakespeare performed by actors in business suits and teatime frocks.

CA: According to Brooks Landon in Dictionary of Literary Biography Yearbook: 1980, Neighbors *was your favorite among your novels at the time it was published, in 1980. Your 1988 book,* The Houseguest, *seems particularly similar to* Neighbors *in its scary kind of comedy and in the perverted way its characters use language. Was there some overflow of comic feeling or intent from* Neighbors *that found its best expression in* The Houseguest? *Do you make a strong connection between the two books?*

BERGER: Neighbors and *Little Big Man* are my own favorites amongst my novels, for the reason that they were the easiest to write, indeed seemed not to require my participation. I couldn't wait to get up in the morning to see what was going to happen in *Neighbors.* In *Little Big Man* I followed history, so I knew the general plot but could never anticipate the details by which it proceeded. As to the possible connection between *Neighbors* and *The Houseguest,* if there is one it was not my conscious intention. But perhaps a very remote association can be traced by a tortuous route: I had admired John Belushi's

work on "Saturday Night Live" long before he was cast in the leading role in the "Neighbors" movie, and one of his best performances was in a sketch called "The Thing That Wouldn't Leave," as a guest who has long since exhausted his welcome but whom his hosts can't force to go home. (An even greater favorite of mine in memory is of John as Rasputin, surviving the many attempts to assassinate him; no matter how decisively he is clubbed, knifed, shot, poisoned, and finally thrown out the window of a Kremlin tower, he soon staggers back into the room, ever the worse for wear, but relentlessly surviving. Images of that sort linger in my imagination and sometimes evoke novels.)

CA: The name of the uninvited guest of The Houseguest, *Chuck Burgoyne, sounds like a play on the name of a famous general or a thrifty variant of a normally fancy beef dish, and that reminds me of how there's often a lot of cooking going on in your books that sounds too real to have come from research. Are you a frequent and accomplished cook?*

BERGER: I wish I could say that my conscious intention with the name Chuck Burgoyne was to make such a play on words as you brilliantly suggest (in *Neighbors* an Italian restaurant is called Caesar's Garlic Wars, which demonstrates that I am capable of anything), but I cannot make that claim. I please myself with the titles of my novels and the names of my characters, but I have no idea where they come from. As to cookery, indeed I do practice it. My wife and I eat one meal a day together, and it is I who have prepared it for the last ten years. I read cookbooks as if they are thrillers, subscribe to every food magazine, have watched all the TV chefs, and am a fearless and dedicated practitioner, but as a veteran of so many memorable meals prepared in kitchens in the great restaurants of the world as well as in the home kitchens of the inspired, I must in all honesty admit to being merely adequate at the stove. My strengths are zeal and endurance: for example I have peeled hundreds of grapes with which to garnish a dish of venison, made *quenelles de homard* the old-fashioned way, sans electrical tools, and performed other such feats of doggedness.

CA: In the case of such settings as the Reinharts' apartment in Reinhart's Women *and the beach house in* The Houseguest, *both of which seemed especially real to me even though they weren't described in photographic detail, do you "construct" them in sketches before you begin writing them down in a book?*

BERGER: Never. I construct them only in sentences. Sometimes I am still adding floorboards, vinyl tiles, plumbing, in the closing lines of the book.

CA: The splendid comedy of your writing, surely one of your finest achievements, has made you the subject of Studies in American Humor. *Do you think of yourself as a comic writer or have well-defined ideas about the role of comedy in your work?*

BERGER: In fact I do not think of myself as a comic writer, and it is rarely my intent to be funny. But this statement itself, which has been made by me repeatedly, is usually taken as being facetious, and if I make it in public, is received with laughter. Years ago, *Esquire* bought a piece of *Little Big Man* because the editors thought it hilarious, and at the same time the *Saturday Evening Post* rejected another segment because it "wasn't funny enough." Yet neither passage, both of which concerned bloodshed, was intended by me to evoke sniggers, still less guffaws, from readers. I spent Christmas Eve of 1944 and the first six hours of Christmas Day as a litter-bearer, carrying fellow countrymen wounded in the Battle of the Bulge, and have never since been moved to smile at gore. But my way of looking at things, which is not humorless, no doubt tends to mislead the careless. If on the other hand the criteria are those of my friend Milos Forman, who calls his fellow Czech Franz Kafka a comic writer, then I happily accept the designation without suggesting that I am in the same league as the author of *Ein Hungerkunstler.*

CA: In the very nice interview you did with Richard Schickel for the New York Times Book Review *you said that "the writer confers only with himself, the Max Perkinses being to my mind obstacles to the creation of literature." Have you been lucky enough in your editors, or stern enough with them, to avoid conflict?*

BERGER: Editors have never been a problem to me. I have simply ignored the nonsense some have felt obliged to dispense, and have stifled others, whom I suspected of the imminent production of twaddle, at the outset of our association. Having said as much, I should lose no time in adding that when I have respected an editor's judgment, a gentle complaint from him that a novel begins a bit slowly (as when Jonathan Dolger, then of Simon & Schuster, first reported on *Sneaky People*) has caused me to delete the opening chapter forthwith and begin with Chapter 2. And when Little, Brown's Roger Donald, my current editor, was less than ecstatic about a novel, I soon discarded it in its entirety of 500-plus pages. But what I seldom do is rewrite in response to the suggestions of another person. My imagination is an altogether private place, which admits no collaborator. Had I been capable of working by committee I should have pursued a legislative or academic career.

CA: In the past you've done stints at various universities as writer in residence or visiting lecturer, and for a while you lived in New York City. Now you appear to maintain strict privacy, which isn't easy for a writer to do. Is the quiet life a condition you've come to need for your writing?

BERGER: My dossier is deceptive. My longest term as writer in residence comprised less than a fortnight, and the visiting lectureships were exercised but one afternoon per week at institutions within commuting distance from my home. Nor did I pursue the literary-social life during my New York City years: I have no memory of attending any gathering of the bookish in Manhattan since the early 1960s, though I lived in that city till the end of 1974. I am not incapable of gregariousness: during my two terms of residence in London, I saw people every evening; and on public-reading tours of universities I have more than once been the Thing That Wouldn't Leave at local parties. But nowadays I'm a recluse because I'm tired of the sound of my own oral voice, and I'm bored with all contemporary phenomena save the exquisite wit to be heard nightly on "The David Letterman Show," the work of whose writers is so often superior to that encountered anywhere in print.

CA: What kind of reading do you enjoy?

BERGER: Narratives of true crime. I pray that my motive is not *Schadenfreude.* Also at any given time I am laboriously but with joy reading in the original some classic—by Cha-

teaubriand or Kleist or of course, eternally, Proust—which I knew in translation as a young man.

CA: The only complaint you've voiced about the reception of your books has to do with their reading by certain—not all— critics. In an ideal readers' and writers' world, what would you like any reader, professional or general, to bring to your books and to take from them?

BERGER: It would be advantageous for a reader of my books to be competent in American English and possess sufficient patience now and again actually to listen to what I am saying, which often will not be what is expected. What I hope he or she takes from my work is something to be valued and not despised. But an author is probably the wrong person to whom to put such a question, unless you want to hear such a phony response as the foregoing. An author, like every other mortal, wants to be adored—and not only *because of,* but also *despite.*

BIOGRAPHICAL/CRITICAL SOURCES:

BOOKS

Cohen, Sarah Blacher, editor, *Comic Relief,* University of Illinois Press, 1978.
Contemporary Literary Criticism, Gale, Volume 3, 1975, Volume 5, 1976, Volume 8, 1978, Volume 11, 1979, Volume 18, 1981, Volume 38, 1986.
Dictionary of Literary Biography, Volume 2: *American Novelists since World War II,* Gale, 1978.
Dictionary of Literary Biography Yearbook: 1980, Gale, 1981.
Landon, Brooks, *Thomas Berger,* Twayne, 1989.
Madden, David, editor, *Proletarian Writers of the Thirties,* Southern Illinois University Press, 1968.
Mitchell, Burroughs, *The Education of an Editor,* Doubleday, 1980.
Schulz, Max F., *Black Humor Fiction of the Sixties: A Pluralistic Definition of Man and His World,* Ohio State University Press, 1973.
Thompson, Raymond H., *The Return from Avalon: A Study of Arthurian legend in Modern Fiction,* Greenwood Press, 1985.

PERIODICALS

American Book Review, March-April, 1982.
Antaeus, Number 61, 1988.
Armchair Detective, Number 14, 1981.
Atlantic, March, 1971, September, 1973.
Audience, Volume 2, number 4, 1972.
Best Sellers, November 1, 1964, October 1, 1967, April 15, 1970.
Books and Bookmen, July, 1968.
Book Week, October 25, 1964.
Centennial Review, Number 13, 1969.
Chicago Tribune Book World, April 13, 1980, September 27, 1981, December 18, 1981, May 29, 1983, May 20, 1984, May 19, 1985, June 16, 1985.
Commentary, July, 1970.
Confrontation, spring/summer, 1976.
Detroit News, October 18, 1981.
Globe and Mail (Toronto), July 20, 1985.
Guardian Weekly (Manchester), April 17, 1971.
Harper's, April, 1970.
Hollins Critic, December, 1983.
Life, March 27, 1970.
Listener, July 11, 1974.
Los Angeles Times, May 11, 1987.

Los Angeles Times Book Review, November 1, 1981, May 15, 1983, April 3, 1988.
Ms., August, 1973.
Nation, August 20, 1977, May 3, 1980, June 11, 1983.
National Review, November 14, 1967, April 21, 1970, October 10, 1975.
New Leader, November 6, 1967, November 12, 1973, May 23, 1977.
New Republic, October 7, 1978, April 26, 1980, May 23, 1983.
Newsweek, April 20, 1970, December 21, 1970.
New Yorker, October 21, 1967.
New York Review of Books, May 26, 1977.
New York Times, September 20, 1967, March 31, 1970, March 18, 1977, April 1, 1980, September 28, 1981, May 2, 1983, April 29, 1985, April 2, 1987.
New York Times Book Review, October 11, 1964, September 17, 1967, March 29, 1970, May 13, 1973, April 20, 1975, March 20, 1977, April 17, 1977, November 12, 1978, April 6, 1980, September 27, 1981, June 6, 1982, June 20, 1982, May 8, 1983, April 7, 1985, May 5, 1985, April 2, 1987, April 12, 1987, April 17, 1988.
Observer Review, May 5, 1968.
Philological Quarterly, Volume 62, number 1, 1983.
Punch, May 15, 1968.
San Francisco Review of Books, summer, 1985.
Saturday Review, March 21, 1970, July 31, 1973, May-June, 1985.
South Dakota Review, Volume 4, number 2, 1966.
Studies in American Humor, spring, 1983, fall, 1983.
Studies in Medievalism, Volume 2, number 4, 1983.
Time, December 21, 1970, April 7, 1980, October 12, 1981, May 23, 1983, June 17, 1985.
Times (London), January 12, 1984.
Times Literary Supplement, September 3, 1982, February 10, 1984, February 21, 1986, June 17, 1988, July 22, 1988.
Tribune Books (Chicago), April 12, 1987.
Wall Street Journal, February 5, 1979.
Washington Post, April 8, 1970, April 14, 1980, September 14, 1981.
Washington Post Book World, April 20, 1975, September 17, 1978, June 27, 1982, May 15, 1983, August 26, 1984, July 7, 1985, April 19, 1987, April 17, 1988.
Western American Literature, Volume 8, numbers 1-2, 1973, Volume 15, number 3, Volume 22, number 4, 1988.
Yale Review, winter, 1981.

—*Sketch by Marilyn K. Basel*

—*Interview by Jean W. Ross*

*   *   *

BERNSTEIN, Philip S(idney)   1901-1985

PERSONAL: Born June 29, 1901, in Rochester, N.Y.; died December 3, 1985 of heart failure; son of Abraham (a manufacturer of trousers) and Sarah (Steinberg) Bernstein; married Sophy Rubin; children: Jeremy, Stephen, Alice (Mrs. Fred Perkins). *Education:* Syracuse University, A.B., 1921; Jewish Institute of Religion, M.H.L. and Rabbi, 1926; attended Columbia University, Cambridge University, and Hebrew University (Jerusalem). *Politics:* Liberal Democrat.

ADDRESSES: Home—2203 East Ave., Rochester, N.Y. 14610. *Office*—Temple B'rith Kodesh, 2131 Elmwood Ave., Rochester, N.Y. 14618.

CAREER: Congregation B'rith Kodesh, Rochester, N.Y., rabbi, 1926-73, rabbi emeritus, 1973-85. Executive director of committee on Army and Navy religious activities for National Jewish Welfare Board (directed entire Jewish religious program for armed forces), 1942-46, adviser to theater commanders in Germany and Austria, 1946-47. President of Central Conference of American Rabbis, 1950-52; member of Monroe County Human Relations Commission; member of board of directors of American Friends of Hebrew University.

MEMBER: American Jewish Congress (vice-president), American-Israel Public Affairs Committee (honorary member), National Rabbinic Organization for Rehabilitation through Training Committee (honorary chairman), Rochester City Club (past president).

AWARDS, HONORS: Rochester Civic Medal, 1962.

WRITINGS:

What the Jews Believe, Farrar, Straus, 1950, reprinted, Greenwood Press, 1978.
Rabbis at War, American Jewish Historical Society, 1971.
To Dwell in Unity: The Jewish Federation Movement in America, 1960-1980, Jewish Publication Society, 1983.

Contributor to *Life, Harper's, Nation, New Republic,* and various Jewish publications.

WORK IN PROGRESS: An autobiography.

SIDELIGHTS: During World War II, Philip S. Bernstein served as adviser on Jewish affairs to U.S. Army commanders in Europe. He was in personal contact with all the Jewish displaced persons installations in Germany and Austria. He also testified before the United Nations Special Committee on Palestine and before the U.S. Congress. After the war, Bernstein assisted in the resettlement of hundreds of thousands of displaced European Jews.*

*   *   *

BERRIDGE, Celia   1943-

PERSONAL: Born September 4, 1943, in Windsor, Berkshire, England; daughter of Jack (an engineer) and Monica (a nurse; maiden name, Browne) Berridge; married William Pell Edmonds (a teacher), January 5, 1967; children: Benjamin, Ceri. *Education:* Cardiff College of Education, Teacher's Certificate, 1965; Central School of Art, London, England, M.A., 1977; doctoral study at University of Sussex.

ADDRESSES: Home—Rodmell, Sussex, England.

CAREER: Primary school teacher in London, England, 1965-71; governor of primary schools in London, 1972-77; Brighton Polytechnic, Brighton, England, research assistant, 1978-79; Central School of Art, London, visiting lecturer in graphic design, 1979—. Member of support group of Lewisham Women's Aid, 1973-75.

MEMBER: National Book League, Society of Authors, Lewes Children's Book Group.

AWARDS, HONORS: Best Children's Books of the Year list, National Book League, 1975, for *Runaway Danny,* 1976, for *Wet-Day Witches,* and 1979, for *What Did You Do in the Holiday?;* Frances Williams Award, National Book League in cooperation with the Victoria and Albert Museum, London, 1977, for illustrations in *Runaway Danny.*

WRITINGS:

SELF-ILLUSTRATED JUVENILES

Runaway Danny, Deutsch, 1975.
On My Way to School, Deutsch, 1976.
Wet-Day Witches, Deutsch, 1976.
What Did You Do in the Holiday?, Deutsch, 1979.
Grandmother's Tales, Deutsch, 1981.

"STEPPING STONES" SERIES

Down the Road, Kingfisher Books, 1987.
In the Playground, Kingfisher Books, 1987.
At Home, Kingfisher Books, 1987.
Going Swimming, Kingfisher Books, 1987.
(With Angela Royston) *Going Shopping*, Kingfisher Books, 1988.
(With Royston) *The Birthday Party*, Kingfisher Books, 1988.
My Family, Kingfisher Books, 1988.
Me and My Friends, Kingfisher Books, 1988.

ILLUSTRATOR

Paul Rogers, *Forget-Me-Not*, Viking Kestrel, 1984.
Rogers, *Sheepchase*, Viking Kestrel, 1986.
Brian Thompson, *Puffin First Picture Dictionary*, Viking Kestrel, 1988.

ILLUSTRATOR; "POSTMAN PAT" SERIES BY JOHN CUNLIFFE

Postman Pat's Treasure Hunt, Deutsch, 1981.
. . . and the Mystery Thief, Deutsch, 1981.
Postman Pat's Rainy Day, Deutsch, 1982.
Postman Pat's Secret, Deutsch, 1982.
Postman Pat's Foggy Day, Deutsch, 1982.
Postman Pat's Difficult Day, Deutsch, 1982.
. . . Takes a Message, Deutsch, 1983.
Postman Pat's Tractor Express, Deutsch, 1983.
Postman Pat's Pressout Village, Deutsch, 1983.
Postman Pat's Greendale Show, Deutsch, 1984.
Postman Pat's Working Day, Deutsch, 1984.
Postman Pat's Thirsty Day, Deutsch, 1984.
. . . Goes Sledging, Deutsch, 1984.
Postman Pat's Letters on Ice, Deutsch, 1985.
Postman Pat's Breezy Day, Deutsch, 1985.
. . . and the Summer Show, Deutsch, 1985.
Postman Pat's Pressout Farm, Deutsch, 1985.
. . . to the Rescue, Deutsch, 1986.
. . . and Greendale Farm: Activity Book, Deutsch, 1986.
Postman Pat's Summer Storybook, Deutsch, 1987.
Postman Pat's Winter Storybook, Deutsch, 1987.
A Day with Postman Pat, Deutsch, 1988.
My Postman Pat Storytime Book, Treasure, 1988.

Also illustrator for various "Postman Pat" bath books, coloring books, and activity books.

OTHER

(Contributor) Treld Pelkey Bicknell and Felicity Trotman, editors, *How to Write and Illustrate Children's Books and Get Them Published*, North Light Books, 1988.

Contributor of articles and reviews to education journals.

WORK IN PROGRESS: Research on pictorial narrative comprehension in children; more picture books; "maybe writing for older children."

SIDELIGHTS: Celia Berridge told *CA:* "My own childhood and my teaching experiences have left me with a firm commitment to writing for ordinary urban children. I try to produce books that are useful to teachers because the children I write for can't usually afford books and will only see my books in libraries and in school. I try to keep my style simple, so that readers can see how the pictures are done, and I try to reflect the real world of ordinary children—both inner and external reality—honestly and accurately both in my texts and my pictures."

BIOGRAPHICAL/CRITICAL SOURCES:

PERIODICALS

Books for Keeps, May, 1981.
Times Literary Supplement, July 11, 1975, October 1, 1976, June 6, 1986.

*   *   *

BIERHORST, John (William)   1936-

PERSONAL: Born September 2, 1936, in Boston, Mass.; son of John William and Sadie Belle (Knott) Bierhorst; married Jane Elizabeth Byers (a graphic designer), June 25, 1965; children: Alice Byers. *Education:* Cornell University, B.A., 1958.

ADDRESSES: Home—Box 566, West Shokan, N.Y. 12494.

CAREER: Former concert pianist; became attracted to the study of native American cultures during a botanical field trip to Peru in 1964; subsequently visited pre-Columbian sites in Yucatan and Mexico.

MEMBER: American Folklore Society, American Anthropological Association.

AWARDS, HONORS: Grants from Center for Inter-American Relations, 1972 and 1979, National Endowment for the Humanities, 1979 and 1986, and National Endowment for the Arts, 1986. American Library Association notable book citations for *In the Trail of the Wind, Black Rainbow: Legends of the Incas and Myths of Ancient Peru, The Girl Who Married a Ghost: Tales from the North American Indian, A Cry from the Earth: Music of the North American Indians, The Whistling Skeleton: American Indian Tales of the Supernatural, The Sacred Path: Spells, Prayers, and Power Songs of the American Indians, Spirit Child: A Story of the Nativity,* and *The Naked Bear: Folktales of the Iroquois.*

WRITINGS:

(Editor) *The Fire Plume: Legends of the American Indians*, Dial, 1969.
(Editor) *The Ring in the Prairie: A Shawnee Legend*, Dial, 1970.
(Editor) *In the Trail of the Wind: American Indian Poems and Ritual Orations*, Farrar, Straus, 1971.
(Editor) *Four Masterworks of American Indian Literature: "Quetzalcoatl," "The Ritual of Condolence," "Cuceb," "The Night Chant,"* Farrar, Straus, 1974.
(Editor) *Songs of the Chippewa*, Farrar, Straus, 1974.
(Editor) *The Red Swan: Myths and Tales of the American Indians*, Farrar, Straus, 1976.
(Editor and translator) *Black Rainbow: Legends of the Incas and Myths of Ancient Peru*, Farrar, Straus, 1976.
The Girl Who Married a Ghost: Tales from the North American Indian, Four Winds, 1978.
A Cry from the Earth: Music of the North American Indians, Four Winds, 1979.
(Translator) *The Glass Slipper: Charles Perrault's Tales of Times Past*, Four Winds, 1981.

(Editor) *The Whistling Skeleton: American Indian Tales of the Supernatural*, Four Winds, 1982.

(Editor and translator) *The Sacred Path: Spells, Prayers, and Power Songs of the American Indians*, Morrow, 1983.

(Editor) *The Hungry Woman: Myths and Legends of the Aztecs*, Morrow, 1984.

(Translator) *Spirit Child: A Story of the Nativity*, Morrow, 1984.

(Editor and translator) *Cantares Mexicanos: Songs of the Aztecs*, Stanford University Press, 1985.

A Nahuatl-English Dictionary, Stanford University Press, 1985.

The Mythology of North America, Morrow, 1985.

(Editor and translator) *The Monkey's Haircut and Other Stories Told by the Maya*, Morrow, 1986.

(Editor) *The Naked Bear: Folktales of the Iroquois*, Morrow, 1987.

(Editor) *Doctor Coyote: A Native American Aesop's Fables*, Macmillan, 1987.

The Mythology of South America, Morrow, 1988.

The Mythology of Mexico and Central America, Morrow, 1990.

WORK IN PROGRESS: A critical edition of the Codex Chimalpopoca.

BIOGRAPHICAL/CRITICAL SOURCES:

PERIODICALS

Los Angeles Times Book Review, March 11, 1984.
New York Times Book Review, January 31, 1982, September 1, 1985, November 22, 1987, October 2, 1988.
Times Literary Supplement, April 18, 1986.
Washington Post Book World, March 14, 1982.

*   *   *

BIGSBY, C(hristopher) W(illiam) E(dgar)   1941-

PERSONAL: Born June 27, 1941, in Dundee, Scotland; son of Edgar Edward Leo and Ivy (Hopkins) Bigsby; married Pamela Lovelady, October 9, 1965; children: Gareth, Kirsten, Juliet, Ewan. *Education:* University of Sheffield, B.A., 1962, M.A., 1964; University of Nottingham, Ph.D., 1966.

ADDRESSES: Home—3 Church Farm, Colney, Norwich, Norfolk, England.

CAREER: University College of Wales, Aberystwyth, lecturer in American literature, 1966-69; University of East Anglia, Norwich, England, lecturer, 1969-73, senior lecturer in American literature, 1973-85, professor, 1985—. Presenter on British Broadcasting Corp. (BBC) radio arts program, "Kaleidoscope," and BBC World Service program, "Meridian."

MEMBER: British Association of American Studies.

WRITINGS:

Confrontation and Commitment: A Study of Contemporary American Drama, 1959-66, MacGibbon & Kee, 1967, University of Missouri Press, 1968.

(Editor) *Edward Albee*, Oliver & Boyd, 1969, published as *Albee*, Prentice-Hall, 1975.

(Contributor) Warren French, editor, *The Forties*, Everett/Edwards, 1969.

(Editor) *The Black American Writer*, two volumes, Everett/Edwards, 1969.

(Editor) *Three Negro Plays*, Penguin, 1969.

(Contributor) French, editor, *The Fifties*, Everett/Edwards, 1970.

(Contributor) Malcolm Bradbury, editor, *The American Novel and the Nineteen Twenties*, Edward Arnold, 1971.

Dada and Surrealism, Methuen, 1972.

(Editor) *Superculture: American Popular Culture and Europe*, Bowling Green University, 1975.

(Contributor) French, editor, *The Twenties*, Everett/Edwards, 1975.

Tom Stoppard, Longman, 1976.

Approaches to Popular Culture, Edward Arnold, 1976, Bowling Green University, 1977.

The Second Black Renaissance: Essays in Black Literature, Greenwood Press, 1980.

(Editor) *Contemporary English Drama*, Arnold, 1981.

Joe Orton, Methuen, 1982.

A Critical Introduction to Twentieth-Century American Drama, Cambridge University Press, Volume 1: *1900-1940*, 1982, Volume 2: *Tennessee Williams, Arthur Miller, Edward Albee*, 1985, Volume 3: *Beyond Broadway*, 1985.

(Editor with Heide Ziegler) *The Liberal Tradition and the Radical Imagination*, Junction Books, 1982.

David Mamet, Methuen, 1985.

(Editor) *Cultural Change in the United States since World War II*, Free University Press, 1986.

(Editor) *Plays by Susan Glaspell*, Cambridge University Press, 1987.

(Editor) *Miller on File*, Methuen, 1988.

Also author with Bradbury, of BBC-TV plays, "The After Dinner Game" and "Stones"; also author of BBC-TV documentaries on John Steinbeck and Arthur Miller. Also author with Bradbury, of BBC radio series "Patterson." General editor with Bradbury, of "Contemporary Writers" series for Methuen.

SIDELIGHTS: C. W. E. Bigsby's critical work on playwright Edward Albee, entitled *Albee*, is "a useful book," according to a *Times Literary Supplement* critic. The critic also adds that while "the interpretative points [Bigsby] makes are always interesting and sometimes illuminating. . . . He detaches ideas from their contexts without examining how they function as integral parts of a play. . . . [However] Dr. Bigsby is more helpful on Albee's early work."

The Second Black Renaissance covers the work of black New Yorkers in the 1960s and early 1970s; Bigsby considers the period similar to artistic outpouring that occurred in Harlem during the 1920s. "An intellectual history, this is work of the first order," praises William S. McFeely in the *Times Literary Supplement*. "Bigsby is neither the guilt-ridden observer who would elevate any black writer into a speaker of a special kind of truth, nor a patronizing one who would subtly convey surprise that black folk can write at all. To be critical is to take seriously, and few books in the field of black cultural history can match the truly critical perspective achieved by the present work."

BIOGRAPHICAL/CRITICAL SOURCES:

PERIODICALS

Times Literary Supplement, February 26, 1970, September 25, 1981, September 3, 1982.

*   *   *

BINYON, T(imothy) J(ohn)   1936-

PERSONAL: Born February 18, 1936, in Leeds, Yorkshire, England; son of Denis Edmund Fynes-Clinton (a university lecturer) and Nancy (Emmerson) Binyon; married Felicity Antonia Roberts (a stenciller), September 11, 1974; children: Polly

Charlotte. *Education:* Exeter College, Oxford, M.A., 1963, D.Phil., 1968.

ADDRESSES: Home—53 Thorncliffe Rd., Oxford, England. *Office*—Wadham College, Oxford University, Oxford, England. *Agent*—Aitken and Stone, 29 Fernshaw Rd., London SW10 0TG, England.

CAREER: University of Leeds, Leeds, Yorkshire, England, lecturer in Russian, 1962-65; Oxford University, Oxford, England, lecturer in Russian, 1965—, senior research fellow of Wadham College, 1968—.

WRITINGS:

Swan Song (novel), Hamish Hamilton, 1982.
Greek Gifts (novel), Hamish Hamilton, 1988.
Murder Will Out (history of detective in fiction), Oxford University Press, 1989.

Contributor of articles and reviews to periodicals, including *Modern Language Review, Times Literary Supplement, Literary Review, Oxford Slavonic Papers,* and *Slavonic Review.*

WORK IN PROGRESS: A biography of the Russian poet Alexander Pushkin; a third novel.

SIDELIGHTS: T. J. Binyon, declares Peter Levi in the *Literary Review,* "is an heir worth watching" to the traditions of the English thriller novel. *Swan Song,* his first novel, drew upon his knowledge of Russian life and culture, while his second, *Greek Gifts,* "shows his powers of invention and suspense at full throttle," according to John Coleman in the *Sunday Times.* "In fact," states Levi, "he offers all you can expect from a thriller, and a good deal more."

BIOGRAPHICAL/CRITICAL SOURCES:

PERIODICALS

Literary Review, January, 1988.
Sunday Times, January 10, 1988.
Times Literary Supplement, October 22, 1982.

*   *   *

BIRSTEIN, Ann   1927-

PERSONAL: Born May 27, 1927, in New York, N.Y.; daughter of Bernard (a rabbi) and Clara (Gordon) Birstein; married Alfred Kazin, June 26, 1952 (divorced, 1981); children: Cathrael. *Education:* Queens College (now of the City University of New York), B.A. (magna cum laude), 1948; graduate work at Kenyon School of English, 1950, and the Sorbonne, Paris, 1951-52.

ADDRESSES: Home—1623 Third Ave., Apt. 27J West, New York, N.Y. 10028. *Office*—Department of English, Columbia University, Barnard College, 606 West 120th St., New York, N.Y. 10027. *Agent*—Joy Harris, 888 Seventh Ave., New York, N.Y. 10106.

CAREER: Writer. Former teacher, State University of New York at Albany, and Iowa Writers Workshop, Iowa City; currently professor of English and director of Writers on Writing, Barnard College, New York, N.Y. Writer in residence and visiting lecturer at various universities and colleges; conductor of writing workshops.

MEMBER: Authors League of America, Authors Guild, PEN (former member of executive board), Phi Beta Kappa (honorary alumni member).

AWARDS, HONORS: Dodd Mead Intercollegiate Literary Fellowship, 1948; Fulbright fellow, 1951-52; National Endowment for the Arts grant, 1982.

WRITINGS:

Star of Glass (novel), Dodd, 1950.
The Troublemaker (novel), Dodd, 1955.
(Co-editor) *The Works of Anne Frank,* Doubleday, 1959.
The Sweet Birds of Gorham (novel), McKay, 1966.
(Contributor) *The Open Form* (essays), Harcourt, 1970.
Summer Situations (novellas), Coward, 1972.
Dickie's List (novel), Coward, 1973.
(Contributor) *On the Job: Fiction about Work by Contemporary American Writers,* Vintage Book, 1977.
American Children (novel), Doubleday, 1980.
The Rabbi on Forty-Seventh Street (biography), Dial, 1982.
The Last of the True Believers (novel), Norton, 1988.

Contributor of short stories, articles, and reviews to *Mademoiselle, New Yorker, Reporter, McCall's, Book World, New York Times Book Review, Vogue, Connoisseur,* and *Confrontation.* Former movie critic for *Vogue;* contributing editor, *Inside.*

SIDELIGHTS: "*Good try, but no cigar:* that actually is the predominant tone of Ann Birstein's writing, and this is precisely what makes her formidable," notes *New York Times Book Review* contributor Sally Beauman in her assessment of Birstein's collection *Summer Situations.* "Choosing a difficult area to explore—the thin line where aspirations teeter over into pretensions—she creates a world of social and sexual disappointments, where almost all her characters are wryly aware of reality's stubborn refusal to live up to their fantasies and expectations." The same tone distinguishes Birstein's novel *American Children,* a post-World War II "collegiate memoir . . . [which is] a modest success story told as circumscribed, incisive satire," remarks Ann Hulbert in the *New Republic.* "Birstein's tone is light and gently satirical, her mode is picaresque," comments the *New York Times*'s Christopher Lehmann-Haupt, "and she writes with such fluidity that her novel seems to end only moments after it has begun." Although she exposes the failings of her characters, Birstein also examines the genuine problems they encounter. In her most recent novel, *The Last of the True Believers,* Birstein follows the career of her protagonist from young mother to faculty wife to independently successful writer. A *Publishers Weekly* reviewer comments that "Birstein is a writer whose intelligence radiates through this engaging narrative. While she pokes fun at everyone involved in producing literature . . . this is primarily a rueful story about the loss of passion."

In addition to her fiction, Birstein has written a biography of her father, Bernard, in *The Rabbi on Forty-Seventh Street.* Leader of a small synagogue in New York City, Rabbi Birstein opened up his congregation to the local population of actors on Broadway during the late 1920s; the synagogue became famous when stars such as Sophie Tucker, Jack Benny, Jimmy Durante, Eddie Cantor, and others staged a benefit to support it. Birstein, who was born shortly after her father took over the temple, includes portraits of her family and friends in this biography; a *New Yorker* critic observes that "Ann Birstein's memories of her father . . . are full of fine details." The critic adds that the author's "occasional lapses into speculation about scenes she could not have witnessed violate only the letter, not the spirit, of biography." "Miss Birstein has written all of this with compassion and affection," asserts Richard F. Shepard in the *New York Times,* "but also in a way that gives us the flavor of a novel—that is, with reasonable objectivity and sensitivity, as well as with touches of cool humor.''

BIOGRAPHICAL/CRITICAL SOURCES:

PERIODICALS

New Republic, April 1, 1972, March 29, 1980.
New Yorker, April 26, 1982.
New York Times, February 27, 1980, April 16, 1982.
New York Times Book Review, March 5, 1972.
Publishers Weekly, April 22, 1988.
Washington Post Book World, March 3, 1980.

*   *   *

BJOERNEBOE, Jens 1920-1976

PERSONAL: Born October 9, 1920, in Kristiansand, Norway; died May 10, 1976, in Oslo, Norway; son of Ingvald a shipowner) and Maja (a shipowner) Bjoerneboe; married Lisl, 1947 (divorced), married Tone Tveteraas (a drama and dance teacher), March, 1961; children: Marianne, Therese, Suzanne. *Education:* Attended University of Oslo and State Academy of Art; studied painting privately under Isaac Gruenewald. *Politics:* ''Anarchistic nihilism.'' *Religion:* ''Perhaps Christian.''

ADDRESSES: Home—3144 Veierland, Norway. *Agent*—Jans Joergen Toming, Montebellobakken 9, Oslo 3, Norway.

CAREER: Went to sea as pantry-boy and became sailor. Worked as a painter and taught at Rudolph Steiner school in Oslo, Norway, before becoming a novelist, dramatist, essayist, and poet in 1957.

MEMBER: PEN (former member of executive committee), Norwegian Authors' Union, Union of Norwegian Dramatists.

AWARDS, HONORS: Norwegian State Prize for Culture, for *Moment of Freedom,* and other Scandinavian prizes.

WRITINGS:

POETRY

Dikt (title means ''Poems''), Aschehoug (Oslo), 1951.
Ariadne, Aschehoug, 1953.
Den store by (title means ''The Big City''), Cappelen (Oslo), 1958.
Aske, vind og jord: Sanger, viser og dikt (title means ''Ashes, Wind, and Earth''), Gyldendal (Oslo), 1968.

NOVELS

Foer hanen galer (title means ''Before the Cock Crows''), Aschehoug, 1952.
Jonas, Aschehoug, 1955, translation by Bernt Jebsen and Douglas K. Stafford published as *The Least of These,* Bobbs-Merrill, 1959.
Under en haardere himmel (title means ''Under a Harder Sky''), Cappelen, 1957.
Vinter i Bellapalma (title means ''Winter in Bellapalma''), Cappelen, 1958.
Blaaman (title means ''Blue Boy''), Aschehoug, 1959, reprinted, Pax, 1974.
Den onde hyrde (title means ''The Evil Shepherd''), Aschehoug, 1960.
Droemmen og hjulet (title means ''The Dream and the Wheel''), Aschehoug, 1964.
Til lykke med dagen (title means ''Many Happy Returns of the Day''), Pax (Oslo), 1965.

Uten en Traad, I, Scala (Oslo), 1966, translation from Norwegian by Walter Barthold published as *Without a Stitch, I,* Grove, 1969.
Frihetens oeyeblikk: Heiligenberg-manuskriptet (first book in ''History of Bestiality'' trilogy), Gyldendal, 1966, translation from the Norwegian by Esther Greenleaf Murer published as *Moments of Freedom: The Heiligenberg Manuscript,* Norton, 1975.
Uten en Traad, II, [Sweden], 1967, (translation published as *Without a Stitch, II*).
Kruttaarnet: La Poudriere (title means ''The Powder Magazine''; second book in ''History of Bestiality'' trilogy), Gyldendal, 1969.
Hertug Hans (title means ''Duke Hans''), Gyldendal, 1972.
Stillheten: En anti-roman og absolutt aller siste protokoll (title means ''The Silence''; third book in ''History of Bestiality'' trilogy), Gyldendal, 1973.
Haiene: Historien om et mannskap og et forlis (title means ''The Sharks''; English translation published as *The Barkship Neptune*), Gyldendal, 1974.

DRAMA

Fugleeskerne (title means ''The Bird Lovers''), Gyldendal, 1966.
Semmelweis: Et anti-autoritaert skuespill, Gyldendal, 1968.
Amputasjon, Gyldendal, 1970.
Samlede skuespill, Pax, 1973.
Til fellet Torgersen (title means ''The Case of Torgersen''), Pax, 1973.
Dongery: En collage om forretningsstanden og om markedsfoerenens liv (title means ''Blue Jeans''), Pax, 1976.

OTHER

(Contributor) Olaf Bull, editor, *Norske studentersamfund,* [Oslo], 1954.
Norge, mitt Norge (essays; title means ''Norway, My Norway''), Pax, 1968.
Vi som elsket Amerika: Essays om formyndermennesket (essays; title means ''We Who Loved America''), Pax, 1970.
Politi og anarki (essays; title means ''Police and Anarchy''), Pax, 1972.
Om Brecht, Pax, 1977.
Om teater, Pax, 1978.

WORK IN PROGRESS: ''Red Emma,'' a play; a novel about whaling; a second trilogy tentatively entitled ''The History of Freedom.''

SIDELIGHTS: Relating a significant moment in his career as a writer, Bjoerneboe once told *CA* that at sixteen he read *Die moorsoldaten (The Rubber Truncheon)*—a book about the concentration camp in Oranienburg, written by Wolfgang Langhoff: ''Almost thirty years later I happened to meet an old man in the restaurant below Bert Brecht's Berliner Ensemble in the Theater am Schiffsbauerdamm in East Berlin. I told him about this book and that it had had an enormous influence upon my whole life and on almost all my writing. He looked paralyzed for a while, then he said: 'I am Langhoff!'''

Bjoerneboe's award-winning novel, *Moment of Freedom,* is an expressionistic work narrated in the first person through memories and reflections of its protagonist, and describes a nightmarish world of ''insanity, violence, and suffering, which must be viewed dispassionately and with laughter to escape an enslavement to its dementia,'' wrote a contributor to *Choice.* ''Bjoerneboe graphically uses memory and hallucination to expand the narrator's . . . probing of mankind under whatever flag,'' observed Roderick Nordel in the *Christian Science Monitor.* Discussing the novel in *Library Journal,* Inge Judd called Bjoerneboe a ''writer known for his passionate attacks against the deficiencies of modern society.''

Bjoerneboe explained to *CA:* ''Almost all my writing has concentrated on 'The Evil.''' In addition to the ''modern, child-killing school system,'' Bjoerneboe listed among his novel's subjects: ''Prison and the mistreatment of prisoners, the abuse of law, and the legal destruction of man.'' Critics tend to disagree on the relative balance of positive and negative forces in Bjoerneboe's work. Judd, for instance, found ''a passionate admiration for its [our civilization's] intellectual and artistic accomplishments,'' where others found pessimism and disconcertion.

The descendant of twelve generations of seafarers, and a former sailor himself, Bjoerneboe lived on a small island of little more than one hundred inhabitants. Although once an international whaling port, the island provided Bjoerneboe with seclusion. He made his home on about 170 acres and shunned radio, telephone, television, and newspapers. Revealing concern about his exhaustion from studying ''bestiality'' and modern politics, Bjoerneboe had planned to work on a major trilogy concentrating on ''The Good.''

AVOCATIONAL INTERESTS: ''Fishing, children, young people, and very old people.''

BIOGRAPHICAL/CRITICAL SOURCES:

PERIODICALS

Atlantic, July, 1975.
Choice, March, 1976.
Christian Science Monitor, August 1, 1975.
Library Journal, May 15, 1975.
Times Literary Supplement, September 10, 1971.
World Literature Today, spring, 1965, spring, 1978, summer, 1978, winter, 1981.

OBITUARIES:

PERIODICALS

AB Bookman's Weekly, June 28, 1976.
New York Times, May 15, 1976.
Washington Post, May 12, 1976.*

*   *   *

BJORNEBOE, Jens
    See BJOERNEBOE, Jens

*   *   *

BLACKSTOCK, Charity
    See TORDAY, Ursula

*   *   *

BLACKSTOCK, Lee
    See TORDAY, Ursula

*   *   *

BLACKWOOD, Alan   1932-

PERSONAL: Born November 23, 1932, in London, England; son of William (an accountant) and Constance (Wingfield) Blackwood; divorced. *Education:* Attended secondary school

in Brighton, England. *Politics:* ''Social Democrat/moderate Labour.'' *Religion:* ''Agnostic.''

ADDRESSES: Home—18 Shelburne Ct., Carlton Dr., London SW15 2DQ, England.

CAREER: Evening Argus, Brighton, England, reporter, 1953-55; Hutchinson Publishing Group Ltd., London, England, editor, 1957-60; Odhams Books Ltd., Feltham, England, editor, 1960; Hamlyn Publishing Group Ltd., Feltham, editor, 1960-69; Thomas Nelson & Sons Ltd., Sunbury-on-Thames, England, children's picture book editor for ''Nelson Young World,'' 1969-76; free-lance writer and editor, 1976—. *Military service:* British Army, 1955-57, instructor in Royal Army Educational Corps; became sergeant.

WRITINGS:

(Translator from the French, and editor) Jean Richartol, Pierre Chardon, and Giuseppe Grazzini, *Famous Battles of World History* (juvenile), Hamlyn, 1970.
(With Johannes Coenraad Van Hunnik) *My Super Book of Baby Animals in Colour* (juvenile), Nelson Young World, 1973.
(Editor) *Mulberry Bush Book of Nursery Rhymes* (juvenile), Thomas Nelson, 1974.
The Pageant of Music, Barrie & Jenkins, 1977.
Dr. Crotchet's Symphony (juvenile), Evans Brothers, 1977.
Ward Lock Encyclopedia of Music, Ward, Lock, 1979.
Gold and Silver (juvenile), Wayland, 1979.
Performing World of the Singer, Hamish Hamilton, 1981.
(Editor) *A-Z of Famous People,* Octopus, 1982.
(Contributor) Simon Adams, editor, *Quest for the Past,* Reader's Digest Press, 1983.
New Encyclopedia of Music, Ward, Lock, 1983.
Musical Instruments (juvenile), Wayland, 1986.
Twenty Names in Classical Music (juvenile), Wayland, 1987.
Twenty Names in Art (juvenile), Wayland, 1987.
Countries of the World: France (juvenile), Wayland, 1988.

Also contributor to encyclopedias, including *The Hamlyn Children's Encyclopedia in Colour;* also contributor to B.B.C. music publications. Contributor to periodicals.

WORK IN PROGRESS: A three-volume guide to western music, initially to be translated and published in Finland.

SIDELIGHTS: Alan Blackwood told *CA:* ''Music is my main interest, and I play the piano, though not professionally. I also have a small house in southern France, where I do some of my work. France is my favorite country, and I read and speak the language quite fluently. As a result, I think there is a slight bias in favor of French composers, notably Debussy and Ravel, in my music books. I have also visited Germany, Italy, Spain, the Soviet Union, the United States, and Sri Lanka.''

*   *   *

BLAKE, Jennifer
    See MAXWELL, Patricia

*   *   *

BLANE, Howard T(homas)   1926-

PERSONAL: Born May 10, 1926, in De Land, Fla.; son of Chesley Thomas and Olive (van Heest) Blane; married Eleanor Peckham (an illustrator), December 27, 1958; children: Benjamin Thomas, Eva Ann. *Education:* Harvard University, A.B.

(cum laude), 1950; Clark University, M.A., 1951, Ph.D., 1957. *Politics:* Independent. *Religion:* None.

ADDRESSES: Office—Research Institute on Alcoholism, 1021 Main St., Buffalo, N.Y. 14201.

CAREER: Massachusetts General Hospital, Boston, research assistant, 1953-54; Children's Medical Center, Boston, clinical research psychologist, 1954-56; Massachusetts General Hospital, research fellow, 1956-57, assistant psychologist, 1957-62, associate psychologist, 1962-70; Harvard University, Medical School, Boston, instructor in psychology, 1957-61, research associate, 1961-65, associate in psychology, 1965-67, assistant professor of psychology, 1968-70; University of Pittsburgh, Pittsburgh, Pa., associate professor, 1970-72, professor of education and psychology, 1972-86, research professor of epidemiology, 1978-86; Research Institute on Alcoholism, Buffalo, N.Y., director, 1986—; State University of New York at Buffalo, research professor of psychology, 1986—, director-designate, Center for Research on Alcoholism and Alcohol Abuse, 1987. Psychotherapist in private practice, 1957-70, 1980-85. Assistant in social work, Simmons College, 1955-58. Field supervisor of research training program for social scientists, Massachusetts Division of Alcoholism, 1961-70; visiting research fellow at Social Science Research Institute, University of Hawaii, 1968-69. Vice president and board member, Health Education Foundation, Washington, D.C., 1975—; member of educational advisory council, Distilled Spirits Council of the United States, Washington, D.C., 1976-79; associate director, National Clearinghouse for Alcohol Information, 1979-80. Manuscript reviewer for Allyn & Bacon, Plenum Press, and University Park Press, all 1976—. Consultant to mental health organizations. *Military service:* 1944-46.

MEMBER: American Psychological Association (fellow), American Association for the Advancement of Science, Research Society on Alcoholism, Society of Psychologists in Addictive Behaviors, New York Academy of Science, Sigma Xi.

AWARDS, HONORS: Recipient of grants from various organizations, including National Institute of Mental Health, National Science Foundation, and National Institute on Alcohol Abuse and Alcoholism.

WRITINGS:

The Personality of the Alcoholic: Guises of Dependency, Harper, 1968.

(With M. E. Chafetz and M. J. Hill) *Frontiers of Alcoholism,* Science House, 1970.

(Editor with Chafetz) *Youth, Alcohol, and Social Policy,* Plenum, 1979.

(Editor with K. E. Leonard) *Psychological Theories of Drinking and Alcoholism,* Guilford, 1987.

CONTRIBUTOR

Jerome M. Seidman, editor, *The Child: A Book of Readings,* Rinehart, 1958.

F. J. McGuigan and A. Calvin, editors, *Current Studies in Psychology,* Appleton-Century-Crofts, 1958.

M. L. Haimowitz and N. R. Haimowitz, editors, *Human Development: Selected Readings,* Cromwell, 1960.

E. W. Eisner and D. W. Ecker, editors, *Readings in Art Education,* Blaisdell, 1966.

J. Muller, editor, *The Clinical Interpretation of Psychological Tests,* Little, Brown, 1966.

J. O. Cole, editor, *Clinical Research in Alcoholism,* American Psychiatric Association, 1968.

R. J. Catanzaro, editor, *Alcoholism,* Thomas, 1968.

N. Mello and J. Mendelson, editors, *Recent Advances in Studies of Alcoholism,* National Institute of Mental Health, 1971.

S. Weitz, editor, *Nonverbal Communication,* Oxford University Press, 1974.

B. Kissin and H. Begleiter, editors, *Biology of Alcoholism,* Plenum, Volume 4: *The Social Aspects of Alcoholism,* 1976, Volume 5: *Treatment and Rehabilitation of the Chronic Alcoholic,* 1977.

R. Room, *Prevention of Alcohol Problems,* University of California, 1976.

N. J. Estes and M. E. Heinemann, editors, *Alcoholism: Developoment, Consequences, and Interventions,* Mosby, 1977, 3rd edition, 1986.

F. A. Nirenberg and P. M. Miller, editors, *Prevention of Alcohol Abuse,* Plenum, 1984.

OTHER

Co-editor of Alcohol Studies Series, Guilford Press, 1979—. Editorial reviewer for over a dozen medical journals since 1966, including *American Psychologist, Journal of Nervous and Mental Disease,* and *Science.* Field editor, *Journal of Studies on Alcohol,* 1983-84; member of editorial board, *Journal of Studies on Alcohol,* 1983—; member of editorial advisory board, *Alcohol Health and Research World,* 1986—.

WORK IN PROGRESS: "A hopefully definitive, comprehensive look at the psychology of alcohol, ranging from the behavioral effects of a drink or two on animals and humans, to the disordering effects of the continued consumption of very large doses of alcohol on humans and the secondary interpersonal effects on family members and others close to the alcoholic."

*   *   *

BLISS, Corinne Demas   1947-

PERSONAL: Born May 14, 1947, in New York, N.Y.; daughter of Nicholas Constantine and Electra (Guizot) Demas; married Matthew G. Roehrig; children: Austin Constantine Bliss, Artemis Demas Roehrig. *Education:* Tufts University, A.B. (magna cum laude), 1968; Columbia University, M.A. (with highest honors), 1969, M.Phil., 1978, Ph.D., 1980.

ADDRESSES: Home—Amherst, Mass. *Office*—Department of English, Mount Holyoke College, South Hadley, Mass. 01075. *Agent*—Ellen Levine, Ellen Levine Literary Agency, Inc., Suite 1205, 432 Park Ave. S., New York, N.Y. 10016.

CAREER: University of Pittsburgh, Pittsburgh, Pa., instructor in English, 1970-78; Mount Holyoke College, South Hadley, Mass., assistant professor, 1978-84, associate professor of English, 1984—. Lecturer at Chatham College, 1977-78; guest writer at Westfield State College, 1979; visiting writer at Goddard College, spring, 1981; gives readings at colleges. Founder and director of Valley Writers; editor for Author's Registry (literary agency), 1967 and 1968.

MEMBER: PEN, Authors Guild, Authors League of America, Bay State Writers Group.

AWARDS, HONORS: National Endowment for the Arts fellowship, 1978, 1983; Andrew W. Mellon Foundation fellowship, 1982; Lawrence Foundation Prize for best short story to appear in *Michigan Quarterly Review,* 1985.

WRITINGS:

(With son, Austin Bliss) *That Dog Melly!* (juvenile; with own
photographs), Hastings House, 1981.
The Same River Twice (novel), Atheneum, 1982.
Daffodils or the Death of Love (short stories), University of
Missouri Press, 1983.

Work represented in anthologies, including *Secrets and Other
Stories by Women,* 1979. Contributor of more than forty sto-
ries, poems, and essays to magazines, including *Michigan
Quarterly Review, McCall's, Redbook, Virginia Quarterly
Review,* and *Esquire.* Fiction editor, *Massachusetts Review,*
1984—.

WORK IN PROGRESS: Alibis, a novel; *Separate Lives,* a collection of short stories.

SIDELIGHTS: Corinne Demas Bliss told *CA:* "Although I've
dabbled in poetry and written nonfiction, I'm most naturally
a fiction writer. I love writing short stories, and am a staunch
defender of the genre. My doctoral dissertation was on the
short story—basically it was an inquiry into how writers make
readers respond the way they want them to and a study of what
makes certain short stories work. At Mt. Holyoke College I
teach both literature and creative writing courses, and the fact
that I'm a working writer influences the way I teach literature,
just as my literature background influences my teaching of
writing.

"My new novel *Alibis* concerns the adoption triangle. I took
a year's leave from teaching to do background research on the
ethical, psychological, and legal questions that are raised when
adopted children search for their biological parents."

AVOCATIONAL INTERESTS: Travel in Greece, music, cross-
country skiing.

*   *   *

BLOM, Karl Arne   1946-
(Bo Lagevi)

PERSONAL: Born January 22, 1946, in Naessjoe, Sweden;
son of Karl Axel (a hotel owner) and Ester (Skoeld) Blom;
married Karin Ann-Marie Gyllen (a nurse), June 29, 1969;
children: Karl Anders Bertil, Kristina Magdalena, Katarina
Elisabet. *Education:* University of Lund, B.A., 1972. *Politics:*
"Liberal, cosmopolitan, anti-Communist." *Religion:* Agnostic.

ADDRESSES: Home and office—Smaaskolevaegen 22, S-223
67 Lund, Sweden. *Agent*—Lennart Sane, Hollaendareplan 9,
S-37434 Karlshamn, Sweden.

CAREER: Free-lance writer, 1970-75.

MEMBER: International Association of Crime Writers, Union
of Swedish Authors, Swedish Academy of Detection, Society
of Detective Story Writers of Skane (honorary chairman),
Mystery Writers of America, Crime Writers Association (England), Poe Club (Denmark).

AWARDS, HONORS: Sherlock Award from *Expressen* (newspaper), 1974, for *The Moment of Truth.*

WRITINGS:

Sanningens oegonblick, AWE/Gebers, 1974, translation by Erik
J. Friis published as *The Moment of Truth,* Harper, 1977.
Smartgransen, AWE/Gebers, 1978, translation by Joan Tate
published as *The Limits of Pain,* Ram Publishing, 1979.

IN SWEDISH

Naagon borde soerja (title means "Somebody Should Mourn"),
AWE/Gebers, 1971.
Naagon aer skyldig (title means "Somebody Is Guilty"), AWE/
Gebers, 1972.
Naagon slog tillbaka (title means "Somebody Hit Back"),
AWE/Gebers, 1973.
Ett gammalt mord (title means "An Old Murder"), Gleerups,
1974.
(Editor) *Brottpunkter* (title means "Murderous Points"),
Lindqvist, 1975.
Vaaldets triumf (title means "Triumph of Violence"), AWE/
Gebers, 1975.
Resan till ingenstans (stories; title means "Journey into No-
where"), Zindermans, 1975.
Lund, Hermods, 1975.
(Editor) *Skaanska Brottstycken* (title means "Pieces of
Crimes"), Bra Deckare, 1976.
Kortaste straaet (title means "Second Best"), Lindqvist, 1976.
Noedhamm (title means "Harbor of Refuge"), Lindqvist, 1976.
Lyckligt lottade (title means "The Happy People"), AWE/
Gebers, 1976.
(Under pseudonym Bo Lagevi) *Allt vad du gjort mot naagon*
(title means "All the Things You Did"), B. Wahlstroem,
1976.
Noedvaern (novel; title means "Self-Defense"), Zinderman,
1977.
40o Kalltli Solen (stories; title means "40 Degrees Cold in the
Sun"), Zindermans, 1977.
Frihetssoekarna (title means "Searchers of Freedom"), AWE/
Gebers, 1977.
(Under pseudonym Bo Lagevi) *Utan personligt ansvar* (title
means "Without Personal Responsibility"), B. Wahls-
troem, 1977.
Det var en gang (title means "Once upon a Time"), AWE/
Gebers, 1978
Mannen i granden (title means "The Man in the Alley"),
AWE/Gebers, 1979.
Gristningspunkten (title means "The Breaking Point"), AWE/
Gebers, 1979.
Kvinnan pa bussen (title means "The Woman on the Bus"),
AWE/Gebers, 1980.
Nodvandigt Ont (title means "Justified Evilness"), AWE/Ge-
bers, 1980.
Mordanglarna (title means "The Murderous Angels"), AWE/
Gebers, 1981.
Med andra ogon (title means "A Point of View"), AWE/
Gebers, 1981.
Nattbok (title means "Nightbrook"), AWE/Gebers, 1982.
Ingenmansland (title means "No Man's Land"), AWE/Ge-
bers, 1982.
Utkagen (title means "The Way Out"), AWE/Gebers, 1983.
Aterresan (title means "The Way Back"), AWE/Gebers, 1983.
Aendamalet (title means "The Purpose"), AWE/Gebers, 1984.
Oevertaget (title means "The Advantage"), AWE/Gerbers,
1985.
Madonna, AWE/Gebers, 1986
Krigsharn (title means "Child of War"), AWE/Gebers, 1987.
Skuggan av en stoevd (title means "The Shadow of a Boot"),
AWE/Gebers, 1988.

TRANSLATOR INTO SWEDISH

Jack Higgins, *Bikten* (title means "A Prayer for the Dying"),
Lindqvist, 1975.

Emilie Gaboriau, *Den lille mannen i Batignolles* (title means "The Little Man in Batignolles"), Lindqvist, 1975.

Arthur Conan Doyle, *En studie i roett* (title means "A Study in Scarlet"), AWE/Gebers, 1977.

Hanning Hjuler, *Raattorna* (title means "The Rats"), Bra Deckare, 1977.

Doyle, *Silverblaesen* (title means "The Memoirs of Sherlock Holmes"), AWE/Gebers, 1977.

Doyle, *Det tomma huset* (title means "The Return of Sherlock Holmes"), AWE/Gebers, 1978.

Doyle, *Den toende detehtiven* (title means "His Last Bow"), AWE/Gebers, 1978.

Doyle, *Den krypande mannen* (title menas "The Casebook of Sherlock Holmes"), AWE/Gebers, 1978.

Translator into Swedish of numerous mystery novels written by Stanley Ellin, R. R. Irvine, Loren Singer, Joe L. Hensley, Newton Thornburg, Lawrence Treat, and Hillary Waugh.

OTHER

Author of material for television series. Contributor of articles and stories to magazines.

SIDELIGHTS: Karl Arne Blom once wrote *CA:* "So far most of what I have written is crime novels . . . because this is the kind of novel by which you can best describe and try to analyze time, society, and human beings. I try to tell about our time—people as they are now and the problems people are facing in a Swedish so-called welfare society. My other novels and most of my short stories are efforts to describe the surrealistic and absurd realities of life.

"I regard the mystery genre as not inferior to so-called real literature. In my opinion a crime novel, a mystery, or whatever it happens to be, can be as good a book as any book of fiction. . . . A good mystery or crime novel is like an iceberg. You see what's on the surface and a lot of things are hidden.

"My first three books deal with crime and murder and violence. But the first one is also a book about how lonely people can be when they are apparently among many others. The second one is about the economic problems students are facing, and the third one is about unemployment among students with degrees. From there on I have dealt with the basic elements of violence among people, with violence in our time and how violence has become almost a natural way of expressing oneself."

*   *   *

BLOUNT, Roy (Alton), Jr. 1941-
(Noah Sanders, C. R. Ways)

PERSONAL: Surname rhymes with "punt"; born October 4, 1941, in Indianapolis, Ind.; son of Roy Alton (a savings and loan executive) and Louise (Floyd) Blount; married Ellen Pearson, September 6, 1964 (divorced March, 1973); married Joan Ackerman, 1976 (separated); children: (first marriage) Ennis Caldwell, John Kirven. *Education:* Vanderbilt University, B.A. (magna cum laude), 1963; Harvard University, M.A., 1964. *Politics:* "Dated white Southern liberalism, with healthy undertones of redneckery and anarchism; nostalgia for Earl Long." *Religion:* "Lapsed Methodist."

ADDRESSES: Home—Mill River, Mass.; and New York, N.Y.

CAREER: Decatur-DeKalb News, Decatur, Ga., reporter and sports columnist, 1958-59; *Morning Telegraph,* New York City, reporter, summer, 1961; *New Orleans Times-Picayune,* New

Orleans, La., reporter, summer, 1963; *Atlanta Journal,* Atlanta, Ga., reporter, editorial writer, and columnist, 1966-68; *Sports Illustrated,* New York City, staff writer, 1968-74, associate editor, 1974-75; free-lance writer, 1975—. Occasional performer for American Humorists' Series, American Place Theatre, 1986, and 1988, and has appeared on "A Prairie Home Companion," "The CBS Morning Show," "The Tonight Show," "The David Letterman Show," "Austin City Limits," "All Things Considered," and many other radio and television programs. Instructor at Georgia State College, 1967-68. Member of usage panel, American Heritage Dictionary. *Military service:* U.S. Army, 1964-66; became first lieutenant.

MEMBER: Phi Beta Kappa.

WRITINGS:

About Three Bricks Shy of a Load, Little, Brown, 1974.
Crackers: This Whole Many-Sided Thing of Jimmy, More Carters, Ominous Little Animals, Sad-Singing Women, My Daddy and Me, Knopf, 1980.
One Fell Soup; or, I'm Just a Bug on the Windshield of Life, Little, Brown, 1982.
What Men Don't Tell Women, Atlantic-Little, Brown, 1984.
Not Exactly What I Had in Mind, Atlantic Monthly Press, 1985.
It Grows on You: A Hair-Raising Survey of Human Plumage, Doubleday, 1986.
"Roy Blount's Happy Hour and a Half" (one-man show), produced Off-Broadway at American Place Theatre, January 22-February 7, 1986.
Soupsongs/Webster's Ark (double book of verse), Houghton, 1987.
Now, Where Were We?, Villard, 1989.

Also author of two one-act plays produced at Actors Theater of Louisville, Ky., November, 1983, and fall, 1984. Contributor to anthologies, including *The Best of Modern Humor,* 1983, *Laughing Matters,* 1987, *The Norton Book of Light Verse,* 1987, *The Oxford Book of American Light Verse, The Ultimate Baseball Book, Classic Southern Humor,* and *Sudden Fiction.* Columnist, *Atlanta Journal,* 1967-70. Contributor of articles, short stories, poems, crossword puzzles, and drawings, sometimes under pseudonyms Noah Sanders and C. R. Ways, to 92 very different publications, including *Sports Illustrated, New Yorker, Atlantic, New York Times Magazine, Esquire, Playboy, Rolling Stone, GQ, Conde Nast Traveler, Spy,* and *Antaeus.* Contributing editor, *Atlantic,* 1983—.

WORK IN PROGRESS: A novel, *First Hubby;* lyrics for musical comedy, "Murder at Elaine's," book by Nora Ephron.

SIDELIGHTS: Roy Blount, Jr., "is Andy Rooney with a Georgia accent, only funnier," declares Larry L. King in the *Washington Post Book World.* Like Rooney, Blount has entertained the American public not only through his multitudinous magazine publications (his articles have appeared in nearly one hundred different magazines) and his books, but also through other media—he has performed on radio and television shows ranging from Minnesota Public Radio's "A Prairie Home Companion" to NBC's "The David Letterman Show." "The unceasing drip-drip-drip of bizarre images, intricate wordplay, droll asides and crazy ideas disorients the reader," states Patrick F. McManus in the *New York Times Book Review,* "until Mr. Blount finally has him at his mercy." His work has been compared to that of Mark Twain, and his "light touch and sense of bemusement," declares Eric Zorn in the *Chicago*

Tribune, "combine with arch intellect to give him the versatility to publish in *Organic Gardening* and *Country Journal* one day and *Harvard Magazine* the next."

Blount's books, says Leslie Bennetts in the *New York Times,* "attest to the breadth of his interests, from 'One Fell Soup, or I'm Just a Bug on the Windshield of Life' (which is also the name of one of the original songs Mr. Blount sings 'unless I'm forcibly deterred') to 'What Men Don't Tell Women' to 'It Grows on You,' a volume about hair." His first book, *About Three Bricks Shy of a Load,* "did for the Pittsburgh Steelers roughly what Sherman did for the South," states Donald Morrison in *Time,* and it "remains the most comic treatise on professional football extinct or extant," reports King. *New York Times Book Review* contributor Robert W. Creamer calls *About Three Bricks Shy of a Load* "a terrific book," and he concludes, "I have never read anything else on pro football, fiction or nonfiction, as good as this."

With his second book, *Crackers: This Whole Many-Sided Thing of Jimmy, More Carters, Ominous Little Animals, Sad-Singing Women, My Daddy and Me,* Blount established his reputation as a humorist. *Crackers* examines the presidency of Jimmy Carter, a Georgian like Blount, and concludes that what the Carter administration needed was a more down-to-earth, redneck, approach to the business of governing the country. "If *Crackers* reveals an overarching thesis, it is that contemporary America, like its president, is too emotionally constrained, too given to artifice, too Northern," explains Morrison. The book was a critical success; Harry Crews, writing in the *Washington Post Book World,* calls *Crackers* "the funniest book I've read in a decade," and labels it "a triumph over subject, proving—if it needed proving again—that there are no dull subjects, only dull writers."

Blount has also achieved success in collections of his magazine articles, including *One Fell Soup; or, I'm Just a Bug on the Windshield of Life, What Men Don't Tell Women, Not Exactly What I Had in Mind, It Grows on You: A Hair-Raising Survey of Human Plumage,* and *Now, Where Were We?* Gathered from sources as diverse as *Esquire,* the *New Yorker,* and *Eastern Airlines Pastimes,* the collections prove Blount's "ability to be amusing on a diversity of topics," according to Beaufort Cranford of the *Detroit News.* After all, he asks, "what other source can prove the existence of God by considering the testicle?"

Although some critics—like *Los Angeles Times* contributor Taffy Cannon, who calls Blount's stories "considerably funnier in a bar at midnight than spread at meandering and pointless length across the printed page"—find that Blount's later works aren't as successful as his earlier ones, many others celebrate his collections. "It gives me great pleasure," King declared after reading *One Fell Soup,* "to here officially designate [Blount] . . . a semi-genius at the very least. I have been reading his stuff for years and he seldom fails to break me up." Ron Givens, writing in *Newsweek,* declares, "It's downright refreshing, then, to read somebody who has taste, intelligence, style and, oh, bless you, wit—qualities that Roy Blount Jr. . . . [has] in abundance."

Blount has also attracted attention as a versifier and songwriter. Despite his claims to be "singing impaired," Blount has performed both his stories and his verses in his one-man show, "Roy Blount's Happy Hour and a Half," and on radio programs such as "A Prairie Home Companion." A recent collection of the comic's verse, *Soupsongs/Webster's Ark,* "contains odes to beets, chitlins, barbeque sauce, catfish and grease ('I think that I will never cease/To hold in admiration grease')," explains Bennetts, "along with a 'Song Against Broccoli' that reads in its entirety: 'The neighborhood stores are all out of broccoli,/Loccoli.'" "Blount's verses may resemble Burma Shave's more than Byron's," declares the *Chicago Tribune*'s Jim Spencer, "but they are bodaciously funny."

Critics have tried to define with varying success the sources of Blount's sense of humor. "I can't tell you what makes Roy Blount such a funny writer," confesses *Washington Post Book World* contributor Dennis Drabelle, "—perhaps a dose of comic afflatus administered by the gods." Another contributing factor, suggests Givens, "derives from his off-center perceptions." Kenneth Turan of *Time* calls Blount's work "in the tradition of the great curmudgeons like H. L. Mencken and W. C. Fields." And the comic "is not of the punch-line school of humor writing," declares McManus. "His humor is cumulative in effect, like Chinese water torture. When you can bear it no longer, you collapse into a spasm of mirth, often at a line that taken by itself would provoke no more than a smile."

Roy Blount, Jr., summed up his life for *CA,* saying, "Raised in South by Southern parents. Couldn't play third base well enough so became college journalist. Ridiculed cultural enemies. Boosted integration. Decided to write, teach. Went to Harvard Graduate School. Didn't like it. Went back to journalism. Liked it. Got a column. Ridiculed cultural enemies. Wrote limericks. Boosted integration. Wanted to write for magazines. Took writing job at *Sports Illustrated.* Have seen country, met all kinds of people, heard all different kinds of talk. Like it. Ready now to write a novel that sums it all up."

CA INTERVIEW

CA interviewed Roy Blount, Jr., by telephone on August 1, 1988, at his home in Massachusetts.

CA: Studying at Vanderbilt and later working on a master's in English at Harvard Graduate School, did you have in mind to become a very funny writer?

BLOUNT: From the time I started, I was writing things more or less along the lines of what I'm writing now. It's not as though I set out to learn how to be a funny writer; I set out to learn how to write as well as I could. I'm not trying just to be funny. But it seems to me that when I'm going best, there's an element of humor involved and it keeps things afloat. I think almost all good writing has a certain amount of humor in it at some level. It seems natural to me to write in a funny way, but I find it impossible to say anything funny about being funny.

The first time I wrote for publication was in high school, and I was satirizing my school. Whenever we'd have to write a theme on some topic like "What I Did Last Summer," I would hate that sort of straightforward assignment, so I'd write about something odd. I had several English teachers who encouraged me, but one in particular, Ann Lewis, in my sophomore year, gave me Perelman and Benchley and Thurber and E. B. White and Wolcott Gibbs to read. They were inspirations to me, and influences. But I'd always read lots of funny writers. I was a big enthusiast of "Pogo" and read Mark Twain and Booth Tarkington—Penrod, Penrod and Sam, all that stuff. I tended to like funny stuff. I could get all analytical about what humor does, at least for me. I think it's a way of resolving contradictions and tensions in a way that people can enjoy. But that's a boring thing to say.

CA: I have a theory that anyone who grew up in the South some years ago (having done so myself) had to see things in a funny way or become entirely crazy.

BLOUNT: That's true. It was difficult to make social and psychological sense out of growing up in the South, but it was a challenge which seemed to me rewarding, and a challenge in which comedy helped. I think Southerners have a sense of the inherent comedy of language that is comparable to the Irish. In the South there is less faith, than in the Northeast, that language can explain things analytically. I never wanted to accept the fact that you could just sort of bullshit your way through culture, and I resented the blathering of southern politicians. On the other hand, there was a whole lot of flavor in the blathering of southern politicians, however benighted. I always wanted to try to make eastern intellectual sense without giving up the richness of southern linguistics.

CA: You're especially good at reproducing in your writing the sounds of actual speech, particularly southern speech but certainly not only that variety. Has that talent been nurtured by heavy listening when you were very young?

BLOUNT: I guess everybody listens pretty heavily when they're very young. I was trying to figure things out. People tend to assume that I was surrounded stereotypically by wonderful storytellers. I don't recall that I was. But my family did take pleasure in figures of speech and turns of phrase, and in being funny, in delighting in the chaos of animals and family.

CA: Going from the South to Harvard, did you suffer a kind of culture shock that brought into sharper focus the southern ways you've written so much about?

BLOUNT: Going to Harvard was in many ways the opposite of culture shock. I was looking for some place where people talked about books and were interested in the things I was interested in. I'd never known anybody my own age who talked about books until I went up North. On the other hand, I was shocked to find that all these people, the ones who knew about the books that I was interested in, had their own areas of elementary ignorance. To be suddenly plunged into the midst of people who read books all the time gave me a perspective on where I came from, but it also gave me a perspective on the kind of people who read books all the time.

CA: After a few years of newspapering you went to Sports Illustrated, *where you worked from 1968 to 1975. And your first book,* About Three Bricks Shy of a Load, *was about the Pittsburgh Steelers. Was sports something you'd really have liked to make a career of?*

BLOUNT: Oh yeah. When I was a kid, before I wanted to be a writer, I wanted to be a sports immortal. A three-sport immortal: baseball, basketball, and football. But I gradually realized that I was not only no immortal, but extremely mediocre.

CA: So often writers get typecast by publishers and find it difficult to prove they can do something other that what they're known for. Was it a struggle for you to begin selling articles to magazines that weren't about sports?

BLOUNT: It was a kind of shift. It took a while before I was able to make a living primarily off of the kinds of things I most wanted to do. When I quit *Sports Illustrated* and started

freelancing, I had a contract with them and kept on writing for them as a freelancer. After a year I started writing a sports column for *Esquire,* which was a good transitional deal because it enabled me to be funny about sports, to write about them in a personal and unorthodox way.

But it still took a lot of work. I kept trying to write things for the *New Yorker,* which is what I grew up wanting to do. They would take one out of three and would quibble about why they weren't taking the other two. There was no way in the world you could make a living like that. I wrote a lot of long pieces about country-music stars and athletes and one thing and another while I was moving toward being the kind of writer I wanted to be.

I wanted to write short, funny pieces for the magazines, and a big step in that direction was when Bill Whitworth left the *New Yorker* to become editor of the *Atlantic.* He urged me to send him funny pieces, and, in fact, I signed a contract with the *Atlantic* to send them my funny pieces first instead of the *New Yorker.* I've found the *Atlantic* a lot less peculiar in its view of what's funny. That helped get me into being able to make a living mostly as a humorist, but by that time I had gotten involved in doing a lot of other things, like writing sports, which I still like to do. I like to write about politics and other things. I grew up wanting to be a humorist, but now that I are one, I wish people wouldn't press it so hard. I don't want people to think that all I can do is write little funny pieces. There's a term that the Library of Congress uses for light essays and such things: facetiae. I don't want to bog down in facetiaism. I've always wanted—in fact I've always been urged by publishers, and I'm responding to those urges—to write a novel. It's hard to do, but I feel that I need to write some kind of long, strange book that's not a collection.

CA: You've had articles published in something like ninety magazines at this point, and of widely varying kinds. Has it been hard to sustain a schedule of writing for so many markets?

BLOUNT: I've never had a schedule; I never wanted one. The main thing I want is to be free. There are all sorts of disadvantages to being a freelancer, but the great advantage is that you're free to do whatever comes up if you can squeeze it in. That's the challenge of freelancing. And if a lot of different people want you to write for them, you're not at the mercies of any one magazine. You don't have to do things any given magazine's way; you've got all sorts of places to go. I have probably overdone it—I take a certain pride in how many magazines I've written for: I think it's up to ninety-two now. And I think I've spread myself a bit thin. I've written things that not many people read, because I wrote them for out-of-the-way magazines. But what I like is to keep an eye out for opportunities to do something unexpected. I don't want to get bogged down in writing for the *New York Times* or for the *New Yorker,* because then you become a *Times* writer or a *New Yorker* writer. It's important for me to write for a lot of people.

CA: Was there any response from Jimmy Carter and his family to your second book, Crackers?

BLOUNT: No. I heard from some people in the White House who liked it, but I never heard from any Carters. And if somebody had written a book like that involving me, I don't think I would have responded either.

CA: There are more and more little songs as your books go on, and yet you say you're singing-impaired. Are any of these songs getting sung anywhere, or going to get sung? It's sad to think of them having a life only on the page.

BLOUNT: I have sung a number of them on "Prairie Home Companion" and on television and one thing and another. But to say that I have sung them is not to say that they have been sung.

CA: You've had two one-act plays produced at Actors Theatre of Louisville and early in 1988 did a one-man show, "Roy Blount's Happy Hour and a Half," at the American Place Theater in New York. How did all the shows come about?

BLOUNT: In the case of the one-act plays, I had been invited to expand something I had written into plays. The first one grew out of a story I had in *Esquire*, which was a baseball player talking on the phone. I just recast it as a monologue for the stage. The other one was a short story from the *New Yorker* in which people were sitting around the television and talking. But the "Happy Hour and a Half" grew up out of doing appearances. I've always liked to get up and talk. I would do that a lot on radio and television promoting my books, and then I started being on "Prairie Home Companion" and other things. The people at the American Place Theater called me up and said they had a series there called the American Humorists' Series, and did I have anything that I thought could be adapted to the stage. I said I didn't know, but I could just get up and talk on the stage. They agreed to that, and I did it two or three years ago for a series called "Laugh at Lunch." It's in a small part of the theater, and people bring their lunches in to eat while they listen to a bit of theater.

That went well and got good reviews, and I did it for six weeks, three or four days a week. Then Wynn Handman, the American Place Theater director, came back a year or so later and asked if I thought I could do that show to a bigger audience in the main theater at night. I mulled it over apprehensively for a while and then thought I shouldn't pass up the chance, so I did it.

CA: Is it in part the immediate response to your material that makes you like getting up in front of an audience?

BLOUNT: Sure. It's lonesome sitting at some typing machine. Also, you can do the same things more than once. I make speeches from time to time, and you can use the same material, which is a great thing. As a writer, you write something once and get paid for it; maybe some anthology will pick it up and pay you another thirty dollars, but that's about it. Performing, you can use the same material and rework it and play around with it. That's sort of like rewriting. Rewriting's more fun than writing, usually, I think, because you've already got something basically there.

CA: You've been doing a lot of travel lately. I gather from my reading about you and from your postcard from Ireland. Do you speak to groups everywhere you go, or do you like to sort of hide away from people when you're traveling?

BLOUNT: I don't have to hide; it's not as though groups form around me waiting to be entertained. I wrote a column for the *Traveler* magazine for a year—I've just finished writing the last couple of columns—so I've traveled a lot for that. I've traveled a lot to make speeches in this country, but I don't

think I've ever made a speech abroad. I go to look. There seems to be a great deal of interest in travel writing lately, and I've been living with an Englishwoman who likes to travel, so I've been in a travel phase.

CA: In "Roy Blount's Happy Hour and a Half" you told about some of the adventures and misadventures you've had in the course of your work. What's been the most truly scary assignment you've undertaken as a writer?

BLOUNT: I did a story about the Ku Klux Klan; I went down and watched them burn a cross. They had guns and stuff. My friend Slick Lawson, the photographer, and I went into the woods with them and watched them burn the cross and make hateful speeches, and we walked along on this march they were on, expecting to be attacked by decent citizens any minute and have gunfire break out. But that was cheap thrills. The Klan seemed to be—thank goodness—a shadow of its former self and sort of a publicity organization. When the Klan was really scary was when it was deep into the infrastructure of the society and people were afraid to say anything about it. But they do shoot people. I was just called by the Justice Department to see if I would testify against some of the guys I interviewed, whom they want to try for shooting demonstrators.

That was scary, I guess, but I think it's less scary than trying to do justice to people I write about and not misrepresent them and rip them off. When you write about real people, you have to talk about them the same way you would behind their back, and yet they're listening. That always bothers me—especially when it's somebody I know. I just wrote a little piece for *Esquire* about the director Jonathan Demme, and I worried and worried about that. We're not close friends, but we've been friendly for a long time, and I was trying to get it right. For the most part, I don't think that I've ripped off people that I've written about, but occasionally somebody is devastated by something I write, and it's usually something I thought they would like. Trying to be objective about somebody you like is iffier than walking around the woods with the Klan.

CA: Do you have a built-in sense of what's off-limits to the humorist, or what has to be handled very delicately?

BLOUNT: I want to try to write about just those things. One of the challenges is getting into embarrassing, shameful, frightening things and trying to convert them to comedy. That's the whole point of comedy, it seems to me. If an alarm goes off and says, You'd better not try to write about this, then I feel honor-bound to write about it.

CA: Your interest in the odd word and the odd fact is particularly evident in the second part of Soupsongs/Webster's Ark, *in which you give an alphabet of strange animal life. Did this part of the book possibly grow out of your work on the* American Heritage Dictionary?

BLOUNT: I've always loved dictionaries, and a lot of the illustrations of the animals in the book came from old dictionaries. I love definitions and I like finding odd juxtapositions of things in dictionaries. The fact that some odd little animal is followed immediately by some bit of architecture or something like that fascinates me. I like the miscellaneity of the dictionary, and I like the fact that the only thing that rules it is language. It's not ordered by any kind of moral or religious system or any sense of propriety except the requirement to alphabetize and be precise. It seems to me that language is the final test of things, and the dictionary is sheer language. I realize the dubiousness of saying that language is the final test of things, but that's what a writer has to believe.

CA: It's evident from what might seem like the most casual writing of yours that you care a great deal about using words correctly and effectively.

BLOUNT: Sure. Painters care about using paint carefully. The only way to be funny or tragic or cogent in any way is to use the language, not just correctly in a conventional way but also at a higher level of correctness that's surprisingly correct. Words are such a mess and a tangle; it's like unraveling a backlash in a fishing line to try to get a single sentence to stay put. It's a frustrating thing. The more you deal with it, the more you try to write a decent sentence, the more you appreciate how sweet a decent sentence is once you've completed it. You have to have an appreciation of language, whether it's instinctive or learned or both, to write a good sentence.

CA: Your career seems to be taking some new directions, including the novel you mentioned earlier. What's close enough or definite enough to talk about at this point?

BLOUNT: I have another collection coming out in March from Villard called *Now, Where Were We?* It's supposed to come out at the end of the Reagan era, and it's a collection of pieces I've been writing the last five years or so. That and the novel I'm working on are the big things. I've got one or two little magazine pieces I'm doing.

CA: Somewhere it was reported that you've been writing lyrics for a musical.

BLOUNT: Yes. Nora Ephron and I and Jess Korman have been working off and on for years on a musical called "Murder at Elaine's." We've written five songs. It keeps being interrupted by the summer and other projects, but it's still in progress; we've still got to talk to directors about it. But I think someday it might actually come to fruition. Then I can become an expert on not only singing- but also dancing-impairment.

BIOGRAPHICAL/CRITICAL SOURCES:

PERIODICALS

Books of the Times, December, 1980.
Chicago Tribune, November 4, 1982, December 24, 1987.
Detroit News, October 17, 1982.
Globe and Mail (Toronto), July 14, 1984.
Los Angeles Times, December 13, 1985.
Newsweek, September 17, 1984.
New York Times, September 27, 1980, November 1, 1982, April 28, 1984, January 25, 1988, January 26, 1988.
New York Times Book Review, December 1, 1974, September 28, 1980, May 13, 1984, November 17, 1985, February 7, 1988, March 26, 1989.
Sports Illustrated, February 10, 1969, June 18, 1973, April 15, 1974, August 5, 1974.
Time, October 20, 1980, June 4, 1984.
Times Literary Supplement, June 3, 1983.
Washington Post, June 19, 1984.
Washington Post Book World, September 28, 1980, November

2, 1980, January 23, 1983, October 13, 1985, February 19, 1989.

—*Sketch by Kenneth R. Shepherd*
—*Interview by Jean W. Ross*

*   *   *

BOARMAN, Patrick M(adigan) 1922-

PERSONAL: Born April 23, 1922, in Buffalo, N.Y.; son of Marcus Daly (a lawyer) and Virginia (Madigan) Boarman; married Katharina Theresa Schumacher, December 12, 1953 (divorced, 1980); children: Thomas, Christopher, Jesse, Barbara. *Education:* Fordham University, A.B., 1943; Columbia University, M.S., 1946; University of Geneva, Ph.D., 1965; also attended University of Amsterdam, 1949-50, University of Michigan, 1958, and University of Virginia, 1965.

ADDRESSES: Home—6421 Caminito Estrellado, San Diego, Calif. 92120. *Office*—National University, 4141 Camino Del Rio S., San Diego, Calif.

CAREER: Doubleday & Co., Inc., New York, N.Y., assistant to advertising manager, 1944-45; Columbia Broadcasting System, correspondent in Geneva, Switzerland, 1947-48; John Carroll University, Cleveland, Ohio, assistant professor of economics, 1948-49; National Catholic Welfare Conference, director of Office of Cultural Affairs in Bonn, Germany, 1951-55; University of Wisconsin—Milwaukee, assistant professor of economics, 1956-62; Bucknell University, Lewisburg, Pa., associate professor of economics, 1962-67; Long Island University, Arthur T. Roth School of Business Administration, Greenvale, N.Y., professor of economics, 1967-72; Pepperdine University, Center for International Business, Los Angeles, Calif., professor of international economics and director of research, 1972-75; Patrick M. Boarman Associates (international business consulting firm), Palos Verdes, Calif., president, 1975—; National University, San Diego, professor of international economics and chairman of international business, 1979—; Supervisor of San Diego County Third District, 1983-85.

Visiting professor of economics, University of Geneva, 1965-66; distinguished visiting professor of economics, Pitzer College, 1977. Director of research, U.S. House of Representatives Republican Conference, 1967-68; member of board of directors, Committee for Monetary Research and Education, New York City, 1970—; senior economist, World Trade Institute, New York City, 1971. Member of California Republican State Central Committee, 1985—. Consultant, General Electric, 1964-65, American Telephone and Telegraph, 1969, U.S. Secretary of the Treasury, 1970-71, and Economic Stabilization Board, 1971-72. *Military service:* U.S. Army, 1943.

MEMBER: American Economic Association, Western Economic Association, World Trade Association of San Francisco, University Club (San Diego), American Conservative Union (founding member), Philadelphia Society (founding member).

AWARDS, HONORS: Distinguished Service Cross of Order of Merit, West German Federal Republic, 1956; Relm Foundation grant, 1966; service plaque, San Diego County Board of Supervisors, 1983-84; award of merit, Southern California Regional Association of County Supervisors, 1983-84.

WRITINGS:

(Editor) *Der Christ und die soziale Marktwirtschaft*, Kohlhammer (Stuttgart), 1955.

(Translator) Wilhelm Roepke, *Economics of the Free Society,* Regnery, 1963.

Union Monopolies and Antitrust Restraints, Labor Policy Association, 1963.

Germany's Economic Dilemma—Inflation and the Balance of Payments, Yale University Press, 1964.

The World's Money: Gold and the Problem of International Liquidity, Bucknell University, 1965.

(Editor) *The Economy of South Vietnam: A New Beginning,* Center for International Business, Pepperdine University, 1973.

(Editor with Jayson Mugar) *Trade with China: Assessments by Leading Businessmen and Scholars,* Praeger, 1974.

(Editor with Hans Schollhammer) *Multinational Corporations and Governments: Business-Government Relations,* Praeger, 1975.

(Editor with David G. Tuerck) *World Monetary Disorder: National Policies vs. International Imperatives,* Praeger, 1976.

The Welfare Juggernaut, Institute for Economic and Legal Analysis, 1976.

Also editor of *Economy in Crisis* and *The Balance of Payments: Proceedings of a Republican Seminar,* both 1968. Contributor to *Modern Age, Challenge, Wall Street Journal,* and other journals and newspapers.

WORK IN PROGRESS: Research on international economic policy, on the significance of cultural factors in national economic performance, and on capitalism and Christianity.

SIDELIGHTS: Patrick M. Boarman told *CA:* "My earliest ambition was to be a writer. But I had to cope with two handicaps in pursuing that ambition: lack of time and a compulsion to do too much research before beginning the act of writing. My life has been full of action. I've been a professor, an elected public official, a diplomat, a consultant to major corporations and governments, and an inveterate traveler to faraway places like China, Africa, and the Soviet Union. I have moved ten times in twenty years. And in my spare time, I've diligently pursued my hobby of playing the piano. In short, my life has been rich in things to write about but woefully lacking in the time to write about them. And with my perfectionism—needing to know more and more about any given subject before starting to write—I ran the risk of never getting anything on paper.

"Here, now, is my method (or rather my ex-wife's method) for coping with these handicaps. Lock husband in bedroom. Deny him food and drink and, yes, the usual pleasures of the married state, *until* he has produced and passed under the locked door at least ten pages of manuscript per day for two days. Also, deny him all further research materials such as books, reports, newspapers, etc. In this situation, after several hours of increasing hunger pangs, I said to myself: Okay, I'll produce ten pages of garbage just to get something to eat and drink. Part of that garbage included a chapter outline of the book I was proposing to write, plus a few phrases about the content of each chapter. Harder was the production of Chapter 1. But since I knew it was garbage, it really didn't matter much what I wrote. My internal perfectionist 'censor' that had inhibited me in the past was, for the moment, banished from the scene.

"So I just wrote stuff. The first ten pages were quickly done and I passed them out under the door. I was duly rewarded with food and drink. Great, I said, this is easy, thinking always that the garbage would ultimately be replaced by a serious writing effort. But lo and behold, the garbage turned out to be not garbage. It was good. And once I had started, the flood of writing could hardly be contained. Moreover, only minor revisions were required in the final press-ready manuscript. The episode illustrates one of the perhaps less touted advantages, for a writer, of marriage. It certainly justified my acknowledgement, at the time, in a preface to my book, that without my wife, it would not have been finished."

*   *   *

BOATENG, E(rnest) A(mano) 1920-

PERSONAL: Born November 30, 1920, in Aburi, Ghana; son of Christian Robert (a clergyman) and Adelaide (Asare) Boateng; married Evelyn K. Danso (a librarian), March 26, 1955; children: Akosua, Akua, Amanobea, Oduraa. *Education:* Attended Achimota College, Ghana; St. Peter's College, Oxford, M.A., 1953, M.Litt., 1954. *Religion:* Presbyterian.

ADDRESSES: Home—3 Aviation Rd., Airport Residential Area, Accra, Ghana.

CAREER: University of Ghana, Legon, Accra, lecturer, 1950-57, senior lecturer, 1958-61, professor of geography, 1961-73, dean of Faculty of Social Studies, 1962-69; University of Cape Coast, Cape Coast, Ghana, principal of University College, 1969-72, vice-chancellor of university, 1972-73; Environmental Protection Council, Accra, executive chairman, 1973-81; currently environmental and educational consultant. Smuts Visiting Fellow, University of Cambridge, 1965-66; visiting professor at University of Pittsburgh, 1966. Chairman of geography committee, Ghana Population Census, 1960; member of Planning Commission of Ghana, 1962-64; Ghana representative, Scientific Council for Africa, 1963-80, and at international conferences, including the thirty-first session of the United Nations General Assembly, 1976. Honorary director of Ghana National Atlas Project, 1965-77. Member of National Economic Planning Council, 1974-78 and National Council for Higher Education, 1975-79. Chairman of West African Examinations Council, 1977-85.

MEMBER: Royal Geographical Society (London), Royal Society of Arts (fellow), Ghana Geographical Association (president, 1959-69), Ghana Academy of Science (president, 1973-76).

AWARDS, HONORS: Henry Oliver Becket Memorial Prize, 1949; Grand Medal of Ghana, 1968; Ghana Book Award, 1978; D.Litt. from University of Ghana, 1979.

WRITINGS:

A Geography of Ghana, Cambridge University Press, 1959, 2nd edition, 1966.

(Editor) *Ghana Junior Atlas,* Thomas Nelson, 1965, revised edition, International Publications Service, 1969.

West African Secondary School Atlas, Thomas Nelson, 1968.

Independence and Nation Building in Africa, Ghana Publishing Corp., 1973.

A Political Geography of Africa, Cambridge University Press, 1978.

African Unity: The Dream and the Reality, Ghana Academy of Arts and Sciences, 1978.

Contributor to *Encyclopaedia Britannica,* 1961—, and to geography journals.

SIDELIGHTS: E. A. Boateng has a reading knowledge of French. He has traveled in the United States, most of Europe, the Soviet Union, Australia, India, and in several tropical African countries.

AVOCATIONAL INTERESTS: Photography, gardening, English literature, architecture, listening to classical music.

*   *   *

BOCOCK, Robert (James) 1940-

PERSONAL: Born September 29, 1940, in Lincoln, England; son of Frank William (a farmer) and Jessie (Drake) Bocock. *Education:* University of London, diploma, 1963; Brunel University, Ph.D., 1973.

ADDRESSES: Home—10, Village Close, Belsize Lane, London N.W. 3, England. *Office*—Department of Sociology, Open University, Milton Keynes, Buckinghamshire, England.

CAREER: Brunel University, Uxbridge, England, lecturer in sociology, 1966-79; Open University, Buckinghamshire, England, currently lecturer in sociology. Annual lecturer at University of Birmingham; consultant to Richmond Fellowship.

MEMBER: International Conference of Sociology of Religion, British Sociological Association, Association of University Teachers, Association of Pastoral Care and Counseling.

WRITINGS:

Ritual in Industrial Society, Allen & Unwin, 1974.
Freud and Modern Society, Thomas Nelson, 1976.
An Introduction to Sociology, Fontana, 1980.
Sigmund Freud, Routledge & Kegan Paul, 1983.
(Editor) *Religion and Ideology,* Manchester University Press, 1985.
Hegemony, Routledge & Kegan Paul, 1986.

Contributor to sociology journals.

WORK IN PROGRESS: Research on relations between psychoanalysis and sociology, on the sociology of morals, and on religion.

SIDELIGHTS: Robert Bocock wrote *CA:* "I'm interested in the use of Freudian ideas to provide a basis for a view of man-in-society. The role of psychoanalysis and therapy in the United States and Europe, especially in religious institutions, is of interest to me. I aim to increase *tolerance of ambiguity* in individuals and organisations and between states."

*   *   *

BODDINGTON, Craig Thornton 1952-

PERSONAL: Born November 12, 1952, in Kansas City, Mo.; son of Edward Mosely (an attorney) and Jeanne (Popham) Boddington; married Paula Lynn Merriman, 1984; children: Brittany Lynn. *Education:* University of Kansas, B.A., 1974. *Politics:* Republican. *Religion:* Presbyterian.

ADDRESSES: Home—10131 Geuesla Ave., Northridge, Calif. 91325. *Office*—*Petersen's Hunting,* 8490 Sunset Blvd., Los Angeles, Calif. 90069.

CAREER: International Hunting Consultants Ltd., Santa Monica, Calif., vice-president, 1978-79; Petersen Publishing Co., Los Angeles, Calif., editorial director of guns and ammunition specialty publications in Outdoor Books Division, 1979-80, executive editor of *Petersen's Hunting,* 1980-83, editor, 1983—. *Military service:* U.S. Marine Corps, 1974-78; became cap-

tain. U.S. Marine Corps Reserve, 1978—; present rank, major.

MEMBER: Amateur Trapshooting Association, National Rifle Association, Outdoor Writers Association of America, African One-Shooters, California Wildlife Federation, Safari Club International (member of board of directors), Ducks Unlimited, Southern California Safari Club, Boone and Crockett Club.

WRITINGS:

(Editor) *America: The Men and Their Guns That Made Her Great,* Caroline House, 1982.
Campfires and Game Trails: Hunting North American Big Game, Winchester Press, 1985.
From Mt. Kenya to the Cape: Ten Years of African Hunting, Safari Press, 1987.
Shots at Big Game, Stackpole, 1989.

Editor with Guns and Ammo Specialty Publications, 1979-83; publications include 1981, 1982, and 1983 editions of *Guns and Ammo Annual* and *Petersen's Hunting Annual* and twenty firearms and hunting-related newsstand books. Contributor to Petersen Publishing's outdoor titles, including *Petersen's Hunting* and *Guns and Ammo,* and to specialty publications, 1979—. Contributor to outdoor magazines, including *Outdoor Life, Sports Afield, Guns, Gun World,* and *Safari.*

WORK IN PROGRESS: Research for a book on rifles and cartridges for African game.

SIDELIGHTS: Craig Thornton Boddington wrote *CA:* "I was raised hunting Kansas quail and pheasants with good bird dogs and as a youngster was an All-American trapshooter. While I still do a fair amount of shotgunning, big game hunting has become my primary interest and hobby and the subject of most of my writing. I have hunted extensively in North America, and to date have made eight African safaris into five different countries.

"As a hunter and as a member of the sporting press, my views on hunting are far from objective. However, the fact is that hunters' dollars—from license fees, taxes on firearms and ammunition, and voluntary contributions—are the primary means of funding the game management efforts that have resulted in the excellent state of America's wildlife resources today. While I love wild game meats and rarely purchase any domestic meats, I can't say that I hunt strictly for food. I'm primarily a trophy hunter and often spend days on end in back country looking for an exceptional specimen—one that I may not find. Like all true hunters, I love wild country and the animals that live there. The enjoyment is to be there, and while the purpose of being there is to harvest an animal, the actual shot—if one is taken—is secondary and anticlimactic.

"I have been fortunate to be able to combine my hobbies of hunting and shooting with my desire to write. Writing and editing are not necessarily the same thing, but, as a full-time editor, I manage to work in a fair amount of writing. Of course, the subject matter in *Hunting* magazine falls right in line with my own interests. This portion of the writing field, outdoor writing, is somewhat limited, but I have found it possible to break into the field, given knowledge of the subject, patience, persistence, and the hide of a rhinoceros.

"To really enjoy writing and editing, I think it is essential to be involved in one's subject. But to avoid becoming too one-tracked, it is a good idea to carry on unrelated outside activities. Aside from helping a writer to maintain his sanity, it allows a greater degree of freshness and objectivity."

BOECKMAN, Patti
(Patti Beckman)

PERSONAL: Born in Chicago, Ill.; daughter of Levi Towle (an accountant) and Juanita (a nurse; maiden name, Vezie) Kennelly; married Charles Boeckman (a writer), July 25, 1965; children: Sharla Tricia. *Education:* Attended Del Mar Junior College, 1958-59; North Texas State University, B.A., 1962; Texas A & I University, M.A., 1972. *Religion:* Protestant.

ADDRESSES: Home and office—322 Del Mar Blvd., Corpus Christi, Tex. 78404.

CAREER: Writer. Secretary to county auditor of Nueces County, Tex., summers, 1958-62; teacher of English and Spanish at public secondary schools in Corpus Christi, 1962-65, 1966-74, and Victoria, Tex., 1965-66; photographer, 1974-76; instructor, Del Mar College, 1986-87. Bass player with Dixieland band, 1970—; sponsor of local jazz festival, 1973-74, 1976. Lecturer at writers' workshops; guest on "Today Show."

MEMBER: Romance Writers of America.

WRITINGS:

NOVELS; UNDER NAME PATTI BECKMAN

Captive Heart, Simon & Schuster, 1980.
The Beachcomber, Simon & Schuster, 1980.
Louisiana Lady, Simon & Schuster, 1981.
Angry Lover, Simon & Schuster, 1981.
Love's Treacherous Journey, Simon & Schuster, 1981.
Spotlight to Fame, Simon & Schuster, 1982.
Bitter Victory, Simon & Schuster, 1982.
Daring Encounter, Simon & Schuster, 1982.
Mermaid's Touch, Simon & Schuster, 1982.
Please Let Me In, Simon & Schuster, 1982.
Tender Deception, Simon & Schuster, 1982.
Forbidden Affair, Simon & Schuster, 1983.
Enchanted Surrender, Simon & Schuster, 1983.
Thunder at Dawn, Simon & Schuster, 1983.
Storm Over the Everglades, Simon & Schuster, 1984.
Nashville Blues, Simon & Schuster, 1984.
Time for Us, Simon & Schuster, 1984.
On Stage, Simon & Schuster, 1984.
With the Dawn, Simon & Schuster, 1984.
The Movie, Simon & Schuster, 1985.
Odds Against Tomorrow, Simon & Schuster, 1985.
Dateline: Washington, Simon & Schuster, 1986.
Summer's Storm, Simon & Schuster, 1986.
Danger in His Arms, Simon & Schuster, 1987.

OTHER

Contributor of several hundred articles to national magazines.

WORK IN PROGRESS: A novel for young people; a family saga; magazine articles.

SIDELIGHTS: Patti Boeckman told *CA:* "Full-time, free-lance professional writing is both a wonderful and a precarious way to make a living. The wonderful aspects include the flexibility: not having to abide by somebody else's rigid schedule, being able to 'knock off' a day now and then to pursue another interest, traveling to do research for backgrounds for books, being my own boss. The precarious parts are knowing every paycheck depends on my personal output, having no company benefits, having to adapt to changing markets, and wondering where the next idea will come from.

"In spite of its pitfalls, writing is a rewarding way of making a living. To me the allure of the writing profession is the wide variety of experience it gives me when I conduct on-site research. Also, almost everything I do has the potential for inclusion in a book or as the focus of an article. For example, I have recently taught myself to draw (something I once thought impossible for me to learn) and am now dabbling in painting. I can use my experiences in both a book and as the catalyst for an article on myths about the necessity for artistic talent.

"A fact that increases my enjoyment of writing is my husband's presence at home. He was a writer long before I took the plunge, and our working together is a source of companionship denied to many writers, who often work alone. My husband and I share an office behind our home. We plot books together and read and criticize each other's manuscripts.

"Another advantage of writing is the opportunity it gives me to homeschool my daughter, who loves the flexible life of a writer. She enjoys school at home, where she learns as much or more than she would in a classroom but has the advantages of a tailor-made schedule and an opportunity to pursue her own interests."

Boeckman's books have been published in England, Japan, France, Brazil, Canada, Spain, Israel, and Switzerland.

AVOCATIONAL INTERESTS: Drawing, painting, travel, home schooling, computers, reading, pets.

*　　　*　　　*

BOGGESS, Louise Bradford 1912-

PERSONAL: Surname is pronounced *Bog*-gess, with hard g's; born March 28, 1912, in Sweetwater, Tex.; daughter of Giles Edward (a banker and rancher) and Hattie (Corbett) Bradford; married William Fannin Boggess, Jr. (an investigator with the U.S. Immigration and Naturalization Service), June 1, 1946; children: Patricia Anne, William Fannin III. *Education:* University of Texas, B.A., 1933, M.A., 1934, graduate study, summers, 1935-39; professional writing courses, University of Oklahoma. *Politics:* Democrat. *Religion:* Episcopalian.

ADDRESSES: Home—4016 Martin Dr., San Mateo, Calif. 94403.

CAREER: Junior high school teacher in Dallas, Tex., 1937-39; high school teacher in Wichita Falls, Tex., 1941-46; Texas College of Arts and Industry (now Texas A & I University), Kingsville, instructor in history and government, 1946-47; *Kingsville Record,* Kingsville, women's editor, 1947-51; College of San Mateo, San Mateo, Calif., instructor in professional writing, 1956-79, teacher of televised courses for KCSM-TV, 1971-79. Teacher of correspondence courses for University of California, Berkeley, and Writer's Digest School. Staff member of fifty-four writers conferences and workshops.

MEMBER: American Cut Glass Association (co-founder; newsletter editor; committee chairman), American Association of University Women, Authors Guild, National Early American Glass Club, California Writers Club (former president), Burlingame Writers Club (former president), Scribblers Club, Phi Beta Kappa, Phi Lambda Theta, Phi Sigma Alpha.

AWARDS, HONORS: Jack London Award for outstanding service, California Writers Club.

WRITINGS:

Fiction Techniques That Sell, Prentice-Hall, 1964.

Writing Articles That Sell, Prentice-Hall, 1965.
Writing Fillers That Sell, Funk, 1967.
Journey to Citizenship, Funk, 1968.
Your Social Security Benefits, Funk, 1969.
(With husband, Bill Boggess) *American Brilliant Cut Glass,* Crown, 1977.
Article Techniques That Sell, 2nd edition, B & B Press, 1978.
Writing Fiction That Sells, 2nd edition, B & B Press, 1978.
(Contributor) *Law and the Writer,* Writer's Digest, 1978, 4th edition, 1988.
How to Write Short Stories That Sell, 3rd edition, Writer's Digest, 1980.
How to Write Fillers and Short Features That Sell, 2nd edition, Harper, 1981, 3rd edition, 1984.
(Contributor) Jean M. Fredette and John Brady, editors, *Fiction Writers Market,* Writer's Digest, 1981, 8th edition, 1988.
(With B. Boggess) *Identifying American Brilliant Cut Glass,* Crown, 1984.
(Contributor) Fredette, editor, *Handbook of Short Story Writing,* 3rd edition, 1988.

Author of columns "Reflections on Glass," *American Collector,* "Pressed Glass," *Antique Reporter,* and "Over the Coffee Cup," *Kingsville Record.* Author of video and audio tapes on "Fiction Techniques That Sell" and "Article Techniques That Sell" for KCSM-TV, College of San Mateo. Contributor to antique magazines.

WORK IN PROGRESS: A third edition of book on article writing; a third book on American brilliant cut glass; articles for antiques magazines on American brilliant cut glass; a fourth edition of *Writing Fiction That Sells;* a suspense novel set in the cut glass background.

SIDELIGHTS: Louise Bradford Boggess told *CA:* "Like many others I began writing because we needed an extra income, and writing enabled me to stay home with my children, a boy and a girl, until they were school age, and I could go back to teaching. I found teaching professional writing and writing myself blended beautifully. In all my books, whether on writing or collecting American cut glass, I try to help others avoid mistakes I made. I always urge anyone who turns to a career in writing to learn how to write, approach writing as a profession. A lawyer or a doctor doesn't practice until he has studied. Neither should a writer try to sell without learning professional techniques. Anyone starting to collect should read and talk to people so as to learn as much as possible about how to buy or sell. Learning to write or collect never ends, but from learning comes the excitement of achievement. Dare to make mistakes once, but not again. Impeccable research leads to success."

*   *   *

BOICE, James Montgomery 1938-

PERSONAL: Born July 7, 1938, in Pittsburgh, Pa.; son of G. Newton (an orthopedic surgeon) and Jean (Shick) Boice; married Linda Ann McNamara, June 9, 1962; children: Elizabeth Anne Horn, Heather Louise, Jennifer Sue. *Education:* Harvard University, A.B. (with high honors), 1960; Princeton Theological Seminary, B.D., 1963; University of Basel, D.Theol. (insigni cum laude), 1966.

ADDRESSES: Home—1935 Pine St., Philadelphia, Pa. 19103. *Office*—Tenth Presbyterian Church, 1700 Spruce St., Philadelphia, Pa. 19103.

CAREER: Licensed in the Presbytery of Pittsburgh, Pa., 1963. *Christianity Today,* Washington, D.C., member of editorial staff, summers, 1962, 1963, assistant editor, 1966-68; Tenth Presbyterian Church, Philadelphia, Pa., pastor, 1968—; City Center Academy, Philadelphia, principal, 1983-87, chairman of board of trustees, 1983—. Speaker on "The Bible Study Hour," radio program originating in Philadelphia, 1969—. Chairman of Philadelphia Conference on Reformed Theology, 1974—. President of Evangelical Ministries, Inc., 1985—.

MEMBER: International Council on Biblical Inerrancy (chairman, 1977-88).

WRITINGS:

Witness and Revelation in the Gospel of John, Zondervan, 1970.
Philippians: An Expositional Commentary, Zondervan, 1971.
The Sermon on the Mount, Zondervan, 1972.
How to Really Live It Up, Zondervan, 1973, published as *How to Live the Christian Life,* Moody, 1982.
The Last and Future World, Zondervan, 1974.
How God Can Use Nobodies, Victor Books, 1974, published as *Ordinary Men Called by God,* 1974.
Commentary on the Gospel of John, five volumes, Zondervan, 1975-79.
(Contributor) Frank E. Gaebelin, editor, *The Expositor's Bible Commentary,* Zondervan, 1976.
Can You Run Away from God?, Victor Books, 1977.
Our Sovereign God, Baker Book, 1977.
The Sovereign God, Inter-Varsity Press, 1978.
God the Redeemer, Inter-Varsity Press, 1978.
Awakening to God, Inter-Varsity Press, 1979.
(Editor) *Making God's Word Plain,* Tenth Presbyterian Church, 1979.
The Epistles of John, Zondervan, 1980.
Does Inerrancy Matter?, Tyndale, 1980.
God and History, Inter-Varsity Press, 1981.
(Editor) *Our Savior God,* Baker Book, 1981.
The Parables of Jesus, Moody, 1983.
The Christ of Christmas, Moody, 1983.
The Minor Prophets, two volumes, Zondervan, 1983-86.
Genesis, three volumes, Zondervan, 1983-87.
Standing on the Rock, Tyndale, 1984.
The Christ of the Empty Tomb, Moody, 1985.
Christ's Call to Discipleship, Moody, 1986.
(Editor) *Transforming Our World: A Call to Action,* Multnomah, 1988.
Daniel: An Expositional Commentary, Zondervan, 1989.
Ephesians: An Expositional Commentary, Zondervan, 1989.
Joshua: We Will Serve the Lord, Revell, 1989.

Contributor to religious periodicals.

*   *   *

BONDI, Joseph C. 1936-

PERSONAL: Born August 15, 1936, in Tampa, Fla.; son of Joseph C. (a teacher) and Virginia (Colie) Bondi; married Patsy Hammer (a teacher), August 6, 1960; children: Pamela Jo, Beth Jana, Bradley Joseph. *Education:* University of Florida, B.S., 1958, M.Ed., 1962, Ed.D., 1968. *Politics:* Democrat. *Religion:* Presbyterian.

ADDRESSES: Home—207 Bannockburn, Temple Terrace, Fla. 33617. *Office*—Department of Education, University of South Florida, Tampa, Fla. 33620.

CAREER: Hillsborough County (Fla.) Public Schools, teacher, administrator, and curriculum director, 1959-65; University of South Florida, Tampa, 1965—, began as assistant professor, became professor of education, former chairman of department of curriculum and instruction. Elected mayor of Temple Terrace, Fla., 1974, re-elected, 1976; member, Temple Terrace City Council, 1970-74; chairman, Tampa metropolitan council of governments. Chairman, State of Florida Middle School Committee. Educational program consultant to schools throughout the United States. *Military service:* U.S. Naval Reserve, 1955-63.

MEMBER: Association for Supervision and Curriculum Development (member of board of directors and executive council; chairman of working group), National Middle School Association, American Educational Research Association, National Education Association, John Dewey Society, Florida Educational Research Association, Florida Association for Supervision and Curriculum Development (vice-president; president), Phi Delta Kappa, Kappa Delta Pi.

WRITINGS:

(Editor with Glen Haas and Kimball Wiles) *Readings in Curriculum,* 2nd edition (Bondi was not associated with earlier edition), Allyn & Bacon, 1970.
Developing Middle Schools: A Guidebook, MSS Information, 1972.
(Compiler with Haas and Jon Wiles) *Curriculum Planning: A New Approach,* Allyn & Bacon, 1974, 2nd edition, 1977.
(With J. Wiles) *Curriculum Development: A Guide to Practice,* C.E. Merrill, 1979, 3rd edition, 1989.
(With J. Wiles) *Supervision: A Guide to Practice,* C.E. Merrill, 1980, 2nd edition, 1986.
(With J. Wiles and David K. Wiles) *Practical Politics for School Administrators,* Allyn & Bacon, 1981.
(With J. Wiles) *The Essential Middle School,* C.E. Merrill, 1981.
(With J. Wiles) *Principles of School Administration,* C.E. Merrill, 1983.
(With J. Wiles) *The School Board Primer,* Allyn & Bacon, 1985.
(With J. Wiles) *Making Middle Schools Work,* Association for Supervision and Curriculum Development, 1987.

Also author of filmscript and study guide "Profile of a Middle School."

Contributor of articles to professional journals, including *Educational Leadership, Journal of Teacher Education, Middle School Journal, National Elementary School Principal,* and *Clearing House.*

*   *   *

BOORSTIN, Daniel J(oseph) 1914-

PERSONAL: Born October 1, 1914, in Atlanta, Ga.; son of Samuel Aaron (an attorney) and Dora (Olsan) Boorstin; married Ruth Carolyn Frankel, April 9, 1941; children: Paul Terry, Jonathan, David West. *Education:* Harvard University, A.B. (summa cum laude), 1934; Oxford University, Balliol College (Rhodes Scholar), B.A. (first class honors), 1936, B.C.L. (first class honors), 1937; Yale University (Sterling fellow), J.S.D., 1940. *Politics:* Independent. *Religion:* Jewish.

ADDRESSES: Home—3541 Ordway St. N.W., Washington, D.C. 20016. *Office*—c/o U.S. News and World Report, 2400 North St. N.W., Washington D.C. 20037.

CAREER: Admitted as barrister-at-law, Inner Temple, London, England, 1937; admitted to the Massachusetts Bar, 1942; Harvard University, Cambridge, Mass., history instructor, 1939-42, Harvard Law School, legal history lecturer, 1939-42; Office of Lend-Lease Administration, Washington, D.C., senior attorney, 1942; Swarthmore College, Swarthmore, Pa., assistant professor of history, 1942-44; University of Chicago, Chicago, Ill., assistant professor, 1944-49, associate professor, 1949-56, Preston and Sterling Morton Distinguished Professor of History, 1956-69; Smithsonian Institution, Washington, D.C., director of National Museum of History and Technology (now National Museum of American History), 1969-73, senior historian, 1973-75; Library of Congress, Washington, D. C., Librarian, 1975-87, Librarian Emeritus, 1987—; Doubleday and Co., New York, N. Y., editor-at-large, 1987—. Fulbright visiting lecturer, University of Rome, 1950-51, and Kyoto University, 1957; visiting lecturer at many institutions, including Cambridge University and University of Paris; international lecturer for U.S. Department of State, 1959-60, 1968, 1974. First occupant of American History Chair, Sorbonne, Paris, 1961-62; fellow of Trinity College, and Pitt Professor of American History and Institutions, Cambridge University, 1964-65; Shelby and Kathryn Cullom Davis Lecturer, Graduate Institute of International Studies, Geneva, Switzerland, 1973-74. Delivered Reith Lectures on radio for British Broadcasting Corp. (BBC), 1975. Member, American Film Institute at Kennedy Center, 1972—, Indo-American Subcommittee for Education and Culture, 1974-81, Japan-American Commission, 1978—, Woodrow Wilson International Center for Scholars, Japan-United States Friendship Commission, Carl Albert Congressional Research and Studies Center, American Academy of Arts and Sciences, and Presidential Task Force on the Arts and Humanities. Trustee, Colonial Williamsburg, 1967-85, and Kennedy Center, 1975-87. Consultant.

MEMBER: Authors Guild, Authors League of America, American Studies Association (president, 1969-70), American Historical Association, American Antiquarian Society, American Philosophical Society, Organization of American Historians, Royal Historical Society (London; fellow and corresponding member), Colonial Society of Massachusetts, International House of Japan, Phi Beta Kappa, Elizabethan Club (Yale University), Cosmos Club (Washington, D.C.).

AWARDS, HONORS: Bancroft Prize, Columbia University, and Friends of American Literature Prize, both 1959, both for *The Americans: The Colonial Experience;* Francis Parkman Prize, Society of American Historians, and Patron Saints Award of Society of Midland Authors, both 1966, both for *The Americans: The National Experience;* Litt.D., Cambridge University, 1968, and numerous other honorary degrees; Distinguished Service Professor, University of Chicago, 1968; Dexter Prize and Pulitzer Prize in Letters—History, both 1974, both for *The Americans: The Democratic Experience;* La decoration d'Officer de l'Ordre de la Couronne from His Majesty the King of the Belgians, 1980; Chevalier de l'Ordre de la Legion d'Honneur from the government of France, 1984; *Los Angeles Times* Book Prize nomination, 1984, Grand Officer of the Order of Prince Henry the Navigator from the government of Portugal, 1985, and Watson-Davis Prize of the History of Science Society, 1986, all for *The Discoverers;* First Class Order of the Sacred Treasure from the government of Japan, 1986; Phi Beta Kappa Prize for distinguished service to the humanities, 1988; honorary fellow, American Geographical Society; honorary member, Academy of Political Science.

WRITINGS:

EDITED BY WIFE, RUTH FRANKEL BOORSTIN

The Mysterious Science of the Law, Harvard University Press, 1941, reprinted, Peter Smith, 1973.

The Lost World of Thomas Jefferson, Holt, 1948, reprinted with new preface, University of Chicago Press, 1981.

The Genius of American Politics (lectures), University of Chicago Press, 1953, reprinted, 1973.

The Americans, Random House, Volume 1: *The Colonial Experience,* 1958, new edition published as *The Americans 1: The Colonial Experience,* 1985, Volume 2: *The National Experience,* 1965, new edition published as *The Americans 2: The National Experience,* 1985, Volume 3: *The Democratic Experience* (Book-of-the-Month Club main selection), 1973, new edition published as *The Americans 3: The Democratic Experience,* 1985.

America and the Image of Europe: Reflections on American Thought, Meridian, 1960.

The Image: What Happened to the American Dream, Atheneum, 1962, paperback edition published as *The Image: A Guide to Pseudo-Events in America,* Harper, 1964, twenty-fifth anniversary edition, Atheneum, 1987.

(With R. F. Boorstin) *Landmark History of the American People* (juvenile), Random House, Volume 1: *From Plymouth to Appomattox,* 1968, Volume 2: *From Appomattox to the Moon,* 1970, revised edition published as boxed set, 1987.

The Decline of Radicalism: Reflections of America Today (essays), Random House, 1969.

The Sociology of the Absurd: or, The Application of Professor X (satiric essay), Simon & Schuster, 1970.

Democracy and Its Discontents: Reflections on Everyday America, Random House, 1974.

Portraits from the Americans: The Democratic Experience, Random House, 1975.

The Exploring Spirit: America and the World, Then and Now (Reith lectures), Random House, 1976 (published in England as *The Exploring Spirit: America and the World Experience,* BBC Publications, 1976).

The Republic of Technology: Reflections on Our Future Community, Harper, 1978.

The Fertile Verge: Creativity in the United States (pamphlet), Library of Congress, 1980.

(With R. F. Boorstin and Brooks Mather Kelley) *A History of the United States* (eleventh-grade textbook), Ginn, 1981, published as *A History of the United States since 1861,* Prentice-Hall, 1986.

The Discoverers: A History of Man's Search to Know His World and Himself (Book-of-the-Month Club main selection), Random House, 1983.

Books in Our Future: A Report from the Librarian of Congress to the Congress (pamphlet), Library of Congress, 1984.

(And editor) *Hidden History: Exploring Our Secret Past,* Harper, 1987.

EDITOR

Delaware Cases, 1792-1830, three volumes, West, 1943.

A Lady's Life in the Rocky Mountains, University of Oklahoma Press, 1960.

An American Primer, two volumes, University of Chicago Press, 1966.

American Civilization: A Portrait from the Twentieth Century, McGraw, 1972.

Technology and Society, fifty-three books, Ayer Co., 1972.

We Americans, National Geographic Society, 1975.

America in Two Centuries: An Inventory, Arno, 1976.

Visiting Our Past: America's Historylands, National Geographic Society, 1977.

Also editor of the thirty-volume *The Chicago History of American Civilization,* University of Chicago Press, 1967—. Editor of American history for *Encylopaedia Britannica,* 1951-55, member of board of editors, 1981—.

OTHER

Also author of pamphlet, *A Nation of Readers.* Contributor to *Harper's, Newsweek, U.S. News & World Report, New York Times Book Review, Commentary, Life, Fortune, Esquire,* and *Look.* Contributing editor, *U.S. News and World Report,* 1987—. Boorstin's books have been translated into many languages, including Korean, Chinese, and Japanese.

WORK IN PROGRESS: The Creators, a sequel to *The Discoverers,* for Random House.

SIDELIGHTS: Pulitzer-Prize-winning author and former Librarian of Congress Daniel J. Boorstin stands out from other contemporary historians through his conservative viewpoint and his unique accounts of American life, which *Washington Post* writer Curtis Suplee claims are "distinguished for their graceful style and a viewpoint that emphasizes individual initiative and social climate over ideology." According to *New York Review of Books* contributor Sheldon S. Wolin, "Boorstin is a prolific and fluent writer, serious and dignified, perceptive, cultivated, and wide-ranging; he has enjoyed both popular success and the highest forms of professional recognition."

In his books, Boorstin reflects his preferences for people, experiences, and inventions over ideology as shapers of history. Dolly Langdon writes in *People:* "A passionate generalist and popularizer, Boorstin has built his reputation on an innovative and compelling idea: that the great engine of American history has been driven by native invention, not political theory. His special heroes are 'the go-getters' whose pragmatism has molded our lives with technology." In the *Dictionary of Literary Biography* Frank Annunziata explains that Boorstin's interpretation of history "represents a shift away from Progressive historiography's emphasis upon economic and class conflicts. Replacing the dichotomies of aristocracy and democracy, capitalists and agrarians, business and labor, he portrayed an America living in essential harmony within a framework of substantive agreement upon democratic capitalism."

Boorstin also emphasizes the importance of heroes. Norman Stone attests in the London *Times,* "Dr. Boorstin has an old-fashioned belief in Progress and in Heroes; mankind, once liberated from 'the prison of Christian Dogma', can achieve anything." And unlike many current historians, Boorstin regards America's past in a positive light. Annunziata believes the author has been "able to see achievements where other historians found deficiencies and inadequacies." *Washington Star* contributor Mary Anne Dolan sees Boorstin as "An anti-historian historian, a lawyer-in-academe.... A proud conservative in the primarily liberal world of American scholars, one who is unafraid of materialism and in fact, builds his view of democracy around entrepreneurs and inventions.... [Boorstin] is one of those rare intellectuals, whose opinions—sometimes outrageous, nearly always against the grain—are carried to classrooms and cocktail parties alike. And whether from friend or enemy, an opinion of Daniel Boorstin is bound to be emphatic."

After twenty-five years of teaching history at the University of Chicago, Boorstin became the director of the National Museum of History and Technology (now the National Museum of American History) at the Smithsonian Institution. Carol Krucoff of the *Washington Post* interviewed Smithsonian historian Silvio Bedini, deputy director of the National Museum of History and Technology from 1969 to 1973. According to Bedini, "the museum was like a brand new toy box to [Boorstin]. He generates ideas so quickly and so innovatively that it was quite an experience to try to keep up with him." It was from this position that Boorstin rose to his post at the Library of Congress, nominated by President Ford despite objections from the American Library Association, who wanted a professional librarian for the post and from the Congressional Black Caucus, who cited the candidate's opposition to affirmative action policies.

But Boorstin found answers to both complaints. Research showed him that former Librarian Archibald MacLeish had not himself been a professional librarian. And as Boorstin explained his position on affirmative action to Dolan: "Efforts to 'compensate' for historical injustices by quotas, by reverse discrimination and other devices were creating a new suspiciousness and resentment in the non-Negro community; this in turn threatened to accentuate and perpetuate the Negro's indelible status, and to create problems which neither good will nor violence gave promise of solving." In the long run, Boorstin won even his opponents' good will. Annunziata states that Boorstin's headship of the Library "has been marked by imaginative administrative leadership and an enhanced visibility for the library in American institutional and intellectual life."

"The Americans" trilogy is among the author's best-known works. As is the case with most of his books, the trilogy's scope is wide: it commences in the early seventeenth century with the Puritans' arrival in America and ends with the Apollo moon landing. Wolin claims, "Like the society it describes, *The Americans* is unique and somewhat unconventional. It is not a detailed account of great and familiar political events. Instead, it addresses the questions of how America became the most dynamic, expansive, productive, affluent, and equalitarian society in history and what this has meant for the quality and texture of everyday life. . . . Accordingly, Boorstin's history is of westward migrations, the flow of immigrants, the appearance of new technologies and techniques of mass production, the democratization of culture and everyday life. Its heroes are the founding fathers of the cattle business, railroads, hotel systems, department and chain stores, and industrial invention and research."

Los Angeles Times Book Review critic Robert Dawidoff praises Boorstin's discernment: "Daniel Boorstin's colophon as a historian has been his ability to discover in the profusion of American civilization themes that at once suggest the order and accident of our history. He has a distinct feeling for what people knew as opposed to what they believed, and how they lived as opposed to how they were supposed to live." However, Wolin also notes the book's shortcomings: "There is little or no place in the American Experience for: the Declaration of Independence, the revolutionary war, the Constitutional Convention." Wolin also sees as a weakness that "Boorstin recognizes the power of the technological order but not its political significance. He sees it mainly as directed at the external world and as determining the trivia of our daily lives; but he mystifies its political significance by garbing it in the pseudoscientific language of 'momentum,' a vast overpowering force beyond our control."

The Colonial Experience is the first volume of the trilogy. In it Boorstin examines the failures and successes of the visionaries and pragmatists who attempted to create a unique civilization in the new world. *Saturday Review* contributor Bruce Lancaster describes the book as "a superb panorama of life in America from the first settlements on through the white-hot days of the Revolution." He also states, "It is a very real—and rare—pleasure to come upon such a book as this. . . . There is a welcome absence of smugly knowing iconoclasm or parading of half-truths. . . . Dr. Boorstin has given us an amazingly stimulating and brilliant study of America's past in which its present may be recognized and its future envisioned. He has thus placed every literate American in his debt." And in the *Yale Review*, Edmund S. Morgan claims the author "has brought to his search a freshness of vision, a lucidity of style, and a breadth of scope that command admiration. His book will delight the layman and provoke the historian in equal measure. . . . Boorstin's originality lies in the application of an old idea to explain a great many things that had not before been connected with it, from the organization of the legal and medical professions to enunciation and spelling."

Many critics, however, disagree with the conservatism Boorstin displays in *The Colonial Experience* and the series as a whole, and dislike how it affects his view of the past. Bernard Bailyn comments on *The Colonial Experience* in the *New Republic*, stating that "on the one hand there is vividness and vigor in the writing, and originality in the selection and analysis of topics in cultural history; but on the other hand there is a continuous foreshortening of the history presented, a disconcerting bobbing from then to now. . . . His book is more a sensitive reaction to the unpredicted whisperings of our present political climate than it is a result of the careful dissecting, ordering, and interpreting of knowledge. Of knowledge Mr. Boorstin has a staggering quantity . . . those who are familiar with his earlier writings . . . will know the intellectual refinement of which he is capable. But seeking in history proof of the necessity and immemorial rightness of his present political views, he has sketched a colorful, occasionally brilliant, but lopsided image of the past."

The National Experience, the trilogy's second volume, follows American expansion and development from the Revolutionary War up to the Civil War. Primary to Boorstin's narrative is his conception of the "upstarts," a group of transients representing American rootlessness. When the upstarts founded new towns and settled in them, they became the "boosters," or city fathers. *New York Times Book Review* contributor George Dangerfield thinks "Mr. Boorstin idealizes his booster businessman, but he makes him a striking paradigm of what was going on in the young nation's economy. . . . This is the history of a nation 'beginning again and again, under men's very eyes.'. . . This is a fine book—controversial certainly, but a courageous, learned and most exciting work." And a *Times Literary Supplement* reviewer concludes, "In discussing the hopes and fears, the swindles and the self-deceptions of the boosters, Professor Boorstin has a subject that lends itself to facile irony in the manner of Dickens or of Sinclair Lewis. But Professor Boorstin sees deeper."

The basis of *The National Experience* is the continual reforming and redefining of American civilization in the process of settling a continent. The *Times Literary Supplement* contributor states what he sees as Boorstin's thesis: "The American is a stripped European in a great and nearly empty country. He is a new man because Nature and Necessity made him so. Professor Boorstin, in one sense, is like Hans Andersen's child; he sees that the Emperor has no clothes.'' The reviewer believes that by answering the question, ''What is American?'' the book provides a good background for European readers: ''The understanding that an intelligent European reader can get, if he wants to, from this brilliant book, makes it a most rewarding and timely investment, to be read in the Elysee, the Kremlin—and in 10 Downing Street.''

New Republic contributor Lawrence Grauman, however, finds the book somewhat flawed: ''This kind of polemical, topical history is at times a hit-or-miss proposition. When Boorstin hits, when his insights are precise and well developed, he is brilliant. Unfortunately he has a tendency to elaborate instead of develop, he is given to sweeping generalizations, and he has a real fondness for negative absolutes. . . . But he has a remarkable knack for coming up with the right institution, however unknown . . . [and] the truly representative character.''

The trilogy's third book, *The Democratic Experience,* won Boorstin the Pulitzer Prize. Elting E. Morison writes in the *New York Times Book Review* that Boorstin ''has written a big book filled with arresting quotations from past observers of the American scene. . . . the range of information is remarkable.'' Yet that very range has proved to some critics a liability. While in the *National Review* Jack Chatfield states, ''It is impossible in a short essay to do justice to the breadth and richness of this work of high scholarship about common things,'' he continues that ''one finishes the book with a curious sense of incompleteness. . . . Boorstin's book is less of an analysis of modern America than a very long list of the things that have happened here since 1865—'one damn thing after another,' as an historian friend described it recently. . . . No criticism can detract from Boorstin's substantial accomplishment. . . . But he has overlooked or decided not to pursue certain matters which are vital to an understanding of our past.'' Morison, however, finds the work ''a big book filled with arresting quotations from past observers of the American scene; delightful portraits of inventors, organizers, go-getters, scholars, conmen, engineers and reformers that he has, often enough, rescued from oblivion; clear and simple description of industrial processes; entertaining reports on customs, habits and states of mind.''

The Discoverers enabled Boorstin to pursue his love of technology and its origins. The book is a popular history of the world, viewed through individual achievements. Over seven hundred pages long, it includes the discoveries of early man as well as modern ones. Stone views the book through one of Boorstin's chapters, ''Cataloguing the Whole Creation,'' which ''more or less sums up his book. It is a romantic, narrative version of discoveries-that-have-shaped-the-world, from ancient times up to the day before yesterday.''

Some reviewers, however, while appreciating Boorstin's ambition, find the work over-inclusive. *New Yorker* reviewer Jeremy Bernstein describes reading the ''brilliant, sometimes frustrating'' book as ''taking a guided tour of a fascinating, difficult, remote place—Tibet, say. The great advantage of such an organized tour is that one gets to see places one would never have imagined seeing by oneself, and the disadvantage is that if one wants to stay longer or dig deeper there may well not be time. This book is full of things that one would not have thought of or learned about on one's own. Yet because

of its immense sweep they go by as if they were seen from a speeding train, and in some places the view seems a little blurred.'' And according to Ivan R. Dee of the *Chicago Tribune Book World,* ''While there is much to marvel at here, one comes away with a sense of unfulfilled energy, an idea undelivered. Intellectual purpose seems to be missing in 'The Discoverers,' but it is a grand voyage nonetheless, a marvelous cornucopia of a book.''

Still, Dee thinks that on the whole, Boorstin's study ''succeeds remarkably. 'The Discoverers' is filled with good writing, wit, keen analysis and a unusually solid grasp of ideas across an incredible range of interest. If nothing else, it is an almost stupefying entertainment.'' And *New Statesman* contributor Stephen Brook believes that time spent reading the book is worthwhile: ''The reader is abundantly rewarded by Boorstin's triumphant chronicling of our intellectual conquest of time and space and the world about us. . . . Given the scope of the book, it's astonishingly readable and presents its narrative with grace and the utmost clarity.''

Hidden History is a collection of Boorstin's essays. Michael Kammen of the *Washington Post Book World* sees the collection as ''highly representative of [Boorstin's] awesome scope: from antiquity to the future, and from law to technology. It is also indicative of his customary strengths and trademarks.'' David E. Scrivens of the Toronto *Globe and Mail* considers the book ''a series of deceptively casual essays which build upon some of his previously published ideas, exploring the dimmer corners of his country's past and recounting anecdotes that illuminate more familiar events.'' And while *Tribune Books* contributor John Kenneth Galbraith finds *Hidden History* ''a trifle didactic in tone,'' and believes ''the reader on finishing these essays will feel he has had some unduly solemn instruction on historical error, including his own,'' he adds: ''It is, nonetheless, a very good book, and I hope that my enjoyment of it is widely shared.''

''In his generation, Boorstin has been one of our most inventive and interesting historians,'' Dee writes. ''His best books . . . compel the reader to consider American history in unexpected ways. By turn of argument and arrangement of facts, he has refreshed our perspectives.'' Boorstin explained himself and his work to Krucoff through this analogy: ''William James, the philosopher and one of my heroes, divided people into two categories—the tough-minded and the tender-minded. I make a different distinction—the single-minded and the many-minded. There are those who look for uniformity and neatness and those who are interested in plurality and variety. I distrust single explanations of anything, including the meaning of truth. The thing that interests me most is the varied, unpredictable contrasts of human nature and of civilization.''

CA INTERVIEW

CA interviewed Daniel J. Boorstin by telephone on May 4, 1988, at his study at the Library of Congress in Washington, D.C.

CA: As teacher, writer, Librarian of Congress, and now an editor at Doubleday, you've led a life centered around books. When and how did you begin to care about them?

BOORSTIN: I don't remember when I first started, but I do remember that one of my earliest hopes was to be a writer. And it's still my hope to be a writer when I grow up. I'm still working at it, and, I hope, getting better. There's nothing more discouraging to an author than to have a reviewer comment that his first book was really his best. I hope no one will ever say that about my writing.

CA: You were admitted as barrister-at-law to London's Inner Temple in 1937 and to the Massachusetts Bar in 1942. How did history get the upper hand in your affections?

BOORSTIN: I suppose it was just a love affair. How does a love affair begin? I do remember some of the books that inspired me to an interest in history. One was Spengler's *Decline of the West,* which I read when I was in high school and which impressed me with its poetic and cosmic view of history and its effort to look at the questions that would interest you about people in any time.

Then when I was a sophomore at Harvard I first read Edward Gibbon's *Decline and Fall of the Roman Empire.* I finally wrote my honors essay on it and won the Bowdoin Prize for it. My title for the essay, and something that still interests me, was "Unspoken Limitations of History." Gibbon has remained an inspiration to me. In fact, I still have in my study at home a late-eighteenth-century engraving of Gibbon with his triple chin and his complacent and slightly quizzical look. I've always thought his kind of history, history which is an enduring work of literature, was the kind of history I wanted to try to write. That's been my effort. And the effort is not simple. It's different from other literary efforts in that you have to be true to the facts and yet find or make a dramatic structure within the facts, something that will not be ephemeral.

CA: You told Carol Krucoff for the Washington Post *that you have never taken a course in American history, that you're an "amateur historian."*

BOORSTIN: The concept of an amateur has been very important in my life. All the positions I've taken on, from which I've made my living, are activities for which I was never properly trained in the conventional sense of the word.

CA: Do you think the amateur status is valuable because it enables one to approach his work with more openness than he might otherwise?

BOORSTIN: Not just openness, but more freedom. Professional training is training in the ways and the *ruts.* If you've not been trained in the ruts, you don't have to be very smart to stay out of them. Instead you simply pursue your interest in what you think is important. You're not worried at the discontinuities that you find, and you also never see any trivia, because you haven't been trained to think that only certain kinds of things are important.

It seems to me that the great historians have been amateurs in the sense that they did it for the love of it and not as a profession. That would include not only Herodotus and Thucydides but also Gibbon, whom I've just mentioned, and the great American historians: Francis Parkman, William Prescott, Henry Adams. It's unfortunate that the word *amateur* has taken on a secondary meaning connected with the rise of professions. An amateur really is a lover. And I think the best reason to write is because you love what you're doing; you can't help it. That's why I consider writing my vocation, whatever my other occupations have been.

CA: In your 1953 book, The Genius of American Politics, *you set forth the concept of this country's "givenness," described in part as "the belief that values in America are in some way or other automatically defined: given by certain facts of geography or history peculiar to us." Would you comment on how that idea developed from your reading and thinking about our history?*

BOORSTIN: That's a difficult question. I think the idea really was hatched when I spent a year in Rome. My wife Ruth and I and our children went around the ruins and saw the layers of history that had covered that country. I had been in Italy before—I'd spent most of my vacations in Italy when I was a student at Oxford—but I was again impressed with those layers of history. America, a vast and relatively uninhabited land with a very few layers of history that we know about, impressed me as a contrast.

I was also impressed with the European preoccupation with ideology: political parties fighting each other, each one standing for the right and the true, and based on some set of theories of politics or philosophy. The American situation struck me more vividly as a contrast. What I saw then, as it's been often remarked, was that our land was a land with a very thin layer of history on which the geography always showed through. That meant that Americans found their opportunity not in the library but on the land.

That's the closest I can come to describing it, and that's what I mean by "givenness." It also fitted with a lifelong antipathy to ideology and a lifelong suspicion of theories and of the notion that you can explain the world by a few attractive theories, whether of economics or politics or religion or anything else.

CA: You're often called the leader of the "consensus" school of American history. How do you feel about the term itself? Is it adequate as a description?

BOORSTIN: I think it's silly, for a lot of reasons. In the first place, I don't think you can talk about historians who are worth talking about under a single label like that. The people who use the labels are the people who usually are looking for some easy way to damn or praise, and to damn or praise a lot of people together without having to distinguish among them. The important historians, it seems to me, are not classifiable in that way.

I think also that one of the reasons these categories grow up is that a lot of people find it easier to write about historians than about history. To write about history, you have to deal with a miscellany of facts and resources that are spread around the place. But if you want to categorize a historian, all you need to do is get his works and start with a few prejudices. And that's easy.

CA: Your prize-winning trilogy The Americans *(subtitled* The Colonial Experience, The National Experience, *and* The Democratic Experience*) is full of interesting and unusual social detail that one doesn't find in most histories.*

BOORSTIN: You may note that each volume has in its title the word *experience.* It's a word I like. It suggests my interests, which are in the elusive miscellany and variety and flow of experience rather than in the punctuated simplicity of a few grand events in the chronology. Also, starting with the advantage of being an amateur, I was not boxed in by certain kinds of things, and therefore was not troubled by the fact that some subjects were not respectable. One of the subjects I have been interested in, for example, is packaging. I consider packaging to be an aspect of epistemology. That may be describing it rather pompously, but I think the attitude of people toward packaging is a way of discovering their concept of reality, the essence of things.

Another aspect of my interest in the multiplicity of experience is expressed in the titles of my books. That work is called *The Americans;* it is not called *American Civilization* or *American Culture* or anything like that. My latest book is not called *Discovery;* it's called *The Discoverers.* I am intrigued and enticed by the elusiveness of human nature, the impossibility of categorizing people, the unpredictability of achievements and of the arts. I've let my interests lead me and have been drawn to all kinds of subjects.

CA: In The Discoverers: A History of Man's Search to Know His World and Himself *you began with time, "the first grand discovery," and dealt with some of the brave people who have broken through "the obstacles of discovery—the illusions of knowledge." Would you like to talk about how the book in progress,* The Creators, *will serve as a companion piece to* The Discoverers?

BOORSTIN: Ever since I read Spangler and Gibbon, I had always wanted to try to write a world history—my kind of world history. My kind of world history would have to be one that interests me. It would not be about empires and economics and politics, but about man's fulfillment, his effort to be all that he was capable of being. In studying mankind, then, I tried to find a way to do that.

The first volume turned out to be *The Discoverers,* which bears the subtitle *A History of Man's Search to Know the World and Himself.* I could call the work as a whole a world history, but it might also be called *The Quest.* That would be a way of describing the boundlessness of my subject and the amorphousness of it, which is centered around a search and not around geographic or chronological boundaries. So *The Discoverers* turned out to be about man's search to know what's out there and what's in here.

The second volume is a companion to it, not a sequel, because it doesn't follow along chronologically. It's about man's search to enhance the world, to add to the world with all the arts—architecture, sculpture, drawing, painting, music, dance, drama, literature. It's a pretty big order, but it's the kind of thing I want to know about. I might almost say that I delimit the subject only by saying it's about all the subjects I don't know anything about, and that's the way to learn something about them. I'm already being rewarded for my own effort to discover.

CA: In his New York Times *review of* The Discoverers, *Christopher Lehmann-Haupt commented on how entertaining the book was, thanks to its master plan and to its dramatic tension. You mentioned dramatic structure earlier in this interview. Would you comment further on its importance in nonfiction?*

BOORSTIN: I've been working at the outline for *The Creators,* reflecting on it to see how I can focus the subject to keep my own quest from getting out of hand and at the same time to give it dramatic structure. The fiction writer has the advantage over the nonfiction writer in that he can *create* the suspense. The reader doesn't know, when he begins a novel, whether the leading character is going to turn out to be a hero or a villain, or in what respects he will be one or the other, or whether the story will turn out to be comedy or tragedy. But when the reader comes to history—unfortunately for the writer—he already knows how it's going to turn out.

The task of the historian is to induce a willing suspension of knowledge, to create a dramatic suspense about something the reader already knows the third act of. That's a tantalizing and interesting enterprise, but it makes the writing of nonfiction more difficult from a literary point of view than the writing of fiction. You not only must provide a dramatic structure, but you must, while being honest to the facts, encourage the reader to feel suspense and to be prepared for the unexpected.

CA: You have dedicated books to your wife, Ruth Frankel Boorstin, credited her in your acknowledgments, and praised her in previous interviews for her ongoing part in your writing. How does your collaboration work on an everyday basis?

BOORSTIN: I would like to underline my dedication, because I think she's been the most important influence in my life so far. She is not a research assistant; she's not a secretary—she's never typed a word for me. She's an intellectual companion and an editor, and a very severe critic of my style—a catalyst and a critic, I would say. Her extracurricular reading interests are rather different from mine; she reads mostly fiction and poetry. She is something of a poet herself. Her work has appeared in the *Wall Street Journal.*

Our collaboration works by our talking together about ideas, and then I show my drafts to Ruth and she criticizes my work. Her awareness of my own kind of quest is helpful in making me discover when I'm being pompous or verbose, and in keeping me on track. She also has a sense of the word as a *thing,* which I think only a person with a poetic feeling has. It's been a wonderful collaboration for me. She's very modest about it and would deny it, but I don't think I could have done my work without her. It's also been fun, because it's been an intellectual companionship, which you can't always have with an editor.

CA: What do you enjoy reading, in fiction and nonfiction, apart from what you read for research?

BOORSTIN: One of the troubles, when you pick a subject with such vague boundaries as I have chosen to write about, is that everything is grist for your mill. You're tempted always to have a note pad beside you, which I do. And that makes it very hard to be vagrant in your thoughts; you're always wondering what this has to do with chapter six or whether this contradicts the suggestions you've made in one of your books or are going to make in your next one.

The fiction book that I've enjoyed the most recently is Tom Wolfe's *Bonfire of the Vanities,* which I think is a wonderful combination of Rabelais and Nabokov. Among historians, there are many whose work I admire: the writings of Arthur Schlesinger, Jr., for example; the writings of Jaroslav Pelikan, who has written about the history of Christianity; and William McNeill's work. I admire historians who write on a large canvas, who choose large subjects and are not intimidated by the mystery of things but instead are willing to admit that mystery and try to explore it. I consider Jacques Barzun a historian. I would define the boundaries of history rather loosely, for obvious reasons. I think we need the works of editors and monograph writers, but I consider them to be the raw materials of history rather than history itself. What I think of as history is always a literary product, something that will command the attention of people when the current fashions in subject matter have dissolved.

CA: You have written about how we should teach history, not social studies and other topics mistakenly called "relevant." As a long-time teacher of history on the university level, do you have thoughts on how it should be taught on the secondary and primary levels?

BOORSTIN: I've written a textbook for the eleventh grade in collaboration with Brooks Kelley called *A History of the United States.* It's published by Prentice-Hall and has been very successful. It seems to me that of all the areas of publishing and authorship, the textbook market has been most corrupted by the determination of publishers to produce something that's just like the competition. In writing our textbook, our effort, our *struggle,* has been to keep it a literary work full of suspense and integrity, not something produced to match the competition. Marketers of textbooks, who are the people who control the materials that people read in history classes, are terribly obsessed with what the competition is doing and are, on the whole, unsympathetic to the efforts of writers who've tried to do a book with a distinctive literary style. Textbook publishers tend to treat books of history as products. I think that's a sacrilege, and it's symbolic of what's wrong with the teaching of history. History teachers don't write their own textbooks, and they have to depend on what the salesmen of publishers tell them.

I think there's nothing more important than the study of history, and among the things that dismays me is the dissolution of the study and teaching of history into so-called social studies, which is the dissolving of the past into the flow of daily newspapers. I also regret the decline of the teaching of geography. It's a wonderful subject, and I think it's an enticing subject. History and geography are concerned with the *when* and the *where.* If people no longer know when they are and where they are, they will no longer know *what* they are and where they're going. That dismays me. I would like to put in a plea for the study of history as chronology and the study of geography as the whereness of our experience. I do think history is a subject that deserves respect in its own right, and not as a handmaiden of anything else. As a great historian once said, history should teach us not what to do tomorrow, but how to be wiser forever.

CA: You've written in "The Historian: 'A Wrestler with the Angel,'" published in the New York Times Book Review, *about the problems of historical evidence, how for example little-used buildings and documents survive while more important, everyday ones perish. Given our wide use of such modern inventions as television and the telephone for communications that were once done in writing, should we be devising special strategies for preserving information?*

BOORSTIN: Yes. And at the Library of Congress we have been working, I think with some effect, on the preservation of books, which is a major problem. It becomes an increasingly important problem as people become more preoccupied with the imperial present, with the media which can cross the oceans but can't cross the centuries. I think it's very important that we be alerted to the problem of the self-destruction of books, and find ways to conserve them.

I also, however, am not one of those who considers the different technologies to be enemies of each other. I don't consider television to be the enemy of the book. On the contrary, I think that every technology is a potential ally of all the others, and what we should search for is to find ways to make television the ally of the book and the book the ally of intelligent and critical television watching. An appalling fact, of course, is that we do have the power to let works die if they're on paper. It's important that we should discover that threat and try to preserve the heritage of books by improving the technology of paper preservation. The Library of Congress has been making great strides in that area; it has been one of the pioneers in finding ways to keep paper from disintegrating.

CA: Is this preservation work related to "The Book in the Future?"

BOORSTIN: That is part of it. "The Book in the Future" was a two-part report that was the product of a joint resolution of the Congress instructing me to have a national committee report to them and the nation on the future of the conventional book in a world of television and the other media. That report was aimed to see in what areas the conventional book was apt to be replaced by the new technologies, and in what area it would survive.

It's interesting how we've forgotten that the book is a product of technology. It's perhaps the *greatest* product of technology, and one which is think is apt to be displaced only in certain limited areas of experience. The temptation, especially in the United States, is to think that the new technology displaces the old. But our history suggests that, instead, the new technology creates new roles for the old. For example, the rise in television news has been an important influence in promoting investigative reporting in the newspapers, and the automobile has created new roles for the radio.

CA: As Librarian of Congress for twelve years (and now Librarian Emeritus), what are you happiest about having achieved during your tenure there?

BOORSTIN: As to what I've accomplished as administrator during those years, I would have to leave that to someone about twenty years from now. What one contributes to an institution can only assessed in retrospect. But I found it a wonderful, fulfilling, and tantalizing experience to be the Librarian of Congress for a lot of reasons. One of them was that I had an opportunity to become acquainted with the members of Congress. Since my interest is less in demography than in biography, I found that opportunity to see the institution through the eyes and in the works of individuals very rewarding. It also gave me a sense of the boundlessness of knowledge and of the mystery which has always attracted me to knowledge in the problems of history. There's no place in the world that will impress you more with the multiplicity and variety of the pieces of human knowledge and of the arts than the Library of Congress.

I also enjoyed working with the people here. I found it certainly the best staff I had ever worked with, although I had been in other institutions. I love institutions—I believe we achieve immortality through institutions—and I have had the good fortune to be associated for much of my life with three great institutions: the University of Chicago, the Smithsonian Institution, and the Library of Congress. I speak to you now from my study in the Library. When I left my post as Librarian of Congress, I didn't go out of the Library, I really walked *into* the Library. The Congress was kind enough to pass a special law creating this new post of Librarian of Congress Emeritus, which provided a study and a secretary and a parking place. The opportunity for this continuing association means a great deal to me.

CA: We've talked about the future of the book. What's in your future that you'd like to mention? Do you have long-range plans beyond The Creators?

BOORSTIN: One of the things that enticed me to the study of history, and I think the only generalization that one can make about history, is the certainty of the unexpected. That's what I like about our future. One of the opportunities I have now that I'm no longer administering the Library but am still in it and exploring it is the opportunity for more and more of the unexpected. I want to continue to work as an author, which is my vocation, and as a historian, and to find other ways to be useful to the republic of letters and to my country.

BIOGRAPHICAL/CRITICAL SOURCES:

BOOKS

Authors in the News, Volume 2, Gale, 1976.
Boorstin, Daniel J., *The Discoverers: A History of Man's Search to Know His World and Himself,* Random House, 1983.
Dictionary of Literary Biography, Volume 17: *Twentieth-Century American Historians,* Gale, 1983.
Cunliffe, M., and Winks, R., editors, *Pastmasters: Some Essays on American Historians,* Harper, 1969.

PERIODICALS

American Historical Review, February, 1971.
Best Sellers, November 1, 1968.
Book Week, March 5, 1967.
Chicago Tribune Book World, December 25, 1983.
Children's Book World, November 3, 1968.
Globe and Mail (Toronto), March 31, 1984, April 2, 1988.
Kenyon Review, January, 1966.
Los Angeles Times Book Review, March 11, 1984.
Nation, January 17, 1959, March 6, 1971.
National Review, April 7, 1970, October 26, 1973.
New Republic, December 15, 1958, October 2, 1965.
New Statesman, August 17, 1984.
New Yorker, March 12, 1984.
New York Review, February 12, 1970.
New York Review of Books, September 19, 1974.
New York Times, July 3, 1973, November 16, 1983, September 21, 1987.
New York Times Book Review, November 9, 1958, October 31, 1965, November 24, 1968, July 29, 1973, November 27, 1983, September 20, 1987.
People, April 19, 1982.
Publishers Weekly, January 4, 1985, January 9, 1987, December 4, 1987.
Saturday Review, November 15, 1958.
Time, December 26, 1983.
Times (London), August 9, 1984.
Times Literary Supplement, May 19, 1966, April 26, 1985.
Tribune Books (Chicago), October 4, 1987.
Village Voice, October 2, 1969.
Washington Post, November 18, 1969, January 29, 1984, December 11, 1986.
Washington Post Book World, December 11, 1983, November 8, 1987.

Washington Star, November 9, 1969, July 27, 1975.
Yale Review, spring, 1959.

—Sketch by Jani Prescott
—Interview by Jean W. Ross

*   *   *

BOOTH, John A(llan)   1946-

PERSONAL: Born December 12, 1946, in Monahans, Tex.; son of George Allan (a clerk) and Grace Emmeline (a teacher; maiden name, Abbott) Booth; married Julie Caroline Murphy (a university professor), May 18, 1970; children: Laura Caroline, Catherine Ann. *Education:* Rice University, B.A., 1970; University of Texas, M.A., 1972, Ph.D., 1975. *Religion:* Religious Society of Friends (Quakers).

ADDRESSES: Home—Denton, Tex. *Office*—Department of Political Science, University of North Texas, Denton, Tex. 76203.

CAREER: University of Texas at San Antonio, assistant professor, 1975-79, associate professor of political science, 1979-84; University of North Texas, Denton, associate professor, 1984-86, professor of political science and chairperson of department, 1986—. Political risk consultant on Mexico and Central America.

MEMBER: American Political Science Association, Latin American Studies Association, American Association of University Professors.

AWARDS, HONORS: Woodrow Wilson fellowship, 1970-71; National Science Foundation trainee, 1970-72; Fulbright fellowship, 1979-80.

WRITINGS:

(Editor with Mitchell A. Seligson) *Political Participation in Latin America,* Holmes & Meier, Volume I: *Citizen and State,* 1978, Volume II: *Politics and the Poor,* 1979.
The End and the Beginning: The Nicaraguan Revolution, Westview, 1982.
(Editor with David R. Johnson and Richard J. Harris) *San Antonio Politics: Community, Progress, and Power,* University of Nebraska Press, 1983.
(Editor with Seligson) *Elections and Democracy in Central America,* University of North Carolina Press, 1989.
(With Thomas W. Walker) *Understanding Central America,* Westview, in press.
Costa Rican Democracy, Westview, in press.

SIDELIGHTS: John A. Booth told *CA:* "Having grown up in a partly Mexican-American neighborhood, I became interested in Spanish and Hispanic culture. My mother was born and reared in Canada and our several visits there as a family stirred my interest in other countries. In 1964 I visited Colombia for two months as an American Field Service exchange student, and I was greatly impressed by the vitality of the culture and people. A Spanish professor in college so intrigued me about Spain that I spent my junior year there to learn the language. I graduated from Rice with the intention of studying Latin American politics in graduate school.

"My selection of Central America as a major research focus was as fortuitous as my decision to study Latin America had been deliberate—my Latin American teaching fellowship was changed suddenly from Bolivia to Costa Rica. The year and a half in Costa Rica working for the National Community Development Agency as a researcher provided me with tremendous amounts of data about social and political participation in Costa Rica. My doctoral dissertation and several scholarly articles were drawn from these data. In 1979 I returned to Costa Rica intending to revise my dissertation for publication as a book. The overthrow of the Somoza regime in neighboring Nicaragua, however, was such an enormously attractive research opportunity that I turned to that topic instead. The Costa Rica book remains unfinished.

"The study of the Nicaraguan revolution, *The End and the Beginning: The Nicaraguan Revolution,* is an in-depth study of the roots and processes of the insurrection that overthrew the Somoza dynasty and the social revolution that has followed it. My studies of revolution and social movements had convinced me that great social upheavals cannot be understood without knowledge of the historical evolution of a society. Indeed the roots of the Nicaraguan insurrection and revolution were easily traced to colonial Nicaragua and to almost two centuries of evolution of the social classes and the political system. While indifference toward the excesses of the Somoza dynasty and foreign intervention in Nicaragua were impossible, I strove to prepare a balanced and factually accurate depiction of events and processes rather than a partisan or ideological interpretation of them. The title refers to the end or overthrow of the Somoza family dictatorship, and to the beginning of a new socio-political and economic system under the new Sandinista regime.

"My side-venture into studying San Antonio politics grew out of the fact that I taught Texas politics courses much of the time. To give my classes some insight into their own community setting—in a state of considerable change and turmoil in the 1970s—I began investigating the city's political history. This became a major study of San Antonio since Texas gained its independence in 1836."

*   *   *

BORENSTEIN, Audrey F(arrell)   1930-

PERSONAL: Born October 7, 1930, in Chicago, Ill.; daughter of Robert C. (a plumbing contractor) and Rose (Schageman) Farrell; married Walter Borenstein (a professor of Spanish language and literature), September 5, 1953; children: Jeffrey Theodore, Shari Rebecca. *Education:* University of Illinois, A.B., 1953, M.A., 1954; Louisiana State University, Ph.D., 1958.

ADDRESSES: Home—4 Henry Court, New Paltz, N.Y. 12561.

CAREER: Louisiana State University, Baton Rouge, assistant professor of sociology, 1958-60; Cornell College, Mt. Vernon, Iowa, assistant professor of anthropology, 1965-69; State University of New York College at New Paltz, adjunct lecturer, 1970-1986. Member of Ulster County Council for the Arts.

MEMBER: International Women's Writing Guild, National League of American Pen Women, Poets and Writers, Hudson Valley Writers Guild, Stone Ridge Poetry Society.

AWARDS, HONORS: First prize in fiction from *Zeitgeist,* 1966, for "Rachel"; creative writing fellowship from National Endowment for the Arts, 1976-77; Rockefeller Foundation humanities fellowship, 1978-79; National League of American Pen Women Fiction Prize for New York State, April, 1988.

WRITINGS:

(Translator) Ferdinand Toennies, *Custom: An Essay on Social Codes,* Free Press, 1961.
Redeeming the Sin: Essays on Social Science and Literature, Columbia University Press, 1978.
Older Women in Twentieth Century America: A Selected Annual Bibliography, Garland, 1982.
Chimes of Change and Hours, Farleigh Dickinson University Press/Associated University Presses, 1983.
(With husband, Walter Borenstein) *Through the Years: A Chronicle of Congregation Ahavath Achim,* Franklin, 1989.

Contributor of articles, stories, poems and reviews to literary journals, including *Antioch Review, South Atlantic Quarterly, The Albany Review, Calyx, Oxalis, Ascent,* and *North Dakota Quarterly.*

WORK IN PROGRESS: From the Palatine Sketchbook, a series of novels; short stories; essays.

SIDELIGHTS: Audrey F. Borenstein told *CA:* "Both a creative writer and a social scientist, I have in the past written works of fiction and nonfiction concurrently. But I began as a poet. And now I want to find my poet's voice and vision again, in writing fiction. I resigned in 1986 from academe to dedicate myself full-time to writing."

*   *   *

BOWEN, Robert Sydney   1900-1977
(James Robert Richard)

PERSONAL: Born in 1900, in Boston, Mass.; died April 11, 1977, in Honolulu, Hawaii; married; wife's name, Mary Ann; children: three sons, one daughter.

ADDRESSES: Home—Honolulu, Hawaii.

CAREER: Author, editor, and journalist. Began working as a journalist, 1918, for *London Daily Mail, Chicago Tribune* in Paris, and for two Boston newspapers; served as editorial director for International Civil Aeronautics Conference in Washington, D.C.; editor-in-chief, *Aviation;* editor of *Flying News* and several motor magazines; free-lance writer of fiction, 1930-77. *Military service:* U.S. Aviation Service, 1914-18; qualified as ace fighter pilot by shooting down eight enemy aircraft.

MEMBER: American Society for Promotion of Aviation (publicity director).

AWARDS, HONORS: Gold medal and certificates from Boys Clubs of America.

WRITINGS:

Flying from the Ground Up, McGraw, 1931.
Red Randall in Burma, Grosset, 1945.
The Winning Pitch, Lothrop, 1948.
Player, Manager, Lothrop, 1949.
Fourth Down, Lothrop, 1949.
Ball Hawk, Lothrop, 1950.
Blocking Back, Lothrop, 1950.
Hot Corner, Lothrop, 1951.
Touchdown Kid, Lothrop, 1951.
Canyon Fury, Lothrop, 1952.
Pitcher of the Year, Lothrop, 1952.
Behind the Bat, Lothrop, 1953.
Infield Spark, Lothrop, 1954.

The Million-Dollar Fumble, Lothrop, 1954.
The Big Inning, Lothrop, 1955.
The Last White Line, Lothrop, 1955.
The 4th Out, Lothrop, 1956.
No Hitter, Lothrop, 1957.
The Big Hit, Lothrop, 1958.
Triple Play, Lothrop, 1959.
Hot Rod Angels, Chilton, 1960.
Pennant Fever, Lothrop, 1960.
Million-Dollar Rookie, Lothrop, 1961.
Bat Boy, Lothrop, 1962.
Flight into Danger, Chilton, 1962.
Wings for an Eagle, Chilton, 1962.
Perfect Game, Lothrop, 1963.
Dirt Track Danger, Doubleday, 1963.
They Found the Unknown: The Stories of Nine Great Discoveries in the Field of Medical Knowledge, Macrae, 1963.
Hot Corner Blues, Lothrop, 1964.
Hot Rod Rodeo, Criterion, 1964.
Rebel Rookie, Lothrop, 1965.
They Flew to Glory: The Story of the Lafayette Flying Corps, Lothrop, 1965.
Hot Rod Patrol, Criterion, 1966.
Man on First, Lothrop, 1966.
Hot Rod Showdown, Criterion, 1967.
Lightning Southpaw, Lothrop, 1967.
Hot Rod Outlaws, Chilton, 1968.
Wipeout, Criterion, 1969.
Hawaii Five-O: Top Secret, Western Publishing, 1969.
Infield Flash, Lothrop, 1969.
Born to Fly, Criterion, 1971.
Hot Rod Doom, Criterion, 1973.

"DAVE DAWSON" SERIES

Dave Dawson at Dunkirk, Crown, 1941.
. . .in Libya, Crown, 1941.
. . .on Convoy Patrol, Crown, 1941.
. . .with the R.A.F., Crown, 1941.
. . .with the Commandos, Crown, 1942.
. . .at Singapore, Crown, 1942.
. . .with the Pacific Fleet, Crown, 1942.
. . .at the Russian Front, Crown, 1943.
. . .at Casablanca, Crown, 1944.
. . .at Truk, Crown, 1946.

UNDER PSEUDONYM JAMES ROBERT RICHARD

The Club Team, Lothrop, 1950.
Fighting Halfback, Lothrop, 1952.
Quarterback, All-American, Lothrop, 1953.
Phantom Mustang, Lothrop, 1954.
The Purple Palomino, Lothrop, 1955.
The Appaloosa Curse, Lothrop, 1956.
Snow King, Lippizan Horse, 1957.
Double M for Morgans, Lothrop, 1958.
Joker, the Polo Pony, Lothrop, 1959.

OBITUARIES:

PERIODICALS

New York Times, April 13, 1977.*

*   *   *

BOWER, Keith
  See BECKETT, Kenneth A(lbert)

BOWERS, Neal   1948-

PERSONAL: Born August 3, 1948, in Clarksville, Tenn.; son of Floyd E. and Willine (Tigart) Bowers; married Nancy Brooker (a writer). *Education:* Austin Peay State University, B.A., 1970, M.A., 1971; University of Florida, Ph.D., 1976.

ADDRESSES: Home—1507 Carroll Ave., Ames, Iowa 50010. *Office*—Department of English, Iowa State University, 203 Ross Hall, Ames, Iowa 50011.

CAREER: Iowa State University, Ames, assistant professor, 1977-83, associate professor, 1983-87, professor of creative writing and modern poetry, 1987—.

MEMBER: Academy of American Poets, Associated Writing Programs.

WRITINGS:

Theodore Roethke: The Journey from I to Otherwise, University of Missouri Press, 1982.
The Golf Ball Drive, New Rivers Press, 1983.
James Dickey: The Poet as Pitchman, University of Missouri Press, 1985.
Lost in the Heartland, Cedar Creek Press, 1988.

Contributor of articles and poems to periodicals, including *New Yorker*, *American Poetry Review*, *Sewanee Review*, *Harper's*, *Hudson Review*, *North American Review*, and *Modern Poetry Studies*. Editor of *Poet and Critic*.

WORK IN PROGRESS: Night Vision, poems; *Legends*, poems.

SIDELIGHTS: Neal Bowers told *CA:* "I consider myself to be a poet and critic, though I can't say the two occupations are always compatible. In fact, I've come to accept the fact that I cannot write poetry when I'm involved in a critical writing project, nor can I write very good criticism when I'm producing poetry. However, I do think the poet and the critic can learn from one another, and that's why I persist in trying to harbor both identities.

"It seems to me that the poet and the critic cover essentially the same ground, but they move in opposite directions. Whereas the critic's business is to take things apart, the poet's job is to put things together. One's stock-in-trade is analysis; the other's is synthesis. When I write poetry, I hope the poet identity will be aware of but not dominated by his alter ego, just as I hope the critic identity will be aware of but not dominated by his. You don't want Jekyll and Hyde to be ignorant of one another's existence, but you hope they will modify each other in useful ways to produce a better identity than either could have alone."

BIOGRAPHICAL/CRITICAL SOURCES:

PERIODICALS

Des Moines Register, October 21, 1984.
Georgia Review, spring, 1986.
Nashville Tennessean, July 1, 1984.
Sewanee Review, spring, 1986.

*   *   *

BOYLE, Deirdre   1949-

PERSONAL: Born July 12, 1949, in New York, N.Y.; daughter of Hubert and Margaret (Mangan) Boyle. *Education:* College of Mount St. Vincent, B.A. (cum laude), 1970; Antioch College, M.A., 1976.

ADDRESSES: Home and office—88 Bleecker St., New York, N.Y. 10012.

CAREER: R.R. Bowker Co., New York City, associate editor, 1973-74; *Sightlines,* New York City, video editor, 1978-86. Senior faculty member at New School for Social Research, 1978—, and Fordham University, College at Lincoln Center, 1979—. Associate producer and writer of cable television series "Ordinary People," 1986-87. Trustee, International Film Seminars. Consultant to "New Television" and various government and private funding agencies, museums, and media festivals.

MEMBER: Authors Guild, Authors League of America, Association of Independent Video and Filmmakers.

AWARDS, HONORS: Writing grant, New York State Council on the Arts, 1982, 1987; Guggenheim fellow, 1983-84; Yaddo fellow, 1984-85; Millay Colony for the Arts fellow, 1986; MacDowell Colony fellow, 1987; Ace Award, 1988, for best documentary series on cable television.

WRITINGS:

Expanding Media, Oryx, 1977.
(Editor with Stephen Calvert) *Children's Media Market Place,* Gaylord, 1978.
Video Classics: A Guide to Video Art and Documentary Tapes, Oryx, 1986.
American Documentary Video: Subject to Change, Museum of Modern Art, 1988.
Guerilla Television Revisited, Oxford University Press, 1989.
(Documentary and video editor) *International Encyclopedia of Communications,* Oxford University Press, 1989.

Contributor of articles and reviews to video, film, art, and library journals. Assistant editor, *Wilson Library Bulletin,* 1978-79.

SIDELIGHTS: Deirdre Boyle told *CA:* "A novelist looks at the pictures in her mind and then writes, as Joan Didion has said, 'entirely to find out what I'm thinking, what I'm looking at, what I see and what it means. What I want and what I fear.' A critic looks at someone else's pictures—in my case, videotapes—for the very same reasons. I scrutinize the glass of shifting shapes in black, white, and color much like a medium gazes into her crystal ball—to discover the past, reveal the elusive present, predict the shadowy future—always searching for a glimpse of myself reflected back in the glass."

*   *   *

BRETT, John Michael
   See TRIPP, Miles (Barton)

*   *   *

BRETT, Michael
   See TRIPP, Miles (Barton)

*   *   *

BROADWELL, Martin M.   1927-

PERSONAL: Born February 15, 1927, in Nashville, Tenn.; son of William Ernest (an engineer) and Jessie (Bell) Broadwell; married Patricia Breeding (an elementary school science teacher), December 29, 1951; children: Martin M., Jr., Timothy W., Patricia Carol. *Education:* George Peabody College for Teachers, B.S., 1948; graduate study at Wittenburg Col-

lege and University of Tennessee; National Christian University, M.A., 1975. *Politics:* Conservative. *Religion:* Conservative.

ADDRESSES: Home—2882 Hollywood Dr., Decatur, Ga. 30033.

CAREER: High school teacher of science and mathematics in Xenia, Ohio, 1948-51; Bell System in Tennessee, Georgia, and Kentucky, engineer, 1951-56, technical writer, 1956-57, in public relations, 1957-59, personnel director, 1959-63, director of technical training, 1964-70; resources for Education and Management, Inc., Decatur, Ga., co-founder and partner, 1968-83; Center for General Management Services, Inc., Decatur, founder and general manager, 1984—. Co-founder and director of Publishing Systems, Inc., 1972—. Consultant to major business firms. *Military service:* U.S. Navy, radarman, 1944-45.

MEMBER: American Society for Training and Development, American Society for Engineering Education, Institute of Electrical and Electronic Engineers, National Society for Performance and Instruction.

AWARDS, HONORS: Blue ribbon from American Film Festival, 1969, for writing and producing "The Managerial Skills"; cited for outstanding contribution to city by a business author, Atlanta, Ga., 1983.

WRITINGS:

The Supervisor as an Instructor: A Guide to Classroom Training, Addison-Wesley, 1968, 4th edition, 1984.
The New Supervisor, Addison-Wesley, 1972, 3rd edition, 1984.
Success at Bible Teaching, Publishing Systems, Inc., 1974.
The Supervisor and On-the-Job Training, Addison-Wesley, 1974, 2nd edition, 1975.
The Lecture Method of Instruction, Educational Technology Publications, 1975.
(With Brij Kapur) *The New Manager,* Shri Ram Centre for Industrial Relations, 1977.
The Practice of Supervising: Making Experience Pay, Addison-Wesley, 1977, 2nd edition, 1984.
(With Nancy Diekelmann) *The New Hospital Supervisor,* Addison-Wesley, 1977.
The New Insurance Supervisor, Addison-Wesley, 1978.
Moving Up To Supervision: For Use in Pre-supervisory Training, Career Planning, Upward Mobility, and Other Human Resource Development Efforts, Wiley, 1985.
Supervising Today: A Guide for Positive Leadership, Wiley, 1985.
Handbook on Supervision, Wiley, 1986.
Supervising Technical and Professional People, Wiley, 1987.

Contributor of about 200 articles to trade journals in the United States and abroad.

WORK IN PROGRESS: Revision of six trade books; three novels.

SIDELIGHTS: Martin M. Broadwell writes: "As a consultant, I've traveled around the world four times, with three trips to Australia. I spent weeks in my favorite outside-the-United States country: India. I have worked and/or traveled in sixty different countries. All this travel is intended to support my fiction writing hobby when I grow up. I have skied in the Canadian Rockies, ridden elephants to the Amber Palace in India, hiked in the Himalayas, boated past the wats of Thailand, walked the Great Wall of China, gazed at the Kremlin, and explored Singapore, Amsterdam, Stonehenge, and the wilds of Alaska.

From the steps of the parthenon to the ruins of Delphi and old Corinth, I've tried to feel at home, know the people and the places. Being a country boy keeps me awed by all that's outside my day-to-day world.''

*   *   *

BROCKMAN, James R(aymond)   1926-

PERSONAL: Born August 3, 1926, in Cincinnati, Ohio; son of Raymond J. and Rose (Gieske) Brockman. *Education:* Xavier University, Litt.B., 1951; West Baden College, Ph.L., 1955, S.T.B., 1961; Loyola University, M.A., 1959.

ADDRESSES: Home—6559 North Glenwood Ave., Chicago, Ill. 60626-5121.

CAREER: Entered Society of Jesus (Jesuits), 1947, ordained Roman Catholic priest, 1960; St. Ignatius High School, Cleveland, Ohio, teacher, 1952-53; Loyola Academy, Chicago, Ill., teacher, 1955-56; St. Ignatius High School, Chicago, teacher, 1956-57; Colegio San Jose, Arequipa, Peru, teacher and administrator, 1963-72; Cook County Hospital, Chicago, chaplain, 1973; *America*, New York, N.Y., associate editor, 1974-80; writer, 1980—. *Military service:* U.S. Army, 1945-46.

WRITINGS:

The Word Remains: A Life of Oscar Romero, Orbis, 1982 (published in England as *Oscar Romero, Bishop and Martyr*, Sheed & Ward, 1982).
(Editor and translator) *The Church Is All of You: Thoughts of Archbishop Romero*, Winston Press, 1984.
(Contributor of translations) Oscar Romero, *Voice of the Voiceless*, Orbis, 1985.
(Editor and translator) *The Violence of Love: The Pastoral Wisdom of Archbishop Oscar Romero*, Harper, 1988.

Also contributor to *The New Catholic Encyclopedia Supplement*. Contributor to periodicals, including *Third World Quarterly, Spirituality Today, Sign, Thought, Christian Century, Mensaje* (Santiago, Chile), and *Accion* (Asuncion, Paraguay).

WORK IN PROGRESS: Editing a volume of selections from writings and sermons of Oscar Romero, for Centro de Estudios y Publicaciones (CEP; Lima, Peru); a revised edition of *The Word Remains*.

SIDELIGHTS: James R. Brockman told *CA:* "In my writing I have tried to make the church and people of Latin America better understood in the United States and the world at large. In recent years my work has centered on Archbishop Oscar Romero, whose life and work symbolize and exemplify the transformation going on in the Latin American church. I think that a better understanding of that renewal can help us all to deepen our own religious dimension and can help the United States to form a more mature relationship with the people of Latin America.''

*   *   *

BRODERICK, Damien (Francis)   1944-

PERSONAL: Born April 22, 1944, in Melbourne, Australia; son of Francis Arthur (a toolmaker) and Pamela Beatrix (Bartels) Broderick. *Education:* Monash University, B.A., 1966; postgraduate research, Deakin University, 1986—.

ADDRESSES: Home—19 Croft Cres., Reservoir, Victoria, Australia.

CAREER: Go-Set, Melbourne, Australia, journalist, 1967; freelance writer, 1967-70; David Syme Pty. Ltd,, Melbourne, journalist, 1970; *Man*, Sydney, Australia, editor, 1971; freelance writer, 1971-73; *Walkabout*, Sydney, assistant editor of *Club*, 1973; free-lance writer, 1973—. Writer in residence, Deakin University, 1986.

AWARDS, HONORS: Fellow, Australia Council Literature Board, 1980 and 1984; Ditmar Award, Australian National Science Fiction Convention, and John W. Campbell Memorial Award runner-up, both 1981, both for *The Dreaming Dragons;* guest of honor, Swancon (science fiction convention), Perth, Australia, 1983; special Ditmar Award, 1985, for *Transmitters*.

WRITINGS:

A Man Returned (science fiction stories), Horwitz, 1965.
Sorcerer's World (science fiction novel; also see below), Signet, 1970.
(Editor) *The Zeitgeist Machine* (science fiction stories), Angus & Robertson, 1977.
The Dreaming Dragons (science fiction novel), Pocket Books, 1980.
The Judas Mandala (science fiction novel), Pocket Books, 1982.
(With Rory Barnes) *Valencies* (science fiction novel), University of Queensland Press, 1983.
Transmitters (novel), Ebony Books, 1984.
(Editor) *Strange Attractors* (stories), Hale & Iremonger, 1985.
The Black Grail (novel; revised version of *Sorcerer's World*), Avon Books, 1986.
(Editor) *Matilda at the Speed of Light* (stories), Angus & Robertson, 1988.
Striped Moles (science fiction novel), Avon Books, 1988.

Contributor to magazines, including *Magazine of Fantasy and Science Fiction, Omni*, and *Isaac Asimov's Science Fiction Magazine*.

SIDELIGHTS: Damien Broderick told *CA:* "I'm a storyteller in a cross-disciplinary universe of discourse. This reduces the transparency of my writing, but adds, I hope, little jokes and jolts for other people with minds as cluttered as mine.'' Broderick's *The Dreaming Dragons* has been translated into German.

BIOGRAPHICAL/CRITICAL SOURCES:

BOOKS

Mattoid 24, Deakin University, 1986.

PERIODICALS

Science Fiction, Volume 4, number 3, 1982.

*   *   *

BURFORD, Eleanor
See HIBBERT, Eleanor Burford

*   *   *

BURKE, James   1936-

PERSONAL: Born December 22, 1936, in Londonderry, Northern Ireland; son of John James (a businessman) and Mary (Gallagher) Burke; married F. Madeline Hamilton. *Education:* Oxford University, B.A. and M.A., both 1961.

ADDRESSES: Agent—Jonathan Clowes, 22 Prince Albert Rd., London N1 7ST, England.

CAREER: British School, Bologna, Italy, lecturer in English and director of studies, 1961-63; English School, Rome, Italy, teacher of English and head of school, 1963-65; Granada Television, Rome, reporter for "World in Action" current affairs program, 1965-66; British Broadcasting Corp. (BBC-TV), London, England, 1966—, writer-host for television series including "Tomorrow's World" and "The Burke Special," writer and host of television documentaries including "The Inventing of America," "Connections," "The Real Thing," and "The Day the Universe Changed," chief reporter for Apollo moon missions, and producer. Managing director, Burke Productions. University lecture circuit, visiting scholar, University of Michigan—Dearborn, 1988. *Military service:* Royal Air Force, 1957-59; became flying officer.

MEMBER: Royal Institution, Savile Club.

AWARDS, HONORS: Royal Television Society, silver medal for creative work on camera, 1973, and gold medal for outstanding program of the year, 1974; USA TV blue ribbon, 1978, 1986.

WRITINGS:

TELEVISION DOCUMENTARIES

"The Inventing of America," first aired on British Broadcasting Corp. (BBC-TV), July 4, 1976, aired on National Broadcasting Co. (NBC-TV), July 3, 1979.
"Connections" (also see below), first aired on BBC-TV, autumn, 1979, aired on Public Broadcasting Service (PBS-TV), autumn, 1979.
"The Real Thing," first aired on BBC-TV, autumn, 1980, aired on PBS-TV, autumn, 1981.
"The Day the Universe Changed" (also see below), first aired on BBC-TV, spring, 1985, aired on PBS-TV, autumn, 1986.

OTHER

(With Raymond Baxter) *Tomorrow's World* (based on the BBC-TV series), British Broadcasting Corp., 1970.
Connections: An Alternate View of Change, Macmillan, 1978, published as *Connections*, Little, Brown, 1979.
The Day the Universe Changed, Little, Brown, 1986.

Contributor to periodicals, including *Vogue, Harpers, Punch, Radio Times, New York Magazine, T.V. Times,* and many others.

WORK IN PROGRESS: "Communications," a ten-part television series, to be broadcast in 1991.

SIDELIGHTS: James Burke has earned a reputation as one of British television's finest writers. In order to prepare his celebrated documentary "Connections," a study of the process of invention, he spent more than three years researching and filming in twenty-three countries. "Connections" proved very popular with television audiences in both Britain and America; it gained the largest audience ever for a PBS network documentary when it was broadcast in 1979.

A companion volume to the series, also entitled *Connections*, goes into greater detail than does the television programs. In the book Burke examines eight recent technological achievements—the computer, the production line, telecommunications, the airplane, the atomic bomb, plastics, the guided rocket, and television—and traces the sequence of events that led to these inventions. Burke's thesis is that technological progress is not usually the result of the work of a few brilliant individuals, but rather is brought about by the creative adaptations and combinations of many people.

The book *Connections* proved to be just as popular as the television series, making bestseller lists in both America and the United Kingdom. Although a few critics expressed some reservations about the book and its conclusions, most greeted the work with the same enthusiasm as did the popular audiences. A *Los Angeles Times* reviewer described it as "marvelously illustrated and written with a lively wit." *Washington Post* contributor Joseph McLellan admired Burke's ability to enliven what might have been a rather dull subject: "There is a deep fascination in the way Burke traces the process and relates technology to everyday life."

Burke returns to the subject of change in *The Day the Universe Changed*, a ten-part television series and companion book that proved fully as popular as *Connections*. Covering Western cultural history from the Middle Ages to the 20th century, the book and series illustrate the origins of modern Western attitudes and institutions through significant shifts in the body of scientific knowledge. When man's concept of the universe changed, everything else—architecture, music, literature, economics, etc.—changed with it, mirroring the new perception. However, Burke points out that each method of understanding the way the universe worked was valid for its own time. In the preface to the book *The Day the Universe Changed*, Burke asks, "If views at all times are valid, which is the right one?. . . Is knowledge merely what we decide it should be? Is the universe what we discover it is, or what we say it is? If knowledge is an artefact, will we go on inventing it, endlessly? And if so, is there no truth to seek?"

Reviewers of *The Day the Universe Changed* found some defects—Rudy Rucker, writing for the *Washington Post Book World*, criticizes the book's "unwillingness to say anything substantive about the world we live in"—but also found much that was praiseworthy. "Burke assails his readers and viewers with facts, history, and beautiful illustrations," declares Paul A. Robinson Jr. in the *Christian Science Monitor*. "The illustrations in the text are interesting and thought-provoking. The progress, or at least the changing scene, of mankind is spread across the text with amazing speed." Rucker concludes, "Despite its weaknesses—which are perhaps not as great as this review suggests—'The Day the Universe Changed' will certainly set people thinking new thoughts."

Burke told *CA:* "I am interested in trying to explain in a very limited way some aspects of why the world is as it is, and I believe that science has the most profound effect on it. Understanding science—even in the most general way—is a step toward understanding the social systems we live by. Some critics mistake my intentions, which are *not* to write definitively, but to provide access to the lay reader to subjects that are closed by nature of their very vocabulary."

BIOGRAPHICAL/CRITICAL SOURCES:

BOOKS

Burke, James, *The Day the Universe Changed*, Little, Brown, 1986.

PERIODICALS

Christian Science Monitor, September 5, 1979, June 16, 1987.
Los Angeles Times, November 2, 1979.
New York Times Book Review, December 30, 1979.

Washington Post, September 20, 1979.
Washington Post Book World, October 4, 1986.

*   *   *

BURMAN, Jose Lionel 1917-

PERSONAL: Born April 10, 1917, in Jagersfontein, South Africa; son of Elias Lewis and Dora (Loewenberg) Burman; married Ruth Valerie Herbert (deceased); married Cecily Kathleen Cheetham Robertson, August 28, 1940; children: (first marriage) Carol Lesley Burman Katz. *Education:* University of South Africa, B.A., 1938, LL.B., 1940. *Religion:* Jewish.

ADDRESSES: Home—P.O. Box 500, Hermanus, South Africa.

CAREER: Solicitor in Cape Town, South Africa, 1945-84; writer, 1960-88. *Military service:* South African Army, 1940-45.

MEMBER: International PEN, Mountain Club of South Africa, South African Spelaeological Association (president, 1967-77), Institute of Directors, South African Camping Club (chairman, 1965-70), British Alpine Club, Historical Society of Cape Town (founder; chairman, 1972), Masons (past district senior grand warden).

AWARDS, HONORS: Gold Medal from South African Spelaeological Association, 1965; award from International Wine Organization, 1980, for *Wine of Constantia*.

WRITINGS:

Safe to the Sea, Human & Rousseau, 1962.
Peninsula Profile, Thomas Nelson, 1963.
So High the Road, Human & Rousseau, 1963.
The Garden Route, Human & Rousseau, 1964.
A Peak to Climb, Struik, 1966.
Great Shipwrecks off the Coast of Southern Africa, Struik, 1967.
Where to Walk in the Cape Peninsula, Human & Rousseau, 1967.
Strange Shipwrecks of the Southern Seas, Struik, 1968.
Cape of Good Intent, Human & Rousseau, 1969.
Who Really Discovered South Africa, Struik, 1969.
Waters of the Western Cape, Human & Rousseau, 1970.
Disaster Struck South Africa, Struik, 1971.
Guide to the Garden Route, Human & Rousseau, 1972.
1652 and So Forth, Human & Rousseau, 1973.
The Saldanha Bay Story, Human & Rousseau, 1974.
Bay of Storms: Story of the Development of Table Bay, 1503-1860, Human & Rousseau, 1976.
The False Bay Story, Human & Rousseau, 1977.
Wine of Constantia, Human & Rousseau, 1979.
Latest Walks in the Cape Peninsula, Human & Rousseau, 1979, revised and expanded edition, 1982.
Early Railways at the Cape, Human & Rousseau, 1984.
Day Walks in the South-Western Cape, Human & Rousseau, 1984.
Rediscovering the Garden Route, Human & Rousseau, 1985.
Hottentots Holland to Hermanus, Human & Rousseau, 1985.
Shipwreck, Human & Rousseau, 1986.

Also author of *Cape Drives and Places of Interest, Coastal Holiday, Trails and Walks in the Southern Cape*, and *The Little Karoo*. Contributor to *Standard Encyclopedia of South Africa* and *Dictionary of South African Biography*.

WORK IN PROGRESS: A definitive history of the ox-wagon in South Africa.

SIDELIGHTS: Jose Lionel Burman told *CA:* ''My interests are basically outdoor activities, and my writings are mostly a combination of the history and geography of South Africa. My driving motive is to let others share in enjoying the wildness and beauty of my country.''

*   *   *

BUTLER, Annie L(ouise) 1920-1979

PERSONAL: Born September 21, 1920, in Huntsville, Ala.; died in 1979; daughter of George B. (a postmaster) and Marilee (Dilworth) Butler. *Education:* Alabama College (now University of Montevallo), B.S., 1943; University of Iowa, M.A., 1944; Columbia University, Ed.D., 1958.

CAREER: St. Cloud Teachers College (now St. Cloud State College), St. Cloud, Minn., supervisor of nursery school, 1944-46; University of Alabama, Tuscaloosa, director of nursery school, 1946-51; Columbia University Teachers College, New York, N.Y., teacher of preschool children at Agnes Russell Center, 1951-53, supervisor of student teaching and part-time instructor, 1953-54; Newark State Teachers College (now Kean College of New Jersey), Union, N.J., assistant professor of early childhood education, 1954-57; New York State Education Department, Albany, associate in child development, 1957-60; Indiana University at Bloomington, assistant professor, 1960-66, associate professor, 1966-72, professor of childhood education, 1972-79, curriculum coordinator, Project Head Start Staff Orientation Program, 1965-67. Consultant, Project Head Start, 1965-69; chairman of board of directors, Child Development Associate Consortium, 1975-76.

MEMBER: Association for Childhood Education International (vice-president, 1967-69; president, 1973-75), International Reading Association, U.S. National Committee on Early Childhood Education (secretary, 1971-73), National Association for the Education of Young Children, American Association of Elementary-Kindergarten-Nursery Educators, American Association of University Women, Association for Supervision and Curriculum Development, Midwest Association for the Education of Young Children, Indiana Association for the Education of Young Children (vice-president, 1966-67; president, 1967-68), Indiana University Women's Faculty Club (vice-president, 1965-66; president, 1966-67), Pi Lambda Theta, Delta Kappa Gamma.

AWARDS, HONORS: Grants from U.S. Office of Education and U.S. Office of Economic Opportunity.

WRITINGS:

(With Lorene Kimball Fox) *All Children Want to Learn*, Grolier Society, 1954.
(Contributor) *Reading in the Kindergarten*, Association for Childhood Education International, 1962.
An Evaluation Scale for Four and Five Year Old Children, School of Education, Indiana University, 1965.
(Contributor) *Social Studies for Young Americans*, Kendall-Hunt, 1970.
(Editor) *Current Research in Early Childhood Education: A Compilation and Analysis for Program Planners*, American Association of Elementary-Kindergarten-Nursery Educators, 1970.
(With Edward Gotts, Nancy Quisenberry, and Robert Thompson) *Literature Search and Development of an Evaluation*

System in Early Childhood Education (series of reports), U.S. Office of Education, 1971.

Early Childhood Education: Planning and Administering Programs, Van Nostrand, 1974.

(With Gotts and Quisenberry) *Early Childhood Programs: Developmental Objectives and Their Uses,* C. E. Merrill, 1975.

(With Gotts and Quisenberry) *Play as Development,* C. E. Merrill, 1978.

(Editor with Natalie P. LeVasseur) *Early Childhood Education in Perspective,* School of Education, Indiana University, 1979.

Contributor to numerous professional journals; contributor of a series of ten articles to the Associated Press, 1972. Chairman of publications committee, *Childhood Education,* 1970-72.

OBITUARIES:

PERIODICALS

Childhood Education, October, 1979.*

C

CABLE, Mary 1920-

PERSONAL: Born January 24, 1920, in Cleveland, Ohio; daughter of Robert Winthrop (an engineer) and Elizabeth (a painter; maiden name, Southwick) Pratt; married Arthur Goodrich Cable, May 25, 1949; children: Cassandra Southwick Dunning. *Education:* Studied at Cas'Alta School, Florence, Italy, 1939; Barnard College, A.B., 1941.

ADDRESSES: Home—1810 Calle de Sebastian (J2), Santa Fe, N.M. 87501. *Agent*—Harriet Wasserman Literary Agency, 137 East 36th St., New York, N.Y. 10016.

CAREER: New Yorker, New York City, member of editorial staff, 1944-49; *Harper's Bazaar,* New York City, member of editorial staff, 1949-51; American Heritage Publishing Co., Inc., New York City, member of editorial staff, 1963-65.

AWARDS, HONORS: National Endowment for the Arts grant, 1977; National Endowment for the Humanities grant, 1978; Louisiana Library Association Award, 1980, for *Lost New Orleans.*

WRITINGS:

Dream Castles, Viking, 1966.
(With the editors of *American Heritage*) *American Manners and Morals,* American Heritage Press, 1969.
The Avenue of the Presidents, Houghton, 1969.
Black Odyssey: The Case of the Slave Ship Amistad, Viking, 1971.
(With the editors of Newsweek Books) *El Escorial,* Newsweek, 1971.
The Little Darlings: A History of Childrearing in America, Scribner, 1975.
Lost New Orleans, Houghton, 1980.
Avery's Knot (novel), Putnam, 1981.
Top Drawer: American High Society from the Gilded Age to the Roaring Twenties, Atheneum, 1984.
The Blizzard of '88, Atheneum, 1988.

Contributor of short stories and articles to *New Yorker, Horizon, Harper's Bazaar, Atlantic, American Heritage, Vogue,* and other periodicals.

SIDELIGHTS: Mary Cable's fact-based novel, *Avery's Knot,* re-creates the case of Sarah Maria Cornell, a twenty-nine-year-old mill worker who was found beaten and hanging from a stake in a Rhode Island field in December of 1832. Her accused murderer was the Reverend Ephraim Avery, a Methodist minister who apparently killed her to hide the fact that she was pregnant with his child. When Avery was brought to trial in Newport, R.I., according to Faith McNulty's *Washington Post* review, "he denied the crime in a few words and then, with eloquent sanctimony, put the dead girl on trial. She was a known fornicator, he said, and afflicted with a foul disease. The court absolved him." As a profile of the treatment and the rights of women in nineteenth-century America, *Avery's Knot* "brings their condition into a sharp focus that has the impact of revelation," asserts McNulty. "Sarah Cornell's life is a case history of what can happen to a woman in a society totally dominated by men." Although the book presents a convincing portrait of early America, *New York Times Book Review* contributor Valerie Miner feels *Avery's Knot* works as "a sad and terrifying novel. . . . The chilly spareness of people and place evokes a haunting psychological tension in this book, which is stronger on mood than narrative. Still," continues Miner, "the story is compelling from the start. We watch, in helpless horror, as Sarah is caught inextricably in Avery's knot." And McNulty concludes that "in bringing Sarah Cornell back to life, Mary Cable has awakened a troubling ghost."

Cable reconstructs another era in *The Blizzard of '88,* an account of a three-day snowstorm which struck the East Coast in March of 1888. The storm consisted of hurricane force winds which sunk or damaged over two hundred ships and killed one hundred sailors, while on land the winds created drifts of twenty to thirty feet, and caused the deaths of more than three hundred. In retelling this story, "Mary Cable intrigues readers with detailed accounts from the correspondence of survivors who 41 years later formed the Society of Blizzard Men and Blizzard Ladies," describes Thomas C. Widner in *America.* Chicago *Tribune Books* writer John Blades, while acknowledging the secondary nature of the disaster, also finds Cable's narrative entertaining: "However low the blizzard may rank on the fatality scale, there's little question that the story is well worth repeating, especially when it's told as swiftly and surely as Cable tells it here. Though nonfiction, the book has the epic cast and the taut construction of a superior disaster novel." The critic adds that Cable's account is "mostly an upbeat survival tale. . . . As a consequence, 'The Blizzard of '88' is almost as much a socioeconomic composite of an age (the so-called 'Age of Confidence') as it is a brisk record of death and transfiguration, heroism and anarchy.'' Denise P. Donavin similarly concludes in *Booklist* that Cable's anecdotes ''render a dramatic, realistic impression of both the blizzard itself and the era in general. A nice dose of history, ingeniously delivered.''

BIOGRAPHICAL/CRITICAL SOURCES:

PERIODICALS

America, February 13, 1988.
Booklist, February 1, 1988.
New Yorker, July 28, 1975, November 24, 1980.
New York Times Book Review, August 24, 1969, January 17, 1982.
Tribune Books (Chicago), February 21, 1988.
Village Voice Literary Supplement, February, 1988.
Washington Post, November 6, 1981.

*   *   *

CAMPBELL, Joseph   1904-1987

PERSONAL: Born March 26, 1904, in New York, N.Y.; died October 30, 1987, in Honolulu, Hawaii; son of Charles William (a hosiery importer and wholesaler) and Josephine (Lynch) Campbell; married Jean Erdman (a dancer and choreographer), May 5, 1938. *Education:* Attended Dartmouth College, 1921-22; Columbia University, A.B., 1925, M.A., 1927, additional graduate study, 1927-28, 1928-29; graduate study at the University of Paris, 1927-28, and the University of Munich, 1928-29.

CAREER: Independent study of mythology, 1929-32; Canterbury School, New Milford, Conn., teacher of French, German, and ancient history, 1932-33; Sarah Lawrence College, Bronxville, N.Y., member of literature department faculty, 1934-72. Lecturer, Foreign Service Institute, U.S. Department of State, 1956-73, and Columbia University, 1959. President, Creative Film Foundation, 1954-63, and Foundation for the Open Eye, beginning 1973. Trustee, Bollingen Foundation, 1960-69.

MEMBER: American Folklore Society, American Oriental Society, American Society for the Study of Religion (president, 1972-75), American Academy of Psychotherapists (honorary member), Century Club, New York Athletic Club.

AWARDS, HONORS: Proudfit fellow, 1927-28, 1928-29; grants-in-aid for editing Zimmer volumes, 1946-55; National Institute of Arts and Letters grant in literature, 1949, for *The Hero with a Thousand Faces;* Distinguished Scholar Award, Hofstra University, 1973; D.H.L., Pratt Institute, 1976; Melcher Award for contribution to religious liberalism, 1976, for *The Mythic Image;* National Arts Club medal of honor for literature, 1985; elected to the American Academy of Arts and Letters, 1987.

WRITINGS:

(With Maud Oakes and Jeff King) *Where the Two Come to Their Father: A Navaho War Ceremonial*, Pantheon, 1943.
(With Henry Morton Robinson) *A Skeleton Key to ''Finnegans Wake,''* Harcourt, 1944, reprinted, Penguin, 1977.
The Hero with a Thousand Faces, Pantheon, 1949, revised edition, Princeton University Press, 1980.
The Masks of God, Viking, Volume 1: *Primitive Mythology*, 1959, Volume 2: *Oriental Mythology*, 1962, Volume 3: *Occidental Mythology*, 1964, Volume 4: *Creative Mythology*, 1968.
The Flight of the Wild Gander, Viking, 1969.

Myths to Live By, Viking, 1972.
(With M. J. Abadie) *The Mythic Image*, Princeton University Press, 1974.
(With Richard Roberts) *Tarot Revelations*, Alchemy Books, 1980, 2nd edition, Vernal Equinox, 1982.
Historical Atlas of World Mythology, Van der Marck, Volume 1: *The Way of the Animal Powers*, 1983, revised edition published in two parts, Part 1: *Mythologies of the Primitive Hunters and Gatherers*, 1988, Part 2: *Mythology of the Great Hunt*, 1988, Volume 2: *The Way of the Seeded Earth*, Part 1: *The Sacrifice*, 1988.
The Inner Reaches of Outer Space: Metaphor as Myth and as Religion, Van der Marck, 1986.
(With Bill Moyers) *The Power of Myth* (also see below; interviews), Doubleday, 1988.
(With Moyers) ''The Power of Myth'' (six-part television series), Public Broadcasting Service, 1988.

EDITOR

Heinrich Robert Zimmer, *Myths and Symbols in Indian Art and Civilization*, Pantheon, 1946, reprinted, Princeton University Press, 1971.
Zimmer, *The King and the Corpse: Tales of the Soul's Conquest of Evil*, Pantheon, 1948, reprinted, Princeton University Press, 1971.
Zimmer, *Philosophies of India*, Pantheon, 1951, reprinted, Princeton University Press, 1969.
The Portable Arabian Nights, Viking, 1952.
(General editor) *Papers from the Eranos Yearbooks*, Princeton University Press, Volume 1: *Spirit and Nature*, 1954, Volume 2: *The Mysteries*, 1955, Volume 3: *Man and Time*, 1957, Volume 4: *Spiritual Disciplines*, 1960, Volume 5: *Man and Transformation*, 1964, Volume 6: *The Mystic Vision*, 1969.
Zimmer, *The Art of Indian Asia*, Pantheon, 1955, 2nd edition in two volumes, Princeton University Press, 1960.
Myths, Dreams, and Religion, Dutton, 1970, reprinted, Spring Publications, 1988.
The Portable Jung, Viking, 1972.
Rato K. Losang, *My Life and Times: The Story of a Tibetan Incarnation*, Dutton, 1977.

Also editor of *The Mountainy Singer* by Seosamh MacCathmhaoil, AMS Press. General editor of ''Myth and Man'' series, Thames & Hudson, 1951-54.

CONTRIBUTOR

The Complete Grimm's Fairy Tales, Pantheon, 1944, reprinted, Random House, 1972.
James Joyce: Two Decades of Criticism, Vanguard, 1948.
Psychoanalysis and Culture, International Universities Press, 1951.
Basic Beliefs, Sheridan, 1959.
Culture in History, Columbia University Press, 1960.
Myth and Mythmaking, Braziller, 1960.
Myths, McGraw, 1974.

Contributor of articles to publications.

WORK IN PROGRESS: Further volumes in the *Historical Atlas of World Mythology*.

SIDELIGHTS: One of the world's leading authorities on mythology and folklore, Joseph Campbell believed that all myth has a common source in the biology of man himself. Mythology is ''a production of the human imagination,'' he told D. J. R. Bruckner of the *New York Times Book Review*, ''which is moved by the energies of the organs of the body operating against each other. These are the same in human beings all over the world and this is the basis for the archetypology of myth." Campbell saw the world's myths, religions, and rituals to be humanity's explanations for the essential mystery of creation. "God," Garry Abrams of the *Los Angeles Times* quoted Campbell explaining, "is a metaphor for a mystery that absolutely transcends all categories of human thought. . . . It's as simple as that." Jeffrey Hart of the *National Review* explained that Campbell "sought out the great overarching patterns of human perception that underlie the stories human beings tell about themselves, that inform the works of art they create and the rites they perform." For modern man, Campbell advocated a new mythology, "a modern, planetary myth," he told Chris Goodrich of *Publishers Weekly,* "not one of this group or that group." Campbell's work made him "known among an avid circle of friends and admirers as the Western world's foremost authority on mythology," K. C. Cole wrote in *Newsweek.* Hart called Campbell "a great modern anthropologist, . . . a great modern artist, . . . [and] one of the last survivors of the heroic age of twentieth-century modernism. Like Goethe, whom he worshipped, he combined science and art."

As a young boy in New York City, Campbell was first drawn to mythology by his interest in the American Indians. After a visit to Buffalo Bill's Wild West Show at Madison Square Garden, Campbell invaded his local library and read every book they had about Indian tribes. He spent his spare time touring the American Museum of Natural History with his brother and sister, enthralled by the Indian exhibits there. In school he studied the primitive cultures of the South Pacific and by the time he entered college, Campbell had a wide knowledge of folklore and mythology. Majoring in English and earning a degree in medieval literature, he dropped out of Columbia University's doctoral program when told that mythology was not a fit subject for his thesis. For several years he studied mythology on his own. A stay in California allowed him to accompany a scientific expedition along the Alaskan coast. For a year and a half he lived in a cabin in rural Woodstock, New York, reading scholarly works on mythology, legends, and folklore. In 1932, he was offered a teaching position with his old preparatory school, the Canterbury School, in New Milford, Connecticut. In 1934, he moved to Sarah Lawrence College, where he was to teach literature until 1972.

During his years as a teacher, Campbell produced a massive body of work in the fields of comparative mythology, folklore, and religion. He began during the 1940s by editing the works of the late Heinrich Zimmer, a friend of his who had been a noted Indologist at Columbia University. With Henry Morton Robinson, Campbell also wrote a literary interpretation of James Joyce's novel *Finnegans Wake* in which the story's origins in ancient myth are explained. The book, *A Skeleton Key to "Finnegans Wake,"* is, Andrew Klavan recounted in the *Village Voice,* "still a standard textbook 44 years after its publication."

Campbell's first book as sole author, *The Hero with a Thousand Faces,* took him four years to write. Campbell felt "that the four years he put into *The Hero* were sublime madness, a passage of joyous creativity he has not matched since," Donald Newlove reported in *Esquire. The Hero with a Thousand Faces* attempts to unite the world's mythologies into what Campbell called a "monomyth," the single underlying story which all the myths tell. This story outlines the proper way for man to live. "In Campbell's view," Cole said of the book's

thesis, "the myths are not merely entertaining tales, but are allegorical instructions that seek to teach us, as he put it, nothing less than 'how to live a human lifetime under any circumstances.'"

The Hero with a Thousand Faces focuses on the many tales of heroes who overcome great odds to perform impossible tasks. Campbell discerns a consistent pattern in these tales: The hero is called to an adventure which he accepts; he is given charms or magical weapons by a protective figure who is older and wiser; the hero then journeys into an unknown land where he meets demons and undergoes great suffering; the hero triumphs over the menace and is reborn in the process; he then returns to his homeland enriched with new insights that will benefit his people. Campbell saw this story as primarily an inner battle in which the hero undergoes a kind of self-psychotherapy, confronts his own darker side, and gains a greater understanding of himself and his culture in the process.

Early reviewers of *The Hero with a Thousand Faces* were put off by Campbell's almost mystical tone. "It is all presented," complained Max Radin of the *New York Times,* "in the mystical and pseudo-philosophical fog of Jung." H. A. Reinhold of *Commonweal* found the book to be "full of inconclusive tales [and] vague and shadowy parallels." The *New Yorker* critic judged *The Hero with a Thousand Faces* to be "one of the most fascinating and maddening books of the season." Despite such critical misgivings, the book was awarded a grant-in-literature from the National Institute of Arts and Letters and went on to sell several hundred thousand copies. And Abrams reported that *The Hero with a Thousand Faces* "still sells 10,000 copies a year."

In the four-volume work *The Masks of God,* Campbell surveyed the world's mythology, arguing on behalf of his idea of the monomyth. The first volume, *Primitive Mythology,* begins with the religious ideas of the Bronze Age, when prehistoric men were still hunters and gatherers. At this time, Campbell believed, mankind was stamped with a basic set of religious beliefs, a coda of responses to his questions about the nature of the universe. These beliefs grew from the daily life of early man, a life that consisted of hunting for food, constant migration, and the observance of the cosmos. Because of this experience, peoples throughout the world developed common rituals and beliefs revolving around the hunt, astronomy, and the cycles of nature.

Primitive Mythology, according to Joseph Bram of the *Library Journal,* is "truly thought-provoking and in some ways path breaking and should be welcomed as a real contribution to the ancient science of mythology." But other critics were less sure about the book's importance. S. P. Dunn, in his review for the *American Anthropologist,* claimed that "Campbell has written a stimulating, disturbing, often quite exasperating book." M. E. Opler of the *New York Herald Tribune Book Review* found himself "alternately exhilarated and puzzled. . . . But if Campbell seems sometimes wrong, he is never dull." Philip Rieff of the *American Sociological Review* called *Primitive Mythology* "highly readable, almost too much so. Campbell cannot resist telling a good story. . . . Not all are necessary to his argument." "This work," the *Kirkus* reviewer commented, "is one of enormous scholarship."

The second volume of *The Masks of God,* entitled *Oriental Mythology,* turns to the East, covering the myths of Egypt, Japan, China, and India. Campbell discusses the particularly Asian ideas of reincarnation and transcendence of the ego, tracing their historical emergence in Eastern culture. Alan Watts, writing of the book for *Saturday Review,* called it "the first time that anyone has put the rich complexities of Asian mythology into a clear historical perspective.... What Mr. Campbell is offering here is not so much a mythological encyclopedia as a thoroughly documented discussion of the development of myth and of its function in human cultures. It is a bold, imaginative, deeply stimulating work."

Campbell followed the same historical approach in *Occidental Mythology,* the third volume in the series. Beginning with the prehistoric belief in a mother-goddess, he follows the course of Western religious belief down through the centuries. A strong contrast in attitude is shown between the beliefs of the East and West, a difference that Campbell felt was due to environment. The harsher landscape of the West "challenged man to shape his own destiny," explained Bram, "whereas India and the Far East have always fostered the attitudes of passivity, resignation, and fatalism." Watts, reviewing the book for *New Republic,* thought it to be "the best and richest" volume in the series.

The Masks of God concludes with the volume *Creative Mythology,* in which Campbell shifts his attention from the myths of the past, created by anonymous authors, to those of the present, which have been created by such artists and writers as Dante, James Joyce, and T. S. Eliot. He argues that a new mythology is needed, one that speaks to the entire human race in modern terms, and one that is created by the individual artist from his own life. The book, the *New Yorker* critic summarized, "deals with the modern 'secular' use of myth to express individual experience." Gerald Sykes of the *New York Times Book Review* saw a "major implication" of the book to be that "although we were once given our myths by the group that nurtured us, now we must mine them painfully from the depths of our own experience." Newlove claimed that in *Creative Mythology* Campbell "is out to show the face of God burning away the received masks of culture and to herald the birth within." The *Choice* reviewer called *Creative Mythology* "a landmark in its field," while Bram concluded that it was "a major work of inspired scholarship that no student of mythology will be able to ignore."

In *The Mythic Image* Campbell turned to the origins of myth, arguing that man's unconscious mind, particularly his dreams, formed the basis of all mythology. Through the use of 400 illustrations drawn from all over the world, and ranging from prehistoric cave paintings to the avant-garde works of the present day, he showed how the relationship between myth and dream was evident in mankind's artistic creations. Peter S. Prescott of *Newsweek* described the book as "an iconography of the human spirit." Although he felt that psychologist Carl Jung had raised the same point earlier with his theory of the universal unconscious, Winthrop Sargeant of the *New Yorker* nonetheless believed that the idea "has never before been given such a clear and splendid demonstration" as in *The Mythic Image.* Prescott concluded that the book's premise "is convincing, and elegantly supported by hundreds of excellent reproductions of art."

In 1983 Campbell published the first of a planned six-volume series entitled *Historical Atlas of World Mythology,* a work meant to relate the world's mythological history in a single, all-encompassing narrative. The initial volume, *The Way of the Animal Powers,* covers the beginnings of human culture and examines the early myth of the Great Hunt, a story common to many prehistoric hunting peoples. Combining an au-

thoritative text with an extensive collection of relevant artwork, *The Way of the Animal Powers* is "a beautiful and informative volume by a world-renowned scholar," as C. Robert Nixon commented in *Library Journal.* Wendy O'Flaherty of the *New York Times Book Review* claimed that "no one but Joseph Campbell could conceive of such a scheme or carry it out as boldly as he does in this extraordinary book.... It is an exhilarating experience." Hart concluded that *The Way of the Animal Powers* is "one of the great works of our time."

The second volume in the *Historical Atlas of World Mythology, The Way of the Seeded Earth,* moves forward in time, focusing on the mythology of the first agricultural communities and contrasting the beliefs of that time with the earlier beliefs of the hunting cultures. As Campbell explained to Goodrich: "In *The Way of the Animal Powers,* ... people are killing animals all the time; that's where the base of the culture rests. This second book is about women's magic—birth and nourishment. The myth shifts from the male-oriented to the gestation-oriented, and the image is of the plant world." At the time of his death in 1987, Campbell had not yet completed the six volumes of the *Historical Atlas of World Mythology.*

Campbell's last project was a number of interviews with Bill Moyers for a special Public Broadcasting Service television program entitled "The Power of Myth." These interviews were broadcast in 1988 as a six-part series, drawing an audience of some two-and-a-half million people for each episode. A best-selling book based on the television program was also released, while a video cassette version has sold over 50,000 copies. "The Power of Myth" allows Campbell to range over a host of topics, including the mythology of many cultures, the role of myth in modern society, and the possibilities for myth-making in the future. "Intermittently provocative and ponderous, the conversations are a rambling, serendipitous intellectual journey," explained Clifford Terry of the *Chicago Tribune.* Ironically, because of the program's popularity, Campbell became known to more people after his death than knew him while he was alive. As Cole noted, "Campbell has become something of a legend himself.... The hero is dead, but the message lives on."

At the time of his death in late 1987 Campbell had become "one of the world's great scholars and teachers of mythology," Terry reported. His prominence rested as much on his scholarly prowess as on his ability to appeal to a mass audience. As Cole remarked, "Campbell has become the rarest of intellectuals in American life: a serious thinker who has been embraced by the popular culture." Among his most fervent disciples has been filmmaker George Lucas, who credited Campbell with inspiring his movie "Star Wars." "If it hadn't been for him," Lucas told Wolfgang Saxon of the *New York Times,* "it's possible I would still be trying to write 'Star Wars' today." Sir Lauren van der Post, writing in the London *Times,* cited Campbell for his efforts to "rediscover for a deprived world the fundamental mythological pattern of the human spirit.... He has done more than any scholar of our time to reconnect modern man to a reality which his mind and spirit were rejecting at great peril to his well-being and sanity." Joseph Coates of the *Chicago Tribune* called Campbell "that rare scholar with something really useful to say about how life should be lived."

MEDIA ADAPTATIONS: "The Power of Myth" television series is available on video cassette from Mystic Fire Video, 1988.

BIOGRAPHICAL/CRITICAL SOURCES:

BOOKS

Campbell, Joseph and Bill Moyers, *The Power of Myth*, Doubleday, 1988.

PERIODICALS

American Anthropologist, December, 1960.
American Sociological Review, December, 1960.
Chicago Tribune, May 23, 1988.
Choice, December, 1968.
Christian Science Monitor, October 9, 1969.
Commentary, December, 1969.
Commonweal, July 8, 1949.
Esquire, September, 1977.
Kirkus, August 15, 1959.
Library Journal, September 1, 1959, January 15, 1964, February 15, 1968, January, 1984.
Los Angeles Times, May 27, 1987.
National Review, July 13, 1984.
New Republic, June 27, 1964.
Newsweek, March 31, 1975, November 14, 1988.
New Yorker, May 7, 1949, February 1, 1969, July 21, 1975.
New York Herald Tribune Book Review, November 22, 1959.
New York Times, June 26, 1949, March 22, 1987.
New York Times Book Review, May 18, 1969, December 18, 1983.
Publishers Weekly, August 23, 1985.
Saturday Review, June 2, 1962.
Times (London), July 12, 1984.
Village Voice, August 1, 1968, May 24, 1988.

FILMS

"A Hero's Journey: The World of Joseph Campbell," William Free, 1987.

OBITUARIES:

PERIODICALS

Chicago Tribune, November 5, 1987.
Los Angeles Times, November 30, 1987.
National Review, December 4, 1987.
New York Times, November 3, 1987.
Parabola, spring, 1988.
Time, November 16, 1987.
Washington Post, November 4, 1987.*

—*Sketch by Thomas Wiloch*

*   *   *

CARLSON, Vada F.   1897-
(Florella Rose)

PERSONAL: Born February 27, 1897, in Cody, Neb.; daughter of Fred Lorenzo (employed in building trades) and Hattie F. (Ditson) Rose; married Albert B. Carlson, July 22, 1917 (divorced, 1937); married Jose C. Rodriguez (an artist), January 29, 1972; children: Lois Rose (Mrs. Earl A. Toburen), Wayne B. *Education:* Attended public schools in Cody and Gordon, Neb.; took correspondence courses; attended Mexico City writing school. *Politics:* Republican. *Religion:* Methodist.

ADDRESSES: Home—123 West Fourth St., Winslow, Ariz. 86047.

CAREER: Began working at age sixteen as a telephone operator in Cody, Wyo.; writer and woman's page editor on papers in Riverton, Wyo., at various intervals, 1915-32, Concord, Calif., 1932-37, and Pittsburg, Calif., 1938-41; Columbia Steel, Pittsburg, secretary to foundry superintendent, 1942-45; newspaper editor, Concord, 1946-48; publisher of own paper in Oakley, Calif., 1948-49; woman's page editor of *Winslow Mail*, Winslow, Ariz., 1955-56, and *Flagstaff Daily Sun*, Flagstaff, Ariz., 1956-57, 1963-64; *Winslow Mail*, editor, 1965-66; A.R.E. Press, Virginia Beach, Va., editor of children's magazine, 1968-70.

MEMBER: National Federation of Press Women (regional director, 1965-67), American Association of Retired Persons, Arizona Press Women (president, 1957-58), Winslow Arts Association (founder; president, 1962-64), Business and Professional Woman's Club, Order of Eastern Star, Soroptimist Club.

AWARDS, HONORS: Business Woman of the Year, Business and Professional Woman's Club, 1965; named Woman of Achievement by National Federation of Press Women, Winslow Woman of the Year by Winslow Chamber of Commerce, and Woman of the Year by Arizona Press Women; holder of more than sixty awards for writing.

WRITINGS:

We Saw the Sundance, Graphic Press, 1948.
The Desert Speaks (poetry), Ranger Press, 1956.
This Is Our Valley (history of Santa Maria Valley), Westernlore, 1959, 3rd edition, 1977.
(Ghost writer for Clara Edge) *Tahirih*, Eerdmans, 1963.
(With Elizabeth W. White [Indian name, Polingaysi Qoyawayma]), *No Turning Back*, University of New Mexico Press, 1964.
Fluffy and the Flyaway Fly (juvenile), Whitman Publishing, 1966.
Little Lamb, Whitman Publishing, 1968.
(With Gary Witherspoon) *Black Mountain Boy* (juvenile), Navajo Curriculum Center Press (Rough Rock, Ariz.), 1968, revised edition, 1972.
(Editor) *Coyote Legends*, Navajo Curriculum Center Press, 1968.
The Vision and the Promise (juvenile), A.R.E. Press, 1969.
The Sacred Summer, A.R.E. Press, 1969.
The Great Migration, A.R.E. Press, 1970.
High Country Canvas, Northland Press, 1972.
East of the Sun (anthology), A.R.E. Press, 1972.
Wanderer in the Wilderness, Harvey House, 1973.
Cochise: Chief of the Chiricahuas, Harvey House, 1973.
John Charles Fremont: Adventurer in the Wilderness (biography), Harvey House, 1973.
John Wesley Powell: Conquest of the Canyon (juvenile), Harvey House, 1974.
Porcelain Pony, privately printed, 1979.
(With husband, Joe Rodriguez) *They Came to the Little Colorado*, privately printed, 1980.
(With Rodriguez) *A Town Is Born: The First Fifty Years of Winslow, Arizona*, privately printed, 1982.
Fred Turley and Promontory Lookout, edited by D. R. Ayres, illustrations by Jerome Breezin, D. R. Ayres, 1987.

JUVENILES; UNDER PSEUDONYM FLORELLA ROSE

Peter Picket Pin, Whitman, 1953.
Yipee Kiyi, Whitman, 1954.
Yipee Kiyi and Whoa Boy, Whitman, 1955.

OTHER

Also author of *Broken Pattern: Sunlight and Shadows of Hopi History,* Naturegraph, of the children's story, *The Adventures of Hop-tee-ma-lou,* 1986, of two anniversary pageants, "A Tale of Todos Santos," 1948, and "And Still the River," and of the introduction to *Arizona History,* 1975. Special writer for golden anniversary edition, *Riverton Ranger,* 1956. Contributor of articles and poetry to magazines.

WORK IN PROGRESS: With Love—To Greece, an account of Carlson's three trips to Greece, 1961, 1966, and 1970; *Battle Butte,* a novel; (with Rodriguez) *Roundup,* a book of poems; (with Rodriguez) a documentary of the Beale Road through Arizona.

SIDELIGHTS: Vada F. Carlson wrote *CA:* "Aside from travel, which I love, [I] relax by doing oil paintings and by reading. One of my greatest pleasures is knowing that my pageant, 'And Still the River,' was shown for the second time in 1981, and is scheduled for the Centennial Celebration of 2006. My first pageant (1948) was 'A Tale of Todos Santos,' a story of the beginning of the town of Concord, California.

"[I] was born near the Rosebud Reservation and have lived near Indians most of my life. . . . When, at Christmas of my fourteenth year, I was taken out of school because my mother was ill, her twelfth child expected that next spring, I thought the world had come to an end for me. I had been taking normal training courses in high school that would make it possible for me to get, and teach, a country school at sixteen. My destination [instead] was the lonely sandhill section of Nebraska where my father had filed on a homestead.

"I had barely celebrated my fifteenth birthday of the next year—1912—when a terrible blizzard blew in, penning us, father, mother, my two little sisters and one brother, into the tiny, tar-papered claim shack. It was during those frightening four days that I began writing my first short story, which I named 'A Tangled Web.' Eventually we dug out and life assumed its usual pace, but that was my first attempt to put my thoughts into story form. The tangled web was never satisfactorily untangled, but it seemed to foreshadow my life, which went from one tangle to the other until 1970 when I settled down and began the task of *seriously* putting my thoughts in order and on paper.

"Now, in the beginning of my nineties, I still hope to see another of my books in print before the little typewriter and I go into storage."

*　　　*　　　*

CARO, Francis G(eorge)　1936-

PERSONAL: Born September 28, 1936, in Milwaukee, Wis.; son of Walter (an engineer) and Elizabeth (Voss) Caro; married Carol Bauer (a librarian), December 28, 1965; children: Paul, David. *Education:* Marquette University, B.S., 1958; University of Minnesota, Ph.D., 1962. *Politics:* Democrat.

ADDRESSES: Home—262 Farrington Ave., North Tarrytown, N.Y. 10591. *Office*—Gerontology Institute, University of Massachusetts—Boston, Boston, Mass. 02125.

CAREER: Community Studies, Inc., Kansas City, Mo., research associate, 1962-64; Community Progress, Inc., New Haven, Conn., research associate, 1964-65; Marquette University, Milwaukee, Wis., assistant professor of sociology, 1965-67; University of Colorado, Boulder, associate professor

of sociology, 1967-70; Brandeis University, Waltham, Mass., associate professor of social welfare, 1970-74; Community Service Society, New York, N.Y., director of Institute for Social Welfare Research, 1974-88; University of Massachusetts—Boston, Gerontology Institute, director of Manning Research Division, 1988—.

MEMBER: American Sociological Association, Society for the Study of Social Problems, Gerontological Society, Evaluation Research Society.

WRITINGS:

(Editor) *Readings in Evaluation Research,* Russell Sage, 1970, 2nd edition, 1977.
(Co-author) *Family Care of the Elderly,* Heath, 1981.
(Contributor) E. M. Goldberg and N. Connelly, *Evaluative Research in Social Care,* Heinemann, 1982.
(Co-author) *Revisiting the Default Debtor,* Community Service Society of New York, 1983.
(Contributor) H. E. Freeman and others, *Applied Sociology,* Jossey-Bass, 1983.
(Co-author) *Quality Impact of Home Care for the Elderly,* Haworth Press, 1988.

Contributor to gerontology and evaluation research journals.

WORK IN PROGRESS: Papers on supports for families with developmentally disabled children and redefinition of poverty standards.

*　　　*　　　*

CARR, Philippa
See HIBBERT, Eleanor Burford

*　　　*　　　*

CASEY, Brigid　1950-

PERSONAL: Born January 11, 1950, in New York, N.Y.; daughter of Michael T. (an educator) and Rosemary (an editor; maiden name, Christmann) Casey; married Dennis R. Meyer; children: Liam Joseph Meyer, Megan Michel Meyer. *Education:* St. Francis College, Brooklyn, N.Y., B.A., 1972; New York University, M.A., 1976.

ADDRESSES: Office—109 Vley Rd., Scotia, N.Y. 12302.

WRITINGS:

(With Sigmund A. Lavine) *Wonders of the World of Horses,* Dodd, 1972.
(With Lavine) *Wonders of Ponies,* Dodd, 1980.
(With Wendy Haugh) *Sled Dogs,* Dodd, 1983.
(With Lavine) *Wonders of Draft Horses,* Dodd, 1983.
(Contributor) Ron Klug and Lyn Klug, *The Christian Family Easter Book,* Augsburg, 1989.

Contributor of stories and articles to *Cobblestone, Friend, Baby Talk, Saratoga Style,* and *Schenectady Magazine.*

*　　　*　　　*

CASSEL, Don　1942-

PERSONAL: Born April 4, 1942, in Galt, Ontario, Canada; son of Kenneth W. (a laborer) and Aleda (Cressman) Cassel; married Barbara Winger, May 20, 1976; children: Carina, Pamela. *Education:* York University, B.A., 1975.

ADDRESSES: Home—8 Markham St., Bramalea, Ontario, Canada L6S 2X7. *Office*—Humber College, Rexdale, Ontario, Canada M9W 5L7.

CAREER: International Business Machines Corp., Toronto, Ontario, 1961-69, began as programmer trainee, became senior programmer and analyst; Humber College, Rexdale, Ontario, instructor and head of department of computer studies, 1969—. Vice-president of Computer Education Group, 1981-83.

WRITINGS:

Programming Language One, Reston, 1972.
BASIC Programming in Real Time, Reston, 1975.
PL/I: A Structured Approach, Reston, 1978.
Introduction to Computers and Information Processing, Reston, 1980.
BASIC Made Easy, Reston, 1980.
Introduction to Computers and Information Processing: Language-Free Edition, Reston, 1981.
Introduction to Computers and Information Processing: With BASIC, COBOL, FORTRAN, PASCAL, Reston, 1981.
The Structured Alternative: An Introduction to Program Design Coding, Style, Debugging, and Testing, Reston, 1983.
FORTRAN Made Easy, Reston, 1983.
BASIC 4.0 Programming for the PET/CBM, W. C. Brown, 1983.
BASIC Programming for the VIC-20, W. C. Brown, 1983.
Computers Made Easy, Reston, 1984.
WordStar Simplified for the IBM Personal Computer, Prentice-Hall, 1984.
Easy Writer Simplified for the IBM Personal Computer, Prentice-Hall, 1985.
dBASE II Simplified for the IBM Personal Computer, Prentice-Hall, 1985.
Lotus 1, 2, 3 Simplified for the IBM Personal Computer, Prentice-Hall, 1985.
WATCOM BASIC Made Easy, Prentice-Hall, 1986.
Introduction to Structured COBOL and Program Design, Prentice-Hall, 1987.
Advanced Structured COBOL and Program Design, Prentice-Hall, 1987.

Also author of "An Introduction to Microcomputers," an audio-visual presentation released by Prentice-Hall Media, 1983.

*   *   *

CATE, Robert L(ouis)   1932-

PERSONAL: Born August 11, 1932, in Nashville, Tenn.; son of George H., Sr. (an attorney) and Lucile (Cowherd) Cate; married Dorothy Wright (a dealer in antiques), August 17, 1951; children: Ruth Cate Ackermann, Robert Louis, Jr., Fred H. *Education:* Vanderbilt University, B.Eng., 1953; Southern Baptist Theological Seminary, B.D., 1956, Ph.D., 1960.

ADDRESSES: Home—562 Storer Dr., Mill Valley, Calif. 94941. *Office*—Dean of Academic Affairs, Golden Gate Baptist Theological Seminary, Mill Valley, Calif. 94941.

CAREER: Ordained Southern Baptist minister, 1952; pastor of Southern Baptist churches in Bethpage, Tenn., 1952-53, and Campbellsville, Ky., 1955-57; Southern Baptist Theological Seminary, Louisville, Ky., instructor in Hebrew, 1959; pastor of Southern Baptist churches in McRae, Ga., 1959-64, and Aiken, S.C., 1964-75; Golden Gate Baptist Theological Seminary, Mill Valley, Calif., associate professor, 1975-78, professor of Old Testament, 1978-84, dean of academic affairs 1984—. Member of General Board of the South Carolina Baptist Convention, 1966-68. Aiken-Barnwell Community Mental Health Center, member of board of directors, 1967-69, chairman of board, 1969-74. Member of board of trustees of Tift College, 1961-63, Furman University, 1970-74, and Southern Baptist Theological Seminary, 1974. Seminar leader.

MEMBER: Society of Biblical Literature, National Association of Professors of Hebrew, Baptist Professors of Religion, Society for Old Testament Studies (England), Tau Beta Pi.

WRITINGS:

(Contributor) Herschel Hobbs and Franklin Paschall, editors, *Teacher's Bible Commentary*, Broadman, 1972.
Layman's Bible Commentary: Exodus, Broadman, 1979.
Old Testament Roots for New Testament Faith, Broadman, 1979.
How to Interpret the Bible, Broadman, 1983.
Help in Ages Past, Hope for Years to Come, Prentice-Hall, 1983.
These Sought a Country: A History of Israel in Old Testament Times, Broadman, 1985.
An Introduction to the Old Testament and Its Study, Broadman, 1987.
Discovering Judges, Ruth, I and II Samuel, Guideposts, 1988.
A History of the New Testament Era, Broadman, 1990.
Discovering Jeremiah and Lamentation, Guideposts, in press.
A History of the Bible Lands in the Interbiblical Period, Broadman, in press.

Author of church school curriculum material. Contributor to religious magazines and denominational newspapers.

SIDELIGHTS: Robert L. Cate wrote: "Because of my earlier ignorance of the Bible in general and the Old Testament in particular, I feel a special responsibility to try to make the Old Testament live for contemporary people. It is not just a book of ancient stories, it is our story as well. Most Christians are weak in their understanding of the Old Testament due to two things. First, they do not realize just how much the New Testament is build upon the Old. Second, the Old Testament covers such a long period of history and deals with such strange cultures and peoples that they have felt it was impossible ever to master. At the same time, there is usually a deep feeling of guilt at failing to understand the Old Testament, since it is a part of our Bible, that people avoid the guilty feeling by avoiding the Old Testament. My years of service as a pastor have led me to a deep belief that laymen both want to be able to deal with the Old Testament and can handle it if they are given the proper tools; therefore, most of my writing is specifically aimed at making the best results of biblical scholarship both available and understandable to lay people. The end result will be a strengthening of the biblical knowledge of the laity.

"Another real need among both ministers and laymen is the development and maintenance of a devotional life. The many demands of our daily schedules increase the problem. Both as a pastor and as a teacher I struggled with this problem for my parishioners and my students. Further, there is a feeling among some people that a thorough knowledge and practice of biblical scholarship is a serious hindrance to reading the Bible devotionally. *Help in Ages Past, Hope for Years to Come* is my response to this. It is a book of daily devotionals based upon Old Testament passages where biblical scholarship is used to enhance the devotional use of the Bible. These were actually used in the classroom in the classes I have taught. My writing has become a ministry with me, where I seek to extend myself to those I cannot serve personally. It is my attempt to help people hear God's good news.''

AVOCATIONAL INTERESTS: Travel (United States, England, Europe, the Middle and Far East).

*   *   *

CELINE, Louis-Ferdinand
   See DESTOUCHES, Louis-Ferdinand

*   *   *

CHANDLER, David (Geoffrey)   1934-

PERSONAL: Born January 15, 1934, in England; son of Geoffrey Edmund (a clergyman) and Joyce Mary (Ridsdale) Chandler; married Gillian Dixon (a part-time indexer), February 18, 1961; children: Paul Geoffrey, John Roger, Mark David. *Education:* Keble College, Oxford, B.A. (with second class honors), 1955, Diploma of Education, 1956, M.A., 1960. *Politics:* Conservative. *Religion:* Church of England.

ADDRESSES: Home—''Hindford,'' Monteagle Lane, Yateley, near Camberley, Surrey, England. *Office*—Department of War Studies, Royal Military Academy Sandhurst, Camberley, Surrey, England.

CAREER: Royal Military Academy Sandhurst, Camberley, Surrey, England, lecturer in politics and modern history, 1960-61, lecturer, 1961-64, senior lecturer in military history, 1964-70, deputy head of department, 1970-80, head of department of war studies and international affairs, 1980—. Visiting professor, Ohio State University, 1970, Virginia Military Institute, 1988; visiting lecturer, Naval War College, 1974 and 1983. *Military service:* British Army, 1957-60; seconded to Nigerian Military Forces; became captain.

MEMBER: International Commission of Military History (international vice-president, 1975—), Royal Historical Society (fellow), Royal Geographical Society (fellow), Society for Army Historical Research (council member), Army Records Society (council member).

WRITINGS:

(Contributor) C. Falls, editor, *Great Military Battles*, Weidenfeld & Nicolson, 1965.
(Editor) *A Traveller's Guide to the Battlefields of Europe*, two volumes, Hugh Evelyn, 1965, Chilton, 1966.
The Campaigns of Napoleon, Macmillan, 1966.
(Contributor) Brian Bond, editor, *Victorian Military Campaigns*, Hutchinson, 1967.
(Contributor) *History of the Second World War*, Purnell & Sons, 1967.
(Editor) Robert Parker and Comte de Merode-Westerloo, *The Marlborough Wars*, Shoe String, 1968.
(Contributor) *New Cambridge Modern History*, Cambridge University Press, 1971.
Marlborough as Military Commander, Scribner, 1973, new edition, 1979.
Napoleon, Saturday Review Press, 1974.
Art of Warfare on Land, Hamlyn, 1974.
Art of War in the Age of Marlborough, Batsford, 1976.
A Dictionary of the Napoleonic Wars, Macmillan, 1979.
An Atlas of Military Strategy, 1618-1878, Free Press, 1980.
Waterloo: The Hundred Days, Macmillan, 1980.

(Editor) John Marshall Deere, *A Journal of Marlborough's Campaigns*, Society for Army Historical Research, 1984.
(Editor) *Napoleon's Marshalls*, Macmillan, 1987.
(Editor) *The Dictionary of Battles*, Holt, 1987.
(Editor) *The Military Maxims of Napoleon*, Macmillan, 1987.

Contributor to military and historical journals.

WORK IN PROGRESS: Battles of the Second World War, for Arms and Armour; revisions for a new edition of *A Traveller's Guide to the Battlefields of Europe*, for Thorsons, and of *Napoleon*, for Paul Press.

SIDELIGHTS: David Chandler has made lecture tours to British bases in the Mediterranean, Far East, Germany, and to universities and other institutions in the United States. He has also made battlefield tours to Flanders, northern Italy, Belgium, Germany, the United States, and France.

AVOCATIONAL INTERESTS: Sailing, war games, model ship construction, gardening, camping.

BIOGRAPHICAL/CRITICAL SOURCES:

PERIODICALS

Guardian (London), December 21, 1981.
St. Louis Post-Dispatch, December 17, 1967.

*   *   *

CHAPMAN, Clark Russell   1945-

PERSONAL: Born May 13, 1945, in Palo Alto, Calif.; son of Seville (a physicist) and Mary (Bried) Chapman; married Jennalyn Weed (a librarian), June, 1966; children: Ginette. *Education:* Harvard University, A.B., 1967; Massachusetts Institute of Technology, M.S., 1968, Ph.D., 1972.

ADDRESSES: Home—6160 North Montebella, Tucson, Ariz. 85704. *Office*—Planetary Science Institute, Suite 201, 2030 East Speedway, Tucson, Ariz. 85719.

CAREER: Illinois Institute of Technology, Chicago, research scientist in astroscience, 1971-72; Science Applications International Corp., Planetary Science Institute, Tucson, Ariz., senior scientist, 1972—. Consultant to National Aeronautics and Space Administration (NASA), 1975-88, University Space Research Association, 1975-78, National Academy of Sciences, 1977-80, Scientists' Institute for Public Information, 1979—, French Space Agency, 1980, Tucson Public Library, 1981-83, and M.I.T. Corp. visiting committee, 1986—.

MEMBER: International Astronomical Union (president of Commission 15, 1982-85), American Association for the Advancement of Science, American Astronomical Society (chairman of Division for Planetary Sciences, 1982-83), American Astronomical Association, American Geophysical Union, American Planning Association, Meteoritical Society.

WRITINGS:

The Inner Planets: New Light on the Rocky Worlds of Mercury, Venus, Earth, the Moon, Mars, and the Asteroids, Scribner, 1977.
(Editor with D. P. Cruikshank) *Observing the Moon, Planets, and Comets*, Shramm & Groves, 1980.
Planets of Rock and Ice: From Mercury to the Moons of Saturn, Scribner, 1982.
(Co-editor) *Mercury*, University of Arizona Press, 1988.
(With David Morrison) *Cosmic Catastrophes*, Plenum, 1989.
The Asteroids, Smithsonian Institution Press, 1989.

Also author of NASA brochure, "Solar System Exploration: Discovering Our Origins and Destiny," 1988. Author of "News and Reviews" column in *Planetary Report*, 1981—. Contributor to periodicals. Associate editor of *Journal of Geophysical Research*, 1976-78; editor of Northwest Homeowners Association newsletter, 1979—.

WORK IN PROGRESS: Planning the Future of a Sun-Belt City, for University of Arizona Press.

SIDELIGHTS: New York Times Book Review writer Henry S. F. Cooper, Jr., welcomed Clark Russell Chapman's first book, *The Inner Planets: New Light on the Rocky Worlds of Mercury, Venus, Earth, the Moon, Mars, and the Asteroids.* "Given the explosion of information returned by NASA spacecraft from various parts of the solar system, it is high time someone thoroughly familiar with it made it seem less imposing, and this is exactly what Chapman has done in his lucid and informal book of essays," Cooper asserts. In addition, continues the critic, "implicit throughout is the fact that science itself is a sociological process, and that not the least interesting aspect of the recent developments is the interaction of the people making them." Chapman told *CA:* "Although my chief professional activity is scientific research, I am very interested in increasing public awareness and understanding of science. To this end I have participated in community educational programs and contributed to newspapers, magazines, and journals, in addition to writing books."

He adds: "My next writing project is to summarize my experiences as a Planning and Zoning Commissioner in Pima County, Arizona, and to address issues of urban growth in the sunbelt."

BIOGRAPHICAL/CRITICAL SOURCES:

PERIODICALS

New York Times Book Review, October 2, 1977.

*   *   *

CHEAPE, Charles Windsor 1945-

PERSONAL: Born October 11, 1945, in Charlottesville, Va.; son of Charles Windsor, Jr. (a telephone company engineer) and Evelyn Florence (a legal secretary) Cheape; married Cheryl Cooper (a physical therapist), August 10, 1974. *Education:* University of Virginia, B.A., 1968; Brandeis University, M.A., 1974, Ph.D., 1976.

ADDRESSES: Home—1425 Putty Hill Ave., Baltimore, Md. 21204. *Office*—Department of History, Loyola College, 4501 North Charles St., Baltimore, Md. 21210.

CAREER: Dartmouth College, Hanover, N.H., assistant professor, 1975-81, associate professor of history, 1981-83; Oklahoma State University, Stillwater, Okla., assistant professor, 1983-84; Loyola College, Baltimore, Md., associate professor, 1984—.

MEMBER: Organization of American Historians, Economic History Association, Business History Conference, Phi Beta Kappa.

WRITINGS:

Moving the Masses: Urban Public Transit in New York, Boston, and Philadelphia, 1880-1912, Harvard University Press, 1980.
Family Firm to Modern Multinational: Norton Company, a New England Enterprise, Harvard University Press, 1985.

Contributor to economic history journals.

WORK IN PROGRESS: A history of top management at DuPont in the twentieth century.

*   *   *

CHOMSKY, (Avram) Noam 1928-

PERSONAL: Born December 7, 1928, in Philadelphia, Pa.; son of William (a Hebrew scholar) and Elsie (Simonofsky) Chomsky; married Carol Schatz (a linguist and specialist on educational technology), December 24, 1949; children: Aviva, Diane, Harry Alan. *Education:* University of Pennsylvania, B.A., 1949, M.A., 1951, Ph.D., 1955. *Politics:* Libertarian socialist.

ADDRESSES: Home—15 Suzanne Rd., Lexington, Mass. 02173. *Office*—Room 20D-219, Massachusetts Institute of Technology, 77 Massachusetts Ave., Cambridge, Mass. 02139.

CAREER: Massachusetts Institute of Technology, Cambridge, assistant professor, 1955-58, associate professor, 1958-62, professor, 1962-65, Ferrari P. Ward Professor of Modern Languages and Linguistics, 1966-76, Institute Professor, 1976—. Visiting professor of linguistics, Columbia University, 1957-58, University of California, Los Angeles, 1966, University of California, Berkeley, 1966-67, and Syracuse University, 1982. Member, Institute of Advanced Study, Princeton University, 1958-59. John Locke lecturer, Oxford University, 1969; Bertrand Russell Memorial Lecturer, Cambridge University, 1971; Nehru Memorial Lecturer, University of New Delhi, 1972; Huizinga Lecturer, University of Leiden, 1977; Woodbridge Lecturer, Columbia University, 1978; Kant Lecturer, Stanford University, 1979.

MEMBER: National Academy of Sciences, American Academy of Arts and Sciences, Linguistic Society of America, American Philosophical Association, American Association for the Advancement of Science, British Academy (corresponding fellow), British Psychological Society (honorary member), Deutsche Akademie der Naturforscher Leopoldina, Utrecht Society of Arts and Sciences.

AWARDS, HONORS: Junior fellow, Harvard Society of Fellows, 1951-55; research fellow at Harvard Cognitive Studies Center, 1964-67; named one of the "makers of the twentieth century" by the London *Times,* 1970; Guggenheim fellowship, 1971-72; distinguished scientific contribution from American Psychological Association, 1984; Gustavus Myers Center Award, 1986 and 1988; George Orwell Award, National Council of Teachers of English, 1987; Kyoto Prize in Basic Sciences, 1988. Honorary degrees include D.H.L., University of Chicago, 1967, Loyola University of Chicago and Swarthmore College, 1970, Bard College, 1971, University of Massachusetts, 1973, and University of Pennsylvania, 1984; D.Litt., University of London, 1967, Delhi University, 1972, Visva-Bharati University (West Bengal), 1980.

WRITINGS:

Syntactic Structures, Mouton & Co., 1957, reprinted, 1978.
Current Issues in Linguistic Theory, Mouton & Co., 1964.
Aspects of the Theory of Syntax, M.I.T. Press, 1965, reprinted, 1986.
Cartesian Linguistics: A Chapter in the History of Rationalist Thought, Harper, 1966.
Topics in the Theory of Generative Grammar, Mouton & Co., 1966, reprinted, 1978.

(With Morris Halle) *Sound Patterns of English,* Harper, 1968.

Language and Mind, Harcourt, 1968, enlarged edition, 1972.

American Power and the New Mandarins, Pantheon, 1969.

At War with Asia, Pantheon, 1970.

Problems of Knowledge and Freedom: The Russell Lectures, Pantheon, 1971.

(With George A. Miller) *Analyse formelle des langues naturelles,* Mouton & Co., 1971.

Studies on Semantics in Generative Grammar, Mouton & Co., 1972.

(Editor with Howard Zinn) *The Pentagon Papers, Volume 5: Critical Essays,* Beacon Press, 1972.

(With Edward Herman) *Counterrevolutionary Violence,* Warner Modular, Inc., 1974.

Peace in the Middle East?, Pantheon, 1975.

The Logical Structure of Linguistic Theory, Plenum, 1975.

Reflections on Language, Pantheon, 1975.

Essays on Form and Interpretation, North-Holland, 1977.

Dialogues avec Mitsou Ronat, Flammarion, 1977, translation published as *Language and Responsibility,* Pantheon, 1979.

Human Rights and American Foreign Policy, Spokesman, 1978.

(With Herman) *The Political Economy of Human Rights,* Volume I: *The Washington Connection and Third World Fascism,* Volume II: *After the Cataclysm: Postwar Indochina and the Construction of Imperial Ideology,* South End, 1979.

Rules and Representations, Columbia University Press, 1980.

Massimo Piattelli-Palmarini, editor, *Language and Learning: The Debate between Jean Piaget and Noam Chomsky,* Harvard University Press, 1980.

Lectures on Government and Binding, Foris, 1981.

Radical Priorities, Black Rose Books, 1981.

Towards a New Cold War: Essays on the Current Crisis and How We Got There, Pantheon, 1982.

Noam Chomsky on the Generative Enterprise: A Discussion with Riny Huybregts and Henk van Riemsdijk, Foris, 1982.

(With Jonathan Steele and John Gittings) *Superpowers in Collision: The Cold War Now,* Penguin Books, 1982.

Some Concepts and Consequences of the Theory of Government and Binding, M.I.T. Press, 1982.

The Fateful Triangle: The United States, Israel, and the Palestinians, South End, 1983.

Turning the Tide: U.S. Intervention in Central America and the Struggle for Peace, South End, 1985.

Barriers, M.I.T. Press, 1986.

Knowledge of Language: Its Nature, Origins, and Use, Praeger, 1986.

Pirates and Emperors: International Terrorism in the Real World, Claremont, 1986.

On Power and Ideology: The Managua Lectures, South End, 1987.

James Peck, editor, *The Chomsky Reader,* Pantheon, 1987.

Language and Problems of Knowledge: The Managua Lectures, M.I.T. Press, 1987

Language in a Psychological Setting, Sophia University (Tokyo), 1987.

Generative Grammar: Its Basis, Development, and Prospects, Kyoto University of Foreign Studies, 1988.

The Culture of Terrorism, South End, 1988.

(With Edward Herman) *Manufacturing Consent,* Pantheon, 1988.

Necessary Illusions: Thought Control in a Democratic Society, South End, 1989.

Contributor of numerous articles to scholarly and general periodicals.

SIDELIGHTS: "Judged in terms of the power, range, novelty and influence of his thought, Noam Chomsky is arguably the most important intellectual alive today," writes Paul Robinson in the *New York Times Book Review.* Chomsky, a professor of linguistics at the Massachusetts Institute of Technology, has attracted worldwide attention with his ground-breaking research into the nature of human language and communication. As the founder of the "Chomskyan Revolution," the scholar has become the center of a debate that transcends formal linguistics to embrace psychology, philosophy, and even genetics. *New York Times Magazine* contributor Daniel Yergin maintains that Chomsky's "formulation of 'transformational grammar' has been acclaimed as one of the major achievements of the century. Where others heard only a Babel of fragments, he found a linguistic order. His work has been compared to the unraveling of the genetic code of the DNA molecule." Yergin further contends that Chomsky's discoveries have had an impact "on everything from the way children are taught foreign languages to what it means when we say that we are human." Chomsky is also an impassioned critic of American foreign policy, especially as it affects ordinary citizens of Third World nations. Many of his books since 1969 concern themselves with "the perfidy of American influence overseas," to quote *Atlantic* essayist James Fallows. In *America,* Kenneth J. Gavin finds a unifying strain in all of Chomsky's various writings. The author's goal, says Gavin, is "to highlight principles of human knowledge and indicate the priority of these principles in the reconstruction of a society. His efforts leave us with more than enough to think about."

Chomsky was born in Philadelphia on December 7, 1928. His father was a Hebrew scholar of considerable repute, so even as a youngster Chomsky "picked up a body of informal knowledge about the structure and history of the Semitic languages," according to David Cohen in *Psychologists on Psychology.* While still in high school Chomsky proofread the manuscript of his father's edition of a medieval Hebrew grammar. Yergin notes: "This backdoor introduction to 'historical linguistics' had considerable impact in the future; it helped fuel his later conviction that the explanation of how language worked, rather than categories and description, was the business of linguistic study." The young Chomsky was more interested in politics than grammar, however. He was especially passionate about the rebirth of a Jewish culture and society in what later became the state of Israel, and for a time he entertained the idea of moving there. In 1945 he enrolled at the University of Pennsylvania, where he came under the influence of Zellig Harris, a noted professor of linguistics. John Lyons observes in *Noam Chomsky* that it was the student's "sympathies with Harris's political views that led him to work as an undergraduate in linguistics. There is a sense, therefore, in which politics brought him into linguistics."

The school of linguistics in which Chomsky took his collegiate training held as its goal the formal and autonomous description of languages without wide reference to the meaning—or semantics—of utterances. Lyons elaborates: "Semantic considerations were strictly subordinated to the task of identifying the units of phonology and syntax and were not involved at all in the specification of the rules or principles governing their permissible combinations. This part of the grammar was to be a purely *formal* study, independent of semantics." Chomsky questioned this approach in his early work in generative grammar as a student at the University of Pennsylvania, and broke with it more radically while in the Harvard Society of Fellows from 1951. There he was immersed in new developments in mathematical logic, the abstract theory of thinking machines, and the latest psychological and philosophical debates. These ideas led him to develop further his earlier work on generative grammar and to ask "precise and formal questions about linguistics and language," to quote Justin Leiber in his work *Noam Chomsky: A Philosophical Overview*. Leiber adds: "His results led him to criticize and discard the prevailing views in linguistics."

What Chomsky began to develop in the 1950s was a mathematically precise description of some of human language's most striking features. Yergin contends that the scholar was "particularly fascinated by 'generative systems'—the procedures by which a mathematician, starting with postulates and utilizing principles and inferences, can generate an infinite number of proofs. He thought that perhaps language was 'generated' from a few principles as well." Yergin claims that this line of reasoning led Chomsky to another salient question, namely: *"How is it possible that, if language is only a learned habit, one can be continually creative and innovative in its use?"* This question—and its explication—would provide a novel and compelling critique of two established fields, traditional structural linguistics and behavioral psychology. Leiber concludes that Chomsky's new theory "explained many features of language that were beyond structuralist linguistics and placed the specific data, and many lower-level generalizations, of the structuralists within a richer theory."

Many of Chomsky's novel ideas saw print in his first book, *Syntactic Structures*, published in 1957. Yergin calls the work "the pale blue book . . . which heralded the Chomskyan Revolution." He adds that the volume "demonstrated that important facts about language could not be explained by either structural linguistics or by computer theory, which was then becoming fashionable in the field. In 'Syntactic Structures,' Chomsky departed from his mentors in stressing the importance of explaining creativity in language and introduces his own transformational grammar as a more 'powerful' explanation of how we make sentences." Webster Schott offers a similar assessment in the *Washington Post Book World*. In *Syntactic Structures*, writes Schott, "Chomsky [presents] and [seems] to demonstrate the proposition that every human being has an innate ability to acquire language, and this ability to learn language is called into use when one hears, at the right age, language for the first time. He also [offers] a concept—it came to be known as 'generative' or 'transformational-generative' grammar—which [has] made it possible to predict ('generate') the sentence combinations in a language and to describe their structure." Lyons states that the short and relatively nontechnical *Syntactic Structures* "revolutionized the scientific study of language."

The proofs Chomsky uses for his theories are complex, but his conclusions are readily accessible. Robinson observes that, put as simply as possible, Chomsky's view holds that "the ability to speak and understand a language cannot be explained in purely empirical terms—that is, purely by induction. When we 'learn' a language, he says, we are able to formulate and understand all sorts of sentences that we've never heard before. What we 'know,' therefore, must be something deeper—a grammar—that makes an infinite variety of sentences possible. Chomsky believes that the capacity to master grammatical structures is innate: It is genetically determined, a product of the evolutionary process, just as the organic structures of our bodies are." A strict "stimulus-response" mechanism cannot adequately account for the way young children master language during the first four years of life; the child, to quote Cohen, "learns . . . to extract the more complex rules of grammar needed for speech." Leiber explains that for Chomsky, then, the primary interest of the linguist should be with specifying the "device of some sort" that *generates* an infinite variety of grammatically-correct sentences. "This device will specify what is somehow 'internalized' in the competent speaker-hearer of the language," Leiber writes. "Though the most usual label for Chomsky's general sort of linguistics is 'transformational-generative linguistics,' the most crucial word is 'generative'—as opposed to 'taxonomical'—since the primary concern is with the 'principles and processes by which sentences are constructed in particular languages,' not with the identification and classification of items found in the surface end product of these principles and processes."

One of the mechanisms Chomsky proposes for sentence generation is the "deep structure-surface structure" scenario. According to Yergin, the surface structure "'faces out' on the world and, by certain phonological rules, is converted into the sounds we hear; it corresponds to the parsing of sentences which we all learned from our indefatigable junior high English teachers. The deep structure 'faces inward' toward the hazy region of conceptualization, is more abstract and related to meaning. It expresses the basic logical relations between nouns and verbs." Transformational grammar therefore "consists of a limited series of rules, expressed in mathematical notation, which transform deep structures into well-formed surface structures. The transformational grammar thus relates meaning and sound." Cohen discusses the applications of this concept. "Chomsky has analysed the necessary constituents of the deep structure and the transformations through which this deep structure is turned into the surface structure we recognize and use as sentences. He has, of course, extended his theory from this point into the implications for our knowledge of man that comes from the fact that our knowledge of language is based upon this deep structure, a structure that we cannot guess or divine just from speaking, and upon the necessary transformations."

Chomsky has argued that all natural human languages possess deep and surface structures and cycles of transformations between them. In the *Nation*, Gilbert Harman writes: "These built-in aspects of grammar will be parts of the grammar of every language. They are, in other words, aspects of 'universal grammar.' We must therefore suppose that people have a specific faculty of language, a kind of 'mental organ' which develops in the appropriate way, given appropriate experience, yielding a knowledge of whatever language is spoken in their community." John Sturrock elaborates in the *New York Times Book Review*: "Chomskyism starts with grammar and finishes in genetics. Drill deep enough into the structure of our sentences, he maintains, and you will come to those ultimate abstractions with which we were born, the grammar of any given language being originally determined by the fairly restricted grammatical possibilities programmed in the brain. . . . DNA sets up to master a syntax, the accident of birth determines which one." Needless to say, not everyone agrees with Chomsky's view. *Psychology Today* contributor Howard Gardner calls the human being in Chomsky's formulation "a totally preprogrammed computer, one that needs merely to be plugged into the appropriate outlet." Lyons, conversely, states that Chomsky "was surely right to challenge 'the belief that the mind must be simpler in its structure than any known physical organ and that the most primitive of assumptions must be adequate to explain whatever phenomena can be observed.'"

Obviously, Chomsky's theory has as much to do with psychology and philosophy as it does with linguistics. For instance, the very premises of the scholar's work have made him one of the most devastating critics of behaviorism, the view that suggests all human responses are learned through conditioning. Sturrock notes: "Chomsky's case is that . . . that fanatical core known as behaviorism, has a theory of learning, all rote and Pavlovian reinforcement, which is deficient and, in the end, degrading. . . . [Behaviorists], given their sinister theory of learning, must be proponents of the view that human nature is not nature at all, but a social product conditioned from outside. Chomsky finds hope and a decisive guarantee of intellectual freedom in the cognitive structures which sit incorruptibly in the fastness of our brains." Chomsky's work reinforces the philosophical tradition of "rationalism," the contention that the mind, or "reason," contributes to human knowledge beyond what is gained by experience. He is opposed by the "empiricists," who claim that all knowledge derives from external stimuli, including language. In the *Nation,* Edward Marcotte declares: "What started as purely linguistic research . . . has led, through involvement in political causes and an identification with an older philosophic tradition, to no less than an attempt to formulate an overall theory of man. The roots of this are manifest in the linguistic theory. . . . The discovery of cognitive structures common to the human race but only to humans (species specific), leads quite easily to thinking of unalienable human attributes." Leiber concludes: "Mind is the software of human psychology, and thought is individuated as instances of the mind's operations. The behaviorist is seen to be insisting . . . on a very minimal sort of software; the rationalist is out to show that much more powerful and abstract, perhaps in good measure innate, software has to be involved. One can feel unhappy with Chomsky's particular way of putting, or productively narrowing, the issue, but it is not an unreasonable viewpoint. Chomsky has an interesting and important sense of *know* at hand. He is looking at men in a way that has an established and well-defined sense when applied to thinking devices."

While establishing his academic reputation, Chomsky continued to be concerned about the direction of American politics and ideology. His moral indignation rose in the 1960s until he became "one of the most articulate spokesmen of the resistance against the Vietnam war," to quote Jan G. Deutsche in the *New York Times Book Review.* Chomsky attacked the war in articles, in books, and from the podium; in the process he became better known for his political views than for his linguistic scholarship. In a *New York Times* piece written during that era, Thomas Lask observes: "Unlike many others, even those who oppose the war, Noam Chomsky can't stand it and his hatred of what we are doing there and his shame, as well as his loathing for the men who defend and give it countenance are tangible enough to touch." *Nation* essayist Brian Morton finds "nothing exotic about his critique of the U.S. role in Vietnam: He attempted no analysis of arcane economic or political structures. All he did was evaluate our government's actions by the same standards that we apply when we evaluate the actions of other governments."

Chomsky's first book-length work on Vietnam, *American Power and the New Mandarins,* offers "a searing criticism of the system of values and decision-making that drove the United States to the jungles of Southeast Asia," according to Michael R. Beschloss in the *Washington Post Book World.* The book's strongest vitriol is directed toward those so-called "New Mandarins"—the technocrats, bureaucrats, and university-trained

scholars who defend America's right to dominate the globe. Deutsch states that Chomsky's concern "is not simply that social scientists have participated widely in designing and executing war-related projects. What he finds disturbing are the consequences of access to power by intellectuals; the difficulties involved in retaining a critical stance toward a society that makes the reward of power available as well as the need to be 'constructive,' the recognition as problems of only those difficulties that are soluble by the means at hand." Inevitably, Chomsky's volume has drawn scathing criticism from those who oppose his views and high praise from those who agree with him. *Chicago Tribune Book World* reviewer Arthur Schlesinger, Jr., claims: "Judging by *American Power and the New Mandarins,* one can only conclude that Chomsky's idea of the responsibility of an intellectual is to forswear reasoned analysis, indulge in moralistic declamation, fabricate evidence when necessary and shout always at the top of one's voice. It need hardly be said that, should the intellectual community follow the Chomsky example, it would betray its own traditions and hasten society along the road to unreason and disaster." In the *Nation,* Robert Sklar feels otherwise about the work. The critic contends: "The importance of *American Power and the New Mandarins* lies in its power to free our minds from old perspectives, to stimulate new efforts at historical, political and social thought."

Subsequent Chomsky books on American foreign policy have explored other political hotbeds around the world, drawing the conclusion that U.S. interests in human rights, justice, and morality are inevitably subordinated to big business profit-taking. As Beschloss notes, Chomsky's "is a portrait of corporate executives manipulating foreign policy for profit motives, of Third World peoples devastated for drifting away from the American 'grand area' of influence; of hand-maiden journalists, politicians, and intellectuals shrouding the darker realities of American statecraft under platitudes about idealism and goodwill with an eye toward their flow of rewards from the Establishment." *Times Literary Supplement* correspondent Charles Townshend observes that Chomsky "sees a 'totalitarian mentality' arising out of the mainstream American belief in the fundamental righteousness and benevolence of the United States, the sanctity and nobility of its aims. The publicly tolerated 'spectrum of discussion' of these aims is narrow." Chomsky himself transcends that narrow spectrum, adducing "example after example to illuminate how American policies have led knowingly to large scale human suffering," to quote Beschloss. In the *New York Times Book Review,* Sheldon S. Wolin suggests that the author "is relentless in tracking down official lies and exposing hypocrisy and moral indifference in the high places. . . . Yet the passion of Chomsky's indictment is always controlled, and while he is harsh toward his opponents, he is never unfair or arrogant."

Other critics have been less sanguine about Chomsky's political views; in fact, some have actually labelled him a pariah and attempted to discredit him on a number of grounds. "It has been Chomsky's singular fate to have been banished to the margins of political debate," writes Steve Wasserman in the *Los Angeles Times Book Review.* "His opinions have been deemed so kooky—and his personality so cranky—that his writings no longer appear in the forums . . . in which he was once so welcome." Wolin offers one dissenting view: "Chomsky's political writings are curiously untheoretical, which is surprising in a writer renowned for his contributions to linguistic theory. His apparent assumption is that politics is not a theoretical subject. . . . One gets the impression from reading

Chomsky that if it were not urgently necessary to expose lies, immorality and the abuse of power, politics would have no serious claim upon the theoretical mind.'' *New York Times Book Review* contributor Paul Robinson notes that in Chomsky's case, ''the popular or accessible [political] works often seem to belie the intellectual powers unambiguously established in the professional works. . . . Indeed, one might argue that the discrepancy is more extreme in his work than in that of any other important intellectual.'' Morton feels that the attacks on Chomsky's historical/political scholarship—and more recently the tendency to ignore his work—have affected his level of stridency. ''His later tone is that of a man who doesn't expect anything to change,'' Morton observes. ''. . . Chomsky is savagely indignant because the values he cherishes are being strangled. But increasingly, the reasons for his indignation—the values he cherishes—are hard to see in his work. Only the indignation is clear.''

Chomsky has his champions, however. Leiber, for one, finds an overriding commitment to freedom in the author's work—''the freedom of the individual to produce and create as he will without the goad of external force, economic competition for survival, or legal and economic restraint on social, intellectual, or artistic experiment; and the freedom of ethnic and national groups to work out their own destinies without the intervention of one or another Big Brother.'' ''From his earliest writings to his latest, Chomsky has looked with astonishment at what the powerful do to the powerless,'' Morton declares. ''He has never let his sense of outrage become dulled. If his voice has grown hoarse over twenty years, who can blame him? And who can feel superior? No one has given himself more deeply to the struggle against the horrors of our time. His hoarseness is a better thing than our suavity.'' Deutsch writes: ''The most convincing indication of the extent to which Chomsky's wide ranging indictment of United States society and policy must be taken seriously is that a man possessed of these sensibilities should have felt compelled to undertake it.'' Morton offers a compelling conclusion. ''Americans are no longer convinced that our government has the right to destroy any country it wants to,'' the essayist states. ''And to the extent that this is true, Chomsky, along with others like him, deserves much of the credit. He did his job well.''

In 1970, the London *Times* named Chomsky one of the thousand ''makers of the twentieth century.'' According to Yergin, his theory ''remains the foundation of linguistics today,'' and ''his vision of a complex universe within the mind, governed by myriad rules and prohibitions and yet infinite in its creative potential, opens up vistas possibly as important as Einstein's theories.'' Yergin adds: ''The impact of Chomsky's work may not be felt for years. . . . Yet this beginning has revolutionized the study of language and has redirected and redefined the broad inquiry into intelligence and how it works.'' Robinson calls the scholar's work ''a prolonged celebration of the enormous gulf that separates man from the rest of nature. He seems overwhelmed by the intellectual powers that man contains within himself. Certainly nobody ever stated the case for those powers more emphatically, nor exemplified them more impressively in his own work. Reading Chomsky on linguistics, one repeatedly has the impression of attending to one of the more powerful thinkers who ever lived.''

Appreciation has likewise attended Chomsky's political writings. According to Christopher Lehmann-Haupt in the *New York Times*, Chomsky ''continues to challenge our assumptions long after other critics have gone to bed. He has become the foremost gadfly of our national conscience.'' *New States-*

man correspondent Francis Hope praises Chomsky for ''a proud defensive independence, a good plain writer's hatred of expert mystification, a doctrine of resistance which runs against the melioristic and participatory current of most contemporary intellectual life.'' Hope concludes: ''Such men are dangerous; the lack of them is disastrous.''

BIOGRAPHICAL/CRITICAL SOURCES:

BOOKS

Cohen, David, *Psychologists on Psychology*, Taplinger, 1977.
Contemporary Issues Criticism, Volume 1, Gale, 1982.
Greene, Judith, *Psycholinguistics: Chomsky and Psychology*, Penguin Books, 1972.
Harman, Gilbert, editor, *On Noam Chomsky: Critical Essays*, Anchor Press, 1974.
Kim-Renaud, Young-Key, *Studies in Korean Linguistics*, Hanshin Publishing, 1986.
Leiber, Justin, *Noam Chomsky: A Philosophical Overview*, Twayne, 1975.
Lyons, John, *Noam Chomsky*, 2nd edition, Penguin Books, 1977.
Mehta, Ved, *John Is Easy to Please*, Farrar, Straus, 1971.
Osiatynski, Wiktor, *Contrasts: Soviet and American Thinkers Discuss the Future*, Macmillan, 1984.
Rieber, Robert W., editor, *Dialogues on the Psychology of Language and Thought: Conversations with Noam Chomsky, Charles Osgood, Jean Piaget, Ulric Neisser, and Marcel Kinsbourne*, Plenum, 1983.
Sampson, Geoffrey, *Liberty and Language*, Oxford University Press, 1979.
Thinkers of the Twentieth Century, Gale, 1983.

PERIODICALS

America, December 11, 1971.
Atlantic, July, 1973, February, 1982.
Book World, March 23, 1969.
Christian Century, July 23, 1969.
Christian Science Monitor, April 3, 1969, May 14, 1970.
Chronicle of Higher Education, May 12, 1982.
Commentary, May, 1969.
Dissent, January-February, 1970.
Economist, November 29, 1969.
Globe and Mail (Toronto), June 16, 1984, July 5, 1986.
Harvard Education Review, winter, 1969.
Horizon, spring, 1971.
International Affairs, January, 1971.
Los Angeles Times Book Review, December 27, 1981, June 8, 1986, August 30, 1987.
Maclean's, August 18, 1980.
Nation, September 9, 1968, March 24, 1969, May 17, 1971, May 8, 1976, March 31, 1979, February 16, 1980, December 22, 1984, December 26, 1987-January 2, 1988, May 7, 1988.
National Review, June 17, 1969.
New Republic, April 19, 1969, October 26, 1974, March 13, 1976, February 17, 1979, September 6-13, 1980, March 24, 1982, March 23, 1987.
New Statesman, November 28, 1969, August 17, 1979, April 25, 1980, July 17, 1981, August 14, 1981, September 11, 1981, January 21, 1983.
Newsweek, March 24, 1969.
New Yorker, November 11, 1969, May 8, 1971.
New York Review of Books, August 9, 1973, January 23, 1975, November 11, 1976, October 23, 1980.

New York Times, March 18, 1969, August 2, 1973, February 5, 1979, March 8, 1982.
New York Times Book Review, March 16, 1969, January 17, 1971, January 9, 1972, September 30, 1973, October 6, 1974, February 15, 1976, February 25, 1979, October 19, 1980, March 21, 1982, April 13, 1986.
New York Times Magazine, May 6, 1968, December 3, 1972.
Progressive, December, 1982.
Psychology Today, July, 1979.
Saturday Review, May 31, 1969.
Science and Society, spring, 1970.
Sewanee Review, winter, 1977.
Times Literary Supplement, March 27, 1969, March 31, 1972, December 21, 1973, December 12, 1975, September 10, 1976, November 21, 1980, February 27, 1981, July 23, 1982, July 15-21, 1988.
Village Voice, June 18, 1980, June 23, 1980, July 13, 1982.
Virginia Quarterly Review, summer, 1969.
Washington Post Book World, March 11, 1979, March 7, 1982, February 21, 1988.

—*Sketch by Anne Janette Johnson*

*   *   *

CLARK, Burton R(obert) 1921-

PERSONAL: Born September 6, 1921, in Pleasantville, N.J.; son of Burton H. (in business) and Cornelia (Amole) Clark; married Adele Halitsky (an editor), August 31, 1949; children: Philip Neil, Adrienne. *Education:* University of California, Los Angeles, B.A., 1949, Ph.D., 1954.

ADDRESSES: Home—201 Ocean Ave., Apt. 1710B, Santa Monica, Calif. 90402. *Office*—Department of Education, University of California, Los Angeles, Calif. 90024.

CAREER: Stanford University, Stanford, Calif., assistant professor of sociology, 1953-56; Harvard University, Cambridge, Mass., research associate and assistant professor of education, 1956-58; University of California, Berkeley, associate professor, 1958-64, professor of education, 1964-66, associate research sociologist, 1958-64, research sociologist, 1964-66; Yale University, New Haven, Conn., professor of sociology, 1966-80, chairman of department, 1969-72, chairman of Higher Education Research Group, 1973-80; University of California, Los Angeles, Allan M. Carter Professor of Higher Education and Sociology, 1980—, chairman of Comparative Higher Education Research Group, 1982—. *Military service:* U.S. Army, 1942-46.

MEMBER: International Sociological Association, American Sociological Association, National Academy of Education, American Educational Research Association, Association for the Study of Higher Education (president, 1979-80), American Association for Higher Education.

AWARDS, HONORS: Research award, American Educational Research Association and American College Testing Program, 1979; Research Achievement Award, Association for the Study of Higher Education, 1985; Distinguished Research Award, American Educational Research Association, Division J, 1988.

WRITINGS:

Adult Education in Transition, University of California Press, 1956.
The Open Door College, McGraw, 1960.
Educating the Expert Society, Chandler, 1962.

The Distinctive College: Antioch, Reed, and Swarthmore, Aldine, 1970.
(With Paul Heist, T. R. McConnell, Martin A. Trow, and George Yonge) *Students and Colleges,* Center for Research and Development in Higher Education, (Berkeley), 1972.
(With James S. Coleman and others) *Youth: Transition to Adulthood,* University of Chicago Press, 1973.
The Problems of American Education, F. Watts, 1975.
(With Ted I. K. Youn) *Academic Power in the United States,* American Association for Higher Education, 1976.
Academic Power in Italy, University of Chicago Press, 1977.
(With John H. Van de Graaff and others) *Academic Power: Patterns of Authority in Seven National Systems of Higher Education,* Praeger, 1978.
The Higher Education System: Academic Organization in Cross-National Perspective, University of California Press, 1983.
(Editor) *Perspectives on Higher Education,* University of California Press, 1984.
(Editor) *The School and the University,* University of California Press, 1985.
(Editor) *The Academic Profession,* University of California Press, 1987.
The Academic Life, Carnegie Foundation for the Advancement of Teaching and Princeton University Press, 1987.

SIDELIGHTS: Burton R. Clark told *CA:* "My work centers on a sociological understanding of higher education. Since 1960, I have specialized in cross-national studies of how national systems of higher education are organized. This work has taken me, as researcher, lecturer, and consultant, to Japan, the United Kingdom, Sweden, the Federal Republic of Germany, France, Italy, Poland, Portugal, Canada, Mexico, Chile, China, Norway, Finland, and the Netherlands.

"I am impressed with the enormous diversity of American higher education, which makes our system open and flexible, but also leaves it with uneven standards and much confusion. I am convinced that international comparisons are the best way to grasp the special nature of our educational system."

*   *   *

CLARK, Lydia Benson
See MEAKER, Eloise

*   *   *

CLARKE, Arthur C(harles) 1917-
(E. G. O'Brien, Charles Willis)

PERSONAL: Born December 16, 1917, in Minehead, Somersetshire, England; son of Charles Wright (a farmer) and Nora (Willis) Clarke; married Marilyn Mayfield, 1953 (divorced, 1964). *Education:* King's College, University of London, B.Sc. (first class honors), 1948.

ADDRESSES: Home—25, Barnes Pl., Colombo 7, Sri Lanka. *Agent*—Scott Meredith Literary Agency, Inc., 845 Third Ave., New York, N.Y. 10022; and David Higham Associates, 5-8 Lower John St., Golden Square, London W1R 4HA, England.

CAREER: British Civil Service, His Majesty's Exchequer and Audit Department, London, England, auditor, 1936-41; Institution of Electrical Engineers, *Science Abstracts,* London, assistant editor, 1949-50; free-lance writer, 1951—. Underwater explorer and photographer, in partnership with Mike Wilson, on Great Barrier Reef of Australia and coast of Sri Lanka,

1954-64. Has appeared on television and radio numerous times, including as commentator with Walter Cronkite on Apollo missions, CBS-TV, 1968-70, and as host of television series "Arthur C. Clarke's Mysterious World," 1980, and "Arthur C. Clarke's World of Strange Powers," 1984. Acted role of Leonard Woolf in Lester James Peries's film "Beddagama" (based on Woolf's *The Village in the Jungle*), 1979.

Director of Rocket Publishing Co., United Kingdom, and Underwater Safaris, Sri Lanka; founder and patron, Arthur C. Clarke Centre for Modern Technologies, Sri Lanka, 1984—. Chancellor of University of Moratuwa, Sri Lanka, 1979—; Vikram Sarabhai Professor, Physical Research Laboratory, Ahmedabad, India, 1980; trustee, Institute of Integral Education, Sri Lanka. Fellow, Franklin Institute, 1971, King's College, 1977, Institute of Robotics, Carnegie-Mellon University, 1981. Lecturer, touring United States and Britain, 1957-74. Board member of National Space Institute, United States, Space Generation Foundation, United States, International Astronomical Union (Search for ExtraTerrestrial Intelligence) Commission 51, International Space University, Institute of Fundamental Studies, Sri Lanka, and Planetary Society, United States. Chairman, Second International Astronautics Congress, London, 1951; moderator, "Space Flight Report to the Nation," New York, 1961. *Military service:* Royal Air Force, radar instructor, 1941-46; became flight lieutenant.

MEMBER: International Academy of Astronautics (honorary fellow), International Science Writers Association, International Council for Integrative Studies, World Academy of Art and Science (academician), British Interplanetary Society (honorary fellow; chairman, 1946-47, 1950-53), Royal Astronomical Society (fellow), British Astronomical Association, Association of British Science Writers (life member), British Science Fiction Association (patron), Royal Society of Arts (fellow), Society of Authors (council member), American Institute of Aeronautics and Astronautics (honorary fellow), American Astronautical Society (honorary fellow), American Association for the Advancement of Science, National Academy of Engineering (United States; foreign associate), Science Fiction Writers of America, Science Fiction Foundation, H. G. Wells Society (honorary vice-president), Third World Academy of Sciences (associate fellow), Sri Lanka Astronomical Society (patron), Institute of Engineers (Sri Lanka; honorary fellow), Sri Lanka Animal Welfare Association (patron), British Sub-Aqua Club.

AWARDS, HONORS: International Fantasy Award, 1952, for *The Exploration of Space;* Hugo Award, World Science Fiction Convention, 1956, for "The Star"; Kalinga Prize, UNESCO, 1961, for science writing; Junior Book Award, Boy's Club of America, 1961; Stuart Ballantine Gold Medal, Franklin Institute, 1963, for originating concept of communications satellites; Robert Ball Award, Aviation-Space Writers Association, 1965, for best aerospace reporting of the year in any medium; Westinghouse Science Writing Award, American Association for the Advancement of Science, 1969; Second International Film Festival special award, and Academy Award nomination for best screenplay with Stanley Kubrick, Academy of Motion Picture Arts and Sciences, both 1969, both for "2001: A Space Odyssey"; *Playboy* editorial award, 1971, 1982; D.Sc., Beaver College, 1971, and University of Moratuwa, 1979; Nebula Award, Science Fiction Writers of America, 1972, for "A Meeting with Medusa"; Nebula Award, 1973, Hugo Award, 1974, John W. Campbell Memorial Award, Science Fiction Research Association, 1974, and Jupiter Award, Instructors of Science Fiction in Higher Education, 1974, all

for *Rendezvous with Rama;* Aerospace Communications Award, American Institute of Aeronautics and Astronautics, 1974; Bradford Washburn Award, Boston Museum of Science, 1977, for "contributions to the public understanding of science"; GALAXY Award, 1979; Nebula and Hugo Awards, both 1980, both for *The Fountains of Paradise;* special Emmy Award for engineering, National Academy of Television Arts and Sciences, 1981, for contributions to satellite broadcasting; "Lensman" Award, 1982; Marconi International Fellowship, 1982; Centennial Medal, Institute of Electrical and Electronics Engineers, 1984; E. M. Emme Astronautical Literature Award, American Astronautical Society, 1984; Grand Master Award, Science Fiction Writers of America, 1986; Vidya Jyothi Medal (Presidential Science Award), 1986; Charles A. Lindbergh Award, 1987; named to Society of Satellite Professionals Hall of Fame, 1987; named to Aerospace Hall of Fame, 1988; D.Litt., University of Bath, 1988.

WRITINGS:

NONFICTION

Interplanetary Flight: An Introduction to Astronautics, Temple, 1950, Harper, 1951, 2nd edition, 1960, reprinted, Berkley Publishing, 1985.

The Exploration of Space (U.S. Book-of-the-Month Club selection), Harper, 1951, revised edition, Pocket Books, 1979.

The Young Traveller in Space, Phoenix, 1953, published as *Going into Space,* Harper, 1954, revised edition (with Robert Silverberg) published as *Into Space: A Young Person's Guide to Space,* Harper, 1971.

The Exploration of the Moon, illustrated by R. A. Smith, Harper, 1954.

The Coast of Coral, Harper, 1956.

The Reefs of Taprobane: Underwater Adventures around Ceylon, Harper, 1957.

The Scottie Book of Space Travel, Transworld Publishers, 1957.

The Making of a Moon: The Story of the Earth Satellite Program, Harper, 1957, revised edition, 1958.

Voice across the Sea, Harper, 1958, revised edition, 1974.

(With Mike Wilson) *Boy beneath the Sea,* Harper, 1958.

The Challenge of the Spaceship: Previews of Tomorrow's World, Harper, 1959, reprinted, Pocket Books, 1980.

(With Wilson) *The First Five Fathoms: A Guide to Underwater Adventure,* Harper, 1960.

The Challenge of the Sea, Holt, 1960.

(With Wilson) *Indian Ocean Adventure,* Harper, 1961.

Profiles of the Future: An Inquiry into the Limits of the Possible, Harper, 1962, revised edition, Holt, 1984.

The Treasure of the Great Reef, Harper, 1964, new edition, Ballantine, 1974.

(With Wilson) *Indian Ocean Treasure,* Harper, 1964.

(With the editors of *Life*) *Man and Space,* Time-Life, 1964.

Voices from the Sky: Previews of the Coming Space Age, Harper, 1965, reprinted, Pocket Books, 1980.

(Editor) *The Coming of the Space Age: Famous Accounts of Man's Probing of the Universe,* Meredith, 1967.

The Promise of Space, Harper, 1968, reprinted, Berkley Publishing, 1985.

(With Neil Armstrong, Michael Collins, Edwin E. Aldrin, Jr., Gene Farmer, and Dora Jane Hamblin) *First on the Moon,* Little, Brown, 1970.

Report on Planet Three and Other Speculations, Harper, 1972.

(With Chesley Bonestell) *Beyond Jupiter,* Little, Brown, 1972.

(Contributor) *Mars and the Mind of Man,* Harper, 1973.

The View from Serendip (autobiography), Random House, 1977.

"Arthur C. Clarke's Mysterious World" (also see below; television series), Yorkshire Television, 1980.

(With Simon Welfare and John Fairley) *Arthur C. Clarke's Mysterious World* (based on television series), A & W Publishers, 1980.

Ascent to Orbit, a Scientific Autobiography: The Technical Writings of Arthur C. Clarke, Wiley, 1984.

1984: Spring—A Choice of Futures, Del Rey, 1984.

(With Welfare and Fairley) *Arthur C. Clarke's World of Strange Powers* (also see below; based on television series of same title), Putnam, 1984.

(With Peter Hyams) *The Odyssey File,* Fawcett, 1985.

Arthur C. Clarke's July 20, 2019: Life in the 21st Century, Macmillan, 1986.

Arthur C. Clarke's Chronicles of the Strange and Mysterious, edited by Welfare and Fairley, Collins, 1987.

Astounding Days (science-fictional autobiography), Bantam, 1989.

Also author of introduction to *Inmarsat History.*

FICTION

The Sands of Mars (also see below), Sidgwick & Jackson, 1951, reprinted, 1976, Gnome Press, 1952.

Prelude to Space (also see below), World Editions, 1951, reprinted, Sidgwick & Jackson, 1980, published as *Master of Space,* Lancer Books, 1961, published as *The Space Dreamers,* Lancer Books, 1969.

Islands in the Sky, Winston, 1952, new edition, Penguin Books, 1972, reprinted, New American Library, 1987.

Childhood's End (also see below), Ballantine, 1953, reprinted, Del Rey, 1981.

Against the Fall of Night (also see below), Gnome Press, 1953, reprinted, Berkley Books, 1983.

Expedition to Earth (also see below; short stories), Ballantine, 1953, reprinted, New English Library, 1987.

Earthlight (also see below), Ballantine, 1955, reprinted, Sidgwick & Jackson, 1973.

Reach for Tomorrow (short stories), Ballantine, 1956, reprinted, Gollancz, 1985.

The City and the Stars (also see below; based on novel *Against the Fall of Night*), Harcourt, 1956, reprinted, New American Library, 1987.

The Deep Range (also see below), Harcourt, 1957, reprinted, New American Library, 1987.

Tales from the White Hart, Ballantine, 1957, reprinted, 1981.

The Other Side of the Sky (short stories), Harcourt, 1958, reprinted, New American Library, 1987.

Across the Sea of Stars (anthology; includes *Childhood's End* and *Earthlight*), Harcourt, 1959.

A Fall of Moondust (also see below), Harcourt, 1961, reprinted, Gollancz, 1987, abridged edition, University of London Press, 1964.

From the Oceans, from the Stars (anthology; includes *The Deep Range* and *The City and the Stars*), Harcourt, 1962.

Tales of Ten Worlds (short stories), Harcourt, 1962, reprinted, New American Library, 1987.

Dolphin Island: A Story of the People of the Sea, Holt, 1963, reprinted, Penguin Books, 1986.

Glide Path, Harcourt, 1963, reprinted, New American Library, 1987.

Prelude to Mars (anthology; includes *Prelude to Space* and *The Sands of Mars*), Harcourt, 1965.

An Arthur C. Clarke Omnibus (contains *Childhood's End, Prelude to Space,* and *Expedition to Earth*), Sidgwick & Jackson, 1965.

(Editor) *Time Probe: The Science in Science Fiction,* Dial, 1966.

The Nine Billion Names of God (short stories), Harcourt, 1967.

A Second Arthur C. Clarke Omnibus (contains *A Fall of Moondust, Earthlight,* and *The Sands of Mars*), Sidgwick & Jackson, 1968.

(With Stanley Kubrick) "2001: A Space Odyssey" (screenplay; also see below), Metro-Goldwyn-Mayer, 1968.

2001: A Space Odyssey (based on screenplay), New American Library, 1968, reprinted, Inner Circle Books, 1983.

The Lion of Comarre; and, Against the Fall of Night, Harcourt, 1968, reprinted, 1986.

The Lost Worlds of 2001, New American Library, 1972.

The Wind from the Sun (short stories), Harcourt, 1972.

(Editor) *Three for Tomorrow,* Sphere Books, 1972.

Of Time and Stars: The Worlds of Arthur C. Clarke (short stories), Gollancz, 1972.

Rendezvous with Rama (also see below), Harcourt, 1973, reprinted, Ballantine, 1988, adapted edition, Oxford University Press, 1979.

The Best of Arthur C. Clarke, edited by Angus Wells, Sidgwick & Jackson, 1973, published as two volumes, Volume 1: *1937-1955,* Volume 2: *1956-1972,* 1977.

Imperial Earth: A Fantasy of Love and Discord, Gollancz, 1975, Harcourt, 1976.

Four Great Science Fiction Novels (contains *The City and the Stars, The Deep Range, A Fall of Moondust,* and *Rendezvous with Rama*), Gollancz, 1978.

The Fountains of Paradise, Harcourt, 1979.

(Editor with George Proctor) *The Science Fiction Hall of Fame,* Volume 3: *The Nebula Winners,* Avon, 1982.

2010: Odyssey Two, Del Rey, 1982.

The Sentinel: Masterworks of Science Fiction and Fantasy (short stories), Berkley Publishing, 1983.

Selected Works, Heinemann, 1985.

The Songs of Distant Earth, Del Rey, 1986.

(Author of afterword) Paul Preuss, *Breaking Strain,* Avon, 1987.

2061: Odyssey Three, Del Rey, 1988.

(With Gentry Lee) *Cradle,* Warner Books, 1988.

(Author of afterword) Paul Preuss, *Maelstrom,* Avon, 1988.

A Meeting with Medusa (bound with *Green Mars* by Kim Stanley Robinson), Tor Books, 1988.

(With Lee) *Rama II,* Bantam, 1989.

OTHER

Opus 700, Gollancz, 1990.

Also author of television series "Arthur C. Clarke's World of Strange Powers" and a movie treatment based on *Cradle.* Contributor of over six hundred articles and short stories, occasionally under pseudonyms E. G. O'Brien and Charles Willis, to numerous magazines, including *Harper's, Playboy, New York Times Magazine, Vogue, Holiday,* and *Horizon.*

Clarke's works have been translated into Polish, Russian, French, German, Spanish, Serbo-Croatian, Greek, Hebrew, Dutch, and over twenty other languages.

WORK IN PROGRESS: Afterwords for "Arthur C. Clarke's Venus Prime Series," Volumes III-VI; *Rama III* and *Rama IV,* with Gentry Lee, for Bantam; *Tales from Planet Earth; Arthur C. Clarke's Century of Mysteries,* with John Fairley and Simon Welfare, for Collins; editing *Project Solar Sail* for the World Space Foundation; consulting on television scripts for a series adaptation of *A Fall of Moondust.*

SIDELIGHTS: Renowned not only for his science fiction, which has earned him the title of Grand Master from the Science Fiction Writers of America, Arthur C. Clarke also has a reputation for first-rate scientific and technical writing. Perhaps best known in this field for "Extraterrestrial Relays," the 1945 article in which he first proposed the idea of communications satellites, Clarke has also published works on such diverse topics as underwater diving, space exploration, and scientific extrapolation. Nevertheless, it is Clarke's science fiction which has secured him his reputation, with such novels as *Childhood's End* and *Rendezvous with Rama* acknowledged as classics in their field. In addition, his story "The Nine Billion Names of God" was named to the science fiction "Hall of Fame," while the movie "2001: A Space Odyssey," written with director Stanley Kubrick, has been called the most important science fiction film ever made.

Often dealing with themes of exploration and discovery, Clarke's fiction almost always conveys to the reader a sense of wonder about the universe. Some critics, seeing the author's detailed descriptions of possible futures, have accused Clarke of ignoring the human element for the sake of science in his work. But while the development of scientific ideas and speculations plays a large role in Clarke's narratives, "what distinguishes Clarke's fictions from the usually more ephemeral examples of science fiction is his vision," asserts Eric S. Rabkin in his study *Arthur C. Clarke.* This vision, writes Rabkin, is "a humane and open and fundamentally optimistic view of humankind and its potential in a universe which dwarfs us in physical size but which we may hope some day to match in spirit."

Born in 1917 in an English seaside town, Clarke first discovered science fiction at the age of 12, when he encountered the pulp magazine *Amazing Stories.* The encounter soon became an "addiction," as Clarke describes in the *New York Times Book Review:* "During my lunch hour away from school I used to haunt the local Woolworths in search of my fix, which cost threepence a shot, roughly a quarter today." The young Clarke then began nurturing his love for the genre on the books of such English writers as H. G. Wells and Olaf Stapledon. He started writing his own stories for a school magazine while in his teens, but was unable to continue his schooling for lack of funds. He consequently secured a civil service job as an auditor, which left him plenty of free time to pursue his "hobby." Alone in London, Clarke joined an association of several science fiction and space enthusiasts, and as he relates in *The View from Serendip,* "my life was dominated by the infant British Interplanetary Society, of which I was treasurer and general propagandist." As part of his involvement with the BIS, Clarke wrote several scientific articles on the feasibility of space travel for the organization's journal; the BIS also gained him contacts with several science fiction editors and writers, which led to the publication of some of his short stories.

In 1941, although his auditor's position was still a reserved occupation, Clarke engaged in "what was probably the single most decisive act of my entire life," as he describes in *Ascent to Orbit: The Technical Writings of Arthur C. Clarke;* he voluntarily enlisted in the Royal Air Force. En route to becoming a radar instructor in a new system called Ground Controlled Approach, Clarke taught himself mathematical and electronics theory. After World War II ended, Clarke entered college and obtained a degree in physics as well as pure and applied mathematics; after graduation he spent two years as an assistant editor for a technical journal. But with publication of the novel *Childhood's End* (1953) and *The Exploration of Space,* which in 1952 was the first science book ever chosen as a Book-of-the-Month Club selection, Clarke began earning enough money to pursue writing full-time.

The Exploration of Space, besides allowing Clarke to leave his job, also broke ground in explaining scientific ideas to a popular audience. As H. H. Holmes describes in the *New York Herald Tribune Book Review,* in "the realm of speculative factual writing . . . Mr. Clarke's new book will serve as the most important yet in its field. Not that it says much that is new," explains Holmes, but because "it is precisely calculated to bring our present knowledge of space travel before a whole new public." What enables the book to reach such an audience is a "charm and magnetism" that is due to "Clarke's ability to reduce complex subjects to simple language and his steadfast avoidance of fantasy as a substitute for factual narration," observes Roy Gibbons in the *Chicago Sunday Tribune.* In contrast, F. L. Whipple writes in a 1952 *Saturday Review* article that the author's "imagination sometimes overwhelms his good resolve, causing him to stray from the narrow path of scientific probability." But Clarke himself "reminds us that in the history of scientific prediction, the wildest flights of fancy have fallen short of subsequent realities," observes Charles J. Rolo in the *Atlantic.* While its overall result might seem fantastic, *The Exploration of Space* is "an exceptionally lucid job of scientific exposition for the layman," concludes Rolo.

Clarke applied the same speculative techniques to other areas in the 1962 book *Profiles of the Future: An Inquiry into the Limits of the Possible.* The author "has a thorough grounding in science, and, in addition has a nimble and most receptive mind," states Isaac Asimov in the *New York Times Book Review.* "Nothing reasonable frightens him simply because it seems fantastic, and—equally important—nothing foolish attracts him simply because it seems fantastic." As his previous books have been, *Profiles of the Future* "is highly entertaining reading," remarks R. C. Cowen in the *Christian Science Monitor.* "It also is informative, for the author is careful to adhere to the yardstick of natural laws that set the bounds of the possible." The critic concludes that Clarke "thus helps a layman to learn the difference between rational speculation and . . . wholly baseless imaginings." Asimov concurs, writing that "this book offers all of us a chance to raise our eyes from the ground and to contemplate the scenery ahead. It is marvelous scenery indeed, and there could scarcely be a better guide to its landmarks than Arthur Clarke."

Although most speculative science texts are soon outdated, Clarke's work has withstood years of technical progress. In *The Promise of Space,* published in 1968 to "replace" *The Exploration of Space,* Clarke "is able to show the manner in which many of his predictions have been fulfilled," notes a *Times Literary Supplement* contributor. But rather than simply cataloging recent discoveries, Clarke's work incorporates them into new ideas: "All through the book Clarke not only recounts what has been done during the last two decades," describes Willy Ley in the *New York Times Book Review,* "but has his eye on both the immediate results and the future." Similarly, *Science* contributor Eugene M. Emme asserts that the book contains "the best available summary of scientific and imaginative theory regarding space potentials. . . . Collectively they offer a most persuasive rationale." A 1984 revision of *Profiles of the Future* also withstands years of advancement: "Testing the limits of technological progress," observes David N. Samuelson in the *Los Angeles Times Book Review,* "it has remained remarkably current since its 1962 book publication.'' Gregory Benford, who calls Clarke ''a vindicated sage in his own time,'' theorizes in the *Washington Post Book World* that while ''books on futurology date notoriously, this one has not, principally because Clarke was unafraid of being adventurous.'' And *New York Times Book Review* writer Gerald Jonas offers this reason for Clarke's success: ''What makes Clarke such an effective popularizer of science is that, without bobbling a decimal point or fudging a complex concept, he gives voice to the romantic side of scientific inquiry.''

Although much of Clarke's early fiction reinforced the idea that space travel was an eventuality, *Childhood's End*, his first successful novel, is ''Clarke's only work—fiction or nonfiction—in which 'The stars are not for Man,''' suggests Thomas D. Clareson in *Voices for the Future*. The novel relates the appearance of the Overlords, a race of devil-shaped aliens who have come to guide Earth to peace and prosperity. Beginning by eliminating all individual governments and thus ending war, the Overlords use their superior technology to solve the problems of poverty, hunger, and oppression. The cost of this utopia is that most scientific research is set aside as unnecessary, and the exploration of space is forbidden. The motives of the Overlords become clear as the youngest generation of humans develops extrasensory powers; the children of Earth are to join the Overmind, a collective galactic ''spirit'' that transcends physical form. The need for science, technology, and space is eliminated with humanity's maturation, and the Earth itself is destroyed as her children join the Overmind.

Some critics view *Childhood's End* as the first manifestation of the theme of spiritual evolution that appears throughout Clarke's fiction. John Huntington, writing in the critical anthology *Arthur C. Clarke*, believes the novel to be Clarke's solution to one of the problems posed by technological progress: how can spiritual development keep pace with scientific development when by making man comfortable, science often takes away man's curiosity and drive. *Childhood's End* solves the problem with a stage of ''transcendent evolution,'' and Huntington proposes that ''it is its elegant solution to the problem of progress that has rightly earned *Childhood's End* that 'classic' status it now enjoys.'' Donald A. Wollheim, however, considers this solution a negative one; writing in *The Universe Makers* he comments that the work ''has always seemed to me to be a novel of despair. Others may see it as offering hope, but this tampering with humanity always struck me as being synthetic.'' But other critics reaffirm the novel as hopeful: *Childhood's End* ''becomes a magnificently desperate attempt to continue to hope for a future for the race in the face of mounting evidence to the contrary,'' writes John Hollow in *Against the Night, the Stars: The Science Fiction of Arthur C. Clarke*. Written in 1953 in the midst of the Cold War, ''it becomes, in fact, a sometimes brilliant attempt to turn the contrary evidence to the positive,'' adds Hollow. ''It becomes nothing less than an effort to make positive the destruction of the race.''

For all its uplifting themes, some critics still fault the novel as imperfect. David N. Samuelson, for example, notes in the anthology *Arthur C. Clarke* that ''the literate reader, especially, may be put off by an imbalance between abstract theme and concrete illustration, by a persistent banality of style, in short, by what may seem a curious inattention to the means by which the author communicates his vision.'' Holmes, reviewing Clarke's book in the *New York Herald Tribune*, calls *Childhood's End* ''at once his least successful and most promising [work].'' The critic elaborates by remarking that the basic

ideas are ''fascinating, but the awkward imbalance between the vast major plot and a series of small-scale subplots makes for a diffuse and distracting novel.'' Nevertheless, the novel ''has a way of lingering in the imagination that suggests it may in time, and defiance of all criticism, find a place in the supreme pantheon of [science fiction] beside such works as [Mary Shelley's] *Frankenstein* and [H. G. Wells's] *The Time Machine*,'' observes Thomas M. Disch in the *Times Literary Supplement*. And *Science Fiction Review* writer Gene DeWeese declares, thirty years after its publication, that *Childhood's End* ''in my opinion [is] the best SF novel ever written.''

Perhaps Clarke's best known work, *2001: A Space Odyssey* was the result of four years work on both the film version and the subsequent novel. The collaboration between Clarke and director Stanley Kubrick began when the filmmaker sought a suitable basis for making the ''proverbial good science fiction movie,'' as he has frequently described it. The two finally settled upon Clarke's 1951 short story ''The Sentinel,'' and developed it ''not [into] a script, which in [Kubrick's] view does not contain enough of the visual and emotional information necessary for filming, but a prose version, rather like a novel,'' relates Michel Ciment in *Focus on the Science Fiction Film*. The result ''was of more help to him in creating the right atmosphere because it was more generous in its descriptions,'' adds Ciment.

The film and the novel have the same basic premise: a large black monolith has been sent to Earth to encourage the development of Man. First shown assisting in the ''dawn of man'' four million years ago, a monolith is next uncovered on the moon, and upon its unveiling sends a strong radio signal toward the outer planets. As a result the spaceship *Discovery*, operated by the intelligent computer HAL 9000, is sent in the direction of the signal to investigate. However, while the human crew is kept ignorant of the ship's true assignment, the HAL 9000 begins to eliminate what it sees as obstacles in the way of the mission—including all of the crew. First captain Dave Bowman manages to survive, however, and upon his arrival at a moon of Saturn (Jupiter in the film) encounters yet a third monolith which precipitates a journey through the infinite, ''into a world where time and space are relative in ways beyond Einstein,'' describes Penelope Gilliatt in the *New Yorker*. Bowman is transformed during this journey, and subsequently arrives at a higher plane of evolution as the Star Child. ''In the final transfiguration,'' notes Tim Hunter in *Film Heritage*, ''director Kubrick and co-author Arthur Clarke . . . suggest that evolutionary progress may in fact be cyclical, perhaps in the shape of a helix formation.'' The critic explains: ''Man progresses to a certain point in evolution, then begins again from scratch on a higher level.''

Because of the film's complexity and length, of which less than one-third was dedicated to dialogue, the early reviews of ''2001'' were mixed. Although ''2001'' is a landmark in the use of special visual effects, many critics find that the abundance of detail overwhelms the plot and character. ''Very quickly we see that the gadgets are there for themselves, not for use in an artwork,'' comments the *New Republic*'s Stanley Kauffmann. By de-emphasizing the human aspects, says Kauffmann, the result is ''a film that is so dull, it even dulls our interest in the technical ingenuity for the sake of which Kubrick has allowed it to become dull.'' Similarly, Joseph Gelmis of *Newsday* states that ''because its characters are standardized, bland, depersonalized near-automatons who have surrendered their humanity to the computers, the film is antidramatic and thus self-defeating. It moves at a slow, smug pace.'' But ''after seeing *2001: A Space Odyssey* a second time,'' Gelmis asserts his conviction that ''it is a masterwork.... This awesome film is light-years ahead of any science fiction you have ever seen.'' The critic explains that upon a second screening, he understands it is the ''dullness'' of the characters and conversation ''that makes the symbolic rebirth of this automaton Everyman of the 21st century so profoundly stirring and such a joyous reaffirmation of life.'' Gilliatt concurs, contending that Clarke and Kubrick ''have found a powerful idea to impel space conquerors whom puny times have robbed of much curiosity. The hunt for the remnant of a civilization ... turns the shots of emptied, comic, ludicrously dehumanized men into something more poignant.'' Later reviews of the film acknowledge its brilliance; a 1984 *New York Times* article by Vincent Canby calls it a ''witty, mind-bending science fiction classic'' that is ''forever separate ... from all [films] that came before and all that have come after.''

''Clarke's *2001: A Space Odyssey* was an extraordinary development in fiction, a novel written in collaboration with the director who was simultaneously filming it,'' writes Colin Greenland of the *Times Literary Supplement*. Clarke himself explains in the epilogue to the 1982 edition of *2001* that during the project he ''often had the strange experience of revising the manuscript *after* viewing rushes based upon an earlier version of the story—a stimulating but rather expensive way of writing a novel.'' Because the book appeared three months after the movie's premiere, it was inevitable that critics would draw comparisons between the two. *New Statesman* contributor Brenda Maddox finds the book lacking beside the movie; the novel ''has all the faults of the film and none of its virtues.'' The critic elaborates: ''The characters still have the subtlety of comic-strip men and, lacking the film's spectacular visual gimmickry ... the story must propel itself with little gusts of scientific explanation.'' In contrast, Eliot Fremont-Smith asserts in the *New York Times* that ''the immense and moving fantasy-idea of '2001' ... is an idea that can be *dramatically* envisioned only in the free oscillations of the delicately cued and stretched mind.'' The critic adds that the film ''is too direct for this, its wonders too unsubtle and, for all their majesty, too confining.'' And where the movie may have been obscure, ''all of it becomes clear and convincing in the novel. It is indeed an odyssey, this story, this exhilarating and rather chilling science fiction fantasy.'' Nevertheless, in comparing the visual genius of the film with the clarity of the book, Clarke himself admits in *Focus on the Science Fiction Film* that both versions ''did something that the other couldn't have done.''

2001 has also been compared to Clarke's other work and has received similar criticisms, such as the accusation that the novel concentrates on science at the expense of story. A *Times Literary Supplement* reviewer, for example, comments that ''too often the whole affair collapses into the science-popularization for which Mr. Clarke is well known.'' But Rabkin, while acknowledging the technical elements of the novel, believes that *2001* blends these elements into a ''mature amalgamation'' with Clarke's ''spiritual commitment to a homocentric and optimistic vision. In many ways,'' concludes Rabkin, ''the book may be his culminating artistic achievement.'' And *New Yorker* contributor Jeremy Bernstein similarly considers *2001* ''one of [Clarke's] best, full of poetry, scientific imagination, and typical wry Clarke wit.'' Claiming that the author's work transcends the typical science fiction novel, the critic writes that ''the Clarke genre is something else again.

By standing the universe on its head, he makes us see the ordinary universe in a different light.'' Summarizing Clarke's work with *2001* in a 1983 article, Jonas declares that '''2001' is not just another science-fiction novel or movie. It is a science-fiction milestone—one of the best novels in the genre and undoubtedly the best s.f. movie ever made.''

''Although it lacks some of the metaphysical fireworks and haunting visionary poetry of [his earlier work],'' Clarke's *Rendezvous with Rama* is nevertheless ''essentially an expression of wonder in the presence of Mystery,'' comments a *Virginia Quarterly Review* contributor. Written in 1973, the novel is the only work to win all four major awards in its genre; Disch calls it ''probably [Clarke's] most considerable work of art.'' The book follows the appearance of an asteroid-like object which is hurtling directly towards the inner solar system—and which turns out to be a cylindrical, obviously unnatural artifact. An Earth ship is dispatched to the object, labelled ''Rama,'' and a team led by commander Bill Norton enters to investigate. The exploration of the many mysterious aspects of Rama is interrupted by several distractions—including the emergence of what appears to be generated life forms and the arrival of a nuclear warhead sent by paranoid colonists from nearby Mercury. The study of Rama is concluded safely, however, although Norton's team has not gathered enough information to discern a purpose to the craft. Seemingly indifferent to a meeting with intelligent life, Rama then exits the solar system and continues its journey. ''This is story-telling of the highest order,'' notes Theodore Sturgeon in the *New York Times Book Review*. ''There are perpetual surprise, constant evocation of the sense of wonder, and occasions of the most breathless suspense.''

Because the emphasis of the novel is on the exploration of Rama, ''Mr. Clarke, according to his custom, is benignly indifferent to the niceties of characterization,'' writes *New York Times* contributor John Leonard. Melody Hardy similarly observes in *Best Sellers* that the book ''is almost totally devoid of human interest,'' although she admits that ''it does possess the enticing characteristics of science fiction at its best.'' Sturgeon suggests, however, that this lack of characterization may be an asset, for ''unbothered by human subtleties one may gaze cleareyed at the horizonless reach of the man's mind, its command of naked Euclidean spectacle.'' Hardy also grants that ''perhaps Clarke's disinterest in characterization results from this view that the universe is indifferent to man.'' Rabkin calls the book's resolution, where man is ignored by an extrasolar intelligence, a ''unique repudiation of his homocentrism,'' an idea common to science fiction that man is important to the universe. ''But having done that,'' continues Rabkin, Clarke creates ''a novel not only of science but of a science dramatized, humanized. In the exploration of Rama, we readers feel the challenge of discovery and the exhilaration of using our minds, of encountering the new.'' Concludes the critic: ''That is one reason why the book, although it defies homocentrism, seems to uplift us.... *Rendezvous with Rama* is Arthur C. Clarke's most mature exploration of his constant theme of the meaning for mankind of science.''

Although classic works such as *Childhood's End* and *Rendezvous with Rama* focus on the effects of extraterrestrial visitation, Clarke's next two works concentrate more on the achievements of humanity. *Imperial Earth: A Fantasy of Love and Discord*, which takes place in the quincentennial year of 2276, most directly ''shows Clarke at the height of his [extrapolative] powers,'' remarks Jonas. The novel includes demonstrations of outer planet mining operations, cloning, and spaceship propulsion systems, all woven into the story of Titan native Duncan Makenzie's visit to Earth. Duncan's trip serves many purposes; ostensibly it is to deliver an address at the quincenntenial celebration, but it is also to investigate political and scientific intrigues, as well as to procure, through cloning, an heir for the sterile Duncan. Through Duncan's eyes "Clarke not only supplies us with a fair number of technological wonders," observes Mark Rose in the *New Republic*, but the author also "makes much of such human matters as the political and psychological isolation of a distant colonial world such as Titan." Nevertheless, "one problem with the full-blown novel of extrapolation is that the author may neglect plot and character," states Jonas. But while he notes some of these faults, *National Review* contributor Steve Ownbey calls *Imperial Earth* "a book nobody should miss. It's an utterly delightful tale, suspenseful and moving, full of unexpected chuckles and stunning surprises." And Rose comments that the novel is "a literary performance conducted with genuine intelligence and grace."

Clarke's Hugo and Nebula-winning *The Fountains of Paradise* is even more technical in its basic premise: the construction of an orbital "space elevator" designed to make escaping the Earth's gravity a simple process. Based on actual scientific treatises, Clarke once again develops his idea "with sufficient technical detail to lend plausibility" says Jonas, "and the more plausible it sounds, the more stupendous it becomes." The novel also concerns Vannevar Morgan, the engineer obsessed with realizing the creation of his space elevator. Providing a "curious backdrop" to Morgan's enterprise is "a highly advanced galactic civilization [which] has already communicated with the human race through a robot probe," summarizes Jonas. In addition, Morgan's story is paralleled by the account of Prince Kalidasa, who two thousand years earlier challenged the gods by attempting to build a garden tower into heaven—on Taprobane, the same island that Morgan wants for his elevator. But while critics commend this parallel, they fault Clarke for not sustaining it: "the direct interweaving of Kalidasa's story should have extended throughout the entire work rather than petering out," comments Paul Granahan in *Best Sellers*. Similarly, *New Republic* contributor Tim Myers criticizes Clarke for ending the parallel: "The Indian king, the only character with nobility, is taken from us. We are left with Morgan, a pathetic egotist who is also hopelessly stereotyped."

In contrast to these criticisms, Algis Budrys praises the author for combining two themes that have marked Clarke's work: mysticism and technology. In the *Magazine of Fantasy and Science Fiction*, Budrys comments that *The Fountains of Paradise* "is the first instance in which all the author's demonstrated capabilities have melded. Not *perfectly*, mind you . . . but more than well enough to constitute a crucial event in Clarke's career, and thus in SF." And Steve Brown expresses the opinion in *Science Fiction Review* that "Clarke's prose hasn't been this good in years, effortless, stripped to the bone, and clear as mylar." Continues the critic: "The Tower is much more impressive than Rama, (or [Larry] Niven's Ringworld, for that matter) because it seems so *real*, something that could, and should, actually be done. . . . [Clarke's] total control of his material illuminates every corner of the landscape, in deft little brushstrokes." "As I read I kept pushing myself further and further back in my chair, squealing with vertigo," recounts *New Statesman* contributor Kingsley Amis. "This is not Arthur Clarke's best novel, . . . [but] it's delightfully written, always interesting, and at times almost unbearably exciting."

Although for several years Clarke (and others) insisted that a sequel to *2001* would be impossible, in 1982 Clarke published *2010: Odyssey Two*. Incorporating elements of both the film and novel versions, as well as new information from the Voyager probes of Jupiter, in *2010* "Clarke sensibly steps back down to our level to tell the story of a combined Russian and American expedition to salvage Bowman's deserted ship, the Discovery, and find out what happened," relates Greenland. Although the expedition finds the remains of the ship and repairs the HAL 9000, the purpose of the black monolith mystifies them. While some critics find this an adequate approach to a sequel, others criticize Clarke for even attempting to follow up a "classic." DeWeese believes a large problem is that *2010* "is not so much a sequel to the original book, which was in many ways superior to the movie, but a sequel to and an explanation of the movie. Unfortunately, many of these explanations already existed [in the novel of *2001*;cb." *Washington Post Book World* contributor Michael Bishop similarly notes a tendency to over-explain: "Ponderous expository dialogue alternates with straightforward expository passages in which Heywood Floyd . . . or the author himself lectures the reader." And Jonas complains that *2010* "violates the mystery [of the original] at every turn."

In addition, observers comment on a lack of emphasis on character; Jonas writes that Clarke "fails to make [the characters] any more interesting as people than they were the first time around." The emotional level seems to be overly subdued, remarks Greenland; Clarke "can't handle any of the real turbulence of human intercourse." But while noting similar flaws in the novel's characterization, Bishop admits that in *2010* "Clarke has striven heroically to outfit his characters with recognizable longings, prejudices, and fears." And Hollow believes that emotional detachment is an important theme of the novel, suggesting that in *2010* "the natural process of maturity—and perhaps of evolution—is away from such fatal attractions."

Despite the various criticisms, *2010* still "has its share of that same sense of wonder, which means that it is one of the dozen or so most enjoyable SF books of the year," says DeWeese. "Clarke deftly blends discovery, philosophy, and a newly acquired sense of play," states *Time* contributor Peter Stoler, creating a work that will "entertain" readers. Cary Neeper presents a similar assessment in the *Christian Science Monitor*, noting that "Clarke's story drives on to an exciting finish in which the mix of fantasy and fact leaves the reader well satisfied with a book masterfully written." And in contrast to the criticisms of the sequel's worthiness, Bud Foote claims in the *Detroit News* that with "the book's penultimate triumph [of] a new, awesome and terrifying world transformation," Clarke has created "a fine book." The critic concludes that *2010* "is better than the original book, and it illuminates and completes the original movie. It is so good, in fact, that even Clarke couldn't write a sequel to it."

Despite this assertion and Clarke's own remarks to the *Washington Post*'s Curt Suplee that "if I ever do write 'Odyssey III'—allowing for the fact that my energies are declining—it won't be before the year 2001," 1988 brought *2061: Odyssey Three*, the next chapter in the saga of the black monolith. 2061 is the year of the next appearance of Halley's comet; *Odyssey Three* follows Heywood Floyd on a survey of the object. While en route, the survey party is redirected to rescue a ship that has crashed on the Jovian moon of Europa—the one celestial object the monoliths have warned humans against visiting. Some critics have been skeptical of a second sequel, such as the *Time* reviewer who finds that "the mix of imagination and anachronism is wearing as thin as the oxygen layer on Mars." Although Jonas also observes that "Mr. Clarke's heart is obviously not in the obligatory action scenes that advance the plot," he concedes that the author "remains a master at describing the wonders of the universe in sentences that combine a respect for scientific accuracy with an often startling lyricism." Clarke "is not to be measured by the same standards we apply to a mundane plot-smith," asserts David Brin in the *Los Angeles Times.* "He is, after all, the poet laureate of the Space Age. He is at his best making the reader feel, along with Heywood Floyd," continues Brin, "how fine it might be to stand upon an ancient comet, out under the stars, knowing that it is those dreams that finally come true that are the best dreams of all." And a *Kirkus Reviews* writer claims that *2061* is "the all-round best *Odyssey* so far. Indeed Clarke, with an absorbing blend of scientific extrapolation and events that generate their own tension, has returned to something like vintage form."

Between the publication of the two *Odyssey* sequels Clarke finished *The Songs of Distant Earth,* an elaborate revision and extension of a short story first published in 1958. The novel takes place on the ocean world of Thalassa, where the few habitable islands there have been populated by descendants of an Earth "seedship," sent to perpetuate humanity even after the nova explosion of the Earth's sun. The Thalassan society is a type of utopia, for superstition, prejudice, and extreme violence no longer exist; the robots who raised the first generations eliminated all religion and art which might encourage these elements. The Thalassans are seemingly content with their world when the starship *Magellan* lands, bringing with it the last survivors (and witnesses) of the Earth's destruction. Although the ship is not permitted to colonize a world that has already been settled, the idyllic setting tempts the crew to a possible mutiny. Further complicating the situation is the emergence of a marine life form that appears to be intelligent, creating a possible conflict on two different fronts.

Although this dilemma "makes for an interesting novel," *Science Fiction Review* contributor Richard E. Geis still faults Clarke's plot as improbable, decrying the lack of individual conflict. Echoing previous criticisms, Geis comments that the "characters are uncomplicated, non-neurotic, with only minor problems to be solved. . . . Clarke has written a story of plausible high-tech future science and peopled it with implausible, idealized,'nice' humans." In contrast, Dan K. Moran of the *West Coast Review of Books* believes that "how Clarke deals with the mutiny is interesting; and his characters come alive throughout." Nevertheless, the critic finds that "the great flaw is the lack of sense-of-wonder. Nothing herein is really new, neither science nor Clarke's synthesis," concludes Moran.

Countering the criticism that the novel lacks conflict, Jonas suggests that "the drama that interests Mr. Clarke is played out on a much larger canvas. It concerns the lures and limitations of knowledge, the destiny of mankind and the fate of the universe. . . . He knows what few philosophers (or poets, for that matter) know—prolixity only diminishes big themes." "It is ultimately not Clarke's ambitious imagination, or his skilful depiction of the joys of reason, that characterizes *The Songs of Distant Earth,*" observes Greenland, "but rather the pathos of his vision of humanity, burdened by knowledge and loss, exiled from innocence and tranquility, forever searching

the stars for the face of God." Jonas similarly notes that "the key to [Clarke's] achievement is to be found not in his utopian fantasies but in his poetic evocation of human dignity in the face of death." Concludes the critic: "This is not a poetry that relies on fresh language or fresh insights; it is a poetry of perspective, of attitude; it invites us to forget our petty problems in the contemplation of a mortality so immense as to mimic immortality in scale." "*The Songs of Distant Earth,* in other words, repeats the question that *Childhood's End, 2001,* and *2010* were meant to answer," declares Hollow. The resolution or "discovery that our species is a part of some near-divine plan [does not] really answer the central difficulty, that each of us will one day have to stop voyaging into the future."

This question or "grand theme" that runs throughout Clarke's fiction "can be stated only in the form of a paradox," suggests Jonas: "Man is most himself when he strives greatly, when he challenges the very laws of the universe; yet man is small and the universe is large, and anything he creates must, in the long run, be dwarfed by the works of others." The science in Clarke's fiction provides a good backdrop for this theme; Benford writes that Clarke "prefers a pure, dispassionate statement of facts and relationships, yet the result is not cold. Instead, he achieves a rendering of the scientific esthetic, with its respect for the universal qualities of intelligence, its tenacity and curiosity. His fiction neglects conflict and the broad spectrum of emotion, which gives it a curiously refreshing honesty." Although Clarke's fiction "may appear to be about science, appear to be about numbers, appear to be about ideas," Rabkin feels that "in fact at bottom whatever Clarke writes is about people and that means it is about the human spirit."

"Science fiction is often called escapism—always in a negative sense," Clarke told Alice K. Turner in a *Publishers Weekly* interview. "Of course it's not true. Science fiction is virtually the only kind of writing that's dealing with real problems and possibilities; it's a concerned fiction." Clarke added that "we know so much more now that we don't have to waste time on the petty things of the past. We can use the enormous technological advances in our work. Vision is wider now, and interest has never been deeper." Although he has been involved with the genre for over half a century, Clarke believes that "today's readers of science fiction are indeed fortunate; this really is the genre's Gold Age," the author writes in a 1983 *New York Times Book Review* article. Nevertheless, Clarke has not greatly changed his style and themes throughout his career. "I guess I'm just an old conservative," the author told Charles Platt in *Dream Makers: The Uncommon Men and Women Who Write Science Fiction.* "Although, really, if I have stayed true to the original form of my writing that's simply because I have a constant commitment to science." Clarke also remarked to Platt that he is proud of retaining the "sense of wonder" in his writing: "I regard it as something of an achievement not to have become cynical. . . . I do remain an optimist, especially in my fiction, because I hope it may operate as a self-fulfilling prophecy." This dedication to the idealism of science is reflected in a 1966 interview with *New York Times Magazine* contributor Godfrey Smith: referring to the consequences of the space race, Clarke commented that "of the many lessons to be drawn from this slice of recent history, the one that I wish to emphasize is this. Anything that is theoretically possible will be achieved in practice, no matter what the technical difficulties, if it is desired greatly enough."

MEDIA ADAPTATIONS: Arthur C. Clarke has made the following sound recordings of his works for Caedmon: *Arthur C.*

Clarke Reads from his 2001: A Space Odyssey, 1976; *Transit of Earth; The Nine Billion Names of God; The Star*, 1978; *The Fountains of Paradise*, 1979; *Childhood's End*, 1979; and *2010: Odyssey Two*. A full-length recording of *A Fall of Moondust* was made by Harcourt in 1976.

2010: Odyssey Two was filmed in 1984 by Metro-Goldwyn-Mayer (Clarke has a cameo in the film); the short story "The Star" was adapted for an episode of "The New Twilight Zone" by CBS-TV in 1985. The following works have been optioned for movies: *Childhood's End*, by Universal; *The Songs of Distant Earth*, by Michael Phillips; *The Fountains of Paradise*, by Robert Swarthe; and *Cradle*, by Peter Guber.

AVOCATIONAL INTERESTS: "Observing the equatorial skies with a fourteen-inch telescope," table-tennis, scuba diving, and "playing with his Rhodesian Ridgeback and his six computers."

BIOGRAPHICAL/CRITICAL SOURCES:

BOOKS

Agel, Jerome, editor, *The Making of Kubrick's 2001*, New American Library, 1970.
Bleiler, E. F., editor, *Science Fiction Writers*, Scribners, 1982.
Clareson, Thomas D., editor, *Voices for the Future: Essays on Major SF Writers*, Bowling Green University Press, 1976.
Clarke, Arthur C., *2001: A Space Odyssey*, New American Library, 1968, published with new afterword, 1982.
Clarke, Arthur C., *The View from Serendip*, Random House, 1977.
Clarke, Arthur C., *Ascent to Orbit, a Technical Autobiography: The Technical Writings of Arthur C. Clarke*, Wiley, 1984.
Clarke, Arthur C., *Astounding Days*, Bantam, 1989.
Contemporary Literary Criticism, Gale, Volume 1, 1973, Volume 4, 1975, Volume 13, 1980, Volume 16, 1981, Volume 18, 1981, Volume 35, 1985.
Hollow, John, *Against the Night, the Stars: The Science Fiction of Arthur C. Clarke*, Harcourt, 1983, expanded edition, Ohio University Press, 1987.
Johnson, William, editor, *Focus on the Science Fiction Film*, Prentice-Hall, 1972.
Magill, Frank N., editor, *Survey of Science Fiction Literature*, Volumes 1-5, Salem Press, 1979.
Malik, Rex, editor, *Future Imperfect*, Pinter, 1980.
Moskowitz, Sam, *Seekers of Tomorrow*, Ballantine, 1967.
Olander, Joseph D., and Martin Harry Greenburg, editors, *Arthur C. Clarke*, Taplinger, 1977.
Platt, Charles, *Dream Makers: The Uncommon Men and Women Who Write Science Fiction*, Volume II, Berkley Publishing, 1983.
Rabkin, Eric S., *Arthur C. Clarke*, Starmont House, 1979.
Samuelson, David N., *Arthur C. Clarke: A Primary and Secondary Bibliography*, G. K. Hall, 1984.
Slusser, George Edgar, *The Space Odysseys of Arthur C. Clarke*, Borgo Press, 1978.
Wollheim, Donald A., *The Universe Makers*, Harper, 1971.

PERIODICALS

Algol, November, 1974.
Atlantic, July, 1952.
Best Sellers, October 1, 1973, May, 1979.
Chicago Sunday Tribune, July 13, 1952.
Christian Science Monitor, February 26, 1963, December 3, 1982.

Commonweal, May 3, 1968.
Detroit News, November 28, 1982.
Kirkus Reviews, November 1, 1987.
Los Angeles Times, December 1, 1982.
Los Angeles Times Book Review, December 19, 1982, March 4, 1984, December 6, 1987.
Magazine of Fantasy and Science Fiction, September, 1979.
Nation, March 5, 1983.
National Review, May 14, 1976.
New Republic, May 4, 1968, March 20, 1976, March 24, 1979.
Newsday, April 4, 1968, April 20, 1968.
New Statesman, December 20, 1968, January 26, 1979.
Newsweek, October 30, 1961.
New Yorker, April 24, 1965, May 27, 1967, April 13, 1968, September 21, 1968, August 9, 1969, December 13, 1982, December 20, 1982.
New York Herald Tribune Book Review, July 13, 1952, August 10, 1952, August 23, 1953.
New York Times, May 29, 1968, July 5, 1968, August 22, 1973, February 26, 1985.
New York Times Book Review, March 14, 1954, April 14, 1963, August 25, 1968, September 23, 1973, January 18, 1976, October 30, 1977, March 18, 1979, January 23, 1983, March 6, 1983, May 11, 1986, December 20, 1987.
New York Times Magazine, March 6, 1966.
Omni, March, 1979.
People, December 20, 1982.
Playboy, July, 1986.
Publishers Weekly, September 10, 1973, June 14, 1976.
Reader's Digest, April, 1969.
Saturday Review, July 5, 1952, April 20, 1968.
Science, August 30, 1968.
Science Fiction Review, March/April, 1979, August, 1981, February, 1983, May, 1984, summer, 1986.
Time, July 19, 1968, November 15, 1982, January 11, 1988.
Times (London), November 25, 1982.
Times Literary Supplement, July 15, 1968, January 2, 1969, December 5, 1975, June 16, 1978, January 21, 1983, October 31, 1986.
Virginia Quarterly Review, winter, 1974.
Washington Post, February 16, 1982, November 16, 1982.
Washington Post Book World, December 26, 1982, March 25, 1984.
West Coast Review of Books, Number 1, 1986.
World Press Review, April, 1985.

—*Sketch by Diane Telgen*

*   *   *

CLEMENT, Wallace 1949-

PERSONAL: Born March 1, 1949, in Niagara-on-the-Lake, Ontario, Canada. *Education:* McMaster University, B.A. (with honors), 1972; Carleton University, M.A., 1973, Ph.D., 1976.

ADDRESSES: Office—Department of Sociology and Anthropology, Carleton University, Ottawa, Ontario, Canada.

CAREER: McMaster University, Hamilton, Ontario, assistant professor of sociology, 1975-80; Carleton University, Ottawa, Ontario, associate professor, 1980-84, professor of sociology and anthropology, 1984—. Guest researcher, Swedish Work Life Center, 1984-85; visiting researcher, University of New England, 1986; visiting professor, University of Augsburg, 1988.

MEMBER: Studies in the Political Economy of Canada (member of executive board; member of board of directors, 1978—).

AWARDS, HONORS: Canada Council grant, 1977-78; grants from Canada's Social Sciences and Humanities Research Council, 1982-89.

WRITINGS:

The Canadian Corporate Elite: An Analysis of Economic Power, McClelland & Stewart, 1975.
Continental Corporate Power: Economic Elite Linkages Between Canada and the United States, McClelland & Steward, 1977.
(With Daniel Drache) *A Practical Guide to Canadian Political Economy,* James Lorimer and Co., 1978, 2nd edition published as *The New Practical Guide to Canadian Political Economy,* 1986.
Hardrock Mining: Industrial Relations and Technological Change at Inco, McClelland & Stewart, 1981.
Class, Power, and Property: Essays on Canadian Society, Methuen, 1983.
The Struggle to Organize: Resistance in Canada's Fishery, McClelland & Stewart, 1986.
The Challenge of Class Analysis, Carleton University Press, 1988.

Contributor of chapters to over seventeen books, including *The Canadian State: The Political Economy and Political Power,* University of Toronto Press, 1977, *People, Power, and Process: Sociology for Canadians,* McGraw, 1980, *Modern Canada, 1930-1980: Readings in Canadian Social History,* McCelland & Stewart, 1984, *Understanding Canadian Society,* McGraw, 1988. Also contributor to *New Canadian Encyclopedia.* Contributor of more than forty articles and reviews to sociology and Canadian studies journals. *Studies in Political Economy,* member of editorial board, 1978—, editorial board coordinator, 1982—; member of editorial board, *Journal of Canadian Studies,* 1979—, and *Australian-Canadian Studies,* 1986—.

WORK IN PROGRESS: A comparative class-structure project.

*   *   *

CLEVERLEY FORD, D(ouglas) W(illiam) 1914-

PERSONAL: Born March 4, 1914, in Sheringham, England; son of Arthur James (a clerk) and Mildred (Cleverley) Ford; married Olga Mary Gilbart-Smith, June 28, 1939. *Education:* London College of Divinity, A.L.C.D. (with first class honors), 1936; University of London, B.D., 1937, M.Th., 1941.

ADDRESSES: Home—Rostrevor, Lingfield, Surrey RH7 6BZ, England.

CAREER: Ordained priest of Church of England in St. Paul's Cathedral, London, England, 1937; London College of Divinity, London, tutor, 1937-39; Bridlington, Yorkshire, England, curate, 1939-42; Holy Trinity, Hampstead, London, vicar, 1942-55; Holy Trinity, South Kensington, London, vicar, 1955-74; senior chaplain to the Archbishop of Canterbury, Canterbury, England, 1975-80; Six Preacher of Canterbury Cathedral, Canterbury, 1982—. Chaplain to Queen Elizabeth II, 1973-84. Honorary director, College of Preachers, 1960-73; rural dean of Westminster, 1965-74; prebendary of St. Paul's Cathedral, 1968, currently prebendary emeritus; provincial canon of York, 1969—. Chairman of Queen Alexandra's House, Kensington

Gore, 1966-74. Member of governing body, Westminster City School and United Westminster Schools, 1965-74.

MEMBER: British and Foreign Bible Society (life governor), Church's Ministry among the Jews, Athenaeum Club (London).

AWARDS, HONORS: Queen's Jubilee Medal, 1977.

WRITINGS:

Why Men Believe in Jesus Christ, Lutterworth, 1950.
A Key to Genesis, S.P.C.K., 1951.
An Expository Preacher's Notebook, Hodder & Stoughton, 1960, Harper, 1961.
A Theological Preacher's Notebook, Hodder & Stoughton, 1962.
(Co-author) *The Churchman's Companion,* Hodder & Stoughton, 1964.
A Pastoral Preacher's Notebook, Hodder & Stoughton, 1965.
A Reading of St. Luke's Gospel, Lippincott, 1967.
Preaching at the Parish Communion, Mobray, Volume 1, 1967, Volume 2: *On the Epistles,* 1968, Volume 3: *On Saints' Days and Holy Days,* 1969, Volume 7, 1975.
Preaching Today, S.P.C.K., 1969.
Preaching through the Christian Year: Sermon Outlines for the Seasons of the Church's Year, Mobray, 1971.
Praying through the Christian Year, Mobray, 1973.
Have You Anything to Declare?, Mobray, 1973.
Preaching on Special Occasions, Mobray, Volume 1, 1975, Volume 2, 1982.
New Preaching from the Old Testament, Mobray, 1976.
New Preaching from the New Testament, Mobray, 1977.
The Ministry of the Word, Hodder & Stoughton, 1979, Eerdmans, 1980.
Preaching through the Acts of the Apostles, Mobray, 1980.
More Preaching from the New Testament, Mobray, 1982.
More Preaching from the Old Testament, Mobray, 1983.
Preaching through the Psalms, Mobray, 1984.
Preaching through the Life of Christ, Mobray, 1985, CBP Press, 1986.
Preaching on Devotional Occasions, Mobray, 1986.
From Strength to Strength, Mobray, 1987.
Preaching the Risen Christ, Mobray, 1988.
Preaching the Great Themes, Mobray, 1989.

Contributor to *Expository Times* (Edinburgh) and *Church Times* (London).

SIDELIGHTS: D. W. Cleverly Ford told *CA* that he began his writing career because people wanted to read what he had said in lectures in sermons. "Since my spoken word had always been carefully prepared, having been written and rewritten," he says, "this was not difficult. Writing for speaking is different from writing for reading, but it is good training in the art of clarity. I believe that a writer's work will be flat if it pays attention only to conveying information couched in a good literary style; it also needs to move the reader. This implies a sense of drama. I suppose a person either has or has not this sense. A rough and ready test of a good piece of writing is whether or not the reader is sorry when he has come to the end."

AVOCATIONAL INTERESTS: Music, the arts, European travel, gardening and carpentry at his house in the country.

BIOGRAPHICAL/CRITICAL SOURCES:

PERIODICALS

Church Times, January 4, 1963.

COCHRANE, Eric W.   1928-1985

PERSONAL: Born May 13, 1928, in Berkeley, Calif.; died following a stroke, November 29, 1985, in Florence, Italy; son of Eric and Adelaide (Griffith) Cochrane; married Lydia Goodwin Steinway (a French teacher), December 23, 1953; children: John, Nicholas. *Education:* Yale University, B.A., 1949, Ph. D., 1954. *Religion:* Roman Catholic.

ADDRESSES: Home—5220 South Greenwood Ave., Chicago, Ill. 60615; via dell'Anguillara 1, 50122 Florence, Italy. *Office*—Department of History, University of Chicago, 1126 East 59th St., Chicago, Ill. 60637.

CAREER: University of Chicago, Chicago, Ill., assistant professor, 1957-61, associate professor, 1961-67, professor of history, 1967-85. Fulbright scholar in Italy, 1951-53; visiting professor at University of Perugia, 1969-70. Member of board of trustees of Newberry Library, Chicago, beginning 1966. *Military service:* U.S. Army, served two years.

MEMBER: American Historical Association, American Catholic Historical Association (vice-president, 1972-73; president, 1973-74), Society for Italian Historical Studies, Societa Colombaria, Renaissance Society of America, Colorado and Utah Society of Chicago (secretary, 1972); Accademia Arte del Disegno, Deputazione Storia Patria Toscana.

AWARDS, HONORS: Guggenheim fellowship, 1961; Llewellyn John and Harriet Manchester Quantrell Award for Excellence in Undergraduate Teaching, from University of Chicago, 1965; Gordon J. Laing Prize, 1975, for *Florence in the Forgotten Centuries, 1527-1800: A History of Florence and Florentines in the Age of the Grand Dukes.*

WRITINGS:

Tradition and Enlightenment in the Tuscan Academies: 1690-1800, University of Chicago Press, 1961.
(Editor) *The Late Italian Renaissance,* Harper, 1970.
Florence in the Forgotten Centuries, 1527-1800: A History of Florence and the Florentines in the Age of the Grand Dukes, University of Chicago Press, 1973.
Historians and Historiography in the Italian Renaissance, University of Chicago Press, 1981.

Contributor to *Journal of Modern History, Archivio Storico Italiano, Commonweal,* and *Catholic Historical Review.*

WORK IN PROGRESS: Manuscript for book to be entitled, *Baroque Italy.*

OBITUARIES:

PERIODICALS

Chicago Tribune, December 4, 1985.
New York Times, December 4, 1985.
Times (London), December 5, 1985.*

*   *   *

COHEN, Morton N(orton)   1921-
(John Moreton)

PERSONAL: Born February 27, 1921, in Calgary, Alberta, Canada; son of Samuel and Zelda (Miller) Cohen. *Education:* Tufts University, B.A., 1949; Columbia University, M.A., 1950, Ph.D., 1958.

ADDRESSES: Home—72 Barrow St., Apt. 3-N, New York, N.Y. 10014. *Agent*—A. P. Watt & Son, 20 John St., London

WC1N 2DR, England; and Brandt & Brandt, 1501 Broadway, New York, N.Y. 10036.

CAREER: West Virginia University, Morgantown, instructor, 1950-51; City College of the City University of New York, New York, N.Y., tutor, 1952-53, lecturer, 1953-59, instructor, 1959-62, assistant professor, 1963-65, associate professor, 1966-70, professor of English, 1971-81, professor emeritus, 1981—, deputy executive officer, Ph.D. program in English, 1976-81. Visiting professor, Syracuse University, 1965-66, 1967-68. Senior Fulbright research fellow, Oxford University, 1974-75. *Military service:* U.S. Army, 1943-45; became sergeant; awarded Bronze Star, three battle stars.

MEMBER: Lewis Carroll Foundation of the United States of America (member of board of directors), Lewis Carroll Society, Modern Language Association of America, Century Association, Kipling Society, Lewis Carroll Birthplace Trust (member of board of directors), American Trust for the British Library (member of advisory council).

AWARDS, HONORS: Ford Foundation faculty fellowship, 1951-52; Fulbright fellowship, England, 1954-55, 1970-71; American Philosophical Society research grants, 1962, 1964; American Council of Learned Societies research grant, 1963; Guggenheim fellow, 1966-67; National Endowment for the Humanities senior fellowships, 1970-71, 1978-79.

WRITINGS:

Rider Haggard: His Life and Works, Hutchinson, 1960, Walker, 1961.
(With Robert Dickson) *A Brief Guide to Better Writing,* Oceana, 1960.
(Under pseudonym John Moreton) *Punky: Mouse for a Day* (juvenile), Faber, 1962, Putnam, 1965.
(Editor) *Rudyard Kipling to Rider Haggard: The Record of a Friendship,* Hutchinson, 1965.
(Adaptor) Sergei Prokofiev, *The Love for Three Oranges* (juvenile), Putnam, 1966.
(Editor) *The Letters of Lewis Carroll,* two volumes, Oxford University Press, 1979.
(Editor and author of introduction) *Lewis Carroll, Photographer of Children: Four Nude Studies,* C. N. Potter, 1979.
(Author of introduction) Lewis Carroll, *Alice's Adventures Under Ground,* Genesis Publications, 1979.
(Editor) *The Russian Journal—II: A Record Kept by Henry Perry Liddon of a Tour Taken with C. L. Dodgson in the Summer of 1867,* Lewis Carroll Society, 1979.
(Editor) *Lewis Carroll and the Kitchins: Containing Twenty-five Letters Not Previously Published and Nineteen of His Photographs,* Lewis Carroll Society, 1980.
(Editor and author of introduction and notes) *The Selected Letters of Lewis Carroll,* Pantheon, 1982.
Lewis Carroll and Alice, 1832-1982, Pierpont Morgan Library, 1982.
(Editor with Anita Gandolfo) *Lewis Carroll and the House of Macmillan,* Cambridge University Press, 1987.
Lewis Carroll: Interviews and Recollections, Macmillan, 1989.

Contributor to professional journals.

SIDELIGHTS: Morton N. Cohen researched for twenty years to compile his book *The Letters of Lewis Carroll.* Assisted by Roger Lancelyn Green, Cohen sifted through 4000 of Carroll's letters (totalling 98,721 by Carroll's count) before choosing 1,305 of them for publication. Concerning this collection, *New York Times Book Review* contributor Richard Ellman feels that "Professor Cohen is a brilliant editor. He has turned up letters in the most unexpected repositories, and the details he generously furnishes in his notes would often have defied any but the most Holmesian detection. . . . The results of Professor Cohen's scholarship are supplied lightheartedly and are no less interesting than the letters they illuminate.''

AVOCATIONAL INTERESTS: Antiques, the theater, travel.

BIOGRAPHICAL/CRITICAL SOURCES:

PERIODICALS

New York Times Book Review, June 17, 1979.
Publishers Weekly, July 2, 1979.
Times Literary Supplement, July 11, 1980.
Washington Post Book World, July 29, 1979.

*   *   *

COOKSON, Catherine (McMullen) 1906-
(Catherine Marchant)

PERSONAL: Born June 20, 1906, in Tyne Dock, South Shields, England; mother's name, Catherine Fawcett; married Thomas H. Cookson (a schoolmaster), June 1, 1940.

ADDRESSES: Home—Bristol Lodge, Langley on Tyne, Northumberland, England. *Agent*—Anthony Sheil Associates Ltd., 43 Doughty St., London WC1N 2LF, England.

CAREER: Writer. Lecturer for women's groups and other organizations.

MEMBER: Society of Authors, PEN (England), Authors Guild (U.S.A.), Authors League of America, Women's Press Club (London).

AWARDS, HONORS: Winifred Holtby Award for best regional novel from Royal Society of Literature, 1968, for *The Round Tower;* Order of the British Empire, 1985; recipient of Freedom of the County Borough of South Shields in recognition of her services to the city.

WRITINGS:

Kate Hannigan, Macdonald & Co., 1950, reprinted, Macdonald & Jane's, 1979.
Fifteen Streets (also see below), Macdonald & Co., 1952, reprinted, Corgi Books, 1979.
Colour Blind, Macdonald & Co., 1953, reprinted, Macdonald & Jane's, 1975, published as *Color Blind,* New American Library, 1977.
Maggie Rowan, Macdonald & Co., 1954, New American Library, 1975.
Rooney, Macdonald & Co., 1957, reprinted, Macdonald & Jane's, 1974.
The Menagerie, Macdonald & Co., 1958, reprinted, Macdonald & Jane's, 1974.
Slinky Jane, Macdonald & Co., 1959, reprinted, Macdonald & Jane's, 1979.
Fenwick Houses, Macdonald & Co., 1960, reprinted, Macdonald & Jane's, 1979.
The Garment, Macdonald & Co., 1962, New American Library, 1974.
The Blind Miller (also see below), Macdonald & Co., 1963, reprinted, Heinemann, 1979.
Hannah Massey, Macdonald & Co., 1964, New American Library, 1973.
The Long Corridor, Macdonald & Co., 1965, New American Library, 1976.

The Unbaited Trap, Macdonald & Co., 1966, New American Library, 1974.
Katie Mulholland, Macdonald & Co., 1967, reprinted, Macdonald & Jane's, 1980.
The Round Tower (also see below), Macdonald & Co., 1968, New American Library, 1975.
The Nice Bloke, Macdonald & Co., 1969, published as *The Husband,* New American Library, 1976.
Our Kate: An Autobiography, Macdonald & Co., 1969, Bobbs-Merrill, 1971, published as *Our Kate: Catherine Cookson—Her Personal Story,* Macdonald & Jane's, 1974.
The Glass Virgin, Macdonald & Co., 1970, Bantam, 1981.
The Invitation, Macdonald & Co., 1970, New American Library, 1974.
The Dwelling Place, Macdonald & Jane's, 1971.
Fanny McBride, Corgi Books, 1971, reprinted, Macdonald & Jane's, 1980.
Feathers in the Fire (also see below), Macdonald & Co., 1971, Bobbs-Merrill, 1972.
Pure as the Lily, Macdonald & Co., 1972, Bobbs-Merrill, 1973.
The Invisible Cord (also see below), Dutton, 1975.
The Gambling Man (also see below), Morrow, 1975.
The Tide of Life, Morrow, 1976.
The Girl (also see below), Morrow, 1977.
The Cinder Path (also see below), Morrow, 1978.
Tilly Trotter, Heinemann, 1978, published as *Tilly,* Morrow, 1980.
Selected Works, Heinemann/Octopus, Volume 1 (contains *Fifteen Streets, The Blind Miller, The Round Tower, Feathers in the Fire,* and *A Grand Man* [also see below]), 1978, Volume 2 (contains *The Mallen Streak* [also see below], *The Invisible Cord, The Gambling Man, The Girl,* and *The Cinder Path*), 1980.
The Man Who Cried, Morrow, 1979.
Tilly Wed, Morrow, 1981 (published in England as *Tilly Trotter Wed,* Heinemann, 1981).
Tilly Alone, Morrow, 1982 (published in England as *Tilly Widowed,* Heinemann, 1982).
The Whip, Summit Books, 1982.
Hamilton (comic), Heinemann, 1983.
The Black Velvet Gown, Summit Books, 1984.
Goodbye Hamilton, Heinemann, 1984.
The Bannaman Legacy, Summit Books, 1985 (published in England as *A Dinner of Herbs,* Heinemann, 1985).
Harold, Heinemann, 1985.
The Moth, Summit Books, 1986.
Bill Bailey, Heinemann, 1986.
Catherine Cookson Country, Heinemann, 1986.
The Parson's Daughter, Summit Books, 1987.
The Harrogate Secret, Summit Books, 1988.

''MARY ANN'' SERIES

A Grand Man, Macdonald & Co., 1954, Macmillan, 1955, reprinted, Morrow, 1975.
The Lord and Mary Ann, Macdonald & Co., 1956, reprinted, Macdonald & Jane's, 1974, Morrow, 1975.
The Devil and Mary Ann, Macdonald & Co., 1958, Morrow, 1976.
Love and Mary Ann, Macdonald & Co., 1961, Morrow, 1976.
Life and Mary Ann, Macdonald & Co., 1962, Morrow, 1977.
Marriage and Mary Ann, Macdonald & Co., 1964, Morrow, 1978.
Mary Ann's Angels, Macdonald & Co., 1965, Morrow, 1978.
Mary Ann and Bill, Macdonald & Co., 1966, Morrow, 1979.

Mary Ann Omnibus (contains all novels in "Mary Ann" series), Macdonald & Jane's, 1981.

"MALLEN NOVELS" TRILOGY

The Mallen Streak (also see below), Heinemann, 1973.
The Mallen Girl (also see below), Heinemann, 1974.
The Mallen Lot, Dutton, 1974 (published in England as *The Mallen Litter* [also see below], Heinemann, 1974).
The Mallen Novels (contains *The Mallen Streak, The Mallen Girl*, and *The Mallen Litter*), Heinemann, 1979.

JUVENILE NOVELS

Matty Doolin, Macdonald & Co.; 1965, New American Library, 1976.
Joe and the Gladiator, Macdonald & Co., 1968.
The Nipper, Bobbs-Merrill, 1970.
Blue Baccy, Macdonald & Jane's, 1972, Bobbs-Merrill, 1973.
Our John Willie, Morrow, 1974.
Mrs. Flanagan's Trumpet, Macdonald & Jane's, 1977, Lothrop, 1980.
Go Tell It to Mrs. Golightly, Macdonald & Jane's, 1977, Lothrop, 1980.
Lanky Jones, Lothrop, 1981.

UNDER PSEUDONYM CATHERINE MARCHANT

Heritage of Folly, Macdonald & Co., 1963, reprinted, Macdonald & Jane's, 1980.
The Fen Tiger, Macdonald & Co., 1963, Morrow, 1979.
House of Men, Macdonald & Co., 1964, Macdonald & Jane's, 1980.
Evil at Roger's Cross, Lancer Books, 1965, revised edition published as *The Iron Facade*, Heinemann, 1976, Morrow, 1980.
Miss Martha Mary Crawford, Heinemann, 1975, Morrow, 1976.
The Slow Awakening, Heinemann, 1976, Morrow, 1977.

SIDELIGHTS: Catherine Cookson is a prolific British author with a large following. Her family sagas, for which she is most noted, are read in some thirty countries, and in the early 1980s she was commemorated by Corgi Books for exceeding the 27 million mark in paperback sales alone. According to Anne Duchene in the *Times Literary Supplement,* "these days there are never fewer than fifty Cookson titles in print in English at any time; they are translated into fifteen languages; and new books are still readily produced." In a London *Times* interview with Caroline Moorehead, Cookson emphasizes that she never has trouble coming up with ideas for her historical novels: "I've always been a jabberer. I just talked. I see everything in images. The plot sort of unfolds. Even the dialogue. In the morning, it's all there to put down." The fact that readers easily identify with Cookson's characters is part of the reason her works have sold so well. As Duchene observes: "[Cookson] writes stories in which her readers can gratefully recognize experiences and emotions of their own—heightened, to be sure, by greater comedy or greater violence than their own lives normally vouchsafe, but based on all their own affections, furies, aspirations and reactions."

BIOGRAPHICAL/CRITICAL SOURCES:

BOOKS

Cookson, Catherine, *Our Kate: An Autobiography,* Macdonald & Co., 1969, Bobbs-Merrill, 1971, published as *Our Kate: Catherine Cookson—Her Personal Story,* Macdonald & Jane's, 1974.

PERIODICALS

Catholic World, June, 1955.
New York Times, January 7, 1955.
New York Times Book Review, October 20, 1974.
Times (London), August 15, 1983.
Times Literary Supplement, January 7, 1955, June 19, 1969, July 24, 1981.

*   *   *

CORCORAN, Barbara 1911-
(Paige Dixon, Gail Hamilton)

PERSONAL: Born April 12, 1911, in Hamilton, Mass.; daughter of John Gilbert (a physician) and Anna (Tuck) Corcoran. *Education:* Wellesley College, B.A., 1933; University of Montana, M.A., 1955; post-graduate study at University of Colorado, Denver, 1965-66. *Politics:* Democrat. *Religion:* Episcopalian.

ADDRESSES: Home—P.O. Box 4394, Missoula, Mont. 59806.

CAREER: Worked at a variety of jobs in New York, N.Y., and Hamilton, Mass., 1933-40, including writing for the Works Progress Administration, working as a theater manager, and working as a playwright and free-lance writer; Celebrity Service, Hollywood, Calif., researcher, 1945-53; Station KGVO, Missoula, Mont., copywriter, 1953-54; University of Kentucky, Covington, instructor in English, 1956-57; Columbia Broadcasting System, Hollywood, researcher, 1957-59; Marlboro School, Los Angeles, Calif., teacher of English, 1959-60; University of Colorado, Boulder, instructor in English, 1960-65; Palomar College, San Marcos, Calif., instructor in English, 1965-69; author of books for children and young adults, 1969—. Instructor in expressive writing, Austin Community College, 1983; instructor in writing for children, Women's Center, University of Missouri, Missoula, 1984—. *Wartime service:* Worked as a Navy inspector at a proximity-fuse factory in Ipswich, Mass., and for the Army Signal Corps in Arlington, Va., 1940-45.

MEMBER: Authors League of America, PEN.

AWARDS, HONORS: Samuel French Award for original play, 1955; children's book of the year citation, Child Study Association, 1970, for *The Long Journey;* William Allen White Children's Book Award, 1972, for *Sasha, My Friend;* Pacific Northwest Book Sellers' Award, 1975; outstanding science trade book for children citation, National Science Teachers Association, 1977, for *Summer of the White Goat.*

WRITINGS:

YOUNG ADULT NOVELS

Sam, illustrated by Barbara McGee, Atheneum, 1967.
(With Jeanne Dixon and Bradford Angier) *The Ghost of Spirit River,* Atheneum, 1968.
A Row of Tigers, illustrated by Richard L. Shell, Atheneum, 1969.
Sasha, My Friend, illustrated by Allan Eitzen, Atheneum, 1969.
The Long Journey, illustrated by Charles Robinson, Atheneum, 1970.
(With Angier) *A Star to the North* (Junior Literary Guild selection), Thomas Nelson, 1970.
The Lifestyle of Robie Tuckerman, Thomas Nelson, 1971.
This Is a Recording, illustrated by Richard Cuffari, Atheneum, 1971.

A Trick of Light (Junior Literary Guild selection), illustrated by Lydia Dabcovich, Atheneum, 1972.

Don't Slam the Door When You Go, Atheneum, 1972.

All the Summer Voices (historical), illustrated by Robinson, Atheneum, 1973.

The Winds of Time, illustrated by Gail Owens, Atheneum, 1973.

A Dance to Still Music, illustrated by Robinson, Atheneum, 1974.

Meet Me at Tamerlane's Tomb (mystery), illustrated by Robinson, Atheneum, 1975.

The Clown, Atheneum, 1975, published as *I Wish You Love,* Scholastic Book Services, 1977.

Axe-Time, Sword-Time (historical), Atheneum, 1976.

The Faraway Island, Atheneum, 1977.

Make No Sound, Atheneum, 1977.

(With Angier) *Ask for Love and They Give You Rice Pudding,* Houghton, 1977.

Hey, That's My Soul You're Stomping On, Atheneum, 1978.

Me and You and a Dog Named Blue, Atheneum, 1979.

Rising Damp, Atheneum, 1980.

The Person in the Potting Shed (mystery), Atheneum, 1980.

Making It, Little, Brown, 1980.

You're Allegro Dead (mystery), Atheneum, 1981.

Child of the Morning (Junior Literary Guild selection), Atheneum, 1982.

A Watery Grave (mystery), Atheneum, 1982.

Strike!, Atheneum, 1983.

Which Witch Is Which? (mystery), Atheneum, 1983.

August, Die She Must (mystery), Atheneum, 1984.

The Woman in Your Life, Atheneum, 1984.

Mystery on Ice (mystery), Atheneum, 1985.

The Shadowed Path (Moonstone Mystery Romance), Archway, 1985.

Face the Music, Atheneum, 1985.

A Horse Named Sky, Atheneum, 1986.

When Darkness Falls (Moonstone Mystery Romance), Archway, 1986.

I Am the Universe (Junior Literary Guild selection), Atheneum, 1986 (also published as *Who Am I Anyway?,* Field Enterprises).

You Put Up with Me, I'll Put Up with You (Junior Literary Guild selection), Atheneum, 1987.

The Hideaway (Junior Literary Guild selection), Atheneum, 1987.

The Sky Is Falling, Atheneum, 1988.

The Private World War of Lillian G. Adams, Atheneum, 1989.

HISTORICAL ROMANCE NOVELS

Abigail, Ballantine, 1981.

Abbie in Love (continuation of *Abigail*), Ballantine, 1981.

A Husband for Gail (conclusion of *Abigail*), Ballantine, 1981.

Beloved Enemy, Ballantine, 1981.

Call of the Heart, Ballantine, 1981.

Love Is Not Enough, Ballantine, 1981.

Song for Two Voices, Ballantine, 1981.

By the Silvery Moon, Ballantine, 1982.

UNDER PSEUDONYM PAIGE DIXON; JUVENILE NOVELS

Lion on the Mountain, illustrated by J. H. Breslow, Atheneum, 1972.

Silver Wolf (wildlife), illustrated by Ann Brewster, Atheneum, 1973.

The Young Grizzly (wildlife), illustrated by Grambs Miller, Atheneum, 1973.

Promises to Keep, Atheneum, 1974.

May I Cross Your Golden River?, Atheneum, 1975, published as *A Time to Love, A Time to Mourn,* Scholastic Book Services, 1982.

The Search for Charlie, Atheneum, 1976.

Cabin in the Sky (historical), Atheneum, 1976.

Pimm's Cup for Everybody, Atheneum, 1976.

Summer of the White Goat (wildlife), Atheneum, 1977.

The Loner: A Story of the Wolverine, illustrated by Miller, Atheneum, 1978.

Skipper (sequel to *May I Cross Your Golden River?*), Atheneum, 1979.

Walk My Way, Atheneum, 1980.

UNDER PSEUDONYM GAIL HAMILTON; JUVENILE NOVELS

Titania's Lodestone, Atheneum, 1975.

A Candle to the Devil (mystery), illustrated by Joanne Scribner, Atheneum, 1975.

Love Comes to Eunice K. O'Herlihy, Atheneum, 1977.

OTHER

"From the Drawn Sword" (play), first produced in Boston, 1940.

"Yankee Pine" (play), first produced at Bard College, Annandale-on-Hudson, N.Y., 1940.

The Mustang and Other Stories (short stories), Scholastic Book Services, 1978.

Contributor of radio scripts to "Dr. Christian" program; contributor of short stories and other pieces to *Glamour, Charm, Woman's Day, Redbook, American Girl,* and *Good Housekeeping.*

WORK IN PROGRESS: Other books for young people.

SIDELIGHTS: Barbara Corcoran, who also has written as Paige Dixon and Gail Hamilton, often fashions novels that feature young men and women who are generally handicapped. Some suffer a physical defect, such as deafness, a learning disability, or a terminal illness. Others must endure social or emotional stigmatas, such as shyness, being a member of a minority group, having eccentric parents, or coming from a broken family. In the end, each character must come to terms with his or her own problems by learning, growing, and maturing.

Margaret, the newly-deaf heroine of *A Dance to Still Music,* serves as a model of Corcoran's protagonists. Having recently recovered from a severe illness, Margaret "is trying in a bitter way to accept her handicap but not to overcome it," explains Jean Fritz in the *New York Times Book Review.* She runs away from her unfeeling mother in Key West, intending to return to her home in Maine. "En route," comments *Dictionary of Literary Biography* contributor Mary Lou White, "she has the good fortune to be cared for by a wonderful woman on a houseboat." She brings Margaret aboard and gradually coaxes her to come to terms with her disability.

A Dance to Still Music includes topics that are characteristic of Corcoran's fiction. "The themes of alienation and self-discovery appear with frequency in contemporary fiction," explains Charity Chang in *Children's Literature,* "[and] in *A Dance to Still Music* these themes are paramount and handled by Barbara Corcoran with finesse." In *A Dance to Still Music,* White declares, "Corcoran grasps the feelings of anger and frustration and skillfully develops the characters." Also, when Margaret first leaves Key West, she finds a fawn that has been hit by a truck. She brings it with her on the houseboat and helps ready it for an independent life in the woods. "Generally there is a wild animal in Barbara Corcoran's books," remarks Fritz; "indeed her stories are played out on the thin line between wilderness and civilization, and the intertwining of the two adds depth to her theme."

May I Cross Your Golden River?, which Corcoran wrote under the pseudonym Paige Dixon, is her "best book," according to White. It tells the story of eighteen-year-old Jordan Phillips, who suffers from amyotrophic lateral sclerosis—Lou Gehrig's disease, a type of muscular paralysis—and must come to terms with the immediate inevitability of his own death. In the story, says White, "Corcoran constructs a portrait of Jordan through the reactions of his friends and family."

While many reviewers enjoyed this book—Beryl Reid in *Publishers Weekly* calls it "one of the most touching and best books of [the winter 1975] season,"—others felt that Corcoran's treatment lacks depth. E. Coston Frederick, writing in the *Journal of Reading,* calls the novel "disappointing," and declares, "There really was no conflict . . . no one became hysterical or overly despondent; no one really approached the question: What are life—and death? And no real answers were found." *New York Times Book Review* contributor Georgess McHargue finds Dixon's depiction of Lou Gehrig's disease cliched; she states that Jordan's "affliction . . . is bloodless, physically almost painless, unequivocally hopeless, and affords its victim a dignity often denied to those of us clods who merely die of cancer or cirrhosis of the liver." Nonetheless, she concludes, "What makes the book worth reading is the warm and careful drawing of the Phillips family, particularly the four brothers. Their jokes are funny, their horseplay and self-mockery ring true, and in the end their lives and relationships are more important and moving than the drama of death."

BIOGRAPHICAL/CRITICAL SOURCES:

BOOKS

Butler, Francelia, editor, *Children's Literature: Annual of the Modern Language Association Seminar on Children's Literature and the Children's Literature Association,* Volume 4, Temple University Press, 1975.
Contemporary Authors Autobiography Series, Volume 2, Gale, 1985.
Contemporary Literary Criticism, Volume 17, Gale, 1981.
Dictionary of Literary Biography, Volume 52: *American Writers for Children since 1960: Fiction,* Gale, 1986.

PERIODICALS

Christian Science Monitor, November 2, 1967.
Horn Book, August, 1969, October, 1969, October, 1970, February, 1971, December, 1971, June, 1978.
In Review: Canadian Books for Children, summer, 1971.
Journal of Reading, February, 1976, March, 1976.
New York Times Book Review, October 3, 1971, November 3, 1974, November 17, 1974, January 4, 1976.

*   *   *

CORDIS, Lonny
  See DONSON, Cyril

*   *   *

COURTWRIGHT, David T(odd)   1952-

PERSONAL: Born April 10, 1952, in Kansas City, Mo.; son of Robert T. (a salesman) and Elizabeth (a nurse; maiden name, Brown) Courtwright; married Shelby Miller (a librarian), December 29, 1976; children: Andrew, Paul. *Education:* University of Kansas, B.A., 1974; Brown University, Ph.D., 1979. *Religion:* Catholic.

ADDRESSES: Home—3871 Arrow Point Tr. W., Jacksonville, Fla. 32211. *Office*—Department of History and Philosophy, University of North Florida, 4567 St. Johns Bluff Rd. S., Jacksonville, Fla. 32216.

CAREER: University of Hartford, West Hartford, Conn., assistant professor, 1979-85, associate professor of history, 1985-88, chairman of history department, 1979-88; University of North Florida, Jacksonville, professor of history and chairman of department, 1988—. Assistant clinical professor of community medicine and health care, University of Connecticut Health Center, Farmington, 1981-88. Trustee of Mark Twain Memorial, 1982-88.

MEMBER: American Historical Association, Organization of American Historians, Phi Beta Kappa.

AWARDS, HONORS: National Endowment for the Humanities fellowship, 1981.

WRITINGS:

(With Howard Barnstone, Stephen Fox, and Jerome Iowa) *The Architecture of John F. Staub: Houston and the South,* University of Texas Press, 1979.
Dark Paradise: Opiate Addiction in America before 1940, Harvard University Press, 1982.
(With Herman Joseph and Don Des Jarlais) *Addicts Who Survived: An Oral History of Narcotic Use in America, 1923-1965,* University of Tennessee Press, 1989.

Contributor of articles to periodicals, including *Journal of Southern History, William and Mary Quarterly,* and *Civil War History.*

WORK IN PROGRESS: A research project, "The Family, Sex, Marriage and Self in America since 1585."

SIDELIGHTS: David T. Courtwright's *Dark Paradise* documents the evolving use of opium during the early twentieth century. He reveals how the shift from medicinal to recreational use resulted in a change in the stereotypical addict, as the bourgeois woman of the late nineteenth century gave way to the lower-class male of pre-World War II America. In *Reviews in American History,* Roger Lane labelled *Dark Paradise* a "more refined product" than David Musto's *The American Disease,* a book which is considered a seminal work in the sociological field of drug use. In her *Times Literary Supplement* review of *Dark Paradise,* book critic Alethea Hayter predicted that this "valuable piece of research . . . will be useful to other social historians, [though] for the general reader, especially on the literary side, *Dark Paradise* is rather too specialized to make easy reading." Courtwright has also published *Addicts Who Survived,* a chronological sequel to *Dark Paradise* based upon extensive oral history interviews with American narcotic users who were active in the mid-twentieth century.

Courtwright told *CA:* "Most of my books and articles have been historical or interdisciplinary studies of drug use and alcoholism. At present I am working on several large-scale projects in demographic, family, and religious history."

BIOGRAPHICAL/CRITICAL SOURCES:

PERIODICALS

British Medical Journal, November 27, 1982.
Journal of the History of Medicine, April, 1983.
Reviews in American History, June, 1983.
Times Literary Supplement, November 5, 1982.

*　　*　　*

COVVEY, H(arry) Dominic J(oseph) 1944-

PERSONAL: Born March 14, 1944, in Philadelphia, Pa.; son of Harry Joseph, Jr., and Florence (Miller) Covvey; married Carol Lynn Patricia Thompson (a radiologist); children: Laura, Beth, Mark. *Education:* Attended St. Norbert College, 1962-65; University of Wisconsin—Madison, B.A., 1967; University of Toronto, M.Sc., 1971.

ADDRESSES: Home—103 Handsart Blvd., Winnipeg, Manitoba, Canada R3P OC4. *Office*—Clinicom International, 208-93 Lombard Ave. East, Winnipeg, Manitoba, Canada R3B 3B1.

CAREER: University of Wisconsin—Madison, technician at Space Astronomy Laboratories, 1966, research assistant in biophysics, 1967-68; Toronto General Hospital, Toronto, Ontario, junior physicist, 1968-71, professional assistant in cardiovascular unit, 1971-74, senior research fellow in cardiology, 1974-83, director of cardiovascular computing group, 1975-83, director of Clinical Research Computing Unit and research computing department, 1982-83; Clinicom International (health care consulting company), president and owner, 1983—; University of Manitoba, assistant professor of medicine, 1986—. University of Western Ontario, lecturer, and coordinator of computer application at university hospital, 1973-77; University of Toronto, lecturer 1975-84, member of computer systems research group, 1977-84, member of Institute of Biomedical Engineering, 1978-83, assistant professor, 1979-84. Member of faculty at Toronto Institute for Medical Technology, 1982. Speaker at more than one hundred scientific meetings; public lecturer.

Owner, Visual Computer Systems, Ltd., Toronto, 1971-79. Chairman of Standard Psychiatric Medical Record Committee, 1973-75, and London Area Psychological Testing Committee, 1974-76; member of professional advisory committee of Health Computer Information Bureau, 1975-80; member of Ontario Provincial Advisory Committee on the Computer Proceedings of Electrocardiograms, 1978-81; member of scientific review committee of Canadian Heart Foundation, 1978-83; director, Clinical Research Computing Ltd., Toronto, 1983—; senior member, Institute of Electrical and Electronic Engineers; member, Toronto Academy of Medicine, Canadian College of Health Service Executives, and Partner of Medical Computing Consultants Ltd., 1971-83. Chairman of workshops and seminars; assistant organizer of Computer Culture Expositions at Photo/Electric Arts Foundation, 1980-81. Consultant, Royal Commission on the Privacy and Confidentiality of Health Records.

MEMBER: Association for Computing Machinery, Healthcare Information and Management Systems Society, American Association for Medical Systems and Informatics, Canadian Cardiovascular Society, Canadian Information Processing Society, Canadian Organization for the Advancement of Computers in Health.

AWARDS, HONORS: Grants from Ontario Heart Foundation, 1971-74, 1974-77, 1976-77, 1977-80, 1980-83, 1981-83, Ontario Ministry of Health, 1972-75, 1975-77, 1980-83, Ivey Foundation, 1976, International Business Machines Foundation, 1977-82, Toronto General Hospital Foundation, 1979, Natural Science Engineering and Research Council, 1980, 1981, 1982, 1983-84, 1983-86, Food and Drug Administration, 1980, and National Health and Welfare, 1983.

WRITINGS:

(With N. H. McAlister) *Computers in the Practice of Medicine,* Volume 1: *Introduction to Computing Concepts,* Volume 2: *Issues in Medical Computing,* Addison-Wesley, 1980.
(With McAlister) *Computer Consciousness: Surviving the Automated Eighties,* Addison-Wesley, 1980.
(With McAlister) *Computer Choices: Beware of Conspicuous Computing,* Addison-Wesley, 1982.
Concepts and Issues in Health Care Computing, C. V. Mosby, 1985.

Also contributor to *Cardiac Pacing,* edited by B. S. Goldman, Jane Wilson, and others, 1982. Contributor of more than one hundred and fifty articles to medical and scientific journals, including *American Journal of Sports Medicine.* Editor of journal, *Healthcare Computing Strategies,* and of newsletter, *Healthcare Computing Tips and Warnings.*

WORK IN PROGRESS: Introduction to Databases for Healthcare Professionals.

SIDELIGHTS: H. Dominic J. Covvey has developed computer applications in a wide variety of medical specialties, ranging from psychiatry to dentistry, nephrology, oncology, and emergency care.

Covvey once told *CA:* "My main interest is to de-obfuscate computing. I prefer a light (slightly humorous) style and believe that technical material can be interesting and absorbing reading. I'm especially concerned about the oversell of high technology and the uncritical acceptance of computerization—and even its use as a status symbol—regardless of social sequels.

"The software crisis is the failure of software to keep up with the revolution in hardware. We are using fifth generation machines with second generation (and often second rate) software. We will continue to put computer systems into situations where even our lives depend on them—but they will be running software that almost certainly contains errors and that is increasingly inefficient and costly to produce, especially if we attempt real quality control.

"In some sense the exposure of children and the lay public to computers is good. What concerns me is that it will be a long time before these machines are really useful to the consumer, and therefore a rip-off is in process. Even businesses are being sold machines and programs that are inadequate—and it is only through use and subsequent recognition of the inadequacy (perhaps seen only after business failure) that the real capabilities and limits of the systems will be known. I believe we must create true consumerists among computer end-users and do so rapidly.

"The social impacts of computer technology also need to be recognized: dependence on unreliable systems (health-monitoring, air traffic control); the dangers to our privacy; the potential for mass joblessness; the 'faceless' centralization that often results; the potential for massive undetectable fraud; war-gaming and the potential for moving even closer to the edge of the nuclear abyss; automated nuclear response (launch on warning); cradle to grave surveillance; and many others. The computer is the ultimate sword and it has more than two edges.''

*　　*　　*

CRAFT, Maurice 1932-

PERSONAL: Born May 4, 1932, in London, England; son of Jack (an upholsterer) and Polly (Lewis) Craft; married Alma Sampson (a principal officer in the U.K. School Curriculum Development Committee), May 19, 1957; children: Anna, Naomi. Education: University of London, B.Sc.Econ., 1953, Academic Diploma in Education, 1959; University of Dublin, H.Dip.Ed., 1956; University of Liverpool, Ph.D., 1972.

ADDRESSES: Office—School of Education, University of Nottingham, University Park, Nottingham NG7 2RD, England.

CAREER: High school teacher in London, England, 1956-60; Edge Hill College of Education, Ormskirk, Lancashire, England, principal lecturer in sociology and head of department, 1960-67; University of Exeter, Exeter, Devon, England, senior lecturer in School of Education, 1967-73; La Trobe University, Melbourne, Australia, professor of education and chairman of Centre for the Study of Urban Education, 1973-75; University of London, London, Goldsmiths' Professor of Education at Institute of Education, 1976-80; University of Nottingham, Nottingham, England, professor of education, chairman of School of Education, dean of Faculty of Education, and Pro-Vice-Chancellor, 1980—.

Member of British delegation to European Economic Community Colloquia on Ethnic Minority Education, 1979, 1982; chairman of East Midlands Regional Consultative Group on Teacher Education, 1980—; United Kingdom delegate to Council of Europe seminars on the intercultural training of teachers, 1981-83. Consultant to numerous organizations, including Devonshire County Council, 1970-72, Australian Federal Poverty Commission, 1974-75, Social Science Research Council, 1974—, Association of Commonwealth Universities, 1976, 1979, Council for National Academic Awards, 1978—, House of Commons Home Affairs Committee, 1981, and British Government Committee on the Education of Children from Ethnic Minority Groups, 1982-83. Military service: British Army, Royal Army Ordnance Corps, 1953-55; served in Suez Canal Zone; became second lieutenant.

MEMBER: British Sociological Association, Association of Teachers in Colleges and Departments of Education (past member of national executive committee; founder and chairman of sociology section, 1967-69).

AWARDS, HONORS: Research grants from Social Science Research Council, 1966-72, 1974-76, Government of the Commonwealth of Australia, 1974-75, Japan Foundation, 1975, and Shell (U.K.) Ltd., 1984.

WRITINGS:

(Chief editor) Linking Home and School, Longmans, Green, 1967, revised edition, 1980.

(Editor with H. Lytton) Guidance and Counselling in British Schools, Edward Arnold, 1969, revised edition, 1974.
(Editor) Family Class and Education: A Reader, Longmans, Green, 1970.
Urban Education: A Dublin Case Study, Open University, 1974.
School Welfare Provision in Australia, Australian Government Public Service, 1976.
(Editor) Teaching in a Multicultural Society, Falmer Press, 1981.
Education for Diversity, University of Nottingham, 1982.
(With M. Atkins) Training Teachers of Ethnic Minority Community Languages, University of Nottingham, 1983.
Education in a Plural Society, Falmer Press, 1984.
Change in Teacher Education, Holt-Saunders, 1984.
Teacher Education in a Multicultural Society, University of Nottingham, 1986.
The Democratisation of Education, University of Nottingham, 1987.

CONTRIBUTOR

W. H. Pedley, editor, Education and Social Work, Pergamon, 1967.
W. Taylor, editor, Towards a Policy for the Education of Teachers, Butterworth, 1969.
J. W. Tibble, editor, The Future of Teacher Education, Routledge & Kegan Paul, 1971.
R. Jackson, editor, Careers Guidance: Practice and Problems, Edward Arnold, 1973.
S. J. Eggleston, editor, Contemporary Research in the Sociology of Education, Methuen, 1974.
R. E. Best, editor, Perspectives on Pastoral Care, Heinemann, 1979.
M. O'Mahony, editor, Young People, School and Society in Ireland, Mental Health Association of Ireland, 1981.
L. Cohen, editor, Educational Research and Development in Britain, 1970-80, NFER-Nelson, 1982.
J. Barlls and T. Lynch, editors, Multicultural Education in Western Societies, Holt, 1986.

OTHER

Joint general editor of ''Aspects of Modern Sociology'' series, Longmans, Green, 1965—; editor of ''Education in a Multicultural Society'' series, Batsford, 1981. Contributor to numerous professional journals. Member of management committee of Sociology of Education Abstracts; member of editorial board of Journal of Multilingual and Multicultural Development and Multicultural Education Abstracts.

WORK IN PROGRESS: Directing a national project in multicultural teacher education.

AVOCATIONAL INTERESTS: Music, walking.

*　　*　　*

CREASY, Rosalind R.

PERSONAL: Born in Boston, Mass.; daughter of Carleton A. (in sales) and Alice (a writer; maiden name, White) Reeves; married Robert J. Creasy (a computer scientist), June 23, 1961; children: Robert William, Laura Lynn. Education: Attended New York University, 1960, and Foothill College, 1970-74; Simmons College, B.S., 1961.

ADDRESSES: Home—P.O. Box 853, Los Altos, Calif. 94022.

CAREER: Arthur D. Little, Inc., Boston, Mass., data analyst, 1961-62; McKendall-Creasy (landscape consultants), Los Altos, Calif., partner, 1974-87; Modern Landscaping, San Jose, Calif., designer, 1977-82. Adult education teacher in Palo Alto, Calif., 1974-78. Lecturer at universities and arboretums; has appeared on numerous radio and television programs. Member of numerous political and conservation groups, including Santa Clara County Planning Commission. Consultant to government resources organizations, and to seed companies and restaurants.

MEMBER: American Institute for Wine and Food, Organization of Women in Architecture, League of Women Voters, Sierra Club, Indoor Citrus Society, Native Seeds Search, Seed Savers Exchange, California Rare Fruit Growers.

WRITINGS:

The Complete Book of Edible Landscaping, Sierra Books, 1982.
Earthly Delights, Sierra Books, 1984.

The Gardener's Handbook of Edible Plants, Sierra Books, 1986.
Cooking from the Garden, Sierra Books, 1988.

Contributor of photographs to *The 1989 Diet and Health Calendar,* Golden Turtle Press. Contributor of articles and photographs to magazines and newspapers.

SIDELIGHTS: Rosalind R. Creasy told *CA:* "The majority of American houses are surrounded with non-productive lawns and shrubs. Edible plants have been considered inappropriate for landscaping. I felt strongly that beautiful agricultural soil was being wasted, along with money at the grocery store. In my books, I seek to legitimize ornamental edible plants."

* * *

CROSS, Amanda
  See HEILBRUN, Carolyn G(old)

D

DAGG, Anne Innis 1933-

PERSONAL: Born January 25, 1933, in Toronto, Ontario, Canada; daughter of Harold Adams (a professor) and Mary (a writer; maiden name, Quayle) Innis; married Ian Ralph Dagg (a professor), August 22, 1957; children: Hugh Eric, Ian Innis, Mary Christine. *Education:* University of Toronto, B.A., 1955, M.A., 1956; University of Waterloo, Ph.D., 1967.

ADDRESSES: Home—81 Albert St., Waterloo, Ontario, Canada. *Office*—University of Waterloo, Waterloo, Ontario, Canada N2L 3G1.

CAREER: Waterloo Lutheran University, Waterloo, Ontario, lecturer in biology, 1962-65; University of Guelph, Guelph, Ontario, assistant professor of zoology, 1967-72; free-lance biology writer and researcher, 1972—; University of Waterloo, Waterloo, integrated studies resource person, 1978-85, academic director of independent studies, 1986—. Director, Harold Innis Foundation.

MEMBER: Writers' Union of Canada (member of national council, 1981-82).

AWARDS, HONORS: Named one of Canada's top female biologists by the National Museums of Canada, 1975, for International Women's Year.

WRITINGS:

(With C. A. Campbell) *Mammals of Waterloo and South Wellington Counties,* Otter Press, 1972.
Canadian Wildlife and Man, McClelland & Stewart, 1974.
Mammals of Ontario, Otter Press, 1974.
(With J. B. Foster) *The Giraffe: Its Biology, Behavior, and Ecology,* Van Nostrand, 1976, revised edition, Robert E. Krieger, 1981.
Wildlife Management in Europe, Otter Press, 1977.
Running, Walking, and Jumping: The Science of Locomotion, Taylor & Francis, 1977.
Camel Quest, York Publishing, 1978.
A Reference Book of Urban Ecology, Otter Press, 1981.
(With H. Gauthier-Pilters) *The Camel: Its Evolution, Ecology, Behavior and Relationship to Man,* University of Chicago Press, 1981.
Harems and Other Horrors: Sexual Bias in Behavioral Biology, Otter Press, 1983.

Tangalooma and Moreton Island: History and Natural History, Tangalooma Island Resort, 1986.
The Fifty Per Cent Solution: Why Should Women Pay for Men's Culture, Otter Press, 1986.
(With Patricia Thompson) *MisEducation: Women and Canadian Universities,* Ontario Institute for Studies in Education, 1988.

WORK IN PROGRESS: Dagg "continues to work on issues related to feminism and education."

SIDELIGHTS: Anne Innis Dagg told *CA:* "Until recently, feminists have worked to include information on women in educational curricula. Currently, they are advocating a complete analysis of all social and humanities disciplines so that they can be restructured as far as possible without gender or other bias."

*   *   *

DAHRENDORF, Ralf 1929-

PERSONAL: Born May 1, 1929, in Hamburg, Germany; naturalized British citizen. *Education:* University of Hamburg, Dr.phil., 1952; University of London, Ph.D., 1956.

ADDRESSES: Office—St. Anthony's College, Oxford OX2 6JF, England.

CAREER: University of Saarbruecken, Saarbruecken, Germany, assistant, 1954-57, Privatdozent, 1957-58; University of Hamburg, Hamburg, Germany, professor, 1958-60; University of Tuebingen, Tuebingen, Germany, professor of sociology, 1960-65; University of Constance, Constance, Germany, professor of sociology, 1965-69; University of London, London, England, director of School of Economics, 1974-84; University of Constance, professor of sociology, 1984-87; St. Anthony's College, Oxford University, Oxford, England, warden, 1987—. Member of German Parliament, 1969-70. Fellow, Center for Advanced Study in the Behavioral Sciences, Palo Alto, Calif., 1957-58. Visiting professor, Columbia University, 1960; visiting scholar, Russell Sage Foundation, 1986-87. Trustee, Ford Foundation, 1976-87. Member of numerous commissions.

MEMBER: International Sociological Association, German Sociological Society (president, 1967-70), American Academy of Arts and Sciences (honorary member), National Academy of Sciences (foreign associate), American Philosophical Society, PEN.

AWARDS, HONORS: Journal Fund Award for learned publication, 1959, 1966; Grand Prix de l'Ordre du Merite du Senegal, 1971; fellow, London School of Economics, 1973; fellow, Imperial College of Science and Technology, 1974; Grand Croix de l'Ordre du Merite du Luxembourg, 1974; Grosses Bundesverdienstkreuz mit Stern und Schulterband, 1974; fellow, St. Anthony's College, 1975; Grosses Goldenes Ehrenzeichen am Bande, 1975; Grand Croix de l'Ordre de Leopold II, 1975; fellow, British Academy, 1977; Knight of the British Empire, 1982. Honorary doctorates from University of Reading, University of Manchester, and New University of Ulster, 1973, Open University and Kalamazoo College, 1974, Trinity College, Dublin, 1975, Wagner College, Universite Catholique de Louvain, and University of Bath, 1977, University of Maryland and University of Surrey, 1978, York University, Ontario, 1979, Queen's University, Belfast, 1984, and Columbia University, 1989.

WRITINGS:

Marx in Perspektive, J. H. W. Dietz, 1953, 2nd edition, 1971.
Industrie und Betriebssoziologie, De Gruyter, 1956, 2nd edition, 1962.
Soziale Klassen und Klassenkonflikt in der industriellen Gesellschaft, F. Enke, 1957, translated, revised and expanded by author as *Class and Class Conflict in Industrial Society,* Stanford University Press, 1959.
Homo Sociologicus, Westdeutscher Verlag, 1958.
Sozialstruktur des Betriebes, T. Gabler, 1959.
Gesellschaft und Freiheit, Piper Verlag, 1961.
Ueber den Ursprung der Ungleichheit unter den Menschen, Mohr, 1961.
Die angewandte Aufklaerung, Piper Verlag, 1963.
Gesellschaft und Demokratie in Deutschland, Piper Verlag, 1965, translation published as *Society and Democracy in Germany,* Doubleday, 1967.
Bildung ist Buergerrecht, Nannen, 1965.
Das Mitbestimmungsproblem in der deutschen Sozialforschung, Piper Verlag, 1965.
Essays in the Theory of Society, Stanford University Press, 1968.
Feur eine Erneuerung der Demokratie in der Bundesrepublik, Piper Verlag, 1968.
Konflikt end Freiheit, Piper Verlag, 1972.
Plaedoyer fuer die Europaeische Union, Piper Verlag, 1973.
The New Liberty: Survival and Justice in a Changing World, Stanford University Press, 1975.
Life Chances, Stanford University Press, 1980.
On Britain, British Broadcasting Corp., 1982.
Die Chancen der Krise, Stuttgart, 1983.
Reisen nach innen und aussen: Aspekteder Zeit, Deutsche Verlags-Anstalt (Stuttgart), 1984.
Law & Order, Stevens & Sons, 1985.
(With Theodore C. Sorensen) *A Widening Atlantic?: Domestic Change and Foreign Policy,* Council on Foreign Relations, 1986.
The Modern Social Conflict: An Essay on the Politics of Liberty, Weidenfeld & Nicolson, 1989.

BIOGRAPHICAL/CRITICAL SOURCES:

PERIODICALS

New York Times Book Review, May 4, 1986.

Times Literary Supplement, June 3, 1983, February 22, 1985.
Washington Post Book World, May 8, 1983.

*   *   *

DALY, Cahal Brendan   1917-

PERSONAL: Born October 1, 1917, in Loughguile, County Antrim, Northern Ireland; son of Charles and Susan Daly. *Education:* Received B.A. (with honors) and M.A. from Queen's University, Belfast, Northern Ireland; received D.D. from St. Patrick's College, Maynooth, Ireland; received L.Ph. from Institut Catholique, France. *Religion:* Roman Catholic.

ADDRESSES: Home—Bishop's House, Lisbreen, 73 Somerton Rd., Belfast BT15 4DE, Ireland.

CAREER: Ordained Roman Catholic priest, 1941; classics master at secondary school in Belfast, Northern Ireland, 1945-46; Queen's University, Belfast, lecturer, 1946-63, reader in scholastic philosophy, 1963-67; St. Michael's, Longford, Ireland, bishop of Ardagh and Clonmacnois, 1967-82; bishop of Down and Connor, 1982—. Member of British Broadcasting Corp. Northern Ireland Religious Advisory Council, 1945-59; committee member, Northern Ireland Independent Television Authority, 1960-65; religious advisor to UTV.

MEMBER: Christus Rex Society (chairman, 1941-66).

WRITINGS:

(Contributor) I. T. Ramsey, editor, *Prospect for Metaphysics,* G. Allen, 1961.
Morals, Law, and Life: An Examination of the Sanctity of Life and the Criminal Law by Granville Llewellyn Williams, Clonmore, 1962, Scepter, 1966.
Natural Law: Morality Today, Burns & Oates, 1965.
(Contributor) T. A. Langford and W. H. Poteat, editors, *Intellect and Hope,* Duke University Press, 1968.
(Contributor) D. M. High, editor, *New Essays in Religious Language,* Oxford University Press, 1969.
Violence in Ireland and Christian Conscience, Veritas Publications, 1973.
Theologians and the Magisterium, Veritas Publications, 1977.
Penance Renewed, Irish Messenger, 1977.
(Editor with A. S. Worrall) *Ballymascanlon: An Irish Venture in Inter-Church Dialogue,* Veritas Publications, 1978.
Peace: The Work of Justice—Addresses on the Northern Tragedy, Veritas Publications, 1979.
Communities without Consensus: The Northern Irish Tragedy, Irish Messenger, 1984.
Renewed Heart for Peace, Irish Messenger, 1984.
Cry of the Poor, Irish Messenger, 1986.

Also contributor to *Understanding the Eucharist,* 1969. Contributor to theology and philosophy journals.

*   *   *

DANA, E. H.
See HAMEL PEIFER, Kathleen

*   *   *

DANK, Milton   1920-

PERSONAL: Born September 12, 1920, in Philadelphia, Pa.; son of Charles (a barber) and Olga (Olessker) Dank; married Naomi Rand (a hospital administrator), March 18, 1954; children: Gloria, Joan. *Education:* University of Pennsylvania,

B.A., 1947, Ph.D., 1953. *Politics:* Democrat. *Religion:* Judaism.

ADDRESSES: Home—1022 Serpentine Lane, Wyncote, Pa. 19095.

CAREER: Writer. Owen-Illinois Glass, Toledo, Ohio, research physicist, 1953-56; General Electric (Aerospace), King of Prussia, Pa., research manager, 1958-72; research consultant in thermonuclear fusion power, laser applications, and space vehicle vulnerability, 1972—. *Military service:* U.S. Army Air Forces, 1940-45; became first lieutenant.

MEMBER: Authors Guild, Authors League of America, American Physical Society, National World War II Glider Pilots Association.

WRITINGS:

The French against the French, Lippincott, 1974.
The Glider Gang, Lippincott, 1977.
The Dangerous Game, Lippincott, 1977.
Game's End, Lippincott, 1979.
Khaki Wings, Delacorte, 1980.
Red Flight Two, Delacorte, 1981.
Albert Einstein, F. Watts, 1983.
(With daughter, Gloria Dank) *The Computer Caper,* Delacorte, 1983.
(With G. Dank) *A UFO Has Landed,* Delacorte, 1983.
D-Day, F. Watts, 1984.
(With G. Dank) *The 3-D Traitor,* Delacorte, 1984.
(With G. Dank) *The Treasure Code,* Delacorte, 1985.

WORK IN PROGRESS: The Gestapo in France: The Case of Klaus Barbie.

SIDELIGHTS: Milton Dank once told *CA* that most of his books were "derived from my wartime experiences. *The French against the French* and *The Dangerous Game* were based on my study of the behavior of the French under the German occupation. As squadron translator and liaison officer, I found the French civilians most reluctant to talk of the fifty months during which the Nazis occupied France.

"*The Glider Gang* is a tribute to the Allied glider pilots, my comrades-in-arm. They flew in fragile canvas and wood motorless craft at low altitudes over enemy guns, and brought in jeeps, howitzers and antitank guns to the paratroopers. Their casualties were high, as much from poor planning and faulty intelligence as from enemy resistance. They wore no parachutes because their passengers wore none. I thought it was wrong that their story should go untold.

"In my next book, I am going back to the theme that fascinated me while researching my first book: the permissable limits of collaboration under a foreign military occupation."

*   *   *

DAVIDSON, Paul 1930-

PERSONAL: Born October 23, 1930, in Brooklyn, N.Y.; son of Charles and Lillian (Janow) Davidson; married Louise Tattenbaum, 1952; children: Robert Alan, Diane Carol, Greg Stuart. *Education:* Brooklyn College (now Brooklyn College of the City University of New York), B.S., 1950; City College (now City College of the City University of New York), M.B.A., 1955; University of Pennsylvavia, Ph.D., 1959.

ADDRESSES: Home—2400 Craghead Lane, Knoxville, Tenn. 37920. *Office*—Department of Economics, University of Tennessee, Knoxville, Tenn. 37996.

CAREER: University of Pennsylvania, Philadelphia, instructor in physiological chemistry, 1951-52, instructor in economics, 1955-58; Rutgers University, New Brunswick, N.J., assistant professor of economics, 1958-60; Continental Oil Co., Houston, Tex., assistant director of Economics Division, 1960-61; University of Pennsylvania, assistant professor, 1961-63, associate professor of economics, 1963-66; Rutgers University, professor of economics, 1966-87, associate director of Bureau of Economic Research, 1966-75, chairman of New Brunswick Department of Economics and Allied Sciences and director of Bureau of Economic Research, 1975-78; University of Tennessee, Knoxville, Tenn., distinguished professor of economics, 1987—. Visiting lecturer, University of Bristol, 1964-65; senior visiting lecturer, Cambridge Universtiy, 1970-71; George Miller Distinguished Lecturer, University of Illinois, 1972; Bernardin Distinguished Visiting Lecturer, University of Missouri, 1979; professor, International Summer School Centro di Studi Economici Avanzati, Trieste, Italy, 1980; visiting professor, Institute for Advanced Studies, Vienna, Austria, 1980, 1984. Member, Brookings Economic Panel, 1974; senior visitor, Bank of England, 1979. Participant in government conferences and witness before numerous Congressional committees. Consultant, Resources for the Future, 1964-66, Ford Foundation energy policy project, 1973, International Communications Agency, U.S. Department of State, 1980, and to numerous public and private organizations, including Western Union, Federal Trade Commission, and the State of Alabama; member of national board of advisors, Public Interest Economics Center, 1972—. *Military service:* U.S. Army, 1953-55.

MEMBER: American Economic Association, Econometric Society, National Association of Business Economists, Royal Economic Society, Epsilon Phi Alpha.

AWARDS, HONORS: Ford Foundation fellow, 1956-57; Fulbright fellow, 1964-65; Rutgers faculty research fellow, 1970-71, 1980; Lindbeck Award for Research, 1975.

WRITINGS:

Theories of Aggregate Income Distribution, Rutgers University Press, 1960.
(With Eugene Smolensky) *Aggregate Supply and Demand Analysis,* Harper, 1964.
(With C. J. Chiccetti and J. J. Seneca) *The Demand and Supply of Outdoor Recreation: An Econometric Study,* Bureau of Economic Research, Rutgers Universtiy, 1968.
Money and the Real World, Macmillan, 1972, 2nd edition, 1978.
(With Milton Friedman and others) *Milton Friedman's Monetary Theory: A Debate with His Critics,* University of Chicago Press, 1974.
International Money and the Real World, Macmillan, 1981.
(With son, Greg S. Davidson) *Economics for a Civilized Society,* Norton, 1987.

CONTRIBUTOR

(With F. G. Adams and Seneca) A. V. Kneese and S. C. Smith, editors, *Water Research,* Johns Hopkins Press, 1966.
M. G. Garnsney and J. Hibbs, editors, *Social Sciences and the Environment,* University of Colorado Press, 1968.
A. Utton, editor, *Towards a National Petroleum Policy,* University of New Mexico Press, 1970.
D. R. Croome and H. G. Johnson, editors, *Money in Britain, 1959-1969,* Oxford University Press, 1970.

R. Dorfman and N. S. Dorfman, editors, *Economics of the Environment,* Norton, 1972.

G. M. Brannon, editor, *Studies in Energy Tax Policy,* Ballinger, 1975.

S. Weintraub, editor, *Modern Economic Thought,* University of Pennsylvania Press, 1977.

G. Harcourt, editor, *Microfoundations of Macroeconomics,* Cambridge University Press, 1977.

V. L. Smith, editor, *Economics of Natural and Environmental Resources,* Gordon & Breach, 1977.

D. J. Teece, editor, *R & D in Energy: Implications of Petroleum Industry Reorganization,* Institute for Energy Studies (Stanford, Calif.), 1977.

Weintraub, editor, *Keynes, Keynesians and Monetarists,* University of Pennsylvania Press, 1978.

Vicens-Vives, editor, *Desquilibrio, Inflacion y Desempleo,* [Madrid], 1978.

(With J. A. Kregal) E. J. Nell, editor, *Growth, Property, and Profits,* Cambridge University Press, 1980.

Stagflation: The Causes, Effects and Solutions, Joint Economic Committee (Washington, D.C.), 1980.

D. Bell and I. Kristol, editors, *The Crisis in Economic Theory,* Basic Books, 1981.

OTHER

Contributor to economic and public finance journals. Editor, *Journal of Post Keynesian Economics,* 1978—; member of editorial board, *Energy Journal,* 1980-83.

* * *

DAVIS, Robert Murray   1934-

PERSONAL: Born September 4, 1934, in Lyons, Kan.; son of Mathew Cary (a dealer) and Elizabeth (Murray) Davis; married Barbara Hillyer, December 28, 1958 (divorced April 3, 1981); children: Megan, Jennifer, John. *Education:* Rockhurst College, B.S., 1955; University of Kansas, M.A., 1958; University of Wisconsin, Ph.D., 1964.

ADDRESSES: Office—Department of English, University of Oklahoma, 760 Van Vleet, Norma, Okla. 73019.

CAREER: Loyola University, Chicago, Ill., assistant professor of English, 1962-65; University of California, Santa Barbara, assistant professor of English, 1965-67; University of Oklahoma, Norman, 1967—, currently professor of English. Visiting professor, University of New Brunswick, St. John, summer, 1981, and Dalhousie University, summers, 1984, 1986. Fulbright lecturer, Eotvos University, Budapest, 1981; visiting lecturer, University of Paris, spring, 1983; United States Information Service lecturer in France, Yugoslavia, Hungary, and Germany, spring, 1983.

MEMBER: Modern Language Association of America, South Central Modern Language Association.

AWARDS, HONORS: National Endowment for the Humanities summer stipend, 1969; DeGolyer Prize for American Studies, 1984.

WRITINGS:

(Editor) *The Novel: Modern Essays in Criticism,* Prentice-Hall, 1969.

(Editor) *Evelyn Waugh,* B. Herder, 1969.

(Editor) *Steinbeck,* Prentice-Hall, 1972.

(Editor) *Modern British Short Novels,* Scott, Foresman, 1972.

(With others) *Evelyn Waugh: A Checklist of Primary and Secondary Material,* Whitston Publishing, 1972.

(With others) *Donald Barthelme: A Bibliography,* Archon, 1977.

A Catalogue of the Evelyn Waugh Collection, Whitston Publishing, 1981.

Evelyn Waugh, Writer, Pilgrim, 1981.

(Editor) *Evelyn Waugh, Apprentice,* Pilgrim, 1985.

A Bibliography of Evelyn Waugh, Whitston Publishing, 1986.

(Editor) *Owen Wister's West,* [New Mexico], 1987.

Evelyn Waugh and the Forms of His Time, Catholic University of America Press, in press.

Contributor to periodicals.

WORK IN PROGRESS: A book on the use of Western motifs in avant-garde fiction; a book on theory of the novel in England in the 1930s; a volume on *Brideshead Revisited,* for Twayne; volumes of poetry and reminiscences.

BIOGRAPHICAL/CRITICAL SOURCES:

PERIODICALS

Times Literary Supplement, August 21, 1981, July 9, 1982.

* * *

DAVIS, William   1933-

PERSONAL: Born March 6, 1933, in Hanover, Germany; married Sylvette Jouclas, April 8, 1967. *Education:* Attended City of London College.

ADDRESSES: Office—Headway Publications, Ltd., Athene House, 66-73 Shoe Lane, London EC4P 4AB, England.

CAREER: London Financial Times, London, England, staff member, 1954-59; *Investor's Guide,* London, editor, 1959-60; *London Evening Standard,* London, financial editor, 1960-65; *Manchester Guardian,* Manchester, England, financial editor, 1965-68; *Punch,* London, editor, 1968-79; currently chairman and editorial director, Headway Publications, Ltd., London and New York. Broadcaster and lecturer.

MEMBER: Hurlington Club and Garrick Club (both London).

WRITINGS:

Three Years Hard Labor: The Road to Devaluation, Deutsch, 1968, published with a foreword by Eliot Janeway, Houghton, 1970.

Merger Mania, Constable, 1970.

Money Talks—William Davis Translates: A Glossary of Money, Deutsch, 1972, published as *The Language of Money: An Irreverent Dictionary of Business and Finance,* Houghton, 1973.

Have Expenses, Will Travel, Deutsch, 1975.

It's No Sin to Be Rich, Osprey, 1976.

Money in the 1980's, Weidenfeld & Nicolson, 1981.

(Editor) *The Best of Everything,* St. Martin's, 1981.

The Rich: A Study of the Species, F. Watts, 1982.

The Corporate Infighter's Handbook, Sidgwick & Jackson, 1985.

The Supersalesman's Handbook, Sidgwick & Jackson, 1986.

The World's Best Business Hotels, Bloomsbury Press, 1987.

The Innovators, American Management Associations, 1987.

Editor of annual *Pick of "Punch,"* Hutchinson, 1969-79; editor of "Punch" series, published by Hutchinson and others, including *"Punch" Book of Golf, Bedside Book,* and *Good Living Book.* Editor of *High Life* (in-flight magazine of British Airways), 1973—; editor of *Business Life,* 1986—.

SIDELIGHTS: William Davis once told *CA:* "People always ask what made an economist and leading financial editor become editor-in-chief of *Punch,* the world's best-known humorous weekly. Natural progression, I tell them. I have always believed in exposing pomposity and pretence, and the business world has more than its share of it. My books are all on various aspects of economics and business, and I [have written essays] in *Punch* on a wide range of subjects—politics, business, and the social scene. An American magazine once called me 'the poor man's Galbraith.'"

AVOCATIONAL INTERESTS: Drinking wine, traveling, thinking about retirement, tennis.

*　　*　　*

DAVIS, William S(terling)　1943-

PERSONAL: Born April 18, 1943, in Pittston, Pa.; son of Sterling Q. (a postal supervisor) and Alice (an accountant; maiden name, Phethean) Davis; married Catherine A. Curcio, July 2, 1966; children: William, Theresa, Carla. *Education:* Lafayette College, B.S., 1965; State University of New York at Binghamton, M.A., 1968. *Politics:* Independent.

ADDRESSES: Home—602 White Oak Dr., Oxford, Ohio 45056. *Office*—Department of Systems Analysis, Miami University, Oxford, Ohio 45056.

CAREER: International Business Machines Corp. (IBM), Vestal, N.Y., industrial engineer, 1965-67; Lafayette College, Easton, Pa., instructor in industrial engineering, 1967-68; International Business Machines Corp., Endicott, N.Y., systems analyst and programmer, 1968-71; Miami University, Oxford, Ohio, assistant professor, 1971-77, associate professor, 1977-81, professor of systems analysis, 1981—. Adjunct professor, U.S. Navy Postgraduate School, 1987. Business consultant.

WRITINGS:

Operating Systems: A Systematic View, Addison-Wesley, 1977, 3rd edition, 1987.
Information Processing Systems, Addison-Wesley, 1978, 2nd edition, 1981.
Business Data Processing, Addison-Wesley, 1978.
(With Richard H. Fisher) *COBOL: An Introduction to Structures Logic and Modular Program Design,* Addison-Wesley, 1979.
(With S. Allison McCormack) *The Information Age,* Addison-Wesley, 1979.
FORTRAN 77: Getting Started, Addison-Wesley, 1981.
BASIC: Getting Started, Addison-Wesley, 1981.
Computers and Business Information Processing, Addison-Wesley, 1981, 2nd edition, 1983.
Tools and Techniques for Structured Systems Analysis and Design, Addison-Wesley, 1983.
Systems Analysis and Design: A Structured Approach, Addison-Wesley, 1983.
The NECEN Voyage, Addison-Wesley, 1985.
True BASIC Primer, Addison-Wesley, 1986.
Fundamental Computer Concepts, Addison-Wesley, 1986.
PC BASIC: Getting Started, Addison-Wesley, 1988.
Computing Fundamentals: Word Perfect, Addison-Wesley, in press.
Computing Fundamentals: Concepts, Addison-Wesley, in press.

SIDELIGHTS: William S. Davis told *CA:* "In 1957, the Russians launched the first artificial satellite, and science and mathematics moved to the fore throughout the United States.

Consequently, when I entered college, there was little question that I would be an engineer. I really wanted to write, though. After several years with IBM, Miami University offered me an academic position. One of my first assignments was to teach operating systems; finding no acceptable text, I decided to write my own. The result, *Operating Systems: A Systematic View,* has since been translated into Russian, Spanish, and Bahasa-Indonesian.

"My writing is influenced by a number of factors. First, perhaps, is my engineering training; I worry about technical accuracy and precision, and tend to present concepts in an applied (rather than theoretical) context. Second, I am a self-taught computer person (academic computer training was not common in the sixties), and my writing tends to document my own learning experiences. Finally, I believe that technical literature should read like a novel, with a careful development of the 'story line' from beginning to end; the fact that a work is technical is no excuse for bad writing.

"I normally start a project by preparing a chapter outline, first at a very high level, and then in detail. I write one chapter at a time, using a word processor. A first draft is prepared in a day or two of intense, almost uninterrupted activity, after which I settle into a more regular work pattern to revise and polish the prose. This is where the word processor helps; I've found that I can complete five or six revisions in the time it used to take to finish two. At key points, for example at the end of a section, I print the material and go through another revision cycle, this time stressing consistency and continuity; similar revisions are made when the entire book is finished. The final steps involve preparing chapter exercises and an instructor's guide. Anyone who claims that writing is easy has never tried it—it's hard work. Still, I can't think of anything I would rather do."

*　　*　　*

DAWOOD, N(essim) J(oseph)　1927-

PERSONAL: Born August 27, 1927, in Baghdad, Iraq; son of Yousef (a merchant) and Muzli (Tweg) Dawood; married Juliet Abraham, September 18, 1949; children: Richard, Norman, Andrew. *Education:* University of London, B.A. (with honors), 1949.

ADDRESSES: Office—Berkeley Square House, Berkeley Sq., London W1X 5LE, England.

CAREER: Arabic Advertising and Publishing Co. Ltd., London, England, managing director, 1959—; Contemporary Translations Ltd., London, director, 1962—. Director, Bradbury Wilkinson (graphics) Ltd., 1975-86. Consultant on the Middle East.

MEMBER: Institute of Linguists (fellow), Hurlingham Club.

AWARDS, HONORS: Iraq State Scholar in England, 1945-49.

WRITINGS:

(Translator and author of introduction) *Tales from the Thousand and One Nights,* Penguin, 1954, reprinted, 1989.
(Translator and author of introduction and notes) *The Koran,* Penguin, 1956, published with parallel Arabic text, 1989.
(Translator and author of introduction) *Aladdin and Other Tales from the Thousand and One Nights,* Penguin, 1957, published as *Puffin Classics: Aladdin and Other Tales,* Puffin, 1989.

(Editor) Ibn Khaldun, *The Muqaddimah: An Introduction to History*, Routledge & Kegan Paul, 1967, Princeton University Press, 1969.

(Translator and adapter) *Tales from the Arabian Nights* (juvenile), Doubleday, 1978.

Translator of numerous technical works into Arabic. Writer and narrator of film commentaries in English and Arabic, including documentary, "In the Name of Allah," hosted by James Mason. Contributor to English-Arabic dictionaries.

AVOCATIONAL INTERESTS: Going to the theater.

*   *   *

DEAK, Istvan   1926-

PERSONAL: Born May 11, 1926, in Szekesfehervar, Hungary; came to United States in 1956, naturalized in 1962; son of Istvan (an engineer) and Anna (Timar) Deak; married Gloria Alfano (a free-lance editor and writer), July 4, 1959; children: Eva. *Education:* Attended University of Budapest, 1945-48, University of Paris, 1949-51, and University of Maryland, 1954-56; Ecole de Documentation, diploma, 1950; Columbia University, M.A., 1958, Ph.D., 1964.

ADDRESSES: Home— 410 Riverside Dr., New York, N.Y. 10025. *Office—* 611 Fayerweather Hall, Columbia University, New York, N.Y. 10027.

CAREER: Free-lance researcher and translator in New York City, 1956-59; Smith College, Northampton, Mass., instructor, 1962-63; Columbia University, New York City, instructor, 1963-64, assistant professor, 1964-67, associate professor, 1967-71, professor of history, 1971—, director of Institute on East Central Europe, 1967-78, acting director, 1979-80, 1983. Lecturer, University of Maryland Overseas Program, West Germany, 1961, and School of General Studies, Columbia University, 1961-62. Visiting lecturer, Yale University, spring, 1966; visiting professor, University of California, Los Angeles, 1975, and Universitaet Siegen, West Germany, 1981. German Academic Exchange fellow, 1960-61, Fulbright-Hays Travel fellow, 1973, 1984-85. Member, Joint Committee on Slavic Studies, 1967-69. International Research and Exchanges Board travel fellow, 1972, 1973, 1984-85, fellowship committee member, 1980-83, program committee member, 1983—. American Council of Learned Societies, committee member, 1972-74, fellow, 1981. Executive secretary, Committee to Promote Studies of the History of the Hapsburg Monarchy, 1974-77. Vice president, Conference Group for Slavic and East European History, 1975-77, president, 1985. Member, Institute for Advanced Study, Princeton, N.J., 1981. Institute for Advanced Study fellow, 1981. Woodrow Wilson International Center for Scholars, Smithsonian Institution, Washington, D.C., fellow, 1985, advisory committee member, 1985—.

MEMBER: American Association for the Advancement of Slavic Studies (president of Mid-Atlantic Association, 1977-78, member of board of directors, 1985—), American Association for the Study of Hungarian History (awards committee chairman, 1974—, vice chairman, 1979-80, chairman, 1980-81).

AWARDS, HONORS: Scudder W. Johnston fellowship, Columbia University, 1959-60; Chamberlain fellow, Columbia University, 1966; study grant, School of International Affairs, Columbia University, 1969; Guggenheim fellowship, 1970-71; Lionel Trilling Book Award, Columbia University, 1977,

for *The Lawful Revolution: Louis Kossuth and the Hungarians, 1848-1849*, and 1979.

WRITINGS:

Weimar Germany's Left-Wing Intellectuals: A Political History of the Weltbuehne and Its Circle, University of California Press, 1968.
The Lawful Revolution: Louis Kossuth and the Hungarians, 1848-1849, Columbia University Press, 1979.

CONTRIBUTOR

Hans Rogger and Eugen Weber, editors, *The European Right: A Historical Profile*, University of California Press, 1965.
Ivan Volgyes, editor, *Hungary in Revolution, 1918-1919*, University of Nebraska Press, 1971.
(And editor with Sylvia Sinanian and Peter C. Ludz) *Eastern Europe in the 1970's* (conference papers), Praeger, 1972.
Situations revolutionnaires en Europe, 1917-1922, University of Montreal, 1977.
German Realism of the Twenties: The Artist as Social Critic, Minneapolis Institute of Arts, 1980.
Jaroslaw Pelenski, editor, *The American and European Revolutions, 1776-1848*, University of Iowa Press, 1980.
Film and Politics in the Weimar Republic, Minnesota University Press, 1982.
Ivo Banac and Paul Bushkovitch, editors, *The Nobility in Russia and Eastern Europe*, Yale Concilium on International and Area Studies, 1983.
John F. Cadzow, Andrew Ludanyi, and Louis J. Elteto, editors, *Transylvania: The Roots of Ethnic Conflict*, Kent State University Press, 1983.
Bela K. Kiraly, editor, *East Central European Society and War in the Era of Revolutions, 1775-1856*, Brooklyn College Press, 1984.
Kiraly, editor, *The Crucial Decade: East Central European Society and National Defense, 1859-1870*, Brooklyn College Press, 1984.
Randolph L. Braham and Bela Vago, editors, *The Holocaust in Hungary Forty Years Later*, Columbia University Press, 1985.
Kiraly and N. F. Dreisziger, editors, *East Central European Society in World War I*, Social Science Monographs, 1985.
K. D. Grothusen, editor, *Ungarn*, Vandenhoeck and Ruprecht (Goettingen, West Germany), 1987.

OTHER

(Editor with Allan Mitchell) *Everyman in Europe: Essays in Social History*, two volumes, Prentice-Hall, 1974, 2nd edition, 1981.

Also contributor to *Encyclopedia Year Book 1973*. Contributor to *New York Review of Books*, *Slavonic and East European Review*, *Austrian History Yearbook*, *Oesterreichische Osthefte*, *East Central Europe*, *New Hungarian Quarterly*, *Romania Bulletin*, and other journals. Author of book reviews for periodicals, including *Slavic Review* and *American Historical Review*. Member of editorial advisory board, *Political Science Quarterly*, 1969-70, of board of editors, *Austrian History Yearbook*, 1971-77, of editorial board, *East Central Europe*, 1972—.

*   *   *

de BEAUVOIR, Simone (Lucie Ernestine Marie Bertrand)

See BEAUVOIR, Simone (Lucie Ernestine Marie Bertrand) de

De FELITTA, Frank (Paul) 1921-

PERSONAL: Born August 3, 1921, in New York, N.Y.; son of Pat and Genevieve (Sibilio) De Felitta; married Dorothy Gilbert, August 4, 1945; children: Eileen, Raymond. *Education:* Attended University of North Carolina, 1939-40, and New School for Social Research, 1947-48.

ADDRESSES: Agent—Tim Seldes, Russell & Volkening, Inc., 50 West 29th St., New York, N.Y. 10001.

CAREER: Columbia Broadcasting System (CBS-TV), New York City, producer, director, writer, 1950-57; National Telefilms Associates, New York City, and Los Angeles, Calif., West Coast director of film programming, 1959-61; National Broadcasting Co. (NBC-TV), New York City, producer, writer, director, 1962—; Universal Studios, Los Angeles, producer, writer, director, 1968-70. Also director of television movie "Dark Night of the Scarecrow," CBS-TV, 1981. *Military service:* U.S. Army Air Forces, 1941-45; served in European theater; became captain; received Distinguished Flying Cross and Air Medal.

MEMBER: Directors Guild of America, Writers Guild of America.

AWARDS, HONORS: Peabody Awards, 1954, for "Adventure," and 1963, for "American Revolution"; Ohio State University Award, 1957, for "Satan in Salem"; George Polk Award for Journalism, 1957, for "Algeria at Large"; Writers Guild award nomination, 1958, for program "They Took a Blue Note"; Thomas Alva Edison Award, 1958, for "Conquest"; Venice Film Festival Award, 1959, for "Waves"; Emmy Awards, National Academy of Television Arts and Sciences, 1962, for "Emergency Ward," and 1966, for "The Battle of the Bulge"; National Education Association School Bell Award, 1963, for "An Experiment in Excellence"; CINE (Council on International Nontheatrical Events) Gold Eagle Awards, 1964, for "An Experiment in Excellence," 1966, for "The Battle of the Bulge," 1966, for "The World of the Teenager," 1967, for "Pearl Harbor," and 1968, for "The American Image"; Robert J. Flaherty Award, 1966, for "The World of the Teenager"; Brotherhood Award, National Conference of Christians and Jews, 1967, for "Mississippi: A Self-Portrait"; George Washington Honor Medal, Freedoms Foundation, 1968, for "The American Image."

WRITINGS:

NOVELS

Oktoberfest, Doubleday, 1973.
Audrey Rose (also see below), Putnam, 1975.
The Entity (also see below), Putnam, 1978.
Sea Trial, Avon, 1980.
For Love of Audrey Rose, Warner Books, 1982.
Golgotha Falls: An Assault on the Fourth Dimension, Simon & Schuster, 1984.

SCREENPLAYS

(Contributor) "Anzio," Columbia Pictures, 1968.
"The Buffalo Soldiers," Cherokee Films, 1968.
(With Max Erlich) "Z.P.G.," Sagittarius/PAR, 1972.
(With Erlich) "The Savage Is Loose," Campbell Devon, 1974.
(And co-producer) "Audrey Rose" (adapted from his novel), United Artists, 1977.

"The Entity" (adapted from his novel), Twentieth Century-Fox, 1983.

Also author of "Boy on a Smokestack," 1967, "Success . . . or Something Like It," 1967, and "The First of January," 1970.

TELEVISION SCRIPTS

"Adventure" (natural science series), Columbia Broadcasting System (CBS-TV), 1953-55.
"Conquest" (science series), CBS-TV, 1957.
(And director) "The Chosen Child" (documentary), National Broadcasting Co. (NBC-TV), 1962.
(And director) "An Experiment in Excellence" (documentary), NBC-TV, 1963.
(And director) "The Stately Ghosts of England" (documentary), NBC-TV, 1964.
(And director) "The Battle of the Bulge" (documentary), NBC-TV, 1964.
(And director) "Mississippi: A Self-Portrait" (documentary), NBC-TV, 1965.
(And director) "Pearl Harbor" (documentary), NBC-TV, 1966.
(And director) "The World of the Teenager" (documentary), NBC-TV, 1966.
(And director) "The American Image" (documentary), NBC-TV, 1967.
(And director) "Trapped," American Broadcasting Co. (ABC-TV), 1973.
(And director) "The Two Worlds of Jennie Logan," CBS-TV, 1979.
(And director) "Killer in the Mirror," NBC-TV, 1986.

Also author of scripts for "Music of the South," 1955, "Odyssey" series, 1958, and "Emergency Ward," 1962.

SIDELIGHTS: A veteran filmmaker and producer who has won numerous awards for his documentaries, Frank De Felitta's most renowned contributions to the field of horror/suspense are marked by development reminiscent of a factual film. In *Audrey Rose,* for example, much of the action is recounted at the kidnapping trial of Elliot Hoover, who believes that the soul of his daughter Audrey Rose has been prematurely reincarnated into the body of young Ivy Templeton. Traditional elements of horror, such as possession of the soul, are present in the novel, but De Felitta demonstrates them through the distance of the witnesses's testimony. Although the work was not well received by critics, it became a bestseller with 2.5 million copies in print; it also inspired a movie and a sequel.

Similarly, much of *The Entity*'s action is reported through the psychiatric sessions of Carlotta Moran, who believes she is being visited by a spectral rapist. In a review of the subsequent movie, which De Felitta scripted, the *Los Angeles Times*'s Kevin Thomas states that "shrewdly, De Felitta eschews conventional exposition and lets us learn about [Carlotta] through her sessions." Because of the psychiatrist's belief that Carlotta's experiences are hysterically induced, "it's 'The Entity's' key strength that we're kept unsure," writes Thomas. Like a documentary, *The Entity* (which was reportedly based on an actual case) "is well researched and offers a mind-challenging look into the paranormal," comments Cassandra Smith in the *West Coast Review of Books*.

Golgotha Falls: An Assault on the Fourth Dimension also contains elements that differentiate it from standard horror fiction. Dealing with a demonic showdown and possible apocalypse, nevertheless the "horror is predominantly philosophical," observes Sam Cornish in the *Christian Science Monitor*. "This is a novel of religious experience within the conventions of genre fiction, and its horror has roots more in the realization of religious and scientific speculation than in explicit depiction of violence," adds Cornish. Similarly, Sue Martin notes in the *Los Angeles Times Book Review* that "what this book has, more of than horror, is great passion and mysticism. . . . This is no cheap thrill; there's an engrossing struggle for redemption that sweeps the reader along."

BIOGRAPHICAL/CRITICAL SOURCES:

PERIODICALS

Christian Science Monitor, December 10, 1984.
Los Angeles Times, February 7, 1983.
Los Angeles Times Book Review, November 18, 1984.
New York Times Book Review, November 25, 1973, April 4, 1976, August 5, 1984.
Washington Post, July 27, 1978, February 9, 1983.
West Coast Review of Books, September, 1978.

*　　*　　*

DENNISON, Sam   1926-

PERSONAL: Born September 26, 1926, in Geary, Okla.; son of Frank Houston (an entrepreneur) and Ada Lee (a fashion designer; maiden name, Williams) Dennison; children: Paul Scott, David Houston, Lee Ann. *Education:* University of Oklahoma, B.M., 1950; University of Southern California, M.M., 1962; Drexel University, M.S.L.S., 1966.

ADDRESSES: Home—Philadelphia, Pa. *Office*—Fleisher Collection, Free Library of Philadelphia, Philadelphia, Pa. 19103.

CAREER: Teacher and free-lance musician in the United States and abroad, 1952-60; Inter-American University, San German, P.R., professor of music, 1960-64; Free Library of Philadelphia, Philadelphia, Pa., music librarian, 1964-75, curator, 1975—. Lecturer and composer. Music consultant and appraiser. *Military service:* U.S. Naval Reserve, active duty, 1944-46.

MEMBER: Sonneck Society, Musical Fund Society of Philadelphia, Sigma Alpha Iota.

WRITINGS:

(Editor) *Catalog of Orchestral and Choral Compositions from the Library of the Musical Fund Society of Philadelphia*, Musical Fund Society of Philadelphia, 1974.
(Chief editor) *The Edwin A. Fleisher Collection of Orchestral Music in the Free Library of Philadelphia*, G. K. Hall, 1977.
Scandalize My Name: Black Imagery in American Popular Music, Garland Publishing, 1982.

MUSICAL COMPOSITIONS

"Thirteen Pieces for Helen," 1948.
"Monologue of a Water Faucet," 1948.
"Mother Wears Army Boots," 1949.
"The Last Man on Earth," 1952.
"Quodlibet," 1953.
"The Days of the Week," 1953.
"Folksong Medley," 1957.
"Brass Sextet," 1963.
"Jesus Christes Milde Moder," 1963.
"The Faucon Hath Taken My Mate Away," 1963.
"Suite for Flute," 1968.

"Epithalamium," 1968.
"Adagio for Horn and Orchestra," 1978.
"Cirrus," 1980.
"Lyric Piece and Rondo," 1982.
Rappaccini's Daughter (one-act opera), Kalmus, 1985.
Short Symphony, Kalmus, 1988.
"*And If Elected . . .*," Kalmus, 1988.

OTHER

Also contributor to *Grove's Dictionary of Music and Musicians;* also composer of film scores for "Good Speech for Gary," 1952, "Penn Relays," 1968, and "History of Delaware." Co-editor of series of biographies of American composers, Scarecrow.

WORK IN PROGRESS: A book on orchestral librarianship, for Scarecrow; "Three Centuries of American Music," a twelve-volume series of musical examples of American music; *Composers of Latin America: A Biographical Dictionary*, for Scarecrow.

SIDELIGHTS: Sam Dennison told *CA* that he wondered whether he spent years researching and writing *Scandalize My Name* because the Jim Crow laws in the Bible Belt where he grew up kept him from blacks and blacks from him. As he (and his black secretary) were cataloging "coon songs," he seemed to face the enormous task of finding out why songwriters would attack a race that already had troubles enough to deal with. As a professional musician, he had played some of this music and was disturbed by it, without fully realizing why.

BIOGRAPHICAL/CRITICAL SOURCES:

PERIODICALS

Pan Pipes of Sigma Alpha Iota, winter, 1982.

*　　*　　*

**DENVER, Walt
See REDDING, Robert Hull
and SHERMAN, Jory (Tecumseh)**

*　　*　　*

**de ROUTISIE, Albert
See ARAGON, Louis**

*　　*　　*

**de SAINT ROMAN, Arnaud
See ARAGON, Louis**

*　　*　　*

**DESTOUCHES, Louis-Ferdinand   1894-1961
(Louis-Ferdinand Celine)**

PERSONAL: Born May 27, 1894, in Courbevoie, France; died July 1, 1961, of a stroke, in Paris, France; son of Ferdinand-Auguste Destouches (an insurance executive) and Marguerite-Louise-Celine Guilloux (a businesswoman); married Suzanne Nebout (a bar maid), 1915 (marriage ended, 1916); married Edith Follet, August, 1919 (divorced, 1926); married Lucette Almanzor (a dancer), February, 1943; children: (second marriage) Colette. *Education:* University of Rennes, baccalaureat degree, 1919; University of Paris, medical degree, 1924.

CAREER: Writer and medical doctor. Worked in passport office of French Consulate in London, England, 1915-16; agent with a French lumber company in Africa, 1916-17; worked for Rockefeller Foundation as a health lecturer in Brittany, 1917-20; in private medical practice, Rennes, France, 1924-25; worked as a doctor with the League of Nations, 1925-28, travelling in the United States, Canada, Cuba, Africa, and Switzerland; in private medical practice, Paris, France, 1928-31; doctor with municipal clinic, Clichy, France, 1931-38; volunteer doctor on French naval vessel, 1939; doctor with municipal clinic, Satrouville, France, 1940-41; doctor-in-charge at municipal clinic, Bezons, France, 1942; left France, 1944, and travelled through Germany to Denmark; arrested in Denmark as a collaborationist, 1945, and imprisoned for fourteen months; lived in Koersor, Denmark, 1947-51; received French government amnesty, 1950; returned to France to practice medicine in the town of Meudon. *Military service:* French Army, 1912-15, served in the cavalry; became sergeant; wounded in action; mentioned in dispatches; received Medaille Militaire.

AWARDS, HONORS: Theophraste Renaudot Prize, 1933, for *Voyage au bout de la nuit.*

WRITINGS:

La Vie et l'oeuvre de Philippe-Ignace Semmelweis (doctoral thesis; also see below), Francis Simon (Rennes), 1924, reprinted, Gallimard, 1952.
La Quinine en therapeutique, Doin (Paris), 1925.

UNDER PSEUDONYM LOUIS-FERDINAND CELINE; IN ENGLISH

Voyage au bout de la nuit, Denoel, 1932, reprinted, Gallimard, 1972, translation by J. P. Marks published as *Journey to the End of the Night*, Little, Brown, 1934, reprinted, New Directions, 1983.
Mort a credit, Denoel, 1936, reprinted, Gallimard, 1969, translation by Marks published as *Death on the Installment Plan*, Little, Brown, 1938, new translation by Ralph Manheim, New Directions, 1966.
Mea culpa, suivi de la vie et l'ouvre de Philippe-Ignace Semmelweis (also see below), Denoel, 1937, translation by Robert A. Parker published as *Mea Culpa and the Life and Work of Semmelweis*, Little, Brown, 1937.
Guignol's Band, Denoel, 1941, Gallimard, 1967, translation by B. Frechtman and J. T. Nile published under same title, New Directions, 1954.
Entretiens avec le professeur Y, Gallimard, 1955, translation published as *Conversations with Professor Y*, University Press of New England, 1986.
D'un chateau a l'autre, Gallimard, 1957, translation by Manheim published as *Castle to Castle*, Delacorte, 1968, reprinted, Carroll & Graf, 1987.
Nord, Gallimard, 1960, translation by Manheim published as *North*, Delacorte, 1972.
Rigodon, Gallimard, 1969, translation by Manheim published as *Rigadoon*, Delacorte, 1974.

UNDER PSEUDONYM LOUIS-FERDINAND CELINE; OTHER

L'Eglise (five-act play), Denoel, 1933.
Secrets dans l'ile, Gallimard, 1936.
Hommage a Zola, Denoel, 1936.
Van Bagaden, Denoel, 1937.
Bagatelles pour un massacre, Denoel, 1937.
L'Ecole des cadavres, Denoel, 1938.
Les Beaux Draps, Nouvelles editions francaises, 1941.
Preface pour Bezons a travers les ages, Denoel, 1944.
A l'agite du bocal, P. L. de Tartas, 1948.
Foudres et fleches, C. de Jonquieres, 1949.

Casse-pipe, F. Chambriand, 1949, reprinted (bound with *Carnet du Cuirassier Destouches*), Gallimard, 1975.
Scandale aux abysses, F. Chambriand, 1950.
Feerie pour un autre fois, Gallimard, 1952, reprinted, 1977.
Normance, Gallimard, 1954.
Ballet sans personne, sans musique, sans rien, Gallimard, 1959.
La Naissance d'une fee (ballet), Gallimard, 1959.
Voyou Paul, Pauvre Virginie, Gallimard, 1959.
Vive l'amnestie Monsieur, Editions Dynamo, 1963.
Le Pont de Londres, Gallimard, 1964.
Oeuvres de Louis-Ferdinand Celine, Balland, five volumes, 1966-69.
Romans, edited by Henri Godard, two volumes, Gallimard, 1973-74, revised one volume edition, 1981.
Semmelweis et autres ecrits medicaux, edited by Jean-Pierre Dauphin and H. Godard, Gallimard, 1977.
Lettres et premiers ecrits d'Afrique (1916-1917), Gallimard, 1977.
Progres, Mercure de France, 1978.
Oeuvres de Celine, edited by Frederic Vitoux, nine volumes, Club de l'Honnete Homme, 1981—.
Lettres a Albert Paraz (1947-1957), Gallimard, 1981.
Chansons, Flute de Pan, 1981.
Arletty, jeune fille dauphinoise, Flute de Pan, 1983.
Lettres a son avocat: 118 lettres inedites a Maitre Albert Naud, Flute de Pan, 1984.
Maudits soupirs pour une autre fois, Gallimard, 1986.

Also author of *Lettres a des amies*, 1980.

SIDELIGHTS: Louis-Ferdinand Celine was among the most distinguished and influential writers of the twentieth century. His five most successful novels—*Journey to the End of the Night, Death on the Installment Plan, Castle to Castle, North,* and *Rigadoon*—introduced a scabrous, hallucinatory approach to fiction that has influenced the work of many writers throughout the world. John Fraser, writing in *Wisconsin Studies in Contemporary Literature,* called Celine "the only genius in French literature since Proust." And yet, for many years Celine faced massive opposition to his work. He was, as David Hayman wrote in his study *Louis-Ferdinand Celine,* "one of the least recognized writers of his generation." The primary reasons for Celine's long obscurity lie in his outspoken political beliefs and the abrasive nature of his literary work. "Celine's harsh style and sordid perspective, his reputation as a collaborationist, his anti-Semitism and racism are largely to blame for this neglect," Hayman contended. Richard Seaver, writing in *Saturday Review,* explained that "political considerations . . . too long deprived Celine of his due." It was not until the 1960s that the literary community began to accept Celine as a major figure and to evaluate his work in unbiased terms.

Celine's controversial novels are marked by misanthropic narrators, free-wheeling invective, ferocious humor, and squalid settings ranging from the jungles of Africa to the factories of Detroit. His unrestrained language is a unique amalgam of French slang, profanity, street grammar, and near-delirium. His episodic plots are rendered in burlesque fashion and are laced with an acidic satire. His work has often been compared to that of such earlier writers as Rimbaud, Baudelaire, and Jarry. Bettina Knapp described Celine's linguistic landscape in her study *Celine: Man of Hate:* "Huge verbal frescoes loom forth, horrendous-looking giants trample about, paraplegics, paralytics, gnomes, bloodied remnants hover over the narrations; scenes of dismemberment, insanity, murder, disease parade before the readers' eyes in all of their sublime and hideous grandeur." Maurice Nadeau, writing in his *The French Novel since the War,* claimed that Celine possessed "a living, colourful language of flesh and blood which translates emotion and feeling in direct terms.... It brings literary expression back to life." Hayman thought that Celine's books were "packed with exclamations of anguish and anger unsurpassed in the literature of any language or any century."

Celine began his career as a writer only after serving in the First World War and spending several years as a medical doctor. His military service began in 1912 when, in apparent reaction to an argument with his family, he enlisted in the French cavalry. When war broke out, Celine's unit saw heavy fighting on the German front. While stationed near the town of Ypres in October of 1914, Celine "volunteered for a dangerous front-line mission in Flanders, carried it out successfully, but was gravely wounded on the way back to base," as Merlin Thomas explained in his study *Louis-Ferdinand Celine.* His battlefield exploits earned him a medal for heroic conduct under fire, and he was featured on the cover of the popular weekly magazine *L'Illustre National.* In January of 1915, Celine underwent surgery on his injured arm, was given a three-month convalescent leave, and later that year was judged unfit for further combat duty and released from his military obligation. His right arm was to remain partially paralyzed for the rest of his life.

Celine worked with the passport office of the French Consulate in London, England during 1915 and 1916. During this time he married a French woman who was also working in London. Because their marriage was never recorded with the French Consulate, it was never legally recognized under French law. When, in 1916, Celine abandoned his wife and left England, it was as if the marriage had never taken place. He spent a year working for a French lumber company in Africa, then returned to France and took a position with the Rockefeller Foundation. On behalf of the foundation, he toured the French province of Brittany, giving lectures on tuberculosis. At the same time, he studied medicine at the University of Rennes, where he received a degree in 1919. He married again that same year. After earning a medical degree in 1924, Celine entered private medical practice and settled in Rennes with his wife and young daughter. But conventional married life did not appeal to him. By 1925, he was working for the League of Nations and travelling throughout Europe and North America on their behalf, while his wife and child were left behind. He never again returned to them. By the late 1920s, Celine was back in France, practicing medicine near Paris. He took a position with a municipal clinic in 1931, where he worked almost exclusively with the poor. From then until the end of his life, Celine practiced medicine only among the needy, despite the financial hardships that choice entailed. He argued that he could not in good conscience make money from the suffering of others.

Celine turned to literature while working as a doctor among the poor. He had already published several works on medicine, including his doctoral thesis on the life and work of Philippe-Ignace Semmelweis, before attempting to write fiction. He said on several occasions that his motivation to write a novel came from his belief that he could make enough money from writing to buy himself a decent apartment. The salary he made from his medical work was too modest to allow him this luxury; few of his patients were able to pay even the small amounts he charged for his services.

His first work, a novel entitled *Journey to the End of the Night* (originally *Voyage au bout de le nuit*), took him five years to write. Inspired in part by the success of Eugene Dabit's novel

Hotel du Nord, which concerned the French underclass Celine knew from his medical work, *Journey to the End of the Night* also focused on the urban poor, drawing from Celine's experiences as a doctor. When it was finally completed in 1932, the 1,000-page manuscript was sent off to two French publishing houses, Gallimard and Denoel. Gallimard found the book too controversial and suggested that its author might need to finance its publication himself. But Robert Denoel, a new publisher who had brought out several other controversial manuscripts, accepted Celine's novel. In an ultimately unsuccessful effort to separate his medical career from his literary one, the author published the work under the pseudonym Louis-Ferdinand Celine while continuing to practice medicine under his given name of Dr. Louis Ferdinand Destouches.

Journey to the End of the Night is told in the first person by Bardamu, a character who closely resembles Celine himself, and whose life in the military during the First World War, in medical school after the war, and as a married doctor among the poor, strongly parallels that of the author. Bardamu fights in the army during the First World War and is wounded in much the same manner as Celine himself was wounded. After the war, he travels around the world, visiting many of the same places Celine visited during his work with the League of Nations. Finally, he becomes a doctor and works among the poor. "The subject of the book in the most general sense," Thomas explained, "could be said to be Bardamu's voyage of discovery through life, ... until through the practice of medicine he comes to understand the futility of so much of human existence and recognize the significance of death."

The novel is composed, according to Irving Howe in his book *A World More Attractive: A View of Modern Literature and Politics,* "as a series of loosely-related episodes, a string of surrealist burlesques, fables of horror and manic extravaganzas, each following upon the other with energy and speed." Some of the incidents are taken from Celine's experiences as a doctor and are little changed. Others use actual experience as a starting point for Celine's acerbic and cynical commentary on life and humanity. Writing in the *New York Times,* Anatole Broyard claimed that "in his first and best book, 'Journey to the End of the Night,' Celine had hardly a good word for anybody, yet you felt that he was in closer touch with the human race, with people in the depths of their souls, than any other author in this century. And though 'Journey' was distilled out of disgust, the aftertaste was not sour—as it so often is with modern French novels—but bittersweet. His disgust was a kind of curdled love."

Journey to the End of the Night was phenomenally popular throughout Europe. Critics of both political extremes hailed it. Leon Daudet of the reactionary newspaper *L'Action Francaise* fought unsuccessfully to have Celine awarded the prestigious Prix Goncourt. Soviet revolutionary Leon Trotsky praised Celine in the highest of terms. Celine, he wrote in the *Atlantic Monthly,* "walked into great literature as other men walk into their own homes." Mavis Gallant, speaking of the book in the *New York Times Book Review,* explained that "Celine's dark nihilism, his use of street language, the undertow of mystery and death that tugs at the novel from start to finish were wildly attractive to both Left and Right; both could read into it a prophecy about collapse, the end of shoddy democracy, the death of sickened Europe." The reading public made *Journey to the End of the Night* a bestseller. "Celine's cynicism and denunciations seemed to speak for everyone....," Allen Thiher wrote in his *Celine: The Novel as Delirium.* "[His] popular, obscene language was like a violent gust of fresh air breaking into the literary climate." And attacks against the book's alleged obscenity merely provoked more interest and increased sales. "It was an immediate, enormous success," Thomas wrote, "and Celine found himself famous overnight and pretty prosperous very soon."

He followed this initial success with *Death on the Installment Plan* (originally *Mort a Credit*), a novel which takes the premises of the first book to their logical extremes. "An even grizzlier testimony than *Journey to the End of the Night*," as Howe believed, "Celine's second novel is written in a fitful and exuberant prose, and its tone is one of joyous loathing. . . . The misanthropy of the earlier novel ripens into outright paranoia; but with such bubbling energy, such a bilious and sizzling rhetoric, such a manic insistence upon dredging up the last recollection of filth! *Death on the Installment Plan* is a prolonged recital of cheating, venality and betrayal."

Featuring a narrator named Ferdinand, *Death on the Installment Plan* largely fictionalizes much of Celine's childhood, transforming it into a horrific and tragicomic story. Thiher stated that *Death on the Installment Plan* "presents a vision of a world in which delirious, comic automatons blindly act out their obsessions with predictably cataclysmic results." Fraser maintained that in this book, Celine "has rendered with a Shakespearean energy and vividness the horrors of an existence in which the 'everyday' bears in upon one monstrously, and one doesn't have even the normal amount of unconsciously assimilated mental procedures, let alone consciously shared theories and value-systems, for ordering it and making it intellectually endurable." Hayman described *Death on the Installment Plan* as "a cruel, a brutal, an explosive book, a Gargantuan burst of hilarity released from the pit. But the rage, hysteria, and hallucination are all controlled and masterfully timed."

In both of these novels, Celine employed a misanthropic, first-person narrator, a device he was to continue in his later works. In an article for the *National Review*, Guy Davenport described Celine's typical narrator: "Reading Celine is the same as falling in with a mad old man of glittering and feverish eye whom, he will shout in your face, the world has treated unfairly. He rambles, borders on an inspired inarticulateness, repeats himself, spits, insults, rolls shoelace-loosening obscenities on his tongue, and damns everything in sight except his wife, his cat Brebert, and himself. He is a thoroughly unsavory old cooter, and he meant to be."

These narrators recount their stories in a language that is highly-charged with venom, cynicism, disgust, and black humor. Their speech is part poetry and part obscenity, possessing what Gillian Tindall of the *New Statesman* called a "genteel crudeness." "It is not slang, as such, that informs almost every sentence of his long works," Tindall explained, "but a subtler and all-pervading coarseness, a lace-matted vulgarity as domestically familiar and unmistakable as human smells. There is no word for this voice, for no one else has written in it, but it is for this that Celine is read, appreciated and remembered." Douglas Johnson of the *Spectator* compared Celine's own conversation to that of his characters. "Celine would talk violently and contemptuously," Johnson wrote. "He sensed disaster everywhere; he saw unhappiness, disease and death; he denounced conspiracy, wickedness and hypocrisy. He had a gift for telling stories and a weakness for telling those which were impossible. . . . And his writing is like that."

These first two novels established Celine as a prominent writer of the 1930s. But this reputation was tarnished by his increasingly political work. This political phase began in 1936, when Celine was obliged to visit the Soviet Union. Soviet law forbade the export of literary royalties to writers who lived outside the country. Soviet law, too, required writers to spend their royalties only in the Soviet Union. To obtain and use the money he had made from the Russian editions of his novels, Celine went to Moscow.

His visit to the Soviet Union was at first enjoyable. Like many other writers and intellectuals of the time, Celine believed that the Soviets were creating a viable alternative society to the capitalist West. But after a short time in the country, he realized how wrong he had been. He found the country to be a police state where the oppression of the masses was even worse than that found in the West. And the Soviet communists were as materialistic as the bourgeoisie that Celine despised. Outraged, he began to speak out against them. Upon his return to France, he published *Mea Culpa*, a book denouncing the Soviet system, and declared himself to be "an avowed enemy of all Communists," as O'Connell reported.

This break with the French political left was detrimental to Celine's literary reputation; many of the critical journals of the 1930s sympathized with the communists. But Celine's reputation was hurt most by his next three books. In these works, he turned his attention from the communists to the Jews, whom he accused of conspiring to start another world war. In *Bagatelles pour un massacre* ("Trifles for a Massacre" in English), published in 1937, Celine spoke of a Jewish plot to involve the Gentiles of Europe in a major war, the "massacre" of the book's title. He argued that both communism and capitalism were materialistic systems invented by Jews, while war was the means by which the Jews weakened their enemies. O'Connell believed that the book's contentions were not coherently argued, and that "this work rambles on and winds around itself, spilling forth hatred, venom, lies, and distortions as it goes."

Celine's second book about the Jews, *Ecole des cadavres* ("School for Cadavers" in English), appeared in 1938 and reiterated his earlier statements about the coming Jewish war, while underlining what Celine called his basically pacifistic reasons for writing about it. He ends the book with a call for a military and political alliance between France and Nazi Germany as a way to keep the peace in Europe. In *Les Beaux Draps* ("A Nice Mess" in English), published in 1941 while Paris was already occupied by the German military, Celine attacks the French bourgeoisie. He sees this class as being primarily Jewish, decidedly materialistic, and a menace to the French Gentile population. He proposes a reorganization of society to abolish the class system and replace it with a form of National Socialism, similar to that established in Hitler's Germany. Speaking of the anti-Semitic books, Broyard noted that they were "murderous, inflammatory, impossible to imagine coming from France's greatest living novelist. To despise everyone is all right—it is not uncommon among French intellectuals—but to narrow it down to the Jews is something else. Especially on the eve of World War II."

Explanations for why Celine wrote these three books vary according to whether the commentator is sympathetic or hostile to the author. Kinder critics attribute his motivations to genuine pacifistic feelings and argue that his anti-Semitism was a simple mistake. Others see psychological reasons for Celine's dislike of Jews, declaring in some cases that he may have been mad or a paranoiac. They point to the vitriol of his novels as a sign of Celine's mental instability. Whatever his reasons for writing these books—and to his credit, Celine refused in later life to allow them to be reprinted—it is undoubtedly true that he spent the war years in occupied France and by all accounts was on friendly, although not close, terms with the Nazis. As Broyard noted in the *New York Times Book Review,* "the relation between [Celine's] genius as a novelist and his anti-Semitism has never been satisfactorily explained."

At war's end, Celine's life was in danger. He was denounced as a collaborationist over BBC radio. The French Resistance marked him for execution and began to send death threats to his house. When France fell to the Allied forces in 1944, Celine and his third wife fled first to Germany and then to Denmark, a country where he had banked a considerable amount of his royalties. The apartment he left behind in Paris was ransacked by the French Resistance, and many of his papers and manuscripts were destroyed.

But even in Denmark Celine was not safe. On Christmas eve of 1945, he was arrested by the Danish authorities. Although the French government wanted to extradite him for trial as a collaborationist, the Danes refused. Instead, they imprisoned him for some fourteen months. He was only released in 1947 because of his failing health. Celine remained in Denmark until receiving an official amnesty from the French government in 1950. At that time, a French court cleared him of any wrongdoing during the war. He spent the remaining years of his life as a doctor in the French town of Meudon.

Celine's postwar career was crippled by his earlier political pronouncements, and he was often the target of political attack. In 1945, Jean Paul Sartre accused Celine of having been paid by the Nazis to write on their behalf. Celine answered him in a book entitled *A l'agite du bocal,* defending his political beliefs and denying that he had been paid to express them. Other leftist spokesmen charged him with having advocated the extermination of the Jews, of having worked with the Gestapo, and of having gotten off far too lightly for his crimes. George Grant, writing in *Queen's Quarterly,* explained that "the French Left were baying for [Celine's] blood." Nadeau argued that "when Celine spoke of the 'witch-hunt' he was subjected to; when, before his return to France, he complained of being a 'scape-goat,' he was not far from the truth."

Celine also had trouble finding a publisher upon his return to France. Robert Denoel had been assassinated in 1945, and the publishing house that bore his name was accused of collaboration with the Nazis. It was not allowed to operate until finally cleared of the charge in 1947. Several of Celine's books appeared from smaller publishers, but they received little critical attention. As O'Connell remarked, "the silence and critical indifference that often follow the death of a major author appeared to be taking place while Celine was still alive and writing."

It was not until the publication of *Castle to Castle* (originally *D'un chateau l'autre*) in 1957 that Celine began once more to attract serious critical attention. He had used a misanthropic, first-person narrator in his earlier fiction. But in *Castle to Castle* he began to openly cast himself as the misanthrope, and the stories he narrated occupy the blurred realm between fiction and autobiography. He thereby satirized his own efforts as a writer while poking fun at the monstrous image his political enemies had given him.

Castle to Castle recounts the problems that Celine had experienced since war's end. It begins with the author at home,

explaining that he is only writing this book because his publisher demands that he write it to justify the advance he has been paid. "He is forever counting the number of pages completed, piling them up seemingly against his will, but knowing all the time that Gallimard will accept nothing less," O'Connell explained. After some seventy pages of grumbling about his relationship with his publisher, Celine settles into a recounting of his war years in France and of his sufferings after the war at a German castle where members of the French occupation government took refuge.

"The reader," John Weightman said in the *New York Review of Books,* "has to surrender himself to an impressionistic, paranoiac monologue, in which more often than not the sentences are left unfinished, the transitions from one idea to the next are not explained, and many of Celine's contemporaries are referred to elliptically and derisively under transparent nicknames." Writing in *Critique: Studies in Modern Fiction,* Haminda Bosmajian called *Castle to Castle* "a novel where the lines between fictional reality and the reality of fiction remain fluid, a novel which reveals with disconcerting honesty not only the human condition of Celine, but also that of ourselves."

Celine followed much the same approach in the novel *North* (originally *Nord*). "Once again," Lee T. Lemon wrote in *Prairie Schooner,* "Celine is the protagonist of his own novel." In this book he traces his travels across Germany and into Denmark at war's end. The book, as a critic for the *Times Literary Supplement* remarked, "does not record the convulsions of the Reich in collapse but recreates them." Thomas found the novel to be a successful blend of humor and danger. "Taking us through a whole series of events and adventures," he wrote, "the book leaves an overall impression of a vividly recollected nightmare. . . . Celine's 'hallucinatory' manner is much in evidence, but never sustained over long sections . . . , and with it there goes a sharp sense of humour and a savage awareness of man's cruelty to man. If the circumstances were not so miserable and depressing, *Nord* would undoubtedly be a very funny book indeed; as it is there are many passages where the sense of absurdity is stronger than the sense of menace and danger, and Celine succeeds in controlling the balance with consummate skill." Hayman claimed that *North* showed Celine to be "at the height of his technical powers" and "is filled with brilliant technical turns, unified but rich in detail and incident, abounding in dramatic sequences, comic tension, irony, and surprise."

Celine concludes the story of his wartime adventures in *Rigadoon,* a book which recounts the trials he suffered in Denmark. It was the last book he was to write. On the very day he completed the manuscript, Celine suffered a stroke and passed away. Grant described the desperate escape across war-torn Europe with which these three final novels are concerned. "The journey," Grant recounted, "takes place while the Russian armies get closer and closer, and while the American and British bombers flatten and reflatten the cities. Roosevelt's unconditional surrender is in full swing. Europe is being demolished by the two great continental empires with the help of the British. Celine's chronicle is of the collapse of that Europe and is laid before us with prodigality." Grant concluded that Celine's final trilogy "is one of the great masterpieces of western art and the greatest literary masterpiece of this era."

By the time of his death in 1961, Celine had reclaimed a place in contemporary French literature. His later novels had won him renewed critical respect, while his early books still commanded a wide and appreciative audience. But he was perhaps more widely known for his pervasive influence on a host of other writers. He is, according to Rima Drell Reck in her *Literature and Responsibility: The French Novelist in the Twentieth Century,* "the strongest subterranean force in the novel today." Among those he is credited with having influenced are Jean Paul Sartre (whose novel *Nausea* was dedicated to Celine), Henry Miller, Albert Camus, Samuel Beckett, Alain Robbe-Grillet, Michel Butor, William Burroughs, Thomas Pynchon, Gunter Grass, and Joseph Heller. Much of this influence was due to Celine's shattering of accepted approaches to the novel through his wild, personal, and aggressively nihilistic style. He created new possibilities for what the novel could be, possibilities which other writers explored. Erika Ostrovsky, writing in her *Celine and His Vision,* outlined what she saw as the author's literary impact. "Essentially," she wrote, "it consists of the creation of a new tone, a literary ambience which pervades an entire sector of modern letters and exceeds the limits of national boundaries or personal orientation and background."

Despite his influence, Celine is still denigrated by some critics. Davenport claimed that Celine's "significance remains to be seen. He was an angry old man talking, talking. It will take a critic more patient than most of us to sift through his ravings and decide if there is anything in it." Even more dubious of Celine's achievement is Henri Peyre who, in his book *French Novelists of Today,* criticized "the monotony of Celine's inspiration, the artificiality of his language and the 'pompierisme' of his tawdry sentimentality." Paul West wrote in *Book World* that "your mature reader dismisses Celine as a barfing werewolf (antihumanist, antihuman, self-obsessed, crypto-war-criminal, etc.)" And some critics still cannot evaluate Celine's literary efforts objectively because of his outspoken political beliefs, anti-Semitism, and racism.

But many critics find great value in his work, claiming that Celine is among the leading figures in the literature of the extreme. Stephen Day, writing in *Queen's Quarterly,* explained: "Observed as a whole, Celine's work is a journey through the events of the twentieth century with its wars, chaos and apprehension. And a great part of Celine's urge to write is the desire to achieve a mode of expression capable of relating them." Milton Hindus argued in an article for *MOSAIC: A Journal for the Comparative Study of Literature and Ideas* that Celine "has long seemed to me one of the masters of the novel of the twentieth century.... His picaresque tales of various underworlds bare the scabrous backside of our civilization." Thiher maintained that "Celine's work stands as a monument to . . . dissonance, rage, and madness." Weightman claimed that "there can be no doubt about the historical importance of Louis-Ferdinand Celine in the literature of anarchistic revolt. He was the first great foul-mouthed rhapsodist of the 20th century to proclaim a satanic vision of a godless world, rolling helplessly through space and infested with crawling millions of suffering, diseased, sex-obsessed, maniacal human beings." In similar terms, Hayman concluded that Celine "is the black magician of hilarity and rage, the perverse mirror of twentieth-century energy—a force so dynamic and diverse that it leads inevitably to overproduction and suicide. His vision supplements in our time that of Kafka, Beckett, or Grass, putting a real gun in the hand of the metaphorical fool, substituting explosion for restraint. He stands next to Proust as the painter of a moribund society, next to Joyce as a liberator of language. He is unmatched as a comic genius, the father of verbal slapstick."

In judging Celine's ultimate worth as a writer, critics point to several aspects of his work which they believe will last. Thiher concluded that, despite the extreme nature of his writings, it is Celine's ultimately liberating energy that will endure. "The Celinian novel is . . . ," Thiher wrote, "one of the most naked revelations of the tormented self in modern literature. . . . Language mimics madness and destruction in Celine. [But] it also mimics a riotous joy, the joy of shouting down all the misery and injustice with which life can crush a man. It is this exuberance that will not allow us to abandon Celine." Thomas argued that Celine's extreme literary vision, because of its basic honesty in reflecting the nature of our time, would last longer than those of other twentieth century writers. Celine was, Thomas wrote, "a witness of our century, of one of the most violent and troublous periods in human history. . . . The testimony this witness gives is bleak and even frightening for the most part, but by no means exclusively so. It may well be that future generations will regard it as a reasonable picture of an age. . . . They will perhaps find it more rewarding than that of most of his contemporaries." Writing in the *Dictionary of Literary Biography,* O'Connell claimed that "in Celine's work a whole civilization is judged deficient, as is perhaps even mankind itself. Such an accusatory image remains popular, generation after generation; despite tremendous social changes in Europe and the rest of the world, present readers can find in Celine outbursts of sarcasm and anger against individuals and institutions that seem timely today."

BIOGRAPHICAL/CRITICAL SOURCES:

BOOKS

Bardeche, Maurice, *Louis-Ferdinand Celine,* Table Ronde, 1986.
Bree, Germaine and Margaret Guiton, *The French Novel from Gide to Camus,* Harcourt, 1962.
Contemporary Literary Criticism, Gale, Volume 1, 1973, Volume 3, 1975, Volume 4, 1975, Volume 7, 1977, Volume 9, 1978, Volume 15, 1980, Volume 47, 1988.
Dauphin, Jean-Pierre and Jacques Boudillet, *Album Celine,* Gallimard, 1977.
Dictionary of Literary Biography, Volume 72: *French Novelists, 1930-1960,* Gale, 1988.
Flynn, James and C. K. Mertz, *Understanding Celine,* Genitron, 1984.
Gibault, Francois, *Celine,* three volumes, Mercure de France, 1977-85.
Hanrez, Marc, *Celine,* Gallimard, 1961.
Hayman, David, *Louis-Ferdinand Celine,* Columbia University Press, 1965.
Hindus, Milton, *The Crippled Giant: A Bizarre Adventure in Contemporary Letters,* Boar's Head Books, 1950.
Howe, Irving, *A World More Attractive: A View of Modern Literature and Politics,* Horizon Press, 1963.
Knapp, Bettina L., *Celine: Man of Hate,* University of Alabama Press, 1974.
Luce, Stanford L. and William K. Buckley, *A Half Century of Celine: An Annotated Bibliography, 1932-1982,* Garland, 1983.
Mahe, Henri, *La Brinquebale avec Celine: Cent lettres inedites,* La Table Ronde, 1969.
Matthews, J. H., *The Inner Dream: Celine as Novelist,* Syracuse University Press, 1978.

McCarthy, Patrick, *Celine: A Critical Biography*, Allen Lane, 1975.

Morand, Jacqueline, *Les Idees politiques de Louis-Ferdinand Celine*, Pichon et Durand-Auzias, 1972.

Nadeau, Maurice, *The French Novel since the War*, Grove, 1969.

O'Connell, David, *Louis-Ferdinand Celine*, Twayne, 1976.

Ostrowsky, Erika, *Celine and His Vision*, New York University Press, 1967.

Ostrowsky, Erika, *Voyeur Voyant: A Portrait of Louis-Ferdinand Celine*, Random House, 1971.

Peyre, Henri, *French Novelists of Today*, Oxford University Press, 1967.

Poulet, Robert, *Mon ami Bardamu: Entretiens familiers avec L.-F. Celine*, Plon, 1971.

Queriere, Yves de la, *Celine et les mots*, University of Kentucky Press, 1973.

Reck, Rima Drell, *Literature and Responsibility: The French Novelist in the Twentieth Century*, Louisiana State University Press, 1969.

Richard, J.-P., *La Nausee de Celine*, Scolies Fata Morgana, 1973.

Roux, Dominique de, *La Mort de L.-F. Celine*, Christian Bourgeois, 1966.

Thiher, Allen, *Celine: The Novel as Delirium*, Rutgers University Press, 1972.

Vandromme, Paul, *Louis-Ferdinand Celine*, Editions Universitaires, 1963.

Vitoux, F., *Louis-Ferdinand Celine: Misere et parole*, Gallimard, 1973.

PERIODICALS

Atlantic Monthly, October, 1935.
Book World, January 30, 1972.
Canadian Review of Comparative Literature, winter, 1981.
Critique: Studies in Modern Fiction, Volume XIV, number 1, 1972.
L'Herne, Number 3, 1963.
L'Illustre National, December 28, 1914.
Modern Fiction Studies, spring, 1970.
MOSAIC: A Journal for the Comparative Study of Literature and Ideas, spring, 1973, spring, 1975.
Nation, May 2, 1934.
National Review, March 31, 1972.
New Statesman, July 11, 1975.
New York Review of Books, June 5, 1969.
New York Times, April 22, 1934, January 12, 1972.
New York Times Book Review, July 18, 1976, August 31, 1986, February 1, 1987.
Queen's Quarterly, autumn, 1983, spring, 1987.
Saturday Review, February 5, 1972, August 7, 1976.
Saturday Review of Literature, April 28, 1934.
Spectator, June 29, 1934, July 5, 1975.
Times Literary Supplement, September 1, 1972, June 6, 1986.
Western Humanities Review, autumn, 1967.
Wisconsin Studies in Contemporary Literature, Volume 8, number 1, 1967.
World Literature Today, autumn, 1986.*

—*Sketch by Thomas Wiloch*

*   *   *

DIAMOND, Jacqueline
   See HYMAN, Jackie (Diamond)

DILLON, Barbara 1927-

PERSONAL: Born September 2, 1927, in Montclair, N.J.; daughter of George Rudolph (a sugar broker) and Janet (Quin) Dinkel; married Harold C. Dillon (an account executive for International Business Machines Corp.), November 22, 1952; children: Lisa Dillon Tullis, Brook, Nina. *Education:* Brown University, B.A., 1949.

ADDRESSES: Home—29 Harbor Rd., Darien, Conn. 06820.

CAREER: New Yorker, New York, N.Y., editorial assistant, 1949-57; writer, 1978—. Volunteer teacher at Mountaintop Day Care Center.

WRITINGS:

JUVENILES

The Good-Guy Cake, Morrow, 1980.
The Beast in the Bed, Morrow, 1981.
Who Needs a Bear?, Morrow, 1981.
What's Happened to Harry?, Morrow, 1982.
The Teddy Bear Tree, Morrow, 1982.
Mr. Chill, Morrow, 1985.
Mrs. Tooly and the Terrible Toxic Tar, Lippincott, 1988.
The Man from Milliken's, Lippincott, 1990.

WORK IN PROGRESS: A children's book, *The House on Park Street*.

SIDELIGHTS: Barbara Dillon told *CA:* "I always thought I might one day attempt juvenile fiction, though when my own three girls were small I had neither the time nor the psychological need to do so. It was only as they grew up that I felt a real desire to return to the world of children's books in which I had dwelt so happily with my children for so many years. My own childhood memories are, for some reason, most vivid at the third and fourth grade level, so it was to this age group that I naturally gravitated.

"Writing is, as the author Colette said, 'a difficult metier.' But once one is hooked on it, there is no turning back. The shape and color of my day usually hinge on how well my work has gone that morning. Letters from young readers are a particular source of pleasure to me, and I shall keep writing for them until I've used up every idea in my head."

*   *   *

DIXON, Paige
   See CORCORAN, Barbara

*   *   *

DOBKIN, Kathy
   See HAMEL PEIFER, Kathleen

*   *   *

DOBKIN, Kaye
   See HAMEL PEIFER, Kathleen

*   *   *

DOBSON, Theodore E(lliott) 1946-

PERSONAL: Born December 4, 1946, in Chicago, Ill.; son of

Theodore Arthur (an artist) and Ruth Virginia (Hacker) Dobson. *Education:* St. Mary of the Lake Seminary, M.Div., 1972.

ADDRESSES: Home—1792 Kline Way, Lakewood, Colo. 80226.

CAREER: Ordained Roman Catholic priest, 1972; associate pastor of Roman Catholic parishes in Chicago, Ill., 1972-78; free-lance lecturer and retreat master, 1978-81; Roman Catholic Archdiocese of Denver, Denver, Colo., director of Spiritual Renewal Services, 1981—.

MEMBER: International Platform Association, Association of Christian Therapists.

AWARDS, HONORS: Say but the Word: How the Lord's Supper Can Transform Your Life was selected book-of-the-month by Spiritual Book Associates, 1984; "Healing Wounded Masculinity through Prayer" was selected best article by Catholic Press Association, 1986.

WRITINGS:

Inner Healing: God's Great Assurance, Paulist Press, 1978.
(Contributor) Robert Heyer, editor, *Healing Family Hurts,* Paulist Press, 1980.
How to Pray for Spiritual Growth: A Practical Handbook of Inner Healing, Paulist Press, 1982.
Say but the Word: How the Lord's Supper Can Transform Life, Paulist Press, 1984.
Understanding the Catholic Charismatic Renewal: A Report on the Charismatic Renewal Today, Easter Publications, 1985.
Catholic and Fundamentalist Approaches to the Bible, Easter Publications, 1988.
The Falling Phenomenon: Discovering Principles of Discernment for "Slaying in the Spirit" and Other Extraordinary Religious Experiences, Dove Books, 1988.

WORK IN PROGRESS: The Secret Wisdom of the Enneagram with Kathleen V. Hurley.

SIDELIGHTS: Theodore E. Dobson wrote to *CA:* "I write on topics which I believe will help people to grow spiritually in their love of God and which help them to become more whole psychologically. I believe psychology and spirituality are connected. If human beings do not learn how to connect with the spiritual world through God, they find it much more difficult to become whole or happy; thus they create sickness, relationship difficulties, and social evils within themselves and around themselves.

"I wrote my first three books to teach and inspire, although by *Say but the Word: How the Lord's Supper Can Transform Your Life* I was already moving into a different genre. The first two books taught people how to pray; *Say but the Word* teaches prayer but also was motivated by an even deeper need I saw in the human soul: transformation.

"The [succeeding] three books [*Understanding the Catholic Charismatic Renewal, Catholic and Fundamentalist Approaches to the Bible,* and *The Falling Phenomenon*] are challenging to people of a religious background because they lead them on a critical appraisal of various aspects of religion: the charismatic renewal in the church, the effects of biblical fundamentalism, and the need to discern religious experience. The message of these books is that religious movements and phenomena are only helpful when they serve a higher goal: the awakening and transformation of the human person. This goal is becoming the focus of my life work, as I can see it presently.

"It seems to me that living in a place like Colorado affects my thinking. A little lake near my house is a place of frequent walks both for exercise and reflection. Sharing a place on the earth with ducks, geese, and gulls, muskrats and rabbits, cattails, flowers, and trees, with a view of the mountains and the ever-changing western sky, have opened my mind to possibilities and potential."

*   *   *

DONSON, Cyril   1919-1986
(Lonny Cordis, Via Hartford, Russ Kidd, Anita Mackin)

PERSONAL: Born May 26, 1919, in Mexborough, Yorkshire, England; died November 13, 1986, of a heart attack in Hartford, Huntingdonshire, England; son of Ernest (a coal miner) and Ada (Wagstaffe) Donson; married Dorothy Denham (a teacher), May 23, 1942; children: Valerie Norma Noble. *Education:* Educated at Bristol College, Loughborough College, and University of Nottingham; received Teacher's Certificates in psychology and education, and Diploma of Loughborough College, 1950. *Politics:* Liberal. *Religion:* Nonconformist.

CAREER: Newspaper journalist in England, 1941-43; schoolmaster, 1944-62, intermittently deputy headmaster and head of handicraft department in a bilateral school; public relations officer for a short period in 1964; writer. *Military service:* Royal Air Force, 1936-40.

MEMBER: Royal Society of Arts, Crime Writers' Association, Western Writers.

AWARDS, HONORS: Nominated for Tom Gallon Trust Award as best short-story writer.

WRITINGS:

(With Armand Georges) *Lonelyland: A Panorama of Loneliness, from Childhood to the "Sunset Years",* Bala Press, 1967.
(With Georges) *Bedsitterland: One-Room Living; A Contribution towards a Greater Understanding and Awareness of the Loneliness Scene and the Problems of the Lonely,* Bala Press, 1967.
Born in Space, R. Hale, 1968.
The Perspective Process, R. Hale, 1969.
Tritonastra: Planet of the Gargantua, R. Hale, 1969.
Draco the Dragon (horror novel), New English Library, 1974.
Make Your Own Wooden Toys, Arrow, 1975.
Guide to Authors, Venton, 1976.

UNDER PSEUDONYM RUSS KIDD

Brannan of the Bar B, Ward, Lock, 1964.
Thunder at Bushwhack, Ward, Lock, 1965, Arcadia House, 1967.
Jinx Ranch, Ward, Lock, 1966.
Gun Law at Concho Creek, Ward, Lock, 1966.
Throw a Tall Shadow, Ward, Lock, 1967.
Fight for Circle C, Ward, Lock, 1967.
Dead Man's Colts, Ward, Lock, 1968.
Ghost Town Marshall, R. Hale, 1982.
Battle for Bear Head Creek, R. Hale, 1982.
The Man from Wyoming, R. Hale, 1982.
Banner's Back from Boothill, R. Hale, 1983.
Vengeance Ride to Mesa, R. Hale, 1983.
Town Tamer from Texas, R. Hale, 1983.
Trouble Brand, R. Hale, 1984.

The Merciless Marshall, R. Hale, 1984.
Borrowed Badge, R. Hale, 1985.
Gunsmoke at Slade, R. Hale, 1985.
Six for Mexico, R. Hale, 1985.
Six-Shooter Sod-Buster, R. Hale, 1985.
Unsmiling Gun, R. Hale, 1985.
Wyoming's Debt to a Dead Man, R. Hale, 1986.
Dakota Feud, R. Hale, 1986.
One-Armed Bandit, R. Hale, 1987.

OTHER

Writer of romantic short stories for women under pseudonym Via Hartford and of other short stories under pseudonyms Lonny Cordis and Anita Mackin. Former editor of various county magazines and author of three crossword puzzles.

SIDELIGHTS: Cyril Donson once told *CA:* "I . . . write to make a living. But were this not necessary I would still be a compulsive writer, as I have been since the age of fourteen years.

"Present day trends in 'literature' I largely deprecate. As I see it, writing today has been desecrated to come down to the general level of human morals, standards, etc. But I do believe, and have always done, that a writer can say what he wants to say in any kind of wrapping, be it of the highest quality or closer to the gutter.

"My advice to aspiring writers would be simply . . . DON'T. There is no lonelier, more difficult occupation. If the would-be writer still persists, I would then warn him or her to watch out for the sharks, ever ready to cream off profit from the author's creative skill. My own experience has sadly included the copyright in one book ignored by a publisher, my work being sold without my knowledge by agents abroad, being left unpaid for work ordered by agents abroad (including some in America). And there is little protection against this."

[Sketch reviewed by wife, Dorothy Donson]

*   *   *

DORF, Richard C. 1933-

PERSONAL: Born December 27, 1933, in New York, N.Y.; son of William Carl (a sales representative) and Marion (a secretary; maiden name, Fraser) Dorf; married Joy McDonald (a Presbyterian minister), 1957; children: Christine, Renee. *Education:* Clarkson College of Technology (now Clarkson Technical University), B.S.E.E., 1955; University of Colorado, M.S.E.E., 1957; U.S. Naval Postgraduate School, Ph.D., 1961. *Religion:* Presbyterian.

ADDRESSES: Home—1124 Bucknell Dr., Davis, Calif. 95616. *Office*—Department of Electrical Engineering, Graduate School of Management, University of California, Davis, Calif. 95616.

CAREER: Clarkson College of Technology (now Clarkson Technical University), Potsdam, N.Y., instructor in electrical engineering, 1956-58; U.S. Naval Postgraduate School, Monterey, Calif., instructor, 1958-61, assistant professor of electrical engineering, 1961-63; University of Santa Clara, Santa Clara, Calif., associate professor, 1963-65, professor of electrical engineering, 1965-69, chairman of department, 1963-69, dean of College of Engineering and vice-president of Education Service, 1969-72; University of California, Davis, professor of electrical engineering, 1972—, dean of extended learning, 1972-81. Research associate at University of New Mexico, 1958-59; lecturer at University of Edinburgh, 1961-

62; vice-president of Ohio University, 1969-72; visiting fellow at Institute of Engineers, Australia, 1983. Member of board of directors of Boyd & Fraser Publishing Co., 1968—, and KVIE-TV, 1979-81.

MEMBER: Institute of Electrical and Electronics Engineers (fellow), American Society for Engineering Education.

WRITINGS:

Time-Domain Analysis and Design of Control Systems, Addison-Wesley, 1965.
(With George Julius Thaler) *Algebraic Methods for Dynamic Systems*, National Aeronautics and Space Administration, 1966.
Matrix Algebra: A Programmed Introduction, Wiley, 1969.
Introduction to Computers and Computer Science, Boyd & Fraser, 1972, abridged edition published as *Computers and Man*, 1974, 3rd edition, 1982.
Technology, Society, and Man, Boyd & Fraser, 1974.
Technology and Society, Boyd & Fraser, 1974.
Energy, Resources, and Policy, Addison-Wesley, 1978.
Appropriate Visions, Boyd & Fraser, 1978.
The Energy Factbook, McGraw, 1981.
Modern Control Systems, 3rd edition (Dorf was not associated with earlier editions), Addison-Wesley, 1981, 4th edition, 1986.
The Energy Answer, 1982-2000, Brick House Publishing, 1982.
Robotics and Automated Manufacturing, Reston, 1983.
A User's Guide to the IBM Personal Computer, Addison-Wesley, 1983.
International Encyclopedia of Robotics, Wiley, 1988.
Introduction to Electric Currents, Wiley, 1989.

*   *   *

DOUGLAS, David C(harles) 1898-1982

PERSONAL: Born January 5, 1898, in London, England; died September 12, 1982, in Bristol, England; son of John Josiah (a physician) and Margaret (Peake) Douglas; married Evelyn Helen Wilson, June 7, 1932; children: Ann Margaret. *Education:* Keble College, Oxford, B.A. (first class honors), 1921.

ADDRESSES: Home—4 Henleaze Gardens, Bristol BS9 4HJ, England.

CAREER: University of Glasgow, Glasgow, Scotland, lecturer in history, 1924-34; University of Exeter, Exeter, England, professor of history, 1934-39; University of Leeds, Leeds, England, professor of medieval history, 1939-45; University of Bristol, Bristol, England, professor of history, 1945-63, professor emeritus, 1963-82. Ford's Lecturer, Oxford University, 1962-63. Member of board of trustees, London Museum, 1945-70.

MEMBER: British Academy (fellow).

AWARDS, HONORS: James Tait Black Prize, 1939, for *English Scholars;* D.Litt., University of Caen, 1957, University of Wales, 1966, and University of Exeter, 1974; honorary fellow, Keble College, Oxford, 1960.

WRITINGS:

The Social Structure of Medieval East Anglia, Clarendon Press, 1927, reprinted, Octagon Books, 1974.
The Age of the Normans, Nelson & Sons, 1929.
(Editor) *Feudal Documents from the Abbey of Bury St. Edmunds*, British Academy, 1932, reprinted, Kraus Reprint (Munich), 1981.

(Contributor) Edward Eyre, general editor, *European Civilization: Its Origin and Development,* seven volumes, Oxford University Press, 1934-39, Volume 3 by Douglas: *The Development of Medieval Europe,* 1935.

English Scholars, Jonathan Cape, 1939, 2nd edition published as *English Scholars, 1660-1730,* Eyre & Spottiswoode, 1951, Greenwood Press, 1975.

(Editor and author of introduction) *The Domesday Monachorum of Christ Church, Canterbury,* Historical Society of Great Britain, 1944.

(Editor with Charles Travis Clay) *The Origins of Some Anglo-Norman Families,* Harleian Society, 1951.

(General editor) *English Historical Documents,* twelve volumes, Eyre & Spottiswoode, 1953-77, Volume 2 (editor with George W. Greenaway): *1042-1189,* 1953, 2nd edition, Oxford University Press, 1981.

(Contributor) Dorothy Whitelock, editor, *The Anglo-Saxon Chronicle: A Revised Translation,* Eyre & Spottiswoode, 1961, Rutgers University Press, 1962, reprinted, Greenwood Press, 1986.

William the Conqueror: The Norman Impact upon England, University of California Press, 1964.

The Norman Achievement, 1050-1154, University of California Press, 1969.

The Norman Fate, 1100-1154, University of California Press, 1976.

Time and the Hour: Some Collected Papers of David C. Douglas, Metheun, 1977.

Contributor of articles and reviews to journals.

BIOGRAPHICAL/CRITICAL SOURCES:

PERIODICALS

Book Week, July 19, 1964.
New Statesman, July 17, 1964.
New York Review of Books, August 20, 1964.
New York Times Book Review, August 16, 1964.
Times (London), August 20, 1964.
Times Literary Supplement, May 21, 1976.

OBITUARIES:

PERIODICALS

Times (London), September 18, 1982.*

* * *

DOWNS, Anthony 1930-

PERSONAL: Born November 21, 1930, in Evanston, Ill.; son of James Chesterfield, Jr. (a real estate consultant) and Florence Glassbrook (Finn) Downs; married Katherine Watson, April 7, 1956; children: Kathy, Christine, Tony, Paul, Carol. *Education:* Carleton College, B.A., 1952; Stanford University, M.A., Ph.D., both 1956. *Politics:* Democrat. *Religion:* Roman Catholic.

ADDRESSES: Home—8483 Portland Pl., McLean, Va. 22102. *Office*—1775 Massachusetts Ave. N.W., Washington, D.C. 20036.

CAREER: University of Chicago, Chicago, Ill., assistant professor of economics and political science, 1959-62; Real Estate Research Corp., Chicago, staff member, 1959-77, chairman of board of directors, 1973-77; Brookings Institution, Washington, D.C., senior fellow, 1977—. Affiliated with Rand Corp., Santa Monica, Calif., 1963-65; member of National

Commission on Urban Problems, 1966-68. Member of board of directors, National Association for the Advancement of Colored People (NAACP) Legal Defense Fund, and Standard Shares. Consultant to various federal agencies, local governments, private real estate developers, and corporations. *Military service:* U.S. Naval Reserve, active duty, 1956-59; became lieutenant junior grade.

MEMBER: American Finance Association, American Economic Association, Urban Land Institute, American Real Estate and Urban Economists Association, Economic Club of Chicago, Commercial Club of Chicago, Lambda Alpha.

WRITINGS:

An Economic Theory of Democracy, Harper, 1957.
Inside Bureaucracy, Little, Brown, 1967.
Who Are the Urban Poor?, Committee for Economic Development, 1968, revised edition, 1970.
Urban Problems and Prospects, Markham, 1970, 2nd edition, Rand McNally, 1976.
(With Al Smith and M. Leanne Lachman) *Achieving Effective Desegregation,* Lexington Books, 1973.
Federal Housing Subsidies: How Are They Working?, Lexington Books, 1973.
Opening up the Suburbs: An Urban Strategy for America, Yale University Press, 1973.
Stimulating Capital Investment in Central City Downtown Areas and Inner-City Neighborhoods, National Urban Coalition, 1973.
(Editor with Katharine L. Bradbury) *Do Housing Allowances Work?,* Brookings Institution, 1981.
Neighborhoods and Urban Development, Brookings Institution, 1981.
(With Bradbury and Kenneth A. Small) *Futures for a Declining City: Simulations for the Cleveland Area,* Academic Press, 1981.
(With Bradbury and Small) *Urban Decline and the Future of American Cities,* Brookings Institution, 1982.
Rental Housing in the 1980s, Brookings Institution, 1983.
(With Bradbury) *Energy Costs, Urban Development, and Housing,* Brookings Institution, 1984.
The Revolution in Real Estate Finance, Brookings Institution, 1985.

Also author of numerous monographs and government and commission reports. Contributor of over three hundred articles and reviews to professional publications.

* * *

DREYFUS, Hubert L(ederer) 1929-

PERSONAL: Born October 15, 1929, in Terre Haute, Ind.; son of Stanley S. (a businessman) and Irene (Lederer) Dreyfus; married Patricia Allen, June 25, 1962 (divorced, 1967); married Genevieve Boissier, December 10, 1974; children: (second marriage) Stephen Daniel, Gabrielle Boissier. *Education:* Harvard University, B.A. (with highest honors), 1951, M.A., 1952, Ph.D., 1964.

ADDRESSES: Home—1116 Sterling Ave., Berkeley, Calif. 94708. *Office*—Department of Philosophy, University of California, Berkeley, Calif. 94720.

CAREER: Brandeis University, Waltham, Mass., instructor in philosophy, 1957-59; Massachusetts Institute of Technology, Cambridge, instructor, 1960-63, assistant professor, 1963-66, associate professor of philosophy, 1966-68; University of California, Berkeley, associate professor, 1968-72, professor of philosophy, 1972—. Visiting professor, Technische Universitaet, May-June, 1986. National Endowment for the Humanities (N.E.H.) Summer Institute, University of California, Berkeley, director, 1980, seminar director, 1981, 1983, and 1984; director, N.E.H. Summer Institute, University of California, Santa Cruz, 1988. Has conducted interviews and made numerous appearances on television and radio.

MEMBER: American Philosophical Association, Society for Phenomenology and Existential Philosophy, Phi Beta Kappa.

AWARDS, HONORS: Sheldon traveling fellowship, Harvard University, 1953-54; Fulbright fellowship, 1956-57; French Government grant, 1959-60; Baker Award, 1966, for outstanding teaching; National Science Foundation grant, 1968; Harbison Prize, 1968, for outstanding teaching; American Council of Learned Societies grant, 1968-69; National Endowment for the Humanities fellow, 1976—; Guggenheim fellow, 1985.

WRITINGS:

(With wife, Patricia Allen Dreyfus, translator and author of preface) Maurice Merleau-Ponty, *Sense and Non-Sense*, Northwestern University Press, 1964.
Alchemy and Artificial Intelligence, RAND Corp., 1965.
What Computers Can't Do: A Critique of Artificial Reason, Harper, 1972, 2nd edition, 1979.
(Editor with Harrison Hall) *Husserl, Intentionality and Cognitive Science* (anthology), MIT Press, 1982.
"Beyond Philosophy: The Thought of Martin Heidegger" (twelve filmed lectures), University of California Extension Media Center, 1982.
(With Paul Rabinow) *Michel Foucault: Beyond Structuralism and Hermeneutics*, University of Chicago Press, 1982, 2nd edition, 1983.
(With brother Stuart Dreyfus) *Mind over Machine: The Power of Human Intuition and Expertise in the Era of the Computer*, Free Press, 1985.
(Editor) Michel Foucault, *Mental Illness and Psychology*, University of California Press, 1987.
Being-in-the-World: A Commentary on Heidegger's "Being and Time," Division I, MIT Press, 1989.

What Computers Can't Do has been translated into Russian, Japanese, Portuguese, Yugoslavian, German, French, and Chinese. Contributor to over thirty books. Contributor of articles and reviews to periodicals, including *Philosophical Review*, *Times Literary Supplement*, and *Vanity Fair*.

SIDELIGHTS: Hubert L. Dreyfus told *CA*: "I write because I am a teacher. Teaching helps me clarify and test my ideas, my line of argument, and writing is the natural thing to do afterward." He added: "At the moment my attention and energy are more than ever focused on the world of Artificial Intelligence. I consider myself to be applying Phenomenology to determine the place of computers in our culture."

Regarding *Mind over Machine: The Power of Human Intuition and Expertise in the Era of the Computer*, written by Dreyfus with his brother Stuart Dreyfus, Jeff Meer notes in *Psychology Today*: "Using clearly reasoned arguments, [the authors] conclude that the goal of the artificial-intelligence, or AI, movement, trying to make computers work out solutions to problems the way that human experts do, is both a philosophical and a practical impossibility." The reviewer comments that the authors' "urge for restraint is a refreshing change from the unbridled optimism that seems to surround AI."

Dreyfus lived in Germany for one year and has spent a total of six years in France.

BIOGRAPHICAL/CRITICAL SOURCES:

PERIODICALS

Book World, January 23, 1972.
Chicago Tribune, September 4, 1986.
Comparative Literature, spring, 1986.
London Review of Books, November 4, 1982, November 1, 1984.
New York Review of Books, November 15, 1973.
Psychology Today, July, 1986.
Times Literary Supplement, July 15, 1983.
USA Today, July 25, 1986.

*   *   *

DUKE, Charles (Richard)   1940-

PERSONAL: Born July 6, 1940, in West Stewartstown, N.H.; son of George T. and Evelyn (Murray) Duke; married Jonquelyn R. Simpson (a teacher), May 20, 1973; married second wife, Leona Blum, June 1, 1983. *Education:* Plymouth State College, B.Ed., 1962; Middlebury College, M.A., 1968; Duke University, Ph.D., 1972.

ADDRESSES: Home—P.O. Box 118, Providence, Utah 84332. *Office*—Department of Secondary Education, Utah State University, Logan, Utah 84322-2815.

CAREER: High school English teacher and department chairman in Sunapee, N.H., 1962-68; Plymouth State College, Plymouth, N.H., instructor, 1968-72, assistant professor, 1972-73, associate professor of English, 1973-78; Murray State University, Murray, Ky., associate professor, 1978-81, professor of English, 1981-84; Utah State University, Logan, professor and head of department of secondary education, 1984—.

MEMBER: International Reading Association, Association for Supervision and Curriculum Development, National Council of Teachers of English, American Association of Colleges for Teacher Education, Conference on English Education, Association of Teacher Educators, Council of Writing Program Administrators, Adolescent Literature Assembly, New England Association of Teachers of English (member of advisory board, 1973-74; publicity chairman, 1974-75; president-elect, 1976-77; president, 1977-78), Kentucky Council of Teachers of English (vice-president, 1979-80; president, 1980-81), New Hampshire Association of Teachers of English (vice-president, 1971; president, 1973-77), Utah Council of Teachers of English.

WRITINGS:

(Editor) *Granite State Writers*, New Hampshire Association of Teachers of English, 1972.
Creative Dramatics and English Teaching, National Council of Teachers of English, 1974.
(Contributor) R. Baird Shuman, editor, *Creative Approaches to the Teaching of English: Secondary*, F.E. Peacock, 1974.
Teaching Fundamental English Today, J. Weston Walch, 1976.
(Contributor) Shuman, editor, *Educational Drama for Today's Schools*, Scarecrow, 1978.
Teaching Literature Today, J. Weston Walch, 1979.
(Contributor) Shuman, editor, *English for the 80's*, National Education Association, 1980.

Writing through Sequence: A Process Approach, Little, Brown, 1983.

(Editor with Sally Jacobsen) *Reading and Writing Poetry: Successful Approaches for the Student and Teacher,* Oryx Press, 1983.

(Editor) *Writing Exercises from Exercise Exchange,* National Council of Teachers of English, 1984.

(With wife, Leona Duke) *Strategies for Teaching Basic Language Skills,* J. Weston Walch, 1987.

Contributor of articles and reviews to English language journals. Editor, *Exercise Exchange.*

WORK IN PROGRESS: Revision of two books, one on creative drama, the other on adolescent literature; developing an 11th-grade American literature anthology; editing a collection of articles on teaching literature.

SIDELIGHTS: Charles Duke told *CA*: "I find that my writing is almost always a direct product of my teaching interests; the books I have done thus far have grown out of classroom experiences and needs. My writing is addressed to definite audiences—the practicing teacher and students—and I derive a good deal of satisfaction from being able to translate theory into practical applications which can be of use to others."

AVOCATIONAL INTERESTS: Camping, fast European cars.

* * *

DUNCAN, Robert (Edward) 1919-1988
(Robert Edward Symmes)

PERSONAL: Born January 7, 1919, in Oakland, Calif.; died January 7, 1988, of a heart attack in San Francisco, Calif.; name at birth, Edward Howard Duncan; son of Edward Howard (a day laborer) and Marguerite (Wesley) Duncan (who died at the time of his birth); adopted, March 10, 1920, by Edwin Joseph (an architect) and Minnehaha (Harris) Symmes; adopted name, Robert Edward Symmes; in 1941 he took the name Robert Duncan; companion of Jess Collins (a painter). *Education:* Attended University of California, Berkeley, 1936-38, 1948-50, studying the civilization of the Middle Ages under Ernst Kantorowicz.

ADDRESSES: c/o New Directions Publishing Corp., 333 Sixth Ave., New York, N.Y. 10014.

CAREER: Poet. Worked at various times as a dishwasher and typist. Organizer of poetry readings and workshops in San Francisco Bay area, California. *Experimental Review,* co-editor with Sanders Russell, publishing works of Henry Miller, Anais Nin, Lawrence Durrell, Kenneth Patchen, William Everson, Aurora Bligh (Mary Fabilli), Thomas Merton, Robert Horan, and Jack Johnson, 1940-41; *Berkeley Miscellany,* editor, 1948-49; lived in Banyalbufar, Majorca, 1955-56; taught at Black Mountain College, Black Mountain, N.C., spring and summer, 1956; assistant director of Poetry Center, San Francisco State College, under a Ford grant, 1956-57; associated with the Creative Writing Workshop, University of British Columbia, 1963; lecturer in Advanced Poetry Workshop, San Francisco State College, spring, 1965. *Military service:* U.S. Army, 1941; discharged on psychological grounds.

AWARDS, HONORS: Ford Foundation grant, 1956-57; Union League Civic and Arts Foundation Prize, *Poetry* magazine, 1957; Harriet Monroe Prize, *Poetry,* 1961; Guggenheim fellowship, 1963-64; Levinson Prize, *Poetry,* 1964; Miles Poetry Prize, 1964; National Endowment for the Arts grants, 1965,

1966-67; Eunice Tietjens Memorial Prize, *Poetry,* 1967; nomination for National Book Critics Circle Award, 1984, for *Ground Work: Before the War;* first recipient of National Poetry Award, 1985, in recognition of lifetime contribution to the art of poetry; Before Columbus Foundation American Book Award, 1986, for *Ground Work: Before the War;* Fred Cody Award for Lifetime Literary Excellence from Bay Area Book Reviewers Association, 1986.

WRITINGS:

Heavenly City, Earthly City (poems, 1945-46), drawings by Mary Fabilli, Bern Porter, 1947.

Medieval Scenes (poems, 1947), Centaur Press (San Francisco), 1950, reprinted with preface by Duncan and afterword by Robert Bertholf, Kent State University Libraries, 1978.

Poems, 1948-49 (actually written between November, 1947, and October, 1948), Berkeley Miscellany, 1950.

The Song of the Border-Guard (poem), Black Mountain Graphics Workshop, 1951.

The Artist's View, [San Francisco], 1952.

Fragments of a Disordered Devotion, privately printed, 1952, reprinted, Gnomon Press, 1966.

Caesar's Gate: Poems, 1949-55, Divers Press (Majorca), 1956, 2nd edition, Sand Dollar, 1972.

Letters (poems, 1953-56), drawings by Duncan, J. Williams (Highlands, N.C.), 1958.

Faust Foutu: Act One of Four Acts, A Comic Mask, 1952-1954 (an entertainment in four parts; first produced in San Francisco, Calif., 1955; produced in New York, 1959-60), decorations by Duncan, Part I, White Rabbit Press (San Francisco), 1958, reprinted, Station Hill Press, 1985, entire play published as *Faust Foutu,* Enkidu sur Rogate (Stinson Beach, Calif.), 1959.

Selected Poems (1942-50), City Lights Books, 1959.

The Opening of the Field (poems, 1956-59), Grove, 1960, revised edition, New Directions, 1973.

(Author of preface) Jess [Collins], *O!* (poems and collages), Hawk's Well Press (New York), 1960.

(Author of preface) Jonathan Williams, *Elegies and Celebrations,* Jargon, 1962.

On Poetry (radio interview, broadcast on WTIC, Hartford, Conn., May 31, 1964), Yale University, 1964.

Roots and Branches (poems, 1959-63), Scribner, 1964.

Writing Writing: A Composition Book of Madison 1953, Stein Imitations (poems and essays, 1953), Sumbooks, 1964.

As Testimony: The Poem and the Scene (essay, 1958), White Rabbit Press, 1964.

Wine, Auerhahn Press for Oyez Broadsheet Series (Berkeley), 1964.

Uprising (poems), Oyez, 1965.

The Sweetness and Greatness of Dante's "Divine Comedy," 1263-1965 (lecture presented at Dominican College of San Raphael, October 27, 1965), Open Space (San Francisco), 1965.

Medea at Kolchis; [or] The Maiden Head (play; first produced at Black Mountain College, 1956), Oyez, 1965.

Adam's Way: A Play on Theosophical Themes, [San Francisco], 1966.

(Contributor) Howard Nemerov, editor, *Poets on Poetry,* Basic Books, 1966.

Of the War: Passages 22-27, Oyez, 1966.

A Book of Resemblances: Poems, 1950-53, drawings by Jess, Henry Wenning, 1966.

Six Prose Pieces, Perishable Press (Rochester, Mich.), 1966.

The Years as Catches: First Poems, 1939-46, Oyez, 1966.

Boob (poem), privately printed, 1966.

Audit/Robert Duncan (also published as special issue of *Audit/ Poetry,* Volume 4, number 3), Audit/Poetry, 1967.

Christmas Present, Christmas Presence! (poem), Black Sparrow Press, 1967.

The Cat and the Blackbird (children's storybook), illustrations by Jess, White Rabbit Press, 1967.

Epilogos, Black Sparrow Press, 1967.

My Mother Would Be a Falconress (poem), Oyez, 1968.

Names of People (poems, 1952-53), illustrations by Jess, Black Sparrow Press, 1968.

The Truth and Life of Myth: An Essay in Essential Autobiography, House of Books (New York), 1968.

Bending the Bow (poems), New Directions, 1968.

The First Decade: Selected Poems, 1940-50, Fulcrum Press (London), 1968.

Derivations: Selected Poems, 1950-1956, Fulcrum Press, 1968.

Achilles Song, Phoenix, 1969.

Playtime, Pseudo Stein; 1942, A Story [and] *A Fairy Play: From the Laboratory Records Notebook of 1953, A Tribute to Mother Carey's Chickens,* Poet's Press, c.1969.

Notes on Grossinger's "Solar Journal: Oecological Sections," Black Sparrow Press, 1970.

A Selection of Sixty-Five Drawings from One Drawing Book, 1952-1956, Black Sparrow Press, 1970.

Tribunals: Passages 31-35, Black Sparrow Press, 1970.

Poetic Disturbances, Maya (San Francisco), 1970.

Bring It up from the Dark, Cody's Books, 1970.

(Contributor) Edwin Haviland Miller, editor, *The Artistic Legacy of Walt Whitman: A Tribute to Gay Wilson Allen,* New York University Press, 1970.

A Prospectus for the Prepublication of Ground Work to Certain Friends of the Poet, privately printed, 1971.

An Interview with George Bowering and Robert Hogg, April 19, 1969, Coach House Press, 1971.

Structure of Rime XXVIII; In Memoriam Wallace Stevens, University of Connecticut, 1972.

Poems from the Margins of Thom Gunn's Moly, privately printed, 1972.

A Seventeenth-Century Suite, privately printed, 1973.

(Contributor) Ian Young, editor, *The Male Muse: Gay Poetry Anthology,* Crossing Press, 1973.

Dante, Institute of Further Studies (New York), 1974.

(With Jack Spicer) *An Ode and Arcadia,* Ark Press, 1974.

The Venice Poem, Poet's Mimeo (Burlington, Vt.), 1978.

Veil, Turbine, Cord & Bird: Sets of Syllables, Sets of Words, Sets of Lines, Sets of Poems, Addressing . . . , J. Davies, c.1979.

Fictive Certainties: Five Essays in Essential Autobiography, New Directions, 1979.

The Five Songs, Friends of the University of California, San Diego Library, 1981.

Towards an Open Universe, Aquila Publishing, 1982.

Ground Work: Before the War, New Directions, 1984.

A Paris Visit, Grenfell Press, 1985.

The Regulators, Station Hill Press, 1985.

Also author of "The H.D. Book," a long work in several parts, published in literary journals. Represented in anthologies, including *Faber Book of Modern American Verse,* edited by W. H. Auden, 1956, *The New American Poetry: 1945- 1960,* edited by Donald M. Allen, 1960, and many others. Contributor of poems, under the name Robert Edward Symmes, to *Phoenix* and *Ritual.* Contributor to *Atlantic, Poetry, Nation, Quarterly Review of Literature,* and other periodicals.

SIDELIGHTS: Though the name Robert Duncan is not well known outside the literary world, within that world it has become associated with a number of superlatives. Kenneth Rexroth, writing in *Assays,* named Duncan "one of the most accomplished, one of the most influential" of the postwar American poets. An important participant in the Black Mountain school of poetry led by Charles Olson, Duncan became "probably the figure with the richest natural genius" from among that group, suggests M. L. Rosenthal in *The New Poets: American and British Poetry since World War II.* Duncan was also, in Rosenthal's opinion, perhaps "the most intellectual of our poets from the point of view of the effect upon him of a wide, critically intelligent reading." In addition, "few poets have written more articulately and self-consciously about their own intentions and understanding of poetry," reports *Dictionary of Literary Biography* contributor George F. Butterick. The homosexual companion of San Francisco painter Jess Collins, Duncan was also one of the first poets to call for a new social consciousness that would accept homosexuality. Largely responsible for the establishment of San Francisco as the spiritual hub of contemporary American poetry, Duncan has left a significant contribution to American literature through the body of his writings and through the many poets who have felt the influence of the theory behind his poetics.

Duncan's poetics were formed by the events of his early life. His mother died while giving him birth, leaving his father, a day-laborer, to care for him. Six months later, he was adopted by a couple who selected him on the basis of his astrological configuration. Their reverence for the occult in general, and especially their belief in reincarnation, and other concepts from Hinduism, was a lasting and important influence on his poetic vision. Encouraged by a high school English teacher who saw poetry as an essential means of sustaining spiritual vigor, Duncan chose his vocation while still in his teens. Though his parents wanted him to have a European education in Medieval history, he remained in San Francisco, living as a recluse so as not to embarrass the academic figure who was his lover. He continued reading and writing, eventually became the student of Middle Ages historian Ernst Kantorowicz, and throughout his life "maintained a profound interest in occult matters as parallel to and informing his own theories of poetry," Michael Davidson reports in another *Dictionary of Literary Biography* essay.

Minnesota Review contributor Victor Contoski suggests that Duncan's essays in *The Truth and Life of Myth* may be "the best single introduction to his poetry," which, for Duncan, was closely related to mysticism. Duncan, says a London *Times* reporter, was primarily "concerned with poetry as what he called 'manipulative magic' and a 'magic ritual', and with the nature of what he thought of (in a markedly Freudian manner) as 'human bisexuality.'" Reports James Dickey in *Babel to Byzantium,* "Duncan has the old or pagan sense of the poem as a divine form of speech which works intimately with the animism of nature, of the renewals that believed-in ceremonials can be, and of the sacramental in experience; for these reasons and others that neither he nor I could give, there is at least part of a very good poet in him." While this emphasis on myth was an obstacle to some reviewers, critic Laurence Liebermann, writing in a *Poetry* review, said of *The Opening of the Field,* Duncan's first mature collection, that it "announced the birth of a surpassingly individual talent: a poet of mysticism, visionary terror, and high romance."

Duncan wrote some of the poems in *The Opening of the Field* in 1956 when he taught at Olson's Black Mountain College.

Olson promoted projective verse, a poetry shaped by the rhythms of the poet's breath, which he defined as an extension of nature. These poems would find their own "open" forms unlike the prescribed measures and line lengths that ruled traditional poetry. "Following Olson's death Duncan became the leading spokesman for the poetry of open form in America," notes Butterick. Furthermore, say some critics, Duncan fulfilled Olson's dictum more fully than Olson had done; whereas Olson projected the poem into a space bounded by the poet's natural breath, Duncan carried this process farther, defining the poem as an open field without boundaries of any kind.

Duncan was a syncretist possessing "a bridge-building, time-binding, and space-binding imagination" in which "the Many are One, where all faces have their Original Being, and where Eternal Love encompasses all reality, both Good and Evil," writes Stephen Stepanchev in *American Poetry since 1945*. A Duncan poem, accordingly, is like a collage, "a compositional field where anything might enter: a prose quotation, a catalogue, a recipe, a dramatic monologue, a diatribe," Davidson explains. The poems draw together into one dense fabric materials from sources as diverse as works on ancient magic, Christian mysticism, and the *Oxford English Dictionary*. Writing in the *New York Times Book Review*, Jim Harrison calls the structure of a typical Duncan poem multi-layered and four-dimensional ("moving through time with the poet"), and compares it to "a block of weaving. . . . *Bending the Bow* is for the strenuous, the hyperactive reader of poetry; to read Duncan with any immediate grace would require Norman O. Brown's knowledge of the arcane mixed with Ezra Pound's grasp of poetics. . . . [Duncan] is personal rather than confessional and writes within a continuity of tradition. It simply helps to be familiar with Dante, [William] Blake, mythography, medieval history, H.D., William Carlos Williams, Pound, [Gertrude] Stein, [Louis] Zukofsky, Olson, [Robert] Creeley and [Denise] Levertov."

Process, not conclusion, drew Duncan's focus. In some pages from a notebook published in Donald Allen's *The New American Poetry: 1945-1960*, Duncan stated: "A longing grows to return to the open composition in which the accidents and imperfections of speech might awake intimations of human being. . . . There is a natural mystery in poetry. We do not understand all that we render up to understanding. . . . I study what I write as I study out any mystery. A poem, mine or another's, is an occult document, a body awaiting vivisection, analysis, X-rays." The poet, he explained, is an explorer more than a creator. "I work at language as a spring of water works at the rock, to find a course, and so, blindly. In this I am not a maker of things, but, if maker, a maker of a way. For the way is itself." As in the art of marquetry (the making of patterns by enhancing natural wood grains), the poet is aware of the possible meanings of words and merely brings them out. "I'm not *putting* a grain into the wood," he told Jack R. Cohn and Thomas J. O'Donnell in a *Contemporary Literature* interview. Later, he added, "I acquire language lore. What I am supplying is something like . . . grammar of design, or of the possibilities of design." The goal of composition, he wrote in a *Caterpillar* essay, was "not to reach conclusion but to keep our exposure to what we do not know."

Each Duncan poem builds itself by a series of organic digressions, in the manner of outward-reaching roots or branches. The order in his poems is not an imposed order, but a reflection of correspondences already present in nature or language. At times, the correspondences inherent in language become insistent so that the poet following an organic method of writing is in danger of merely recording what the language itself dictates as possible. Duncan was highly susceptible to impressions from other literature—perhaps too susceptible, he said in a *Boundary 2* interview. In several interviews, for example, Duncan referred to specific early poems as "received" from outside agents, "poems in which angels were present." After reading Rainer Marie Rilke's *Duino Elegies,* he came to dread what he called "any angelic invasion"—or insistent voice other than his own. One poem that expresses this preference is "Often I Am Permitted to Return to a Meadow," the first poem in *The Opening of the Field*. He told Cohn and O'Donnell, "When I wrote that opening line, . . . I recognized that this was my permission, and that this meadow, which I had not yet identified, would be the thematic center of the book. In other words, what's back of that opening proposition I understood immediately: twice *you* wanted to compel me to have a book that would have angels at the center, but *now* I am permitted, often you have permitted me, to return to a mere meadow." His originality consisted of his demand that the inner life of the poem be his own, not received from another spiritual or literary source. "Whether he is working from Dante's prose Renaissance meditative poems, or Thom Gunn's *Moly* sequence, he works *from* them and *to* what they leave open or unexamined," explains Thomas Parkinson in *Poets, Poems, Movements.*

At the same time, Duncan recognized his works as derivative literature for several reasons. He said, "I am a traditionalist, a seeker after origins, not an original," reports Herbert Mitgang in the *New York Times*. Often he claimed Walt Whitman as his literary father, seeking in poetry to celebrate the experiences common to all men and women of all times, trying to manifest in words the underlying unity of all things that was essential to his beliefs. Complete originality is not possible in such a cosmos. In fact, the use of language—an inherited system of given sounds and symbols—is itself an imitative activity that limits originality. Even so, the poet, he believed, must be as free as possible "from preconceived ideas, whether structural or thematic, and must allow the internal forces of the composition at hand to determine the final form," Robert C. Weber observes in *Concerning Poetry*. This position, Duncan recognized, was bequeathed to him by Whitman and Pound, who viewed a poet's life work as one continuous "unfinished book," Parkinson notes.

Duncan's works express social and political ideals conversant with his poetics. The ideal environment for the poet, Duncan believed, would be a society without boundaries. In poetry, Duncan found a vocation where there was no prohibition against homosexuality, James F. Mersmann observes in *Out of the Viet Nam Vortex: A Study of Poets and Poetry against the War*. Duncan's theory, he goes on, "not only claims that the poem unfolds according to its own law, but envisions a compatible cosmology in which it may do so. It is not the poem alone that must grow as freely as the plant: the life of the person, the state, the species, and indeed the cosmos itself follows a parallel law. All must follow their own imperatives and volition; all activity must be free of external coercion."

Political commitment is the subject of *Bending the Bow*. Duncan was "one of the most astute observers of the malpractices of Western governments, power blocs, etc., who [was] always on the human side, the *right* side of such issues as war, poverty, civil rights, etc., and who therefore [did] not take an easy way out," though his general avoidance of closure sometimes weakened his case, Harriet Zinnes remarks in a *Prairie Schooner* review. Highly critical of the Viet Nam war, pollution, nuclear armament, and the exploitation of native peoples and natural resources, the poems in *Bending the Bow* include "Up-Rising," "one of the major political poems of our time," according to Davidson. For Duncan, the essayist continues, "the American attempt to secure *one* meaning of democracy by eliminating all others represents a massive violation of that vision of polis desired by John Adams and Thomas Jefferson and projected through Walt Whitman." Though such poems voice an "essentially negative vision," says Weber, "it is a critical part of Duncan's search for the nature of man since he cannot ignore what man has become. . . . These themes emerge from within the body of the tradition of the poetry he seeks to find; politics are a part of the broad field of the poet's life, and social considerations emerge from his concern with the nature of man."

The difference between organic and imposed order, for Duncan, says Mersmann, "is the difference between life and death. The dead matter of the universe science dissects into tidy stacktables; the living significance of creation, the angel with which the poet wrestles, is a volatile whirlwind of sharp knees and elbows thrashing with a grace beyond our knowledge of grace." The only law in a dancing universe, he goes on, is its inherent "love of the dance itself." Anything opposed to this dance of freedom is seen as evil. Both Duncan's poetics and his lifestyle stem from "a truly different kind of consciousness, either a very old or a very new spirituality," Mersmann concludes.

Duncan's method of composition based on this spirituality results in several difficulties for even the sympathetic reader. Duncan's "drifting conglomerations" are an exercise of poetic freedom that sometimes inspires, "but more often I feel suicidal about it," Dickey comments. Davidson notes that Duncan "never courted a readership but rather a special kind of reader, who grants the poet a wide latitude in developing his art, even in its most extreme moments. . . . The number of such readers is necessarily limited, but fierce in devotion." A large number of Duncan's poems are most accessible to an inner circle familiar with the personal and literary contexts of his writings, observes a *Times Literary Supplement* reviewer, who points out that "not everyone can live in California."

Duncan's method of composition presents some difficulties for the critic, as well. The eclectic nature of *Bending the Bow*, for example, remarks Hayden Carruth in the *Hudson Review*, excludes it from "questions of quality. I cannot imagine my friends, the poets who gather to dismember each other, asking of this book, as they would of the others in this review, those narrower in scope, smaller in style, 'Is it good or is it bad?' The question doesn't arise; not because Duncan is a good poet, though he is superb, but because the comprehensiveness of his imagination is too great for us."

After the publication of *Bending the Bow* in 1968, Duncan announced he would not publish a major collection for another fifteen years. During this hiatus he hoped to produce process-oriented poems instead of the "overcomposed" poems he wrote when he thought in terms of writing a book. In effect, this silence kept him from receiving the widespread critical attention or recognition he might otherwise have enjoyed. However, Duncan had a small but highly appreciative audience among writers who shared his concerns. Distraught when *Ground Work: Before the War*, the evidence of nearly twenty years of significant work, did not win the attention they thought it deserved from the publishing establishment, these poets founded the National Poetry Award and honored Duncan by

making him the first recipient of the award in 1985. The award, described in a *Sagetrieb* article, was "a positive action affirming the admiration of the poetic community for the dedication and accomplishment of a grand poet."

BIOGRAPHICAL/CRITICAL SOURCES:

BOOKS

Allen, Donald M., *The New American Poetry, 1945-1960*, Grove, 1960.
Allen, Donald M., *The Poetics of the New American Poetry*, Grove, 1973.
Bertholf, Robert J. and Ian W. Reid, editors, *Robert Duncan: Scales of the Marvelous*, New Directions, 1979.
Charters, Samuel, *Some Poems/Poets: Studies in American Underground Poetry since 1945*, Oyez, 1971.
Contemporary Literary Criticism, Gale, Volume 1, 1973, Volume 2, 1974, Volume 4, 1975, Volume 7, 1977, Volume 15, 1980, Volume 41, 1987.
Dickey, James, *Babel to Byzantium*, Farrar, Straus, 1968.
Dictionary of Literary Biography, Gale, Volume 5: *American Poets since World War II*, 1980, Volume 16: *The Beats: Literary Bohemians in Postwar America*, 1983.
Faas, Ekbert, editor, *Towards a New American Poetics: Essays and Interviews*, Black Sparrow Press, 1978.
Fass, Ekbert, *Young Robert Duncan: Portrait of the Homosexual in Society*, Black Sparrow Press, 1983.
Fauchereau, Serge, *Lecture de la poesie americaine*, Editions de Minuit, 1969.
Mersmann, James F., *Out of the Viet Nam Vortex: A Study of Poets and Poetry against the War*, University Press of Kansas, 1974.
Parkinson, Thomas, *Poets, Poems, Movements*, University of Michigan Research Press, 1987.
Pearce, Roy Harvey, *Historicism Once More: Problems and Occasions for the American Scholar*, Princeton University Press, 1969.
Rexroth, Kenneth, *Assays*, New Directions, 1961.
Rexroth, Kenneth, *American Poetry in the Twentieth Century*, Herder and Herder, 1971.
Rosenthal, M. L., *The New Poets: American and British Poetry since World War II*, Oxford University Press, 1967.
Stepanchev, Stephen, *American Poetry since 1945*, Harper, 1965.
Tallman, Warren, *Godawful Streets of Man*, Coach House Press, 1976.
Weatherhead, Kingsley, *Edge of the Image: Marianne Moore, William Carlos Williams, and Some Other Poets*, University of Washington Press, 1967.

PERIODICALS

Agenda, autumn/winter, 1970.
Audit/Poetry (special Duncan issue), Number 3, 1967.
Boundary 2, winter, 1980.
Caterpillar, number 8/9, 1969.
Centennial Review, fall, 1975, fall, 1985.
Concerning Poetry, spring, 1978.
Contemporary Literature, spring, 1975.
Hudson Review, summer, 1968.
Maps (special Duncan issue), 1974.
Minnesota Review, fall, 1972.
New York Review of Books, June 3, 1965, May 7, 1970.
New York Times Book Review, December 20, 1964, September 29, 1968, August 4, 1985.
Poetry, March, 1968, April, 1969, May, 1970.

Sagetrieb, winter, 1983, (special Duncan issue) fall/winter, 1985.
Saturday Review, February 13, 1965, August 24, 1968.
Southern Review, spring, 1969, winter, 1985.
Sulfur 12, Volume 4, number 2, 1985.
Times Literary Supplement, May 1, 1969, July 23, 1971.
Unmuzzled Ox, February, 1977.
Voice Literary Supplement, November, 1984.

OBITUARIES:

PERIODICALS

New York Times, February 2, 1988.
Times (London), February 11, 1988.*

—*Sketch by Marilyn K. Basel*

*　　*　　*

DUPREE, Louis (Benjamin) 1925-1989

PERSONAL: Born August 23, 1925, in Greenville, N.C.; died March 21, 1989; son of Chauncey Leary (a postal clerk) and Luna (Tripp) Dupree; married Ann Bradford Kirschner, September 15, 1949 (divorced, 1965); married Nancy Marie Shakuntula Hatch (a writer), February 20, 1966; children: (first marriage) Julie, Louis F. R., Sara G. *Education:* Harvard University, A.B. (cum laude), 1949, A.M., 1953, Ph.D., 1955. *Politics:* Liberal. *Religion:* Muslim.

ADDRESSES: Home—Willow Grove Rd., Stony Point, N.Y. 10980. *Office*—Universities Field Staff International, P.O. Box 150, Hanover, N.H. 03755.

CAREER: Member of American Museum of Natural History expeditions in West Pakistan and Afghanistan, 1949, 1950-51, and University of Pennsylvania Museum expedition in Iran, 1951; Harvard University, Cambridge, Mass., assistant to dean of scholarships, 1953; Air University, Maxwell Air Force Base, Ala., area study contractor, 1953-54, assistant professor, 1954-57, associate professor of Middle Eastern studies, 1957; Pennsylvania State University, University Park, associate professor of anthropology, 1957-66, adjunct professor, 1966-89; Universities Field Staff International, Hanover, N.H., associate with joint teaching-research appointments at eleven universities, 1959-83. Research associate, American Museum of Natural History, 1959-71; director, Archaeological Mission to Afghanistan, 1959-78. Visiting professor, Kabul University, 1962, 1964-66, Pennsylvania State University, winter, 1981-82, Princeton University, Woodrow Wilson School of Public and International Affairs, 1983-84, and U.S. Military Academy, 1984-85; visiting distinguished professor, University of Nebraska, 1981; visiting scholar, Ramapo College of New Jersey, 1983. Lecturer at intervals for U.S. Department of State, Foreign Service Institute, 1967-89; visiting lecturer, University of Chicago, spring, 1968, Semester-at-Sea, spring, 1982; Walter A. Edge Distinguished Lecturer, Princeton University, 1980; distinguished lecturer, Mary Washington College of University of Virginia, and Saul O. Sidmore Lecturer, Plymouth State College, both 1981; Taft Distinguished Lecturer, University of Cincinnati, 1984. Faculty associate, Columbia University seminar on the archaeology of the eastern Mediterranean, eastern Europe, and the Near East, 1966-89; research associate, Center of Afghanistan Studies, University of Nebraska, 1974-89. Member, Near and Middle East Committee, Social Science Research Council, 1958-59, Eisenhower Exchange Fellowship Committee for Afghanistan, 1971, and Commission Internationale d'Enquete Humanitaire sur les Personnes Deplacees en Afghanistan, 1984-89. Member of board of directors, American Friends of Afghanistan, and Afghanistan Relief Committee, both 1979-89, and Afghanistan Forum, Inc., 1983-89. Member of Advisory board, Center of Textile and Rug Studies, Carnegie Institute, 1978-80, Afghan Freedom Organization, 1979-89, and Committee for a Free Afghanistan, 1980. Member of advisory committee, American Aid for Afghans, 1979-89. Sponsor, American Council for the Study of Islamic Societies, 1983-89. Foreign affairs consultant, American University, 1958, 1960-61, 1967; consultant, U.S. Operations Mission-Pakistan, 1963, 1966; Peace Corps, director of area studies in Afghanistan, 1966, consultant on Afghanistan, 1970, cross-cultural coordinator, 1976. Consultant to U.S. Agency for International Development, 1976, United Nations Development Programme, United Nations Educational, Scientific, and Cultural Organization (UNESCO), 1977, Ford Foundation, 1979, Woodrow Wilson International Center for Scholars, 1983, and Helsinki Watch, 1984. *Military service:* U.S. Merchant Marine Reserve, 1943-44. U.S. Army, Paratroopers, 1944-47; served in Philippines, Okinawa, Japan; became first lieutenant.

MEMBER: American Anthropological Association (fellow), American Association for the Advancement of Science (fellow), Society for Applied Anthropology (fellow), American Oriental Society (fellow), American Ethnological Society (fellow), American Geographical Society (fellow), Society for American Archeology (fellow), Archaeological Institute of America, Middle East Institute, Royal Central Asian Society, Royal Society for Asian Affairs, Societe Prehistorique Francaise, Asia Society (member of Afghanistan council), British Institute of Persian Studies, Society for Afghan Studies (founding member), Afghanistan Studies Association, Friends of the National Army Museum, Society of World War I Aero Historians, North Carolina Archeological Society, Campaign for Real Ale, Gamma Alpha, Explorers Club (New York; fellow), Harvard Travellers Club.

AWARDS, HONORS: Meritorious service commendation from U.S. Air Force, 1956, for field work on survival test in the Libyan Sahara; grants for field work in Afghanistan from Wenner-Gren Foundation, 1959-60, 1965, 1978-80, Social Science Research Council, 1964, American Philosophical Society, 1964-65, 1966, Rockefeller Fund, 1965, American Museum of Natural History, 1968, National Science Foundation, 1969-70, and Heinze Foundation, 1970-71; National Endowment for the Humanities fellow and American Council of Learned Societies fellow at King's College (Cambridge), 1972-73; grants from John D. Rockefeller III Fund, L. S. B. Leakey Foundation, and Archaeological Institute of America for research trip to People's Republic of China, 1978, Ford Foundation, 1982-83, 1984-85, and from American Institute for Pakistan Studies, 1984.

WRITINGS:

The Jungle Survival Field Test, Air University, 1956.
The Desert Survival Field Test, Air University, 1956.
The Warm Water Survival Field Test, Air University, 1958.
Shamshir Ghar: Historic Cave Site in Kandahar Province, Afghanistan (based on doctoral thesis), Volume 46, Anthropological Papers of American Museum of Natural History, 1958.
(Editor) *Anthropology in the Armed Forces,* Social Science Research Center, Pennsylvania State University, 1959.
Deh Morasi Ghundai: A Chalcolithic Site in South-Central Afghanistan, Volume 50, Anthropological Papers of American Museum of Natural History, 1963.

(With former wife, Ann Dupree, and A. A. Motamedi) *A Guide to the Kabul Museum*, National Museum of Afghanistan, 1964, 2nd edition, 1968.

(With others) *Prehistoric Research in Afghanistan: 1959-1966*, Volume 62, Transactions of American Philosophical Society, 1972.

Afghanistan, Princeton University Press, 1973.

(Editor) George Scott Robertson, *Kaffirs of the Hindu Kush*, Oxford University Press, 1974.

(Editor with L. Albert) *Afghanistan in the 1970's*, Praeger, 1974.

(With wife, Nancy Hatch Dupree) *The National Museum of Afghanistan: A Pictorial Guide*, [Kabul], 1974.

(Editor and author of introduction) G. B. Malleson, *History of Afghanistan*, 1984.

(Editor and author of introduction) Charles Marvin, *The Russian Advance towards India*, Saeed Book Bank, 1984.

CONTRIBUTOR

L. P. Vidyarthi, editor, *Anthropology and Tribal Welfare in India*, Bihar University, 1959.

Vidyarthi, editor, *Aspects of Religion in Indian Society*, [Meerut], 1961.

K. H. Silvert, editor, *Expectant Peoples: Nationalism and Development*, Random House, 1963.

Robert B. Textor, editor, *Cultural Frontiers of the Peace Corps*, MIT Press, 1965.

Donald N. Wilber, editor, *The Nations of Asia*, Hart Publishing, 1966.

The Developing World: AUFS Readings, Volume 1, American Universities Field Staff, 1966.

Silvert, editor, *Churches and States: The Religious Institution and Modernization*, American Universities Field Staff, 1967.

City and Nation in the Developing World: AUFS Readings, Volume 2, American Universities Field Staff, 1968.

Louise Sweet, editor, *Peoples and Cultures of the Middle East*, Volume 2, Natural History Press, 1970.

(Author of notes and illustrations) G. F. Debets, *Physical Anthropology of Afghanistan*, Volumes 1 and 2, edited by Henry Field and translated by Eugene V. Prostov, Peabody Museum of Archaeology and Ethnology, Harvard University, 1970.

(Author of foreword) Hasan Kakar, *Afghanistan: A Study in International Political Developments, 1880-1896*, Punjab Educational Press, 1971.

Harrison Brown and Alan Sweezy, editors, *Population: Perspective, 1971*, Freeman, Cooper, 1972.

Peoples of the Earth, Volume 15: *Western and Central Asia*, Danbury, 1973.

T. C. Grondahl, editor, *A Select Bibliography: Asia, Africa, Eastern Europe, Latin America*, cumulative supplement, 1961-71, American Universities Field Staff, 1973.

Commoners, Climbers, and Notables, E. J. Brill, 1977.

Clarence Maloney, editor, *Contributions to Asian Studies*, Volume 11: *Language and Civilization Change in South Asia*, Leiden, 1978.

Norman N. Miller and Manon Spitzer, editors, *Faces of Change: Five Rural Societies in Transition*, Wheelock Educational Resources, 1978.

Abdul Hasan Dani, editor, *Indus Civilisation: New Perspectives*, Islamabad, 1981.

Archaeological Gazetteer of Afghanistan, two volumes, Editions Recherche sur les Civilisations, 1982.

Akbar Ahmed and David Hart, editor, *Islam in Tribal Societies*, [London], 1984.

OTHER

Author of book-length reports for U.S. Air Force, including *Cultural Study of Afghanistan*, 1953, *... of Iran*, 1954, *... of West Pakistan and Kashmir*, 1954, *... of North India, Nepal, Bhutan and Sikkim*, 1957. Author of film essays for American Universities Field Staff film project. Contributor of about seventy articles to *American Universities Field Staff Reports: South Asia Series*, 1959-89. Project officer for U.S. Government "Ethnic Card Study: A Description of the Peoples of the World," 1954-57. Contributor to *Collier's Encyclopedia, Encyclopaedia Brittanica, Cowles Comprehensive Encyclopedia, Cowles Encyclopedia of Nations, Americana Annual*, and other annuals. Contributor of more than 150 articles and thirty reviews to *Time, American Antiquity, Nation, Illustrated London News, Arts Asiatiques, U.S. Lady, Afghanistan, Muslim World, Economist, Middle East Journal*, and other periodicals and newspapers. Occasional columnist, *Kabul Times*, 1962-89; corresponding member, International News Rights and Royalties (London), 1963-89.

*   *   *

DYE, Thomas R(oy)   1935-

PERSONAL: Born December 16, 1935, in Pittsburgh, Pa.; son of James C. and Marguerite A. (Dewan) Dye; married Joan G. Wohleber, June, 1957; children: Roy Thomas, Cheryl Price. *Education:* Pennsylvania State University, B.A., 1957, M.A., 1959; University of Pennsylvania, Ph.D., 1961.

ADDRESSES: Home—2321 Killarney Way, Tallahassee, Fla. 32308. *Office*—Policy Sciences Program, Florida State University, Tallahassee, Fla. 32306.

CAREER: University of Wisconsin—Madison, assistant professor of political science, 1962-63; University of Georgia, Athens, assistant professor, 1963-65, associate professor of political science and chairman of department, 1965-68; Florida State University, Tallahassee, professor of government, 1968—, chairman of department, 1969-72, director of Policy Sciences Program, 1978—. Visiting professor at Bar Ilan University, 1972, and University of Arizona, 1976; visiting scholar, Brookings Institution, 1984. *Military service:* U.S. Air Force Reserve, 1957-62; became first lieutenant.

MEMBER: American Political Science Association (secretary, 1969-72), Southern Political Science Association (member of executive council; president, 1976-77), Phi Beta Kappa, Omicron Delta Kappa.

AWARDS, HONORS: U.S. Office of Education research grants, 1966-67, 1969-70; National Science Foundation grants, 1967, 1970-71; National Institutes of Health research grant, 1973-76; Lynde and Harry Bradley Foundation grant, 1986-88; Harold D. Lasswell Award, American Political Science Association, for contributions to the study of public policy.

WRITINGS:

(With Oliver P. Williams, S. Charles Liebman, and Harold Herman) *Suburban Differences and Metropolitan Policies*, University of Pennsylvania Press, 1965.

Politics, Economics, and the Public, Rand McNally, 1966.

(Editor with Brett W. Hawkins) *Politics in the Metropolis: A Reader in Conflict and Cooperation,* C.E. Merrill, 1967.

Politics in States and Communities, Prentice-Hall, 1969, 6th edition, 1988.

(With Lee Greene and George S. Parthemos) *American Government: Theory, Structure, and Process,* Wadsworth, 1969.

(Compiler) *American Public Policy,* C.E. Merrill, 1969.

(With Harmon Zeigler) *The Irony of Democracy,* Wadsworth, 1970, 7th edition, 1987.

The Politics of Equality, Bobbs-Merrill, 1971.

Understanding Public Policy, Prentice-Hall, 1972, 6th edition, 1987.

Power and Society, Brooks/Cole, 1975, 4th edition, 1986.

Who's Running America?: Institutional Leadership in the United States, Prentice-Hall, 1976, 2nd edition published as *Who's Running America?: The Carter Years,* 1979, 3rd edition published as *Who's Running America?: The Reagan Years,* 1983, 4th edition published as *Who's Running America?: The Conservative Years,* 1986.

Policy Analysis: What Governments Do, Why They Do It, and What Difference It Makes, University of Alabama Press, 1976.

(Editor with Virginia Gray) *Determinants of Public Policy,* Heath, 1980.

(With Zeigler) *American Politics in the Media Age,* Brooks/Cole, 1983, 2nd edition, 1986.

(Editor with G. William Domhoff) *Power Elites and Organizations,* Sage Publications, 1987.

CONTRIBUTOR

The Legislative Process in Congress and the States, Institute of Public Administration, Pennsylvania State University, 1961.

Robert E. Crew, editor, *State Politics,* Wadsworth, 1966.

Michael N. Danielson, editor, *Metropolitan Politics,* Little, Brown, 1966.

Samuel C. Patterson, editor, *American Legislative Process: A Reader,* Van Nostrand, 1967.

Peter Woll, editor, *American Government: Readings and Cases,* Little, Brown, 1968.

Aaron Wildavsky and Nelson Polsby, editors, *American Governmental Institutions,* Rand McNally, 1968.

Donald P. Sprengel, editor, *Comparative State Politics: A Reader,* Wadsworth, 1970.

Ira Sharkansky and Richard I. Hofferbert, editors, *Politics and Policies in States and Communities,* Little, Brown, 1970.

Walter G. Hack, editor, *Educational Administration: Selected Readings,* Allyn & Bacon, 1970.

David A. Morgan and Samuel Kirkpatrick, editors, *Urban Political Analysis: A Systems Approach,* Free Press, 1970.

Oliver Walter, editor, *Political Scientists at Work,* Duxbury, 1971.

Robert N. Spadaro, editor, *The Policy Vacuum,* Lexington Books, 1975.

Frank P. Scioli and Thomas J. Cook, editors, *Methodologies for Analyzing Public Policies,* Lexington Books, 1975.

Stuart Nagel, editor, *Policy Studies and the Social Sciences,* Lexington Books, 1975.

Robert J. Waste, editor, *Community Power,* Sage Publications, 1986.

OTHER

Editor of ''Policy Analysis'' series, Bobbs-Merrill. Contributor of numerous articles, essays, and reviews to social science journals.

WORK IN PROGRESS: Writing on state politics, on equality, political leadership, and political systems, and on public policy.

E

EASTMAN, Frances W(hittier) 1915-

PERSONAL: Born January 9, 1915, in Indianapolis, Ind.; daughter of Fred Wilson and Ethel (Richardson) Eastman. *Education:* University of Tulsa, B.A., 1935; Chicago Theological Seminary, M.A., 1941; Andover-Newton Theological School, B.D., 1958.

CAREER: First Presbyterian Church, Topeka, Kan., director of Christian education, 1941-43; Westminster Presbyterian Church, Minneapolis, Minn., director of Christian education, 1943-44; Hawaiian Evangelical Association of Congregational Churches, Honolulu, territorial director of Christian education, 1944-50; United Church of Christ, Board of Homeland Ministries, Division of Christian Education, New York City, editor of *Children's Religion,* 1950-63, secretary of education program, beginning 1963. Visiting instructor in religious education, Andover-Newton Theological School, 1964-70; adjunct instructor, Defiance College, 1973-78.

MEMBER: Amnesty International, Religious Education Association of North America, American Association of University Women, Pi Gamma Mu, Kappa Delta Pi, Pi Kappa Delta, Delta Delta Delta.

AWARDS, HONORS: Litt.D., Chicago Theological Seminary, 1958.

WRITINGS:

A Junior Teacher's Guide on Africa (guide to *New Magic* by Esma Booth), Friendship, 1959.
We Belong Together, Friendship, 1960.
A Junior Teacher's Guide on New Nations, Friendship, 1964.
Good News, United Church Press, 1964.
God Speaks through the Bible, United Church Press, 1964.
Bigger Than All of Us, Friendship, 1965.
(With Elaine Lubbers) *A Guide for Early Teens on Mission: The Christian's Calling,* Friendship, 1965.
(Contributor) C. L. Laymon, editor, *One Volume Interpreter's Commentary on the Bible,* Abingdon, 1966.
(With Carolyn E. Goddard) *Reclaiming Christian Education,* United Church Press, 1970.
(Editor) *Developing an Educational Consultant Service: A Notebook for Area and Middle Judicatory Personnel,* 2nd edition, United Church Press, 1976.

Also author of *Christ, the Church, and Race* and *Africa,* both published for Friendship. Contributor to *Westminster Dictionary of Christian Education;* contributor to professional journals.

AVOCATIONAL INTERESTS: Photography, travel, collecting letter openers.*

*   *   *

ECKLEY, Grace 1932-

PERSONAL: Born November 30, 1932, in Alliance, Ohio; daughter of Clyde L. and Wilma (Hahn) Williamson; married Wilton Eckley, Jr. (a professor), September 12, 1954; children: Douglas, Stephen, Timothy. *Education:* Mount Union College, A.B., 1955; Case Western Reserve University, M.A., 1964; Kent State University, Ph.D., 1970.

ADDRESSES: Home—744 Chimney Creek Dr., Golden, Colo. 80401. *Office*—Department of English, Drake University, Des Moines, Iowa. 50311.

CAREER: Simpson College, Indianola, Iowa, instructor in English, 1965-68; Drake University, Des Moines, Iowa, assistant professor of English, 1968—.

MEMBER: Stead Memorial Society, Titanic Historical Association.

AWARDS, HONORS: National Endowment for the Humanities fellow, 1984-85.

WRITINGS:

Benedict Kiely, Twayne, 1972.
(Contributor) Eric Rothstein, editor, *Literary Monographs,* Volume 5, University of Wisconsin Press, 1973.
Edna O'Brien, Bucknell University Press, 1974.
(Contributor) Michael Begnal and Fritz Senn, editors, *A Conceptual Guide to "Finnegans Wake,"* Pennsylvania State University Press, 1974.
(With Begnal) *Narrator and Character in "Finnegans Wake,"* Bucknell University Press, 1975.
Finley Peter Dunne, Twayne, 1981.
Children's Lore in "Finnegans Wake," Syracuse University Press, 1985.

Contributor to *Dictionary of Literary Biography,* Volume 9: *American Novelists, 1910-1945,* Gale, 1981; contributor to scholarly and literary journals, including *Modern Fiction Studies, Modern Drama, James Joyce Quarterly,* and *Studies in the Novel.*

*   *   *

ECKLEY, Wilton Earl, Jr. 1929-

PERSONAL: Born June 25, 1929, in Alliance, Ohio; son of Wilton Earl and Louise (Bert) Eckley; married Grace Ester Williamson (a professor), September 12, 1954; children: Douglas, Stephen, Timothy. *Education:* Mount Union College, A.B., 1952; Pennsylvania State University, M.A., 1955; additional graduate study at Kent State University, 1958-60; Case Western Reserve University, Ph.D., 1965; also studied at Yale University and DePauw University.

ADDRESSES: Home—744 Chimney Creek Dr., Golden, Colo. 80401. *Office*—Department of Humanities and Social Science, Colorado School of Mines, Golden, Colo. 80401.

CAREER: French teacher in public school in Ravenna Township, Ohio, 1952-54; Euclid Senior High School, Euclid, Ohio, teacher of English and head of department, 1955-63; Hollins College, Hollins College, Va., assistant professor of English and director of teacher training, 1963-65; Drake University, Des Moines, Iowa, associate professor, 1965-68, professor of English, 1968-84, chairman of department, 1967-80; Colorado School of Mines, Golden, Colo., head of department of humanities and social sciences, 1984—. Visiting associate professor, University of Northern Iowa, summer, 1965; Fulbright professor of American literature, University of Ljubljana, Yugoslavia, 1972-73, and University of Veliko, Bulgaria, 1981-82; has lectured at many universities all over the world, including University of Heidelberg, University of Belgrade, University of Sarajevo, University of Warsaw, University of Iowa, and Kent State University. Member of board of directors, Colorado Endowment for the Humanities. Coe fellow in American studies, 1957—; John Hay Fellow, Yale University, 1961-62.

MEMBER: Modern Language Association of America, American Association of University Professors, Circus Historical Society, Phi Kappa Tau.

WRITINGS:

(Contributor) Louis Rubin, editor, *Guide to the Study of Southern Literature,* Louisiana State University Press, 1969.
Guide to e. e. cummings, C. E. Merrill, 1970.
Checklist of e. e. cummings, C. E. Merrill, 1970.
(Contributor) James Austin and Donald Kach, editors, *Popular Literature in America,* Bowling Green University Press, 1971.
Harriette Arnow, Twayne, 1974.
T. S. Stribling, Twayne, 1975.
(Contributor) Kieth Neilson, editor, *Survey of Science Fiction,* Salem, 1979.
Bret Harte, Scribner, 1980.
Herbert Hoover, G. K. Hall, 1980.
The American Circus, G. K. Hall, 1984.

Also author, with Mirko Jurak, of *Selected Lectures in English and American Literature,* Ljubljana Press. Contributor to *Encyclopedia of Short Fiction,* Salem, 1980; contributor to *Dictionary of Literary Biography,* Volume 9: *American Novelists, 1910-1945,* Gale, 1981. Contributor to journals, including *Ex-*

plicator, Language Arts News, Perspectives, ADE Bulletin, Iowa English Yearbook, and *College Literature.*

*   *   *

EDEN, Laura
See HARRISON, Claire (E.)

*   *   *

EDMONSON, Munro Sterling 1924-

PERSONAL: Born May 18, 1924, in Nogales, Ariz.; son of Everett Sterling and Lillian (Munro) Edmonson; married Barbara Bay Wedemeyer, August 1, 1953; children: Evelyn Mila, Ann Munro, Sallie Ross. *Education:* Harvard University, B.A., 1945, M.A., 1948, Ph.D., 1952.

ADDRESSES: Home—901 Cherokee St., New Orleans, La. 70118. *Office*—Department of Anthropology, Tulane University, New Orleans, La. 70118.

CAREER: Washington University, St. Louis, Mo., instructor in anthropology, 1951; Tulane University, New Orleans, La., assistant professor, 1951-57, associate professor, 1957-60, professor of anthropology, 1960—, chairman of department, 1969-72, staff associate, Urban Life Research Institute, 1951-57, research associate, Middle American Research Institute, 1954—. Visiting professor at University of San Carlos, Quezaltenango, Guatemala, 1960-61, Purdue University, 1964, Harvard University, 1965-66, University of Arizona summer school in Guadalajara, 1972, and Stanford University; professor in charge, Tulane University Junior Year Abroad program, Paris, 1972-73. Member of fellowship committee, National Science Foundation, 1967-69; member of joint committee on Latin American studies, American Council of Learned Societies-Social Science Research Council, 1968-72. Consultantships include Educational Testing Service, 1967-71, and National Endowment for the Humanities, 1976-79. *Military service:* U.S. Naval Reserve, 1944-46; served in the Pacific; became lieutenant junior grade.

MEMBER: American Anthropological Association (fellow; chairman of membership committee, 1968-69), American Association for the Advancement of Science, American Ethnological Society (president, 1966), American Association of University Professors (member of national council, 1971-75), Southern Anthropological Society, Louisiana Academy of Sciences, New Orleans Academy of Sciences.

AWARDS, HONORS: National Endowment for the Humanities research grants, 1976 and 1980.

WRITINGS:

Status Terminology and the Social Structure of North American Indians, University of Washington Press, 1958.
(Editor with John H. Rohrer) *The Eighth Generation: Cultures and Personalities of New Orleans Negroes,* Harper, 1959, reprinted as *The Eighth Generation Grows Up: Cultures and Personalities of New Orleans Negroes,* Harper, 1964.
Quiche-English Dictionary, Middle American Research Institute, Tulane University, 1965.
Lore: The Science of Folklore and Literature, Holt, 1970.
(Translator) *The Book of Counsel: The Popol Vuh of the Quiche Maya of Guatemala,* Middle American Research Institute, 1971.
(Editor) *Meaning in Mayan Languages,* Mouton, 1973.

(Editor) *Sixteenth Century Mexico: The Work of Sahagun,* University of New Mexico Press, 1974.
(Translator) *The Ancient Future of the Itza: The Book of Chilam Balam of Tizimin,* University of Texas Press, 1982.
(Editor with Victoria R. Bricker) *Supplement to the Handbook of Middle American Indians,* University of Texas Press, Volume 2: *Linguistics,* 1984, Volume 3: *Literatures,* 1985.
(Translator) *Heaven Born Merida and Its Destiny: The Book of Chilam Balam of Chumayel,* University of Texas Press, 1986.
The Book of the Year: Middle American Calendrical Systems, University of Utah Press, 1988.

CONTRIBUTOR

Harold I. Lief and others, editors, *The Psychological Basis of Medical Practice,* Harper, 1963.
Evon Z. Vogt and Alberto Ruz Lhuiller, editors, *Desarrollo Cultural de los Mayas,* National University of Mexico, 1964.
Guy Hunter, editor, *Industrialization and Race Relations,* Oxford University Press, 1965.
Vogt and Ethel M. Albert, editors, *People of Rimrock: A Study of Values in Five Cultures,* Harvard University Press, 1966.
Robert Wauchope, editor, *Handbook of Middle American Indians,* University of Texas, 1967.
John B. Orr and Lydia Pulsipher, editors, *Education and Social Change,* Southwest Educational Development Laboratory, 1967.
Vogt and John L. Fischer, editors, *The Anthropology of Clyde Kluckhohn,* University of Southern Illinois Press, 1973.
Walter W. Taylor, Fischer, and Vogt, editors, *Culture and Life,* Southern Illinois University Press, 1973.
Marco Giardino, Barbara Edmonson, and Winifred Creamer, editors, *Codex Wauchope: A Tribute Roll,* Human Mosaic, 1978.
John A. Grahan, editor, *Ancient Mesoamerica,* Peek Publications, 1981.
Elizabeth Benson, editor, *Dumbarton Oaks Symposium,* University of Texas Press, 1984.

OTHER

Contributor to *Caribbean Quarterly, Western Folklore,* and other folklore, anthropology, and history journals. Member of editorial board, *Annual Review of Anthropology,* 1971-75.

SIDELIGHTS: "How exactly the Maya themselves have chosen to represent their history and experience of the world, in the corpus of the alphabetic literature, is vividly brought out in Munro [Sterling] Edmonson's edition and translation" of *The Ancient Future of the Itza: The Book of Chilam Balam of Tizimin,* notes *Times Literary Supplement* contributor Gordon Brotherston. A professor of anthropology, Edmonson throws new light on the civilization of the ancient Mayan tribes by using his knowledge of their culture and history to help interpret the texts. In creating an accurate translation, Edmonson had "to face the difficulties typical of texts from that area," including "the *intent* to be obscure and beyond the reach of outsiders," continues Brotherston. In his rendition of the *Chilam Balam,* "Edmonson excels chiefly in unravelling the immensely sophisticated calendrics," or calendar references and reforms, "and in doing so he considerably modifies the readings of previous scholars," adds the critic. "His mastery of technical detail comes through on several points," while the entire work "vindicates the historical continuity of the ancient Maya count."

Edmonson told *CA:* "The common thread in my writing is to recognize the familiarity in what is alien and the alien in what is familiar, and to describe that recognition in a way that is intelligible to other people—whose experience of this polarity is inevitably different from my own. Such an endeavor may be based, as it is in my work, on scientific methods. But it must also transcend them. The challenge of writing lies to me in an awareness that one may know things he cannot communicate and communicate things he doesn't know. The act of writing like that of reading cultivates and develops this awareness. Even when it is only partially successful it is the most important form of creativity; it creates light out of mystery."

Edmonson speaks Spanish and French, and has a reading knowledge of Russian, German, Italian, Portuguese, Quiche, and Yucatec Maya.

BIOGRAPHICAL/CRITICAL SOURCES:

PERIODICALS

Times Literary Supplement, December 3, 1982.

*   *   *

EGAN, Gerard   1930-

PERSONAL: Born June 17, 1930, in Chicago, Ill. *Education:* Loyola University, Chicago, A.B., 1953, M.A. (philosophy), 1959, M.A. (clinical psychology), 1963, Ph.D., 1969.

ADDRESSES: Office—Center for Organization Development, Loyola University, Chicago, Ill. 60611.

CAREER: Loyola University of Chicago, Chicago, Ill., 1969—, began as assistant professor, currently professor of psychology. Consultant to various organizations and institutions.

MEMBER: American Psychological Association, American Association for Counseling and Development.

WRITINGS:

Encounter: Group Processes for Interpersonal Growth, Brooks/Cole, 1970.
(Editor) *Encounter Groups: Basic Readings,* Brooks/Cole, 1971.
Face to Face: The Small Group Experience and Interpersonal Growth, Brooks/Cole, 1973.
The Skilled Helper: A Model for Helping and Human Relations Training, Brooks/Cole, 1975, 2nd edition published as *The Skilled Helper: Model, Skills, and Methods for Effective Helping,* 1982.
Exercises in Helping Skills, Brooks/Cole, 1975, 2nd edition, 1981.
Interpersonal Living: A Skills/Contract Approach to Human Relations Training in Groups, Brooks/Cole, 1976, instructor's manual (with M. Bacchi), 1978.
You and Me: The Skills of Human Communication in Everyday Life, Brooks/Cole, 1977, instructor's manual (with J. W. Bryer, Jr.) published as *Training the Skilled Helper,* Brooks/Cole, 1979.
(With M. Cowan) *People in Systems: A Model Development for the Human Services Professions and Education,* Brooks/Cole, 1979.
(With Cowan) *Moving into Adulthood: Themes and Variations in Self-Directed Development,* Brooks/Cole, 1980.
Change Agent Skill for Helping and Human-Service Professionals, Brooks/Cole, 1985.
Change Agent Skills A: Assessing and Designing Excellence, University Associates, 1988.

Change Agent Skills B: Managing Innovation and Change, University Associates, 1988.

Contributor to numerous books, including *Human Behavior and Its Encounter Groups,* Schenkman, 1971, *The Cutting Edge: Current Theory and Practice in Organization Development,* University Associated, 1978, and *Teaching Psychological Skills: Models for Giving Psychology Away,* Brooks/Cole, 1983. Also contributor of articles to various professional journals.

SIDELIGHTS: Gerald Egan wrote *CA:* "I teach, write, and consult to a wide variety of organizations, with writing and consulting taking the lion's share of my time. Consulting takes me all over the world and includes both not-for-profit institutions and Fortune 500 companies."

*   *   *

EHRLICH, Paul R(alph)   1932-

PERSONAL: Born May 29, 1932, in Philadelphia, Pa.; son of William (a salesman) and Ruth (a Latin teacher; maiden name, Rosenberg) Ehrlich; married Anne Fitzhugh Howland (a biological research associate and writer), December 18, 1954; children: Lisa Marie. *Education:* University of Pennsylvania, B.A., 1953; University of Kansas, M.A., 1955, Ph.D., 1957. *Politics:* Independent.

ADDRESSES: Home—Pine Hill, Stanford, Calif. 94305. *Office*—Department of Biological Sciences, Stanford University, Stanford, Calif. 94305.

CAREER: Field officer on Northern Insect Survey, summers, 1951-52; associate investigator on United States Air Force research project in Alaska, 1956-57; Chicago Academy of Science, Chicago, Ill., research associate, 1957-58; University of Kansas, Lawrence, research associate, 1958-59; Stanford University, Stanford, Calif., assistant professor, 1959-62, associate professor, 1962-66, professor of biological sciences, 1966—, Bing Professor of Biological Sciences, 1976—, director of biological science graduate study department, 1966-69, 1974-76. Editor in population biology and consultant in biology, McGraw-Hill Book Co., 1964—. Has conducted field work in Africa, Latin America, Antarctica, Australia, and in Southeast Asia. Associate of Center for the Study of Democratic Institutions. Consultant, Behavioral Research Laboratories, 1963-67.

MEMBER: International Association for Ecology, National Academy of Sciences, American Academy of Arts and Sciences (fellow), Zero Population Growth (founder; president, 1969-70), Society for the Study of Evolution (vice-president, 1970), American Institute of Biological Science, Society of Systematic Zoology, American Society of Naturalists, Lepidopterists Society (secretary, 1957-63), American Museum of Natural History (honorary life member), American Association of University Professors, Airplane Owners and Pilots Association, California Academy of Sciences (fellow), Sigma Xi, Royal Aero Club of New South Wales.

AWARDS, HONORS: National Science Foundation fellow at University of Sydney, 1965-66; Bestseller's Paperback of the Year Award, 1970, for *The Population Bomb.*

WRITINGS:

(With wife, Anne H. Ehrlich, and others) *How to Know the Butterflies,* W. C. Brown, 1961.

(With Richard W. Holm) *The Process of Evolution,* McGraw, 1963, 2nd edition, also with Dennis R. Parnell, 1974.

Principles of Modern Biology, Addison-Wesley, 1968.

(Compiler with Holm and Peter H. Raven) *Papers on Evolution,* Little, Brown, 1968.

The Population Bomb, Ballantine, 1968, revised and expanded edition, 1971.

(With A. H. Ehrlich) *Population, Resources, Environment: Issues in Human Ecology,* W. H. Freeman, 1970, 2nd edition, 1972.

(With Richard L. Harriman) *How to Be a Survivor: A Plan to Save Spaceship Earth,* Ballantine, 1970.

(Editor and compiler with John P. Holdren) *Global Ecology: Readings toward a Rational Strategy for Man,* Harcourt, 1971.

(Compiler with Holdren and Holm) *Man and the Ecosphere: Readings from Scientific American,* W. H. Freeman, 1971.

(With A. H. Ehrlich and Holdren) *Human Ecology: Problems and Solutions,* W. H. Freeman, 1973.

(With Holm and Michael E. Soule) *Introductory Biology,* McGraw, 1973.

(With A. H. Ehrlich) *The End of Affluence: A Blueprint for Your Future,* Ballantine, 1974.

(With Dennis Pirages) *Ark II: Social Response to Environmental Imperatives,* W. H. Freeman, 1974.

(With Holm and Irene L. Brown) *Biology and Society,* McGraw, 1976.

(With S. Shirley Feldman) *The Race Bomb: Skin Color, Prejudice, and Intelligence,* New York Times Co., 1977.

(With A. H. Ehrlich and Holdren) *Ecoscience: Population, Resources, Environment,* W. H. Freeman, 1977.

(With A. H. Ehrlich and Loy Bilderback) *The Golden Door: International Migration, Mexico, and the United States,* Ballantine, 1979.

(With A. H. Ehrlich) *Extinction: The Causes and Consequences of the Disappearance of Species,* Random House, 1981.

(With Carl Sagan, Donald Kennedy, and Walter Orr Roberts) *The Cold and Dark,* Norton, 1984.

The Machinery of Nature, Simon & Schuster, 1986.

(With Jonathan Roughgarden) *The Science of Ecology,* Macmillan, 1987.

(With A. H. Ehrlich) *Earth,* F. Watts, 1987.

(Editor with Holdren) *The Cassandra Conference: Resources and the Human Predicament,* Texas A & M University Press, 1988.

(With others) *The Birder's Handbook: A Field Guide to the Natural History of North American Birds,* Simon & Schuster, 1988.

CONTRIBUTOR

Garrett DeBell, editor, *The Environmental Handbook,* Ballantine, 1970.

Harold W. Helfrich, Jr., editor, *The Environmental Crisis,* Yale University Press, 1970.

OTHER

Also author with others of, *The Collected Papers: Index and Bibliography,* Volume IV, Pergamon. Contributor of articles to periodicals. Member of editorial board, *Systematic Zoology,* 1964-67, and *International Journal of Environmental Science,* 1969—.

SIDELIGHTS: Reviewing *The Golden Door: International Migration, Mexico, and the United States, Washington Post Book World* writer Christopher Dickey comments that the book "brings into focus virtually all the crucial problems [of immigrants] and explains, as must be done, why some of the most troubling issues related to international migration remain blurred by ignorance." Dickey also notes the authors' "skill and patience" in examining immigration and commends the book's "many virtues." Robert Sherrill of the *New York Times Book Review* terms the work a "fascinating book," adding: "The solutions to the immigration crisis that [the authors] offer as possibilities are vague and not very hopeful. But never mind. In most respects, *The Golden Door* is a first-rate book, an excitingly scary book that sizes up a mammoth problem that the politicians appear determined to ignore for as long as possible."

In *Extinction: The Causes and Consequences of the Disappearance of Species,* Anne H. and Paul R. Ehrlich alert readers to the hazards of allowing any species of life to die out, and in particular, identify potential dangers to mankind when other species become extinct. *New York Times Book Review* critic Bayard Webster observes, "In *Extinction,* Paul and Anne Ehrlich, members of Stanford University's department of biological sciences, explain in dramatic, definitive, and entertaining fashion the reason for the general alarm, and then present their strategy for the prevention of further extinctions, including our own." Webster concludes that the Ehrlichs "have produced a very readable volume that, in addition to demonstrating the importance of preserving species, is an invaluable compendium of facts, events, and theories of evolution, biology, environmental history, and ecology."

MEDIA ADAPTATIONS: Metro-Goldwyn-Mayer has purchased documentary rights to *The Population Bomb.*

BIOGRAPHICAL/CRITICAL SOURCES:

BOOKS

Cox, Donald W., *Pioneers of Ecology,* Hammond, 1971.

PERIODICALS

Los Angeles Times, May 6, 1986.
Nation, January 5, 1980.
New Republic, August 1, 1981.
New York Review of Books, April 23, 1970.
New York Times, October 1, 1977.
New York Times Book Review, January 26, 1975, July 17, 1977, November 18, 1979, June 21, 1981.
Saturday Review, July 3, 1971.
Washington Post Book World, December, 16, 1979.

*   *   *

EICHER, Joanne B(ubolz) 1930-

PERSONAL: Born September 18, 1930, in Lansing, Mich.; daughter of George C., Sr., and Stella L. (Mangold) Bubolz; married Carl K. Eicher (a professor), June 8, 1952 (divorced December, 1974); children: Cynthia, Carolyn, Diana. *Education:* Michigan State University, B.A., 1952, M.A., 1956, Ph.D., 1959. *Politics:* Democrat. *Religion:* Lutheran.

ADDRESSES: Home—2179 Folwell St., St. Paul, Minn. 55108. *Office*—Department of Textiles and Clothing, College of Home Economics, University of Minnesota, St. Paul, Minn. 55108.

CAREER: Boston University, Boston, Mass., 1957-61, began as instructor, became assistant professor of social sciences; Michigan State University, East Lansing, assistant professor, 1961-69, associate professor, 1969-72, professor of human

ecology, 1972-77; University of Minnesota, St. Paul, professor of textiles and clothing, 1977—, department head, 1977-83, department head of design, housing, and apparel, 1983—. Research associate, University of Nigeria, Enugu, 1963-66. Consultant, Time-Life, Inc., Prentice-Hall, Inc., and Howard University. Director, Goldstein Gallery, 1983—.

MEMBER: American Home Economics Association, American Sociological Association, African Studies Association, Association of College Professors of Textiles and Clothing, Costume Society of America, Costume Society (London), Nigeria National Museum Society, Walker Art Center, Minneapolis Institute of Art, Gamma Sigma Delta, Phi Kappa Phi, Alpha Kappa Delta, Tau Sigma, Alpha Gamma Delta.

AWARDS, HONORS: Research grants, International Programs, Michigan State University, 1963-64, African Studies Center, 1965-66, Midwest University consortium for International Affairs, 1968, and Buguma International Affairs Society, 1982, 1984; Ford Foundation grant, 1973; resident scholar at Rockefeller Foundation Study and Conference Center (Bellagio, Italy), 1973.

WRITINGS:

(With Mary Ellen Roach) *Dress, Adornment, and the Social Order,* Wiley, 1965.
(Compiler) *African Dress: A Select and Annotated Bibliography of Subsaharan Countries,* Michigan State University Press, Volume 1, 1970, Volume 2 (with Pokornowski, Thieme, and Harris), 1985.
(With Roach) *The Visible Self: Perspectives on Dress,* Prentice-Hall, 1973.
(With Eleanor Kelley and Betty Wass) *A Longitudinal Study of High School Girls' Friendship Patterns, Social Class, and Clothing,* Michigan Agricultural Experiment Station, 1973.
Nigerian Handcrafted Textiles, University of Ife Press, (Ile-Ife, Nigeria), 1976.
(Contributor) *Living Arts of West Africa* (exhibition catalogue), University Gallery, University of Minnesota, 1978.
(With Erekosima and Thieme) *Pelete Bite: Kalabari Cut-Thread Cloth,* Goldstein Gallery, University of Minnesota, 1982.

Contributor to periodicals, including *Social Forces, Journal of Home Economics, Journal of Psychology, Adolescence,* and *Kresge Art Center Bulletin.*

WORK IN PROGRESS: The Sociology of Dress (with Roach); *African Costume* (with Roy Sieber).*

*   *   *

EISENBERG, Dennis (Harold) 1929-

PERSONAL: Born October 3, 1929, in Lichtenburg, South Africa; son of Sam (a chemist) and Anne (Gordon) Eisenberg; married Paule Germaine Escoubes, November 9, 1958; children: Nadine, Stephane. *Education:* Witwatersrand Pharmacy School, diploma, 1950. *Politics:* "Free thinker." *Religion:* Jewish.

CAREER: Pharmacist in Johannesburg, South Africa, 1950-52; journalist in England, 1956-67, writing for *Derby Evening Telegram,* 1956-57, *Birmingham Post,* 1958, *News Chronicle,* 1959, and as foreign correspondent and foreign editor for *Daily Herald* and *Sun,* both London, England, 1960-67; free-lance writer, 1967—. Director, World Wide Exclusive Press Service.

WRITINGS:

Fascistes et Nazis d'aujourd'hui, Albin Michel (Paris), 1963, revised and updated edition published as *The Re-emergence of Fascism*, MacGibbon & Kee, 1967, A. S. Barnes, 1968.

(With Eli Landau) *Carlos: Terror International*, Corgi Books, 1976.

(With Landau and Uri Dann) *The Mossad Inside Stories: Israel's Secret Intelligence Service*, Paddington Press, 1978.

(With Landau and Menahem Portugali) *Operation Uranium Ship*, New American Library, 1978.

(With Landau and Dann) *Meyer Lansky: Mogul of the Mob*, Paddington Press, 1979.

Contributor to periodicals, including *Look*, *McCall's*, *Chatelaine*, *Elle*, *Woman*, *Stern* (Germany), and *Woman's Own*.

SIDELIGHTS: Dennis Eisenberg once told *CA:* "Covered wars, upheavals, etc., in Congo, Algeria, and South Africa. Speak French. Interested in modern history and legends and the Royal family. Write about anything which takes my fancy."

BIOGRAPHICAL/CRITICAL SOURCES:

PERIODICALS

Christian Science Monitor, June 7, 1969.
Commonweal, July 25, 1969.
Nation, May 12, 1969.
National Review, May 6, 1969.
New Republic, March 22, 1969.
New Yorker, April 5, 1969.
New York Times, April 10, 1969.*

*   *   *

EISENBERG, Ronald L(ee) 1945-

PERSONAL: Born July 11, 1945, in Philadelphia, Pa.; son of Milton (a physician) and Betty (Klein) Eisenberg; married Zina Leah Schiff (a concert violinist), September 19, 1970; children: Avlana Kinneret, Cherina Carmel. *Education:* University of Pennsylvania, A.B., 1965, M.D., 1969.

ADDRESSES: Home—14 Tealwood, Shreveport, La. 71104. *Office*—Department of Radiology, Louisiana State University Medical Center, P.O. Box 33932, Shreveport, La. 71130.

CAREER: Mount Zion Hospital, San Francisco, Calif., intern, 1969-70; Massachusetts General Hospital, Boston, Mass., resident in radiology, 1970-71; University of California, San Francisco, resident in radiology, 1973-75, assistant professor of radiology, 1975-80; Louisiana State University Medical Center, Shreveport, professor of radiology and chairman of department, 1980—. Chief of gastrointestinal radiology at Veterans Administration Hospital (San Francisco), beginning 1975. *Military service:* U.S. Army, 1971-73; became major.

MEMBER: American Roentgen Ray Society, San Francisco Radiology Society, Phi Beta Kappa, Alpha Omega Alpha.

WRITINGS:

The Iguana Corps of the Haganah, Bloch Publishing, 1977.
Critical Diagnostic Pathways in Radiology, Lippincott, 1981.
Gastrointestinal Radiology, Lippincott, 1983.
Atlas of Signs in Radiology, Lippincott, 1984.
Veterans Compensation: An American Scandal, Pierremont, 1985.
Diagnostic Imaging in Internal Medicine, McGraw, 1985.

Diagnostic Imaging in Surgery, McGraw, 1986.
Clinical Imaging: Atlas of Differential Diagnosis, Aspen, 1988.
Diagnostic Imaging: An Algorithmic Approach, Lippincott, 1988.

Contributor to professional journals.

WORK IN PROGRESS: Book on history of radiology.

SIDELIGHTS: Ronald L. Eisenberg writes: "The idea of writing seriously (other than medical articles) arose during my years in the Army. When I was on call every fourth night I had to remain on the base. Rarely was I called on to see a patient. With a great deal of time on my hands, I began to write.

"The subject of my writing was iguanas—primarily because we had one named Waverly. This, coupled with a visit to Israel and the reading of a work about a dog-parachutist by [a former] head of the Israeli Army, led me to write . . . *The Iguana Corps of the Haganah*. It is a story, probably fictitious, about the use of the large lizards to carry messages, guns, and explosives to the Israeli agents behind Arab lines."

AVOCATIONAL INTERESTS: Playing the piano, collecting Israeli stamps (almost a complete set).

*   *   *

ELBOW, Peter (Henry) 1935-

PERSONAL: Born April 14, 1935, in New York, N.Y.; son of William C. and Helen (Platt) Elbow; married Linda Smickle, September 1, 1964 (divorced March, 1968); married Caroline Cambell Pelz (a divorce mediator), July 8, 1972; children: two. *Education:* Williams College, B.A. (magna cum laude), 1957; Exeter College, Oxford, B.A., 1959, M.A., 1963; graduate study at Harvard University, 1959-60; Brandeis University, Ph.D., 1969.

ADDRESSES: Home—47 Pokeberry Ridge, Amherst, Mass. 01002. *Office*—Department of English, University of Massachusetts at Amherst, Amherst, Mass. 01003.

CAREER: Massachusetts Institute of Technology, Cambridge, instructor in humanities, 1960-63; Franconia College, Franconia, N.H., member of English faculty and chairman of core curriculum, 1963-65, associate dean of faculty, 1964-65; Massachusetts Institute of Technology, lecturer, 1968-69, assistant professor of literature, 1969-72; Evergreen State College, Olympia, Wash., member of faculty, 1972-81; State University of New York at Stony Brook, director of writing programs, beginning 1982; University of Massachusetts at Amherst, currently member of faculty in department of English. Teacher of evening writing classes in Roxbury, Mass., 1968-72. Consultant to writing programs at various colleges and universities.

MEMBER: National Council of Teachers of English, Society for Values in Higher Education, Phi Beta Kappa.

AWARDS, HONORS: Honorary Woodrow Wilson fellowship, 1957; Danforth fellowship, 1957; essay prize, English Institute, 1966; Kent postdoctoral fellowship, Wesleyan University Center for Writing, 1981-82.

WRITINGS:

Writing without Teachers, Oxford University Press, 1973.
Oppositions in Chaucer, Wesleyan University Press, 1975.
Writing with Power: Techniques for Mastering the Writing Process, Oxford University Press, 1981.

Embracing Contraries: Explorations in Learning and Teaching, Oxford University Press, 1986.
(With Pat Belanoff) *A Community of Writers,* Random House, 1988.

CONTRIBUTOR

Philip Damon, editor, *Literary Criticism and Historical Understanding,* Columbia University Press, 1967.
Don Flourney, editor, *The New Teachers,* Jossey-Bass, 1971.
Writing: Voice and Thought, National Council of Teachers of English, 1971.
Henry B. Maloney, editor, *Goal-Making for English Teaching,* National Council of Teachers of English, 1973.
Gerald Grant, editor, *On Competence: An Analysis of a Reform Movement in Higher Education,* two volumes, Syracuse Research Corp., 1978.
Jack Noonan and Kenneth Eble, editors, *New Directions for Teaching and Learning,* Jossey-Bass, 1981.
Richard Martin and Eble, editors, *Sourcebook for College Teachers,* Jossey-Bass, 1981.
Toby Fulwiler, *The Journal Book,* Boynton Cook, 1987.
Chris Anderson, *Literary Nonfiction: Theory, Criticism, Pedagogy,* Southern Illinois University Press, 1988.

OTHER

Contributor to writing, education, and literature journals, and to *Christian Century.*

SIDELIGHTS: Peter Elbow told *CA,* "I got interested in writing because of my own difficulties with it."

*   *   *

ELIAV, Arie L(ova)   1921-
(Ben Ami)

PERSONAL: Born November 21, 1921, in Moscow, U.S.S.R.; immigrated to Palestine (now Israel) in 1924; son of Joseph and Matilda Eliav; married Tania Zvi, October 12, 1947; children: Zvi, Ofra, Eyal. *Education:* Attended University of Reading and Cambridge University, both 1953; Hebrew University of Jerusalem, diploma (cum laude), 1959.

ADDRESSES: Home—3 Karl-Netter St., 65202 Tel Aviv, Israel. *Office*—International Center for Peace in the Middle East, 107 Hahashmonaim St., Tel Aviv 67011, Israel.

CAREER: Israeli government official in Settlement Department, Ministry of Agriculture, and Ministry of Finance, 1949-53; instructor in immigrants' village of Moshav Nevatim, 1954; first director of Lachish regional project, 1955-57, and of Arad and Chazvin projects, 1960-63; Israeli Embassy, Moscow, U.S.S.R., first secretary, 1958-60; head of Israeli aid and rehabilitation team to earthquake stricken Ghazvin region of Iran, 1962-64; Knesset (Israeli Parliament), head of Mapai Organization Department, 1965-79, deputy minister of Commerce and Industry, 1966-67, and of Immigration and Absorption, 1967-70; Center for International Affairs, Harvard University, Cambridge, Mass., lecturer and fellow, 1979-80; scholar-in-residence, American Jewish Committee of Greater Boston, 1979-80; adult education teacher in Or-Akiva and Caesarea, Israel, 1980-81; Tel Hai Regional College, Galilee, Israel, teacher, 1981-82; International Center for Peace in the Middle East, Tel Aviv, chairman of board of trustees, 1982-84; Regional College of the Negev, Israel, teacher, 1984-85; Israel Prison Service, teacher, 1985-86; head of educational project in Nitzana, Negev, 1987-88.

Labor Party, Tel Aviv, Israel, secretary general, 1970-72. Member of mission on behalf of Beit Hillel to the United States, 1964, to Morocco, 1964-65, and to Mullah Mustafa Barzani (head of Kurdish national movement), 1966; represented Israel at Council of Europe in Strasbourg, 1965-73; participated in talks with Palestinian-Arab leaders in Paris, 1976-77; chairman of Sheli (Israeli Peace movement), 1977-79; negotiated exchange of Israeli prisoners of war (Lebanese War), 1982-87. Served as emergency room volunteer at Hadassah Hospital, Tel Aviv, 1974-75. *Military service:* Served in Hagana (Jewish underground defense organization), 1936-40. British Army, served in artillery and engineering united during World War II. Served in Mossad illegal immigration operations, 1945-47. Israeli Defense Forces, 1948-49; became lieutenant colonel; commanded during Sinai campaign, 1956.

AWARDS, HONORS: Ussishkin Prize for Zionist literature (Jerusalem), 1966; Dr. Bruno Kreisky Prize for peace (Vienna), 1979; Love of Israel Prize (Jerusalem), 1983; Adult Education Prize, 1985; "Planning of Israel" Prize, 1986; D.Phil., Hebrew University of Jerusalem, 1987; "Prize of Israel," 1988.

WRITINGS:

Some Observations on Regional Planning Practice, Tahal, 1964.
(Under pseudonym Ben Ami) *Ben ha-patish veha-magal,* Am Oved Publishers, 1965, translation published as *Between Hammer and Sickle,* Jewish Publication Society of America, 1967, revised edition, New American Library, 1969.
(With Galia Yardeni) *Sipurah shel sefinat ma'pilim* (title means "The Story of an 'Illegal' Immigrants Ship"), World Zionist Organization, 1965.
Ha-Sefinah Ulu'ah Seporo shel Artor, Am Oved Publishers, 1967, translation by Israel I. Taslitt published as *The Voyage of the Ulua,* Funk, 1969.
Ye'adim hadashim le-Yisrael (political essays), Lewin-Epstein, 1969, translation published as *New Targets for Israel,* Jerusalem Post Publications, 1969, 3rd Hebrew edition, Lewin-Epstein, 1971.
Kefitsat ha-derekh, Am Oved Publishers, 1970, translation by Dov Chaikin published as *No Time for History: A Pioneer Story,* Sabra Books, 1970.
Erets ha-tsvi, Am Oved Publishers, 1972, translation by Judith Yalon published as *Land of the Hart: Israelis, Arabs, the Territories, and a Vision of the Future,* Jewish Publication Society of America, 1974.
Ha-Ruah lo yikah (title means "The Wind Shall Not Carry Them Away"), Am Oved Publishers, 1974.
Shalom, Massada, 1975, translation by Misha Louvish published as *Shalom: Peace in Jewish Tradition,* Massada, 1977.
Sulam Yisrael (political and social analysis; title means "Israel's Ladder"), Zmora, Beitan, Modan Press, 1977.
An Entire World (in Hebrew), Am Oved Publishers, 1980.
Rings of Dawn (autobiographical; in Hebrew), Am Oved Publishers, 1983.
Rings of Faith (autobiographical; in Hebrew), Am Oved Publishers, 1984.
A New Heart and a New Spirit (in Hebrew), Am Oved Publishers, 1986, translation published by Jewish Publication Society of America, 1988.

Also author of *Ba-yam, be-derekh mahteret,* 1964. Contributor to periodicals in Israel and abroad.

SIDELIGHTS: Arie L. Eliav served as commander of the rescue ship "Ulua" which carried two thousand Jewish refugees from Europe to Palestine. He participated in the Sinai Campaign, and in the rescue evacuation of Jews from Port Said. After bringing thousands of refugees into Israel, he continued thereafter to help them adjust to their new homes. His books, which have also been translated into French and Spanish, reflect his ongoing concern for these Jewish immigrants and for the country which they have helped to shape.

BIOGRAPHICAL/CRITICAL SOURCES:

PERIODICALS

Christian Science Monitor, August 19, 1969.
Time, January 26, 1970.
Washington Post, May 31, 1969.

*   *   *

ELLIN, Stanley (Bernard)   1916-1986

PERSONAL: Born October 6, 1916, in Brooklyn. N.Y.; died of a heart attack, July 31, 1986, in Brooklyn; son of Louis and Rose (Mandel) Ellin; married Jeanne Michael (a free-lance editor), 1937; children: Susan. *Education:* Brooklyn College (now Brooklyn College of the City University of New York), B.A., 1936.

ADDRESSES: Agent—Curtis Brown Ltd., 10 Astor Place, New York, N.Y. 10003.

CAREER: Writer. Until World War II, worked as a "push-manager" for a newspaper distributor, taught at a junior college, managed a dairy farm, and was a steelworker. *Military service:* U.S. Army, one year.

MEMBER: PEN American Center, Mystery Writers of America (former president), Crime Writers Association (England).

AWARDS, HONORS: Ellery Queen Awards for best story of the year, 1948, for "The Specialty of the House," 1949, for "The Cat's Paw," 1950, for "Orderly World of Mr. Appleby," 1951, for "Fool's Mate," 1952, for "Best of Everything," 1953, for "The Betrayers," 1954, for "The House Party," 1955, for "Moment of Decision," 1956, for "The Blessington Method," and 1957, for "Faith of Aaron Memfee"; Edgar Allan Poe Awards, Mystery Writers of America, 1954, for "The Blessington Method," 1956, for "The House Party," and 1958, for *The Eighth Circle;* short story "The Day of the Bullet" included in *Best American Short Stories, 1960;* Grand Prix de Litterature Policiere (France), 1975, for *Mirror, Mirror on the Wall;* Grand Master Award, Mystery Writers of America, 1981, for lifetime writing accomplishment.

WRITINGS:

NOVELS

Dreadful Summit: A Novel of Suspense, Simon & Schuster, 1948, published as *The Big Night: A Novel of Suspense* (also see below), New American Library, 1966, reprinted under original title, Countryman Press, 1981.
The Key to Nicholas Street, Simon & Schuster, 1952, published with new introduction, Garland, 1983.
The Eighth Circle, Random House, 1958, published with new introduction by Otto Penzler, Gregg Press, 1979.
The Winter after This Summer, Random House, 1960.
The Panama Portrait, Random House, 1962, reprinted, Foul Play Press, 1981.
House of Cards, Random House, 1967.
The Valentine Estate, Random House, 1968.

The Bind, Random House, 1970 (published in England as *The Man from Nowhere*, J. Cape, 1970).
Mirror, Mirror on the Wall, Random House, 1972.
Stronghold, Random House, 1974.
The Luxembourg Run, Random House, 1977.
Star Light, Star Bright, Random House, 1979.
The Dark Fantastic, Mysterious Press, 1983.
Very Old Money (Book-of-the-Month Club selection), Arbor House, 1985.

SHORT STORIES

Mystery Stories, Simon & Schuster, 1956, published as *Quiet Horror*, Dell, 1959, and as *The Specialty of the House, and Other Stories*, Penguin, 1968.
The Blessington Method, and Other Strange Tales, Random House, 1964.
Kindly Dig Your Grave and Other Wicked Stories, edited by Ellery Queen, Random House, 1975.
The Specialty of the House and Other Stories: The Complete Mystery Tales, 1948-1978, Mysterious Press, 1979.

SHORT STORIES REPRESENTED IN ANTHOLOGIES

David C. Cooke, editor, *Best Detective Stories of the Year, 1950*, Dutton, 1950.
Cooke, editor, *Best Detective Stories of the Year, 1951*, Dutton, 1951.
Cooke, editor, *Best Detective Stories of the Year, 1956*, Dutton, 1956.
Alfred Hitchcock, editor, *Alfred Hitchcock Presents Stories They Wouldn't Let Me Do on TV*, Simon & Schuster, 1957.
Martha Foley and David Burnett, editors, *The Best American Short Stories, 1960*, Houghton, 1960.
Leonora Hornblow and Bennett Cerf, editors, *Bennett Cerf's Take Along Treasury*, Doubleday, 1963.
Elizabeth Lee, editor, *Murder Mixture: An Anthology of Crime Stories*, Elek, 1963.
Howard Haycraft and John Beecroft, editors, *Three Times Three: Mystery Omnibus*, Doubleday, 1964.
Dorothy Parker and Frederick B. Shroyer, editors, *Short Story: A Thematic Anthology*, Scribner, 1965.
Basil Davenport, editor, *13 Ways to Kill a Man: An Anthology*, Dodd, 1965.
Joan Kahn, editor, *The Edge of the Chair*, Harper, 1967.
Ross Macdonald, editor, *Great Stories of Suspense*, Knopf, 1974.
Arthur Liebman, compiler, *Tales of Horror and the Supernatural: The Occult in Literature*, Richards Rosen Press, 1975.
Otto Penzler, editor, *Whodunit? Houdini?: Thirteen Tales of Magic, Murder, Mystery*, Harper, 1976.
John Ball, editor, *Cop Cade*, Doubleday for the Crime Club, 1978.
Helen Hoke, editor, *Terrors, Torments and Traumas: An Anthology*, Nelson, 1978.
Charles G. Waugh, Martin Harry Greenburg, and Joseph Olander, editors, *Mysterious Visions: Great Science Fiction by Masters of the Mystery*, St. Martin's, 1979.
Hoke, editor, *Terrors, Terrors, Terrors*, illustrations by Bill Prosser, F. Watts, 1979.
Eric Potter, editor, *A Harvest of Horrors*, illustrations by Hank Blaustein, Vanguard, 1980.
Carol-Lynn Roessel Waugh, Greenburg, and Isaac Asimov, editors, *The Twelve Crimes of Christmas*, Avon Books, 1981.

Bill Pronzini, Barry N. Maltzburg, and Greenburg, editors, *The Arbor House Treasury of Mystery and Suspense,* Arbor House, 1981.

Great Short Tales of Mystery and Terror, illustrations by Leo and Diane Dillon, Reader's Digest, 1982.

Thomas Godfrey, editor, *Murder for Christmas,* illustrations by Gahan Wilson, Mysterious Press, 1982.

Josh Pachter, editor, *Top Crime: The Authors' Choice; Selected and Introduced by the Authors Themselves,* St. Martin's, 1983.

Barry Woelfel, editor, *Through Glass Darkly: 13 Tales of Wine and Crime,* Beaufort Books, 1984.

Edward D. Hoch, editor, *The Year's Best Mystery and Suspense Stories, 1984,* Walker & Co., 1984.

Julian Symonds, editor, *The Penguin Classic Crime Omnibus,* Penguin Books, 1984.

Hugh Hood and Peter O'Brien, editors, *Fatal Recurrences: New Fiction in English from Montreal,* Vehicule Press, 1984.

Marcia Muller and Pronzini, editors, *The Wickedest Show on Earth: A Carnival of Circus Suspense,* Morrow, 1985.

Francis M. Nevins, Jr., and Greenburg, editors, *Hitchcock in Prime Time,* Avon Books, 1985.

Marvin Kaye and Saralee Kaye, compilers, *Masterpieces of Terror and the Supernatural: A Treasury of Spellbinding Tales Old and New,* Doubleday, 1985.

Pronzini and Muller, editors, *The Deadly Arts,* Arbor House, 1985.

Scott Walker, editor, *Buying Time: An Anthology Celebrating 20 Years of the Literature Program of the National Endowment for the Arts,* introduction by Ralph Ellison, Graywolf Press, 1985.

Daniel Halpern, editor, *The Art of the Tale: An International Anthology of Short Stories, 1945-1985,* Viking, 1986.

SHORT STORIES REPRESENTED IN "ELLERY QUEEN" ANTHOLOGIES

Queen's Awards, 1948 (3rd annual), Little, 1948.

Queen's Awards, 1949 (4th annual), Little, 1949.

Queen's Awards (5th annual), Little, 1950.

Queen's Awards (6th annual), Little, 1951.

Queen's Awards (7th annual), Little, 1952.

Queen's Awards (8th annual), Little, 1953.

Ellery Queen's Awards (9th annual), Little, 1954.

Ellery Queen's Awards (10th annual), Simon & Schuster, 1955.

Ellery Queen's Awards (11th annual), Simon & Schuster, 1956.

Ellery Queen's Awards (12th annual), Simon & Schuster, 1957.

Ellery Queen's Annual (13th annual), Simon & Schuster, 1958.

Ellery Queen's Mystery Annual (14th annual), Random House, 1959.

Ellery Queen's Mystery Annual (15th annual), Random House, 1960.

Ellery Queen's Mystery Annual (16th annual), Random House, 1961.

Anthony Boucher, editor, *The Quintessence of Queen: Best Prize Stories from Twelve Years of Ellery Queen's Mystery Magazine,* Random House, 1962.

To Be Read before Midnight (17th annual), Random House, 1962.

Ellery Queen's Mystery Mix (18th annual), Random House, 1963.

Ellery Queen's Double Dozen (19th annual), Random House, 1964.

Ellery Queen's 20th Anniversary Annual (20th annual), Random House, 1965.

Ellery Queen's Crime Carousel (21st annual), New American Library, 1966.

Ellery Queen's All-Star Lineup (22nd annual), New American Library, 1967.

Ellery Queen's Mystery Parade (23rd annual), New American Library, 1968.

Ellery Queen's Murder Menu (24th annual), World Publishing, 1969.

Ellery Queen's Grand Slam (25th annual), World Publishing, 1970.

Ellery Queen's The Golden 13: 13 First Prize Winners from Ellery Queen Mystery Magazine, World Publishing, 1970.

Ellery Queen's Headliners (26th annual), World Publishing, 1971.

Ellery Queen's Mystery Bag (27th annual), World Publishing, 1972.

Ellery Queen's Crookbook (28th annual), Random House, 1974.

Ellery Queen's Murdercade (29th annual), Random House, 1975.

Ellery Queen's Magicians of Mystery, Davis Publications, 1976.

Searches and Seizures (31st annual), Davis Publications, 1977.

Ellery Queen's A Multitude of Sins (32nd annual), Davis Publications, 1978.

Ellery Queen's Scenes of the Crime (33rd annual), Davis Publications/Dial Press, 1979.

Ellery Queen's Circumstantial Evidence (34th annual), Davis Publications/Dial Press, 1980.

Ellery Queen's Crime Cruise Round the World (35th annual), Davis Publications/Dial Press, 1981.

Ellery Queen and Eleanor Sullivan, editors, *Ellery Queen's Book of First Appearances,* Davis Publications/Dial Press, 1982.

Queen and Sullivan, editors, *Ellery Queen's Lost Ladies,* Dial Press/Davis Publications, 1983.

Sullivan, editor, *Ellery Queen's Lost Men,* Dial Press/Davis Publications, 1983.

Sullivan and Karen A. Prince, editors, *Ellery Queen's Memorable Characters,* Dial Press/Davis Publications, 1984.

SHORT STORIES REPRESENTED IN "MYSTERY WRITERS OF AMERICA" ANTHOLOGIES

Maiden Murders, Harper, 1952.

George Hamilton Coxe, editor, *Butcher, Baker, Murder-maker,* Knopf, 1954.

Dorothy Salisbury Davis, editor, *A Choice of Murders,* Scribner, 1958.

Rex Stout, editor, *For Tomorrow We Die,* Macdonald & Co., 1958.

David Alexander, editor, *Tales for a Rainy Night,* Holt, 1961.

Cream of the Crime, Holt, 1962.

Thomas B. Dewey, editor, *Sleuths and Consequences,* Simon & Schuster, 1966.

Robert L. Fish, editor, *With Malice toward All,* Putnam, 1968.

Lucy Freeman, editor, *Killers of the Mind,* Random House, 1974.

Fish, editor, *Every Crime in the Book,* Putnam, 1975.

Arthur Maling, *When Last Seen,* Harper, 1977.

Joe Gores and Pronzini, editors, *Tricks and Treats,* Doubleday for the Crime Club, 1976.

Michele Slung, editor, *Women's Wiles,* Harcourt, 1979.

Pronzini, editor, *The Edgar Winners,* Random House, 1980.

Lawrence Treat, editor, *A Special Kind of Crime,* Doubleday for the Crime Club, 1982.

Brian Garfield, editor, *The Crime of My Life,* Walker & Co., 1984.

OTHER

(With Joseph Losey) "The Big Night" (screenplay; based on Ellin's novel *Dreadful Summit: A Novel of Suspense*, also published as *The Big Night: A Novel of Suspense*), United Artists, 1951.

Contributor of chapter on crime writing to *Writers Handbook*. Also contributor of short stories to periodicals, including *Ellery Queen's Mystery Magazine*, and of nonfiction to *Writer*. Ellin's manuscripts are collected at Boston University's Mugar Memorial Library.

SIDELIGHTS: Stanley Ellin received numerous awards for excellence in mystery writing, including the prestigious Grand Master Award from the Mystery Writers of America for lifetime writing accomplishment. Widely considered a master who transcended the bounds of his genre, Ellin was most highly regarded for his short stories; however, his novels were also well received. Several of his stories and novels have been adapted for television or motion pictures, testifying to the visual immediacy of Ellin's writing as well. "From his earliest days," wrote a London *Times* contributor, "it was apparent to reviewers that a talent capable of raising that much-abused genre, the thriller, to the level of, at least, minor art, had made its appearance."

Asked by Matthew J. Bruccoli in *Conversations with Writers II* why he became a mystery writer, Ellin recalled that after reading Dashiell Hammett and Graham Greene, he found himself "gravitating more or less toward the idea of a crime being the most dramatic thing you could write about," but thought he had been "hijacked into the mystery field." Launching his career in 1948 with a much anthologized classic short story about cannibalism entitled "The Specialty of the House," Ellin also published his first novel, *Dreadful Summit: A Novel of Suspense,* a psychological study about a youth who seeks to avenge the humiliation that his father suffered by murdering the man responsible. Ellin told Bruccoli that he considered the book a straight novel, but the publisher believed that its "emphasis on crime made it a novel in the mystery field." Ellin added that because the publisher felt its "particular treatment didn't put it squarely in the field . . . a new category was created . . . 'suspense specials.'" Financially compelled to publish his first novel within the mystery genre, Ellin remarked to Bruccoli: "I have all along, by the way, been uneasily balanced between the genre and the straight novel."

Praised for an essential veracity in his work, Ellin was especially credited for his ability to realistically render a sense of time and place. Ellin told Bruccoli that he regarded the mystery novel as a sociological document: "They mark—I hit on this long ago—their times very clearly, as Holmes and his people marked London at that period. You had in the twenties Hammett coming along—the cynical era . . . and Chandler picking that up. You had Mickey Spillane coming along at the McCarthy time, because Spillane's Mike Hammer was the quintessential McCarthy hero: the 'I-am-the-judge-jury-and-executioner' thing was implicit in that time. And during the nadir of the Cold War Bond came along, but Bond had to be transformed as social events were transformed. . . . So that there is always a picture of the time and place." The sense of authenticity in Ellin's own work resulted from thorough research. "I also enjoy, and I think readers enjoy, novels which are set in what to a local person is an exotic place," he told Bruccoli, adding that while travelling in Europe, he and his wife Jeanne, who was also his editor, would "settle down in a city and every day simply walk in the city, live the city."

His wife would make extensive notes during their travels while Ellin would be "enjoying the local television, whatever language," absorbing the atmosphere and "enjoying the experience." Ellin remarked to Bruccoli, "It's only when bit by bit as I go along, usually near the end of a trip, that pieces start falling together—that I become acutely aware that I now have the makings of my story material."

According to Edwin McDowell in the *New York Times*, Otto Penzler, owner and publisher of the Mysterious Press, said of Ellin, "He was probably the most highly rated among his peers of any mystery writer I know." Noting that Ellin's work has been translated into twenty-two languages, Penzler added that in some European countries, Ellin is considered "a major literary figure." Despite his established reputation, though, Ellin experienced great difficulty in finding a publisher for his *The Dark Fantastic*, a novel about a retired white, and once liberal, professor who is dying from cancer and whose mind has slipped into insanity. Espousing bigotry, he also harbors a suicidal plot to blow up the Brooklyn apartment house in which he was born, thereby killing its black inhabitants as well as himself. Publishers were apparently reluctant to publish the novel because of the racist tenor of some of its segments: "No fewer than 10 commercial presses rejected the manuscript," wrote David Lehmann in *Newsweek*, "evidently underestimating the ability of readers to distinguish the author from the hate-riddled Kirwan." In the *Washington Post Book World*, Michele Slung discussed Ellin's reaction: "'You'd have to read the book with an astigmatic eye in order to come out thinking I'm a racist,' Ellin says, with a flicker of bitterness at the lack of understanding he ran into." According to Anthony Olcott's report of the controversy in the *Chicago Tribune Book World*, Ellin admitted: "I knew I was taking some risks when I did the book, but I never expected rejection."

Once published though, *The Dark Fantastic* was favorably received. For instance, in the *Los Angeles Times Book Review*, Charles Champlin wrote that the novel "has all the requisites of the successful thriller: The characters are vivid, the dialogue has the authentic ring of silver dollars on marble, the scenes are remarkably envisionable (no wonder Ellin's work has been so often seized for film), the suspense escalates with what can be called a terrible efficiency." Ellin's hate-consumed character is balanced by the characterization of the white detective who falls in love with a black resident of the apartment building; and, according to Olcott: "Their courtship is a masterpiece of erotic, racial and social tension, as the two lurch toward what Ellin sees as the only possible hope for racial harmony, a one-to-one relationship between human beings." Calling it "a book by one of the truth-tellers," H. R. F. Keating added in the London *Times:* "The nasty equally with the good are depicted so you believe this is what such people are like through and through."

Ellin's last book, *Very Old Money*, "falls somewhere between a mystery and a serious work of fiction," Jonathan Yardley commented in the *Washington Post Book World*, adding that Ellin managed to achieve that "difficult balance" with "ease and aplomb." The novel is about a couple of unemployed teachers who become domestic servants in the Manhattan mansion of an elderly wealthy recluse. Although T. J. Binyon suggested in the *Times Literary Supplement* that *Very Old Money* is a "disappointing successor to the author's previous books," Yardley concluded that "it is intelligent, good-humored, thoughtful and sophisticated: adult entertainment, in the best sense of both words." A *New Yorker* contributor praised Ellin's "special ability to create an almost imperceptible spiral of suspense.'' However, Yardley maintained that the suspense was ''incidental to the setting and the characters he creates. At this more serious work Ellin . . . is most accomplished.'' Although Ellin's work is often characterized by inventive plotting, in the *New York Times Book Review,* Melik Kaylin found that the plot of *Very Old Money* ''lacks suspense'' and that Ellin ''strays too far from the exigencies of the genre in pursuit of a moral, which is that very old money is corrupt and alluring.'' Ellin did not believe that a work should revolve around plot, though: ''I always have the feeling in all mystery writing that you must have a sound and valid plot, and that is the skeleton,'' Ellin told Bruccoli. ''But as you build and as you work, the skeleton should properly and will properly sort of disappear.''

Describing Ellin's books as ''densely woven and subtly timed adventures,'' the London *Times* contributor indicated that ''both his prose and his play of mind were things of elegance.'' Ellin wrote six hours a day, six days a week, and a novel would take him fourteen or sixteen months to complete; but he acknowledged to Bruccoli that his method of writing was ''atrocious'' and ''damaging to productivity'' because he was unable to abandon a page until it was in its final form: ''It's a compulsion. . . . I find that when I try to just gallop ahead, I am frozen with the thought that there's something wrong on that preceding page and I will work and rework it at length, until I am as satisfied as I can be with it.'' He found, however, that the method did have its advantages, though: ''When I read my own stuff back, I find that each page has a tension in manuscript, and if they all interlock properly they create tension throughout a book.''

MEDIA ADAPTATIONS: Several of Ellin's stories have been adapted for television and broadcast on ''Alfred Hitchcock Presents,'' including ''Specialty of the House,'' which featured Robert Morely, in 1959; *The Key to Nicholas Street* was made into a film starring Jean-Paul Belmondo, released in France in 1959 as ''Leda,'' and in 1961 as ''Web of Passion''; Ellin's story ''The Best of Everything'' provided the basis for the film ''Nothing but the Best,'' starring Alan Bates, produced by Royal and released in Britain in 1964; *House of Cards* was made into a film of the same title by Universal in 1968, starring Orson Welles and George Peppard; ''Sunburn,'' a 1979 film by Paramount starring Farrah Fawcett, Charles Grodin, Art Carney, and Joan Collins, was based on Ellin's novel *The Bind.*

BIOGRAPHICAL/CRITICAL SOURCES:

BOOKS

Conversations with Writers II, Gale, 1978.

PERIODICALS

Books and Bookmen, June, 1971.
Chicago Tribune Book World, December 18, 1983.
Los Angeles Times Book Review, June 22, 1980, July 10, 1983, February 1, 1985.
National Observer, March 20, 1967, November 11, 1968.
New Republic, May 30, 1981.
Newsweek, July 11, 1983.
New Yorker, April 9, 1979, April 8, 1985.
New York Times, August 8, 1970, November 15, 1977, August 1, 1986.
New York Times Book Review, February 26, 1967, July 12, 1970, September 24, 1972, October 16, 1977, April 8, 1979, May 6, 1979, April 5, 1981, September 11, 1983, March 17, 1985.

Punch, November 16, 1983, August 21, 1985.
Saturday Review, August 1, 1970, August 26, 1972, March, 1985.
Spectator, June 23, 1973, April 8, 1978, February 11, 1984.
Time, September 18, 1972.
Times (London), December 8, 1983, August 4, 1986.
Times Literary Supplement, June 29, 1967, October 18, 1985.
Washington Post Book World, March 18, 1979, July 20, 1980, April 19, 1981, June 5, 1983, February 17, 1985.

OBITUARIES:

PERIODICALS

AB Bookman's Weekly, September 8, 1986.
Detroit Free Press, August 1, 1986.
Globe and Mail (Toronto), August 2, 1986.
Newsweek, August 11, 1986.
New York Times, August 1, 1986.
Publishers Weekly, August 15, 1986.
Rochester Times-Union, August 1, 1986.
Time, August 11, 1986.
Times (London), August 4, 1986.
Washington Post, August 2, 1986.
Writer, November, 1986.*

—*Sketch by Sharon Malinowski*

*   *   *

ELLIS, Howard S(ylvester)   1898-

PERSONAL: Born July 2, 1898, in Denver, Colo.; son of Sylvester Eldon (a Protestant clergyman) and Nellie Blanche (Young) Ellis; married Lilah Priscilla Whetstine, January, 1925 (divorced, 1934); married Hermine Johanna Hoerlesberger, July 6, 1945; children: (first marriage) Audrey Elinor; (second marriage) Dorothy Margaret, Martha Josephine. *Education:* State University of Iowa, A.B., 1920; University of Michigan, A.M., 1922; Harvard University, A.M., 1924, Ph.D., 1929; also studied at University of Heidelberg, 1924-25, and University of Vienna, 1933-35.

ADDRESSES: Home—936 Cragmont Ave., Berkeley, Calif. 94708.

CAREER: University of Michigan, Ann Arbor, instructor, 1920-22, 1925-29, assistant professor, 1929-35, associate professor, 1935-37, professor of economics, 1937-38; University of California, Berkeley, professor of economics, 1938-43; Federal Reserve System, Board of Governors, Washington, D.C., economic analyst, 1943-44, assistant director of research and statistics, 1944-45; University of California, Berkeley, Flood Professor of Economics, 1946-65, professor emeritus, 1965—. Visiting professor at Columbia University, 1944-45, 1949-50, in Tokyo, Japan, summer, 1951, in Bombay, India, 1958-59, and at Claremont Graduate School, 1969; research professor at Center of Economic Research (Athens), 1963; Knapp Visiting Professor at University of Wisconsin—Milwaukee, 1972. Director of Marshall Aid Research Project for Council on Foreign Relations, 1949-50; head of joint UNESCO-Economic Commission for Latin America (ECLA)—Organization of American States (OAS) Mission on Economic Education in Latin America, 1960; chief of party for U.S. Agency for International Development (U-SAID)—University of California program in Rio de Janeiro, 1965-67; member of economic policy committee of U.S. Chamber of Commerce, 1945-46; consultant to U.S. House of Representatives Committee on

Postwar Planning, 1944-45, and U.S. Department of State, 1952-53.

MEMBER: International Economic Association (member of council, 1950-53, 1956-63; president, 1953-56; honorary president, 1957—, executive committee, 1956-62), American Academy of Arts and Sciences, American Economic Association (member of executive committee, 1945-48, 1950-53; president, 1949), Royal Economic Society, Mont Pelerin Society, Phi Beta Kappa.

AWARDS, HONORS: David A. Wells Award from Harvard University, 1930; fellowship from Social Science Research Council, 1933-35, for study in Europe; M.A., Yale University, 1946; LL.D., University of Michigan, 1951; distinguished service award from American Economic Association, 1966; LL.D, University of California, Berkeley, 1968.

WRITINGS:

German Monetary Theory: 1905-1933, Harvard University Press, 1934.
(With others) *Explorations in Economics,* Macmillan, 1936.
Exchange Control in Central Europe, Harvard University Press, 1941, reprinted, Greenwood Press, 1978.
(With others) *Postwar Economic Problems,* McGraw, 1943.
(With others) *Financing American Prosperity,* Twentieth Century Fund, 1945.
(With others) *Economic Reconstruction,* McGraw, 1945.
(Editor) *A Survey of Contemporary Economics,* Blakeston, 1948, reprinted, Irwin, 1978.
(Editor with Lloyd A. Metzler) *Readings in the Theory of International Trade,* Volume 1, Blakeston, 1949.
The Economics of Freedom: The Progress and Future of Aid to Europe, Harper, 1950.
(With N. S. Buchanan) *Approaches to Economic Development,* Twentieth Century Fund, 1955, reprinted, Greenwood Press, 1978.
(With others) *United States Monetary Policy,* American Assembly, Columbia University, 1958, 2nd edition, 1964.
(With others) *Economic Development and International Trade,* Southern Methodist University Press, 1959.
(Editor with Henry C. Wallich) *El Desarrollo economico y America Latina* (title means "Economic Development and Latin America"), Fondo de Cultura Economico, 1960.
(With Benjamin Cornejo and Luis Escobar Cerda) *The Teaching of Economics in Latin America,* Organization of American States, 1961.
(With Diomedes D. Psilos, Richard M. Westebbe, and Calliope Nicolaou) *Industrial Capital in Greek Development,* Center of Economic Development (Athens), 1964.
(Editor) *The Economy of Brazil,* University of California Press, 1969.
Private Enterprise and Socialism in the Middle East, American Enterprise Institute, 1970.
(With others) *Ensaios economics: Homenagema Octavio Gouvea de Bulhoes* (title means "Economic Essays in Honor of O. Gouvea de Bulhoes"), APEC Editora (Rio de Janiero), 1972.
Notes on Stagflation, American Enterprise Institute for Public Policy Research, 1978.

OTHER

Contributor of articles on economic theory, money and banking, fiscal policy, and international finance to economic journals. Member of board of editors of American Economic As-

sociation, 1940-43; co-editor of *Kyklos: International Journal of the Social Sciences,* 1950—.

SIDELIGHTS: Howard S. Ellis's books have been published in Japanese, Arabic, Persian, Indonesian, Bengali, and Spanish.

AVOCATIONAL INTERESTS: Music, gardening.*

*   *   *

ELLMANN, Richard (David)   1918-1987

PERSONAL: Born March 15, 1918, in Highland Park, Mich.; died May 13, 1987 of pneumonia brought on by amyotrophic lateral sclerosis (Lou Gherig's disease) in Oxford, England; son of James I. (a lawyer) and Jeanette (Barsook) Ellmann; married Mary Donahue (a writer), August 12, 1949; children: Stephen, Maud, Lucy. *Education:* Yale University, B.A., 1939, M.A., 1941, Ph.D., 1947; Trinity College, Dublin, B.Litt., 1947.

ADDRESSES: Home—39 St. Giles, Oxford OX1 3LW, England.

CAREER: Harvard University, Cambridge, Mass., instructor, 1942-43, 1947-48, Briggs-Copeland Assistant Professor of English Composition, 1948-51; Northwestern University, Evanston, Ill., professor of English, 1951-63, Franklin Bliss Snyder Professor, 1963-68; Yale University, New Haven, Conn., professor of English, 1968-70; Oxford University, Oxford, England, Goldsmiths' Professor of English Literature, 1970-84, New College, fellow, 1970-84, honorary fellow, 1984-87; Wolfson College, extraordinary fellow, 1984-87. Frederick Ives Carpenter Visiting Professor, University of Chicago, 1959, 1967, and 1975-77; Emory University, visiting professor, 1978-81, Woodruff Professor of English, 1982-87. Member of United States/United Kingdom Educational Commission, 1970-85. Consultant to "The World of James Joyce," Public Broadcasting Service, 1983. *Military service:* U.S. Navy and Office of Strategic Services, 1943-46.

MEMBER: British Academy (fellow), Modern Language Association of America (chairman of English Institute, 1961-62; member of executive council, 1961-65), English Institute (chairman, 1961-62), Royal Society of Literature (fellow), American Academy and Institute of Arts and Letters (fellow), Phi Beta Kappa, Chi Delta Theta, Signet.

AWARDS, HONORS: Rockefeller Foundation fellow in humanities, 1946-47; Guggenheim fellow, 1950, 1957-58, and 1970; grants from American Philosophical Society and Modern Language Association of America, 1953; *Kenyon Review* fellowship in criticism, 1955-56; School of Letters fellow, Indiana University, 1956 and 1960, senior fellow, 1966-72; National Book Award for nonfiction, Friends of Literature Award in biography, Thormond Monson Award from Society of Midland Authors, and Carey-Thomas Award for creative book publishing to Oxford University Press, all for *James Joyce,* 1960, and Duff Cooper Prize and James Tair Black Prize for new and revised edition, 1982; George Polk Memorial Award, 1970, for *The Artist As Critic: Critical Writings of Oscar Wilde;* M.A., Oxford University, 1970; D.Litt. from National University of Ireland, 1975, Emory University, 1979, and Northwestern University, 1980; National Endowment for the Humanities research grant, 1977; Ph.D., University of Gothenburg (Sweden), 1978; D.H.L. from Boston College and University of Rochester, both 1979; National Book Critics Circle Award for best biography/autobiography, 1989, for *Oscar Wilde.*

WRITINGS:

Yeats: The Man and the Masks, Macmillan, 1948, reprinted, Norton, 1978, corrected edition with new preface, Oxford University Press, 1979.

The Identity of Yeats, Oxford University Press, 1954, 2nd edition, 1964, reprinted, 1985.

James Joyce, Oxford University Press, 1959, new and revised edition with corrections, 1982.

Edwardians and Late Victorians, Columbia University Press, 1960.

(With E. D. H. Johnson and Alfred L. Bush) *Wilde and the Nineties: An Essay and an Exhibition,* edited by Charles Ryskamp, Princeton University Library, 1966.

Eminent Domain: Yeats among Wilde, Joyce, Pound, Eliot, and Auden, Oxford University Press, 1967.

Ulysses on the Liffey, Oxford University Press, 1972, corrected edition, Faber and Faber, 1984.

Golden Codgers: Biographical Speculations, Oxford University Press, 1973.

(With John Espey) *Oscar Wilde: Two Approaches* (Papers Read at a Clark Library Seminar, April 17, 1976), Williams Andrews Clark Memorial Library, 1977.

The Consciousness of Joyce, Oxford University Press, 1977.

Four Dubliners: Wilde, Yeats, Joyce, and Beckett, U.S. Government Printing Office, 1986.

Oscar Wilde, Hamish Hamilton, 1987, Knopf, 1988.

a long the riverrun: Selected Essays, Hamish Hamilton, 1988.

EDITOR

(And translator, and author of introduction) Henri Michaux, *Selected Writings,* Routledge & Kegan Paul, 1952.

James Joyce, *Letters of James Joyce,* Volumes 2-3, Viking, 1966.

Stanislaus Joyce, *My Brother's Keeper: James Joyce's Early Years,* Viking, 1958.

(With others) *English Masterpieces,* 2nd edition, two volumes, Prentice-Hall, 1958.

Arthur Symons, *The Symbolist Movement in Literature,* Dutton, 1958.

(With Ellsworth Mason) *The Critical Writings of James Joyce,* Faber and Faber, 1959, reprinted, 1979.

(With Charles Feidelson, Jr.) *The Modern Tradition: Backgrounds of Modern Literature,* Oxford University Press, 1965.

(Of corrected holograph) James Joyce, *A Portrait of the Artist As a Young Man,* drawings by Robin Jacques, Cape, 1968.

Oscar Wilde, *The Artist As Critic: Critical Writings of Oscar Wilde,* Random House, 1969.

Oscar Wilde: A Collection of Critical Essays, Prentice-Hall, 1969.

(With Robert O'Clair) *The Norton Anthology of Modern Poetry,* Norton, 1973.

James Joyce, *Selected Letters of James Joyce,* Viking, 1975.

(With O'Clair) *Modern Poems: An Introduction to Poetry,* Norton, 1976.

The New Oxford Book of American Verse, Oxford University Press, 1976.

(And author of introduction) Oscar Wilde, *The Picture of Dorian Gray and Other Writings,* Bantam, 1982.

OTHER

(Contributor of "A Chronology on the Life of James Joyce") James Joyce, *Letters,* Volume 1, edited by Stuart Gilbert, Viking, 1957.

Ulysses the Divine Nobody (monograph), Yale University Press, 1957, reprinted, 1981.

Joyce in Love (monograph), Cornell University Library, 1959.

(Contributor of "Overtures to Wilde's Salome") *Twentieth Anniversary, 1968,* Indiana University School of Letters, 1968.

(Author of introduction and notes) James Joyce, *Giacomo Joyce,* Faber, 1968, reprinted, 1984.

(Contributor of "Ulysses: A Short History") James Joyce, *Ulysses,* Penguin, 1969.

James Joyce's Tower (monograph), Eastern Regional Tourism Organisation (Dublin), 1969.

Literary Biography (monograph; inaugural lecture, University of Oxford, May 4, 1971), Clarendon Press, 1971.

The Poetry of Yeats (phono tape), BFA Educational Media, 1974.

James Joyce's Hundredth Birthday, Side and Front Views (monograph), Library of Congress, 1982.

Oscar Wilde at Oxford (monograph), Library of Congress, 1984.

(Author of introduction) Michael Moscato and Leslie LeBlanc, *The United States of America vs. One Book Entitled Ulysses by James Joyce; Documents and Commentary: 50-Year Retrospective,* University Publications of America, 1984.

Henry James among the Aesthetes (lectures), Longwood Publishing Group, 1985.

W. B. Yeats' Second Puberty (monograph), Library of Congress, 1985.

Samuel Beckett, Nayman of Noland (monograph), Library of Congress, 1986.

Also author of monographs *Wallace Stevens' Ice-Cream,* 1957, and *The Background of Joyce's The Dead,* 1958.

SIDELIGHTS: Renowned biographer, literary critic, and educator Richard Ellmann held professorial posts at such universities as Harvard, Northwestern, and Yale before becoming the first American to teach English literature at Oxford University, a position he held for many years. Ellmann devoted most of his distinguished academic career to the study of the Irish literary renaissance. "It is difficult to think of the great writers of Irish literature—W. B. Yeats, James Joyce, or Oscar Wilde—without thinking of Ellmann," remarked Steven Serafin in a *Dictionary of Literary Biography Yearbook, 1987* essay. Ellmann's scholarship on Yeats remains a standard reference, and he is widely acknowledged as having been the foremost authority on Joyce. His much heralded, National Book Award-winning biography *James Joyce,* not only represents the definitive work on the artist but, in the opinion of many, casts its shadow as the best literary biography ever written. Referring to him as "an extraordinary individual of rare and exceptional talent," Serafin believed that "Ellmann essentially redefined the art of biography." And in a *Times Literary Supplement* review of Ellmann's National Book Critics Circle Award-winning final work, the biography *Oscar Wilde,* Gore Vidal deemed him "our time's best academic biographer."

Ellmann's scholarship sought the literary influences upon and connections among writers and their work. Calling Ellmann "particularly sensitive to the impingement of one talent upon another," Denis Donoghue added in a *New York Times Book Review* essay about *Eminent Domain: Yeats among Wilde, Joyce, Pound, Eliot, and Auden:* "As critics we look for corresponding moments in the work, moments of representative force and definition. Mr. Ellmann is a keen student of these epiphanies in life and art. He finds them more often than not in the pressure of one mind upon another, and he delights in these occasions." In Ellmann's *Eminent Domain*, "Yeats's greatness as a poet is seen as illustrated by his gift for expropriating or confiscating, from youth to age, ideas or tactics from other writers," stated a *Times Literary Supplement* contributor.

Ellmann, whose work on Yeats "set the tone of much subsequent criticism," stated Kevin Sullivan in *Nation* review of *Eminent Domain*, believed that as "a young poet in search of an aesthetic," Yeats was significantly indebted to Wilde, whose "professional reputation rested . . . on his skill as a talker before all else." Yeats "pillaged freely" of this talk during their London meetings and believed that "Wilde's dazzling conversation was an aristocratic counterpart to the oral culture that had persisted among the Irish peasantry at home," explained Sullivan. "But what really attracted him was Wilde's easy assumption of the superiority of imagination to reason and intellect, and the corollary that followed almost at once upon that assumption—the primacy and autonomy of art." And about the relationship between Yeats and Joyce, the *Times Literary Supplement* contributor noted that while "Joyce's attitude to Yeats was that of a rebel in the Irish literary movement," according to Sullivan, Ellmann believed that "Joyce turned from verse to prose out of an awareness of Yeats's unchallengeable mastery as a poet." Praised by Sullivan for describing "a wide and graceful arc that encompasses many of the major developments in English poetry during a full half-century," *Eminent Domain* was labeled "lucid, perceptive, urbane, in itself a graceful occasion" by Donoghue.

James Joyce, Ellmann's masterwork, was hailed with critical superlatives. "This immensely detailed, massive, completely detached and objective, yet loving biography, translates James Joyce's books back into his life," wrote Stephen Spender in the *New York Times*. "Here is the definitive work," assessed Dwight Macdonald in *New Yorker*, "and I hope it will become a model for future scholarly biographies." And according to Mark Schorer in the *San Francisco Chronicle*, "This is not only the most important book that we have had on James Joyce until now (and the only reliable biography), it is also, almost certainly, one of the great literary biographies of this century, a book that will last for years, probably for generations." A few critics, however, faulted the biography for the enormity of its detail. A *Times Literary Supplement* contributor, for example, contended that "much of the difficulty with Mr. Ellmann's book is in seeing the wood for the trees." But in the *Saturday Review*, Stuart Gilbert echoed the widely shared critical recognition that Ellmann performed commendably, calling *James Joyce* "a masterpiece of scholarly objectivity and exact research, in which the facts are marshaled and set forth with fine lucidity, and the imposing mass of detail never clogs the analysis."

In 1982, more than twenty years after the publication of *James Joyce*, Ellmann marked the centennial year of Joyce's birth with a new and revised edition of his biography. Having had access to Joyce's private library and other previously unavailable material, Ellmann was able to define the influences upon Joyce's art, especially *Ulysses*. "Ellmann's task was a dual one," wrote Thomas Flanagan in the *Washington Post Book World*. "He re-created for the reader what had become one of the exemplary lives of modern literature, conveying its color and its textures, its characterizing movements and stances, by the adroit but unobtrusive deployment of many thousands of details." The *New York Time*'s Christopher Lehmann-Haupt, who felt that this minutely detailed new material was "entirely appropriate and desirable, considering the obsessive sort of

attachment that Joyce's art inspires," remarked: "And the effect of this experience is fairly stunning, not alone because of the remarkable wealth of details that the author has gathered up and artfully pieced together. What also strikes the reader is the number of those details that wound up in Joyce's fiction, or, to put it the other way around, the degree to which Joyce's art was grounded in actuality."

Although *Newsweek*'s Peter S. Prescott regarded it "a pleasure to salute this masterly book as it marches past again," critcs such as Hugh Kenner in the *Times Literary Supplement* acknowledged the book's achievement while pondering its veracity. Kenner suggested that because much of Ellmann's data was based upon interviews with those who claimed a link to Joyce, it was essentially unreliable, citing in particular Ellmann's use of "Irish Fact, definable as anything you get told in Ireland, where you get told a great deal." Kenner further maintained: "'Definitive' in 1959, was a word that got thrown around rather thoughtlessly by reviewers stunned beneath an avalanche of new information. But there can be no 'definitive' biography. Biography is a narrative form: that means, a mode of fiction. Many narratives can be woven from the same threads. Biography incorporates 'facts', having judged their credibility. Its criteria for judgment include assessment of sources . . . and, pervasively, assessment of one's man." Moreover, Kenner also questioned whether Ellmann's detachment from his subject was sufficient: "Tone is a delicate matter; we don't want a hagiography. We'd like, though, to feel the presence of the mind that made the life worth writing and makes it worth reading." Conversely, Flanagan concluded that it was "because of the unsparing scrupulousness of his own methods," that Ellmann wrote "the kind of book which has become unhappily rare—a work of exacting scholarship which is also a humane and liberating document. Joyce found the proper biographer, and there can be no higher praise." John Stallworthy concurred in the *Times Literary Supplement*, "Speaking with his master's voice, his master's elegance, and his master's wit, Ellmann has produced a biography worth its place on the shelf beside *Dubliners, Ulysses,* and *Finnegans Wake*."

James Joyce marked a turning point for Ellmann, even though he was encouraged by its critical reception, said Serafin: "Shortly after its publication he ruminated about the future of his career: 'There really aren't any other modern writers that measure up to Yeats or Joyce. I can't think of anyone else I'd want to work on the way I've worked on them.'" Vidal suggested that "since Ellmann had already written magisterial works on two of the four [subjects of his essays, *Four Dubliners: Wilde, Yeats, Joyce, and Beckett*], symmetry and sympathy plainly drew him to a third." Ellmann spent the last twenty years of his life working on *Oscar Wilde*. Suffering from Lou Gherig's disease, "during the last weeks of his life, with the help of small machines on which he typed out messages that were then printed on a screen or on paper, he made final revisions on his long-awaited biography," reported Walter Goodman in the *New York Times*.

"While the literary world will continue to mourn his passing, we must all be grateful that he lived long enough to complete his magnificent life of Oscar Wilde . . . ," wrote Robert E. Kuehn in *Tribune Books*. "Like his earlier life of James Joyce, this book is biography on the grand scale: learned, expansive, judicious, magnanimous, and written with care and panache." Ellmann perceived Wilde, said Michael Dirda of the *Washington Post Book World*, "chiefly as a fearless artist and social critic who, like a kamikaze pilot, used himself as the bomb to explode the bourgeois values, pretentions and hypocrisies of late Victorian society.'' Likening Wilde's fate to that of ''a hero of classic tragedy [who] plummeted from the heights of fame to utter ruin,'' Dirda pointed out that although Wilde has been the subject of several biographies, ''they cannot compete with this capacious, deeply sympathetic and vastly entertaining new life of Richard Ellmann.''

''There's no question that *Oscar Wilde* is brilliant,'' declared Walter Kendrick in the *Voice Literary Supplement;* ''its post-humous publication splendidly caps Ellmann's career and, like his *James Joyce,* it belongs on the short shelf of biographies correctly labeled definitive.'' Although praising Ellmann as ''a masterful biographer,'' Elspeth Cameron continued in the Toronto *Globe and Mail* that ''no biography is definitive, and this one is not without its flaws. Ellmann's intellectual grasp of Wilde is firmer than his comprehension of Wilde's emotional life.'' However, Kuehn found that ''when it comes to interpretation, the psychological patterns he traces tend to be all the more persuasive for his refusal to overstate the case.'' Declaring that ''Oscar Wilde is not easily led,'' Richard Eder acknowledged in the *Los Angeles Times Book Review* that ''Ellmann does everything a biographer could do, and some things that few biographers have the courage and talent to do. He refuses to net the butterfly Wilde; he flies with him instead.''

Regarding Ellmann as ''unusually intelligent, a quality seldom found in academe or, indeed, on Parnassus itself,'' Vidal felt that Wilde did ''not quite suit his schema or his talent.'' Wilde does not require ''explication or interpretation,'' assessed Vidal. ''He needs only to be read, or listened to.'' Noting that ''Wilde provides little occasion for Ellmann's formidable critical apparatus,'' Vidal added that ''where Ellmann showed us new ways of looking at Yeats and, above all, at Joyce, he can do nothing more with Wilde than fit him into a historical context and tell, yet again, the profane story so well known to those who read.'' Concluding, however, that ''nobody could do better than Ellmann,'' Eder questioned how does one ''deliver up a figure who lived and wrote under such polymorphous signs of evasion?''

In Serafin's estimation, Ellmann's *Oscar Wilde* has ''rekindled interest in both the subject and the biographer. Virtually assured a permanent position in the history of literary biography, Ellmann has given new and sustained meaning to an ancient art.'' Serafin also credited Ellmann with ''establishing a standard of excellence in the art of contemporary life writing'' by fulfilling '''the ideal of sympathetic intuition' in re-creating and virtually reliving the lives of his subjects.'' As Seamus Heaney observed in *Atlantic,* ''There is an overall sense of Wilde's being tolerantly supervised by an intelligence at once vigilant and dignified.'' Remarking that ''Joyce as well as his Irish compatriot Oscar Wilde might have agonized less in knowing Ellmann would write the story of his life,'' Serafin recalled: ''It was Wilde who professed every great man has his disciples, and it is usually Judas who writes the biography. Surely no Judas, Ellmann would neither deceive nor deny.''

''He loved language as he loved life,'' said Serafin, ''and never failed in his work, as Anthony Burgess would astutely observe, 'to stimulate, instruct, amuse, and, for this writer, reawaken a sleeping belief in the glory of making literature.''' Critics and colleagues alike unanimously admired Ellmann's intelligence as well as his humility. ''He carries much learning with lightness and illumination,'' wrote Stephen Spender in a

New York Review of Books piece on Ellmann's book of essays, *Golden Codgers: Biographical Speculations.* And in the *Chicago Sun Times,* Bob Hergath observed: ''The nice thing about Ellmann, for all his scholarship and erudition, he was a regular guy. He had a terrific sense of humor.'' Referring to Ellmann's ''notable sense of humor and a donnishly droll way with a punchline,'' Goodman remarked that ''his wit remained intact throughout his illness; with speech difficult, he typed out jokes and repartee with visitors.'' As his brother, William Ellmann, is quoted in the *Detroit Free Press,* ''Dick Ellmann was a literary giant whose first question might be, 'How are the Tigers doing?'''

BIOGRAPHICAL/CRITICAL SOURCES:

BOOKS

Contemporary Literary Criticism, Volume 50, Gale, 1988.
Dictionary of Biography Yearbook, 1987, Gale, 1988.

PERIODICALS

Antioch Review, spring, 1972, winter, 1978.
Chicago Sun Times, May 15, 1987.
Contemporary Literature, winter, 1969.
Detroit Free Press, May 14, 1987.
Globe and Mail (Toronto), December 26, 1987.
Guardian, October 30, 1959.
Hudson Review, spring, 1968.
Los Angeles Times, May 16, 1987.
Los Angeles Times Book Review, November 14, 1982, February 14, 1988, November 27, 1988.
Maclean's, December 21, 1987.
Nation, October 17, 1959, November 13, 1967, June 23, 1969, June 19, 1972, November 20, 1982, February 13, 1988.
New Republic, June 3, 1972, February 15, 1988.
Newsweek, September 27, 1982.
New Yorker, December 12, 1959, March 21, 1988.
New York Review of Books, August 26, 1965, October 18, 1973, September 19, 1974, October 13, 1977, February 18, 1988.
New York Times, October 25, 1959, January 1, 1968, October 25, 1969, November 25, 1969, May 17, 1972, December 15, 1975, June 1, 1977, September 21, 1982, May 14, 1987.
New York Times Book Review, December 10, 1967, January 21, 1968, May 14, 1972, June 19, 1977, April 19, 1981, February 21, 1988.
San Francisco Chronicle, November 1, 1959.
Saturday Review, October 24, 1959, May 24, 1969, March 28, 1970, May 13, 1972.
Sewanee Review, winter, 1969.
South Atlantic Quarterly, winter, 1968, winter, 1973, summer, 1978.
Spectator, November 13, 1959, February 12, 1977, October 23, 1982.
Time, January 4, 1988.
Times (London), November 20, 1959, January 5, 1967, July 25, 1968, March 17, 1972, February 18, 1977, October 8, 1987.
Times Literary Supplement, December 30, 1965, July 25, 1968, April 2, 1970, March 17, 1972, October 26, 1973, January 24, 1975, December 17, 1982, March 23, 1984, November 14, 1986, October 2-8, 1987, November 4-10, 1988, December 2, 1988.
Tribune Books (Chicago), February 7, 1988.
Virginia Quarterly Review, spring, 1968.

Washington Post Book World, May 21, 1972, March 29, 1981, October 31, 1982, October 30, 1983, January 24, 1988, November 20, 1988.
World Literature Today, winter, 1979, summer, 1983.

OBITUARIES:

PERIODICALS

Chicago Sun Times, May 15, 1987.
Cincinnati Post, May 14, 1987.
Detroit Free Press, May 14, 1987.
International Herald Tribune, May 16-17, 1987.
Long Island Newsday, May 15, 1987.
Los Angeles Times, May 16, 1987.
Newsweek, May 25, 1987.
New York Times, May 14, 1987.
Time, May 25, 1987.
Times (London), May 15, 1987.*

—*Sketch by Sharon Malinowski*

* * *

ESOHG, Lama
See GHOSE, Amal

* * *

ESSAME, Hubert 1896-1976

PERSONAL: Born December 2, 1896, in Exeter, England; died March 2, 1976, in England; son of Ernest Horatio and Phoebe (Salter) Essame; married Hilda Mary Kennedy, July 3, 1926 (died, 1964); married Dorothy Fox, June 6, 1964; children: (first marriage) Peter Kennedy, Robin Stephen Kennedy, Primrose Mary (Mrs. Edgar Joseph Feuchtwanger). *Education:* Army Staff College, Quetta, Pakistan, graduate, 1930. *Religion:* Anglican.

ADDRESSES: Home—The Courtyard, West Wittering, North Chichester P020 8LQ, England.

CAREER: British Army, career officer, 1915-49, retiring as major general; Ministry of Information, England, lecturer for army classes at University of Oxford, University of Southampton, University of Leeds, University of London, and University of Exeter, 1952-72. Chairman of Honiton Division of Conservative Party, 1952-57; chairman of Friends of Marlpits Hospital, 1952-64; governor of Royal School for Daughters of Officers of the Army, Bath, England, 1962-76.

MEMBER: Royal United Services Institute for Defense Studies, United Service Club.

AWARDS, HONORS: Military Cross, Distinguished Service Order, Commander of Order of British Empire.

WRITINGS:

The Forty-third Wessex Division at War, Clowes, 1952.
The North-West Europe Campaign, 1944-1945, Gale & Polden, 1962, reprinted, 1986.
(With Eversley M. G. Belfield) *The Battle for Normandy,* Batsford, 1965, reprinted, 1983.
The Battle for Germany, Batsford, 1969.
Normandy Bridgehead, Ballantine, 1970.
The Battle for Europe, 1918, Scribner, 1972.

Patton: A Study in Command, Scribner, 1974 (published in England as *Patton: The Commander,* Batsford, 1974).
(With Brian Horrocks) *Corps Commander,* Scribner, 1977.

Contributor to military journals.

WORK IN PROGRESS: The Art of Command—the Human Side: Hannibal to Eisenhower.

SIDELIGHTS: Historian, educator, and author Hubert Essame was a retired British Army general who served in both world wars and wrote several books on military subjects. According to John Toland in a *New York Times Book Review* assessment of *The Battle for Germany,* a study of "Field Marshal Montgomery's 21st Army Group through Holland to the Baltic," Essame treated "an area largely neglected by historians who have concentrated on the mainstream of the conflict—Omar Bradley's drive." Toland credited Essame with knowing how to tell a good story and how to infuse his battle scenes with human interest: "He also enlivens the proceedings by his personal views of the continuing controversy between Montgomery and the Americans on strategy and tactics." Although Elbridge Colby suggested in *Best Sellers* that the study is somewhat less than impartial, a *Times Literary Supplement* contributor observed that "General Essame is scrupulously fair in his judgments," and if they "are sometimes delivered with an unmistakable whiff of grapeshot, they are invariably sound and well conceived."

"He is surprisingly free of pro-British bias," wrote J. C. Dougherty in a *Best Sellers* review of *Patton: A Study in Command,* a study of General George S. Patton's achievements on the battlefield during World War II. "Essame's discussion, always lucid and set forth in laymen's terms, is essentially a professional soldier's appraisal of Patton as a military man in his military environment," commented Martin Blumenston in the *New York Times Book Review.* "Writing with authority and grace Essame concludes that in mobile operations Patton outclassed his Allied contemporaries 'in imagination, technique and achievement.'" And Blumenton further remarked that Patton "would certainly have agreed . . . with Essame's sympathetic presentation of his operational role."

AVOCATIONAL INTERESTS: Georgian and Victorian painting, history of British India.

BIOGRAPHICAL/CRITICAL SOURCES:

PERIODICALS

Best Sellers, October 1, 1969, May 15, 1974.
New York Times Book Review, October 5, 1969, May 19, 1974.
Times Literary Supplement, November 13, 1969.

OBITUARIES:

PERIODICALS

AB Bookman's Weekly, April 26, 1976.*

* * *

ETEROVICH, Francis Hyacinth 1913-1980

PERSONAL: Surname is pronounced A-*tare*-o-vich; born October 4, 1913, in Pucisca, Croatia (now part of Yugoslavia); naturalized U.S. citizen; died in 1980; son of Lovro (a mailman) and Marija (Petrovic) Eterovich. *Education:* Dominican School of Philosophy and Theology, Dubrovnik, Yugoslavia, diploma in philosophy, 1937; Dominican School of Theology,

Louvain, Belgium, lectorate, 1939; Croatian State University, classics diploma, 1944; Dominican University, Le Saulchoir, France, Ph.D., 1948; University of Chicago, A.M., 1965.

ADDRESSES: Office—Department of Philosophy, DePaul University, Chicago, Ill. 60604.

CAREER: College of St. Joseph (now University of Albuquerque), Albuquerque, N.M., instructor in sociology, 1953-56; College of St. Teresa, Winona, Minn., assistant professor of philosophy, 1957-61; DePaul University, Chicago, Ill., professor of philosophy, 1962-78.

MEMBER: American Philosophical Association, American Academy of Political and Social Science, American Association for the Advancement of Slavic Studies, Croatian Academy of America (vice-president, 1973-74, 1976-78), Croatian Foundation of America (chairman, 1968-74), Center for the Study of Democratic Institutions.

WRITINGS:

(Editor, compiler, and publisher) *Hrvati profesori na americkim i kanadskim visokim skolama,* [Chicago], 1963, 2nd edition published as *Directory of Scholars, Artists, and Professionals of Croatian Descent in the United States and Canada,* 1965, 3rd edition, 1970.

(Editor with Christopher Spalatin) *Croatia—Land, People, Culture,* University of Toronto Press, Volume I, 1964, Volume II, 1970, Volume III, 1978.

(Co-author) *Approaches to Morality,* Harcourt, 1966.

Approaches to Natural Law from Plato to Kant, Exposition Press, 1972.

(Author of analysis and commentary) Aristotle, *Nicomachian Ethics,* University Press of Washington, 1978.

Aristotle's Nicomachian Ethics: Commentary and Analysis, University Press of America, 1980.*

F

FATCHEN, Max 1920-

PERSONAL: Born August 3, 1920, in Adelaide, South Australia; son of Cecil William (a farmer) and Isabel (Ridgway) Fatchen; married Jean Wohlers (a teacher), May 15, 1942; children: Winsome Genevieve, Michael John, Timothy James. *Education:* Attended schools in South Australia. *Religion:* Uniting Church of Australia.

ADDRESSES: Home—Jane St., Smithfield, South Australia. *Office*—c/o *Advertiser,* 121 King William St., Adelaide, South Australia. *Agent*—John Johnson, Clerkenwell House, 54-57 Clerkenwell Green, London EC1R 0HT, England.

CAREER: Adelaide News and *Sunday Mail,* Adelaide, South Australia, journalist and special writer, 1946-55; *Advertiser,* Adelaide, special writer, 1955-71, 1982-84, literary editor, 1971-82. *Military service:* Royal Australian Air Force, World War II.

AWARDS, HONORS: The River Kings received a commendation and *The Spirit Wind* received a high commendation in annual book-of-the-year awards from Australian Children's Book Council; made member of Order of Australia, 1980, for services to journalism and literature.

WRITINGS:

JUVENILES

The River Kings, Methuen, 1966, St. Martin's, 1968.
Conquest of the River, Methuen, 1970.
The Spirit Wind, Methuen, 1973.
Chase through the Night, Methuen, 1976.
The Time Wave, Methuen, 1978.
Songs for My Dog (verse), Kestrel Books, 1980.
Closer to the Stars, Methuen, 1981.
Wry Rhymes for Troublesome Times, Kestrel Books, 1983.
A Paddock of Poems (verse), Omnibus Books, 1987.
Had Yer Jabs, Methuen, 1987.
Pass Me a Poem, Omnibus Books, 1989.

OTHER

Contributor of light verse to *Denver Post.*

SIDELIGHTS: Max Fatchen, who has made two trips to the United States for the *Advertiser,* is "very fond of America and Americans," and has "warm links with Denver and the *Denver Post.*" He explains that his light verse first found its way into the *Post* through a long friendship with that newspaper's former cartoonist, Pulitzer Prize-winner Pat Oliphant, who began his career on the Adelaide *Advertiser* illustrating Fatchen's lighter pieces.

"I have a great interest in rivers," Fatchen told *CA,* "and know the Murray [on which *The River Kings* is based] intimately. My forays into the Australian Outback have included a mapping expedition with Army surveyors and Naval support group to the Gulf of Carpentaria and Arnhem Land—a wild and remote area. . . . [I] have also travelled on mailman's truck on Birdsville Track, one of Australia's loneliest trails, landed on many offshore islands on the Australian coast, and travelled with trains supplying settlers on outback lines such as the trans-Australia line."

MEDIA ADAPTATIONS: Chase through the Night has been filmed for the Australian Broadcasting Corp.

* * *

FAUST, Irvin 1924-

PERSONAL: Born June 11, 1924, in New York, N.Y.; son of Morris (in insurance business) and Pauline (Henschel) Faust; married Jean Satterthwaite, August 29, 1959. *Education:* Attended Queens College of the City of New York (now Queens College of the City University of New York); City College of New York (now City College of the City University of New York), B.S., 1949; Columbia University, M.A., 1952, Ed.D., 1960.

ADDRESSES: Home—417 Riverside Dr., New York, N.Y. 10025. *Office*—Garden City High School, Garden City, N.Y. *Agent*—Gloria Loomis, Watkins Loomis Agency Inc., 150 East 35th St., Suite 530, New York, N.Y. 10016.

CAREER: Author. Manhattan Junior High School, New York, N.Y., teacher, 1949-53; Lynbrook High School, Lynbrook, N.Y., guidance counselor, 1956-60; Garden City High School, Garden City, N.Y., director of guidance and counseling, 1960—. Teacher at Columbia University, summer, 1963, New School for Social Research, 1975, Swarthmore College, 1976, City College of the City University of New York, 1977, and University of Rochester, summer, 1978. *Military service:* U.S.

Army, 1943-46; served in European theater and in Southwest Pacific.

MEMBER: PEN, New York State Personnel and Guidance Association.

AWARDS, HONORS: New York Times list of best books of the year included *Roar Lion Roar and Other Stories,* 1965, *Willy Remembers,* 1971, and *Newsreel,* 1980; *Book World* list of best books of 1971 included *Willy Remembers;* O. Henry Award, 1983 and 1986.

WRITINGS:

Entering Angel's World: A Student-Centered Casebook (nonfiction), Teachers College Press, Columbia University, 1963.

FICTION

Roar Lion Roar and Other Stories, Random House, 1965.
The Steagle, Random House, 1966.
The File on Stanley Patton Buchta, Random House, 1970.
Willy Remembers (Book-of-the-Month Club alternate selection), Arbor House, 1971.
Foreign Devils, Arbor House, 1973.
A Star in the Family, Doubleday, 1975.
Newsreel, Harcourt, 1980.
The Year of the Hot Jock and Other Stories, Dutton, 1985.

OTHER

(Author of afterword) Paul Cain, *Fast One,* University of Southern Illinois Press, 1978.

Contributor of short stories to *Atlantic, Esquire, Saturday Evening Post, Paris Review, Carleton Miscellany, New York Magazine, Sewanee Review,* and *Northwest Review;* contributor of reviews to *Esquire, New Republic,* and *New York Times Book Review.*

SIDELIGHTS: Like other successful writers, Irvin Faust divides his time between two careers. By day, Faust is director of guidance and counseling at a New York high school; by night he writes fiction. "I guess I belong to the European tradition of the writer who has to be involved with reality, rather than contemplating his navel and just being a confessional writer over and over and over again. I find that this doesn't necessarily give me material that I use, but it keeps me in touch with what's going on in the world," quotes George DeWan in *Newsday.* Faust has written several novels and two short story collections, and though he admits he is not a best-selling author, critics enjoy his humor, his disturbing yet often admirable characters, and his storehouse of information about American history—both the trivial and the critical.

Faust had little intention of becoming a writer. His undergraduate education was mainly in physical education, and afterwards he taught at a public school in Harlem. He later studied guidance and counseling at Teachers College of Columbia University and received his Ed.D. degree in 1960. Surprising to Faust, Teachers College published one of his case studies in 1956, and then his doctoral thesis as *Entering Angels World* in 1963. In an interview conducted by Matthew J. Bruccoli in 1977 and published in *Conversations with Writers II,* Faust claims that the interest Teachers College showed in his writing prompted him to believe in his own talent for the first time. Soon after, Faust enrolled in a short story writing course and sold his first story, "Into the Green Night." From that point on, interest in Faust's fiction has been steady.

Like some contemporary American writers, Faust is Jewish, and his name has become associated with the phrase "Jewish-American writer." According to Frank Campenni in the *Dictionary of Literary Biography: American Novelists since World War II,* Faust's Jewish-American heritage is significant. From Faust's early short story "Jake Bluffstein and Adolph Hitler" to the later novel *Foreign Devils,* writes Campenni, "Faust deals with the theme of Jews who identify obsessively with non-Jewish, even anti-Jewish, culture heroes. . . . In this theme of self-hatred (only one of Faust's Jewish themes), the Jew must exorcise his 'foreign devils' and accept his Jewish heritage. Only then can he further assimilate and understand his other heritage of American history and culture." Ivan Gold also proclaims in his *New York Times Book Review* assessment of Faust's novel *Newsreel* that, among other things, Jews have been a common "ingredient" and "theme" in Faust's writing to date.

Faust, however, does not consider himself a Jewish-American writer. In speaking with Bruccoli, Faust declared: "I have this Jewish-American base, but I don't think of myself in that sense as I think perhaps people refer to Malamud or Bellow, whose heroes are almost consistently Jews. . . . No, I don't see myself as a stereotype Jewish-American writer, and yet I suppose that out of that wellspring much has developed." Julia B. Boken comments in her *Dictionary of Literary Biography: Twentieth-Century American Jewish Fiction Writers* article that the majority of Faust's protagonists are Jewish, but "religion or ethnicity does not play a highly significant role in their portraiture. All of his protagonists suffer angst . . . [which is] not necessarily an ethnic manifestation."

Faust's published successes began with his short story collection *Roar Lion Roar and Other Stories.* Of the ten stories, most focus on the alienated and confused youth in New York City. As noted by Webster Schott in the *New York Times Book Review,* the stories "rise from Manhattan, isle of illusions, and all deal with the consequences of placing faith in fantasies." The title story, which derives its name from the fight song of Columbia University, relates the tragedy of a displaced Puerto Rican high school dropout who, upon becoming a janitor at the university, strives to become an accepted part of this Ivy League world. The young man identifies so completely with the university football team that he commits suicide when the team loses. In another story entitled "Philco Baby," a pocket radio is the lifeblood of an adolescent shipping clerk named Morty. Stanley Kauffmann explains in the *New Republic* that the radio "is not a safeguard against loneliness; there is evidence that [Morty] need not be alone. He *chooses* to live alone in the ambience of that radio, he wants it to be his Baby, his love, he wants it to dictate his gestures, his idioms, how he feels about his brand of beer and his filter cigarette. The little radio is his pocket priest."

As these two examples indicate, one of *Roar Lion Roar's* important themes concerns the issue of conformity. According to Kauffmann, several of the stories in Faust's collection contain protagonists who are most happy when they see themselves fitting into society. "Philco Baby," Kauffmann explains, expounds "not the horrors but the joys of conformity, the fullness that ad-mass jargon and jingle supplies to otherwise frantically self-dependent lives. . . . [And,] the same hunger for communion with something more golden than one's own life, the same ecstasy in embracing large publicity images, is the core of the title story, ['Roar Lion Roar']." *New York Review of Books* contributor Philip Rahv, however, stresses that in nine of the ten stories in *Roar Lion Roar* the characters fail to overcome their helplessness and their delusions primarily because of their overwhelming desire to fit in. "Faust's people," says Rahv, "are cast as types well below the level of alienation, which, for all the anxieties it induces, might make them feel far more alive and at least conscious of their plight than their frantic efforts to belong to their society by conforming, in the most literal possible manner, to its shoddiest dreams and images." In contrast to both Kauffmann and Rahv, Boken believes the issue at hand is not whether conformity is to be desired. Instead, she claims Faust's characters act within the parameters of the world as they have come to know it: "As outsiders might view them, many of the characters in *Roar Lion Roar* hold unorthodox views of America. They can be seen as maladjusted, even psychotic, but their methods of dealing with their lives stem from their cultural bedrock—urban life, poverty, unexamined perceptions, cultural artifacts, especially the radio, music, and the mass media television and the cinema."

For a first publishing endeavor, *Roar Lion Roar* was well received by critics. Ivan Gold called it a "brilliant collection" in his *New York Times Book Review* assessment of *Newsreel,* one of Faust's later novels. According to *Saturday Review* contributor Granville Hicks, "Faust uses the urban vernacular with authority.... The boldest stylistic venture . . . is in the title story, which is written entirely in the third person but uses the vocabulary and phraseology of the Puerto Rican hero." Rahv appreciates Faust's "unusual ear for the vernacular," but considers some of the stories "a bit too ingenious and anecdotal." Nevertheless, Kauffmann and others believe that "opening [Faust's] book is like clicking on a switch; at once we hear the electric hum of talent."

Following *Roar Lion Roar,* Faust published several novels that reflect a preoccupation with popular culture, an emphasis on the objective analysis of America's history, and a portrayal of characters who are no more heroic than the rest of us. Faust's first novel *The Steagle* is, according to critic Stephen Kroll in *Commonweal,* "but a short step" from *Roar Lion Roar* with its emphasis on living out one's pop culture fantasies. In the novel, Harold Aaron Weissburg, college professor and suburban family man, suddenly lets go of his conventional existence when President Kennedy announces the onset of the Cuban missile crisis. "The missile crisis releases [Weissburg], just as it makes all the women he knows grow big-eyed and warm, and off he goes to explore the make-out scene of Pop American, border to border, coast to coast," remarks Eliot Fremont-Smith in his *New York Times* commentary. "He goes physically, but what he explores is fantasy." Weissburg treks westward, seducing women, taking on numerous aliases—including those of Andy Hardy and Humphrey Bogart—and getting into barroom brawls. As *Commonweal* reviewer Irving Malin succinctly explains, during his odyssey, Weissburg "*becomes the hero of his own movie.*" But Weissburg is more real than the aliases he adopts, and the simpler world of the past that Weissburg wildly seeks is just that—a memorable segment of history. As the Cuban missile crisis winds down, so too does Weissburg's psychological crisis. He returns East to his suburban lifestyle.

Critics consider *The Steagle* Faust's record of one man's psychological or sociological breakdown in hostile circumstances. Reviewing the book in *Commonweal,* Richard Kostelanetz deems Faust a "master" in this regard: "In comparison, other novelists of madness seem distinctly amateur." Jack Ludwig, writing in the *New York Times Book Review,* finds *The Steagle* a "sadly accepting" novel because it ultimately professes that

"as long as reality is what it is, fantasy must serve man as refuge." According to Ludwig, Weissburg's fantasy existence is gradually eroded by his "recurring image of . . . a fallible President or an oversimplifying populace pushing the nightmare fantasy of nuclear annihilation into . . . reality. . . . From page to page, the touch-and-go realities of the Cuban missile crisis contrast with the inadequacies of popular language and popular culture. Gary Cooper is not the guide to how one behaves in an international crisis."

The Steagle, in contrast to *Roar Lion Roar,* received a mixed critical response. Though a number of reviewers found the book entertaining and ambitious, they felt it failed on certain grounds. "There is no doubt that Faust captures the frantic atmosphere in which Weissburg moves. . . ," writes Malin, "[but] although he can push us into certain adventures, he cannot completely characterize Weissburg. What do we learn about him. . .? Can we *care* about his divided longings? Faust merely uses him." In a second *New Republic* review, Kauffmann describes the book as "extraordinarily entertaining . . . but from the first page it starts to slip from a position of consequence into a pigeon-hole. That first page begins to tell us that this is, yet again, a novel about a perplexed contemporary urban American Jew. . . . The principal defect . . . is a lack of relation between action and theme. Partially, this is because [Weissburg] is not a realized character." But Hicks maintains in a second *Saturday Review* critique of Faust's work that, "as in [*Roar Lion Roar*], the writing is vigorous, often surprising, and full of wit. It beautifully serves Faust's purpose, which is the revelation of a man who is completely unique and yet a good deal like the rest of us."

After a lukewarm response to Faust's second novel, *The File on Stanley Patton Buchta,* Faust received much acclaim for his third, *Willy Remembers.* R. V. Cassill introduces this novel in the *New York Times Book Review* with somewhat of a fanfare: "I assume I'm in agreement with most of the front-line fiction critics in calling *Roar Lion Roar* one of the best short-story collections of the 1960's—and in feeling what neither 'The Steagle' nor 'The File on Stanley Patton Buchta' quite met the promise of Faust's first book. But—double-happy ending—those two novels now appear as projected lines that close in the fulfillment of 'Willy Remembers.'" Ninety-three-year-old Willy Kleinhans is a veteran of the Spanish-American War and has never been able to forget it. The lively, opinionated Willy, viewed by critics as sometimes bigoted, sometimes ignorant, but always likeable, recounts his life as he relaxes in the Old Soldiers Home in Washington. Willy's memories, however, have become blurred through the years. Writing in the *Saturday Review,* Joseph Catinella deems *Willy Remembers* "a great, big, beautiful hunk of Americana—a luscious novel that re-creates a vernal period in our nation's history when war was believed to be a test of strength and courage, and a man's love of country competed only with pride in his family. . . . In a style notable for its wide range of color and tone, the author evokes the imperialist spirit of late nineteenth-century America." *New York Times* contributor Richard R. Lingeman similarly comments: "I suspect that in [Faust's] latest book all his gifts—the ear for colloquial speech, the catch-basin memory for American trivia, the sheer verbal dazzlement, the gushing imagination—have coalesced into something stronger and more artistically coherent. In 'Willy Remembers' . . . Faust moulds the clay of 90 years of American popular culture into one archetypal hero who is a sort of Vox Pop man of the century. . . . Yet, 'Willy Remembers' is more than trivia-dropping, or garrulous, rambling reminiscences, it has a structure of steel.''

President Nixon's trip to China in the early 1970s inspired Faust's fourth novel, *Foreign Devils*. In this novel within a novel, Faust, Campenni maintains, "comes closest to achieving mastery of his own particular form, the blending of popular history and the disintegrating personality." In the book, Sidney Benson is a Jewish, New York writer with writer's block (four years of it), a crumbling marriage, and a myriad of other problems. Though continually nagged by his "Captain Bligh" alter ego, Benson begins writing a novel about reporter Norris Blake, a correspondent for the *New York World* who covers the Boxer Rebellion of 1900, the incident in which China purged itself of its "foreign devils." In much the same vein, Benson strives to eliminate the "foreign devils" in his own life. In alternating chapters of *Foreign Devils*, the affairs of both men are presented—Blake's in the somewhat florid prose of the nineteenth century, which leads some critics to consider this work a parody of the period's journalistic style. Campenni, for one, believes the "novel-within-the-novel is a nearly perfect parody, [as] captivating as outrageous melodrama and [as] revealing as wishful psychodrama. Faust sustains the stilted rhythms and arrogant ideology of the Richard Harding Davis school of foreign correspondence while projecting [Benson's] longings for sex and danger."

In the opinion of *Commonweal* critic Stephen Kroll, *Foreign Devils* is the first time in which all of Faust's "themes and obsessions have been brought together." As in previous novels, *Foreign Devils* illustrates a fixation with the past. According to Christopher Lehmann-Haupt in the *New York Times*: "The more [Benson's] need for bygone history and the game of trivia becomes evident, and the longer it goes unexplained, the more we are forced to think about its meaning. The more we do so, the more we can sense the desperation with which both he and his creator are seeking an identity in history, even if only in the junk of history." In the end, apart from its "search for the self in the rubbish of mass culture," Campenni says this "tour de force" novel touches on such themes as "the American attempt to find a usable, acceptable past; the ethnic yearning to belong and the Jew's need to survive as a Jew; the wounded male ego in the turbulent city," and more. Not only does Faust intermingle several themes in his fourth novel, but, according to Campenni, Faust personally considers it his best-structured novel. Its structure allows Faust many literary freedoms, including the opportunity to experiment with very different writing styles when moving back and forth across the decades.

After *Foreign Devils*, Faust took it upon himself in his novel *A Star in the Family* to present the rise and fall of Jewish-American comic Bart Goldwine. Unfortunately, Faust's novel came out almost simultaneously with "Lenny," a movie about comedian Lenny Bruce. The critics identified Faust's protagonist with Bruce and essentially ignored the book. "Very clearly my man was not Lenny. . . ," Faust told Bruccoli. "My comic was the all-American straight Jewish-American kid who stood for all the old-fashioned virtues and was the stand-up comic who is perhaps best represented by people like Jerry Lester[,] . . . Morey Amsterdam, a little of Berle, perhaps. . . . And, of course, what I was trying to do was to show the rise and fall of this nation of the last forty years, using as a vehicle the most vulnerable kind of person in our society—somebody whose business it is to try and stand up and make people laugh. In my judgment, after 1963 there wasn't a hell of a lot to laugh about in America."

A Star in the Family is a biography of Goldwine, containing interviews with people who had known Goldwine as well as the comedian's own words. Because the story is told by a multitude of persons, its structure is what Boken considers "fractured and disjunctive. . . . Its disjunctive style makes the reader leap from time present to World War II and back again as Goldwine shuttles between that which was and that which is now with his biographer, the fractured structure mirroring the emotional breakdown of the comic." "That which was" included Goldwine's Hollywood stardom, his performances in movies, on radio, and on television. "That which is now" is, according to Boken, Goldwine "look[ing] back on his life with a masked cynicism of one who is aware of his final failure and who shrouds his self-hatred with wry wit." In the novel's chronicling of Goldwine's rise and fall, Boken finds a "coalescing in the gold and the wine of the Kennedy days when Americans felt charmed and warmed by the White House and, like their president, could laugh easily." But, as Faust notes in his interview with Bruccoli, Kennedy was assassinated and the implications behind America as superpower were "not a hell of a lot to laugh about."

Campenni claims Faust has not been entirely successful in paralleling the rise and fall of Goldwine with that of the United States before and after President Kennedy's assassination. Rather, "the strength of the novel lies mainly in the character of Goldwine. . . . He cares about his family and his country in a way that Faust makes us feel is redeeming, old-fashioned and, presumably, disappearing." Whereas *New York Times Book Review* commentator Gilbert Millstein claims he was not moved in any way by Faust's fifth novel—"I wanted to smell the flop sweat on Bart Goldwine and to feel his exaltation when an audience succumbed to him. And to know why. But I did not feel, and I do not know why. And I regret it."— Lingeman remarks that Faust's "sense of the past as tributary to the present, his deep feeling for family ties expanding into ties to large entities of city and country, his underlying sadness in whatever promise it is that isn't quite working out for us any more leave a touching after-resonance. There is something savingly likable about [Goldwine]—and . . . Faust as a writer."

Some reviewers question why Faust is not better known as one of the literary scene's urban wits. According to Herbert Gold in his *New York Times Book Review* assessment of Faust's second story collection, *The Year of the Hot Jock and Other Stories*, "perhaps a certain ornery going his own way is the most substantial [reason]." Gold suggests that Faust's insistence on advertising on his dust jackets his position as guidance director of a New York high school might be partly responsible. Nevertheless, Gold considers Faust "one of the finer, more dogged American writers, absolutely unconcerned with any 'career planning' on his behalf, unmoved by the winds of fashion." As for Boken, "the hallmarks of Faust's writing are many. . . . Above all, his characters are survivors. . . . [They] do not build empires, but they fight wars, report on them, teach the country's young, record America, dream the American dream that never was. . . . [And] Faust, somewhat like Dr. Faustus, commands the historical moment to stay and be meaningful, to blend that which was heroic with the present moment to make it not only fulfilling but also touched with dynamic possibilities."

MEDIA ADAPTATIONS: The Steagle was made into a movie of the same title, starring Richard Benjamin, by Avco Embassy in 1971.

AVOCATIONAL INTERESTS: Yoga, jogging, bicycling.

BIOGRAPHICAL/CRITICAL SOURCES:

BOOKS

Contemporary Literary Criticism, Volume 8, Gale, 1978.
Conversations with Writers II, Gale, 1978.
Dictionary of Literary Biography, Gale, Volume 2: *American Novelists since World War II*, 1978, Volume 28: *Twentieth-Century American Jewish Fiction Writers*, 1984.
Dictionary of Literary Biography Yearbook, 1980, Gale, 1981.

PERIODICALS

Books of the Times, June, 1980.
Book World, September 5, 1971.
Commonweal, October 28, 1966, December 2, 1966, August 24, 1973.
Library Journal, August, 1971, May 15, 1973.
Los Angeles Times, August 6, 1980.
New Republic, January 30, 1965, July 16, 1966, September 11, 1971, June 9, 1973.
Newsday, June 18, 1980.
New York Review of Books, April 8, 1965, August 13, 1980.
New York Times, January 30, 1965, July 11, 1966, July 6, 1970, August 30, 1971, July 11, 1973, July 3, 1975, April 8, 1980.
New York Times Book Review, March 7, 1965, July 17, 1966, June 28, 1970, August 29, 1971, May 20, 1973, March 30, 1975, April 13, 1980, July 14, 1985.
Saturday Review, January 23, 1965, July 16, 1966, September 11, 1971.

—*Sketch by Cheryl Gottler*

*   *   *

FEDIN, Konstantin A(lexandrovich)   1892-1977

PERSONAL: Born February 27, 1892, in Saratov, Russia (now U.S.S.R.); died July 15, 1977, in the U.S.S.R. *Education:* Attended Moscow Commercial Institute.

ADDRESSES: Office—U.S.S.R. Writers' Union, 52 Ul. Vorovskogo, Moscow, U.S.S.R.

CAREER: Interned in Germany, 1914-18; employed by Commissariat of Education; editor, journalist and war correspondent during Russian civil war; full-time writer, 1921-77. Deputy to U.S.S.R. Supreme Soviet. *Military service:* Served in Red Army in Leningrad, 1919.

MEMBER: Writers' Union of U.S.S.R. (first secretary, 1959-71; chairman, 1971-77), Union of Soviet Writers (member of Secretariat, 1953-77), U.S.S.R. Academy of Sciences, Soviet-German Cultural and Friendship Society (chairman), Deutsche Akademie der Kuenste, Moscow Union of Soviet Writers (chairman, 1955-59).

AWARDS, HONORS: Named Hero of Socialist Labor, 1967; received Order of Lenin and Order of Red Banner of Labor; honorary doctorate from Humbolt University; awarded Silver Medal of World Peace Council.

WRITINGS:

IN ENGLISH TRANSLATION

Goroda i gody, [Moscow], 1924, reprinted, Sovetskai Rossila, 1982, translation by Michael Scammell published as *Cities and Years*, Dell, 1962.
Sanatorii Arktur, [Moscow], 1940, reprinted, 1983, translation by O. Shartse published as *Sanitorium Arktur*, Foreign Languages Publishing (Moscow), 1957.

Pervye radosti (first volume of historical trilogy), [Moscow], 1944, reprinted, 1982, translation by Hilda Kazanina published as *Early Joys*, Foreign Languages Publishing, 1948, Progress Publishers, 1967.
Neobyknovennoe leto (second volume of historical trilogy), [Moscow], 1949, reprinted, 1984, translation by Margaret Wettlin published as *No Ordinary Summer: A Novel*, Foreign Languages Publishing, 1950.
Koster (third volume of historical trilogy; translated in part as "The Bonfire"), [Moscow], 1962, reprinted, 1985.
(With others) *Maxim Gorky, Vladimir Mayakovsky, Alexei Tolstoy, Konstantin Fedin on the Art and Craft of Writing*, translated by Alex Miller, Progress Publishers (Moscow), 1972.

Work represented in anthologies, including *Great Soviet Short Stories*, 1962, *Soviet Literature 1 and 2*, 1962, and *Soviet Literature 8*, 1965. Contributor to *Atlantic* and other periodicals.

IN RUSSIAN

Pustyr (stories; title means "The Wasteland"), [Moscow], 1923.
Bakunin v Drezdene (selections), 1928, [Moscow], 1982.
Brat'ia (title means "The Brothers"), [Moscow], 1928, reprinted, 1983.
Pokhishchenie Evropy (also see below; title means "The Rape of Europa"), two volumes, 1933, 1935, reprinted, [Moscow], 1983.
Povesti i rasskazy, [Moscow], 1936.
Gor'kii sredi nas (title means "Gorky among Us"), two volumes, [Moscow], 1943-44, reprinted in one volume, 1977.
Mal'chiki (booklet), [Moscow], 1944.
Izbrannye proizvedeniia, [Moscow], 1947.
Carp (booklet), edited by G. A. Birkett, Oxford University Press, 1950, reprinted, Irvington, 1966.
IA byl akterom, [Moscow], 1956.
Pisatel, iskusstvo, vremia (essays), [Moscow], 1957, 3rd edition, 1973.
Fedin und Deutschland, Aufbau-Verlag, 1962.
Kak my pishem, [Moscow], 1966.
Malenkie romany, povesti, rasskazy, [Moscow], 1975.
(Contributor) *Slovo k molodym*, [Moscow], 1975.
Pravda o pravakh cheloveka, [Moscow], 1977.
Koster: Kniga vtoraia, [Moscow], 1985.

Also author of *Anna Timofsevna*, 1922, *Narovcatskaja chronika*, 1926, *Transvaal* (stories), 1927, *Ispytanie*, 1942, *Davno i nedavno*, 1947, *Rasskazy mnogikh let*, 1957, and *Sobranie sochinenii* (ten-volume collected works), 1972. Contributor to *Novy Satirikon* and other periodicals. The first chapter of the second book of *Koster* has been recorded on disc by the author.

SIDELIGHTS: Martin Weil discussed Konstantin A. Fedin's contribution to Soviet literature: "While living under a system not known for fostering artistic freedom, [Fedin] succeeded in creating works of widely recognized artistic merit. . . . While evincing the optimism about Soviet life that characterized members of [the] officially approved school [of Soviet Realism], Mr. Fedin avoided the sentimentalism and woodenly simplistic psychology that plagued the work of many of them."

OBITUARIES:

PERIODICALS

New York Times, July 18, 1977.
Washington Post, July 18, 1977.*

FERRER, Aldo 1927-

PERSONAL: Born April 15, 1927, in Buenos Aires, Argentina; son of Antonio and Isabel (Agretti) Ferrer; married Susana Lustig (a physician and psychoanalyst), December 23, 1958; children: Carmen, Amparo, Lucinda. *Education:* University of Buenos Aires, Dr.Econ., 1949.

ADDRESSES: Home—Libertador 1750, Buenos Aires, Argentina.

CAREER: United Nations Secretariat, New York, N.Y., economist, 1950-53; Argentine Embassy, London, England, economic counselor, 1956-57; Province of Buenos Aires, Buenos Aires, Argentina, minister of economics, 1958-60; University of Buenos Aires, Buenos Aires, professor of economics, 1963-66; National Government of Argentina, Buenos Aires, minister of works and public services, 1970, minister of economy and labour, 1970-71; Bank of the Province of Buenos Aires, Buenos Aires, president, 1983-87; University of Buenos Aires, professor of economics, 1987—. Member of panel of experts, Inter-American Committee of Alliance for Progress, 1967-70; member of South Commission, Geneva; executive secretary, Latin American Social Science Council, 1967-70.

MEMBER: National Academy of Economic Sciences of Argentina.

WRITINGS:

El Estado y el desarrollo economico, Editorial Raigal, 1956.
La economia argentina: Las etapas de su desarrollo y problemas actuales, Fondo de Cultura Economica Mexico, 1963, 15th edition, 1982, translation by Marjory M. Urquidi published as *The Argentine Economy,* University of California Press, 1967.
Industrialization in Argentina and Australia: A Comparative Study, Centro de Investigaciones Economicas, Instituto Torcuatodi Tilla, 1966.
Desarrollo sin dependencia, Quadrante Latino, 1974.
Tecnologia y politica economica en America Latina, [Buenos Aires], 1974.
Economia internacional contemporanea: Texto para latino-americanos, Fondo de Cultura Economica, 1976.
Crisis y alternativas de la politica economica argentina, Fondo de Cultura Economica, 1977, 2nd edition, 1981.
(Contributor) *America Latina y el sistema internacional,* Montvideo Centro Latinoamericano de Economica Humana, 1979.
La posguena, El Cid (Buenos Aires), 1982.
Puede Argentina pagar su deuda externa?, El Cid, 1982.
Nacionalismo y orden constitucional, Fondo de Cultura Economica, 2nd edition, 1983.
Vivir con lo nuestro, El Cid, 1983, translation by M.I. Alvarez and N. Caistor published as *Living within Our Own Means,* Westview, 1985.
Poner la casa en orden, El Cid, 1984.
El pais nuestro de cada dia, Hyspamerica (Buenos Aires), 1985.

Also author of numerous published papers.

*   *   *

FIGUEROA, Loida
See FIGUEROA-MERCADO, Loida

FIGUEROA-MERCADO, Loida 1917-
(Loida Figueroa)

PERSONAL: Born October 6, 1917, in Yauco, P.R.; daughter of Agustin (a cane cutter) and Emeteria (Mercado) Figueroa; married third husband, Jose Nelson Castro, November 14, 1953 (divorced, 1957); children: Eunice, Maria Antonia, Rebeca, Avaris (daughters). *Education:* Polytechnic Institute, San German, P.R., B.A. (magna cum laude), 1941; Columbia University, M.A., 1952; Universidad Central de Madrid, Ph.D., 1963. *Politics:* "Independentist." *Religion:* Protestant.

ADDRESSES: Home—Box 456, San Antonio, Aguadilla, P.R. 00752.

CAREER: Teacher in elementary and high schools, 1942-57; Guanica High School, Guanica, P.R., acting principal, 1947, 1955; University of Puerto Rico, Mayaguez, professor of Puerto Rican history, 1957-74; Brooklyn College of the City University of New York, Brooklyn, N.Y., professor of Puerto Rican history, 1974-77. Writer and lecturer.

MEMBER: PEN, Associacion Historica Puertorriquena, Association of Caribbean Historians, Associacion de Historiadores Latinoamericanos y del Caribe, Sociedad de Autores Puertorriquenos, Club de Puerto Rico, National Audubon Society, Phi Alpha Theta.

AWARDS, HONORS: Yale University fellow, 1975.

WRITINGS:

Acridulces (poems), Rodriquez Lugo, 1947.
Arenales (novel), Ediciones Rumbos, 1961, 2nd edition, 1985.
Breve Historia de Puerto Rico, Editorial Edil, Volume 1: *Desde sus comienzos hasta 1800,* 1968, Volume 2: *Desde 1800 a 1892,* 1969, 4th edition of Volumes 1 and 2 published together as *Breve Historia de Puerto Rico,* Part 1, 1971, Part 2: *Desde 1892-1900,* 1976, translation of Part 1 published as *History of Puerto Rico from the Beginning to 1892,* Anaya Book Co., 1972.
Tres puntos claves: Lares, idioma, soberania, Editorial Edil, 1972.
La Histografia de Puerto Rico, Ediciones Paraninfo (Madrid), 1975.
El Caso de Puerto Rico a nivel international, Editorial Edil, 1980.
(Biographical editor) Emilio Godinez Sosa, editor, *Hostos, ensayos ineditos* (booklet), Editorial Edil, 1987.
(With Vicente Reynal) *Biografias de hombres y mujeres ilustres de Puerto Rico,* Editorial Edil, 1988.
(With Jim Blaut) *La cuestion nacional y el colonialismo,* Editorial Claridad, 1988.

Contributor to *Revista de Historia.* Editor of *Atenea* (journal).

WORK IN PROGRESS: Mesa revuelta, an essay anthology (includes "Una Isla en el mar de los caribes" and "Conociendo a Vieques," a travel chronicle).

SDIELIGHTS: Loida Figueroa-Mercado once told *CA:* "A speech by the late Juan B. Soto, Chancellor of the University of Puerto Rico, given during my high school commencement exercises in 1934 induced me to change my purpose to be a nurse, prompting me instead to continue studying all the way to Ph.D. The aim was attained in 1963.

"I wrote poems when I was young, but I have abandoned this genre since 1958. I have written one novel, but others rumble in my brain. I cannot direct my pen to write them on account of my involvement in historical writings. I have continued in this track because the majority of our people do not know their own history, and historians in Puerto Rico are few.''

She added: ''I began to write *Breve Historia de Puerto Rico* (not so brief now) because there was no adequate textbook for the course I was asked to teach in the University. I continued writing it and will continue again soon, because even persons on the street ask me when I am going to publish the next volume.''

* * *

FINE, Elsa Honig 1930-

PERSONAL: Born May 24, 1930, in Bayonne, N.J.; daughter of Samuel M. (a lawyer) and Yetta (Suskind) Honig; married Harold J. Fine (a psychologist), December 23, 1951; children: Erika Susan, Amy Minna. *Education:* Syracuse University, B.F.A., 1951; Temple University, M.Ed. in Art, 1967; University of Tennessee, Ed.D., 1971.

ADDRESSES: Home—7008 Sherwood Dr., Knoxville, Tenn. 37919. *Office*—Department of Art, Knoxville College, Knoxville, Tenn. 37921.

CAREER: Writer. Knoxville College, Knoxville, Tenn., assistant professor of art, 1971-75. Currently editor, *Woman's Art Journal*.

MEMBER: College Art Association, Women's Caucus for Art, Southeastern Women's Caucus for Art.

WRITINGS:

The Afro-American Artist: A Search for Identity, Holt, 1973, reprinted, Hacker Art Books, 1987.
Women and Art: A History of Women Painters and Sculptors from the Renaissance to the 20th Century, Allanheld & Schram/Prior, 1978.
(Editor) *Women's Studies and the Arts*, Women's Caucus for Art, 1978, revised edition, 1980.

Also contributor to *Feminist Collage: Educating Women in the Visual Arts*, edited by Judy Loeb.

WORK IN PROGRESS: Kathe Kollwitz: A Self-Portrait.

* * *

FISK, Nicholas 1923-

PERSONAL: Born October 14, 1923, in London, England; married Dorothy Antoinette, 1949; children: Moyra and Nicola (twins), Steven, Christopher. *Education:* Educated in private secondary school in Sussex, England.

ADDRESSES: Home—59 Elstree Rd., Bushey Heath, Hertfordshire WD2 3QX, England. *Agent*—Laura Cecil, 17 Alwyne Villas, Canonbury, London N1 2HG, England.

CAREER: Writer and illustrator. Former advertising creative director, head of creative groups, and consultant. Has worked as an actor, publisher, musician, and speaker, to children and adults. *Military service:* Royal Air Force.

MEMBER: Savile Club.

WRITINGS:

Look at Cars (self-illustrated juvenile), Hamish Hamilton, 1959, revised edition, Panther, 1970.

(Illustrator) Philip Joubert, *Look at Aircraft*, Hamish Hamilton, 1960.
Look at Newspapers (juvenile), Hamish Hamilton, 1962.
The Young Man's Guide to Advertising, Hamish Hamilton, 1963.
Cars, Parrish, 1963.
The Bouncers (self-illustrated), Hamish Hamilton, 1964
The Fast Green Car, illustrations by Bernard Wragg, Hamish Hamilton, 1965.
Making Music, Crescendo, 1966.
There's Something on the Roof, illustrations by Dugald Macdougall, Hamish Hamilton, 1966.
Space Hostages (juvenile), Hamish Hamilton, 1967, Macmillan, 1969.
(With Raymond Briggs) *Lindbergh the Lone Flier* (juvenile), illustrations by Briggs, Coward, 1968.
Richthofen the Red Baron, illustrations by Briggs, Hamish Hamilton, 1968.
(Editor and contributor of photographs) Eric Fenby, *Menuhin's House of Music*, Icon Books, 1970.
Trillions (juvenile), Hamish Hamilton, 1971, Pantheon, 1973.
Grinny (juvenile science fiction), Heinemann, 1973.
High Way Home, Hamish Hamilton, 1973.
(Illustrator) W. Mayne, *Skiffy*, Hamish Hamilton, 1973.
Der Ballon, Junior Press (Germany), 1974.
(With Carol Barker) *Emma Borrows a Cup of Sugar* (juvenile), Heinemann, 1974.
Little Green Spaceman, illustrations by Trevor Stubley, Heinemann, 1974.
(Contributor) Edward Blishen, editor, *The Thorny Paradise* (juvenile anthology), Viking Kestrel, 1975.
The Witches of Wimmering, illustrations by Stubley, Pelham Books, 1976.
Time Trap, Gollancz, 1976.
Wheelie in the Stars, Heinemann, 1976.
Escape from Splatterbang, Pelham Books, 1977, Macmillan, 1978, published as *Flamers*, Knight, 1979.
Antigrav, Viking Kestrel, 1978.
(Contributor) D. J. Denney, editor, *Young Winter's Tales*, Macmillan (London), 1978.
Monster Maker, Pelham Books, 1979, Macmillan, 1980.
Leadfoot, Pelham Books, 1980.
A Rag, a Bone and a Hank of Hair, Viking Kestrel, 1980.
Robot Revolt, Pelham Books, 1981.
Sweets from a Stranger and Other SF Stories, illustrations by David Barlow, Viking Kestrel, 1982.
Snatched, Hodder and Stoughton, 1983.
You Remember Me!, Viking Kestrel, 1983, G. K. Hall, 1987.
Bonkers Clocks, illustrations by Colin West, Kestrel, 1984.
On the Flip Side, Viking, 1985.
(Contributor) Dennis Pepper, editor, *An Oxford Book of Christmas Stories*, Oxford University Press, 1986.
(Contributor) *I Like This Story*, Puffin, 1986.
Dark Sun, Bright Sun, illustrations by Brigid Marlin, Blackie, 1987.
Living Fire (short stories), Corgi, 1987.
Mindbenders, Viking Kestrel, 1987.
(Contributor) Mick Gowar, editor, *Twisted Circuits*, Beaver Books, 1987.
Backlash, Walker Books, 1988.
(Contributor) Gowar, editor, *Electric Heroes*, Bodley Head, 1988.
The Talking Car, illustrations by Ann John, Macdonald, 1988.
The Telly's Watching You!, Macdonald, 1989.

STARSTORMER SAGA

Starstormers, Knight, 1980.
Sunburst, Knight, 1980.
Catfang, Knight, 1981.
Evil Eye, Knight, 1982.
Volcano, Knight, 1985.

OTHER

Also writer for television. Author of cassettes. General editor of "Hamish Hamilton Monographs," Hamish Hamilton, 1964. Contributor, "Take Part" series, Ward Lock, 1977. Contributor to *Junior Pears Encylopaedia*. Contributor of articles and science fiction stories to magazines.

WORK IN PROGRESS: Children's novels and collected short stories; television scripts.

SIDELIGHTS: Nicholas Fisk told *CA:* "I cannot escape the buzzword 'communications.' [While] my main interest lies in writing books for children, I am also an illustrator and photographer and often an impresario of adult printed works. But, increasingly, writing for children dominates. They have wide, generous minds. They are quick to accept and master a computer or a new skill, and, similarly, quick to accept such premises as domestic robots, dual existences, alien worlds, [or] a viciously inclined teddy bear. Children no longer form a separate tribe. They live among adults and share adult amusements and preoccupations. They are separated only by size, experience, and power to command. So I like my readers, and like the tautness and pace of children's books. Of course I write for TV, but books are what matter to me, so books are my main products."

"Nicholas Fisk keeps his readers guessing," writes a *Times Literary Supplement* reviewer. "All one can forecast with confidence is that his next [book] will be stimulating and startlingly original." Gillian Cross, also writing in the *Times Literary Supplement*, states that Fisk "has a gift for combining the fantastic with the down-to-earth. In books like *Grinny* and *Trillions*, the interest comes not merely from the central events, but also from the effect of those events on recognizable characters."

Similarly, another *Times Literary Supplement* critic comments on the tale of *Grinny*, a metal and plastic alien who invades an ordinary middle-class household. "[While] the materials of the story . . . are commonplace, the treatment [is] startlingly original and in parts downright nasty. . . . Fisk—a master in this genre—makes the fantasy of his invention horribly real by putting it into an everyday contemporary setting."

BIOGRAPHICAL/CRITICAL SOURCES:

BOOKS

Blishen, Edward, editor, *The Thorny Paradise*, Pelham Books, 1975.

PERIODICALS

Times Literary Supplement, April 6, 1973, June 15, 1973, December 10, 1976, July 7, 1978.

*　　　*　　　*

FOON, Dennis   1951-

PERSONAL: Born November 18, 1951, in Detroit, Mich.; son of Alvin Nathan (in business) and Shirley (a teacher; maiden name, Weiss) Foon; married Jane Howard Baker, May 2, 1975

(divorced June, 1982); children: Rebecca Howard. *Education:* University of Michigan, B.A. (with honors), 1973; University of British Columbia, M.F.A., 1975.

ADDRESSES: Home—647 East 12th Ave., Vancouver, British Columbia, Canada V5T 2H7. *Agent*—Great North Artists Management, 350 Dupont St., Toronto, Ontario, Canada M5R 1V9 (for adult plays and media); Green Thumb Theatre, 1885 Venables, Vancouver, British Columbia, Canada V5L 2H6 (for plays for young people).

CAREER: University of British Columbia, Centre for Continuing Education, Vancouver, instructor in playwriting, 1974-79; Green Thumb Theatre for Young People, Vancouver, co-founder and artistic director, 1975-88. Playwright in residence at Young People's Theatre, Toronto, 1983-84. Lecturer and workshop director. Consultant to Canada Council, Provincial Educational Media Centre, and National Film Board of Canada.

MEMBER: International Association of Children's Theatre (vice-president, 1979-82), Professional Association of Canadian Theatres (member of board, 1978-79), Composers, Authors, and Publishers Association of Canada, Performing Artists for Nuclear Disarmament.

AWARDS, HONORS: Avery Hopwood Award, University of Michigan, 1972, for story "The Quivering Scarecrow Flinch"; *Writer's Digest* Award, 1973, for story "Putting It to Linda on a Sunday Afternoon"; Jesse Awards for best production for young audiences, Vancouver Theatre Awards, 1984, for directing "One Thousand Cranes," 1985, for directing "Not So Dumb," 1986, for directing "Skin," and 1987, for directing "Night Light"; CBC Literary Award, 1985, for *The Short Tree and the Bird That Could Not Sing;* British Theatre Award for best production for young adults, 1986, for "Invisible Kids"; Chalmers Award for best children's play, 1987, for "Skin."

WRITINGS:

PUBLISHED PLAYS

The Last Days of Paul Bunyan (one-act), Playwrights Canada, 1977.
The Windigo (one-act; first produced in Vancouver, British Columbia, at Green Thumb Theatre, May 1977), Talonbooks, 1978.
Raft Baby (one-act; first produced at Green Thumb Theatre, March 25, 1978), Talonbooks, 1978.
Heracles (one-act; first produced on tour in British Columbia and Alberta by Axis Mime Theatre and Green Thumb Theatre, May 22, 1978), Talonbooks, 1978.
New Canadian Kid (one-act; first produced on tour in British Columbia by Green Thumb Theatre, October, 1981; also see below), Pulp Press, 1982.
The Hunchback of Notre Dame (adapted from the novel by Victor Hugo; two-act; first produced at Vancouver Playhouse Mainstage, November, 1981), Playwrights Canada, 1983.
"Trummi Kaput" (adapted from the German play by Volker Ludwig; two-act; produced on tour in Canada by Grips Theatre, Berlin, and Green Thumb Theatre, May, 1982), published in *Canadian Theatre Review*, May, 1983.
Skin [and] *Liars* ("Skin" first produced at Project One, Vancouver, 1984; "Liars" first produced by Green Thumb Theatre, 1986), Playwrights Canada, 1988.

New Canadian Kid [and] *Invisible Kids* ("Invisible Kids" first produced at Unicorn Theatre, London, England, 1985), Pulp Press, 1989.

UNPUBLISHED PLAYS

"Peach" (one-act), first produced at Vancouver East Cultural Centre, April 28, 1976.

(Co-creator) "Hotsy Totsy," first produced at Arts Club Theatre, 1978.

"La Malice, Voyageur" (one-act), first produced at Green Thumb Theatre, May, 1979.

"Dr. Smyrichinsky's Brother" (two-act), first produced in Montreal, Quebec, at Montreal Playwright's Workshop, May, 1982.

"Children's Eyes" (monologue), first produced in Vancouver at New Play Centre, March, 1983.

"Afternoon Tea," first produced at New Play Centre, 1986.

"Bedtimes and Bullies" (adaptation of Ludwig's play), first produced by Young People's Theatre, 1987.

"ZAYDOK: A Comedy for Adults," first produced at New Play Centre by Touchstone Theatre, October, 1987.

"Mirror Game," produced at La Quinzaine International Theatre Festival, Quebec City, by Green Thumb Theatre, 1988.

OTHER

(Contributor) Cathy Ford, editor, *The Canadian Short Fiction Anthology,* Intermedia Press, 1976.

(With Judith Mastai, Brian Thorpe, Fran Gebhard, and Wendy Van Reisen) "Feeling Yes, Feeling No: A Child Sexual Abuse Prevention Program," produced by Green Thumb Theatre, 1982.

(With Brenda Wright) *Am I the Only One? A Child's Book on Sexual Abuse,* Douglas & McIntyre, 1985.

"Differences," National Film Board of Canada, 1986.

The Short Tree and the Bird That Could Not Sing (Book-of-the-Month Club selection), illustrated by John Bianchi, Groundwood, 1986.

"Wheels" (television drama), Canadian Broadcasting Corp. (CBC-TV), 1987.

"Boogeymen" (television drama), CBC-TV, 1987.

Also author of "Loss," a television drama commissioned by KCTS, and of "Baby," a television drama for CBC-TV. Contributor of articles, fiction, and poems to periodicals, including *GRAIN, Afterthoughts,* and *ANON.*

SIDELIGHTS: Dennis Foon told *CA:* "Over the last eight years I have been deeply involved in child advocacy theatre, writing and/or directing plays for the young that help give them some tools to better cope with a complex and confusing world. This work with Green Thumb Theatre has taken me across North America and Europe and has led to a number of international collaborations."

MEDIA ADAPTATIONS: "Feeling Yes, Feeling No" has been produced on film by the National Film Board of Canada. "Skin," was filmed by Intercom Films in 1988. "New Canadian Kid" was produced as a videoplay by Hy Perspectives Media Production in 1982, and "Invisible Kids" was produced in the same format by Winnipeg Videon in 1987. "La Malice, Voyageur" was produced for radio by the Provincial Educational Media Centre, Vancouver, British Columbia, in March, 1979, and "Children's Eyes" was broadcast on CBC Radio's "Vanishing Point" series in December, 1985.

BIOGRAPHICAL/CRITICAL SOURCES:

PERIODICALS

Canadian Theatre Review, spring, 1983.

Chimo!, September, 1982.
Montreal Sunday Express, July 11, 1982.
Vancouver Sun, November 29, 1983.

*　　　*　　　*

FORBES, Malcolm S(tevenson) 1919-

PERSONAL: Born August 19, 1919, in Brooklyn, N.Y.; son of Bertie Charles (an editor and publisher) and Adelaide (Stevenson) Forbes; married Roberta Remsen Laidlaw, September 21, 1946 (divorced, 1985); children: Malcolm S., Jr., Robert Laidlaw, Christopher Charles, Timothy Carter, Moira Hamilton. *Education:* Woodrow Wilson School of Public and International Affairs, Princeton University, A.B., 1941. *Politics:* Republican. *Religion:* Episcopalian.

ADDRESSES: Home—Timberfield, Old Dutch Rd., Far Hills, N.J. 07931. *Office*—Forbes Bldg., 60 Fifth Ave., New York, N.Y. 10011.

CAREER: Fairfield Times (weekly newspaper), Lancaster, Ohio, owner and publisher, 1941-42; *Lancaster Tribune* (weekly newspaper), Lancaster, owner and publisher, 1942; *Forbes* magazine, New York City, associate publisher, 1946-54, publisher, 1954-60, editor, 1954-57, editor in chief, 1957—; Forbes Inc., New York City, vice-president, 1947-64, president, 1964—. Founder of *Nation's Heritage* (bimonthly historical magazine), 1948. Chief executive officer, Forbes International, Inc., Investors Advisory Institute, Forbes Trinchera, Inc., Forbes Europe, Inc., Fiji Forbes, and Sangre de Cristo Ranchers, Inc.; chairman of the board, 60 Fifth Avenue Corp. Bernardsville Borough councilman, 1949-51; New Jersey state senator, 1951-58; founder and chairman, New Jersey Ike-Nixon clubs, 1951; unsuccessful Republican candidate for governor of New Jersey, 1957; delegate-at-large to Republican National Convention, 1960. Vestryman, St. John's-on-the-Mountain Episcopal Church, 1948-65; member of board of advisors, Naval War College, 1975-77; trustee, St. Mark's School, 1976-80; director, Coast Guard Academy Foundation, 1976—; chairman, New Jersey Rhodes Scholarship Committee, 1976, 1978, and 1979; member of board of trustees, Princeton University, 1982-86. Founder of the world's first balloon museum, located at the Forbes-owned Chateau de Balleroy in Normandy, France. *Military service:* U.S. Army, 1942-45; became staff sergeant; received Bronze Star and Purple Heart.

MEMBER: International Balloonists Association, International Society of Balloonpost Specialists, National Aeronautic Association of the United States of America (member of board of directors, 1975—; executive vice-president, 1976—), Balloon Federation of America (member of board of directors, 1974-76), Lighter Than Air Society, British Balloon and Airship Club, New Jersey Historical Society, St. Andrew's Society, Newcomen Society, Essex Fox Hounds, New York Yacht Club, New York Racquet and Tennis Club, Staniel Cay Yacht Club, Jockey Club, Explorers Club, Links, Pilgrims of the United States.

AWARDS, HONORS: Freedom Foundation Medal, 1949; Harmon Trophy for aeronaut of the year, 1975; Forbes was named Paramount Chief of the Nimba Tribe of Liberia in 1976; Eaton Corporation award for business spokesmanship, International Platform Association, 1979; American Image Award ("Adam") for Business and Industry, Men's Fashion Association of America, 1979; University of Southern California Journalism Alumni Association distinguished achievement award in periodical journalism, 1979; French Order of Merit, 1980; Columbia University Business School award for business leadership, 1980; Man of Conscience Award, Appeal of Conscience Foundation, 1980; Franklin Award for distinguished service, Printing Industries of Metropolitan New York, 1981; Commander of the Order of Ouissam Alaoyite, presented by King Hassan II of Morocco, 1981; Sacred Cat Award, Milwaukee Press Club, 1981; Yale Management School award for entrepreneurial excellence, 1982; "Superstar of the Year," Police Athletic League, 1982; Gentleman's Quarterly Manstyle Award, 1983; President's Medal of Achievement, presented by President Zia ul-Haq of Pakistan, 1983; 33rd Annual Enterprise Award, Area Council for Economic Education in Philadelphia, 1983; Communicator of the Year, Business/Professional Advertising Association, 1983; Community Service Award, Greenwich Village Chamber of Commerce, 1983. Forbes has received twenty-five honorary degrees from various colleges and universities, including the American Graduate School of International Management, Pace University, Ball State University, Ohio University, University of Vermont, University of Colorado, and University of Denver.

WRITINGS:

Fact and Comment, Knopf, 1974.
The Sayings of Chairman Malcolm, Harper, 1978.
Around the World on Hot Air and Two Wheels, Simon & Schuster, 1985.
How to Use the Power of the Printed Word: Thirteen Articles Packed with Facts and Practical Information Designed to Help You Read Better, Write Better, Communicate Better, Anchor Press, 1985.
The Further Sayings of Chairman Malcolm, Harper, 1986.
(With Jeff Bloch) *They Went That-a-Way: How the Famous, the Infamous, and the Great Died*, Simon & Schuster, 1988.

Also author of "Fact and Comment" column in *Forbes*, 1950—.

SIDELIGHTS: "Not since antitrust spoilsports put the kibosh on the Gilded Age has an American capitalist reveled so openly in the pleasures that money can buy," says Arthur Lubow of *People* magazine about Malcolm S. Forbes. As editor in chief and sole stockholder of the magazine his father began and which now grosses over $10 million annually, Forbes has built up a private fortune which, though not the largest in the country, has provided him with the means to be perhaps the most flamboyant millionaire alive today. Over the years he has amassed collections of both monetary and historical worth, as well as collections that are for pure enjoyment, like his collection of approximately 75,000 toy soldiers, "the largest collection of military miniatures in the world," according to *Saturday Review* contributor Alice Hess. In addition to his miniatures, Forbes owns ten of the 53 famous bejeweled Faberge eggs (worth about $10 million), a collection of French military and Victorian paintings, a French chateau, one of the Fiji islands, 400 square miles of Colorado, and a yacht which is, as Christopher Buckley of the *Washington Post Book World* describes it, "large enough to invade the Falklands with."

Forbes takes any criticism of his extravagance in stride. Arthur Lubow captures this attitude by quoting the millionaire's anticipation of a reporter's question about the expense of his balloon trips: "What in hell has [ballooning] to do with a business magazine? The answer is, 'Nothing at all.' It's just for the fun-ness of it." His fascination with ballooning and motorcycling have led him to establish several firsts. He was the first balloonist to fly coast-to-coast in a single hot air balloon. While performing the feat in 1973, he set six world

records. Also in 1973, he founded the world's first balloon museum in Normandy, France. In October, 1982, Forbes was the first person to make a free flight in a hot air balloon over Peking. He also was the first to conduct a motorcycle tour of 1,600 miles (from Xian to Peking) of China. In April, 1983, he introduced ballooning to the Republic of Pakistan. These adventures, along with his extravagant nature, have made the magazine mogul one of the most talked about millionaires of our day. In addition, his book *They Went That-a-Way: How the Famous, the Infamous, and the Great Died* is drawing even more attention to Forbes by making the October, 1988, *New York Times Book Review* best seller list. A *Publishers Weekly* reviewer calls it an "undeniably fascinating" work, concluding that the "profiles are entertaining and informative." Whenever Forbes is asked what formula he used to become so successful, he frequently replies: "sheer ability (spelled i-n-h-e-r-i-t-a-n-c-e)."

AVOCATIONAL INTERESTS: Art collecting, motorcycling, ballooning, boating.

BIOGRAPHICAL/CRITICAL SOURCES:

PERIODICALS

Chicago Tribune, September 6, 1988, October 2, 1988.
People, July 19, 1982.
Publishers Weekly, May 6, 1988.
Saturday Review, August, 1980.
Washington Post, June 5, 1983.
Washington Post Book World, December 12, 1985.

*   *   *

FORD, D(ouglas) W(illiam) Cleverley
    See CLEVERLEY FORD, D(ouglas) W(illiam)

*   *   *

FORD, Elbur
    See HIBBERT, Eleanor Burford

*   *   *

FORNES, Maria Irene   1930-

PERSONAL: Born May 14, 1930, in Havana, Cuba; came to United States in 1945, naturalized in 1951; daughter of Carlos Luis (a public servant) and Carmen Hismenia (Collado) Fornes. *Education:* Attended Escuela Publica No. 12, Havana, Cuba. *Politics:* Democrat. *Religion:* Catholic.

ADDRESSES: Home—1 Sheridan Sq., New York, N.Y. 10014. *Agent*—Helen Merrill, 435 West 23rd St. #1A, New York, N.Y. 10011.

CAREER: Playwright, 1960—. Painter in Europe, 1954-57; textile designer in New York City, 1957-60. Director of her plays, including "The Successful Life of 3," "The Annunciation," "Molly's Dream," "Aurora," "Cap-a-Pie," "Fefu and Her Friends," "Washing," "Eyes on the Harem," "Evelyn Brown (A Diary)," "Life Is a Dream," "A Visit," "The Danube," "Abingdon Square," "Sarita," "Mud," "Cold Air," "The Conduct of Life," "A Matter of Faith," and "Lovers and Keepers." Founding member and president, New York Theatre Strategy, 1973-78. Teacher with Theatre for the New City, New York City, 1972-73, Padua Hills Festival, Claremont, Calif, 1978—, and INTAR (International Arts Relations), New York City, 1981—, and at numerous universities in the United States.

MEMBER: Dramatists Guild, ASCAP, League of Professional Theatre Women, Society of Stage Directors and Choreographers.

AWARDS, HONORS: John Hay Whitney Foundation fellowship, 1961; Centro Mexicano de Escritores fellowship, 1962; Obie Award (Off-Broadway theatre award) for distinguished playwriting (and direction), 1965, for "Promenade" and "The Successful Life of 3," 1977, for "Fefu and Her Friends," 1984, for "The Danube," "Mud," and "Sarita," and 1988, for "Abingdon Square"; Yale University fellowship, 1967, 1968; Cintas Foundation fellowship, 1967; Boston University-Tanglewood fellowship, 1968; Rockefeller Foundation grant, 1971, 1984; Guggenheim fellowship, 1972; Creative Artist Public Service grants, 1972, 1975; National Endowment for the Arts grants, 1974, 1984; Obie Award for distinguished direction, 1979, for "Eyes on the Harem"; Obie Award for sustained achievement, 1982; American Academy and Institute of Arts and Letters Award in Literature, 1985; Obie Award for best new play, 1985, for "The Conduct of Life"; Playwrights U.S.A. Award, 1986, for translation of "Cold Air."

WRITINGS:

PLAYS

"The Widow," published as "La Viuda" in *Cuatro Autores Cubanos,* Casa de las Americas (Havana), 1961.

"There! You Died," first produced in San Francisco at Actor's Workshop, November 19, 1963; produced under title "Tango Palace" (also see below) on double bill with "The Successful Life of 3" in Minneapolis at Firehouse Theatre, January 22, 1965; produced in New York City at Theatre Genesis, 1973.

"The Successful Life of 3" (also see below), first produced on double bill with "Tango Palace" in Minneapolis at Firehouse Theatre, January 22, 1965; produced Off-Broadway at Sheridan Square Playhouse, Theatre, March 15, 1965.

"Promenade" (musical; also see below), music by Al Carmines, first produced Off-Off Broadway at Judson Poets' Theatre, April 9, 1965; produced Off-Broadway at Promenade Theatre, June 4, 1969.

The Office (first produced on Broadway at Henry Miller's Theatre, April 21, 1966 [preview performances; never officially opened]), Establishment Theatre Co., 1965.

"A Vietnamese Wedding" (also see below), first produced in New York City at Washington Square Methodist Church, February 4, 1967; produced Off-Broadway at La Mama Experimental Theater, April 12, 1969.

"The Annunciation," first produced on double bill with "The Successful Life of 3" Off-Off Broadway at Judson Poets' Theater, May, 1967.

"Dr. Kheal" (also see below), first produced Off-Off Broadway at Judson Poets' Theater, April 3, 1968; produced in London, 1969.

"The Red Burning Light: or Mission XQ" (also see below), first produced in Zurich, Switzerland, for Open Theatre European Tour, June 19, 1968; produced Off-Off Broadway at La Mama Experimental Theatre, April 12, 1969.

"Molly's Dream" (also see below), music by Cosmos Savage, first produced Off-Off Broadway at New York Theatre Strategy, 1968.

Promenade and Other Plays (includes "Tango Palace," "The Successful Life of 3," "Promenade," "A Vietnamese Wedding," "Dr. Kheal," "The Red Burning Light: or Mission XQ3," and "Molly's Dream"), Winter House, 1971, reprinted, PAJ Publications, 1987.

"The Curse of the Langston House," first produced in Cincinnati at Playhouse in the Park, October, 1972.

"Aurora," first produced Off-Off Broadway at New York Theatre Strategy, 1974.

"Cap-a-Pie," music by Jose Raul Bernardo, first produced Off-Off Broadway at INTAR (International Arts Relations), May, 1975.

"Washing," first produced Off-Off Broadway at Theatre for the New City, November 11, 1976.

"Lolita in the Garden," first produced Off-Off Broadway at INTAR, 1977.

"Fefu and Her Friends," first produced Off-Off Broadway at New York Theatre Strategy, May 5, 1977; produced Off-Broadway at American Place Theater, January 6, 1978; published in *Wordplays 1,* PAJ Publications, 1981.

"In Service," first produced in Claremont, Calif., at the Padua Hills Festival, 1978.

"Eyes on the Harem," first produced Off-Off Broadway at INTAR, April 23, 1979.

"Evelyn Brown (A Diary)," first produced Off-Off Broadway at Theatre for the New City, April 3, 1980.

(Adaptor) Federico Garcia Lorca, "Blood Wedding," produced Off-Off Broadway at INTAR, May 15, 1980.

(Adaptor) Pedro Calderon de la Barca, "Life Is Dream," produced Off-Off Broadway at INTAR, May 28, 1981.

"A Visit," first produced at the Padua Hills Festival, 1981; produced Off-Off Broadway at Theatre for the New City, December 24, 1981.

"The Danube" (also see below), first produced at the Padua Hills Festival, 1982; produced Off-Off Broadway at Theatre for the New City, February 17, 1983; produced Off-Broadway at the American Place Theater, March 11, 1984.

"Mud" (also see below), first produced at the Padua Hills Festival, 1983; produced Off-Off Broadway at Theatre for the New City, November 10, 1983.

"Sarita" (musical; also see below), music by Leon Odenz, first produced Off-Off Broadway at INTAR, January 18, 1984.

"No Time," first produced at the Padua Hills Festival, 1984.

"The Conduct of Life" (also see below), first produced Off-Off Broadway at Theatre for the New City, February 21, 1985.

(Adaptor and translator) Virgilio Pinera, *Cold Air* (produced Off-Off Broadway at INTAR, March 27, 1985), Theatre Communications Group, 1985.

Maria Irene Fornes: Plays (includes "Mud," "The Danube," "Sarita," and "The Conduct of Life"), preface by Susan Sontag, PAJ Publications, 1986.

"A Matter of Faith," first produced Off-Off Broadway at Theatre for the New City, March 6, 1986.

Lovers and Keepers (three one-act musicals; music by Tito Puente and Fernando Rivas; first produced Off-Off Broadway at INTAR, April 4, 1986), Theatre Communications Group, 1987.

"Drowning" (adapted from Anton Chekhov's story of the same title; one act play; produced with six other one-act plays under collective title "Orchards"), first produced Off-Broadway at Lucille Lortel Theater, April 22, 1986; published in *Orchards,* Knopf, 1986.

"Art," first produced Off-Off Broadway at Theatre for the New City, 1986.

"The Mothers" (also see below), first produced at the Padua Hills Festival, 1986.

"Abingdon Square," first produced Off-Broadway at the American Place Theatre, 1987.

(Adaptor) Chekhov, "Uncle Vanya," produced Off-Broadway at Classic Stage Company, December, 1987.

"Hunger" (also see below), first produced Off-Off Broadway by En Garde Productions, 1989.

"And What of the Night" (includes "Hunger," "Springtime," "Lust," and "Charlie" [previously "The Mothers"]), first produced in Milwaukee, Wis., at Milwaukee Repertory, 1989.

SIDELIGHTS: "One would almost think," writes the *Chicago Tribune*'s Sid Smith, that playwright and director Maria Irene Fornes "was a hot young New York experimentalist—indeed, in a sense, she is and always will be. Her work spans decades, but she endures as a refreshing influence." Smith comments that although Fornes has won six "Obie" awards for her plays Off-Broadway, she is "one of the art form's most cherished secrets. Ask playgoers about her, and they are apt to answer with a blank look. Mention Fornes to those who work in the theater, and their faces light up." As Wynn Handman of the American Place Theatre told *New York*'s Ross Wetzsteon, "She's clearly among the top five playwrights in America today. [But] playwrights like Irene, whose work haunts and resonates rather than spelling everything out, almost never receive immediate recognition." Although they frequently deal with human and even "political" issues, "Fornes's plays are whimsical, gentle and bittersweet, and informed with her individualistic intelligence," state Bonnie Marranca in *American Playwrights: A Critical Survey*. "Virtually all of them have a characteristic delicacy, lightness of spirit, and economy of style. Fornes has always been interested in the emotional lives of her characters, so human relationships play a significant part in the plays." The critic adds that Fornes "apparently likes her characters, and often depicts them as innocent, pure spirits afloat in a corrupt world which is almost absurd rather than realistic. . . . Political consciousness is present in a refined way."

It is not Fornes's subjects, however, that make her work unconventional; as the playwright told Kathleen Betsko and Rachel Koenig in *Interviews with Contemporary Women Playwrights*, "I realized that what makes my plays unacceptable to people is the form more than the content. My content is usually not outrageous. . . What makes people vicious must be the form." This form is influenced by diverse factors, "neither theatre nor literature but certain styles of painting and the movies," notes Susan Sontag in her preface to *Maria Irene Fornes: Plays*. "But unlike similarly influenced New York dramatists, her work did not eventually become parasitic on literature (or opera, or movies). It was never a revolt against theatre, or a theatre recycling fantasies encoded in other genres." The critic continues by remarking that "Fornes is neither literary nor anti-literary. These are not cerebral exercises or puzzles but the real questions."

Fornes's first major critical success was "Promenade," a musical which first debuted in 1965 and contributed to her first Obie Award. "The play mixes wit and compassion, humor and tenderness, zaniness and social satire as prisoners named 105 and 106 journey from prison out into the world and back again," describes Phyllis Mael in a *Dictionary of Literary Biography* essay. While much of the play's action concerns the comic conflict between the prisoners and the rich and powerful people they meet, it is Fornes's lyrics that "comment on unrequited love, the abuse of power, the injustice of those who are supposed to uphold the law, and the illogical and

random nature of life," adds Mael. "In a work that is really more a choreographed oratorio than a conventional musical," comments Stephen Holden in the *New York Times*, "the music and language are reduced to artful basics, as in the Virgil Thomson-Gertrude Stein operas." Because of this lack of conventional plot, "there may be those who will question the slightness of the story line," maintains *New York Times* critic Clive Barnes, "but there will be more, many, many more who will glory in the show's dexterity, wit and compassion. Miss Fornes's lyrics, like her book, seem to have a sweetly irrelevant relevance." Marranca similarly observes that "*Promenade* has the joie de vivre, the disregard for external logic and spatial convention, the crazy-quilt characters that one associates with the plays of Gertrude Stein. . . . The satire seems almost effortless because the playwright's touch is so playful and laid back. Yet Fornes makes her point, and there's no confusion as to whose side she is on in this comedy of manners." As Barnes concludes in his review: "One definition of 'Promenade' might be that it is a protest musical for people too sophisticated to protest."

"Fefu and Her Friends," Fornes's next major success, ventures even farther into new dramatic forms. Set in one house where eight women are meeting, "the play has no plot in the conventional sense, and the characters are presented as fragments," remarks Marranca. "Though there is much about them that Fornes keeps hidden, the play—seeming at first like realism—is purposely set in the realm of the mysterious and abstract. By setting the play in a home, and then offering a narrative that subverts realistic conventions, Fornes plays ironically with domestic space, and the notion of domestic drama." The playwright presents a further innovation by having the audience separate and move out of the main theatre to view four separate scenes in different areas of the house. "[But] the conceit is more than just a gimmick," writes David Richards in the *Washington Post*. "Fornes, you see, is literally asking her audience to 'track down' her characters. . . . Theater-goers are being transformed into sleuths." The result of this fragmentation, claims Richard Eder in the *New York Times,* is that "'Fefu' is the dramatic equivalent of a collection of poems. Each conversation, each brief scene tries to capture an aspect of the central, anguished vision."

This reformation of traditional staging has disturbed some critics, however. Walter Kerr believes that there is too much emphasis on the structure of the play; he states in the *New York Times* that while "everyone finally gets to see every scene, though not in the same sequence . . . this does not matter for the play is not going anywhere; *you* are." The critic also comments that "if I lasted as long as I did, it was because I kept hoping during my constant journeyings that I *might* find a play in the very next room." But others, such as *Washington Post* contributor Lloyd Grove, find that this complicated staging is effective: "You're close enough to touch the characters in action, and suddenly on intimate-enough terms with them to grasp what they're about." Mael similarly believes that "these close-ups (another example of Fornes's use of cinematic style) enable members of the audience to experience the women's relationship in a more intimate manner than would be possible on a proscenium stage." And Richards feels that "the strength of this production is that it has you thinking, 'If only I could look into one more room, catch one more exchange, come back a minute later.' In short, it lures you into a labyrinth of the mind." "*Fefu and Her Friends* has the delicacy of tone and economical style of Fornes's earlier plays," concludes Marranca. "[But] what makes this play stand apart—and ahead—of the others is, more than the inclusiveness of the experiment in text and performance, the embodiment of a deeply personal vision."

"Ever since *Fefu and Her Friends* Maria Irene Fornes has been writing the finest realistic plays in this country," asserts Maranca in *Performing Arts Journal*. "In fact, one could say that *Fefu* and the plays that followed it . . . have paved the way for a new language of dramatic realism, and a way of directing it." The critic explains: "Fornes brings a much needed intimacy to drama, and her economy of approach suggests another vision of theatricality, more stylized for its lack of exhibitionism." Calling Fornes "America's truest poet of the theatre," a *Village Voice* critic observes that in 1985 Obie-winner "The Conduct of Life," the author "takes on a subject so close to the bones of our times you'd think it unapproachable." "The Conduct of Life" follows the family life of a torturer who works for a fascist Latin American government. Although "we don't think of the fascist classes in Latin America bothering with disgust or introspection or moral concern," remarks Paul Berman in the *Nation*, ". . . of course they do, and no doubt they ask [questions] much the way Fornes shows this officer's unhappy wife asking in *The Conduct of Life*, with agonies of soul and eventually with a gun. And what is this, by the way, if not the spirit of our time?"

In presenting the internal and external conflicts of these characters, Fornes uses "a dozen or so vignettes, some lasting only a moment or two, that are punctuated by lighting that fades slowly," describes Herbert Mitgang of the *New York Times*. The critic adds that "these theatrical punctuation marks are the equivalent of the ellipses that some poets and novelists use, and abuse, to tell the reader: At this point it's time to think about the wisdom of what is being said." Thus "the play conjures a lot of tension, mostly by keeping the scenes tight and disciplined and unsettlingly short," states Berman. "The dialogue and staging seem almost to have been cropped too close . . . [but] sometimes the cropping pares away everything but the musing of a single voice, and these monologues are the most effective aspect of all." Although he finds some faults with the play, Berman concludes that "*The Conduct of Life* is incomparably more serious than any of the new plays on Broadway and will surely stand out in memory as a bright spot of the season." And another *Village Voice* critic presents a comparable assessment, calling Fornes's work "as important and as entertaining as any you're likely to see this year."

"Fornes's work goes to the core of character," writes Marranca. "Instead of the usual situation in which a character uses dialogue or action to explain what he or she is doing and why, her characters exist in the world by their very act of trying to understand it. In other words, it is the characters themselves who appear to be thinking, not the author having thought." Sontag also praises the playwright, commenting that "Fornes's work has always been intelligent, often funny, never vulgar or cynical; both delicate and visceral. Now it is something more. . . . The plays have always been about wisdom: what it means to be wise. They are getting wiser." "Working for more than [thirty] years in Off-Broadway's unheralded spaces," declares Marranca, "Fornes is an exemplary artist who through her writing and teaching has created a life in the theatre away from the crass hype that attends so many lesser beings. How has she managed that rare accomplishment in this country's theatre—a career?" Explains the critic: "What is admirable about Fornes is that she is one of the last real bohemians among the writers who came to prominence in the sixties. She never changed to fit her style to fashion. She has simply been

writing, experimenting, thinking. Writers still have to catch up to her." The critic concludes that "if there were a dozen writers in our theatre with Fornes's wisdom and graciousness it would be enough for a country, and yet even one of her is sometimes all that is needed to feel the worth of the enormous effort it takes to live a life in the American theatre."

A manuscript collection of Fornes's work is located at the Lincoln Center Library of the Performing Arts in New York City.

CA INTERVIEW

CA interviewed Maria Irene Fornes by telephone on March 16, 1988, at her home in New York, New York.

CA: You were a painter originally, but began writing plays around 1960, inspired partly, as you told Ross Wetzsteon for New York, *by seeing Zero Mostel's "Ulysses." How did that play prompt such a change in your work?*

FORNES: It was not a conscious inspiration. It wasn't that I saw the play and thought, I'm going to write plays. And even when I was writing my first play, "Tango Palace," I wasn't thinking that I wanted to write plays like that. But the character of Isidore in "Tango Palace" in my mind *was* Zero Mostel. Originally I had thought of writing a play about a young man and a computer—what we called at that time an IBM machine, which was a different kind of thing from the computers we have now—and this is the reason why in "Tango Palace" there are these cards that Isidore flips toward Leopold. It was going to be not a human being but a machine that communicated to Leopold through these cards. But soon after I started writing I realized that wasn't the best way to do it; I don't think I wrote more than a page or two with that idea. I soon thought it should be a person, and it immediately became someone so much like Zero Mostel that gradually I started seeing Zero Mostel playing it. Even then, though, I didn't realize I was influenced by his performance in "Ulysses." You can see something that has such a profound impact on you that it changes your work dramatically, and yet you're not aware of what was the reason for the change.

CA: Did you immediately stop painting when you began writing plays—or do you still paint?

FORNES: Before I started writing it had become harder and harder for me to get myself to work in my painting. It had always been difficult. I always had to force myself to work— I had to promise myself that I would work and then I had to force myself to do it. I thought that was normal for a young person to prefer being in coffee houses to working at home, but when I started writing plays, I realized that wasn't so, because I preferred writing to doing anything else. I think the reason I was having a hard time painting was that it wasn't the form of art that was best suited for me.

CA: How do you feel your concept of structure in drama is related to your background as a painter?

FORNES: That too is something that I have only recently become aware of. I have been quite aware from my very early writing that my writing had a connection with films and with silent comedies; for example, the quick scenes and time transitions in "The Successful Life of 3," which are like film. Things just happen rather than making the play lead to the event. Plays or those who write them seem to find it difficult to have a time lapse unless they do it between acts. They seem to feel they need an intermission, that is, actual time to best suggest the passage of time.

CA: Maybe because audiences expect that kind of structure on the stage?

FORNES: Audiences don't expect anything. In fact, I think audiences get tired of seeing the same thing over and over. But playwrights and directors and other people who do theater don't know what they're doing unless they follow a familiar structure. I think it's their fault, not the fault of the audiences.

CA: I interrupted your thought earlier. You were leading up to how your background in painting may have influenced your dramatic structure.

FORNES: Yes. Only recently I was talking with someone who asked me something about my painting, and suddenly it came to my mind how Hans Hofmann always talked about push-and-pull, as he called it: the dynamics created between colors when you place one color very close to another or anywhere else in the canvas. It was push-and-pull sideways but also in terms of depth: a color would go inside the canvas and the other colors would come out. The color and shape of the form would create this tension, and he always spoke of that almost as if it were the main thing that guided his work and his teaching. I realized only recently that that had a very strong impact on my playwriting, because I compose my plays guided not by story line but more by energies that take place within each scene, and also the energies that take place between one scene and the scene that follows. It's like Hofmann's push-and-pull in that the narrative doesn't control how the play proceeds, but the development of the energies within the play.

CA: You began writing and getting your work produced at a time when there was a great deal of experimentation in the theater, and your plays are often thought of as experimental. Do you think experimental *is a valid and useful term? Does it have a specific meaning to you as a writer and director?*

FORNES: I don't think any term is right; that's why I don't object to one term more than another. I just do theater. But I know that there is a difference between traditional work and work that is not so traditional, and work that has forms that are not traditional but deals with traditional or mainstream or middle-class concerns. I know that my work is different, so I accept whatever term people choose to use for it. I think my work is experimental because every time I write a play I feel I'm entering an experiment. When I start I never know what I'm going to do or how I'm going to do it. That is what thrills me about writing a play, discovering the subject, the characters and the form as I write the play, and having no idea how to do it, just as if I'd never written a play before. That is, I suppose, what an experiment is.

CA: In the case of the musicals, such as "Promenade" and "Lovers and Keepers," how does the collaboration between you and your composers usually work?

FORNES: I think the way I work with the composer was set by Al Carmines, who is able to write music to almost anything you give him. It could be lyrics, a page of narrative where he could find something lively, or a scene. When he's working with someone on a musical, he will turn the lyrics into songs.

But he will also just look at a page where there is a narrative and compose a song for that narrative. He doesn't use the conventional song form, where the melody is repeated and the words have to fit into it several times. Because he was the first composer I worked with, I thought that was how everybody wrote songs. Then I worked with different composers, and sometimes they would say "Oh, no; you have to stick to the formal scheme." And that's why the lyrics tend to be very boring.

CA: People who write about your plays often comment on your tenderness toward your characters. Do they become very much real people to you, whether or not they are fully developed in the traditional sense?

FORNES: Yes, I feel they're all real. I was just thinking the other day that maybe I should write a play where all my characters meet. I have plays that have very different styles and very different periods, and I thought, not every single character, but the central characters of the plays should meet each other and I should do a play with all of them.

CA: Regional theater has been important in the production of your plays. Generally speaking, what do you think regional theater should be doing for playwrights and audiences, and how well do you think it's functioning?

FORNES: Actually, regional theater hasn't done very many productions of my plays until recent years. In the '60s, there were more productions of my work than in the '70s and early '80s. In the '60s there were several anthologies of plays by the Off-Off Broadway playwrights, and because of those anthologies, lots of universities did those plays. There weren't that many regional theaters then. They hadn't really started yet. There were a few theaters that did experimental plays, like the Firehouse Theater in Minneapolis, which later moved to San Francisco, and a few others like that. It was mostly universities. There were a few major theaters but they didn't do experimental work, although my first play received its first production at one of the few major theaters. Herbert Blau did it at the San Francisco Actors Workshop. My work started being done in regional theater again after I wrote "Fefu and Her Friends," in the late '70s. In '78 a few regional theaters did "Fefu." But I think now there's a renewed interest in my work.

CA: Do you have favorite theaters for staging your plays, or specific physical qualities in a theater that you feel are important for your productions?

FORNES: The atmosphere in the theater is very important in getting an audience involved. The space can completely take possession of a production. Working with people who understand the work and have the same values that you have makes a production so much more exciting. I mean the management. I will put up with all kinds of physical inconvenience to have that. The actors and designers of course—that goes without saying. But I haven't had that much experience in the thrust theater. I think I've only done "Lovers and Keepers" at the New City Theater in Pittsburgh and "Hedda Gabler" at the Milwaukee Rep in thrust. I like proscenium; I like seeing pictures.

Even more than proscenium, though, I like working in a real place. For example, at the Padua Hills Festival in California, we used to write plays for a particular spot. We usually did our festival on the campus of a university, and we had lots of places where we could go and work outdoors. We would do our plays either against a building or in an orchard or on a hill or against some kind of structure, like the side of a loading dock. To me, that is the most mysterious and beautiful way of working, writing a play for a particular spot so that the set is whatever the place is.

I'm doing that right now here in New York. I'm doing a play I wrote that takes place in an empty warehouse, and there are three different areas on this floor. They are like lofts, but with connecting doors or archways. The play starts in one room and moves to the second room, where the audience moves with it, and then the play and audience move to the third room. The audience just walks into the next room and sits around wherever the chairs are. There's no real front, though there is something like a front, because I put more chairs in one direction that in the others. I find it exquisite to work that way.

CA: You very often direct your own plays. Would you prefer always to do that, if it were possible, rather than turn them over to other people's interpretation?

FORNES: Not always. It depends on who the director is. People think I don't like to have other people direct my plays, but that is not true. I don't like bad directors to direct my work, but I like to have good directors do it.

CA: Is it a question of trust?

FORNES: No, it's a question of quality. To start with, I always think it's going to be good. When I see it, I either like what they've done and feel delighted that they've done something good, or I'm horrified by it.

People feel quite suspicious of a writer who directs. They feel that there's a kind of selfishness involved. Just the other night I was talking with a friend and another person who saw a production of a play of mine that was directed by someone else. I didn't like it very much. I didn't think it was terrible, but I objected to some things. I didn't think I was going to go around recommending it. When I was saying this, the second fellow was kind of smiling, suspecting that the reason I didn't like it was because I wished I had directed it myself. He had seen that production, but he had not seen the same play directed by me. My friend had seen both productions, and he said that when I directed the play, the main character was very luminous and the play was luminous, and he didn't see that at all in this other production.

When my friend said that, the other young man was convinced that the current production was not as good as it could be. But when *I* was saying it, he suspected me of bias. I think anytime I say the slightest critical thing about another director, it seems as if I just want to direct all my productions. It's not so.

CA: Do you find that audiences vary widely across the country?

FORNES: I think they do, audiences and critics too. The Acting Company did an evening called "Orchards," made up of short dramatizations of Chekhov stories done by seven American playwrights. One of these was a piece of mine, "Drowning." "Orchards" toured all over the country, and I was quite interested in seeing the reviews. It was the same group of actors, the same set, traveling through the United States, and it was amazing how different the reviews were. But what was

more amazing was that in each city the different critics seemed to agree on which plays they preferred. It was as if one town liked certain plays while another town liked others.

CA: Tell me about the New York Theatre Strategy, in which you were instrumental in getting experimental American plays produced.

FORNES: The Theatre Strategy's last season was in 1980. The organization was formed by a group of Off-Off Broadway playwrights at a point when we felt we were being a little bit ignored by the Off-Off Broadway theater. We felt that the directors were becoming the ones who made the choices about productions—and I mean by that not directors who direct plays, but directors who would create a piece in collaboration or they would do very singular productions of classics.

So we formed this organization because artistic directors in the Off-Off Broadway theater had become a little bit uppity and they were appointing themselves judges of work and making decisions that they shouldn't have made. First of all, nobody knows for sure when a play is excellent or not so good. There are extraordinary plays that have been neglected, and very bad plays that are done. This happens all the time. I never wanted to be in the position of making decisions about what should be produced; I just knew that the writers who formed the organization were all good, and whenever one of them felt a play was ready to be done, they should do it. It should be up to them.

People have the idea that it's the theater that loses or gains, therefore it has to decide what will be produced. That is not so. A playwright has more at stake than the theater does. If playwrights don't hold the reins to their work, they are being robbed of something that belongs to them. Naturally I'm talking about good writers who have proven that they know what they're doing and that their work is interesting. In these cases I think a theater can take a chance, even if the person running the theater thinks that a play is not as good as other plays by the same writer. Maybe the director is wrong. Even if he's right, he should consider that maybe the playwright is right and that a playwright may need to change directions, and this play that's not so good might be a necessary part of the playwright's development. Later on it may proven to be an important work, or maybe because that play was done the playwright's next play will be a masterpiece.

CA: You have also been very active as a teacher, especially of young Hispanic writers. You told Sylvie Drake for the Los Angeles Times *that you see in Hispanic theater in America "an enormous potential rather than something that's been realized." Do young Hispanic playwrights face particular obstacles in their work beyond those of aspiring playwrights in general?*

FORNES: Yes. There's a very rich Spanish tradition of classic theater, but there hasn't been a strong modern Hispanic theater—by that I mean since the turn of the century. A Spanish playwright who lives in the United States necessarily has to look to the American or English or German or Italian theater for models. It's very important to try to work with Hispanic playwrights at a level where they are just beginning to write, so that they don't dismiss possibilities of ways of writing that would be very original to them but ways they would not see models for in the active American or English or German theater.

That has happened with the Latin-American novelists, who have created a very diverse and yet very particular Latin-American voice. Certainly it is a very singular Latin-American voice.

The Hispanic American doesn't have a model yet. They are in this country, and they have a vast void in front of them. They have to enter that void and create their own way. What I'm talking about is not writing about Hispanics. That is not enough. It is not calling the characters Pedro and Josefa, because anybody can do that. I am talking about the way that a culture creates an aesthetic, the imagery and the things that relate to that culture, to their memory, smells, sounds, what things are important, what things come first, what is the cadence of Hispanic life. All that is something that has to be captured. And to do that, it's very important that a playwright not be rushed into writing a play that would be acceptable as a play by commercial standards. I think that applies to any writer, any creative person, anyway; but it applies more to people who don't have a world of creativity which corresponds to their own sensibility.

CA: You keep doing new things, trying out new ideas, encouraging other people in theater. With all the frustration that it must entail, do you still find it an exciting career?

FORNES: Oh yes, because to me the most interesting thing is the creation of the work. Writing it and rehearsing it for the first time is the most exciting thing. Of course, if people come to see it and they like it and then there are other productions, I am very, very happy. In no way do I disdain all of that. But I find more pleasure in the creating part of it, and I think that's the reason why I am always willing to keep experimenting and inventing things. You see, what happens otherwise is that people become afraid to fail and they start repeating themselves because they know what they've done has been successful. Or they have not been successful and they're afraid to try anything else, because they have no reason to think that anything else they do is going to be successful either.

BIOGRAPHICAL/CRITICAL SOURCES:

BOOKS

Betsko, Kathleen and Rachel Koenig, *Interviews with Contemporary Women Playwrights*, Beech Tree Books, 1987.
Contemporary Literary Criticism, Volume 39, Gale, 1986.
Dictionary of Literary Biography, Volume 7: *Twentieth-Century American Dramatists*, Gale, 1981.
Fornes, Maria Irene, *Maria Irene Fornes: Plays*, preface by Susan Sontag, PAJ Publications, 1986.
Marranca, Bonnie and Gautam Dasgupta, *American Playwrights: A Critical Survey*, Volume I, Drama Books Specialists, 1981.

PERIODICALS

Chicago Tribune, June 14, 1969, February 8, 1988.
Los Angeles Times, July 9, 1987.
Nation, April 6, 1985.
Newsweek, June 4, 1969.
New York, June 23, 1969, March 18, 1985.
New York Times, April 17, 1968, June 5, 1969, June 6, 1969, February 22, 1972, January 14, 1978, January 22, 1978, April 25, 1979, December 30, 1981, October 25, 1983, March 13, 1984, March 20, 1985, April 17, 1986, April 23, 1986, October 17, 1987, December 15, 1987.
Performing Arts Journal, Number 1, 1984.

Village Voice, April 21, 1966, April 17, 1969, March 19, 1985, March 26, 1985.
Washington Post, July 9, 1983, July 15, 1983.

—Sketch by Diane Telgen

—Interview by Jean W. Ross

*　　*　　*

FORTMAN, Edmund J. 1901-

PERSONAL: Born July 21, 1901, in Chicago, Ill.; son of Fred and Louise (Smith) Fortman. *Education:* Loyola University, A.B., 1922; St. Louis University, M.A., 1927; Gregorian University, S.T.D., 1937. *Politics:* Democrat.

ADDRESSES: Home and office—Loyola University, 6525 North Sheridan Rd., Chicago, Ill. 60626.

CAREER: Roman Catholic priest, member of Society of Jesus; professor of dogmatic theology for 40 years at Bellarmine School of Theology (formerly West Baden College, West Baden Springs, Ind.), North Aurora, Ill., and at Jesuit School of Theology, Hyde Park, Ill.

WRITINGS:

(Editor) *The Theology of Man and Grace*, M.M. Bruce, 1966.
(Editor) *The Theology of God*, M.M. Bruce, 1968.
The Triune God: A Historical Study of the Doctrine of the Trinity, Westminster, 1971.
Everlasting Life after Death, Alba House, 1976.
Activities of the Holy Spirit, Franciscan Herald, 1984.
Everlasting Life, Alba House, 1986.
Ne obliviscamur, Loyola University Press, 1986.
Come, Follow Me, Loyola University Press, 1987.
Lineage, Loyola University Press, 1987.

SIDELIGHTS: The Theology of God has been published in Spanish.

*　　*　　*

FOWLER, David Covington 1921-

PERSONAL: Born January 3, 1921, in Louisville, Ky.; son of Earl Broadus and Susan (Covington) Fowler; married Mary Gene Stith, 1943; children: Sandra, Caroline. *Education:* University of Florida, B.A., 1942; University of Chicago, M.A., 1947, Ph.D., 1949. *Religion:* Presbyterian.

ADDRESSES: Home—6264 Nineteenth Ave. N.E., Seattle, Wash. 98115. *Office*—Department of English/International Studies, University of Washington, Seattle, Wash. 98195.

CAREER: University of Pennsylvania, Philadelphia, instructor of English, 1949-51; University of Washington, Seattle, instructor, 1952-53, assistant professor, 1953-59, associate professor, 1959-62, professor of English, 1963—, associate dean of Graduate School, 1960-62. *Military service:* U.S. Navy, 1942-46; served in Pacific area, participating in invasions of Marianas and Philippines; became lieutenant.

MEMBER: American Association of University Professors, Modern Language Association of America, American Folklore Society.

AWARDS, HONORS: American Council of Learned Societies Scholars Award, 1951-52; Guggenheim fellow, 1962-63, 1975-76.

WRITINGS:

(Editor with Thomas A. Knott) William Langland, *Piers the Plowman: A Critical Edition of the A-Version*, Johns Hopkins Press, 1952.

Prowess and Charity in the Perceval of Chretien de Troyes, University of Washington Press, 1959.

Piers the Plowman: Literary Relations of the A- and B-Texts, University of Washington Press, 1961.

A Literary History of the Popular Ballad, Duke University Press, 1968.

The Bible in Early English Literature, University of Washington Press, 1976.

The Bible in Middle English Literature, University of Washington Press, 1984.

Contributor to *A Manual of the Writings in Middle English*, Volume 6, 1979; contributor to scholarly journals.

*   *   *

FRANK, Andre Gunder   1929-

PERSONAL: Born February 24, 1929, in Berlin, Germany; son of Lenhard and Elena (Pevsner) Frank; married Marta Fuentes Enberg (a librarian), December 21, 1962; children: Paulo Rene, Miguel Leonardo. *Education:* Swarthmore College, B.A. (with honors), 1950; University of Michigan, graduate study, 1951; University of Chicago, M.A., 1952, Ph.D., 1957; University of Paris, Doctorat d'Etat, 1978.

ADDRESSES: Office—University of Amsterdam, Jodenbreestraat 23, kr. 2296, 1011 NH Amsterdam, Netherlands.

CAREER: Iowa State University, Ames, Iowa, instructor, 1956-57; Michigan State University, East Lansing, began as lecturer, became assistant professor, 1957-61; University of Brasilia, Brasilia, Brazil, associate professor, 1963; UNESCO Latin American Center for Research in the Social Sciences, Rio de Janeiro, Brazil, visiting research fellow, 1963-64; National Autonomous University of Mexico, Obregon, professor extraordinario, 1965; Sir George Williams University, Montreal, visiting professor, 1966-68; University of Chile, Santiago, professor, 1968-73, research professor, 1970-73; Max Planck Institute, Starnberg, Germany, visiting research associate and fellow of the German Society for Peace and Conflict Research, 1974-78; University of East Anglia, Norwich, England, professor of development studies department, 1978-83; University of Amsterdam, Amsterdam, Netherlands, professor of development economics, 1981—, director of Institute for Socio-Economic Studies of Developing Regions, 1981—. Visiting professor to colleges and universities, including Free University of Berlin, fall, 1973, Boston University, summer, 1979, and New School for Social Research, spring, 1981. Consultant, United Nations Economic Commission for Latin America, Santiago, Chile, 1964.

WRITINGS:

Capitalism and Underdevelopment in Latin America: Historical Essays of Chile and Brazil, Monthly Review Press, 1967, revised edition, 1969.

Latin America: Underdevelopment or Revolution, Monthly Review Press, 1969.

Sociology of Development and Underdevelopment of Sociology, Zenit foerlag (Stockholm), 1969.

Lumpenbourgeoisie: Lumpendevelopment; Dependency, Class and Politics in Latin America, Monthly Review Press, 1972.

(With R. Puiggros and E. Laclau) *America Latina: Feudalismo o Capitalismo?*, Ediciones Oveja Negra (Bogota), 1972.

(With D. Johnson and J. Cockcroft) *Dependence and Underdevelopment: Latin America's Political Economy*, Doubleday, 1972.

(With O. Caputo, R. Pizarro, and A. Quijano) *Aspectos de la Realidad Latinoamericana*, Quimantu Editora (Santiago), 1973.

Carta Abierta en el Aniversario del Golpe Militar en Chile, edited by Alberto Corazon, [Madrid], 1974.

Raices del Desarrollo y del Subdesarrollo en el Nuevo Mundo, Universidad Central de Venezuela, Facultad de Ciencias Economicas y Sociales, 1974.

On Capitalist Underdevelopment, Oxford University Press (Bombay), 1975.

Economic Genocide in Chile, Spokesman Books, 1976.

(With S. Amin and H. Jaffe) *Quale 1983/No Esperar a 1984*, Ediciones Zero (Madrid), 1976.

Critica y Anti-Critica, Ediciones Zero, 1978, translated edition published as *Critique and Anti-Critique*, Macmillan, 1984.

World Accumulation, 1492-1789, Monthly Review Press, 1978.

Dependent Accumulation and Underdevelopment, Macmillan (London), 1978, Monthly Review Press, 1979.

Mexican Agriculture, 1521-1630: Transformation of the Mode of Production, Cambridge University Press, 1979.

(With Amin) *Pa Vei Mot 1984*, Gyldendal Norsk Forlag (Oslo), 1979.

Crisis: In the World Economy, Holmes & Meier, 1980.

Crisis: In the Third World, Holmes & Meier, 1981.

Reflections on the World Economic Crisis, Monthly Review Press, 1981.

(With Amin, Immanuel Wallerstein, and G. Arrighi) *Dynamics of Global Crisis*, Monthly Review Press, 1982.

The European Challenge, Spokesman Books, 1983.

El Desafio de la Crisis, Editorial Nueva Sociedad, 1988.

Contributor to over 100 anthologies; contributor to numerous professional journals and magazines.

WORK IN PROGRESS: A book providing a historical perspective on "the new world capitalist crisis"; an ancient and modern history of the world system; a work on contemporary social movements and their history.

*   *   *

FRIDAY, Nancy   1937-

PERSONAL: Born August 27, 1937, in Pittsburgh, Pa.; daughter of Walter (a financier) and Jane (Colbert) Friday; married W. H. Manville (a writer), October 20, 1967 (marriage ended); married Norman Pearlstine (an editor), July, 1988. *Education:* Attended Wellesley College.

ADDRESSES: Home—1108 Southard St., Key West, Fla. 33040. *Agent*—Betty Anne Clarke, International Creative Management, 20 West 51st St., New York, N.Y. 10019.

CAREER: San Juan Island Times, San Juan, Puerto Rico, reporter, 1960-61; editor, *Islands in the Sun* (magazine), 1961-63; free-lance writer, 1963—.

WRITINGS:

NONFICTION

My Secret Garden: Women's Sexual Fantasies, Trident, 1973.

Forbidden Flowers: More Women's Sexual Fantasies, Pocket Books, 1975.

My Mother/My Self: The Daughter's Search for Identity, Delacorte, 1977.
Men in Love: Men's Sexual Fantasies; The Triumph of Love over Rage, Delacorte, 1980.
Jealousy, Perigord, 1985.

SIDELIGHTS: Nancy Friday entered the ranks of "pop-psychology" in the early 1970s with her books *My Secret Garden: Women's Sexual Fantasies* and *Forbidden Flowers: More Women's Sexual Fantasies*. Though non-scientific, both books broke ground as forums for women who might not otherwise suspect that their fantasies could be shared by others. But even before these works were published, Friday had been researching questions on the theme of mother-daughter relationships in contemporary times. In 1978, after interviewing three hundred mothers and daughters nationwide, Friday published perhaps her best-known book to date, *My Mother/My Self: The Daughter's Search for Identity*.

A quick bestseller, *My Mother/My Self* generated controversy because of the frank and often disturbing conclusions the author offered. "In effect, Friday is saying that our mothers molded us to fit the preliberation ideal of woman, and thus burdened us with the task of freeing ourselves," according to Amy Gross, writing in a *Village Voice* review. "She is also saying that until we do free ourselves, we will define happiness in terms of the symbiotic relationship we had with mother, no matter how unhappy that was." Gross faults *My Mother/My Self* for the author's "demands that we accept her every point as the truth about our lives," adding that in this book Friday's "focus is on the psychologically pathological. Her focus is on rage." But to *New York Times Book Review* critic Doris Grumbach, *My Mother/My Self* is "rich in anecdote, memories, testimonials, confessions, opinions by experts. What [the author] tells us that we inherit from our mothers much of what we are: our physical selves, our capacities, our whole baggage of repressions, insecurities and guilts," continues Grumbach. "Friday instructs us to look at ourselves not so much as the victims of a discriminatory patriarchy, but of an inevitable and unavoidable and destructive maternalism."

Friday followed *My Mother/My Self* with *Men in Love: Men's Sexual Fantasies; The Triumph of Love over Rage*. Similar in format to her first two books (the author solicited responses by including a mailing address within the two volumes) *Men in Love* includes two hundred male fantasies culled from three thousand letters. As the book was being released, Friday predicted it would be more controversial than her previous works because "people found it easy to talk about [female fantasies]; they're easily dismissed as trivial. This time you're dealing with *men*, the bedrock of society, you're talking about the deepest vulnerabilities of the so-called powerful sex," as Friday told John F. Baker in a *Publishers Weekly* interview. In the same article, the author revealed that *Men in Love* deals with "very powerful, primitive feelings, which arouse deep anxiety. The way I see it, the fantasies and feelings don't need an intellectual response; they need a gut-level deeply felt reaction, and that's how I treat them."

A number of critics fault Friday's analytics in *Men in Love*. *Newsweek*'s Peter S. Prescott, for one, reports that the volume features a "stupefying quantity of testimony to various agitated states of mind interleaved with brief essays in which the author repeats what we have just read and ventures her interpretations. . . . Her thesis, that men's love of women is filled with rage, is pretty enough, but entirely unsupported by any

of the evidence she has assembled." But Prescott does confess his "affection for this woman. Her charm, surely has much to do with her lack of credentials, with her distrust of statistical method, with her conviction that she has become in our society a liberating force, and with her refusal to disbelieve whatever her excited informers tell her to be true. I particularly like her just-folks prose style," the critic adds.

Jealousy, Friday's 1985 publication, postulates that jealousy and envy, two emotions that may seem synonymous, are in fact vastly different. The author makes an important distinction in this respect, says Susan Wood of *Washington Post Book World*. Jealousy "arises from a fear of losing something we have," while envy "is a desire to have something someone else has," as Wood relates. "Envy is by far the most destructive emotion and it is envy that is most often at work when we spoil what we love."

Again, critical reaction proved mixed. *Los Angeles Times* reviewer Carolyn See, taking the negative viewpoint, calls *Jealousy* "long, too long, way too long" at 524 pages, and adds that the author's "own diligent work habits may have finally betrayed her. She may have worked so long on 'Jealousy' that her . . . finger has slipped off the pulse of the nation: While she was working the temper of the times may have changed." Noting a passage in the book's introduction, where Friday describes a lustful encounter with a man who "introduced her [later on] to *huevos rancheros*, See remarks that "no woman in the 1980s—when the rest of the nation is contemplating monogamy, children, 'the new chastity' and the sinister specter of AIDS—can hope to establish authority and credibility with tales of picking up other women's underwear and eating Mexican breakfasts." Wood, while sharing See's opinion that the book's length "might seem daunting," nonetheless adopts a more positive viewpoint overall. In *Jealousy*, she says, "nearly every page is readable, intelligent and full of insight and information. Most of all, *Jealousy* is big in importance. Relatively little has been written on the subject, certainly for the general reader, and Friday is convincing in her argument of jealousy's central role in our lives and the ways in which our lack of understanding, even our denial of the 'green-eyed monster' often cripples our most intimate relationships."

BIOGRAPHICAL/CRITICAL SOURCES:

BOOKS

Friday, Nancy, *My Mother/My Self: The Daughter's Search for Identity*, Delacorte, 1977.
Friday, Nancy, *Jealousy*, Perigord, 1985.

PERIODICALS

Chicago Tribune Book World, May 18, 1980.
Esquire, March, 1980.
Los Angeles Times, November 26, 1985.
Ms., May, 1980.
Nation, May 31, 1980.
Newsweek, March 17, 1980.
New York Review of Books, May 13, 1976.
New York Times, December 30, 1977.
New York Times Book Review, October 7, 1973, February 12, 1978, February 22, 1981, October 6, 1985.
People, December 19, 1977.
Publishers Weekly, February 28, 1980.
Times Literary Supplement, October 24, 1975.
Village Voice, November 28, 1977.

Washington Post Book World, August 19, 1973, March 23, 1980, September 29, 1985.*

—*Sketch by Susan Salter*

*   *   *

FRYE, John   1910-

PERSONAL: Born September 27, 1910, in Chicago, Ill.; son of Harry C. and Lida G. (Frow) Frye; married Harriet Bennitt (an artist), August 18, 1934; children: Keith, Ann (Mrs. James W. Meyer), Ellen. *Education:* Antioch College, B.A., 1934.

CAREER: Associated Press, reporter and editor in Cincinnati and Columbus, Ohio, 1934-48; Scripps-Howard, wire-chief in Columbus, 1949-54; advertising and free-lance public relations work in Columbus and Dayton, Ohio, 1955-62; free-lance newspaper and magazine writer in Kilmarnock, Va., beginning 1962.

WRITINGS:

Skipper, What's That Light?, [Kilmarnock, Va.], 1969.

The Search for the Santa Maria, Dodd, 1973.
(Contributor) R. Gordon Pirie, editor, *Oceanography,* 2nd edition, Oxford University Press, 1977.
The Men All Singing: The Story of Menhaden Fishing, Donning, 1978.
(With wife, Harriet Frye) *North to Thule: An Imagined Narrative of the Famous "Lost" Voyage of Pytheas of Massalia of the 4th Century B.C.,* Algonquin Books, 1985.

Associate editor of *National Fisherman,* 1970—.

WORK IN PROGRESS: Further research in Spanish-Portuguese discovery, colonization, and prehistoric trade; editing a book by Hein Zenker on circumnavigation in twenty-foot sloop.

SIDELIGHTS: John Frye once told *CA* that he hoped to travel to Europe for further historical research on the discovery era. He speaks Spanish in addition to limited French and German.

BIOGRAPHICAL/CRITICAL SOURCES:

PERIODICALS

Times Literary Supplement, December 13, 1985.

G

GARCIA MARQUEZ, Gabriel (Jose) 1928-

PERSONAL: Born March 6, 1928, in Aracataca, Colombia; son of Gabriel Eligio Garcia (a telegraph operator) and Luisa Marquez Iguaran; married Mercedes Barcha, 1958; children: Rodrigo, Gonzalo. *Education:* Attended Universidad Nacional de Colombia, 1947-48, and Universidad de Cartagena, 1948-49.

ADDRESSES: Home—P.O. Box 20736, Mexico City D.F., Mexico. *Agent*—Agencia Literaria Carmen Balcells, Diagonal 580, Barcelona 21, Spain.

CAREER: Worked as a journalist, 1947-65, including jobs with *El heraldo,* Baranquilla, Colombia, *El espectador,* Bogota, Colombia, and Prensa Latina news agency, Bogota, 1959, and New York City, 1961; writer, 1965—. Fundacion Habeas, founder, 1979, president, 1979—.

MEMBER: American Academy of Arts and Letters (honorary fellow).

AWARDS, HONORS: Colombian Association of Writers and Artists Award, 1954, for story "Un dia despues del sabado"; Premio Literario Esso (Colombia), 1961, for *La mala hora;* Chianciano Award (Italy), 1969, Prix de Meilleur Livre Etranger (France), 1969, and Romulo Gallegos prize (Venezuela), 1971, all for *Cien anos de soledad;* LL.D., Columbia University, 1971; Books Abroad/Neustadt International Prize for Literature, 1972; Nobel Prize for Literature, 1982; *Los Angeles Times* Book Prize nomination for fiction, 1983, for *Chronicle of a Death Foretold; Los Angeles Times* Book Prize for fiction, 1988, for *Love in the Time of Cholera.*

WRITINGS:

FICTION

La hojarasca (novella; title means "Leaf Storm"; also see below), Ediciones Sipa (Bogota), 1955, reprinted, Bruguera (Barcelona), 1983.

El coronel no tiene quien le escriba (novella; title means "No One Writes to the Colonel"; also see below), Aguirre Editor (Medellin, Colombia), 1961, reprinted, Bruguera, 1983.

La mala hora (novel; also see below), Talleres de Graficas "Luis Perez" (Madrid), 1961, reprinted, Bruguera, 1982,

English translation by Gregory Rabassa published as *In Evil Hour,* Harper, 1979.

Los funerales de la Mama Grande (short stories; title means "Big Mama's Funeral"; also see below), Editorial Universidad Veracruzana (Mexico), 1962, reprinted, Bruguera, 1983.

Cien anos de soledad (novel), Editorial Sudamericana (Buenos Aires), 1967, reprinted, Catedra, 1984, English translation by Rabassa published as *One Hundred Years of Solitude,* Harper, 1970.

Isabel viendo llover en Macondo (novella; title means "Isabel Watching It Rain in Macondo"; also see below), Editorial Estuario (Buenos Aires), 1967.

No One Writes to the Colonel and Other Stories (includes "No One Writes to the Colonel," and stories from *Big Mama's Funeral*), translated by J. S. Berstein, Harper, 1968.

La increible y triste historia de la candida Erendira y su abuela desalmada (short stories), Barral Editores, 1972.

El negro que hizo esperar a los angeles (short stories), Ediciones Alfil (Montevideo), 1972.

Ojos de perro azul (short stories; also see below), Equisditorial (Argentina), 1972.

Leaf Storm and Other Stories (includes "Leaf Storm," and "Isabel Watching It Rain in Macondo"), translated by Rabassa, Harper, 1972.

La increible y triste historia de la candida Erendira y su abuela desalmada (novella; title means "Innocent Erendira and Her Heartless Grandmother"; also see below), Libreria de Colegio (Buenos Aires), 1975.

El otono del patriarca (novel), Plaza & Janes Editores (Barcelona), 1975, translation by Rabassa published as *The Autumn of the Patriarch,* Harper, 1976.

Todos los cuentos de Gabriel Garcia Marquez: 1947-1972 (title means "All the Stories of Gabriel Garcia Marquez: 1947-1972"), Plaza & Janes Editores, 1975.

Innocent Erendira and Other Stories (includes "Innocent Erendira and Her Heartless Grandmother" and stories from *Ojos de perro azul*), translated by Rabassa, Harper, 1978.

Dos novelas de Macondo (contains *La hojarasca* and *La mala hora*), Casa de las Americas (Havana), 1980.

Cronica de una muerte anunciada (novel), La Oveja Negra (Bogota), 1981, translation by Rabassa published as *Chronicle of a Death Foretold,* J. Cape, 1982, Knopf, 1983.

Viva Sandino (play), Editorial Nueva Nicaragua, 1982, 2nd edition published as *El asalto: el operativo con que el FSLN se lanzo al mundo*, 1983.

El rastro de tu sangre en la nieve: El verano feliz de la senora Forbes, W. Dampier Editores (Bogota), 1982.

El secuestro: Guion cinematografico (unfilmed screenplay), Oveja Negra, 1982.

"Erendira" (filmscript; adapted from his novella *La increible y triste historia de la candida Erendira y su abuela desalmada*), Les Films du Triangle, 1983.

Collected Stories, Harper, 1984.

El amor en los tiempos del colera, Oveja Negra, 1985, English translation by Edith Grossman published as *Love in the Time of Cholera*, Knopf, 1988.

"A Time to Die" (filmscript), ICA Cinema, 1988.

"Diatribe of Love against a Seated Man" (play), first produced at Cervantes Theater, Buenos Aires, 1988.

NONFICTION

(With Mario Vargas Llosa) *La novela en America Latina: Dialogo*, Carlos Milla Batres (Lima), 1968.

Relato de un naufrago (journalistic pieces), Tusquets Editor (Barcelona), 1970, English translation by Randolph Hogan published as *The Story of a Shipwrecked Sailor*, Knopf, 1986.

Cuando era feliz e indocumentado (journalistic pieces), Ediciones El Ojo de Camello (Caracas), 1973.

Cronicas y reportajes (journalistic pieces), La Oveja Negra, 1978.

Periodismo militante (journalistic pieces), Son de Maquina Editores (Bogota), 1978.

De viaje por los paises socialistas: 90 dias en la "Cortina de hierro" (journalistic pieces), Ediciones Macondo (Colombia), 1978.

(Contributor) *Los sandanistas*, Oveja Negra, 1979.

(Contributor) Soledad Mendoza, editor, *Asi es Caracas*, Editorial Ateneo de Caracas, 1980.

Obra periodistica (journalistic pieces), edited by Jacques Gilard, Bruguera, Volume 1: *Textos constenos*, 1981, Volumes 2-3: *Entre cachacos*, 1982, Volume 4: *De Europa y America (1955-1960)*, 1983.

El olor de la guayaba: Conversaciones con Plinio Apuleyo Mendoza (interviews), La Oveja Negra, 1982, English translation by Ann Wright published as *The Fragrance of Guava*, Verso, 1983.

(With Guillermo Nolasco-Juarez) *Persecucion y muerte de minorias: dos perspectivas*, Juarez Editor (Buenos Aires), 1984.

(Contributor) *La Democracia y la paz en America Latina*, Editorial El Buho (Bogota), 1986.

La aventura de Miguel Littin, clandestino en Chile: Un reportaje, Editorial Sudamericana, 1986, English translation by Asa Zatz published as *Clandestine in Chile: The Adventures of Miguel Littin*, Holt, 1987.

OTHER

Author of weekly syndicated column.

SIDELIGHTS: "I knew [*One Hundred Years of Solitude*] would please my friends more than my other [books] had," said Gabriel Garcia Marquez in a *Paris Review* interview with Peter H. Stone. "But when my Spanish publisher told me he was going to print eight thousand copies, I was stunned because my other books had never sold more than seven hundred. I asked him why not start slowly, but he said he was convinced that it was a good book and that all eight thousand copies would be sold between May and December. Actually they were sold within one week in Buenos Aires."

Winner of the 1982 Nobel Prize for Literature, Garcia Marquez "is one of the small number of contemporary writers from Latin America who have given to its literature a maturity and dignity it never had before," asserts John Sturrock in the *New York Times Book Review*. *One Hundred Years of Solitude* is perhaps Garcia Marquez's best-known contribution to the awakening of interest in Latin American literature, for the book's appearance in Spanish in 1967 prompted unqualified approval from readers and critics. It has sold more than ten million copies, has been translated into over thirty languages and, according to an *Antioch Review* critic, the popularity and acclaim for the novel "mean that Latin American literature will change from being the exotic interest of a few to essential reading and that Latin America itself will be looked on less as a crazy subculture and more as a fruitful, alternative way of life." So great was the novel's initial popularity, writes Mario Vargas Llosa in *Garcia Marquez: Historia de un deicido*, that not only was the first Spanish printing of the book sold out within one week, but for months afterwards Latin American readers alone would exhaust each successive printing. Translations of the novel similarly elicited enthusiastic responses from critics and readers around the world.

In this outpouring of critical opinion, which *Books Abroad* contributor Klaus Muller-Bergh refers to as "an earthquake, a maelstrom," various reviewers have termed *One Hundred Years of Solitude* a masterpiece of modern fiction. For example, Chilean poet Pablo Neruda, himself a Nobel laureate, is quoted in *Time* as calling the book "the greatest revelation in the Spanish language since the *Don Quixote* of Cervantes." Similarly enthusiastic is William Kennedy, who writes in the *National Observer* that "*One Hundred Years of Solitude* is the first piece of literature since the Book of Genesis that should be required reading for the entire human race." And Regina Janes, in her study *Gabriel Garcia Marquez: Revolutions in Wonderland*, describes the book as "a 'total novel' that [treats] Latin America socially, historically, politically, mythically, and epically," adding that *One Hundred Years of Solitude* is also "at once accessible and intricate, lifelike and self-consciously, self-referentially fictive."

The novel is set in the imaginary community of Macondo, a village on the Colombian coast, and follows the lives of several generations of the Buendia family. Chief among these characters are Colonel Aureliano Buendia, perpetrator of thirty-two rebellions and father of seventeen illegitimate sons, and Ursula Buendia, the clan's matriarch and witness to its eventual decline. Besides following the complicated relationships of the Buendia family, *One Hundred Years of Solitude* also reflects the political, social, and economic troubles of South America. Many critics believe that the novel, with its complex family relationships and extraordinary events, is a microcosm of Latin America itself. But as *Playboy* contributor Claudia Dreifus states in her interview with the author, Garcia Marquez has facetiously described the plot as "just the story of the Buendia family, of whom it is prophesied that they shall have a son with a pig's tail; and in doing everything to avoid this, the Buendias *do* end up with a son with a pig's tail."

The mixture of historical and fictitious elements that appear in *One Hundred Years of Solitude* places the novel within that type of Latin American fiction that critics term magical or marvelous realism. Janes attributes the birth of this style of writing to Alejo Carpentier, a Cuban novelist and short story writer, and concludes that Garcia Marquez's fiction follows ideas originally formulated by the Cuban author. The critic notes that Carpentier "discovered the duplicities of history and elaborated the critical concept of 'lo maravilloso americano' the 'marvelous real,' arguing that geographically, historically, and essentially, Latin America was a space marvelous and fantastic . . . and to render that reality was to render marvels." Garcia Marquez presents a similar view of Latin America in his *Paris Review* interview with Stone: "It always amuses me that the biggest praise for my work comes for the imagination while the truth is that there's not a single line in all my work that does not have a basis in reality." The author further explained in his *Playboy* interview with Dreifus: "Clearly, the Latin American environment is marvelous. Particularly the Caribbean. . . . The coastal people were descendants of pirates and smugglers, with a mixture of black slaves. To grow up in such an environment is to have fantastic resources for poetry. Also, in the Caribbean, we are capable of believing anything, because we have the influences of all those different cultures, mixed in with Catholicism and our own local beliefs. I think that gives us an open-mindedness to look beyond apparent reality."

The first line of *One Hundred Years of Solitude* introduces the reader into this world of imagination. According to James Park Sloan in the *Chicago Tribune Book World:* "Few first lines in literature . . . have comparable force: 'Many years later, as he faced the firing squad, Colonel Aureliano Buendia was to remember that distant afternoon when his father took him to discover ice.' It contains so much of what [makes] the work magical, including a steadily toneless background in which everyday events become marvelous and marvelous events are assimilated without comment into everyday life. Equally important, it establishes a time scheme," continues the critic, which "simultaneously [looks] backward at a present seen as memory in light of that future." Gordon Brotherson also notes the magical quality of *One Hundred Years of Solitude* and the book's relationship with Carpentier's fiction. In *The Emergence of the Latin American Novel,* Brotherson refers to the "skillful vagueness" of the opening sentence and writes, "Phrases like 'many years later' and 'that distant afternoon' lead back through the prehistoric stones to a timeless world where (in an allusion to Carpentier and his magic realism) we are told many things still needed to be named."

Muller-Bergh believes that Garcia Marquez's particular gift for inserting the magical into the real is responsible for his popularity as a writer. The critic comments that "Latin American and Spanish readers . . . as well as European critics who have heaped unprecedented praise on the author" have found that this "penchant for plausible absurdities [is] one of Garcia Marquez's most enduring qualities." Alan Weinblatt explains the novelist's technique in the *New Republic,* noting that for Garcia Marquez "the key to writing *One Hundred Years of Solitude* was the idea of saying incredible things with a completely unperturbed face." The author credits this ability to his maternal grandmother: "She was a fabulous storyteller who told wild tales of the supernatural with a most solemn expression on her face," he told Dreifus. "As I was growing up, I often wondered whether or not her stories were truthful. Usually, I tended to believe her because of her serious, deadpan facial expression. Now, as a writer, I do the same thing; I say extraordinary things in a serious tone. It's possible to get away with *anything* as long as you make it believable. That is something my grandmother taught me." The straightforward manner in which the author tells of Aureliano Buendia and his

father going out "to discover ice" is repeated throughout the novel and throughout Garcia Marquez's fiction. For example, in *One Hundred Years of Solitude* Remedios the Beauty ascends into heaven while outside shaking out some sheets, yellow flowers fall all night when a family patriarch dies, and when a young man dies, his blood runs through the streets of the town and into his parents' house where, avoiding the rugs, it stops at the feet of his mother. In other works, Garcia Marquez tells of a woman "so tender she could pass through walls just by sighing" and of a general who sires five thousand children.

But along with the fantastic episodes in Garcia Marquez's fiction appear the historical facts or places that inspired them. An episode involving a massacre of striking banana workers is based on a historical incident; in reality, Garcia Marquez told Dreifus, "there were very few deaths . . . [so] I made the death toll 3000 because I was using certain proportions in my book." But while *One Hundred Years of Solitude* is the fictional account of the Buendia family, the novel is also, as John Leonard states in the *New York Times,* "a recapitulation of our evolutionary and intellectual experience. Macondo is Latin America in microcosm." Robert G. Mead, Jr. similarly observes in *Saturday Review* that "Macondo may be regarded as a microcosm of the development of much of the Latin American continent." Adds the critic: "Although [*One Hundred Years of Solitude*] is first and always a story, the novel also has value as a social and historical document." Garcia Marquez responds to these interpretations in his interview with Dreifus, commenting that his work "is not a history of Latin America, it is a *metaphor* for Latin America."

The "social and historical" elements of *One Hundred Years of Solitude* reflect the journalistic influences at work in Garcia Marquez's fiction. Although known as a novelist, the author began as a reporter and still considers himself one. As he remarked to Stone, "I've always been convinced that my true profession is that of a journalist." Janes believes that the evolution of Garcia Marquez's individual style is based on his experience as a correspondent; in addition, this same experience leads Janes and other critics to compare the Colombian with Ernest Hemingway. "[The] stylistic transformation between *Leaf Storm* and *No One Writes to the Colonel* was not exclusively an act of will," Janes claims. "Garcia Marquez had had six years of experience as a journalist between the two books, experience providing practice in the lessons of Hemingway, trained in the same school." And George R. McMurray, in his book *Gabriel Garcia Marquez,* maintains that Hemingway's themes and techniques have "left their mark" on the work of the Colombian.

Garcia Marquez has also been compared to another American Nobel-winner, William Faulkner, who also elaborated on facts to create his fiction. Faulkner based his fictional territory Yoknapatawpha County on memories of the region in northern Mississippi where he spent most of his life; Garcia Marquez based Macondo, the town appearing throughout his fiction, on Aracataca, the coastal city of his birth. A *Time* reviewer calls Macondo "a kind of tropical Yoknapatawpha County" while *Review* contributor Mary E. Davis points out further resemblances between the two authors. Davis notes: "Garcia Marquez concentrates on the specific personality of place in the manner of the Mississippean, and he develops even the most reprehensible of his characters as idiosyncratic enigmas." Concludes the critic: "Garcia Marquez is as fascinated by the capacity of things, events, and characters for sudden metamorphosis as was Faulkner."

Nevertheless, *Newsweek* writer Peter S. Prescott maintains that it was only after Garcia Marquez shook off the influence of Faulkner that he was able to write *One Hundred Years of Solitude;* in this novel the author's "imagination matured: no longer content to write dark and fatalistic stories about a Latin Yoknapatawpha County, he broke loose into exuberance, wit and laughter." Thor Vilhjalmsson similarly observes in *Books Abroad* that while "Garcia Marquez does not fail to deal with the dark forces, or give the impression that the life of human beings, one by one, should be ultimately tragic, . . . he also shows every moment pregnant with images and color and scent which ask to be arranged into patterns of meaning and significance while the moment lasts." While the Colombian has frequently referred to Faulkner as "my master," Luis Harss and Barbara Dohmann add in their *Into the Mainstream: Conversations with Latin-American Writers* that in his later stories, "the Faulknerian glare has been neutralized. It is not replaced by any other. From now on Garcia Marquez is his own master."

In *The Autumn of the Patriarch* Garcia Marquez uses a more openly political tone in relating the story of a dictator who has reigned for so long that no one can remember any other ruler. Elaborating on the kind of solitude experienced by Colonel Aureliano Buendia in *One Hundred Years,* Garcia Marquez explores the isolation of a political tyrant. "In this fabulous, dream-like account of the reign of a nameless dictator of a fantastic Caribbean realm, solitude is linked with the possession of absolute power," describes Ronald De Feo in the *National Review.* Rather than relating a straightforward account of the general's life, however, *The Autumn of the Patriarch* skips from one episode to another, using dense and detailed descriptions. *Times Literary Supplement* contributor John Sturrock finds this approach appropriate to the author's subject; calling the work "the desperate, richly sustained hallucination of a man rightly bitter about the present state of so much of Latin America," Sturrock notes that "Garcia Marquez's novel is sophisticated and its language is luxuriant to a degree. Style and subject are at odds because Garcia Marquez is committed to showing that our first freedom—and one which all too many Latin American countries have lost—is of the full resources of our language." *Time* writer R. Z. Sheppard similarly comments on Garcia Marquez's elaborate style, observing that "the theme is artfully insinuated, an atmosphere instantly evoked like a puff of stage smoke, and all conveyed in language that generates a charge of expectancy." The critic concludes: "Garcia Marquez writes with what could be called a stream-of-consciousness technique, but the result is much more like a whirlpool."

Some critics, however, find both the theme and technique of *The Autumn of the Patriarch* lacking. J. D. O'Hara, for example, writes in the *Washington Post Book World* that for all his "magical" realism Garcia Marquez "can only remind us of real-life parallels; he cannot exaggerate them. For the same reason," adds the critic, "although he can turn into grisly cartoons the squalor and paranoia of actual dictatorships, he can scarcely parody them; reality has anticipated him again." *Newsweek*'s Walter Clemons similarly finds the novel somewhat disappointing: "After the narrative vivacity and intricate characterization of the earlier book [*The Autumn of the Patriarch*] seems both oversumptuous and underpopulated. It is—deadliest of compliments—an extended piece of magnificent writing," concludes Clemons. But other critics believe that the author's skillful style enhances the novel; referring to the novel's disjointed narrative style, Wendy McElroy comments

in *World Research INK* that "this is the first time I have seen it handled properly. Gabriel Garcia Marquez ignores many conventions of the English language which are meant to provide structure and coherence. But he is so skillful that his novel is not difficult to understand. It is bizarre; it is disorienting," continues the critic. "But it is not difficult. Moreover, it is appropriate to the chaos and decay of the general's mind and of his world." Similarly, De Feo maintains that "no summary or description of this book can really do it justice, for it is not only the author's surrealistic flights of imagination that make it such an exceptional work, but also his brilliant use of language, his gift for phrasing and description." Concludes the critic: "Throughout this unique, remarkable novel, the tall tale is transformed into a true work of art."

"With its run-on, seemingly free-associative sentences, its constant flow of images and color, Gabriel Garcia Marquez's last novel, *The Autumn of the Patriarch,* was such a dazzling technical achievement that it left the pleasurably exhausted reader wondering what the author would do next," comments De Feo in the *Nation.* This next work, *Chronicle of a Death Foretold* "is, in miniature, a virtuoso performance," states Jonathan Yardley of the *Washington Post Book World.* In contrast with the author's "two masterworks, *One Hundred Years of Solitude* and *The Autumn of the Patriarch,*" continues the critic, "it is slight; . . . its action is tightly concentrated on a single event. But in this small space Garcia Marquez works small miracles; *Chronicle of a Death Foretold* is ingeniously, impeccably, constructed, and it provides a sobering, devastating perspective on the system of male 'honor.'" In the novella, describes Douglas Hill in the Toronto *Globe and Mail,* Garcia Marquez "has cut out an apparently uncomplicated, larger-than-life jigsaw puzzle of passion and crime, then demonstrated, with laconic diligence and a sort of concerned amusement, how extraordinarily difficult the task of assembling the pieces can be." The story is based on a historical incident in which a young woman is returned after her wedding night for not being a virgin; her brothers then set out to avenge the stain on the family honor by murdering the man she names as her "perpetrator." The death is "foretold" in that the brothers announce their intentions to the entire town; but circumstances conspire to keep all but Santiago Nasar, the condemned man, from this knowledge, and he is brutally murdered.

"In telling this story, which is as much about the townspeople and their reactions as it is about the key players, Garcia Marquez might simply have remained omniscient," observes De Feo. But instead "he places himself in the action, assuming the role of a former citizen who returns home to reconstruct the events of the tragic day—a day he himself lived through." This narrative maneuvering, claims the critic, "adds another layer to the book, for the narrator, who is visible one moment, invisible the next, could very well ask himself the same question he is intent on asking others, and his own role, his own failure to act in the affair contributes to the book's odd, haunting ambiguity." This recreation after the fact has an additional effect, as Gregory Rabassa notes in *World Literature Today:* "From the beginning we know that Santiago Nasar will be and has been killed, depending on the time of the narrative thread that we happen to be following, but Garcia Marquez does manage, in spite of the repeated foretelling of the event by the murderers and others, to maintain the suspense at a high level by never describing the actual murder until the very end." The critic explains: "Until then we have been following the chronicler as he puts the bits and pieces together ex post facto, but he has constructed things in such a way that we are still hoping for a reprieve even though we know better.'' ''As more and more is revealed about the murder, less and less is known,'' writes Leonard Michaels in the *New York Times Book Review.* ''Yet the style of the novel is always natural and unselfconscious, as if innocent of any paradoxical implication.''

In approaching the story from this recreative standpoint, Garcia Marquez is once again making use of journalistic techniques. As *Chicago Tribune Book World* editor John Blades maintains, ''Garcia Marquez tells this grisly little fable in what often appears to be a straight-faced parody of conventional journalism, with its dependence on 'he-she-they told me' narrative techniques, its reliance on the distorted, contradictory and dreamlike memories of 'eyewitnesses.' '' Blades adds, however, that ''at the same time, this is precision-tooled fiction; the author subtly but skillfully manipulates his chronology for dramatic impact.'' The *New York Times*'s Christopher Lehmann-Haupt similarly notes a departure from the author's previous style: ''I cannot be absolutely certain whether in 'Chronicle' Gabriel Garcia Marquez has come closer to conventional storytelling than in his previous work, or whether I have simply grown accustomed to his imagination.'' The critic determines that ''whatever the case, I found 'Chronicle of a Death Foretold' by far the author's most absorbing work to date. I read it through in a flash, and it made the back of my neck prickle.'' ''It is interesting,'' remarks *Times Literary Supplement* contributor Bill Buford, that Garcia Marquez has chosen to handle ''a fictional episode with the methods of a journalist. In doing so he has written an unusual and original work: a simple narrative so charged with irony that it has the authority of political fable.'' Concludes the critic: ''If it is not an example of the socialist realism [Garcia] Marquez may claim it to be elsewhere, *Chronicle of a Death Foretold* is in any case a mesmerizing work that clearly establishes [Garcia] Marquez as one of the most accomplished, and the most 'magical' of political novelists writing today.''

Despite this journalistic approach to the story, *Chronicle of a Death Foretold* does contain some of the ''magical'' elements that characterize Garcia Marquez's fiction. As Robert M. Adams observes in the *New York Review of Books,* there is a ''combination of detailed factual particularity, usually on irrelevant points, with vagueness, confusion, or indifference on matters of more importance.'' The result, suggests Adams, is that ''the investigation of an ancient murder takes on the quality of a hallucinatory exploration, a deep groping search into the gathering darkness for a truth that continually slithers away.'' But others find that this combination of journalistic detail and lack of explanation detracts from the novel; D. Keith Mano, for example, comments in the *National Review* that because the narrator ''has been sequestered as a juror might be . . . , he cannot comment or probe: and this rather kiln-dries the novel.'' The critic elaborates by noting that the primary characters ''are left without development or chiaroscuro. They seem cryptic and surface-hard: film characters really. . . . Beyond a Warren Report-meticulous detective reconstruction, it is hard to care much for these people. Emotion, you see, might skew our clarity.'' But Edith Grossman asserts in *Review* that this reconstruction is meant to be enigmatic: ''Garcia Marquez holds onto the journalistic details, the minutiae of the factual, that constitute the great novelistic inheritance of Western realism, and at the same time throws doubt on their reliability through his narrative technique and by means of the subtle introduction of mythic elements.'' Concludes the critic: ''Once again Garcia Marquez is an ironic chronicler who dazzles the reader with uncommon blendings of fantasy, fable and fact.''

Another blending of fable and fact, based in part on Garcia Marquez's recollections of his parents's marriage, *Love in the Time of Cholera* ''is an amazing celebration of the many kinds of love between men and women,'' characterizes Elaine Feinstein in the London *Times.* ''In part it is a brilliantly witty account of the tussles in a long marriage, whose details are curiously moving; elsewhere it is a fantastic tale of love finding erotic fulfilment in aging bodies.'' The novel begins with the death of Dr. Juvenal Urbino, whose attempt to rescue a parrot from a tree leaves his wife of fifty years, Fermina Daza, a widow. Soon after Urbino's death, however, Florentino Ariza appears on Fermina Daza's doorstep; the rest of the novel recounts Florentino's determination to resume the passionate courtship of a woman who had given him up over half a century ago. In relating both the story of Fermina Daza's marriage and her later courtship, *Love in the Time of Cholera* ''is a novel about commitment and fidelity under circumstances which seem to render such virtues absurd,'' recounts *Times Literary Supplement* contributor S. M. J. Minta. ''[It is] about a refusal to grow old gracefully and respectably, about the triumph sentiment can still win over reason, and above all, perhaps, about Latin America, about keeping faith with where, for better or worse, you started out from.''

Although the basic plot of *Love in the Time of Cholera* is fairly simple, some critics accuse Garcia Marquez of overembellishing his story. Calling the plot a ''boy-meets-girl'' story, Chicago *Tribune Books* contributor Michael Dorris remarks that ''it takes a while to realize this core [plot], for every aspect of the book is attenuated, exaggerated, overstated.'' The critic also notes that ''while a Harlequin Romance might balk at stretching this plot for more than a year or two of fictional time, Garcia Marquez nurses it over five decades,'' adding that the ''prose [is] laden with hyperbolic excess.'' In addition, some observers claim that instead of revealing the romantic side of love, *Love in the Time of Cholera* ''seems to deal more with libido and self-deceit than with desire and mortality,'' as Angela Carter terms it in the *Washington Post Book World.* Dorris expresses a similar opinion, writing that while the novel's ''first 50 pages are brilliant, provocative, . . . they are overture to a discordant symphony'' which portrays an ''anachronistic'' world of machismo and misogyny. In contrast, Toronto *Globe and Mail* contributor Ronald Wright believes that the novel works as a satire of this same kind of ''hypocrisy, provincialism and irresponsibility of the main characters' social milieu.'' Concludes the critic: ''Love in the Time of Cholera is a complex and subtle book; its greatest achievement is not to tell a love story, but to meditate on the equivocal nature of romanticism and romantic love.''

Other reviewers agree that although it contains elements of his other work, *Love in the Time of Cholera* is a development in a different direction for Garcia Marquez. Author Thomas Pynchon, writing in the *New York Times Book Review,* comments that ''it would be presumptuous to speak of moving 'beyond' 'One Hundred Years of Solitude' but clearly Garcia Marquez has moved somewhere else, not least into deeper awareness of the ways in which, as Florentino comes to learn, 'nobody teaches life anything.' '' Countering criticisms that the work is overemotional, Minta claims that ''the triumph of the novel is that it uncovers the massive, submerged strength of the popular, the cliched and the sentimental.'' While it ''does not possess the fierce, visionary poetry of 'One Hundred Years of Solitude' or the feverish phantasmagoria of 'The Autumn of the Patriarch,' '' as *New York Times* critic Michiko Kakutani describes it, *Love in the Time of Cholera* ''has revealed how the extraordinary is contained in the ordinary, how a couple of forgotten, even commonplace lives can encompass the heights and depths of grand and eternal passion. The result," concludes the critic, "is a rich commodious novel, a novel whose narrative power is matched only by its generosity of vision." "The Garcimarquesian voice we have come to recognize from the other fiction has matured, found and developed new resources," asserts Pynchon, "[and] been brought to a level where it can at once be classical and familiar, opalescent and pure, able to praise and curse, laugh and cry, fabulate and sing and when called upon, take off and soar." Concludes the critic: "There is nothing I have read quite like [the] astonishing final chapter, symphonic, sure in its dynamics and tempo. . . . At the very best [this remembrance] results in works that can even return our worn souls to us, among which most certainly belongs 'Love in the Time of Cholera,' this shining and heartbreaking novel."

Although he has earned literary fame through his fiction, Garcia Marquez has also gained notoriety as a reporter; as he commented to Stone, "I always very much enjoy the chance of doing a great piece of journalism." The Colombian elaborated in his interview with Dreifus: "I'm fascinated by the relationship between literature and *journalism*. I began my career as a journalist in Colombia, and a reporter is something I've never stopped being. When I'm not working on fiction, I'm running around the world, practicing my craft as a reporter." His work as a journalist, however, has produced some controversy, for in it Garcia Marquez not only sees a chance to develop his "craft," but also an opportunity to become involved in political issues. His self-imposed exile from Colombia was prompted by a series of articles he wrote in 1955 about the sole survivor of a Colombian shipwreck, for the young journalist related that the government ship had capsized due to an overloading of contraband. Garcia Marquez has more recently written *Clandestine in Chile: The Adventures of Miguel Littin*, a work about an exile's return to the repressive Chile of General Augusto Pinochet; the political revelations of the book led to the burning of almost 15,000 copies by the Chilean government. In addition, Garcia Marquez has maintained personal relationships with such political figures as Cuban President Fidel Castro, French President Francois Mitterand, and the late Panamanian leader General Omar Torrijos.

Because of this history of political involvement, Garcia Marquez has often been accused of allowing his politics to overshadow his work; he has also encountered problems entering the United States. When asked by the *New York Times Book Review*'s Marlise Simons why he is so insistent on becoming involved in political issues, the author replied that "If I were not a Latin American, maybe I wouldn't [become involved]. But underdevelopment is total, integral, it affects every part of our lives. The problems of our societies are mainly political." The Colombian further explained that "the commitment of a writer is with the reality of all of society, not just with a small part of it. If not, he is as bad as the politicians who disregard a large part of our reality. That is why authors, painters, writers in Latin America get politically involved."

Despite the controversy that his politics and work stir, Garcia Marquez's *One Hundred Years of Solitude* is enough to ensure the author "a place in the ranks of twentieth century masters," claims Curt Suplee of the *Washington Post*. The Nobel-winner's reputation, however, is grounded in more than this one masterpiece; as the Swedish Academy's Nobel citation states, "Each new work of his is received by critics and readers as an event of world importance, is translated into many languages and published as quickly as possible in large editions." "At a time of dire predictions about the future of the novel," observes McMurray, Garcia Marquez's "prodigious imagination, remarkable compositional precision, and wide popularity provide evidence that the genre is still thriving." And as *Chicago Tribune Book World* contributor Harry Mark Petrakis describes him, Garcia Marquez "is a magician of vision and language who does astonishing things with time and reality. He blends legend and history in ways that make the legends seem truer than truth. His scenes and characters are humorous, tragic, mysterious and beset by ironies and fantasies. In his fictional world, anything is possible and everything is believable." Concludes the critic: "Mystical and magical, fully aware of the transiency of life, his stories fashion realms inhabited by ghosts and restless souls who return to those left behind through fantasies and dreams. The stories explore, with a deceptive simplicity, the miracles and mysteries of life."

MEDIA ADAPTATIONS: A play, "Blood and Champagne," has been based on Garcia Marquez's *One Hundred Years of Solitude.*

BIOGRAPHICAL/CRITICAL SOURCES:

BOOKS

Brotherson, Gordon, *The Emergence of the Latin American Novel,* Cambridge University Press, 1979.
Contemporary Literary Criticism, Gale, Volume 2, 1974, Volume 3, 1975, Volume 8, 1978, Volume 10, 1979, Volume 15, 1980, Volume 27, 1984, Volume 47, 1988.
Dictionary of Literary Biography Yearbook: 1982, Gale, 1983.
Fernandez-Braso, Miguel, *Gabriel Garcia Marquez,* Editorial Azur (Madrid), 1969.
Gabriel Garcia Marquez, nuestro premio Nobel, La Secretaria de Informacion y Prensa de la Presidencia de la Nacion (Bogota), 1983.
Gallagher, David Patrick, *Modern Latin American Literature,* Oxford University Press, 1973.
Guibert, Rita, *Seven Voices,* Knopf, 1973.
Harss, Luis and Barbara Dohmann, *Into the Mainstream: Conversations with Latin-American Writers,* Harper, 1967.
Janes, Regina, *Gabriel Garcia Marquez: Revolutions in Wonderland,* University of Missouri Press, 1981.
Mantilla, Alfonso Renteria, compiler, *Garcia Marquez habla de Garcia Marquez,* Renteria (Colombia), 1979.
McGuirk, Bernard and Richard Cardwell, editors, *Gabriel Garcia Marquez: New Readings,* Cambridge University Press, 1988.
McMurray, George R., *Gabriel Garcia Marquez,* Ungar, 1977.
Porrata, Francisco E. and Fausto Avedano, *Explicacion de Cien anos de soledad [de] Garcia Marquez,* Editorial Texto (Costa Rica), 1976.
Pritchett, V. S., *The Myth Makers,* Random House, 1979.
Rodman, Selden, *Tongues of Fallen Angels,* New Direction, 1974.
Vargas Llosa, Mario, *Garcia Marquez: Historia de un deicido,* Barral Editores, 1971.

PERIODICALS

Books Abroad, winter, 1973, summer, 1973, spring, 1976.
Book World, February 22, 1970, February 20, 1972.
Chicago Tribune, March 6, 1983.
Chicago Tribune Book World, November 11, 1979, November 7, 1982, April 3, 1983, November 18, 1984, April 27, 1986.
Christian Science Monitor, April 16, 1970.

Commonweal, March 6, 1970.

Detroit News, October 27, 1982, December 16, 1984.

El Pais, January 22, 1981.

Globe and Mail (Toronto), April 7, 1984, September 19, 1987, May 21, 1988.

Hispania, September, 1976.

London Magazine, April/May, 1973, November, 1979.

Los Angeles Times, October 22, 1982, January 25, 1987, August 24, 1988.

Los Angeles Times Book Review, April 10, 1983, November 13, 1983, December 16, 1984, April 27, 1986, June 7, 1987, April 17, 1988.

Nation, December 2, 1968, May 15, 1972, May 14, 1983.

National Observer, April 20, 1970.

National Review, May 27, 1977, June 10, 1983.

New Republic, April 9, 1977, October 27, 1979, May 2, 1983.

New Statesman, June 26, 1970, May 18, 1979, February 15, 1980, September 3, 1982.

Newsweek, March 2, 1970, November 8, 1976, July 3, 1978, December 3, 1979, November 1, 1982.

New York Review of Books, March 26, 1970, January 24, 1980, April 14, 1983.

New York Times, July 11, 1978, November 6, 1979, October 22, 1982, March 25, 1983, December 7, 1985, April 26, 1986, June 4, 1986, April 6, 1988.

New York Times Book Review, September 29, 1968, March 8, 1970, February 20, 1972, October 31, 1976, July 16, 1978, September 16, 1978, November 11, 1979, November 16, 1980, December 5, 1982, March 27, 1983, April 7, 1985, April 27, 1986, August 9, 1987, April 10, 1988.

Paris Review, winter, 1981.

Playboy, February, 1983.

Publishers Weekly, May 13, 1974, December 16, 1983.

Review, Number 24, 1979, September/December, 1981.

Saturday Review, December 21, 1968, March 7, 1970.

Southwest Review, summer, 1973.

Time, March 16, 1970, November 1, 1976, July 10, 1978, November 1, 1982, March 7, 1983, December 31, 1984, April 14, 1986.

Times (London), November 13, 1986, June 30, 1988.

Times Literary Supplement, April 15, 1977, February 1, 1980, September 10, 1982, July 1, 1988.

Tribune Books (Chicago), June 28, 1987, April 17, 1988.

Washington Post, October 22, 1982.

Washington Post Book World, February 22, 1970, November 14, 1976, November 25, 1979, November 7, 1982, March 27, 1983, November 18, 1984, July 19, 1987, April 24, 1988.

World Literature Today, winter, 1982.

World Press Review, April, 1982.

World Research INK, September, 1977.*

—*Sketch by Marian Gonsior and Diane Telgen*

*   *   *

GARRETT, Gerald R.   1940-

PERSONAL: Born September 21, 1940, in Mount Vernon, Wash.; son of Kenneth J. and Pearl Odessa (Wells) Garrett; married Marcia Pope (a professor of sociology and a lawyer), June 10, 1967 (divorced June 10, 1976). *Education:* Whitman College, A.B., 1962; Washington State University, M.A., 1966, Ph.D., 1970.

ADDRESSES: Office—Department of Sociology, University of Massachusetts—Boston, Harbor Campus, Boston, Mass. 02125-3393.

CAREER: University of Wisconsin, Whitewater, instructor in sociology, 1966-67; Carroll College, Waukesha, Wis., assistant professor of sociology, 1967-68; Washington State University, Pullman, research fellow in sociology, 1968-70; University of Massachusetts—Boston, Harbor Campus, professor of sociology, 1970—, director, Graduate Program in Applied Sociology, 1982-85. Research associate at Columbia University, 1969, 1970; lecturer at University of Maryland, European Division, Heidelberg, Germany, 1976-77, and Boston University Overseas Programs, Seckenheim, West Germany, 1978-84; visiting associate professor at Washington State University, 1977-78, and University of Alaska, Fairbanks, 1978; visiting professor, Troy State University/Europe, Wiesbaden, West Germany, 1978-79. Member of National Task Force on Higher Education and Criminal Justice, 1975-76. Consultant, National Institute on Alcohol Abuse and Alcoholism, Rockville, Md., 1988-89.

MEMBER: Academy of Criminal Justice Sciences, Society for the Study of Social Problems (program chairman, 1980-81), American Sociological Association, American Society of Criminology, Eastern Sociological Society (program chairman, 1981-82), Massachusetts Academy of Criminal Justice Sciences.

WRITINGS:

(With H. M. Bahr) *Disaffiliation among Urban Women*, Columbia, 1971.

(With Bahr) *Women Alone*, Heath, 1976.

(With Richard Rettig and Manuel J. Torres) *Manny: A Criminal-Addict's Story*, Houghton, 1977.

(With R. Schutt) *Working with the Homeless: A Video-Based Training Experience* (video and guidebook), Center for Communications Media, 1987.

(With Schutt and B. Blakeney) *Responding to the Homeless*, Plenum, 1989.

CONTRIBUTOR

Bahr, editor, *Skid Row: An Introduction to Disaffiliation*, Oxford University Press, 1973.

Jack Kinton, editor, *Professionalization in America: Police Roles in the 1970s*, Social Science & Sociological Resources, 1975.

Jack and Joann Delora, editors, *Intimate Life Styles*, Goodyear Publishing, 1976.

Joseph Scott and Simon Dinitz, editors, *Criminal Justice Planning*, Praeger, 1978.

E. J. Hunter and Steven Nice, editors, *Military Families: Adaptation to Stress*, Praeger, 1979.

C. Ford and J. Eddy, editors, *Women and Alcohol*, W. C. Brown, 1980.

C. Larson, *Crime, Correction and Society*, General Hall, 1984.

Homelessness: Critical Issues in Policy and Practice, Boston Foundation, 1987.

J. Baumohl, editor, *Research Agenda: The Homeless with Alcohol and Drug Problems*, National Institute on Alcohol Abuse and Alcoholism, 1987.

(With Schutt) M. Robertson and M. Greenblatt, editors, *Homelessness: The National Perspective*, Plenum, 1988.

(With Schutt) J. Momeni, editor, *Homelessness in the United States*, Greenwood, Volume 1, 1989, Volume 2, 1989.

Also contributor to numerous professional journals.

WORK IN PROGRESS: Research on alcoholism among the homeless; alcohol prevention and education, and correctional education; evaluations research; training in substance abuse for social services and criminal justice professionals.

SIDELIGHTS: Gerald R. Garrett wrote *CA:* "The crisis of homelessness in the 1980s touches the lives of every American. It is a social problem that cuts across the fabric of American life—social services and welfare, criminal justice, health care, employment, education, housing, and federal, state and local government. Most of all, homelessness offends our sense of humanity and compassion for others. For both personal and professional reasons, my work in the 1980s has focused on issues related to homelessness and on how we can return the homeless to stable and productive lifestyles. My research interest in alcohol problems and substance abuse are especially relevant, since as many as half of the homeless suffer from alcohol and other drug disorders. In the course of my research work, it is increasingly clear to me that alcohol and drug dependency among the homeless is not just a treatment issue. It is also a political and economic issue. Therapeutic successes are short-lived without efforts that provide opportunities for education, job training and placement, access to health care services, and affordable housing. The homelessness-addiction cycle will continue unless we adopt a broader approach in our recovery programs."

*   *   *

GASCOIGNE, Bamber   1935-

PERSONAL: Born January 24, 1935, in London, England; married Christina Ditchburn (a photographer), 1965. *Education:* Attended Magdalene College, Cambridge.

ADDRESSES: Home—London, England. *Agent*—Curtis Brown, 1 Craven Hill, London W2 3EW, England.

CAREER: Author and lyricist. Drama critic of *Spectator*, London, England, 1961-63, and *Observer*, London, 1963-64; also writes for television, and appeared weekly as chairman of "University Challenge" program, Granada Television, Manchester, England, 1962-87; presenter of thirteen-part television documentary series, "The Christians," 1977, and of eighteen-part series, "Man and Music," 1986-87.

WRITINGS:

NONFICTION

Twentieth-Century Drama, Hutchinson, 1962.
World Theatre: An Illustrated History, Little, Brown, 1968.
The Great Moghuls (history), photographs by wife, Christina Gascoigne, Harper, 1971.
The Dynasties and Treasures of China (history), photographs by C. Gascoigne and Derrick Witty, Viking, 1973 (published in England as *The Treasures and Dynasties of China,* Cape, 1973).
The Christians, photographs by C. Gascoigne, Morrow, 1977.
(With Jonathan Ditchburn) *Images of Richmond: A Survey of the Topographical Prints of Richmond in Surrey up to the Year 1900,* St. Helena Press, 1978.
(With Ditchburn and Harriet and Peter George) *Images of Twickenham: With Hampton and Teddington,* St. Helena Press, 1981.
Quest for the Golden Hare, Cape, 1983.
How to Identify Prints, Thames and Hudson, 1987.

FICTION

Murgatreud's Empire, Viking, 1972.
The Heyday, Cape, 1973, Viking, 1974.

Ticker Khan, Cape, 1974, Simon & Schuster, 1975.
(With C. Gascoigne) *Why the Rope Went Tight* (juvenile), illustrations by C. Gascoigne, 1981.
Fearless Freddie's Magic Wish (juvenile), illustrations by C. Gascoigne, Methuen, 1982.
Fearless Freddie's Sunken Treasures, illustrations by C. Gascoigne, Methuen, 1982.
Cod Streuth, Cape, 1986.

OTHER

"The Feydeau Farce of 1909" (play), first produced in Greenwich, England, revised version retitled "Big in Brazil," first produced on the West End at Old Vic, September, 1984.

Also author of "Share My Lettuce," first produced at Cambridge University, England.

SIDELIGHTS: In *The Great Moghuls,* author and critic Bamber Gascoigne retraces the more than two-hundred-year history of the Moghul Empire in India. Critics liked the photographs, contributed by Gascoigne's wife, Christina, as well as the text. According to *New Statesman* contributor Christopher Wordsworth, *The Great Moghuls* is "a digest of the first six Moghul emperors that feasts the eye and should not seriously affront the pundits.... [Gascoigne] avoids equally the trite and the ornate, preserving the outline of personality and achievement through a great melting-pot of intrigue and skirmish that could have boiled the shape out of any book." A *Virginia Quarterly Review* critic praises the way Gascoigne's narrative "moves smoothly through the matrix of intersecting plots and counterplots, through the welter of military campaigns and disguised tiger-hunts, through the complex of petty jealousies and magnanimous gestures." And Christopher Hibbert concludes in *Book World* that "in recording the lives and achievements of this remarkable family, Bamber Gascoigne has written a well-researched and valuable book. Combined with its splendid illustrations, including many fine photographs by his wife, his text vividly recalls the strange, lost world of the Moghuls and the timeless beauty of India."

Gascoigne's socio-religious farce *Cod Streuth* also takes place far from British society. In Brazil, a travelling monk is captured by cannibals who are awaiting a copy of the Bible promised by an earlier missionary. However, the monk's manuscript is not the expected document but a portion of Rabelais. The ten pages of Rabelais becomes Holy Writ for the Tupinili tribe, and the former monk becomes their king, accepting, as well as other responsibilities, the mandated twenty wives. *Times Literary Supplement* contributor Peter Reading comments that Gascoigne relates his tale "with entertaining bibliophilic plausibility." He continues, "there is bawdry in this well-balanced book ... there is tenderness.... there is unpresumptuous shrewdness in its apophthegms." And Gary Krist in the *New York Times Book Review* calls the book a "wonderful little fiction with just the right balance of ironic restraint and unbuttoned vulgarity. One of the most unusual books to appear in a long time, 'Cod Streuth' ('God's Truth') is literary entertainment of a high order."

BIOGRAPHICAL/CRITICAL SOURCES:

PERIODICALS

Books Abroad, summer, 1969.
Book World, December 1, 1968, December 5, 1971.
New Statesman, November 5, 1971.
New York Times Book Review, May 3, 1987.

Spectator, December 20, 1968.
Times Literary Supplement, December 5, 1971, March 19, 1982, May 30, 1986.
Virginia Quarterly Review, winter, 1972.

*   *   *

GASCOYNE, David (Emery) 1916-

PERSONAL: Born October 10, 1916, in Harrow, England; son of Leslie Noel (a bank official) and Winfred Isabel (Emery) Gascoyne; married Judy Tyler Lewis, May 17, 1975; children: 2 stepsons, 2 stepdaughters. *Education:* Attended Salisbury Cathedral Choir School ("this had a lasting influence on my life") and Regent Street Polytechnic.

ADDRESSES: Home—48 Oxford St., Northwood, Cowes, Isle of Wight PO31 8PT, England. *Agent*—Alan Clodd, 22 Huntington Rd., London N29 DV, England.

CAREER: Poet and writer. Has given poetry reading tours in the United States, 1951-52, and 1981, and in Ireland, 1984. Representative on international committee, *Nuova Revista Europa*, Milan; president, Third European Festival of Poetry, Belgium, 1981. Attended poetry festivals in Rome, Paris, Amsterdam, Florence, Belgrade, and other cities. 1978-88.

MEMBER: Royal Society of Literature (fellow), World Organization for Poets (member of cultural committee), Committee of Belgian Biennales Internationales de Poesi (honorary member).

AWARDS, HONORS: Rockefeller-Atlantic Award, 1949; the British Council and the Centre Georges Pompidou presented an "Homage to David Gascoyne" in 1981; Biella European Poetry Prize, 1982, for *La Mano de Poeta*.

WRITINGS:

POEMS

Roman Balcony, and Other Poems, Lincoln Williams, 1932.
Man's Life Is This Meat, Parton Press, 1936.
Hoelderlin's Madness, Dent, 1938.
Poems, 1937-1942, Editions Poetry, 1943.
A Vagrant, and Other Poems, Lehmann, 1950.
Night Thoughts (verse play; first broadcast on radio by the British Broadcsting Corp., December 7, 1955), Grove, 1956.
Collected Poems, edited and with an introduction by Robin Skelton, Oxford University Press, 1965, enlarged edition published as *Collected Poems, 1988*, 1988.
The Sun at Midnight: Aphorisms, with Two Poems, Enitharmon Press, 1970.
Three Poems, Enitharmon Press, 1976.
Early Poems, Greville Press, 1980.
La Mano de Poeta, Edizioni S. Marco dei Giustiniani, 1982.
Tankens Doft, Ellerstroms, 1988.

TRANSLATOR

Salvador Dali, *Conquest of the Irrational*, J. Levy, 1935.
(With Humphrey Jennings) Benjamin Peret, *A Bunch of Carrots: Twenty Poems*, Roger Roughton, 1936, revised edition published as *Remove Your Hat*, 1936. (With others) Paul Eluard, *Thorns of Thunder*, Europa/Nott, 1936.
Andre Breton, *What Is Surrealism?*, Faber, 1936.
Collected Verse Translations, edited by Skelton and Alan Clodd, Oxford University Press, 1970.
(With others) Paul Auster, editor, *The Random House Book of 20th Century French Poetry*, Random House, 1982.

Breton and Philippe Soupault, *The Magnetic Fields*, Atlas Press, 1985.

CONTRIBUTOR

Poets of Tomorrow, Hogarth Press, 1942.
Penguin Modern Poets, No. 17, Penguin, 1970.
A Garland of Poems for Leonard Clark on His 75th Birthday, Lomond Press/Enitharmon Press, 1980.
Free Spirits I, City Lights, 1982.

Also contributor to anthologies published in France, Germany, Italy, Yugoslavia, Argentina, and Hong Kong.

OTHER

Opening Day (novel), Cobden-Sanderson, 1933.
A Short Survey of Surrealism, Cobden-Sanderson, 1935, City Lights, 1982.
(Editor and author of introduction) Kenneth Patchen, *Outlaw of the Lowest Planet*, Grey Walls Press, 1946.
"The Hole in the Fourth Wall; or, Talk, Talk, Talk" (play), first produced in London at the Watergate Theatre, 1950.
Thomas Carlyle, Longmans, Green, 1952.
Paris Journal, 1937-1939, preface by Lawrence Durrell, Enitharmon Press, 1978.
Journal, 1936-1937, Enitharmon Press, 1980.
Rencontres avec Benjamin Fondane, Editions Arcane, 1984.

Contributor to *New English Weekly, Partisan Review, Cahiers du Sud, Times Literary Supplement, Literary Review, Two Rivers, Ambit, Poetry Review, PN Review, Temenos, Malahat Review, Botteghe Oscure*, and other publications in England, France, Belgium and Italy.

SIDELIGHTS: The poetry of David Gascoyne has undergone several major changes during his long career. At first an imagist, then a dedicated surrealist, Gascoyne's early poems were visionary, fantastic works filled with hallucinatory images and symbolic language. By the 1940s, he was writing mystical poems in which Christian imagery played a large part and the ecstatic pain of the religious seeker was paramount. Since publishing a few more poems in the late 1940s, Gascoyne has published little new work. Since the 1950s, his writing has been curtailed due to a mental breakdown and continuing bouts of severe depression. But Gascoyne's place in modern British poetry is secure; writing in *Twentieth Century*, Elizabeth Jennings describes Gascoyne as the "only living English poet in the true tradition of visionary or mystical poetry." In an article for the *Dictionary of Literary Biography*, Philip Gardner calls Gascoyne's *Poems, 1937-1942* "among the most distinguished and powerful collections of the last fifty years."

According to Gardner, in an article for the *Times Literary Supplement*, Gascoyne "was the literary prodigy of the 1930s." *Roman Balcony, and Other Poems*, Gascoyne's first book of poetry, appeared when the author was sixteen, and was followed by a novel, a nonfiction study entitled *A Short Survey of Surrealism*, several volumes of work translated from the French, and, before Gascoyne was twenty, a second volume of poems. This initial burst of activity was never to be repeated.

Roman Balcony, and Other Poems was published in 1936 while Gascoyne was still attending school. He had received a small legacy and used the money to finance the book's publication. Strongly influenced by the imagist poets and the fin-de-siecle writings of the 1890s, these early poems are "highly impressionistic, introspective, and word-conscious," Gardner explains in the *Dictionary of Literary Biography*. Robin Skelton, in his introduction to Gascoyne's *Collected Poems,* calls *Roman Balcony* "an astonishing performance for an adolescent. . . . Already in this book there is that interest in hallucinatory obsessive symbolism which gave so many of [Gascoyne's] poems of the later thirties their individual and disturbing quality."

Gascoyne's early interest in symbolism and the hallucinatory led him to study the surrealist writers of the 1930s, a school little known in England at that time. He was one of the first British poets to take note of the surrealists, and is generally credited with introducing their work to the English-speaking world. In 1935 and 1936, Gascoyne translated collections by the surrealists Salvador Dali, Benjamin Peret, and Andre Breton. His nonfiction introduction to the group's beliefs, *A Short Survey of Surrealism,* is described by Stephen Spender in the *Times Literary Supplement* as "a delightful book conveying, almost for the first time in English, the fascination of this movement."

This interest in surrealism is evident in the second collection of Gascoyne's poems, *Man's Life Is This Meat,* a book which contains works dedicated to such surrealists as Max Ernst, Rene Magritte, and Salvador Dali. The poems utilize the juxtapositions, intense imagery, and dream logic found in many surrealist works. Skelton says of the poems in this collection that "Gascoyne employed surrealist techniques to good effect. . . . Some poems look like products of a free-association game, [but] a second glance shows them to be full of profound implications."

With *Poems, 1937-1942,* published during the Second World War, Gascoyne first won widespread critical acclaim. "It was with with publication of *Poems, 1937-1942* . . . that Gascoyne's stature became fully apparent," Skelton believes. The book, Derek Stanford maintains in *Poetry Review,* represents "the high-water-mark of Gascoyne's career." Containing poems which are more mystical than those he wrote during his brief association with the surrealists, the book is the first expression, according to Jennings, of Gascoyne's mature poetic voice. "I do not think, . . . that he really found his own voice or his own individual means of expression until he started writing the poems which appeared in the volume entitled *Poems, 1937-42,*" Jennings writes.

In these mystical poems Gascoyne writes as an agonized Christian seeker desperate for a transcendent realm beyond the mortal world. "The theme which emerges most clearly . . . ," Skelton states, "is that of man's despair at his mortality, and his confusion; but often it seems that some illumination of the darkness is imminent." Speaking of the poem series entitled "Miserere" which forms part of the book, Kathleen Raine of the *Sewanee Review* explains that these works "are in praise of the 'Eternal Christ'; the poet speaks from those depths into which the divine Presence has descended in order to redeem our fallen world, in a voice of sustained eloquence, as if at last the angel spoke." Commenting on this same group of poems, Spender explains that Gascoyne was inspired to write these works by the outbreak of the Second World War. Gascoyne, Spender states, "employs the Christian theme of the Miserere to express and transform the agony of war. . . . The poems which Gascoyne wrote early in the war have the immediacy of terrifying events which, acting upon the poet's sensibility like a hand upon an instrument, produce music and images that become part of the larger religious history of mankind."

Gascoyne's ability to combine his visionary poetry with an awareness of the real world around him is remarked upon by Skelton, who states that in *Poems, 1937-1942,* Gascoyne "achieved a religious poetry which combines powerful symbolism with contemporary relevance." Writing in *The Freedom of Poetry: Studies in Contemporary Verse,* Stanford believes that "the poetry of Gascoyne creates a world that is no escape from or substitute for the world we already know. All the problems reality makes us face, we face again in this poetry; and meeting them here for a second time we find them no longer modified by the small distractions of daily life, or the comic relief which existence offers. In this verse we are made to experience the total impact of wickedness—evil itself assumes an image. So, without mercy or mitigation, we are forced to look on this picture of our guilt and inhabit a sphere that seems to be sealed against the possible entry of hope."

Gascoyne's affiliation with the surrealists of the 1930s left its mark on these later poems, although the works are not strictly in the surrealist style. As Michael Schmidt writes in *A Reader's Guide to Fifty Modern British Poets,* "Gascoyne, in his mature work, adapted elements of surrealist technique to an English tradition." Raine comments that "from the surrealists Mr. Gascoyne learned to find, everywhere mirrored in objective reality, subjective states." Writing in *The Ironic Harvest: English Poetry in the Twentieth Century,* Geoffrey Thurley finds that Gascoyne's "capacity for feeling in the presence of rare affinities . . . springs from the same sensibility as created the Surrealist poems, tutored by the Surrealist discipline." Schmidt sees two major influences from the surrealists: "In [Gascoyne's] later poems the surreal elements serve to intensify a mental drama which is powerful for being rooted in the real. . . . The tension is between what he can say and what a language, wrenched and disrupted, can only hope to imply. . . . The main lesson he learned from surrealism was rhythmical. Throughout his work, his sense of line and rhythm units is subtle. In the surreal poems, it is rhythm alone that renders the distorted imagery effective, that fuses disparate elements into an apparent whole."

Beginning with *Poems, 1937-1942,* Gascoyne began to write in a distinctive narrative voice. As a writer for the *Times Literary Supplement* observes, "what makes Gascoyne's poetry so remarkable is its oracular quality." Raine believes that Hoelderlin's work inspired Gascoyne. She cites the metaphysical poems in the *Poems, 1937-1942* volume as bearing "the evident mark of Holderlin's influence; whose imaginative flights David Gascoyne from this time dared, finding in his own wings an eagle-strength upon which he outsoared, in sublimity, all his contemporaries.

A Vagrant, and Other Poems appeared in 1950 and contains works written between 1943 and 1950. "Though it contains nothing finer than [the poems found in *Poems, 1937-1942*], the high level of pure poetry, the perfect command of language, never falters," Raine states. "The tone," Skelton notes, "is generally more quiet. The same beliefs are expressed, but with greater delicacy, and often with humor." Gardner, too, sees a quieter mood in *A Vagrant, and Other Poems.* Many of the poems in this collection, he states in the *Dictionary of Literary Biography,* "transmit a quiet inner beauty one would call mellow, if that word did not carry overtones of a temperament too easily satisfied. Perhaps one may suggest their spiritual quality by saying that they convey a new acceptance of human limitations, a reconciliation."

Several critics believe that *Night Thoughts,* Gascoyne's lone attempt at a dramatic verse play, is among his finest works. Skelton, for example, calls it "his single greatest achievement." The play, written for and first broadcast on radio, is meant to "break through to those other islands of humanity, to reach the drifting rafts of those who, being alone, are also ready to make contact," as Thurley explains. This attempted union with members of the listening audience has a mystical connotation. Stanford believes that the most successful section of *Night Thoughts* is called "Encounter with Silence." This section of the play "is one of the most subtle expositions of man as a spiritually communicative animal to be found in contemporary literature," Stanford writes. "The voice we hear speaking is that of the Solitary, who slowly realises that silence is the music not of the Void but of the Spirit."

During the 1960s and 1970s, Gascoyne published little new work. His *Collected Poems* appeared in 1965 to general critical appreciation, and two volumes of his journals appeared in the late 1970s and early 1980s. But problems in his personal life prevented Gascoyne from writing new work. Bouts of severe depression and paranoia, along with a brief drug addiction, hindered his efforts. He suffered, too, Gardner notes in the *Dictionary of Literary Biography,* "three serious breakdowns in the course of his life." During one such episode in 1973, Gascoyne met Judy Tyler Lewis, a part-time hospital worker. They married in 1975. Gascoyne has said that since that time, his life has vastly improved.

Gascoyne's *Paris Journal, 1937-1939* and *Journal, 1936-37* were written just after his intitial burst of creative activity. They record his move to Paris in the mid-1930s, his break with the surrealists and brief affiliation with communism, and provide a fascinating insight into his thoughts and observations of the time. As Spender notes about *Paris Journal,* "On several levels, Gascoyne's journal is a classic example of this genre." "Taken together," Gardner writes in the *Times Literary Supplement,* "the two journals offer admirers of Gascoyne's work an engrossing record of his self-realization and artistic growth."

Especially noted by critics was Gascoyne's success at rendering the tone and flavor of the time, as well as his revealing expression of his own moods and thoughts. "Few at 20, which was Gascoyne's age when he began [*Paris Journal, 1937-1939*], could have known themselves so fully or have had the literary maturity for such a self-portrait . . . ," Ronald Blythe comments in the *Listener.* "The *Journal* certainly charms, but with something more than talent—perhaps by its ability to describe, with neither conceit nor tedium, all the initial *longeur* of a writer's existence." Spender finds in *Paris Journal* "some beautiful passages of prose poetry evoking Paris street scenes and the French countryside—and also some very somber ones. The young Gascoyne is a marvellously truthful and exact recorder of impressions made on him at concerts and art exhibitions." Alan Ross, writing in *London Magazine,* sees the appearance of Gascoyne's journals as a hopeful sign that the poet may soon begin writing new work. "What is encouraging about the journals," he states, "is that they suggest a shrewd and amusing observer of contemporary foibles, to the extent that one could envisage a late period in the poetry that might be more anecdotal and idiomatic as well as lighter in mood. Gascoyne's literary career, after so long and distressing an interruption, deserves a happy ending. There are few writers from whom one would more welcome poems out of the blue."

In a letter to *CA,* Gascoyne comments on the possibility of his writing new poetry: "After about 15 years of complete nonproduction, and hospitalizations following three severe mental breakdowns, I have at the age of 72 recovered sufficient self-confidence to make me feel I may be entering a new, closing period of creativity."

BIOGRAPHICAL/CRITICAL SOURCES:

BOOKS

Bedford, Colin, *David Gascoyne: A Bibliography of His Works (1929-1985),* Heritage Books, 1986.
Contemporary Literary Criticism, Volume 45, Gale, 1987.
Dictionary of Literary Biography, Volume 20: *British Poets, 1914-1945,* Gale, 1983.
Gascoyne, David, *Collected Poems,* Oxford University Press, 1965.
Gascoyne, David, *Paris Journal, 1937-1939,* Enitharmon Press, 1978.
Gascoyne, David, *Journal, 1936-37,* Enitharmon Press, 1980.
Raine, Kathleen, *Defending Ancient Springs,* Oxford University Press, 1967.
Remy, Michel, *David Gascoyne, ou l'urgence de l'inexprime,* Presses Universitaires de Nancy, 1984.
Scarfe, Francis, *Auden and After: The Liberation of Poetry, 1930-1941,* Routledge, 1942.
Schmidt, Michael, *A Reader's Guide to Fifty Modern British Poets,* Heinemann Educational, 1979.
Stanford, Derek, *The Freedom of Poetry: Studies in Contemporary Verse,* Falcon Press, 1947.
Stanford, Derek, *Inside the Forties: Literary Memoirs, 1937-1957,* Sidgwick & Jackson, 1977.
Thurley, Geoffrey, *The Ironic Harvest: English Poetry in the Twentieth Century,* Edward Arnold, 1974.

PERIODICALS

Book Forum, fall, 1978.
Listener, September 7, 1978.
London Magazine, July, 1957, November, 1965, June, 1981.
New Statesman, September 22, 1978.
Observer, December, 1950.
Poetry, September, 1966.
Poetry Review, Volume LVI, 1965.
Sewanee Review, spring, 1967.
Temenos, Number 7.
Times Literary Supplement, August 12, 1965, October 1, 1971, October 27, 1978, February 6, 1981, August 26, 1988.
Twentieth Century, June, 1959.

—*Sketch by Thomas Wiloch*

*   *   *

GHOSE, Amal 1929-
(Lama Esohg)

PERSONAL: Born May 19, 1929, in Undivided Old Bengal (now Bangladesh); son of Manmatha Nath and Sarala Devi Ghose; married Prity Chakraborty (a dance and music academy principal), 1956; children: Dipankar, Nabarun. *Religion:* "Universalism."

ADDRESSES: Home—Diparun, T-29 Seventh Ave., Besant Nagar, Madras 600 090, India. *Office*—Laser Services, National Biographical Centre, India-Asia.

CAREER: Special correspondent for *Jungantar* and *Amarita Bazar Patrika* newspapers in Calcutta, India, 1950-74. Founder and director of Laser Services. Consultant. Member of Eurasian Institute of Human Resources Development.

MEMBER: World Assembly of Literature and Languages Lovers (founder and director), Cinque Ports Poet (England), Leonardo da Vinci Academy (Rome).

AWARDS, HONORS: D. Litt. from World Academy of Languages and Literature, 1972, for Ruby and Rouge and So Many Roses; Ph.D. from Academy of Philosophy (U.S.A.).

WRITINGS:

(In Bengali) Debabhumi Dahshin (travel book), A. Mukherj, 1961.
Ruby and Rouge (poems), Diparun, 1969.
Pebbles and Pearls (novel), Diparun, 1971.
So Many Roses (poems), Diparun, 1972.
Flames of Agonies (poems), Diparun, 1973.
Art: I Adore (art book), Diparun, 1973.
The Depth (five-act drama), Diparun, 1976.
Bouquet of Amaranths (poems), Diparun, 1976.
Living-Loving-Green (poems), Tagore Institute of Creative Writing International, 1981.
(Co-author) Beauty that Never Fades (travel book), Rajesh Publications, 1981.
The Winged Gods (short stories), Tagore Institute of Creative Writing International, 1986.
Freshness of the Ancient, Tagore Institute of Creative Writing International, 1987.
Creative Quality Leads to Perfection, Tagore Institute of Creative Writing International, 1988.

EDITOR

Who's Who of Indian Women, International, National Biographical Centre, 1977.
(With Sandra Fowler) The Album of International Poets (anthology), Tagore Institute of Creative Writing International, 1981.
(With Fowler and Stella Browning) Eve's Eden (anthology), Tagore Institute of Creative Writing International, 1983.
The Wholeness of Dream, Tagore Institute of Creative Writing International, 1988.

OTHER

Editor of "Friendship Bridge" anthology series, including Friendship Bridge, The Japonica Sings, The Eastern Sun Is So Inviting, Flowers of Great Southland, Life and Love, The Bloom, and Perfume and Fragrance. Also author of poems and reviews under pseudonym Lama Esohg. Editor of Ocarina: English Poetry Journal of International Poems, 1969—.

WORK IN PROGRESS: Two research projects involving Indian history and Indo-American basic commitment to democracy and democratic living.

SIDELIGHTS: Amal Ghose, who is conversant in four languages, told CA that his "entire motivation is aimed at universal manhood and inspiring others to give their best to bring reality to intellectual friendship, to remove (as far as is practicable) pettiness from creative minds, and to flood the world with a beacon of the heart's greatness, not merely in words but in creative action.

"To serve humanity and mankind without any reservation or bias has been the most important factor in my career. From a tender age I have had the feeling that nothing equals creativity in the subtlest sense of the word. Men and women may earn riches and wealth and employ them to grab power, but crea-

tivity alone stands above all for all time. This prompted me to begin writing, not for making money, but for superb ecstacy.

"I write like passing through nature's wonders at ease, without any routine or plan. Anytime is good for my writing, either by day or by night. Sometimes, when I begin writing a novel or essay, I feel restless until I bring the piece to a satisfactory conclusion.

"I have been influenced by Shakespeare, Rabindranath Tagore, Dostoevski, and a few French authors, but I have always been interested in going ahead in exploring the depth and magnitude, mysteries and majestic traits, and feeling and potentiality of the human mind. No doubt, epic authors' unbounded love for humanity and the ever-living presence of their concepts inspire me to add a little more to the treasure of civilization's store.

"Nowadays most of our contemporary writers try to fool the readers in general and intellectuals in particular by mere superlatives and tall talk. Huge promises and often betrayals remind the ultimate surpassing the end of 'Pied Piper of Hamelin.' The super addiction to patico-gene, it seemed has overawed elitist exquisite perusers in general. Very few contemporary writers are truly keen about developing international understanding and wiping out narrowness of so-called educated and power-mad minds that always exploit the mean tendencies dwelling in ordinary human beings. Many things go marching on in the name of world organizations, but very few keep their aim fixed at unspoiled universalism. Creative quality is the first victim, closely followed by the slaughter of real humanism and pure compassion. I wish that writers would search their own hearts and seek feelings rather than parade pollutions purchased from trash as best-sellers."

*   *   *

GILBERT, Michael (Francis) 1912-

PERSONAL: Born July 17, 1912, in Billinghay, Lincolnshire, England; son of Bernard Samuel (a writer) and Berwyn Minna (Cuthbert) Gilbert; married Roberta Mary Marsden, July 26, 1947; children: Harriett Sarah, Victoria Mary, Olivia Margaret, Kate Alexandra, Richard Adam St. John, Laura Frances, Gerard Valentine Hugo. Education: University of London, LL.B., 1937. Politics: "Me-ist." Religion: Church of England.

ADDRESSES: Home—Luddesdown Old Rectory, Cobham, Kent, DA13 0XE, England. Agent—Curtis Brown Ltd., 162-168 Regent St., London W1R 5TA, England.

CAREER: Schoolmaster in Salisbury, 1931-38; Ellis, Bickersteth, Aglionby & Hazel, London, England, articled clerk, 1938-39; Trower, Still & Keeling, London, solicitor, 1947-51, partner, 1952-73. Legal advisor, government of Bahrain, 1960. Military service: British Army, Royal Horse Artillery, 1939-45; served in North Africa and Italy; held for a time in an Italian prisoner of war camp; escaped; became major; mentioned in dispatches.

MEMBER: Law Society, Society of Authors, Crime Writers Association (founder; member of committee, 1985-87), Mystery Writers of America, British Film Association, Garrick Club.

AWARDS, HONORS: Commander, Order of the British Empire, 1980; Grand Master Award, Mystery Writers of America, 1987, for lifetime achievement.

WRITINGS:

NOVELS

Close Quarters, Hodder & Stoughton, 1947, Walker & Co., 1963, reprinted, Hamlyn, 1981.

He Didn't Mind Danger, Harper, 1948 (published in England as *They Never Looked Inside,* Hodder & Stoughton, 1948).

The Doors Open, Hodder & Stoughton, 1949, Walker & Co., 1962.

Smallbone Deceased, Harper, 1950, reprinted, Garland Publishing, 1976.

Death Has Deep Roots, Hodder & Stoughton, 1951, reprinted, 1975, Harper, 1952.

The Danger Within, Harper, 1952, reprinted, 1978 (published in England as *Death in Captivity,* Hodder & Stoughton, 1952).

Fear to Tread, Harper, 1953, reprinted, 1978.

The Country-House Burglar, Harper, 1955 (published in England as *Sky High,* Hodder & Stoughton, 1955).

Be Shot for Sixpence, Harper, 1956.

Blood and Judgement, Hodder & Stoughton, 1959, Harper, 1978.

After the Fine Weather, Harper, 1963.

The Crack in the Teacup, Harper, 1966.

The Dust and the Heat, Hodder & Stoughton, 1967, published as *Overdrive,* Harper, 1968.

The Family Tomb, Harper, 1969 (published in England as *The Etruscan Net,* Hodder & Stoughton, 1969).

The Body of a Girl (also see below), Harper, 1972.

The Ninety-Second Tiger, Harper, 1973.

Flash Point (also see below), Harper, 1974.

The Night of the Twelfth, Harper, 1976.

The Empty House, Harper, 1979.

The Killing of Katie Steelstock, Harper, 1980 (published in England as *Death of a Favourite Girl,* Hodder & Stoughton, 1980).

End Game, Harper, 1982 (published in England as *The Final Throw,* Hodder & Stoughton, 1982).

The Black Seraphim, Harper, 1984.

The Long Journey Home, Harper, 1985.

Trouble, Harper, 1987.

STORY COLLECTIONS

Game without Rules (also see below), Harper, 1967.

Stay of Execution and Other Stories of Legal Practice, Hodder & Stoughton, 1971.

Amateur in Violence, Davis Publications, 1973.

Petrella at Q, Harper, 1977.

Mr. Calder and Mr. Behrens, Harper, 1982.

The Young Petrella: Stories, Harper, 1988.

PLAYS

A Clean Kill (also see below; first produced in London on the West End, 1959), Constable, 1961.

The Bargain (first produced in London on the West End, 1961), Constable, 1961.

The Shot in Question (first produced in London on the West End, 1963), Constable, 1963.

Windfall (first produced in London on the West End, 1963), Constable, 1963.

EDITOR

Crime in Good Company: Essays on Criminals and Crime-Writing, Constable, 1959.

Best Detective Stories of Cyril Hare, Faber, 1959, Walker & Co., 1961.

The Oxford Book of Legal Anecdotes, Oxford University Press, 1986.

Editor, "Classics of Detection and Adventure" series, Hodder & Stoughton.

CONTRIBUTOR

Herbert Brean, editor, *The Mystery Writers' Handbook,* Harper, 1956.

George Hardinge, editor, *Winter's Crimes I,* St. Martin's, 1969.

John Ball, editor, *The Mystery Story,* University of California Extension, 1976.

Miriam Gross, editor, *The World of Raymond Chandler,* Weidenfeld & Nicolson, 1977.

H. R. F. Keating, editor, *Agatha Christie: First Lady of Crime,* Weidenfeld & Nicolson, 1977.

Dilys Winn, editor, *Murder Ink: The Mystery Reader's Companion,* Workman Publishing, 1977.

Otto Penzler, editor, *The Great Detectives,* Little, Brown, 1978.

Julian Symons, editor, *Verdict of Thirteen,* Harper, 1979.

Hilary Watson, editor, *Winter's Crimes 12,* St. Martin's, 1980.

Alice Laurance and Isaac Asimov, editors, *Who Done It?,* Houghton, 1980.

After Midnight Ghost Book, Hutchinson, 1980.

Crime Wave, Collins, 1980.

OTHER

Dr. Crippen, Odhams Press, 1953.

The Claimant, Constable, 1957.

The Law, David & Charles, 1977.

Also author of radio scripts: "Death in Captivity," 1953, "The Man Who Could Not Sleep," 1955, "Crime Report" (also see below), 1956, "Doctor at Law," 1956, "The Waterloo Table," 1957, "You Must Take Things Easy," 1958, "Stay of Execution," 1965, "Game without Rules" (based on his story of the same title), 1968, "The Last Chapter," 1970, "Black Light," 1972, "Flash Point" (based on his novel of the same title), 1974, "Petrella," 1976, "In the Nick of Time," 1979, "The Last Tenant," 1979, and "The Oyster Catcher," 1983. Also author of television scripts: "The Crime of the Century," 1956, "Wideawake," 1957, "The Body of a Girl" (based on his novel of the same title), 1958, "Fair Game," 1958, "Crime Report" (based on his radio script of the same title), 1958, "Blackmail Is So Difficult," 1959, "Dangerous Ice," 1959, "A Clean Kill" (based on his play of the same title), 1961, "The Men from Room 13" (adapted from a story by Stanley Firmin), 1961, "Scene of the Accident," 1961, "The Betrayers" (adapted from a story by Stanley Ellin), 1962, "Trial Run," 1963, "The Blackmailing of Mr. S.," 1964, "The Mind of the Enemy," 1965, "The Man in Room 17," 1966, "Misleading Cases" (adapted from a story by A. P. Herbert), 1971, "Hadleigh," 1971, "Money to Burn" (adapted from the novel by Margery Allingham), 1974, and "Where There's a Will," 1975. Contributor of short stories to *Ellery Queen's Mystery Magazine.*

SIDELIGHTS: Michael Gilbert has written some thirty novels of mystery and adventure, a similar number of works for radio and television, and four successful plays for the West End, all while working full time as a solicitor. Incredibly, Gilbert wrote most of his books during the train ride to and from his office in London. He tells Rosemary Herbert of *Publishers Weekly:* "The journey lasted 45 or 50 minutes, and I know it doesn't *sound* like a great deal of time, but it's true.... The train started; I started writing. The train pulled into Victorian station and I stopped.'' This method allowed Gilbert, writing some two-and-a-half pages a day, to finish a novel in about five or six months' time. In 1987 his efforts earned him a Grand Master Award from the Mystery Writers of America, the mystery genre's highest honor.

Before writing mysteries, Gilbert served in the British Army during the Second World War and was stationed in Canada and North Africa. He was captured by the Germans and held for a time in a prisoner of war camp in Italy. This experience was later re-created in the novel *The Danger Within*, the story of British prisoners who must uncover the traitor among them while they plot their escape. Following the war, Gilbert followed the advice of his uncle, who was the Lord Chief Justice of India, and joined a law firm in London, where he became a partner in 1952. At one time he served as mystery writer Raymond Chandler's legal advisor, and drew up the late author's will. Gilbert retired from the legal profession in 1983.

Gilbert's first novel, *Close Quarters*, is a traditional mystery story set in a small English cathedral town, a setting Gilbert has used in many of his stories. His early novels follow the conventional pattern of classic English mystery fiction, presenting Agatha Christie-type puzzles that must be solved by the reader. They are noted, too, for their realistic depiction of police procedures and the workings of the legal system, subjects well known to Gilbert from his own law career.

As he became more comfortable with the writing of mysteries, Gilbert began to move away from the courtroom and police station. He began to explore other settings and characters and to develop plots that are more than just puzzles. In *Fear to Tread*, Gilbert writes of a school headmaster who turns detective, while in *The Doors Open*, he writes of illegal activities in the insurance business. In other novels he has written of counterintelligence agents, the French resistance, and British diplomatic missions on the Continent. His work began to include more humor, as well. His *Smallbone Deceased*, for example, concerns a corpse that is discovered in a bank's safe deposit box. M. H. Oakes of the *New York Times* calls the novel an ''agreeably understated satire,'' while L. G. Offord of the *San Francisco Chronicle* praises the ''excellent plot and characters, high literacy and that inimitable English trick of submerged humor.''

Among the many strengths of Gilbert's stories, Anthony Boucher writes in the *New York Times Book Review*, are ''the smooth ingenuity of plotting [and] the manner of telling, which disconcertingly combines elegance and harshness.'' ''From Gilbert one expects supercivilized writing,'' Newgate Callendar explains in the *New York Times Book Review*, ''and he does not disappoint.''

Reviewing the 1987 book *Trouble*, John Gross of the *New York Times* notes that ''Gilbert published his first novel some 40 years ago, but you would never guess it from 'Trouble.' The writing is as crisp as ever; there is the same professionalism, the same firm balance between atmosphere and plot.''

Several critics especially praise Gilbert for his ability to take his readers behind the scenes of a respected profession and show how it operates. T. J. Binyon of the *Times Literary Supplement*, for example, remarks on ''how expert he is at creating the atmosphere of a profession.'' Speaking of the novel *Trouble*, Jon L. Breen of the *Armchair Detective* notes that it ''demonstrates [Gilbert's] ability to impart specialized information and to deploy a large cast of characters effec-

tively.'' The realism of Gilbert's stories has also been remarked upon by several reviewers. Boucher, for one, claims that the espionage stories found in the collection *Game without Rules* are ''short works of art in social realism.''

Gilbert has created several memorable detective characters who reappear from time to time in his novels. Perhaps his most popular has been Patrick Petrella, a detective chief inspector with the South London Division of the Metropolitan Police. Petrella's father was a police lieutenant in Franco's Spain, while his mother is a proper Englishwoman. He is fond of quoting from the classics of literature as well as from the police manual of English law. His only full-length adventure was recounted in 1959's *Blood and Judgement*, a novel in which then-sergeant Petrella investigated the murder of a convict's wife on the bank of a London reservoir. The novel earned high accolades as one of the best police novels of the year.

Writing in his contribution to *The Great Detectives*, Gilbert recalls how he invented his character. ''Petrella,'' he writes, ''was conceived in church. The moment of his conception is as clearly fixed in my mind as though it had happened yesterday. . . . It was a drowsy summer evening and the preacher had reached what appeared to be only the midpoint of his sermon. It was not an inspired address, and I turned, as I sometimes do in such circumstances, to the hymn book for relief.'' There, Gilbert found the words of a poem by Christina Rosetti and an idea for a story came to him. More importantly, the picture of the police officer who played the central role in the story came to him. ''In that short sequence, which cannot have lasted for more than a few seconds,'' Gilbert comments, ''a complete character was encapsulated.'' Since his initial case in the late 1950s, Petrella has gone on to solve a number of baffling mysteries and has appeared in many short stories.

Over the more than three decades that Gilbert had been writing mystery stories, he has earned the praise of many critics in the field. Gross calls Gilbert ''one of the acknowledged masters of the contemporary crime story,'' while Anatole Broyard of the *New York Times* describes him as ''a master of the classic English murder mystery.'' In an article for the *Times Literary Supplement*, Julian Symons maintains that Gilbert ''has been writing intelligent, well-crafted detective stories and thrillers'' for more than thirty years. ''When at the top of his form,'' Symons concludes, ''nobody excels Mr. Gilbert in posing and developing a mystery.''

AVOCATIONAL INTERESTS: Cricket, contract bridge, walking.

BIOGRAPHICAL/CRITICAL SOURCES:

BOOKS

Penzler, Otto, editor, *The Great Detectives*, Little, Brown, 1978.
Twelve Englishmen of Mystery, Popular Press, 1984.

PERIODICALS

Armchair Detective, summer, 1988.
Best Sellers, February 15, 1966.
New Republic, October 16, 1976.
New Yorker, July 1, 1967.
New York Times, November 5, 1950, December 10, 1983, May 17, 1985, June 19, 1987.
New York Times Book Review, February 6, 1966, July 2, 1967, August 20, 1976.
Publishers Weekly, October 25, 1985.
San Francisco Chronicle, October 22, 1950.

Times (London), May 16, 1985.
Times Literary Supplement, May 23, 1980, August 21, 1987.

—*Sketch by Thomas Wiloch*

*   *   *

GILL, Jerry H.   1933-

PERSONAL: Name legally changed, 1965; born February 7, 1933, in Lynden, Wash.; son of Walter and Virginia (McGinnis) Gauthier. *Education:* Westmont College, B.A., 1956; University of Washington, Seattle, M.A., 1957; New York Theological Seminary, B.D., 1960; Duke University, Ph.D., 1966.

ADDRESSES: Office—Department of Philosophy, College of St. Rose, Albany, N.Y. 12203.

CAREER: Clergyman; ordained, 1956; Seattle Pacific College, Seattle, Wash., assistant professor of philosophy and religion, 1960-64; Southwestern at Memphis (now Rhodes College), Memphis, Tenn., assistant professor of philosophy, 1966-69; Eckerd College, St. Petersburg, Fla., 1969-77, began as associate professor, became professor of philosophy; Eastern College, St. Davids, Pa., professor of Christianity and culture, 1977-83; Barrington College, Barrington, R.I., professor of philosophy, 1983-85; College of St. Rose, Albany, N.Y., professor of philosophy and religious studies, 1985—.

MEMBER: American Philosophical Association, American Academy of Religion.

WRITINGS:

Ingmar Bergman and the Search for Meaning, Eerdmans, 1967.
(Editor) *Philosophy and Religion,* Burgess, 1968.
(Editor) *Philosophy Today,* Macmillan, Number 1, 1968, Number 2, 1969, Number 3, 1970.
(Editor) *Essays on Kierkegaard,* Burgess, 1969.
The Possibility of Religious Knowledge, Eerdmans, 1971.
Ian Ramsey, Allen & Unwin, 1976.
Wittgenstein and Metaphor, University Press of America, 1981.
On Knowing God, Westminster, 1981.
Toward Theology, University Press of America, 1982.
Metaphilosophy, University Press of America, 1982.
Faith in Dialogue, Word Books, 1985.
Language, Truth, and Body, Mellan, 1989.
Meditated Transcendence, Mercer University Press, 1989.

Contributor to theology and philosophy journals.

*   *   *

GILLIES, John   1925-

PERSONAL: Born December 15, 1925, in Chicago, Ill.; son of Anton J. (a clergyman) and Anna (a social worker; maiden name, Batutis) Gillies; married Carolyn Young (a librarian), March 18, 1950; children: Laurie Gillies Yarbrough, Stephen, Andrew. *Education:* Attended Wheaton College, 1945, 1947, Northwestern University, 1947-49, and University of Texas, 1956-57. *Politics:* Independent. *Religion:* Presbyterian.

ADDRESSES: Home—9303 Hunters Trace E., Austin, Tex. 78758.

CAREER: Presbyterian Church of the United States, Atlanta, Ga., audiovisual director, 1961-65; Christian Rural Overseas Program/Church World Service, Elkhart, Ind., communication director, 1965-72; communications consultant, 1972-74; State

Department of Public Welfare, Austin, Tex., regional director for Texas, 1977-79; free-lance writer, 1979—. Interim director, Texas Conference of Churches, 1982. Has also worked as mass communications missionary in Brazil, advertising executive, announcer, television director, and newscaster. *Military service:* U.S. Army, 1945-46.

MEMBER: Authors Guild, Authors League of America, American Federation of Television and Radio Artists, Screen Actors Guild, Religious Public Relations Council (past member of board of governors).

AWARDS, HONORS: Blue ribbon, Educational Film Library Association, 1964, for filmstrip script "Gold D. Lox and the Five Bears"; bronze medal, Religious Arts Festival, 1973, for "The Retreat."

WRITINGS:

A Primer for Christian Broadcasters, Moody, 1955.
The Martyrs of Guanabara, Moody, 1976.
A Guide to Caring for and Coping with Aging Parents, Thomas Nelson, 1981, new edition published as *Caregiving: When Someone You Love Grows Old,* Harold Shaw, 1988.
(With Walter Price) *Antiochus,* Moody, 1982.
A Guide to Compassionate Care of the Aging, Thomas Nelson, 1985.
Soviet Union: The World's Largest Country, Dillon, 1985.
Senor Alcalde: A Biography of Henry G. Cisneros, Dillon, 1988.

PLAYS

"The Firemakers" (musical play), first produced in Bristol, Ind., at the Frontier Theatre, July 1, 1974.
The Retreat (one-act; first produced in Sacramento, Calif., at Religious Arts Festival, 1973), Contemporary Drama Service, 1980.
Give Us a Sign (one-act; first produced as "The Sign Painter"), Contemporary Drama Service, 1980.

OTHER

Also author of numerous radio, film, filmstrip, and television scripts.

WORK IN PROGRESS: Research on Hannah More and other nineteenth-century evangelical Anglican social reformers in England, for a novel.

SIDELIGHTS: John Gillies told *CA:* "I am vitally interested in history, believing that there are authentic heroes and heroines yet to be described and popularized. I have found many of these in church history, particularly in script assignments; I am infatuated with the sometimes not-so-saintly saints who have made our life and our world more livable. I am a first-generation American, and I still have hope and excitement about this country."

*   *   *

GILPIN, Alan   1924-

PERSONAL: Born August 20, 1924, in Whitley Bay, Northumberland, England; son of George and Clara M. (Dobeson) Gilpin; married Sheila Margaret Humphries, April 3, 1954; children: Elizabeth Mary, Alan Stuart, David Anthony. *Education:* Attended Rutherford College of Technology, 1940-43, 1947-49; University of London, B.Sc. (with honors), 1953; University of Queensland, Ph.D., 1974.

ADDRESSES: Office—Office of Commissioners of Inquiry, Level 13 Wynyard House, 301 George St., Sydney, New South Wales 2000, Australia.

CAREER: County Borough of Wallasey, Cheshire, England, chief environmental health officer, 1958-61; Central Electricity Generating Board, London, England, planning engineer, 1961-65; Queensland State Government, Brisbane, Australia, director of air pollution control, 1965-72; Environment Protection Authority, Victoria, Australia, chairman, 1972-74; Department of Environment, Housing and Community Development, Canberra, Australia, director of Natural Resources Branch, 1974-77; Office of Commissioners of Inquiry, Sydney, New South Wales, New South Wales Pollution Control Commission, assistant director of environmental control, 1977-80, Environment and Planning, commissioner of inquiry, 1980—. Part-time lecturer at University of Queensland; occasional lecturer at University of Sydney. Chartered engineer, United Kingdom and Australia. *Military service:* British Army, 1943-47; served in Middle East.

MEMBER: Institute of Energy (United Kingdom; fellow), Institution of Engineers (fellow), St. Paul's College Union and Foundation (University of Sydney).

WRITINGS:

Control of Air Pollution, Butterworth & Co., 1963.
Dictionary of Economic Terms, Butterworth & Co., 1965, 5th edition, 1986.
Dictionary of Fuel Technology, Philosophical Library, 1969.
Air Pollution, University of Queensland Press, 1971.
Dictionary of Environmental Terms, University of Queensland Press, 1976.
Environmental Policy in Australia, University of Queensland Press, 1980.
The Australian Environment: Twelve Controversial Issues, Macmillan, 1981.
Dictionary of Energy Technology, Butterworth & Co., 1982.
Environmental Planning: A Condensed Encyclopedia, Noyes, 1987.
Australian Dictionary of Environment and Planning, Oxford University Press, 1988.

General editor, "Australian Environment" series, University of Queensland Press, 1972-82.

AVOCATIONAL INTERESTS: Bushwalking.

*   *   *

GINSBURG, Mirra

PERSONAL: Born in Bobruisk, Russia (now U.S.S.R.); daughter of Joseph and Bronia (Geier) Ginsburg. *Education:* Attended schools in Russia, Latvia, Canada, and the United States.

ADDRESSES: Home and office—150 West 96th St., Apt. 9-G, New York, N.Y. 10025.

CAREER: Free-lance writer, editor, and translator from Russian and Yiddish.

MEMBER: PEN, American Literary Translators Association.

AWARDS, HONORS: National Translation Center grant, 1967; Lewis Carroll Shelf Award, 1972, for *The Diary of Nina Kos-terina;* Mildred L. Batchelder nomination, 1973, for *The Kaha Bird: Tales from Central Asia,* and 1974, for *The White Ship;* Children's Book Showcase Title, 1973, for *The Chick and the Duckling;* Guggenheim fellow, 1975-76.

WRITINGS:

TRANSLATOR

Roman Goul, *Azef,* Doubleday, 1962.
Vera Alexandrova, *A History of Soviet Literature,* Doubleday, 1963.
(And author of introduction) Mikhail Bulgakov, *Master and Margarita,* Grove, 1967, reprinted, 1987.
(And author of introduction) *The Diary of Nina Kosterina,* Crown, 1968.
Bulgakov, *Heart of a Dog,* Grove, 1968, 3rd edition, 1987.
(And author of introduction) Bulgakov, *Flight* (play; also see below), Grove, 1969.
(And author of introduction) Bulgakov, *The Life of Monsieur de Moliere,* Funk and Wagnalls, 1970, New Directions, 1986.
(And author of introduction) Chingiz Aitmatov, *The White Ship,* Crown, 1972.
(And author of introduction) Yevgeny Zamyatin, *We,* Viking, 1972.
Fyodor Dostoyevsky, *Notes from Underground,* introduction by Donald Fanger, Bantam, 1974.
Lydia Obukhova, *Daughter of Night: A Tale of Three Worlds* (science fiction), Macmillan, 1974.
(And author of introduction) Andrey Platonov, *The Foundation Pit,* Dutton, 1975.
(And author of introduction) Bulgakov, *Flight and Bliss* (two plays), New Directions, 1985.

EDITOR AND TRANSLATOR

(And author of introduction) *The Fatal Eggs and Other Soviet Satire,* Macmillan, 1965, Grove, 1987.
(And author of introduction) *The Dragon: Fifteen Stories by Yevgeny Zamyatin,* Random House, 1966, 2nd edition, University of Chicago Press, 1986.
(And author of introduction) *The Last Door to Aiya: Anthology of Soviet Science Fiction,* S. G. Phillips, 1968.
A Soviet Heretic: Essays by Yevgeny Zamyatin, introduction by Alex Shane, University of Chicago Press, 1970.
(And author of introduction) *The Ultimate Threshold: Anthology of Soviet Science Fiction,* Holt, 1970.
The Air of Mars (Soviet science fiction anthology), Macmillan, 1976.
Kirill Bulychev, *Alice* (science fiction), Macmillan, 1977.

FOLK TALE COLLECTIONS; EDITOR, ADAPTOR, TRANSLATOR

Three Rolls and One Doughnut: Fables from Russia, illustrations by Anita Lobel, Dial, 1970.
The Master of the Winds: Folk Tales from Siberia, illustrations by Enrico Arno, Crown, 1970.
The Kaha Bird: Folk Tales from Central Asia, illustrations by Richard Cuffari, Crown, 1971.
One Trick Too Many: Tales about Foxes, illustrations by Helen Siegl, Dial, 1973.
The Lazies: Folk Tales from Russia, illustrations by Marian Parry, Macmillan, 1973.
How Wilka Went to Sea: Folk Tales from West of the Urals, Crown, 1974.
The Twelve Clever Brothers and Other Fools: Folk Tales from Russia, illustrations by C. Mikolaycak, Lippincott, 1979.

PICTURE BOOKS; AUTHOR, ADAPTOR, TRANSLATOR

The Fox and the Hare, Crown, 1969.

Vladimir Grigor'evich Suteyev, *The Chick and the Duckling,* illustrations by Jose Aruego and Ariane Dewey, Macmillan, 1972, reprinted, 1988.

What Kind of Bird Is That? (Weekly Reader Book Club selection), illustrations by Guilio Maestro, Crown, 1973.

Suteyev, *The Three Kittens* (Junior Literary Guild selection), illustrations by Maestro, Crown, 1973.

Mushroom in the Rain: Adapted from the Russian of V. Suteyev, illustrations by Aruego and Dewey, Macmillan, 1974.

The Proud Maiden, Tungak, and the Sun, illustrations by Igor Galanin, Macmillan, 1974.

How the Sun Was Brought Back to the Sky: Adapted from a Slovenian Folk Tale (Weekly Reader Book Club and Children's Choice Book Club selections), illustrations by Aruego and Dewey, Macmillan, 1975.

The Two Greedy Bears: Adapted from a Hungarian Folk Tale, illustrations by Aruego and Dewey, Macmillan, 1976.

Pampalche of the Silver Teeth, illustrations by Rocco Negri, Crown, 1976.

Pyotr Dudochkin, *Which Is the Best Place?,* illustrations by Roger Duvoisin, Macmillan, 1976.

The Strongest One of All: Based on a Caucasian Folktale, illustrations by Aruego and Dewey, Greenwillow, 1977.

Little Rystu, illustrations by Tony Chen, Greenwillow, 1978.

Striding Slippers, illustrations by Sal Murdocca, Macmillan, 1978.

The Fisherman's Son, illustrations by Chen, Greenwillow, 1979.

The Night It Rained Pancakes, illustrations by Douglas Florian, Greenwillow, 1979.

Ookie-Spooky, illustrations by Emily McCully, Crown, 1979.

Good Morning, Chick (Young Parents Book Club, Book-of-the-Month Club, and Scholastic Magazine Book Club selections), illustrations by Byron Barton, Greenwillow, 1980.

Kitten from One to Ten, illustrations by Maestro, Crown, 1980.

Where Does the Sun Go at Night?, illustrations by Aruego and Dewey, Greenwillow, 1980.

The Sun's Asleep behind the Hill, illustrations by Paul O. Zelinsky, Greenwillow, 1982.

Across the Stream, illustrations by Nancy Tafuri, Greenwillow, 1982.

The Magic Stove, illustrations by Linda Heller, Putnam, 1983.

Four Brave Sailors, illustrations by Tafuri, Greenwillow, 1987.

The Chinese Mirror, illustrations by Margot Zemach, Harcourt, 1988.

OTHER

Also translator of stories by Isaac Bashevis Singer, Alexey Remizov, Isaac Babel, and Zoshchenko, for various anthologies, collections and periodicals; co-translator of Isaac Babel's play, "Sunset," produced in 1966 and 1972.

SIDELIGHTS: Mirra Ginsburg writes: "I have loved folktales since childhood, and have gone on collecting them and delighting in them ever since. I place folktales among the greatest works of literature. To me they are a distillation of man's deepest experience into poetry, wisdom, truth, sadness, and laughter."

Many of Ginsburg's books have been translated into various languages, including Japanese, Swedish, Afrikaans, Portuguese, French, German, and Danish.

AVOCATIONAL INTERESTS: Poetry, cats (big and little), birds, ballet, baroque, folk and early music, early and primitive art.

*   *   *

GIRARD, Rene N(oel)   1923-

PERSONAL: Born December 25, 1923, in Avignon, France; son of Joseph and Therese (Fabre) Girard; married Martha V. McCullough, June 18, 1951; children: Martin J., Daniel C., Mary P. *Education:* Ecole Nationale des Chartres, Sorbonne, University of Paris, Archiviste-paleographe, 1947; Indiana University, Ph.D., 1950.

ADDRESSES: Office—Department of French and Italian, Stanford University, Stanford, Calif. 94305.

CAREER: Indiana University, Bloomington, instructor in French, 1947-52; Duke University, Durham, N.C., instructor in French, 1952-53; Bryn Mawr College, Bryn Mawr, Pa., assistant professor of French, 1953-57; Johns Hopkins University, Baltimore, Md., associate professor, 1957-61, professor of French, 1961-68; State University of New York at Buffalo, professor of arts and letters, 1968-76; Johns Hopkins University, James M. Beall Professor of French and Humanities, 1976-80; Stanford University, Stanford, Calif., Andrew B. Hammond Professor of French, 1980—. Professor at Institut d'Etudes Francaises d'Avignon, 1962—.

MEMBER: Modern Language Association of America (member of executive council, 1969-72).

AWARDS, HONORS: William Riley Parker Prize, 1964, for essay "Camus's Stranger Retried."

WRITINGS:

Mensonge romantique et verite romanesque, Grasset, 1961, translation by Yvonne Freccero published as *Deceit, Desire and the Novel: Self and Other in Literary Structure,* Johns Hopkins University Press, 1965.

(Editor) *Proust: A Collection of Critical Essays,* Prentice-Hall, 1962, reprinted, Greenwood Press, 1977.

Dostoievsky: Du double a l'unite, Plon, 1963.

La Violence et le sacre, Grasset, 1972, translation by Patrick Gregory published as *Violence and the Sacred,* Johns Hopkins University Press, 1977.

Critique dans un souterrain, L'Age d'Homme, 1976.

Des Choses cachees depuis la fondation du monde, Grasset, 1978, translation by Stephen Bann and Michael Metteer published as *Things Hidden since the Foundation of the World,* Stanford University Press, 1987.

To Double Business Bound: Essays on Literature, Mimesis, and Anthropology, Johns Hopkins University Press, 1978.

Le Bouc emissaire, Grasset, 1982, translation by Freccero published as *The Scapegoat,* Johns Hopkins University Press, 1986.

La Route antique des hommes pervers, Grasset, 1985, translation by Freccero published as *Job: The Victim of His People,* Stanford University Press, 1987.

(Editor with Brigitte Cazelles) *Alphonse Juilland: D'une passion l'autre,* Anma Libri, 1987.

BIOGRAPHICAL/CRITICAL SOURCES:

BOOKS

Deguy, Michel and Jean-Pierre Dupuy, editors, *Rene Girard et le probleme du Mal,* Grasset, 1982.

Dumouchel, Paul, editor, *Violence and Truth: On the Work of Rene Girard*, Stanford University Press, 1988.

PERIODICALS

Berkshire Review, Volume 14, 1979.
Diacritics, spring, 1978.
Modern Language Journal, April, 1979.
New Republic, April 1, 1978.
Partisan Review, fall, 1968.
Semeia, Volume 33, 1985.
Times Literary Supplement, December 22, 1966, October 5, 1973, March 20, 1987.

*   *   *

GIROUX, Robert   1914-

PERSONAL: Born April 8, 1914, in New Jersey; son of Arthur J. (a weaver and cabinetmaker) and Katharine (a teacher; maiden name, Lyons) Giroux; married Carmen de Arango, August 30, 1952 (divorced, 1969). *Education:* Columbia College (now University), A.B. (with honors), 1936. *Politics:* Democrat. *Religion:* Roman Catholic.

ADDRESSES: Office—Farrar, Straus & Giroux, Inc., 19 Union Sq. W., New York, N.Y. 10003.

CAREER: Columbia Broadcasting System, Inc., New York City, editor of program book, 1936-39; Harcourt, Brace & Co. (now Harcourt Brace Jovanovich, Inc.), New York City, editor, 1940-47, editor-in-chief of trade books, 1948-55; Farrar, Straus & Giroux, Inc., New York City, vice-president, editor-in-chief, and member of board of directors, 1955-79, chairman of board of editors, 1979—. President of National Board of Review of Motion Pictures, Inc., 1975-82. *Military service:* U.S. Naval Reserve, active duty, 1942-45; became lieutenant commander.

MEMBER: Phi Beta Kappa, Century Club, Players Club.

AWARDS, HONORS: Ivan Sandrof Award for "distinguished contribution to the enhancement of American literary and critical standards" from National Book Critics Circle, 1987; Alexander Hamilton Medal from Columbia University, 1987; Campion Award for service in the cause of Christian letters from *America*, 1988.

WRITINGS:

(Contributor) Allen Tate, editor, *T. S. Eliot: The Man and His Work*, Delacorte, 1966.
(Author of introduction) *The Complete Stories of Flannery O'Connor*, Farrar, Straus, 1971.
(Author of preface) John Berryman, *The Freedom of the Poet*, Farrar, Straus, 1976.
The Education of an Editor, Bowker, 1982.
The Book Known as Q: A Consideration of Shakespeare's Sonnets, Atheneum, 1982.
The Future of the Book, Grolier Club, 1984.
(Editor and author of introduction) Elizabeth Bishop, *The Collected Prose*, Farrar, Straus, 1984.
(Editor and author of introduction) Robert Lowell, *Robert Lowell: Collected Prose*, Farrar, Straus, 1987.

Also author of the radio drama "Delia Bacon: The Yankee Seeress and the Stratford Booby," for British Broadcasting Corporation (BBC-Radio), 1987. Contributor of articles to periodicals, including *Atlantic* and *Yale Review*.

SIDELIGHTS: After four decades of working with such writers as Carl Sandburg, Flannery O'Connor, Bernard Malamud,

T. S. Eliot, Jack Kerouac, Robert Lowell, Susan Sontag, and Walker Percy, Robert Giroux has become, in the words of Donald Hall for the *New York Times Book Review*, "the only living editor whose name is bracketed with Maxwell Perkins." Giroux began his publishing career at Harcourt Brace (now Harcourt Brace Jovanovich) and his first book was Edmund Wilson's treatise on nineteenth-century socialist thinkers entitled *To the Finland Station*. Giroux observes in his 1981 Bowker Memorial Lecture, later published as *The Education of an Editor*, that Wilson's manuscript was almost flawless: "Thus at the start of my life as an editor I experienced the rarest and most ideal situation: a manuscript needing few or no changes. This is what every editor, and author, really wants."

Giroux has discovered many young authors, including Jean Stafford, whose first novel, *Boston Adventure*, came to Harcourt in 1943. Giroux took the manuscript with him on a train one afternoon and became so engrossed in the story that he missed his stop. Stafford, in turn, brought the work of her husband, the poet Robert Lowell, to the publisher's attention, and later Giroux edited Lowell's stories and essays in *Robert Lowell: Collected Prose*. Giroux also discovered Bernard Malamud, accepting his first novel, *The Natural*, for Harcourt after it had been rejected by another publisher. After Giroux moved to the Farrar, Straus publishing company in 1955, Harcourt rejected Malamud's novel *The Assistant;* accepted by Giroux, it won a National Book Award.

Giroux's taste is renowned in the book trade. He was granted the Ivan Sandrof Award from the National Book Critics Circle in 1987 for his "distinguished contribution to the enhancement of American literary and critical standards." He is also a recipient of the Alexander Hamilton Medal from Columbia University and the Campion Award from *America* for service in the cause of Christian letters. Ted Morgan for the *Saturday Review* maintains that "[Giroux's] standards can be held up as an example in today's publishing industry, where the bottom line often takes precedent over the printed word.... As an editor who relies on his taste, the strongest statement he can make about a book is not its earn-out figure or its subrights potential, but simply 'I like it.'" Giroux, who deplores the many diet, self-help, financial, and beauty books that are prevalent in today's market, insists that if a publisher cannot find quality books to publish, he or she should not resort to publishing junk. Giroux quipped in his Bowker Memorial Lecture that "editors used to be known by their authors; now some of them are known by their restaurants." Furthermore, Giroux explained to Morgan: "To keep going, publishers must make money, and they like to make it as much as authors do. Commercial success is not only desirable, it's necessary. What I dislike is the great number of what I call *ooks*, publications that are almost but not quite books. You have trouble remembering them two weeks after they come out."

In *The Book Known as Q: A Consideration of Shakespeare's Sonnets*, Giroux examines the evidence for various theories about the date of composition and the autobiographical content of Shakespeare's sonnets, which were published in 1609. Scholars have long debated the identity of the young man who is the subject of many of the poems; Giroux identifies him as the third Earl of Southampton and offers his explanation of why the sonnets were not published until more than fifteen years after most of them were written and why they were virtually unknown until nearly a century after Shakespeare's death. Michael Dirda for the *Washington Post Book World* writes: "*The Book Known as Q* beguiles with the charm of a well-told historical detective story," whereas Christopher Lehmann-Haupt of the *New York Times* is somewhat more analytical; he identifies the thesis of the book as "highly inferential. Practically everything we know about Shakespeare is inferential. . . . Giroux goes out on a limb when he assumes that the sonnets must be autobiographical. . . . . [He] . . . feels strongly on the subject and attacks what he calls 'the antibiographical fallacy' at length. But however strong or weak his thesis, its value lies in this: It offers us a plausible and coherent explanation of what the sonnets, personal statements that they formally are, might actually be referring to. This, in turn, gives them an added dimension of dramatic life." Finally, according to Frances Taliaferro for the *New York Times Book Review, The Book Known as Q* "makes no flamboyant claims; it is a modest, fair-minded introduction to the history and scholarship of the sonnets and to that period when, in Colette's words, 'Shakespeare worked without knowing that he would become Shakespeare'. . . . [Giroux's] enthusiasm inspires the reader to intimacy with the sonnets themselves; as is fitting, the last section of this book is a facsimile of 'Q.'"

AVOCATIONAL INTERESTS: Films, attending the opera, walking, sailing.

BIOGRAPHICAL/CRITICAL SOURCES:

BOOKS

Giroux, Robert, *The Education of an Editor*, Bowker, 1982.

PERIODICALS

New York Times, May 31, 1982.
New York Times Book Review, January 6, 1980, August 29, 1982.
Saturday Review, September 1, 1979.
Washington Post Book World, June 13, 1982.

*　　　*　　　*

GLASSFORD, Wilfred
See McNEILLY, Wilfred (Glassford)

*　　　*　　　*

GODDARD, Donald   1934-

PERSONAL: Born April 16, 1934, in Cortland, N.Y.; son of Don Gay (a newspaperman) and Adele (Letcher) Goddard. *Education:* Princeton University, A.B., 1956. *Politics:* Independent.

ADDRESSES: Home—62 Greene St., New York, N.Y. 10012.

CAREER: Editor and writer of books on art. American Archives of World Art, New York City, editor, 1958-65; McGraw-Hill Book Co., New York City, editor, 1966-68; director, Editorial Photocolor Archives, 1968-74; managing editor, *ARTnews*, 1974-78; Harry N. Abrams, Inc., New York City, editor, 1979-82; New York Zoological Society, New York City, public affairs editor, 1981—.

WRITINGS:

(Editor) *American Library Compendium and Index of World Art*, American Archives of World Art, 1961.
Lecture Notes for the Study of Art History, American Archives of World Art, 1961—.
Tschacbasov, American Archives of World Art, 1964.
(Editor) *The McGraw-Hill Dictionary of Art*, McGraw, 1969.
(Editor) *Encyclopedia of Painting*, Crown, 1970.
(Editor) *Ad Reinhardt*, Abrams, 1979.

(With Robert Farber) *Moods*, Amphoto, 1980.
(Editor) *Olitski*, Abrams, 1980.
(With Farber) *The Fashion Photographer*, Amphoto, 1981.
(With John Walker and others) *Harry Jackson, Forty Years of His Art, 1941-1981*, Wyoming Foundry Studios, 1981.
(With Larry Pointer) *Harry Jackson*, Abrams, 1981.
(Editor) *Yves Klein*, Abrams, 1982.
(Editor) *Watercolors and Drawings of the French Impressionists and Their Parisian Contemporaries*, Abrams, 1982.
Sound Art, SoundArt Foundation, 1983.
(Editor) *Special Effects: Creating Movie Magic*, Abbeville Press, 1984.
(Editor) *Elegant New York*, Abbeville Press, 1985.
(Editor) *Edward Hicks*, Abbeville Press, 1985.
(Editor) *American Independents*, Abbeville Press, 1987.

Also author of *New York Zoological Society Annual Report*, 1981-88. Contributor to periodicals. Contributing editor, *ARTnews*, 1978—.

WORK IN PROGRESS: Writing on contemporary art.

*　　　*　　　*

GOFFSTEIN, (Marilyn) Brooke   1940-
(M. B. Goffstein)

PERSONAL: Born December 20, 1940, in St. Paul, Minn.; daughter of Albert A. (an electrical engineer) and Esther (Rose) Goffstein; married Peter Schaaf (a photographer and concert pianist), August 15, 1965; married David Allender, July 8, 1986. *Education:* Bennington College, B.A., 1962. *Religion:* Jewish.

ADDRESSES: Home—697 West End Ave., New York, N.Y. 10025.

CAREER: Author and artist; Parsons School of Design, New York City, instructor, 1985—; University of Minnesota, Duluth, Minn., summer workshop instructor, 1987—; has had several one-woman exhibitions of pen and ink and watercolor drawings in New York City, and St. Paul, Minn.

AWARDS, HONORS: Book Week's Children's Spring Book Festival honor book, 1966, for *The Gats!;* New York Times Outstanding Children's Book, 1968, for *Across the Sea*, 1969, for *Goldie the Dollmaker*, 1974, for *Me and My Captain;* New York Times Best Illustrated Children's Book, 1972, for *A Little Schubert*, 1978, for *Natural History*, 1980, for *An Artist;* American Library Association Notable Book, 1976, for *Fish for Supper*, 1978, for *Family Scrapbook* and *My Noah's Ark*, 1986, for *Our Snowman;* Caldecott Honor Book, 1977, for *Fish for Supper;* Jane Adams Peace Award Special Certificate, 1979, for *Natural History;* National Book Award nomination, 1980, for *An Artist; Sleepy People, Across the Sea, My Noah's Ark, An Artist, A Writer, School of Names* and *Our Snowman* were selected for American Institute of Graphic Arts' Children's Book Shows.

WRITINGS:

An Actor (juvenile; self-illustrated), Harper, 1987.
Our Prairie Home: A Picture Album (juvenile), Harper, 1988.

UNDER NAME M. B. GOFFSTEIN

The Underside of the Leaf (young adult novel), Farrar, Straus, 1972.

A Little Schubert (juvenile; includes record of five Schubert waltzes performed by Peter Schaaf), Harper, 1972.
Daisy Summerfield's Style (young adult novel), Delacorte, 1975.
Lives of the Artists (juvenile), Farrar, Straus, 1981.
My Editor (for adults), Farrar, Straus, 1985.
An Artists Album (juvenile), Harper, 1985.

SELF-ILLUSTRATED; UNDER NAME M. B. GOFFSTEIN

The Gats! (juvenile; also see below), Pantheon, 1966.
Sleepy People (juvenile; also see below), Farrar, Straus, 1966, revised edition, 1979.
Brookie and Her Lamb (juvenile; also see below), Farrar, Straus, 1967, revised edition, 1981.
Across the Sea (juvenile short stories; also see below), Farrar, Straus, 1968.
Goldie the Dollmaker (juvenile; also see below), Farrar, Straus, 1969.
Two Piano Tuners (juvenile; also see below), Farrar, Straus, 1970.
Me and My Captain (juvenile; also see below), Farrar, Straus, 1974.
The First Books (juvenile; trade paperback collection; includes *The Gats!, Sleepy People, Brookie and Her Lamb, Across the Sea, Goldie the Dollmaker, Two Piano Tuners,* and *Me and My Captain*), Farrar, Straus, 1974.
Fish for Supper (juvenile), Dial, 1976.
My Crazy Sister (juvenile), Dial, 1976.
Family Scrapbook (juvenile), Farrar, Straus, 1978.
My Noah's Ark (juvenile), Harper, 1978.
Natural History (juvenile), Farrar, Straus, 1979.
Neighbors (juvenile), Harper, 1979.
An Artist (juvenile), Harper, 1980.
Laughing Latkes (juvenile), Farrar, Straus, 1980.
A Writer (juvenile), Harper, 1984.
School of Names (juvenile), Harper, 1986.
Our Snowman (juvenile), Harper, 1986.
Rosa Lee and Doc Watson, *Your Lone Journey,* Harper, 1986.
Artists Helpers Enjoy the Evening (juvenile), Harper, 1987.

WORK IN PROGRESS: A House, a children's book.

SIDELIGHTS: "It is not simple to simplify. [Brooke] Goffstein is a miniaturist recording different aspects of the world, large and little. Like a whittler she eliminates excess in order to extract an essence," Karla Kuskin writes in the *New York Times Book Review.* A prolific artist, Goffstein has won almost as much recognition for the quality of her illustrations as for her writing. Several of her works have been named either *New York Times*'s Outstanding Children's Books or Best Illustrated Children's Books, as well as receiving many other honors. The themes of her juvenile books cover such subjects as "friendship, family, the rituals of holidays and every day, natural history, and the importances of finding and following one's vocation," according to Janice Alberghene in a *Dictionary of Literary Biography* entry on Goffstein. Writing in the *Washington Post Book World,* Maggie Stern calls the author "one of the finest illustrator/writers of our time. Like porcelain, there is more to her work than meets the eye. Beneath the delicacy and fragility is a core of astounding strength."

BIOGRAPHICAL/CRITICAL SOURCES:

BOOKS

Children's Literature Review, Volume 3, Gale, 1978.
Dictionary of Literary Biography, Volume 61: *American Writers for Children since 1960: Poets, Illustrators, and Nonfiction Writers,* Gale, 1987.

PERIODICALS

New York Times Book Review, December 16, 1979, January 11, 1981.
Washington Post Book World, September 9, 1979.

*   *   *

GOFFSTEIN, M. B.
See GOFFSTEIN, (Marilyn) Brooke

*   *   *

GORDIMER, Nadine   1923-

PERSONAL: Born November 20, 1923, in Springs, South Africa; daughter of Isidore (a jeweler) and Nan (Myers) Gordimer; married Gerald Gavronsky, March 6, 1949 (divorced, 1952); married Reinhold H. Cassirer (owner and director of art gallery), January 29, 1954; children: (first marriage) Oriane Taramasco; (second marriage) Hugo. *Education:* Attended private schools and the University of the Witwatersrand.

ADDRESSES: Home—7 Frere Rd., Parktown West, Johannesburg 2193, South Africa. *Agent*—Russell & Volkening, Inc., 50 West 29th St., New York, N.Y. 10001.

CAREER: Writer. Ford Foundation visiting professor, under auspices of Institute of Contemporary Arts, Washington, D.C., 1961. Lecturer, Hopwood Awards, University of Michigan, Ann Arbor, 1970. Writer in residence, American Academy in Rome, 1984. Has also lectured and taught writing at Harvard, Princeton, Northwestern, Columbia, and Tulane Universities.

MEMBER: International PEN (vice-president), Congress of South African Writers, Royal Society of Literature, American Academy of Arts and Sciences (honorary member), American Academy of Literature and Arts (honorary member).

AWARDS, HONORS: W. H. Smith and Son Literary Award, 1961, for short story collection, *Friday's Footprint, and Other Stories;* Thomas Pringle Award, 1969; James Tait Black Memorial Prize, 1973, for *A Guest of Honour;* Booker Prize for Fiction, National Book League, 1974, for *The Conservationist;* Grand Aigle d'Or, 1975; CNA Award, 1975; Neil Gunn fellowship, Scottish Arts Council, 1981; Common Wealth Award for Distinguished Service in Literature, 1981; Modern Language Association of America award, 1982; Premio Malaparte, 1985; Nelly Sachs Prize, 1985; Bennett Award, *Hudson Review,* 1986; Officier de l'Ordre des Arts et des Lettres (France), 1986. D. Litt., University of Leuven, 1980, Smith College, City College of the City University of New York, and Mount Holyoke College, all 1985; honorary degrees from Harvard University and Yale University, both 1987, and New School for Social Research, 1988.

WRITINGS:

NOVELS

The Lying Days, Simon & Schuster, 1953, published with new introduction by Paul Bailey, Virago, 1983.
A World of Strangers, Simon & Schuster, 1958, reprinted, J. Cape, 1976.
Occasion for Loving, Viking, 1963, published with new introduction by Bailey, Virago, 1983.
The Late Bourgeois World, Viking, 1966, reprinted, Penguin, 1982.
A Guest of Honour, Viking, 1970, reprinted, Penguin, 1988.
The Conservationist, J. Cape, 1974, Viking, 1975.

Burger's Daughter, Viking, 1979.
July's People, Viking, 1981.
A Sport of Nature (Book-of-the-Month Club dual selection), Knopf, 1987.

SHORT STORIES

Face to Face (also see below), Silver Leaf Books (Johannesburg), 1949.
The Soft Voice of the Serpent, and Other Stories (contains many stories previously published in *Face to Face*), Simon & Schuster, 1952.
Six Feet of the Country (also see below), Simon & Schuster, 1956.
Friday's Footprint, and Other Stories, Viking, 1960.
Not for Publication, and Other Stories, Viking, 1965.
Livingstone's Companions, Viking, 1971.
Selected Stories (contains stories from previously published collections), J. Cape, 1975, Viking, 1976 (published in England as *No Place Like: Selected Stories*, Penguin, 1978).
Some Monday for Sure, Heinemann Educational, 1976.
A Soldier's Embrace, Viking, 1980.
Town and Country Lovers, Sylvester and Orphanos (Los Angeles), 1980.
Six Feet of the Country (contains stories from previously published collections; selected for television series of same title), Penguin, 1982.
Something Out There, Viking, 1984.

CONTRIBUTOR OF SHORT STORIES TO ANTHOLOGIES

Stories from the New Yorker, 1950-1960, Simon & Schuster, 1960.
David Wright, editor, *South African Stories*, Faber, 1960.
Gerda Charles, *Modern Jewish Stories*, Prentice-Hall, 1963.
C. L. Cline, editor, *The Rinehart Book of Short Stories*, alternate edition, Holt, 1964.
Penguin Modern Stories 4, Penguin, 1970.
James Wright, editor, *Winter's Tales 22*, St. Martin's, 1977.
Robert and Roberta Kalechofsky, editors, *Echad 2: South African Jewish Voices*, Micah Publications, 1982.
Marie R. Reno, editor, *An International Treasury of Mystery & Suspense*, Doubleday, 1983.
Short Story International 46: Tales by the World's Great Contemporary Writers, International Cultural Exchange, 1984.
Chinua Achebe and C. L. Innes, editors, *African Short Stories*, Heinemann, 1985.
Nancy Sullivan, editor, *The Treasury of English Short Stories*, Doubleday, 1985.
Stephen Gray, editor, *The Penguin Book of Southern African Stories*, Penguin, 1985.
Clifton Fadiman, editor, *The World of the Short Story: A Twentieth Century Collection*, Houghton, 1986.
Daniel Halpern, editor, *The Art of the Tale: An International Anthology of Short Stories*, Viking, 1986.
Alberto Manguel, editor, *Dark Arrows: Great Stories of Revenge*, Potter, 1987.

Also contributor of previously published short stories to numerous other anthologies.

OTHER

(Editor with Lionel Abrahams) *South African Writing Today*, Penguin, 1967.
African Literature: The Lectures Given on This Theme at the University of Cape Town's Public Summer School, February, 1972, Board of Extra Mural Studies, University of Cape Town, 1972.

The Black Interpreters: Notes on African Writing, Spro-Cas/Ravan (Johannesburg), 1973.
On the Mines, photographs by David Goldblatt, C. Struik (Cape Town), 1973.
(Author of appreciation) *Kurt Jobst: Goldsmith and Silversmith; Art Metal Worker*, G. Bakker (Johannesburg), 1979.
(With others) *What Happened to Burger's Daughter; or, How South African Censorship Works*, Taurus (Johannesburg), 1980.
Lifetimes under Apartheid, photographs by Goldblatt, Knopf, 1986.
The Essential Gesture: Writing, Politics and Places, edited and introduced by Stephen Clingman, Knopf, 1988.

Also author of television plays and documentaries, including "A Terrible Chemistry," 1981, "Choosing for Justice: Allan Boesak," with Hugo Cassirer, 1985, "Country Lovers," "A Chip of Glass Ruby," "Praise," and "Oral History," all part of "The Gordimer Stories" series adapted from stories of the same titles, 1985. Contributor to periodicals, including *Atlantic, Encounter, Granta, Harper's, Holiday, Kenyon Review, Mother Jones, New Yorker, Paris Review*, and *Playboy*.

SIDELIGHTS: "Nadine Gordimer has become, in the whole solid body of her work, the literary voice and conscience of her society," declares Maxwell Geismar in *Saturday Review*. In numerous novels, short stories, and essays, she has written of her South African homeland and the apartheid under which its blacks, coloreds, and whites subsist; and from her prolific pen has flowed a cultural collage upon which readers worldwide have gazed sentiently for decades. "This writer, several times rumored to be under consideration for the Nobel Prize in Literature, has made palpable the pernicious, pervasive character of that country's race laws, which not only deny basic rights to most people but poison many relationships," maintains Miriam Berkley in *Publishers Weekly*. Her insight, integrity, and compassion inspire unreserved and unabated critical admiration; and, internationally honored for having written what some critics consider social history, she is acclaimed as well for the elegance and meticulousness with which she records it. "She has mapped out the social, political and emotional geography of that troubled land with extraordinary passion and precision," says Michiko Kakutani of the *New York Times*, observing in a later essay that "taken chronologically, her work not only reflects her own evolving political consciousness and maturation as an artist—an early lyricism has given way to an increased preoccupation with ideas and social issues—but it also charts changes in South Africa's social climate." As Merle Rubin remarks in the *Los Angeles Times Book Review*, "Gordimer is a voice worth listening to."

Born in South Africa to Jewish emigrants from London, Gordimer experienced a typical European middle-class colonial childhood, the solitude of which was relieved by extensive and eclectic reading at her local library—an activity she delighted in "like a pig in clover," she recalls in a *Los Angeles Times* interview with Berkley. She settled into political awareness slowly, explaining to Carol Sternhell in *Ms.:* "I think when you're born white in South Africa, you're peeling like an onion. You're sloughing off all the conditioning that you've had since you were a child." Having begun to write as a child, she published her first short story at the age of fifteen, and gained an American audience from fiction appearing in such periodicals as the *New Yorker* and *Harper's*. "Her extraordinary gifts," writes Rubin, "were evident from the start: a precise ear for spoken language that lent great authenticity to her dialogue; a sensitivity to the rhythms and texture of the written word that gave her prose the power of poetry; a keen eye that made her a tireless observer; an even keener sense of social satire based upon her ability to see through appearances to the heart of the matter, and a strong feeling of moral purpose, composed in equal parts of her indignation at the sheer injustice of South Africa's entrenched racial oppression and of her commitment to speak the truth as she saw it.''

Much of Gordimer's fiction focuses upon white middle-class lives and frequently depicts what Geismar describes as ''a terrified white consciousness in the midst of a mysterious and ominous sea of black humanity''; but the ''enduring subject'' of her writing has been ''the consequences of apartheid on the daily lives of men and women, the distortions it produces in relationships among both blacks and whites,'' says Kakutani. Margo Jefferson finds the pieces in *Selected Stories* ''marked by the courage of moral vision and the beauty of artistic complexity,'' adding in *Newsweek* that ''Gordimer examines, with passionate precision, the intricacies both of individual lives and of the wide-ranging political and historical forces that contain them.'' Culling from several of her previously published collections of the early fifties through the middle seventies, *Selected Stories* opens with ''Is There Nowhere Else We Can Meet?,'' a glimpse of a white woman's fears of sexual attack during a mugging by a black male, and closes with ''Africa Emergent,'' a candid exploration of reluctance to assist a politically imprisoned black artist. Noting in the introduction that the collection's ''chronological order turns out to be an historical one,'' Gordimer continues that ''the change in social attitudes unconsciously reflected in the stories represents both that of the people in my society—that is to say, history—and my apprehension of it; in the writing, I am acting upon my society, and in the manner of my apprehension, all the time history is acting upon me.''

''Gordimer splendidly observes the remnants of persons beneath the repulsive stereotypes, an imaginative effort paralleled by her view of Africa itself, its extraordinary beauty showing through the obscene mess that has been dumped on it,'' writes Frank Kermode in the *New York Review of Books* about *Selected Stories*. Anatole Broyard concurs in a *New York Times* review of *A Soldier's Embrace:* ''Nobody else writes about contemporary Africa as well as Nadine Gordimer does. . . . She, almost alone, achieves what Saul Bellow called 'the esthetic consumption of the environment.' Her Africa does not disappear into metaphors: in her books, metaphors disappear into Africa, like the early explorers and missionaries.'' Despite avowed attempts to avoid ''adulation'' in his critical study of her shorter work, *Nadine Gordimer*, Robert F. Haugh nonetheless recognizes that ''her gifts are so diverse, her range so astonishingly broad, her gallery of places and people so various, that one cannot speak of her world in a phrase, as one would say Faulkner's South, or Hardy's Wessex.'' Haugh maintains that ''to read her stories is to know Africa.''

From the first, reviewers hailed her promise as a writer—a promise quickly realized, for each successive novel or collection of stories elicits critical accolades and further enhances her literary stature. In a *New York Times* review of *The Lying Days*, about a young white woman raised in a mining suburb of Johannesburg, James Stern deems her first novel ''as void of conceit and banality, as original and as beautifully written as a novel by Virginia Woolf.'' Particularly esteemed, though, as a master of short fiction, Gordimer is called ''one of the most gifted practitioners of the short story anywhere in English'' by Edward Weeks in an *Atlantic* review of the award-winning *Friday's Footprint, and Other Stories*. As Robert E.

Kuehn proclaims in a *Chicago Tribune Book World* review of her most recent collection, *Something Out There*, ''Her best stories . . . deserve a place on the same shelf as the masterpieces of the genre. And even her less than perfect pieces command attention and admiration for their characteristic chastity of language, emotion and gesture.''

Critics praise Gordimer's prose for its sustained poetic elegance and clarity, but they occasionally detect in her early work what Irving Howe refers to as ''literary self-consciousness'' in a *New Republic* review of Gordimer's second novel, *A World of Strangers*, in which a young Oxford-educated publishing employee on assignment in Johannesburg confronts the disparity in lives of privilege and deprivation decided solely by skin pigmentation. Although Edmund Fuller contends in a *Chicago Sunday Tribune* review that ''Gordimer is an artist of marked skill and control, with perceptive insights into character and moral dilemmas,'' Howe observes that ''she spins her sentences immaculately; she never drops into anger or vital passion; the satiny flow of similies and metaphors, modestly calling attention to themselves, survives every pressure of her subject.'' As Whitney Balliett describes it in the *New Yorker*, ''One is always conscious of a pleased deliberation, as if her prose were continually hugging itself.''

However, in a *Washington Post Book World* review of *A Soldier's Embrace*, Lynne Sharon Schwartz describes Gordimer's technique as ''this elliptical poet's way with metaphor as a shortcut to meaning, together with a compression of language that can render the core of a life or a situation in a few sentences,'' sentences which, according to Vivian Gornick in the *Village Voice*, ''accumulate slowly into a concentrate of thoughtful feeling that is reserved and quiet.'' *Newsweek*'s Peter S. Prescott suggests that despite Gordimer's ''occasionally eccentric'' syntax, her ''stories are so thickly textured and of such high specific gravity as to demand, and repay, a second reading.'' Calling her prose ''meticulous yet earthily sensual, a blend of metaphor and minute detail,'' Eric Redman of the *Washington Post Book World* thinks that ''while her writing is oblique, it is never obscure.'' In Gornick's opinion, ''Gordimer's work—like that of a good doctor trying to find out where it hurts—applies steady pressure to external circumstance until the live places beneath the surface stir with surprised feeling.''

Critics also point to what they perceive to be a certain detachment or stoicism in Gordimer's early work; but her fourth novel *The Late Bourgeois World*, which transpires during a weekend in which a divorced woman must explain to her child the suicide of his father, a man who betrayed the cause of African nationalism to which he was once committed, prompts a *Newsweek* reviewer to acknowledge, ''In this slim, nervous novel about tensions in racially torn South Africa, Miss Gordimer—usually so cool and distant—bristles openly with angry frustration.'' A *Times Literary Supplement* contributor thinks that despite its atmosphere of horror, the novel is not an overtly political one, ''Only incidentally, and after one has put down the book, does one reflect on the situation out of which so fine, compassionate, and exquisitely written a work has emerged.'' Stuart Evans suggests in the London *Times* that ''Gordimer's achievement is the way in which the importance of personal feelings are represented in the context of real and present political and social malaise; and more broadly in the light of moral and ethical questions which complacency and comfort, exemplary nannies of another age, ensure are heard but not noticed.'' Noting that Gordimer includes in her work ''the heroic and the base, the public and the private, politics and love and the clashes endemic to both," Schwartz proposes that "for Gordimer, the public and private zones are not neatly separable; perhaps this integrity is one source of her artistic strength."

The essence of Gordimer's value as an artist rests in "her ability to meet the demands of her political conscience without becoming a propagandist and the challenges of her literary commitment without becoming a disengaged esthete," as J. B. Breslin determines in an *America* review of *A Soldier's Embrace*. "She is never trivial, she never rejoices, she never groans," states Kuehn. "She is above all a truthful writer. Her abiding subject is the politics of everyday life." And she is particularly praised for the way in which she politicizes her fiction. Veronica Geng suggests in *Ms.* that the manner in which "Gordimer's fiction connects to her political views and activities" illustrates "what the literary critic Leslie Fiedler has called 'the relationship between the truth of art, the truth of conscience, and the truth of facts.'" Although her work is political, it is neither didactic, nor propagandistic. "I was writing before politics impinged itself upon my consciousness," Gordimer remarks in a *Paris Review* interview, adding: "But the real influence of politics on my writing is the influence of politics on people. Their lives, and I believe their very personalities, are changed by the extreme political circumstances one lives under in South Africa. I am dealing with people; here are people who are shaped and changed by politics. In that way my material is profoundly influenced by politics."

Newsweek's Walter Clemons notes that "she says she tries to make the political implications of her works grow out of the lives of particular characters"; and she is especially commended for those characters that epitomize specific aspects of South African society itself. In *The Conservationist*, for instance, Gordimer explores the rapacity of white rule through the characterization of Mehring, a wealthy South African industrialist whose interests are clearly material and whose privilege as a white in a country of suppressed blacks denies him little. Calling the novel "an evocation of the whole South African nightmare," Paul Theroux declares in the *New Statesman* that "it is not often that lyrical intelligence and political purpose are combined in so effective a way."

In *Burger's Daughter*, Gordimer examines white ambivalence about apartheid through the characterization of Rosa, whose irresolution about the anti-apartheid cause of her imprisoned Afrikaner father surfaces when he dies and she leaves the country to establish a new life. The novel provides "multiple views of a complex, uncertain person and of the complex cause that formed her," comments Anne Tyler in the *Saturday Review*. Calling it her "most political and most moving novel, going to the heart of the racial conflict in South Africa," Anthony Sampson points out in the *New York Times Book Review:* "Its politics come out of its characters, as part of the wholeness of lives that cannot evade them." And in a *Christian Science Monitor* review of this novel, David Winder indicates that "what ennobles Gordimer's riveting poetic prose is her intellectual and political honesty—the scrupulous unsentimentality with which she affixes blame or despair, irrespective of color, status, or political orientation."

Referring to Gordimer as "the most influential home-grown critic of her country's repressive racial policies," Paul Gray continues in a *Time* review of *Something Out There:* "But that reputation tends to blur some of the finer distinctions of her art. She is not really a polemicist. The portraits of her native

land shade softly into irony and indirection; an overriding injustice must be deduced from small, vividly realized details." Deeming this to be particularly true about *Burger's Daughter*, Tyler thinks that Gordimer "has a special reverence for the particular, for that one small, glittering facet that will cast light on the whole." Observing, also, that in *Burger's Daughter*, "the political moments are always illuminated by the intense observation of people and places," Sampson feels that this universalizes Gordimer's writing: "People, landscapes and politics are blended in this evocative style, and through the eyes of the young, bewildered daughter the wide arc of South African politics comes into sudden focus." In the *Hudson Review*, Joseph Epstein compares reading this novel to "looking at a mosaic very close up, tile by tile; and it is only toward the end that one gets a feel for the whole—that one stands back and says, My, this is really quite impressive."

"Microscopic observation, language so sharp it stings" is how Edmund Morris, in the *New York Times Book Review*, expresses the way in which Gordimer's "writing lingers in the mind." However, some critics believe that her writing merely iterates the dilemma without offering alternatives to it. For example, although Melvyn Hill finds Gordimer "truly passionate in her loyalty to experience and dedication to craft," he suggests in a *Voice Literary Supplement* discussion of *Something Out There*, that her "premises are not truly revolutionary. She shows the structure of apartheid but cannot offer a vision of the future." Alice Digilio, though, contends in the *Washington Post Book World* that "Gordimer's role as an artist is not to offer answers or scenarios for the future. She goes on telling her stories, finding new ways to present them and recording through the imagination the personal sides of political and historical journeys." Yet, Gordimer's fiction, especially her most recent work, does envision and convey a South African future.

In *A Guest of Honour*, for example, Gordimer sketches a newly independent African country and a former colonial administrator whose invitation to return is complicated by the opposing factions of two of his former proteges; the conflicts are no longer between black and white, but among blacks themselves. In an *Encounter* review, Derwent May especially admires Gordimer's description of Africa—"a wonderfully rich description, drawing on a fine feeling both for nature and history, and an exceptional knowledge of individual African character." And in the *New York Times Book Review*, Theroux suggests that "Gordimer's vision of Africa is the most complete one we have, and in time to come, when we want to know everything there is to know about a newly independent black African country, it is to this white South African woman and 'Guest of Honour' that we will turn."

"It is a commonplace to say of serious writers that they have only one tale to tell, and they write it again and again," comments Cynthia Propper Seton in the *Washington Post Book World*. "But the mind of Nadine Gordimer has a reach so wide, that each of her books, indeed each of her stories, seems to be new ground, freshly observed." In *July's People*, Gordimer peers into South Africa's future to discover a toppled government, besieged cities, and a liberal white family rescued from the wreckage of their suburban Johannesburg home by their black house servant, July, who takes them to his own village home. In this novel, Gordimer "shows us convincingly, rather than tells us, that black rule *must* come to South Africa, and even with the best will in the world on both sides, when it does come it won't be easy," remarks Bruce Cook in the *Detroit News*. As Bette Howland assesses it in the *Chicago*

Tribune Book World: "When Nadine Gordimer imagines and creates a situation, you are going to experience it—like it or not. Her gift is not particularly ingratiating, but it is commanding. 'July's People' does something that novels used to do, before newspapers, radio, TV, and movies took over; and it proves that the novel still does it better. It shows us how things are; the privilege of experience." And Seton numbers the novel "among those seemingly slighter novels that become a benchmark in one's understanding, not only of South African realities, but of all good people in Western society, and how we buckle."

In Gordimer's most recent novel, *A Sport of Nature,* she offers "a panoramic view not only of what has already taken place in South Africa but of what the future, inevitably or at least imaginatively, will become," writes *Time*'s Paul Gray, adding that once again, Gordimer "has fused her native land's agonies and contradictions into intense portraits of ordinary lives." The novel, which is about a white woman who is raised in South Africa and inherits the revolutionary cause of her assassinated black husband, "imagines, in its triumphal ending, a black African state in the place of South Africa, with Hillela and her second husband, a revolutionary general and reinstated president, standing for the wished-for integration within it," summarizes Patricia Craig in the *Times Literary Supplement.* And although Stuart Evans of the London *Times* feels that *A Sport of Nature* is flawed by Gordimer's projection of a "South African future which few of us can really believe in," Gray considers her novel to be "both richly detailed and visionary, a brilliant reflection of a world that exists and an affirmation of faith in one that could be born."

Rubin suggests that "as Gordimer's reputation has steadily and deservedly risen, there have been signs of falling off in her most recent work." Considering *A Sport of Nature* "as weak in purely literary terms as it is lacking in positive political wisdom," the critic also ponders whether these weaknesses could possibly be "reflections of her deepening pessimism about the future of her country and a growing disillusionment, not only with liberalism, which she dismissed decades ago, but with all kinds of human endeavor from rationalism to radicalism." Although similarly referring to Gordimer as a writer "who has been developing an apparently justifiable contempt for her own kind," Marq de Villiers adds in the Toronto *Globe and Mail* that she "has not given up on them altogether." Despite "the pessimism and the contempt, this is not a book with hopelessness as its tone," says de Villiers. As Maureen Howard observes in the *New York Times Book Review,* "Never a polemic, the novel is the mature achievement of the once isolated provincial child, the once politically uninvolved writer of accomplished New Yorker stories."

Finding her work "exhilarating," Mark Abley writes in the Toronto *Globe and Mail* about *Something Out There:* "One of Gordimer's extraordinary qualities as a writer is her knack of seeming authoritative about nearly all classes and social groups—young and old; rural and urban; female and male; Afrikaans, English and black. She works with her formidable intelligence and all her senses at full pitch." This is especially evidenced by her depiction of Mehring in *The Conservationist,* for in Jonathan Raban's estimation in *Encounter,* Gordimer "writes about being a man with more curiosity, passion and intelligence than any man could bring to the subject." In a *Times Literary Supplement* review of *A Soldier's Embrace,* Frank Tuohy suggests that "on one level her writing can be seen as the most sensitive record we have of the various shifts in attitude—breaths, rather than winds, of change—as they

have occurred in South Africa throughout the past forty or so years," but adds that "we see her world most clearly and movingly as it affects women, especially good-hearted young girls."

According to a *People* contributor, Gordimer "suggests that only people like Hillela, shrewd and perceptive and infinitely adaptable, can survive the insanity." Regarding her fascination with people like the character of Hillela, Gordimer tells Sternhell: "There *are* people who live instinctively, who act first and think afterward. And they are great survivors. And I think that cerebral people like myself have often been inclined to look down on them. And then you find that really you've been quite wrong." Yet, "Gordimer is not a feminist," Sternhell points out: "The Women's Movement, she says, 'doesn't seem irrelevant to me in other places in the world, but it does seem at the present time to be kind of a luxury in South Africa. Every black woman has more in common with a black man than she has with her white sisters.'" Commenting on her belief that writers are "androgynous beings," Gordimer tells Sternhell that "the real thing that makes a writer a writer is the ability to intuit other people's states of mind. . . . I think there is a special quality a writer has that is not defined by sex."

According to Brigitte Weeks in the *Washington Post Book World,* "Gordimer insists that her readers face South African life as she does: with affection and horror." And noting Gordimer's perception of apartheid as "a personal as well as a political tragedy," Weeks feels that "her characters define her moral position with devastating clarity: humanity and apartheid cannot coexist. Inevitably, one must destroy the other." Noting that Gordimer's books are no longer banned by the South African government, Dan Bellm indicates in *Mother Jones,* "A deeper dilemma thus comes to light: a white writer is committed to black liberation, but is in no more than a marginal position to help bring it about and is declared harmless by apartheid itself. Now what?" Gordimer tells Beth Austin in a *Chicago Tribune* interview that her greatest hope is that blacks gain political power and "come into their own in South Africa, come into their own heritage." She cares little whether whites will survive as a group in that country, indicating: "But if you're a white born in South Africa, I believe that there is a place for you—if you prove it, by your actions, by the way you live—primarily by the fight you put up against oppressive government. If you do this, you then prove that it is possible to opt out of class and color. . . . You can be part of the new South Africa."

In her introduction to *Selected Stories,* Gordimer considers the "tension between standing apart and being fully involved" as that which at once creates and serves as a writer's point of departure. However, as she indicates to Austin, "I feel that as a citizen, as a human being, I also have other responsibilities. I can't say that these are all discharged by my work." Noting in a *U.S. News & World Report* conversation with Alvin P. Sanoff that she admires those individuals with "that extra passion and courage" who have sacrificed their own careers and have "put every energy into the struggle," Gordimer points out: "Everybody treads a kind of line of how far they will go and measures that against what use they can be. Yet, I think that anybody who is still lucky enough to be able to go out of the country, who still has a passport, couldn't come out and refuse to be interviewed about these things."

Kakutani states that Gordimer, who has helped establish the South African Anti-Censorship Action Group, and has granted numerous interviews, proposes that the essential question is how much influence do writers have at all: "My observation is that writers are not taken seriously in America—they're regarded as entertainers. And in Eastern Europe and the Soviet Union, they're taken so seriously that sometimes they can't be published at all. In South Africa, as writers, I doubt whether we have any influence on the Government at all. But I do think South African fiction writers, if we've been of any use at all, have helped rouse and raise the consciousness of the outside world to the longterm effects of life in our country. To put it very simplistically, a newspaper account, however good, tells you what happened. But it's the playwright, the novelist, the poet, the short-story writer who gives you some idea of why."

"I began to write, I think, out of the real source of all art, and that is out of a sense of wonderment about life, and a sense of trying to make sense out of the mystery of life," Gordimer tells Austin. "That hasn't changed in all the years that I've been writing. That is the starting point of everything that I write." Gordimer explains that in writing, one attempts to "build the pattern of his own perception out of chaos," continuing in the introduction to *Selected Stories,* "To make sense of life: that story, in which everything, novels, stories, the false starts, the half-completed, the abandoned, has its meaningful place, will be complete with the last sentence written before one dies or imagination atrophies."

MEDIA ADAPTATIONS: "City Lovers," based on Gordimer's short story of the same title, was filmed by TeleCulture Inc./TelePool in South Africa in 1982.

CA INTERVIEW

CA interviewed Nadine Gordimer by telephone on January 11, 1988, at her home in Johannesburg, South Africa.

CA: In A Sport of Nature, *you followed Hillela Capran over the course of forty years to an elevated position in a free South African state. You seem to have found your heroine both fascinating and shocking at the same time, judging from comments you've made in previous interviews. How did she form in your mind before you began to write her story?*

GORDIMER: I think she began to form in my mind because I realized that so many of us who reject racism have a fixed idea of how one may deal with the situation of being born a white South African. There are various ways—realistically, that is; I'm not talking about the people who decide that it hasn't any special meaning at all, or any special responsibility. I've often thought that for a young person of each generation, including myself when I was young, the "solutions" that were offered were in practice shown to have many flaws, and that these were always the solutions of the cerebral people, thinkers. And we thinkers are inclined to despise people who live instinctually. Then I began picking up a little information here or there or bumping into people who had somehow begun to live here—or partly here and partly in exile—in a meaningful fashion that we would never have thought of. They were following other instincts, another line of life. So maybe the house of liberation has many mansions, just as the New Testament house has.

Also, I've always been fascinated with women who use their femininity in a special way—more than their femininity: their *femaleness*—going back in history to the Madame de Pompadours up to Eva Peron and later, and some lesser lights you see around you, people who have an extraordinary power over others and who also make a mark in the world, sometimes a very useful one, but not in the cerebral way. That's how I came to Hillela. I've also found such people often very attractive in their naturalness, their warmth, their life-giving attitudes.

CA: Where does Hillela stand among your characters, in your own estimation? Is she a favorite of yours?

GORDIMER: I've never graded my characters on a scale. I think that some of my favorites are in an old book of mine called *A Guest of Honour,* and I would say that Rosa Burger, from *Burger's Daughter,* is top of the list with me. But of course I'm fascinated by Hillela, and I was fascinated as I went along making her, so to speak, by how much there was to her, how much to puzzle out.

CA: How has A Sport of Nature *been received in South Africa?*

GORDIMER: I think it's been much misunderstood. Irony is a method that I'm very fond of, and it's very much present in this book. My whole attitude toward Hillela is one of regarding, smiling irony. And I think there's a kind of priggish attitude toward irony as a mode in South Africa at present. I think it's felt perhaps by my own friends and colleagues to be something that doesn't sit with a revolutionary. Hillela is not clearly enough a heroine; she's too compromised in many ways, and too individualistic. I don't know what the others think, but I feel that they really want a book about goodies and baddies, not about people who are complex and who, in some unexpected way, manage to make themselves useful in the world.

I've had some strange reactions, and not only at home. A friend of mine, an academic from Canada, happened to be here on a visit and came to see me. He liked the book very much but was absolutely infuriated by Hillela because, he said, she was so cruel to men. I was amazed. I think this is a projection of some kind. Hillela isn't cruel to anybody, really. She's a very life-giving character: everybody whose life she goes into she enriches for the time she's there, whether it's the ambassador, whom she makes happy as a mistress, or the ambassador's wife and children, for whom she's so helpful in the household. She's such an adaptable person, and she always seems to be adaptable in a way that's helpful to other people. Even when she deserts the American who wants to marry her, Brad, it's for his own good. She would never have fitted into the kind of life he could offer her. Really, she's best off with the General, who is as much of a rogue as she is and a bit more.

CA: In the introduction to Selected Stories, *you said, "The tension between standing apart and being fully involved; that is what makes a writer." Has your increasing involvement in political activities made an ideal balance hard to maintain?*

GORDIMER: It's not an ideal balance; it's a difficult balance, because the tension gets drawn tighter and tighter just in terms of time and that withdrawal into oneself that you need when you are writing. For me, it's a constant battle with so many calls on my time, but I can't live in an ivory tower and not take part in anything political in this country, so I just have to work it out. I also think that I'm like many writers in that perhaps I always require some opposition, some difficulty, something that makes it hard for me to get on with my work and forces me to be defiantly getting on with it.

CA: Though some of your themes are the same from novel to novel, you manage to make each one unique. Do you continue to find the novel form as exciting a challenge as your books would indicate?

GORDIMER: Absolutely. It's only the country and the people that are same, with the one exception of *A Guest of Honour*, which was not set in South Africa at all. As long as you're alive, life is changing you as an individual. If you're a writer, it is changing, widening, broadening your knowledge of what life is about. It works that way for me.

CA: You've acknowledged as influences D. H. Lawrence, Henry James, Ernest Hemingway, and later Albert Camus. Would you say a bit about what each has contributed to your own ideas on writing?

GORDIMER: Those are names plucked from earlier interviews, and really it's an astonishing list. I think I may have remarked long ago that when I was young and first started to read Henry James, I admired him greatly and still do. But I think he's a terrible influence on a young writer, because one gets tangled up in his immensely long sentences. Whatever influence he had on me, I sloughed off. D. H. Lawrence was a very early influence when I started to write short stories. He has not been a sustaining influence, and I don't see how he can be, because he was a writer belonging to a particular class, country, time. He was a very sensuous and sensual writer. That sensuousness is something that I think belongs more to youthful writers. Not *sensuality,* of course; that stays on. I've always said that, to me, the strongest motivations in life are sexual and political, and I think that comes out in my books. Camus I don't think of as having been an influence except for a short time. But there again, I admire him very much. You can admire writers who are very different from you.

Marcel Proust has been an enduring influence, I think. One can hardly imagine any modern novelist who has not been influenced by Marcel Proust. There are other writers I've tremendously admired in my mature life. For instance, I appreciate Thomas Mann more and more. But I could never say that he's been an influence on me. When I brought Hemingway up in an earlier interview, I was saying that I didn't think anybody who wrote short stories could be without the influence, primarily and most importantly, of Chekhov, who really created the modern short story for all of us. But probably for people in the English-literature culture like myself, which of course includes the American one, Hemingway's stories did have an influence. But I no longer really admire him; I can't reread him. I can reread Chekhov endlessly—the best bedside books in the world.

In the end, influences only last, I think, until you're 'round about thirty, mid-thirties perhaps. You have to find your own voice, and if you don't do that, then you're never going to be able to write what you want to write. I hope that about that stage in my life I found my own voice.

CA: Reviewing The Conservationist *in* Encounter, *Jonathan Raban noted that to create the protagonist Mehring and write the book, you had to "reconstruct, piece by piece, a sensibility, even a historical consciousness, quite alien" to your own. Was Mehring a hard character to capture?*

GORDIMER: No, he really wasn't. And it's a book that I wrote in a burst, rather more quickly than my other books. Of course that may have something to do with the fact that much

of it is in the historic present tense, which is a sort of breath-holding mode. But it seemed to be right for that book. Jonathan Raban was quite right: it was a sensibility very far from my own, which had nothing to do with the fact that the main character was a man. But you must remember that I've been around such people all my life. I've been listening to them. I've even watched the young ones grow into middle-aged ones, getting more and more like that. It's a whole ethos, a whole world of values, that I've long, long known. And it's not unusual for writers to be able to portray a sensibility alien to their own. In a sense it was almost as big a shift with Rosa Burger's family, though there were links there with the sort of people that I know. Also, I've always described that book as a kind of homage to people like the Burger family. I've known people like that intimately, whereas the Mehrings, the characters in *The Conservationist,* have been observed more from the outside, and from the way they reveal themselves in their actions and in their words.

CA: You started in The Conservationist *writing dialogue without quotation marks, a form you've continued. I'm curious about why you made that change.*

GORDIMER: First of all, of course, it's nothing new. You can go back to Laurence Sterne. He never used a quotation mark in his life, as far as I know—you certainly won't find one in *Tristram Shandy*. Our friend Hemingway didn't use them either, very often. There have been many other writers who didn't use them. But I didn't take it up as an intimate thing, or as any kind of fashion. Indeed, if I had, one could see that it was already out of date. I did it, and I cling to it, because there's something to me actually physical, visual, about those strange little double commas (or single commas, in some cases) that seems to set what somebody says apart in a kind of artificial framework. It always suggested to me that now the author is putting these words into the character's mouth.

I've long ago given up the "he said" and "she said," which is more important, because that is difficult to do. I did it as a kind of challenge to try and see whether I could make the voice of each character so unmistakable and individual that the reader would know who was speaking. I think I've probably succeeded eighty percent of the time. Occasionally, no doubt, I'll puzzle my readers and they'll have to go over a line or two.

CA: Quotation marks can be distracting to the reader.

GORDIMER: Yes. Other people say you don't notice them because they're the convention. And of course the dash is a convention. But to me the dash is much quicker, more intimate. I feel that there is that pause between one person speaking and the other responding to which the visual symbol of the dash corresponds more than these little double commas.

CA: When Burger's Daughter *was banned, you published* What Happened to Burger's Daughter; or, How South African Censorship Works, *a pamphlet consisting of the opinions of the banning board. For people who can't easily get a copy, would you talk about the publication and what it revealed?*

GORDIMER: *Burger's Daughter* was my third book to be banned. There is a process whereby you can, within fourteen days, challenge the ban and then you will get a hearing—not in a court of law, but in a sort of court put up by the censors themselves, called the Publications Control Appeal Board. I had never done this. First, I felt it was a case of *I'll be judge, I'll be jury* from the point of view of the censors themselves. Secondly, I object to this evasion of the normal legal processes whereby the author, if he offends by obscenity or by a threat to state security, would have the right to state his case and defend himself in a normal court of law or before a properly qualified judge. Thirdly, since I don't recognize the right of the government to censor what I read or what I write, I don't want to collaborate with them even to the extent of appealing against a ban on one of my books. So I followed the same course with *Burger's Daughter*.

But I discovered—I had been rather careless about reading the small print before—that in the censorship laws, the writer or the publisher, within that same fourteen days, without appealing, can ask for a transcript of the opinions of the people who decided that the book is undesirable. I duly asked for this and got the dossier, which was really quite something. Here were the opinions of the people who had read the book and had recommended that it be banned. Of course, they're all anonymous. And the reasons were so extraordinary—in some cases so ludicrous and in others so offensive—and showing no literary understanding at all. You could see that they were written by people who don't understand how far literature goes.

I thought, I just can't keep this to myself as an item of interest, and I had the idea of publishing the full transcript, which I found that I had the right to do, and publishing alongside it letters that I got from various people—from International PEN, from prominent writers like Heinrich Boell, Iris Murdoch and others—protesting against this book's being banned. So I put it together, and it is my first and last vanity press book; I decided I would publish it myself. In the end I did publish it myself, but it was the collaboration of a small and sort of half-underground publishing house of friends of mine.

I think it was a good idea. People simply say, Oh, well, a book is banned; that's the law. But here they could read between the lines the caliber of mind of the people who are judging what we may read and what we may not. I think it did good from that point of view. It had a novel form of distribution: the bookshops took it gladly and displayed it on the counter where you pay, so people could pick it up with their purchases. And it had quite a wide distribution that way. It resulted in (though it wasn't admitted that it did) the Publications Control Board's reviewing their decision and releasing the book. And it established a kind of principle. After that there were a number of other writers who didn't actually publish booklets about what happened to them, but would ask for the reasons their books were banned, and these were quite often published in literary journals here.

CA: Is there a solid core of writers there who also act as book reviewers, as is the case here in the States?

GORDIMER: Unfortunately not, and reviewing is absolutely pathetic here. It hardly exists, and personally I don't bother to read the reviews. The way it seems to be done is that whoever is acting as what's called literary editor—I'm talking about the big dailies now—gets a pile of books from publishers and then, one feels, goes around the office and asks, Who'd like to read this; who'd like to read that? Any cub reporter can go off with a book to review. And very often books by authors with a whole body of work behind them are reviewed by somebody who's come upon the author for the first time, who's got no idea of the development of the writer. I used to write angry letters to the papers about this. I once saw a Graham Greene

book reviewed by somebody who'd obviously never read anything by Graham Greene before. The space is minimal, and it's very often given over partly to how-to books, which should be in the gardening section or homebody section or something like that. This is the general standard in the dailies. In the weeklies, and especially in the alternative weeklies, there is an attempt at serious reviewing, but nowhere else.

CA: You've been instrumental in the organization of the Anti-Censorship Action Group in South Africa. How does the group work against censorship, and how successfully is it functioning?

GORDIMER: It's just a year old. The main thrust of its activity is indeed to expose what happens, to show people what they're missing. We have concentrated, since we were formed, on the terrible conditions under which journalists work. In the case of fiction, poetry, and even essays, very few books are censored now. You'd be amazed at some of the things that get published. The reason is that they don't reach a massive grass-roots readership, and it's felt that they're read by the kind of people for whom the damage—from the point of view of the government wanting compliance—is already done; the people who read these books are *not* compliant. But when it comes to the daily press, and even more when it comes to television and radio both at home and all over the world, this is another matter altogether. These are the masses' source of information. Since the two states of emergency, the second of which is still in operation, there's an unbelievable clampdown on the press here, as you might have noticed. We've disappeared off your television screens, and there's less and less about us in your papers. We at home are in much the same position. There's so much that cannot be written about on the day-to-day basis on which journalists operate.

ACAG has concentrated on this. We've held debates between editors and journalists. The situation should produce fellow feeling, but it often produces frustrations and bad feelings. The journalist goes off, brings back a story; the editor looks at it, consults his lawyer. Every newspaper has more or less a resident lawyer, who disagrees with what the newspaper editor thinks would pass the censors, and the journalist feels his story is cut to pieces. It's a very, very difficult way to work, in addition to which many journalists actually suffer physical danger with the situation as it is now.

And now, of course, our alternative press is under terrible threat of being closed down altogether—notably the *Weekly Mail* and the *New Nation*, both of which are very important to us. The editor of the *New Nation*, Zwelakhe Sisulu, has been in detention for a year and a month now. The paper continues to be published, but the *New Nation*, the *Weekly Mail*, and three other publications have received warnings from the relevant minister about the nature of the reports they publish and the tone of the papers. One fears they may be closed down. There's a great deal of protest about that. The protest, ironically, is in those very papers. But it is also in the daily press. I must say that the *Star*, which is the biggest English-language daily, has taken a strong stand against the threat to the alternative press.

CA: What's the situation there now with PEN and other writers' groups?

GORDIMER: PEN doesn't exist here. We have close relations with PEN International, and, of the branches, PEN in America has been most generous and helpful and concerned about us. We have a new organization since July, 1987—the Congress of South African Writers. It's a nonracial national organization, and we're very excited about it.

CA: How much closeness is there between white and black writers in South Africa?

GORDIMER: They have gone through a time when black separatism parted them. But now, in this new organization, they're very close indeed. This depends simply upon the white writers. The organization goes out of its way to make them feel welcome. But many seem to have reservations about belonging to an organization that (*a*) has a majority of black members, and (*b*) is closely allied to the cultural movements of the trade unions and has as its avowed aim the formation of a new culture in South Africa based on a worker's culture. These are principles that some white writers seem to be uneasy with.

CA: In an interview with Edmund Morris for the New York Times Book Review, *you talked about the rich oral tradition in Africa and its survival despite its suppression and debasement by the European missionaries. How is that oral tradition in evidence today?*

GORDIMER: I believe that oral tradition has found new life in the theater, the liveliest branch of literature—and I regard the theater as a branch of literature since it's so concerned with the word as well as movement and all the other things. The theater is immensely lively in the big centers like Johannesburg and Capetown—particularly in Johannesburg, with its vast population of black and white people in the surrounding areas, but also in Durban and in other places as well. There's a great upsurge of talent and activity, workshopped plays where actors begin to bloom indeed as playwrights in an informal way. In this, in the new style of acting, in the new mode of what theater is and what drama means, the mode appropriate to our society has been found. It includes in the framework of what we think of as drama a great deal of mime, music, dance, and declaimed poetry, which have all come together as a dramatic form. It's really great.

There've been wonderful plays in New York that have grown out of this movement, notably a whole season at the Vivian Beaumont Theatre at Lincoln Center. Now there's another one independent of that particular grouping, a big musical called *Sarafina* with a huge case of black school children who have never acted before. Then there are the more formal plays, such as the very good one called *Bopha!* and one called *Asinamali*, devised and acted by blacks. There are many plays like *Born in the RSA*, the work of one of our best white director-writers, Barney Simon, in collaboration with black actors and actresses. And of course there are Athol Fugard's seminal plays, which are constantly revived. There's *Sophiatown*, which is music and dancing and satire, with a mixed cast. And I could go on and on.

There are lots of small theater groups, and there are children's groups which are very good. The black children don't get this sort of thing at school the way white children do, and there are now a number of alternative or supplementary educational organizations where they can learn drama and painting and all the lovely life-expanding things they don't get in their rotten schools. It makes a tremendous difference; you can see such confidence in these young people who've had the opportunity to enjoy alternative activities. That is the good side of a terrible situation.

CA: I know you don't talk about work in progress. Can you say anything about your hopes for your writing, any goals you may have for it, anything different you might like someday to explore in it?

GORDIMER: Every time I finish a book I think, Well, now I've said all I have to say. Then, of course, you go on living and something else comes up—another goal, as you call it, something else that you feel you must say. But one has to wait to fill up. I published *A Sport of Nature* only last year, and I am doing all sorts of other things. I am bringing out this year, for the first time, a book of nonfiction pieces. These are pieces of mine written over thirty years. Some of them are political pieces, some are literary criticism, and there are a few travel pieces. The book is called *The Essential Gesture*, which is a quote from Roland Barthes. The essential gesture is what I think a writer's writing means in terms of his society, the way a writer puts out his hand to his society—through the writing.

BIOGRAPHICAL/CRITICAL SOURCES:

BOOKS

Clingman, Stephen R., *The Novels of Nadine Gordimer: History from the Inside*, Allen & Unwin, 1988.
Contemporary Literary Criticism, Gale, Volume 3, 1975, Volume 5, 1976, Volume 7, 1977, Volume 10, 1979, Volume 18, 1981, Volume 33, 1985, Volume 51, 1989.
Gordimer, Nadine, *Selected Stories*, Viking, 1976.
Haugh, Robert F., *Nadine Gordimer*, Twayne Publishers, 1974.
Heywood, Christopher, *Nadine Gordimer*, Profile, 1983.
Nell, Racilia Jilian, *Nadine Gordimer, Novelist and Short Story Writer: A Bibliography of Her Works*, University of the Witwatersrand, 1964.
Tucker, Martin, *Africa in Modern Literature: A Survey of Contemporary Writing*, Ungar, 1967.
Wade, Michael, *Nadine Gordimer*, Evans, 1978.

PERIODICALS

America, April 17, 1976, October 11, 1980.
Atlantic, January, 1960.
Best Sellers, December 15, 1970, November 15, 1971, March 15, 1975.
Booklist, October 1, 1958, January 10, 1960.
Chicago Sunday Tribune, September 21, 1958.
Chicago Tribune, May 18, 1980, December 7, 1986, November 12, 1987.
Chicago Tribune Book World, September 9, 1979, June 7, 1981, July 29, 1984.
Christian Science Monitor, January 10, 1963, November 4, 1971, May 19, 1975, September 10, 1979.
Commonweal, October 23, 1953, July 9, 1965, November 4, 1966.
Detroit News, September 2, 1979, June 7, 1981, May 31, 1989.
Encounter, August, 1971, February, 1975.
Globe and Mail (Toronto), July 28, 1984, June 6, 1987.
Harper's, February, 1963, April, 1976.
Hudson Review, spring, 1980.
Library Journal, September 1, 1958.
London Magazine, April/May, 1975.
Los Angeles Times, July 31, 1984, December 7, 1986.
Los Angeles Times Book Review, August 10, 1980, April 19, 1987, April 3, 1988.
Modern Fiction Studies, summer, 1987.
Mother Jones, December, 1988.
Ms., July, 1975, September, 1987.

Nation, June 18, 1971, August 18, 1976, May 2, 1987.

New Republic, July 7, 1952, November 10, 1958, May 8, 1965, September 10, 1966, September 13, 1975.

New Statesman, May 24, 1958, May 14, 1971, November 8, 1974, November 28, 1975.

New Statesman and Nation, August 18, 1956.

Newsweek, May 10, 1965, July 4, 1966, March 10, 1975, April 19, 1976, September 22, 1980, June 22, 1981, July 9, 1984, May 4, 1987.

New Yorker, June 7, 1952, November 21, 1953, November 29, 1958, May 12, 1975.

New York Herald Tribune Book Review, May 25, 1952, October 4, 1953, October 21, 1956, September 21, 1958, January 10, 1960, April 7, 1963.

New York Review of Books, June 26, 1975, July 15, 1976.

New York Times, June 15, 1952, October 4, 1953, October 7, 1956, September 21, 1958, May 23, 1965, October 30, 1970, September 19, 1979, August 20, 1980, May 27, 1981, July 9, 1984, January 14, 1986, April 22, 1987, December 28, 1987.

New York Times Book Review, January 10, 1960, September 11, 1966, October 31, 1971, April 13, 1975, April 18, 1976, August 19, 1979, August 24, 1980, June 7, 1981, July 29, 1984, May 3, 1987.

Paris Review, summer, 1983.

People, May 4, 1987.

Publishers Weekly, March 6, 1987, April 10, 1987, September 30, 1988.

San Francisco Chronicle, May 26, 1952, November 9, 1953, January 24, 1960.

Saturday Review, May 24, 1952, October 3, 1953, September 13, 1958, January 16, 1960, May 8, 1965, August 20, 1966, December 4, 1971, March 8, 1975, September 29, 1979.

Sewanee Review, spring, 1977.

Spectator, February 12, 1960.

Time, October 15, 1956, September 22, 1958, January 11, 1960, November 16, 1970, July 7, 1975, June 8, 1981, July 23, 1984, April 6, 1987.

Times (London), December 16, 1982, March 22, 1984, April 2, 1987.

Times Literary Supplement, October 30, 1953, July 13, 1956, June 27, 1958, February 12, 1960, March 1, 1963, July 22, 1965, July 7, 1966, May 14, 1971, May 26, 1972, January 9, 1976, July 9, 1976, April 25, 1980, September 4, 1981, March 30, 1984, April 17, 1987, September 23-29, 1988.

Tribune Books (Chicago), April 26, 1987.

U.S. News & World Report, May 25, 1987.

Village Voice, September 17, 1980.

Voice Literary Supplement, September, 1984.

Washington Post, December 4, 1979.

Washington Post Book World, November 28, 1971, April 6, 1975, August 26, 1979, September 7, 1980, May 31, 1981, July 15, 1984, May 3, 1987, November 20, 1988.

World Literature Today, autumn, 1984.

Yale Review, winter, 1988.

—*Sketch by Sharon Malinowski*

—*Interview by Jean W. Ross*

*   *   *

GORDON, Diana R(ussell) 1938-

PERSONAL: Born July 18, 1938, in North Adams, Mass.; daughter of Hallett Darius (an English professor) and Mary Elizabeth (Earl) Smith; married James D. Lorenz, August 20, 1960 (divorced, 1965); married David M. Gordon (an economist), September 7, 1967. *Education:* Attended Goucher College, 1954-56; Mills College, B.A., 1958; Radcliffe College, M.A., 1959; Harvard University, LL.B., 1964. *Politics:* Democrat. *Religion:* Protestant.

ADDRESSES: Home—317 East Tenth St., New York, N.Y. 10009. *Office*—Department of Political Science, City College of New York, New York, N.Y. 10031.

CAREER: Beardsley, Hufstedler & Kemble, Los Angeles, Calif., law clerk, 1964-65; Office of Economic Opportunity, Washington, D.C., program analyst, 1965-66; City of New York, N.Y., Budget Bureau, legislative assistant, 1966-70; Harvard University, Kennedy School of Government, Cambridge, Mass., research fellow of Institute of Politics, 1970-71; Fund for the City of New York, consultant, 1971-73; State Charter Revision Commission, New York City, consultant, 1973; Citizens' Inquiry on Parole and Criminal Justice, New York City, director, 1973-78; National Council on Crime and Delinquency, Hackensack, N.J., vice-president, 1978-81, president, 1982-83; City College of New York, New York City, associate professor of political science, 1984—. Member of board of directors, Green Hope Residence for Women, 1975-85, Legal Action Center, 1979—, Prisoner's Legal Services, 1982—, and Manhattan Country School, 1984—. Consultant to various urban affairs organizations, 1971-84.

WRITINGS:

City Limits: Barrier to Change in Urban Government, Charterhouse, 1973.

Toward Realistic Reform: A Commentary on Proposals for Change in New York City's Criminal Justice System, National Council on Crime and Delinquency, 1981.

The Justice Juggernaut: Getting Tough with Common Criminals in the 1980s, Rutgers University Press, 1990.

Contributor to *New York Affairs, Ms., Village Voice, Political Science Quarterly,* and *Nation.*

*   *   *

GORES, Joe
See GORES, Joseph N(icholas)

*   *   *

GORES, Joseph N(icholas) 1931-
(Joe Gores)

PERSONAL: Surname rhymes with "roars"; born December 25, 1931, in Rochester, Minn.; son of Joseph Mathias (an accountant) and Mildred Dorothy (Duncanson) Gores; married Dori Jane Corfitzen, May 16, 1976; children: Timothy, Gillian. *Education:* University of Notre Dame, A.B., 1953; Stanford University, M.A., 1961. *Politics:* Republican. *Religion:* Roman Catholic.

ADDRESSES: Home—401 Oak Crest Rd., San Anselmo, Calif. 94960. *Office*—DOJO, Inc., P.O. Box 446, Fairfax, Calif. 94930. *Agent*—(Books) Henry Morrison, P.O. Box 235, Bedford Hills, N.Y. 10507; (scripts) Bettye McCartt, McCartt-Oreck-Barrett Agency, 10390 Santa Monica Blvd., Suite 310, Los Angeles, Calif. 90025.

CAREER: Novelist, short story writer, film and television script writer. Has worked as hod carrier, laborer, logger, stock clerk, truck driver, carnival worker, and assistant motel manager; Floyd Page's Gymnasium, Palo Alto, Calif., instructor, 1953-55; L. A. Walker Co., San Francisco, Calif., private investigator, 1955-57, 1959; David Kikkert & Associates, San Francisco, private investigator, 1959-62, 1965-66; Kakamega Boys Secondary School, Kakamega, Kenya, East Africa, English teacher, 1963-64; Automobile Auction Co., San Francisco, manager and auctioneer, 1968-76; currently affiliated with DOJO, Inc., Fairfax, Calif. *Military service:* U.S. Army, 1958-59.

MEMBER: Mystery Writers of America (secretary, 1966, 1968; vice-president, 1967, 1969-70; member of board of directors, 1967-70, 1975-76; general awards chairman, 1976-77; president, 1986), Writers Guild of America West, Crime Writers Association.

AWARDS, HONORS: Edgar Allen Poe Award, Mystery Writers of America, 1969, for best first mystery novel, *A Time of Predators,* 1969, for best mystery short story, "Goodbye, Pops," and 1975, for best episode, "No Immunity for Murder," in a television dramatic series, "Kojak"; Falcon Award, Maltese Falcon Society of Japan, 1986, for best hard-boiled mystery novel, *Hammett.*

WRITINGS:

NOVELS; UNDER NAME JOE GORES

A Time of Predators, Random House, 1969.
Dead Skip, Random House, 1972.
Interface (also see below), M. Evans, 1974.
Hammett (also see below), Putnam, 1975.
Gone, No Forwarding, Random House, 1978.
Come Morning (also see below), Mysterious Press, 1986.

FILM SCRIPTS; UNDER NAME JOE GORES

"Interface," Cinema Entertainment, 1974.
"Deadfall," Twentieth-Century Fox, 1976.
"Hammett," Zoetrope Studios, 1977-78.
"Paper Crimes," P.E.A./United Artists, 1978.
"Paradise Road," Paramount, 1978.
"Golden Gate Memorial" (television film), Universal, 1978.
"A Wayward Angel," Solofilm/United Artists, 1981.
(With Kevin Wade) "Cover Story," Columbia, 1985.

Also author of films (with Arthur M. Kaye) "Force Twelve," 1971, (with Kaye) "Game without Rules," 1972, and "Come Morning," 1980.

OTHER; UNDER NAME JOE GORES

Marine Salvage (nonfiction), Doubleday, 1971.
(Editor) *Honolulu: Port of Call* (anthology), Comstock, 1974.
(Editor with Bill Pronzini) *Tricks and Treats* (anthology), Doubleday, 1975.

Contributor of scripts to television series "Kojak," "Eischeid," "Kate Loves a Mystery," "The Gangster Chronicles," "Strike Force," "Magnum, P.I.," "Mike Hammer," "Remington Steele," "Scene of the Crime," "Eye to Eye," "Hell Town," and "T. J. Hooker." Also contributor to anthologies, including *Mystery Writers of America Annual Anthology, Boucher's Choicest,* and *Best Detective Stories of the Year.* Contributor of stories and articles to *Ellery Queen's Mystery Magazine, Argosy, Adam, Negro Digest,* and other periodicals.

WORK IN PROGRESS: 32 Cadillacs and *Wind Time, Wolf Time,* two novels; three short stories.

SIDELIGHTS: Joe Gores writes his detective stories from a unique perspective; he worked as a private detective in San Francisco for more than ten years, beginning in 1955. Winner of three Edgar Allan Poe Awards, Gores is probably best known for his novel *Hammett,* which sets the real-life detective and mystery writer Dashiell Hammett in a fictional murder case in 1928. Although *Newsweek* reviewer Peter S. Prescott finds fault with Gores's narrative technique and *New York Times* critic Richard R. Lingeman believes Gores's portrayal of Hammett is superficial, according to Max Byrd, *Hammett* is "a splendid story, a candy-apple to the connoisseur." Reviewing the novel in the *New Republic,* Byrd writes that Gore's protagonist "sets out to clean up a corrupt society,... but his civic aim is constantly deflected by a revenge *motif* worthy of Jacobean drama and by Gores' obvious delight in the conventions of his genre." Byrd adds that "perhaps, but not likely, Gores had even more fun writing this book than we do reading it."

In his *Washington Post Book World* assessment of Gores's *Come Morning,* Lawrence Block claims "Gores is one of the better-kept secrets in crime fiction.... *Come Morning* is a pure pleasure to read. Please understand that the basic ingredients are nothing new. One man has something—spy secrets, a black bird, a fortune in diamonds. Others want to take it from him.... [Yet,] the plot is a honey, intricate, logical, fair, and constantly surprising.... Within the mystery field, Gores has won awards and fans. He deserves a wider audience, and this book should get it for him." According to Brian Garfield for the *Chicago-Sun Times, Come Morning* is the work of a novelist who has matured—"[Gores] has absolute control of his material: the book inspires a chill on the back of the neck—the short hairs are raised by a thrill of confidence that we are in the hands of a master who *knows*.... Although metaphors do not flood his pages (he won't stoop to that sort of pretentiousness), nevertheless there are images, doled out at frugal intervals—striking, apt, stunningly effective. They do what good prose is supposed to do: they show us new ways of perceiving things." Even within the novel's rush of action, Garfield senses a "convincing warmth," and concludes that the work is the major event Gores's publishers claimed it would be: "Like a handful of previous writers ... Gores brings a vivid new voice to America's literatures of the criminal on the run."

Gores wrote to *CA:* "I entered college thinking I wanted to be a cartoonist in a Milton Caniff-Hal Foster moe. But I soon realized I was intrigued by storytelling, so I quit drawing and started writing short stories, averaging 300 rejection slips a year until my first sale (to *Manhunt* for $65) four years after graduation. It was only years later, when I added film and TV to the novel and the short story, that I realized I had come full circle: I was back to telling stories in words *and* pictures.

"In 1968, Lee Wright of Random House wrote that if I ever wanted to write a novel she'd probably want to publish it. I immediately wrote *A Time of Predators,* Wright published it, and it won an Edgar. In 1974, Jack Laird, supervising producer of 'Kojak,' wrote that if I ever wanted to write a 'Kojak' episode, he'd probably want to buy it. I immediately wrote 'No Immunity for Murder,' Laird bought it, and it won an Edgar. I seem to keep backing into my career moves.

"While living in Africa I read Robert Ardrey's *African Genesis,* and a few years later Joseph Campbell's *The Hero with a Thousand Faces.* From these I came to understand what my basic fictional theme was: A hero who has been stripped of society's defenses must overcome danger and death armed only with the genetic survival skills inherited from his prehuman ancestors.

"Writing is all I do and all I want to do. I try to write every day but [I] don't always make it—travel, for instance, makes the work schedule disappear."

MEDIA ADAPTATIONS: Hammett was adapted into a film by Ross Thomas and Dennis O'Flaherty, produced by Francis Ford Coppola, and released by Warner Brthers in 1982.

AVOCATIONAL INTERESTS: Skin diving, handball, weight-lifting, hiking, African prehistory, travel.

BIOGRAPHICAL/CRITICAL SOURCES:

PERIODICALS

Chicago-Sun Times, March 2, 1986.
Listener, November 25, 1976.
Los Angeles Times, March 13, 1981.
New Republic, May 22, 1979.
Newsweek, September 8, 1975.
New York Times, September 4, 1975, July 1, 1983, February 19, 1986.
New York Times Book Review, August 24, 1969, August 11, 1972, May 14, 1978.
Times Literary Supplement, October 10, 1975.
Washington Post Book World, August 23, 1970, December 17, 1972, May 19, 1974, March 2, 1986.

*   *   *

GOTTSCHALK, Laura Riding
See JACKSON, Laura (Riding)

*   *   *

GRAHAM-YOOLL, Andrew M(ichael)   1944-

PERSONAL: Born January 5, 1944, in Buenos Aires, Argentina; son of Douglas Noel (a farmer) and Ines Louise (Tovar) Graham-Yooll; married Micaela Meyer (an architect), January 17, 1966; children: Ines, Luis, Isabel.

ADDRESSES: Home—10 Rotherwick Rd., London NW11 7DA, England. *Office—South,* New Zealand House, 80 Haymarket, London SW1Y 4TS, England.

CAREER: Buenos Aires Herald, Buenos Aires, Argentina, news editor and political writer, 1966-76; *Daily Telegraph,* London, England, sub-editor, 1976-77; *Guardian,* London, sub-editor, 1977-84; *South,* London, deputy editor, 1984-85, editor, 1985—.

MEMBER: International PEN (press officer; member of committee of English Center), National Union of Journalists, Writers Guild of Great Britain.

AWARDS, HONORS: Poetry prize from *El Vidente Ciego* magazine, 1975; Nicholas Tomalin Memorial Award from *Sunday Times,* 1977.

WRITINGS:

IN ENGLISH

Day to Day (poetry), Ediciones de la Flor, 1973.
The Press in Argentina, 1973-78, Writers and Scholars Educational Trust, 1979.

A Matter of Fear: Portrait of an Argentinian Exile (memoir), Lawrence Hill, 1981 (published in England as *Portrait of an Exile,* Junction Books, 1981).
The Forgotten Colony: A History of the English-Speaking Communities in Argentina (nonfiction), Hutchinson, 1981.
Small Wars You May Have Missed (nonfiction), Junction Books, 1983.
A State of Fear: Memories of Argentina's Nightmare (memoir), Eland, 1986.

IN SPANISH

Se habla spangles (poetry), Ediciones de la Flor, 1972.
Tiempo de tragedia: Argentina 1966-1971 (nonfiction; title means "Time of Tragedy: Argentina 1966-1971"), Ediciones de la Flor, 1972.
Tiempo de violencia: Argentina 1972-1973 (nonfiction; title means "Time of Violence: Argentina 1972-1973"), Granica, 1974.
Lancelot Holland: Viaje al Plata en 1807 (nonfiction; title means "Lancelot Holland: Journey to the River Plate, 1807"), EUDEBA, 1976.
Arthur Koestler: Del infinito al cero (biography; title means "Arthur Koestler: From Infinity to Zero"), Altalena, 1978.
La censura en el mundo (nonfiction; title means "Censorship in the World"), Libros de Hoy, 1980.
Asi vieron a Rosas los ingleses (nonfiction; title means "Thus the English Saw Rosas"), Rodolfo Alonso, 1980.
La independencia de Venezuela vista por "The Times" (nonfiction; title means "Venezuelan Independence as Seen by *The Times*"), Libros de Hoy, 1980.
Pequenas guerras britanicas en America latina (nonfiction; title means "Small British Wars in Latin America"), Legasa, 1985.

OTHER

Contributor of short stories, poems, and articles to newspapers and magazines, including the *San Francisco Chronicle, Miami Herald, Baltimore Sun, Kansas City Star, New York Times, Newsweek, London Magazine, Literary Review, Los Andes, El Vidente Ciego, Descant, Index on Censorship,* and *New Edinburgh Review.*

WORK IN PROGRESS: A biographical omnibus of anecdotes and interviews; commentary on twentieth-century Argentina.

SIDELIGHTS: Andrew M. Graham-Yooll was born into the British community in Argentina, where he lived for thirty-two years. In 1976, when Isabel Peron's government was overthrown by a military coup and the armed forces began arresting "subversives"—including several journalists—Graham-Yooll left his job as news editor of the English-language *Buenos Aires Herald* and went with his family to England. In *Portrait of an Exile,* which was published in the United States as *A Matter of Fear: Portrait of an Argentinian Exile,* Graham-Yooll describes his experiences of the political chaos in Argentina, as well as his first encounter with English life.

A contributor to *Contemporary Review* calls the book "a frightening account of political life in Argentina during the seventies.... Graham-Yooll tells vividly of many experiences, including secret guerrilla press conferences and attempted investigations into political murders and abductions. It is a story of terror and violence in which law and order had collapsed." *Encounter* critic James Nielson designates *Portrait of an Exile* as "by far the best description of Argentina in the 1970s," and further notes that "this very interesting book is more than the reflections of a sensitive man whose home is always somewhere else. It is also an elegy for the Argentina he knew.''

Graham-Yooll told *CA:* ''My work is too uneven for me to give any constructive advice. I think all writing is a search for public notice and therefore an expression of vanity.''

BIOGRAPHICAL/CRITICAL SOURCES:

BOOKS

Graham-Yooll, Andrew M., *A Matter of Fear: Portrait of an Argentinian Exile,* Lawrence Hill, 1981 (published in England as *Portrait of an Exile,* Junction Books, 1981).
Graham-Yooll, Andrew M., *A State of Fear: Memories of Argentina's Nightmare,* Eland, 1986.

PERIODICALS

Contemporary Review, August, 1981.
Encounter, November, 1981.
London Magazine, January, 1982.
New Statesman, November 6, 1981.
Observer (London), November 30, 1986.
Times Literary Supplement, November 20, 1981, August 15, 1986.

*   *   *

GRANT, J(ohn) B(arnard) 1940-
(Jack Grant)

PERSONAL: Born March 23, 1940; son of Ellsworth S. (a historical writer and maker of documentary films) and Marion (a historical writer; maiden name, Hepburn) Grant; married Ann Halterman, May 28, 1965; children: Jason, Schuyler. *Education:* University of California, Berkeley, B.A., 1965.

ADDRESSES: Home—Sebastopol, Calif.

CAREER: High school teacher during 1960s; skipper of a charter sailing boat for a private school in Florida, 1968-70; writer and editor, 1970—. *Military service:* U.S. Marine Corps, 1960-64.

MEMBER: Musicians Union, local 292.

WRITINGS:

(And editor) *The Geocentric Experience,* Lamplighters Roadway Press, 1972.
(With Katharine Houghton) *Two Beastly Tales,* Lamplighters Roadway Press, 1975.

UNDER NAME JACK GRANT

(With Stanley Keleman) *Your Body Speaks Its Mind,* Simon & Schuster, 1975.
Skateboarding: A Complete Guide to the Sport, Celestial Arts, 1976.
(With Jim Gault) *The World of Women's Gymnastics,* Celestial Arts, 1976.
Soccer: A Personal Guide for Players, Coaches, and Parents, Celestial Arts, 1978.
Ins and Outs of Soccer, Prentice-Hall, 1983.
(With Laeh Maggie Garfield) *Companions in Spirit,* Celestial Arts, 1985.
The Unamericans in Paris, Celestial Arts, 1988.
''Joan Rainbow'' (three-act play), first performed at Sonoma State University Center for Performing Arts, 1989.

OTHER

Also author of three novels and a volume of short stories, all unpublished. Contributor of numerous stories and poems to magazines; contributor of essays to *San Francisco Review of Books.*

WORK IN PROGRESS: Two novels; two full-length plays; stories; poems.

SIDELIGHTS: J. B. Grant told *CA:* ''Writing seems to be the main way I'm able to explore and celebrate life, especially anything whose whole is greater than the sum of its parts: humor, paradox, glory and misery, an atom, an apple tree, a marriage. Whatever form I write in, I'm most satisfied when able to convey inner quirks and qualities along with accurate portrayals and descriptions. Relative to the rest of my life, I'm continually grateful for writing's odd, unbiddable capacity to reveal what I need to develop or reconsider or let go altogether.''

AVOCATIONAL INTERESTS: Playing and coaching soccer, rollerskating, caring for house and orchard, playing rhythm-and-blues piano.

*   *   *

GRANT, Jack
See GRANT, J(ohn) B(ernard)

*   *   *

GREENE, Mott T(uthill) 1945-

PERSONAL: Born December 2, 1945, in Syracuse, N.Y.; son of Lynne Tuthill (a physician) and Irene (Button) Greene; married Jo Leffingwell (an actress), November 21, 1978; children: one. *Education:* Columbia University, B.A., 1967, graduate study, 1967-69; University of Washington, Seattle, M.A., 1974, Ph.D., 1978.

ADDRESSES: Home—2218 3rd Ave. N., Seattle, Wash. 98109. *Office*—105 Howarth, University of Puget Sound, 1500 N. Warner, Tacoma, Wash. 98416.

CAREER: Iowa State University, Ames, visiting assistant professor, 1978-79; University of Washington, Seattle, visiting assistant professor, 1979; Portland State University, Portland, Ore., visiting assistant professor, 1980; Lewis and Clark College, Portland, visiting assistant professor, 1980; free-lance editor in New York City, 1981; Skidmore College, Saratoga Springs, N.Y., assistant professor of history, 1981-83; University of Washington, visiting associate professor, 1984-85; University of Puget Sound, Tacoma, Wash., John B. Magee Distinguished Professor in Honors, 1985—. Instructor at Cornell University, summers, 1981-82; visiting professor, Stanford University, 1988. Sigma Xi national lecturer, 1987-89. *Wartime service:* Conscientious objector in alternative civilian service at Columbia Presbyterian Hospital, New York City, 1969-71.

MEMBER: History of Science Society, History of Earth Sciences Society, Bonnet Institute.

AWARDS, HONORS: Fellowship from National Endowment for the Humanities, 1983-84; MacArthur Foundation prize fellowship, 1983-88.

WRITINGS:

Geology in the Nineteenth Century: Changing Views of a Changing World, Cornell University Press, 1982.

Myths or Nature and the Nature of Myths: Essays on Natural Knowledge in Pre-Classical Antiquity, Cornell University Press, 1989.

WORK IN PROGRESS: A biography of Alfred Wegener (1880-1930), the German geophysicist and polar explorer who developed the concept of continental drift, for Cornell University Press; annotated translation of Wegener's 1915 work, *The Origin of Continents and Oceans.*

SIDELIGHTS: Mott T. Greene once told *CA:* "I'm very grateful to the MacArthur Foundation for the opportunity to spend five years working completely free of institutional obligations on whatever projects interest me. My current project is a biography of Alfred Wegener and allows me to continue my work in the history of modern earth science while exploring a form (biography) I have wanted to try, and a subject whose life and work raise a number of interesting questions about scientific innovation. I hope to follow that work with something on formalistic theorizing in modern physical science and on the sharing of metaphors and analogies by different sciences. I also plan to spend time studying the relationship of Greek thought in the pre-Socratic period to Indian philosophy. The combination of metempsychosis, dietary restrictions, and mathematics in Pythagoreanism suggests some contact with India in the sixth century B.C. I have felt for some time that India's philosophical influence on the West has been systematically undervalued, and I would like to do something to rectify that slight.

"As for the views reflected in my writing, what comes to mind is my conviction that nonfiction authors, particularly historians, should stand far in the background of their own writing and make themselves as inconspicuous as possible. They should also avoid taking sides in any current controversy (unless that's the point of the book), as such partisanship hastens the date when the book is out-of-date and lessens its usefulness. Finally, good writing, like great art, is grounded in specificity. A work that generalizes itself leaves nothing for the reader."

BIOGRAPHICAL/CRITICAL SOURCES:

PERIODICALS

Times Literary Supplement, August 26, 1983.

*   *   *

GREGG, Martin
See McNEILLY, Wilfred (Glassford)

*   *   *

GRETZ, Susanna   1937-

PERSONAL: Born September 27, 1937, in New York, N.Y.; daughter of George G. (a lawyer) and Helen (White) Tennant; married Guenter Gretz (an industrial designer), 1966. *Education:* Smith College, B.A., 1959.

ADDRESSES: Home—6 Frankfurt 90, Damaschke-Anger 51, West Germany.

CAREER: Writer and illustrator.

AWARDS, HONORS: Smarties Prize for Under 7's, National Book League (Great Britain), 1985, for *It's Your Turn, Roger!*

WRITINGS:

SELF ILLUSTRATED

Teddy Bears 1 to 10, Follett, 1969, reprinted, Four Winds Press, 1986.
The Bears Who Stayed Indoors, Follett, 1970, 2nd edition (with Alison Sage), A. & C. Black, 1986, published as *Teddy Bears Stay Indoors,* Four Winds Press, 1987.
The Bears Who Went to the Seaside, Benn, 1972, Follett, 1973.
Teddy Bears ABC, Follett, 1975.
Ten Green Bottles, Penguin, 1976.
(With Sage) *Teddybears Cookbook,* Doubleday, 1978.
Teddy Bears' Moving Day, Four Winds Press, 1981.
Teddy Bears Go Shopping, Four Winds Press, 1982.
(With Sage) *Teddy Bears Cure a Cold,* Four Winds Press, 1984 (published in England as *Teddy Bears and the Cold Cure,* Benn, 1984).
It's Your Turn, Roger!, Dial Books for Young Readers, 1985.
Hide-and-Seek, A. & C. Black, 1985, Four Winds Press, 1986.
I'm Not Sleepy, A. & C. Black, 1985, Four Winds Press, 1986.
Ready for Bed, A. & C. Black, 1985, Four Winds Press, 1986.
Too Dark!, A. & C. Black, 1985, Four Winds Press, 1986.
Roger Takes Charge!, Dial Books for Young Readers, 1987.
(With Sage) *Teddy Bears Take the Train,* Four Winds Press, 1987.
Roger Loses His Marbles, Dial Books for Young Readers, 1988.

OTHER

Also illustrator of numerous children's books, including books by Helen Cresswell and Neil Hollander.*

*   *   *

GUINTHER, John   1927-

PERSONAL: Born April 3, 1927, in Reading, Pa.; son of Earl (a bookkeeper) and Mary Guinther; married Elaine McCabe, September 3, 1954 (deceased); children: Carol. *Education:* Kutztown State Teachers College (now Kutztown University), B.S., 1948.

ADDRESSES: Office—1422 Chestnut St., Suite 709, Philadelphia, Pa. 19102.

CAREER: Writer. Previously held various jobs ranging from raising show dogs to selling advertising. Instructor in investigative journalism at Charles Morris Price School, Philadelphia, 1977—; visiting professor at Temple University, 1974, 1976, 1977, 1982, and 1983. Active in early civil rights movement in Washington, D.C., late 1940s and early 1950s; active in political reform movements in Philadelphia, 1950s until 1971; co-founder of New Democratic Coalition, Philadelphia, 1968-69.

AWARDS, HONORS: Robert F. Kennedy Memorial Award for best magazine article of the year on the problems of the disadvantaged American, Robert F. Kennedy Foundation, 1973, for "The Only Good Indian"; four Silver Gavel Awards, American Bar Association, 1974-80, for articles on the justice system; Best Magazine Article Award, Sigma Delta Chi, 1975, for two-part study on investigative grand juries; Gerald Loeb Award for distinguished writing on business and finance, Loeb Memorial Foundation, 1976, for article "Don't Worry, It's Only Money"; Louis Apothaler Award, 1986, for Philadelphia non-lawyer having done most to advance justice system.

WRITINGS:

Moralists and Managers: Public Interest Movements in America, Doubleday, 1976.
The Malpractitioners, Doubleday, 1978.
Winning Your Personal Injury Suit, Doubleday, 1980.
Philadelphia: A Dream for the Keeping (history), Continental Heritage, 1982.
The Jury in America, Facts on File, 1987.
(With Thomas Martinez) *Brotherhood of Murder,* McGraw, 1988.

Also author of documentary scripts for WCAU-CBS Television. Contributor of more than 200 articles to newspapers and magazines. Associate editor, *Welcomat;* contributing editor, *Philadelphia.*

WORK IN PROGRESS: Advocates for the Injured; the law and personal injury litigation.

H

HAGEDORN, Robert (Bruce) 1925-

PERSONAL: Surname is pronounced Hega-dorn; born November 2, 1925, in Menlo Park, Calif.; son of Edward E. Hagedorn; married former wife Elizabeth Masterson, November 9, 1962; children: Gerald, Richard. *Education:* San Francisco State College (now University), B.A., 1950; University of Washington, Seattle, M.A., 1953; University of Texas at Austin, Ph.D., 1963.

ADDRESSES: Office—Department of Sociology, University of Victoria, Victoria, British Columbia, Canada.

CAREER: City College of San Francisco, San Francisco, Calif., instructor in sociology, 1954-55; Ventura College, Ventura, Calif., instructor in psychology and sociology, 1955-60; Washington State University, Pullman, assistant professor of sociology, 1963-66; California State University, Fullerton, associate professor, 1966-69; University of Victoria, Victoria, British Columbia, associate professor, 1969-75, professor of sociology, 1975—. *Military service:* U.S. Army Air Forces, 1944-46; became sergeant.

MEMBER: American Sociological Association, Pacific Sociological Association.

AWARDS, HONORS: National Science Foundation research grant, 1965-66.

WRITINGS:

(With Sanford I. Labovitz) *An Introduction to Social Research*, McGraw, 1971, 3rd edition, 1981.
(With Labovitz) *An Introduction into Sociological Orientation*, Wiley, 1973.
(Contributor) Labovitz, editor, *An Introduction into Sociological Concepts*, Wiley, 1977.
(Editor and contributor) *Sociology*, Holt (Toronto), 1980, W. C. Brown, 1983, 2nd edition, Holt, 1983.
(Editor) *Essentials of Sociology*, Holt (Toronto), 1981, 2nd edition, 1983.

Contributor to professional journals.

*   *   *

HAGOPIAN, Mark N. 1940-

PERSONAL: Born March 21, 1940, in Cambridge, Mass.; son of Jerry and Mary (Semonian) Hagopian; married Alice V. Aghababian, November 20, 1966; children: Berj Nishan. *Education:* Boston University, A.B., 1961, A.M., 1963, Ph.D., 1969.

ADDRESSES: Home—89 Westwood Dr., Westfield, Mass. 01085. *Office*—Department of Political Science, American International College, Springfield, Mass. 01109.

CAREER: Part-time instructor in political science at Calvin Coolidge College, 1964-66; American International College, Springfield, Mass., instructor, 1966-67, assistant professor, 1967-71, associate professor, 1971-79, professor of political science, 1979—.

MEMBER: American Political Science Association, New England Political Science Association.

WRITINGS:

The Phenomenon of Revolution, Dodd, 1974.
Regimes, Movements, and Ideologies: A Comparative Introduction to Political Science, Longman, 1978.
Ideals and Ideologies of Modern Politics, Longman, 1985.

WORK IN PROGRESS: Books on contemporary ideologies and political theory.

*   *   *

HALL, Kendall
See HEATH, Harry E(ugene), Jr.

*   *   *

HAMEL DOBKIN, Kathleen
See HAMEL PEIFER, Kathleen

*   *   *

HAMEL PEIFER, Kathleen 1945-
(Kathy Dobkin, Kaye Dobkin, Kathleen Hamel Dobkin; pseudonyms: E. H. Dana, James Labrador, Judy Labrador, G. F. Moody, Joanna Wharton)

PERSONAL: Born May 18, 1945, in Marshfield, Wis.; daughter of Louis Mahlon (a musician, educator, and health care administrator) and Gladys (an interior decorator; maiden name, Schulfer) Hamel; married Carl S. Dobkin, September, 1969 (divorced, 1975); married Edward Peifer, September, 1985. *Education:* Attended Lakeland College, Sheboygan, Wis., 1963-64; University of Wisconsin—Madison, B.A., 1969.

ADDRESSES: Home—Hudson Valley, N.Y. *Agent*—Barbara Lowenstein Associates, Inc., 250 West 57th St., New York, N.Y. 10107.

CAREER: Penn Books, New York City, began as bookkeeper, became clerk, then assistant manager, 1969-71; Lancer Books, Inc., New York City, associate editor, 1971, editor, 1971-73; free-lance editorial consultant, 1973-75; Berkley Publishing Corp., New York City, editor of nonfiction and women's fiction, 1975-76; free-lance editorial consultant and writer, 1976-78; Boswell-Franz Associates (public relations firm), New York City, chief copywriter, 1978-81; free-lance writer, 1981—. Consultant, McPherson & Co. (publishers), 1987—.

AWARDS, HONORS: Resident fellow of Helene Wurlitzer Foundation, 1985.

WRITINGS:

UNDER NAME KAYE DOBKIN

The Red Room (young adult novel), Scholastic Book Services, 1982.
The Queen of Hearts (novel), Dell, 1983.
The White Rabbit (novel), Dell, 1983.
Valentine for Betsy (young adult novel), New American Library, 1984.
Desire and Dream, Avon, 1984.
Promise Me Tomorrow, Avon, 1986.

UNDER PSEUDONYM JOANNA WHARTON; "CAMPUS FEVER" YOUNG ADULT SERIES

Making the Grade, New American Library, 1985.
All-Nighter, New American Library, 1985.
Illegal Notion, New American Library, 1985.
Time Out, New American Library, 1986.
Fast Lane, New American Library, 1986.
Class Act, New American Library, 1986.
Wild Moves, New American Library, 1986.

OTHER

Author of columns. Contributor of articles and poems to magazines, including *Woman's World, Argosy, Eros, Swank, At Home,* and *One Shot: A Literary Review,* under name Kathy Dobkin and pseudonyms E. H. Dana, G. F. Moody, James Labrador, and Judy Labrador.

SIDELIGHTS: Kathleen Hamel Peifer told *CA:* "One either talks about writing, or one sits down and writes. I prefer doing the latter, as the former, to my ears, has a way of making one sound silly."

*   *   *

HAMEROW, Theodore S(tephen) 1920-

PERSONAL: Born August 24, 1920, in Warsaw, Poland; came to United States, 1930; naturalized, 1930; son of Chaim Shneyer (an actor) and Bella (an actress; maiden name, Rubinlicht) Hamerow; married Margarete Lotter, August 16, 1954; children: Judith Margarete, Helena Francisca. *Education:* City College (now City College of the City University of New York), B.A., 1942; Columbia University, M.A., 1947; Yale University, Ph.D., 1951.

ADDRESSES: Home—466 South Segoe Rd., Madison, Wis. 53711. *Office*—Department of History, University of Wisconsin, Madison, Wis. 53706.

CAREER: Wellesley College, Wellesley, Mass., instructor in history, 1950-51; University of Maryland, College Park, instructor in history, 1951-52; University of Illinois at Champaign-Urbana, instructor, 1952-54, assistant professor, 1954-57, associate professor of history, 1957-58; University of Wisconsin—Madison, associate professor, 1958-61, professor of history, 1961—, G. P. Gooch Professor of History, 1978—, chairman of department, 1973-76. Fulbright research professor, Erlangen University, 1962-63. Member, Council for International Exchange of Scholars, 1983-86. *Military service:* U.S. Army, 1943-46.

MEMBER: American Historical Association, Conference Group for Central European History (secretary-treasurer, 1960-62; chairman, 1976-77).

AWARDS, HONORS: Social Science Research Council fellow, 1962-63; Fulbright scholar, 1962-63.

WRITINGS:

Restoration, Revolution, Reaction: Economics and Politics in Germany, 1815-1871, Princeton University Press, 1958.
(With Chester G. Starr and others) *A History of the World,* Rand McNally, 1960.
(Editor) *Otto Von Bismarck: A Historical Assessment,* Heath, 1962, 2nd edition, 1972.
(Editor) *Otto Von Bismarck: Reflections and Reminiscences,* Harper, 1968.
Social Foundations of German Unification, 1858-1871, Princeton University Press, Volume 1: *Ideas and Institutions,* 1969, Volume 2: *Struggles and Accomplishments,* 1972.
The Age of Bismarck, Harper, 1973.
The Birth of a New Europe: State and Society in the Nineteenth Century, University of North Carolina Press, 1983.
Reflections on History and Historians, University of Wisconsin Press, 1987.

Member of board of editors, *Journal of Modern History,* 1962-64, and *Central European History,* 1966-69. Consulting editor, Dorsey Press, 1961-71.

WORK IN PROGRESS: An analytical history of revolutions in the twentieth century.

*   *   *

HAMILTON, Gail
See CORCORAN, Barbara

*   *   *

HANES, Frank Borden 1920-

PERSONAL: Born January 21, 1920, in Winston-Salem, N.C.; son of Robert March and Mildred (Borden) Hanes; married Barbara Mildred Lasater, 1942; children: Frank Borden, Jr., Nancy, Robin. *Education:* University of North Carolina, A.B., 1942. *Religion:* Methodist.

ADDRESSES: Home—1057 West Kent Rd., Winston-Salem, N.C. 27104.

CAREER: Twin City Sentinel, reporter, and *Winston-Salem Journal & Sentinel,* columnist, both Winston-Salem, N.C., both 1946-49; Chatham Manufacturing Company, Elkin, N.C., director, 1960-87; Merchant's Development Company, Winston-Salem, director, 1961—; director, Hanes Dye & Finishing Company, 1971-86. President, Winston-Salem Operetta Association, 1949, Winston-Salem Arts Council, 1957; former president, Friends of Library of University of North Carolina; former chairman, Old Salem, Inc.; chairman, Summit School; University of North Carolina, chairman of special gifts committee, 1961—, Board of Visitors, 1973-86, and Arts and Science Foundation; chairman of special gifts committee, Friends of Salem College Library; trustee, John Motley Morehead Foundation, 1965—, and North Carolina Zoological Society. *Military service:* U.S. Navy, three years; became lieutenant; served as destroyer officer in South Pacific. Received Presidential Unit citation, four battle stars.

MEMBER: PEN, Authors League of America, North Carolina Writers Conference (former chairman), North Carolina Literary and Historical Association (former president), Winston-Salem Rotary Club (acting president, 1961), Sigma Alpha Epsilon, Order of Minotaurs (former president), Order of Gimghoul (former president), Old Town Club, Cane River Club, Rainbow Springs Club, Roaring Gap Club (former president), Rancheros Visitordores.

AWARDS, HONORS: First Roanoke-Chowan Award for poetry, 1951; Sir Walter Raleigh Award for fiction, 1961, for *The Fleet Rabble: A Novel of the Nez Perce War;* honorary cum laude degree, Woodberry Forest School, 1961; distinguished alumnus award, University of North Carolina, 1975; Ragan Award, St. Andrews College, 1988, for contributions to fine arts.

WRITINGS:

Abel Anders: A Narrative, Farrar, Straus, 1951.
The Bat Brothers, Farrar, Straus, 1953.
Journey's Journal, Winston Pub., 1956.
The Fleet Rabble: A Novel of the Nez Perce War, L. C. Page, 1961.
Jackknife John, Naylor, 1964.
The Seeds of Ares (war poems), Briarpatch Press (Davidson, N.C.), 1977.

Also author of *The Garden of Nonentities,* 1983.

SIDELIGHTS: Frank Borden Hanes once told *CA:* "I believe that most writing is done by people with the same compunctions as those have who carve names on trees; that good writing requires craftsmanship about equal to that of cabinet making; that great writing is as scarce as wisdom and concerns, in part, a diabolical and angelic view into the seethings of the spirit, the disputations of the genes, and the deep, beautiful threnodies of the earth."

BIOGRAPHICAL/CRITICAL SOURCES:

BOOKS

Hoyle, Bernadette, *Tar Heel Writers I Have Known,* Blair, 1956.

PERIODICALS

Raleigh News and Observer, April 2, 1961.

*   *   *

HANNIBAL, Edward   1936-

PERSONAL: Born August 24, 1936, in Manchester, Mass.;
son of Joseph Leary (a ship's machinist) and Loretta (McCarthy) Hannibal; married Margaret Twomey, June 14, 1958; children: Mary Ellen, Edward J., Eleanor, John, Julia. *Education:* Boston College, B.A., 1958. *Religion:* Roman Catholic.

ADDRESSES: Home—118 Pantigo Rd., East Hampton, N.Y. 10022. *Office*—Grey Advertising, Inc., 777 Third Ave., New York, N.Y. 10017.

CAREER: Writer. Kenyon & Eckhardt (advertising agency), New York City, copywriter, 1962-64; Norman, Craig & Kummel (advertising agency), New York City, copywriter, 1964-65; Benton & Bowles (advertising agency), New York City, associate creative director, 1965-68; Wayne Jervis & Associates (advertising agency), New York City, creative director, 1968-69; Grey Advertising, Inc., New York City, associate creative director, 1975—. *Military service:* U.S. Army, Intelligence Corps, 1958-62; became first lieutenant.

AWARDS, HONORS: Houghton Mifflin Literary fellowship, 1970, for manuscript of novel *Chocolate Days, Popsicle Weeks;* Bread Loaf Writers' Conference fellowship, 1971.

WRITINGS:

Chocolate Days, Popsicle Weeks (novel), Houghton, 1970.
Dancing Man (novel), Simon & Schuster, 1973.
Liberty Square Station (novel), Putnam, 1977.
(With Robert Boris) *Blood Feud* (documentary novel), Ballantine, 1979.
A Trace of Red (suspense novel), Dial, 1982.

SIDELIGHTS: Edward Hannibal draws upon his own experience in the field of advertising for his critically well-received first novel, *Chocolate Days, Popsicle Weeks.* It is the story about a factory worker who becomes a well-paid copywriter in a New York City advertising agency and must decide whether to save a crumbling marriage or pursue "further triumphs on Mad Ave.," writes Peter Rowley in *Book World.* Praised for an "often imaginative and highly fresh style" by P. A. Doyle in *Best Sellers,* Hannibal is especially commended for the precision with which he characterizes his protagonist. Suggesting that Hannibal's "awareness of the personality of his hero is deep and almost flawless," Rowley finds that there is a cumulative effect to "his portrait . . . built up of hundreds of devastating brush strokes." Calling the portrayal "a study of egocentricity and ambition," David Dempsey adds in the *New York Times Book Review* that despite being "a rather objectionable young man," the character is basically decent and likeable: "In bringing him to life, Mr. Hannibal works close to the bone—and he works very well."

Hannibal worked with screenwriter Robert Boris for *Blood Feud,* a documentary novel about the mutual animosity that existed between Robert F. Kennedy and James R. Hoffa. A congressional subcommittee's investigations into labor's connections with organized crime, plus Kennedy's relentless pursuit of Hoffa, led to the eventual conviction of the former Teamster president. The book, which later became a two-part television movie, began as a "six-page television idea," notes Aljean Harmetz in the *New York Times,* and its dialogue was "based on conversations . . . known to have taken place." However, critics such as Martin Levin in the *New York Times Book Review* suggest that "the facts are likely to be more tantalizing than a fictional rearrangement such as this." Discussing the unresolved questions that still enshroud both of the principals' deaths, Jeffrey Gillenkirk acknowledges in the *Los Angeles Times Book Review* that the book fails to document implications of conspiracy on both sides. Gillenkirk, though, deems the book "more American myth than documentary," adding, "And like most myths, it tells a good story. Jimmy Hoffa, German and Irish working class, versus the bright and scrappy son of an Irish Brahmin." As Gillenkirk concludes, it is a story of "the fight between two men and more—the battle between two different sides of the American dream embodied in those men."

In his suspenseful novel *A Trace of Red*, Hannibal returns to the world of Madison Avenue advertising for the background of a story about a man who, in an emotionally-scarring incident, is forced to kill a fellow soldier gone "dangerously . . . berserk," says Stanley Ellin in the *New York Times Book Review*. Twenty years later, he is asked to assassinate an American agent who has become romantically involved with his Soviet counterpart. While praising Hannibal's "biting and knowledgeable" descriptions of the advertising world, as well as his dialogue and "vividly sketched" minor characters, Michael Hutchinson suggests in the *Chicago Tribune Book World* that "Hannibal is clearly after bigger game here, chasing the 'trace of red' that runs through our society, and exploring that strange intermingling of the red of passion with the red of violence." As Ellin proclaims: "This is a narrative of substance and profound humanity, written in prose unobtrusively graceful. It is, in every sense, an exceptionally fine novel."

Hannibal once told *CA:* "Just as there's no longer any such thing as a 'B' movie, you can't just write 'a novel' any more. If it isn't a blockbuster, forget it. But, as serious fiction shrinks steadily toward 'endangered species' status, the committed novelist does not despair. He begins to feel—Underground. It's a good place from which to write. Also, Underground has a way of turning Exotic, then, gradually, vaguely, Forbidden. Which is when it becomes Attractive again, and the cycle begins anew, freshened by the process. So, to save literature in our time, stop reading the hard stuff now."

MEDIA ADAPTATIONS: In 1983, *Blood Feud* was adapted for television in a two-part film that featured Robert Blake and Cotter Smith.

BIOGRAPHICAL/CRITICAL SOURCES:

PERIODICALS

Best Sellers, October 15, 1970.
Book World, October 4, 1970.
Chicago Tribune Book World, April 18, 1982.
Los Angeles Times Book Review, July 8, 1979.
New York Times, January 2, 1978, June 11, 1979.
New York Times Book Review, October 4, 1970, November 18, 1973, June 10, 1979, February 28, 1982.

*　　*　　*

HAPPE, Peter 1932-

PERSONAL: Born June 22, 1932, in Folkestone, Kent, England; son of Frederick (a bank official) and Nellie (Fisher) Happe; married Eileen Fisher, August 6, 1955; children: Paul, Katharine, Sara. *Education:* Queens' College, Cambridge, B.A. (with honors), 1955; Birkbeck College, London, M.A., 1961, Ph.D., 1966.

ADDRESSES: *Home*—Woodlands, Goscombs Lane, Gundleton, Alresford, Hampshire SO24 9SP, England. *Office*—Barton Peveril College, Eastleigh, Hampshire SO5 5ZA, England.

CAREER: Cannock Grammar School, Cannock, England, head of English, 1961-66; lecturer in English, Madeley College of Education, 1966-67; Yateley Comprehensive School, Camberley, England, deputy head, 1967-71; Rutland Sixth Form College, Oakham, England, headmaster, 1972-80; Barton Peveril College, Eastleigh, England, principal, 1980—. Taught in Nigeria, 1964. *Military service:* Royal Air Force, 1950-52.

MEMBER: Secondary Heads Association, Societe Internationale pour l'Etude du Theatre Medievale.

AWARDS, HONORS: Schoolmaster fellow, University of Exeter, 1965, and Jesus College, Cambridge, 1978.

WRITINGS:

(Editor) William Shakespeare, *The Winter's Tale*, Ginn, 1969.
(Editor and author of introduction and notes) *Tudor Interludes*, Penguin (Harmondsworth), 1972.
(Editor and author of introduction and notes) *English Mystery Plays: A Selection*, Penguin, 1975, revised edition, 1980.
(Editor and author of introduction and notes) *Four Morality Plays*, Penguin, 1979, revised edition, 1987.
Medieval English Drama, Macmillan, 1984.
(Editor) John Bale, *The Complete Plays of John Bale*, two volumes, Boydell & Brewer, 1986.
(Editor with John N. King) *The Vocacyon of Johan Bale*, Renaissance English Text Society of America, 1989.

Contributor to *Folklore, Research Opportunities in Renaissance Drama, English Literary Renaissance, Renaissance Drama Newsletter, Modern Language Quarterly,* and *Studies in English Literature.*

*　　*　　*

HARDING, Harry (Jr.) 1946-

PERSONAL: Born December 21, 1946, in Boston, Mass.; son of Harry (an executive) and Vernette (Vickers) Harding; married Roca Lau, July 5, 1971; children: James V. L. *Education:* Princeton University, A.B. (summa cum laude), 1967; Stanford University, M.A., 1969, Ph.D., 1974.

ADDRESSES: *Home*—Bethesda, Md. *Office*—Brookings Institution, 1775 Massachusetts Ave. N.W., Washington, D.C. 20036.

CAREER: Swarthmore College, Swarthmore, Pa., instructor in political science, 1970-71; Stanford University, Stanford, Calif., acting assistant professor, 1971-73, assistant professor, 1973-79, associate professor of political science, 1979-83; Brookings Institution, Washington, D.C., senior fellow, 1983—. Visiting assistant professor, University of California, Berkeley, spring, 1977. National fellow, Hoover Institution on War, Revolution, and Peace, 1977-78; coordinator of East Asia program, Woodrow Wilson International Center for Scholars, 1979-80; member, United States-People's Republic of China Joint Commission on Scientific and Technological Cooperation, 1981—.

MEMBER: American Political Science Association, Association of Asian Studies, Asia Society (co-chairman of China Council, 1983—), National Committee on U.S.-China Relations (director, 1983—), Council of Foreign Relations, Research Council of the Pacific Forum, Phi Beta Kappa.

AWARDS, HONORS: Walter J. Gores Award, Stanford University, 1975, for excellence in teaching; Masayoshi Ohira Memorial Prize, 1986, for *Organizing China: The Problem of Bureaucracy, 1949-1976.*

WRITINGS:

China: The Uncertain Future, Foreign Policy Association, 1974.
China and the United States: Normalization and Beyond, China Council of the Asia Society, 1979.
Organizing China: The Problem of Bureaucracy, 1949-1976, Stanford University Press, 1981.
China's Foreign Relations in the 1980s, Yale University Press, 1984.
China's Second Revolution: Reform after Mao, Brookings Institution, 1987.
China and Northeast Asia: The Political Dimension, Asia Society and University Press of America, 1988.

Contributor of articles and reviews to scholarly compendia, professional journals, and newspapers.

WORK IN PROGRESS: A chapter on the Cultural Revolution, to be included in *Cambridge History of China,* edited by John K. Fairbank and Roderick MacFarquhar, Cambridge University Press.

SIDELIGHTS: In his 1987 book *China's Second Revolution: Reform after Mao,* China scholar Harry Harding "provides the first comprehensive analysis of the demise of revolutionary ideology and the accompanying political and economic advances of the post-Mao decade," writes *Los Angeles Times Book Review* contributor Carolyn Wakeman, adding that the book is a "thorough and insightful examination of China's reconstruction." Andrew J. Nathan comments in *New Republic* that "much misunderstanding has attended China's reforms" and that "Harding's new book is a reassuring guide for the perplexed." Nathan adds: "Harding is broadly informed and shows remarkable skill in bringing order to the welter of data that overwhelms students of China. His 'midcourse assessment' of the reforms is comprehensive and clear."

Harding commented to *CA:* "I cannot imagine a more important topic than the fate of one quarter of humankind, nor a more interesting one than the evolution of modern China. In my own writings, I have tried not only to advance our scholarly understanding of Chinese politics and foreign relations, but also to communicate those findings to a broader audience. American attitudes toward China have, over the last century, oscillated wildly between the extremes of idealization and hostility. The challenge for China specialists interested in public affairs is to help dampen these oscillations, and to produce a more objective and balanced understanding of China and the Chinese."

BIOGRAPHICAL/CRITICAL SOURCES:

PERIODICALS

Economist, January 9, 1988.
Los Angeles Times Book Review, January 31, 1988.
New Republic, April 18, 1988.

*   *   *

HARE, William 1944-

PERSONAL: Born February 7, 1944, in Leicester, England; son of Francis and Rose Olive (MacShane) Hare; married Niki Liasi (a teacher), August, 1966; children: Andrew, Antony, Stephen. *Education:* University of London, B.A., 1965; University of Leicester, M.A., 1968; University of Toronto, Ph.D., 1971.

ADDRESSES: Home—74 Doull Ave., Halifax, Nova Scotia, Canada. *Office*—School of Education, Dalhousie University, Halifax, Nova Scotia, Canada B3H 3J5.

CAREER: University of Alberta, Edmonton, assistant professor, 1969-74, associate professor, 1974-79, professor of education and philosophy, 1979—, chairperson of department of education, 1977-80.

MEMBER: Canadian Society for the Study of Education, Philosophy of Education Society (England), Philosophy of Education Society (United States).

AWARDS, HONORS: Canada Council fellow, 1976-77; fellow of Social Science and Humanities Research Council of Canada, 1981.

WRITINGS:

Open-Mindedness and Education, McGill-Queen's University Press, 1979.
Controversies in Teaching, Althouse/Harvester, 1985.
In Defence of Open-Mindedness, McGill-Queen's University Press, 1985.
(Editor with John Portelli) *Philosophy of Education: Introductory Readings,* Detselig, 1988.

Contributor to education and philosophy journals. Editor of Nova Scotia's *Journal of Education,* 1981.

SIDELIGHTS: William Hare once told *CA:* "I became interested in the concept of open-mindedness as a result of asking the question: what are the aims of education in a culturally diverse country like Canada? It occurred to me that the attitude of open-mindedness is particularly important in this context, but it was only after extensive analysis that I came to realize that it is a fundamental aim of education *per se.*"

Hare recently added: "My central interest remains the notion of open-mindedness and related ideas, and I continue to write papers exploring this idea in the context of moral education, the education of young children, etc. I am also interested in the problem of bias in textbooks and teaching."

*   *   *

HARRIS, Janet 1932-1979

PERSONAL: Born April 17, 1932, in Newark, N.J.; died December 6, 1979, in Freeport, N.Y.; daughter of Nathan (an attorney) and Ida (Lachow) Urovsky; formerly married to Martin Harris; children: Michael, Clint. *Education:* Ohio University, Athens, B.S.Ed., 1951.

ADDRESSES: Agent—Dorothy Markinko, McIntosh & Otis, Inc., 310 Madison Ave., New York, N.Y. 10017.

CAREER: Worked as a fund raiser and in public relations and wrote for radio, 1952-60; full-time writer, 1960-79. Lecturer in English, C. W. Post College, Long Island University, 1969, and Glen Cove Community College, State University of New York, 1970. Chairman for South Nassau, Women's Strike for Peace, 1964-65.

MEMBER: Authors League, Congress of Racial Equality (secretary of Long Island chapter, 1966-69).

AWARDS, HONORS: Women's Press Club of New York City Award, 1969, for "contribution to the literature of social protest."

WRITINGS:

The Long Freedom Road: The Civil Rights Story, foreword by
　　Whitney Young, McGraw, 1967.
(With Julius Hobson) *Black Pride: A People's Struggle* (ju-
　　venile), McGraw, 1969.
Students in Revolt, McGraw, 1970.
A Single Standard, McGraw, 1971.
Crisis in Corrections, McGraw, 1973.
The Prime of Ms. America: The American Woman at Forty,
　　Putnam, 1975.
*A Century of American History in Fiction: Kenneth Roberts'
　　Novels,* Gordon Press, 1976.
*Thursday's Daughters: The Story of Women Working in Amer-
　　ica,* Harper, 1977.
*The Woman Who Created Frankenstein: A Portrait of Mary
　　Shelley* (juvenile biography), Harper, 1979.

Reviewer, *New York Times Book Review,* 1970-71.

SIDELIGHTS: Janet Harris once told *CA:* "The theme of all
my writing centers around my belief in the rights of the individual for freedom and self-expression, at the cost of non-
violent revolution against authority. I am opposed to racism,
sexism, to war, to the placing of property rights above human
rights. I believe we are in the midst of a social revolution in
which authoritarian values are being replaced with humane
concepts and my work and my life are dedicated to this change
in consciousness."

BIOGRAPHICAL/CRITICAL SOURCES:

PERIODICALS

Commonweal, May 23, 1969.
Listener, May 16, 1968.
New York Times Book Review, May 7, 1967, May 4, 1969,
　　November 9, 1969.
Young Readers Review, October, 1969.

OBITUARIES:

PERIODICALS

Publishers Weekly, January 18, 1980.*

*　　　*　　　*

HARRISON, Barbara 1941-

PERSONAL: Born January 22, 1941, in New York, N.Y.;
daughter of Alexander (in hotel management) and Ann (Su-
kulak) Harrison. *Education:* Attended schools in New York
and Vermont. *Politics:* Independent. *Religion:* Roman Catholic.

ADDRESSES: Home and office—400 East 57th St., New York,
N.Y. 10022.

WRITINGS:

The Pagans, Avon, 1970.
City Hospital, Avon, 1975.
The Gorlin Clinic, Avon, 1975.
Rhinelander Center, Zebra Books, 1980.
This Cherished Dream, Zebra Books, 1984.
Passion's Price, Zebra Books, 1985.
Impulse, Zebra Books, 1987.
Society Princess, Zebra Books, 1989.

Also author of *The Wildings,* for Dell.

WORK IN PROGRESS: A family saga.

SIDELIGHTS: Barbara Harrison told *CA:* "I hope that my
books are entertaining—brief respites from the terrors of today's world. I'm always happy to hear from my readers, and
especially happy to hear what they like in my work, and what
they don't like." Her books have been published in England,
Australia, Ireland, Norway, and Israel as well as the United
States.

*　　　*　　　*

HARRISON, Claire (E.) 1946-
(Laura Eden)

PERSONAL: Born February 12, 1946, in Brooklyn, N.Y.;
daughter of Martin and Betty (Kerzner) Wisoff; married John
Harrison, April 11, 1965; children: Lisa, Rebecca. *Education:*
Carleton University, Ottawa, Ontario, B.A. (with distinction),
1978.

ADDRESSES: Home—136 Brighton Ave., Ottawa, Ontario,
Canada K1S 0T4. *Agent*—Steven Axelrod, 126 Fifth Ave.,
New York, N.Y. 10011.

CAREER: Writer. Pennysaver Publications Ltd., Ottawa, Ontario, owner and operator, 1973-74; *ARC* (magazine), Ottawa,
assistant editor, 1978-79; Open University, Washington, D.C.,
instructor of writing romance novels, 1981-82. Consultant to
Ontario Ministry of Community and Social Services, Ottawa,
Secretary of State, Ottawa, and National Academy of Sciences, Washington, D.C. Guest speaker and instructor at colleges and conferences.

MEMBER: Writers Union of Canada, Alliance of Canadian
Television and Radio Artists, Romance Writers of America,
Washington Romance Writers (co-founder; chairman, 1982-
83), Ottawa Independent Writers (co-founder; president, 1987-
88).

AWARDS, HONORS: Finalist in mainstream category, Romance Writers of America annual awards, 1985, for *Arctic
Rose,* and 1986, for *Wildflower;* awards for best radio documentary and best radio program, and nomination for best writer
of radio documentary, Alliance of Canadian Television and
Radio Artists (ACTRA), all 1984, for "Love at First Sight:
Romance Novels and the Romantic Fantasy"; grant from Ontario Arts Council, 1988.

WRITINGS:

ROMANCE FICTION

Prophecy of Desire, Harlequin, 1984.
Dance While You Can, Harlequin, 1984.
Leading Man, Harlequin, 1984.
Once a Lover, Harlequin, 1984.
An Independent Woman, Harlequin, 1984.
One Last Dance, Harlequin, 1985.
Dragon's Point, Harlequin, 1985.
Arctic Rose, Worldwide Romance, 1985.
Love Is a Distant Shore, Harlequin, 1986.
Diplomatic Affair, Harlequin, 1986.
Wildflower, Worldwide Romance, 1986.
Fantasy Unlimited, Harlequin, 1987.

UNDER PSEUDONYM LAURA EDEN; ROMANCE FICTION

Mistaken Identity, Silhouette Books, 1981.
Summer Magic, Silhouette Books, 1982.
Flight of Fancy, Silhouette Books, 1983.

OTHER

"Love at First Sight: Romance Novels and the Romantic Fantasy" (radio documentary), broadcast as part of "Ideas" series, Canadian Broadcasting Corp. (CBC-Radio), 1985.
Somebody's Baby (mainstream adult fiction), Doubleday, 1989.

Contributor of poems, stories, and reviews to magazines, including *Ladies' Home Journal*, and to newspapers, including *Ottawa Journal*, Toronto *Globe and Mail*, *Washington Post*, and *Detroit Free Press*. Newsletter editor, Ottawa Independent Writers.

WORK IN PROGRESS: Bye for Now (contemporary adult mainstream).

*   *   *

HARTFORD, Via
   See DONSON, Cyril

*   *   *

HARTLEY, Robert F(rank)   1927-

PERSONAL: Born December 15, 1927, in Beaver Falls, Pa.; son of Frank H. (a merchant) and Eleanor (Theis) Hartley; married Dorothy Mayou, June 30, 1962; children: Constance, Matthew. *Education:* Drake University, B.B.A., 1949; University of Minnesota, M.B.A., 1962, Ph.D., 1967.

ADDRESSES: Home—17405 South Woodland Rd., Shaker Heights, Ohio 44120. *Office*—Department of Marketing, Cleveland State University, Cleveland, Ohio 44115.

CAREER: Management employee for national department store chains, 1949-59; Dayton Corp., Minneapolis, Minn., in merchandise management, 1959-63; University of Minnesota, Minneapolis, instructor in marketing, 1963-65; George Washington University, Washington, D.C., assistant professor, 1965-69, associate professor of marketing, 1969-72; Cleveland State University, Cleveland, Ohio, professor of marketing, 1972—.

MEMBER: American Marketing Association, Case Research Association, Southern Marketing Association, Midwest Business Administration Association.

WRITINGS:

Marketing Management and Social Change, International Textbook Co., 1972.
Retailing: Challenge and Opportunity, Houghton, 1975, 3rd edition, 1984.
Marketing for Responsive Management, Dun Donnelly, 1976.
Marketing Mistakes, Grid Publishing, 1976, 4th edition, 1989.
Sales Management, Houghton, 1979, 2nd edition, C.E. Merrill, 1988.
(Co-author) *Essentials of Marketing Research*, PennWell, 1983.
Management Mistakes, Grid Publishing, 1983, 2nd edition, Wiley, 1986.
Marketing Fundamentals, Harper, 1983.
Marketing Successes, Wiley, 1985.
Bullseyes and Blunders, Wiley, 1987.
Pricing for Export, International Trade Centre, 1987.
Export Channel Management, International Trade Centre, 1987.

Contributor to business and marketing journals.

WORK IN PROGRESS: A book on classic examples of corporate irresponsibility, for Wiley.

SIDELIGHTS: Robert F. Hartley told *CA:* "I have attempted in my writings, aimed primarily at the college market, to blend the practical with the conceptual. An underlying theme in all my books has been the desirability of business to be responsive to the needs and dictums of society and the environment, rather than strictly corporate short-term self-interest. We need to inspire as well as instruct."

*   *   *

HAVIS, Allan   1951-

PERSONAL: Born September 26, 1951, in New York, N.Y.; son of Meyer (in business) and Estelle (Heitner) Havis. *Education:* City College of the City University of New York, B.A., 1973; Hunter College of the City University of New York, M.A., 1976; Yale University, M.F.A., 1980.

ADDRESSES: Home—289 Third Ave., Brooklyn, N.Y. 11215. *Agent*—Helen Merrill, 435 West 23rd St., New York, N.Y. 10011.

CAREER: Guggenheim Museum, New York City, film instructor in children's program, 1974-76; Case Western Reserve University, Cleveland, Ohio, writer in residence, 1976; *Our Town*, New York City, theatre critic, 1977; Foundation of the Dramatist Guild, New York City, playwriting instructor, 1985-87; Ulster County Community College, Stone Ridge, N.Y., playwriting instructor, 1985-87; Old Dominion University, Norfolk, Va., playwriting instructor, 1987; Sullivan County Community College, Loch Sheldrake, N.Y., instructor in playwriting, 1987.

MEMBER: Dramatists Guild, Authors League of America, Circle Rep Writers Lab, Yale Club of New York.

AWARDS, HONORS: John Golden Award for playwriting, 1974 and 1975; Marc A. Klein Award, Case Western Reserve University, 1976, for "Oedipus Again"; Foundation of the Dramatist Guild/CBS Award, 1985; Playwrights USA Award, 1986, for "Morocco"; National Endowment for the Arts fellowship, 1986; Rockefeller fellowship, 1987; Guggenheim fellowship, 1987; New York State Foundation for the Arts fellowship, 1987; Edward Albee Foundation for the Arts fellowship, 1987; Kennedy Center/American Express Production grant, 1987.

WRITINGS:

PLAYS

"The Boarder and Mrs. Rifkin" (two-act), first produced in New York Ctiy at Hunter Playwrights, December, 1974.
"Oedipus Again" (two-act), first produced in Cleveland, Ohio, at Case Western Reserve University, February, 1976.
"Watchmaker" (one-act), first produced in New York City at Kuku Ryku Theatre Lab, November, 1977.
"Heinz" (two-act), first produced in New Haven, Conn., at Yale Drama School, April, 1978.
"Interludes" (one-act), first produced in New Haven at Yale Cabaret, December, 1978.
"Family Rites" (one-act), first produced in New Haven, Conn., at Yale Drama School, December, 1979.
"The Road from Jerusalem," first produced in New York City at American Repertory Theatre, 1984.
Morocco, (first produced in New York City at American Repertory Theatre, 1984), published in *Plays in Process*, Volume 6, number 5, Theatre Communications Group, 1985.
Haut Gout, (first produced in New York City at American Repertory Theatre, 1984), published in *Plays in Process*,

Volume 8, number 5, Theatre Communications Group, 1987.
''Mink Sonata'' (two-act), first produced at Baca Downtown, New York City, 1986.
''Duet for Three,'' first produced at West Bank Cafe, New York City, 1986.
''Mother's Aria,'' first produced at West Bank Cafe, New York City, 1986.

Also author of ''Einstein for Breakfast,'' 1986, and ''Approaching Chimera.''

OTHER

Albert the Astronomer (juvenile novel), Harper, 1979.

WORK IN PROGRESS: A full-length play, tentatively entitled ''Virgin Moon''; *Thirteen,* a juvenile novel.

SIDELIGHTS: Allan Havis once told *CA:* ''In several of my plays I have attempted to build a drama without the mechanics of plotting. I wanted to deal with little scenes, as if I were working in a film editing room, organizing odd anti-climatic dialogues, putting them together in stories that begin harmlessly and end wickedly. These plays were meant to shock the casual audience. 'Interludes,' a one-act play, contains murder, incest, and self-mutilation—and still I would call it a comedy. Why? The story is presented in a series of absurd cabaret blackouts and hallucinatory revelations. Obviously, the events of the play are not meant to be taken literally or in a naturalistic vein.

''These plays were also an experiment in economy. I wanted to take out as much verbiage as possible, leaving only essential—almost subliminal—dialogue that comes from looking inside people's minds. This can tease an audience and invite participation. And, minimalism can be very accurate if employed skillfully. We admire Samuel Beckett for such brevity.''

AVOCATIONAL INTERESTS: Foreign travel, Spanish, horseback and motorcycle riding.

* * *

HEATH, Harry E(ugene), Jr. 1919-
(Kendall Hall)

PERSONAL: Born May 17, 1919, in Iola, Kan.; son of Harry Eugene (a machinist) and Lois Rebecca (McNally) Heath; married Audrey Joan Cass (a child development specialist), October 20, 1942; children: Harry Eugene III, Rebecca Jean Heath Schaefer. *Education:* University of Tulsa, B.A., 1941; Northwestern University, M.S.J., 1947; Iowa State University, Ph.D., 1956; also attended University of Iowa and Oklahoma State University. *Religion:* Methodist.

ADDRESSES: Home—3512 North Washington, Stillwater, Okla. 74075. *Office*—Journalism and Broadcasting Building, Oklahoma State University, Stillwater, Okla. 74078.

CAREER: Sporting News, St. Louis, Mo., correspondent, 1936-37; *Tulsa Tribune,* Tulsa, Okla., education writer, 1938-40; *Tulsa World,* Tulsa, sports writer, 1940-41; National Broadcasting Co., Chicago, Ill., news editor, 1941-42; University of Tulsa, Tulsa, instructor in journalism, assistant director of public relations, and director of News Bureau, 1946-47; *Daily Oklahoman,* Oklahoma City, Okla., staff correspondent, 1946-47; University of Oregon, Eugene, instructor in journalism, 1947-48; Iowa State University, Ames, assistant professor,

1948-56, associate professor of journalism, 1956-61; WOI-TV, Ames, writer and producer, 1952; Oklahoma State University, Stillwater, professor of journalism, 1961-65; University of Florida, Gainesville, professor of journalism, 1965-67; Oklahoma State University, professor of journalism and director of School of Journalism and Broadcasting, 1967-82, Regents Service Professor, 1982—, director emeritus, 1982—. Lecturer at colleges and universities, including the Center for the Advanced Training of Journalists and University of Strasbourg, and at professional meetings. Consultant on public relations, typography, and design to newspapers and magazines. *Military service:* U.S. Army, Chemical Corps, 1942-46, 1950-52; became captain; major in Chemical Corps reserve.

MEMBER: International Society for General Semantics, Society of Professional Journalists, Association for Education in Journalism (former president of National Council on Radio and Television Journalism), Oklahoma Press Association, Oklahoma Education Association, Oklahoma Historical Society, Oklahoma Heritage Association, Phi Kappa Phi, Phi Delta Kappa, Pi Delta Epsilon, Theta Alpha Phi, Alpha Phi Omega, Gamma Sigma Delta, Kappa Tau Alpha.

AWARDS, HONORS: Beachy Mussleman Award, Oklahoma Press Association; Friend of Journalism Award, Society of Professional Journalists (Central Oklahoma chapter); Oklahoma Journalism Hall of Fame.

WRITINGS:

Guide to Newspaper Page Makeup (pamphlet), Iowa State University Press, 1950.
(With Lawrence R. Campbell and Ray Johnson) *A Guide to Radio-TV Writing,* Iowa State University Press, 1950.
(With Louis I. Gelfand) *How to Cover, Write, and Edit Sports,* Iowa State University Press, 1951, 2nd edition published as *Modern Sportswriting,* 1969.
(Editor) *Broadcast Journalism,* Iowa State University Press, 1953.
Tell Me Now Love (poetic story), Journalistic Services (Stillwater, Okla.), 1973.
Pieces of String (poems), Journalistic Services, 1977.
Growin' Time (poems), Journalistic Services, 1979.

Author of booklets and pamphlets. Author of ''Critique,'' a monthly column in *Oklahoma Publisher,* 1964-65, 1967—. Contributor to journalism and education journals, sometimes under pseudonym Kendall Hall, and to *Science of Mind.* Religion editor, *Stillwater News-Press,* 1963-65; book review editor, *Publishers' Auxiliary,* 1982—; member of editorial advisory board, *Journalism Quarterly* and *Journalism Abstracts.*

WORK IN PROGRESS: A centennial history of Oklahoma State University; a book-length poem; a book of miscellaneous poems; a book of real-life vignettes; research on journalistic interviewing and typography and design.

SIDELIGHTS: Harry E. Heath, Jr., once told *CA:* ''I believe in the therapeutic value of poetry, and would like to see both young and old encouraged to practice this creative art. Most people have the poetry locked up inside, and with a little instruction and encouragement it can be coaxed out. I favor free verse for this purpose.''

* * *

HEILBRUN, Carolyn G(old) 1926-
(Amanda Cross)

PERSONAL: Born January 13, 1926, in East Orange, N.J.;

daughter of Archibald (an accountant) and Estelle (Roemer) Gold; married James Heilbrun (a professor of economics), February 20, 1945; children: Emily, Margaret, Robert. *Education:* Wellesley College, B.A., 1947; Columbia University, M.A., 1951, Ph.D., 1959.

ADDRESSES: Home—151 Central Park W., New York, N.Y. 10023. *Office*—613 Philosophy Hall, Columbia University, New York, N.Y. 10027. *Agent*—Ellen Levine Literary Agency, 432 Park Ave. S., Suite 1205, New York, N.Y. 10016.

CAREER: Brooklyn College of the City University of New York, Brooklyn, N.Y., instructor in English, 1959-60; Columbia University, New York, N.Y., instructor, 1960-62, assistant professor, 1962-67, associate professor, 1967-72, professor of English, 1972—, Avalon Foundation professor in the humanities, 1986—. Visiting lecturer at Union Theological Seminary, 1968-70, Swarthmore College, 1970, and Yale University, 1974; visiting professor at University of California, Santa Cruz, 1979, and Princeton University, 1981. Member of policy advisory council, Danforth Foundation, 1978—.

MEMBER: Modern Language Association of America (member of executive council, 1976-79, 1982-84; president, 1984), Mystery Writers of America (member of executive board, 1982-84), Authors Guild.

AWARDS, HONORS: Scroll from Mystery Writers of America, 1964, for *In the Last Analysis;* Guggenheim fellow, 1965-66; Rockefeller fellow, 1976; Radcliffe Institute fellow, 1976; Nero Wolfe Award for Mystery Fiction, 1981, for *Death in a Tenured Position;* National Endowment for the Humanities fellow, 1983; Alumnae Achievement Award, Wellesley College, 1984; honorary degrees from University of Pennsylvania, 1984, Bucknell University, 1985, Rivier College, 1986, and Russell Sage College, 1987.

WRITINGS:

The Garnett Family, Macmillan, 1961.
Christopher Isherwood, Columbia University Press, 1970.
Toward a Recognition of Androgyny: Aspects of Male and Female in Literature, Knopf, 1973 (published in England as *Toward Androgyny,* Gollancz, 1973).
(Contributor) R. T. Francoeur and A. K. Francoeur, editors, *The Future of Sexual Relations,* Prentice-Hall, 1974.
(Contributor) T. Lewis, editor, *Essays on Virginia Woolf,* McGraw, 1975.
(Contributor) M. Springer, editor, *Portrayal of Women in British and American Literature,* Princeton University Press, 1975.
(Editor) *Lady Ottoline's Album,* Knopf, 1976.
Reinventing Womanhood, Norton, 1979.
(Editor with Margaret R. Higgonet) *The Representation of Women in Fiction,* Johns Hopkins University Press, 1983.
Writing a Woman's Life, Norton, 1988.
(Contributor) Boose and Flowers, editors, *Daughter and Fathers,* Johns Hopkins University Press, 1988.

MYSTERY NOVELS; UNDER PSEUDONYM AMANDA CROSS

In the Last Analysis, Macmillan, 1964, reprinted, Garland Publishing, 1983.
The James Joyce Murder, Macmillan, 1967, reprinted, Ballantine, 1982.
Poetic Justice, Knopf, 1970.
The Theban Mysteries, Knopf, 1972.
The Question of Max, Knopf, 1976.

Death in a Tenured Position, Dutton, 1981 (published in England as *A Death in the Faculty,* Gollancz, 1981).
Sweet Death, Kind Death, Dutton, 1984.
No Word from Winifred, Dutton, 1986.
A Trap for Fools, Dutton, 1989.

OTHER

Also editor, with Nancy K. Miller, of *The New Gender and Culture Series,* Columbia University Press. Contributor to anthologies. Contributor to *New York Times Book Review, Saturday Review, Texas Quarterly,* and other publications. Member of editorial boards of *Virginia Woolf Newsletter,* 1971-72, *Virginia Woolf Quarterly,* 1971-73, *Twentieth Century Literature,* 1973—, and *Signs,* 1975—.

SIDELIGHTS: When Columbia University professor Carolyn G. Heilbrun revealed her alter ego as mystery writer Amanda Cross, it came as no great surprise to the fans of Cross's amateur sleuth Kate Fansler. Like her creator, Kate is a professor of English literature and a committed feminist; the mysteries in which she appears are peppered with social commentary and solutions requiring the analysis of literary texts. Although her mysteries have been well received, such as 1967's *The James Joyce Murder,* "Heilbrun kept her identity as Cross hidden from the members of Columbia's English Department until after she got tenure for fear of tarnishing her reputation as a serious scholar," reports Anne C. Roark in the *Los Angeles Times.* This concern for one's reputation is just one aspect of university life that Heilbrun often illuminates in her novels. *Death in a Tenured Position,* for example, explores the death of the first tenured woman in the Harvard University English department; resented and disliked by her colleagues, the professor's death provides Heilbrun and her protagonist with ample opportunity for cutting comment. Kate's encounter with the faculty is told "in a civilized, witty, and learned fashion with an observant eye on society's pretensions and pomposities," observes Jean M. White of the *Washington Post Book World.* The author's portrait of university politics is so scathing that she printed a disclaimer with the book; nevertheless, notes Carolyn See of the *Los Angeles Times,* "the reader with a liberal arts education will see a great many familiar-seeming faces."

This kind of satiric wit plays a great role in the Kate Fansler mysteries; Art Seidenbaum observes in the *Los Angeles Times* that "the killing is almost incidental to the social commentary" in *The James Joyce Murder.* "More than one-third of the book is consumed in clever conversation before the victim falls dead," explains the critic. Kate has time for such talk, for, as See relates, in *Death in a Tenured Position* "she solves the mysterious death of her hated, isolated female counterpart, the poor girl in the tenured position, by scholarship alone." See elaborates: "Kate's detective work, besides the prerequisite interviews of suspects, consists of going to parties . . . and reading books." Heilbrun's ninth Kate Fansler mystery, *No Word from Winifred,* takes this combination of social and detective work even further: "Although the ostensible object of Kate's investigation is a missing woman named Winifred," states Maureen T. Reddy in the *Women's Review of Books,* "the real subjects of the book are women's changing social position and women's relationships with each other; in some ways," adds the critic, "this book is about the effect of twenty-odd years of contemporary feminism on women's lives."

Some critics object to the emphasis on wit, allusion, and conversation in these mysteries; Newgate Callendar, for instance, asserts in the *New York Times Book Review* that *The Question* of Max "wears this kind of Beautiful Writing like a great purple badge." But Margaret Cannon, writing in the Toronto *Globe and Mail,* proposes that "Cross's literary mother is Dorothy L. Sayers, who has also been accused of creating a world of snootiness and intellectual privilege. To be sure, there's more than a little of the snob in Kate Fansler. But this shouldn't deter any reader, since there's also some excellent writing." Similarly, White suggests in her review of *No Word from Winifred* that "those who think Cross is too stuffy should read her witty observations on academics in convention." "Kate Fansler is the treasure at the center of all Cross's cerebral puzzles," comments Katrine Ames in *Newsweek,* "intelligent and self-doubting, one of those rare people who can quote scores of writers unself-consciously and to the point."

Kate's devotion to literature and her observations on social conditions reflect Heilbrun's scholarly work, which includes *Toward a Recognition of Androgyny* and *Reinventing Womanhood,* two studies that investigate women's roles through an analysis of literary texts. In *Toward a Recognition of Androgyny,* Heilbrun proposes the abandonment of fixed sex roles in favor of an ideal that combines the best of both. "Heilbrun's is an interesting, lively, and valuable general introduction to a new way of perceiving our Western cultural tradition," notes Joyce Carol Oates in the *New York Times Book Review.* In creating this new viewpoint, relates Oates, Heilbrun "has done a fantastic amount of reading: she attempts a re-evaluation of the role of women in practically everything ever written." The critic states, however, that this wide focus makes it "easy to lose one's equilibrium"; other reviewers have also faulted the author's approach. But a *Times Literary Supplement* contributor asserts that Heilbrun "does not claim that this [type of approach] can be anything but superficial. . . . This kind of wide-ranging survey depends on scattered insights and lively writing rather than on critical rigour, and there are many such insights here."

In *Reinventing Womanhood,* Heilbrun similarly uses literary examples to develop her thesis: "that women have neither been thought of nor have thought of themselves as autonomous, fully developed selves," details Ann Hulbert in the *New Republic.* Heilbrun continues by arguing, as Hulbert summarizes, that "assertiveness, achievement, autonomy, ambitious engagement in the public sphere do not threaten feminine identity, but fulfill it." The author also uses autobiographical examples to help expand her theory; Sara Ruddick, writing in the *Harvard Educational Review,* asserts that "by refusing to separate personal history from impersonal truth, [Heilbrun] engages us fully in her work, and we understand its particular origins in her life." As with *Toward a Recognition of Androgyny,* some critics accuse Heilbrun of distorting her examples; Hulbert, for example, writes that the author's "arguments tend to be loose and her emphases skewed." The critic admits, however, that "Heilbrun sets an inspiring goal: autonomy for the self and imaginative sympathy for a community—of women." And Ruddick praises the book's open-minded approach: "It is written with an openness and generosity that invites disagreement as well as assent. *Reinventing Womanhood* is a challenging gift: Heilbrun's questions are central, her answers sensitive and intelligent." Concludes the critic: "She writes out of a commitment to *women* with a compassion and courage we would do well to emulate."

BIOGRAPHICAL/CRITICAL SOURCES:

BOOKS

Bargannier, Earl F., editor, *Ten Women of Mystery,* Bowling Green University, 1981.

Contemporary Literary Criticism, Volume 25, Gale, 1983.
Cooper-Clark, Diana, *Designs of Darkness: Interviews with Detective Novelists,* Bowling Green University, 1983.

PERIODICALS

Chicago Tribune, April 22, 1979.
Globe and Mail (Toronto), July 19, 1986.
Harper's, July, 1981.
Harvard Educational Review, November, 1979.
Los Angeles Times, April 6, 1981, March 31, 1982, February 18, 1983.
Los Angeles Times Book Review, May 20, 1984, July 6, 1986.
New Republic, June 9, 1979.
Newsweek, October 4, 1976.
New York Times, March 24, 1973, March 20, 1981.
New York Times Book Review, April 15, 1973, October 3, 1976, May 13, 1979, March 22, 1981.
Times Literary Supplement, October 12, 1973, July 3, 1981.
Washington Post Book World, April 22, 1979, March 15, 1981, June 17, 1984, June 15, 1986.
Women's Review of Books, December, 1986.

—*Sketch by Diane Telgen*

*   *   *

HEINEMAN, Benjamin Walter, Jr.   1944-

PERSONAL: Born January 25, 1944, in Chicago, Ill.; son of Benjamin Walter (a businessman) and Natalie (a civic leader; maiden name, Goldstein) Heineman; married Jeanne Cristine Russell (a journalist), June 7, 1975; children: Zachary R., Matthew R. *Education:* Harvard University, B.A. (magna cum laude), 1965; Balliol College, Oxford, B.Letters, 1967; Yale University, J.D., 1971.

ADDRESSES: Home—43 Huckleberry Ln., Darien, Conn. 06820. *Office*—General Electric Co., 3135 Easton Turnpike, Fairfield, Conn. 06431. *Agent*—Rafael Sagalyn, 1120 19th St. N.W., Washington, D.C. 20036.

CAREER: Admitted to the Bar of District of Columbia, 1973, and U.S. Supreme Court, 1973. *Chicago Sun Times,* Chicago, Ill., reporter, 1968; U.S. Supreme Court, Washington, D.C., law clerk to associate justice Potter Stewart, 1971-72; Center for Law and Social Policy, Washington, D.C., staff attorney, 1973-75; Williams, Connolly & Califano (attorneys), Washington, D.C., lawyer, 1975-76; U.S. Department of Health, Education and Welfare, Washington, D.C., executive assistant to Secretary of Health, Education and Welfare, 1977-78, assistant secretary for planning and evaluation, 1978-79; Califano, Ross & Heineman (attorneys), Washington, D.C., partner, 1979-82; Sidley & Austin (attorneys), Washington, D.C., partner, 1982-87; General Electric Co., Fairfield, Conn., senior vice-president and general counsel, 1987—.

MEMBER: Phi Beta Kappa.

AWARDS, HONORS: Rhodes scholar at Oxford University, 1965-67.

WRITINGS:

The Politics of the Powerless: A Study of the Campaign against Racial Discrimination, Oxford University Press, 1972.
(With Curtis A. Hessler) *Memorandum for the President: A Strategic Approach to Domestic Affairs in the Eighties,* Random House, 1980.
(With others) *Work and Welfare: The Case for New Directions in National Policy,* University Press of America, 1987.

Editor in chief, *Yale Law Journal,* 1970-71.

SIDELIGHTS: "If an incoming Chief Executive wants the best available advice on how to organize his office and his time," Benjamin Walter Heineman, Jr.'s *Memorandum for the President: A Strategic Approach to Domestic Affairs in the Eighties,* authored with Curtis A. Hessler, "is it," notes Aaron Wildavsky in the *New York Times Book Review.* "Though addressed to the Chief Executive in the second person, the book is not really directed toward [a specific individual]; it provides a good guide to the future because it covers the constraints acting on all Presidents." The book is commendable, according to *New Republic* contributor Charles Peters, "because in the process of making its case that presidential strategy in domestic affairs should concentrate on a handful of issues which are either likely to be manageable or are truly unavoidable, it says much that is useful about the problems and choices confronting a new administration." But while he calls *Memorandum for the President* "a book of shrewd insights into politics and government," Edward Cowan adds in his *New York Times* review that "it is not a successful book." The critic explains: "It is too long, too repetitive, too cluttered with details and lists. Some of the book is worth reading, so it is unfortunate that much of it is unlikely to hold the attention of most general readers."

Peters notes that although Heineman and Hessler work from their knowledge as former assistant secretaries in the Carter administration, they fail to capitalize on this experience. "Former government officials should realize," comments the critic, "that if they aren't willing to kiss and tell, then they aren't going to be able to tell—really tell, in the sense of giving the full, human story behind the events they describe." Cowan presents a similar criticism, observing that "what is missing is the human dimension, the anecdotal detail that would make the abstractions come alive." Nevertheless, the reviewer believes that *Memorandum for the President* contains "an excellent critique of the news media, which the authors find preoccupied with 'conflict' and 'electoral politics' to the exclusion of informing the public about issues." In addition, Cowan observes that "the authors perceptively describe the conflict between campaign politics and the constraints of governing." And Peters, while acknowledging that the authors' *Memorandum* "will never make your blood boil or your heart break," admits that the work "[is] must reading."

BIOGRAPHICAL/CRITICAL SOURCES:

PERIODICALS

New Republic, May 16, 1981.
New York Times, April 2, 1981.
New York Times Book Review, February 22, 1981.
Washington Post Book World, January 18, 1981.

* * *

HELLMANN, Donald C(harles) 1933-

PERSONAL: Born June 24, 1933, in Rochester, N.Y.; son of Charles F. (a city employee and businessman) and Agnes A. (Genrich) Hellmann; married Margery Holburne Saunders, July 6, 1960; children: Jane Alison, Thomas Maxwell, John Christopher. *Education:* Princeton University, A.B., 1955; University of California, Berkeley, M.A., 1960, Ph.D., 1964. *Politics:* Independent.

ADDRESSES: Home—4154 42nd Ave. N.E., Seattle, Wash. 98105. *Office*—Department of Political Science/International Studies, University of Washington, Seattle, Wash. 98195.

CAREER: Vanderbilt University, Nashville, Tenn., instructor in political science, 1963-64; Swarthmore College, Swarthmore, Pa., instructor, 1964-66, assistant professor of political science, 1966-67; University of Washington, Seattle, associate professor, 1967-72, professor of political science and international studies, 1972—, Institute for Comparative and Foreign Area Studies, 1967-72, acting director, 1971-72, acting chairman, 1975-76, 1980-81. American Enterprise Institute, adjunct scholar, 1973—, member of academic advisory board, 1975—; director, Asia Commission on Critical Choices for Americans, 1974-76. Consultant to U.S. Department of State, National Security Council, Arms Control and Disarmament Agency, Research Analysis Corp., Brookings Institution, and Committee for Economic Development. *Military service:* U.S. Army, 1955-57.

MEMBER: American Political Science Association, Association for Asian Studies, International Studies Association, International House of Japan.

AWARDS, HONORS: Ford Foundation fellow, 1961-63; Council on Foreign Relations International Affairs fellow, 1970-71; Fulbright-Hayes fellow, 1970-71.

WRITINGS:

Japanese Foreign Policy and Domestic Politics: The Peace Agreement with the Soviet Union, University of California Press, 1969.
Japan and the New East Asian International System (monograph), Research Analysis Corp., 1970.
(Contributor) Steven L. Spiegel and K. N. Waltz, editors, *Conflict in World Politics,* Winthrop, 1971.
Japan and East Asia: The New International Order, Praeger, 1972.
(Contributor) J. W. Morley, editor, *Forecast for Japan,* Princeton University Press, 1972.
Japanese-American Relations: The American View, American Enterprise Institute, 1975.
(Editor and contributor) *China and Japan: A New Balance of Power,* Lexington Books, 1976.

Contributor to *Asian Survey, International Studies Quarterly, Europa-Archiv,* and Japanese journals. Editor, *Japan Newsletter,* Association of Asian Studies, 1964—; member of editorial boards, *Asian Survey,* 1969—, and *Journal of Japanese Studies,* 1974—.

WORK IN PROGRESS: The Emergence of Postwar Japan; research on Japanese nationalism, postwar Japanese defense policy, American foreign policy in East Asia, and Japanese foreign policy.*

* * *

HIBBERT, Eleanor Burford 1906-
(Eleanor Burford; pseudonyms: Philippa Carr, Elbur Ford, Victoria Holt, Kathleen Kellow, Jean Plaidy, Ellalice Tate)

PERSONAL: Born 1906, in London, England; daughter of Joseph and Alice (Tate) Burford; married G. P. Hibbert. *Education:* Privately educated.

ADDRESSES: Agent—A. M. Heath & Co., Ltd., 35 Dover St., London W.1, England.

WRITINGS:

UNDER NAME ELEANOR BURFORD

House at Cupid's Cross, Jenkins, 1949.
Passionate Witness, Jenkins, 1949.
Believe the Heart, Jenkins, 1950.
Love Child, Jenkins, 1950.
Saint or Sinner?, Jenkins, 1951.
Dear Delusion, Jenkins, 1952.
Bright Tomorrow, Jenkins, 1952.
Leave Me My Love, Jenkins, 1953.
When We Are Married, Jenkins, 1953.
Castles in Spain, Jenkins, 1954.
Heart's Afire, Jenkins, 1954.
When Other Hearts, Jenkins, 1955.
Two Loves in Her Life, Jenkins, 1955.
Begin to Live, Mills & Boon, 1956.
Married in Haste, Mills & Boon, 1956.
To Meet a Stranger, Mills & Boon, 1957.
Pride of the Morning, Mills & Boon, 1958.
Dawn Chorus, Mills & Boon, 1959.
Red Sky at Night, Mills & Boon, 1959.
Blaze of Noon, Mills & Boon, 1960.
Night of the Stars, Mills & Boon, 1960.
Now That April's Gone, Mills & Boon, 1961.
Who's Calling?, Mills & Boon, 1962.

UNDER PSEUDONYM PHILIPPA CARR

The Miracle at St. Bruno's, Putnam, 1972.
The Lion Triumphant, Putnam, 1973.
The Witch from the Sea, Putnam, 1975.
Saraband for Two Sisters, Putnam, 1976.
Lament for a Lost Lover, Putnam, 1977.
The Love Child, Putnam, 1978.
Song of the Siren, Putnam, 1979.
Will You Love Me in September, Putnam, 1980.
The Adulteress, Putnam, 1981.

UNDER PSEUDONYM ELBUR FORD

Poison in Pimlico, Laurie, 1950.
Flesh and the Devil, Laurie, 1950.
Bed Disturbed, Laurie, 1952.
Such Bitter Business, Heinemann, 1953, published as *Evil in the House*, Morrow, 1954.

UNDER PSEUDONYM VICTORIA HOLT

Mistress of Mellyn, Doubleday, 1960.
Kirkland Revels, Doubleday, 1962.
Bride of Pendorric (also see below), Doubleday, 1963.
The Legend of the Seventh Virgin, Doubleday, 1965.
Menfreya in the Morning, Doubleday, 1966 (published in England as *Menfreya*, Collins, 1966).
The King of the Castle, Doubleday, 1967.
Queen's Confession: A Biography of Marie Antoinette, Doubleday, 1968, published as *The Queen's Confession*, Fawcett, 1974.
The Shivering Sands, Doubleday, 1969.
The Secret Woman, Doubleday, 1970.
The Shadow of the Lynx, Doubleday, 1971.
On the Night of the Seventh Moon, Doubleday, 1972.
The Curse of the Kings, Doubleday, 1973.
The House of a Thousand Lanterns, Doubleday, 1974.
Lord of the Far Island, Doubleday, 1975.
Pride of the Peacock, Doubleday, 1976.
The Devil on Horseback, Doubleday, 1977.

My Enemy the Queen, Doubleday, 1978.
The Spring of the Tiger, Doubleday, 1979.
The Mask of the Enchantress, Doubleday, 1980.
The Judas Kiss, Doubleday, 1981.
The Demon Lover, Doubleday, 1982.
The Landower Legacy, Doubleday, 1985.

UNDER PSEUDONYM KATHLEEN KELLOW

Danse Macabre, R. Hale, 1952.
Rooms at Mrs. Olivers', R. Hale, 1953.
Lilith (also see below), R. Hale, 1954.
It Began in Vauxhall Gardens (also see below), R. Hale, 1955.
Call of the Blood, R. Hale, 1956.
Rochester, the Mad Earl, R. Hale, 1957.
Milady Charlotte, R. Hale, 1959.
The World's a Stage, R. Hale, 1960.

UNDER PSEUDONYM JEAN PLAIDY

Beyond the Blue Mountains, Appleton, 1947, new edition, R. Hale, 1964.
Murder Most Royal, R. Hale, 1949, Putnam, 1972, published as *King's Pleasure*, Appleton, 1949.
The Goldsmith's Wife, Appleton, 1950.
Madame Serpent (first novel in "Catherine de Medici" trilogy; also see below), Appleton, 1951.
The Italian Woman (second novel in "Catherine de Medici" trilogy; also see below), R. Hale, 1952.
Daughter of Satan, R. Hale, 1952, Putnam, 1973.
Queen Jezebel (third novel in "Catherine de Medici" trilogy; also see below), Appleton, 1953.
The Spanish Bridegroom, R. Hale, 1953, Macrae Smith, 1956.
St. Thomas's Eve, R. Hale, 1954, Putnam, 1970.
The Sixth Wife, R. Hale, 1954, Putnam, 1969.
Gay Lord Robert, R. Hale, 1955, Putnam, 1972.
Royal Road to Fotheringay, R. Hale, 1955, Fawcett, 1972, published as *Royal Road to Fotheringay: A Novel of Mary, Queen of Scots*, Putnam, 1956.
The Wandering Prince (first novel in "Charles II" trilogy; also see below), R. Hale, 1956, Putnam, 1971.
Health unto His Majesty (second novel in "Charles II" trilogy; also see below), R. Hale, 1956, published as *A Health unto His Majesty*, Putnam, 1972.
Flaunting, Extravagant Queen, R. Hale, 1957.
Here Lies Our Sovereign Lord (third novel in "Charles II" trilogy; also see below), R. Hale, 1957, Putnam, 1973.
Madonna of the Seven Hills, R. Hale, 1958, Putnam, 1974.
Triptych of Poisoners, R. Hale, 1958.
Light on Lucrezia, R. Hale, 1958.
Louis, the Well-Beloved, R. Hale, 1959.
The Rise of the Spanish Inquisition (first novel in "Spanish Inquisition" trilogy; also see below), R. Hale, 1959.
Road to Compiegne, R. Hale, 1959.
Castile for Isabella (first novel in "Isabella and Ferdinand" trilogy; also see below), R. Hale, 1960.
The Growth of the Spanish Inquisition (second novel in "Spanish Inquisition" trilogy; also see below), R. Hale, 1960.
Spain for the Sovereigns (second novel in "Isabella and Ferdinand" trilogy; also see below), R. Hale, 1960.
Daughters of Spain (third novel in "Isabella and Ferdinand" trilogy; also see below), R. Hale, 1961.
The Young Elizabeth, Roy, 1961.
Meg Roper: Daughter of Sir Thomas More, Constable, 1961, Roy, 1964.
The End of the Spanish Inquisition (third novel in "Spanish Inquisition" trilogy; also see below), R. Hale, 1961.

Katharine, the Virgin Widow (first novel in "Katharine of Aragon" trilogy; also see below), R. Hale, 1961.

The King's Secret Matter (third novel in "Katharine of Aragon" trilogy; also see below), R. Hale, 1962.

The Young Mary, Queen of Scots, Parrish, 1962, Roy, 1963.

The Shadow of the Pomegranate (second novel in "Katharine of Aragon" trilogy; also see below), R. Hale, 1962.

The Captive Queen of Scots, R. Hale, 1963, Putnam, 1970.

The Thistle and the Rose, R. Hale, 1963, Putnam, 1973.

Mary, Queen of France, R. Hale, 1964.

The Murder in the Tower, R. Hale, 1964, Putnam, 1974.

Evergreen Gallant, R. Hale, 1965, Putnam, 1973.

The Three Crowns, R. Hale, 1965.

The Haunted Sisters, R. Hale, 1966.

The Queen's Favourites, R. Hale, 1966.

Lilith (originally published under pseudonym Kathleen Kellow), R. Hale, 1967.

Queen in Waiting, R. Hale, 1967.

The Princess of Celle, R. Hale, 1967.

The Spanish Inquisition: Its Rise, Growth, and End (trilogy; contains *The Rise of the Spanish Inquisition, The Growth of the Spanish Inquisition,* and *The End of the Spanish Inquisition*), Citadel, 1967.

The Prince and the Quakeress, R. Hale, 1968.

Caroline, the Queen, R. Hale, 1968.

It Began in Vauxhall Gardens (originally published under pseudonym Kathleen Kellow), R. Hale, 1968.

Katharine of Aragon (trilogy; contains *Katharine, the Virgin Widow, The Shadow of the Pomegranate,* and *The King's Secret Matter*), R. Hale, 1968.

The Scarlet Cloak (originally published under pseudonym Ellalice Tate; also see below), R. Hale, 1969.

The Third George, R. Hale, 1969.

Perdita's Prince, R. Hale, 1969.

Catherine de Medici (trilogy; contains *Madame Serpent, The Italian Woman,* and *Queen Jezebel*), R. Hale, 1969.

Sweet Lass of Richmond Hill, R. Hale, 1970.

Indiscretions of the Queen, R. Hale, 1970.

Isabella and Ferdinand (trilogy; includes *Castile for Isabella, Spain for the Sovereigns,* and *Daughters of Spain*), R. Hale, 1970.

The Regent's Daughter, R. Hale, 1971.

Goddess of the Green Room, R. Hale, 1971.

The Captive of Kensington Palace, R. Hale, 1972.

Victoria in the Wings, R. Hale, 1972.

Charles II (trilogy; contains *The Wandering Prince, Health unto His Majesty,* and *Here Lies Our Sovereign Lord*), R. Hale, 1972.

The Queen's Husband, R. Hale, 1973.

The Queen and Lord M., R. Hale, 1973.

The Widow of Windsor, R. Hale, 1974.

The King's Mistress, Pyramid Publications, 1974.

Uneasy Lies the Head, R. Hale, 1982.

Myself My Enemy, Putnam, 1984.

Queen of the Realm: The Story of Elizabeth I, Putnam, 1985.

Victoria Victorious, R. Hale, 1986.

UNDER PSEUDONYM ELLALICE TATE

Defenders of the Faith, Hodder & Stoughton, 1956.

The Scarlet Cloak, Hodder & Stoughton, 1957.

Queen of Diamonds, Hodder & Stoughton, 1958.

Madame du Barry, Hodder & Stoughton, 1959.

This Was a Man, Hodder & Stoughton, 1961.

OTHER

(Contributor) *Three Great Romantic Stories* (contains *Bride of Pendorric*), Collins, 1972.

Contributor to newspapers and magazines, at times under a number of undisclosed pseudonyms.

SIDELIGHTS: "I think people want a good story and this I give them," Eleanor Burford Hibbert told *CA.* "They like something which is readable and you can't really beat the traditional for this. I write with great feeling and excitement and I think this comes over to the reader." Hibbert is perhaps best known for the pseudonyms Victoria Holt and Jean Plaidy, under which she has prolifically crafted most of her fiction. Doubleday kept the Holt pseudonym a well-guarded secret when it first appeared, and many thought that Holt was actually Daphne du Maurier. "I have heard her name mentioned in connection with mine," Hibbert indicated to *CA,* "and I think it is because we have both lived in Cornwall and have written about this place. *Rebecca* is the atmospheric suspense type of book which mine are, but I don't think there is much similarity between her others and mine."

Critics have been generous to the Gothic tales bearing the Holt name. In the *Chicago Sunday Tribune,* for instance, Genevieve Casey says of *Kirkland Revels:* "Murder, intrigue, threats of insanity, family skeletons rattling in closets and ghosts who walk in the moonlight keep the reader credulous and turning pages fast in this absorbing story." Reviewing *The Legend of the Seventh Virgin* for *Best Sellers,* Casey writes: "Among the clamour of novels by angry young men, among the probings and circumlocution of psychological novels, the works of Victoria Holt stand out, unpretentious, sunny, astringent, diverting." Even about work not as critically well-received as others, reviewers still praise the author's ability to engage a reader's interest. In the *New York Times Book Review,* for example, Anthony Boucher says of *Menfreya in the Morning:* "It's hard to say objectively, just why . . . [this] is so intensely readable and enjoyable. . . . It is Holt's weakest and slightest plot to date, and equally certainly nothing much happens in the way of either action or character development for long stretches. But somehow the magic . . . is still there." And more recently, in a *Washington Post Book World* review of *The Landower Legacy,* Susan Dooley calls the author "a very competent escape artist."

Hibbert's historical novels under the Plaidy pseudonym are also well regarded by critics. Writing about *The Captive of Kensington Palace* in *Books and Bookmen,* for instance, Jean Stubbs remarks that "Jean Plaidy never fails to provide what may be termed 'a good read,'" and refers to the novel as a "compulsive good read." Concluding that the author's "gift is that of being a literary confidante: the best kind of gossip, neither malicious nor lacivious," Stubbs adds that "one feels one has experienced a genuine heart-to-heart talk: refreshing, informative, enlightening, and always entertaining."

"Dickens, Zola, Brontes (particularly), and nearly all the Victorians" have influenced her writings, Hibbert says. "I write regularly every day. I think this is important. As in everything else, practice helps to make perfect. Research is just a matter of reading old records, letters, etc., in fact everything connected with the period one is researching. I can only say that I love writing more than anything else. I find it stimulating and I never cease to be excited about it."

Hibbert has traveled widely throughout the world and plans to visit Australia and the Pacific Islands.

MEDIA ADAPTATIONS: Mistress of Mellyn, Hibbert's first novel under her pseudonym Victoria Holt, was adapted for the stage by Mildred C. Kuner; *Daughter of Satan,* written under the pseudonym Jean Plaidy, is being filmed.

BIOGRAPHICAL/CRITICAL SOURCES:

BOOKS

Contemporary Literary Criticism, Volume 7, Gale, 1977.

PERIODICALS

Atlanta Journal-Constitution, July 4, 1966.
Best Sellers, February 1, 1965, July 1, 1971, August 15, 1974.
Books and Bookmen, January, 1973.
Chicago Sunday Tribune, January 14, 1962.
Los Angeles Times Book Review, June 16, 1985.
New York Times Book Review, April 17, 1966, January 15, 1984.
Times (London), January 2, 1986.
Washington Post Book World, November 7, 1982.

*   *   *

HIGHET, Helen
See MacINNES, Helen (Clark)

*   *   *

HILDEBRAND, Verna   1924-

PERSONAL: Born August 17, 1924, in Dodge City, Kan.; daughter of Carrell E. (a farmer) and Florence Butcher; married John R. Hildebrand (an economist), June 24, 1946; children: Carol, Steve. *Education:* Kansas State University, B.S., 1945, M.S., 1957; University of California, Berkeley, graduate study, 1946-48; Texas Woman's University, Ph.D., 1970.

ADDRESSES: Home—308 Michigan, No. 8, East Lansing, Mich. 48823. *Office*—College of Human Ecology, Michigan State University, East Lansing, Mich. 48824-1030.

CAREER: Kansas State University, Manhattan, instructor in family relations, 1953-54, instructor in student counseling center, 1958; Oklahoma State University, Stillwater, instructor in family relations and child development, 1955-56; Texas Technological College (now Texas Tech Unviersity), Lubbock, assistant professor of home and family life, 1962-67; Michigan State University, East Lansing, 1967—, currently professor of family and child economy.

MEMBER: National Association for the Education of Young Children, American Home Economics Association (chairman of family relations and child development section, 1975-77), World Association for Early Childhood Education, National Association of Early Childhood Teacher Educators (president, 1982-84).

WRITINGS:

Introduction to Early Childhood Education, with laboratory workbook, Macmillan, 1971, 4th edition, 1986.
Guiding Young Children, Macmillan, 1975, 4th edition, 1990.
Parenting and Teaching Young Children, McGraw, 1981, 3rd edition, 1990.
(With husband, John R. Hildebrand) *China's Families: Experiment in Societal Change,* Burgess, 1981.
(Contributor) *Patterns of Supplementary Parenting,* Plenum, 1982.
Management of Child Development Centers, Macmillan, 1984, 2nd edition, 1990.

Contributor of articles to journals.

SIDELIGHTS: Verna Hildebrand writes: "I am strongly committed to improving the quality of early childhood schools, child care centers, and kindergartens. Quality care and education for young children is an investment in our future."

*   *   *

HIMMELFARB, Gertrude   1922-

PERSONAL: Born August 8, 1922, in New York, N.Y.; daughter of Max and Bertha (Lerner) Himmelfarb; married Irving Kristol (a professor and editor), January 18, 1942; children: William, Elizabeth. *Education:* Attended Jewish Theological Seminary, 1939-42; Brooklyn College (now Brooklyn College of the City University of New York), B.A., 1942; University of Chicago, M.A., 1944, Ph.D., 1950; attended Girton College, Cambridge, 1946-47.

ADDRESSES: Office—City University of New York, 33 West 42nd St., New York, N.Y. 10036.

CAREER: Brooklyn College and Graduate School of the City University of New York, professor, 1965-78, distinguished professor of history, 1978-88, professor emerita of history, 1988—. Member of board of trustees, National Humanities Center, 1976—; council member, National Endowment for the Humanities, 1982—; council of scholars, Library of Congress, 1984—; member of board of trustees, Woodrow Wilson Center, 1985—; member of board of directors, British Institute of the United States, 1985—, and Institute for Contemporary Studies, 1986—; associate scholar, Ethics and Public Policy Center, 1986—. Member of council of academic advisors, American Enterprise Institute; member of Presidential Advisory Commission on Economic Role of Women.

MEMBER: British Academy (fellow), American Academy of Arts and Sciences, Society of American Historians, American Historical Association, Royal Historical Society (fellow), American Philosophical Society.

AWARDS, HONORS: American Association of University Women fellowship, 1951-52; American Philosophical Society fellowship, 1953-54; Guggenheim fellowships, 1955-56, 1957-58; Rockefeller Foundation grants, 1962-63, 1963-64; National Endowment for the Humanities senior fellowship, 1968-69; American Council of Learned Societies fellowship, 1972-73; Phi Beta Kappa visiting scholarship, 1972-73; Woodrow Wilson Center fellowship, 1976-77; Rockefeller Humanities fellowship, 1980-81.

WRITINGS:

Lord Acton: A Study in Conscience and Politics, University of Chicago Press, 1952.
Darwin and the Darwinian Revolution, Doubleday, 1959, revised edition, Norton, 1968.
Victorian Minds: Essays on Nineteenth Century Intellectuals, Knopf, 1968.
On Liberty and Liberalism: The Case of John Stuart Mill, Knopf, 1974.
The Idea of Poverty: England in the Industrial Age, Knopf, 1984.
Marriage and Morals among the Victorians and Other Essays, Random House, 1987.
The New History and the Old, Harvard University Press, 1987.

EDITOR

Lord Acton, *Essays on Freedom and Power,* Free Press, 1948.
Thomas R. Malthus, *On Population,* Modern Library, 1960.

John Stuart Mill, *Essays on Politics and Culture,* Doubleday, 1962.

John Stuart Mill, *On Liberty,* Penguin, 1975.

CONTRIBUTOR

Bernard Wishy and others, editors, *Chapters in Western Civilization,* Columbia University Press, 3rd edition (Himmelfarb was not included in earlier editions), 1962.

R. H. Browne, editor, *The Burke-Paine Controversy,* Harcourt, 1963.

Robin Winks, editor, *British Imperialism,* Holt, 1963.

Leonard M. Marsak, editor, *The Rise of Science in Relation to Society,* Macmillan, 1964.

Richard Herr and Harold T. Parker, editors, *Ideas in History: Essays in Honor of Louis Gottschalk,* Duke University Press, 1965.

Donald N. Baker and G. W. Fasel, editors, *Landmarks in Western Culture,* Prentice-Hall, 1967.

T. W. Wallbank and others, editors, *Civilization Past and Present,* Scott, Foresman, 6th edition (Himmelfarb was not included in earlier editions), 1969.

John B. Conacher, editor, *The Emergence of British Parliamentary Democracy in the Nineteenth Century,* Wiley, 1971.

Michael Wolff and H. J. Dyos, editors, *The Victorian City: Images and Realities,* Routledge & Kegan Paul, 1973.

Quentin Anderson and others, editors, *Art, Politics, and the Will,* Basic Books, 1977.

OTHER

Contributor to journals, including *Journal of Contemporary History, Victorian Studies, Journal of British Studies, Journal of Modern History, Commentary, Encounter, American Scholar, New Republic,* and *Harper's.* Member of editorial board of *Albion, American Historical Review, American Scholar, Journal of British Studies, Jewish Social Studies, Reviews in European History,* and *This World.*

SIDELIGHTS: As a writer of history books, professor Gertrude Himmelfarb "is almost as much a critic of historiography as a historian—a critic, too, with a strong revisionist impulse, an urge to correct (with some asperity) the errors of her predecessors," as John Gross of the *Observer* describes her. Her books focus upon the history of thought of Victorian England, a period which she defines as extending from the late eighteenth century (and the life of Edmund Burke) to the early twentieth century (ending roughly around the time of John Buchan). In these texts she covers a wide diversity of noteworthy figures, including Thomas Malthus, John Stuart Mill, Thomas Macauley, Walter Bagehot, and Jeremy Bentham, while also discussing historical issues such as the Reform Act of 1867 and Social Darwinism.

With an emphasis on the many ambiguities in philosophy which were present in the Victorian Age, Himmelfarb nevertheless manages to unify the whole with what she calls the "moral imagination" of the Victorians (a phrase that Burke first coined). This is a general term which Gross defines as "a set of characteristic Victorian convictions—a belief in human dignity, a respect for human complexity, a sense of common responsibility based on sympathetic insight rather than textbook rules." Although she is able to tie her subjects together with this motif, she does not fall into the trap of "smoothing over contradictions or bringing [a person's] thought into an erroneous uniformity," observes Thomas Lask of the *New York Times.* Himmelfarb feels that modern critics tend to form a consensus on how history is to be treated based upon whatever school of criticism is popular at the time, and that this seriously clouds their ability to analyze facts properly. *New Statesman* contributor A. S. Byatt phrases the historian's attitude this way: "She deprecates current intellectual fashions of simplicity and commitment, pointing out that subtleties, complications, and ambiguities—once the mark of serious thought—are now taken to signify a failure of nerve." This attitude has drawn both positive and negative reactions from critics.

For example, in a review of Himmelfarb's *Victorian Minds: Essays on Nineteenth Century Intellectuals,* Carleton Miscellany contributor Robert E. Bonner writes: "The problem is that the intelligent historian here changes garb rapidly and often becomes a scourge of idealogues past and, by implication, present. The result is at best misconceived or misdirected history or criticism, and at worst is history in the service of a particular modern American 'liberal' orthodoxy." On the other hand, Robert A. Nisbet of *Commentary* writes that Himmelfarb's "knowledge of the century is vast, but it rarely if ever swamps her judgment . . . which remains . . . precise and discriminating."

Continuing to break down the walls of pat historical interpretation, the historian brings to our attention in *The Idea of Poverty: England in the Industrial Age* not only the subject of England's nineteenth-century poor laws, but also how the very concept of poverty changed over time to include an ever narrower segment of the population. She shows us, according to *Times Literary Supplement* reviewer Harold Perkin, how the awareness of the poverty problem and its relation to ideas about poverty changed over time. Perkin asserts that she cuts "through the mouldy rags of interpretation which have been piled upon the poor and their interpreters for generations."

Marriage and Morals among the Victorians and Other Essays is also a fresh viewpoint of the Victorian Age, this time with an emphasis on the sense of morality of the period. *New York Times Book Review* contributor Neil McKendrick feels that she "offers a more sympathetic response than is usual to late Victorian morality." This book has drawn some negative criticism from reviewers like Rosemary Ashton of the *Times Literary Supplement,* who notes: "If one has a complaint, it is that [the idea of a 'precarious' late Victorian morality] is less argued than assumed, that Himmelfarb spends more time disapproving than approving." Overall, however, critics tend to agree with McKendrick that *Marriage and Morals among the Victorians and Other Essays* "is an important book that deserves a wide readership."

Himmelfarb's criticism of modern historians culminates in her book *The New History and the Old* in which she attacks the prevalent acceptance of social history (a science that studies the history of ordinary people and ignores politics). Her fear here, *Los Angeles Times Book Review* contributor Paul Johnson summarizes, is that "when traditional history is completely displaced, what takes over is often not history at all but forms of covert left-wing propaganda." It is not, as Himmelfarb herself proclaims, that she objects "to social history as such," but she does dispute "its claims of dominance, superiority, even 'totality.'" Himmelfarb manages in this book, as well as in her other books, to maintain a unique perspective of history, avoiding the popular, often transient, schools of history. Her preoccupation with the thoughts behind the actions in history is what probably makes her, as Gross says, "one of the most gifted and trenchant interpreters of the Victorian scene."

BIOGRAPHICAL/CRITICAL SOURCES:

PERIODICALS

Carleton Miscellany, fall, 1968.
Commentary, November, 1968.
Los Angeles Times Book Review, September 27, 1987.
New Statesman, December 6, 1968.
New York Times, February 28, 1986.
New York Times Book Review, March 23, 1986.
Observer, October 6, 1968.
Times Literary Supplement, May 25, 1984, July 25, 1986, January 15, 1988.

—*Sketch by Kevin S. Hile*

*   *   *

HIRSCH, Fred   1931-1978

PERSONAL: Born July 6, 1931, in Vienna, Austria; died January 11, 1978, in Leamington Spa, England, following a long illness; married Ruth Weissrock (a teacher), July 15, 1956; children: Philip, Donald, Timothy. *Education:* London School of Economics and Political Science, B.Sc. (first class honors), 1953. *Politics:* Left. *Religion:* None.

ADDRESSES: Home—11 Leam Terr., Leamington Spa, Warwickshire, England. *Office*—Department of International Studies, University of Warwick, Coventry CV4 7AL, England.

CAREER: Economist, London, England, reporter, 1953-63; financial editor, 1963-66; International Monetary Fund, Washington, D.C., senior adviser, 1966-72; Oxford University, Nuffield College, Oxford, England, research fellow, 1972-74; University of Warwick, Coventry, England, professor of international studies, 1975-78.

MEMBER: Royal Economic Society.

WRITINGS:

The Pound Sterling: A Polemic, Gollancz, 1965.
Money International, Allen Lane, 1967, Doubleday, 1969, revised edition, Penguin, 1969.
An Analysis of Our AFL-CIO Role in Latin America; or, Under the Covers with the CIA, privately printed, 1974.
(With David Gordon) *Newspaper Money: Fleet Street and the Search for the Affluent Reader*, Hutchinson, 1975.
Social Limits to Growth, Harvard University Press, 1976.
(With Michael Doyle and Edward L. Morse) *Alternatives to Monetary Disorder*, McGraw, 1977.
(With Richard Fletcher) *The CIA and the Labour Movement*, Spokesman Books, 1977.
(Editor with John H. Goldthorpe) *The Political Economy of Inflation*, Harvard University Press, 1978.
Dilemmas of Liberal Democracies, Tavistock Publications, 1983.

Also author of several pamphlets, including *Money for Growth*, 1962, *An SDR Standard: Impetus, Elements, and Impediments*, 1973, *Reform of the International Monetary System*, 1973, and *The Bagehot Problem*, 1975. Contributor to financial journals.

WORK IN PROGRESS: Research in various aspects of international political economy.

SIDELIGHTS: Austrian-born, British economist, author, and former financial editor of the British weekly *Economist*, Fred Hirsch also served as an economic adviser to the International Monetary Fund in Washington, D.C., for six years. Having written several books and pamphlets on economics and finance, Hirsch was perhaps best known for his *Social Limits to Growth*. Calling it a "brilliant and important book," a *Choice* reviewer described it as an examination of the weaknesses of theories of such founders of liberal capitalism as Adam Smith, who believed that the "prescription for increasing the wealth of nations linked the pursuit of individual self-interest with the promotion of the interests of all." An *Economist* contributor explained that in economic theory, "there is, on the one hand, the view that decentralised market capitalism is a prerequisite to freedom and on the other that actual capitalism leads inevitably to social conflict." And according to G. R. Laczniak in *Library Journal*, "The thesis of Hirsch's work is that there are also social limits that may disrupt the economy long before physical limits are reached." Although Joe Klein remarked in the *New York Times Book Review* that "unfortunately, the book suffers from a case of pernicious academia," the *Economist* reviewer found that what Hirsch wrote would appeal to a general audience as well as the specialized one, and added that "it is to be hoped that one consequence of this brilliant book is that public discussion of the issue is stimulated."

BIOGRAPHICAL/CRITICAL SOURCES:

PERIODICALS

Choice, March, 1977.
Economist, December 11, 1976.
Library Journal, January 15, 1977.
New York Times Book Review, February 13, 1977.

OBITUARIES:

PERIODICALS

New York Times, January 12, 1978.
Washington Post, January 14, 1978.*

*   *   *

HIVNOR, Robert   1916-
(Jack Askew, Osbert Pismire)

PERSONAL: Born May 19, 1916, in Zanesville, Ohio; son of Harry Franklin and Glovinna (Jones) Hivnor; married Mary Otis, August 11, 1947; children: James, Margaret, Henry. *Education:* University of Akron, A.B., 1936; Yale University, M.F.A., 1946; additional graduate study, Columbia University, 1952-54; studied painting privately. *Politics:* Democrat. *Religion:* "Raised as a Presbyterian."

ADDRESSES: Home—420 East 84th St., New York, N.Y. 10028; and Box 58, Old Mystic, Conn. 06372 (summers).

CAREER: Political cartoonist and commercial artist, 1934-38; Craftsman Press, Akron, Ohio, office manager, 1936-37; University of Minnesota, Minneapolis, instructor in English, 1946-48; Reed College, Portland, Ore., instructor in humanities, 1954-55; Bard College, Annandale-on-Hudson, N.Y., assistant professor of literature, 1956-59; writer. Member of the President's Commission on the Teaching of English, 1966. *Military Service:* U.S. Army, cryptanalyst, 1942-45.

MEMBER: PEN, Dramatists Guild, Theatre for Ideas, American Association of University Professors.

AWARDS, HONORS: Yaddo fellowship, 1940; Rockefeller Foundation grants, 1951, 1968.

WRITINGS:

PLAYS

"Martha Goodwin" (comedy; adapted from a story by Katherine Anne Porter), first produced in New Haven, Conn., at Yale University, 1942, revised version broadcast in 1959.

Too Many Thumbs (comedy; first produced in Minneapolis, Minn., at University of Minnesota, 1948; produced in New York at Cherry Lane Theatre, 1949; produced in London, 1951), University of Minnesota Press, 1949.

"The Ticklish Acrobat," produced Off Broadway, 1954, published in *Playbook: Five Plays for a New Theatre,* New Directions, 1956.

"The Assault upon Charles Sumner," produced in New York, 1964, published in *Plays for a New Theatre: Playbook 2,* New Directions, 1966.

"'I' 'Love' 'You'" (also see below), produced in New York, 1968, published in *Anon,* 1971.

"Love Reconciled to War," produced in Baltimore, Md., 1968, published in *Break Out! In Search of New Theatrical Environments,* edited by James Schevill, Swallow Press, 1973.

(Under pseudonyms Jack Askew and Osbert Pismire) "DMZ" (three plays; includes "Uptight Arms, How Much?," and "'I' 'Love' 'You'"), first produced in New York at DMZ Cafe, 1969.

"A Son Is Always Leaving Home," published in *Anon,* 1971.

OTHER

Also author of several radio plays. Contributor of poems to literary journals.

WORK IN PROGRESS: Plays; a comic novel; a novel set during World War II.

SIDELIGHTS: "There is no doubt, in my judgment," writes Richard Kostelanetz in *Contemporary Dramatists,* "that Robert Hivnor has written two of the best and most original American postwar dramas." Unfortunately, the critic continues, "our knowledge of them, as well as his reputation, must be based more upon print than performance." Hivnor's plays often pose considerable production problems (in costuming and set design, for example), and thus are rarely performed. While the playwright, whom Kostelanetz calls "a dark satirist who debunks myths and permits no heroes," has written works frequently classified as "absurdist," the critic believes that "unlike other protagonist-less playwrights, he is less interested in absurdity than comprehensive ridicule. . . . Hivnor feasts upon episodes and symbols of both personal and national failure."

BIOGRAPHICAL/CRITICAL SOURCES:

BOOKS

Contemporary Dramatists, St. James Press, 1988.

Esslen, Martin, *The Theatre of the Absurd,* Doubleday, 1961, revised edition, 1969.

Kostelanetz, Richard, *The New American Arts,* Horizon Press, 1965.

Weales, Gerald, *American Drama since World War II,* Harcourt, 1962.

PERIODICALS

New Leader, 1966.

Partisan Review, May, 1954.

Southern Review, summer, 1970.*

HOFFMAN, Paul   1934-1984

PERSONAL: Born September 27, 1934, in Chicago, Ill.; died March 26, 1984, in New York, N.Y., from injuries suffered in a fire at his apartment; son of William S. (a physician) and Miriam (Berliner) Hoffman; married Kathleen Scarlett, March 30, 1965 (deceased, 1978). *Education:* University of Chicago, A.B., 1957, A.M., 1958.

ADDRESSES: Home—205 West 10th St., New York, N.Y. 10014. *Agent*—Edward J. Acton, 17 Grove St., New York, N.Y. 10014.

CAREER: City News Bureau, Chicago, Ill., reporter, 1958-60; United Press International, Detroit, Mich., reporter, 1960-61; *Stars & Stripes,* New York City, reporter, 1962; *New York Post,* New York City, reporter, 1962-69; writer, 1969-84. *Military service:* U.S. Army Reserve, 1958-64, active duty, 1958-59.

WRITINGS:

Moratorium: An American Protest, Tower, 1970.

The New Nixon, Tower, 1970.

Spiro!, Tower, 1970.

Lions in the Street: The Inside Story of the Great Wall Street Law Firms, Saturday Review Press, 1973, updated edition published as *Lions of the Eighties: The Inside Story of the Powerhouse Law Firms,* Doubleday, 1982.

Tiger in the Court, Playboy Press, 1973.

What the Hell Is Justice?, Playboy Press, 1974.

To Drop a Dime, Putnam, 1976.

Courthouse, Hawthorn, 1979.

The Dealmakers: Inside the World of Investment Banking, Doubleday, 1984.

Contributor to magazines, including *Good Housekeeping, Nation,* and *Saturday Review,* and to New York City area newspapers.

SIDELIGHTS: Paul Hoffman, who as a reporter for the *New York Post* covered the court system and for a time worked as correspondent from the New York State capital in Albany, was also the author of nonfiction books that depicted New York's legal, financial, and corporate establishment. Among his best-known of such works are *Lions in the Street: The Inside Story of the Great Wall Street Law Firms,* and its updated edition, *Lions of the Eighties: The Inside Story of the Powerhouse Law Firms.* Both books profile the day-to-day activities of leading New York law firms, while highlighting the maneuverings of star lawyers and big-name corporate clients. Hank Greely in the *Los Angeles Times* praised *Lions of the Eighties,* calling the book "well-written in a smooth, fast-paced style without slighting the reassuring legal niceties." He added: "If tales of vast and hoary firms pursuing multi-billion-dollar cases—and grinding up millions of dollars of fees and scores of young lawyers in the process—intrigues you, this is your book." Hoffman's *The Dealmakers: Inside the World of Investment Banking,* published after the author's death in 1984, offers a glimpse into another bastion of New York establishment. Lincoln Caplan wrote in the *New York Times Book Review* that although the book will probably be most useful to readers who follow investment banking, since it provides "comment[s] in a blithe mix of news clips, social history and investment-banking stories without really instructing how or why these things happen," the reviewer also noted that "even novices may be charmed by the book's store of facts, some of which are telling."

BIOGRAPHICAL/CRITICAL SOURCES:

PERIODICALS

Los Angeles Times, July 19, 1982.
New York Times Book Review, July 8, 1973, May 27, 1979,
    September 5, 1982, September 16, 1984.
Washington Post, June 29, 1982.
Washington Post Book World, December 16, 1973.

OBITUARIES:

PERIODICALS

Chicago Tribune, March 29, 1984.
New York Times, March 28, 1984.*

*   *   *

HOFFMAN, Phyllis M(iriam)   1944-

PERSONAL: Born September 7, 1944, in Brooklyn, N.Y.; daughter of Morris and Bertha (Levine) Hoffman. *Education:* State University of New York at Binghamton, B.A. (magna cum laude), 1965; Bank Street College of Education, M.A., 1974.

ADDRESSES: Home and office—49 Eighth Ave., New York, N.Y. 10014.

CAREER: Harper & Row Publishers, Inc., New York City, children's book editor, 1966-70; Abelard-Schuman Ltd., New York City, children's book editor, 1970-72; Little Star of Broome Day Care Center, New York City, group teacher, 1975-77; Harcourt Brace Jovanovich, Inc., New York City, editor in reading department, 1978-82; Scholastic Book Services, New York City, senior editor, club and trade books, 1982-87; free-lance editor and writer, 1988—.

WRITINGS:

JUVENILES

Steffie and Me, Harper, 1970.
(Editor of German translation) Hans Christian Andersen, *The Ugly Duckling,* Abelard, 1972.
Happy Halloween, Atheneum, 1982.
Play Ball with the Yankees, Atheneum, 1983.
Baby's Day, Scholastic, Inc., 1985.
Baby's Kitchen, Scholastic, Inc., 1985.
The Robot Book, Scholastic, Inc., 1986.
The Train Book, Scholastic, Inc., 1986.
Baby's First Year, Harper, 1988.
We Play, Harper, 1989.

Also editor of *Peanut Butter* magazine.

WORK IN PROGRESS: Meatball!, for Harper, "about a little girl in a day care center, with other 3 and 4 year old children. This book came out of my own teaching experiences on the Lower East Side in Manhattan"; *Grandma Guthry,* "about my own mother and her relationship to her granddaughter, Rebecca, my niece. It is a family portrait, so to speak, and a homage to Grandmas everywhere!"

*   *   *

HOLENSTEIN, Elmar   1937-

PERSONAL: Born January 7, 1937, in St. Gallen, Switzerland; son of Adolf and Johanna (Fuerer) Holenstein; married Kae Ito (a psychologist), December 1, 1981. *Education:* Attended University of Louvain, Belgium, 1964-67, Ph.D., 1970;

graduate study at University of Heidelberg, 1967-69, and University of Zurich, 1969-71.

ADDRESSES: Home—Hustadtring 139, D 4630 Bochum, West Germany. *Office*—Institut fuer Philosophie, Ruhr-Universitaet, D 4630 Bochum, West Germany.

CAREER: Husserl Archives, Louvain, Belgium, scientific collaborator, 1971-73; University of Cologne, Cologne, Germany, scientific collaborator, 1975-77; University of Zurich, Zurich, Switzerland, lecturer, 1976-77; Ruhr-Universitaet, Bochum, West Germany, professor, 1977—. Visiting professor, University of Tokyo, 1986-87. Fellow, Japan Foundation, 1983-84.

MEMBER: Allgemeine Gesellschaft fuer Philosophie in Deutschland, Deutsche Gesellschaft fuer Phaenomenologische Forschung, Deutsche Gesellschaft fuer Semiotik.

AWARDS, HONORS: Bourse Burrus, Swiss National Foundation for Scientific Research, 1974.

WRITINGS:

Phaenomenologie der Assoziation (title means "Phenomenology of Association"), Nijhoff (The Hague), 1972.
Roman Jakobsons phaenomenologischer Strukturalismus, Suhrkamp (Frankfurt), 1975, translation by Catherine Schelbert and Tarcisius Schelbert published as *Roman Jakobson's Approach to Language,* Indiana University Press, 1976.
(Editor) *Edmund Husserl: Logische Untersuchungen I* (title means "Logical Investigations I"), Nijhoff, 1975.
(Editor) *Roman Jakobson: Hoelderlin-Klee-Brecht,* Suhrkamp, 1976.
Linguistik, Semiotik, Hermeneutik, Suhrkamp, 1976.
(Editor with T. Schelbert) *Roman Jakobson: Poetik,* Suhrkamp, 1979.
Von der Hintergehbarkeit der Sprache, Suhrkamp, 1980.
(With Roman Jakobson and Hans-Georg Gadamer) *Das Erbe Hegels II* (title means "Hegel's Heritage II"), Suhrkamp, 1984.
Menschliches Selbstverstaendnis (title means "Human Self-Understanding"), Suhrkamp, 1985.
Sprachliche Universalien (title means "Universals of Language"), Brockmeyer (Bochum), 1985.
(Editor) Jakobson, *Semiotik,* Suhrkamp, 1988.

WORK IN PROGRESS: Research in philosophy of language (universals) and in philosophy of mind (relationship between mind and body and between knowledge and language).

*   *   *

HOLSTI, Ole R(udolf)   1933-

PERSONAL: Born August 7, 1933, in Geneva, Switzerland; became American citizen, 1954; son of Rudolf W. (a diplomat) and Liisa (Franssila) Holsti; married Ann Wood, September 20, 1953; children: Eric Lynn, Maija. *Education:* Stanford University, B.A., 1954, Ph.D., 1962; Wesleyan University, Middletown, Conn., M.A.T., 1956.

ADDRESSES: Home—608 Croom Ct., Chapel Hill, N.C. 27514. *Office*—Department of Political Science, Duke University, Durham, N.C. 27706.

CAREER: Stanford University, Stanford, Calif., instructor, 1962-63, acting assistant professor, 1963-65, assistant professor of political science, 1965-67, research coordinator and associate director of Studies in International Conflict and Integration, 1962-67; University of British Columbia, Vancouver, associate professor, 1967-71, professor of political science, 1971-74; Duke University, Durham, N.C., George V. Allen Professor of Political Science, 1974—, chairman of department, 1978-83; University of California, Davis, professor of political science, 1978-79. National Science Foundation, chairman of oversight committee, 1981-84. Member of advisory committee on historical diplomatic documentation, U.S. Department of State, 1983-86. Member of advisory board, University Press of America, 1976—. *Military service:* U.S. Army, 1956-58. U.S. Army Reserve, 1954-56, 1958-62; became staff sergeant.

MEMBER: International Institute of Strategic Studies (London), Peace Science Society (southern section president, 1975-77), International Studies Association (western secretary-treasurer, 1967-68, 1968-69; president, 1969-70; southern president, 1975-76; president, 1979-80; member of communications committee, 1988—), American Political Science Association (council member, 1982-85), Western Political Science Association (executive council member, 1971-74), Inter-university Consortium for Political Research, Fleet Feet Running Club, Carolina Godiva Track Club, North Carolina Road Runners, Duke Master Runners, Phi Beta Kappa.

AWARDS, HONORS: Owen D. Young Fellowship, General Electric Foundation, 1960-61; research fellowship, Haynes Foundation, 1961-62; Canada Council, research grant, 1969, leave fellowship, 1970-71; fellowship, Center for Advanced Study in the Behavioral Sciences, 1972-73; faculty research fellowship, Ford Foundation, 1972-73; research grants, National Science Foundation, 1975-77, 1979-81, 1983-85, 1988-90; Best Published Paper award, *International Studies Quarterly,* 1979-81, for "The Three Headed Eagle"; Guggenheim fellowship, 1981-82; runner of the year award, Carolina Godiva Track Club, 1987; Neritt Sanford Award, International Society for Political Psychology, 1988, for professional contributions to political psychology.

WRITINGS:

(With Robert C. North, M. George Zaninovich, and Dina A. Zinnes) *Content Analysis: A Handbook with Application for the Study of International Crisis,* Northwestern University Press, 1963.

(With David J. Findlay and Richard R. Fagen) *Enemies in Politics,* Rand McNally, 1967.

Content Analysis for the Social Sciences and Humanities, Addison-Wesley, 1969.

(With George Gerbner, Klaus Krippendorff, Philip J. Stone and William Paisley) *The Analysis of Communication Content: Developments in Scientific Theories and Computer Techniques,* Wiley, 1969.

Crisis, Escalation, War, McGill-Queens University Press, 1972.

(With Terrence Hopmann and John D. Sullivan) *Unity and Disintegration in International Alliances,* Wiley, 1973.

(With James N. Rosenau) *Vietnam, Consensus, and the Belief Systems of American Leaders,* Institute for Transnational Studies, University of Southern California, 1977.

(Editor with Alexander L. George and Randolph M. Siverson, and contributor with Rosenau) *Change in the International System,* Westview, 1980.

The Three-Headed Eagle: Who Are the Cold War Internationalists, Post-Cold War Internationalists, and Isolationists?, Duke University, 1981.

(With Rosenau) *American Leadership in World Affairs: The Breakdown of Consensus,* Allen & Unwin, 1984.

CONTRIBUTOR

The Grand Design, University of Southern California Press, 1964.

Davis B. Bobrow, editor, *Components of Defence Policy,* Rand McNally, 1965.

Computers for the Humanities, Yale University Press, 1965.

Elton B. McNeil, editor, *The Nature of Human Conflict,* Prentice-Hall, 1965.

Stone, editor, *The General Inquirer: A Computer Approach to Content Analysis in the Behavioral Sciences,* MIT Press, 1966.

(With North) Richard Merritt and Stein Rokkan, editors, *Comparing Nations,* Yale University Press, 1966.

John C. Farrell and Asa P. Smith, editors, *Image and Reality in World Politics,* Columbia University Press, 1967.

Edmund A. Bowles, editor, *Computers in Humanistic Research,* Prentice-Hall, 1967.

K. J. Holsti, *International Politics: A Framework for Analysis,* Prentice-Hall, 1967, 4th edition, 1982.

(With North and Richard A. Brody) J. David Singer, editor, *Quantitative International Politics: Insights and Evidence,* Free Press, 1967.

Peter Toma and Andrew Gyorgy, editors, *Basic Issues in International Relations,* Allyn & Bacon, 1967.

John H. Bunzel, editor, *Issues of American Public Policy,* Prentice-Hall, 2nd edition, 1968.

Louis Kriesberg, editor, *Social Process in International Relations,* Wiley, 1968.

Bobrow and Judah L. Schwartz, editors, *Computers and the Policy Making Communities,* Prentice-Hall, 1968.

Gardner Lindzey and Elliot Aronson, editors, *The Handbook of Social Psychology,* Addison-Wesley, 2nd edition, 1968.

Charles F. Hermann, editor, *Foreign Policy Crisis: A Simulation Analysis,* Bobbs-Merrill, 1969.

John E. Mueller, editor, *Approaches to Measurement in International Relations,* Appleton-Century-Crofts, 1969.

Richard C. Snyder and Dean Pruitt, editors, *Theory and Research on the Causes of War,* Prentice-Hall, 1969.

Jan F. Triska, editor, *Communist Party-States: International and Comparative Studies,* Bobbs-Merrill, 1969.

The World Communist System: International and Comparative Studies, Bobbs-Merrill, 1969.

Rosenau, editor, *International Politics and Foreign Policy,* Free Press, 2nd edition, 1969.

Rosenau, editor, *Linkage Politics: Essays on the Convergence of National and International Systems,* Free Press, 1969.

Naomi Rosenbaum, editor, *Readings in International Political Behavior,* Prentice-Hall, 1970.

George Cole, John H. Kessel, and Robert G. Seddig, editors, *Micropolitics,* Holt, 1970.

Leroy Graymer, editor, *Systems and Actors in International Politics,* Chandler & Sharp, 1971.

William D. Coplin and Charles W. Kegley, editors, *A Multi-Method Introduction to International Politics,* Markham, 1971.

Samuel A. Kirkpatrick and Lawrence K. Pettit, editors, *The Social Psychology of Political Life,* Duxbury, 1972.

Ivo D. Duchacek, editor, *Discord and Harmony,* Holt, 1972.

Hermann, editor, *International Crises: Insights from Behavioral Research,* Free Press, 1972.

Cornelius P. Cotter, editor, *Political Science Annual,* Volume VI, Bobbs-Merrill, 1975.

William D. Coplin and Charles W. Kegley, editors, *Analyzing International Relations*, Praeger, 1975.

William C. Vocke, editor, *American Foreign Policy: An Analytical Approach*, Free Press, 1976.

Robert Axelrod, editor, *The Structure of Decision*, Princeton University Press, 1976.

I. William Zartman, editor, *The 50% Solution: How to Bargain Successfully with Hijackers, Strikers, Bosses, Oil Magnates, Arabs, Russians, and Other Worthy Opponents in This Modern World*, Anchor Books, 1976.

Rosenau, editor, *In Search of Global Patterns*, Free Press, 1976.

Rosenau, Kenneth Thompson, and Gavin Boyd, editors, *World Politics*, Free Press, 1976.

(With North and Nazli Choucri) Francis W. Hoole and Zinnes, editors, *Quantitative International Politics: An Appraisal*, Praeger, 1976.

Donald Freeman, editor, *Political Science: History, Scope and Methods*, Free Press, 1977.

G. Matthew Bonham and Michael J. Shapiro, editors, *Thought and Action in Foreign Policy*, Birkhauser Verlag, 1977.

Daniel Heradstveit and Ove Narvasen, editors, *Decision-Making Research: Some Recent Developments*, Norwegian Institute of International Affairs, 1977.

C. F. Smart and W. T. Stanbury, editors, *Studies on Crisis Management*, Butterworths, 1978.

David W. Orr and Marvin Soroos, editor, *The Global Predicament: Ecological Perspectives on World Order*, University of North Carolina Press, 1979.

G. W. Keeton and C. Schwarzenberger, editors, *The Year Book of World Affairs*, London Institute of World Affairs, 1979.

Paul Gordon Lauren, editor, *Diplomacy: New Approaches in History, Theory, and Policy*, Free Press, 1979.

Charles W. Kegley, Jr., and Patrick T. McGowan, editors, *Challenges to America: United States Foreign Policy in the 1980s*, Sage Publications, 1979.

Richard A. Falk and Samuel S. Kim, editors, *The War System: An Interdisciplinary Approach*, Westview, 1980.

Rosenau, *The Study of Political Adaptation*, Frances Pinter Publishers, 1981.

Ellen Boneparth, editor, *Women, Power, and Policy*, Pergamon, 1982.

Crister Jonsson, editor, *Cognitive Dynamics and International Politics*, Pinter, 1982.

Kegley and E. R. Wittkopf, editors, *The Sources of American Foreign Policy*, St. Martin's, 1983.

Robert O. Matthews, Arthur G. Ribinoff, and Janice Gross Stein, editors, *International Conflict and Conflict Management*, Prentice-Hall, 1984.

Melvin Small and J. David Singer, editors, *International War*, Dorsey, 1985.

John A. Vasquez, editor, *Classics of International Relations*, Prentice-Hall, 1986.

Terry Deibel and John Lewis Gaddis, editors, *Containment: Concept and Policy*, Washington National Defense University Press, 1986, revised edition, Pergamon, 1987.

Ralph K. White, editor, *Psychology and the Prevention of Nuclear War*, New York University Press, 1986.

James M. McCormick, editor, *A Reader in American Foreign Policy*, F. E. Peacock, 1986.

Paul Viotti and Mark V. Kauppi, editors, *International Relations Theory*, Macmillan, 1987.

Kinhide Mushakoji and Hisakuzu, editors, *Theoretical Frameworks in the Contemporary World in Transition*, Yu Shindo Kobunsha Publishers, 1987.

Jong Youl Yoo, editor, *World Encyclopedia of Peace*, Pergamon, 1987.

OTHER

Also author, with Rosenau, of *Does Where You Stand Depend on When You Were Born? The Impact of Generation on Post-Vietnam Foreign Policy Beliefs*, 1978. Contributor to "Peace Research Society Papers," 1964-65; contributor of articles and reviews to professional journals. Associate editor, *Journal of Conflict Resolution*, 1969-72, *International Studies Quarterly*, 1970-75, and *Western Political Quarterly*, 1970-79. Member of board of editors, *International Studies Quarterly*, 1967-70, 1975-80, and 1985—, *Computer Studies in the Humanities and Verbal Behavior*, 1968-76, *American Journal of Political Science*, 1975-80, and *International Interaction*, 1980—. Corresponding editor, *Running Journal*, 1985—; correspondent, *Racing South*.

WORK IN PROGRESS: Articles on crisis decision-making, and models of international relations and foreign policy; a book on the domestic and foreign policy attitudes of American leaders.

*   *   *

HOLT, Victoria
    See HIBBERT, Eleanor Burford

*   *   *

HOMANS, Peter   1930-

PERSONAL: Born June 24, 1930, in New York, N.Y.; married Celia Ann Edwards (an associate director, National Opinion Research Center); children: Jennifer, Patricia, Elizabeth. *Education:* Princeton University, A.B., 1952; Protestant Episcopal Theological Seminary, B.D., 1957; University of Chicago, M.A., 1962, Ph.D., 1964.

ADDRESSES: Office—1025 East 58th St., University of Chicago, Chicago, Ill. 60637.

CAREER: Institute for Juvenile Research, Chicago, Ill., supervisor of residential treatment for children, 1961-62; University of Toronto, Trinity College, Toronto, Ontario, instructor in department of religion, 1962-64; Hartford Seminary Foundation, Hartford, Conn., assistant professor of theology and psychology, 1964-65; University of Chicago, Divinity School, Chicago, associate professor, 1965-78, professor of religion and psychological studies, 1978—, and professor of social sciences in the college.

MEMBER: American Psychological Association, American Historical Association.

WRITINGS:

(Editor) *The Dialogue between Theology and Psychology*, University of Chicago Press, 1968.

Theology after Freud: An Interpretive Inquiry, Bobbs-Merrill, 1970.

(Editor and contributor) *Childhood and Selfhood: Essays on Tradition, Religion and Modernity in the Thought of Erik H. Erikson*, Bucknell University Press, 1978.

Jung in Context: Modernity and the Making of a Psychology, University of Chicago Press, 1979.

The Ability to Mourn: The Social Origins of the Psychoanalytic Movement, University of Chicago Press, 1989.

WORK IN PROGRESS: A book on the psychological and social meanings embedded in film experiences.

SIDELIGHTS: Peter Homans told *CA:* "Through all my writing I seek to realize a single desire: to understand and describe how the inner, psychological experiences which all persons have, although these vary and change throughout life, relate to the social forms and forces which surround and shape these experiences. Therefore, I have always felt free—and also obliged—to range around a lot and have written about 'Westerns,' religious ideas, TV shows like 'M.A.S.H.,' and even on psychological movements and their founders, because this 'outer,' social world shapes the 'inner' world of the contemporary person. But how does it do that?"

Jung in Context has been translated into Italian and Japanese.

*   *   *

HOPKINS, Raymond F(rederick)   1939-

PERSONAL: Born February 15, 1939, in Cleveland, Ohio; son of William Edward (in advertising) and Ada Elizabeth (Cornwall) Hopkins; married Carol Lynnette Robinson (a computer programmer), June 5, 1962; children: Mark Raymond, Kathryn Carol. *Education:* Ohio Wesleyan University, B.A., 1960; attended Yale Divinity School, New Haven, 1960-61; Ohio State University, M.A., 1963; Yale University, M.A., 1965, Ph.D., 1968. *Politics:* Democrat. *Religion:* Presbyterian.

ADDRESSES: Home—308 Ogden Ave., Swarthmore, Pa. 19081. *Office*—Department of Political Science, Swarthmore College, Swarthmore, Pa. 19081.

CAREER: Assistant pastor of Methodist church, 1960-61; University College, Dar es Salaam, Tanganyika (now part of Tanzania), research associate, 1965-66; Swarthmore College, Swarthmore, Pa., instructor, 1967-68, assistant professor, 1968-73, associate professor, 1973-78, professor of political science, 1978—, acting chairman of department, 1983-84. Visiting scholar at University of Michigan, 1968; research associate at Center for International Affairs, Harvard University, summer, 1969, Indiana University and University of Nairobi, 1970-71; visiting scholar, Food Policy Research Institute, Stanford University, 1982-83; visiting fellow, International Food Policy Research Institute, Washington, D.C., 1984. Consultant to food policy and research organizations and governments in the United States and abroad.

MEMBER: American Political Science Association, African Studies Association, International Studies Association, American Association of University Professors (president, Swarthmore chapter, 1971-72), Inter-University Consortium for Political Research, Phi Beta Kappa.

AWARDS, HONORS: Social Science Research Council fellow, 1969-70; American Philosophical Society grant at University of Nairobi, 1970-71; National Endowment for the Humanities fellow, 1973; Guggenheim fellow, 1974-75; Woodrow Wilson International Center fellow, 1975; Rockefeller foundation fellow, 1979; Mellon faculty fellow, 1982; Heinz endowment recipient, 1982; Yale International Relations grant.

WRITINGS:

Political Roles in a New State: Tanzania's First Decade, Yale University Press, 1971.
(With Richard W. Mansbach) *Structure and Process in International Politics,* Harper, 1973.

(Editor with Donald J. Puchala) *The Global Political Economy of Food,* University of Wisconsin Press, 1978.
(Editor with Puchala and and Ross B. Talbot) *Food, Politics, and Agricultural Development: Case Studies in the Public Policy of Rural Modernization,* Westview Press, 1979.
(With Puchala) *Global Food Interdependence: Challenge to United States Policy,* Columbia University Press, 1980.
(Editor and contributor with others) *Food in the Global Arena: Actors, Values, Policies and Futures,* Holt, 1982.

Contributor to anthologies on political science. Contributor to *Social Forces, World Politics,* and other journals.*

*   *   *

HORNIK, Edith Lynn
See BEER, Edith Lynn

*   *   *

HORNIK-BEER, Edith Lynn
See BEER, Edith Lynn

*   *   *

HOURS, Madeleine   1915-
(Madeleine Hours-Miedan, Magdeleine Hours-Miedan)

PERSONAL: Sometimes indexed in biographical sources under surname Hours-Miedan, with given name listed as Magdeleine; born August 5, 1915, in Paris, France; daughter of Lucien (an exporter) and Suzanne (Ricard) Miedan; married Jacques Hours, January 10, 1935 (separated, 1965); children: Antoine, Emmanuel, Laurent. *Education:* Ecole du Louvre, Diploma, 1942; attended Ecole des Hautes Etudes d'Histoire et de Philologie, Sorbonne. *Religion:* Roman Catholic.

ADDRESSES: Home—10 bis rue du Pre-aux-Clercs, 75007 Paris, France. *Office*—Musee du Louvre, Paris, France.

CAREER: Louvre, Paris, France, member of staff, scientific laboratory, 1936-40, member of staff in department of Oriental archaeology, 1940-44, director of research laboratory, 1946—; National Museums of France, curator, 1959-72, curator-in-chief, 1972—, inspector general, 1980. Head of research, Centre National de la Recherche Scientifique (National Center of Scientific Research), 1966—; producer of regular television program, "Les Secrets des chefs-d'oeuvre" ("The Secrets of Masterpieces"), O.R.T.F., 1959-72; lecturer. Member of field trip to Africa to study monuments from the cult of Tophet of Salamba, Carthage, 1945-47.

MEMBER: Societe des Gens de Lettres, International Council of Museums, Racolta Vinciana (Milan, Italy), European Council of Universities, PACT.

AWARDS, HONORS: Chevalier of Legion of Honor, 1959, Officier, 1972; Commandeur of Arts and Letters; Silver Medal for Research, 1969; Commandeur du Merite National, 1974; International Institute of Conservators (fellow).

WRITINGS:

Carthage, Presses universitaires de France, 1949, 2nd edition, 1959.
A la decouverte de la peinture par les methodes physiques, Arts et metiers graphiques, 1957.
Etude photographique et radiographique de quelques tableux de Nicolas Poussin, Editions des musees nationaux, 1961.

Les Secrets des chefs-d'oeuvre, R. Laffont, 1964, new edition, 1988, translation published as *Secrets of the Great Masters: A Study in Artistic Techniques*, Putnam, 1968.
Analyse et Conservation des Peintures, [Fribourg], 1968.
Jean-Baptiste-Camille Corot, Abrams, 1972, reprinted as *Corot*, 1987.
L'Analyse par microflourescence x apliquee a l'archaeologie, Conseil de L'Europe, 1977.
Musee du Bardo, Unesco (Paris), 1979.
Un Vie au Louvre, R. Laffont (Paris), 1987.

Author of television scripts, ''Les Secrets des chefs-d'oeuvre,'' and ''Tresors de la ville.'' Contributor to periodicals in various countries. Editor, *Annales du Laboratoire de Recherche des Musees de France*, 1959—.

WORK IN PROGRESS: More research on scientific analysis, especially on radiography.

SIDELIGHTS: Madeleine Hours, also known as Magdeleine Hours-Miedan, is well-known for applying scientific methods of study to the masterpieces left to us by Leonardo da Vinci, Rembrandt, and Titian, among many others. Director of the Research Laboratory at the Louvre Museum and curator-in-chief of the National Museums of France, she was one of the first to use X-ray photography to detect features in famous paintings that are hidden from the unaided eye. With the help of X-rays, for instance, she found that da Vinci's *Mona Lisa* is painted on wood instead of canvas, and that he added figures to paintings by his teacher, Andrea del Verrocchio. Rembrandt, she discovered, was apparently not pleased with the head in his painting *Bathsheba*, and had covered it with a second one in a slightly altered position. Hours shares numerous discoveries such as these with viewers of the monthly television show ''Les secrets of des chefs-d'oeuvres'' (title means ''The Secrets of Great Masterpieces''), broadcast from Paris. Her books, which explain the application of science to the understanding and appreciation of fine art, have been translated into English and German. Mme. Hours once told *CA* that the scientific study of works of art transcends both art history and scientific expertise, for it reveals the intimate relationship between the material and the process of creation.

BIOGRAPHICAL/CRITICAL SOURCES:

PERIODICALS

Christian Science Monitor, November 29, 1968.
France-Illustration, December 1, 1950.
New Yorker, December 21, 1968.*

*   *   *

HOURS-MIEDAN, Madeleine
See HOURS, Madeleine

*   *   *

HOURS-MIEDAN, Magdeleine
See HOURS, Madeleine

*   *   *

HUGHES, Erica   1931-

PERSONAL: Born February 21, 1931, in London, England; daughter of Frederick Noel (a journalist) and Nancie (a dancer; maiden name, Hill) Brace; married Peter Hughes (an actor), August 14, 1958; children: Simon Peter, Bettany Mary. *Ed-*

ucation: Attended Royal Academy of Music, 1950-53. *Religion:* Church of England.

ADDRESSES: Home—21 Madeley Rd., Ealing, London W.5, England.

CAREER: Professional actress, 1954-65; writer.

WRITINGS:

(With Peter Watkins) *Here's the Church*, Julia MacRae Books, 1980.
(With Watkins) *Here's the Year* (juvenile), illustrated by Gill Tomblin, Julia MacRae Books, 1982.
(With Watkins) *A Book of Prayer*, Julia MacRae Books, 1982.
(With Watkins) *Here Are the People*, Julia MacRae Books, 1984.
(With Watkins) *A Book of Animals*, Julia MacRae Books, 1985.
(With Watkins) *The Good Samaritan and Other Stories*, Julia MacRae Books, 1987.
(With Watkins) *A Book of Birds*, Julia MacRae Books, in press.

*   *   *

HUNTER, Joe
See McNEILLY, Wilfred (Glassford)

*   *   *

HUNTER, Valancy
See MEAKER, Eloise

*   *   *

HUXLEY, Elspeth (Josceline Grant)   1907-

PERSONAL: Born July 23, 1907, in London, England; daughter of Major Josceline and Eleanor Lillian (Grosvenor) Grant; married Gervas Huxley (a tea commissioner), December 12, 1931 (died, 1971); children: Charles. *Education:* Reading University, Diploma in Agriculture, 1927; attended Cornell University, 1927-28. *Politics:* ''Variable, mainly disillusioned.'' *Religion:* ''Vague.''

ADDRESSES: Home—Green End, Oaksey, Malmesbury, Wiltshire SN16 9TL, England. *Agent*—London Management, 235 Regent St., London W1A 2JT, England.

CAREER: Author and broadcaster. Assistant press officer, Empire Marketing Board, London, England, 1929-32; member of general advisory council, British Broadcasting Corp. (BBC), 1952-59. Member, Monckton Advisory Commission on Central Africa, 1959-60. Justice of the peace for Wiltshire, 1946-77.

MEMBER: National Trust (conservationist organization), Royal Society for Protection of Birds, World Wildlife Fund, Council for the Protection of Rural England, Fauna and Flora Preservation Society, Rhino Rescue, The Woodland Trust, Wiltshire Trust for Nature Conservation, London Library.

AWARDS, HONORS: Companion of the British Empire, 1960.

WRITINGS:

NOVELS

Murder at Government House, Harper, 1937, reprinted, Viking/Penguin, 1988.

Murder on Safari, Harper, 1938, reprinted, Perennial Library, 1982.

Red Strangers, Harper, 1939.

Death of an Aryan, Methuen, 1939, published as *The African Poison Murders*, Harper, 1940, reprinted, Viking, 1988.

The Walled City, Lippincott, 1948.

I Don't Mind If I Do, Chatto & Windus, 1951.

A Thing to Love, Chatto & Windus, 1954.

The Red Rock Wilderness, Morrow, 1957.

The Flame Trees of Thika: Memories of an African Childhood (autobiographical fiction; first book in trilogy), Morrow, 1959, reprinted, Penguin, 1974, illustrated edition, Chatto & Windus, 1987.

On the Edge of the Rift (autobiographical fiction; second book in trilogy), Morrow, 1962, reprinted, Penguin, 1982 (published in England as *The Mottled Lizard*, Chatto & Windus, 1962).

The Merry Hippo, Chatto & Windus, 1963, published as *The Incident at the Merry Hippo*, Morrow, 1964.

A Man from Nowhere, Chatto & Windus, 1964, Morrow, 1965.

Love among the Daughters: Memories of the Twenties in England and America (autobiographical fiction; third book in trilogy), Morrow, 1968.

The Prince Buys the Manor: An Extravaganza, Chatto & Windus, 1982.

Last Days in Eden, Harvill, 1984.

NONFICTION

White Man's Country: Lord Delamere and the Making of Kenya, two volumes, Macmillan, 1935, 2nd edition, Chatto & Windus, 1953, Praeger, 1967, reprinted with new preface, Chatto & Windus, 1968.

Atlantic Ordeal: The Story of Mary Cornish, Chatto & Windus, 1941, Harper, 1942.

(With Margery Perham) *Race and Politics in Kenya: A Correspondence between Elspeth Huxley and Margery Perham*, introduction by Lord Lugard, Faber, 1944, revised edition, 1956, reprinted, Greenwood, 1975.

Settlers of Kenya, Longmans, Green, 1948, reprinted, Greenwood, 1975.

The Sorcerer's Apprentice: A Journey through East Africa, Chatto & Windus, 1954, reprinted, Greenwood, 1975.

Four Guineas: A Journey through West Africa, Chatto & Windus, 1954, reprinted, Greenwood, 1974.

No Easy Way, [Nairobi], 1957.

A New Earth, Morrow, 1960.

Suki, Morrow, 1964.

With Forks and Hope, Morrow, 1964 (published in England as *Forks and Hope*, Chatto & Windus, 1964).

Back Street New Worlds: A Look at Immigrants in Britain, Chatto & Windus, 1964, Morrow, 1965.

Brave New Victuals: An Inquiry into Modern Food Production, Chatto & Windus, 1965.

Their Shining El Dorado: A Journey through Australia, Morrow, 1967.

The Challenge of Africa, Aldus, 1971.

(Editor and compiler) *The Kingsleys: A Biographical Anthology*, Allen & Unwin, 1973.

Livingstone and His African Journeys, Saturday Review Press, 1974.

Florence Nightingale, Putnam, 1975.

Gallipot Eyes: A Wiltshire Diary, Weidenfeld & Nicolson, 1976.

Scott of the Antarctic, Weidenfeld & Nicolson, 1977, Atheneum, 1978.

(Editor with Arnold Curtis) *Pioneers' Scrapbook: Reminiscences of Kenya, 1890-1968*, foreword by Princess Alice, Duchess of Glouchester, Evans Brothers, 1980.

(Author of introduction) Isak Dineson, *Out of Africa*, Folio Society, 1980.

(Editor) Nellie Grant, *Nellie: Letters from Africa*, Weidenfeld & Nicolson, 1980, new edition, 1984, published as *Nellie's Story: With a Memoir by Her Daughter Elspeth Huxley*, Morrow, 1981.

Whipsnade: Captive Breeding for Survival, Collins, 1981.

Out in the Midday Sun: My Kenya, Chatto & Windus, 1985, Viking, 1988.

WORK IN PROGRESS: An anthology of writings about Kenya, covering the years 100-1988 A.D., tentatively titled "Seven Faces of Kenya."

SIDELIGHTS: Travel has always been a major part of Elspeth Huxley's life. At the age of five she moved with her family to Kenya, where her father had started a coffee plantation about forty miles from Nairobi. She spent most of her childhood and adolescence in Africa, although she returned to England during World War I to attend school. Upon receiving her degree from Reading University in 1927, she went to the United States for a year. After her marriage, she continued traveling with her husband, whose work in tea sales promotion took them all over the globe. In 1939 they bought a farm in Wiltshire, England, and, after World War II, settled down to produce milk, pigs, and roses.

Because she grew up in Africa, Huxley made this the setting of most of her work. Her most widely appreciated work is her semi-autobiographical trilogy. The first two volumes, *The Flame Trees of Thika* and *On the Edge of the Rift*, each of which concerns her childhood in Kenya, were bestsellers. With the third volume, *Love among the Daughters: Memories of the Twenties in England and America*, she abandoned Africa as a subject and focused her skills on recapturing the spirit of her student days both at Reading in England and Cornell in the United States. Anne Freemantle reviewed *Love among the Daughters* in the *New York Times Book Review*. She writes: "With the clarity of thought of a brilliant and witty mind scientifically trained, Elspeth Huxley expresses herself in scalpel-precise language." And Peggy Shonbrun, in *Book World*, likens the volume to "the accounts of the several Mitfords" about their youth in England, and concludes that Huxley's "eye for the patterns of English country manners and morals is so sharp and her writing so pleasant that a more deserved comparison might be with Jane Austen."

In *Out in the Midday Sun: My Kenya*, Huxley returns to the subject of the first two novels of her trilogy. With this book she tidies "up the loose ends of her own story, fills in the gaps, and sketches in her own intermittent but intense involvement with East Africa and the gifted, often eccentric men and women who made their lives in colonial Kenya," according to *Washington Post Book World* reviewer Brigitte Weeks. And although some critics like Robert Baldock of the *Times Literary Supplement* have found this book to be somewhat disorganized and, therefore, not on a par with her earlier stories of Kenya, *Out in the Midday Sun* completes the author's lifelong dedication to writing about this country. As *New York Times* contributor Michiko Kakutani puts it: "It makes us appreciate the peculiar mixture of courage, rashness, perseverance, idealism, and opportunism that brought such a varied group of people to this beautiful, dangerous land."

BIOGRAPHICAL/CRITICAL SOURCES:

BOOKS

Dictionary of Literary Biography, Volume 77: *British Mystery Writers, 1920-1939,* Gale, 1989.

PERIODICALS

Atlantic, July, 1967.
Book World, November 3, 1968.
Nature, August 3, 1935.
New York Times, March 18, 1987.
New York Times Book Review, September 22, 1968.
Observer, May 21, 1967, September 29, 1969.
Punch, July 19, 1967, October 9, 1968.
Times Literary Supplement, December 2, 1965, May 25, 1967, January 31, 1987.
Washington Post Book World, March 22, 1987.

*   *   *

HYMAN, Jackie (Diamond)   1949-
(Jacqueline Diamond; pseudonyms: Jacqueline Jade, Jacqueline Topaz)

PERSONAL: Born April 3, 1949, in Menard, Tex.; daughter of Maurice S. (a psychiatrist) and Sylvia (a ceramist; maiden name, Risman) Hyman; married Kurt L. Wilson (a realtor), October 8, 1978; children: Ari Mark Wilson. *Education:* Received B.A. from Brandeis University.

ADDRESSES: Office—316 West Erna Ave., La Habra, Calif. 90631. *Agent*—Jane Jordan Browne, Multimedia Product Development, Inc., 410 South Michigan Ave., Room 724, Chicago, Ill. 60605.

CAREER: Writer. Gloria Zignor & Associates (public relations firm), Newport Beach, Calif., copywriter, 1973-74; *Orange Coast Daily Pilot,* Costa Mesa, Calif., staff writer, 1974-80; Associated Press, Los Angeles, Calif., staff writer, 1980-84.

MEMBER: American Society of Composers, Authors and Publishers, American Theatre Critics Association, Fictionaires, Romance Writers of America, Mystery Writers of America, Science Fiction Writers of America.

AWARDS, HONORS: Franklin Giddon Award in Playwriting from Brandeis University, 1970; Thomas Watson Foundation fellowship for Europe, 1971; Bronze Medallion, Romance Writers of America, 1985, for *The Forgetful Lady;* finalist for Golden Medallion, Romance Writers of America, 1985, for *Swept Away.*

WRITINGS:

The Eyes of a Stranger (suspense novel), St. Martin's Press, 1987.

UNDER NAME JACQUELINE DIAMOND

Lady in Disguise, Walker & Co., 1982.
Song for a Lady, Walker & Co., 1983.
A Lady of Letters, Walker & Co., 1983.
The Dream Never Dies, Harlequin, 1984.
The Forgetful Lady, Walker & Co., 1985.
The Day-Dreaming Lady, Walker & Co., 1985.
An Unexpected Man, Harlequin American, 1987.
Unlikely Partners, Harlequin American, 1987.
The Cinderella Dare, Harlequin American, 1988.

Capers and Rainbows (working title), Harlequin American, 1988.

UNDER PSEUDONYM JACQUELINE TOPAZ

Deeper Than Desire, To Have and To Hold, 1984.
Swept Away, Second Chance at Love, 1985.
Rites of Passion, Second Chance at Love, 1985.
Lucky in Love, Second Chance at Love, 1985.
Golden Girl, Second Chance at Love, 1986.
A Warm December, Second Chance at Love, 1988.

OTHER

(Under name Jacqueline Diamond) "Fantasies" (three-act play), first produced in Irvine, Calif., at Irvine Harvest Festival, September, 1977.
(Under name Jacqueline Diamond) "The Song of the Unicorn" (three-act play), first produced in Garden Grove, Calif., at Garden Grove Youth Musical Theatre, July, 1978.
(Under pseudonym Jacqueline Jade) *A Lucky Star* (novel), Silhouette Desire, 1986.

Also ghostwriter for *Kiss and Make Up,* for "Seniors" series of young adult books.

WORK IN PROGRESS: A horror-suspense novel.

SIDELIGHTS: "When I was in high school," Jackie Hyman commented to *CA,* "a psychologist came to administer a creativity test to us, which I enjoyed, although I expected him to decide I was nuts. For example, one of the challenges was to take an imaginary teddy bear and think of as many uses as possible for it; we were allowed to make it bigger, stronger, and so on.

"I came up with the usual stuff—making a hand puppet out of it, using it as a backrest. Then I suggested a few other more or less normal things, like sticking it on the end of a broom and using it to clean the toilet. Finally I said, 'Well, if you're going to make it bigger and stronger and everything, why not turn it into a ham and eat it?'

"A few months later, I met that psychologist by chance through my father, who was a psychiatrist. He remembered me. He said that what was most unusual about my test was that my answers were almost equally divided between the conventional and the unconventional.

"In a way, that's how my life has been, and my writing. On the one hand, I've never been very unconventional. I never worked as a lumberjack. I was never a go-go girl in a gay bathhouse. I went to high school and college, worked at a newspaper, got married, and finally, at the age of thirty-three, had my first book published.

"But somewhere on my trail through Nashville, where I grew up, I learned fluent French, and came out of Brandeis with a somewhat eclectic repertoire, ranging from fluent Italian to papers on the sociology of Nazi Germany to reams of poetry, written and improved under the influence of Howard Nemerov. I also wrote some pretty terrible plays, which got a little better with the help of William Gibson, who wrote 'The Miracle Worker.'

"Off I went to Europe for a year. I worked on an awful play about Lorenzo de Medici and a bizarre book about a girl who was raised by a banshee and fell in love with a knight from the court of King Arthur. It's been through three rewrites and someday may get published.

"I bumbled into Southern California because my brother offered me a free place to live, fell tail-first into a job in public relations, and fought my way into a position on a newspaper and later a wire service. I learned newspapering the hard way, which means mostly in print.

"And now? I have a handsome husband, a house, a son. And I write novels about love and death and taking chances. And I still think that if you could make a teddy bear bigger and stronger, and so on, you could probably turn it into a ham and eat it."

I

IANNI, Francis A(nthony) J(ames) 1926-

PERSONAL: Born March 29, 1926, in Wilmington, Del.; son of Conte Innocenzo and Rose (Novellino) Ianni; married Elizabeth Reuss (an anthropologist), July 17, 1971; children: Juan, Anthony, Andrew. *Education:* Pennsylvania State University, B.S., 1949, M.A., 1950, Ph.D., 1952; New York Psychoanalytic Institute, graduate, 1981.

ADDRESSES: Home—Villa L'Aquila, 24 Clover Rd., Newfoundland, N.J. 07435. *Office*—Department of Education, Teachers College, Columbia University, 525 West 121st St., New York, N.Y. 10027.

CAREER: Licensed psychologist, State of New York; board certified in psychoanalysis, American Psychoanalytic Association. Russell Sage College, Troy, N.Y., instructor, 1952-53, assistant professor, 1954-55, associate professor of anthropology and psychology, 1955-56; Yale University, New Haven, Conn., assistant professor, 1956-57; University College, Addis Ababa, Ethiopia, professor, 1958-61; U.S. Department of Health, Education, and Welfare, Washington, D.C., director of cooperative research program, 1961-64, associate commissioner for research, Office of Education, 1964-66; University of Florence, Florence, Italy, professor of psychology, 1965; Columbia University Teachers College, New York City, professor and director of Horace Mann-Lincoln Institute, 1965-80, Klingenstein fellow, 1965—. Member, National Commission on Criminal Justice Standards and Goals, 1974-75; member, Mayor's Task Force on Organized Crime, New York City, 1974-79. Consultant to U.S. Department of Education, 1966—, and U.S. Department of Justice, 1974—; consultant in medical psychology to St. Luke's-Roosevelt Psychiatric Center, 1977—. *Military service:* U.S. Naval Reserve, active duty, 1943-46; became lieutenant commander.

MEMBER: American Anthropological Association (fellow), African Studies Association (fellow), Society for Applied Anthropology, American Sociological Association (fellow), American Psychological Association, American Psychoanalytic Association, American Orthopsychiatric Association, American Ethnological Society, New York Psychoanalytic Association.

AWARDS, HONORS: Ford Foundation fellow, 1951-52; Fulbright resident grant to Italy and Ethiopia, 1955; Carnegie teaching fellow, Yale, 1956-57; New York State Department of Health and National Foundation of Infantile Paralysis grant, 1957; Fulbright and Smith-Mundt grants to Rome and Ethiopia, 1959-61; Fulbright grants, 1971, 1974; named Cavaliere by Italian government.

WRITINGS:

(With John D. Hogan) *American Social Legislation,* Harper, 1956, reprinted, Greenwood Press, 1973.
(With David Gottlieb) *Adolescent Culture,* Dorsey, 1963.
Culture, System and Behavior: The Behavioral Sciences and Education, Little, Brown, 1972.
(With wife, Elizabeth Reuss-Ianni) *A Family Business: Kinship and Social Control in Organized Crime,* Russell Sage, 1972.
(Editor with Edward Story) *Cultural Relevance and Educational Issues: Readings in Anthropology and Education,* Little, Brown, 1973.
Black Mafia: Ethnic Succession in Organized Crime, Simon & Schuster, 1974.
(Editor) *Conflict and Change in Education,* Scott, Foresman, 1975.
(Editor with Craig J. Calhoun) *The Anthropological Study of Education,* Aldine, 1976.
(Editor with Reuss-Ianni) *The Crime Society: Organized Crime and Corruption in America,* New American Library, 1976.
Home, School, and Community in Adolescent Education, ERIC Clearinghouse on Urban Education, 1983.
The Search for Structure: A Report on American Youth Today, Free Press, 1989.

Contributor to numerous texts on sociology, education, and anthropology; contributor to *Encyclopedia of Education, World Year Book of Education,* and to anthropology, sociology, and education journals.

WORK IN PROGRESS: Research on adolescence and on organizational stress.

SIDELIGHTS: Francis A. J. Ianni "is an anthropologist who succeeded in gaining enough of the confidence of an Italian-American organized-crime 'family' to be able to make an extensive field study," describes a *Times Literary Supplement* reviewer. The result of this study, written with Elizabeth Reuss-Ianni, is *A Family Business: Kinship and Social Control in Organized Crime;* in the work Ianni traces the origins of Mafia organizations and investigates how they operate in the United

States. "What Dr. Ianni says, and proves, is revolutionary," claims Fred Ferretti in the *New York Times Book Review.* "Italian-American crime, he tells us, is a family business. It is rooted in kinship, nurtured by inheritance and birthright, and welded by intermarriage; and there exists no supportable evidence that this family business is, or can be, part of a national conspiracy." While the author gives an in-depth view of the history of organized crime, "what Dr. Ianni does above all is to humanize the subject of the vexed and obscure subject," claims the *Times Literary Supplement* writer. In addition, "Dr. Ianni's scholarship is scrupulous, his knowledge deep and wide, but he clearly also has important personal qualities which made it possible for him to engineer a three-year interaction with his subjects." Calling *A Family Business* a pioneering study, the critic adds that "it is good to have this clear, candid, knowledgeable description, which also does good service by demonstrating that criminal sub-cultures are governed by older and more universal factors than modern mythmongers have understood."

Ianni uses similar procedures in *Black Mafia: Ethnic Succession in Organized Crime;* S. K. Oberbeck notes in *Newsweek* that "Ianni provides vivid profiles and pungent background on the black and Hispanic 'networks' that are fast replacing the Italian 'families' that once had a hammer-lock on the $200 billion business of organized crime." The author maintains that organized crime is a means by which the lowest socioeconomic group can climb the American ladder of success, and that once one group progresses enough to become involved in "legitimate" business, the next group will move in to take its place. Ianni once again traces the history of organized crime in the United States, and then presents a view of the "new" groups. With the support of eight research assistants tied to the underworld, Ianni "has emerged with tape-recorded interviews, candidly stated personal histories, frank inside accounts of crime, crime networks, criminal methods, and revelations of the life-styles of men and women engaged in narcotics traffic, prostitution, illegal gambling, and the grand theft of property," observes Alan Green in *Saturday Review/World.* The critic adds that "all of this information has come from individuals who live by the first principle of crime: silence." *New York Times Book Review* contributor Jane Kramer, however, finds Ianni's use of these interviews disturbing, citing in particular his trips "inside the head of a junkie ([we are] wondering how in God's name Ianni got there). . . . As the book goes on," continues Kramer, "Ianni takes more and more liberties with his method and our credulity." Oberbeck also sees some of the material as "overdramatized," but recognizes that the author's "general thesis of ethnic take-over is confirmed by other sociologists who are working in the fields of crime, and, like Studs Terkel or Oscar Lewis, he has recorded a vivid gallery of types that ring loud and true." "[Ianni] has written an important, carefully researched, coolly reasoned work," concludes Green, "that could easily become the basis for half a dozen chilling screenplays."

BIOGRAPHICAL/CRITICAL SOURCES:

PERIODICALS

Commentary, February, 1975.
New Statesman, December 22, 1972.
Newsweek, June 17, 1974.
New York Times Book Review, July 16, 1972, September 1, 1974.
Saturday Review/World, June 1, 1974.
Times Literary Supplement, January 26, 1973.

INALCIK, Halil 1916-

PERSONAL: Born May 26, 1916, in Istanbul, Turkey; came to the United States, 1972; son of Seyit Osman (a businessman) and Ayshe (Bahriye) Nuri; married wife, Sevkiye, January 18, 1945; children: Guenhan (Mrs. Tezgoer Ertan). *Education:* University of Ankara, M.A., 1940, Ph.D., 1942. *Religion:* Muslim.

ADDRESSES: Home—5000 East End Ave., Chicago, Ill. 60615. *Office*—Department of History, University of Chicago, 5801 South Ellis Ave., Chicago, Ill. 60637.

CAREER: University of Ankara, Ankara, Turkey, professor of history, 1943-72; University of Chicago, Chicago, Ill., professor of Ottoman history, 1972—. Visiting professor of Turkish history, Columbia University, 1953-54, Princeton University, 1967-68. Co-chairman, First International Congress on the Social and Economic History of Turkey, 1977; co-director, *Turcica,* 1979—; director of studies, Ecole des Hautes Etudes, 1983. *Military service:* Turkish Army, 1943-46.

MEMBER: International Association of South East European Studies (president, 1971-74), American Academy of Arts and Sciences, American Historical Society, Historical Society of America, American Oriental Society, Royal Historical Society (corresponding member), Royal Asiatic Society (honorary member), Turkish Historical Society.

AWARDS, HONORS: Fellow of the Rockefeller Foundation, 1956; Social Science Research Fellowship, 1975; honorary doctorate, University of Bosphorus, 1986, and University of Athens, 1988.

WRITINGS:

The Ottoman Reforms (Tanzimat) and the Bulgarian Question (in Turkish), Turkish Historical Society, 1943.
Studies and Documents on the Reign of Mehmed the Conqueror (in Turkish), Turkish Historical Society, 1954.
Ottoman Population and Land Survey of Albania, 1432 (in Turkish), Turkish Historical Society, 1954.
The Ottoman Empire: The Classical Age, 1300-1600, translated by Norman Itzkowitz and Colin Imber, Praeger, 1973, 2nd edition, Caratzas Publishing, 1989.
The Ottoman Empire: Conquest, Organization, and Economy, Variorum Reprints, 1978.
(Translator with Rhoads Murphey) Tursun Beg, *The History of Mehmed the Conqueror,* Bibliotheca Islamica, 1978.
(Editor with Osman Okyar) *International Congress on the Social and Economic History of Turkey,* Meteskan (Turkey), 1980.
Studies in Ottoman Social and Economic History, Variorum Reprints, 1985.

Contributor to *Ottomans and the Crusades,* Volume 5, edited by K. Setton. Co-editor, *Archivum Ottomanicum,* 1969—.

WORK IN PROGRESS: Editing *The Social and Economic History of the Ottoman Empire,* for Cambridge University Press; co-directing Volume 5 of *A Scientific and Cultural History of Mankind,* a UNESCO project.

SIDELIGHTS: Halil Inalcik once told *CA:* "The Ottoman period in Turkish history is particularly interesting. It embraced the whole Middle East, and the Balkans between 1300 and 1900. There is no modern history of it, [since] the Ottoman archives, unusually rich, have not been exploited. . . . A truly scientific book on the Ottoman empire is badly needed." Inalcik does research study in French, German, Italian, Arabic, and Persian, as well as English and his native Turkish.

* * *

INMAN, Billie (Jo) Andrew 1929-

PERSONAL: Born May 16, 1929, in Thurber, Tex.; daughter of Robert A. and Gussie (Oyler) Andrew; married George D. Inman, May 23, 1950; children: Paul David, Laura Lou. *Education:* Midwestern University, B.A., 1950; Tulane University, M.A., 1951; Texas Technological College (now Texas Tech University), graduate study, summer, 1954; University of Texas at Austin, Ph.D., 1961. *Religion:* Unitarian-Universalist.

ADDRESSES: Home—5531 East North Wilshire Dr., Tucson, Ariz. 85711. *Office*—Department of English, University of Arizona, Tucson, Ariz. 85721.

CAREER: Teacher of English in public schools in Lubbock, Tex., and Borger, Tex., 1951-54; West Texas State College (now University), Canyon, instructor in English, 1955-57; University of Texas at Austin, special instructor, 1961-62; University of Arizona, Tucson, instructor, 1962-63, assistant professor, 1963-68, associate professor, 1968-72, professor of English, 1972—, director of freshman English, 1967-71, director of graduate studies, 1973-74. Director of National Defense Education Act Institute in English, University of Arizona, 1965; director of humanities program, 1986—.

MEMBER: Modern Language Association of America.

AWARDS, HONORS: National Endowment for the Humanities fellowship, 1982-83.

WRITINGS:

(With Ruth Gardner) *Aspects of Composition,* Harcourt, 1970, 2nd edition, 1979.
Walter Pater's Reading, 1858-1873, Garland Publishing, 1981.
(Contributor) Philip Dodd, editor, *Walter Pater: An Imaginative Sense of Fact,* Frank Cass & Co., 1981.
(Contributor) Alan Sullivan, editor, *British Literary Magazines,* Volume III, Greenwood Press, 1984.
Walter Pater and His Reading, 1874-1877, with a Bibliography of His Library Borrowings, 1878-1894, Garland Publishing, 1989.
(General editor) *The Collected Works of Walter Pater,* eight volumes, University of California Press, in press.

WORK IN PROGRESS: "Researches during the summer of 1988 in the Gell Family Papers, Hopton Hall, Wirksworth, Derbyshire, England, which will be published by *English Literature in Transition,* are dramatically altering perceptions of the personality of Walter Pater."

SIDELIGHTS: "In this age of postmodern and new historicist literary criticism," Billie Inman told *CA,* "my delight is still in the type of basic literary research that discovers facts about a writer's life, his/her methods of composition, and the circumstances that prompted the writing of a specific work. I am compelled by desire to fit another piece of evidence into a real story."

BIOGRAPHICAL/CRITICAL SOURCES:

PERIODICALS

Papers of the Bibliographical Society of America, Volume 76, number 4, 1982.
Pater Newsletter, spring, 1982.

IRVING, John (Winslow) 1942-

PERSONAL: Born March 2, 1942, in Exeter, N.H.; son of Colin F. N. (a teacher) and Frances (Winslow) Irving; married Shyla Leary, August 20, 1964 (divorced, 1981); married Janet Turnbull, June 6, 1987; children: (first marriage) Colin, Brendan. *Education:* University of New Hampshire, B.A. (cum laude), 1965; University of Iowa, M.F.A., 1967; additional study at University of Pittsburgh, 1961-62, and University of Vienna, 1963-64.

ADDRESSES: c/o William Morrow, 105 Madison Ave., New York, N.Y. 10016.

CAREER: Novelist. Mount Holyoke College, South Hadley, Mass., assistant professor of English, 1967-72, 1975-78; University of Iowa, Iowa City, writer in residence, 1972-75. Teacher and reader at Bread Loaf Writers Conference.

AWARDS, HONORS: Rockefeller Foundation grant, 1971-72; National Endowment for the Arts fellowship, 1974-75; Guggenheim fellow, 1976-77; *The World According to Garp* was nominated for a National Book Award in 1979, and won an American Book Award in 1980; named one of ten "Good Guys" honored for contributions furthering advancement of women, National Women's Political Caucus, 1988, for *Cider House Rules.*

WRITINGS:

Setting Free the Bears (also see below), Random House, 1969.
The Water-Method Man (also see below), Random House, 1972.
The 158-Pound Marriage (also see below), Random House, 1974.
The World According to Garp, Dutton, 1978.
Three by Irving (contains *Setting Free the Bears, The Water-Method Man,* and *The 158-Pound Marriage*), Random House, 1980.
The Hotel New Hampshire (Book-of-the-Month Club main selection), Dutton, 1981.
The Cider House Rules, Morrow, 1985.
A Prayer for Owen Meany (Book-of-the-Month Club main selection), Morrow, 1989.

Also contributor of short stories to *Esquire, Playboy,* and other magazines.

SIDELIGHTS: Novelist John Irving is a gifted storyteller with a remarkably fertile imagination and a penchant for meshing the comic and the tragic. *Saturday Review* critic Scot Haller describes Irving's work this way: "Fashioning wildly inventive, delightfully intricate narratives out of his sense of humor, sense of dread and sense of duty, Irving blends the madcap, the macabre, and the mundane into sprawling, spiraling comedies of life." Irving is perhaps best known for his critically acclaimed bestseller *The World According to Garp,* which has sold more than three million copies in hardback and paperback together since its 1978 publication. *Garp* achieved a cult status complete with T-shirts proclaiming "I Believe in Garp," and received serious critical attention which ultimately propelled the author "into the front rank of America's young novelists," according to *Time* critic R. Z. Sheppard.

Though a contemporary novelist, Irving's concerns are traditional ones, a characteristic that, critics note, distinguishes his work from that of other contemporary fiction. *Dictionary of Literary Biography* contributor Hugh M. Ruppersburg, for example, writes, "The concerns of Irving's novels are inherently contemporary. Yet often they bear little similarity to other recent fiction, for their author is more interested in affirming certain conventional values—art and the family, for instance—than in condemning the status quo or heralding the arrival of a new age. . . . What is needed, [Irving] seems to suggest, is a fusion of the compassion and common sense of the old with the egalitarian openmindedness of the new." Irving himself likens his fictional values and narrative technique to those of 19th-century writers. "I occasionally feel like a dinosaur in my own time because my fictional values are terribly old-fashioned," Irving states in the *Los Angeles Times.* "They go right back to the deliberately sentimental intentions of the 19th-Century novelist: Create a character in whom the reader will make a substantial emotional investment and then visit upon that character an unbearable amount of pain." Like those nineteenth-century novelists, Irving also believes that he is responsible for entertaining the reader. "I think, to some degree, entertainment is the responsibility of literature," Irving told Haller. "I really am looking upon the novel as an art form that was at its best when it was offered as a popular form. By which I probably mean the 19th century."

Irving's nineteenth-century values are reflected in *The World According to Garp,* a work he describes in the *Washington Post Book World* as "an artfully disguised soap opera." Irving adds: "The difference is that I write well, that I construct a book with the art of construction in mind, that I use words intentionally and carefully. I mean to make you laugh, to make you cry; those are soap-opera intentions, all the way." A lengthy family saga, *Garp* focuses on nurse Jenny Fields, her illegitimate son, novelist T. S. Garp, and Garp's wife and two sons. Described as a "disquieting" work by *New Republic* contributor Terrence Des Pres, *Garp* explicitly explores the violent side of contemporary life. Episodes involving rape, assassination, mutilation, and suicide abound, but these horrific scenes are always infused with comedy. As Irving notes in the *Los Angeles Times,* "No matter how gray the subject matter or orientation of any novel I write, it's still going to be a comic novel."

"A true romantic hero," according to *Village Voice* critic Eliot Fremont-Smith, Garp is obsessed with the perilousness of life, and wants nothing more than to keep the world safe for his family and friends. Ironically, Garp is the one who ultimately inflicts irreversible harm on his children, illustrating Irving's point that "the most protective and unconditionally loving parents can inflict the most appalling wounds on their children," writes Pearl K. Bell in *Commentary.* While Garp is obsessed with protecting his family and friends, his mother's obsession involves promoting her status as a "sexual suspect"—a woman who refuses to share either her life or her body with a man. Through her bestselling autobiography, *A Sexual Suspect,* Jenny becomes a feminist leader. Her home evolves into a haven for a group of radical feminists, The Ellen James Society, whose members have cut out their tongues as a show of support for a young girl who was raped and similarly mutilated by her attackers. Both Garp and Jenny eventually are assassinated—she by an outraged anti-feminist convinced that Jenny's influence ruined his marriage, he by an Ellen Jamesian convinced that Garp is an exploiter of women because of a novel he wrote about rape. Discussing these characters in a *Publishers Weekly* interview with Barbara A. Bannon, Irving remarks, "It mattered very fiercely to me that [Garp and Jenny] were people

who would test your love of them by being the extremists they were. I always knew that as mother and son they would make the world angry at them."

Critics note that *Garp* demonstrates a remarkable sensitivity to women, because it deals sympathetically with issues such as rape, feminism, and sexual roles. *Nation* contributor Michael Malone writes, "With anger, chagrin and laughter, Irving anatomizes the inadequacies and injustices of traditional sex roles. . . . The force behind a memorable gallery of women characters—foremost among them, Garp's famous feminist mother and his English professor wife—is not empathy but deep frustrated sympathy." A similar opinion is expressed by *Ms.* contributor Lindsy Van Gelder, who expresses admiration for Irving's ability to explore "feminist issues from rape to sexual identity to Movement stardom . . . minus any Hey-I'm-a-man-but-I-really understand self-conscious fanfare." Irving explains in the *Los Angeles Times,* however, that his "interest in women as a novelist is really very simple. . . . I see every evidence that women are more often victims than men. As a novelist I'm more interested in victims than in winners." In fact, Irving flatly disagrees with critics who describe *Garp* in sociological or political terms. He states in the *Contemporary Literature* interview with Larry McCaffery: "Obviously now when people write about *Garp* and say that it's 'about' feminism and assassination and the violence of the sixties, they're ignoring the fact that I lived half of the sixties in another country. I don't know anything about the violence of the sixties; it's meaningless to me. I'm not a sociological writer, nor should I be considered a social realist in any way."

Nor does Irving concur with critics who, noting several significant similarities between Garp and Irving, describe *Garp* as a semi-autobiographical work. Bell, for example, writes: "[Irving] indulges in elaborate games of allusion to his own life and career, as though taunting the reader to guess what has been made up, what taken whole from life. A little of this can be useful and funny, but Irving tends to let it go on too long, and the peekaboo can become much too coy." In a *New York Times Book Review* interview with Thomas Williams, however, Irving maintains: "I make up all the important things. I've had a very uninteresting life. I had a happy childhood. I'm grateful for how ordinary my life is because I'm not ever tempted to think that something that happened to me is important simply because it happened to me. I have no personal axes to grind; I'm free, therefore, to imagine the best possible ax to grind—and I really mean that: that's a significant freedom from the tyranny and self-importance of autobiography in fiction."

The World According to Garp was heralded as Irving's finest and most original work; Des Pres observes that "nothing in contemporary fiction matches it." The critic continues: "Irving tells the story of Garp's family with great tenderness and wisdom. By tracing the relationship between wife and husband, and then again between parents and children (and how these two sets intersect to cause catastrophe), Irving is able to handle a large range of human hope and fear and final insufficiency. He is excellent in his portrait of Garp's sons, Duncan and Walt, whose view of their father is often hilarious, whose dialogue is true without fail, and whose vulnerability in a world of numberless hurtful things causes Garp a brooding, prophetic dread."

Several reviewers compliment in particular the narrative flow of *Garp.* "Reading *Garp* was like listening to Homer's account of the Trojan War told in a singsong monotone," writes

Doris Grumbach in *Saturday Review*. "I relished every page, every line, of the imaginative feast. To paraphrase Alexander Pope, it has all the force of many fine words." *New York Times Book Review* critic Richard Locke comments: "What is most impressive about the book . . . is its narrative momentum: Irving has a natural narrative gift, and even when the plot is not as cosmic as it tries to be, one can't help wondering what will happen to these people next and reading on." *Times Literary Supplement* contributor Thomas M. Disch similarly notes, "*The World According to Garp* is a novel about the novel, and the novelist, as seducer. . . . What raises the book above its own conundrums is . . . the personality of its author. It is a seductive personality, not in any opprobrious sense, but in the way that John Ridd, the narrator of *Lorna Doone*, is seductive—by the sweetness of his disposition and the lilt of his voice, which, as it rises from the turning pages, commands not just attention but affection." *New York Times Book Review* contributor Julian Moynahan comments that while Irving's "new novel contains some febrile fabulations (the wrong sort of exaggeration) in its handling of the feminist theme, . . . his instincts are so basically sound, his talent for storytelling so bright and strong, that he gets down to the truth of his time in the end."

Other reviewers praise the originality and credibility of Irving's characterizations. "What does matter about *The World According to Garp* is the captivating originality of the characters, the closely drawn entirety of the life that Irving bestows upon them, and the infectious love he feels for these emanations of his head," writes Bell. Concurs Locke, "The characters . . . compel our sympathy. We feel with them—strongly—in the midst of their family lives and lusts and disasters." *New York Times* reviewer Christopher Lehmann-Haupt adds, "The way he filters [the book's violent events] through his hero's unique imagination, we not only laugh at the world according to Garp, but we also accept it and love it."

However, "not everyone who read *Garp* responded to the novel's fun and games," remarks R. Z. Sheppard in *Time*. "Many readers were offended by Irving's mating of the truly tragic and grotesquely comic." Irving responds in the *Saturday Review*, "People who think *Garp* is wildly eccentric and very bizarre are misled about the real world. . . . I can't imagine where they've been living or what they read for news. Five out of seven days I find things in the *New York Times* that seem to me far less explainable than the rather human behavior in *Garp*." He similarly remarks in a *New York Times Book Review* interview with Thomas Williams, "In just the same way that I don't see comedy and tragedy as contradictions . . . I don't see that unhappy endings undermine rich and energetic lives."

The majority of reviewers embrace Irving's fictional world—violence and all. "If the events seem at times to be too brutal and terrible, if too many violences seem to have been heaped upon already suffering and bloodied persons, that is the way it is," writes Grumbach. "Garp writes and lives as he finds the world. And because John Irving is so subtle and persuasive a writer, we believe in his fictional world." Locke comments, "The horrible violence that plagues this family elicits in the reader something of the large sympathy for the doomed that novelists in the great tradition can summon up." A *Newsweek* reviewer observes, "Irving here deals out Grand Guignol shocks leading to a hushed, heart-stopping revelation of irreparable grief. This is brilliant work." Bell concludes: "Remarkably, none of the slaughter and mayhem that erupt with such bloody frequency in *The World According to Garp* seems sensationalistic or even melodramatic. Irving has taken a capacious and demanding view of his task as a storyteller, and carried it out with sober compassion, adventurous ingenuity, and great intelligence." Ruppersburg determines that "whether [Irving's] future novels climb to the best-seller lists or not, his peculiar synthesis of dark humor, social upheaval, and the tragic tenor of modern life with realistic and likable characters may well exert a profound influence on the fiction of the 1980s. What Irving will ultimately achieve for himself remains to be seen; but his fiction so far—especially his fourth novel—has heralded the arrival of an indisputably significant figure on the American literary scene."

Tucked into the pages of *The World According to Garp* is one of Garp's works, "The Pension Grillparzer," which Locke describes as "a short narrative, given in full, . . . [that] glows at the heart of 'The World According to Garp' like some rich gem or flower." This brief but compelling tale formed the outline for Irving's next work, *The Hotel New Hampshire*. Irving explains in *New York* magazine: "I realized while writing 'Pension' that I wanted to write about hotels—not realistically, as I was doing at the time, but metaphorically. I also wanted to keep the voice of 'Pension,' a straightforward first-person narrative told from a child's point of view that a child could understand. It would be a novel about childhood, about growing up and how the impressions children have of themselves and those closest to them change as they grow older. It is the most fairytale-like novel I have done in that it relies the least on one's understanding of the real world."

Despite its fairytale-like qualities, *The Hotel New Hampshire* explores adult issues like incest, terrorism, suicide, freakish deaths, and gang rape, all infused with Irving's trademark macabre humor. A family saga like *Garp*, *The Hotel New Hampshire* spans nearly four generations of the troubled Berry family. Headed by Win, a charming but irresponsible dreamer who is ultimately a failure at innkeeping, and Mary, who dies in the early stages of the novel, the Berry family includes five children: Franny, Frank, Egg, Lilly, and John, the narrator. While Egg perishes along with his mother, the remaining children are left to struggle through childhood and adolescence. Irving describes the family this way in *New York*: "[The Hotel New Hampshire] takes a large number of people and says in every family we have a dreamer, a hero, a late bloomer, one who makes it very big, one who doesn't make it at all, one who never grows up, one who is the shit detector, the guide to practicality, and often you don't know who these people will be, watching them in their earlier years."

The Berrys, along with an array of subsidiary characters—human and animal—eventually inhabit three hotels: one in New Hampshire, one in Vienna, and one in Maine. According to Irving, the hotels are symbols for the passage from infancy to maturity. "The first hotel is the only real hotel in the story," states Irving in *New York*. "It is childhood. The one in Vienna is a dark, foreign place, that phase called adolescence, when you begin leaving the house and finding out how frightening the world is. . . . The last one is no hotel at all. . . . It is a place to get well again, which is a process that has been going on throughout the novel."

Since it followed such a phenomenally successful work, *The Hotel New Hampshire* naturally invited comparisons to its predecessor. "There is no question in my mind it's better than *The World According to Garp*," Irving maintains in *New York*. "It certainly is every bit as big a book, and it means much more. It's a more ambitious novel symbolically but with a different point of view, deliberately narrower than *Garp.*" Irving nevertheless anticipated that critics would reject the novel. As he states in the *Chicago Tribune Book World:* "There will be people gunning for me—they'll call the book lazy, or worse—sentimental. But getting bad press is better than no press. It's better to be hated than to be ignored—even children know that."

In fact, critics' opinions largely fulfilled Irving's dismal prediction. *Chicago Tribune Book World* contributor Judith Rossner, for example, notes, "I found an emptiness at the core of 'The Hotel New Hampshire' that might relate to the author's having used up his old angers and familiar symbols without having found new reasons for his rage and different bodies to make us see it." *Saturday Review* critic Scot Haller writes: "*The Hotel New Hampshire* could not be mistaken for the work of any other writer, but unfortunately, it cannot be mistaken for Irving's best novel, either. It lacks the urgency of *Setting Free the Bears,* the bittersweet wit of *The 158-Pound Marriage,* the sly set-ups of *Garp.* The haphazardness that afflicts these characters' lives has seeped into the storytelling, too." *Time* critic R. Z. Sheppard offers this view: "[Unlike Garp's story,] John Berry's story is not resolved in violent, dramatic action, but in a quiet balancing of sorrow and hope. It is a difficult act, and it is not faultless. The dazzling characterizations and sense of American place in the first part of the novel tend to get scuffed in transit to Europe. There are tics and indulgences. But the book is redeemed by the healing properties of its conclusion. Like a burlesque *Tempest, Hotel New Hampshire* puts the ordinary world behind, evokes a richly allusive fantasy and returns to reality refreshed and strengthened."

Critics also note that *The Hotel New Hampshire* reflects the influence of numerous other writers, notably J. D. Salinger, Vladimir Nabokov, and Kurt Vonnegut. Discussing this issue at length in *Esquire,* James Wolcott writes, "Imagine Salinger's Glass family with fouler mouths and lower brows and you have some notion of how precociously darling and fragile these Berrys are." The critic adds that "Nabokov holds a particularly potent sway over *The Hotel New Hampshire,*" but concludes, "Perhaps the presiding influence, however, is that of Kurt Vonnegut. Irving is a passionate admirer of Vonnegut's . . . and he seems to share Vonnegut's flip sense of doom and irony." Although he concedes that *The Hotel New Hampshire* "can be devilishly readable," Wolcott believes that Irving is ultimately unsuccessful in his attempt to imitate such "modernist" writers. "Whatever its lapses, *The World According to Garp* was an original affront; *The Hotel New Hampshire* is ultratrendy and nakedly—almost desperately—derivative," Wolcott remarks. "By trying to storm the ranks of the modernist giants, Irving only betrays how far he lags behind their lyricism and expressive brilliance. He kneels like a camp follower in the shadows of their greatness, combing the grass for strands of gold."

According to *Newsweek* critic Peter S. Prescott: "The bad news about 'The Hotel New Hampshire' . . . is that the new novel suffers from a terminal case of the cutes. . . . Irving is determined to charm us; he applies charm to his pages as relentlessly as a mason applies cement to an arch he suspects may collapse." Prescott concludes: "Novels don't need messages, but 'The Hotel New Hampshire' is so incessantly didactic, so portentous, that I found myself quite ready to grapple with ideas and furious that Irving offered me only marshmallow whip. 'LIFE IS SERIOUS BUT ART IS FUN!' he writes at the end, and I guess that's what he intends his

story to mean, but here he offers little to demonstrate either argument." On the other hand, *New Republic* contributor Jack Beatty compliments Irving's narrative technique. "John Irving is a talented but facile writer. His prose never encounters those resistances—emotional, moral, epistemological—that energise memorable statement. It never strains at meaning; it just sweeps you along, its easy momentum lulling your critical faculty and rocking you back to a childlike state of wonder." Beatty concludes: "We all want to check in to the Hotel New Hampshire. It is 'the sympathy space' where we can be fully known and yet fully loved, and where a powerful imagination holds us fast and won't let us die."

Originally intended to be a saga of orphanage life in early twentieth-century Maine, Irving's sixth novel *The Cider House Rules* became, instead, a statement on abortion. The issue of abortion arose during Irving's research for the novel, when he "discovered that abortion was an integral part of the life of an orphanage hospital at that time," as he remarks in the *Los Angeles Times.* He concedes in that same article, "This is in part a didactic novel, and in part a polemic. I'm not ashamed of that. . . . But I remain uncomfortable at the marriage between politics and fiction. I still maintain that the politics of abortion came to this book organically, came to it cleanly."

Evoking the works of Victorian novelists such as Charles Dickens and Charlotte Bronte, Irving's *The Cider House Rules* is set in an orphanage in dreary St. Cloud, Maine, where the gentle, ether-addicted Dr. Larch and his saintly nurses preside lovingly over their orphans. Larch also provides illegal but safe abortions, and although he is painfully aware of the bleak existence that many of the orphans endure, he doesn't encourage expectant mothers to abort. As he puts it, "I help them have what they want. An orphan or an abortion." One unadopted orphan in particular, Homer Wells, becomes Larch's spiritual son and protege. Larch schools Homer in birth and abortion procedures and hopes that Homer will one day succeed him at the orphanage. When Homer comes to believe that the fetus has a soul, however, he refuses to assist with abortions. A conflict ensues, and Homer seeks refuge at Ocean View apple orchard, located on the coast of Maine.

The book's title refers to the list of rules posted in Ocean View's cider house regarding migrant workers' behavior. Several critics acknowledge the significance of rules, both overt and covert, in the lives of the characters. Toronto *Globe and Mail* contributor Joy Fielding, for example, comments, "*The Cider House Rules* is all about rules; the rules we make and break; the rules we ignore; the rules we post for all to see; the invisible rules we create for ourselves to help us get through life; the absurdity of some of these rules and the hypocrisy of others, specifically our rules regarding abortion." Similarly, *Los Angeles Times* critic Elaine Kendall writes, "Much is made of the literal Cider House Rules, a typed sheet posted in the migrant workers dormitory, clearly and politely spelling out the behavior expected by the owners of the orchard. Sensible and fair as these rules are, they're made to be broken, interpreted individually or ignored entirely, heavily symbolic of the social and moral codes Irving is exploring." *New York Times* reviewer Christopher Lehmann-Haupt similarly notes that Dr. Larch follows his own rules, and that "the point—which is driven home with the sledgehammer effect that John Irving usually uses—is that there are always multiple sets of rules for a given society. Heroism lies in discovering the right ones, whether they are posted on the wall or carved with scalpels, and committing yourself to follow them no matter what."

Despite the multiplicity of rules and moral codes explored by Irving, critics tend to focus on abortion as the crucial issue of *The Cider House Rules*. They express different opinions, however, concerning Irving's position on the abortion issue. *Time* critic Paul Gray comments that *The Cider House Rules* "is essentially about abortions and women's right to have them," and Susan Brownmiller describes the work in the *Chicago Tribune* as "a heartfelt, sometimes moving tract in support of abortion rights." Kendall, on the other hand, maintains, "Though Dr. Larch's philosophy justifying his divided practice is exquisitely and closely reasoned, the abortion episodes are graphic and gruesome, as if Irving were simultaneously courting both pro-choice and right-to-life factions." *New York Times Book Review* contributor Benjamin DeMott offers this view: "The knowledge and sympathy directing Mr. Irving's exploration of the [abortion] issue are exceptional. Pertinent history, the specifics of surgical procedure, the irrecusable sorrow of guilt and humiliation, the needs and rights of children—their weight is palpable in these pages."

With a few exceptions, *The Cider House Rules* was favorably reviewed; several critics, including DeMott, believe it is Irving's most worthwhile novel. "By turns witty, tenderhearted, fervent and scarifying, 'The Cider House Rules' is, for me, John Irving's first truly valuable book," writes DeMott. "The storytelling is straightforward—not the case with his huge commercial success, 'The World According to Garp'.... The theme is in firm focus—not the case with 'The Hotel New Hampshire'.... The novelist's often-deplored weakness for the cute and trendy, although still evident, is here less troubling." Christopher Lehmann-Haupt concurs in the *New York Times*: "[Irving's] novels have tended to sprawl both in tone and focus, but in 'The Cider House Rules' he has positively streamlined his form.... The familiar elements of the macabre, the violent and the cute all seem more controlled and pointed, more dedicated to the end of advancing Mr. Irving's story toward a definite and coherent resolution.... 'The Cider House Rules' has greater force and integrity than either of its two immediate predecessors. It's funny and absorbing and it makes clever use of the plot's seeming predictability."

Spectator reviewer David Profumo, however, comments that while "there are moments of outstanding writing in the book," the novel "proves to be something of a phantom pregnancy in itself, promising to deliver so much more than it does." *Washington Post Book World* critic Jonathan Yardley similarly observes that Irving has "assembled his customary cast of mildly eccentric characters and trotted them through the customary paces, but at the end there is no feeling that they—and therefore you, the reader—have been anywhere or done anything interesting. It's not so much that the trip is unpleasant as that it's pointless." Fielding concurs, "The novel, despite many wonderful moments, is never quite as good as it promises to be. Ultimately it fails to engage our emotions, surprising in light of its volatile subject matter. Often Irving is lecturing, telling readers what to feel, instead of allowing them to draw their own conclusions, to feel things for themselves." Gray, on the other hand, attributes the novel's weaknesses to the cynicism of our times. He writes: "Although Irving admires and emulates the expansive methods of Victorian fiction, he is, after all, a product of this century and all its horrors. He cannot, like Dickens, honestly trick out a story with coincidences that will allow good people to triumph; the best Irving can offer is a tale that concludes with a few survivors who are not entirely maimed or deranged by what they have been through."

Remarking in a *Time* interview that he is "moved and impressed by people with a great deal of religious faith," Irving explains to Michael Anderson in the *New York Times Book Review*, "Jesus has always struck me as a perfect victim and a perfect hero." What impresses him most is that Christ is aware of his own destiny: "That is truly a heroic burden to carry," he tells Phyllis Robinson in the *Book-of-the-Month Club News*. Similarly, in *A Prayer for Owen Meany*, a novel that examines the good and evil—especially the capacity of each to be mistaken for the other, Irving's memorable Christ-like hero knows his destiny, including the date and circumstances of his death. Small in size but large in spirit, Owen Meany has a distinctive but ineffable voice caused by a fixed larynx; and throughout the novel, Irving renders Owen's speech in upper case—suggested to him by the red letters in which Jesus's utterances appear in the New Testament. Believing that nothing in his life is accidental or purposeless, Owen professes himself an instrument of God. Although the foul ball hit off Owen's bat kills the mother of his best friend, Johnny Wheelwright, it ultimately reveals to Johnny the identity of his father. The story of their adolescence and friendship is recalled and narrated by Johnny, who eventually comes to a belief in God because of Owen and his sacrifice. "No one has ever done Christ in the way John Irving does Him in *A Prayer for Owen Meany*," writes Stephen King in the *Washington Post Book World*. "This is big time, friends and neighbors."

In a *Time* review, Sheppard points out that "anyone familiar with Irving's mastery of narrative technique, his dark humor and moral resolve also knows his fiction is cute like a fox." Sheppard suggests that despite its theological underpinnings, the novel "scarcely disguise[s] his indignation about the ways of the world," and actually represents "a fable of political predestination." Although finding the book flawed in terms of its structure and development, Robert Olen Butler suggests in Chicago *Tribune Books* that it nevertheless contains "some of the elements that made 'The World According to Garp' so attractive to the critics and the bestseller audience alike: flamboyant, even bizarre, characters; unlikely and arresting plot twists; a consciousness of contemporary culture; and the assertion that a larger mechanism is at work in the universe." In the estimation of Brigitte Weeks in the *Book-of-the-Month Club News*, "John Irving is a reader's writer, and *A Prayer for Owen Meany* is a reader's novel, a large, intriguing grab bag of characters and ideas that moves the spirit and fascinates the mind.... There is no one quite like him."

Sheppard offers this assessment of Irving's work: "Irving's philosophy is basic stuff: one must live willfully, purposefully and watchfully. Accidents, bad luck, undertoads and open windows lurk everywhere—and the dog really bites. It is only a matter of time. Nobody gets out alive, yet few want to leave early. Irving's popularity is not hard to understand. His world is really the world according to nearly everyone."

MEDIA ADAPTATIONS: "The World According to Garp" was released by Warner Bros./Pan Arts in 1982, and starred Robin Williams, Glenn Close, and Mary Beth Hurt, and featured cameo performances by Irving and his sons; "The Hotel New Hampshire" was released by Orion Pictures in 1984, and starred Rob Lowe, Jodie Foster, and Beau Bridges.

BIOGRAPHICAL/CRITICAL SOURCES:

BOOKS

Contemporary Literary Criticism, Gale, Volume 13, 1980, Volume 23, 1983, Volume 38, 1986.

Dictionary of Literary Biography, Volume 5: *American Novelists since World War II,* Second Series, Gale, 1980.
Dictionary of Literary Biography Yearbook: 1982, Gale, 1983.

PERIODICALS

Book-of-the-Month Club News, April, 1989.
Chicago Tribune, May 12, 1985.
Chicago Tribune Book World, May 11, 1980, September 13, 1981.
Christian Century, October 7, 1981.
Commentary, September, 1978, June, 1982.
Contemporary Literature, winter, 1982.
Detroit News, August 30, 1981.
Esquire, September, 1981.
Globe and Mail (Toronto), March 10, 1984, July 6, 1985.
Los Angeles Times, September 16, 1982, March 20, 1983, June 4, 1985, July 10, 1985.
Maclean's, June 11, 1979.
Ms., July, 1979.
Nation, June 10, 1978.
New Republic, April 29, 1978, September 23, 1981.
Newsweek, April 17, 1978, September 21, 1981.

New York, August 17, 1981.
New Yorker, May 8, 1978, October 12, 1981, July 8, 1985.
New York Times, April 13, 1978, August 31, 1981, May 20, 1985.
New York Times Book Review, April 23, 1978, May 21, 1978, May 26, 1985, March 12, 1989.
People, December 25, 1978.
Prairie Schooner, fall, 1978.
Publishers Weekly, April 24, 1978.
Rolling Stone, December 13, 1979.
Saturday Review, May 13, 1978, September, 1981.
Spectator, June 22, 1985.
Time, April 24, 1978, August 31, 1981, June 3, 1985, April 3, 1989.
Times (London), June 20, 1985.
Times Literary Supplement, October 20, 1978, June 21, 1985.
Tribune Books (Chicago), March 19, 1989.
Village Voice, May 22, 1978.
Washington Post, August 25, 1981.
Washington Post Book World, April 30, 1978, May 19, 1985, March 5, 1989.

—Sketch by Melissa Gaiownik

J

JACKSON, Laura (Riding) 1901-
(Laura Riding, Laura Riding Gottschalk; Madeleine Vara, a pseudonym)

PERSONAL: Born January 16, 1901, in New York, N.Y.; name originally Laura Reichenthal; adopted the surname Riding, 1926; daughter of Nathaniel S. and Sarah (Edersheim) Reichenthal; married Louis Gottschalk (a professor of history), 1920 (divorced, 1925); married Schuyler Brinckerhoff Jackson (a poet, critic, and former poetry editor of *Time* magazine), June 20, 1941 (died, 1968). *Education:* Attended Cornell University, 1918-21; further study at University of Illinois, Urbana, and University of Louisville.

ADDRESSES: Home—Box 35, Wabasso, Fla. 32970. *Agent*—A. P. Watt & Son, 26/28 Bedford Row, London WC1R 4HL, England.

CAREER: Poet, critic, and author in various fields "with progressive concern with language as the natural human truth-system." Regular member of "The Fugitives," a group of Southern poets of the 1920s; lived abroad, 1926-39, mainly in England and Spain; worked at "furthering sensitivity of writer-associates, poets especially, to the importance of linguistic integrity as the basis of literary integrity." Founder, with Robert Graves, and managing partner of Seizin Press, 1927-38; founder, with Graves, and editor of *Epilogue* (a series of volumes in which new principles of general criticism were explored), 1935-38. Returned to the United States, 1939; beginning 1943, involved in citrus farming in Florida with husband, Schuyler B. Jackson, and in working with him "towards the enlargement of the knowledge of words and capability of using them in truthfully exact consciousness of their meanings—towards the initiating of a new lexicography."

AWARDS, HONORS: Nashville prize, 1924, and honorary membership (regular and participating), 1925, both from "The Fugitives" group; Mark Rothko Appreciation award, 1971; Guggenheim fellowship, 1973; National Endowment for the Arts fellowship, 1979.

WRITINGS:

POETRY

(Under name Laura Riding Gottschalk) *The Close Chaplet,* Adelphi, 1926.

(Under name Laura Riding Gottschalk) *Voltaire: A Biographical Fantasy,* Hogarth Press, 1927, Folcroft Editions, 1969, reprinted, Norwood Editions, 1977.
(Under name Laura Riding) *Love as Love, Death as Death,* Seizin Press (London), 1928.
(Under name Laura Riding) *Poems: A Joking Word,* J. Cape, 1930.
(Under name Laura Riding) *Twenty Poems Less,* Hours Press (Paris), 1930.
(Under name Laura Riding) *Though Gently,* Seizin Press (Majorca), 1930.
(Under name Laura Riding) *Laura and Francisca,* Seizin Press (Majorca), 1931.
(Under name Laura Riding) *The Life of the Dead* (in French and English), illustrated by John Aldridge, Barker, 1933.
(Under name Laura Riding) *The First Leaf,* Seizin Press (Majorca), 1933.
(Under name Laura Riding) *Poet: A Lying Word,* Barker, 1933.
(Under name Laura Riding) *Americans,* Primavera, 1934.
(Under name Laura Riding) *The Second Leaf,* Seizin Press (Majorca), 1935.
(Under name Laura Riding) *Collected Poems,* Random House, 1938, revised edition, under name Laura (Riding) Jackson, published as *The Poems of Laura Riding: A New Edition of the 1938 Collection,* Persea, 1980.
(Under name Laura Riding) *Selected Poems: In Five Sets,* Faber, 1970, Norton, 1973.

NOVELS

(Under name Laura Riding, with George Ellidge) *14A,* Barker, 1934.
(Under pseudonym Madeleine Vara) *Convalescent Conversations,* Seizin Press (Majorca), 1936.
(Under name Laura Riding) *A Trojan Ending,* Random House, 1937, new edition, Carcanet, 1984.

EDITOR; UNDER NAME LAURA RIDING

Everybody's Letters, Barker, 1933.
Epilogue: A Critical Summary, three volumes, Seizin Press (Majorca), 1935-37.
The World and Ourselves, Chatto & Windus, 1938.

OTHER

(Translator under name Laura Riding Gottschalk) Marcel le Goff, *Anatole France at Home,* Adelphi, 1926.

(Under name Laura Riding, with Robert Graves) *A Survey of Modernist Poetry*, Heinemann, 1927, Doubleday, 1928, reprinted, R. West, 1977.

(Under name Laura Riding, with Robert Graves) *A Pamphlet against Anthologies*, Doubleday, 1928, reprinted, AMS Press, 1970.

(Under name Laura Riding) *Contemporaries and Snobs*, J. Cape, 1928, reprinted, Scholarly Press, 1971.

(Under name Laura Riding) *Anarchism Is Not Enough*, Doubleday, 1928.

(Under name Laura Riding) *Four Unposted Letters to Catherine*, Hours Press (Paris), 1930.

(Under name Laura Riding) *Experts Are Puzzled* (essays and short stories), J. Cape, 1930.

(Under name Laura Riding) *Pictures*, [London], 1933.

(Under name Laura Riding) *Progress of Stories* (short stories), Seizin Press (Majorca), 1935, Books for Libraries, 1971, revised edition, Dial Press, 1982.

(Translator under name Laura Riding, with Robert Graves) Georg Schwarz, *Almost Forgotten Germany*, Random House, 1936.

(Under name Laura Riding) *Len Lye and the Problem of Popular Films*, Seizin Press (London), 1938.

(Under name Laura Riding) *The Covenant of Literal Morality*, Seizin Press (London), 1938.

(Under name Laura Riding, with Harry Kemp and others) *The Left Heresy in Literature and Life*, Methuen, 1939, reprinted, Folcroft Editions, 1974, Norwood Editions, 1977.

(Under name Laura Riding) *Lives of Wives* (historical fiction), Random House, 1939.

The Telling, Athlone Press, 1972, Harper, 1973.

(With husband, Schuyler B. Jackson) *From the Chapter "Truth" in "Rational Meaning: A New Foundation for the Definition of Words" (Not Yet Published)*, Priapus, 1975.

It Has Taken Long: From the Writings of Laura (Riding) Jackson, Chelsea Associates, 1976.

How a Poem Comes to Be, Lord John Press, 1980.

Description of Life, Targ Editions, 1980.

Some Communications of Broad Reference, Lord John Press, 1983.

Also contributor, under names Laura Riding Gottschalk, Laura Riding, and Laura (Riding) Jackson, to periodicals, including *Wilson Library Bulletin, Art and Literature, Civilta Delle Macchine, Massachusetts Review, Denver Quarterly, Glasgow Magazine, PN Review, Ms., Antaeus, Stand*, and *Chelsea. Chelsea* no. 35 (1976) was devoted solely to her writings.

The authorized Laura and Schuyler B. Jackson Collection is held at Cornell University. Letters from Laura (Riding) Jackson's period with "The Fugitives" are at the Joint University Libraries in Nashville, Tenn. Letters from the 1930s are in the collection of the State University of New York at Buffalo, and galleys, page proofs, and letters from the 1960s are in the Northwestern University Library.

WORK IN PROGRESS: Rational Meaning: A New Foundation for the Definition of Words, in revision; a book, *The Failure of Poetry; The Ends of Literature*, a collection of miscellaneous writings; a book of personal narrative and comment on things literary; a book on the English poet Charles M. Doughty, embracing her late husband's work on this subject; *A Century of Loss: Literature and the Cultivation of the Incomplete*, a book of essays.

SIDELIGHTS: Laura Riding, now known as Laura (Riding) Jackson, "was still in her thirties when she published her 477-page *Collected Poems* in 1938," reports Paul Auster in the *New York Review of Books*. "At an age when most poets are just beginning to come into their own," he continues, "she had already reached maturity." A prolific writer, Riding's oeuvre includes volumes of poetry, collections of critical essays and short fiction, novels, and the founding of her own small publishing firm, Seizin Press. In the 1920s and '30s, as Auster relates, she "became an important force of the international avant-garde." Her work was highly praised by some distinguished critics, including Robert Fitzgerald, who wrote in the *Kenyon Review*, "Of all the contemporary poems I know, these seem to me the furthest advanced, the most personal and the purest."

Laura Riding first came to public notice when she attracted the attention of "The Fugitives," a group of American Southern writers centered at Vanderbilt University. Members of the group included John Crowe Ransom, Allen Tate, and Robert Penn Warren. Their activities included meetings for the reading and discussion of poetry and philosophy, and they published their own poetry magazine, *The Fugitive*, which appeared from 1922 to 1925. They were searching for new criteria to apply to poetry, and Laura Riding's work suited them perfectly. In 1923 *The Fugitive* commended her first published poem for its "quality of originality," and in 1924 hailed her work as "the discovery of the year." She was soon invited to join the group, and her acceptance was announced in March 1925 as cause for "general felicitations."

Several years later, working with the English poet and novelist Robert Graves, Riding furthered the aims of the group with *A Survey of Modernist Poetry*, "the implicit critical and theoretical principles of which," notes A. T. K. Crozier in *The Fontana Biographical Companion to Modern Thought*, "she developed in two works of dazzling argument, *Contemporaries and Snobs* (1928) . . . and *Anarchism Is Not Enough* (1928)." The *Survey* introduced a new method for close textual criticism, showing that minute examination of a good poem finds within it truths not communicable in any other way. Its influence contributed greatly to the school of thought that became known as "The New Criticism."

It is for her poetry, however, that Laura Riding is best known, and her poems reflect her commitment to write with truth. "In poem after poem," declares Auster, "we witness her trying somehow to peel back the skin of the world in order to find some absolute and unassailable place of permanence, and because the poems are rarely grounded in a physical perception of that world, they tend, strangely, to exist in an almost purely emotional climate, created by the fervor of this metaphysical quest." Her poems "are highly compressed, intellectual, disciplined, and possess a number of other virtues no longer much in evidence. . . . At their best, they have some of the concentration of language so memorable in Emily Dickinson, while the syntactic difficulty and elaborate conceits [T. S.] Eliot did so much to revive have been practiced in her poems with remarkable effect," remarks James Atlas in *Poetry* magazine.

Laura Riding gave up poetry after her marriage to critic Schuyler B. Jackson because she found it incompatible with truth. Donald Davie, reviewing anonymously for the *Times Literary Supplement*, states that "once Keats had declared 'Beauty is Truth, Truth Beauty,' seeming to affirm an *indissoluble* unity [between the two], it was inevitable that sooner or later there would appear a poet who, having believed in Keats's assurance, would find that it didn't square with experience, and would be honest enough to say so." Her major aim in writing, according to Harry Mathews in the *New York Review of Books,* "was to make articulate in the experience of her readers a knowledge of life that is both true and nonconceptual. It was as if she wanted to make the mechanisms of language, usually so approximate and reductive, accurate enough in the effect of their working to initiate the reader willy-nilly into an awareness of what she felt to be the pure, unmediated truth." Poetry, she felt, could no longer do this. After her husband's death in 1968, she continued the linguistic work alone, completing in 1974 the as yet unpublished book, *Rational Meaning: A New Foundation for the Definition of Words.* In recent years she has resumed publishing articles on poetry, language, woman, and story.

Laura (Riding) Jackson wrote the following summary for *CA:* "At the beginning of the 'forties, [I] made the drastic decision that [I] must renounce poetry, as imposing irremovable obstacles to the realizing of the full potential afforded by language, when words are used faithfully, as they mean, of general human speaking, writing, in what [I] called, in an introduction to a reading of [my] poems in 1962 on a British Broadcasting programme, 'the style of truth.' [My] work on language was accompanied by a long look at not only poetry and literature but the entire human scene, historical and contemporary, with clarifying perception of the so far largely unfulfilled responsibility that human beings have of telling the 'one story' of their being, and the world—the central theme of all [my] earlier work. [I] came to think that this story required a personal truth exceeding literary, poetic, and all other categorically professionalized intellectual points of view, and linguistic styles. [My] book, *The Telling,* which sets forth this 'personal gospel,' as [I call] it, has . . . been received in some quarters with devoted excitement, but with almost total 'patently deliberate avoidance of notice' in the literary press of both countries in which it was published."

BIOGRAPHICAL/CRITICAL SOURCES:

BOOKS

Bullock, Alan, and R. B. Woodings, editors, *The Fontana Biographical Companion to Modern Thought,* Collins, 1983.
Contemporary Literary Criticism, Gale, Volume 3, 1975, Volume 7, 1977.
Murphy, Gwendolen, editor, *The Modern Poet,* Sidgwick, 1938.
Rosenthal, M. L., and Sally M. Gall, *The Modern Poetic Sequence: The Genius of Modern Poetry,* Oxford University Press, 1983.
Southworth, James G., *More Modern American Poets,* Basil Blackwell, 1954.
Wexler, Joyce Piell, *Laura Riding's Pursuit of Truth,* Ohio University Press, 1979.

PERIODICALS

Chelsea, September, 1962, September, 1974.
Chicago Tribune Book World, February 7, 1982.
Encounter, July, 1987.
Fugitive, December, 1923, December, 1924, December, 1925.
Hiroshima Studies in English Language and Literature, Number 21, 1976.
Kenyon Review, summer, 1939.
Los Angeles Times, April 22, 1982.
Los Angeles Times Book Review, June 30, 1985.
Nation, March 27, 1929, September 11, 1937, November 30, 1974.
New Statesman, September 24, 1982.

New Yorker, December 24, 1938, September 9, 1939.
New York Review of Books, August 7, 1975, April 29, 1982.
New York Times, June 23, 1929, August 15, 1937, September 24, 1939.
PN Review, Number 22, 1981.
Poetry, February, 1975.
Quill & Quire, May, 1982.
Review, September, 1970.
Saturday Review, December 10, 1927, July 7, 1928.
Saturday Review of Literature, April 20, 1929, August 31, 1929, February 9, 1935, September 11, 1937, September 9, 1939.
Spectator, December 24, 1927, April 2, 1937, September 22, 1939, August 28, 1982.
Stand, Number 15, 1973.
Time, August 16, 1937, December 26, 1938, September 11, 1939.
Times Literary Supplement, January 19, 1928, April 5, 1928, August 2, 1928, August 16, 1928, March 27, 1937, October 8, 1938, October 21, 1939, February 9, 1973, October 1, 1982.
World Literature Today, autumn, 1981.

*   *   *

JACKSON, R(ichard) Eugene   1941-

PERSONAL: Born February 25, 1941, in Helena, Ark.; son of Howard L. (a steamfitter) and Edna (Warren) Jackson; children: Brandon D. *Education:* Memphis State University, B.S., 1963; Kent State University, M.A., 1964; Southern Illinois University, Ph.D., 1971.

ADDRESSES: Home—1901 Oakleaf Ct., Mobile, Ala. 36609. *Office*—Drama Department, University of South Alabama, Mobile, Ala. 36688.

CAREER: Teacher of English, speech, and drama at high school in Antwerp, Ohio, 1964-65; Wisconsin State University—Eau Claire (now University of Wisconsin—Eau Claire), instructor of drama, 1967-68; San Francisco State University, San Francisco, Calif., assistant professor of drama, 1968-70; University of South Alabama, Mobile, assistant professor, 1971-75, associate professor, 1975-78, professor of drama, 1980—, chairman of department of dramatic arts, 1978—. Director of numerous local and university theater productions, including "The Imaginary Invalid," "Promises, Promises," and "Cat on a Hot Tin Roof."

MEMBER: American Theatre Association, Dramatists Guild, Southeastern Theatre Conference (chairman of children's theatre division, 1979-80), Alabama Theatre League, Mobile Jaycees, Phi Kappa Phi.

AWARDS, HONORS: Winner of several local and university contests; first alternate, O'Neill Playwriting Contest, 1973, for "No Way"; winner of Pioneer Drama Service national playwriting contest, 1979, for "Brer Rabbit's Big Secret," and 1980, for "Snowhite and the Space Gwarfs."

WRITINGS:

PUBLISHED PLAYS; FOR CHILDREN

Ferdinand and the Dirty Knight (two-act comedy; first produced in Kent, Ohio, at Kent State University, June, 1964), Pioneer Drama Service, 1968.
Little Red Riding Wolf (three-act; first produced in Mobile, Ala., at Pixie Playhouse), I. E. Clark, 1973.

Who Can Fix the Dragon's Wagon (two-act; first produced in Eau Claire, Wis., at the University of Wisconsin—Eau Claire, November, 1967), I. E. Clark, 1974.

Triple Play (one-act), Dramatic Publishing, 1974.

The Creepy Castle Hassle (three-act; first produced in Mobile at Pixie Playhouse), Performance Publishing, 1975.

The Crazy Paper Caper (three-act; first produced in Mobile at Pillans School Theatre), Performance Publishing, 1976.

"Snowballs and Grapevines" (one-act; first produced in Mobile at Bethel Theatre, 1973), published in *Dekalb Literary Arts Journal,* summer, 1976.

The Wonderful Wizard of Oz (three-act; first produced in Mobile at Pixie Playhouse, 1975), I. E. Clark, 1976.

(And lyricist) *The Sleeping Beauty* (two-act musical; first produced by Children's Musical Theatre in Mobile, 1975), Pioneer Drama Service, 1976.

Rumpelstiltskin Is My Name (two-act), I. E. Clark, 1977.

(With Susan Snider Osterberg) *Bumper Snickers* (two-act), I. E. Clark, 1978.

(And lyricist) *Brer Rabbit's Big Secret* (two-act musical; first produced by Children's Musical Theatre in Mobile, October 1, 1978), Pioneer Drama Service, 1979.

Superkid (three-act), I. E. Clark, 1980.

A Golden Fleecing (three-act; first produced in Gulf Shores, Ala., at State Park Theatre, June 1, 1980), Pioneer Drama Service, 1980.

(And lyricist) *Snowhite and the Space Gwarfs* (two-act musical; first produced by Children's Musical Theatre in Mobile, October 1, 1980), Pioneer Drama Service, 1980.

Rag Dolls (two-act), I. E. Clark, 1981.

(And lyricist) *Lindy* (three-act musical), Performance Publishing, 1981.

The Adventures of Peter Cottontail (two-act; first produced by Children's Musical Theatre in Mobile, summer, 1979), Pioneer Drama Service, 1981.

(And lyricist) *The Hatfields and the McFangs* (two-act musical; first produced by Children's Musical Theatre in Mobile, October 1, 1981), Performance Publishing, 1982.

Unidentified Flying Reject (three-act), I. E. Clark, 1982.

Coffee Pott and the Wolf Man (three-act), I. E. Clark, 1982.

Animal Krackers (two-act; first produced by Children's Musical Theatre in Mobile, October 1, 1981), Pioneer Drama Service, 1983.

(And lyricist) *Boogie Man Rock* (three-act musical), Baker's Plays, 1984.

(And lyricist) *Popeye the Sailor* (full-length musical), Pioneer Drama Service, 1984.

(And lyricist) *Pinocchio*, I. E. Clark, 1985.

(And lyricist) *Arnold* (full-length musical), Pioneer Drama Service, 1985.

Babes in Toyland, I. E. Clark, 1987.

Christmas Crisis at Mistletoe Mesa, Pioneer Drama Service, 1987.

(And lyricist) *The Hunting of the Snark,* I. E. Clark, 1987.

(And lyricist) *The Life and Adventures of Santa Claus,* Pioneer Drama Service, 1988.

PRODUCED PLAYS

"Carbolic Acid Is Not as Sweet as White Ribbons" (two-act; for adults), first produced in Memphis at Memphis Little Theatre, August, 1963.

"A Thousand and One Spells to Cast" (two-act; for children), first produced in Kent at Kent State University, 1964.

"Sticks and Stones" (two-act; for children), first produced at Memphis Little Theatre, August, 1964.

"Mother Goose Follies" (two-act; for children), first produced by Southern Illinois University in Carbondale, September, 1971.

(And lyricist) "The Jumping off Place," first produced by Children's Musical Theatre in Mobile, 1985.

(And lyricist) "Wild Pecos Bill," first produced by Children's Musical Theatre in Mobile, summer, 1985.

(Librettist) "The Cantor of Vilna" (short opera), first produced by Sha'arai Shomayin Temple in Mobile, April, 1986.

(And lyricist) "The Song of Hiawatha," first produced by Children's Musical Theatre in Mobile, 1988.

Also author of "Felicia and the Magic Pinks" (two-act), first produced in Mobile at Pixie Playhouse.

OTHER

Author of several as yet unpublished and unproduced plays, including "No Way." Also author of lyrics for numerous musical plays produced by Children's Musical Theatre, Mobile, Ala. Contributor of articles to *Children's Theatre Review.*

WORK IN PROGRESS: My Dog Ate My Homework, a novel for teens; "You're a Grand Old Flag," a new play using the music of George M. Cohan; book and lyrics for "The Dancing Snowman."

SIDELIGHTS: R. Eugene Jackson told *CA:* "Teaching on the university level is an exciting and fulfilling vocation. Having the opportunity to write, especially for the youngsters, is frosting on the cake. To that I have added a new hobby: playing the violin which, through all the squeaking and scratching, is relaxing and challenging."

* * *

JACKSON, W. A. Douglas
See JACKSON, William Arthur Douglas

* * *

JACKSON, William Arthur Douglas 1923-
(W. A. Douglas Jackson)

PERSONAL: Born November 25, 1923, in Toronto, Ontario, Canada; naturalized U.S. citizen; son of Joseph Walter and Sara Justine (Palmer) Jackson. *Education:* Royal Conservatory of Music, Toronto, A.T.C.M., 1941, L.T.C.M., 1944; University of Toronto, B.A., 1946, M.A., 1949; University of Maryland, Ph.D., 1953; also studied at University of Wisconsin, 1948-49, and Columbia University, 1952-53.

ADDRESSES: Home—18308 84th Place W., Edmonds, Wash. 98020. *Office*—Department of Geography, University of Washington, Seattle, Wash. 98195.

CAREER: University of Iowa, Iowa City, assistant professor of geography, 1953-54; University of Washington, Seattle, assistant professor, 1955-58, associate professor, 1958-60, professor of geography, 1960—.

MEMBER: American Geographical Society, Association of American Geographers, American Association for the Advancement of Slavic Studies, English Speaking Union, Canadian Association of Geographers, Western Slavic Association.

AWARDS, HONORS: Ford Foundation, fellowship, 1954-55, grant, 1963; grant, Social Science Research Council, 1957;

fellowship, Russian Research Center, Harvard University, 1958; grant, Inter-University Committee, 1959; grants, American Council of Learned Societies, 1961, 1966-67, 1968; grants, American Philosophical Society, 1963, 1972; grant, National Science Foundation, 1967; grant, National Defense Education Act Institute for Advanced Study in Geography, 1967-68; fellowship, Japan Society for the Promotion of Science, 1977.

WRITINGS:

Soviet Union (textbook), Fideler, 1962, revised edition, Gateway Press, 1988.

The Russo-Chinese Borderlands: Zone of Peaceful Contact or Potential Conflict?, Van Nostrand, 1962, 2nd edition, 1968.

(Editor) *Politics and Geographic Relationships: Readings on the Nature of Political Geography*, Prentice-Hall, 1964, 2nd edition (with Marwyn S. Samuels) published as *Politics and Geographic Relationships: Toward a New Focus*, 1971.

(Editor) *Agrarian Problems of Communist and Non-Communist Countries*, University of Washington Press, 1971.

(Editor; also translator with Jacek Romanowski) *Natural Resources of the Soviet Union: Their Use and Renewal*, W. H. Freeman, 1971.

(With Virginia Creed) *Man in Europe: France and Soviet Union* (Soviet Union section by Jackson; France section by Creed), Fideler, 1972, reprinted as *Europe: France and Soviet Union*, 1977.

(With Edward F. Bergman) *A Geography of Politics*, W. C. Brown, 1973.

Introduction to the Study of Geographic Problems and Patterns, Toyon, 1974.

(Editor) *Soviet Resource Management and the Environment*, American Association for the Advancement of Slavic Studies, 1978.

Soviet Manganese Ores: Output and Export, Association of American Geographers, 1980.

The Shaping of Our World: A Human and Cultural Geography, Wiley, 1985.

Also author of *Philadelphia Waterfront Industry: Industrial Land and Its Potentials on the Delaware River*, 1955; also contributor to several books. Contributor to organization annals and to encyclopedias. Contributor to journals.

WORK IN PROGRESS: Colonization and Agricultural Development in the Central Black Earth, a monograph, with Ihor Stebelsky; *Political Geography* (in Japanese), with Shoichi Yokoyama.

* * *

JADE, Jacqueline
  See HYMAN, Jackie (Diamond)

* * *

JEANNIERE, Abel 1921-

PERSONAL: Born August 28, 1921, in Saint-Paul-en-Pareds, Vendee, France; son of Etienne and Celine (Gonnord) Jeanniere. *Education:* Sorbonne, University of Paris, licence, 1949; Gregoriana, Rome, docteur en philosophie, 1957.

ADDRESSES: Home—15 rue Raymond Monsieur, 75007 Paris, France. *Office*—Centre Sevres, 35 rue de Sevres, 75006, Paris, France.

CAREER: Institut d'Etudes Sociales, Institut Catholique, Paris, professor, 1960—; *Projet*, Vanves, France, assistant editor, 1970-84; Centre Sevres, Paris, professor of philosophy, 1984—.

WRITINGS:

La pensee d'Heraclite d'Ephese, Aubier-Montaigne, 1959.

Anthropologie sexuelle, Aubier-Montaigne, 1964, 2nd edition, 1972, translation of first edition by Julie Kernan published as *The Anthropology of Sex*, Harper, 1967.

Sexualite Humaine, Lethielleux, 1966, 2nd edition, Aubier-Montaigne, 1967.

(With Pierre Antoine) *Espace mobile et temps incertains*, Aubier-Montaigne, 1970.

(Editor and author of introduction) *Heraclite: Traducion integrale des fragments*, 2nd revised edition, Aubier-Montaigne, 1977, 3rd edition, 1987.

Liberte sans modeles, Aubier-Montaigne, 1980.

Les Fins du monde, Aubier-Montaigne, 1987.

Anthropologie sociale et politique, Media Sevres (Centre Sevres), 1987.

* * *

JENKINS, John (Robert Graham) 1928-

PERSONAL: Born June 20, 1928, in Pontypridd, Wales; son of J. Henry (a businessman) and Olwen (Prys-Jones) Jenkins. *Education:* Cambridge University, B.A., 1950, M.A., 1955; University of Toronto, M.B.A., 1953; Harvard University, D.B.A., 1968; Oxford University, D.Phil., 1981.

ADDRESSES: Office—School of Business and Economics, Wilfrid Laurier University, Waterloo, Ontario, Canada N2L 3C5.

CAREER: Marketing supervisor, Procter & Gamble of Canada, 1953-56; account executive, Foster Advertising, 1956-57; media director, McKim Advertising, 1957-59; director of market and media planning, Batten, Barton, Durstine & Osborn (Canada), 1959-62; director of marketing research, Canadian Television Network, 1962-64; Northeastern University, Boston, Mass., associate professor of marketing, 1967-70; Wilfrid Laurier University, Waterloo, Ontario, dean of School of Business and Economics, 1970-74, professor of business administration, 1970—. Visiting scholar, Manchester Business School, 1975-76; visiting professor, University of Waikato, New Zealand, 1983, University of New South Wales, Australia, 1984, Monterey Institute of International Studies, 1985-86, and Huazhong University, People's Republic of China, 1989. Appointed public member of Advertising Standards Council, Canadian Advertising Federation, 1988—.

MEMBER: Academy of International Business, International Council for Small Business, American Academy of Advertising, American Marketing Association (former vice-president, Boston chapter), Administrative Sciences Association of Canada.

WRITINGS:

(With J. J. Zif) *Planning the Advertising Campaign* (player's manual and instructor's guide; business simulation game), Macmillan, 1971.

Marketing and Customer Behavior, Pergamon, 1973.

(Contributor) *Marketing Management*, Wiley, 1976.

(Contributor) *Advertising in Canada*, McGraw-Hill Ryerson, 1980.

(With Robert D. Wilson) *Planning the Advertising Campaign: A Canadian Simulation Game* (player's manual and instructor's guide), Collier Macmillan (Canada), 1983.
(Editor with Walter B. Herbert) *Public Relations in Canada: Some Perspectives*, Fitzhenry & Whiteside, 1984.
Jura Separatism in Switzerland, Clarendon Press, 1985.

Author of over fifty research articles and papers. Contributor to numerous academic and professional journals.

*   *   *

JOHNSON, Jane 1951-

PERSONAL: Born February 28, 1951, in London, England; daughter of Eric (an accountant) and Sheila (a painter; maiden name, Myer) Conrad; married Robin Johnson (divorced). *Education:* University of East Anglia, B.A. (with honors), 1973. *Politics:* Liberal. *Religion:* None.

ADDRESSES: Home—32 King Henry's Rd., London NW3 3RP, England.

CAREER: Medici Society (publisher), London, England, advertising assistant, 1973-74; Hodder & Stoughton (publisher), London, book designer, 1974-76; Jonathan Cape, Ltd. (publisher), London, book designer, 1976-81; children's book writer and illustrator. Part-time teacher of illustration at art schools in London.

MEMBER: Association of Illustrators.

AWARDS, HONORS: Sybil and the Blue Rabbit was named among fifty best-designed books in the United Kingdom by National Book League, won the Mother Goose Award first runner-up prize, and won the Owl Prize in Japan, all in 1980.

WRITINGS:

(Illustrator) Serghei Aksakov, *A Russian Gentleman*, Folio Society, 1977.
(And illustrator) *Sybil and the Blue Rabbit* (juvenile), Benn, 1979.
(And illustrator) *Bertie on the Beach* (juvenile), Benn, 1981.
(Compiler and illustrator) *A Book of Nursery Riddles*, Benn, 1984.
(And illustrator) *Today I Thought I'd Run Away* (juvenile), A. & C. Black, 1985.
(Illustrator) David Lloyd, *Pirates* (juvenile), Walker Books, 1985.
(Illustrator) Lloyd, *Dragon Catchers* (juvenile), Walker Books, 1985.
(Illustrator) Lloyd, *Explorers* (juvenile), Walker Books, 1985.
(Contributing illustrator) *The Children's Book* (juvenile), Walker Books, 1985.
(And illustrator) *My Bedtime Rhyme* (juvenile), Anderson Press, 1987.
(And illustrator) *Duck Charlie* (juvenile), Walker Books, 1987.
(And illustrator) *Pig George* (juvenile), Walker Books, 1987.
(Illustrator) Paul Rogers, *From Me to You* (juvenile), Orchard Books, 1987.
(Illustrator) Rosemary Sutcliff, *A Little Dog like You*, Orchard Books, 1987.
(And illustrator) *Our Garden Year*, Orchard Books, 1989.

SIDELIGHTS: Jane Johnson commented: "I was very slow learning to read, so I looked at picture books for hours instead. A lonely childhood and sedentary habits led to my drawing to amuse myself. Because I have vivid memories of the sensa-

tions of being a child, I have no difficulty in returning to that world when I am starting a new book.

"My childhood was not happy, so it has remained very real to me. My books reflect the preoccupations I can remember, wanting to be the center of attention, feeling lonely, bored, uncomprehending, lost. Because I know how vulnerable a child can feel, the books are meant to comfort and encourage, to be fun rather than to seem dangerous and frightening."

AVOCATIONAL INTERESTS: Live theatre, opera, cinema, the history of fashion, the visual arts, collecting antique furniture.

*   *   *

JOHNSON, L. D. 1916-1981

PERSONAL: Born February 18, 1916, in Walters, Okla.; died December 20, 1981; son of Ray (a farmer) and Maude (Goodman) Johnson; married Marion Ervin (a librarian), September 2, 1937; children: Elaine (Mrs. Archer L. Yeatts III), Roland. *Education:* George Washington University, A.B., 1937; Southern Baptist Theological Seminary, Th.M., 1940, Th.D., 1942.

ADDRESSES: Home—306 Chantilly Dr., Greenville, S.C. 29615.

CAREER: Pastor of Baptist church in Danville, Va., 1943-59; University of Richmond, Richmond, Va., professor of religion, 1959-62; pastor of Baptist church in Greenville, S.C., 1962-67; Furman University, Greenville, professor of religion and chaplain, 1967-81.

MEMBER: Association of Baptist Professors of Religion, National Association of College and University Chaplains.

AWARDS, HONORS: George Washington Honor Medal of Freedoms Foundation, 1964, for newspaper column; faculty of the year award, 1975; posthumously elected to Furman University Hall of Fame, 1982.

WRITINGS:

An Introduction to the Bible, Convention Press, 1969.
Out of the Whirlwind: The Major Message of Job, Broadman, 1971.
Israel's Wisdom: Learn and Live, Broadman, 1975.
The Morning after Death, Broadman, 1978.
Moments of Reflection, edited by Mary Neal Jones, Broadman, 1980.
Layman's Bible Book Commentary, Volume 9: *Proverbs, Ecclesiastes, Song of Solomon*, Broadman, 1982.
Images of Eternity, compiled by wife, Marion Johnson, Broadman, 1984.

Author of weekly column appearing in Sunday newspapers in Virginia, 1955-81, and in South Carolina and North Carolina, 1962-81.

[Sketch reviewed by wife, Marion E. Johnson]

*   *   *

JOHNSON, Pamela Hansford 1912-1981
(Nap Lombard, a joint pseudonym)

PERSONAL: Born May 29, 1912, in London, England; died of emphysema, June 18, 1981, in London; daughter of Reginald Kenneth (a civil servant) and Amy Clotilda (an actress; maiden name, Howson) Johnson; married Gordon Neil Stewart (a historian and journalist), 1936 (divorced); married Charles Percy Snow (a scientist and author), July 14, 1950 (died July 1, 1980); children: (first marriage) Andrew Morven, Lindsay Jean; (second marriage) Philip Charles Hansford. *Education:* Attended Clapham County Secondary School.

ADDRESSES: Home—85 Eaton Ter., London S.W. 1, England. *Agent*—Curtis Brown Ltd., 575 Madison Ave., New York, N.Y. 10022.

CAREER: Central Hanover Bank & Trust Co., London, England, stenographer, 1930-34; author, 1935-81; literary critic, 1936-81.

MEMBER: PEN, Royal Society of Literature (fellow), Society for European Culture.

AWARDS, HONORS: Sunday Referee Award, 1933, for poetry; fellow, Center for Advanced Studies, Wesleyan University (Middletown, Conn.), and Timothy Dwight College, Yale University, both 1961; Litt.D., Temple University, Philadelphia, 1963, York University, Toronto, 1967, Widener College, Chester, Penn., 1970; Commander, Order of the British Empire, 1975; D.H.L., University of Louisville.

WRITINGS:

NOVELS

This Bed Thy Centre, Harcourt, 1935, reprinted, Macmillan (London), 1963.
Blessed above Women, Harcourt, 1936.
Here Today, Chapman & Hall, 1937.
World's End, Chapman & Hall, 1937, Carrick & Evans, 1938.
The Monument, Carrick & Evans, 1938.
Girdle of Venus, Chapman & Hall, 1939.
Too Dear for My Possessing (first novel in trilogy), Carrick & Evans, 1940, reprinted, Penguin, 1976, Scribner, 1973.
The Family Pattern, Collins, 1942.
Winter Quarters, Collins, 1943, Macmillan (New York), 1944.
The Trojan Brothers, M. Joseph, 1944, Macmillan, 1945.
An Avenue of Stone (second novel in trilogy), M. Joseph, 1947, Macmillan, 1948, reprinted, Scribner, 1973.
A Summer to Decide (third novel in trilogy), M. Joseph, 1948, Scribner, 1975.
The Philistines, M. Joseph, 1949.
Catherine Carter (first novel in trilogy), Knopf, 1952, reprinted, Macmillan (London), 1969, new edition, Penguin, 1971.
An Impossible Marriage (second novel in trilogy), Macmillan (London), 1954, Harcourt, 1955.
The Last Resort (third novel in trilogy), St. Martin's, 1956, published as *The Sea and the Wedding,* Harcourt, 1957.
The Humbler Creation, Macmillan, 1959, Harcourt, 1960.
An Error of Judgement, Harcourt, 1962.
The Survival of the Fittest, Scribner, 1968.
The Honours Board, Scribner, 1970.
The Holiday Friend, Macmillan, 1972, Scribner, 1973.
The Good Listener, Scribner, 1975.
The Good Husband, Scribner, 1978.
The Bonfire, Scribner, 1981.

"DOROTHY MERTON COMEDIES" TRILOGY

The Unspeakable Skipton, Harcourt, 1959, reprinted, Scribner, 1981.
Night and Silence, Who Is Here? An American Comedy, Scribner, 1963.
Cork Street, Next to the Hatter's: A Novel in Bad Taste, Scribner, 1965.

WITH GORDON NEIL STEWART UNDER JOINT PSEUDONYM NAP LOMBARD; MYSTERY NOVELS

Tidy Death, Cassell, 1940.
The Grinning Pig, Simon & Schuster, 1943 (published in England as *Murder's a Swine,* Hutchinson, 1943).

PLAYS

Corinth House: A Play in Three Acts (produced in London at New Lindsay Theatre, May, 1948), Evans Brothers, 1951, reprinted with an essay on the future of prose drama, St. Martin's, 1954.
(With husband, C. P. Snow) *The Supper Dance,* Evans Brothers, 1951.
(With Snow) *Family Party,* Evans Brothers, 1951.
(With Snow) *Spare the Rod,* Evans Brothers, 1951.
(With Snow) *To Murder Mrs. Mortimer,* Evans Brothers, 1951.
(With Snow) *Her Best Foot Forward,* Evans Brothers, 1951.
(With Snow) *The Pigeon with the Silver Foot: A Legend of Venice* (one-act), Evans Brothers, 1951.
(Adapter with Kitty Black) Jean Anouilh, *The Rehearsal* (produced in London, 1961; produced on Broadway at Royale Theatre, September 23, 1963), Methuen, 1961, Coward, 1962.
(Adapter with Snow) Georgi Dzhagarov, *The Public Prosecutor* (produced in London at Hampstead Theatre Club, 1967), translated from the Bulgarian by Marguerite Alexieva, University of Washington, 1969.

CONTRIBUTOR

Reginald Moore and Woodrow Wyatt, editors, *Stories of the Forties,* Nicolson & Watson, 1945.
Winter's Tales 1, Macmillan, 1955.
George D. Painter, editor and translator, *Marcel Proust: Letters to His Mother,* Rider, 1956, Citadel Press, 1958.
Winter's Tales 3, Macmillan, 1957.
Joan Kahn, editor, *Some Things Strange and Sinister,* Harper, 1973.
John Halperin, *C. P. Snow: An Oral Biography; Together with a Conversation with Lady Snow (Pamela Hansford Johnson),* St. Martin's, 1983.

OTHER

Symphony for Full Orchestra (poems), Sunday Referee-Parton Press, 1934.
Thomas Wolfe: A Critical Study, Heinemann, 1947, published as *Hungry Gulliver: An English Critical Appraisal of Thomas Wolfe,* Scribner, 1948, published as *The Art of Thomas Wolfe,* 1963.
I. Compton-Burnett, Longmans, Green, 1951, reprinted, 1973.
Proust Recaptured: Six Radio Sketches Based on the Author's Characters (radio plays; based on *Remembrance of Things Past* by Marcel Proust; contains "The Duchess at Sunset," broadcast, 1948; "Swan in Love," broadcast, 1952; "Madame de Charlus," broadcast, 1954; "Albertine Regained," broadcast, 1954; "Saint-Loup," broadcast, 1955; "A Window at Montjaurain," broadcast, 1956), University of Chicago Press, 1958 (published in England as *Six Proust Reconstructions,* Macmillan, 1958).
(Editor with Snow) *Winter's Tales 7: Stories from Modern Russia,* St. Martin's, 1961, published as *Stories from Modern Russia,* 1962.
(Author of introduction) Cecil Woolf and Brocard Sewell, editors, *Corvo, 1860-1960,* St. Albert's Press, 1961, published as *New Quests for Corvo,* Icon, 1965.

(Author of introduction) Anthony Trollope, *Barchester Towers,* Norton, 1962.

Africa, 2nd edition, Oxford University Press, 1966.

On Iniquity: Some Personal Reflections Arising out of the Moors Murder Trial, Scribner, 1967.

Important to Me: Personalia (autobiography), Macmillan, 1974, Scribner, 1975.

Also contributor to *Essays and Studies* of the English Association, 1960, and 1963, and to *Transactions* of the Royal Society of Literature, 1963. Contributor of short stories, articles, and critical reviews to numerous periodicals, including *Washington Post, Liverpool Post, John O'London's Weekly, Sunday Chronicle, English Review,* and *Spectator.*

WORK IN PROGRESS: Adelaide Bartlett, a novel.

SIDELIGHTS: Pamela Hansford Johnson was "one of England's best-known novelists, whom many American critics regarded as greatly underrated in the United States," according to her obituary in *Publishers Weekly.* Although perhaps better known in America for her marriage to Lord C. P. Snow, the famous scientist, novelist, and social theorist, Johnson was also renowned as a popular author and critic in her own right. She published her first novel, *This Bed Thy Centre,* when she was only twenty-two, and, in a career covering more than forty years, eventually produced twenty-nine others. "Anthony Burgess, the novelist and critic," said her *New York Times* obituary, "once described Miss Johnson's novels as 'witty, satirical and deftly malicious—some of her books characterized by a sort of grave levity, others by a sort of light gravity.'"

In her books Johnson examined ordinary people, in a wide variety of social classes, who are psychologically impaired in some way, unable to cope with everyday life, people who fall in and out of love, and people who are bound by a philosophy of duty or some other moral concept. According to Ishrat Lindblad in her book *Pamela Hansford Johnson,* "her protagonists are usually intelligent young men and women from the 'middle-middle' class, with literary or artistic ability, whose experience has much in common with her own. She also makes frequent use of a dominant mother and a weak or absent father, and the relationships between mother and child, teacher and pupil are among the most poignantly drawn in her fiction. At the same time she displays an interest in the bizarre and abnormal: nymphomaniacs, homosexuals, old men and women painfully in love with the young, crazed passion, and murder all fall within her range."

Johnson favored the psychological novel early in her career, using counterpoint, stream of consciousness, and interior monologues to examine people under stress. She later turned to more traditional English models, rejecting the experimental forms developed and used by James Joyce and others in the early decades of the twentieth century. Reviewers compared her work to that of George Eliot, Anthony Trollope, and Marcel Proust. In the 1940s, said Lindblad, she adopted an objective voice for narration, using it to explore "the perspective that distance and the passing of time lend to an experience, and it is this aspect of her work that most readily comes to mind as evidence of her debt to Marcel Proust." Later, Lindblad continued, she "moved over to the method of the great nineteenth-century novelists with an implied third-person narrator and a traditional chronological sequence of events." In these later works, stated her London *Times* obituary, "she revealed herself as a novelist in the central English tradition of broad realism. They were works which, in their sad, lucid,

honest acceptance of life, were in the direct line of descent from George Eliot's fiction and were concerned, as that fiction was, with problems of right doing, of duty."

This Bed Thy Centre, although mild by today's standards, caused a sensation when it was first published because of its forthright examination of sex. It is a character study of Elsie Cotton, a young girl from a lower middle-class family growing up in a London suburb, who is trying to come to terms with her sexual inhibitions. She is attracted to Roly, the son of the town councilor, who returns her affections and eventually marries her. "Instead of the 'happily ever after' ending of the fairy tale, however," stated Lindblad, "the last few pages of the novel record the frightened thoughts of the young bride as she waits for her husband on her wedding night." Isabel Quigly in her study *Pamela Hansford Johnson* regarded *This Bed Thy Center* as showing "nearly all the basic characteristics of [Johnson's] later writing: its realism, its seriousness without solemnity, its use of social colour and atmosphere, its examination of love in many aspects, with very varied lovers and reactions to love, its lifelike dialogue—abrupt, easily embarrassed, totally 'unliterary.'"

Novels which followed *This Bed Thy Center* explore the psychological problems of people living in the nineteen twenties and thirties. *World's End* and *The Monument,* for instance, tell of young men and women struggling to survive amid the political and financial unrest of the 1930s, while *Blessed above Women* traces the disintegration of an elderly woman into insanity through sexual frustration. In these volumes Johnson successfully examined the problems resulting from "psychic deprivation and suffering, the exploitation of working-class labor, the unemployment of the thirties, the rise of fascism, and the impending war," declared *Dictionary of Literary Biography* contributor Susan Currier. Although these books were not intended to be didactic, stated Marigold Johnson in the *Times Literary Supplement,* Johnson's "sense of the serious moral duty of the novelist, her concern with the consequences of sin, the torture of bad conscience, the retributive agony of guilt, are still observable even in the plethora of surface domestic detail." Currier explained, "Without blurring the fluid, clear contours of her characters and situations, she bares their irrational and intolerable interiors."

"Possibly the three volumes of the trilogy [*Too Dear for My Possessing, An Avenue of Stone,* and *A Summer to Decide*] are together Pamela Hansford Johnson's most impressive achievement," declared Quigley. "In them, for the first time," the essayist continued, "she used the public and private lives—the outer and inner worlds—of her characters with complete assurance, and manipulated a large number of these characters and worlds, covering a wide social field, without any sense of strain." The narrator of the sequence is Claud Pickering, a young man relating the story of his life and of the lives of those closest to him. However, the dominant character, and the one after whom Johnson named the trilogy, is not Claud but his stepmother Helena Shea, an Irish singer and his father's former mistress. Other major characters include Charmian, Helena's daughter and Claud's half-sister, Sir Daniel Archer, whom Helena marries after Claud's father dies, and Cecil, Archer's daughter.

Johnson pursued a Proustian theme of love and memory in *Too Dear for My Possessing,* said Quigley. In it, Claud relates the story of his early years from the perspective of a grown man. When the novel opens, Claud's parents have separated. Unable to obtain a divorce, Claud's father has taken Helena and his teenaged son to live in Belgium. When Claud turns thirteen he receives a visit from his mother, accompanied by her friend Archer and Cecil. "Cecil awakens Claud's dormant sexuality but circumstances work against their relationship developing," explained Lindblad. Claud grows up, marries a girl who works in his office, "is successful; but [he is] haunted, always, by a dream, a vision, a reality that life—or he himself or the girl who was the heart of the dream—forces into the background," declared *New York Times Book Review* contributor Jane Spence Southron. Although Claud eventually declares his love to Cecil and discovers that it is returned, Cecil dies before Claud is free to marry her. He then sits down to write the story of his love for Cecil, pondering "man's romantic nature and his tendency to fall in love with an unattainable dream," stated Lindblad.

Claud continues his family's story in *An Avenue of Stone* and *A Summer to Decide*. "More Helena's book than either of the other two," according to Currier, *An Avenue of Stone* tells of the widowed Lady Archer's infatuation with a worthless young man and of her inability to accept her own aging. *A Summer to Decide* traces Claud's progress into a new, successful relationship at the same time as it reveals the failure of Charmian's marriage. In both books, said Currier, "Claud finds himself torn between desires to intervene on Helena's or Charmian's behalf and painful acknowledgement of their rights to their own degrading passions." "Claud's anger and fidelity, frustration and love, and finally his decision to withdraw," she concluded, "—these are precisely what Johnson is best at—psychological process, attached to ordinary life, in motion."

Johnson wrote about women who shared Charmian's problem in three related novels: *Catherine Carter, An Impossible Marriage,* and *The Last Resort.* Each of these books features women whose desires conflict with their concept of marital duty. Although they are quite different in plot and setting—*Catherine Carter* is a story of the Victorian theater, while the other two depict modern domestic life—Johnson examined in them the same situation in three different ways, and with three different results. For example, the heroine and title character in *Catherine Carter* ends her unhappy marriage by divorcing her husband and gains professional acceptance on equal terms with her second husband. Christine Jackson, the protagonist of *An Impossible Marriage,* also chooses divorce to escape her unfaithful and unloving first husband, but she relates her story in the same way Claud did his in *Too Dear for My Possessing,* said Lindblad. *The Last Resort,* on the other hand, features a woman who adopts marriage as a refuge from guilt; it is the story of Celia Baird, "a well-to-do girl who is rejected by her lover after the death of his invalid wife, and marries a homosexual in the desperate need to obtain at least a new name and an unseparate life," according to a *Times Literary Supplement* reviewer.

In the late 1950s and early 1960s, Johnson changed the direction of her work, moving away from mainstream fiction. Books produced during these years include the "Dorothy Merton Comedies"—*The Unspeakable Skipton, Night and Silence, Who Is Here? An American Comedy,* and *Cork Street, Next to the Hatter's: A Novel in Bad Taste*—a series of satirical novels commenting on the literary life of England and America. The first of these, Lindblad stated, "attracted more attention than any of the author's books since *This Bed Thy Centre.* Critics were impressed by her ability to write a successful comic novel so different from her previous work." They were especially impressed with her characterization of a paranoid artist. Daniel

Skipton himself, "a superb comic creation," according to Walter Allen in the *New Statesman,* is an English-born writer living in Belgium who is fully convinced that he is an unappreciated genius. He has written a single, largely ignored, decadent novel, and must earn a living by "scroung[ing] on gullible tourists and pimp[ing]" to supplement his income, Lindblad explained. "He exploits everyone he can," remarked Currier, "including relatives and publishers to whom he owes more gratitude than venom; and he rationalizes his behavior with fantasies of persecution and his own undervalued worth." In the period covered by the novel—the last few weeks of Skipton's life—he joins a group of pseudo-literati English tourists led by Dorothy Merton, a poetic dramatist and self-proclaimed literary expert. Skipton's attempts to embezzle the tourists end in his own ruin. "Insufferable in victory, magnificently spiteful and enraged in defeat, Skipton on his death bed conquers, but only esthetically, his gross tormentors," declared *Commonweal* contributor Thomas Curley.

Johnson published her last novel, *A Bonfire,* only a few weeks before she died. Its central image is the bonfire fourteen-year-old Emma Sheldrake watches the night she learns about sexual contact; reviewer Marigold Johnson explained, "Emma thinks she'd prefer being a nun." That same night her father dies. Emma marries Stephen Hood several years later and finds release from many of her inhibitions, but that relationship is doomed. Emma's life from then on is dominated by the "half-real fear of the eternal bonfire at the end of the primrose path of sexual self-indulgence," stated *New Statesman* contributor Gillian Wilce. Before she turns twenty-six, she loses Stephen in an automobile accident, has a brief affair with a younger man, remarries, and her second husband commits suicide. Is it any wonder, asked Marigold Johnson, that Emma is convinced "that her sexual gratifications, blessed or unblessed, have irrevocably destined her for 'the everlasting bonfire'?" In her final book, said R. L. Widman in the *Washington Post Book World,* "Johnson writes with depth, compassion and perspicuity about Emma's feelings, sexual desires and thoughts while avoiding graphic descriptions."

Critical opinion suggests that Johnson's abilities were strongest in the creation of realistic characters and the examination of meaningful themes. Throughout Johnson's career as a novelist, stated Lindblad, "she has demonstrated the seriousness of her commitment to her art and explored those aspects of life that touch upon the experience of most readers with a great deal of lucidity and humaneness." Her talent "is not the mild talent called character-drawing," said Quigly; "it is the creation of people who live outside the novels' pages, who enrich our knowledge of others. It is probably the most creative—the most importantly creative—of the novelist's gifts: the ability to fashion people we come to know more vividly and closely and fruitfully than we know most of our friends, people full grown, credible, feeling, responsive, whose unmentioned feelings we can gauge, whose undescribed reactions we can always imagine, who do not fade and diminish when we shut the book."

AVOCATIONAL INTERESTS: Travel, history, and the philosophy of art.

BIOGRAPHICAL/CRITICAL SOURCES:

BOOKS

Allen, Walter, *The Modern Novel,* Dutton, 1964.
Burgess, Anthony, *The Novel Now: A Guide to Contemporary Fiction,* Norton, 1967.

Contemporary Literary Criticism, Gale, Volume 1, 1973, Volume 7, 1977, Volume 27, 1984.

Dictionary of Literary Biography, Volume 15: *British Novelists, 1930-1959,* Gale, 1983.

Halperin, John, *C. P. Snow: An Oral Biography; Together with a Conversation with Lady Snow (Pamela Hansford Johnson),* St. Martin's, 1983.

Johnson, Pamela Hansford, *Important to Me: Personalia,* Macmillan, 1974, Scribner, 1975.

Karl, Frederick R., *A Reader's Guide to the Contemporary English Novel,* Farrar, Straus, 1962.

Lindblad, Ishrat, *Pamela Hansford Johnson,* Twayne, 1982.

Newquist, Roy, *Counterpoint,* Rand McNally, 1984.

Quigly, Isabel, *Pamela Hansford Johnson,* Longmans, Green, 1968.

Snow, Philip, *Stranger and Brother: A Portrait of C. P. Snow,* Macmillan, 1982, Scribner, 1983.

PERIODICALS

Atlantic, November, 1965.

Chicago Tribune, February 1, 1959, September 16, 1962.

Christian Science Monitor, October 22, 1970, August 3, 1979.

Commonweal, October 21, 1938, February 20, 1959, February 11, 1966.

Drama, fall, 1969.

Kirkus Reviews, January 1, 1960.

Listener, May 16, 1968.

Los Angeles Times Book Review, August 19, 1979, September 13, 1981.

Manchester Guardian, January 23, 1959.

Nation, August 19, 1968.

National Review, August 13, 1968, August 3, 1973.

New Leader, November 16, 1971.

New Republic, March 21, 1960, March 25, 1967.

New Statesman, January 10, 1959, October 1, 1965, March 24, 1967, May 17, 1968, August 14, 1970, October 27, 1972, September 20, 1974, April 25, 1975, July 4, 1975, October 27, 1978, May 1, 1981.

New Statesman and Nation, October 9, 1937, August 31, 1940, February 2, 1952.

Newsweek, May 27, 1968.

New Yorker, March 21, 1959, December 11, 1965, May 25, 1968, April 28, 1973, April 21, 1975, June 30, 1975, November 3, 1975, September 14, 1981.

New York Times, February 25, 1967, May 28, 1968.

New York Times Book Review, February 27, 1938, September 11, 1938, July 28, 1940, July 1, 1945, July 20, 1952, February 24, 1957, February 28, 1960, September 16, 1962, November 14, 1965, July 7, 1968, September 20, 1970, December 6, 1970, September 14, 1975, September 28, 1975.

Observer Review, March 12, 1967.

Publishers Weekly, November 30, 1959.

Reporter, May 18, 1967.

Saturday Evening Post, January 14, 1967.

Saturday Review, July 20, 1963, October 9, 1965, April 15, 1967, August 3, 1968, October 24, 1970, February 22, 1975.

Saturday Review of Literature, June 16, 1945.

Spectator, May 30, 1947, June 21, 1975, May 30, 1981.

Time, November 19, 1965, April 7, 1967, January 3, 1969, September 28, 1970.

Times Literary Supplement, May 31, 1947, November 16, 1956, January 9, 1959, July 20, 1962, September 30, 1965, May 16, 1968, August 14, 1970, October 27, 1972, January 3, 1975, May 2, 1975, June 20, 1975, November 3, 1978, May 1, 1981.

Washington Post, July 14, 1979.

Washington Post Book World, January 28, 1973, September 3, 1981.

OBITUARIES:

PERIODICALS

AB Bookman's Weekly, July 13-20, 1981.

Bookseller, July 4, 1981.

Daily Telegraph (London), June 20, 1981, August 5, 1981.

Guardian (London), June 20, 1981.

Newsweek, June 29, 1981.

New York Times, June 20, 1981.

Publishers Weekly, July 3, 1981.

Sunday Times (London), June 21, 1981.

Time, June 29, 1981.

Times (London), June 20, 1981.

Washington Post, June 21, 1981.

—*Sketch by Kenneth R. Shepherd*

[Sketch reviewed by brother-in-law, Philip Snow]

*   *   *

JOHNSTON, Basil H.   1929-

PERSONAL: Born July 13, 1929, in Parry Island, Ontario, Canada; son of Rufus Francis and Mary (Lafreniere) Johnston; married Lucie Bella Desroches, July 29, 1959; children: Miriam Gladys, Elizabeth Louise, Geoffrey Lawrence. *Education:* Loyola College, Montreal, Quebec, graduated (cum laude), 1954; Ontario College of Education, secondary school teaching certificate, 1962. *Politics:* "Apolitical."

ADDRESSES: Home—253 Ashlar Rd., Richmond Hill, Ontario, Canada. *Office*—Royal Ontario Museum, 100 Queens Park, Toronto, Ontario, Canada.

CAREER: History teacher in secondary school, Toronto, Ontario, 1962-69; Royal Ontario Museum, Toronto, lecturer in North, Central, and South American history, 1969-72, member of ethnology department, 1972—. Night school teacher of English, 1965-70; lecturer in Indian culture. Vice-president of Canadian Indian Centre of Toronto, 1963-69; secretary of Indian consultations with Canadian Government, 1968; committee member of Indian Hall of Fame, 1968-70.

MEMBER: Indian Eskimo Association, Toronto Indian Club (president, 1957).

AWARDS, HONORS: Samuel J. Fels literary award from Coordinating Council of Literary Magazines, 1976.

WRITINGS:

(Contributor) *The Only Good Indian,* New Press, 1970.

(Contributor) *Travel Ontario,* New Press, 1971.

(Contributor) *Teacher's Manual for History,* Ginn, 1972.

(Contributor) *Starting Points in Reading,* Ginn, 1974.

Ojibway Heritage, Columbia University Press, 1976.

Moose Meat and Wild Rice, McClelland & Stewart, 1978.

How the Birds Got Their Colors, Kids Can Press, 1978.

Ojibway Language Course Outline, Indian Affairs Branch, Canadian Department of Indian Affairs and Northern Development, 1979.

Ojibway Language Lexicon for Beginners and Others, Indian Affairs Branch, Canadian Department of Indian Affairs and Northern Development, 1979.

Tales Our Elders Told, Royal Ontario Museum, 1981.
Ojibway Ceremonies, McClelland & Stewart, 1983.
By Canoe and Moccasin, Waapone, 1987.
Indian School Days, Key Porter, 1988.

Also contributor of stories, essays, articles, and poems to educational readers, literary magazines, and newspapers. Translator of brochures and travel guides into Ojibway. Guest editor of *Tawow,* publication of Indian Affairs Branch of Canadian Department of Indian Affairs and Northern Development.

BIOGRAPHICAL/CRITICAL SOURCES:

BOOKS

Dictionary of Literary Biography, Volume 60: *Canadian Writers since 1960, Second Series,* Gale, 1987.

PERIODICALS

Globe and Mail, April 16, 1988.

*   *   *

JONES, Adrienne 1915-

PERSONAL: Born July 28, 1915, in Atlanta, Ga.; daughter of Arthur Washington and Orianna (Mason) Applewhite; married Richard Morris Jones, 1939; children: Gregory, Gwen. *Education:* Educated at Theosophical School of the Open Gate and in Beverly Hills, Calif., public schools; attended University of California, Los Angeles, 1958-59, and University of California, Irvine, 1972. *Politics:* Liberal. *Religion:* Raised a Theosophist; later Episcopalian; more recently Unitarian-Universalist.

ADDRESSES: Home—24491 Los Serranos Dr., Laguna Niguel, Calif. 92677.

CAREER: Professional free-lance writer and novelist; has also worked as an office and managerial worker, cattle rancher, and with youth groups. Speaker at colleges, universities, conferences, schools, libraries, and writers groups.

MEMBER: PEN International, American Civil Liberties Union, Society of Children's Book Writers, Southern California Council on Literature for Children and Young People.

AWARDS, HONORS: University of California, Irvine, Outstanding Book Award, 1968, for *Sail, Calypso!,* 1972, for *Another Place, Another Spring,* 1975, for *So, Nothing Is Forever,* and 1979, for *The Hawks of Chelney;* Southern California Council on Children and Young People Award for best book by a Southern California author, 1972, for *Another Place, Another Spring,* and 1975, for *So, Nothing Is Forever; The Hawks of Chelney* was named to the American Library Association's (ALA) Best Books for Young Adults List, 1979; Southern California Council on Literature for Children and Young People Award for a distinguished body of work, 1984; PEN International USA West Award, 1988, for *Street Family.*

WRITINGS:

Thunderbird Pass, Lippincott, 1952.
Where Eagles Fly, Putnam, 1957.
Ride the Far Wind (juvenile), Little, Brown, 1964.
Wild Voyageur: Story of a Canada Goose (juvenile), Little, Brown, 1966.
Sail, Calypso! (juvenile), Little, Brown, 1968.
Another Place, Another Spring, Houghton, 1971.
Hawk (short story), Bank Street College of Education, 1972.

My Name Is Gnorr with an Unsilent G (short story), Bank Street College of Education, 1972.
Old Witch Hannifin and Her Shoonaget (short story), Bank Street College of Education, 1972.
Niki and Albert and the Seventh Street Raiders, Bank Street College of Education, 1972.
Who Needs a Hand to Hold?, Bank Street College of Education, 1973.
The Mural Master, Houghton, 1974.
So, Nothing Is Forever, Houghton, 1974.
The Hawks of Chelney, Harper, 1977.
The Beckoner, Harper, 1980.
Whistle down a Dark Lane, Harper, 1982.
A Matter of Spunk, Harper, 1983.
Street Family, Harper, 1987.
Long Time Passing, Harper, 1990.

Excerpts of work included in various anthologies.

WORK IN PROGRESS: A sequel to the two novels *Whistle down a Dark Lane* and *A Matter of Spunk,* tentative title *The Climbers.*

SIDELIGHTS: Adrienne Jones told *CA:* "For many years I wrote for children who fall into the category sometimes referred to as 'the middle age child.' This term always amuses me in the same way that the classification 'young adult' amuses me when it comes to writing. I think that many writers who work in the truly creative form do not think of writing for a certain age reader. Each story must find its own level, speak in its own voice.

"It's impossible for me to say why it is that my books gradually moved from the younger audience to that of the young adult. My latest three or four novels are often referred to as 'crossover novels'—books that are enjoyed by the more mature junior high and high school reader as well as those of us who are referred to, rather loosely, as adults. Please note, we never seem to say 'old adults.'

"I consider it a great privilege to write for young people. Writing for them is the nearest one can come to touching the future. As a writer, I want my books to amuse and mystify and delight and move my young readers. But beyond that, one hopes to help them become more sensitive to the wonderful diversity of people everywhere, to inspire them, to stir them to thought and to argument, to add to their wisdom. This generation seems to have inherited the results of the human race's accumulated hostilities and destructive inventiveness. If they are to save themselves, as well as our miraculously beautiful planet, they must reach beyond intelligence to understanding and compassion and, most especially, to wisdom. It seems to me that really fine books of the past and present help greatly in this endeavor."

Jones's books have been published in Germany, Austria, Denmark, Italy, Great Britain, Japan, and the Netherlands.

AVOCATIONAL INTERESTS: Travel, books, music, beach-rambling, conservation activities, mountaineering, golf, conversation.

*   *   *

JONES, David (Michael) 1895-1974

PERSONAL: Born November 1, 1895, in Brockley, Kent, England; died October 28, 1974, in Harrow, London, England; son of James (a printer's overseer) and Alice Ann (Bradshaw)

Jones. *Education:* Attended Camberwell School of Art, 1909-14, and 1919, and Westminster Art School, 1919-21. *Religion:* Roman Catholic.

ADDRESSES: Home—c/o Monksdene Hotel, 2 Northwick Park Rd., Harrow, London, England.

CAREER: Engraver, book illustrator, painter, poet, and water colorist, 1921-74; worked with craftsman Eric Gill at Ditchling Common, Sussex, 1922-24, and at Capel-y-ffin, Wales, 1925-27. Represented at Venice Biennale International Exhibition of the Fine Arts, 1934; exhibitions of work include shows at the Goupil Gallery, 1929, the National Gallery, London, 1940, 1941, 1942, in Paris, 1945, in Brooklyn, N.Y., 1952-53, and one-man shows at St. George's Gallery, 1927, the Tate Gallery, London, 1954-55, the National Book League, London, 1972, and in Edinburgh, Scotland, and Aberystwyth and Swansea, Wales. Works are found in the collections of the Tate Gallery and the Victoria and Albert Museum in London, the Whitworth Gallery, University of Manchester, the Museum of London, the Walker Gallery, the Liverpool Laing Gallery, Newcastle Kelly's Yard, the National Museum of Wales, Cardiff, the Sydney Art Gallery, the Toronto Art Gallery, the Arts Council of Great Britain, London, and the British Council, London. *Military service:* Royal Welch Fusiliers, infantryman, 1915-18; served with 15th Battalion.

MEMBER: Honorable Society of Cymmrodorion, Society for Nautical Research, Royal Society of Painters in Watercolours (honorary member), Royal Society of Literature (fellow).

AWARDS, HONORS: Royal Society Drawing Prize, 1904; Hawthornden Prize, 1938, for *In Parenthesis;* Russell Loines Memorial Award for poetry, National Institute and American Academy of Arts and Letters, 1954, for *The Anathemata;* Commander, Order of the British Empire, 1955; Harriet Monroe Memorial Prize, *Poetry* magazine, 1956, for poem "The Wall"; D.Litt., University of Wales, 1960; Welsh Arts Council Committee prize, 1960, for *Epoch and Artist,* and 1969; Levinson Prize, *Poetry* magazine, 1961, for poem "The Tutelar of Place"; Royal National Eisteddfod of Wales, Visual Arts Section, Gold Medal for Fine Arts, 1964; Midsummer Prize, Corporation of London, 1968; Companion of Honour, 1974.

WRITINGS:

In Parenthesis, Faber, 1937, 2nd edition with an introduction by T. S. Eliot, Viking, 1961.
The Anathemata: Fragments of an Attempted Writing (poetry), Faber, 1952, 2nd edition, 1955, Chilmark, 1963.
Epoch and Artist: Selected Writings, edited by Harman Grisewood, Chilmark, 1959.
The Fatigue: A.V.C. DCCLXXIV, Tantus labor non sit cassus, Rampant Lions Press, 1965.
The Tribune's Visitation (poetry), Fulcrum Press, 1969.
An Introduction to "The Rime of the Ancient Mariner," Clover Hill Editions, 1972.
The Sleeping Lord and Other Fragments, Faber, 1974.
Use and Sign, Golgonooza Press, 1975.
The Kensington Mass, edited by Rene Hague, Agenda Editions, 1975.
The Dying Gaul and Other Writings, edited and with an introduction by Grisewood, Faber, 1978.
The Roman Quarry and Other Sequences, Agenda Editions, 1981, Sheep Meadow Press, 1982.

ILLUSTRATOR

A Child's Rosary Book, St. Dominic's Press, 1924.

Eleanor Farjeon, *The Town Child's Alphabet,* Poetry Bookshop, 1924.
H. D. C. Pepler, *Libellus Lapidum,* St. Dominic's Press, 1924.
Jonathan Swift, *Gulliver's Travels into Several Remote Nations of the World,* two volumes, Golden Cockerel Press, 1925.
The Book of Jonah, Golden Cockerel Press, 1926.
Francis Coventry, *Pompey the Little,* Golden Cockerel Press, 1926.
Llyfr y pregeth-wr (Welsh translation of Book of Ecclesiastes), Gwasg Gregynog, 1927.
J. Isaacs, editor, *The Chester Play of the Deluge,* Golden Cockerel Press, 1927.
Samuel Taylor Coleridge, *The Rime of the Ancient Mariner,* Douglas Cleverdon, 1929.
Gwen Plunket Green, *The Prophet Child,* Longmans, 1935, Dutton, 1937.
David Jones (paintings), Penguin, 1949.
David Jones Exhibition, National Book League (London), 1972.
David Jones (exhibition catalogue), The Tate Gallery, 1981.

Also illustrator of R. H. J. Stewart, *March, Kind Comrade,* 1931. Contributor of illustrations to magazines and periodicals, including *The Game.*

OTHER

(Contributor) Elizabeth Jennings, editor, *An Anthology of Modern Verse, 1940-1960,* Methuen, 1961.
Excerpts from The Anathemata, In Parenthesis, [and] *The Hunt* (recording; read by the author), Argo, 1967.
David Jones: Letters to Vernon Watkins, edited and with notes by Ruth Pryor, University of Wales Press, 1976.
Letters to William Hayward, edited by Colin Wilcockson, Agenda Editions, 1979.
Introducing David Jones: A Selection of His Writings, edited by John Matthias with an introduction by Stephen Spender, Faber, 1980.
Dai Greatcoat: A Self-Portrait of David Jones in His Letters, edited by Hague, Faber, 1980.
Letters to a Friend, edited by Aneirin Talfan Davies, Triskele, 1980.
Inner Necessities: Letters of David Jones to Desmond Chute, edited by Thomas R. Dilworth, Anson-Cartwright, 1984.

Contributor to publications, including *Anglo-Welsh Review, Poetry, Listener, Agenda, Times* (London), *Times Literary Supplement,* and others.

The manuscripts of *In Parenthesis, The Anathemata* and *The Sleeping Lord,* along with Jones's personal library, are in the National Library of Wales at Aberystwyth. Jones's letters to Rene Hague are in the Fisher Rare Book Library of the University of Toronto, and his letters to Harman Grisewood are held in the collection of the Beinecke Rare Book Library of Yale University. Various prose manuscripts are in the Boston College library.

SIDELIGHTS: While not as well known as other modernist writers such as T. S. Eliot, Ezra Pound, and James Joyce, David Jones "is increasingly regarded as an important, innovative poet, who has extended and refined the techniques of literary modernism," according to *Dictionary of Literary Biography* contributor Vincent B. Sherry, Jr. A graphic artist as well as a poet, Jones is best known for his long narrative poems *In Parenthesis* and *The Anathemata,* and for his engravings and paintings, which have won many awards. "The supreme quality of his art," both literary and graphic, reports

Kathleen Raine in the *Sewanee Review*, ". . . has long been apparent to an inner circle of his friends," but, she adds, "he has never at any time been a widely-read, still less a fashionable, writer, nor is he ever likely to become so, for his work is too subtle and learned for popular tastes."

Much of Jones's oeuvre evokes his Welsh heritage and echoes the events of his own life. "At the time of my birth," he once told *CA*, "my father was a printer's overseer and that meant that I was brought up in a home that took the printed page and its illustration for granted. I began drawing when I was aged five and regarded it as a natural activity which I would pursue as I grew older. I was backward at lessons, could not read til I was about seven or eight, and did not take to writing in the sense of writing books until I was thirty-three years old." In January 1915, Jones enlisted in the Royal Welch Fusiliers as an infantryman, and he served on the Western front from December of that year to March of 1918. After the war he embraced Roman Catholicism and joined a small community of Catholic artists headed by craftsman Eric Gill, among whom he began to develop a unique concept of art and the function of the artist. He did not begin to write *In Parenthesis*, a fictionalized account of his activities in the war, until 1928 and almost a decade passed before it was published. Jones's war experiences and his religious conversion permeate his first long poem. Like Jones, John Ball, the protagonist of *In Parenthesis*, served in the British army on the Western Front during World War I. Both Jones and Ball began training late in 1915, and both were wounded in the battle of the Somme in June of 1916. His second long poem, *The Anathemata*, reflects the poet's Catholic faith and understanding of his art. Set during the Consecration of the Mass, it encompasses the entire history of mankind. Other works display Jones's eclectic tastes, depicting scenes from Celtic literature and mythology, Arthurian legend, Greek and Roman antiquity, and scripture.

Complex in organization, rich in vocabulary, *In Parenthesis* demonstrates the intricacies of Jones's work. David M. Blamires points out in *David Jones: Artist and Writer* that "in length and overall structure . . . [it] may be said to be a novel, but in its use of language it is more akin to poetry." The poem is divided into seven parts, and tells the story of Private John Ball and his company from their embarkation from England in December 1915 to their participation in the Somme battle of July 1916. "But though Ball is usually present as protagonist-spectator," declares Monroe K. Spears in *Contemporary Literature*, "the poem expresses not his thoughts alone but, most of the time, a kind of collective consciousness; and hence many different forms and levels are necessary. . . . All the details of speech and everything else are vivid, precise, and evocative: but literal realism is immediately transcended." "*In Parenthesis* varies in medium from straightforward prose to prose that is highly elliptical, condensed, dislocated, and discontinuous and to verse with a rhythm that is sometimes very strong—allusive, liturgical, or incantory—but that never employs rhyme or any regular pattern," Spears explains. "The result is a profound and shattering disclosure of combat's physical destruction and spiritual outrage," asserts Thomas Dilworth in the *Georgia Review*, "which is sustained by a controlled and variegated tone lacking in the work of the combatant poets who wrote during the war."

Jones draws on his Welsh literary heritage to describe his experiences. Each of the seven parts of the poem is prefaced with a quotation from an ancient Welsh heroic epic, *Y Gododdin*, which commemorates the destruction of a three-hundred-man raiding party by the English at the battle of Catraeth. The poet also takes images from Shakespeare's history plays and Malory's *Morte d'Arthur*, as well as from T. S. Eliot's *The Waste Land*, mingling with them expressions from the early twentieth century and soldiers' slang from the war. Paul Fussell points out in *The Great War and Modern Memory* that at the end of the first section of the poem the newly trained soldiers "set toward France," just as Henry V does in Shakespeare's play. Part IV is titled "King Pellam's Launde," in reference to the desolate country in which King Arthur's knights find the Holy Grail in the *Morte d'Arthur*. Also drawn from Malory is Ball's fellow soldier Dai Greatcoat, who rises after the platoon's meal and delivers a warrior's boast, patterned after those that appear in epic poetry, in which he claims to have participated in every major battle in history and legend from the fall of Lucifer to the present. He declares that his fathers were present at Edward III's victory over the French at Crecy, and asserts that he took part in Arthur's wars and was a member of the Roman legion that crucified Jesus.

Many critics hold that the archetypal figure Dai Greatcoat and indeed all Jones's soldiers represent the human experience in war throughout the ages. *New York Review of Books* contributor D. S. Carne-Ross maintains, "Jones came in retrospect to see the first of our 'great' modern wars (at least up to the battle of the Somme) as the last action of an older world, the last time that the ancient usages still just held, hence it represented what he and his friends called the Break, the point at which man stepped clear of his past and turned his back on all the previous history of the race." "Faced with the disintegration brought about by the First World War, David Jones sought to recover roots, not just for an individual, but for a whole people," declares Atholl C. C. Murray in *Critical Quarterly*. "This he attempted by constantly emphasising the continuity of history, by showing that the present derives from the past and that both are part of the one process. Thus it is that at various times his Londoners and Welshmen may be assimilated to the three hundred who fought at Catraeth, or to the troops under Henry V at Agincourt, or even to the Roman legionaries." Samuel Rees, writing in *David Jones*, states that "the racial or mythic ancestry that Jones provides for [the soldiers] places them in the whole history of recorded time; they share the human psyche of the soldiers at Catraeth, at the Crucifixion, at Malplaquet, at Harfleur, wherever man has organized war against his own kind."

While all commentators recognize *In Parenthesis* as an important literary achievement, they are divided in their assessments of its success in representing the experience of the First World War. Some believe, as does Michael Mott of *Poetry* magazine, that "*In Parenthesis* seems an astonishingly successful combining of epic myth and actuality." Yet Jones's verse is decidedly understated compared to that of the heroic bards. "In chronicling the action of which he was a part, [Jones] does not seek to be an epic poet singing hymns of battle in which new heroes reenact the earth-shaking deeds of their ancestors," reports Rees. "Without apology or special pleading, he details from intimate firsthand acquaintance with the present—and from affectionate intimacy with historical man—the minds and actions of those compelled, for whatever reason, whatever 'accidents' of history and geography, to go 'once more into the breach.'" Yet John H. Johnson, writing in *English Poetry of the First World War*, argues that the poem is indeed an epic, and Dilworth agrees; in *The Shape of Meaning in the Poetry of David Jones*, he states that *In Parenthesis* "is the only authentic and successful epic poem in the language since *Paradise Lost*."

In some critics' opinions, *In Parenthesis* presents an ambiguous vision of the war. Carne-Ross remarks, "What is largely missing is the note of protest, the sense of war as an aberration, something that must never be allowed to happen again." Nonetheless, he concludes, the poet's perspective is understandable: "War is hell, certainly, but Jones never doubted that there is a good deal of hell around and this aspect of the matter did not greatly surprise him." Dilworth acknowledges that the poem is not primarily interested in promoting pacifism but, he declares, "Its ironies are double-edged; they indict war but also stress the essential goodness of the individual combatant." Rees concludes that "*In Parenthesis* is not a poem either to provoke or to end a war . . . except as it adds to the accumulation of testimony to the stupidities and brutality of history that each age much learn from or, more likely, ignore."

Critics also disagree in their interpretations of the poem's attempt to understand the war. Murray, for instance, calls *In Parenthesis* "a book about how man, even in the most appalling circumstances, can still discern beneath the surface of experience an ultimate significance in life." "If one is ready to perceive it," he concludes, "then there is order and beauty to be discovered even in the lice-ridden marshes of Flanders." On the other hand, Fussell believes that *In Parenthesis* suggests, by placing the suffering of modern British soldiers in an epic, heroic context, "that the war, if ghastly, is firmly 'in the tradition.' It even implies that, once conceived to be in the tradition, the war can be understood. The tradition to which the poem points holds suffering to be close to sacrifice and individual effort to end in heroism; it contains, unfortunately, no precedent for an understanding of war as a shambles and its participants as victims."

"And yet for all these defects," Fussell admits, "*In Parenthesis* remains in many ways a masterpiece impervious to criticism." The poem, he concludes, is "profoundly decent. When on his twenty-first birthday Mr. Jenkins [the commander of Ball's platoon] receives both his promotion to full lieutenant and a nice parcel from Fortnum and Mason's, we are pleased. Details like these pull the poem in quite a different direction from that indicated by its insistent invocation of myth and ritual and romance. Details like these persuade us with all the power of art that the Western Front is not King Pellam's Land, that it will not be restored and made whole, ever, by the expiatory magic of the Grail. It is too human for that."

In Parenthesis was recognized at the time of its publication in 1937 as a work of immense literary importance and continues to be celebrated as such today. In *The Long Conversation: A Memoir of David Jones,* William Blisset reports that, at a party following the poem's winning the Hawthornden Prize, William Butler Yeats "bowed and intoned: 'I salute the author of *In Parenthesis.*'" T. S. Eliot also praised the work, and many critics acclaimed it highly. "Herbert Read, writing for the *London Mercury,*" relates Sherry, "found it 'as near a great epic of the war as ever the war generation will reach,' displaying 'the noble ardour of the *Chanson de Roland* and the rich cadences of the *Morte d'Arthur.*'" More recently, *New York Times Book Review* contributor Stephen Spender has called *In Parenthesis* "the most monumental work of poetic genius to come out of World War I." Dilworth echoes this assessment, saying, "By most accounts, *In Parenthesis* . . . is the finest work of literature to emerge from combat experience in the First World War."

Between 1937 and 1952 Jones worked on a variety of poems, but published very little. A nervous disorder developing from his war experiences prevented his holding a steady job, and his income depended mainly on the generosity of his friends. Pressures from his uncertain earnings aggravated his condition, and in 1946 he suffered a mental collapse that required seven months of treatment in a psychiatric clinic. In the interim Jones worked on his painting and poetry and further developed his theory of art and artistry, expressing his views in letters and essays. It was not until 1952, with the encouragement of T. S. Eliot and other friends, that he published his second long poem, *The Anathemata,* which partly expounds his aesthetic philosophy and partly expresses his personal faith.

Like *In Parenthesis, The Anathemata* is modernistic, allusive, and fragmentive, but it lacks the chronological storyline that characterizes the earlier work. Instead, it consists of eight separate sections, tracing various traditions of British and European culture, and unified by the image of the Mass. "It is the only epic-length work in any language, as far as I know," declares Dilworth in *The Shape of Meaning,* "in which structure successfully replaces narrative as the primary principle of order. And more than merely ordering content, the structure of *The Anathemata* gives it powerful symbolic focus." "*The Anathemata* does not have the confined narrative structure or the clear identification with classical epic of *In Parenthesis,*" asserts Rees. "More ambitious, certainly, than that work, it attempts something approaching the whole cultural history of the British Isles." Nicholas Jacobs declares in *Agenda,* "Whereas in *In Parenthesis* Jones uses a single major theme, the ideal of comradeship in arms from Aneirin through Malory to Shakespeare, in an attempt to give sense and meaning to the terrible waste of the Western Front, in *The Anathemata* he is concerned much more to recall and celebrate a whole tradition which threatens to slip through his fingers." "*In Parenthesis* tested the military and liturgical forms of order and found them lacking, with neither efficacy for salvation nor effectiveness for survival," Rees reminds us. "The Queen of the Woods, the great earth-goddess, the eternal female principle venerated by myth throughout the centuries, alone could restore order—but *post mortem.* In *The Anathemata* Jones renominates and celebrates the liturgy as the redemptive order for the living, as an art form." The critic concludes, "In intention and scope Jones's poem is truly epic and might be said to rival in ambition Milton's attempt to 'justify the ways of God to Men' for an age which urges art to be at the service of the ego, the State, or itself."

"Clearly," Rees asserts, "it is the whole of human history and prehistory as perceived and experienced by Western man that is Jones's province." The "anathemata" of the poem's title refers to the artifacts that an artist produces, including the graphic and plastic arts, poetry, literature, legend—all the things that help define a culture. The work examines the accumulation of these artifacts from earliest times to the present, with special attention paid to that which has had the greatest influence on the poet: the history, both legendary and factual, "of the Island of Britain as a whole, whose various origins, Celtic, Imperial Roman, Western Christian and Saxon, appear there in the form in which the poet himself, by birth, upbringing and conversion a product of the composite tradition, experiences them," Jacobs explains. "To read [the poem]," declares Rees, "is to engage, in a rare, esoteric way, from a most learned and demanding tutor, in a course in Western Civilization, which is something other than learning the sites of famous battles in Greece and being able to recite, in order, the rulers of Rome and the kings and queens of England.''

The Anathemata was Jones's attempt to reestablish contact with these roots of British culture, states Seamus Heaney in the *Spectator*, roots that modern Britain had neglected, especially in the years after the First World War. Heaney explains: ''His effort has been to graft a healing tissue over that wound in English consciousness inflicted by the Reformation and the Industrial Revolution.'' Jones felt that modern man had lost his understanding of the past by neglecting the history of his culture. Drawing information from the sciences of archaeology and anthropology, he set out to recover the roots of his heritage. The poem, Rees declares, tells the history of the artist from ''his emergence from the reaches of prehistory, from rocks and caves that he decorated, as at Lascaux, adorning burial sites gratuitously, creating objects that are beautiful to an extrautile degree, and continuing, still an artmaker, to the wasted present, 'at the sagging end and chapter's close.'''

Jones uses his traditions in such a way that they become understandable even to those who do not share the poet's background. Kathleen Raine states in her book *David Jones and the Actually Loved and Known:* ''The poet does not thrust his facts upon us, but rather uses these to remind us of our own, often untreasured but none the less precious, fragments of the same totality.'' Jones also concentrates on the universal legacies of mankind. ''In the larger sense,'' Rees explains, ''man's 'anathemata' defines all that legacy of man that is his, that is he.'' The critic concludes that the poet's ideal aim ''is to discover via surviving art and artifact and written word, and with application of all the modern insights and methods of literary study, anthropology, comparative religion, and linguistics, the essential human heritage that is ours.'' He says, ''David Jones's life work is finally his testimony to this central credo: 'We were then *homo faber, homo sapiens* before Lascaux and we shall be *homo faber, homo sapiens* after the last atomic bomb has fallen.'''

Closely tied to Jones's concept of man-as-artist is his understanding of Christianity. *The Anathemata* demonstrates his belief that art should be a form of worship, and that worship is itself a form of art. Guy Davenport remarks in the *New York Times Book Review,* ''For David Jones art was a sacred act and he expected the reading of his work to be as much a rite as he performed in the composing of it.'' ''Art, as Jones's impractical temperament would have it,'' explains Sherry, ''is essentially gratuitous, intransitive; it serves no social purpose; it is, ideally, a free hymn of praise to God, and as such resembles the gift offerings of sacrament.''

But if art can be considered a type of sacrament, the sacraments themselves are a form of art—perhaps, in Jones's opinion, the highest form. ''At the center of *The Anathemata* is that cross, the 'Axile Tree,''' Rees reports. ''Christ being lifted up made an efficacious sign, made 'anathemata' of his own body.'' Belief in the veracity of the Christian gospel is not necessary for the reader, he continues, because ''Western man's whole being, his history, his ancestry, his '*res,*' is wholly bound up in that myth.'' ''The art of the first Eucharist at the Last Supper redefines all preceding art, even as it was an act that with all its reverberations and implications transformed succeeding events and imparted a unique and new order to Western myth, legend, and history,'' he concludes. ''The priest lifting the wafer of bread in the Mass is the supreme artist,'' Sherry declares. ''The Mass thus provides a kind of infinite moment; its sacrament is the timeless archetype of all the ar-

tifacts catalogued in the poem.'' ''Like Joyce, [Jones] has made a total anachronism of all history, so that the Crucifixion is both an event in time, upon which all perspectives converge, and an event throughout time,'' Davenport states. ''The purpose of the evolution of the world was to raise the hill Golgotha, grow the wood for the cross, form the iron for the nails and develop the primate species Homo sapiens for God to be born a member of,'' he asserts. ''The paleolithic Willendorf 'Venus' is therefore as valid and eloquent a Madonna as one by Botticelli, and all soldiers belong to the Roman legion that detailed a work group to execute, by slow torture, the Galilean visionary troublemaker.''

The Anathemata met with mixed reactions from its reviewers. Some critics felt that the complexity of the poem made it too difficult to understand. Many others, however, agreed with W. H. Auden, who declared in *Encounter* that *The Anathemata* ''is one of the most important poems of our time.'' According to Blamires, it had been ''hailed by one critic as one of the five 'major poetic efforts of our era' in English.'' As Sherry relates, Jones particularly enjoyed Raine's assessment of *The Anathemata* which appeared in the *New Statesman:* ''Such is the paradox of our time that the more a poet draws on objective tradition, the less on subjective experiences, the more obscure he will seem.'' Contemporary reviewers continue to appreciate the power of its language. N. K. Sandars, writing in *Agenda*, states, ''We have become numbed, anaesthetized to the power and purpose of words and require to be jolted awake, to feel their recessions and transformations. This is exactly what David Jones has done in *The Anathemata* ... where juxtapositions of English, Welsh and Latin give, not only an incomparable richness of texture and of reference, but also give words the life of icons, 'images not made with hands.'''

In the remaining years of his life, Jones continued to refine his theory of art and the function of the artist, often in letters to friends, but also in his essays collected in *Epoch and Artist.* He also worked on shorter poems and essays, some of which were collected in the books *The Sleeping Lord and Other Fragments, The Dying Gaul and Other Writings,* and *The Roman Quarry and Other Sequences.* Many of them echo the problems that Jones confronted in *The Anathemata:* some reveal the unrest of Roman legionaries on the borders of the decaying Empire, reflecting ''the problems of a political order removed from its local origins,'' says Sherry. Others—many of which are based on figures from Celtic myth and legend— ''praise the virtues of local, rooted culture,'' he continues. Often these poems were published in a consciously unfinished state as works in progress, but even in their fragmentary condition reviewers recognized the power of Jones's work. Heaney concludes his review of *The Sleeping Lord* by calling Jones ''an extraordinary writer'' who has ''returned to the origin and brought something back, something to enrich not only the language but people consciousness of who they have been and who they consequently are.''

Despite his acclaim in poetic circles—Dilworth calls him ''the most important native British poet of the twentieth century'' in *The Shape of Meaning*—David Jones continues to be unknown to the public at large. This is partly due to the demands the poet's work makes on readers, but also partly the result of his own preference; Rees explains, ''There have been few writers of this or any other age so resolutely uninterested in matters of public reputation or recognition.'' He spent the last years of his life quietly working, trying to salvage the remnants of traditional Western culture from the onslaught of the twentieth century. "Like Thoreau, Melville and Hopkins," Spender concludes, "he was one of literature's saints who speak with an authority that comes more from religion than from the world of letters."

BIOGRAPHICAL/CRITICAL SOURCES:

BOOKS

Bergonzi, Bernard, *Heroes' Twilight: A Study of the Literature of the Great War*, Constable, 1965.

Blamires, David M., *David Jones: Artist and Writer*, Manchester University Press, 1971.

Blisset, William, *The Long Conversation: A Memoir of David Jones*, Oxford University Press, 1981.

Cleverdon, Douglas, *The Engravings of David Jones*, Clover Hill Editions, 1981.

Contemporary Literary Criticism, Gale, Volume 2, 1974, Volume 4, 1975, Volume 7, 1977, Volume 13, 1980, Volume 42, 1987.

David Jones, Tate Gallery (London), 1981.

Deutsch, Babbette, *Poetry in Our Time*, Holt, 1952.

Dictionary of Literary Biography, Volume 20: *British Poets, 1914-1945*, Gale, 1983.

Dilworth, Thomas R., *The Liturgical Parenthesis of David Jones*, Golgonooza Press, 1979.

Dilworth, Thomas R., *The Shape of Meaning in the Poetry of David Jones*, University of Toronto Press, 1988.

Fussell, Paul, *The Great War and Modern Memory*, Oxford University Press, 1975.

Gray, Nicolete, *The Painted Inscriptions of David Jones*, Fraser, 1981.

Hague, Rene, *David Jones*, University of Wales Press, 1975.

Hague, Rene, *A Commentary on The Anathemata of David Jones*, University of Toronto Press, 1977.

Hooker, Jeremy, *David Jones: An Exploratory Study of the Writings*, Enitharmon, 1975.

Ironside, Robin, *David Jones*, Penguin, 1949.

Johnson, John H., *English Poetry of the First World War*, Princeton University Press, 1964.

Lectures on Modern Novelists, Department of English, Cambridge University, 1963, Books for Libraries Press, 1972.

Mathias, Roland, editor, *David Jones: Eight Essays on His Work as Writer and Artist*, Gomer, 1976.

Matthias, John, editor, *David Jones, Man and Poet*, National Poetry Foundation (Orono, Me.), 1988.

Nemerov, Howard, *Poetry and Fiction*, Rutgers University Press, 1963.

Pacey, Philip, *David Jones and Other Wonder Voyagers*, Poetry Wales Press, 1982.

Raine, Kathleen, *David Jones and the Actually Loved and Known*, Golgonooza Press, 1978.

Rees, Samuel, *David Jones*, Twayne, 1977.

Rosenthal, M. L. and Sally M. Gall, *The Modern Poetic Sequence: The Genius of Modern Poetry*, Oxford University Press, 1983.

Thwaite, Anthony, *Poetry Today 1960-1973*, British Council, 1973.

Selections II, Sheed, 1954.

PERIODICALS

Agenda, spring-summer, 1967 (special David Jones issue), autumn-winter, 1973-74, (special David Jones issue), winter-spring, 1975.

America, December 19, 1981.

Anglo-Welsh Review, 1981, 1984, 1987.

Antigonish Review, summer, 1984.

Apollo, February, 1963.

Atlantic, July, 1962, October, 1963.

Atlantic Monthly, February, 1975.

Blackfriars, April, 1951.

Books and Bookmen, September, 1971.

Chicago Review, Volume 27, number 1, 1975.

Chicago Sunday Tribune, April 8, 1962.

Christian Century, June 6, 1962, October 2, 1963.

Commonweal, October 19, 1962, October 18, 1963, June 19, 1964.

Contemporary Literature, autumn, 1971, spring, 1973.

Critical Quarterly, autumn, 1973, autumn, 1974.

Dublin Review, fourth quarter, 1952.

Encounter, February, 1954, February, 1970.

English, summer, 1982.

English Language Notes, December, 1977.

Georgia Review, summer, 1981.

Iowa Review, summer-fall, 1975.

Listener, May 14, 1959.

Mercury (London), July, 1937.

New Republic, May 21, 1962, October 16, 1971.

New Statesman, November 22, 1952, May 24, 1974, January 5, 1979, June 27, 1980.

New Yorker, August 17, 1963, August 22, 1964.

New York Herald Tribune Books, July 8, 1962, June 9, 1963.

New York Review of Books, October 9, 1980.

New York Times Book Review, April 15, 1962, July 21, 1963, February 18, 1979, October 17, 1982.

Partisan Review, winter, 1978.

Poetry, May, 1971, January, 1975.

Poetry Wales, winter, 1972.

San Francisco Chronicle, April 29, 1962.

Saturday Review, April 7, 1962, October 26, 1963.

Sewanee Review, autumn, 1967.

Spectator, May 4, 1974, May 27, 1978, May 31, 1980.

Stand, Volume 16, number 3, 1975.

Studio, April, 1955.

Time, April 6, 1962.

Times Literary Supplement, August 6, 1954, July 22, 1965, July 27, 1967, August 20, 1971, May 10, 1974.

Twentieth Century, July, 1960.

University of Toronto Quarterly, April, 1967, spring, 1973, spring, 1985.

Western Humanities Review, spring, 1981.

OBITUARIES:

PERIODICALS

American Bookman, November 18, 1974.

New York Times, October 30, 1974.

Times (London), October 29, 1974.

Washington Post, October 31, 1974.

[Sketch reviewed by Thomas R. Dilworth]

—*Sketch by Kenneth R. Shepherd*

*　　　*　　　*

JONES, Jeanne 1937-

PERSONAL: Born May 17, 1937, in Los Angeles, Calif.; daughter of Jesse Ross (a manufacturer) and Kathryn (Jones) Castendyck; married Joseph Bush (a physician), November 4, 1965 (died July 2, 1968); married Robert Letts Jones, April 15, 1972; children: Thomas Barton Beek, David Benjamin Beek. *Education:* Attended Northwestern University and University of Southern California. *Religion:* Episcopal.

ADDRESSES: Home—P.O. Box 1212, La Jolla, Calif. 92038. *Agent*—Margaret McBride Literary Agency, Box 8730, La Jolla, Calif. 92038.

CAREER: Writer. President and founder of Angelitos del Campo (auxiliary to American Diabetes Association).

MEMBER: National Federation of Press Woman, Authors Guild, Authors League of America, San Diego Opera Association (member of board of directors).

AWARDS, HONORS: National Federation of Press Women, first place in adult books, 1972, for *The Calculating Cook: A Gourmet Cookbook for Diabetics and Dieters;* first place in adult books, nonfiction, instructional, 1988, for *Cook It Light.*

WRITINGS:

The Calculating Cook: A Gourmet Cookbook for Diabetics and Dieters, 101 Productions, 1972.
Diet for a Happy Heart, 101 Productions, 1975, revised edition published as *Diet for a Happy Heart: A Low-Cholesterol, Low-Saturated Fat, Low-Calorie Cookbook,* 1981, revised edition, Ortho Books, 1989.
Fabulous Fiber Cookbook, 101 Productions, 1977, revised edition, 1979.
Jeanne Jones' Party Planner and Entertaining Diary, 101 Productions, 1979.
Secrets of Salt-Free Cooking: A Complete Low Sodium Cookbook, 101 Productions, 1979.
(With James Thomas Cooper) *The Fabulous Fructose Recipe Book,* M. Evans, 1979.
(With Karma Kientzler) *Fitness First: A Fourteen-Day Diet and Exercise Program,* 101 Productions, 1980.
Ambition's Woman (novel), M. Evans, 1980.
More Calculated Cooking: Practical Recipes for Diabetics and Dieters, 101 Productions, 1981.
Jeanne Jones' Food Lovers' Diet, Scribner, 1982.
Stuffed Spuds: One Hundred Meals in a Potato, M. Evans, 1982.
(With Dick Duffy) *Best Restaurants in San Diego County,* 101 Productions, 1983.
(With Donna Swajeski) *The Love in the Afternoon Cookbook: Recipes from Your Favorite ABC-TV Soap Operas, Ryan's Hope, One Life to Live, All My Children,* M. Evans, 1983.
Jet Fuel: New Food Strategy for the High Performance Person, Villard, 1984.
Mocha Mix Cookbook, Presto Food Products, 1986.
Cook It Light, Macmillan, 1987.

*   *   *

JONSEN, Albert R(upert)   1931-

PERSONAL: Born April 4, 1931, in San Francisco, Calif.; son of Albert R. (an advertising executive) and Helen (Sweigert) Jonsen; married Mary Elizabeth Carolan. *Education:* Gonzaga University, B.A. and M.A., 1956; Santa Clara University, S.T.M., 1963; Yale University, Ph.D., 1967. *Politics:* Democrat.

ADDRESSES: Home—2233 38th Pl. E., Seattle, Wash. 98112. *Office*—Department of Medical History and Ethics, School of Medicine-51320, University of Washington, Seattle, Wash. 98195.

CAREER: Roman Catholic priest, member of Society of Jesus (S.J.), 1949-76. University of San Francisco, San Francisco,

Calif., associate professor of ethics and moral theology, 1967-72, president of the university, 1969-72; University of California, San Francisco, School of Medicine, professor of ethics in medicine and chief of Division of Medical Ethics, 1972-87; University of Washington, School of Medicine, Seattle, professor of ethics in medicine and chairman of department of medical history and ethics, 1987—. Director, American Society of Law and Medicine. Member, Institute of Medicine, National Academy of Sciences. Fellow, Institute for Society, Ethics, and the Life Sciences. Commissioner, National Commission for Protection of Human Subjects of Biomedical and Behavioral Research, 1974-78, and President's Commission for Study of Ethical Problems in Medicine and in Biomedical and Behavioral Research, 1979-83.

MEMBER: Society for Christian Ethics, Society for Health and Human Values (president, 1986-87).

WRITINGS:

Responsibility in Modern Religious Ethics, Corpus Books, 1968.
Patterns in Moral Behavior, Corpus Books, 1969.
Christian Decision and Action, Bruce Publishing, 1970.
Ethics of Newborn Intensive Care, University of California, 1973.
Clinical Ethics, Macmillan, 1983, 2nd edition, 1987.
The Abuse of Casuistry, University of California, 1987.

Also associate editor, *Encyclopedia of Bioethics.* Contributor to numerous periodicals, including *America, Religious Education, Sciences Ecclesiastiques, New England Journal of Medicine, Journal of the American Medical Association, Journal of Medicine and Philosophy,* and *Theoretical Medicine.*

*   *   *

JORDAN, Gilbert John   1902-

PERSONAL: Born December 23, 1902, in Mason County, Tex.; son of Daniel (a rancher) and Emilie (Willmann) Jordan; married Vera Tiller, 1926; children: Janice (Mrs. Thomas W. Shefelman), Terry G. *Education:* Southwestern University, Georgetown, Tex., A.B., 1924; University of Texas, M.A., 1928; University of Wisconsin, graduate study, 1930-33; Ohio State University, Ph.D., 1936. *Politics:* Independent. *Religion:* Methodist.

ADDRESSES: Home—4100 Jackson Ave. #216, Austin, Tex. 78731-6002.

CAREER: Teacher and administrator in public schools in Texas, 1924-30; Southern Methodist University, Dallas, Tex., assistant professor, 1930-38, associate professor, 1938-43, professor of German, 1943-68; Sam Houston State University, Huntsville, Tex., professor of German, 1968-73.

MEMBER: Modern Language Association of America, American Association of Teachers of German, American Association of University Professors, South Central Modern Language Association, Texas State Teachers Association.

AWARDS, HONORS: Order of Merit, Federal Republic of Germany, 1960.

WRITINGS:

(Editor) *Southwest Goethe Festival* (collection of papers), Southern Methodist University, 1949.
(Editor and author of introduction and notes) *Four German One-Act Plays,* Holt, 1951.

(Translator) Friedrich von Schiller, *Wilhelm Tell* (verse translation), Bobbs-Merrill, 1964.

(Co-author) *Ernst and Lisette Jordan: German Pioneers in Texas,* Von Boeckmann-Jones, 1971.

The Morning Is Not Far: Some Poems, Southern Methodist University Press, 1974.

Yesterday in the Texas Hill Country, Texas A & M University Press, 1979.

German Texana: A Bilingual Collection, Eakin Press, 1980.

Faces of Texas, Eakin Press, 1983.

Author of feature "Essays and Poems" in *German Texan Heritage Society Newsletter,* 1979-89; author of narration for filmstrips "Wilhelm Tell," 1971, and "The Romantic Road," 1972, both in German and English, and both produced by Educational Film Strip Co.; translator of W. Steinert's *North America,* published in installments as "Steinert's View of Texas" in the *Southwestern Historical Quarterly,* Volumes 80-81, 1976-77. Contributor to *PMLA, Rice University Studies, Perkins School of Theology Journal, Southwestern Historical Quarterly, German Review, Journal of English and German Philology, Monatshefte,* and *South-Central Bulletin.*

AVOCATIONAL INTERESTS: Photography, writing poetry, gardening.

K

KARGON, Robert Hugh 1938-

PERSONAL: Born October 18, 1938, in New York, N.Y.; son of Ira C. (a musician) and Inez (Schulman) Kargon; married Marcia Rose (a dietician), July 14, 1962; children: Jeremy, Dina. *Education:* Duke University, B.S., 1959; Yale University, M.S., 1960; Cornell University, Ph.D., 1964.

ADDRESSES: Home—2407 Everton Rd., Baltimore, Md. 21209. *Office*—Department of History of Science, Johns Hopkins University, 3400 North Charles St., Baltimore, Md. 21218.

CAREER: University of Illinois at Urbana-Champaign, assistant professor of history, 1964-65; Johns Hopkins University, Baltimore, Md., assistant professor, 1965-67, associate professor, 1967-72, professor of history of science, 1972-79, Willis K. Shepard Professor of History of Science, 1979—, chairman of department, 1972-75, 1982-85.

MEMBER: History of Science Society.

AWARDS, HONORS: American Philosophical Society grants, 1971-72, 1980; National Endowment of the Humanities grant, 1972-73, and fellowship, 1976-77; National Science Foundation grants, 1975-79, 1985-88.

WRITINGS:

Atomism in England from Hariot to Newton, Oxford University Press, 1966.
(Editor with W. R. Coleman and George Basalla) *Victorian Science,* Doubleday, 1970.
The Maturing of American Science, 1920-1970, American Association for the Advancement of Science, 1973.
Science in Victorian Manchester: Enterprise and Expertise, Johns Hopkins University Press, 1977.
The Rise of Robert Millikan: Portrait of a Life in American Science, Cornell University Press, 1982.
(Editor with Peter Achinstein) *Kelvin's Baltimore Lectures and Modern Theoretical Physics: Historical and Philosophical Perspectives,* MIT Press, 1987.

Contributor to academic journals.

WORK IN PROGRESS: History of science-technology regions.

KAUFMAN, Martin 1940-

PERSONAL: Born December 6, 1940, in Boston, Mass.; son of Irving (a meatmarket proprietor) and Rose (Langbort) Kaufman; married Henrietta Flax, December 22, 1968; children: Edward Brian, Richard Lee (deceased), Linda Gail. *Education:* Boston University, A.B., 1962; University of Pittsburgh, M.A., 1963; Tulane University, Ph.D., 1969.

ADDRESSES: Home—666 Western Ave., Westfield, Mass. 01085. *Office*—Department of History, Westfield State College, Westfield, Mass. 01085.

CAREER: High school history teacher in Winter Haven, Fla., 1964-65; Worcester State College, Worcester, Mass., instructor in history, 1968-69; Westfield State College, Westfield, Mass., assistant professor, 1969-72, associate professor, 1973-76, professor of history, 1977—, director of Institute for Massachusetts Studies, 1981—. *Military service:* U.S. Army Reserve, 1964-70.

MEMBER: Organization of American Historians, American Association for the History of Medicine, National Education Association.

AWARDS, HONORS: Distinguished service award, Westfield State College, 1981.

WRITINGS:

Homeopathy in America: The Rise and Fall of a Medical Heresy, Johns Hopkins University Press, 1971.
American Medical Education: The Formative Years, 1765-1910, Greenwood Press, 1976.
University of Vermont College of Medicine, University Press of New England, 1979.
(Editor in chief) *Dictionary of American Medical Biography,* Greenwood Press, 1984.
(Editor in chief) *Dictionary of American Nursing Biography,* Greenwood Press, 1988.
A Guide to the History of Massachusetts, Greenwood Press, 1988.

Contributor of articles to periodicals.

WORK IN PROGRESS: History of American School Health, with John Duffy, completion expected in 1990; *South Side Sisters,* a children's book.

SIDELIGHTS: Martin Kaufman told *CA:* "I am far from a brilliant historian and writer; I am a hard worker who does diligent research, tries to ask the right questions, analyzes material, and tries to develop a coherent synthesis. I try to write for the intelligent layman rather than for scholars, and I am most proud of the fact that I have had articles published in *Sports Illustrated, American History Illustrated,* and *Yankee.* Indeed, in one week, millions of people read my article in *Sports Illustrated,* as compared to the thousand who perhaps have read any of my books over a fifteen year period.

"In any discussion of my life and work, there must be mention of the impact of the birth of Richard Lee Kaufman, my son. Ricky was multiply-handicapped, being unable to either walk or talk, and the care he required, combined with his severe behavior problem, resulted in a great turmoil within the house and conflict within the family. From 1976, when we realized that Ricky had a serious problem, to 1981, when he was admitted into the Berkshire Children's Community in Great Barrington, Massachusetts, it was difficult to work, knowing how difficult it was at home. My wife had it much worse, however, since she was at home with the problem twenty-four hours a day, while I could escape by teaching, or by doing research and writing. Yet, many of my accomplishments during these years were achieved under duress.

"With Ricky at a fine residential school, the home life improved, but I thought I would never be able to resume a normal scholarly life, as we were to visit Ricky at least weekly, and there were always problems related to his needs. Ricky contracted pneumonia and died in April of 1984. Yet, life must go on. I am a better person for having been blessed with Ricky, although at times I was certain that it was more of a punishment than a 'blessing.'

"Since Ricky's death, my scholarly life has returned to something resembling 'normalcy,' although I don't think I, or my family, will ever get over his passing. It was much easier, however, to complete the *Dictionary of American Nursing Biography* and *A Guide to the History of Massachusetts,* although I have felt that I would like to make more of a contribution to humanity than is possible through scholarly writing. During the winter vacation of 1987-1988, I had that opportunity, when my daughter Linda, age eleven, complained that I never wrote anything that she could understand. As a result of her complaints (and the fact that I was destined to be with her for more than three weeks), I began a children's book, tentatively entitled *South Side Sisters.* I still cannot believe how it flowed from the computer; in three weeks it was substantially completed, and after revision I sent it to an agent who specializes in placing children's books. Linda and I were both pleased and surprised when the agent, Sidney Kramer, phoned to let us know that he liked the book and wanted to represent it. This may provide an opportunity to make a more substantial contribution to humanity, by writing books for children which will help eradicate racism, anti-Semitism, and which will bring about a greater sensitivity to the needs of the handicapped. I hope to continue writing children's books, and eventually to write one which will portray a multiply-handicapped youngster like our own Ricky.

"I only hope that this new interest in children's literature will not prevent me from completing *History of American School Health,* which I agreed to co-author with John Duffy, who recently retired from a chair at the University of Maryland. Since Dr. Duffy has been my inspiration over the years, the person who first interested me in the history of medicine and the one who taught me how to write, I wouldn't want to do anything to disappoint him in any way."

BIOGRAPHICAL/CRITICAL SOURCES:

PERIODICALS

American Historical Review, autumn, 1973, June, 1977, April, 1980.

*   *   *

KELLOW, Kathleen
    See HIBBERT, Eleanor Burford

*   *   *

KENNER, (William) Hugh   1923-

PERSONAL: Born January 7, 1923, in Peterborough, Ontario, Canada; son of Henry Rowe Hocking (a high school principal) and Mary Isabel (Williams) Kenner; married Mary Josephine Waite, August 30, 1947 (died, 1964); married Mary Anne Bittner, August 13, 1965; children: (first marriage) Catherine, Julia, Margaret, John, Michael; (second marriage) Robert, Elizabeth. *Education:* University of Toronto, B.A., 1945, M.A., 1946; Yale University, Ph.D., 1950. *Religion:* Roman Catholic.

ADDRESSES: Home—103 Edgevale Rd., Baltimore, Md. 21210. *Office*—Department of English, Johns Hopkins University, Baltimore, Md. 21218.

CAREER: Assumption College (now University of Windsor), Windsor, Ontario, assistant professor, 1946-48; University of California, Santa Barbara, instructor, 1950-51, assistant professor, 1951-56, associate professor, 1956-58, professor of English, 1958-73, department chairman, 1956-62; Johns Hopkins University, Baltimore, Md., professor of English, 1973-75, Andrew W. Mellon Professor of Humanities, 1975—, department chairman, 1980-84. Visiting professor, University of Michigan, 1956, University of Chicago, 1962, and University of Virginia, 1963. Alexander Lecturer, University of Toronto, 1973; T. S. Eliot Memorial Lecturer, University of Kent, 1975; Christian Gauss Lecturer, Princeton University, 1975; F. W. Bateson Memorial Lecturer, Oxford University, 1987. Northrop Frye Chair, University of Toronto, 1985; Ames Professor, University of Washington, 1988.

MEMBER: Royal Society of Literature (fellow), American Academy of Arts and Sciences (fellow).

AWARDS, HONORS: American Council of Learned Societies fellow, 1949; Porter Prize, 1950; American Philosophical Society fellow, 1956; Guggenheim fellow, 1957-58, 1963; National Institute of Arts and Letters/American Academy of Arts and Letters prize, 1969; Christian Gauss Award, 1972, for *The Pound Era;* D.H.L., University of Chicago, 1976, Trent University, 1977, Marlboro College, 1978, and University of Windsor, 1983; LL.D., University of Notre Dame, 1984.

WRITINGS:

Paradox in Chesterton, introduction by Marshall McLuhan, Sheed & Ward, 1947.
The Poetry of Ezra Pound, New Directions, 1951, reprinted, University of Nebraska Press, 1985.
Wyndham Lewis, New Directions, 1954.
Dublin's Joyce, Chatto & Windus, 1955, Indiana University Press, 1956, reprinted, Columbia University Press, 1987.

Gnomon: Essays in Contemporary Literature, McDowell, Obolensky, 1958.

The Invisible Poet: T. S. Eliot, McDowell, Obolensky, 1959.

Samuel Beckett, Grove, 1962, revised edition published as *Samuel Beckett: A Critical Study,* University of California Press, 1968.

Flaubert, Joyce and Beckett: The Stoic Comedians, Beacon Press, 1962, published as *The Stoic Comedians: Flaubert, Joyce and Beckett,* University of California Press, 1974.

The Counterfeiters: An Historical Comedy, Indiana University Press, 1968, reprinted, University of California Press, 1987.

The Pound Era, University of California Press, 1971.

A Reader's Guide to Samuel Beckett, Farrar, Straus, 1973.

Bucky: A Guided Tour of Buckminster Fuller, Morrow, 1973.

A Homemade World: The American Modernist Writers, Knopf, 1975.

Geodesic Math and How to Use It, University of California Press, 1976.

Joyce's Voices, University of California Press, 1978.

Ulysses, Allen & Unwin, 1980, revised edition, Johns Hopkins University Press, 1987.

A Colder Eye: The Modern Irish Writers, Knopf, 1983.

Heath-Zenith Z-100 User's Guide, Brady, 1984.

The Mechanic Muse, Oxford University Press, 1987.

A Sinking Island: The Modern English Writers, Knopf, 1988.

Magics and Spells (chapbook), Bennington, 1988.

Mazes (essays), North Point Press, in press.

EDITOR

The Art of Poetry, Rinehart, 1959.

T. S. Eliot: A Collection of Critical Essays, Prentice-Hall, 1962.

Seventeenth Century Poetry: The Schools of Donne and Jonson, Holt, 1964.

Studies in Change: A Book of the Short Story, Prentice-Hall, 1965.

(And author of introduction) *The Translations of Ezra Pound,* Faber, 1970.

(With Seamus Cooney, Bradford Morrow, and Bernard Lafourcade) *Blast 3,* Black Sparrow Press, 1985.

CONTRIBUTOR

Essays by Divers Hands, [London], 1958.

A. Walton Litz, editor, *Eliot in His Time,* Princeton University Press, 1973.

Frank Brady, John Palmer, and Martin Price, editors, *Literary Theory and Structure: Essays Presented to William K. Wimsatt,* Yale University Press, 1973.

Gary Lane, editor, *Sylvia Plath: New Views on the Poetry,* Johns Hopkins University Press, 1979.

Leonard Michaels and Christopher Ricks, editors, *The State of the Language,* University of California Press, 1980.

WORK IN PROGRESS: Historical Fictions, for North Point Press.

SIDELIGHTS: Hugh Kenner is one of the nation's leading literary critics, particularly known for his works on this century's modernist writers. As Michiko Kakutani states in the *New York Times,* "Kenner has earned a well-deserved reputation as our pre-eminent expert on modernism in English." His books on Ezra Pound, T. S. Eliot, Wyndham Lewis, Samuel Beckett, and James Joyce have been received as important contributions to modern literary criticism. Joann Gardner, in an article for the *Dictionary of Literary Biography,* explains that Kenner "has put his hand to most of the major modern

writers, defining their positions historically and offering unique perspectives on difficult and essential works."

In analyzing the works of modernist writers, Kenner often relies on the methods proposed by the writers themselves. He takes their literary criteria as the standard by which to judge their work. As Gardner notes, "Kenner invests the artist with an authority and stature often disallowed by modern criticism." This approach has been well received. Douglas Baiz of the *Chicago Tribune* maintains that "Kenner gives literary criticism a good name. His writing is muscular: clean, direct, free of jargon and obscurities. He wears his considerable learning lightly, even wittily. . ., and he displays an obvious sympathy for the writers he is examining. He flays no dead horses, scatters no red herrings, demolishes no straw men, and when he enters a lecture hall, he comes to praise Caesar, not to bury him."

Kenner's works on Ezra Pound in particular have been pivotal in establishing the author's reputation. A poet, critic, editor, and translator, Pound was the catalytic force behind much of modern literature. In addition to publishing books of poetry, criticism, and translation, he also edited the works of many other writers who later achieved prominence, such as T. S. Eliot, and worked to get the talents of promising writers appreciated by the literary community. But during the Second World War, Pound lost what respect and position he had in the literary world. Convinced that the government of Italian strongman Benito Mussolini was successfully overcoming the economic problems caused by the depression, and in the process circumventing the dire influences of bureaucracy and the banking community, Pound broadcast a series of radio messages on behalf of the Italian government during the war. At war's end, Pound was charged with treason. Found to be unfit for trial, he was hospitalized for some fourteen years in a mental asylum.

In 1951, Kenner's *The Poetry of Ezra Pound* was the first book to be published in the United States to decry Pound's political beliefs and yet argue persuasively on behalf of his literary achievement. Bonamy Dobree of the *Spectator* believes that in this book "Kenner has gone far to achieve what he set out to do, make the reader see Mr. Pound as a poet possibly great, and certainly important to our time." Kenner's argument for taking Pound's literary work seriously proved to be influential. Writing in the *Saturday Review,* C. David Heymann notes that since the publication of Kenner's study, "the first published in this country, . . . the traffic of detailed and far-reaching investigations of and about Pound in the way of exegetical studies and explications, theses and dissertations, memoirs and biographies, has been practically non-stop." Gardner believes that Kenner's studies of Pound and British writer Wyndham Lewis have "done much to establish these figures as central to the modern tradition."

In *The Pound Era,* published in 1971, Kenner examines the course of twentieth-century literary history, tracing how the modernist writers created an aesthetic divorced from the artistic values of the nineteenth century. He sees Pound as an essential part of this development. "He sets out," Gardner explains, "to discover how the twentieth century had extricated itself from the influence of fin-de-siecle literature, and he places Ezra Pound at the vortex of the cultural movement." As Heymann notes, this movement "produced the likes of Eliot, Joyce, Wyndham Lewis, and their contemporaries, and . . . Pound was unquestionably the central and moving force."

Although some observers questioned the centrality of Pound's influence and felt that Kenner had exaggerated his importance, *The Pound Era* won praise for its depiction of Pound's role in twentieth century literature. Charles Molesworth, reviewing the book for the *Nation,* calls it "clearly the capstone of [Kenner's] illustrious career" and maintains that it "clarifies our reading of Pound and his era better than any single book of criticism. Kenner's book is, quite simply, a work of art." Writing in the *New York Review of Books,* Michael Wood terms *The Pound Era* "a brilliant, fascinating, and otherwise altogether satisfactory book," while the reviewer for the *New Republic* describes Kenner himself as "our most knowing and enthusiastic Pound scholar, a true disciple who partakes of the Pound conciseness, lives the Pound vision of art and language."

Kenner's analysis of the works of James Joyce has also proven to be influential. He has written two books about the author, *Dublin's Joyce* and *Joyce's Voices,* and a study of Joyce's most famous book, *Ulysses.* Kenner has also written of Joyce in several critical surveys. In all of these works, he has succeeded in rendering comprehensible Joyce's often difficult prose. A. Walton Litz of the *Times Literary Supplement* claims that "for over thirty years [Kenner] has been our finest reader of *Ulysses.*" In his study of *Ulysses,* also entitled *Ulysses,* Kenner "shows the reader how to read [the novel] —and shows him how exciting the experience can be," as the reviewer for the *South Atlantic Quarterly* remarks. Kenner has also turned his critical attention to other experimental writers, like Samuel Beckett, and presented their ideas and concerns in clear, understandable prose. Gardner maintains that Kenner's "analyses of Joyce, Beckett, and others have made the literary avant-garde accessible to a generation of scholars and students."

When writing of the major authors of the twentieth century, Kenner employs a witty and accessible prose that shows a great concern for the proper use of language. Thomas R. Edwards comments on Kenner's style in the *New York Times Book Review.* "It's always an unexpected pleasure," he states, "to find serious literary criticism written as if the English language still mattered, as Hugh Kenner's writing insists that it does. In book after book ... strong and supple thought finds its proper medium in a style of uncommon wit and pungency, writing whose powers of intellectual entertainment brazenly violate the first law of academic criticism: Be Thou Dull." Kenner's work also possesses an enthusiasm that several observers appreciate for its energy and willingness to take chances. As Richard Eder writes in the *Los Angeles Times Book Review,* "Kenner doesn't write about literature; he jumps in, armed and thrashing. He crashes it, like a party-goer who refuses to hover near the door but goes right up to the guest of honor, plumps himself down, sniffs at the guest's dinner, eats some, and begins a one-to-one discussion. You could not say whether his talking or his listening is done with greater intensity."

Following the example of Pound, Kenner often unites disparate elements of information in a single work in order to show connections between events and ideas that a more conventional approach may not reveal. Speaking in particular of Kenner's method in his critical surveys of British, Irish, and American modernists, John W. Aldridge of the *New York Times Book Review* calls it a "curious but on the whole effective amalgam of anecdotes, character portraits, textual analysis, intellectual history and what Gore Vidal likes spenetically to call 'book chat'." Wood finds that Kenner "combs the world like a critical Sherlock Holmes, isolating details, making distinctions, collecting verbal and technological specimens." "Like Pound,"

Thomas Flanagan observes in the *Washington Post Book World,* "[Kenner] knows how to argue by juxtaposition and surprise, how to use wit as a form of logic. He knows the value of the exact image and the resonant anecdote. And like Pound, he is a skilled swordsman; reading Kenner is a lively and illuminating experience but it is best to keep one's guard up."

For some four decades, Kenner's literary criticism has illuminated many of the major works and authors of twentieth century literature. "He is both the scholar and the celebrant of the Modernist movement, and has written well and instructively about its masters," Flanagan observes. Jane Larkin Crain of the *Saturday Review* ranks Kenner "among the most distinguished of contemporary literary critics, justly celebrated for the felicity and the accessibility of his prose." Michael Rosenthal, writing in the *New York Times Book Review,* claims that "Kenner bestrides modern literature if not like a colossus then at least a presence of formidable proportions." Aldridge notes that for "over 40 years, [Kenner] has written authoritatively and at length about most of the major 20th-century writers ... and has established himself as one of the most distinguished critics now at work in the field."

BIOGRAPHICAL/CRITICAL SOURCES:

BOOKS

Dictionary of Literary Biography, Volume 67: *Modern American Critics since 1955,* Gale, 1988.

PERIODICALS

Book World, August 4, 1968.
Chicago Tribune, March 3, 1987, January 29, 1988.
Denver Quarterly, spring, 1977.
Los Angeles Times Book Review, January 31, 1988.
Nation, March 20, 1972.
New Republic, March 25, 1972, November 29, 1975.
New York Review of Books, February 13, 1969, February 8, 1973, April 17, 1975, May 12, 1983.
New York Times, March 28, 1972, February 4, 1975, November 29, 1986.
New York Times Book Review, March 26, 1972, November 25, 1973, February 9, 1975, July 31, 1983, February 21, 1988.
Saturday Review, May 13, 1972, April 5, 1975.
South Atlantic Quarterly, winter, 1983.
Spectator, November 16, 1951, September 9, 1978.
Times Literary Supplement, May 5, 1978, December 12, 1980.
Village Voice, May 24, 1983.
Voice Literary Supplement, December, 1983.
Washington Post Book World, May 8, 1983, April 3, 1988.

—*Sketch by Thomas Wiloch*

*   *   *

KEPPEL, Charlotte
See TORDAY, Ursula

*   *   *

KERNAGHAN, Eileen   1939-

PERSONAL: Born January 6, 1939, in Enderby, British Columbia, Canada; daughter of William Alfred (a dairy farmer) and Belinda Maude (Pritchard) Monk; married Patrick Walter Kernaghan (a corrections officer), 1959; children: Michael, Susan, Gavin. *Education:* Attended University of British Columbia, 1956-59.

ADDRESSES: Home—Burnaby, British Columbia, Canada. *Office*—5512 Neville St., Burnaby, British Columbia, Canada V5J 2H7.

CAREER: Elementary school teacher in British Columbia, 1959-62; Burnaby Arts Council, Burnaby, British Columbia, secretary, office worker, and coordinator, 1979-84; free-lance writer, 1984—. Operates Neville Books, a secondhand bookstore, with her husband in Burnaby.

MEMBER: Writers Union of Canada, Science Fiction Writers of America, Federation of British Columbia Writers, Burnaby Writers Society.

AWARDS, HONORS: Silver Medal Award for original fantasy from *West Coast Review of Books*, 1980, for *Journey to Aprilioth;* Canadian Science Fiction and Fantasy Award (''Caspar''), 1984, for *Songs from the Drowned Lands: A Novel of High Fantasy.*

WRITINGS:

(Co-author) *The Upper Left-Hand Corner: A Writer's Guide for the Northwest,* J. D. Douglas, 1975, 3rd edition, 1986.
Journey to Aprilioth (fantasy novel; first novel in trilogy), Ace Books, 1980.
Songs from the Drowned Lands: A Novel of High Fantasy (second novel in trilogy), Ace Books, 1983.
(Contributor) Judith Merril, editor, *Tesseracts* (anthology), Press Porcepic, 1985.
(Contributor) Mary Alice Downie and others, editors, *The Window of Dreams* (anthology), Methuen, 1986.
The Sarsen Witch (fantasy novel; third novel in trilogy), Ace Books, 1989.

Contributor of poems and short stories to magazines, including *Galaxy, Space and Time, Womanspace, Room of One's Own, Northern Journey,* and *Canadian Review.*

WORK IN PROGRESS: Winter on the Plain of Ghosts, a prehistoric fantasy set in the bronze-age Indus Valley.

SIDELIGHTS: In an interview with Frank Garcia for *Cross-Canada Writers,* Eileen Kernaghan indicates that she began writing for publication when she was approximately twelve years old. She started in science fiction but switched to fantasy when she realized her background in ''the rules of the real world''—like biology, chemistry, and physics—were lacking. When asked why the fantasy genre appeals to her, she told Garcia: ''I suppose, because in mainstream fiction, you know that the bad guys are probably going to win; whereas Fantasy good is still able to conquer evil. When your life, the country, and the whole world are in a mess, it's nice to read a book in which Order wins over Chaos. From a writer's point of view, what other genre allows you to create, populate and make up all the rules for an entire universe? It's the ultimate act of self-indulgence.''

Journey to Aprilioth, the first novel in Kernaghan's fantasy trilogy, is set in 1970 B.C. It is the story of Nhiall, a religious novice forced to flee his land after accidentally killing a man. While traveling across the terrain of ancient Europe, Nhiall attempts to discover the last survivors of an even older civilization. This journey, however, is disrupted by numerous encounters with bandits and barbarians. According to *Vancouver Sun* contributor Leslie Peterson, the novel is ''plausible'' and ''well balanced.''

Kernaghan's second trilogy novel entitled *Songs from the Drowned Lands: A Novel of High Fantasy* won a Canadian Science Fiction and Fantasy Award in 1984. Events in this novel are set in an even earlier time than that of *Journey to Aprilioth,* with some people calling it a ''prequel.'' As Melanie Conn explains in *Kinesis,* ''*Songs from the Drowned Lands* is a pre-historic disaster novel which explores the mystery of Stonehenge and the disappearance of the Grey Isles beneath the sea. Each of the four ''Songs''—or novelettes—focuses on one character's response to foreknowledge of the coming disaster: What do people do when they know that the world is about to end?'' When Conn heard Kernaghan read parts of *Songs from the Drowned Lands* aloud, she was ''struck by the imagery and emotion of [Kernaghan's] writing.''

Kernaghan wrote to *CA* that ''my major theme is a traditional one in fantasy: the eternal struggle between order and chaos; the message, one of guarded, and long-term, optimism: civilizations rise as well as fall. Essentially, I just enjoy telling a good story. But people whose opinions I respect tell me that my books are about making choices, accepting responsibility, seeking values in something larger than oneself. Perhaps that's because I'm looking at the world of 2000 B.C. through twentieth-century A.D. eyes: a time when we must continue to make choices, with fewer and fewer real choices remaining to us.''

BIOGRAPHICAL/CRITICAL SOURCES:

PERIODICALS

Cross-Canada Writers, Number 2, 1988.
Kinesis, July-August, 1988.
Vancouver Sun, June 26, 1981.

*   *   *

KESSLER, Ronald (Borek)   1943-

PERSONAL: Born December 31, 1943, in New York, N.Y.; son of Ernest Borek (a biochemist) and Minuetta (a pianist; maiden name, Shumiatcher) Kessler; married second wife, Pamela Johnson (a reporter), 1969; children: Greg, Rachel. *Education:* Attended Clark University, 1962-64.

ADDRESSES: Home and office—2516 Stratton Dr., Potomac, Md. 20854.

CAREER: Worcester Telegram, Worcester, Mass., reporter, 1964; *Boston Herald,* Boston, Mass., editorial writer and reporter, 1964-67; *Wall Street Journal,* New York, N.Y., reporter, 1967-70; *Washington Post,* Washington, D.C., investigative reporter, 1970-87. Notable stories include Nixon finances, F.B.I. wiretapping investigations, General Services Administration scandal, and problem loans at New York banks.

AWARDS, HONORS: United Press International first prize award in newswriting, 1965; Associated Press Sevellon Brown Award, 1965; Freedoms Foundation Award, 1966; American Political Science Association public affairs award, 1967; American Dental Society science award, 1968; *Washingtonian* Magazine Washingtonian of the Year award, 1972; Baltimore-Washington Newspaper Guild Front Page Award, 1972; George Polk Memorial awards, 1972, for community service, 1979, for national reporting; American Association of University Women public affairs award, 1973; top prize for business and financial reporting, Washington Chapter of Sigma Delta Chi; first place award in investigative reporting, Association of Area Business Publications.

WRITINGS:

The Life Insurance Game, Holt, 1985.

The Richest Man in the World: The Story of Adnan Khashossi, Warner, 1986.
Spy vs. Spy: Stalking Soviet Spies in America, Scribner, 1987.
Moscow Station: How the KGB Penetrated the American Embassy, Scribner, 1989.

SIDELIGHTS: Ronald Kessler contends an investigative journalist's role is "to find the truth as nearly as it can be determined."

*   *   *

KETCHUM, William C(larence), Jr.   1931-

PERSONAL: Born March 29, 1931, in Columbia, Mo.; son of William Clarence and Mildred Ann (Roberts) Ketchum; married Erica Stoller, August 9, 1982; children: Rachael Forbes, Aaron Roberts. *Education:* Union College (Schenectady, N.Y.), B.A., 1953; Columbia University, J.D., 1956.

ADDRESSES: *Home*—241 Grace Church St., Rye, N.Y. 10580.

CAREER: Member of Bar of State of New York; attorney with law firms in New York City, prior to 1969; Civil Court, New York City, attorney, 1969-76; New School for Social Research, New York City, instructor in fine arts, 1971-87; New York University, New York City, member of faculty, 1984—; Museum of American Folk Art, New York City, curator for special projects, 1984—; Marymount College, Tarrytown, N.Y., member of faculty, 1987—. *Military service:* U.S. Naval Reserve, active duty, 1956-60; became lieutenant.

MEMBER: New York Historical Society, New York State Bar Association, Association of the Bar (New York City).

AWARDS, HONORS: Ambassador of Honor book award, English Speaking Union, 1983, for *American Folk Art of the 20th Century.*

WRITINGS:

Early Potters and Potteries of New York State, Funk, 1970.
The Pottery and Porcelain Collector's Handbook, Funk, 1971.
American Basketry and Woodenware, Macmillan, 1974.
A Treasury of American Bottles, Bobbs-Merrill, 1975.
Hooked Rugs, Harcourt, 1976.
The Catalog of American Antiques, Rutledge Books, 1977.
The Catalog of American Collectibles, Mayflower Books, 1979.
Collecting American Craft Antiques, Dutton, 1980.
Auction, Sterling, 1980.
Western Memorabilia, Hammond, 1980.
Toys and Games, Smithsonian Institution, 1981.
Furniture, Volume II: Post Federal, Smithsonian Institution, 1982.
American Furniture, Cupboards, Chests and Related Pieces, Knopf, 1982.
Pottery and Porcelain, Knopf, 1983.
American Folk Art of the 20th Century, Rizzoli, 1983.
Collecting Bottles for Fun and Profit, HP Books, 1985.
Collecting Toys for Fun and Profit, HP Books, 1985.
Collecting the '40s and '50s for Fun and Profit, HP Books, 1985.
Collecting Sports Memorabilia for Fun and Profit, HP Books, 1985.
All-American: Folk Art and Craft, Rizzoli, 1986.
America's Homespun Ceramics: Yellowware and Spongeware, Knopf, 1987.
Potters and Potteries of New York State: 1650-1900, Syracuse University Press, 1987.

Contributor to *Better Homes & Gardens, Country Home, Western Collector, Spinning Wheel, Antiques Journal, Early American Life,* and *Americana;* also contributor to newsletters *Pontil* and *Pottery Collectors.*

WORK IN PROGRESS: A book on holiday collectibles.

SIDELIGHTS: William C. Ketchum, Jr., told *CA:* "I have just completed installation of a major exhibition of American Folk Art at Tokyo's Isetan Museum and anticipate working with the Japanese on future installations and related projects." Ketchum has travelled and resided in many countries abroad, including Spain, France, the British Isles, Portugal, Italy, Morocco, Switzerland, Canada, Mexico, Chile, Japan, Taiwan, the Philippines, Korea, and Hong Kong.

AVOCATIONAL INTERESTS: Antique collecting and dealing, fishing, historical research.

BIOGRAPHICAL/CRITICAL SOURCES:

PERIODICALS

Los Angeles Times Book Review, December 14, 1980.

*   *   *

KIDD, Russ
See DONSON, Cyril

*   *   *

KLEIN, Daniel M(artin)   1939-

PERSONAL: Born April 20, 1939, in Wilmington, Del.; son of David Xavier (a chemist) and Sophia (a teacher; maiden name, Posner) Klein; married Freke Quirine Vuijst, 1976. *Education:* Harvard University, A.B., 1961. *Religion:* Jewish.

ADDRESSES: *Home*—P.O. Box 629, Great Barrington, Mass. 01230. *Agent*—Mel Berger, William Morris Agency, 1350 Avenue of the Americas, New York, N.Y. 10019.

CAREER: Social worker and welfare worker in New York City, 1962-63; high school teacher in Boiceville, N.Y., 1963-64; television writer in New York City, 1963-65; free-lance writer, 1965—.

WRITINGS:

Everything You Wanted to Know about Marijuana, Tower, 1972.
(With Susan Haven) *Seven Perfect Marriages That Failed,* Stein & Day, 1975.
Embryo: A Novel, Doubleday, 1980.
Wavelengths (novel), Doubleday, 1982.
Magic Time (novel), Doubleday, 1984.
(Ghostwriter) Dagmar O'Connor, *How to Make Love to the Same Person for the Rest of Your Life,* Doubleday, 1985.
How to Put the Love Back into Making Love, Doubleday, 1989.

Contributor of articles and stories to magazines, including *Realist, Saturday Evening Post, McCall's, Eye, Cavalier,* and *Nation.*

WORK IN PROGRESS: *Makeover,* a novel for St. Martin's.

SIDELIGHTS: Daniel M. Klein wrote to *CA:* "Somehow it took me until I was forty to write a novel and here I am at fifty at work on my fourth and actually making a living doing exactly what I've always wanted to do."

BIOGRAPHICAL/CRITICAL SOURCES:

PERIODICALS

Los Angeles Times, June 1, 1984.
Los Angeles Times Book Review, October 10, 1982.
New York Times Book Review, February 8, 1981, May 13,
　　1984.

*　　　*　　　*

KLUGER, Richard 1934-

PERSONAL: Born September 18, 1934, in Paterson, N.J.; son of David (a business executive) and Ida (Abramson) Kluger; married Phyllis Schlain, March 23, 1957; children: Matthew Harold, Leonard Theodore. *Education:* Princeton University, B.A. (cum laude), 1956.

ADDRESSES: Home—Back Brook Rd., Ringoes, N.J. 08551. *Agent*—Georges Borchardt, Inc., 136 East 57th St., New York, N.Y. 10022.

CAREER: Author, editor, critic. *Wall Street Journal*, New York City, city editor, 1956-57; *County Citizen*, New City, N.Y., editor and publisher, 1958-60; *New York Post*, New York City, staff writer, 1960-61; *Forbes* magazine, New York City, associate editor, 1962; *New York Herald Tribune*, New York City, general book editor, 1962-63, book editor, 1963-66; *Book Week*, New York City, editor, 1963-66; Simon & Schuster, New York City, managing editor, 1966-68, executive editor, 1968-70; Atheneum Publishers, New York City, editor in chief, 1970-71; Charterhouse Books, New York City, president and publisher, 1972-73.

MEMBER: Princeton Club of New York.

AWARDS, HONORS: National Book Award nomination and Sidney Hillman Prize, both 1976, both for *Simple Justice: A History of Brown v. Board of Education;* American Book Award nomination, 1986, and George Polk Prize, 1987, both for *The Paper: The Life and Death of the New York Herald Tribune.*

WRITINGS:

NOVELS

When the Bough Breaks, Doubleday, 1964.
National Anthem, Harper, 1969.
Members of the Tribe (Book-of-the-Month Club alternate selection), Doubleday, 1977.
Star Witness, Doubleday, 1979.
Un-American Activities, Doubleday, 1982.

NONFICTION

Simple Justice: A History of Brown v. Board of Education, Knopf, 1976.
(With wife, Phyllis Kluger) *Good Goods*, Macmillan, 1982.
The Paper: The Life and Death of the New York Herald Tribune, Knopf, 1986.

OTHER

Contributor to *Partisan Review, New Republic, Harper's, Nation, New York Times Book Review*, and other periodicals.

SIDELIGHTS: In keeping with his claim that the quest for social justice in America is a unifying theme in his writing, Richard Kluger's acclaimed nonfiction work *Simple Justice: A History of Brown v. Board of Education* relates a crucial event in the black population's struggle for equal rights in America. *Simple Justice* is Kluger's detailed analysis of the landmark U.S. Supreme Court case of 1954 which decided against segregation in the public school system. In the *New York Times Book Review*, Robert Conot finds Kluger's account "intriguing, encyclopedic and deeply researched. . . . Kluger tells the story in terms of the people involved, and so turns what might have been a dry text into an exceedingly human drama." Although Conot feels the book is too long and too detailed, he says, "In the final third of the book, when the focus is on the Supreme Court, the story is gripping." Additionally, *Time* reviewer Melvin Maddocks concludes that Kluger's "collage of facts and events, institutions and people eventually documents nothing less than a national change of heart."

After directing attention to the struggle of blacks for equal opportunity education in *Simple Justice*, "a similar impetus on behalf of American Jews led to [Kluger's] writing *Members of the Tribe*," notes Lincoln Caplan in the *Saturday Review*. In this novel, set in the South in the late nineteenth and early twentieth centuries, Kluger draws on incidents of the Leo M. Frank trial which took place in Atlanta, Georgia, from 1913 to 1915. Accordingly, in *Members of the Tribe*, Seth Adler, a young Jewish lawyer originally from New York, defends a Jewish man accused of killing a fourteen-year-old Christian girl. As Caplan maintains, "Though mainly a work of imagination, the narrative draws on historical events and personalities to describe the growing pains of the postbellum South and its awkwardness in accommodating not just blacks and Northerners but also Jews, who had special anxieties about assimilation." Likewise, *New York Times Book Review* critic Eli N. Evans expresses that Kluger "has written the best novel yet about the Jews who settled in the South. . . . Over the past [several decades] there has been just a handful of novels written about Jews of the South, and the Frank case is one of the reasons why: Southern Jews learned to keep a low profile; they were conditioned by an instinctive wariness against passing for white in that mysterious underland of America. . . . [Perhaps] Kluger's provocative fictionalization of the Frank trial and lynching is an appropriate first step toward dispelling the phantoms that have held back novels about this fascinating aspect of Jews in America as one example of the varieties of the white experience in the South."

Kluger worked as a book editor for the *New York Herald Tribune* during its final four years from 1962 to 1966. His 1986 account, or obituary, as it has been called, of the *Tribune* is said by *Chicago Tribune* reviewer W. A. Swanberg to be a "Grade-A journalistic cliffhanger." According to Don Cook in the *Los Angeles Times Book Review*, Kluger, in *The Paper: The Life and Death of the New York Herald Tribune*, "has performed a vast labor of love and research on 131 years of Herald Tribune history, written with verve, style and skill. For myself, a veteran of 23 years on the Herald Tribune through the best of times and the worst of times, reading Kluger was like walking into that grubby old city room once again with its clattering Underwood typewriters. . . . But happily, this is not just a book of nostalgic fluff for old newspaper buffs. It is an absorbing, serious and colorful picture of social, political and journalistic life in an era when newspapers across America were family businesses, and reporters and writers were the television of the times because there was no television. . . . In Kluger's warm, witty, wonderful obituary, the Trib still lives." As has been the case with *Simple Justice, The Paper*'s success is in part derived from its attention to individuals. Notes David Shaw in the *New York Times Book Review:* "The Paper was always far more a collection of individuals—and a reflection of their special sensibilities—than it was an institution, and Mr. Kluger does a remarkable job of bringing these people to life on the printed page." Included among those Kluger brings to life are the original founder and editor of the *New York Herald*, James Gordon Bennett, the original founder and editor of the *New York Tribune*, Horace Greeley, and James Bellows, the last editor of the merged *New York Herald Tribune*. *New York Times* reviewer Christopher Lehmann-Haupt believes Kluger's enthusiasm for his subject, "which is apparent everywhere," has made *The Paper* a success.

Kluger told *CA* that his quest for social justice in his writing is a "preoccupation which affects my fiction at least as much as my books of social history; novels of exquisite sensibility are not my metier. I believe that my country has thrived not because of its brash arrogance alone but because many of its people naively hold to the precepts with which the United States was endowed. The most patriotic of our citizens are not those who say, 'My country, right or wrong,' but those who call upon it to meet the high promise of its rhetoric and are willing, indeed compelled, to criticize it for its shortcomings and to act with compassion and strength toward that end. The true subversives, I think, are those who mindlessly cheer our every action and fear those—even hate those—who dissent or demur."

BIOGRAPHICAL/CRITICAL SOURCES:

PERIODICALS

Best Sellers, May 1, 1969.
Chicago Tribune, March 4, 1979, November 30, 1986.
Detroit News, August 15, 1982.
Los Angeles Times Book Review, November 23, 1986.
Nation, May 12, 1979.
Newsweek, July 13, 1964, January 26, 1976.
New York Times, February 22, 1977, September 23, 1977, February 28, 1979, July 22, 1982, October 30, 1986.
New York Times Book Review, January 18, 1976, September 25, 1977, February 25, 1979, July 25, 1982, October 26, 1986.
Observer Review, October 26, 1969.
Saturday Review, October 15, 1977.
Time, February 9, 1976, October 10, 1977, October 27, 1986.
Virginia Quarterly Review, autumn, 1969.
Washington Post, March 1, 1979.
Washington Post Book World, June 16, 1982, October 26, 1986.

*   *   *

KRISTOL, Irving   1920-

PERSONAL: Born January 22, 1920, in New York, N.Y.; son of Joseph Kristol; married Gertrude Himmelfarb (a professor), January 18, 1942; children: William, Elizabeth. *Education:* City College (now City College of the City University of New York), B.A. (cum laude), 1940.

ADDRESSES: Office—*Public Interest*, 1112 16th Street N.W., Suite 530, Washington, D.C. 20036.

CAREER: Commentary, New York City, managing editor, 1947-52; *Encounter*, London, England, founder and editor with Stephen Spender, 1953-59; *Reporter*, New York City, editor, 1959-60; Basic Books, Inc., New York City, executive vice presi-

dent, 1960-69, consulting editor, 1969—; *Public Interest* (quarterly), New York City, founder and editor with Nathan Glazer, 1965—; New York University, New York City, Henry R. Luce Professor of Urban Values, 1969-83, Graduate School of Business Administration, John M. Olin Professor of Social Thought, 1983—. Regents lecturer, University of California, Riverside, 1964. Member of study group on urban problems, RAND Corp., 1967; member, President-Elect's Task Force on Voluntary Urban Action, 1968-69; research associate, Russell Sage Foundation, 1968-69; chairman with Daniel P. Moynihan, Conference on the Future of New York City, sponsored by National Affairs, Inc., Ford Foundation, and Carnegie Foundation, 1968; member, President's Commission on White House Fellowships, 1981-84. *Military service:* U.S. Army, World War II.

MEMBER: American Enterprise Institute (distinguished fellow), American Political Science Association, American Academy of Arts and Sciences (fellow), Council on Foreign Relations, Century Club, Phi Beta Kappa.

WRITINGS:

(Editor with Stephen Spender and Melvin Lasky) *Encounters*, Basic Books, 1963.
(Editor with Daniel Bell) *Confrontation: The Student Rebellion and the Universities*, Basic Books, 1969.
(Editor with Bell) *Capitalism Today*, Basic Books, 1971.
On the Democratic Idea in America, Harper, 1972.
(Editor with Nathan Glazer) *The American Commonwealth—1976*, Basic Books, 1976.
(Editor with Paul Weaver) *The Americans, 1976: An Inquiry into Fundamental Concepts of Man Underlying Various U.S. Institutions*, Lexington Books, 1976.
Two Cheers for Capitalism, Basic Books, 1978.
(Editor with Bell) *The Crisis in Economic Theory*, Basic Books, 1981.
Reflections of a Neoconservative: Looking Back, Looking Ahead, Basic Books, 1983.
(With Fernando Moran, Michael D. Barnes, Alois Mertes, and Daniel Oduber) *Third World Instability: Central America as a European-American Issue*, edited by Andrew J. Pierre, Council on Foreign Relations (New York), 1985.

OTHER

(Contributor) *Essays on Personal Knowledge*, Routledge & Kegan Paul, 1962.
(Contributor) *A Nation of Cities*, Rand McNally, 1968.

Contributor to *New York Times*, *Harper's*, *Atlantic*, *Fortune*, *Foreign Affairs*, *Yale Review*, and other publications. Member of board of contributors, *Wall Street Journal*.

BIOGRAPHICAL/CRITICAL SOURCES:

PERIODICALS

Christian Science Monitor, June 27, 1969.
Commonweal, September 26, 1969.
New Leader, May 26, 1969.
New Yorker, May 24, 1969.
New York Times, May 10, 1972.
New York Times Book Review, October 2, 1983, May 19, 1985.
Washington Post Book World, January 1, 1984.

L

LABRADOR, James
See HAMEL PEIFER, Kathleen

*　　*　　*

LABRADOR, Judy
See HAMEL PEIFER, Kathleen

*　　*　　*

LaCAPRA, Dominick 1939-

PERSONAL: Born July 13, 1939, in New York, N.Y.; son of Joseph and Mildred (Sciascia) LaCapra; married Anne-Marie Hlasny, 1965 (divorced, 1970); children: Veronique. *Education:* Cornell University, B.A., 1961; Harvard University, Ph.D., 1969.

ADDRESSES: Home—119 Terrace Place, Ithaca, N.Y. 14850. *Office*—Department of History, Cornell University, Ithaca, N.Y. 14850.

CAREER: Cornell University, Ithaca, N.Y., assistant professor, 1969-74, associate professor, 1974-79, professor of history, 1979—, Goldwin Smith Professor of European Intellectual History, 1985—.

MEMBER: International Association of Philosophy and Literature, American Historical Association.

AWARDS, HONORS: Fulbright fellow, 1961; Woodrow Wilson fellow, 1962; Harvard University fellow, 1963, 1964; Foreign Area Studies fellow, 1965, 1966; National Endowment for the Humanities senior fellow, 1976; Cornell Society for the Humanities senior fellow, 1979.

WRITINGS:

Emile Durkheim: Sociologist and Philosopher, Cornell University Press, 1972.
A Preface to Sartre, Cornell University Press, 1978.
(Editor with Steven L. Kaplan) *Modern European Intellectual History: Reappraisals and New Perspectives,* Cornell University Press, 1982.
"Madame Bovary" on Trial, Cornell University Press, 1982.
Rethinking Intellectual History: Texts, Contexts, Language, Cornell University Press, 1983.
History and Criticism, Cornell University Press, 1985.

History, Politics, and the Novel, Cornell University Press, 1987.

Contributor to journals, including *American Historical Review, Journal of Modern History, Diacritics, Philosophical Review,* and *Modern Language Notes.*

WORK IN PROGRESS: A study of nineteenth- and twentieth-century historical writing.

SIDELIGHTS: Dominick LaCapra's *Emile Durkheim: Sociologist and Philosopher* is a "serious, intelligent, and important study" concerning one of sociology's foremost pioneers, comments Philip Rosenberg in the *New York Times Book Review.* Durkheim, whose works *Suicide* and *The Elementary Forms of the Religious Life* helped define and explain the behavior of nineteenth-century humanity, is represented in LaCapra's work as both an innovator within the budding field of sociology, and as a perceptive analyst of his own society. Rosenberg asserts that "Durkheim, as LaCapra interprets him, emerges as a social critic who recognized that it is not merely the case that our social system is subject to pathological distortions; rather, the system itself is, for its members, pathogenic." LaCapra traces Durkheim's contention that the disorder within society has reached crisis proportions, but faults the sociologist for his refusal to acknowledge Karl Marx's observations on social conflict; nevertheless, the author contends that Durkheim's work has provided the foundation for modern-day sociology.

"For almost a decade, Dominick LaCapra has been urging intellectual historians to pay closer attention to developments in literary criticism and philosophy in order to 'acquire the conceptual means to come to terms with problems in their own field,'" summarizes John E. Toews in the *American Historical Review.* LaCapra believes that fields such as intellectual and social history need to become less objective and less technical; he is "among the few historians currently prepared to rethink the assumptions underlying the craft," states Peter Burke in the *Times Literary Supplement.* In his review of *History and Criticism, Times Literary Supplement* contributor Hayden White observes that LaCapra "openly defines his purpose as an attempt to 'revive a Renaissance ideal of historiography'" which utilizes interpretative techniques from disciplines such as literary criticism and philosophy. The author wants to depart from "the ideal of the historian as writer of 'realistic' narrative prose whose sole concern is to tell the true story of what really happened in the past,'' describes White. Instead, LaCapra ''implies that, if there is a literary dimension to historical discourse, it might well be expressed in the writing of historical narratives in the manner of modernist or even post-modernist novels, as well as in that of the nineteenth century 'realists.''' Toews similarly notes that ''LaCapra perceives the intellectual historian's vocation of historical scholar to be a crucial element in the more general vocation as cultural critic.'' As the author once described his work to *CA*, ''My primary objective has been to reconceptualize the way intellectual history is written, in part by employing approaches developed in recent literary criticism and philosophy. My focus has been upon complex texts and the various contexts that inform them.''

BIOGRAPHICAL/CRITICAL SOURCES:

PERIODICALS

American Historical Review, February, 1983, October, 1987.
Contemporary Review, June, 1979.
Los Angeles Times Book Review, February 18, 1979.
New York Times Book Review, July 15, 1973.
Times Literary Supplement, July 28, 1972, December 14, 1979, July 8, 1983, January 31, 1986, November 6, 1987, February 12, 1988.

*   *   *

LACOLERE, Francois
   See ARAGON, Louis

*   *   *

La COLERE, Francois
   See ARAGON, Louis

*   *   *

LAGEVI, Bo
   See BLOM, Karl Arne

*   *   *

LAMM, Norman 1927-

PERSONAL: Born December 19, 1927, in Brooklyn, N.Y.; son of Samuel and Pearl (Baumol) Lamm; married Mindella Mehler, February 23, 1954; children: Chaye Lamm Warburg, Joshua B., Shalom E., Sarah Rebecca Lamm Dratch. *Education:* Yeshiva University, B.A. (summa cum laude), 1949, Rabbi, 1951; Bernard Revel Graduate School, Ph.D., 1966.

ADDRESSES: Home—101 Central Park W., New York, N.Y. 10023. *Office*—Office of the President, Yeshiva University, 500 West 185th St., New York, N.Y. 10033.

CAREER: Congregation Kehillath Jeshurun, New York City, assistant (Orthodox) rabbi, 1952-53; Congregation Kodimoh, Springfield, Mass., rabbi, 1954-58; Jewish Center, New York City, rabbi, 1958-76; Yeshiva University, New York City, Jakob and Erna Michael Professor of Jewish Philosophy, 1959—, president, 1976—. Visiting professor, Brooklyn College, 1974-75. Member of President's Commission on the Holocaust, 1978-88. Director of the Union of Orthodox Jewish Congregations of America; member of Halakhah (Jewish Law) Commission of the Rabbinical Council of America; former chairman of New York Conference on Soviet Jewry. Has lectured in nine countries on five continents, including India,

Pakistan, South Africa, Israel, Australia, and New Zealand; has testified as an expert in Jewish law before the U.S. Senate Judiciary Committee.

MEMBER: Association of Orthodox Jewish Scientists (charter member; member of board of governors), American Zionist Youth Foundation (member of board of trustees), Federation of Jewish Philanthropists (trustee-at-large), Yavneh (National Religious Jewish Students Association; former chairman of advisory board), American Friendship Alliance (member of board of directors), Israelite Universelle, Association for a Better New York (executive committee member).

AWARDS, HONORS: Abramowitz-Zeitlin Award for Religious Literature (Jerusalem), 1973, for *The Royal Reach: Discourses on the Jewish Tradition and the World Today* and *Faith and Doubt: Studies in Traditional Jewish Thought;* Bernard Revel Award for Religion and Religious Education from Yeshiva College Alumni Association, 1974; Doctor of Hebrew Letters, Hebrew Theological College, 1977.

WRITINGS:

(Editor with Menachem M. Kasher and Leonard Rosenfeld) *The Leo Jung Jubilee Volume,* Jewish Center (New York), 1962.
A Hedge of Roses: Jewish Insights into Marriage and Married Life, Feldheim, 1966, 5th edition, 1977.
(Editor with Walter S. Wurzburger) *A Treasury of Tradition,* Hebrew Publishing, 1967.
The Royal Reach: Discourses on the Jewish Tradition and the World Today, Feldheim, 1970, 2nd edition, 1977.
Faith and Doubt: Studies in Traditional Jewish Thought, KTAV, 1971, 2nd edition, 1986.
Torah Lishmah, Mossad Harav Kook (Jerusalem), 1972, English language edition by Lamm published as *Torah Lishmah: The Study of the Torah for Torah's Sake in the Work of Rabbi Hayyim of Volozhin and His Contemporaries,* KTAV, 1989.
The Good Society, Viking/B'nai B'rith, 1974.
(Co-editor) *The Joseph B. Soloveitchik Jubilee Volume,* Mossad Harav Kook and Yeshiva University (Jerusalem), 1984.

Contributor to Hebrew and English language journals in the United States and abroad. Founder and editor of *Tradition: A Journal of Orthodox Jewish Thought;* associate editor of *Hadarom,* 1957-60, and of the *Library of Jewish Law and Ethics,* 1975—.

WORK IN PROGRESS: Anthology of Hasidic Theology; Interface: Religious Learning and Worldly Wisdom in the Jewish Tradition; Halakhot ve'Halikhot, essays on Jewish law.

SIDELIGHTS: Norman Lamm's books have been translated into Spanish, Hebrew, Portuguese, and Marathi.

*   *   *

LANCASTER, Lydia
   See MEAKER, Eloise

*   *   *

LAWFORD, J(ames) P(hilip) 1915-1977

PERSONAL: Born December 29, 1915, in Peking, China; died November, 1977; son of Lancelot Henry (an officer in the Chinese Maritime Customs) and Laura Hamilla (Taylor) Lawford; married Joan Mary Spencer, December 16, 1944; children: Nigel Philip Charles, Diana Mary, Sylvia Hamilla. *Education:* Cambridge University, M.A., 1937. *Religion:* Church of England.

CAREER: Indian Army, infantry officer, 1937-47, served in India and Far East; British Army officer, 1947-61, served in North Africa and Middle East, retired as lieutenant colonel; Royal Military Academy, Sandhurst, Camberly, England, 1967-77, began as senior lecturer in international affairs, became senior lecturer in communication.

MEMBER: Royal Commonwealth Society, Officers' Club (Aldershot).

AWARDS, HONORS: Military Cross.

WRITINGS:

(Editor with W. E. Catto) *Solah Punjab: The History of the 16th Pubjab Regiment,* Gale & Polden, 1967.
(With Peter Young) *Charge; or, How to Play War Games,* A. S. Barnes, 1969, new edition, Athena Books, 1986.
(Editor with Young) *History of the British Army,* Putnam, 1970.
History of the 30th Punjabis, Osprey, 1972.
(With Young) *Wellington's Masterpiece: The Battle and Campaign of Salamanca,* Allen & Unwin, 1972.
History of the Battle of Salamanca, Allen & Unwin, 1973.
Wellington's Peninsula Army, Osprey, 1973.
The Battle of Vitoria 1813, Knight & Co., 1973.
Clive: Proconsul of India, Allen & Unwin, 1976.
(Editor and contributor) *The Cavalry,* Bobbs-Merrill, 1976.
(With Young) *Napoleon: The Last Campaigns, 1813-15,* Crown, 1977.
Britain's Army in India: From Its Origins to the Conquest of Bengal, Allen & Unwin, 1978.*

[Date of death provided by wife]

*   *   *

LAWRENCE, Helen M(ary)   1925-

PERSONAL: Born May 14, 1925, in Terre Haute, Ind.; daughter of George (a harness maker) and Goldie (Randall) James; married Robert Lawrence (in labor relations), April 20, 1948; children: Debbi, Margaret, Christopher, Jennifer, Shawn, Joshua, Jason. *Education:* University of Michigan, A.B., 1947. *Religion:* Christian.

ADDRESSES: Home—9568 Columbia, Redford, Mich. 48239.

CAREER: Free-lance writer, 1967—. Speaker at churches, high schools, retreats.

AWARDS, HONORS: Mother of the Year, 1968, Genesee County (Michigan) Junior League.

WRITINGS:

Call Me Gertrude—Anything but Mom! (autobiography), Geneva Press, 1967.
Life As You Know It Will Never Be the Same: Meditations for New Mothers, B. B. Butler, 1970, reprinted as *Motherhood Guide for Moms Who Miss the Office,* 1988.
The Virginia Rose (poems), Robson, 1978.
Strawberry Sundays (short stories), Deano D. Press, 1982.
How to Make Your Teenagers Mind Without Losing Yours, Pleasant Press, 1984.
Peaceful Horizons (short stories and poems), Pleasant Press, 1985.

WORK IN PROGRESS: A self-help book on coping with family gatherings.

SIDELIGHTS: Helen M. Lawrence wrote *CA:* "Now that my last child has graduated from college (on the seven-year plan), I am contemplating a quiet life with my husband, who has recently retired. This may remain only contemplation, however, as I now have a total of ten grandchildren, and the number keeps growing. I'm considering writing a guide on finding a good baby-sitter. Of course, the grandchildren are a constant joy; especially since I can always send them home."

*   *   *

LEAR, Peter
See LOVESEY, Peter (Harmer)

*   *   *

LECALE, Errol
See McNEILLY, Wilfred (Glassford)

*   *   *

LECHT, Leonard A.   1920-

PERSONAL: Born October 16, 1920, in Providence, R.I.; son of Harry (a meat packer) and Sarah (Finkle) Lecht; married Jane A. Gillespie (a writer and editor), September 15, 1950; children: David Jonathan. *Education:* University of Minnesota, B.A., 1942; Columbia University, Ph.D., 1953.

ADDRESSES: Home—P.O. Box 3105, Taos, N.M. 87571.

CAREER: Columbia University, New York City, lecturer in economics, 1947-49; University of Texas, Main University (now University of Texas at Austin), Austin, assistant professor of economics, 1949-53; Carleton College, Northfield, Minn., assistant professor of economics, 1953-54; Long Island University, Brooklyn, N.Y., associate professor, 1954-56, professor of economics and sociology, 1956-63, chairman of department, 1954-63; National Planning Association, Washington, D.C., director of national goals project, 1963-67, director of Center for Priority Analysis, 1967-74; Conference Board, New York City, director of special project research, 1974-80; economic consultant, 1980—. Adjunct professor at City University of New York, 1982—. Principal researcher, Taos County Economic Development Department, 1982—. Consultant on merger of New York Central and Pennsylvania railroads, 1962-63, and to a number of government agencies and private groups concerned with manpower, education, and planning. *Military service:* U.S. Army, 1943-45.

MEMBER: American Economic Association, Phi Beta Kappa.

WRITINGS:

Experience under Railway Labor Legislation, Columbia University Press, 1956.
The Dollar Cost of Our National Goals, National Planning Association, 1965.
Goals, Priorities and Dollars: The Next Decade, Macmillan, 1966.
Manpower Needs for National Goals in the 1970s, Praeger, 1969.
Dollars for National Goals: Looking ahead to 1981, Wiley, 1974.

Evaluating Vocational Education Policies and Plans for the 1970s, Praeger, 1974.

(With others) *Changes in Occupational Characteristics,* Conference Board, 1976.

Occupational Choices and Training Needs: Prospects for the 1980s, Praeger, 1977.

Occupational Programs for National, State, and Local Areas, National Commission on Employment Objectives, 1978.

Expenditures for Retirement and Other Age-Related Programs, Academy for Educational Development, 1981.

Contributor to economics journals. Editor, *Employment and Unemployment,* 1977.

* * *

LECKER, Robert 1951-

PERSONAL: Born December 9, 1951, in Montreal, Quebec, Canada; son of Nat (in business) and Dorothy (in business; maiden name, Campbell) Lecker; children: Emily Autumn. *Education:* York University, B.A., 1974, M.A., 1976, Ph.D., 1980; Concordia University, Montreal, Quebec, C.E.G.E.P., 1972.

ADDRESSES: Home—729 Cote Ste. Catherine, Outremont, Quebec, Canada H3T 1A4. *Office*—Department of English, McGill University, 853 Sherbrooke St. W., Montreal, Quebec, Canada H3A 2T6. *Agent*—Canadian Literary Research Foundation, 48 Maclean Ave., Toronto, Ontario, Canada M4E 3A1.

CAREER: York University, Toronto, Ontario, lecturer in English, 1976-78; University of Maine at Orono, assistant professor of English, 1978-82; McGill University, Montreal, Quebec, associate professor, 1982-88, professor of English, 1988—. Publisher of ECW Press, 1975—.

MEMBER: Association of Canadian University Teachers of English, Association for Canadian and Quebec Literature, Association for Canadian Studies, Modern Language Association of America, Association for Canadian Studies in the United States.

AWARDS, HONORS: H. Noel Fieldhouse Award for Distinguished Teaching from McGill University, 1985.

WRITINGS:

(Editor with Jack David) *The Annotated Bibliography of Canada's Major Authors,* ECW Press, Volume 1, 1979, Volume 2, 1980, Volume 3, 1981, Volume 4, 1983, Volume 5, 1984, Volume 6, 1986, Volume 7, 1988.

(Editor with David) *Introduction to Poetry: British, American, Canadian,* Holt, 1981.

(Editor with David) *Introduction to Fiction,* Holt, 1982.

(Editor with David) *Canadian Poetry,* two volumes, General Publishing, 1982.

(Editor with Kathleen Brown) *An Anthology of Maine Literature,* University of Maine at Orono Press, 1982.

(Editor and contributor) *On the Line: Readings in the Short Fiction of Clark Blaise, John Metcalf, and Hugh Hood,* ECW Press, 1982.

(Editor with David and Ellen Quigley) *Canadian Writers and Their Works: Essays on Form, Context, and Development,* twenty volumes, ECW Press, 1983-89.

Robert Kroetsch, Twayne, 1986.

An Other I: The Fictions of Clark Blaise, ECW Press, 1988.

CONTRIBUTOR

David, editor, *Brave New Wave,* Black Moss, 1978.

J. R. Struthers, editor, *Before the Flood: Hugh Hood's Work in Progress,* ECW Press, 1979.

John Moss, editor, *The Canadian Novel: Beginnings,* NC Press, 1980.

Arnold E. Davidson and Cathy N. Davidson, editors, *The Art of Margaret Atwood: Essays in Criticism,* House of Anansi Press, 1981.

OTHER

General editor of "Masterwork Studies and Critical Essays on World Literature" series, 1980—; Canadian editor of "Twayne's World Authors" series, G. K. Hall. Contributor of more than fifty articles and reviews to magazines. Editor of *Critical Essays on World Literature;* co-editor of *Essays on Canadian Writing,* 1975—.

WORK IN PROGRESS: A study of literary value in Canadian poetry and fiction; a collection of essays on canonization in Canadian literature.

SIDELIGHTS: Robert Lecker told *CA:* "My concerns as a writer, editor, and publisher are strongly aligned with those of Jack David, who invited me to join him in editing *ECW* in 1975. David and I felt that a new direction was needed in Canadian criticism—a direction that would emphasize the evaluation and analysis of Canadian literature from a formal, as opposed to thematic, perspective. The principles that guide our selection of critical material for *ECW* also inform my own criticism. I still uphold my statement in *On the Line: Readings in the Short Fiction of Clark Blaise, John Metcalf, and Hugh Hood:* 'My commitment . . . is to the belief that the critic should not generalize, that what we need in Canada is not classification, but identification based on the distinguishing features of an individual author's work. My attempt has not been to reduce the texts [I study] to an exegetical formula, but to suggest how their profound, and very different use of metaphor, imagery, pattern, and language affects me.'

"In my most recent studies, I have become involved with questions pertaining to the nature and formation of literary value in Canada. My exploration of these questions also represents an inquiry into my nationalist stance. My own critical beliefs prompted me to found (again with Jack David) ECW Press, which I would like to think is publishing some of the most worthwhile contemporary Canadian criticism. Now that Canada and the U.S. have signed the free trade agreement, I am concerned about the prospects for the future of Canadian literature. I hope that I will be able to contribute to whatever remains of that future."

BIOGRAPHICAL/CRITICAL SOURCES:

BOOKS

Lecker, Robert, editor, *On the Line: Readings in the Short Fiction of Clark Blaise, John Metcalf, Hugh Hood,* ECW Press, 1982.

* * *

LEDESERT, (Dorothy) Margaret 1916-

PERSONAL: Born September 21, 1916, in Oxford, England; daughter of Edgar Percy Clifford (a schoolmaster) and Ethel Rhoda (Draper) Smith; married Rene Pierre Louis Ledesert (a publisher), August 23, 1941. *Education:* Attended University of Caen, 1936-37; University College of Wales, B.A. (first class honors), 1938, M.A., 1940.

ADDRESSES: Home—Rails, Holyport, Maidenhead, Berkshire SL6 2JL, England.

CAREER: French teacher in Pontypridd, Glamorgan, Wales, 1940-41; Ministry of Economic Welfare, London, England, economic intelligence officer, 1942-45; Foreign Office, London, economic intelligence officer, 1945-50; Lynton House School, Maidenhead, Berkshire, England, teacher of French and geography, 1950-60.

AWARDS, HONORS: Chevalier de l'Ordre des Palmes Academiques, 1971; co-recipient with husband, R. P. L. Ledesert of Whitbread Franco-British Award, 1976.

WRITINGS:

(With husband, R. P. L. Ledesert) *Histoire de la litterature francaise*, Edward Arnold, Volume 1, 1946, Volume 2, 1947.
(With R. P. L. Ledesert and Muriel Holland Smith) *La France*, Harrap, 1952, 4th revised edition, 1971.
(Translator) Andre Siegfried, *America at Mid-Century*, Harcourt, 1955.
(Translator) Claude Aveline, *The Bird That Flew into the Sea*, Harrap, 1961.
(Translator) Jean Filliozat, *India: The Country and Its Traditions*, Harrap, 1962.
(Translator) Pierre Birot, *General Physical Geography*, Harrap, 1966.
Introducing France, Harrap, 1967.
(Editor with R. P. L. Ledesert) Jean E. Mansion, *Harrap's New Shorter French and English Dictionary: French-English, English-French*, Harrap, 1967, revised edition published as *Harrap's New Collegiate French and English Dictionary: French-English, English-French*, National Textbook, 1978, 2nd revised edition published as *Harrap's Shorter French and English Dictionary*, Harrap, 1982.
(Editor with R. P. L. Ledesert and Patricia Forbes) *Harrap's New Pocket French and English Dictionary*, Harrap, 1969, revised edition, 1981.
(Reviser with R. P. L. Ledesert and others) Mansion, editor, *Harrap's New Standard French and English Dictionary*, Harrap, Volume 1: *French-English: A-I*, 1972, Volume 2: *French-English: J-Z*, 1972, Volume 3: *English-French: A-K*, 1980, Volume 4: *English-French: L-Z*, 1980.
Harrap's Mini Pocket French and English Dictionary: French-English, English-French in One Volume, Harrap, 1977, abridged edition (with Forbes) published as *Harrap's Super-Mini French and English Dictionary*, National Textbook, 1977.

FRENCH READERS; WITH R. P. L. LEDESERT

Le Gai Voyage, Harrap, 1954.
Aventure sous-marine, Harrap, 1955.
Aventure sous-terre, Harrap, 1956.
Les Astronautes, Harrap, 1956.
Trafic d'Armes, Harrap, 1957.
Au Voleur, Harrap, 1958.
Le Tresor de Rommel, Harrap, 1961.
Promenades en Normandie, Harrap, 1962.
Promenades dans Paris, Harrap, 1963.

AVOCATIONAL INTERESTS: Travel, medieval architecture, art galleries, museums, cooking.

LEDESERT, R(ene) P(ierre) L(ouis)   1913-1984

PERSONAL: Born April 26, 1913, in Calais, France; died November 26, 1984; son of Andre (a marine engineer), and Denise (Braillon) Ledesert; married Dorothy Margaret Smith (a lexicographer and writer under name Margaret Ledesert), August 23, 1941. *Education:* University of Caen, Licence en Droit, 1934, Licence-es-Lettres, 1935; University of Birmingham, graduate research, 1935-36.

ADDRESSES: Home—Rails, Holyport, Maidenhead, Berkshire SL6 2JL, England. *Office*—George G. Harrap & Co. Ltd., 182 High Holborn, London WC1, England.

CAREER: Eton College, Eton, England, modern language master, 1940-45; George G. Harrap & Co. Ltd. (publishers), London, England, modern language editor, 1946-56, member of board of directors, beginning 1956.

AWARDS, HONORS: Chevalier de l'Ordre des Palmes Academiques, 1962, for contribution to the teaching of the French language; Gold Medal of Institute of Linguists (London), 1972; co-recipient with wife, Margaret Ledesert, of Whitbread Franco-British Award, 1976.

WRITINGS:

(With wife, Margaret Ledesert) *Histoire de la litterature francaise*, Edward Arnold, Volume 1, 1946, Volume 2, 1947.
(Editor) Moliere, *Les Precieuses Ridicules*, Harrap, 1948.
(Editor) Moliere, *Le Malade Imaginaire*, Harrap, 1949, reprinted, 1975.
(Editor) Moliere, *Tartuffe*, Harrap, 1949, reprinted, 1977.
(Editor) Moliere, *Les Fourberies de Scapin*, Harrap, 1949.
(Compiler of supplements) Jean E. Mansion, editor, *Harrap's Standard French and English Dictionary*, Harrap, 1950, revised edition (with P. H. Collins), 1966.
(With M. Ledesert and Muriel Holland Smith) *La France*, Harrap, 1952, 4th revised edition, 1971.
(Editor with M. Ledesert) Mansion, *Harrap's New Shorter French and English Dictionary: French-English, English-French*, Harrap, 1967, revised edition published as *Harrap's New Collegiate French and English Dictionary: French-English, English-French*, National Textbook, 1978, 2nd revised edition published as *Harrap's Shorter French and English Dictionary*, Harrap, 1982.
(Editor with M. Ledesert and Patricia Forbes) *Harrap's New Pocket French and English Dictionary*, Harrap, 1969, revised edition, 1981.
(Reviser with M. Ledesert and others) Mansion, editor, *Harrap's New Standard French and English Dictionary*, Harrap, Volume 1: *French-English, A-I*, 1972, Volume 2: *French-English, J-Z*, 1972, Volume 3: *English-French, A-K*, 1980, Volume 4: *English-French, L-Z*, 1980.

FRENCH READERS; WITH M. LEDESERT

Le Gai Voyage, Harrap, 1954.
Aventure sous-marine, Harrap, 1955.
Aventure sous-terre, Harrap, 1956.
Les Astronautes, Harrap, 1956.
Trafic d'Armes, Harrap, 1957.
Au Voleur, Harrap, 1958.
Le Tresor de Rommel, Harrap, 1961.
Promenades en Normandie, Harrap, 1962.
Promenades dans Paris, Harrap, 1963.

AVOCATIONAL INTERESTS: History of art and architecture.

OBITUARIES:

PERIODICALS

Times (London), December 7, 1984.

[Sketch reviewed by wife, Margaret Ledesert]

*   *   *

LEONARD, Constance (Brink) 1923-

PERSONAL: Born April 27, 1923, in Pottsville, Pa.; daughter of Harry William (an educator) and Dorothy (Jessop) Brink; married John D. Leonard (a journalist), June 21, 1949 (divorced, 1969); children: Gillian. *Education:* Wellesley College, B.A., 1944.

ADDRESSES: Home—Box 126, Francestown, N.H. 03043.

CAREER: Writer.

WRITINGS:

The Great Pumpkin Mystery (novel), Random House, 1971.
The Other Maritha (novel), Dodd, 1972.
Steps to Nowhere (novel), Dodd, 1974.
Hostage in Illyria (novel), Dodd, 1976.
Shadow of a Ghost (young adult novel), Dodd, 1978.

"TRACY JAMES" MYSTERY SERIES

The Marina Mystery, Dodd, 1981.
Stowaway (Junior Literary Guild selection), Dodd, 1983.
Aground, Dodd, 1984.
Strange Waters, Dodd, 1985.

WORK IN PROGRESS: A novel.

SIDELIGHTS: Constance Leonard once told *CA:* "I have 'always' written—stories, verse, anything—but not for publication until the last few years when I've been settled in an old house in a tiny old village in the New Hampshire mountains. As a longtime mystery addict I thought it would be fun to try writing one, and then another, and then another. Aside from writing and reading and friends and good food, I find travel the one essential and have enjoyed using foreign backgrounds in many of my books."

*   *   *

LEONARD, Elmore (John, Jr.) 1925-

PERSONAL: Born October 11, 1925, in New Orleans, La.; son of Elmore John (a salesman) and Flora Amelia (Rive) Leonard; married Beverly Cline, July 30, 1949 (divorced May 24, 1977); married Joan Shepard, September 15, 1979; children: (first marriage) Jane Jones, Peter, Christopher, William, Katherine. *Education:* University of Detroit, Ph.B., 1950. *Religion:* Roman Catholic.

ADDRESSES: Home—Birmingham, Mich. *Agent*—H. N. Swanson, 8523 Sunset Blvd., Los Angeles, Calif. 90069.

CAREER: Writer. Campbell-Ewald Advertising Agency, Detroit, Mich., copywriter, 1950-61; free-lance copywriter and author of educational and industrial films, 1961-63; head of Elmore Leonard Advertising Company, 1963-66. *Military service:* U.S. Naval Reserve, 1943-46.

MEMBER: Writers Guild of America, West, Mystery Writers of America, Western Writers of America, Authors League of America, Authors Guild.

AWARDS, HONORS: Hombre was named one of the twenty-five best western novels of all time by the Western Writers of America, 1977; Edgar Allan Poe Award, Mystery Writers of America, 1984, for *LaBrava.*

WRITINGS:

WESTERN NOVELS

The Bounty Hunters, Houghton, 1953, reprinted, Bantam, 1985.
The Law at Randado, Houghton, 1955, reprinted, Bantam, 1985.
Escape from 5 Shadows, Houghton, 1956, reprinted, Bantam, 1985.
Last Stand at Saber River, Dell, 1957, reprinted, Bantam, 1985 (published in England as *Lawless River,* R. Hale, 1959, and as *Stand on the Saber,* Corgi, 1960).
Hombre, Ballantine, 1961, reprinted, 1984.
Valdez Is Coming, Gold Medal, 1970.
Forty Lashes Less One, Bantam, 1972.
Gunsights, Bantam, 1979.

CRIME NOVELS

The Big Bounce, Gold Medal, 1969, revised edition, Armchair Detective, 1989.
The Moonshine War (also see below), Doubleday, 1969, reprinted, Dell, 1988.
Mr. Majestyk (also see below), Dell, 1974.
Fifty-Two Pickup (also see below), Delacorte, 1974.
Swag (also see below), Delacorte, 1976, published as *Ryan's Rules,* Dell, 1976.
Unknown Man, No. 89, Delacorte, 1977.
The Hunted (also see below), Dell, 1977.
The Switch, Bantam, 1978.
City Primeval: High Noon in Detroit (also see below), Arbor House, 1980.
Gold Coast (also see below), Bantam, 1980, revised edition, 1985.
Split Images, Arbor House, 1981.
Cat Chaser (also see below), Arbor House, 1982.
Stick (also see below; Book-of-the-Month Club alternate selection), Arbor House, 1983.
LaBrava, Arbor House, 1983.
Glitz (Book-of-the-Month Club selection), Arbor House, 1985.
Bandits, Arbor House, 1987.
Touch, Arbor House, 1987.
Freaky Deaky (Book-of-the-Month Club selection), Morrow, 1988.
Killshot (Literary Guild selection), Morrow, 1989.

OMNIBUS VOLUMES

Elmore Leonard's Dutch Treat (contains *The Hunted, Swag,* and *Mr. Majestyk*), introduction by George F. Will, Arbor House, 1985.
Elmore Leonard's Double Dutch Treat (contains *City Primeval: High Noon in Detroit, The Moonshine War,* and *Gold Coast*), introduction by Bob Greene, Arbor House, 1986.

SCREENPLAYS

"The Moonshine War" (based on Leonard's novel of the same title), Metro-Goldwyn-Mayer, 1970.
"Joe Kidd," Universal, 1972.
"Mr. Majestyk" (based on Leonard's novel of the same title), United Artists, 1974.
"High Noon, Part 2: The Return of Will Kane," Columbia Broadcasting System (CBS), 1980.

(With Joseph C. Stinson) "Stick" (based on Leonard's novel of the same title), Universal, 1985.

(With John Steppling) "52 Pick-Up" (based on Leonard's novel of the same title), Cannon Group, 1986.

(With Fred Walton) "The Rosary Murders" (based on the novel by William X. Kienzle), New Line Cinema, 1987.

"Desperado," National Broadcasting Corp. (NBC), 1988.

(With Joe Borrelli) "Cat Chaser" (based on Leonard's novel of the same title), Viacom, 1989.

Also author of filmscripts for Encyclopaedia Britannica Films, including "Settlement of the Mississippi Valley," "Boy of Spain," "Frontier Boy," and "Julius Caesar," and of a recruiting film for the Franciscans.

OTHER

(Contributor) Dennis Wholey, editor, *The Courage to Change: Personal Conversations about Alcoholism*, Houghton, 1984.

Contributor of about 30 short stories and novelettes to *Dime Western, Argosy, Saturday Evening Post, Zane Grey's Western Magazine*, and other publications during the 1950s.

SIDELIGHTS: "After writing 23 novels, Elmore Leonard has been discovered," Herbert Mitgang remarked in the *New York Times* in 1983. Following three decades of moderate success with his novels and short stories, Leonard began in the early 1980s to receive the kind of attention from reviewers befitting an author whom Richard Herzfelder in the *Chicago Tribune* calls "a writer of thrillers whose vision goes deeper than thrill." While the plots of Leonard's books remain inherently action-packed and suspenseful, he is, says *Washington Post Book World* critic Jonathan Yardley, now being "praised for accomplishments rather more substantial than that of keeping the reader on tenterhooks." These accomplishments, which Yardley describes as raising "the hard-boiled suspense novel beyond the limits of genre and into social commentary," have led critics previously inclined to pigeonhole Leonard as a crime or mystery novelist to dispense with such labels in their assessments of his work. In the process, several critics have chosen to mention Leonard's name alongside those of other writers whose literary works transcend their genre, among them Ross Macdonald and Dashiell Hammett. Such comparisons are "flattering, but hardly accurate," according to Grover Sales in the *Los Angeles Times Book Review*. "Leonard is an original," Sales believes. "His uncanny sense of plot, pace and his inexhaustible flair for the nervous rhythms of contemporary urban speech have caught the spirit of the '80s."

Leonard began his career in the early 1950s as a writer of western stories for magazines. His first sale was a novelette entitled "Apache Agent" to *Argosy* magazine for $90. He eventually turned his hand to novels in the genre, publishing five of them while pursuing a career as an advertising copywriter for a firm in Detroit. Copywriter was not an occupation much to Leonard's liking. "He says matter-of-factly that he hated the work," notes Bill Dunn in a *Publishers Weekly* interview, "but it allowed him precious time and a steady paycheck to experiment with fiction, which he did in the early morning before going off to work." Leonard told Dunn: "Sometimes I would write a little fiction at work, too. I would write in my desk drawer and close the drawer if somebody came in."

Western fiction appealed to Leonard for two reasons: he had always liked western movies, and he was determined that his writing should be a lucrative as well as a creative pursuit. "I

decided I wasn't going to be a literary writer, that I wouldn't end up in the quarterlies," he tells Beaufort Cranford in *Michigan Magazine*. "So if I was going to be a commercial writer, I had to learn how to do it." His decidedly professional approach to writing paid off. During the 1950s Leonard sold some thirty short stories and five novels. And two of his stories were also sold to Hollywood: "3:10 to Yuma," a novelette that first appeared in *Dime Western* magazine, starred actor Glenn Ford; "The Tall T" starred Randolph Scott and Richard Boone.

By the early 1960s the western genre had peaked in popularity, and Leonard found that the market for his fiction had dried up. For several years he wrote no fiction at all, devoting his time to free-lance copywriting, primarily for Hurst gear shifters, a popular feature in hot rod cars. He also wrote industrial films for Detroit-area companies and educational films for Encyclopaedia Britannica at a thousand dollars apiece. Finally in 1965, when his agent sold the film rights to his last western novel, *Hombre*, for ten thousand dollars, Leonard had the financial leeway to write fiction again. This time he focused on the mystery-suspense genre. As he tells Gay Rubin of *Detroiter*: "I began writing westerns because there was a market for them. Now of course there is an interest in police stories . . . suspense, mystery, crime."

Despite the shift in genre, Leonard's fiction has remained in many ways the same. In both his western and crime fiction there is an overriding interest in seeing that justice is done. Leonard's prose, lean and hard, has consistently been of the same high quality. And his gunfighters and urban detectives approach their work with the same glib, wisecracking attitude. Writing in *Esquire*, Mike Lupica claims that despite their apparent diversity, all of Leonard's main characters are essentially the same, but "with a different name and a different job. . . . They have all been beat on by life, they all can drop a cool, wise-guy line on you, they are all tough, don't try to push them around."

Leonard's first crime novel, *The Big Bounce*, was rejected by some eighty-four publishers and film producers before being published as a paperback original by Gold Medal. Unsure about his switch to crime writing because of the trouble he had selling the book, Leonard turned again to westerns, publishing two more novels in the genre. But when the film rights to *The Big Bounce* were sold for $50,000, Leonard abandoned the western genre for good. Since making that decision, all of his subsequent novels have enjoyed both hardcover and paperback editions and have been sold to Hollywood.

The typical Leonard novel, Michael Kernan of the *Washington Post* maintains, is distinguished by "guns, a killing or two or three, fights and chases and sex. Tight, clean prose, ear-perfect, whip-smart dialogue. And, just beneath the surface, an acute sense of the ridiculous." Leonard has said on several occasions that he has been less influenced by other crime writers than by such writers as Ernest Hemingway, John Steinbeck, and John O'Hara. Their lean, unadorned writing style and ability to remain in the background of their stories appealed to Leonard. He tells Charles Champlin of the *Los Angeles Times*: "I became a stylist by intentionally avoiding style. When I go back and edit and something sounds like *writing*, I rewrite it. I rewrite constantly, four pages in the basket for every one that survives." The result impresses Ken Tucker of the *Village Voice*, who calls Leonard "the finest thriller writer alive primarily because he does his best to efface style."

To get his dialogue right, Leonard listens to the way people really talk and copies it down as faithfully as possible. When writing the novel *City Primeval: High Noon in Detroit*, Leonard even sat in at the Detroit police department's homicide squad room for several months, listening to the way that police officers, lawyers, and suspects spoke. His writing is full of slang terms and peculiarities of speech that mark each of his characters as a one-of-a-kind individual. More importantly, he captures the speech rhythms of his characters. Leonard recreates speech so well, Alan Cheuse writes in the *Los Angeles Times Book Review*, that "it's difficult to say . . . who among this novelist's contemporaries has a better ear." Herbert Mitgang of the *New York Times* agrees. The conversations in Leonard's books, Mitgang writes, "sound absolutely authentic." Avoiding narration and description, Leonard moves his novels along with dialogue, letting his characters' conversations tell the story. Speaking of the novel *Freaky Deaky*, Jonathan Kirsch writes in the *Los Angeles Times* that the book "is all dialogue—cool banter, jive talk, interior monologue. Virtually everything we learn about the plot and the characters is imparted through conversation, and so the book reads like a radio script."

When plotting his novels, Leonard allows his characters full rein to create their own story. Before beginning a new book, Leonard creates a handful of vividly imagined characters, the relationships between them, and their basic situation, and then he sets them in action. Leonard has, Michael Kernan remarks in the *Washington Post*, "no idea how it will end." He tells Michael Ruhlman in the *New York Times Book Review*: "I see my characters as being most important, how they bounce off one another, how they talk to each other, and the plot just sort of comes along." This spontaneous plotting technique works well for Leonard but has caused at least one reviewer occasional difficulty. Ben Yagoda of the *Chicago Tribune* describes Leonard's crime novels as being "smoky improvisations grouped around a set of reliable elements. . . . Eventually, the elements congeal into a taut climax, but for the first two-thirds or so of the book, the characters, the reader and, it turns out, the author simmer on the low burner and, in Huckleberry Finn style, 'swap juices,' trying to figure out what's going on."

Many of Leonard's crime novels feature lower class characters trying to make fast money with a big heist or quick scam. They "fall into crime," according to Tucker, "because it's an easier way to make money than that tedious nine-to-five." George Stade of the *New York Times Book Review* calls Leonard's villains "treacherous and tricky, smart enough to outsmart themselves, driven, audacious and outrageous, capable of anything, paranoid-cunning and casually vicious—and rousing fun." Dick Roraback of the *Los Angeles Times Book Review* claims that "it is the mark of the author's craft that his characters do not seem to be created, 'written.' They simply are there, stalking, posturing, playing, loving, scheming, and we watch and listen and are fascinated. And appalled, yes, or approving, but always absorbed. They never let us off the hook."

Often partially set in Leonard's hometown of Detroit, his stories can range from Florida, where Leonard vacations and where his mother owns a motel, to New Orleans, where he was born. But Leonard shows only the seedy parts of these towns, the places where his characters are likely to be conducting their criminal business or avoiding their pursuers. He has, according to Marcel Berlins of the London *Times*, "a feel for the losers of this world, and for the shabby world they inhabit, with its

own rules and its own noble principles." As Yardley explains, "Leonard's viewpoint is not exactly cynical, inasmuch as he admits the possibility of something approximating redemption, but it certainly is worldly and unsentimental. In his world nobody gets a free ticket and the victories that people win, such as they are, are limited and costly; which is to say that his world bears a striking resemblance to the real one."

Although he had been writing critically-acclaimed crime novels for a decade, and his work was being adapted for the screen, Leonard had only a small cadre of fans until the early 1980s when his novels began to attract the attention of a larger audience. With the novel *Stick* in 1982, Leonard suddenly became a bestselling writer. One sign of this sudden success can be seen in the agreeable change in Leonard's finances that year. The paperback rights for *Split Images* earned him $7,000 in 1981; the rights for *Stick* a year later earned $50,000. Then, in 1983, *LaBrava* won an Edgar Award from the Mystery Writers of America as the best novel of the year. And the book sold over 400,000 copies. Leonard's next novel, *Glitz*, hit the bestseller lists in 1985 and was a Book-of-the-Month Club selection. All of his novels since then have also been bestsellers.

Now enjoying popular as well as critical acclaim, Leonard is usually ranked as one of the best crime writers in the country. Donald E. Westlake, writing in the *Washington Post Book World*, calls Leonard "an awfully good writer," while James Kaufmann of the *Christian Science Monitor* reports that "nobody brings the illogic of crime and criminals to life better." Yagoda credits him with having "created a gallery of compelling, off-the-wall villains unequaled in American crime fiction." Tucker praises the absolute realism of Leonard's fictional violence: "The violence in his books is quick, quiet, and brutal; it's the kind that can strike you as being true and realistic even though the actions are utterly beyond your experience. Can an artist receive a higher compliment than that?" Writing in the *New York Times Book Review*, Stephen King goes so far as to find that Leonard's "wit, his range of effective character portrayal and his almost eerily exact ear for the tone and nuances of dialogue suggest [Charles] Dickens to me." Margaret Cannon of the Toronto *Globe and Mail* simply describes Leonard as "one of the finest American writers of hard-boiled detective fiction."

CA INTERVIEW

CA interviewed Elmore Leonard by telephone on June 17, 1988, at his home in Birmingham, Michigan.

CA: The desire to write books survived the years of working for an ad agency, when you had to get up at five in the morning to devote two hours a day to fiction, and later the years after you quit the agency to write full-time but had to take on freelance commercial work to pay the bills. Was doing the fiction then always a pleasure on some level, despite the pain?

LEONARD: No, it wasn't a pleasure *yet*, and I wasn't sure that it was ever going to be anything but work, which I don't consider it now. It was hard. I had an idea what kind of sound I wanted, and I pretty much had it in my westerns, in the fifties. But I hadn't yet discovered what I think you might call my most natural sound, which is a little more easygoing and laid back. I was more serious then. I hadn't yet discovered that if I didn't try to write, it would come out better.

I was determined, for some reasons, to tell stories, to write stories and novels—I'm not sure why; I've just always liked stories. And I liked movies. I chose westerns in the fifties as a genre in which to learn because I liked western movies a lot. I don't think I was too depressed in that early sixties period when I had to give up writing, because I really hadn't, in my mind, said, OK, I'm giving it up; I won't be able to write again. It was just that I was busy making a living, and I was doing something new and different for me, and interesting—freelancing, running my own ad agency, in a way, since it was a one-man shop. That was all kind of exciting. But I still couldn't wait, really, for an opportunity to have enough money at one time to get back into a book, and finally the sale of *Hombre* to Fox for a movie gave me that chance.

CA: Do you think writing the ad copy and doing the commercial filmscripts for Encyclopaedia Britannica helped in some way with the fiction writing?

LEONARD: No, not at all, because I had sold at least a dozen short stories before I ever got a job as a writer in advertising. And I knew, as I said, what kind of sound I wanted, kind of a lean, deadpan delivery. I knew that from having studied Hemingway in the early fifties.

CA: Everybody who reads your books agrees that you're a master of dialogue, and you've said that you spend a lot of time just listening to people talk. What sort of process does the talk undergo between what you hear and what the reader finally gets on the printed page?

LEONARD: It's very seldom a phrase or a sentence; it's more just the rhythms of speech. Sometimes it's an expression. Yesterday I was talking to a guy on the phone that I hadn't seen in a long time, and he referred to martinis as "see-throughs." I'd never heard that expression before. My wife had. He said something like, "If you have three or four of those see-throughs, they'll get you in trouble." And I can hear one of my characters using that same expression. Every once in a while something like that will come along. The same friend used to refer to certain people as "chickenfat," which I used in one of my books. I'll pick up something like that. And there's a certain attitude that the character has who uses a word like chickenfat.

CA: Peter Prescott said in his Newsweek *cover story about you that you don't begin with a plot, but rather "with a situation and a handful of characters." How do you go about developing those characters to the point of beginning to write their story?*

LEONARD: I do spend some time with the characters. I may very well write down a character's background, or the way the character talks. Or, for example, in *Bandits*, the way Lucy Nichols referred to her father. Her attitude about her father I put into dialogue in a notebook, trying to get her style, what she was like. I did the same thing with Jack Delaney. I have to get their names right before they'll talk. That's a very big part of them. Jack Delaney was originally Frank Matisse, and he didn't come off the way I wanted him to. He acted older. I *saw* him as older, even though I don't see characters clearly. He was older, and he just wasn't outgoing enough. I had already started to write him. I changed his name to Jack Matisse, and he opened up a little bit; then Jack Delaney, and I had him, the guy I wanted.

CA: Have you ever tried to create a character that just didn't work out?

LEONARD: No. Usually it's the name. If I get the name right, the character will talk. The best kind of character, though, is the one who isn't planned but just kind of comes forth—a character who was going to be minor, let's say a second- or third-string heavy—and he gets into his scene. The Miskito Indian is that character in *Bandits*. In *Freaky Deaky* Donnell Lewis was going to be, not a minor character, but a very menacing character; he was going to be The Heavy. But in the scene where I introduced him, I liked him. I was doing the scene from the point of view of the main character. He sees this black guy in a chauffeur's uniform, and he likes him. I had a lot of fun with Donnell, and I saw the opportunity to do that very early on, though he wasn't planned that way at all.

CA: Do you ever get ideas from real stories in the news, the kind of grim things we read or hear about once or twice a week now?

LEONARD: I make reference to things that are in the paper. In *Bandits*, for example, the two Contra money-raisers are watching the Ferdinand Marcos home movies on television, with Imelda Marcos singing to her husband at his birthday party. Then they're distracted by something and when they look back they think it's more of the home movies, but it's "Wheel of Fortune" going on. In the book that I just finished, there's a reference to whether Elvis Presley is still alive, whether he's coming back—which interests some people, especially my kind of characters.

CA: You manage to get some of your research done by employing an assistant. How does that process work? And does it ever cause problems, having somebody else do that part of the work for you?

LEONARD: On the contrary. My researcher works for a film company in town that does automotive-comparison slide films and movies. He does a lot of computer work for them. But he has an understanding with them that he'll do my work first, because he likes it. So anytime I need anything at all, he'll get it immediately. In the case of the book that I just finished in April, I'd been curious about Cape Girardeau, Missouri. That's a port town on the Mississippi; what's a cape doing there? He was going down to Nashville to see George Jones, one of his favorite performers. So I said, "Go on over to Cape Girardeau and take a look at it. Find out what it's like." He came back with pictures, and what caught my eye was this floodwall that runs three or four thousand yards along the Mississippi River. It looks like a prison wall. That got me started on a way to use Cape Girardeau in that book.

CA: You developed steady and diligent work habits early on, maybe by necessity. Do you give yourself a break between books?

LEONARD: Yeah. I'm between books right now, and I'm reading.

CA: What do you like to read?

LEONARD: I'm reading *Character: America's Search for Leadership*, by Gail Sheehy. It's profiles of those people who were prominent most recently in the presidential campaigns.

Since I've finished that last book I've read Jim Harrison's *Dalva,* Gabriel Garcia Marquez's *Love in the Time of Cholera,* William Boyd's *The New Confessions,* Doris Lessing's *The Fifth Child,* and a new book by Glendon Swarthout that's coming out in the fall, called *The Homesman,* a wonderful story.

CA: Women sometimes get treated pretty roughly in your books, and there's a growing concern about the violence done to women in current fiction. Do you have any thoughts about it? Do you see it as a sexist approach on the part of male writers?

LEONARD: I treat women now as persons. I don't think of them as women per se, in the sense of saying, I need a woman in this book, or I need a girlfriend for this guy. I try and flesh them out as people as well as I can, just as I do the men. In my newest book, the one I just finished, a woman is the main character. I started with a husband and wife who get involved in the Federal Witness Protection program. He's an iron-worker, and he was going to be the main character—he's a very macho kind of a guy. She sells real estate. They've been married for twenty years. She takes over; she becomes the main character, and I was very happy to see it happen.

CA: You have a lot of female readers, haven't you?

LEONARD: I do; in fact I would say that most of the letters I get are from women.

CA: An important part of publisher Donald Fine's campaign to promote your work was getting the attention of reviewers. Do you think crime and mystery fiction is getting to be less categorized and better treated by reviewers generally?

LEONARD: I would say so. And I've been asked that enough to think it must be a fact. When I was on "Today" with Ed McBain, we were asked what we thought was the reason for the resurgence of the popularity of crime fiction. We probably kind of looked blank, because we didn't know that it ever *wasn't* popular. And there are so many books that deal with crime that aren't considered crime novels on the bestseller list.

CA: It's too bad there's as much categorization as there is. You've noted before that your own books aren't mysteries, though they're sometimes put in that category.

LEONARD: They're definitely not mysteries in the classic sense of being puzzles. They're certainly not whodunits. The reader knows everything that's going on—very often more than the main character.

CA: The movie version of Stick, *one of several you've done a screenplay for, was a major disappointment for you, on top of some earlier disappointments. Will you stay involved in the movies made from your books?*

LEONARD: To some extent I will. *Glitz* is being produced right now as an NBC movie. I did three drafts of a script for it as a feature, the last one with Sidney Lumet, but Lorimar then decided it would cost too much money to make it that way. It would probably cost fifteen or sixteen million dollars, and they didn't think it would gross enough. Their rule-of-thumb is that you have to gross three times the production cost to make a profit, and they didn't think it would do that, at least at that time. So it was rewritten for television. I'm not sure when it will be on. Jimmy Smits from "L.A. Law" is

the star. *Freaky Deaky* has been optioned by Richard Brooks, who made "In Cold Blood" and "Looking for Mr. Goodbar." He'll write the screenplay himself.

CA: Have you played with the idea of producing movies on your own so that you could have control over your original stories?

LEONARD: I did play with the idea, and I got involved in it with a screenplay I did back about eight years ago, "The Hunted," from the 1977 book. I got together with a friend of mine who's a local film producer to raise the money to produce it independently. RKO had been out of the picture business about twenty-five years at that time, and they were talking about coming back in, so we made a deal with them. Then it was a question of our coming up with the actors, and they disagreed with us. There was quite a lot of disagreement. Finally they just broke the contract, and that was that. I wasted some time doing it, and I had no business, really, getting involved to the degree that I did. What I do is write, and that's what I should stick to. I don't know of any writer who has control of his material when it goes to the movies. There aren't even that many directors who have final cut, and that's the whole thing.

CA: Do you think the crime and detective shows on television cut down the market for books, or are there two separate audiences involved?

LEONARD: It certainly hurt the sale of western fiction when there were about thirty western series on prime-time television. But I don't think it hurts the crime and detective books. So many more people are interested in police and crime stories than in westerns. The stories are so much more sensational on television, for the most part, with the car chases and the explosions, which you don't get in the books.

CA: Has the popularity that started building in the mid-eighties brought many more readers to the older books?

LEONARD: Definitely. All my titles, including the westerns, are now in print. The thing is that there are reviewers who will say, "I like his older stuff better, his paperbacks." For some reason these reviewers think I started out doing original paperbacks, which I didn't; even my first westerns were hardcover, from Houghton Mifflin. Out of twenty-six books, twenty-seven counting the new one, I'd say maybe seven or eight were original paperbacks. But since *Glitz,* in 1985, they have picked up the ones that were written in the late seventies and early eighties in paperback, because that's the only form in which they're available, and they think that these books were original paperbacks. One reviewer in particular felt that's what I should be writing—"those paperbacks," kind of well worn, with corners turned down and coffee stains on the covers. The thing is, those reviewers weren't reading me in the late seventies; they only read me after *Glitz.* Where were they when I needed them?

CA: Is there something you'd like to write about, or some kind of book you'd like to do, that's completely unlike anything you've done before?

LEONARD: No. I don't know what I'm going to do next, ever. I'm thinking of the next one right now, and I think it'll be set in Hollywood, but the same kinds of situations will develop as far as the good-versus-evil theme goes. There will be crime involved.

CA: You seem so comfortable with that kind of story. Your books read like the work of somebody who has a good time writing them.

LEONARD: Well, I do. That's what I didn't have before I finally developed the way I write best, most efficiently, the kind of attitude I have to have when I sit down to write. John D. MacDonald said you have to write a million words before you have a sense of knowing what you're doing. I certainly agree with that. It takes about ten years.

CA: Success was a much longer time coming to you than it should have been. Now that you've got it, what's the best part of it?

LEONARD: I never thought I was unsuccessful, because everything I wrote sold; and practically everything—all my books except two—sold to the movies. And though I did have to write screenplays and I did need those movie sales to support my novel writing, perhaps more than ninety percent of writers are in that boat. I didn't see anything unusual in that. I didn't think that what I was writing was bestseller material; I didn't write the big book, I'm not writing *literature*—it's commercial fiction. It's to entertain. I felt that I didn't write well enough or poorly enough to get that big bestseller. And I was kind of surprised when it did hit the list.

CA: Do you like the public attention that's come with it?

LEONARD: Notoriety was never my goal. But to be received well by people I respect—yeah, that's a goal. To get the kind of response that I'm getting from respected reviewers, and letters from people thanking me for a good time—that's really satisfying.

MEDIA ADAPTATIONS: The novelette "3:10 to Yuma" was filmed by Columbia Pictures, 1957; the story "The Tall T" was filmed by Columbia, 1957; *Hombre* was filmed by Twentieth Century-Fox, 1967; *The Big Bounce* was filmed by Warner Bros., 1969; *Valdez Is Coming* was filmed by United Artists, 1970; *Glitz* is being filmed for television by the National Broadcasting Corp.; and the film rights to most of Leonard's other novels have been sold.

BIOGRAPHICAL/CRITICAL SOURCES:

BOOKS

Authors in the News, Volume 1, Gale, 1976.
Contemporary Literary Criticism, Gale, Volume 28, 1984, Volume 34, 1985.
Wholey, Dennis, editor, *The Courage to Change: Personal Conversations about Alcoholism,* Houghton, 1984.

PERIODICALS

American Film, December, 1984.
Armchair Detective, winter, 1986, spring, 1986, winter, 1989.
Chicago Tribune, February 4, 1981, April 8, 1983, December 8, 1983, February 7, 1985.
Chicago Tribune Book World, April 10, 1983, October 30, 1983.
Christian Science Monitor, November 4, 1983.
Detroiter, June, 1974.
Detroit News, February 23, 1982, October 23, 1983.
Esquire, April, 1987.

Globe and Mail (Toronto), December 14, 1985.
Los Angeles Times, June 28, 1984, May 4, 1988.
Los Angeles Times Book Review, February 27, 1983, December 4, 1983, January 13, 1985.
Maclean's, January 19, 1987.
Michigan Magazine (Sunday magazine of the *Detroit News*), October 9, 1983.
Newsweek, March 22, 1982, July 11, 1983, November 14, 1983, April 22, 1985.
New York Times, June 11, 1982, April 28, 1983, October 7, 1983, October 29, 1983, April 26, 1985, May 2, 1988.
New York Times Book Review, May 22, 1977, September 5, 1982, March 6, 1983, December 27, 1983, February 10, 1985, January 4, 1987.
People, March 4, 1985.
Publishers Weekly, February 25, 1983.
Rolling Stone, February 28, 1985.
Times (London), April 23, 1987.
U.S. News & World Report, March 9, 1987.
Village Voice, February 23, 1982.
Washington Post, October 6, 1980, February 6, 1985.
Washington Post Book World, February 7, 1982, July 4, 1982, February 20, 1983, November 13, 1983, May 1, 1988.

—Sketch by Thomas Wiloch

—Interview by Jean W. Ross

*   *   *

LESLIE, Robert Franklin 1911-

PERSONAL: Born October 21, 1911, in Dublin, Tex.; son of Frank (a builder) and Ana May (Morison) Leslie; married Lea Rochat, September 13, 1937. *Education:* University of California, Santa Barbara, B.A., 1939; University of Southern California, M.A., 1942. *Politics:* Republican. *Religion:* Episcopalian.

ADDRESSES: Home and office—1270 Coe St., Camarillo, Calif. 93010.

CAREER: Teacher of French and Spanish in public schools in Carpinteria, Calif., 1940-45, and Pasadena, Calif., 1949-53; Harvard School, North Hollywood, Calif., teacher of French, Spanish, and photography, 1953-70. Conductor of photographic tours throughout Latin America, Canada, the American Southwest, Europe, and Asia, 1946-68. *Wartime service:* American Red Cross, field director associated with U.S. Marine Corps, 1945-46; served in the Philippines and Japan.

MEMBER: PEN (treasurer of Los Angeles chapter, 1972).

AWARDS, HONORS: Notable Book award from Southern California Council on Literature for Children and Young People, 1969, for *The Bears and I: Raising Three Cubs in the North Woods of British Columbia.*

WRITINGS:

Green Hell, Macfadden, 1962.
Read the Wild Water: 780 Miles by Canoe down the Green River, Dutton, 1966.
High Trails West, Crown, 1967.
The Bears and I: Raising Three Cubs in the North Woods of British Columbia, illustrated by Theodore A. Karas, Dutton, 1968.
Wild Pets: Firsthand Account of Wild Animals as Pets, Guests, and Visitors, Crown, 1970.
Wild Burro Rescue (juvenile), Children's Press, 1974.

Wild Courage (juvenile), Children's Press, 1974.
In the Shadow of a Rainbow: The True Story of a Friendship between Man and Wolf, Norton, 1974.
Miracle on Squaretop Mountain, Dutton, 1979.
Ringo the Robber Raccoon: The Story of a Northwood Rogue, Dodd, 1984.
Lorenzo the Magnificent: The Story of an Orphaned Blue Jay, illustrated by Patti Ann Harris, Norton, 1985.
In One of Your Moods Again, Herman?, New American Library, 1985.

Also author of *Emil of the Lighthouse,* 1985, and *Queen Wolf.* Contributor to popular magazines, including *Reader's Digest, Argosy, Westways,* and *Defenders of Wildlife.*

WORK IN PROGRESS: Two historical novels; animal books for children.

SIDELIGHTS: Robert Franklin Leslie, of Scottish and Cherokee Indian ancestry, has explored the wilderness regions of western Canada, the United States, and Mexico, living for long periods of time in remote woodland, desert, and mountain areas. He has canoed most rivers and many back-country lakes in the western United States and Canada, hiked thousands of miles along western trail systems, and climbed mountains in North America, Japan, and Europe, including the Schwartz face of the Matterhorn.

As an amateur archaeologist, Leslie has amassed a large collection of Indian relics and lore. As an ecologist, he lectures and writes about preservation of desert, mountain, and forest wilderness areas. As a photographer, he has shown movies nationally on television and has conducted photography tours in Southwestern Indian reservations, Mexico, Canada, Asia, and Europe.

MEDIA ADAPTATIONS: The Bears and I: Raising Three Cubs in the North Woods of British Columbia has been made into a movie by Walt Disney, Inc., and has also been translated into all the European languages and Japanese.

AVOCATIONAL INTERESTS: Leather carving, wood sculpture.*

*   *   *

LESSER, Alexander   1902-1982

PERSONAL: Born October 4, 1902, in New York, N.Y.; died August 7, 1982, in Nassau County, New York; son of Harris and Rachel (Barnett) Lesser; married Virginia M. Hirst (an artist and teacher), 1940; children: Ann (Mrs. Desmond Margetson), Stephen Alexander, Katherine Maren. *Education:* Columbia University, A.B., 1923, Ph.D., 1929; attended New School for Social Research, 1920-25.

ADDRESSES: Home—39 Elmtree Ln., Levittown, N.Y. 11756. *Office*—Department of Anthropology, Hofstra University, Hempstead, N.Y. 11550.

CAREER: Employed in father's garment business, New York City, 1923-25; Columbia University, New York City, lecturer, 1934-39, field leader for Laboratory of Anthropology, Santa Fe, N.M., 1935; Brooklyn College (now Brooklyn College of the City University of New York), Brooklyn, N.Y., instructor, 1939-46; Association on American Indian Affairs, New York City, executive director, 1947-59; Hofstra University, Hempstead, N.Y., professor of anthropology, 1960-64, professor emeritus, 1964-82, chairman of department of anthropology and sociology, 1960-65. Visiting associate professor, Univer-

sity of Pennsylvania, 1931, Northwestern University, 1938, and Brandeis University, 1956-59; visiting professor at University of California, Berkeley, 1964, Columbia University, 1964-68, John Jay College of the City University of New York, 1968-69, and New School for Social Research, 1969; distinguished visiting professor, Brooklyn College of the City University of New York, 1974. Lecturer at institutions, organizations, and conferences, including New York University, 1935, Young Men's Hebrew Association, 1937-39, Brooklyn Academy of Arts and Sciences, 1938, and Cooper Union Institute, 1940. Social science analyst, Office of Coordinator for Inter-American Affairs, 1943-44; chief of economic studies section, Latin American Division, Office of Strategic Services, 1944-45; chief of north and northeast branch, Division of Research on American Republics, U.S. Department of State, 1945-47.

MEMBER: Association on American Indian Affairs (executive director, 1947-55), American Anthropological Association (fellow), American Ethnological Society (secretary-treasurer, 1933-39; vice-president, 1939-41; director, 1942-44), American Folklore Society (life member), American Council of Learned Societies (fellow, 1931-32), Society for Applied Anthropology, Current Anthropology (associate), African Studies Association, Sigma Xi.

AWARDS, HONORS: Committee on American Indian Languages research fellow, 1929, 1933-34; Social Science Research Council fellow, 1929-30; Columbia University Council for Research in the Social Sciences grant, 1930-33; American Council of Learned Societies fellow, 1931-32; certificate of merit from Office of Strategic Services, 1946; Bollingen Foundation fellow, 1960-62; American Philosophical Society grant, 1970-72.

WRITINGS:

(With Paul Radin) *Social Anthropology,* McGraw, 1932.
Pawnee Ghost Dance Hand Game: A Study of Cultural Change, Columbia University Press, 1934, revised edition published as *The Pawnee Ghost Dance Hand Game: Ghost Dance Revival and Ethnic Identity,* University of Wisconsin Press, 1978.
(Editor) Franz Boas, *Race, Language, and Culture,* Macmillan, 1940.
Survey of Research in the United States on Latin America, National Research Council, 1946.
(Contributor) Morton Fried, Marvin Harris, and Robert Murphy, editors, *War: The Anthropology of Armed Conflict,* Natural History Press, 1968.
(Contributor) Sydel Silverman, editor, *Totems and Teachers: Perspectives on the History of Anthropology,* Columbia University Press, 1981.
History, Evolution, and the Concept of Culture, Cambridge University Press, 1985.

Contributor to *International Encyclopedia of Social Sciences* and to professional journals. Contributing editor, *American Year Book,* 1935-38, and *New International Year Book,* 1936-39; editor and member of board of editors, American Ethnological Society, 1937-40; editor, *American Indian,* 1947-59.

BIOGRAPHICAL/CRITICAL SOURCES:

BOOKS

Lowie, Robert Harry, *History of Ethnological Theory,* Farrar & Rinehart, 1937.

OBITUARIES:

PERIODICALS

New York Times, August 8, 1982.*

* * *

LESTER, Godfrey Allen 1943-

PERSONAL: Born September 18, 1943, in Bristol, England; son of Cyril Allen and Alice Rose (Jouxson) Lester; married Margaret Lynas (a teacher), February 12, 1966; children: Amy, Nancy, Jack. *Education:* University of Sheffield, B.A., 1965, M.A., 1968, Ph.D., 1982.

ADDRESSES: Office—Department of English Language, University of Sheffield, Sheffield S10 2TN, England.

CAREER: University of Sheffield, Sheffield, England, lecturer in English, 1967—.

WRITINGS:

Brasses and Brass Rubbing in the Peak District, Midsummer Publications, 1971.
The Anglo-Saxons, David & Charles, 1976.
(Editor) *Three Late Medieval Morality Plays,* Benn, 1981.
Sir John Paston's ''Grete Boke,'' Boydell & Brewer, 1984.
Index of Middle English Prose, Handlist II, Boydell & Brewer, 1985.
Chaucer's Pardoner's Tale, Macmillan, 1987.
(Editor) Vegetius, *De Re Militari,* Winter, 1988.

Contributor to scholarly periodicals.

WORK IN PROGRESS: Research on Old and Middle English literature.

SIDELIGHTS: Godfrey Allen Lester told *CA:* ''My interest in early literature and archaeology reflects a strong belief in the value of an interdisciplinary approach to medieval studies.''

* * *

LEWIN, L.
See LEWIN, Leonard

* * *

LEWIN, Leonard 1919-
(L. Lewin)

PERSONAL: Born July 22, 1919, in Southend, England; came to the United States in 1968; son of Abraham (a printer) and Leza (Roth) Lewin; married Daphne Dorothy June Smith (a dental nurse), July 10, 1943; children: David Ian, Wendy Patricia (Mrs. John Collins). *Education:* Attended public schools in Southend, England.

ADDRESSES: Home—980 McIntire, Boulder, Colo. 80303.

CAREER: British Admiralty, Witley, England, engineering officer, 1940-46; Standard Telecommunication Laboratories, Harlow, England, beginning 1946, head of microwave department, 1950-60, assistant manager of transmission research, 1960-66, senior principal research engineer, 1967-68; University of Colorado at Boulder, professor of electrical engineering, 1968-86. Founder and president, Institute for Research on the Dissemination of Human Knowledge, 1969-74. National Prestige Lecturer for Institution of Electrical Engineers, New Zealand, 1986. Member, Accountability Committee of Boulder Valley Schools, 1979-81. Consultant, Standard Telecommunication Laboratories, 1968—, Medion Ltd., 1970—, National Bureau of Standards, 1978—, Nuclear Protection Advisory Group, 1980—, Massachusetts Institute of Technology Lincoln Laboratories, 1984—, and National Oceanic and Atmospheric Administration, 1984—.

MEMBER: Institution of Electrical Engineers (senior member), Institute of Electrical and Electronics Engineers (fellow), Colorado Association for the Gifted and Talented.

AWARDS, HONORS: Premium Award from Institution of Electrical Engineers, 1952, 1960; Microwave Prize from Institute of Electrical and Electronic Engineers, 1962; W. G. Baker Award, 1962; D.Sc., University of Colorado at Boulder, 1967; grants from United Kingdom Science Research Council, 1973, 1975; grant from Fulbright Commission, 1981.

WRITINGS:

(Under name L. Lewin) *Advanced Theory of Waveguides,* Iliffe, 1951.
(Under name L. Lewin) *Dilogarithms and Associated Functions,* foreword by J. C. P. Miller, Macdonald, 1959, revised edition published under name Leonard Lewin as *Polylogarithms and Associated Functions,* North-Holland, 1981.
(Contributor) Leo Young, editor, *Advances in Microwaves,* Academic Press, 1965.
(Under name L. Lewin) *Theory of Waveguides: Techniques for the Solution of Waveguide Problems,* Wiley, 1975.
(With David C. Chang and Edward F. Kuester) *Electromagnetic Waves and Curved Structures,* P. Peregrinus, 1977.
(Editor under name L. Lewin) *Telecommunications: An Interdisciplinary Survey,* Artech House, 1979.
(Editor) *Telecommunications in the U.S.: Trends and Policies,* Artech House, 1981.
Telecommunications: An Interdisciplinary Text, Artech House, 1984.

Also author of a monograph, *Science and the Paranormal.*

WORK IN PROGRESS: Research on optical fiber communication, antenna theory, waveguides, and field theory; books on polylogarithms and telecommunications.

AVOCATIONAL INTERESTS: Entomology; education, particularly of gifted children.

* * *

LEWIS, Jean 1924-

PERSONAL: Born June 2, 1924, in Shanghai, China, of American parents; daughter of David and Nettie Craig (Lambuth) Lewis. *Education:* Tutored at home. *Politics:* Republican. *Religion:* Protestant.

ADDRESSES: Home—Apt. 13H, 601 East 20th St., New York, N.Y. 10010.

CAREER: Writer of children's books. Actress and singer in radio, television, and theater, mainly in New York City, 1940-53; American Theatre Wing's Hospital Committee, New York City, program director, 1947-51; Volunteer Service Photographers (now Rehabilitation Through Photography, Inc.), New York City, executive director, 1953—. Writer of sales promotion and continuity for women's television shows.

WRITINGS:

JUVENILES

(Adapter) *Swiss Family Robinson*, Artists & Writers Press, 1961.
Pebbles Flintstone, Artists & Writers Press, 1963.
Bamm-Bamm and Pebbles Flintstone, Artists & Writers Press, 1963.
Jane and the Mandarin's Secret, Hawthorn, 1970.
Hot Dog, Grosset, 1971.
Dr. Leo's Pet Patients, American Heritage Press, 1971.
Shag Finds a Kitten, Grosset, 1983.
The Teddy Bear Clan from Evergreen Woods, Grosset, 1984.
Planet Animals—Mission Zapton, Grosset, 1985.
The Dragon and the Tiger, Macmillan, 1986.
Raggedy Ann and Andy Meet Raggedy Cat, Macmillan, 1988.
The Big Book of Dogs, Grosset, in press.

PUBLISHED BY WHITMAN PUBLISHING

Touche Turtle and the Fire Dog, 1963.
The Flintstones at the Circus, 1963.
(Adapter) *The Tortoise and the Hare*, 1963.
Boo Boo Bear and the V.I.V., 1965.
The Flintstones's Picnic Panic, 1965.
(Contributor) *Golden Prize, and Other Stories about Horses*, 1965, revised edition, 1972.
Hoppity Hooper versus Skippity Snooper, 1966.
Alvin and the Chipmunks and the Deep Sea Blues, 1966.
The Road Runner and the Bird Watchers, 1968.
Frankenstein, Jr. and the Devilish Double, 1968.
Tom and Jerry Scairdy Cat, 1969.
Tom and Jerry under the Big Top, 1969.

PUBLISHED BY WESTERN PUBLISHING/GOLDEN PRESS

The Flintstones Meet the Gruesomes, 1965.
(Adapter) *The Jungle Book*, 1967.
(Adapter) *Old Yeller*, 1968.
(Adapter) *The Absent-Minded Professor*, 1968.
(Adapter) *Chitty Chitty Bang Bang*, 1968.
Gumby and Pokey to the Rescue, 1969.
H. R. Pufnstuf, 1970.
Wacky Witch and the Royal Birthday, 1971.
Wacky Witch and the Mystery of the King's Gold, 1973.
Lassie and the Busy Morning, 1973.
Nancy and Sluggo and the Big Surprise, 1974.
Scooby Doo and the Pirate Treasure, 1974.
Bullwinkle's Casserole, 1975.
Bugs Bunny: Too Many Carrots, 1976.
Mickey Mouse and the Pet Show, 1976.
Benji, the Detective, 1978.
Donald Duck in It's Play Time, 1980.
Around the Year with Pooh, 1980.
Little Golden Book of Dogs, 1982.
Rainbow Brite: Starlight Saves the Day, 1985.
Rainbow Brite: Twink's Magic Carpet Ride, 1985.
Tom and Jerry's Big Move, 1985.
Bugs Bunny Rides Again, 1986.
Little Golden Book of Holidays, 1986.
Lady Lovelylocks: Silky Pup's Butterfly Adventure, 1987.
Tweety and Sylvester: A Visit to the Vet, 1987.
Tabitha Tabby's Fantastic Flavor, 1988.

PUBLISHED BY RAND MCNALLY

Kathi and Hash San and the Case of Measles, 1972.
The Sleeping Tree Mystery, 1975.

Hong Kong Phooey and the Fortune Cookie Caper, 1975.
Scooby Doo and the Haunted Dog House, 1975.
Scooby Doo and the Mystery Monster, 1975.
Santa's Runaway Elf, 1977.
Mumbley to the Rescue, 1977.

OTHER

Contributor to periodicals, including *Professional Photographer* and *Human Services*.

WORK IN PROGRESS: *The Temple Summer*, young adult fiction set in China during the Boxer Rebellion of 1900; *I Remember Amah*, memoirs of her childhood in China.

AVOCATIONAL INTERESTS: Animals, particularly cats.

*   *   *

LEYNER, Mark   1956-

PERSONAL: Born January 4, 1956, in Jersey City, N.J.; son of Joel (a lawyer) and Muriel (a real estate agent; maiden name, Chasan) Leyner; married Arleen Portada (a psychotherapist). *Education:* Brandeis University, B.A., 1977; University of Colorado, M.A., 1979. *Religion:* Jewish.

ADDRESSES: *Home*—937 Washington St., Hoboken, N.J. 07030.

CAREER: Panasonic Co., Secaucus, N.J., advertising copywriter, 1981-82; Brooklyn College of the City University of New York, Brooklyn, N.Y., lecturer in English, 1982; Jersey City State College, Jersey City, N.J., lecturer, 1982-84; freelance copywriter, 1984—.

WRITINGS:

I Smell Esther Williams, and Other Stories, Fiction Collective, 1983.
(Editor with Curtis White and Thomas Glynn) *American Made*, Fiction Collective, 1986.
My Cousin, My Gastroenterologist, Fiction Collective, 1989.

Contributor of stories, articles, plays, and poems to magazines, including *Fictional International*, *Mississippi Review*, *Semiotexte*, and *Between C and D*.

WORK IN PROGRESS: *In the Kingdom of Boredom, I Wear the Royal Sweatpants*, a novel.

SIDELIGHTS: Mark Leyner told *CA:* "My work isn't animated by a desire to be experimental or post-modernist or aesthetically subversive or even 'innovative'—it is animated by a desire to craft a kind of writing that is at every single moment exhilarating for the reader; where each phrase, each sentence is an event. That's what I'm trying for, at least. This, I think, is what gives my work its peculiar shape and feel— it's because I want every little surface to shimmer and gyrate that I haven't patience for those lax transitional devices of plot, setting, character, and so on, that characterize a lot of traditional fiction. I'm after the gaudiness, self-consciousness, laughter, encoded sadness of public language (public because language is the sea in which all our minds swim).

"I don't feel part of any artistic movement or 'ism'. But I feel linked to artists who launched their careers reading billboards aloud in the back seats on family trips, who spent their formative Saturday mornings cemented to their television screens with crazy glue, who grew up fascinated by the rhetoric of pentecostal preachers, dictators, game show hosts, and other assorted demagogues, who were entranced by the outlandishly superfluous chatter of baseball announcers filling air-time during rain delays, and who could never figure out the qualitative difference between Thackeray's *Vanity Fair* and E. C. Segar's *Popeye the Sailor.*

"I said in an article once that we need a kind of writing that the brain can dance to. Well, that's the kind of writing I'm trying to write—thrashing the smoky air of the cerebral ballroom with a very American ball-point baton."

*　　*　　*

LIPMAN, Jean

PERSONAL: Born in New York, N.Y.; married Howard Lipman; children: Peter. *Education:* Wellesley College, B.A.; New York University, M.A.

ADDRESSES: Home—Carefree, Ariz.

CAREER: Art in America (magazine), New York City, associate editor, 1938-40, editor, 1941-71; Whitney Museum of American Art, New York City, editor of publications, 1971.

AWARDS, HONORS: American Folk Painters of Three Centuries was named a notable book of 1980 by American Library Association; *Alexander Calder and His Magical Mobiles* was named an English-Speaking Union Books-Across-the-Sea Ambassador Honor Book, 1984.

WRITINGS:

American Primitive Painting, Oxford University Press, 1942.
American Folk Art in Wood, Metal and Stone, Pantheon, 1948.
(With Alice Winchester) *Primitive Painters in America,* Dodd, 1950, reprinted, Books for Libraries, 1971.
(Editor) *The Collector in America,* Viking, 1961.
(Editor) *What Is American in American Art,* McGraw, 1963.
(With Eve Meulendyke) *American Folk Decoration,* Oxford University Press, 1951, reprinted, Dover, 1972.
(With Mary Black) *American Folk Painting,* C. N. Potter, 1967.
Rufus Porter, Yankee Pioneer, C. N. Potter, 1968, revised edition, Hudson River Museum, 1980.
Calder's Circus, Dutton, 1972.
Rediscovery: Jurgan Frederick Huge, Archives of American Art, 1973.
(With Winchester) *The Flowering of American Folk Art,* Viking, 1974.
Provocative Parallels, Dutton, 1975.
(With Helen Franc) *Bright Stars,* Dutton, 1976.
Calder's Universe, Viking, 1976.
(With Richard Marshall) *Art about Art,* Dutton, 1978.
(Editor with Tom Armstrong) *American Folk Painters of Three Centuries,* Hudson Hills Press, 1980.
(With Margaret Aspinwall) *Alexander Calder and His Magical Mobiles,* Hudson Hills Press, 1981.
(With Doris Palca) *Calder's Calendar,* Whitney Museum, 1981.
(With Armstrong) *American Folk Art Address Book,* C. N. Potter, 1981.
(With Cyril Nelson) *The Indian Calendar,* Dutton, 1983.
Nevelson's World, Hudson Hills Press/Whitney Museum of American Art, 1983.
(With Margi Conrads) *Calder Creatures Great and Small,* Dutton, 1985.
(With Robert Bishop and Elizabeth V. Warren) *Young America: A Folk-Art History,* Museum of American Folk Art/ Hudson Hills Press, 1986.

(With Bishop, Warren, Sharon Eisenstat, and Didi Barrett) *Five-Star Folk Art,* Abrams, 1990.

Contributor to art journals and national magazines.

BIOGRAPHICAL/CRITICAL SOURCES:

PERIODICALS

New York Times, February 19, 1974.
New York Times Book Review, July 23, 1972, December 4, 1983, February 22, 1987.
Saturday Review, November 27, 1976.

*　　*　　*

LIPSKI, Alexander   1919-

PERSONAL: Born July 29, 1919, in Berlin, Germany; naturalized U.S. citizen; son of Jack (an exporter) and Margaret (Gollust) Lipski; married Ruth-Maria Kuenkel (a school psychologist), 1949; children: Beatrice Carolyn, Irene Dorothea, Sophia Christine. *Education:* University of California, Berkeley, B.A., 1950, M.A., 1951, Ph.D., 1953. *Religion:* Roman Catholic.

ADDRESSES: Home—7127 Rosebay St., Long Beach, Calif. 90808.

CAREER: Michigan State University, East Lansing, instructor, 1954-55, assistant professor of history, 1955-58; California State University at Long Beach, associate professor, 1961-65, professor of history, beginning 1965, director of religious studies program, beginning 1974, and professor of religious studies, 1978-83; ordained permanent deacon of Roman Catholic Church, Archdiocese of Los Angeles, Calif., 1982—.

MEMBER: Association for Asian Studies, American Academy of Religion, Phi Beta Kappa.

AWARDS, HONORS: American Council of Learned Societies research grant, 1960.

WRITINGS:

(Editor) *Bengal East-West,* Center for Asian Studies, Michigan State University, 1970.
Life and Teachings of Sri Anandamayi Ma, Motilal Banarsidas (Delhi), 1977.
(Editor) Raimohana Samanta, *Letters to Lipski; or, Bijay Krishna Explained,* H. Devi, c. 1977.
Thomas Merton & Asia: His Quest for Utopia, Cistercian Publications, 1983.

Contributor to *Mount Carmel* (magazine).

*　　*　　*

LLOYD, Norman   1909-1980

PERSONAL: Born November 8, 1909, in Pottsville, Pa.; died July 31, 1980, of leukemia in Greenwich, Conn.; buried in Pottsville, Pa.; son of David (a businessman) and Annie Sarah (Holstein) Lloyd; married Ruth Dorothy Rohrbacher (a musician and educator), April 10, 1933; children: David Walter, Alex. *Education:* New York University, B.S., 1932, M.A., 1936; studied music composition with Vincent Jones and Aaron Copland.

ADDRESSES: Home—Greenwich, Conn.

CAREER: Pianist for silent films; instructor at Ernest Williams Band School, 1935-37; New York University, New York City, lecturer in music, 1936-45; Sarah Lawrence College, Bronxville, N.Y., professor of music, 1936-46, conductor of chorus, 1945-48; Juilliard School of Music, New York City, professor of music, 1946-63, director of education, 1946-49; Oberlin College, Oberlin, Ohio, dean of conservatory, 1963-65; Rockefeller Foundation, New York City, director for arts and humanities, 1965-72; free-lance consultant in the arts, beginning 1973. Faculty member at many schools and conservatories. Professional performer. Composer and conductor of dance scores for Martha Graham, 1935, Hanya Holm, 1937, Doris Humphrey, 1941-46, 1949, and Jose Limon, 1949. Composer and conductor of film scores. Helped establish North Carolina Dance Theater at University of North Carolina, 1970. Committee member, Massachusetts Institute of Technology, 1973-75, and Tufts University, 1976-80; member of board of directors, National Music Council.

MEMBER: American Society of Composers, Authors, and Publishers (ASCAP), American Federation of Musicians, Pi Kappa Lambda.

AWARDS, HONORS: Annual awards from American Society of Composers, Authors, and Publishers, 1962-72; Mus.D., Philadelphia Conservatory of Music, 1963, New England Conservatory, 1965, and Peabody Institute, 1973.

WRITINGS:

(Arranger for piano) *Fireside Book of Folk Songs,* edited by Margaret Boni, illustrations by Alice and Martin Provensen, Simon & Schuster, 1947, reprinted, 1974.
(With Boni) *Fireside Book of American Songs,* Simon & Schuster, 1952.
(With Arnold Fish) *Fundamentals of Sight Singing and Ear Training,* Dodd, 1963.
Golden Encyclopedia of Music, Western Publishing, 1968.
(With wife, Ruth Lloyd) *American Heritage Songbook,* American Heritage, 1971.
(Contributor) Margaret Mahoney, editor, *Arts on the Campus,* Graphic Arts Press, 1971.
(With R. Lloyd) *Keyboard Improvisation,* Dodd, 1973.
(With R. Lloyd and Jan DeGaetani) *The Complete Sightsinger: A Stylistic and Historic Approach,* Harper, 1980.

Also author of *Golden Encyclopedia of Music,* 1968, and *Creative Keyboard Musicianship,* 1975. Compiler of *Fireside Book of Love Songs,* 1954, *Favorite Christmas Carols,* 1957, and *Songs of the Gilded Age,* 1960. Composer of "Song for Summer's End," 1951, "Nocturne for Voices," 1953, and other musical works.

OBITUARIES:

PERIODICALS

New York Times, August 1, 1980.*

* * *

LOBDELL, Jared C(harles) 1937-

PERSONAL: Born November 29, 1937, in New York, N.Y.; son of Charles E. (an investment analyst) and Jane (Hopkins) Lobdell. *Education:* Yale University, B.A., 1961; University of Wisconsin—Madison, M.B.A., 1966, M.S., 1975. *Politics:* Republican. *Religion:* Episcopalian.

CAREER: University of Wisconsin, Green Bay, instructor in business, 1970-72; Pace University, Graduate School, Pleasantville, N.Y., assistant professor of finance, 1972-75; Suffolk University, Boston, Mass., assistant professor, 1976-77; Marist College, Poughkeepsie, N.Y., 1977-78; Carnegie-Mellon University, Pittsburgh, Pa., research associate, beginning 1979.

MEMBER: Mory's Association, Elizabethan Club.

AWARDS, HONORS: New Jersey Historical Commission grant, 1973, 1980.

WRITINGS:

(Editor) *A Tolkien Compass,* Open Court, 1974.
England and Always: Tolkien's World of the Rings, Eerdman's, 1981.
(Translator and author of introduction) C. W. Larison, *Silvia Dubois: A Biografy of the Slav Who Whipt Her Mistres and Gand Her Fredom,* Oxford University Press, 1987.

Contributor to *Missouri Historical Review, National Review,* and *New Jersey History.* Associate editor of *Rally,* 1966-67; editor for American Enterprise Institute for Public Policy Research, 1973-79.

WORK IN PROGRESS: Revolutionary War Journal and Letters of Major William Croghan, 1779-1782; Student Attitudes: A Study in Structural Change in American Society; Investor Behavior and Stock Market Profits; a book on the revision of the Pennsylvania state tax.*

* * *

Lo BELLO, Nino 1921-

PERSONAL: Born September 8, 1921, in Brooklyn, N.Y.; son of Joseph and Rosalie (Moscarelli) Lo Bello; married Irene Helen Rooney, February 22, 1948; children: Susan, Thomas. *Education:* Queens College (now Queens College of the City University of New York), B.A., 1947; New York University, M.A., 1948, graduate study, 1948-50. *Politics:* Liberal. *Religion:* Roman Catholic.

ADDRESSES: Home—24 Lenaugasse, 3400 Weidling bei Vienna, Austria. *Agent*—McIntosh & Otis, Inc., 310 Madison Ave., New York, N.Y. 10017.

CAREER: Newspaper reporter in Brooklyn, N.Y., 1946-50; University of Kansas, Lawrence, instructor in sociology, 1950-56; Rome correspondent for *Business Week* and McGraw-Hill's *World News,* 1957-62, and *New York Journal of Commerce,* 1962-64; *New York Herald Tribune,* New York, N.Y., economic correspondent in Vienna, Austria, 1964-66; free-lance journalist. Visiting professor at Denison University, 1956, and University of Alaska, 1974. *Military service:* U.S. Army, 1942-46.

MEMBER: Overseas Press Club of America, Foreign Press Club, Foreign Press Club of Rome.

WRITINGS:

The Vatican Empire, Simon & Schuster, 1968.
The Vatican's Wealth, Bruce & Watson, 1971.
Vatican, U.S.A., Simon & Schuster, 1972.
European Detours, Hammond, Inc., 1981.
The Vatican Papers, New English Library, 1982.
Vatikan im Zwielicht, Econ-Verlag, 1983.
Nino Lo Bello's Guide to Offbeat Europe, Chicago Review Press, 1985.
English Well Speeched Here, Price, Stern, 1986.
Nino Lo Bello's Guide to the Vatican, Chicago Review Press, 1987.

Der Vatikan, HPT-Verlagsgesellschaft, 1988.

WORK IN PROGRESS: Two nonfiction books and an anthology.

SIDELIGHTS: Nino Lo Bello once told *CA:* "It has not been my purpose, in writing frequently about the Vatican, to demean the Roman Catholic religion (the one I grew up with and practice), either in the eyes of Catholics or non-Catholics. I make no judgment on the validity of the faith, for I recognize that the religion gives many people solace and joy. Furthermore, though I have not sought to rebut any Catholic tenets, I have concerned myself with certain imperfections and failings among the men who run the Church. As a journalist I have attempted in my books always to be as professionally objective as is humanly possible and let the facts speak for themselves.

"Whoever takes it upon himself to write about the Vatican could easily give the impression that he is an expert. There are, in my opinion, no experts on the Vatican. There are, indeed, Vatican-watchers, Vatican theorists, and Vaticanologists—but there are no Vatican experts. This reminds me of a story: During an audience one day when a dozen cardinals, bishops, and assorted clerics were present, and Pope Pius XII was in one of his rare good moods, he asked two young priests the same question: 'How long have you been in the Vatican?' The first man replied, 'Three weeks.' 'Then,' said the pope, 'you are an expert on the Vatican!' The second man gave as his reply, 'Three years.' 'Then,' said the pope, 'you know nothing about the Vatican!'"

AVOCATIONAL INTERESTS: Opera ("opera buff supreme").

BIOGRAPHICAL/CRITICAL SOURCES:

PERIODICALS

Christian Science Monitor, July 31, 1969.
Commonweal, February 28, 1969.
New York Times, February 3, 1969.
New York Times Book Review, June 29, 1969.
Saturday Review, February 8, 1969.

*   *   *

LOCHMAN, Jan Milic   1922-

PERSONAL: Born April 3, 1922, in Nove Mesto, Czechoslovakia; son of Josef and Marie (Jelinek) Lochman; married Eliska Jerabek, September 19, 1952; children: Vera, Tomas, Marek. *Education:* Studied at Hus Faculty of Theology, Prague, 1945-46, University of St. Andrews, 1946-47, and University of Basel, 1947-48; Hus Faculty of Theology, Th.D., 1948.

ADDRESSES: Home—Heuberg 33, 4051, Basel, Switzerland. *Office*—University of Basel, 4003, Basel, Switzerland.

CAREER: Clergyman of Czech Brethren Church; Comenius Faculty of Theology, Prague, Czechoslovakia, professor of theology, 1950-68; Union Theological Seminary, New York, N.Y., professor of theology, 1968-69; University of Basel, Basel, Switzerland, professor of theology, beginning 1969, Rector Magnificus, 1981-83. Noble Lecturer, Harvard University, 1971-71; visiting lecturer at other universities throughout the United States and Europe. Member of central committee, World Council of Churches; chairman of theological department, World Alliance of Reformed Churches, 1970-82.

AWARDS, HONORS: D.D., University of Aberdeen, 1973; Jacob Burckhardt Prize (Basel), 1987.

WRITINGS:

Nabozenske mysleni ceskeho obrozeni (title means "Religious Thought of the Czech Enlightenment"), Kalich, 1952.
Theologie und kalter Krieg (booklet), Hefte aus Burgscheidungen, 1960.
Die Bedeutung geschichtlicher Ereignisse fuer ethische Entscheidungen, EVZ Verlag, 1963.
Die Not der Versoehung, Herbert Reich Evangelischer Verlag, 1963.
(With Gerhard Bassarak) *Gemeinde in der veraenderten Welt,* Evangelische Verlagsanstalt, 1963.
Duchovni odkaz obrozeni: Dobrovsky, Bolzano, Kollar, Palacky (title means "Legacy of the Enlightenment"), Kalich, 1964.
Herrschaft Christi in der saekularisierten Welt (booklet), EVZ Verlag, 1967.
(With M. R. Shaull and Charles C. West) *Zur Theologie der Revolution,* Kaiser Verlag, 1967.
Church in a Marxist Society: A Czechoslovak View, Harper, 1970.
Perspektiven politischer Theologie, TVZ Verlag, 1971.
Das radikale Erbe, TVZ Verlag, 1972.
Christus oder Prometheus?, Furche Verlag, 1972, translation published as *Christ and Prometheus?,* WCC (Geneva), 1988.
(With Fritz Buri and Heinrich Ott) *Dogmatik im Dialog,* three volumes, Guetersloher Verlagshaus, 1973-76.
Traegt oder truegt die christliche Hoffnung?, TVZ Verlag, 1974.
Marx begegnen, Guetersloher Verlagshaus, 1975, translation by Edwin H. Robertson published as *Encountering Marx,* Fortress, 1977.
Living Roots of Reformation, Augsburg, 1979.
Reconciliation and Liberation, Fortress, 1980.
Signposts to Freedom, Augsburg, 1982.
Theology of Praise, Knox, 1982.
Das Glaubensbekenntnis, Guetersloher Verlagshaus, 1982.
Vom Sinn der Feste, Reinhardt, 1982.
Comenius, Imba, 1983.
The Faith We Confess—An Ecumenical Dogmatics, Fortress, 1984.
Unser Vater, Guetersloher Verlagshaus, 1988.

WORK IN PROGRESS: An English translation of *Unser Vater,* for Eerdmans.

*   *   *

LOMBARD, Nap
See JOHNSON, Pamela Hansford

*   *   *

LONG, Wesley
See SMITH, George O(liver)

*   *   *

LONGMATE, Norman Richard   1925-

PERSONAL: Born December 15, 1925, in Newbury, Berkshire, England; son of Ernest (a photographer) and Margaret (Rowden) Longmate; married Elizabeth Jean Taylor (a teacher), August 8, 1953; children: Jill. *Education:* Attended Christ's Hospital, Horsham, England, 1936-43; Worcester College, Oxford, B.A. (with honors), 1950, M.A., 1954. *Religion:* Anglican.

ADDRESSES: c/o Century Hutchinson, 62-65 Chandos Pl., London WC2N 4NW, England.

CAREER: Daily Mirror, London, England, feature writer, 1953-57; Electricity Council, London, administrator in industrial relations department, 1957-63; British Broadcasting Corp., London, radio producer, 1963-65, administrator in secretariat, 1965-83; writer. Historical consultant to television and film companies and to Imperial War Museum, London. *Military service:* British Army, 1944-47.

MEMBER: Society of Authors, Royal Historical Society (fellow), National Trust, Historical Association, Prayer Book Society, Fortress Study Group, Oxford Society, Worcester College Society, Society of Sussex Downsmen, Ramblers' Association, U.K. Fortifications Club.

WRITINGS:

HISTORY

King Cholera: The Biography of a Disease, Hamish Hamilton, 1966.
The Waterdrinkers: A History of Temperance, Hamish Hamilton, 1968.
Alive and Well: Medicine and Public Health, 1830 to the Present Day, Penguin, 1970.
How We Lived Then: A History of Everyday Life during the Second World War, Hutchinson, 1971, reprinted, Arrow Books, 1988.
If Britain Had Fallen, Hutchinson, 1972, Stein & Day, 1974.
The Real Dad's Army: The Story of the Home Guard, Arrow Books, 1974.
The Workhouse, St. Martin's, 1974.
Milestones in Working Class History, BBC Publications, 1975.
The G.I.s: Americans in Britain 1942-1945, Hutchinson, 1975, Scribner, 1976.
(Author of historical postscript) Jimmy Perry and David Croft, *Dad's Army,* Elm Tree Books, 1975.
Air Raid: The Bombing of Coventry, 1940, Hutchinson, 1976, McKay, 1978.
When We Won the War: The Story of Victory in Europe, 1945, Hutchinson, 1977.
The Hungry Mills: The Story of the Lancashire Cotton Famine 1861-1865, Temple Smith, 1978.
The Doodlebugs: The Story of the Flying-Bombs, Hutchinson, 1981.
(Editor) *The Home Front: An Anthology of Personal Experience, 1938-1945,* Chatto & Windus, 1981, Salem House, 1982.
The Bombers: The RAF Offensive against Germany 1939-1945, Hutchinson, 1983.
The Breadstealers: The Fight against the Corn Laws, 1838-1846, St. Martin's, 1984.
Hitler's Rockets: The Story of the V-2s, Hutchinson, 1985.
Defending the Island: From Caesar to the Armada, Century Hutchinson, 1989.

DETECTIVE STORIES

Death Won't Wash, Cassell, 1957.
A Head for Death, Cassell, 1958.
Strip Death Naked, Cassell, 1959, reprinted, Garland Publishing, 1983.
Vote for Death, Cassell, 1960.
Death in Office, R. Hale, 1961.

OTHER

(Editor and author of historical introduction) *A Socialist Anthology and the Men Who Made It,* Phoenix House, 1953.

Oxford Triumphant (documentary), Phoenix House, 1954.
Keith in Electricity (juvenile career book), Chatto & Windus, 1961.
Electricity Supply (juvenile career book), Sunday Times Publications, 1961.
Electricity as a Career (juvenile), Batsford, 1964.
(Editor and author of introduction) *Writing for the BBC,* BBC Publications, 1966, (author) 8th edition, 1988.

Contributor of articles to periodicals, including *Observer, Spectator, Listener, New Society, Sunday Mirror,* and *Daily Telegraph.* Contributor to British Broadcasting Corp. radio and television programs.

WORK IN PROGRESS: The second volume of *Defending the Island,* covering the period 1603-1945, entitled *After the Armada.*

SIDELIGHTS: Norman Richard Longmate told *CA:* "My special field of interest is relating major events (e.g. a cholera epidemic or a war) to the individual human experience. I have tried to find unexplored aspects of important subjects, e.g. civilian experience during World War II, or the human story of workhouse inmates, not merely the legal and administrative facts about the setting up of the institution. The books which best illustrate my distinctive technique are *How We Lived Then* and *The Bombers.*"

For *How We Lived Then,* an account of civilian wartime experiences, Longmate queried hundreds of people about their memories of World War II. "For me, as for so many people," Longmate added, "the war is still far more vivid in my recollection than anything which has happened since then." Focusing on the "everyday life" of people on the home front, the book brings together a variety of personal war experiences. In a *Spectator* review, Angus Maude praises the book as being "minutely detailed, accurate, skilfully marshalled and engagingly written." The critic recommends the book to both social historians and general readers: "Its compilation is a real *tour-de-force,* most brilliantly done. For the young, it will provide a new slant on what their parents went through. For the parents themselves, it will provide a total and nostalgic recall."

AVOCATIONAL INTERESTS: Reading and country walking.

BIOGRAPHICAL/CRITICAL SOURCES:

PERIODICALS

Listener, November 24, 1966, March 25, 1971, August 22, 1974, November 27, 1975.
Reading Evening Post, July 9, 1986.
Spectator, April 10, 1971, June 29, 1974.
Times (London), November 17, 1966.
Times Literary Supplement, December 11, 1966, April 9, 1971, August 30, 1974, June 3, 1977, June 9, 1978, July 3, 1981, August 12, 1983, July 13, 1984, September 13, 1985.

*   *   *

LONGWORTH, Philip   1933-

PERSONAL: Born February 17, 1933, in London, England. *Education:* Balliol College, Oxford, B.A., 1956, M.A., 1960. *Politics:* "Varies according to the particular issue." *Religion:* Jewish.

ADDRESSES: Office—Department of History, McGill University, 855 Shoolwooke St. W., Montreal, Quebec, Canada

H3A 2T7. *Agent*—A. M. Heath & Co., Ltd., St. Martin's Lane, London WC2N 4AA, England.

CAREER: Central Asian Research Centre, London, England, researcher, 1962-65; Commonwealth War Graves Commission, London, historian, 1965-67; University of Birmingham, Birmingham, England, lecturer in Russian history, 1967-68; University of London, London, visiting fellow at School of Slavonic and East European Studies, 1973-74; McGill University, Montreal, Canada, professor of history, 1984—. *Military service:* British Army, 1951-53.

WRITINGS:

(Translator) M. Lermontov, *A Hero of Our Time,* New English Library, 1962, New American Library, 1964.
The Art of Victory, Constable, 1964, Holt, 1966.
The Unending Vigil: A History of the Commonwealth War Graves Commission, 1917-1967, Constable, 1967, reprinted, Secker & Warburg, 1985.
The Cossacks, Constable, 1969, Holt, 1970.
The Three Empresses: Catherine I, Anne, and Elizabeth of Russia, Constable, 1972, Holt, 1973.
The Rise and Fall of Venice, Constable, 1974.
(Contributor) H. A. Landsberger, editor, *Rural Protest,* Macmillan, 1975.
(Contributor) A. G. Cross, editor, *Great Britain and Russia in the Eighteenth Century,* Oriental Research Partners, 1979.
(Contributor) B. Kiraly and G. Rothenberg, editors, *War and Society in East Central Europe,* Brooklyn College Press, 1979.
(Contributor) Kiraly, Rothenberg, and P. Sugar, editors, *Social Science Monographs,* Boulder Book Co., 1982.
Alexis: Tsar of All the Russias, Secker & Warburg, 1984, F. Watts, 1985.

Also contributor to *Encyclopaedia Britannica.* Contributor to journals, including *Past and Present, Russia* (Milan, Italy), *Slavonic and East European Review, Race,* and *History Today.*

AVOCATIONAL INTERESTS: Music, bibliophilia.

BIOGRAPHICAL/CRITICAL SOURCES:

PERIODICALS

Los Angeles Times, January 11, 1985.
Times Literary Supplement, December 7, 1984.

*　　*　　*

LORD MANCROFT
　　See MANCROFT, Stormont Mancroft Samuel

*　　*　　*

LOVESEY, Peter (Harmer) 1936-
　　(Peter Lear)

PERSONAL: Born September 10, 1936, in Whitton, Middlesex, England; son of Richard Lear (a bank official) and Amy (Strank) Lovesey; married Jacqueline Ruth Lewis, May 30, 1959; children: Kathleen Ruth, Philip Lear. *Education:* University of Reading, B.A. (honors), 1958.

ADDRESSES: Agent—John Farquharson Ltd., 162-168 Regent St., London W1R 5TB, England.

CAREER: Thurrock Technical College, Grays, Essex, England, senior lecturer, 1961-69; Hammersmith College for Further Education, London, England, head of general education department, 1969-75; currently full-time writer. *Military service:* Royal Air Force, 1958-61; served as education officer; became flying officer.

MEMBER: Crime Writers' Association, Writers Guild, Detection Club.

AWARDS, HONORS: Macmillan/Panther First Crime Novel award, 1970, for *Wobble to Death;* Silver Dagger, 1979, and Gold Dagger, 1983, both from Crime Writers' Association; Grand Prix de Litterature Policiere, 1985; Prix du Roman d'Adventures, 1986; Veuve Clicquot/Crime Writers Association Short Story Award, 1986.

WRITINGS:

CRIME NOVELS

Wobble to Death (Sergeant Cribb mystery), Dodd, 1970.
The Detective Wore Silk Drawers (Sergeant Cribb mystery), Dodd, 1971.
Abracadaver (Sergeant Cribb mystery), Dodd, 1972.
Mad Hatter's Holiday: A Novel of Murder in Victorian Brighton (Sergeant Cribb mystery), Dodd, 1973.
Invitation to a Dynamite Party (Sergeant Cribb mystery), Macmillan, 1974, published as *The Tick of Death,* Dodd, 1974.
A Case of Spirits (Sergeant Cribb mystery), Dodd, 1975.
Swing, Swing Together (Sergeant Cribb mystery), Dodd, 1976.
Waxwork (Sergeant Cribb mystery), Pantheon, 1978.
The False Inspector Dew, Pantheon, 1982.
Keystone, Pantheon, 1983.
Rough Cider, Bodley Head, 1986, Mysterious Press, 1987.
Bertie and the Tinman, Mysterious Press, 1988.
On the Edge, Mysterious Press, 1989.

NONFICTION

The Kings of Distance: A Study of Five Great Runners, Eyre & Spottiswoode, 1968, published as *Five Kings of Distance,* St. Martin's Press, 1981.
(With Tom McNab) *The Guide to British Track and Field Literature 1275-1968,* Athletics Arena (London), 1969.
The Official Centenary History of the Amateur Athletic Association, Guinness Superlatives (London), 1979.

CONTRIBUTOR

Virginia Whitaker, editor, *Winter's Crimes 5,* St. Martin's Press, 1973.
Dilys Winn, editor, *Murder Ink: The Mystery Reader's Companion,* Workman, 1977.
Hilary Watson, editor, *Winter's Crimes 10,* St. Martin's Press, 1978.
John Waite, editor, *Mystery Guild Anthology,* Constable, 1980.
Edward D. Hoch, editor, *Best Detective Stories of the Year 1981,* Dutton, 1981.
Watson, editor, *Winter's Crimes 14,* St. Martin's Press, 1982.
Josh Pachter, editor, *Top Crime,* St. Martin's Press, 1983.
George Hardinge, editor, *Winter's Crimes 15,* St. Martin's Press, 1983.
Herbert Harris, editor, *John Creasey's Crime Collection, 1983,* St. Martin's Press, 1983.
Hardinge, editor, *Winter's Crimes 17,* St. Martin's Press, 1985.
Harris, editor, *John Creasey's Crime Collection, 1985,* St. Martin's Press, 1985.
Hardinge, editor, *The Best of Winter's Crimes,* St. Martin's Press, 1986.

Harris, editor, *John Creasey's Crime Collection, 1986,* St. Martin's Press, 1986.

Hoch, editor, *The Year's Best Mystery and Suspense Stories, 1986,* Walker, 1986.

Hilary Hale, editor, *Winter's Crimes 19,* St. Martin's Press, 1987.

Harris, editor, *John Creasey's Crime Collection, 1987,* St. Martin's Press, 1987.

Martin H. Greenberg and Carol-Lynn Waugh, editors, *The New Adventures of Sherlock Holmes,* Carroll & Graf, 1987.

Hale, editor, *Winter's Crimes 20,* St. Martin's Press, 1988.

Harris, editor, *John Creasey's Crime Collection, 1988,* St. Martin's Press, 1988.

OTHER

(Under pseudonym Peter Lear) *Goldengirl,* Cassell, 1977, Doubleday, 1978.

(Under pseudonym Peter Lear) *Spider Girl,* Viking, 1980.

Butchers and Other Stories of Crime (short stories), Macmillan (London), 1985, Mysterious Press, 1987.

(Under pseudonym Peter Lear) *The Secret of Spandau,* M. Joseph, 1986.

Also author with wife, Jacqueline Ruth Lovesey, of "Sergeant Cribb" teleplays for Granada television and the Public Broadcasting Service's "Mystery!" program, including "The Last Trumpet," "Murder, Old Boy?" "Something Old, Something New," "The Horizontal Witness," and "The Choir That Wouldn't Sing." Contributor to periodicals, including *Armchair Detective, Ellery Queen's Mystery Magazine, Harper's,* and *Company.*

SIDELIGHTS: Peter Lovesey's interest in sport led him to write his prize-winning first Victorian crime novel *Wobble to Death.* He told Diana Cooper-Clark in the *Armchair Detective,* "At this time, I didn't regard myself as an authority or expert on the Victorian period. But I had become interested in Victorian sport as a school boy because I wasn't a very good athlete and would have liked to have been. I was flat-footed and butter-fingered and couldn't really perform very well in any team game, so I tried to take up the more individual sports, like high jumping." While researching the life of an American Indian athlete, he found a description of the Victorian "wobble," a walking endurance contest. Later, while "perusing the personals columns of the [London] *Times* as Sherlock Holmes used to do," he states, he discovered an advertisement for a crime novel contest. *Wobble to Death* was the result.

Wobble to Death is the first of a series of novels featuring Detective Sergeant Cribb and his assistant Constable Thackeray. Critics have praised these books for their authentic evocation of Victorian atmosphere and restrained characterization. Lovesey explains to Cooper-Clark: "I was looking in *Wobble to Death* for a realistic Victorian detective. I was conscious that the great detectives were super figures, the omniscient Sherlock Holmes, the sophisticated Lord Peter Wimsey, and even Hercule Poirot, with the little grey cells. These were not really for me. I wanted somebody who would have to struggle to solve a crime and have to work against the limitations of the period." Marcel Berlins of the London *Times* states: "Peter Lovesey has written eight [Sergeant Cribb] detective novels set in late Victorian times, and not one has fallen short on factual accuracy or ratiocinative skill. . . . Mr. Lovesey's strength is to place those subdued characters into a meticulously researched historical reality, and produce a supremely satisfying novel of detection." All eight novels featuring Cribb and Thackeray proved very popular. They were adapted and broad-

cast in America on the Public Broadcasting Service's "Mystery!" program, and Lovesey later collaborated with his wife Jacqueline to produce six new "Sergeant Cribb" stories for the series.

Besides his "Sergeant Cribb" novels Lovesey has written detective fiction set in a variety of other times and places. He left the Victorian period for *The False Inspector Dew,* bringing his evocative talents to a 1920s transatlantic cruise. A reviewer for the London *Times* reports, "Lovesey has researched his setting not merely just enough to have plenty of local colour to push in when there's some excuse, but so thoroughly that he had at his fingertips a dozen facts to choose from at any instant." This, along with a gripping story line, the reviewer adds, is part of "the charge that powers his book." Other stories include *Keystone,* a mystery set in Hollywood just before the First World War, which involves the Keystone Kops and many of the period's actors, and *Rough Cider,* a novel of psychological suspense.

More recently Lovesey has returned to the Victorian era with *Bertie and the Tinman.* This time the author features a rather unusual detective—Albert Edward, Prince of Wales, Queen Victoria's son and heir, who later became Edward VII of England. Bertie, as he is known to his intimates, tells the story of the apparent suicide of his favorite jockey Fred Archer, popularly known as the Tinman. Doubting that Archer was suicidal, the Prince becomes suspicious and launches a personal investigation that takes him all over Victorian London, from the coarsest fleshpots to the most elegant salons. "The rueful, candid voice [Lovesey] gives to the fleshy prince rings true," declares *Time* magazine contributor William A. Henry III, "the details of the horse-racing and music-hall worlds are vivid, and much of the tale is sweetly funny." "This is an affectionate look at Prince Albert, a likable chap even with his pomposities and one-sided view of life," reports Newgate Callendar in the *New York Times Book Review.* "And the racetrack scenes and backgrounds crackle with authenticity. There is a great deal of humor in the book, even a strong dash of P. G. Wodehouse. 'Bertie and the Tinman' is a delightful romp."

MEDIA ADAPTATIONS: Peter Lovesey's *Goldengirl,* written under the pseudonym Peter Lear, was filmed by the Avco Embassy Pictures Corp. in 1979. It starred James Coburn as Dryden, the shrewd sports agent, and Susan Anton as Goldengirl, the woman bred to win three gold medals in track events at the 1980 Moscow Olympics. Lovesey's "Sergeant Cribb" novels were filmed for Granada Television and broadcast in America by the Public Broadcasting Service (PBS-TV) on its "Mystery!" program, 1980-82, featuring Alan Dobie as Sergeant Cribb and William Simons as Constable Thackeray.

BIOGRAPHICAL/CRITICAL SOURCES:

BOOKS

Barnes, Melvin, *Murder in Print: A Guide to Two Centuries of Crime Fiction,* Barn Owl Books, 1986.

Benstock, Bernard, editor, *Art in Crime Writing,* St. Martin's Press, 1983.

Burack, Sylvia K., *Writing Mystery and Crime Fiction,* The Writer, 1985.

Carr, John C., *The Craft of Crime: Conversations with Crime Writers,* Houghton, 1983.

Cooper-Clark, Diana, *Designs of Darkness: Interviews with Detective Novelists*, Bowling Green State University Popular Press, 1983.

Dove, George N., and Earl F. Bargainner, *Cops and Constables: American and British Fictional Policemen*, Bowling Green State University Popular Press, 1986.

Keating, H. R. F., *Crime and Mystery: The One Hundred Best Books*, Carroll & Graf, 1987.

PERIODICALS

Armchair Detective, summer, 1981.
New Republic, March 3, 1982.
Newsweek, July 3, 1978, April 5, 1982.
New York Times, June 15, 1979, October 14, 1983.
New York Times Book Review, October 25, 1970, October 15, 1972, February 15, 1976, May 28, 1978, October 3, 1982.
Publishers Weekly, October 25, 1985.
Saturday Review, October 28, 1972.
Spectator, March 28, 1970, April 10, 1982.
Times (London), March 1, 1980, March 18, 1982, December 31, 1987.
Times Literary Supplement, April 9, 1970, June 25, 1982.
Washington Post Book World, September 17, 1972, May 16, 1982, March 20, 1988.

*   *   *

LUCAS, Henry C(ameron), Jr. 1944-

PERSONAL: Born September 4, 1944, in Omaha, Neb.; son of Henry Cameron (an advertising executive) and Lois (a teacher; maiden name, Himes) Lucas; married Ellen Kuhbach, June 8, 1968; children: Scott Cameron, Jonathan Gerdes. *Education:* Yale University, B.S. (magna cum laude), 1966; Massachusetts Institute of Technology, M.S., 1968, Ph.D., 1970.

ADDRESSES: Home—18 Portland Rd., Summit, N.J. 07901. *Office*—Information Systems Area, School of Business, New York University, New York, N.Y. 10003.

CAREER: Arthur D. Little, Inc., Cambridge, Mass., consultant on information systems, 1966-70; Stanford University, Stanford, Calif., assistant professor of computer and information systems, 1970-74; New York University, New York, N.Y., associate professor, 1974-78, professor of computer applications and information systems and chairman of department, both 1978-85.

MEMBER: Association for Computing Machinery, Institute of Management Sciences, Phi Beta Kappa, Tau Beta Pi.

WRITINGS:

Computer-Based Information Systems in Organizations, Science Research Associates, 1973.

Toward Creative Systems Design (monograph), Columbia University Press, 1974.

Why Information Systems Fail (monograph), Columbia University Press, 1975.

The Implementation of Computer-Based Models (monograph), National Association of Accountants, 1976.

The Analysis, Design, and Implementation of Information Systems, McGraw, 1976, 2nd edition, 1981.

(With C. F. Gibson) *Casebook for Management Information Systems*, McGraw, 1976, 2nd edition, 1981.

Information Systems Concepts for Management, McGraw, 1978, 2nd edition, 1982.

(Editor with F. Land, T. J. Lincoln, and K. Supper) *The Information Systems Environment*, North-Holland, 1980.

Implementation: The Key to Successful Information Systems (monograph), Columbia University Press, 1981.

Coping with Computers: A Manager's Guide to Controlling Information Processing, Free Press, 1982.

Introduction to Computers and Information Systems, Macmillan, 1987.

Managing Information Services, Macmillan, 1989.

CONTRIBUTOR

F. Gruenberger, editor, *Efficient versus Effective Computing*, Prentice-Hall, 1973.

R. Schultz and D. Slevin, editors, *Implementing Operations Research/Management Science: Research Findings and Implications*, American Elsevier, 1975.

R. Goldberg and H. Lorin, editors, *The Economics of Information Processing*, Volume 2, Wiley, 1982.

G. Salvendi, editor, *The Handbook of Industrial Engineering*, Wiley, 1982.

H. Ansoff, A. Bosman, and P. Storms, editors, *Understanding and Managing Strategies Change*, North-Holland, 1982.

OTHER

Contributor of over forty articles and reviews to information systems and management journals. Editor in chief of *Systems, Objectives, Solutions;* associate editor of *MIS Quarterly;* editor of *Industrial Management* (now *Sloan Management Review*), 1967-68, and *Performance Evaluation Review*, 1972-73; member of editorial board of *Sloan Management Review*.

WORK IN PROGRESS: Research on the implementation of information systems; the impact of systems on the organization; and the management of information processing and expert systems.

SIDELIGHTS: Henry C. Lucas, Jr., wrote to *CA:* ''Information processing is the least well managed part of most organizations. Recent books and research attempt to improve the effectiveness of information processing through better management.''

M

MACAROV, David 1918-

PERSONAL: Born November 20, 1918, in Savannah, Ga.; son of Isaac (a manufacturer) and Fannie (Schoenberg) Macarov; married Frieda Rabinowitz (a registered nurse), December 5, 1946; children: Varda, Frances, Raanan, Annette. *Education:* University of Pittsburgh, B.Sc., 1951; Western Reserve University (now Case Western Reserve University), M.Sc., 1954; Brandeis University, Ph.D., 1968. *Religion:* Jewish.

ADDRESSES: Home—Nayot 8, Jerusalem, Israel. *Office*—Paul Baerwald School of Social Work, Hebrew University, Jerusalem, Israel.

CAREER: Hebrew University of Jerusalem, Paul Baerwald School of Social Work, Jerusalem, Israel, professor of social welfare and planning, 1959—, director of Joseph J. Schwartz Graduate Program for Training Directors and Senior Personnel for Community Centers, 1970-75. Visiting professor at Adelphi University, 1975-77, and University of Melbourne, 1977. *Military service:* U.S. Army Air Forces, 1942-45; served in China, Burma, and India; received Distinguished Unit Citation and battle cluster. Israel Defence Forces, 1947-49; became squadron leader.

MEMBER: International Association of Social Workers, International Society for Social Economics (member of board), World Future Society (Israel coordinator), Society for the Reduction of Human Labor (chairman), National Association of Social Workers, American Council on Social Work, National Conference of Jewish Communal Service, Council on Social Work Education, Society for Human Development, Industrial Relations Research Association.

WRITINGS:

Incentives to Work: The Effects of Unearned Income, Jossey-Bass, 1970.

The Short Course in Development Training, Massada, 1973.

(Contributor) D. Thursz and J. L. Vigilante, editors, *Meeting Human Needs: An Overview of Nine Countries,* Sage Publications, Volume 1, 1975, Volume 2, 1977.

Administration in the Social Work Curriculum, Council on Social Work Education, 1976.

Work and Welfare: The Unholy Alliance, Sage Publications, 1980.

Worker Productivity: Myths and Reality, Sage Publications, 1982.

(Editor and contributor) *People, Work, and Human Services in the Future,* School of Social Work, Adelphi University, 1982.

(Contributor) H. Didsbury, editor, *Working Now and in the Future,* World Future Society, 1983.

(Contributor) *The Global Economy: Today, Tomorrow, and the Transition,* World Future Society, 1985.

(Contributor) O. Riihinen, editor, *Social Policy and Post-Industrial Society,* International Council on Social Welfare, 1985.

(Contributor) Didsbury, editor, *Challenges and Opportunities: from Now to 2001,* World Future Society, 1986.

(Contributor) J. Dixon, editor, *Social Welfare in the Middle East,* Croom Helm, 1987.

(Contributor) J. Eaton, editor, *Colleges of Choice: The Enabling Impact of the Community College,* Macmillan, 1987.

(Contributor) E. Cornish, editor, *Careers Tomorrow: The Outlook for Work in a Changing World,* World Future Society, 1988.

Quitting Time: The End of Work, MCB University Press, 1988.

(Editor) *Social Welfare in Socialist Countries,* Croom Helm, in press.

*   *   *

MacINNES, Helen (Clark) 1907-1985
(Helen Highet)

PERSONAL: Born October 7, 1907, in Glasgow, Scotland; died September 30, 1985, following a stroke, in New York, N.Y.; came to United States in 1937, naturalized in 1951; daughter of Donald and Jessica (McDiarmid) MacInnes; married Gilbert Highet (a scholar and critic), September 22, 1932 (died January 20, 1978); children: Keith. *Education:* Glasgow University, M.A., 1928; University College, London, Diploma in Librarianship, 1931. *Religion:* Presbyterian.

ADDRESSES: Home—15 Jefferys Lane, East Hampton, N.Y. 11937.

CAREER: Acted with Oxford University Dramatic Society and with Experimental Theatre, both Oxford, England; writer, 1941-1985.

AWARDS, HONORS: Wallace Award, America-Scottish Foundation, 1973.

WRITINGS:

TRANSLATIONS FROM THE GERMAN

(With husband, Gilbert Highet; under name, Helen Highet) Otto Kiefer, *Sexual Life in Ancient Rome,* Routledge & Kegan Paul, 1934, Dutton, 1935, reprinted, AMS Press, 1972.

(With G. Highet; under name, Helen Highet) Gustav Mayer, *Friedrich Engels,* Chapman & Hall, 1936.

NOVELS

Above Suspicion (also see below), Little, Brown, 1941, reprinted, Fawcett, 1978.

Assignment in Brittany (also see below), Little, Brown, 1942, reprinted, Fawcett, 1978.

While Still We Live, Little, Brown, 1944 (published in England as *The Unconquerable,* Harrap, 1944), reprinted, Fawcett, 1964.

Horizon (also see below), Harrap, 1945, Little, Brown, 1946, reprinted, Fawcett, 1979.

Friends and Lovers, Little, Brown, 1947, reprinted, Fawcett, 1978.

Rest and Be Thankful, Little, Brown, 1949, reprinted, Fawcett, 1978.

Neither Five Nor Three, Harcourt, 1951, reprinted, Fawcett, 1978.

I and My True Love, Harcourt, 1953, reprinted, Fawcett, 1978.

Pray for a Brave Heart, Harcourt, 1955, reprinted, Fawcett, 1979.

North from Rome (also see below), Harcourt, 1958, reprinted, Fawcett, 1979.

Decision at Delphi, Harcourt, 1960.

Assignment: Suspense (contains *Above Suspicion, Horizon,* and *Assignment in Brittany),* Harcourt, 1961.

The Venetian Affair, Harcourt, 1963, reprinted, Fawcett, 1978.

Home Is the Hunter (two-act play), Harcourt, 1964.

The Double Image (also see below; Book-of-the-Month Club alternate selection), Harcourt, 1966.

The Salzburg Connection, Harcourt, 1968.

Message from Malaga, Harcourt, 1971.

Triple Threat (contains *Above Suspicion, North from Rome,* and *The Double Image),* Harcourt, 1973.

Snare of the Hunter, Harcourt, 1974.

Agent in Place, Harcourt, 1976.

Prelude to Terror, Harcourt, 1978.

The Hidden Target, Harcourt, 1980.

Cloak of Darkness, Harcourt, 1982.

Ride a Pale Horse, Harcourt, 1984.

SIDELIGHTS: Helen MacInnes's novels of international intrigue have long been regarded as among the most entertaining in the genre. As P. L. Buckley explains in the *National Review:* "In the long ago, before Ian Fleming's sex 'n' sadists and John Le Carre's weary professionals took over the espionage field, a young English woman carved herself out a following.... [Her] formula, a quarter of a century later, remains much the same, a couple of non-professionals inveigled into taking a hand from—hold your breath—patriotic motives with the good guys against the bad [and] the adventure taking place in some attractive foreign part." A *Christian Science Monitor* reviewer notes: "Novels that blot out our environment can hardly be measured by those that reveal it, but they have their place all the same. There is nothing quite like 'a good

read' to take us out of all our waiting-rooms. In her mysteries, Helen MacInnes has hit on just the formula, carefully combining a European countryside, much suspense, a little romance, and any number of likable, sensible characters."

MacInnes once commented on the objectives of her writing: "I'm continually interested in the question of how an ordinary guy of intelligence and guts resists oppression.... My basic characters have a certain decency and honesty. They still believe in standards of human conduct, and they rise to the occasion without fear.... [In my stories,] suspense is not achieved by hiding things from the reader [who]. . . always would know who did it. The question is, when is the event going to take place and how can you stop it? A reader may know everything, but still be scared stiff by the situation."

MacInnes painstakingly researched her books, wanting them to be as accurate—and credible—as possible. A typical MacInnes novel, for example, begins with a kernel of truth, usually drawn from a brief newspaper clipping which has caught the author's eye and imagination. Around this seemingly insignificant fact, MacInnes would build her story, embellishing it with information discovered in the course of extensive reading (which she insisted was "the best training" for a would-be-writer) or from personal experience and observation (she visited and became thoroughly familiar with nearly every place she wrote about). To add even more authenticity to her novels, MacInnes made sure that such things as street names and directions were correct, though she occasionally invented a town or street for the purposes of plot. "Underlying everything," MacInnes once explained, "is the fact that I'm interested in international politics [and] in analyzing news, [for I try] to read newspapers both on and between the lines, to deduct and add, to utilize memory."

Some reviewers find the inclusion of such detail to be overwhelming at times; many of these same reviewers also criticize MacInnes for what they perceive as shallow and cliche-ridden characterization. A *National Observer* critic, though admitting that MacInnes is probably "second to none in her power to evoke and employ a setting," feels that her heroes and heroines "are rather flimsy stuff, curiously untouched by the deep drama in which the author involves them." In addition, the critic reports, "there is the matter of length, sometimes a difficulty with MacInnes books. [*The Salzburg Connection,* for example,] could well have been about 100 pages shorter. Not that it seems padded—merely overanalytical, a bit too discursive: The lady tells us perhaps a bit *too* much." A reviewer for *Spectator* agrees with this evaluation: "[MacInnes's] plots are invariably as twisty and opaque as her heroes are broad-shouldered and thoroughly transparent.... After 380 pages the enemy are routed and [the hero] drives into the sun.... I found the novel far too long, but Miss MacInnes's fans will not be disappointed."

Anatole Broyard of the *New York Times* similarly comments that, unlike "the new suspense movies, in which nothing is explained; in which there are no transitions and the actors never change expressions," in a MacInnes book, "everything is slow—talk, talk, talk,—and the burden of [interpretation] is on you too." In addition, Broyard notes, "it would not be unreasonable to say that [she]. . . ought to avoid portraying desperate men who will stop at nothing. But her women are not much better.... [The author's] forte—her intimate evocation of the glamorous cities of Europe—is so overlaid with her characters' cliches that we see them as if through a chill rain. . . . Though [MacInnes] obviously knows these places well, we can't enjoy them in the company she has given us.''

Joseph McLellen of *Book World,* however, is convinced that there is much more to admire in a Helen MacInnes novel than there is to criticize: ''One reads Helen MacInnes for a good story well-told, of course, but also for reassurance that some things remain unchanged. . . . She has been writing her kind of novel for nearly 40 years, and her writing has reflected the realities of a changing world, but the basic approach has remained refreshingly the same. She writes of decent people in bad situations. There are certain truths to be learned, certain things awry to be set right, and her sympathetic characters go about what must be done, a bit clumsily and not without pain— but goodness wins out, and (a growing rarity in this kind of writing) it is recognizable as goodness. . . . Beyond the plot lie the values without which a good plot is merely a meaningless spinning of wheels. . . . [Her novels are] full of the things that make life worthwhile—not a perfectly mixed martini or an invigorating tumble in the hay, but works of art, dreams, the feelings of home, family, specially cherished places, friendship and (the only crime unthinkable in most suspense fiction) love. . . . Partly because she is a woman and much more because she is determinedly a bit old-fashioned, Helen MacInnes insists that [the good guys *do* differ from the bad guys] and that the difference is important.''

MacInnes's novels have sold over twenty-three million copies in their various American editions and have been translated into twenty-two languages. Just before MacInnes's death in 1985, her novel *Ride a Pale Horse* appeared on the *New York Times* paperback bestseller list for the first time.

MEDIA ADAPTATIONS: Several of MacInnes's novels have been made into films, including *Above Suspicion,* 1943, *Assignment in Brittany,* 1943, and *The Venetian Affair,* 1967, all by Metro-Goldwyn-Mayer, Inc., and *The Salzburg Connection,* 1972, by Twentieth Century-Fox Film Corp.

AVOCATIONAL INTERESTS: The American West, travel, music.

BIOGRAPHICAL/CRITICAL SOURCES:

BOOKS

Breit, Harvey, *The Writer Observed,* World Publishing, 1956.
Contemporary Literary Criticism, Gale, Volume 27, 1984, Volume 39, 1986.
Newquist, Roy, *Counterpoint,* Rand McNally, 1964.
Writer's Yearbook, Writer's Digest, 1967.

PERIODICALS

Atlantic Monthly, June, 1944.
Best Sellers, September 13, 1968.
Book World, September 21, 1978.
Chicago Tribune Magazine, May 4, 1980.
Christian Science Monitor, October 3, 1968, March 27, 1974, September 27, 1978.
Commonweal, August 8, 1941, May 26, 1944.
Cosmopolitan, January, 1967.
Harper's, December, 1968.
National Observer, November 11, 1968.
National Review, January 14, 1969.
New York Herald Tribune Book Review, August 7, 1949, October 30, 1960.
New York Herald Tribune Books, July 13, 1941, July 12, 1942, October 30, 1960.

New York Times, January 8, 1966, September 16, 1971, August 13, 1976, September 26, 1980, October 1, 1985.
New York Times Book Review, May 26, 1946, August 17, 1947, November 29, 1963, January 9, 1966, December 17, 1978, January 11, 1981, September 26, 1982, November 11, 1984.
Punch, March 5, 1969.
Saturday Review, February 14, 1953.
Spectator, February 21, 1969.
Times (London), October 2, 1985.
Times Literary Supplement, October 1, 1976.
Washington Post, October 20, 1963, February 9, 1969, October 12, 1984.

OBITUARIES:

PERIODICALS

Chicago Tribune, October 3, 1985.
Los Angeles Times, October 2, 1985.
New York Times, October 1, 1985.
Times (London), October 2, 1985.
Washington Post, October 2, 1985.*

*   *   *

MACKIN, Anita
See DONSON, Cyril

*   *   *

MacLEAN, Alistair (Stuart)   1922(?)-1987
(Ian Stuart)

PERSONAL: Born 1922 (some sources say 1923), in Glasgow, Scotland; died of heart failure following a stroke, February 2, 1987, in Munich, West Germany; married Gisela Hinrichsen (divorced, 1972); married Mary Marcelle Georgeus (a film production company executive), October 13, 1972 (divorced, 1977); children: Lachlan, Michael, and Alistair; Curtis (stepson). *Education:* University of Glasgow, M.A., 1953.

ADDRESSES: Office—c/o William Collins & Sons, Ltd., 8 Grafton St., London W1X 3LA, England.

CAREER: Writer, 1955-87. Former teacher of English and history at Gallowflat Secondary School in Glasgow, Scotland. *Military service:* Royal Navy, 1941-46; served as torpedo man on convoy escorts.

WRITINGS:

NOVELS

H.M.S. Ulysses, Collins, 1955, Doubleday, 1956.
The Guns of Navarone (also see below), Doubleday, 1957.
South by Java Head, Doubleday, 1958.
The Secret Ways, Doubleday, 1959 (published in England as *The Last Frontier,* Collins, 1959).
Night without End, Doubleday, 1960.
Fear Is the Key, Doubleday, 1961.
The Golden Rendezvous (also see below), Doubleday, 1962.
Ice Station Zebra, Doubleday, 1963.
When Eight Bells Toll (also see below), Doubleday, 1966.
Where Eagles Dare (also see below; Companion Book Club and Readers' Book Club selections), Doubleday, 1967.
Force 10 from Navarone (also see below), Doubleday, 1968.
Puppet on a Chain (also see below), Doubleday, 1969.
Caravan to Vaccares (also see below), Doubleday, 1970.
Bear Island, Doubleday, 1971.

The Way to Dusty Death, Doubleday, 1973.
Breakheart Pass (also see below), Doubleday, 1974.
Circus, Doubleday, 1975.
The Golden Gate, Doubleday, 1976.
Seawitch, Doubleday, 1977.
Goodbye, California, Collins, 1977, Doubleday, 1978.
Athabasca, Doubleday, 1980.
River of Death, Collins, 1981, Doubleday, 1982.
Partisans, Collins, 1982, Doubleday, 1983.
Floodgate, Collins, 1983, Doubleday, 1984.
San Andreas, Collins, 1984, Doubleday, 1985.
Santorini, Collins, 1986, Doubleday, 1987.

OMNIBUS VOLUMES

Five War Stories, Collins, 1978.
Four Great Adventure Stories, Collins, 1981.

UNDER PSEUDONYM IAN STUART

The Black Shrike, Scribner, 1961 (published in England as *The Dark Crusader,* Collins, 1961, published under name Alistair MacLean, Collins, 1963).
The Satan Bug, Scribner, 1962.

SCREENPLAYS

"The Guns of Navarone" (based on novel of same title), Columbia, 1959.
"Where Eagles Dare" (based on novel of same title), Metro-Goldwyn-Mayer, 1969.
"When Eight Bells Toll" (based on novel of same title), Rank, 1971.
"Puppet on a Chain" (based on novel of same title), Scotia-Barber, 1971.
"Caravan to Vaccares" (based on novel of same title), Rank, 1974.
"Breakheart Pass" (based on novel of same title), United Artists, 1976.
"The Golden Rendezvous" (based on novel of same title), Rank, 1977.
"Force 10 from Navarone" (based on novel of same title), American-International, 1978.

Also author of "Deakin."

OTHER

Lawrence of Arabia (juvenile), Random House, 1962 (published in England as *All About Lawrence of Arabia,* W. H. Allen, 1962).
Captain Cook (nonfiction), Doubleday, 1972.
Alistair MacLean Introduces Scotland, McGraw-Hill, 1972.
(With John Denis) *Hostage Tower,* Fontana, 1980.
(With Denis) *Air Force One Is Down,* Fontana, 1981.
The Lonely Sea (story collection), Collins, 1985, Doubleday, 1986.

Also author of *A Layman Looks at Cancer,* for the British Cancer Council.

SIDELIGHTS: Alistair MacLean once claimed that he wrote fast, taking only thirty-five days to complete a novel, because he disliked writing and didn't want to spend much time at it. He also claimed never to re-read his work once it was finished and to never read reviews of his books. According to the *New York Post,* MacLean once explained: "I'm not a novelist, I'm a storyteller. There's no art in what I do, no mystique." Despite his disclaimers, MacLean's many adventure novels sold over 30 million copies and were translated into a score of languages. He was, Edwin McDowell noted in the *New York Times,* "one of the biggest-selling adventure writers in the world."

MacLean's first success as a writer came while he was teaching school in his native Glasgow, Scotland, in the mid-1950s. A local newspaper, the *Glasgow Herald,* sponsored a story contest and MacLean's entry about a fishing family in the West Highlands won first prize. The story attracted the interest of an editor at the publishing house of William Collins & Sons when he noticed his wife crying over a short story in the local newspaper and asked to see it for himself. It was MacLean's winning entry. The editor, Ian Chapman, enjoyed the story so much that he called MacLean and suggested that he try his hand at a novel. MacLean agreed. Over the next three months he worked evenings on the novel, *H.M.S. Ulysses,* drawing upon his years as a torpedo man in the Royal Navy. The novel came out in September of 1955 and sold a record 250,000 copies in hardcover in its first six months. It was to be the first in a long string of best-selling novels.

H.M.S. Ulysses is based on MacLean's own experiences during World War II. For much of the war he worked on convoy ships delivering much-needed supplies to Britain, the Soviet Union, and other Allied nations. The work was perilous. MacLean was wounded twice by the Nazis and captured by the Japanese. The Japanese tortured him, pulling out his teeth "without benefit of anesthetic," as MacLean once remarked. The ordeal, Bob McKelvey noted in the *Detroit Free Press,* "left him bearing a grudge against the Japanese until his death."

The pain and hardship of the war at sea is evident in *H.M.S. Ulysses,* the story of a convoy in the North Atlantic which battles German submarines as well as the treacherous weather. "Even in his first novel," Robert A. Lee wrote in his *Alistair MacLean: The Key Is Fear,* "MacLean has an acute sense of plot and structure, and it is clear that he understands quite well the consequences of action as defined by the necessities of story-telling." Reviewers of the time found faults with MacLean's work, citing a melodramatic tendency, for example, but saw the novel as a forceful and realistic portrayal of the war at sea. E. B. Garside of the *New York Times* claimed that "this novel is a gripping thing. . . . Mr. MacLean, former torpedoman, now a Scottish schoolmaster, has caught the bitter heart of the matter." Writing in the *Saturday Review,* T. E. Cooney maintained that "Mr. MacLean's true achievement [is] that of setting down in print the image of war, so that any reader, regardless of his experience, can say, That is what it was like."

This "first and greatest work," as Martin Sieff of the *Washington Times* called *H.M.S. Ulysses,* was MacLean's personal favorite and the novel which he believed was his best work. It also set the pattern for much of his later novels. Its emphasis on men battling the elements as well as the immoral machinations of other men was to recur in all of MacLean's later books. Speaking of the clear demarcation between good and evil to be found in MacLean's work, Sieff explained that MacLean's "novels are imbued with a powerful, uncompromising moral vision—that there is wickedness in the world and that it must be recognized and fought to the death, come what may."

Despite the success of his first novel, MacLean was too cautious to leave his teaching job. He suspected that the book's success might prove to be only a fluke. It wasn't until his second novel, *The Guns of Navarone,* appeared in 1957 to popular acclaim that he became a full-time writer. This novel, telling of a mission to destroy an enemy gun installation during the Second World War, proved to be "MacLean's most famous and popular novel." as Lee observed. It is, William Hogan remarked in the *San Francisco Chronicle,* "a tense, compelling, extraordinarily readable adventure." The book sold some 400,000 copies in its first six months and is still a worldwide best-seller. In 1959, it was adapted as a successful motion picture starring Gregory Peck and David Niven and produced by Carl Forman.

After the success of *The Guns of Navarone,* MacLean moved to Switzerland, where he found the climate and tax laws to his liking. For a time he wrote one new novel every year. His usual writing schedule began early in the morning and lasted until early afternoon, working away on an IBM electric typewriter. "He never rewrote anything," Caroline Moorehead revealed in the London *Times,* "and resisted, with considerable stubbornness, even minor editorial changes proposed by [his publisher] Collins." MacLean's faith in his work proved to be justified. Once, after receiving the manuscript for a MacLean novel and judging it unsatisfactory, his publisher dispatched a representative to speak with MacLean about rewriting it. By the time the agent arrived in Switzerland, however, film rights to the book had already been sold and the rewrite idea was quietly shelved. "I don't write the first sentence," MacLean told Moorehead, "until I have the last in mind. . . . I don't even re-read. One draft and it's away." MacLean never kept copies of any of his books, preferring to give them away to friends and admirers. "I don't think any are very good," he explained to Moorehead. "I'm slightly dissatisfied with all of them. I'm pleased enough if at the end of the day I produce a saleable product—and that I do."

By the early 1970s, MacLean's books had sold over 20 million copies and had been made into several popular films. He was one of the top ten best-selling writers in the world and arguably the one whose books were most often adapted for the screen. MacLean made enough money from his writing that at one point in the 1960s he gave it up and went into business as a hotelier, buying the famous Jamaica Inn and three other hotels. But he found running a hotel chain too boring. When a filmmaker offered him the chance to write a screenplay in 1967, MacLean accepted. The resulting work, *Where Eagles Dare,* was a bestseller and a successful film and MacLean returned to his book-a-year schedule again.

The enormous amount of money that his adventure novels earned him never seemed to alter MacLean's lifestyle. Several observers noted that he lived frugally, content with few of the luxuries one might associate with such a successful writer. MacLean's frugality was in part the result of his innate caution. He had been raised in poverty and was always aware that his wealth might prove to be transitory. And, as Moorehead noted, he always felt "that it is morally wrong to earn so much." A writer for the London *Times* claimed that MacLean's "vast wealth lay uncomfortably on his conscience." At the time of his death in 1987, MacLean was living in a modest apartment in Switzerland, where he bought his own food and prepared his own meals.

Evaluations of MacLean's career are often colored by the sheer popularity of his books, which moved some critics to see him as nothing more than a writer who catered to mass tastes. And MacLean's flippant dismissals of his work abet this view. One such critic is Reg Gadney. Writing in *London Magazine,* Gadney described a typical MacLean adventure as "a hero, a band of men, hostile climate, a ruthless enemy. . . . The pace of the narrative consists in keeping the hero or heroes struggling on

in the face of adversity. There's little time for reflection upon anything which does not contribute to the race: no characterization, merely the odd caricature; no subtlety of ploy, anything other than a fatuous one would get in the way. So the refinements are discarded and the narrative is a sprint from start to finish."

Yet, at his best, MacLean moved other critics to praise his work. Tim Heald of the London *Times* called him the "Yarn-spinner Laureate" and "one of the country's most distinguished old thriller writers." Heald affectionately explained that MacLean "is at his best on the bridge of an indomitable British craft fighting its way through stupendous seas. The crew—and part of the plot—will resemble one of those stories in which an Englishman, a Scotsman, an Irishman, and a Welshman say or do something incredibly characteristic. They will be united, not only against the appalling gale, but also against a number of perfectly filthy foreigners." According to Sieff, MacLean's strong points included his "unmatched narrative drive, his complex plots and his—in the earlier novels—powerfully compelling characters." Sieff maintained that MacLean "was also a master of black, biting wit—a quality for which he was seldom given credit."

Most reviewers did credit MacLean with writing absorbing adventure novels, a task he performed with particular skill in such books as *H.M.S. Ulysses, The Guns of Navarone, Ice Station Zebra,* and *Where Eagles Dare.* In a review of *Ice Station Zebra,* the story of a nuclear submarine in peril under the Arctic ice cap, a *Times Literary Supplement* critic maintained that "the story evolves in a succession of masterful puzzles as astonishing as they are convincing. . . . There is so much swift-moving action, so much clever innuendo and such a feeling for relevant detail that one cannot help but be fascinated by the mind at work here." Speaking of *Where Eagles Dare,* Anthony Boucher of the *New York Times Book Review* described it as "a real dazzler of a thriller, with vivid action, fine set pieces of suspense, and a virtuoso display of startling plot twists."

Despite such appreciation of his work, MacLean always dismissed the value of his accomplishment. According to McKelvey, the author once claimed: "I am just a journeyman. I blunder along from one book to the next, always hopeful that one day I will write something really good." This appraisal of his work was not shared by Sieff, who ranked MacLean's *H.M.S. Ulysses* with "Nicholas Montsarrat's 'The Cruel Sea' as the greatest novel to come out of the maritime war." Lee concluded that "MacLean's books work best when he allies evil and the natural forces of violence, when he makes the structure of his novels an undulation of tension, release, and tension, when he manages to twist his plots in such a way as to reveal parts of the mystery bit by bit, until a final stunning denouement at the end. When all these elements mesh together in one harmonious whole, the result is adventure writing at its best." MacLean, according to Linda Bridges of the *National Review,* was "one of the best suspense writers around."

MEDIA ADAPTATIONS: South by Java Head was filmed by Twentieth Century-Fox, 1959; *The Secret Ways* was filmed by Universal, 1961; *The Satan Bug* was filmed by United Artists, 1964; *Ice Station Zebra* was filmed by Metro-Goldwyn-Mayer, 1968; *Fear Is the Key* was filmed by Metro-Goldwyn-Mayer—EMI, 1972. *H.M.S. Ulysses* and *Bear Island* were also filmed.

AVOCATIONAL INTERESTS: Science and astronomy.

BIOGRAPHICAL/CRITICAL SOURCES:

BOOKS

Contemporary Literary Criticism, Gale, Volume 3, 1975, Volume 13, 1980.
Lee, Robert A., *Alistair MacLean: The Key Is Fear*, Borgo Press, 1976.

PERIODICALS

Books and Bookmen, May, 1968, November, 1971.
Glasgow Herald, March 6, 1954, September 27, 1955.
Life, November 26, 1971.
London Magazine, December-January, 1972-73.
National Review, January 31, 1975.
New Statesman, February 20, 1976.
New York Times, January 15, 1956, March 2, 1984.
New York Times Book Review, December 31, 1967, March 12, 1978.
San Francisco Chronicle, February 3, 1957.
Saturday Review, January 14, 1956.
Spectator, January 22, 1977.
Times (London), September 8, 1983, December 13, 1984, October 7, 1985, December 4, 1986.
Times Literary Supplement, August 9, 1963, September 14, 1973.
Washington Post, March 6, 1982, March 12, 1984.

OBITUARIES:

PERIODICALS

AB Bookman's Weekly, February 23, 1987.
Chicago Sun-Times, February 3, 1987.
Chicago Tribune, February 3, 1987.
Detroit Free Press, February 3, 1987.
Los Angeles Times, February 3, 1987.
New York Post, February 3, 1987.
New York Times, February 3, 1987.
San Francisco Examiner, February 3, 1987.
Times (London), February 3, 1987.
Washington Post, February 3, 1987.
Washington Times, February 3, 1987.*

—Sketch by Thomas Wiloch

*　　　*　　　*

MAILER, Norman 1923-

PERSONAL: Born January 31, 1923, in Long Branch, N.J.; son of Isaac Barnett (an accountant) and Fanny (owner of a small business; maiden name, Schneider) Mailer; married Beatrice Silverman, 1944 (divorced, 1952); married Adele Morales (an artist), 1954 (divorced, 1962); married Lady Jeanne Campbell, 1962 (divorced, 1963); married Beverly Rentz Bentley (an actress), 1963 (divorced, 1980); married Carol Stevens, 1980 (divorced, 1980); married Norris Church (an artist), 1980; children: (first marriage) Susan; (second marriage) Danielle, Elizabeth Anne; (third marriage) Kate; (fourth marriage) Michael Burks, Stephen McLeod; (fifth marriage) Maggie Alexandra; (sixth marriage) John Buffalo. *Education:* Harvard University, S.B. (cum laude), 1943; graduate studies at Sorbonne, Paris, France, 1947-48. *Politics:* "Left Conservative."

ADDRESSES: Home—142 Columbia Heights, Brooklyn, N.Y.; and Provincetown, Mass. *Agent*—Scott Meredith, Inc., 580 Fifth Ave., New York, N.Y. 10022.

CAREER: Writer. Producer and director of, and actor in, films, including "Wild 90," 1967, and "Maidstone: A Mystery," 1968; producer, "Beyond the Law," 1967; actor, "Ragtime," 1981; director, "Tough Guys Don't Dance," 1987. Lecturer at colleges and universities, 1950-89; University of Pennsylvania Pappas Fellow, 1983. Candidate for democratic nomination in mayoral race, New York, N.Y., 1960 and 1969. Founder, Fifth Estate (merged with Committee for Action Research on the Intelligence Community), 1973. *Military service:* U.S. Army, 1944-46, field artillery observer; became infantry rifleman serving in the Philippines and Japan.

MEMBER: PEN (president of American Center, 1984-86), American Academy and Institute of Arts and Letters.

AWARDS, HONORS: Story magazine college fiction prize, 1941, for "The Greatest Thing in the World"; National Institute and American Academy grant in literature, 1960; elected to National Institute of Arts and Letters, 1967; National Book Award nomination, 1967, for *Why Are We in Vietnam?;* National Book Award for nonfiction, 1968, for *Miami and the Siege of Chicago;* National Book Award for nonfiction, Pulitzer Prize in letters-general nonfiction, and George Polk Award, all 1969, all for *Armies of the Night;* Edward MacDowell Medal, MacDowell Colony, 1973, for outstanding service to arts; National Arts Club Gold Medal, 1976; National Book Critics Circle nomination and Notable Book citation, American Library Association, Pulitzer Prize in letters, all 1979, and American Book Award nomination, 1980, all for *The Executioner's Song;* Emmy nomination for best adaptation, for script for "The Executioner's Song"; Rose Award, Lord & Taylor, 1985, for public accomplishment.

WRITINGS:

NOVELS

The Naked and the Dead, Rinehart, 1948, limited deluxe edition, Collector's Book Club (London), 1949, reprinted with introduction by Chester E. Eisenger, Holt, c.1968, limited edition with illustrations by Alan E. Corber, Franklin Library, 1979.
Barbary Shore, Rinehart, 1951, reprinted, Fertig, 1980.
The Deer Park (also see below), Putnam, 1955, reprinted with preface and notes by Mailer, Berkley, 1976.
An American Dream (first written in serial form for *Esquire*, January-August, 1964), Dial, 1965, reprinted, Holt, 1987.
Why Are We in Vietnam?, Putnam, 1967, reprinted with preface by Mailer, Putnam, 1977.
A Transit to Narcissus: A Facsimile of the Original Typescript with an Introduction by the Author (limited edition of unpublished 1944 manuscript), Fertig, 1978.
The Executioner's Song (excerpted in *Playboy* in 1979; also see below), Little, Brown, 1979.
Ancient Evenings, Little, Brown, 1983.
Tough Guys Don't Dance (also see below), Random House, 1984, signed edition, Franklin Library, 1984.

Also author of *No Percentage*, 1941.

NONFICTION NARRATIVES

The Armies of the Night: History as a Novel, the Novel as History, New American Library, 1968.
Miami and the Siege of Chicago, New American Library, 1968, reprinted, D. I. Fine, 1986 (published in England as *Miami and the Siege of Chicago: An Informal History of the American Political Conventions of 1968*, Weidenfeld and Nicolson, 1969).

Of a Fire on the Moon (first appeared in *Life* magazine), Little, Brown, 1970, reprinted, Grove, 1985 (published in England as *A Fire on the Moon*, Weidenfeld & Nicolson, 1970).

King of the Hill: On the Fight of the Century (also see below), New American Library, 1971.

St. George and the Godfather, New American Library, 1972.

The Fight, Little, Brown, 1975.

NONFICTION

The Bullfight: A Photographic Narrative with Text by Norman Mailer (with record of Mailer reading from text; also see below), CBS Legacy Collection/Macmillan, 1967.

The Prisoner of Sex (first published in *Harper's* magazine), Little, Brown, 1971, Primus, c.1985.

Marilyn: A Biography, Grosset and Dunlap, 1973, reprinted with new chapter by Mailer, Warner, 1975.

The Faith of Graffiti (also see below), photographs by Jon Naar, Praeger, 1974 (published in England as *Watching My Name Go By*, Matthews Miller Dunbar, 1974).

(Editor and author of introductions) *Genius and Lust: A Journey through the Major Writings of Henry Miller*, Grove, 1976.

Of a Small and Modest Malignancy, Wicked and Bristling with Dots (essay; also see below), limited edition, Lord John, 1980.

Huckleberry Finn: Alive at 100 (booklet; criticism), limited edition, Caliban Press, 1985.

SCREENPLAYS

"Wild 90" (adaptation of *The Deer Park*; 16mm film), Supreme Mix, 1967.

"Beyond the Law" (16mm film), Supreme Mix/Evergreen Films, 1968.

"Maidstone: A Mystery" (16mm film; also see below), Supreme Mix, 1971.

"The Executioner's Song," Film Communication Inc. Productions, 1982.

"Tough Guys Don't Dance," Zoetrope, 1987.

Also author of movie script for a modern version of King Lear.

COLLECTIONS

The White Negro: Superficial Reflections on the Hipster (essays; includes "Communications: Reflections on Hipsterism"; "The White Negro" first published in *Dissent* magazine, summer, 1957; also see below), City Lights, 1957.

Advertisements for Myself (short stories, verse, articles, and essays, with narrative; includes "The White Negro," "The Man Who Studied Yoga," and "The Time of Her Time"), Putnam, 1959, reprinted with preface by Mailer, Berkley, 1976.

The Presidential Papers (also see below), Putnam, 1963, reprinted with preface by Mailer, 1976.

Cannibals and Christians (also see below), Dial, 1966, abridged edition, Panther, 1979.

Some Honorable Men: Political Conventions 1960-1972 (collection of previously published nonfiction narratives), Little, Brown, 1976.

The Short Fiction of Norman Mailer (also see below), Dell, 1967, reprinted, Fertig, 1980.

The Idol and the Octopus: Political Writings on the Kennedy and Johnson Administrations (includes selections from *The Presidential Papers* and *Cannibals and Christians*), Dell, 1968.

The Long Patrol: 25 Years of Writing from the Work of Norman Mailer, edited by Robert F. Lucid, World, 1971.

Existential Errands (includes *The Bullfight: A Photographic Narrative with Text by Norman Mailer*, "A Course in Filmmaking," and *King of the Hill;* also see below), Little, Brown, 1972.

The Essential Mailer (includes *The Short Fiction of Norman Mailer* and *Existential Errands*), New English Library, 1982.

Pieces and Pontifications (essays and interviews first appearing 1973-77; includes *The Faith of Graffiti* and *Of a Small and Modest Malignancy, Wicked and Bristling with Dots*), edited by Michael Lennon, Little, Brown, 1982, published as *Pieces*, 1982, published as *Pontifications: Interviews*, 1982.

OTHER

Deaths for the Ladies and Other Disasters: Being a Run of Poems, Short Poems, Very Short Poems, and Turns of Prose, Putnam, 1962, reprinted with introduction by Mailer, New American Library, 1971.

Gargoyle, Guignol, False Closets (booklet; first published in *Architectural Forum*, April, 1964), privately printed, 1964.

The Deer Park: A Play (two-act; adaptation of novel *The Deer Park;* first produced Off-Broadway at Theater De Lys, January 31, 1967), Dell, 1967.

Maidstone: A Mystery (film script; includes essay "A Course in Filmmaking"), New American Library, 1971.

The Pulitzer Prize for Fiction, Little, Brown, 1967, reprint, 1980.

Of Women and Their Elegance (fictional interview), photographs by Milton H. Greene, Simon and Schuster, 1980.

"The Executioner's Song" (two-part television movie), Film Communications Inc. Productions, 1982.

The Last Night: A Story (first published in "Esquire," 1962), limited, signed edition, Targ Editions, 1984.

"Strawhead" (play), first produced at Actors Studio, January 3, 1985.

CONTRIBUTOR

Writers at Work, Third Series, Viking, 1967.

Running Against the Machine: The Mailer-Breslin Campaign, edited by Peter Manso, Doubleday, 1969.

(Author of introduction and captions) *The 1974 Marilyn Monroe Datebook*, photographs by Eve Arnold and others, Simon and Schuster, 1973.

Writer's Choice, edited by Rust Hills, McKay, 1974.

(Author of preface) Hallie and Whit Burnett, *A Fiction Writer's Handbook*, Harper, 1975.

(Author of foreword) Eugene Kennedy, *St. Patrick's Day with Mayor Daley and Other Things Too Good to Miss*, Seabury, 1976.

(Author of introduction) Abbie Hoffman, *Soon To Be a Major Motion Picture*, Putnam, 1980.

Black Messiah, Vagabond, 1981.

(Author of introduction) Jack Henry Abbott, *In the Belly of the Beast: Letters from Prison*, Random House, 1981.

(Author of foreword) Harold Conrad, *Dear Muffo: 35 Years in the Fast Lane*, Stein & Day, 1982.

Also contributor to anthologies. Author of column for *Esquire*, "The Big Bite," 1962-63; columnist for *Village Voice*, January-May, 1946, and for *Commentary*, 1962-63. Contributor to numerous periodicals, including *Harper's, Rolling Stone, New Republic, Playboy, New York Times Book Review*, and

Parade. Contributing editor of *Dissent,* 1953-69; co-founding editor of *Village Voice,* 1955.

SIDELIGHTS: When *The Naked and the Dead,* drawing on Norman Mailer's experiences in the Pacific theater of World War II, was published in 1948, *New York Times* critic Orville Prescott called it "the most impressive novel about the Second World War that I have ever read." The large, ambitious book was number one on the *New York Times* bestseller list for eleven consecutive weeks and was the object of continuing critical admiration. The twenty-five-year-old literary novice was suddenly famous and at the dawn of a prolific career in which he would henceforth be forever a public figure and measured, by others as well as himself, against his precocious success. "I had the freak of luck to start high on the mountain, and go down sharp while others were passing me," wrote the author in *Advertisements for Myself,* in which he shows himself determined from the outset "to hit the longest ball ever to go up into the accelerated hurricane air of our American letters."

Mailer's second novel, *Barbary Shore,* centers on a young leftist, Michael Lovett, who lives in a Brooklyn Heights boarding house and who discovers revolutionary socialism as the only alternative to contemporary barbarism. Hilary Mills reports in *Mailer: A Biography* that the book was dismissed by Mailer's French mentor, Jean Malaquais, as "a political tract, not a novel"; and *Time* labeled it "paceless, tasteless and graceless." Still suffering from what he called in *Advertisements for Myself* "the peculiar megalomania of a young writer who is determined to become an important writer," Mailer was devastated by the novel's hostile reception and became more preoccupied than ever not only with attaining his grandiose literary goals but also with establishing himself as an important public figure.

Mailer became part of a circle of prominent cultural figures in New York and began conceiving an ambitious cycle of eight novels centering on a universal mythical hero named Sergius O'Shaugnessy. The short story "The Man Who Studied Yoga" was designed as a prologue to the series, and *The Deer Park,* published in 1955, was its first installment. Three years in the making, *The Deer Park,* which Mailer later adapted for theater, also proved to be the cycle's only volume. Primarily because of the work's overt sexuality, Rinehart, Mailer's original publisher, backed out of an agreement to publish the novel, a study in the powers of art, sex, and money in a hedonist resort in southern California. Several other houses rejected the manuscript before it was accepted by G. P. Putnam's. Reviews of *The Deer Park* were mixed, with Brendan Gill asserting in the *New Yorker:* "Only a writer of the greatest and most reckless talent could have flung it between covers."

Mailer continued recklessly throughout the 1950s, attempting to embody the values of "the hipster" as he defined them in a defiant essay "The White Negro": "energy, life, sex, force, the Yoga's *prana,* the Reichian's orgone, Lawrence's blood, Hemingway's 'good,' the Shavian life-force; 'It'; God; not the God of the churches but the unachievable whisper of the mystery within the sex." His own flirtations with the frontiers of sex, drugs, violence, and belligerency culminated in a boisterous party on the evening of November 19, 1960, at the conclusion of which the drunken author stabbed his wife Adele. Mailer was arrested, but, after Adele refused to press charges, he received a suspended sentence.

It took a decade after *The Deer Park* for Mailer to publish his next novel, *An American Dream,* in 1965. The book, about a prominent professor of existential psychology who murders his wealthy wife, was a great commercial success and the object of intense critical controversy. Elizabeth Hardwick described it in *Partisan Review* as "a very dirty book—dirty and extremely ugly," while John Adlridge's review in *Life* called the novel "a major creative breakthrough." The protagonist of *An American Dream,* Stephen Rojack, was loosely modeled after Mailer himself, and his strongest writing now included explicitly autobiographical elements. In *Advertisements for Myself,* he brashly anthologized a selection of his own writings and interpolated a running, and pugnacious, personal commentary. As co-founding editor of the *Village Voice* and as a regular contributor of nonfiction to it and to *Dissent* and *Esquire,* Mailer found an effective arena for his combative ego. It is arguably in his nonfiction writing, directly engaging contemporary issues in his own distinctive voice, that Mailer's special talents as antic public gadfly are most effectively exploited. His provocative self-portrait as philosophical "existentialist" and political "left conservative" ensured that his own personality would be a continuing stage for dramatic conflict.

Mailer cultivated the mystique of personal violence through a close friendship with professional boxer Jose Torres. As a writer and public figure, Mailer increasingly placed himself at the epicenter of contemporary trends and events—political campaigns, space exploration, feminist polemics, boxing, peace demonstrations. He became a familiar, notorious presence on television talk shows and, in 1969, a very unconventional candidate for the Democratic nomination for mayor of New York, advocating that the city secede from the state. He and his running mate the writer Jimmy Breslin finished fourth in a field of five. Mailer was also producer, director, writer, and star of three low-budget improvisational films that he and his friends made in rapid succession—"Wild 90," "Beyond the Law," and "Maidstone." His many marriages and progeny added to the publicity surrounding the author who in 1968 described himself as "a warrior, presumptive general, expolitical candidate, embattled enfant terrible of the literary world, wise father of six children, radical intellectual, existential philosopher, hard-working author, champion of obscenity, husband of four battling sweet wives, amiable bar drinker, and much exaggerated street fighter, party giver, hostess insulter. . . ." Though the number of wives and children would soon change, the summary accurately reflects his protean personality.

This self-portrait appears in *The Armies of the Night,* a literary triumph that redeemed Mailer in the eyes of critics who were convinced he had squandered his talents in playing the part of a national celebrity. In this book, a very personal account of a massive demonstration against the Vietnam War staged in front of the Pentagon on October 21, 1967, Mailer joined his artistic skills with his own compulsive involvement in the event to create a work that is more than insightful reportage of a momentous phenomenon. Mailer's status as both participant and observer resulted in a night in jail and a book that won both the Pulitzer Prize and the National Book Award. *The Armies of the Night* comically inflates Mailer's role in the proceedings to create both a bracing portrait of individual orneriness in combat against the tyranny of modern mass society and a meditation on the relationship between the self and history. Subtitled *History as a Novel, the Novel as History,* the work is likely to be among the most enduring of many contemporary attempts to contest the boundaries between fiction and chronicle. Richard Gilman's review in the *New Republic* applauded "the central, rather wonderful achievement of the book, that in it history and personality confront each other with a new sense of liberation."

In *The Armies of the Night*, Mailer himself quotes Alfred Kazin's observation in *Bright Book of Life* "that Mailer was as fond of his style as an Italian tenor is fond of his vocal chords," and it is the congruence of the author's stylistic bravura with his acute perceptions of political realities that makes that "nonfiction novel" so compelling. *Miami and the Siege of Chicago* contains fresh observations of 1968, but lacks the rich conjunction of incident and personal style found in *The Armies of the Night*. Mailer's account of the 1972 national political conventions, *St. George and the Godfather*, was not nearly as successful as the earlier nonfiction novels. The whimsically titled novel *Why Are We in Vietnam?*, a disk jockey's violent, vulgar narrative of a bear hunt in Alaska, is an ostentatiously inventive allegory of American foreign policy.

Though he had received a B.S. in engineering from Harvard, Mailer was notorious as a scourge of modern technology. Nevertheless, *Life* magazine commissioned him to write a book about the first moon landing in July, 1969. NASA was wary of Mailer's antibureaucratic attitudes, and he was denied access to the astronauts themselves. *Of a Fire on the Moon* is the product of months spent in Houston and Cape Canaveral and in technical research into the space program. Calling himself "Aquarius," Mailer characteristically writes of himself in the third person and as a central character at odds with the triumphant antisepsis of the technocrats. "I liked the book in a lot of ways," Mailer later told the *New York Times Book Review*, "but I didn't like my own person in it—I felt I was highly unnecessary." Depressed over the collapse of his marriage to actress Beverly Bentley (his fourth marriage), Aquarius confessed in *Of a Fire on the Moon*, "He was weary of his own voice, own face, person, persona, will, ideas, speeches, and general sense of importance." But it was to be only a transient weariness.

When Mailer found himself portrayed as the archetypal male chauvinist pig in Kate Millett's 1970 literary study *Sexual Politics*, he participated in a raucous debate on feminism at New York's Town Hall, and he wrote *The Prisoner of Sex*, which, when first published in *Harper's*, accounted for the widest sales of any issue in the magazine's history and for the departure of its editors because of a dispute with its publisher over the work's offensive language. The book was another chapter in Mailer's continuing obsession with the mysteries of sexuality, pursued later in his passionate meditations on Marilyn Monroe in *Marilyn* and *Of Women and Their Elegance*. Praising *The Prisoner of Sex* as "Mailer's best book," *New York Times* critic Anatole Broyard declared: "What Mailer has tried to do here is write a love poem." But Gore Vidal in the *New York Review of Books* found: "There has been from Henry Miller to Norman Mailer to Charles Manson a logical progression." The remark ignited a sensational public feud between rival novelists Mailer and Vidal. Mailer attracted further controversy when he successfully petitioned the Utah State Prison parole board to release Jack Henry Abbott, for whose book *In the Belly of the Best* he had helped find a publisher. One month after leaving the penitentiary, Abbott, who had spent much of his life incarcerated, killed another man, and Mailer was again sparring with the press.

Mailer had met Abbott while conducting exhaustive research for *The Executioner's Song*, a self-described "true life novel" about the sad, bizarre life and death of Gary Gilmore, who,

on January 17, 1977, became the first convict to be executed in the United States in more than a decade. What is most remarkable about this long and detailed narrative is the patient self-effacement of its author. Gone from *The Executioner's Song* are the familiar, patent Mailerisms—the baroque syntax, the hectoring tone, the outrageous epigrams, the startling bravura imagery, the political/metaphysical digressions, the self-conscious presence of the author in every line. Instead, from its first crisp, limpid sentence, Mailer's prose assumes the coloration of its huge cast of characters—lawyers, policemen, doctors, journalists, as well as relatives, friends, and victims of Gary Gilmore—and immerses the reader in the alarmingly ordinary world of its main character. *The Executioner's Song* was an extraordinary triumph, the second Mailer work to win a Pulitzer Prize and an enormous success.

For all of his best sellers, Mailer was, as a result of his many failed marriages, in dire financial straits, and it was only through lucrative but demanding multi-book contracts that he was able to remain solvent while supporting his large extended family. *The Executioner's Song* is, possibly, the big, important book that he had aspired to write throughout his career, but he wrote it, on assignment, in a mere fifteen months. Mailer was, meanwhile, planning a boldly immense fictional creation, a vast trilogy that would encompass the distant past, the future, and the present in each successive volume. After ten years of intermittent work on it, in 1983 he published the first installment, a seven hundred-page novel set in ancient Egypt. By turns dense, overwrought, self-indulgent, forbidding, daring, and brilliant, *Ancient Evenings* follows the four lives of the courtier Menenhetet through three reincarnations during the nineteenth and twentieth dynasties of Egypt. The book is rich in researched details about daily life, beliefs, and battles of the period. Mailer's intoxication with grandiose ideas, his delight in stylistic flourishes, and his preoccupation with sex and violence are again on ostentatious display, and *Ancient Evenings* once more polarized critics in their assessment of his achievement. George Stade in the *New Republic* called it "a new and permanent contribution to the possibilities of fiction and our communal efforts of self-discovery," while Benjamin DeMott dismissed it in the *New York Times Book Review* as "pitiably foolish in conception" and "a disaster." Mailer characteristically taunted his critics with a full-page advertisement for *Ancient Evenings* juxtaposing scathing reviews of his novel with similar attacks on Herman Melville's *Moby Dick*, Leo Tolstoy's *Anna Karenina*, Walt Whitman's *Leaves of Grass*, and Charles-Pierre Baudelaire's *Les Fleurs du mal*.

Mailer was critical of Little, Brown's limited zeal in marketing his ambitious book and was disappointed with their paperback and foreign sales of it. In 1983, he signed a $4 million contract with Random House to deliver four novels to them within nine years. His new publisher also took on an additional novel that Mailer had written, a short, seamy murder mystery called *Tough Guys Don't Dance*. He also returned to the cinema when he chose to write a screenplay for *Tough Guys Don't Dance* and to direct it himself. In 1981, Mailer had had some experience with mainstream commercial movie production when he was cast in the minor role of architect Stanford White in Milos Forman's adaptation of E. L. Doctorow's novel *Ragtime*. The film noir "Tough Guys Don't Dance," in contrast to "Wild 90," "Beyond the Law," and "Maidstone," received studio backing, and Mailer cast a bankable star, Ryan O'Neal, in the lead role of Tim Madden. "Tough Guys Don't Dance" was well received at the 1987 Cannes film festival.

In his sixties, Mailer was increasingly positioning himself in the role of elder statesman of American letters. The feistiness was still there, ready to erupt over fools he would not suffer gladly, but the aging *enfant terrible* was growing perceptibly more mellow and even courtly. Active in the writers' organization PEN, he became president of its American center in 1984, in time to serve as host for the 1986 international PEN Congress in New York. The gathering of some seven hundred authors from throughout the world proved to be a tumultuous event, and, while cherishing the role of executive conciliator, Mailer was again the lightning rod for public controversy. He assailed United States foreign policy, but he invited Secretary of State George Schultz to address the assembly of writers, a decision that provoked fierce opposition. President Mailer was also angrily attacked for his alleged sexism in assigning men a dominant position in the program for the PEN meeting. The author who, in *Advertisements for Myself,* had declared, ''I have been running for President these last ten years in the privacy of my mind,'' relished this very public and pugnacious presidency and the opportunity to do battle again with his literary rivals.

''The sour truth,'' wrote Mailer in the same book, ''is that I am imprisoned with a perception which will settle for nothing less than a revolution in the consciousness of our time.'' Few American writers of his time have had such magisterial aspirations and such genuine claims to public attention. The self presented in *Advertisements for Myself* is ''an actor, a quick-change artist, as if I believe I can trap the Prince of Truth in the act of switching a style.'' Thus, it is appropriate that one scholar of Mailer's protean career titled a collection of essays about her subject *Will the Real Norman Mailer Please Stand Up?*

Throughout all the artist's quick changes, the real Norman Mailer has been an author of enormous, agonistic energies and elaborate initiative. Though he finds much of Mailer's writing unreadable after it has lost the immediacy of the occasion, Harold Bloom, in *Norman Mailer,* characterizes him as ''a historian of the moral consciousness of his era, and as the representative writer of his generation.'' A self-styled nice Jewish boy from Brooklyn who has lived for most of his life within close proximity to his adoring mother, Mailer has been animated by transgression. His career has thrived on risk and friction and has undergone as many incarnations as his Egyptian character Menenhetet. Fond of pugilistic metaphors for the writing life, as he is of boxing itself (as spectator and participant), Norman Mailer is the contemporary American author for whom a literary Golden Glove would be most fitting.

MEDIA ADAPTATIONS: The Naked and the Dead was made into a film by Warner Brothers in 1958; *An American Dream* became the film ''See You in Hell, Darling,'' produced by Warner Brothers in 1966.

AVOCATIONAL INTERESTS: Skiing, sailing, hiking.

BIOGRAPHICAL/CRITICAL SOURCES:

BOOKS

Adams, Laura, *Norman Mailer: A Comprehensive Bibliography,* Scarecrow, 1974.

Adams, Laura, editor, *Will the Real Norman Mailer Please Stand Up?,* Kennikat Press, 1974.

Adams, Laura, *Existential Battles: The Growth of Norman Mailer,* Ohio University Press, 1976.

Authors in the News, Volume 2, Gale, 1976.

Bailey, Jennifer, *Norman Mailer: Quick-Change Artist,* Harper, 1979.

Begiebing, Robert J., *Acts of Regeneration: Allegory and Archetype in the Works of Norman Mailer,* University of Missouri Press, 1980.

Bloom, Harold, editor, *Norman Mailer,* Chelsea House, 1986.

Braudy, Leo Beal, editor, *Norman Mailer: A Collection of Critical Essays,* Prentice-Hall, 1972.

Bufithis, Philip H., *Norman Mailer,* Ungar, 1978.

Contemporary Authors Bibliographical Series, Volume 1: *American Novelists,* Gale, 1986.

Contemporary Literary Criticism, Gale, Volume 1, 1973, Volume 2, 1974, Volume 3, 1975, Volume 4, 1975, Volume 5, 1976, Volume 8, 1978, Volume 11, 1979, Volume 14, 1980, Volume 28, 1984, Volume 39, 1986.

Dictionary of Literary Biography, Gale, Volume 2: *American Novelists since World War II,* 1978, Volume 16, part 2: *The Beats: Literary Bohemians in Postwar America,* 1983, Volume 28: *Twentieth-Century American-Jewish Fiction Writers,* 1984.

Dictionary of Literary Biography Documentary Series, Gale, Volume 3, 1983.

Dictionary of Literary Biography Yearbook:, Gale, *1980, 1981, 1983,* 1984.

Ehrlich, Robert, *Norman Mailer: The Radical as Hipster,* Scarecrow Press, 1978.

Gordon, Andrew, *An American Dreamer: A Psychoanalytic Study of the Fiction of Norman Mailer,* Farleigh Dickinson University Press, 1980.

Gutman, Stanley T., *Mankind in Barbary: The Individual and Society in the Novels of Norman Mailer,* University Press of New England, 1975.

Jackson, Richard, *Norman Mailer,* University of Minnesota Press, 1968.

Kazin, Alfred, *Bright Book of Life: American Novelists and Storytellers from Hemingway to Mailer,* Little, Brown, 1973.

Kellman, Steven, G., *Loving Reading: Erotics of the Text,* Archon, 1985.

Leeds, Barry H., *The Structured Vision of Norman Mailer,* New York University Press, 1969.

Lennon, J. Michael, editor, *Critical Essays on Norman Mailer,* G. K. Hall, 1986.

Lucid, Robert F., editor, *Norman Mailer: The Man and His Work,* Little, Brown, 1971.

Mailer, Norman, *The Armies of the Night: History as a Novel, the Novel as History,* New American Library, 1968.

Mailer, Norman, *Advertisements for Myself,* Berkley, 1976.

Mailer, Norman, *Of a Fire on the Moon,* Grove, 1985.

Mailer, Norman, *The White Negro: Superficial Reflections on the Hipster,* City Lights, 1957.

Manso, Peter, *Mailer: His Life and Times,* Simon and Schuster, 1985.

Merrill, Robert, *Norman Mailer,* G. K. Hall, 1978.

Middlebrook, Jonathan, *Mailer and the Times of his Time,* Bay Books (San Francisco), 1976.

Millett, Kate, *Sexual Politics,* Doubleday, 1970.

Mills, Hilary, *Mailer: A Biography,* Empire, 1982.

Poirier, Richard, *Norman Mailer,* Viking, 1972.

Radford, Jean, *Norman Mailer: A Critical Study,* Harper, 1975.

Sokoloff, B. A., *A Biography of Norman Mailer,* Darby Books, 1969.

Solotaroff, Robert, *Down Mailer's Way,* University of Illinois Press, 1974.

Weatherby, William J., *Squaring Off: Mailer vs. Baldwin,* Mason/Charter, 1977.

PERIODICALS

Atlantic, July, 1971, September, 1984.
Chicago Tribune, December 20, 1982, September 21, 1987.
Chicago Tribune Book World, October 7, 1979, November 30, 1980, June 13, 1982, April 10, 1983, August 5, 1984, July 14, 1985.
Cosmopolitan, August, 1963.
Esquire, June, 1966, December, 1968, June, 1986.
Life, March 19, 1965, September 24, 1965, February 24, 1967, September 15, 1967.
Look, May, 1969.
Los Angeles Times, September 23, 1984.
Los Angeles Times Book Review, December 14, 1980, July 11, 1982, April 24, 1983, August 19, 1984.
Nation, May 27, 1968, June 25, 1983, September 15, 1984.
National Review, April 20, 1965.
New Republic, February 9, 1959, February 8, 1964, June 8, 1968, January 23, 1971, May 2, 1983, August 27, 1984.
New Statesman, September 29, 1961.
Newsweek, December 9, 1968, April 18, 1983, August 6, 1984.
New Yorker, October 23, 1948, October 22, 1955.
New York Review of Books, May 6, 1971, June 15, 1972.
New York Times, October 27, 1968, April 28, 1983, December 23, 1985.
New York Times Book Review, May 7, 1948, September 17, 1967, May 5, 1968, October 27, 1968, January 10, 1971, February 18, 1972, October 7, 1979, September 20, 1980, December 7, 1980, June 6, 1982, January 30, 1983, April 10, 1983, July 20, 1984, July 29, 1984, April 11, 1985.
New York Times Sunday Magazine, September, 1979.
Partisan Review, spring, 1965, fall, 1965, summer, 1967, July, 1980.
People, May 30, 1983, October 5, 1987.
Publishers Weekly, March 22, 1965, October 8, 1979.
Saturday Review, January, 1981.
Time, May 28, 1951, June 28, 1982, April 18, 1983, January 27, 1986.
Times (London), June 10, 1983.
Times Literary Supplement, October 3, 1968, January 11, 1980, March 6, 1981, December 10, 1982, June 10, 1983, October 19, 1984.
Village Voice, February 18, 1965, January 21, 1971.
Washington Post Book World, July 11, 1970, October 14, 1979, November 30, 1980, July 11, 1982, April 10, 1983, August 12, 1984, November 24, 1985.

—*Sidelights by Steven G. Kellman*

*   *   *

MALABRE, Alfred L(eopold), Jr.   1931-

PERSONAL: Surname is pronounced Ma-*larb;* born April 23, 1931, in New York, N.Y.; son of Alfred L. and Marie (Cassidy) Malabre; married Mary Patricia Wardropper; children: Richard, Ann, John. *Education:* Yale University, B.A., 1952; Columbia University, M.S., 1953. *Politics:* Independent.

ADDRESSES: Home—150 East 73rd St., New York, N.Y. 10021. *Office*—*Wall Street Journal,* 200 Liberty St., New York, N.Y. 10281.

CAREER: U.S. Navy, career officer, 1953-56, retiring as lieutenant; rewrite man for *Hartford Courant,* 1957-58; *Wall Street*

Journal, New York City, worked on Midwest edition in Chicago, Ill., 1958-60, worked with London bureau, 1960-61, Bonn bureau chief, 1961-62, economics reporter with New York City bureau, 1962-68, news editor for economics, 1968-72, news editor, 1972—.

MEMBER: Pilgrims Society of the United States.

AWARDS, HONORS: Poynter fellow at Yale University, 1976; Eccles Prize from Columbia University, 1988.

WRITINGS:

Understanding the Economy: For People Who Can't Stand Economics, Dodd, 1976.
America's Dilemma: Jobs vs. Prices, Dodd, 1978.
Investing for Profit in the Eighties, Doubleday, 1982.
Beyond Our Means: How America's Long Years of Debts, Deficits and Reckless Borrowing Now Threaten to Overwhelm Us, Random House, 1987.
Understanding the New Economy, Dow Jones-Irwin, 1989.

Also contributor to anthologies, including *Here Comes Tomorrow* and *The World of the Wall Street Journal.* Author of column "Outlook" in *Wall Street Journal.* Contributor to *Encyclopaedia Britannica* and *Dow Jones Investors Handbook,* and to popular magazines, such as *Harper's, Money, Saturday Review, Reporter, Science Digest,* and *Reader's Digest.*

SIDELIGHTS: Reviewing Alfred L. Malabre, Jr.'s, book *Investing for Profit in the Eighties,* Karen Arenson for the *New York Times Book Review* finds it "a readable book that explains how the economy shrinks and expands in periodic business cycles and how you can plan investments around those cycles." Of particular value, notes Michael M. Thomas for the *Washington Post Book World,* is Malabre's recounting of his less successful investment experiences. "Here's a man who's been burned by investmentdom's best and brightest; he displays his scars, tells us wherefrom they came, and thereby teaches a lesson to be ignored at our peril." Malabre told *CA* that an "understanding of our economic system and the forces that move our economy is vital to the country's well-being."

Also vital to this country's well-being, according to Malabre, is the ability of its citizens, corporations, and governments to put a restraint on borrowing—if it is not already too late. As Toronto *Globe and Mail* reviewer Philip DeMont explains it, Malabre's book *Beyond Our Means: How America's Long Years of Debts, Deficits and Reckless Borrowing Now Threaten to Overwhelm Us* "is the embodiment of [the] borrowing-as-original-sin attitude . . . [and] warns that the United States hangs on the edge of a severe depression, the result of the postwar borrowing binge. . . . Remedial action can only assuage, not prevent, what Mr. Malabre likens to a coming storm." In *Beyond Our Means* Malabre predicts three possible outcomes of the nation's growing debts—hyperinflation, deflation, or government intervention on a grand scale.

On the whole, reviewers feel Malabre's arguments have a basis but that he tends to be somewhat of an alarmist, somewhat too portentous. In the opinion of DeMont, "Malabre uses a mountain of statistics to tell his tale of woe. . . . And he may have a point. The plethora of Third World nations facing economic ruin because of excessive debt is evidence that a country cannot continue to increase borrowing forever. Mr. Malabre is, however, unable to take his gloomy scenario beyond the level of the economic alarmists such as Eliot Janeway and Howard Ruff, people who seem to say every week that a depression is around the corner." Additionally, writes De-

Mont, "although [Malabre] nibbles around the edges of the argument, he never explains why too much debt is a problem." Peter Cook likewise expresses concern in his *Globe and Mail* assessment that Malabre's "kind of treatment of America-the-bankrupt comes across, at times, like a medieval morality play.... The reality is that the U.S. problem is not unique; the country faces a balance-of-payments crisis of the kind that other countries—Britain, Canada, Brazil and France—have gone through in the past. In such circumstances, a wrenching economic adjustment is needed. But not a lobotomy." In turn, *Washington Post Book World* critic John H. Makin questions what he sees as Malabre's "careless recitations of statistics" and also Malabre's scorn for current economic theories and economists: "As much as Malabre dislikes economists in general, supply siders seem to be a lightning rod for his disdain. Supply-side theory 'is in reality nothing more than the ultimate ideological expression of our extravagance, our effort to keep on living beyond our means.'" Despite the fact that *New York Times Book Review* contributor Adam Smith describes *Beyond Our Means* as a "sober account of our fiscal and monetary sins that is scarier than anything by Stephen King," he says Malabre "is not one of the doomsday kooks we used to read in the 1970's," and that even though it may be too late to do anything, "they should issue this book to Congress before they issue parking stickers."

BIOGRAPHICAL/CRITICAL SOURCES:

BOOKS

Malabre, Alfred L., Jr., *Beyond Our Means: How America's Long Years of Debts, Deficits and Reckless Borrowing Now Threaten to Overwhelm Us,* Random House, 1987.

PERIODICALS

Globe and Mail (Toronto), August 22, 1987, January 16, 1988.
Los Angeles Times Book Review, April 19, 1987.
New York Times Book Review, October 17, 1982, April 12, 1987.
Washington Post Book Review, March 6, 1983, March 8, 1987.

*   *   *

MALAMUD, Bernard   1914-1986

PERSONAL: Born April 28, 1914, in Brooklyn, N.Y.; died of natural causes, March 18, 1986, in New York, N.Y.; son of Max (a grocery store manager) and Bertha (Fidelman) Malamud; married Ann de Chiara, November 6, 1945; children: Paul, Janna. *Education:* City College of New York (now City College of the City University of New York), B.A., 1936; Columbia University, M.A., 1942.

ADDRESSES: Home—New York, N.Y.; and Bennington, Vt. *Agent*—Russell & Volkening, 50 West 29th St., New York, N.Y. 10001.

CAREER: Worked for Bureau of Census, Washington, D.C., 1940; Erasmus Hall High School, New York, N.Y., evening instructor in English, beginning 1940; instructor in English, Harlem High School, 1948-49; Oregon State University, 1949-61, began as instructor, became associate professor of English; Bennington College, Bennington, Vt., Division of Language and Literature, member of faculty, 1961-86. Visiting lecturer, Harvard University, 1966-68. Honorary consultant in American letters, Library of Congress, 1972-75.

MEMBER: National Institute of Arts and Letters, American Academy of Arts and Sciences, PEN American Center (president, 1979).

AWARDS, HONORS: Partisan Review fellow in fiction, 1956-57; Richard and Hinda Rosenthal Foundation Award, and Daroff Memorial Award, both 1958, both for *The Assistant;* Rockefeller grant, 1958; National Book Award in fiction, 1959, for *The Magic Barrel,* and 1967, for *The Fixer;* Ford Foundation fellow in humanities and arts, 1959-61; Pulitzer Prize in fiction, 1967, for *The Fixer;* O. Henry Award, 1969, for "Man in the Drawer"; Jewish Heritage Award of the B'nai B'rith, 1976; Governor's Award, Vermont Council on the Arts, 1979, for excellence in the arts; American Library Association Notable Book citation, 1979, for *Dubin's Lives;* Brandeis University Creative Arts Award in fiction, 1981; Gold Medal for fiction, American Academy and Institute of Arts and Letters, 1983; Elmer Holmes Bobst Award for fiction, 1983; honorary degree from City College of the City University of New York.

WRITINGS:

NOVELS

The Natural, Harcourt, 1952, reprinted, Avon, 1980.
The Assistant, Farrar, Straus, 1957, reprinted, Avon, 1980.
A New Life, Farrar, Straus, 1961, reprinted, 1988.
The Fixer, Farrar, Straus, 1966, reprinted, Pocket Books, 1982.
Pictures of Fidelman: An Exhibition (includes "Last Mohican," "A Pimp's Revenge," and "Glass Blower of Venice"), Farrar, Straus, 1969, reprinted, New American Library, 1985.
The Tenants, Farrar, Straus, 1971, reprinted, 1988.
Dubin's Lives, Farrar, Straus, 1979.
God's Grace, Farrar, Straus, 1982.

SHORT STORIES

The Magic Barrel (includes "The Magic Barrel" and "The First Seven Years"), Farrar, Straus, 1958, reprinted, Avon, 1980.
Idiots First (includes "Idiots First" and "The Maid's Shoes"), Farrar, Straus, 1963.
Rembrandt's Hat (includes "The Silver Crown" and "Man in the Drawer"), Farrar, Straus, 1973.
The Stories of Bernard Malamud, Farrar, Straus, 1983.

OTHER

(Contributor) John Fisher and Robert B. Silvers, editors, *Writing in America,* Rutgers University Press, 1960.
A Malamud Reader, edited by Philip Rahv, Farrar, Straus, 1967.

Contributor of short stories to various magazines, including *American Preface, Atlantic, Commentary, Harper's, New Threshold,* and *New Yorker.* Contributor of articles to *New York Times* and *New York Times Book Review.* Manuscripts, typescripts, and proofs of *The Natural, The Assistant, A New Life, The Fixer, Pictures of Fidelman,* and various stories from *The Magic Barrel* and *Idiots First* are in the collection of the Library of Congress.

SIDELIGHTS: Novelist and short story writer Bernard Malamud often drew on the New York East Side where his Russian-Jewish immigrant parents worked in their grocery store sixteen hours a day. Malamud attended high school and college during the height of the Depression. His own and his family's experience is clearly echoed in his fiction, much of which chronicles, as Mervyn Rothstein declares in the *New York Times,* "simple people struggling to make their lives better in a world of bad luck." His writings also are strongly influenced by classic nineteenth-century American writers, especially Nathaniel Hawthorne, but also Henry David Thoreau, Herman

Melville, and Henry James. In addition his works reflect a post-Holocaust consciousness in addressing Jewish concerns and employing literary conventions drawn from earlier Jewish literature.

The first major period of Malamud's work extended from 1949 to 1961 when he was teaching composition at Oregon State College. Producing three novels and a collection of short stories during this period, he won five fiction prizes, including the National Book Award. Each of the first three novels features a schlemiel figure who tries to restore a Wasteland to a Paradise against a Jewish background. The setting varies in the novels, but in the short fiction is most often the East Side of New York. "The Prison" portrays a small New York grocery store based on that of Malamud's parents, in which a young Italian, Tommy Castelli, is trapped. Similarly "The Cost of Living"—a predecessor of *The Assistant*—and "The Bill" both present the grocery store as a sort of prison. As Leslie and Joyce Field observe in *Bernard Malamud: A Collection of Critical Essays,* "In Malamud's fictional world, there is always a prison," and in a 1973 interview with the Fields, Malamud said: "Necessity is the primary prison, though the bars are not visible to all." Beneath most Malamudian surfaces lie similar moral and allegorical meanings.

Malamud's first novel, *The Natural,* is, as Earl R. Wasserman declares in *Bernard Malamud and the Critics,* "the necessary reference text for a reading of his subsequent fiction." The work is a mythic novel, based on the Arthurian legends, in which the Parsifal figure, Roy (King) Hobbs, restores fertility to the Fisher King, Pop Fisher, the manager of a baseball team called The Knights. Pitcher Roy appears as an Arthurian Knight modeled in part on Babe Ruth, but his character also probably is drawn from Chretien de Troye's medieval tale, *Lancelot of the Cart,* featuring a Lancelot who is most often unhorsed and frequently humiliated. As Peter L. Hays has said in *The Fiction of Bernard Malamud,* "Like Lancelot, Malamud's heroes are cut to ribbons in their quests for love and fortune."

The novel's title is baseball slang for a player with natural talent, but it can also mean, as it did in the Middle Ages, an innocent fool. As Philip Roth has said in *Reading Myself and Others,* this is "not baseball as it is played in Yankee Stadium, but a wild, wacky game." Roy thinks of himself as "Sir Percy lancing Sir Maldemer, or the first son (with a rock in his paw) ranged against the primitive papa." Even more Freudian is Roy's lancelike bat, Wonderboy, which droops when its phallic hero goes into a slump and finally splits at the novel's conclusion.

In an echo of the Black Sox scandal of 1919, Roy is bribed to throw the pennant game by evil-eyed Gus Sands, whose Pot of Fire nightclub and chorus girls wielding pitchforks suggest hell itself. Though there are few obvious Jewish traces in *The Natural,* the prank Roy plays on Gus is a retelling of a Yiddish prankster tale, with the challenge by the prankster, the foil or victim's reaction, and the retort or prank—here Roy's pulling silver dollars out of Gus's ears and nose. Yet Roy's success is only temporary. As Glenn Meeter notes in *Bernard Malamud and Philip Roth: A Critical Essay,* "From the grail legend also we know that Roy will fail; for the true grail seeker must understand the supernatural character of his quest, and Roy does not." In the end Roy, defeated, throws his bribe money in the face of Judge Banner, who is a dispenser of "dark wisdom, parables and aphorisms which punctuate his conversation, making him seem a cynical Poor Richard," as Iska Alter remarks in *The Good Man's Dilemma:*

Social Criticism in the Fiction of Bernard Malamud. This dramatic scene, and others in Malamud's work, accord with his statement in a 1973 interview: "My novels are close to plays."

Other influences are also clearly at work in Malamud's first novel. *The Natural* has significant references to birds and flowers and steady reminders of the passage of the seasons. The simplicity of this pastoral style at its best allows the presentation of complex ideas in a natural way. A second influence, as Malamud acknowledged, is film technique. For example, there are quick movie-like changes of scene, called jump cuts, when Roy and Memo Paris are tricked into sleeping with each other. In addition, the portrayal of Roy has a Chaplinesque quality of humor to it. Though Malamud would never again write non-Jewish fiction, *The Natural* was a treasure house of reusable motifs and methods for all his subsequent work.

In 1954 Malamud published one of his greatest short stories, "The Magic Barrel," which Sanford Pinsker, in *Bernard Malamud: A Collection of Critical Essays,* calls "a nearly perfect blend of form and content." In this story the matchmaker Pinye Salzman, using cards listing eligible women and drawn from his magic barrel, tricks student rabbi Leo Finkle into a love match with Salzman's daughter, Stella, a streetwalker. In *Judaism,* Marcia Booher Gealy describes the structural essence of such Hasidic-influenced stories: (1) the inward journey; (2) the older man tutoring the younger; (3) the triumph of love; (4) the reality of evil; and (5) transformation through the tale itself. This structure merges with another influence, that of nineteenth-century American romanticism, for Malamud often joins the Hasidic and Hawthornian in his fables. As Renee Winegarten comments in *Bernard Malamud: A Collection of Critical Essays,* "His magic barrels and silver crowns, whatever their seal, firmly belong in the moral, allegorical realm of scarlet letters, white whales and golden bowls."

Concerning Salzman, as Irving Howe has said in *World of Our Fathers,* "The matchmaker, or *shadkhn,* is a stereotypic Yiddish figure: slightly comic, slightly sad, at the edge of destitution." Such confidence men reappear in Malamud's fiction, in "The Silver Crown," for example. And Salzman shows Malamud's early perfection of a Jewish-American speech, which is neither pure Yiddish dialect nor mere literary chat, but an imaginative combination of both. Kathryn Hellerstein observes in *The State of the Language,* that Yiddish speakers in Malamud are "elderly, static, or declining" and concludes that for Malamud, Yiddish figures are "a spectral presence of the constraining, delimited, stultified past."

What many critics have referred to as Malamud's finest novel, *The Assistant,* appeared in 1957. As Ihab Hassan has said in *The Fiction of Bernard Malamud,* "*The Assistant,* I believe, will prove a classic not only of Jewish but of American literature." Frank Alpine, "the assistant," suggests St. Francis of Assisi, whose biography, *The Little Flowers,* is Alpine's favorite book and whose stigmata he at one point seems to emulate. Like Roy in *The Natural,* Frank is the Parsifal figure who must bring fertility, or at least new life, to the Fisher King, here the grocery store owner Morris Bober. Some critics have contended that Bober may parallel philosopher Martin Buber whose I-THOU philosophy of human relations he seems, however instinctively, to share, though Malamud himself denied any use of Buber in this novel.

When he stands under a "No Trust" sign, Bober also recalls Melville's novel, *The Confidence Man.* Giving food to a drunk woman who will never pay, Morris teaches Frank to have compassion for others. Yet Frank cannot control his passion for Morris's daughter, Helen. Thus when Frank saves Helen from an attempted rape, he fails the trial of the Perilous Bed, rapes her just as she is about to admit her love for him, and loses her.

Frank and Morris represent a familiar motif in Malamud's works, that of the father-son pair, the schlemiel-schlimazel twins. Malamud likes these doublings and there are three other father/son pairs in the novel. A favorite definition of these types is that the schlemiel spills his teacup, and the schlimazel is the one he spills it on. Norman Leer, thinking perhaps of Russian novelist Feodor Dostoevsky's *Crime and Punishment,* speaks in *Mosaic: A Journal for the Comparative Study of Literature and Ideas* of "the notion of the divided self, and the attraction of two characters who mirror a part of each other, and are thereby drawn together as doubles."

Another recurrent feature of Malamudian narrative, the Holocaust, is never far from the surface, though it appears almost always in an oblique way. Morris, in despair over his luckless grocery store/prison, turns on the gas to commit suicide, a reminder of the gas chambers of the Holocaust. And here Malamud introduces from the world of fantasy a professional arsonist who is like a figure from hell—recalling the night club women and their pitchforks in *The Natural.* At Morris's funeral, Frank halts the ceremony by falling into the open grave, while trying to see the rose Helen had thrown into it. In Malamud's fiction, the characters frequently dream, and in Frank's dream, St. Francis successfully gives Frank's rose to Helen. Rachel Ertel declares in *Le Roman juif americain: Une Ecriture minoritaire,* "By going constantly from the real to the supernatural, Bernard Malamud deadens, nullifies the disbelief of the reader and gives himself elbow room to narrate the fables, the parables that make up his novels and short stories."

In 1958, with the publication of his first collection of short stories, *The Magic Barrel,* Malamud received national recognition and in 1959 won the National Book Award for the collection. All the stories in the volume display Malamud's continuing debt to Hawthorne; as Jackson J. Benson says in *The Fiction of Bernard Malamud,* the two writers "possess the ability to combine, with great skill, reality and the dream, the natural and supernatural." Thus there is a kinship between Malamud's "Idiots First," "The Silver Crown," and "The Magic Barrel" and Hawthorne's short stories "My Kinsman, Major Molineux," "Young Goodman Brown," and "The Birthmark." Moreover, "The First Seven Years," featuring Feld, a Polish immigrant shoemaker who refuses to speak Yiddish and who wants his daughter Miriam to marry a rising young suitor, Max, rather than his middle-aged but devoted helper, Sobel, is reminiscent of Hawthorne's "Ethan Brand," with its warning about "hardness of the heart." However, "The First Seven Years" is Hawthorne plus Holocaust, for Sobel had barely escaped Hitler's incinerators.

In the years from 1949 to 1961 Malamud slowly became "one of the foremost writers of moral fiction in America," as Jeffrey Helterman comments in *Understanding Bernard Malamud.* Of his last work in this first period, Sheldon J. Hershinow remarks in *Bernard Malamud:* "*A New Life* is Malamud's first attempt at social satire, and much of the novel is given over to it." Its hero, marginal Jew Sy Levin, shows the complexity behind the names of practically all major characters in Malamud. In *City of Words: American Fiction 1950-1970,* Tony Tanner explains that the name Levin means the east, or light; it is also associated with lightning. Tanner writes: "I have it direct from Mr. Malamud that by a pun on 'leaven' he

is suggesting what the marginal Jew may bring in attitude to the American scene." Levin, whose fictional career resembles that of Malamud, is a former high school teacher who joins the faculty at Cascadia University in Easchester, Oregon, a name that suggests a castle of ease. According to Mark Goldman, in a *Critique* review, "Early in the novel, Levin is the tenderfoot Easterner, the academic sad sack, or schlimazel of Yiddish literature, invoking nature like a tenement Rousseau." Levin, then is the schlemiel as lecturer, who teaches his first class with his fly open, then bumbles his way into an affair with a coed, Nadalee, a lady of the lake who has written an essay on nude bathing. As Sandy Cohen says in *Bernard Malamud and the Trial by Love,* "Malamud's favorite method of portraying a protagonist's struggle to overcome his vanity is to symbolize it in terms of the Grail myth. Thus Levin's journey to meet Nadalee takes on certain aspects of the grail quest." Indeed, Levin journeys "in his trusty Hudson, his lance at his side."

Later Levin makes love in the woods to Pauline Gilley; in an echo of English novelist D. H. Lawrence's *Lady Chatterley's Lover,* Pauline also has an impotent husband, Gerald Gilley, future chairman of the English Department. Against this pastoral background, complete with the passage of the seasons, Levin is also the American Adam: as Hershinow observes, "Immersed in the writings of Emerson, Thoreau, and Whitman, Levin believes wholeheartedly the metaphors about America as a New-World Garden of Eden. By going west he feels he can recapture his lost innocence and escape the past— become the New-World Adam."

This major love affair is also Hawthornian: as Paul Witherington notes in *Western American Literature,* "Levin's affair with Pauline matures in Hawthorne fashion to an inner drama of the ambiguities of paradise." In fact, Levin sees himself as "Arthur Dimmesdale Levin, locked in stocks on a platform in the town square, a red A stapled on his chest." From Levin's point of view, Pauline, whose love earned him his scarlet letter A, is also the tantalizing *shiksa,* the Gentile temptress of so many Jewish-American novels, not only those of Malamud but also of Saul Bellow and Philip Roth among others. As Frederick Cople Jaher points out in the *American Quarterly,* to Jewish men, such women seem to be "exotic insiders" and so represent "tickets of admission into American society."

At the conclusion of the novel, Gilley asks Levin why he wants to take on two adopted children and Gilley's apparently barren wife. Levin replies, "Because I can, you son of a bitch." And Levin, defeated in academe, but having impregnated the barren Pauline, whose flat breasts are beginning to swell, drives away with his new family, having agreed with Gilley never again to teach in a university. This ending, as so often in Malamud, is ambiguous, for Levin is no longer in romantic love with Pauline. Here is what *Critique* contributor Ruth B. Mandel calls "ironic affirmation"—"The affirmation itself is ironic in that the state of grace is unaccompanied by paradise."

After Malamud's move back east to Bennington College, his second period (roughly 1961-1970) began, and both his stories and his next two novels took a more cosmopolitan and international direction. In *Bernard Malamud,* Sidney Richman perceptively observes that the title story in *Idiots First* is "a morality [play] *a la Everyman* in which the sense of a real world (if only the sense of it) is utterly absorbed by a dream-landscape, a never-never-land New York City through which an elderly Jew named Mendel wanders in search of comfort and aid." Mendel is indeed a Jewish Everyman, who tries to dodge the Angel of Death (here named Ginzburg) to arrange for the future of his handicapped son, Isaac.

Another short story, "The Maid's Shoes," reveals the new subject matter and style. Professor Orlando Krantz, who plays the part of the comparatively wealthy American as Everyman, tries to give a small gift to his poor Italian maid, Rosa, but it is a gift without the understanding that the impoverished European needs: "But though they shared the same roof, and even the same hot water bottle and bathtub, they almost never shared speech." Here, failures of the heart, common to the fiction of the first period, are extended to complete failures of empathy. Furthermore, the story is no longer fantastic, as in Malamud's first period, but realistic. Of Rosa, Malamud writes: "She was forty-five and looked older. Her face was worn but her hair was black, and her eyes and lips were pretty. She had few good teeth. When she laughed she was embarrassed around the mouth." Finally, the story has a single consistent point of view instead of the omniscient point of view of the earlier stories. Yet since that omniscient narration contained Malamud's often compassionate comments that are a part of his first period manner, these newer stories have a bleaker cast to them.

Next to *The Assistant* in critical reputation comes *The Fixer,* winner of the Pulitzer Prize and the National Book Award in 1967. In a search for a suffering Everyman plot, Malamud had thought of several subjects—the trial of Alfred Dreyfus and the Sacco-Vanzetti case, among others—before deciding on a story he had heard from his father as a boy, that of the trial of Mendel Beiliss for ritual bloodletting and murder in 1913 in Russia. Through this story, Malamud also tries to answer the question of how the death camps in Germany had been possible. Hero Yakov Bok's last name suggests a scapegoat, and also the goat mentioned in the song chanted for the end of the Passover Seder as a symbol of Jewish survival. As Malamud said in an interview with Christopher Lehmann-Haupt in the *New York Times Book Review,* it was necessary "to mythologize—that is, to make metaphors and symbols of the major events and characters."

The novel itself covers two years, spring 1911 to winter 1913, during which Bok is imprisoned after being falsely accused of the ritual murder of a Gentile boy. Without legal counsel Bok suffers betrayal, gangrene, poison, and freezing cold, and finally turns inward to develop a sense of freedom. In prison this Everyman fixer learns through suffering to overcome, at least in part, his initial agnosticism, and his doubts of what is meant by the Chosen People. He rejects both suicide and a pardon, and accepts his Jewishness. Finally, in a dream encounter with Tsar Nicholas II, Bok shoots the Tsar. As John F. Desmond writes in *Renascence: Essays on Values in Literature,* "Yakov has come to understand that no man is apolitical, especially as a Jew; consequently, if his chance came, as it does in the imaginary meeting with the Tsar, he would not hesitate to kill the ruler as a beginning step towards purging that society of its agents of repression and injustice, and thus strike a blow for freedom and humanity." Bok, at least in his dream, is no longer the passive suffering servant of Isaiah, portrayed in many of Malamud's first period fictions, but one who seeks revenge. Has Bok lost more important values? The dream setting leaves the ending ambiguous, but Malamud's real subject is not so much Bok himself, as those, like the Germans, other Europeans, and Americans during the Holocaust, who either participate in, or passively observe, the treatment of Everyman as victim. As the Fields remark, Malamud

repeatedly tried to make clear, especially in this second period, that Jewish victims are Everyman as victim, for history, sooner or later, treats all men as Jews.

The final major work of this second period was *Pictures of Fidelman: An Exhibition.* As Leslie A. Field has written in *Bernard Malamud: A Collection of Critical Essays,* "Of all the Malamud characters, early and late, one must return to Arthur Fidelman as the Malamud *schlemiel par excellence.*" The Fidelman stories appeared both separately in magazines and in two story collections from 1958 to 1969, and they were not originally thought of as a unity. But the last three stories are tightly linked, and as Robert Ducharme asserts in *Art and Idea in the Novels of Bernard Malamud: Toward "The Fixer,"* Malamud deliberately saved the last story for the book because he didn't want to let readers know the ending. Three genres merge in *Pictures of Fidelman,* that of the *Kunstlerroman* or artist novel, the *Bildungsroman* or education novel, and the *Huckleberry Finn*-like picaresque novel, in which the main character wanders through a series of adventures. Fidelman (faith man) encounters Susskind (sweet child) in the first story or chapter, "Last Mohican." Susskind is a Jewish folktale type, a *chnorrer,* or as Goldman terms him, "a beggar with style," who wants the second of Fidelman's two suits. Rebuffed, Susskind steals the first chapter of Fidelman's book on Italian artist Giotto di Bondone. Hershinow suggests that "Susskind becomes for Fidelman a kind of dybbuk (demon) who inhabits his conscience, destroying his peace of mind." As Cohen remarks, "So Fidelman begins an active search for Susskind who begins to take on the roles of alter-ego, superego, and symbol for Fidelman's true heritage and past." Here again is the familiar Malamud motif of the journey that changes a life.

In pursuit, Fidelman visits a synagogue, a Jewish ghetto, and a graveyard that contains victims of the Holocaust. Both at the cemetery and in his crazy pursuit of Susskind, Schlemiel Fidelman recalls Frank Alpine in *The Assistant,* for Fidelman too is linked to St. Francis. In a dream Fidelman sees Susskind, who shows him a Giotto fresco in which St. Francis gives his clothing to a poor knight. As Sidney Richman affirms in *Bernard Malamud and the Critics,* "In the same fashion as Frankie Alpine, Fidelman must discover that the way to the self is paradoxically through another; and the answer is heralded by a sudden alteration of the pursuit." At the end of this artistic pilgrim's progress, "against his will, Fidelman learns what the ancient rabbis taught and what Susskind has always known: Jews—that is, human beings, *menschen,* in Malamud's terms—are responsible for each other. That is the essence of being human," Michael Brown relates in *Judaism.*

Fidelman must learn in the next stories what makes a great artist. For example, in the fourth story, "A Pimp's Revenge," Fidelman returns his mistress, Esmeralda, to prostitution to pay for his constantly repainted masterwork, a portrait of her, first as Mother and Son, then as Brother and Sister, and finally as Prostitute and Procurer. "The truth is I am afraid to paint, like I might find out something about myself," Fidelman says. Esmeralda knows the secret: "If I have my choice, I'll take life. If there's not that there's no art." Barbara Lefcowitz justly argues in *Literature and Psychology,* "Where Malamud excels is in his subtle and nearly always comical juxtaposition of a neurotic character against a deeper and wider moral and historical context." Fidelman finally produces a masterpiece, but, second-rate artist that he is, can't let it alone, and mars it. The genius knows when to stop, but Everyman does not, and Esmeralda calls him a murderer.

In the final story, "Glass Blower of Venice," Fidelman tries to play artist once more, under the reluctant teaching of his homosexual lover Beppo, but at last gives up art for craftsmanship and returns to America. Fidelman, the craftsman, no longer the inadequate artist, has finally achieved the goals toward which Susskind—and later Esmeralda—pointed him. Samuel I. Bellman argues in *Critique* that "more than any other Malamudian character Fidelman is constantly growing, realizing himself, transforming his unsatisfactory old life into a more satisfactory new one." In *Bernard Malamud: A Collection of Critical Essays,* Sheldon N. Grebstein praises the juxtaposition of "the coarsely sexual and the sublimely aesthetic." Indeed, no other work of Malamud shows so much appetite for life; as Helterman has argued: "[Fidelman] also seeks, and occasionally participates in, a richness of passion not typical of Malamud's urban heroes." The epigraph for *Pictures of Fidelman* is from Yeats: "The intellect of man is forced to choose Perfection of the life or of the work." However, the new Fidelman chooses "both."

The Tenants inaugurated Malamud's third and final period. In the works of this period the heroic structuring of the first period is gone, as are the Wandering Jews and the Everyman motifs of the second. Beneath differing surface plots, though, a new structural likeness appears. Before 1971 Malamud's typical Jewish characters tend to move towards responsibility rather than towards achievement; but from 1971 on, they become extraordinary achievers, or *machers*.

In *The Tenants* Harry Lesser, a minor Jewish novelist, is writing a novel about being unable to finish a novel, in a kind of infinite regression. He keeps on living in the apartment building that landlord Levenspiel (leaven game) wants to tear down; then a squatter, black writer Willie Spearmint (Willie Shakespeare), moves into the building. Willie and Harry are the kind of doubled pair (drawn from Edgar Allan Poe and Dostoevsky) that Malamud is fond of, for Harry's writing is all form, and Willie's is all vitality. Harry takes over Irene, Willie's Jewish girl; Willie burns Harry's manuscript; Harry axes Willie's typewriter; and in a final burst of overachievement, Willie brains Harry and Harry castrates Willie. *The Tenants* "ends in a scream of language," reports Malcolm Bradbury in *Encounter*. Though the novel hints at two other possible endings—by fire, or by Harry's marriage to Irene—Levenspiel has the last word, which is *Rachmones,* or mercy.

Though *The Tenants* did little for Malamud's reputation, he continued to place stories in top American magazines. Mervyn Rothstein reported in the *New York Times* that Malamud said at the end of his life, "With me, it's story, story, story." In Malamud's next-to-last collection, *Rembrandt's Hat,* only one story, "The Silver Crown," is predominantly Jewish, in sharp contrast to his first collection, while other stories are more reminiscent of Chekhov. There is even a visit to the Chekhov Museum in "Man in the Drawer," a story that shows the fascination with achievement so dominant in Malamud's final period. Howard Harvitz, an intellectual tourist in Russia and a marginal Jew, has changed his name from Harris back to Harvitz. Hardly a creative writer himself, he is doing a piece on museums. A Russian writer, Levitansky—also a marginal Jew, but a determined achiever in spite of official opposition—intends to smuggle his stories out of Russia. Harvitz at first doesn't want this charge, but discovers that four of the stories show heroes not taking responsibility. After reading them, Harvitz timorously takes the stories out of Russia.

Dubin's Lives took Malamud over five years to write, twice as long as any previous novel. Ralph Tyler in the *New York Times Book Review* reports that Malamud said *Dubin's Lives* was "his attempt at bigness, at summing up what he . . . learned over the long haul." In the novel, the biographer Dubin is an isolated achiever, no mere recorder of biographical facts but a creative, even fictionalizing biographer: "One must transcend autobiographical detail by inventing it after it is remembered." Dubin is trying to write a biography of D. H. Lawrence, a writer who made passion his religion, yet was impotent. There had been a glancing counterpointing of Lawrence's career in *A New Life,* but here this motif is much enlarged; as David Levin observes in *Virginia Quarterly Review,* "The complexities of Dubin's subsequent adventures often run parallel to events in Lawrence's life."

In the kind of psychomachia, or inner struggle, which some critics see as the essence of American fiction, Dubin, as Helterman notes, "loses his memory, his sexual powers, his ability to work, even his ability to relate to his family. At first, the only compensation for these losses is a kind of high-grade nostalgia brought about by a process called reverie." These reveries lead Dubin to a liaison with young Fanny Bick, whose first name comes from English novelist Jane Austen's heroine in *Mansfield Park,* Fanny Price; Fanny Bick is an Austen heroine with glands. Like a number of heroines in Malamud's fiction, she is significantly associated with wildflowers, fruit, and bird flights. Chiara Briganti remarks in *Studies in American Jewish Literature* that "all the female characters in Malamud's fiction share a common shallowness and common values: they all respect marriage and family life, and, whatever their past, they all seek fulfillment through a permanent relationship with a man." But Fanny breaks this stereotypical pattern, for at the end of *Dubin's Lives* she ambitiously intends to become a lawyer.

Dubin's affair in Venice, where the youthful Fanny almost immediately betrays him with their gondolier, is that of the schlemiel lover seen before in Frank Alpine and Sy Levin. Barbara Quart, in *Studies in American Jewish Literature,* has seen a further problem: "While Malamud's central characters try to break out of their solitude, they appear to fear love and women as much as they long for them." But dominant among familiar motifs is the character of Dubin as the isolated overachiever, who moves his study from his country house into the barn to devote all possible energy and space to his biography. Dubin even begrudges time wasted thinking about Fanny, with whom he is genuinely in love.

Malamud's last finished novel, *God's Grace,* treats both the original Holocaust and a new, imagined Holocaust of the future. In *Immigrant-Survivors: Post-Holocaust Consciousness in Recent Jewish-American Literature,* Dorothy Seldman Bilik has pointed out that the question of why God permitted the Holocaust has been an issue in Malamud's fiction for thirty years; indeed, for Malamud the Holocaust has been the ultimate mark of inhumanity, and *God's Grace* treats the Holocaust not only as man's inhumanity to man, but as God's inhumanity to man. The novel is a wild, at times brilliant, at times confusing description of a second Noah's Flood. Calvin Cohn, a paleologist and the son of a rabbi-cantor, had been doing underseas research when the Djanks and the Druzhkies (Yanks and Russians) launched an atomic Holocaust and destroyed every other human. Calvin recalls many Biblical and literary figures: Parsifal, Romeo, Prospero, Robinson Crusoe, Gulliver, and Ahab. His Eve and Juliet is Mary Madelyn, a chimpanzee. An albino ape appears (possibly an oblique reference to Moby Dick) with other apes as Yahoos from Jonathan Swift's *Gulliver's Travels,* and the chimpanzee Buz serves as Cohn's Isaac, Caliban, and man Friday. There is even an Arthurian spear used to harpoon the albino ape.

On Cohn's Island Calvin turns into an overachiever, and even an un-Job-like defier of God, in spite of God's pillars of fire, showers of lemons, and occasional warning rocks. The foundation of *God's Grace* is Biblical in part, but also characteristically American, for it is the story of the Americanized—and reversed—Fortunate Fall. The idea conveyed by the Fortunate Fall is that Adam and Eve, driven from Paradise by eating of the tree of Knowledge, in fact obtained benefits from their fall, notably free will and a consciousness of good and evil. Cohn has treated the chimpanzees as his inferiors; as a schlemiel lecturer he has imposed his admonitions and teachings on them, rather than encouraging them to learn for themselves. He has promised but never given Mary Madelyn the marriage she has wanted, and he has prevented the marriage or mating of Buz and Mary Madelyn, which could have been just as desirable for the future gene stock as Cohn's half-chimpanzee child Rebekah. In short, over-achieving Calvin Cohn has eaten from the tree of hubris, or sinful pride, rather than knowledge.

This complex novel baffled its first reviewers; for example, Joseph Epstein wrote in *Commentary:* "Much of the humor in the novel is of the kind known as faintly amusing, but the chimp humor, on the scale of wit, is roughly three full rungs down from transvestite jokes." Part of the difficulty in the novel is that *God's Grace* does not fall into a clear genre category; in a 1982 *Christian Science Monitor* article, Victor Howes called it "somewhat east of sci-fi, somewhat west of allegory." However, like much of Malamud's work, *God's Grace* not only reflects the Jewish Old Testament but also partakes of an American colonial genre, the Jeremiad, or warning of future disaster.

Malamud's final, but unfinished work, "The Tribe," concerns the adventures of a Russian Jewish pedlar, Yozip, among the western Indians. As Nan Robertson recounts in the *New York Times,* the schlemiel hero Yozip becomes a marshal, is kidnapped by a tribe of Indians, and has a dialogue with an Indian chief about obtaining his freedom.

Malamud gave few interviews, but those he did grant provided the best commentary on his work, as when he told Michiko Kakutani in the *New York Times:* "People say I write so much about misery, but you write about what you write best. As you are grooved, so you are grieved. And the grieving is that no matter how much happiness or success you collect, you cannot obliterate your early experience." Yet perhaps Malamud's contribution is clearest in his greatest invention, his Jewish-American dialect, comic even at the height of tragedy. For example, Calvin Cohn, sacrificed by the chimpanzee Buz in a wild inversion of the story of Abraham and Isaac, reflects that God after all has let him live out his life; Cohn then asks himself—forgetting his educated speech and reverting to the Yiddish rhythms of his youth—"Maybe tomorrow the world to come?" In such comic-serious questionings, Malamud captures the voice of the past and gives it relevance to the present.

MEDIA ADAPTATIONS: The Fixer was filmed by John Frankenheimer for Metro-Goldwyn-Mayer and released in 1969. "The Angel Levine" starred Zero Mostel and Harry Belafonte and was adapted by William Gunn for United Artists in 1970. *A New Life* and *The Assistant* were both optioned in the early 1970s, and producer Sidney Glazier planned a filmscript based on "Black Is My Favorite Color." "The Natural," starring Robert Redford as Roy Hobbs, Robert Duvall as Max Mercy, Glenn Close as Iris Gaines, and Kim Basinger as Memo Paris, was directed by Barry Levinson for Tri-Star Pictures and released in 1984.

AVOCATIONAL INTERESTS: Reading, travel, music, walking.

BIOGRAPHICAL/CRITICAL SOURCES:

BOOKS

Alter, Iska, *The Good Man's Dilemma: Social Criticism in the Fiction of Bernard Malamud,* AMS Press, 1981.

Astro, Richard, and Jackson J. Benson, editors, *The Fiction of Bernard Malamud,* Oregon State University Press, 1977.

Avery, Evelyn G., *Rebels and Victims: The Fiction of Richard Wright and Bernard Malamud,* Kennikat, 1979.

Baumbach, Jonathan, *The Landscape of Nightmare: Studies in the Contemporary American Novel,* New York University Press, 1965.

Bilik, Dorothy Seldman, *Immigrant-Survivors: Post-Holocaust Consciousness in Recent Jewish-American Literature,* Wesleyan University Press, 1981.

Bloom, Harold, *Bernard Malamud,* Chelsea House, 1986.

Cohen, Sandy, *Bernard Malamud and the Trial by Love,* Rodopi (Amsterdam), 1974.

Concise Dictionary of American Literary Biography: The New Consciousness, 1941-1968, Gale, 1987.

Contemporary Authors Bibliographical Series, Volume 1: *American Novelists,* Gale, 1986.

Contemporary Literary Criticism, Gale, Volume 1, 1973, Volume 2, 1974, Volume 3, 1975, Volume 5, 1976, Volume 8, 1978, Volume 9, 1978, Volume 11, 1979, Volume 18, 1981, Volume 27, 1984, Volume 44, 1987.

Dictionary of Literary Biography, Gale, Volume 2: *American Novelists since World War II,* 1978, Volume 28: *Twentieth-Century American-Jewish Fiction Writers,* 1984.

Dictionary of Literary Biography Yearbook, Gale, *1980,* 1981, *1986,* 1987.

Ducharme, Robert, *Art and Idea in the Novels of Bernard Malamud: Toward "The Fixer,"* Mouton, 1974.

Ertel, Rachel, *Le Roman juif americain: Une Ecriture minoritaire,* Payot (Paris), 1980.

Fiedler, Leslie, *Love and Death in the American Novel,* Criterion, 1960.

Field, Leslie A., and Joyce W. Field, editors, *Bernard Malamud and the Critics,* New York University Press, 1970.

Field, Leslie A., and Joyce W. Field, editors, *Bernard Malamud: A Collection of Critical Essays,* Prentice-Hall, 1975.

Helterman, Jeffrey, *Understanding Bernard Malamud,* University of South Carolina Press, 1985.

Hershinow, Sheldon J., *Bernard Malamud,* Ungar, 1980.

Howe, Irving, *World of Our Fathers,* Harcourt, 1976.

Kosofsky, Rita Nathalie, *Bernard Malamud: An Annotated Checklist,* Kent State University Press, 1969.

Malamud, Bernard, *The Natural,* Harcourt, 1952, reprinted, Avon, 1980.

Malamud, Bernard, *A New Life,* Farrar, Straus, 1961, reprinted, 1988.

Malamud, Bernard, *Idiots First,* Farrar, Straus, 1963.

Malamud, Bernard, *Pictures of Fidelman: An Exhibition,* Farrar, Straus, 1969, reprinted, New American Library, 1985.

Malamud, Bernard, *Dubin's Lives,* Farrar, Straus, 1979.

Malamud, Bernard, *God's Grace,* Farrar, Straus, 1982.

Meeter, Glen, *Bernard Malamud and Philip Roth: A Critical Essay*, Eerdmans, 1968.
Michaels, Leonard, and Christopher Ricks, editors, *The State of the Language*, University of California Press, 1980.
Radical Innocence: Studies in the Contemporary American Novel, Princeton University Press, 1961.
Richman, Sidney, *Bernard Malamud*, Twayne, 1966.
Roth, Philip, *Reading Myself and Others*, Farrar, Straus, 1975.
The Schlemiel as Metaphor: Studies in the Yiddish and American Jewish Novel, Southern Illinois University Press, 1971.
Tanner, Tony, *City of Words: American Fiction 1950-1970*, Harper, 1971.

PERIODICALS

American Quarterly, Volume 35, number 5, 1983.
Centennial Review, Volume 9, 1965, Volume 13, 1969.
Chicago Tribune Book World, February 11, 1979, September 5, 1982, October 30, 1983.
Christian Science Monitor, September 10, 1982.
Commentary, October, 1982.
Commonweal, October 28, 1966.
Critique, winter, 1964/65.
Detroit News, December 25, 1983.
Encounter, Volume 45, number 1, 1975.
Judaism, winter, 1979, fall, 1980.
Linguistics in Literature, fall, 1977 (special Malamud number).
Literature and Psychology, Volume 20, number 3, 1970.
Los Angeles Times Book Review, September 12, 1982, December 25, 1983.
Mosaic: A Journal for the Comparative Study of Literature and Ideas, spring, 1971.
New Leader, May 26, 1969.
New Republic, September 20, 1982, September 27, 1982.
Newsweek, September 6, 1982, October 17, 1983.
New Yorker, November 8, 1982.
New York Review of Books, September 30, 1973.
New York Times, May 3, 1969, February 2, 1979, July 15, 1980, August 23, 1982, October 11, 1983, February 23, 1985, July 15, 1985.
New York Times Book Review, September 4, 1964, May 4, 1969, October 3, 1971, February 18, 1979, August 29, 1982, August 28, 1983, October 16, 1983, April 20, 1986.
Paris Review, spring, 1975.
Partisan Review, winter, 1962, summer, 1964.
Renascence: Essays on Values in Literature, winter, 1975.
Saturday Review, May 10, 1969.
Studies in American Jewish Literature, spring, 1978 (special Malamud number), number 3, 1983.
Time, May 9, 1969, September 13, 1982, October 17, 1983.
Times Literary Supplement, October 16, 1969, October 29, 1982, February 24, 1984.
Virginia Quarterly Review, winter, 1980.
Washington Post, August 27, 1982.
Washington Post Book World, February 25, 1979, August 29, 1982, October 16, 1983.
Western American Literature, August, 1975.
Western Humanities Review, winter, 1968, winter, 1970.
Writer's Digest, July, 1972.

OBITUARIES:

PERIODICALS

Chicago Tribune, March 20, 1986.
Detroit News, March 23, 1986.
Los Angeles Times, March 19, 1986.

New Republic, May 12, 1986.
Newsweek, March 31, 1986.
New York Times, March 20, 1986.
Times (London), March 20, 1986.
Washington Post, March 20, 1986.*

—*Sidelights by John Ashmead*

*   *   *

MALTIN, Leonard 1950-

PERSONAL: Born December 18, 1950, in New York, N.Y.; son of Aaron I. (a lawyer) and Jacqueline (a singer; maiden name Gould) Maltin; married Alice Tlusty (a researcher), March 15, 1975. *Education:* New York University, B.A., 1972. *Religion:* Jewish.

ADDRESSES: Office—c/o "Entertainment Tonight," 5555 Melrose Ave., Hollywood, Calif. 90038. *Agent*—Richard Curtis Associates, Inc., 164 East 64th St., Suite 1, New York, N.Y. 10021.

CAREER: Film Fan Monthly (magazine), Teaneck, N.J., editor and publisher, 1966-77; New School for Social Research, New York City, member of faculty, 1973-82; film correspondent and segment producer for syndicated television series "Entertainment Tonight," 1982—. Curator, American Academy of Humor, 1975-76; guest curator, film department, Museum of Modern Art, New York City, 1975-76. Consultant and writer, Showtime Entertainment, Inc., Los Angeles, Calif., 1976-80.

MEMBER: Authors Guild, Society of Cinephiles, Sons of the Desert.

WRITINGS:

Movie Comedy Teams, New American Library, 1970, revised edition, 1985.
Behind the Camera: The Cinematographer's Art, New American Library, 1971, published as *The Art of the Cinematographer*, Dover, 1978.
The Great Movie Shorts, Crown, 1972, published as *Selected Short Subjects*, Da Capo Press, 1983.
The Disney Films, Crown, 1973, revised edition, 1984.
Carole Lombard, Pyramid Publications, 1976.
(With Richard W. Bann) *Our Gang: The Life and Times of the Little Rascals*, Crown, 1977.
The Great Movie Comedians, Crown, 1978.
Of Mice and Magic: A History of American Animated Cartoons, McGraw, 1980, revised edition, New American Library, 1987.
(With Allan Greenfield) *The Complete Guide to Home Video*, Crown, 1981.

EDITOR

TV Movies, New American Library, 1969, revised annually as *Leonard Maltin's TV Movies and Video Guide*, 1984—.
The Real Stars, Curtis Books, 1973.
The Laurel and Hardy Book, Curtis Books, 1973.
The Real Stars #2, Curtis Books, 1973.
Hollywood: The Movie Factory, Popular Library, 1976.
Hollywood Kids, Popular Library, 1977.
The Real Stars #3, Popular Library, 1979.
The Whole Film Sourcebook, New American Library, 1983.

CONTRIBUTOR

A Concise History of the Cinema, A. S. Barnes, 1971.

The Compleat Guide to Film Study, National Council of Teachers of English, 1972.
The American Film Heritage, Acropolis Books, 1972.
Directors in Action, Bobbs-Merrill, 1973.
The Encyclopedia of Jazz in the Seventies, Horizon, 1976.
The Movie Buff's Book, Volume 2, Pyramid Publications, 1977.

OTHER

General editor of "Curtis Film Series," 1973-74, and "Popular Library Film Series," 1975-78. Contributing editor and columnist for *Video Review.* Contributor to periodicals, including *Esquire, Smithsonian, Saturday Review, TV Guide, Film Comment, Variety, American Film, Millimeter,* and *Print;* contributor to newspapers, including the *New York Times* and *New York Post.*

WORK IN PROGRESS: A book about the golden age of radio, for New American Library.

SIDELIGHTS: Few movie buffs have turned their enthusiasm for films into a lucrative career as effectively as Leonard Maltin has. At age fifteen Maltin assumed editorship of *Film Fan Monthly* and within a short time increased the magazine's circulation dramatically. By the time he was contracted to produce the popular series *TV Movies,* his editor, Patrick O'Connor, had to conceal Maltin's age "lest the [New American Library] brass suspect that O'Connor had taken leave of his senses" in hiring a seventeen-year-old, according to *Los Angeles Times* writer Charles Champlin.

"No, I haven't seen 15,000 movies," states Maltin, noting in *Film Comment* the first question he is often asked when people learn about his association with *TV Movies,* the latest edition of which contains about 18,000 reviews. He is, however, an avid movie-viewer. "I used to be considered a freak, in that I saw three or four movies a day or in a weekend," he tells Patricia Brennan in the *Washington Post.* "Now everyone is doing it." According to Maltin, videos are responsible for the increase in movie sales, but he feels that this is not necessarily a postive development. "Videos only hurt movies that aren't 'hot,'" he explains to Brennan. But he also remarks that at "the same time, movie attendance is up, theaters have done just fine, there are a lot of theaters being built. I think what it's done is it's turned the nation into a country of movie nuts."

Maltin credits some of his success as an author to good timing. "I became involved with film history before publishers (and readers) were inundated with movie books, and the field was oversaturated," he told *CA.* "I managed to break some new ground, conduct original research, and reach an appreciative audience of film buffs." He sees this work as not "simply a livelihood, but as a way to reach people who haven't yet appreciated a film or an actor." As for his own tastes, Maltin prefers the old classics, such as "Casablanca," "Singin' in the Rain," and "A Night at the Opera." "Old movies just push certain buttons for me," he explains to Brennan. "I just don't have the same affection for recent movies, although I thought 'The Untouchables' was terrific."

Despite his success as a film critic on television's "Entertainment Tonight," Maltin prefers to think of himself as an author. With this in mind, he told *CA* that he finds no small irony in the fact that more people see one of his appearances on any given evening than have purchased all his books put together. His greatest satisfactions in life, he added, are "seeing all my books restored to print during the past few years (like children getting a new lease on life) . . . having my publisher of sixteen years standing put my name above the title on my last volume

(without my asking) . . . and being anthologized this past year, not in a book about movies, but a book on prose writing, which may be the highest compliment I've ever received."

BIOGRAPHICAL/CRITICAL SOURCES:

PERIODICALS

Chicago Tribune, November 12, 1980.
Film Comment, September-October, 1982.
Los Angeles Times, December 2, 1982.
Los Angeles Times Book Review, October 12, 1980.
New York Times, May 6, 1976.
New York Times Book Review, December 21, 1980.
Saturday Review, September 17, 1967.
Washington Post, July 5, 1987.

*　　　　*　　　　*

MANCROFT, Stormont Mancroft Samuel　1914-
(Lord Mancroft)

PERSONAL: Succeeded father to title of Lord Mancroft as second baron of Mancroft, 1942; born July 27, 1914, in London, England; son of Arthur Michael Samuel (1st Baron Mancroft) and Phoebe (Fletcher) Mancroft; married Diana Elizabeth Lloyd Quarry, 1951; children: Victoria, Jessica Rosetta, Benjamin Lloyd Quarry. *Education:* Christ Church, Oxford, M.A., 1937.

ADDRESSES: Home—29 Margaretta Terrace, London SW3 5NU, England.

CAREER: Called to Bar of Inner Temple, London, England, 1938; member of Bar Council, London, 1947-51; member of St. Marylebone Borough Council, 1947-53; lord-in-waiting to Queen Elizabeth II, 1952-54; parliamentary under-secretary of state, British Home Office, 1954-57; parliamentary secretary, British Ministry of Defence, 1957; minister without portfolio, 1957-58; Great Universal Stores Ltd., London, deputy chairman, 1966-71; also worked for Cunard Steamship Co. President, Institute of Marketing, 1959-63; member, Council of Industrial Design, 1960-63; chairman, Committee for Exports to the United States. President, London Tourist Board, 1963-73; chairman, British Greyhound Racing Board, 1977-85. *Military service:* Territorial lieutenant colonel; twice mentioned in dispatches.

MEMBER: Pratt's Club, West Ham Boys' Club.

AWARDS, HONORS: Member of Order of the British Empire, 1945, Knight Commander, 1959; Croix de Guerre, 1945.

WRITINGS:

Booking the Cooks (collection of essays from *Punch*), Mason Publishing, 1969.
Chinaman in My Bath, Bachman & Turner, 1979.
Bees in Some Bonnets, Bachman & Turner, 1979.

*　　　　*　　　　*

MANN, David Douglas　1934-

PERSONAL: Born September 13, 1934, in Oklahoma City, Okla.; son of Loftin Harry and Jeannette (Kneer) Mann; married Jane McKenzie, August 12, 1962 (divorced); married Cathy Hoyser, June 18, 1972 (divorced); married Susan Garland, August 15, 1983. *Education:* Oklahoma State University, B.S., 1956, M.A., 1963; Indiana University, Ph.D., 1969.

ADDRESSES: Home—327 East Vine St., Oxford, Ohio 45056. *Office*—Department of English, Miami University, Oxford, Ohio 45056.

CAREER: Wabash College, Crawfordsville, Ind., instructor in English, 1965-67; Miami University, Oxford, Ohio, instructor, 1968-69, assistant professor, 1969-73, associate professor, 1973-79, professor of English, 1979—. Scholar in residence, University of Luxembourg, 1978-80. *Military service:* U.S. Navy, 1956-59; became lieutenant commander.

MEMBER: Modern Language Association of America, American Society for Eighteenth-Century Studies, Samuel Johnson Society Midwest.

AWARDS, HONORS: Folger Shakespeare Library fellowship, 1970; National Endowment for the Humanities grant, 1976; Bibliographic Society of America fellowship, 1988; Beinecke Library fellowship, 1989.

WRITINGS:

(Editor) *A Concordance to the Plays of William Congreve,* Cornell University Press, 1973.
(Editor and author of introduction) *The Plays of Theophilus and Susannah Cibber,* Garland Press, 1981.
Sir George Etherege: A Reference Guide, G. K. Hall, 1981.
(Editor) *A Concordance to the Plays and Poems of Sir George Etherege,* Greenwood Press, 1985.

Contributor to *An Encyclopedia of British Women Writers* and *Beecham's Guide to Literature and Biography for Young Adults.* Also contributor to journals, including *Analytical & Enumerative Bibliography, Essays in Literature, PMLA, Computers and the Humanities, Mississippi Valley Review, Studies in Scottish Literature, Wabash Review, Old Northwest, Journal of Narrative Technique,* and *Eighteenth-Century Studies.* Assistant editor, *Old Northwest,* 1975-78.

WORK IN PROGRESS: A critical edition of *The Wrong Box* by Robert Louis Stevenson and Samuel Lloyd Osborne.

*   *   *

MANN, W(illiam) Edward 1918-

PERSONAL: Born April 4, 1918, in Toronto, Canada; son of Charles Edward (a transfer agent) and Laura Louise (Wainwright) Mann; married Madeleine Helen Bear, March 16, 1951 (divorced); married Elizabeth Dianne Hughes, August 27, 1983; children: Jocelyn, Gwynneth, Christopher, Allison, Andrew, Portia. *Education:* University of Toronto, B.A., 1942, M.A., 1943, Ph.D., 1953. *Politics:* "Social anarchist." *Religion:* Anglican.

ADDRESSES: Home—39 Lehar Crescent, North York, Ontario, Canada M2H 1J4. *Agent*—Susan Protter, 565 Fifth Ave., New York, N.Y. 10017.

CAREER: University instructor, 1945-47; Anglican parish priest in Ontario, 1949-53; Toronto Anglican Diocesan Council for Social Service, Toronto, Ontario, executive secretary, 1953-58; Ontario Agricultural College, Guelph, assistant professor of sociology, 1959-61; University of Western Ontario, London, assistant professor of sociology, 1961-65; York University, Atkinson College, Toronto, associate professor, 1965-68, professor of sociology, 1969-83, chairman of sociology department, 1965-68. Special lecturer, Trinity College, University of Toronto, 1945-46. Assistant secretary, Canadian Council of Churches, 1948-49; director, Social Science Pub-

lishers, 1967-69; president, Life Energy Action and Research Network, 1978-82; president, Creative Solutions Consulting, 1987. Consultant, Community Relations Services, 1968-72. Research sociologist. *Military service:* Royal Canadian Air Force, instructor in navigation and flying officer, 1943-45.

MEMBER: Canadian Anthropological and Sociological Association, Science for Peace (Canada).

AWARDS, HONORS: Canada Council fellowships and awards, 1946-47, 1958-59, 1961-62, 1968-69, 1970-71, 1972-73; Motoyama-Bentov fellowship for research in Japan, 1985; two Canadian Social Science Research awards; three research awards from Atkinson College, York University.

WRITINGS:

The Rural Church in Canada, Canadian Council of Churches, 1948.
Sect, Cult and Church in Alberta, University of Toronto Press, 1955, reprinted, 1972.
Society behind Bars, Social Science Publishers, 1967.
Canadian Trends in Premarital Behavior, Anglican Church of Canada, 1967.
Canada: The Way It Is and Could Be, Willowdale Press, 1968.
Orgone, Reich, and Eros, Simon & Schuster, 1973.
(With John Alan Lee) *The R.C.M.P. vs. the People: Inside Canada's Security Service,* General Publishing, 1979.
(With Edward Hoffman) *The Man Who Dreamed of Tomorrow: A Conceptual Biography of Wilhelm Reich,* J. P. Tarcher, 1980.

EDITOR

Canada: A Sociological Profile, Copp Clark, 1968, 3rd edition, with Leslie Wheatcroft, 1976.
Deviant Behavior in Canada, Social Science Publishers, 1968.
The Underside of Toronto, McClelland & Stewart, 1970.
Poverty and Social Policy in Canada, Copp Clark, 1970.
Social and Cultural Change in Canada, two volumes, Copp Clark, 1970.
Social Deviance in Canada, Copp Clark, 1971.

OTHER

Author with Earle Beattie of a television series on urbanism for Canadian Broadcasting Corp. Contributor to *Encyclopedia Canadiana.* Contributor to periodicals, including *Canadian Review of Sociology, Continuous Learning, Christian Century, MacLean's Magazine, Toronto Star Weekly,* and *Chatelaine.* Editor of *International Journal of Life Energy,* 1978-81.

WORK IN PROGRESS: The Quest for Total Bliss, a sociological analysis of the Rajneesh Cult; *Jesus of Nazareth—The Christian's Guru; They Were First,* on the sociology of great innovators; *Activist Sociology in Canada,* an autobiographical account.

AVOCATIONAL INTERESTS: Travel, squash, volleyball, tennis, gardening.

BIOGRAPHICAL/CRITICAL SOURCES:

PERIODICALS

Financial Post, May 1, 1974.
Los Angeles Times, November 27, 1980.
Washington Post, January 29, 1981.

MANUS, Willard 1930-

PERSONAL: Born September 28, 1930, in New York, N.Y.; son of Isidore (a merchant) and Henriette (Lewine) Manus; married Mavis Ross (a cookbook writer), October 26, 1960; children: Lisa Jennifer, Ross Saul. *Education:* Adelphi College (now University), B.A., 1952. *Politics:* Independent. *Religion:* Jewish.

ADDRESSES: Home and office—248 Lasky Dr., Beverly Hills, Calif. 90212; Lindos, Rhodes, Greece. *Agent*—Carole Abel, Literary Agent, 160 West 87th St., New York, N.Y. 10024.

CAREER: Yonkers Daily Times, Yonkers, N.Y., reporter, 1953; Columbia Broadcasting System, Inc. (CBS-Radio), New York City, writer for "John Henry Faulk Show," 1953-54; *Bounty* (magazine), New York City, managing editor, 1955; Cecilwood Summer Playhouse, Fishkill, N.Y., publicity director, 1956-59; Macmillan Publishing Co., Inc., New York City, publicity director, 1962-64; free-lance writer in Lindos, Rhodes, Greece, 1965-70; *Financial Post,* Toronto, Ontario, foreign correspondent in the Mediterranean, 1970-78; film and theatre critic for *Century City News, Daily News, Star News, Evening Outlook,* and *Northeast Newspapers,* 1980—.

MEMBER: Writers Guild of America (West), American Theatre Critics Association, Los Angeles Film Critics Association, Los Angeles Playwright's Group.

WRITINGS:

This Is Lindos (nonfiction), Anglo-Hellenic (Athens), 1974.

ADULT NOVELS

The Fixers, Ace Books, 1957.
Mott the Hoople, McGraw, 1967, reprinted, Pinnacle Books, 1980.
The Fighting Men, Panjandrum, 1982.
Pornography Begins at Home, Panjandrum, 1988.

FOR CHILDREN

The Proud Rebel, Teenage Book Club, 1959.
Sea Treasure, illustrations by Lee J. Ames, Doubleday, 1962.
The Mystery of the Flooded Mine, illustrations by James Dwyer, Doubleday, 1964.
The Island Kids, Anglo-Hellenic, 1974.

PLAYS

"Creatures of the Chase"(also see below), published in *Adelphi Quarterly,* summer, 1967.
"The Bleachers" (one-act), first produced in New York at Public Theatre, March, 1975.
"Junk Food" (new version of "Creatures of the Chase"; one-act), first produced in Los Angeles, Calif., at Actors Theatre, June, 1981, revised and produced as a three-act play, first produced in Los Angeles at Actors Theatre, December, 1982.
(With Brian Maeda) "The Kendo Master" (one-act), first produced in Los Angeles at Company of Angels Theatre, October, 1981.
"The Deepest Hunger" (adapted from David Ray's *The Orphans of Mingo*), first produced in North Hollywood, Calif., at Group Repertory Theatre, 1984.
"Bon Appetit" (one-act), first produced in North Hollywood at Group Repertory Theatre, 1984.
"Walt—Sweet Bird of Freedom," first produced in Los Angeles at Chamber Theatre, 1985.

"Diamonds," first produced in Los Angeles at Richmond Shepard Theatre, 1986.
"The Love Boutique"(one-act), first produced in Los Angeles at Skylight Theatre, 1987.
(With Ed Metzger) "Hemingway," first produced in Ottawa, Kan., at Ottawa Theatre, 1987.

TELEVISION SCRIPTS

"Secrets of Midland Heights," first broadcast by Columbia Broadcasting System (CBS-TV), October, 1980.
"Shannon," first broadcast by CBS-TV, November, 1981.
"Too Close for Comfort," first broadcast by American Broadcasting Company (ABC-TV), February, 1984.

OTHER

Unproduced motion picture scripts include "Vendetta," "The Blues Kid," "Evil Heart," "Roller Devils," "P.S., I Love You," and "A Mermaid's Daughter." Contributor of stories and articles to numerous periodicals, including *Argosy* (United Kingdom), *Blackwood's Magazine, Holiday, Nation, New Leader, Observer, Quest,* and *Venture.* Also contributor to newspapers, including *Chicago Tribune, Denver Post, New York Times, San Francisco Chronicle,* and *Washington Post.*

WORK IN PROGRESS: Book for the musical comedy "Central Avenue"; a novel.

SIDELIGHTS: Willard Manus told *CA:* "For me—a writer who has not yet won important critical or financial recognition—one of the few sustaining pleasures of the craft is to be able to do something new each time out. Each of my published novels is different from the last, and intentionally so, because I cannot understand how and why a writer would want to go on writing and publishing the same kind of work year after year the way many of our so-called best writers do. What a failure of nerve and imagination.

"*The Fixers,* my first novel, was based on the college basketball scandals of the 1950s and dealt with my deep disillusionment with the way sport has been corrupted in this society. Next time around, in *Mott the Hoople,* a book on which I labored for seven years, I went for wild, Rabelasian comedy and a bigger-than-life hero who could laugh at the insanities he encountered during his brief, bizarre stay on earth. Number three was *The Fighting Men,* a tough, gritty story about a bunch of men who were in Vietnam together and who meet for a reunion in an unnamed South American country and get caught up in a gunfight with a left-wing guerilla band.

"My book *Pornography Begins at Home* bears no relation whatsoever to any of the above. It is a tragicomic exploration of sexual obsession.

"As for my plays, they too look radically unlike each other. Their settings range from a sex shop to a dirt farm in Oklahoma to a garbage dump in Pittsburgh. In the future I hope to change gears even more and write a series of short stories—or perhaps a novel—dealing with my experiences living on a Greek island from 1965 to 1978. Enough, though. I shouldn't go on talking about my work because, to paraphrase Samuel Beckett, I doubt whether I'm qualified to do so."

BIOGRAPHICAL/CRITICAL SOURCES:

PERIODICALS

Los Angeles Times, June 21, 1985.
Observer, August 6, 1967.

MARCHANT, Catherine
  See COOKSON, Catherine (McMullen)

*   *   *

MARCUS, Jacob Rader   1896-

PERSONAL: Born March 5, 1896, in Connellsville, Pa.; son of Aaron (a merchant) and Jennie (Rader) Marcus; married Antoinette Brody (a musician), December 30, 1925 (deceased); children: Merle Judith (deceased). *Education:* University of Cincinnati, A.B., 1917; Hebrew Union College, Rabbi, 1920; additional study at University of Kiel, 1923; University of Berlin, Ph.D., 1925; postgraduate study at Ecole Rabbinique, 1925, and University of Jerusalem, 1926. *Politics:* Democrat. *Religion:* Reform Jew.

ADDRESSES: Home—401 McAlpin Ave., Cincinnati, Ohio 45220. *Office*—Hebrew Union College, Clifton Ave., Cincinnati, Ohio 45220.

CAREER: Hebrew Union College—Jewish Institute of Religion, Cincinnati, Ohio, instructor in Bible and rabbinics, 1920-26, assistant professor, 1926-29, associate professor, 1929-34, professor of Jewish history, 1934-46, Adolph S. Ochs Professor of American Jewish History, 1946-65, Milton and Hattie Kutz Distinguished Service Professor of American Jewish History, 1947—, founding director, American Jewish Archives, 1947—, director, American Jewish Periodical Center, 1956—. *Military service:* U.S. Army, Infantry, 1917-19; served in France; became second lieutenant.

MEMBER: American Academy for Jewish Research, American Jewish Historical Society (president, 1956-59), Central Conference of American Rabbis (president, 1949-50, honorary president, 1978—), B'nai B'rith.

AWARDS, HONORS: LL.D., University of Cincinnati, 1950, Dropsie College, 1955, Spertus College of Judaica, 1977, Gratz College, 1978, Brandeis University, 1978, and Xavier University, 1985; Frank L. Weil Award of National Jewish Welfare Board, 1955; National Service Award, Phi Epsilon Pi, 1955; Lee M. Friedman Medal for distinguished service in history, 1961.

WRITINGS:

The Rise and Destiny of the German Jew, Union of American Hebrew Congregations, Department of Synagogue and School Extension (Cincinnati), 1934, 2nd edition, Ktav, 1973.
A Brief Introduction to the Bibliography of Modern Jewish History, Hebrew Union College, 1935.
(With A. T. Bilgray) *An Index to Jewish Festschriften,* Hebrew Union College, 1937, 2nd edition, [New York], 1970.
The Jew in the Medieval World: A Source Book, 315-1791, Union of American Hebrew Congregations, 1938, reprinted, Atheneum, 1983.
Communal Sick-Care in the German Ghetto, Hebrew Union College Press, 1947.
Early American Jewry, Jewish Publication Society of America (Philadelphia), Volume 1: *The Jews of New York, New England, and Canada, 1649-1794,* 1951, Volume 2: *The Jews of Pennsylvania and the South, 1655-1790,* 1953, 2nd edition published in single volume, Ktav, 1974.
(Editor) *Memoirs of American Jews, 1775-1865,* three volumes, Jewish Publication Society of America, 1955, 2nd edition published in two volumes, Ktav, 1974.

(Editor) *American Jewry—Documents, Eighteenth Century,* Hebrew Union College Press, 1958.
On Love, Marriage, Children . . . and Death, Too: Intimate Glimpses into the Lives of American Jews in a Bygone Age as Told in Their Own Words, Society of Jewish Bibliophiles, 1964, 2nd edition, American Jewish Archives, 1980.
Studies in American Jewish History: Studies and Addresses, Hebrew Union College Press, 1969.
The Colonial American Jew, three volumes, Wayne State University Press, 1970.
Critical Studies in American Jewish History, three volumes, Ktav, 1971.
An Index to Scientific Articles on American Jewish History, American Jewish Archives, 1971.
Mavo Le-Toldot Yahadut Amerikah Bitkufat Reshita, Magnes Press (Jerusalem), 1971.
Israel Jacobson: The Founder of the Reform Movement in Judaism, revised 2nd edition, Hebrew Union College Press, 1972 (originally published in *Central Conference of American Rabbis Yearbook,* 1928).
(Editor with S. F. Chyet) *Historical Essay on the Colony of Surinam, 1788,* Ktav, 1974.
An Index to the Picture Collection of the American Jewish Archives, American Jewish Archives, 1978.
The American Jewish Woman, 1654-1980, Ktav, 1981.
The American Jewish Woman: A Documentary History, Ktav, 1981.

CONTRIBUTOR

A. T. E. Olmstead, *Syria-Palestine,* [Chicago], 1932.
K. S. Pinson, editor, *Essays on Antisemitism,* [New York], 1942.
Encyclopaedia Britannica, Encyclopaedia Britannica, 1943.
Irving I. Katz, *The Beth El Story,* Wayne University Press, 1955.
Moshe Davis and Isidore S. Meyer, *The Writing of American Jewish History,* American Jewish Historical Society (New York), 1957.
In the Time of Harvest: Essays in Honor of Abba Hillel Silver, [New York], 1963.

OTHER

(Author of foreword) Bernard Postal and Lionel Koppman, *A Jewish Tourist's Guide to the U.S.,* [Philadelphia], 1954, 2nd edition, Jewish Publication Society of America, 1974.
(Author of introduction) Martin M. Weitz, *Year without Fear,* [New York], 1955.
(Author of foreword) Isaac S. Emmanuel, *Precious Stones of the Jews of Curacao: Curacaon Jewry, 1656-1957,* [New York], 1957.
(Author of preface) Martin M. Weitz, *Life without Strife,* [New York], 1957.
(Author of foreword) Julius Nodel, *The Ties Between: A Century of Judaism on America's Last Frontier,* [Portland, Ore.], 1959.
(Author of preface) Fedora S. Frank, *Five Families and Eight Young Men: Nashville and Her Jewry, 1850-1861,* [Nashville], 1962.
(Author of preface) Abraham Cronbach, *Reform Movements in Judaism,* [New York], 1963.
(Author of foreword) Anita de Sola Lazaron, *De Sola Odyssey: A Thousand and One Years,* [Richmond, Va.], 1966.
(Author of foreword) Rudolf Glanz, *Studies in Judaica Americana,* Ktav (New York), 1970.

(Author of introduction) *Critical Studies in American Jewish History,* three volumes, American Jewish Archives/Ktav, 1971.

(Author of preface) Frank J. Adler, *Roots in a Moving Stream: The Centennial History of Congregation B'nai Jehudah of Kansas City, 1870-1970,* [Kansas City, Mo.], 1972.

(Author of introduction) Isaac S. Emmanuel, *The Jews of Coro, Venezuela,* American Jewish Archives, 1973.

(Author of introduction) Joseph Levine, *John Jacob Hays: The First Known Jewish Resident of Fort Wayne,* [Fort Wayne, Ind.], 1973.

(Author of foreword) Mark H. Elovitz, *A Century of Jewish Life in Dixie: The Birmingham Experience,* University of Alabama, 1974.

(Author of foreword) Fedora S. Frank, *Beginnings on Market Street: Nashville and Her Jewry, 1861-1901,* [Nashville], 1974.

(Author of foreword) Samuel Rezneck, *Unrecognized Patriots: The Jew in the American Revolution,* [Westport, Conn.], 1975.

(Author of foreword) Malcolm H. Stern, *First American Jewish Families: 600 Genealogies, 1654-1977,* Ktav, 1977.

(Author of foreword) Rudolf Glanz, *Aspects of the Social, Political, and Economic History of the Jews in America,* Ktav, 1978.

Also contributor to numerous journals and periodicals, including *Hebrew Union College Monthly, American Hebrew, Jewish Tribune, Central Conference of American Rabbis Yearbook, Jewish Quarterly Review, American Scholar, Review of Religion, Liberal Judaism, William and Mary Quarterly,* and *Jewish Digest.* Also editor of and contributor to *American Jewish Archives,* 1948—; member of editorial board, *Studies in Bibliography and Booklore,* 1953—.

WORK IN PROGRESS: United States Jewry, four volumes, for Wayne State University Press.

SIDELIGHTS: Ordained a rabbi and trained in European Jewish history, distinguished author and educator Jacob Rader Marcus pioneered the field of American Jewish history. Having prolifically recorded this history for several decades, Marcus is also primarily responsible for the collection and preservation of the materials that document it. "He above all others has mastered the wide-flung materials relating to colonial American Jewry, their life during the American Revolution, and their flowering during the early National period," states Bertram Wallace Korn in the preface of his *A Bicentennial Festschrift for Jacob Rader Marcus.* "His achievement has been as monumental as his knowledge is encyclopedic."

Praising Marcus for his "requisite ability, vision and indefatigibility," Allan Tarshish writes in his *Dr. Jacob R. Marcus and His Work in American Jewish History:* "As the first professional historian of any stature to devote himself to the subject, he has been largely responsible for bringing objectivity and scientific methodology to the study of American Jewish history at a crucial period." Marcus began his career at Hebrew Union College where, during the 1940s, he taught the first course in American Jewish history and founded the American Jewish Archives, which he continues to direct. Stanley F. Chyet, in a biographical sketch published in *Essays in American Jewish History,* a volume commemorating the tenth anniversary of the founding of the American Jewish Archives, writes of Marcus: "Alive to the challenge of the past, Marcus has never lost sight of the future. Whatever the devotion and concentration which he has summoned to his study of the Jew-

ish past, it has, all of it, been motivated by devotion and concern for the Jewish future. That future will be immeasurably the richer for his labors in its behalf."

BIOGRAPHICAL/CRITICAL SOURCES:

BOOKS

Essays in American Jewish History, American Jewish Archives, 1958.

Korn, Bertram Wallace, editor, *A Bicentennial Festschrift for Jacob Rader Marcus,* American Jewish Historical Society/Ktav, 1976.

Tarshish, Allan, *Dr. Jacob R. Marcus and His Work in American Jewish History,* Rabbi's Fund of Temple Emanuel (Grand Rapids, Mich.), 1960.

Zafren, Herbert C. and Abraham J. Peck, compilers, *The Writings of Jacob Rader Marcus,* American Jewish Archives, 1978.

*   *   *

MARKHAM, Robert
See AMIS, Kingsley (William)

*   *   *

MARNEY, Dean   1952-

PERSONAL: Born December 30, 1952, in Waterville, Wash.; son of Keith S. (a realtor) and Alice (a musician; maiden name, Osborne) Marney; married Susan Carr (an actress and health consultant), July 12, 1975; children: Blythe, Dylan, Luke. *Education:* University of Washington, Seattle, B.A., 1975; University of Oregon, M.L.S., 1977.

ADDRESSES: Home—2996 Riviera Blvd., Malaga, Wash. 98828. *Office*—North Central Regional Library, 238 Olds Station Rd., Wenatchee, Wash. 98801.

CAREER: North Central Regional Library, Wenatchee, Wash., assistant director, 1985—.

WRITINGS:

YOUNG ADULT NOVELS

Just Good Friends, Addison-Wesley, 1982.
The Computer That Ate My Brother, Houghton, 1985.
The Trouble with Jake's Double, Scholastic, Inc., 1988.
You, Me, and Gracie Makes Three, Scholastic, Inc., 1989.

WORK IN PROGRESS: A young adult novel concerning "love, death, and raisins," for Scholastic, Inc.

SIDELIGHTS: Dean Marney's *Just Good Friends* centers on the relationship of three seventh graders: Boyd, the thirteen-year-old narrator whose prepubscent status embarrasses him, and his two best friends—an intellectual and an athlete—who both happen to be girls. A *Seattle Times* review declares that Marney "has produced a delightful first book" and judges the story "wonderfully amusing" as well as "poignant." Will Manley commends the work in *School Library Journal* as "one of the few novels available at this level that looks at changing sex roles from a boy's perspective."

Marney told *CA:* "My manuscripts tend to be short and funny. They have no relationship to me physically, for I am six feet tall and can be quite serious if I have to be. I seem to like to write about being confused, being forced to make decisions, and finding ways to not be at war with yourself. It seems that we are taking a healthier view of how hard it can be to grow up male in this world. I think *Just Good Friends* does a good job of speaking for that movement. Besides, it brings pubic hair out of the closet. If you're going to read a young adult novel with pubic hair in it—this is the one. *The Computer that Ate My Brother* links computers, brothers, forgiveness, and infinite intelligence, all done with tremendous humor; no easy feat but one that needs to be done.''

Marney also wrote *CA:* "You are what you think you are is the point of my fantasy, *The Trouble with Jake's Double.* A teacher told me she read it aloud to her sixth grade class and they laughed their way into deeper self-appreciation. That teacher made me feel wonderful. My new book is about love, death, and raisins. What more is there to write about?''

BIOGRAPHICAL/CRITICAL SOURCES:

PERIODICALS

School Library Journal, November, 1982.
Seattle Times, June 6, 1982.

*   *   *

MARR, David G(eorge)   1937-

PERSONAL: Born September 22, 1937, in Macon, Ga.; son of Henry George (an auditor) and Louise M. (a teacher; maiden name, Brown) Marr; married Phan Thi Ai, April 15, 1963; children: Daniel G., Aileen T., Andrew P. *Education:* Dartmouth College, B.A. (magna cum laude), 1959; University of California, Berkeley, M.A., 1966, Ph.D., 1968.

ADDRESSES: Office—Australian National University, Research School of Pacific Studies, GPO Box 4, Canberra, ACT 2601, Australia.

CAREER: University of California, Berkeley, lecturer in history, 1968-69, assistant professor of Vietnamese studies, 1969-72, research associate at Center for South and Southeast Asian Studies, 1971-75; Cornell University, Ithaca, N.Y., co-director of Indochina Resource Center, 1971-75; Australian National University, Canberra, research fellow and senior fellow, 1975—. *Military service:* U.S. Marine Corps, 1959-64; became captain.

MEMBER: Association for Asian Studies, Social Science Research Council/American Council of Learned Societies Joint Committee on Southeast Asia, Asian Studies Association of Australia, Australia-Vietnam Society, Phi Beta Kappa.

AWARDS, HONORS: Woodrow Wilson fellowship, 1964; Fulbright-Hays grant, 1968; National Endowment for the Humanities grant, 1971-72.

WRITINGS:

(Contributor) Donald Emmerson, editor, *Students and Politics in Emerging Nations,* Praeger, 1969.
Vietnamese Anticolonialism: 1885-1925, University of California Press, 1971.
(Contributor) Noam Chomsky and Howard Zinn, editors, *Critical Essays on the Pentagon Papers,* Beacon, 1972.
(Editor) Phan Boi Chau and Ho Chi Minh, *Reflections from Captivity: Phan Boi Chau's "Prison Notes" and Ho Chi Minh's "Prison Diary,"* translated by Christopher Jenkins, Ohio University Press, 1977.
(Editor with Anthony Reid) *Perceptions of the Past in Southeast Asia,* Heinemann Educational, 1979.

(Contributor) Mary Kaldor and Asbjorn Eide, editors, *The World Military Order,* Macmillan, 1979.
(Contributor) Alfred McCoy, editor, *Southeast Asia under Japanese Occupation,* Yale Southeast Asia Studies, 1980.
Vietnamese Tradition on Trial, 1920-1945, University of California Press, 1981.
(Contributor) Robin Jeffrey, editor, *Asia: The Winning of Independence,* Macmillan, 1981.
(Co-editor) *Society and the Writer: Essays on Literature in Modern Asia,* Australian National University Press, 1981.
(With Carlyle A. Thayer) *Vietnam since 1975: Two Views from Australia,* Griffith University Press, 1982.
(Editor) Tran Tu Binh, *The Red Earth: A Vietnamese Memoir of Life on a Colonial Rubber Plantation,* translated by John Spragens, Jr., Ohio University Center for International Studies, Center for Southeast Asian Studies, 1985.
(Contributor) Ben Kiernan, editor, *Burchett: Reporting the Other Side of the World,* Quartet Books, 1986.
(Editor with A. C. Milner) *Southeast Asia in the Ninth to Fourteenth Centuries,* Gower, 1986.
(Contributor) Norman G. Owen, editor, *Death and Disease in Southeast Asia,* Oxford University Press (Singapore), 1987.
(Editor with Christine White) *Postwar Vietnam: Dilemmas in Socialist Development,* Cornell University Southeast Asia Program, 1988.

Also editor of *Tradition and Revolution in Vietnam,* 1974. Contributor to professional journals. Editor of quarterly journal *Vietnam Today.*

WORK IN PROGRESS: Vietnam 1940-45: The Quest for Power; An Institutional History of the Early Democratic Republic of Vietnam, 1945-46.

AVOCATIONAL INTERESTS: Tennis, computerized information systems.

*   *   *

MARRINER, Ernest (Cummings)   1891-1983

PERSONAL: Born October 16, 1891, in Bridgton, Me.; died February 8, 1983; son of Willis E. (a grocer) and Margie (Whitney) Marriner; married Eleanor Creech, June 17, 1917 (deceased); children: Ernest C., Jr., Ruth Eleanor (Mrs. Eugene Szopa). *Education:* Colby College, A.B., 1913; Suffolk University, A.M., 1937. *Politics:* Republican. *Religion:* Baptist.

ADDRESSES: Home—17 Winter St., Waterville, Me. 04901. *Office*—Colby College, Waterville, Me. 04901.

CAREER: Hebron Academy, Hebron, Me., teacher, 1913-20; Maine representative, Ginn & Co., 1921-23; Colby College, Waterville, Me., professor of bibliography, 1923-29, librarian, 1923-29, professor of English, 1929-60, historian, 1960-83, dean of men, 1929-46, dean of faculty, 1946-57. Trustee, Thomas College, 1963-83; member of State Archives Board of Maine; member of State Board of Education of Maine, 1949-72. Presented weekly radio program devoted to history of Maine communities.

MEMBER: American Association for State and Local History, New England Association of College Deans, Maine League of Historical Societies, Maine Folklore Society, Waterville Historical Society (president, 1962-76).

AWARDS, HONORS: L.H.D., Colby College, 1954, University of Maine, 1957; award of merit from American Association for State and Local History, 1966; Litt.D., Thomas College, 1975; Marriner Hall of Colby College, Marriner Library of Thomas College, and Marriner Assembly Room of Waterville Historical Society were named in Marriner's honor.

WRITINGS:

Kennebec Yesterdays, Colby College Press, 1954.
Remembered Maine, Colby College Press, 1957.
The History of Colby College, Colby College Press, 1962.
Man of Mayflower Hill, Colby College Press, 1966.
The Strider Years: An Extension of "The History of Colby College," Colby College Press, 1980.

Also author of *Jim Connally and the Fishermen of Gloucester,* 1948. Contributor to *Down East.*

OBITUARIES:

PERIODICALS

New York Times, February 10, 1983.*

* * *

MARTIN, Cort
See SHERMAN, Jory (Tecumseh)

* * *

MARTIN, Kevin
See PELTON, Robert W(ayne)

* * *

MARTIN, Robert W.
See PELTON, Robert W(ayne)

* * *

MASER, Edward A(ndrew)   1923-1988

PERSONAL: Surname is pronounced *Mase*-er; born December 23, 1923, in Detroit, Mich.; died October 7, 1988; son of Andrew J. (an electrician) and Bozena (Slezak) Maser; married Inge Besas, March 31, 1956. *Education:* Attended University of Michigan, 1941-43; University of Chicago, M.A., 1948, Ph.D., 1958; also attended University of Frankfurt, 1949-50, and University of Florence, 1950-52.

ADDRESSES: Home—5318 South Hyde Park Blvd., Chicago, Ill. 60615. *Office*—Department of Art, University of Chicago, 5801 South Ellis, Chicago, Ill. 60637.

CAREER: Northwestern University, Evanston, Ill., instructor in art history, 1952-53; University of Kansas, Lawrence, instructor, 1953-55, assistant professor, 1955-57, associate professor of art history, 1957-61, director of Museum of Art, 1953-61; University of Chicago, Chicago, Ill., professor of art history, beginning 1961, chairman of department, 1961-64, director of David and Alfred Smart Gallery of Art, 1972-83. Lecturer at art schools and galleries. Consultant to Samuel H. Kress Foundation. *Military service:* U.S. Army Air Forces, 1943-45; served in Mediterranean theater.

MEMBER: College Art Association, Renaissance Society of America, American Association of University Professors, Phi Beta Kappa.

AWARDS, HONORS: Fulbright fellowships, 1950-53, 1965-66; Guggenheim fellowship, 1969-70; Cross of Honor for Literature and Art, first class, Republic of Austria, 1974.

WRITINGS:

(With Lando Bartoli) *Il Museo dell'opificio delle pietre dure di Firenze* (title means "The Museum of the Manufactory of Florentine Mosaic"), Museo del Opificio delle Pietre Dure, 1954.
Gian Domenico Ferretti, Marchi & Bertolli (Florence, Italy), 1968.
(Author of introduction) *Baroque Cartouches for Designers and Artists: 136 Plates from the "Historische Bilder-Bibel" Designed and Engraved by Johann Ulrich Krauss,* Dover, 1969.
(Author of introduction, translations, and commentaries) Cesare Ripa, *Baroque and Rococo Pictorial Imagery: The 1758-60 Hertel Edition of Ripa's "Iconologia,"* Dover, 1971.
Disegni inediti di Johann Michael Rottmayr (title means "Unpublished Drawings by Johann Michael Rottmayr"), Monumenta Bergomensia (Bergamo, Italy), 1971.
German and Austrian Painting of the Eighteenth Century: An Exhibition, David and Alfred Smart Gallery, University of Chicago, 1978.
Drawings by Johann Michael Rottmayr (1654-1730): An Exhibition of Drawings by the Austrian Painter from an Italian Private Collection, David and Alfred Smart Gallery, University of Chicago, 1980.
(Author of foreword) *Alumni Who Collect I: Drawings from the Sixteenth Century to the Present,* David and Alfred Smart Gallery, University of Chicago, 1982.
(With Gert Schiff) *Adolf-Hiremy-Hirschl: The Beauty of Decline,* R. Ramsay Gallery, 1984.

Contributor to journals.

WORK IN PROGRESS: Studies on Franz Anton Maulbertsch, Johann Michael Rottmayr, Giuseppe Zocchi, and 18th-century Austrian decorative arts.

SIDELIGHTS: Edward A. Maser once told *CA:* "I have hoped to enrich the literature on art and art history with books, articles, and exhibition catalogues on periods either little-known or little-studied in America today. This has been, perhaps, my main motivation, and has led me into such abstruse areas of research as Baroque and Rococo Florentine art, the Baroque art of Central Europe, and the decorative arts of the Baroque period. Such was the lack of interest in English-speaking countries at the time I wrote them that two of my three major books were in Italian and a number of my articles in German."*

* * *

MASIA, Seth   1948-

PERSONAL: Surname rhymes with "Asia"; born September 25, 1948, in New York, N.Y.; son of Bertram Bernard (an educational psychologist) and Phyllis (a teacher and librarian; maiden name, Acselrod) Masia. *Education:* University of Chicago, B.A., 1970.

ADDRESSES: Home—P.O. Box 8279, Truckee, Calif. 95737. *Office—Ski,* 380 Madison Ave., New York, N.Y. 10017.

CAREER: Skier in Steamboat Springs, Colo., 1970-73; *Backpacker,* New York City, equipment editor, 1973-75; *Ski,* New York City, senior editor, 1974-85, technical editor and West Coast editor, 1986—. Ski instructor, Squaw Valley, Calif., 1985—. Host and co-producer of "Weekend Skier," a series on WBTB-TV, 1978; reporter on "Ski World," ESPN-TV, 1986—. Editorial assistant for Science Research Associates, summer, 1966; editor for Greater Cleveland Science Foundation, summer, 1967; writer and artist for Hough Parent-Child Center, summer, 1969.

WRITINGS:

Choosing a College, Science Research Associates, 1970.
(With John Monroe Bennet) *Walking in the Catskills,* East Woods Press, 1974.
(With William Kemsley) *Backpacking Equipment,* Macmillan, 1975.
(With Peter Miller) *Peter Miller's Ski Almanac,* Doubleday, 1979.
The Ski Maintenance and Repair Handbook, Contemporary Books, 1982, new edition, 1987.
Cross Country Ski Maintenance, Contemporary Books, 1987.
(With Bob Jonas) *Total Skiing,* Putnam, 1987.

Also contributor to videotapes, including "Ski Magazine's Learn to Ski," 1986, and "Beginning Ski Tuning," 1987. Contributor of articles and photographs to numerous periodicals, including *Outdoor Life, Ski, American West, Outside, Pacific Flyer,* and *Passages.* Associate editor of *Argosy,* 1973-74; editor of *Ski Business,* 1974-80.

WORK IN PROGRESS: A novel about professional skiers; outdoor writing.

SIDELIGHTS: Seth Masia told *CA:* "I love wilderness sports, and I'm delighted to make a living writing about them. A decade of reporting on the ski industry has made me, willy-nilly, an authority in the field, particularly regarding ski equipment and its manufacture.

"I started skiing in college and have skied all over the world: the U.S. and Canadian Rockies, Sierra Nevada, New England, and the French, Swiss, Italian, and Austrian Alps. I enjoy both alpine and nordic skiing. My most memorable experiences were skiing the supersteep couloirs above Les Arcs and Val d'Isere in France, solo touring at midsummer on the Beartooth Plateau in Montana, skiing from town to town through the Vanoise region of France, climbing the high bowls of Idaho's Sawtooth Range, skiing the downhill racecourses of St. Anton, Sarajevo, and Lake Placid, glacier skiing near Chamonix, and helicopter skiing in Canada.

"I love speed, adrenalin, and silence."

AVOCATIONAL INTERESTS: Motorcycle racing, whitewater canoeing, rock climbing, boardsailing, flying.

*   *   *

MAXWELL, Patricia   1942-
(Patricia Ponder; pseudonyms: Jennifer Blake, Maxine Patrick; Elizabeth Treahearne, a joint pseudonym)

PERSONAL: Born March 9, 1942, in Winn Parish, La. (one source lists Goldonna, La.); daughter of John H. (an electrician) and Daisy (Durbin) Ponder; married J. R. Maxwell (a retail automobile dealer), August 1, 1957; children: Ronnie, Ricky, Delinda, Kathy.

ADDRESSES: Home—R.R. 1, Box 133, Quitman, La. 71268.

CAREER: Writer.

MEMBER: National League of American Pen Women, Romance Writers of America.

AWARDS, HONORS: "Best Historical Romance Novelist of the Year" citation, *Romantic Times,* 1985; "Best Historical Romance with a Southern Background" citation, Georgia Romance Writers in association with Waldenbooks, 1985, for *Midnight Waltz,* and 1987, for *Southern Rapture;* Golden Treasure Award, Romance Writers of America, 1987, for lifetime achievement in the romance genre.

WRITINGS:

The Secret of Mirror House, Fawcett, 1970.
Stranger at Plantation Inn, Fawcett, 1971.
(With Carol Albritton, under joint pseudonym Elizabeth Treahearne) *Storm at Midnight,* Ace Books, 1973.
Dark Masquerade, Fawcett, 1974.
The Bewitching Grace, Popular Library, 1974.
The Court of the Thorn Tree, Popular Library, 1974.
Bride of a Stranger, Fawcett, 1974.
The Notorious Angel, Fawcett, 1977, reprinted under pseudonym Jennifer Blake, 1983.
(Under name Patricia Ponder) *Haven of Fear,* Manor Books, 1977.
(Under name Patricia Ponder) *Murder for Charity,* Manor Books, 1977.
Sweet Piracy, Fawcett, 1978.
Night of the Candles, Fawcett, 1978.

UNDER PSEUDONYM JENNIFER BLAKE; HISTORICAL ROMANCES

Love's Wild Desire, Popular Library, 1977.
Tender Betrayal, Popular Library, 1979.
The Storm and the Splendor, Fawcett, 1979.
Golden Fancy, Fawcett, 1980.
Embrace and Conquer, Fawcett Columbine, 1981.
Royal Seduction, Fawcett Columbine, 1983.
Surrender in Moonlight, Fawcett Columbine, 1984.
Midnight Waltz, Fawcett Columbine, 1985.
Fierce Eden, Fawcett Columbine, 1985.
Royal Passion, Fawcett Columbine, 1986.
Prisoner of Desire, Fawcett Columbine, 1986.
Southern Rapture, Fawcett Columbine, 1987.
Louisiana Dawn, Fawcett Columbine, 1987.
Perfume of Paradise, Fawcett Columbine, 1988.
Love and Smoke, Fawcett Columbine, 1989.

UNDER PSEUDONYM MAXINE PATRICK

The Abducted Heart, Signet, 1978.
Bayou Bride, Signet, 1979.
Snowbound Heart, Signet, 1979.
Love at Sea, Signet, 1980.
Captive Kisses, Signet, 1980.
April of Enchantment, Signet, 1981.

OTHER

Contributor to *Vignettes of Louisiana History* and *Louisiana Leaders;* contributor of poetry, short stories, and articles to newspapers.

SIDELIGHTS: Patricia Maxwell once told *CA:* "I write for the classic reason, to entertain, but also for the joy of the mental exercise and for that rare moment of euphoria that comes when the writer's subconscious takes over and pours out the story with little interference from the conscious mind. The [Jennifer] Blake historical romances give me particular pleasure because of a love affair with history that is of long standing. I like to recreate the past as closely as possible. If I can take readers with me back in time, if I can make them see what I see, feel what I feel, even if only for a brief moment, then I am satisfied.''

BIOGRAPHICAL/CRITICAL SOURCES:

BOOKS

Falk, Kathryn, editor, *Love's Leading Ladies*, Pinnacle Books, 1982.

*   *   *

MAY, Derwent (James)   1930-

PERSONAL: Born April 19, 1930, in Eastbourne, England; son of Herbert and Nellie (Newton) May; married Jolanta Sypniewska, September 22, 1961; children: Orlando James, Miranda Izabella. *Education:* Lincoln College, Oxford, B.A., 1952, M.A., 1956.

ADDRESSES: Home—201 Albany St., London N.W.1, England. *Office*— *Sunday Telegraph*, 181 Marsh Wall, London E.14, England.

CAREER: Continental Daily Mail, Paris, France, drama critic, 1952-53; University of Indonesia, Djakarta, lecturer in English, 1955-58; lecturer in English at University of Lodz and University of Warsaw in Poland, 1959-63; *Times Literary Supplement*, London, England, leader-writer and poetry editor, 1963-65; *Listener*, London, literary editor, 1965-86; *Sunday Telegraph*, London, literary and arts editor, 1986—. Member of literature advisory panel, Arts Council of Great Britain, 1967-70.

WRITINGS:

(Editor with James Price) *Oxford Poetry 1952*, Basil Blackwell, 1952.
The Professionals (novel), Chatto & Windus, 1964, David White, 1968.
(Editor) *Good Talk: An Anthology from BBC Radio*, Gollancz, 1968, Taplinger, 1969.
Dear Parson (novel), Chatto & Windus, 1969.
(Editor) *Good Talk, 2*, Gollancz, 1969, Taplinger, 1970.
The Laughter in Djakarta (novel), Chatto & Windus, 1973.
A Revenger's Comedy (novel), Chatto & Windus, 1979.
(Editor) *The Music of What Happens: Poems, 1965-1980*, BBC Publications, 1981.
Proust, Oxford University Press, 1983.
The Times Nature Diary, Robson, 1983.
Hannah Arendt, Penguin, 1986.

Also contributor of critical articles to *Essays in Criticism*. Contributor to periodicals, including *Times Literary Supplement*.

WORK IN PROGRESS: A volume of short stories.

BIOGRAPHICAL/CRITICAL SOURCES:

PERIODICALS

Punch, June 24, 1981.
Times Literary Supplement, May 29, 1981, May 27, 1983.

*   *   *

MAYER, Ralph   1895-1979

PERSONAL: Born August 11, 1895, in New York, N.Y.; died August 3, 1979 of a heart attack in New York, N.Y.; son of Moritz (a manufacturer) and Leonora (Toch) Mayer; married Bena Frank (an artist), July 25, 1927. *Education:* Studied

chemical engineering at Rensselaer Polytechnic Institute, 1913-16; studied painting at Art Students' League of New York, 1926-28.

ADDRESSES: Home—207 West 106th St., New York, N.Y. 10025.

CAREER: Chemist with industrial firms manufacturing paints, pigments, and varnishes, 1917-27; lecturer and teacher in art schools and colleges, beginning 1932; conductor of courses in materials and techniques of creative painting at Columbia University, 1944-64, and at New School for Social Research, 1959-65. Co-founder and director, with wife, Artists Technical Research Institute, 1959-79. Consultant in conservation of paintings to museums and private collectors. *Military service:* U.S. Army, Chemical Warfare Service, 1917-18.

MEMBER: American Institute of Chemists (fellow), American Society of Contemporary Artists (member of board of directors), International Institute for Conservation (fellow), Artists Equity Association.

AWARDS, HONORS: Guggenheim fellowship, 1952; painting fellowships from Yaddo, MacDowell Colony, and Huntington Hartford Foundation; Grumbacher Awards for paintings in 1966, 1974, and 1975 exhibitions of American Society of Contemporary Artists; Named ''Man of the Year in Art,'' National Art Materials Trade Association, 1969; cited by Artists Equity Association of New York for ''longtime contribution to the technical background of American painting,'' 1976.

WRITINGS:

The Artists Handbook of Materials and Techniques, Viking, 1940, 4th revised edition, 1981.
The Painter's Craft: An Introduction to Artists' Methods and Materials, Van Nostrand, 1948, 3rd edition, 1975.
A Dictionary of Art Terms and Techniques, Crowell, 1969, reprinted, Harper, 1981.
Ralph Mayer Answers 101 Questions Most Frequently Asked by Artists, American Artist, 1977.

Contributor to *Encyclopaedia Britannica* and to art journals and periodicals. Technical editor, *Arts* (formerly *Arts Digest*), 1950-55, and *American Artist*, 1962-79.

OBITUARIES:

PERIODICALS

AB Bookman's Weekly, October 8, 1979.
New York Times, August 4, 1979.*

*   *   *

MAZZEO, Guido E(ttore)   1914-1984

PERSONAL: Born August 14, 1914, in New York, N.Y.; died of cancer, June 5, 1984, in Washington, D.C.; son of Vincenzo C. (a tailor) and Margherita (Cavuoto) Mazzeo; married Avelina Solorzano Munoz, December 31, 1941; children: Margarita (Mrs. Michael B. Miller). *Education:* City College (now City College of the City University of New York), B.A., 1936; Columbia University, M.A., 1938, Ph.D., 1961. *Politics:* Democrat. *Religion:* Roman Catholic.

ADDRESSES: Home—6902 Highland St., Springfield, Va. 22150. *Office*—Department of Romance Languages, George Washington University, Washington, D.C. 20052.

CAREER: Fordham University, New York City, instructor in Spanish, 1938-42, and 1946; United States Naval Academy,

Language Division, Postgraduate School, Washington, D.C., assistant professor of Spanish, 1946-50; Inter-American Defense Board, Washington, D.C., conference-document specialist and simultaneous interpreter, 1950-58; George Washington University, Washington, D.C., associate professor, 1958-68, professor of Spanish, 1968-84, professor emeritus, 1984; chairman of department of Romance languages, 1977-83. Part-time instructor in Spanish, City College (now City College of the City University of New York), 1939-40, and Columbia University, 1940-42, and 1946; part-time assistant professor of Spanish, George Washington University, 1946-58. Director of National Affiliation of Spanish Clubs in the United States, 1938-50. *Military service:* U.S. Army, military intelligence, 1942-45; became sergeant.

MEMBER: American Associaton of Teachers of Spanish and Portuguese, Modern Language Association of America, American Association of University Professors, American Society for Eighteenth-Century Studies, Sigma Delta Pi.

WRITINGS:

The Abate Juan Andres: Literary Historian of the XVIII Century, Hispanic Institute in the United States, Columbia University, 1965.
(Contributor) *New Catholic Encyclopedia,* McGraw, 1967.
(Editor) *Ensayos espanoles* (anthology; title means ''Spanish Essays''), Prentice-Hall, 1973.
Los jesuitas espanoles y la cultura hispanoitaliana del sigo XVII (title means ''The Spanish Jesuits and Spanish-Italian Culture in the Seventeenth Century''), Centro Asociacion Tortosa, 1977.

Contributor of articles and book reviews to journals, including *Hispania.*

OBITUARIES:

PERIODICALS

Washington Post, June 9, 1984.*

*   *   *

McALLISTER, Amanda
See MEAKER, Eloise

*   *   *

McCOMB, David G(lendinning)   1934-

PERSONAL: Born October 26, 1934, in Kokomo, Ind.; son of John F. (in civil service) and Jennie (Glendinning) McComb; married Mary Alice Collier, September 6, 1957; children: Katherine, Susan, Joe. *Education:* Southern Methodist University, B.A., 1956; Stanford University, M.B.A., 1958; Rice University, M.A., 1962; University of Texas, Ph.D., 1968. *Religion:* Unitarian Universalist.

ADDRESSES: Home—2024 Manchester Dr., Fort Collins, Colo. 80523. *Office*—Department of History, Colorado State University, Fort Collins, Colo. 80523.

CAREER: South Texas Junior College (now University of Houston Downtown College), Houston, instructor in history, 1962; San Antonio College, San Antonio, Tex., assistant professor of history, 1962-66; University of Houston, Houston, instructor in history, 1966-68; University of Texas at Austin, research associate in oral history, 1968-69; Colorado State University, Fort Collins, assistant professor, 1969-72, asso-

ciate professor, 1972-77, professor of history, 1977—, chairman of department, 1975-80.

MEMBER: World History Association, North American Association for Sports History, Oral History Association, Society for the History of Technology, Western History Association, State Historical Association of Colorado, Texas State Historical Association (fellow).

AWARDS, HONORS: Tullis Prize from Texas Historical Association, 1969, for *Houston: The Bayou City;* award of merit for oral history work in Colorado from American Association for State and Local History; Danforth associate, 1978; Pennock Distinguished Service Award from Colorado State University, 1986; Texas State Historical Commission Book Award, 1987, for *Galveston: A History.*

WRITINGS:

Houston: The Bayou City, University of Texas Press, 1969, revised edition published as *Houston: A History,* 1981.
Big Thompson: Profile of a Natural Disaster, Pruett, 1980.
Agricultural Technology and Society in Colorado: A History of the Centennial State, Colorado Associated University Press, 1982.
Galveston: A History, University of Texas Press, 1986.
(Editor) *World History* (two volumes), Dushkin, 1988.
Lone Star Adventure: A History of Texas, University of Texas Press, 1989.

WORK IN PROGRESS: A history of Dallas-Fort Worth; a biography of Henry M. Robert.

SIDELIGHTS: David McComb wrote *CA:* ''In the academic world there exists a division between teaching and writing, but I have always looked upon writing as an extension of teaching beyond the classroom. I have begun to reconsider this attitude, however, as my books go out of print. It is a sort of death. No writer, I think, wants that kind of early retirement.''

*   *   *

McGOVERN, Robert   1927-

PERSONAL: Born December 2, 1927, in Minneapolis, Minn.; son of Frank Raymond (a cook) and Mary (Weimer) McGovern; married Barbara Male (a professor and manager of a symphony orchestra), October 3, 1964; children: Nicholas Robert, Brigid Johanna, James Patrick Shannon, Tara Gwendolyn. *Education:* University of Minnesota, B.A., 1951, M.A., 1957; University of London, further graduate study, 1960; Case Western Reserve University, Ph.D., 1968. *Politics:* Liberal Democrat. *Religion:* Roman Catholic.

ADDRESSES: Home—935 County Rd./1754, R.D. 6, Ashland, Ohio 44805. *Office*—Department of English, Ashland College, Ashland, Ohio 44805.

CAREER: Moorhead Daily News, Moorhead, Minn., editor, 1951-52; Radford College, Radford, Va., assistant professor of English, 1957-65; Ashland College, Ashland, Ohio, assistant professor, 1966-68, professor of English and creative writing, 1969—. Leader of jazz band; editor of Ashland Poetry Press; president of Radford Human Relations Council, 1964. *Military service:* U.S. Army, 1951-52.

MEMBER: American Association of University Professors, Poets in the Schools Program, Ohio Poets Association (co-director), Society for Ashland's Preservation.

WRITINGS:

A Feast of Flesh and Other Occasions, Ashland Poetry Press, 1971.
The Way of the Cross in Time of Revolt, Ashland Poetry Press, 1971.
A Poetry Ritual for Grammar School, Ashland Poetry Press, 1974.

EDITOR OF ANTHOLOGIES; WITH RICHARD SNYDER

A Consort of Poets, Ashland Poetry Press, 1969.
Sixty on the Sixties: A Decade's History in Verse, Ashland Poetry Press, 1970.
Poets on the Platform, Ashland Poetry Press, 1970.
Read Out Read-in, Ashland Poetry Press, 1971.
Our Only Hope is Humor: Some Public Poems, Ashland Poetry Press, 1972.
The Young Voice, Ashland Poetry Press, 1972.
The Young Voice Two, Ashland Poetry Press, 1973.
The Strong Voice Two, Ashland Poetry Press, 1973.
The Young Voice Three, Ashland Poetry Press, 1974.
The Strong Voice Three, Ashland Poetry Press, 1974.
Seventy on the Seventies: A Decade's History in Verse, Ashland Poetry Press, 1981.

OTHER

(Contributor) *National Poets' Anthology,* Dekalb University Press, 1974.

Contributor of articles, poems, and reviews to *Nation, Hollins Critic, Kansas City Star,* and to other literary journals and newspapers.

WORK IN PROGRESS: The Wild World of Home, a collection of poems.*

*　　*　　*

McHUGH, Heather 1948-

PERSONAL: Born August 20, 1948, in California; daughter of John Laurance (a marine biologist) and Eileen Francesca (Smallwood) McHugh. *Education:* Radcliffe College, B.A., 1970; University of Denver, M.A., 1972. *Politics:* Independent. *Religion:* "No -isms."

ADDRESSES: Office—Department of English, GN-30, University of Washington, Seattle, Wash. 98195.

CAREER: State University of New York at Binghamton, associate professor of English, 1976-82; University of Washington, Seattle, professor of English and Milliman Writer in Residence, 1983—. Visiting appointments at Columbia University and as Holloway Lecturer at University of California at Berkeley, both 1987. Judge, National Poetry Series book award, 1986, and Poetry Society of America book award, 1987. Member of Italian exchange program, Poetry Society of America, 1988. Core faculty member of M.F.A. writing program, Warren Wilson College.

AWARDS, HONORS: Fellow of Cummington Community for the Arts, 1970, and Provincetown Fine Arts Work Center, 1972; Academy of American Poets prize, 1972; MacDowell Colony fellowships, 1973, 1974, 1976; National Endowment for the Arts grant in poetry, 1974, 1981; winner of New Poetry Series Competition, Houghton Mifflin Co., 1976, for *Dangers;* Yaddo Colony fellowship, 1980; Rockefeller Foundation Bellagio grant, 1986; winner of several Pushcart Prizes.

WRITINGS:

Dangers (poems), Houghton, 1977.
A World of Difference (poems), Houghton, 1981.
(Translator) *D'Apres Tout: Poems by Jean Follain,* Princeton University Press, 1981.
(Editor) Mitchell Toney, *The Matter with Stairs,* Lynx, 1986.
To the Quick (poems), Wesleyan University Press, 1987.
Shades (poems), Wesleyan University Press, 1988.
(Translator with Niko Boris) *Because the Sea is Black: Poems by Blaga Dimitrova,* Wesleyan University Press, 1989.

Contributor to anthologies, including: *American Poetry Anthology,* edited by Daniel Halpern, Avon, 1976; *Poets Teaching: The Creative Process,* edited by Alberta Turner, Longman, 1980; *Forty-five Contemporary Poems,* edited by Turner, Longman, 1985; *The Morrow Anthology of Younger American Poets,* edited by Dave Smith and David Bottoms, Morrow, 1985; and *Antaeus Anthology,* edited by Halpern, Ecco Press, 1986.

WORK IN PROGRESS: More poems.

SIDELIGHTS: "Heather McHugh is likable," writes Alfred Corn of the poet's first collection, *Dangers,* in the *New York Times Book Review.* "The virtues—and weaknesses—of her first book are: personality, energy, and immediacy." Further remarking on her style, another *New York Times Book Review* critic, Hugh Seidman, says the verses in *A World of Difference* are "terse, well-wrought, often ironic poems. She manipulates language to produce resonances of meaning without necessarily creating a psychological depth that might justify her insights and conclusions." In contrast to this, McHugh's more recent collection, *Shades,* sometimes has an "emotional directness [that] is uncharacteristic of Ms. McHugh's style," remarks J. D. McClatchy in the *New York Times Book Review.* McClatchy concludes that "there is a good deal of wheel-spinning in her poems, a nervous need to chatter and charm. But when they are focused by an intriguing subject she can be delightful, inventive and surprising."

From her own standpoint, McHugh told *CA:* "I have a feel for graphics, shapes in sight and sound; but they ripple out beyond our ken. Among poets, [Rainer Maria] Rilke is my spirit's meat: Rilke, as I read him, keeps sailing past customs, out of habit-harbors, toward near unknowns. (It isn't to identify or locate that we look into mirrors: it is to get lost. Who said that?) For myself, I can say 'finding myself' is no goal. If I am given to write, it is rather to explore than to explain." She later added: "I write poems to wake myself up, or to preserve a suddenly lit awakened state. Of dreams, as of taste, too many sweets spoil the sense. It's not sweet dreams I'm yearning for; it's true dreams."

BIOGRAPHICAL/CRITICAL SOURCES:

PERIODICALS

New York Times Book Review, July 7, 1977, September 13, 1981, April 17, 1988.

*　　*　　*

McLAURIN, Melton A(lonza) 1941-

PERSONAL: Born July 11, 1941, in Fayetteville, N.C.; son of A. Merrill (an insurance agent) and Thelma (Melton) McLaurin; married Sandra Cockrell (a teacher), November 23, 1961; children: Natasha Olivia, Shena Nicole. *Education:* East Carolina University, B.S., 1962, M.A., 1964; University of

South Carolina, Ph.D., 1967. *Religion:* Unitarian-Universalist.

ADDRESSES: Home—6241 Teal St., Wilmington, N.C. 28403. *Office*—Department of History, University of North Carolina, Wilmington, N.C. 28403.

CAREER: University of South Alabama, Mobile, assistant professor, 1967-72, associate professor, 1972-76, professor of history, 1976-77; University of North Carolina, Wilmington, professor of history and chairman of department, 1977—.

MEMBER: Organization of American Historians, Southern Historical Association, North Carolina Historical Society.

WRITINGS:

Paternalism and Protest: Southern Cotton Mill Workers and Organized Labor, 1875-1905, Greenwood Press, 1971.
(With Michael Thomason) *Mobile: American River City,* Easter Publishers, 1975.
The Knights of Labor in the South, Greenwood Press, 1978.
(With Thomason) *The Image of Progress: Alabama Photographs, 1872-1917,* University of Alabama Press, 1980.
Mobile: The Life and Times of a Great Southern City, Windsor Publications, 1981.
Separate Pasts: Growing Up White in the Segregated South, University of Georgia Press, 1987.

Contributor to *Phylon, Labor History, Southern Exposure, South Today, North Carolina Historical Review,* and *South Carolina Historical Magazine.*

WORK IN PROGRESS: Research on the impact of segregation on Southern whites; research on the themes of country music as expressions of a continuing Southern culture.

SIDELIGHTS: Historian Melton A. McLaurin once commented to *CA* on his work: "My major motivation is to probe the past of the southern United States, the region in which I live. Some subjects which I feel need to be explored are the life of the southern Negro after slavery and before the second Reconstruction, the uses of photography in history, and the cultural life of the South's working people."

McLaurin evokes the American South of the 1950s in his autobiographical *Separate Pasts: Growing Up White in the Segregated South,* an account of the author's youth in the small town of Wade, North Carolina. McLaurin, who worked in his grandfather's general store near the black section of town, depicts a variety of characters who helped to dispel the socially ingrained notions of racism. "Part remembrance, part sociology, the book makes an adolescent's confusions illuminate much of the moral confusion of white society," Anthony Borden writes in *Nation.* "Through portraits of dozens of acquaintances, white and black, family members and transients, McLaurin explains the lessons he learned—and unlearned—from each." Jonathan Yardley writes in the *Washington Post* that McLaurin's story, with regards to the majority of literature on Southern race relations that focuses on black deprivation and white suppression, "is another story, an important one, that is told less frequently: the story of those whites, raised in unquestioning acceptance of a racist system, who for whatever reason came to challenge that system and eventually to make their private rebellions against it."

Separate Pasts is praised by Alison Friesinger in the *New York Times Book Review* for its "vivid" details, yet the critic also feels that McLaurin "often explains and analyzes too much." Borden comments that "one of the book's main strengths comes

from its being, in many places, as textured as a novel," yet also points out that "McLaurin is a historian, not a novelist, and he resolutely checks his narrative at every turn." Critics have also commented on the insightful details of McLaurin's account. Heinz R. Kuehn remarks in *American Scholar:* "McLaurin, whether he stands behind the counter of the store dispensing soda pop, candy, or canned goods, or whether he is playing basketball on the playground of the black elementary school as a member of an integrated team, is at all times a keen observer of human nature and actions, and he reflects mercilessly. In vignette after vignette, we encounter all the basic stereotypes, prejudices, cliches, and assumptions elevated by a racist society to anthropological dogma and social norms sanctified by tradition."

BIOGRAPHICAL/CRITICAL SOURCES:

PERIODICALS

American Scholar, spring, 1988.
Nation, January 30, 1988.
New York Times Book Review, October 11, 1987.
Washington Post, October 7, 1987.

*   *   *

McLURE, Charles E., Jr. 1940-

PERSONAL: Born April 14, 1940, in Sierra Blanca, Tex.; son of Charles E. (a retailer) and Dessie (Evans) McLure; married Patsy Nell Carroll, September 17, 1962. *Education:* Attended Texas Western College (now University of Texas at El Paso), 1961; University of Kansas, B.A., 1962; Princeton University, M.A., 1964, Ph.D., 1966.

ADDRESSES: Home—250 Yerba Santa Ave., Los Altos, Calif. 94022. *Office*—Hoover Institution, Stanford University, Stanford, Calif. 94022.

CAREER: Rice University, Houston, Tex., assistant professor, 1965-69, associate professor, 1969-72, professor of economics, 1972-73, Allyn R. and Gladys M. Cline Professor of Economics and Finance, 1973-79; National Bureau of Economic Research, Cambridge, Mass., executive director for research, 1977-78, vice-president, 1978-81, research associate, 1978—; Stanford University, Hoover Institution, Stanford, Calif., senior fellow, 1981—. Honorary research associate, Harvard University, 1967-68, 1977-79, and University of California, Berkeley, 1975; senior staff economist, Council of Economic Advisors, 1969-70; adjunct scholar, American Enterprise Institute, 1972—. Visiting lecturer, St. Thomas University, 1968-70; John S. Burgas Visiting Distinguished Lecturer in Economics, University of Wyoming, 1972; visiting professor, Stanford University, 1973. Deputy assistant secretary for tax analysis, U.S. Treasury Department, 1983-85. Organizer of economics conferences. Member of academic advisory board, International Center for Economic Growth. Consultant to private and governmental agencies, including U.S. Treasury Department, the United Nations, and the governments of Panama, Jamaica, and Malaysia.

MEMBER: American Economic Association, National Tax Association (board of directors, 1978-81), Phi Beta Kappa, Omnicron Delta Kappa.

AWARDS, HONORS: Woodrow Wilson fellowship, 1962-63; Ford Foundation fellowship, 1964-65, 1967-68; exceptional service award, U.S. Treasury Department, 1985.

WRITINGS:

Fiscal Failure: Lessons of the Sixties, American Enterprise Institute, 1972.

(With Norman B. Ture) *Value Added Tax: Two Views,* American Enterprise Institute, 1972.

(With others) *Inflation in the 1960s,* American Enterprise Institute, 1972.

(With others) *A New Look at Inflation,* American Enterprise Institute, 1973.

(With others) *Perspectives on Tax Reform: Death Taxes, Tax Loopholes, and the Value Added Tax,* Praeger, 1974.

(With Malcolm Gillis) *La reforma tributaria colombiana de 1974* (title means "The Colombian Tax Reform of 1974"), Biblioteca Banco Popular (Bogata), 1977.

Once Is Enough: The Taxation of Corporate Equity Income, Institute for Contemporary Studies, 1977.

Must Corporate Income Be Taxed Twice?, Brookings Institution, 1979.

(Editor with Peter Mieszkowski) *Fiscal Federalism and the Taxation of Natural Resources,* Lexington Books, 1983.

(Editor) *Tax Assignment in Federal Countries,* Centre for Research on Federal Financial Relations, 1983.

(Editor) *The State Corporation Income Tax: Issues in Worldwide Unitary Combination,* Hoover Institution Press, 1984.

The Value Added Tax: Key to Deficit Reduction?, American Enterprise Institute, 1987.

Economic Perspectives on State Taxation of Multijurisdictional Corporations, Tax Analysts (Arlington, Virginia), 1987.

CONTRIBUTOR

Gillis, editor, *Fiscal Reform for Columbia: The Final Report and Staff Papers of the Columbian Commission on Tax Reform,* Part II, Harvard Law School, 1971.

Richard A. Musgrave, editor, *Broad-Based Taxes: New Options and Sources,* Johns Hopkins University Press, 1973.

La politica tributaria como instrumento del desarrollo (title means "Tax Policy as an Instrument of Development"), Organization of American States, 1973.

The Impact of Multinational Corporations on Development and on International Relations, United Nations, 1974.

Richard M. Bird and Oliver Oldham, editors, *Readings on Taxation in Developing Countries,* 3rd edition (McLure was not associated with earlier editions), Johns Hopkins University Press, 1975.

Erwin N. Griswold and Michael J. Graetz, editors, *Cases and Materials on Federal Income Taxation,* Foundation Press (Mineola, N. Y.), 1975.

Amacher, Tollison, and Willett, editors, *The Economic Approach to Public Policy,* Cornell University Press, 1976.

Wallace E. Oates, editor, *The Political Economy of Fiscal Federalism,* Lexington Books, 1977.

Joseph A. Pechman, editor, *Comprehensive Income Taxation,* Brookings Institution, 1977.

Tax Policies in the 1979 Budget, American Enterprise Institute, 1978.

(With J. Gregory Ballentine) *1978 Compendium of Tax Research,* U.S. Government Printing Office, 1978.

Roy W. Bahl, editor, *The Taxation of Urban Property in Less Developed Countries,* University of Wisconsin Press, 1979.

John R. Moroney, editor, *Income Inequality: Trends and International Comparisons,* Lexington Books, 1979.

Sijbren Cnossen, editor, *Beschouwingen over het verrekingsstelsel* (title means "Reflections on the Imputation System"), Kluwer (Netherlands), 1979.

R. Albert Berry and Ronald Soligo, editors, *Economic Policy and Income Distribution in Colombia,* Westview, 1980.

Henry J. Aaron and Michael J. Boskin, editors, *The Economics of Taxation,* Brookings Institution, 1980.

Felicity Skidmore, editor, *Financing Social Security,* MIT Press, 1981.

Wayne Thirsk and John Whalley, editors, *Tax Policy Options in the 1980s,* Canadian Tax Foundation, 1982.

Supreme Court Economic Review: The 1980 Term, Volume 1, Macmillan, 1983.

Charles E. Walker and Mark A. Bloomfield, editors, *New Directions in Federal Tax Policy for the 1980's,* Ballinger Publishing, 1983.

Musgrave, editor, *Aspectos regionales de la politica fiscal,* Instituto de Estudios Fiscales, 1984.

George Break, editor, *State and Local Finance: The Pressure of the 80's,* University of Wisconsin Press, 1984.

John Moore, editor, *To Promote Prosperity: U.S. Domestic Policy in the Mid 1980s,* Hoover Institution Press, 1984.

Joseph A. Pechman, editor, *Options for Tax Reform,* Brookings Institution, 1984.

Alicia Munnell, editor, *Economic Consequences of Tax Simplification,* Federal Reserve Bank of Boston, 1986.

James R. Follain, editor, *Tax Reform and Real Estate,* Urban Institute, 1986.

The Consumption Tax: A Better Alternative?, Ballinger Publishing, 1987.

Martin Feldstein, editor, *Behavioral Simulation in Tax Policy Analysis,* University of Chicago Press, in press.

John Shoven and Herb Scarf, editors, *Applied General Equilibrium Models,* Cambridge University Press, in press.

Also contributor to *Budgetwirkungen und Budgetpolitik,* edited by Klaus Mackscheidt, Gustave Fischer Verlag (West Germany).

OTHER

Contributor to journals, including *National Tax Journal, Canadian Journal of Economics, Public Finance Quarterly,* and *American Economic Review.* Referee for numerous journals, including *Public Policy, American Economic Review, Journal of Political Economy, Growth and Change, Journal of Public Economics,* and *Journal of Money, Credit, and Banking.* Invited reader, *Quarterly Journal of Economics,* 1972-77. Member of editorial advisory board, *National Tax Journal,* 1972-83, and *Texas Business Review,* 1982-83; member of editorial board, *Public Finance Quarterly,* 1975-77, 1977-79, and *Southern Economic Journal,* 1977-79.

WORK IN PROGRESS: Research on tax policy, tax reform in developing countries, taxation of natural resources, and tax incidence; contributing to numerous volumes on taxation.

AVOCATIONAL INTERESTS: Backpacking, ski touring.

*   *   *

McNEILLY, Wilfred (Glassford)   1921-
    (Wilfred Glassford; pseudonyms: William Howard Baker, W. A. Ballinger, Martin Gregg, Joe Hunter, Errol Lecale; house pseudonyms: Desmond Reid, Peter Saxon)

PERSONAL: Born March 8, 1921, in Renfrewshire, Scotland; son of William Henry and Christina Glassford (Aitkenhead) McNeilly; married Margaret Ferguson Macdonald Miller, March 7, 1946; children: Colin J. R. G., John H. R., Christopher A.

P., Duncan F. S., Quentin K. C. *Education:* "Some." *Politics:* "Presbyterian/Agnostic."

ADDRESSES: Home and office—Glassford House, Ardglass, County Down, Northern Ireland. *Agent*—Albert Zuckerman, Writer's House, 132 West 31st St., New York, N.Y. 10001.

CAREER: Journalist for *Northern Whig*, Belfast, Northern Ireland, 1938-40; "a snake charmer with an Indian circus," 1946-47; journalist for *Belfast Newsletter*, Belfast, and part-time author, 1947-52; full-time author, occasional fisherman, and cameraman (film and still), for British Broadcasting Corp., 1952—. Founder and first honorary secretary, Ardglass Town Committee; member of East Down development and tourist committees. *Military service:* British Army, later Indian Army, and then Royal Indian Navy, 1940-46; became captain in Second Royal Lancers, Indian Army, and lieutenant commander in Royal Indian Navy.

MEMBER: PEN, Downe Society, Royal Naval Sailing Association, Irish Kennel Club, British Legion.

WRITINGS:

The Case of the Stag at Bay, Mayflower Books, 1965.
Death in the Top Twenty, Mayflower Books, 1965.
The Case of the Muckrakers, Mayflower Books, 1966.
No Way Out (contains *Storm over Rockall;* also see below), World Distributors, 1966.
Land of the Free, Howard Baker, 1968.
The War Runners, New English Library, 1970.

UNDER NAME WILFRED GLASSFORD

Alpha-Omega (also see below), New English Library, 1977.
The Sea People, J. A. S. Books Ltd., 1980.

UNDER PSEUDONYM WILLIAM HOWARD BAKER

The Cellar Boys, World Distributors, 1965.
Cry from the Dark, World Distributors, 1965.
Departure Deferred (also see below), World Distributors, 1965.
Destination Dieppe, Mayflower Books, 1965.
The Fugitive, Mayflower Books, 1965.
No Place for Strangers, World Distributors, 1965.
Storm over Rockall, World Distributors, 1965.
Strike North, Mayflower Books, 1965.
Take Death for a Lover, World Distributors, 1965.
The Rape of Berlin, World Publishers, 1965, published as *The Girl, the City, and the Soldier*, Howard Baker, 1968.
Blood Trail, Mayflower Books, 1966.
The Dogs of War, Mayflower Books, 1966.
Every Man an Enemy, Mayflower Books, 1966.
Fire over India, Mayflower Books, 1966.
The Inexpendable, World Distributors, 1966.
The Big Steal, Howard Baker, 1967.
The Dead and the Damned, Mayflower Books, 1967.
The Girl in Asses' Milk, Mayflower Books, 1967.
The Guardians, Mayflower Books, 1967, published as *The Dirty Game*, Howard Baker, 1968.
Treason Remembered, Mayflower Books, 1967.
Night of the Wolf, Howard Baker, 1969.
Quintain Strikes Back, Howard Baker, 1969.
The Judas Diary, Howard Baker, 1969.
The Treasure Hunters, Mayflower Books, 1970.
The Charge is Treason, Lancer Books, 1971.
(Editor) *Howard Baker Holiday Annual*, Howard Baker, 1973.
(Editor and compiler) *Tiger Tim's Own Comic Collection*, Howard Baker, 1977.
(Editor) *Howard Baker Easter Omnibus*, Howard Baker, 1978.

Also editor, under pseudonym William Howard Baker, of *The Greyfriars Holiday Annual*, 1972, 1974, 1976, and 1977.

UNDER PSEUDONYM W. A. BALLINGER

Unfriendly Persuasion, World Distributors, 1964.
I, the Hangman, Mayflower Books, 1965.
Call It Rhodesia, Mayflower Books, 1966.
Drums of the Dark Gods, Mayflower Books, 1966.
Rebellion, Mayflower Books, 1966.
A Starlet for a Penny, Mayflower Books, 1966.
Women's Battalion, Mayflower Books, 1967.
The Galaxy Lot, Mayflower Books, 1967.
The Exterminator (contains *Departure Deferred*), World Distributors, 1968.
Down among the Ad Men, Mayflower Books, 1968.
The Green Grassy Slopes, Corgi Books, 1969.
Congo, Mayflower Books, 1970.
The Six-Day Loving, Mayflower Books, 1970.
The Shark Hunters, Howard Baker, 1970.
The Carrion Eaters, M. Joseph, 1971.
The Waters of Madness, New English Library, 1974.
The Voyageurs: A Novel, New English Library, 1976.
The Voyagers: There and Back Again, New English Library, 1977.
Alpha-Omega, Severn House, 1979.

UNDER PSEUDONYM MARTIN GREGG

Dark Amazon, illustrations by Stuart Tresilian, St. Martin's, 1957.
Dhow Patrol, Hale, 1983, Walker & Co., 1984.

"ATTACK FORCE" SERIES; UNDER PSEUDONYM JOE HUNTER

French Assignment, New English Library, 1976.
Mission to the Gods, New English Library, 1976.
Roman Holiday, New English Library, 1976.
Vampire Mission, New English Library, 1977.

"SPECIALIST" SERIES; UNDER PSEUDONYM ERROL LECALE

The Tigerman of Terrahpur, New English Library, 1973.
Castledoom, New English Library, 1974.
The Death Box, New English Library, 1974.
The Severed Hand, New English Library, 1974.
Zombie, New English Library, 1975.
Blood of My Blood, New English Library, 1976.

UNDER HOUSE PSEUDONYM DESMOND REID

The Babcock Boys, Mayflower Books, 1966.
The Deadlier of the Species, Mayflower Books, 1966.
Death Waits in Tucson, Mayflower Books, 1966.
Frenzy in the Flesh, Mayflower Books, 1966.
The Man from Pecos, Mayflower Books, 1966.
The Snowman Cometh, Mayflower Books, 1966.
Dead Respectable, Mayflower Books, 1967.
(Editor) Peter Saxon, *The Slave Brain*, Mayflower Books, 1967.
The Abductors, Mayflower Books, 1968.
The Case of the Renegade Agent, Mayflower Books, 1968.
The Slaver, Mayflower Books, 1969.

UNDER HOUSE PSEUDONYM PETER SAXON

The Darkest Night, Mayflower Books, 1966.
The Torturer, Mayflower Books, 1966.
Satan's Child, Mayflower Books, 1967.

OTHER

(Contributor) *Danger Man Omnibus*, Number 1, Howard Baker, 1965.

(Contributor) *Sexton Blake Omnibus,* Howard Baker, Number 2, 1968, Number 3, 1968, Number 5, 1969, (under name Wilfred McNeilly) Number 8, 1970, (under name Wilfred McNeilly and pseudonym W. A. Ballinger) Number 9, 1972.

Also author of verse, and radio and television plays.

WORK IN PROGRESS: "Too many books in progress to list."

SIDELIGHTS: Wilfred McNeilly told *CA:* "I don't have a vocation, I just write books [and] I get better at it as I go along. Mostly I'm interested in sailing boats, archery, Irish wolfhounds, Siamese cats and sitting around boozers talking to people instead of working. I am motivated better by a pile of bills than anything else though occasionally I strike a vein of pure lyric genius that has to be carefully excised afterwards. The vital thing for a writer to do is to write. A paragraph on paper beats the hell out of a chapter in the mind."

BIOGRAPHICAL/CRITICAL SOURCES:

PERIODICALS

Best Sellers, May 1, 1969.
New York Times Book Review, May 26, 1968, July 11, 1971.*

*   *   *

McPHERSON, William (Alexander) 1933-

PERSONAL: Born March 16, 1933, in Sault Sainte Marie, Mich.; son of Harold Agnew and Ruth (Brubaker) McPherson; married Elizabeth Mosher, July 7, 1959 (divorced, 1979); children: Jane Elizabeth. *Education:* Attended University of Michigan, 1951-55, Michigan State University, 1956-58, and George Washington University, 1960-62.

ADDRESSES: c/o Alice E. Mayhew, editor, Simon & Schuster, Inc., 1230 Avenue of the Americas, New York, N.Y. 10020.

CAREER: Literary critic, editor, journalist, and novelist. *Washington Post,* Washington, D.C., copyperson, 1958, staff writer and editor, 1959-66; William Morrow & Co., senior editor, 1966-69; *Washington Post,* daily book editor, 1969-72, editor of *Book World,* 1972-78, book critic, 1978-79, member of editorial page staff, 1981-85, columnist, 1983-85. American University, lecturer, 1971, adjunct professor, 1975. Member of New York County Democratic Committee, 1969.

MEMBER: PEN, Authors Guild.

AWARDS, HONORS: Pulitzer Prize for Distinguished Criticism, 1977.

WRITINGS:

Testing the Current (novel), Simon & Schuster, 1984.
To the Sargasso Sea (novel), Simon & Schuster, 1987.

Ghost writer in early 1960s for two books on political subjects. Also author of poetry. Contributor of book reviews, poems, and articles to periodicals, including *Nation, New Republic, New Yorker, Esquire, Sun and Moon,* and *Life.*

WORK IN PROGRESS: A third book about Tommy MacAllister.

SIDELIGHTS: William McPherson is an established and very well respected editor and literary critic who had no intention of writing a novel until the idea came to him when he was in his mid-forties. Editor of works ranging from Patrick Dennis'

How Firm A Foundation to a biography of his grandfather, a Pulitzer Prize winning book reviewer and book editor for the *Washington Post,* as well as the founder of its current *Book World* publication, McPherson told Sam Staggs in a *Publishers Weekly* interview that he at one time felt that "there's no need for me to write a novel and add another tree to the pulp mill."

However, one day what he described to Staggs as a "vision" appeared. McPherson said: "I saw a scene on a golf course, saw it with a clarity and intensity, every leaf on the trees. It wasn't a flashback or a memory or hallucination—more like a vision, a *tableau vivante.*" He wrote down the scene and soon others followed and McPherson found himself writing *Testing the Current.* But finishing the book was not as easy for McPherson as the idea of inspirational visions might indicate. Staggs reports: "It's growth was long and arduous; he worked on the book for five and a half years, obsessed by it even when he wasn't actually writing. Then . . . in a feverish surge of energy, McPherson wrote the last two-fifths of his story in 30 days."

Set in a small town in the North in 1939, *Testing the Current* explores the loss of childhood innocence by chronicling a year in the life of eight-year-old Tommy MacAllister. Born to an upper middle-class family, Tommy enjoys a life that is similar to those of many other children his age—a life that is simple, and yet complicated at the same time. The reader sees Tommy celebrating holidays, attending school, and enjoying the fun and games of an ordinary summer—his life barely effected by the depression that is sweeping the country. However, he is also faced with new feelings that interrupt his cozy and peaceful existence when he experiences the death of his grandmother, the drowning of a schoolmate, the suspected adultery of his mother, and the repercussions of an explosion at his father's chemical plant.

"McPherson's first novel is an extraordinarily intelligent, powerful and, I believe, permanent contribution to the literature of family, childhood and memory," declares Russell Banks. In a review of *Testing the Current* published in the *New York Times Book Review* Banks continues: "From the first sentence . . . to the last, there is not one false note, one forced image. It is a novel written with great skill, and with love. It's what most good first novels merely aspire to be."

Calling McPherson's first book an "unusually fine first novel" David Lehman explains in *Newsweek* that *Testing the Current* "works its magic on us largely because of its precise rendering of the world as seen by an exceptionally likable, exceptionally perceptive eight-year-old boy. [McPherson] sets out here to recover a time (the late 1930s), a place (the impeccably genteel Midwestern community he calls Grande Rivere) and, above all, the lost paradise that is every boy's legacy from Huckleberry Finn."

Many reviewers believe *Testing the Current* "works its magic on us," as Lehman writes, because of McPherson's skillful use of the third person narrative. Tommy MacAllister tells his story in his own words and the reader sees events through Tommy's eyes. "Life reveals itself in sharpest detail to children which is probably why it's so mysterious to them," remarks Wyatt Wyatt in the *Detroit News.* "One forgets what an amazing amount of information a young boy has. Of course there is a lot Tommy can't understand, but almost nothing he doesn't see. It is the pure clarity and honesty of his observations that give this book its power." A critic for *Progressive* comments that "if you let yourself be absorbed into this richly textured pre-war world [of Tommy MacAllister], you will wonder about the puzzling vagaries of grownups and delight in treasures and discoveries, empathizing with those who are in pain or ostracized. Charming but not precocious, the Tommy so sensitively portrayed by Pulitzer Prize-winner McPherson makes you believe that the old moneyed bourgeoisie rejected by many of its literary progeny couldn't have been all bad.''

Testing the Current has also been widely praised for its rich detail and its sensitive portrayal of a child's growth toward adulthood. Stefan Kanfer remarks in *Time* that "the slow awakening of youth is noted in minutely observed and somewhat magnified detail, but at a third-person remove, almost as if the author were examining his cast through binoculars." Kanfer continues: "Through Tommy's wide eyes, most of humanity's sins and sorrows pass in review.... There is no escaping from natural law. Tommy learns to place the comforting theories of his teachers and parents alongside the facts of the human predicament as he sees and hears them. The result is irony, a tone that McPherson manages with untiring subtlety and poignancy."

Perhaps as a result of McPherson's ability to so accurately capture the thoughts and emotions of a young boy, many readers believed that *Testing the Current* was based on events in the author's own life. While McPherson has stated that his book is pure fiction, he told interviewer Herbert Mitgang of the *New York Times Book Review*, "I'm writing from the imagination—but it's my imagination."

As he was completing *Testing the Current*, McPherson realized he had already begun his second novel, *To the Sargasso Sea*. McPherson felt so compelled to start this book, that he began writing sections even before he finished the manuscript of *Testing the Current*.

In *To the Sargasso Sea*, the reader is reintroduced to Tommy MacAllister, who is now a forty-year-old writer awaiting the opening of his second play in London. Tommy, who is also the central character and narrative voice for this novel as he was in *Testing the Current*, has since changed his name to Andrew, is married, and with an eight-year-old daughter of his own. The reader watches as MacAllister is confronted with a series of moral conflicts that threaten his secure and well balanced life. This mid-life crisis causes MacAllister confusion, triggers erratic and inconsistent behavior, and eventually results in soul searching on his part. Catherine Petroski notes in the *Chicago Tribune* that "as much as [*Testing the Current*] was about childhood, so [*To the Sargasso Sea*] is about adulthood."

As a reviewer for *Time* writes: "Sailors once dreaded the blue Sargasso Sea, believing its gulfweed could entangle them forever. The protagonist of William McPherson's novel fears entrapment in other currents.... Andrew learns to trust that he is 'lost in the weeds, but swimming.' McPherson allows a few jarring coincidences to intrude, but his wise story of longing and limitations show the disturbances that lie close beneath reflecting surfaces."

And Petroski summarizes *To the Sargasso Sea* in this manner: "Andrew's life is complex, sometimes troubling.... In [*To the Sargasso Sea*], Andrew outgrows Tommy and accepts the adult task of focusing his energies on his work, trying to make something coherent of experience. As he tells us at the end the struggle is sometimes bewildering, but one that must continue."

While most reviewers agree that it is not necessary to read both *Testing the Current* and *To the Sargasso Sea* to com-

pletely follow MacAllister's personal growth, many critics remark that reading both novels only enhances the reader's enjoyment of the continuing story. "One needn't have read the first novel in order to enjoy or understand *To the Sargasso Sea*," explains Russell Banks in the *Washington Post Book World*, "but it adds resonance and pleasure if one has because the earlier book limns the later nicely, focuses the themes and gives weight and meaning to the dark moral crisis faced by Andrew MacAllister at what should be his moment in the sun." In seeming agreement, Janet Maslin points out in *New Republic*: "*To the Sargasso Sea* shares with *Testing the Current* an abundance of rich detail and close observation.... *To the Sargasso Sea* echoes its predecessor to such a degree that the earlier book is virtually required reading. This makes *To the Sargasso Sea* incomplete in some ways, though it also gives it the added weight and resonance of the familiar."

CA INTERVIEW

CA interviewed William McPherson by telephone on October 19, 1987, at his home in Washington, D.C.

CA: Not least among the good things about your first novel, Testing the Current, *is its being told from the point of view of a small boy. How hard was it to find that eight-year-old character and to put yourself into his mind as an observer?*

McPHERSON: I didn't realize when I first got the idea for the book, or even when I started writing the book, that it was going to be told from that point of view. But after I had written about five pages, I did. And once I heard the voice, or got the tone, it wasn't all that hard. I would have to think about it occasionally, but really I just slipped into it.

CA: One way Testing the Current *is made so authentic is through the accumulation of details and objects such as the shoe buckles, the arrow pin, the pearls, the child's desk, the beloved book* Fingerfins—*which are carried over into the second novel,* To the Sargasso Sea. *Were many of them special objects from your own childhood?*

McPHERSON: I did have a book called *Fingerfins*, though I altered the title slightly for *Testing the Current*. But I wouldn't say that I was pulling magical objects from my own childhood.

CA: How soon in the writing of Testing the Current *did you know that the story would go on beyond that book?*

McPHERSON: There are two possible ways to answer that question, and they're both true. One is that I was quite far into it, close to the end. Certainly by the time I was finishing the book I realized it. And in fact I had a title for the next book before I had a title for *Testing the Current;* even the beginning of it—what I'd thought was a short story begun some years before. The other response, equally correct, is that I knew it from the beginning, but not in the form of a conscious thought.

CA: In To the Sargasso Sea, *Tommy is a forty-year-old playwright, now called Andrew. Did you have to work through that time in some way mentally, or did you make the leap more or less automatically?*

McPHERSON: I had a vision of something I wanted to write about, then an evolving story that I wanted to tell.

CA: Is this the vision you spoke of to Sam Staggs for Publishers Weekly, *the vision of the character Daisy on the golf course?*

McPHERSON: Yes. I hate to talk about that because it sounds either weird or pretentious, but it was very important to me. It changed the direction of my life. Unfortunately, I did mention it on a couple of occasions, and now it keeps coming back to me—like a boomerang, and often with a certain skeptical spin. But it did happen. I saw this picture, this tableau, and then it began to move and I began to work.

CA: In addition to essays and book reviews, you'd had some poems published before the novels. Poetry also figures very importantly in To the Sargasso Sea. *Was it an early love of yours?*

McPHERSON: I've always read poetry. I've always read books. But I've written very, very few poems and published even fewer—four, I think. I don't consider myself a poet, though I'd like to. Writing poetry cannot be a hobby. It's not a sideline, it's an art. Some novelists—Thomas Hardy, for instance—write poetry and write it well, but I don't. I just plug away at my novels.

CA: Were there writers who made you want to write?

McPHERSON: When I was a kid, fourteen or fifteen, I read Thomas Wolfe, and I was knocked off my feet. So I started writing stuff in imitation of Thomas Wolfe. But that passed very quickly, thank God. That's appropriate only for fourteen-year-olds. Later I was influenced by James Joyce. When I was in college I was influenced by Hemingway, the way everybody else was then, and Fitzgerald, and Chekhov. I had a Henry James period. I had a Faulkner period, a Tolstoy period, a Flaubert period. I had a "junk" period too. Every author I've read has influenced me in some way, but I didn't pattern myself after any one of them. I didn't start writing when I was twenty-two, after all, when those influences are much stronger and more immediate because you're just discovering them. It's quite overwhelming to read some of these people when you're young—that's how it should be—and they do influence you for a while, not just in the way you write but in the way you think, in the way you live, in the way you are. With any luck, it's quite overwhelming to read them when you're older too, but the influence then is less direct. By the time I actually got around to writing—years later; I never started out intending to become a novelist—I'd found my own voice, for better or worse.

CA: What were the other advantages of coming to writing fiction relatively late?

McPHERSON: You go into it with your eyes open. I never thought, Golly, this is going to be glamorous. I had, after all, worked for a time as an editor in a publishing house in New York, where you spend a couple of years cajoling a book out of an author, and once you've gotten it out of him you spend the next nine months trying to prepare him for the shock of publication: that nothing much is going to happen. Publication day is just another day. Maybe your editor remembers; maybe not. It's not likely to change your life. It's not likely that you'll suddenly find yourself rich or famous. But the real advantage of coming to fiction relatively late is that you've got a lot of experience behind you, a lot more than experience in a writer's workshop. You hope you've acquired some knowledge and some depth.

CA: Also according to the Publishers Weekly *interview, you had ghostwritten two political books. Was that writing any help at all to you when it came to doing fiction?*

McPHERSON: I don't know that I would call it anything so grand. I was fortunate because I ran the book review section at the *Washington Post*, and I could choose the books I wanted to review. I don't like reviewing books that don't interest me, that I have nothing to say about. I like to review books that are a challenge. With a few notable exceptions, the standard of reviewing in this country is abysmally low, but I suppose it is everywhere and always has been. One problem is that reviewing doesn't pay well, so if you're trying to make money at it, or just trying to keep your name in print, you have to do it quickly, without much time for reflection, for questions, for thought. You're expected to come up with a snap, readable judgment, not necessarily a good judgment. To anyone who has written a book—or indeed to anyone who had *read* a book—it's often quite clear from the reviews that a reviewer has not done his homework—but he had found a formula. Some formulas are better than others.

As to my philosophy of book reviewing, I'd say *read* the book, then get the facts straight. Look first at the text, not at yourself. That's basic. It's basic, but it's not always the case. What is the book actually trying to say? Explain that to the reader and make a judgment on it. But be honest, and be a little humble. Reviews can come back to haunt you. Particularly when you start out reviewing books, you tend to throw in a lot of superlatives—this is the greatest, or this is the worst, depending on your disposition. You have to get over that very quickly, especially when you see your words flung back at you two years later and you don't even remember the book you once thought so great. There are people who really delight in reviewing books they hate because it makes them sound clever. We all enjoy a little malice, and in some cases malice may be earned. Still, it's easy to get a few laughs at the expense of a book you're destroying, but cheap shots are just that—cheap and easy. They're to be avoided. Unless a book is bad in some serious and important way, destroying it is not worth the effort, at least for me. And reviewing does take a lot of effort, or ought to.

CA: You have taught criticism also. What aspects of it do you think can be learned, and what qualities do potential critics have to bring with them?

McPHERSON: They should come with an open mind, and they have to bring with them a background of reading. You can't criticize books in a vacuum, without a context. You can't come to any informed judgment about a poem, say, if you've never read other poems—and you certainly can't write one—any more than you can understand mathematics if you're still trying to figure out fractions. I think criticism *can* be taught. You can teach other critics; you can study the history of criticism; you can study the works being criticized. When I was in college I had a course called "Practical Criticism" that really opened my eyes. The teacher, Herbert Barrows, had a great influence on me. His course was modeled more or less on I. A. Richard's book of the same name. Mr. Barrows would give us four or five poems a week, their authors unknown to us, and we'd have to read—really read—the poems and write a short paper on each telling what it said, whether it was good or bad, and why. That's harder than it may sound.

Taste is another matter. If you're writing about painting or music, you've got to have an eye for paintings or an ear for music. The same is true of literature. Some people have keener eyes and ears for these things, that's all.

CA: Do you miss writing regularly for the Post *since you've been doing fiction full-time?*

McPHERSON: Yes. I wrote a column on the Op-Ed page for a couple of years, and I do miss that. It's quick, you get an immediate response (insofar as you get one), and it's over with. You go in Monday and write the column and it appears Tuesday, and then you do another one the next week. Also you feel as if you're an active participant in the world—not a constant feeling here at the desk at home, mucking around in the imagination. Obviously, if you write a column you have to believe in what you're writing, and you hope that maybe a couple of other people will come to believe it too and, if you're writing on a political issue, will act on it; will respond, in any event. When they do, that's gratifying. Also, the audience for a column in the *Post* is vastly greater than exists for a book. But on the other hand, the satisfaction you get from writing a book is different and for me considerably greater. So is the challenge. It's harder. Lots harder. The response you get is different too.

CA: It must be great to hear from people who've read one of your books carefully and been moved enough by it to sit down and write to you.

McPHERSON: You bet it is. That someone you don't know, someone you've never seen or heard of, and something you've done has affected them enough to move them to write you— and intelligently, too—that's definitely a good feeling.

CA: According to what I've read, two people wrote to you to say they remembered the explosion in Testing the Current, *although it was strictly fiction.*

McPHERSON: True. People of course are very selective with their facts. They see some event they think they recognize— like that explosion that never took place—and they extrapolate everything from there. I suppose it's flattering in a way, that they find the story so convincing, so "real" in some sense, but it's also disconcerting. And it is definitely not the point. It is not the way to read a novel.

CA: Do you keep a rigid writing schedule?

McPHERSON: I get up in the morning and I go to work. And I do it seven days a week. Boring life, not glamorous at all. But of course you're free—except for being chained to your word processor. I suppose that's rigid.

CA: There's the water imagery in the titles of both novels and in the story in each: in Testing the Current, *the tricky river that has to be crossed from the Island, the summer place, to the mainland; in the second novel, the attractive and very dangerous Sargasso Sea. Will you continue that pattern in the third book?*

McPHERSON: Well, the third book does begin in Maine. There's water, there's the ocean. People have asked me what I'm going to title my third book, how it will relate to water. I think I'll avoid water. Maybe fire this time.

CA: Have you thought of doing any other kind of writing? Would you like, for example, to do plays, like your character Andrew?

McPHERSON: I have never thought about it until I started *Sargasso* and decided the character would be a playwright. That made me think about the theater. I don't have a play in mind, but sure, it would be fun to write one sometime. On second thought, "fun" is probably not the right word. I'd like to do critical writing again too—but not now, not when I'm writing these books. I'd like to be able to write long pieces on subjects that interest me. That would be wonderful. It would also be hard work. Those pieces take a long time to do, and they're a real luxury because you're not paid enough to compensate for the hours you spend on them, even assuming someone wants to publish in some small magazines—so you're talking about doing something essentially for nothing. It would be pleasant to be in that position.

BIOGRAPHICAL/CRITICAL SOURCES:

BOOKS

Contemporary Literary Criticism, Volume 34, Gale, 1985.

PERIODICALS

American Spectator, October, 1984.
Booklist, March 15, 1984.
Chicago Tribune, May 17, 1987.
Detroit News, May 13, 1984.
Los Angeles Times Book Review, May 6, 1984, July 26, 1987.
New Republic, April 30, 1984, July 27, 1987.
Newsweek, May 14, 1984.
New York Times, June 3, 1987.
New York Times Book Review, March 18, 1984, June 14, 1987.
Progressive, September, 1984.
Publishers Weekly, May 22, 1987.
Time, April 2, 1984.
Times Literary Supplement, March 22, 1985.
Washington Post Book World, June 7, 1987.

—*Sketch by Margaret Mazurkiewicz*
—*Interview by Jean W. Ross*

*   *   *

McSHERRY, James E(dward)   1920-

PERSONAL: Born January 15, 1920, in Johnston City, Ill.; son of Patrick H. and Edna E. (Spence) McSherry; married, 1948 (divorced, 1958). *Education:* Southern Illinois University, B.A., 1951, M.A., 1952; graduate study at University of Illinois, 1954, and George Washington University, 1959.

ADDRESSES: Home and office—4201 South 31st St., Apt. 848, Arlington, Va. 22206.

CAREER: Editor and writer for U.S. Department of State, U.S. Department of Defense, and U.S. Air Force, 1952-60; university press editor at Southern Illinois University, Carbondale, 1960-64, and Pennsylvania State University, University Park, 1964-69; free-lance editor and indexer in Arlington, Va., 1969—. *Military service:* U.S. Army, 1938-40, 1942-48; Canadian Army, 1940-42; twice wounded in action.

WRITINGS:

Stalin, Hitler, and Europe, World Publishing, Volume I: *The Origins of World War II, 1933-1939*, 1968, Volume II: *The Imbalance of Power, 1939-1941*, 1970, reprinted, Open Door Press, 1986.
Khrushchev and Kennedy in Retrospect, Open Door Press, 1971.

Documents on German Foreign Policy, 1918-1945, Series D, Volume XIV (index), Open Door Press, 1976.
Computer Typesetting, Open Door Press, 1984.

Contributor to United States Naval Institute *Proceedings* and *American Historical Review.**

*   *   *

McWHINNEY, Edward Watson   1926-

PERSONAL: Born May 19, 1926, in Sydney, New South Wales, Australia; son of Matthew Andrew and Evelyn Annie (Watson) McWhinney; married Emily Ingalore (an economist and stockbroker), June 27, 1951. *Education:* University of Sydney, LL.B., 1949; Yale University, LL.M.,1951, Sc.Jur.D., 1953; Academy of International Law, Diploma in International Law, 1951.

ADDRESSES: Home—1949 Beach Ave., Vancouver, British Columbia, Canada V6G 1Z2. *Office*—Department of Politics, Simon Fraser University, Burnaby, Vancouver, British Columbia, Canada V5A 1SG.

CAREER: Yale University, New Haven, Conn., lecturer in law, 1951-53, assistant professor of political science and fellow of Silliman College, 1953-55; University of Toronto, Toronto, Ontario, professor of international and comparative law and member of Centre for Russian Studies, 1955-66; McGill University, Montreal, Quebec, professor of law and director of Institute of Air and Space Law, 1966-71; Indiana University—Bloomington, professor of law and director of international and comparative legal studies, 1971-74; Simon Fraser University, Burnaby, Vancouver, British Columbia, professor of international law and relations and chairman of department of politics, 1974—. Visiting professor at Ecole Libre des Hautes Etudes, 1952, University of Heidelberg and Max-Planck Institut, 1960-61, National University of Mexico, 1965, University of Paris and University of Madrid, 1968, University d'Aix-Marseille, 1969, Institut Universitaire, Luxembourg, 1972, 1974, 1976, Academy of International Law, 1973, Aristotelian University of Thessaloniki, 1975, 1978, 1982, University of Nice, 1976-77, Jagellonian University of Cracow, 1976, University of Paris, 1982, 1985, College of France, Paris, 1983, Meiji University, 1987, and Institute of Contemporary International Relations, 1987. Queen's counsel, Canada, 1967—; royal commissioner, Quebec, 1968-72; royal commissioner, British Columbia, 1974-75. Legal consultant to United Nations, 1953-54, U.S. Naval War College, 1961-68, government of Ontario, 1965-71, government of Quebec, 1969-70, 1974-75, and government of Canada, 1979. Special advisor, Canadian delegation to the United Nations, 1981-83. *Military service:* Australian Air Force, 1943-45; became flying officer (first lieutenant).

MEMBER: Institut de Droit International (membre titulaire), Academie International de Droit Compare, Canadian Society of International Law (chairman of executive committee, 1972-75), American Society of International Law (member of executive council, 1965-68), American Foreign Law Association, Institut Grand-Ducal.

AWARDS, HONORS: Rockefeller Foundation fellowship, 1960-61, 1966-68; Canada Council fellowship, 1960-61.

WRITINGS:

Judicial Review in the English-Speaking World, University of Toronto Press, 1956, 4th edition, 1969.

(Editor and contributor) *Canadian Jurisprudence: The Civil Law and Common Law in Canada,* University of Toronto Press, 1958.
Foederalismus und Bundesverfassungsrecht, Quelle & Meyer, 1961.
Constitutionalism in Germany, Sijthoff, 1962.
Comparative Federalism, University of Toronto Press, 1962, 2nd edition, 1965.
Peaceful Coexistence and Soviet-Western International Law, Sijthoff, 1964.
(Editor and contributor) *Law, Foreign Policy, and the East-West Detente,* University of Toronto Press, 1964.
Federal Constitution-Making for a Multi-National World, Sijthoff, 1966.
International Law and World Revolution, Sijthoff, 1967.
(Editor with Martin A. Bradley) *The Freedom of the Air,* Oceana, 1968.
Conflit ideologique et Ordre public mondial, A. Pedone (Paris), 1969.
(Editor with Bradley) *New Frontiers in Space Law,* Oceana, 1969.
(Editor and contributor) *The International Law of Communications,* Oceana, 1971.
(Editor and contributor) *Aerial Piracy and International Law,* Oceana, 1971.
(Editor and contributor with P. Pescatore) *Federalism and Supreme Courts and the Integration of Legal Systems,* Editions UGA (Brussels), 1973.
The Illegal Diversion of Aircraft and International Law, Sijthoff, 1975.
The International Law of Detente, Sijthoff, 1978.
The World Court and the Contemporary International Law-Making Process, Sijthoff, 1979.
Quebec and the Constitution, 1960-1978, University of Toronto Press, 1979.
Constitution-Making: Principles, Process, Practices, University of Toronto Press, 1981.
Conflict and Compromise: International Law and World Order in a Revolutionary Age, Holmes & Meier, 1981.
Supreme Courts and Judicial Law-Making, Holmes & Meier, 1986.
Aerial Piracy and International Terrorism, Martinus Nijhoff, 1987.
The International Court of Justice and the Western Tradition of International Law, Martinus Nijhoff, 1987.
(With Nagendra Singh) *Nuclear Weapons and Contemporary International Law,* Martinue Nijhoff, 1988.

Author of *Canada and the Constitution,* 1982, and *United Nations Law-Making,* 1983. Contributor to *International Encyclopaedia of the Social Sciences* and *Encyclopaedia Britannica.* Also contributor of articles and essays to *Harvard Law Review, Revue Generale de Droit/International Public,* and other journals in the United Kingdom, United States, France, Germany, Spain, and India.

WORK IN PROGRESS: Federalism and Nationalism; studies on relations between the West, the Communist countries, and the Third World; science and technology and international law; communications and broadcasting and international law.

SIDELIGHTS: Edward Watson McWhinney is fluent in French and German and competent in Russian, Italian, and Spanish.

AVOCATIONAL INTERESTS: Golf, tennis, swimming, walking.

McWILLIAMS, John P(robasco), Jr.   1940-

PERSONAL: Born July 22, 1940, in Cleveland, Ohio; son of John P. and Brooks (Barlow) McWilliams; married Margot Helen Brown, April 15, 1967; married Mireille Barbaud, July 13, 1985; children: (first marriage) Andrew, Suzannah, Kirsten, Elizabeth; (second marriage) Christopher, Isabel. *Education:* Princeton University, A.B. (summa cum laude), 1962; Harvard University, Ph.D., 1968.

ADDRESSES: Home—42 Seminary St., Middlebury, Vt. 05753. *Office*—Department of American Literature, Middlebury College, Middlebury, Vt. 05753.

CAREER: University of California, Berkeley, assistant professor of English, 1968-74; University of Illinois at Chicago Circle, associate professor of English, 1974-77; Middlebury College, Middlebury, Vt., professor of American literature, 1978—.

MEMBER: Modern Language Association of America, American Studies Association, Phi Beta Kappa.

AWARDS, HONORS: Woodrow Wilson fellow, 1962-63; National Endowment for the Humanities fellowships, 1982-83, 1988-89.

WRITINGS:

Political Justice in a Republic: James Fenimore Cooper's America, University of California Press, 1972.
(Editor with George Dekker) *Fenimore Cooper: The Critical Heritage,* Routledge & Kegan Paul, 1973.
Law and American Literature, Knopf, 1983.
Hawthorne, Melville and the American Character: A Looking Glass Business, Cambridge University Press, 1986.
American Epic: Changes of a Genre, Cambridge University Press, 1989.
(Editor) James Fenimore Cooper, *The Last of the Mohicans,* Oxford University Press, 1989.

Contributor of essays to journals, including *American Quarterly, New England Quarterly,* and *Studies in Romanticism.*

*   *   *

MEAKER, Eloise   1915-
(Lydia Benson Clark, Valancy Hunter, Lydia Lancaster, Amanda McAllister)

PERSONAL: Born July 13, 1915, in Auburn, N.Y.; daughter of James S. (a merchant) and Elizabeth (Smith) Case; married Charles Meaker, April 2, 1935; children: Cynthia A. *Education:* Attended high school in Auburn, N.Y.

ADDRESSES: Home—Glendale, Ariz. *Agent*—Shirley Burke, 370 East 76th St., Suite B-704, New York, N.Y. 10021.

CAREER: Writer, 1972—. Worked as grocery clerk and in print shop bindery.

WRITINGS:

UNDER PSEUDONYM LYDIA LANCASTER; NOVELS

Passion and Proud Hearts, Warner Books, 1978.
Stolen Rapture, Warner Books, 1978.
Desire and Dreams of Glory, Warner Books, 1979.
The Temptation, Warner Books, 1979.
Her Heart's Honor, Warner Books, 1980.
To Those Who Dare, Warner Books, 1982.
Love's Hidden Glory, Warner Books, 1982.

Heaven's Horizon, Warner Books, 1983.
The Arms of a Stranger, Pocket Books, 1985.
Always the Dream, Pocket Books, 1987.

OTHER

(Under pseudonym Valancy Hunter) *Devil's Double,* Dell, 1973.
(Under pseudonym Lydia Benson Clark) *Yesterday's Evil,* Ace Books, 1974.
(Under pseudonym Valancy Hunter) *The Namesake,* Dell, 1974.
(Under pseudonym Lydia Benson Clark) *Demon Cat,* Zebra Books, 1975.
(Under pseudonym Valancy Hunter) *The Rebel Heart,* Dell, 1976.
(Under pseudonym Amanda McAllister) *Waiting for Caroline,* Playboy Press, 1976.
(Under pseudonym Amanda McAllister) *Look over Your Shoulder,* Playboy Press, 1976.

Also author of weekly newspaper column during the 1950s for the *Phoenix Sun Valley Sun.*

WORK IN PROGRESS: The Chameleons; Bitter Seeds of Storm.

SIDELIGHTS: Eloise Meaker told *CA:* "I write because I love to write, and I write historical novels because history has always been my first love. The research involved in writing an historical romance is a joy in itself, there is always something new to learn. Writing demands a great deal of self-discipline. I would warn any would-be writer that the hours are long, and that it demands total dedication. It is, in other words, hard work and it requires regular working hours, the same as any job. But the satisfaction of turning out a completed book, written to the best of your ability, is more than enough compensation.

"I make it a rule to answer all my letters from my readers. If anyone is kind enough to read my books and then even more kind, taking the time to write to me, that person is entitled to the courtesy of a personal reply. Criticism is always welcome, especially if mistakes are pointed out. Everyone has something to learn.

"Like the delightful character in 'Arsenic and Old Lace,' who if he couldn't be Teddy Roosevelt refused to be anybody, if I couldn't be a writer, I wouldn't be anything. I think that this drive is inborn. If you are a writer, you write."

AVOCATIONAL INTERESTS: Square dancing, swimming, needlepoint, oil painting, horseback riding.

*   *   *

MEEHAN, Thomas Edward   1932-

PERSONAL: Born August 14, 1932, in Ossining, N.Y.; son of Thomas Edward (a businessman) and Helen (O'Neill) Meehan; married Karen Termohlen (a writer and editor), June 22, 1963. *Education:* Hamilton College, B.A., 1951.

ADDRESSES: Office—*New Yorker,* 25 West 43rd St., New York, N.Y., 10036. *Agent*—Candida Donadio, 111 West 57th St., New York, N.Y. 10019.

CAREER: Writer. *New Yorker,* New York, N.Y., staff writer for "Talk of the Town." Staff writer for television program "That Was the Week That Was," 1964-65. *Military service:* U.S. Army, 1951-53; counterintelligence agent in Germany.

AWARDS, HONORS: Antoinette Perry ("Tony") Award, 1977, for "Annie."

WRITINGS:

Yma, Ava; Yma, Abba; Yma, Oona; Yma, Ida; Yma, Aga . . . and Others, Simon & Schuster, 1967.
(Adaptor, and author of stage production book) ''Annie'' (musical comedy based on comic strip ''Little Orphan Annie'' by Harold Gray; also see below), first produced on Broadway at the Alvin Theatre, April 21, 1977.
(Adaptor, and author of stage production book) ''I Remember Mama'' (based on 1944 musical comedy of same title by John van Druten, from stories and novel *Mama's Bank Account* by Kathryn Forbes), first produced on Broadway at the Majestic Theatre, June, 1979.
Annie: An Old-Fashioned Story, illustrations by Julia Noonan, Macmillan, 1980.
(With Ronny Graham) ''To Be or Not to Be'' (screenplay; based on 1942 screenplay of same title by Edwin Justin Mayer, from story by Melchior Lengyel), Brooksfilms/Twentieth Century-Fox, 1983.
''One Magic Christmas'' (screenplay; based on story by Meehan, Phillip Borsos, and Barry Healey), Disney-Silver Screen Partners II/Buena Vista, 1985.
(With Mel Brooks and Graham) ''Spaceballs'' (screenplay), Metro-Goldwyn-Mayer/United Artists, 1987.
(Librettist) Cyma Rubin, ''Mike'' (musical; based on life of producer Mike Todd), first produced in Philadelphia, Pa., at the Walnut Street Theater, March 30, 1987.
(With Martin Charmin, Marvin Hamlisch, Marshall Brickman, and others) ''No Frills Revue'' (musical), first produced in New York City at Musical Theater Works, 1987.

SIDELIGHTS: Thomas Edward Meehan, a versatile writer associated with several successful stage productions, is perhaps best known for his ''Tony'' Award-winning work on the long-lived Broadway musical comedy ''Annie,'' which ran for more than twenty-three hundred performances. ''Thomas Meehan's book, artfully adapted and economically plotted from the old comic strip adventures of 'Little Orphan Annie,' appeals to all ages with its combination of ingenuous charm and sophisticated wit,'' states Richard Christiansen, critic at large for the *Chicago Tribune.* In addition to authoring the stage production book for ''Annie,'' which served in part as the basis for the equally successful film adaptation, Meehan has also penned the fictional account, *Annie: An Old-Fashioned Story.*

An active screenwriter as well, whose work includes two Mel Brooks comedies, ''To Be or Not to Be'' and ''Spaceballs,'' Meehan has written the screenplay for a film that some critics believe will surely become a Christmas classic. ''One Magic Christmas,'' based upon a story on which Meehan also collaborated, centers around a suburban wife and mother whose Christmas spirit is tried by the family's various financial woes. Contemplating suicide, she is escorted by an angel to the North Pole where her belief in Santa Claus is restored. Although Gene Siskel, movie critic for the *Chicago Tribune,* found it a depressing film despite its happy ending, Michael Wilmington suggests in a *Los Angeles Times* review of the film that despite certain problems with script, ''it has plenty of magical moments as well.'' And as Paul Attanasio proclaims in the *Washington Post,* '' 'One Magic Christmas' is a film that, whatever its immediate commercial prospects, promises to become a fixture in our holiday film library—already, it ages well in the mind.''

MEDIA ADAPTATIONS: ''Annie,'' a musical comedy based in part upon the stage production book by Meehan, was filmed by Columbia in 1982, and featured Albert Finney, Carol Burnett, and Bernadette Peters.

BIOGRAPHICAL/CRITICAL SOURCES:

PERIODICALS

Chicago Tribune, December 19, 1983, November 25, 1985, June 24, 1987.
Christian Science Monitor, December 7, 1967.
Los Angeles Times, January 11, 1984, November 22, 1985.
Los Angeles Times Book Review, September 7, 1980.
National Observer, December 4, 1987.
Newsweek, June 29, 1987.
New Yorker, December 9, 1967.
New York Times, June 1, 1979, June 10, 1979, December 16, 1983, January 1, 1984, November 22, 1985, August 21, 1987, October 9, 1987.
Washington Post, December 16, 1983, November 22, 1985.*

*　　　*　　　*

MEEKER, Joseph W(arren)   1932-

PERSONAL: Born August 4, 1932, in Iowa; son of Russell E. and Annamae (Block) Meeker; married Marlene Rae Rundell, December 27, 1956; children: Benjamin, Kurt. *Education:* Occidental College, B.A., 1954, M.A., 1961, Ph.D., 1963; also studied at University of California, Berkeley, 1956, and University of Oregon, 1959.

ADDRESSES: Office—c/o Frederick Garber, International Comparative Literature Association, State University of New York, Binghamton, N.Y. 13901.

CAREER: Deep Springs College, Deep Springs, Calif., assistant professor of languages and literature, 1962-63; University of Alaska, Fairbanks, assistant professor, 1963-65, associate professor of English and chairman of department, 1965-67; Hiram Scott College, Scottsbluff, Neb., professor of English and comparative literature, 1967-71, chairman of humanities division, 1969-71; University of California, Santa Cruz, lecturer in environmental studies at Kresge College, and fellow in comparative literature, 1971-73; Athabasca University, Edmonton, Alberta, senior tutor in humanities, 1973. Conference coordinator of World Law Fund Workshop on Global Environment, 1972; consultant to National Park Service Academy, and to Thorne Ecological Institute. Visiting professor, University of Montana, summer, 1967. *Military service:* U.S. Army, program director of Armed Forces Radio Network, 1954-56; served in Korea.

MEMBER: International Comparative Literature Association, Modern Language Association of America, National Council of Teachers of English, American Comparative Literature Association, American Association of University Professors, American Association for the Advancement of Science.

AWARDS, HONORS: National Endowment for the Humanities fellowship in literature, philosophy, and ecology, 1971-72; Ford Foundation fellowship in innovative education, Kresge College of University of California, Santa Cruz, 1972-73.

WRITINGS:

The Comedy of Survival: Studies in Literary Ecology, Scribner, 1973.
The Spheres of Life: An Introduction to World Ecology, Scribner, 1974.
(Editor) *The New Natural Philosophy Reader,* Guild of Tutors Press, 1980.

The Comedy of Survival: In Search of an Environmental Ethic, illustrations by William Berry, Guild of Tutors Press, 1980.
Minding the Earth: Thinly Disguised Essays on Human Ecology, Latham Foundation (Alameda, Calif.), 1988.

Contributor of numerous articles and reviews to journals, including *Canadian Fiction, North American Review, Ecologist, Journal of Environmental Education, Thymos, Inquiry,* and *Not Man Apart.* Environment editor for *North American Review;* editorial consultant for U.S. Forest Service research publications, 1964-67.

WORK IN PROGRESS: The Rights of Non-Human Nature; research on environmental ethics; *Nature and Other Mothers: Sexuality and Environmental Crisis.**

*   *   *

MEEKS, Wayne A.   1932-

PERSONAL: Born January 8, 1932, in Aliceville, Ala.; son of Benjamin LaFayette (a stationmaster) and Winnie (Gavin) Meeks; married Martha Fowler (a free-lance artist), June 10, 1954; children: Suzanne, Edith, Ellen. *Education:* University of Alabama, B.S., 1953; Austin Presbyterian Theological Seminary, B.D., 1956; University of Tuebingen, graduate study, 1956-57; Yale University, M.A., 1963, Ph.D., 1965.

ADDRESSES: Office—Department of Religious Studies, Yale University, P.O. Box 2160, New Haven, Conn. 06520.

CAREER: Ordained Presbyterian minister, 1956; Presbyterian Campus Christian Life, Memphis, Tenn., university pastor, 1957-61; Dartmouth College, Hanover, N.H., instructor in religion, 1964-65; United Ministry to Yale, New Haven, Conn., university pastor, 1965-66; Indiana University at Bloomington, assistant professor, 1966-68, associate professor, 1968-69; Yale University, New Haven, Conn., associate professor, 1969-73, professor of religious studies, 1973—, Woolsey Professor of Biblical Literature, 1985—, chairman of department, 1972-75.

MEMBER: American Academy of Religion, Studorium Novi Testamenti Societas, Society of Biblical Literature (president, 1985), Society for Values in Higher Education, Phi Beta Kappa.

AWARDS, HONORS: Fulbright fellowship to University of Tuebingen, 1956-57; Kent fellowship, 1962-65; National Endowment for the Humanities senior fellow, 1975-76; Guggenheim fellow, 1979-80.

WRITINGS:

Go from Your Father's House, John Knox, 1964.
The Prophet-King, E. J. Brill, 1967.
(Editor) *The Writings of St. Paul,* Norton, 1972.
(Editor with F. O. Francis) *Conflict at Colossae,* Society of Biblical Literature, 1973.
(Editor with J. Jervell) *God's Christ and His People,* Universitetsforlaget (Oslo), 1977.
(With R. L. Wilken) *Jews and Christians in Antioch in the First Four Centuries of the Common Era,* Scholars Press (Missoula, Mont.), 1978.
(Editor) *Zur Soziologie des Urchristentums,* Kaiser (Munich), 1979.
The First Urban Christians: The Social World of the Apostle Paul, Yale University Press, 1982.
The Moral World of the First Christians, Westminster John Knox, 1986.

(Editor) Grant, Robert M., *Gods and the One God,* Westminster John Knox, 1986.
(Editor) Stambaugh, John E. and Balch, David L., *The New Testament in Its Social Environment,* Westminster John Knox, 1988.

Also contributor to various symposia and festschrifts. Contributor of articles to *Journal of Biblical Literature, History of Religions,* and *Journal for Study of the New Testament.*

WORK IN PROGRESS: A further book on early Christian ethics.

SIDELIGHTS: Wayne A. Meeks, the professor of religious studies at Yale University, began to write *The First Christians: The Social World of the Apostle Paul* in 1965. Grants from the National Endowment for the Humanities and the Guggenheim foundation helped him to complete the nearly twenty-year project, reports *New York Times Book Review* contributor Robert McAfee Brown, who remarks, "It was worth the extended investment." Similarly appreciative of *The First Urban Christians* is *Times Literary Supplement* reviewer J. L. Houlden, who calls it "a much-needed authoritative study of the churches founded by or in association with Paul in relation to their social setting. It is admirably documented and indexed, and with lucidity and conciseness it not only gives a great deal of information but also discusses the many debated issues in the field. Above all, it asks persistently what it felt like to believe and worship as a member of those first Christian groups in Greece and Asia Minor." Brown elaborates, "[Readers] with any historical bent will be intrigued by the way a story usually overlaid with thick layers of theological speculation is unraveled as an account of ordinary first-century citizens dealing with a series of claims and loyalties that put them out of step with their time."

Estimating that "there will be no lack of praises" for "the book's many fine passages and observations on the Greco-Roman and Jewish backgrounds and the day-to-day practices of Christianity," Morton Smith (author of *Jesus the Magician*) uses his *Washington Post Book World* review to emphasize the book's shortcomings, as he sees them. Smith feels the author's "outstanding" common-sense approach to Paul's teachings is misapplied, since Paul made claims and value judgments that no one with common sense would make, in Smith's opinion. In addition, Smith faults Meeks for omitting to draw parallels between Christian practices (speaking in tongues, the sacraments) and similar practices of their contemporaries who employed ritual magic. "In sum," according to Smith, "Meeks' exegesis is that of a conscientious, . . . modern man, who has blundered into this world of ancient magic . . . , and does not understand what is going on." In contrast, other reviewers emphasize Meeks's contribution to a more accurate view of the sociological facets of the early church. For instance, though it was previously thought that Christianity spread quickly among the dissatisfied poor, evidence compiled by Meeks shows that church members came from a wide variety of status and income levels. For placing the early church "more firmly than ever in historical focus," Houlden and others consider *The First Urban Christians* a significant contribution to literature about the early Christians.

BIOGRAPHICAL/CRITICAL SOURCES:

PERIODICALS

New York Times Book Review, April 3, 1983.
Times Literary Supplement, October 7, 1983.
Washington Post Book World, April 10, 1983.

MENDELSOHN, Everett (Irwin) 1931-

PERSONAL: Born October 28, 1931, in Yonkers, N.Y.; son of Morris H. and May (Albert) Mendelsohn; married Mary B. Anderson, September 13, 1974; children: (previous marriage) Daniel L., Sarah E., Joanna M.; stepchildren: Jesse Marshall Wallace. *Education:* Antioch College, A.B., 1953; Harvard University, Ph.D., 1960.

ADDRESSES: Home—26 Walker St., Cambridge, Mass. 02138. *Office*—Harvard University, Science Center 235, Cambridge, Mass. 02138.

CAREER: Harvard University, Cambridge, Mass., assistant professor, 1960-65, associate professor, 1965-69, professor of history of science, 1969—, chairman of department, 1971-78. Director of research group on bio-medical sciences. Conducted university program on technology and society, Harvard University, 1966-68. President, International Council for Science Policy Studies, 1980—, and Institute for Peace and International Security; chairman of executive committee, American Friends Service Committee; chairman, Harvard-Radcliffe Child Care Council. Member of board of directors, Institute for Defense and Disarmament Studies, 1980—; trustee, Cambridge Friends School.

MEMBER: International Academy of the History of Medicine, Academie Internationale d'Histoire des Sciences, History of Science Society (council member), American Association for the Advancement of Science (fellow; council member, 1961-62; vice-president, chairman, section L), American Academy of Arts and Sciences (fellow).

AWARDS, HONORS: Bowdoin Prize, 1957; D.H.L., Rhode Island College, 1977; overseas fellow, Churchill College, Cambridge University; fellow, Wissenschafts-kolleg (Berlin), 1983-84.

WRITINGS:

(Editor with I. B. Cohen and H. M. Jones) *Treasury of Scientific Prose: A Nineteenth-Century Anthology*, Little, Brown, 1963.
Heat and Life: The Development of the Theory of Animal Heat, Harvard University Press, 1964.
(Editor) *Human Aspects of Biomedical Innovation*, Harvard University Press, 1971.
(Editor with Arnold Thackray) *Science and Values: Patterns of Tradition and Change*, Humanities, 1974.
(Editor with Marjorie Grene) *Topics in the Philosophy of Biology*, D. Reidel, 1976.
(Editor with Peter Weingart and Richard Whitley) *The Social Production of Scientific Knowledge*, D. Reidel, 1977.
(Editor with Yehuda Elkana) *Sciences and Cultures: Anthropological and Historical Studies of the Sciences*, D. Reidel, 1981.
A Compassionate Peace: A Future of the Middle East, Hill & Wang, 1982.
(Editor with Helga Nowotny) *1984: Science between Utopia and Dystopia*, D. Reidel, 1984.
(Editor) *Transformation and Tradition in the Sciences*, Cambridge University Press, 1984.
(Editor with M. Roe Smith and Weingart) *Science, Technology and the Military*, D. Reidel, 1988.

Editor, *Journal of the History of Biology*, 1967—; member of editorial board, *Science*, 1965-70, *Social Studies of Science*, 1970-82, *Ethics in Science and Medicine*, 1973-81, *Philosophy and Medicine*, 1974-86, *Sociology of Sciences*, 1976—, *Social Sciences and Medicine*, 1981—, *Synthese*, 1985—, and *Scientia*, 1987—.

*   *   *

MILLGATE, Michael (Henry) 1929-

PERSONAL: Born July 19, 1929, in Southampton, England; son of Stanley (a civil servant) and Marjorie Louisa (Norris) Millgate; married Eunice Jane Barr (a university teacher), February 27, 1960. *Education:* St. Catharine's College, Cambridge, B.A., 1952, M.A., 1956; University of Michigan, graduate study, 1956-57; University of Leeds, Ph.D., 1960.

ADDRESSES: Home—75 Highland Ave., Toronto, Ontario, Canada M4W 2A4. *Office*—Department of English, University of Toronto, Toronto, Ontario, Canada M5S 1A1. *Agent*—Peter H. Matson, Literistic Ltd., 264 Fifth Ave., New York, N.Y. 10001.

CAREER: Workers' Educational Association, tutor and organizer in South Lindsey, England, 1953-56; University of Leeds, Leeds, England, lecturer in English literature, 1958-64; York University, Downsview, Ontario, professor of English and chairman of the department, 1964-67; University of Toronto, Toronto, professor of English, 1967—. *Military service:* Royal Air Force, 1947-49.

AWARDS, HONORS: Killam Senior Research scholarship, 1974-76; Guggenheim fellowship, 1977-78; Fellow of Royal Society of Canada, 1981; Fellow of Royal Society of Literature, 1983; Killam Research fellowship, 1986-88; University Professorship, University of Toronto, 1987.

WRITINGS:

William Faulkner, Grove, 1961.
American Social Fiction: James to Cozzens, Barnes & Noble, 1964.
The Achievement of William Faulkner, Random House, 1966.
(Author of introduction) Edith Wharton, *The House of Mirth*, Constable, 1966.
Thomas Hardy: His Career as a Novelist, Random House, 1971.
Thomas Hardy: A Biography, Random House, 1982.

EDITOR

(And author of introduction) Alfred Tennyson, *Selected Poems*, Oxford University Press, 1963.
(And author of introduction) Theodore Dreiser, *Sister Carrie*, Oxford University Press, 1965.
(With Paul F. Mattheisen) *Transatlantic Dialogue: Selected American Correspondence of Edmund Gosse*, University of Texas Press, 1965, UMI Publications, 1988.
(With James B. Meriwether) *Lion in the Garden: Interviews with William Faulkner, 1926-1962*, Random House, 1968.
(With Richard L. Purdy) *The Collected Works of Thomas Hardy*, Oxford University Press, Volume 1: *1840-92*, 1978, Volume 2: *1893-1901*, 1980, Volume 3: *1902-08*, 1982, Volume 4: *1909-13*, 1984, Volume 5: *1914-19*, 1985, Volume 6: *1920-25*, 1987, Volume 7: *1926-27*, 1988.
The Life and Work of Thomas Hardy, Macmillan (London), 1984, University of Georgia Press, 1985.
(And author of introduction) William Faulkner, *William Faulkner Manuscripts 20: A Fable*, Garland Publishing, 1986.

(And author of introduction) Faulkner, *William Faulkner Manuscripts 21: The Town*, Garland Publishing, 1986.
(And author of introduction) Faulkner, *William Faulkner Manuscripts 22: The Mansion*, Garland Publishing, 1987.
(And author of introduction) Faulkner, *William Faulkner Manuscripts 23: The Rivers*, Garland Publishing, 1987.
(And author of introduction) *New Essays on "Light in August,"* Cambridge University Press, 1987.

OTHER

Contributor of articles on English and American literature and reviews to journals.

SIDELIGHTS: A scholar of English and American literature, Michael Millgate is frequently noted for his extensively researched writing and editing concerning the life and works of William Faulkner and Thomas Hardy. His book, *Thomas Hardy: A Biography,* has received praise from critics such as *New York Times* reviewer Anatole Broyard, who writes: "Mr. Millgate is the kind of biographer writers dream of. He gives us all the necessary details; but none of the gratuitous ones." Robert E. Keuhn appraises the biography in a *Chicago Tribune Book World* article as being "a magnificent biography—learned, thorough, judicious, sympathetic, in every sense definitive."

BIOGRAPHICAL/CRITICAL SOURCES:

PERIODICALS

Chicago Tribune Book World, May 23, 1982.
Los Angeles Times, June 4, 1982, October 13, 1985.
New Yorker, June 15, 1968.
New York Times, May 12, 1982.
New York Times Book Review, June 30, 1968, May 9, 1982.
Times Literary Supplement, July 16, 1982, September 10, 1982, March 23, 1984, June 7, 1985, July 3, 1987.

*   *   *

MILTON, Mark
    See PELTON, Robert W(ayne)

*   *   *

MITCHUM, Hank
    See SHERMAN, Jory (Tecumseh)

*   *   *

MONTRESOR, Beni   1926-

PERSONAL: Born March 31, 1926, in Bussolengo, Italy; came to the United States, 1960; son of Angelo Silvino (a furniture manufacturer) and Maria (Fantin) Montresor. *Education:* Attended Liceo Artistico, Verona, Italy, 1942-45, Academia di Belle Arti, Venice, 1945-49, and Centro Sperimentale di Cinematografia, Rome, 1950-52.

ADDRESSES: Home—31 West 12th St., New York, N.Y. 10011.

CAREER: Newspaper film critic and author of radio plays, including adaptations of children's fairy tales, in Verona, Italy, 1945-49; set and costume designer, 1952-59, for twenty European films, including "Siegfried," 1958, and several European stage productions, such as Alberto Moravia's "Beatrice Cenci" and Paddy Chayefsky's "Middle of the Night"; illustrator of children's books, 1961—; set and costume designer in the United States, England, and Italy, 1961—, for

operas including Samuel Barber's "Vanessa," 1961, Claude Debussy's "Pelleas et Melisande," 1962, Gian-Carlo Menotti's "The Last Savage," 1964, Gioacchino Rossini's "La Cenerentola," 1965, Amilcare Ponchielli's "La Gioconda," 1966, Hector Berlioz's "Benvenuto Cellini," 1966, Menotti's "Amahl and the Night Visitors," 1968, Giacomo Puccini's "Turandot," 1969, Jean-Philippe Rameau's "Platee," 1977, Richard Wagner's "Lohengrin," 1978, Giuseppi Verdi's "Nabucco," 1979, Richard Strauss's "Salome," 1979, Jules Massenet's "Esclarmonde," 1983, George Friedrich Handel's "Alcina," 1983, Francesco Cavalli's "L'Ormindo," 1984, and Sergei Prokofiev's "The Love for Three Oranges," 1984, ballets including Anthony Tudor's "Dim Lustre," 1964, musicals including Richard Rodgers and Stephen Sondheim's "Do I Hear a Waltz?," 1965, plays including August Strindberg's "Ghost Sonata," 1976, and many others; debuted as director/designer with staging of Mozart's "The Magic Flute" at Lincoln Center, New York, N.Y., 1966; writer and director of movies, "Pilgrimage" (selected for the Cannes Film Festival), 1972, "The Golden Mass," 1975, and "Daybreak," 1984. Exhibitions include: Knoedler Gallery, New York City, 1965; Rizzoli Gallery, New York City, 1967; "The Magic of Montresor," New York City's Library and Museum of Performing Arts at Lincoln Center, 1981; Wildenstein Gallery, New York City, 1982.

MEMBER: New York Theatre Scenic Designers Union.

AWARDS, HONORS: Radio Critics Prize (Italy), 1948, for radio play "Angelina e Le Beate"; book of the year citation, American Institute of Graphic Arts, 1961-62, for *Mommies at Work;* best illustrated book of the year citation, *New York Times,* 1962, for *The Princesses: Sixteen Stories about Princesses;* Caldecott Medal, 1965, for *May I Bring a Friend?;* knighted by Italian government, 1966, for services to the arts; best illustrated book of the year citation, *New York Times,* 1966, for *The Magic Flute;* American Society of Illustrators gold medal, 1967, for *I Saw a Ship A-Sailing; or, The Wonderful Games That Only Little Flower-Plant Children Can Play;* Leonide Massine Prize, 1979, for best ballet design of the year for *Homage to Picasso;* first prize from the French Ministry of Culture, 1980, for the best opera design of the 1979-80 season, for the Tolouse Opera Company's production of Richard Strauss's "Salome"; Order of Gran Cavaliere (Italy), for distinguished contributions to the arts.

WRITINGS:

JUVENILES; SELF-ILLUSTRATED

House of Flowers, House of Stars (picture book), Knopf, 1962.
The Witches of Venice, Knopf, 1963.
Cinderella (English adaptation of Gioacchino Rossini's opera "La Cenerentola"), Knopf, 1965.
I Saw a Ship A-Sailing; or, The Wonderful Games That Only Little Flower-Plant Children Can Play (Italianate fantasy based on Mother Goose rhymes), Knopf, 1967.
A for Angel, Knopf, 1969.
Bedtime, Harper, 1978.

ILLUSTRATOR; JUVENILES

Margaret Wise Brown, *On Christmas Eve,* W. R. Scott, 1961.
Mary Stolz, *Belling the Tiger,* Harper, 1961.
Stolz, *The Great Rebellion,* Harper, 1961.
Eve Merriam, *Mommies at Work,* Knopf, 1961.
Sally P. Johnson, editor, *The Princesses: Sixteen Stories about Princesses,* Harper, 1962.
Stolz, *Siri the Conquistador,* Harper, 1963.

Rose L. Mincielli, *Old Neapolitan Fairy Tales,* Knopf, 1963.

May Garelick, *Sounds of a Summer Night,* W. R. Scott, 1963.

Beatrice Schenk deRegniers, *May I Bring a Friend?* (verse; also see below), Atheneum, 1964.

Gian-Carlo Menotti, *The Last Savage* (narrative version of opera), New York Graphic Society, 1964.

Stephen Spender, adapter, *The Magic Flute* (based on the opera by Wolfgang Amadeus Mozart), Putnam, 1966.

deRegniers, *Willy O'Dwyer Jumped in the Fire* (variations on a folk rhyme), Atheneum, 1968.

Oscar Wilde, *The Birthday of the Infanta and Other Tales,* Atheneum, 1982.

Hans Christian Andersen, *The Nightingale,* retold by Alan Benjamin, Crown, 1985.

OTHER

(Adapter with deRegniers) "May I Bring a Friend?," produced in Albany, N.Y., at Empire State Institute for the Performing Arts, 1983.

WORK IN PROGRESS: Writing and illustrating *Don't Wake Me Up* (tentative title); a movie script, "In the House of the Lord"; a ballet adaptation of *The Birthday of the Infanta.*

SIDELIGHTS: Beni Montresor's fascination with color was evident at an early age. In an article for *Holiday* entitled "My Verona," he tells of his childhood in that old and lovely city of "warm colors . . . soft yellows, pinks, terra cotta." His grandfather often drove him "to the stationers, the little *carteleria* near the Della Pietra Bridge. It was a dark place filled with rolls of paper and books and colored pencils and many other things that seemed strange to me then (even though I had decided to be a painter when I was three)." Montresor mentions another major childhood influence in an interview with Joan Barthel of the *New York Times:* "Being Italian, I was practically born in the Church. . . . I grew up surrounded by pageantry, imagery, fantasy."

Now an internationally known set and costume designer for films, operas, and stage plays, Montresor has worked on location all over the world with directors like Frederico Fellini, Roberto Rosselini, and Vitorrio de Sica. Difficulty in finding employment as a stage designer when he came to the U.S. in 1960 led him to illustrating children's books, a medium which has proved as much a showcase for his talents as the stage has been. His first self-illustrated picture book, *House of Flowers, House of Stars,* is, according to *Publishers Weekly,* "still a favorite with American children." Montresor won the Caldecott Medal for illustrating Beatrice Schenk deRegniers's *May I Bring a Friend?,* a verse fantasy of a boy who brings animal friends to visit the king and queen, who in turn are invited to tea at the zoo. His second solo children's book, *The Witches of Venice,* inspired a San Francisco Ballet Company production at the New York State Theatre in 1965.

Montresor seems to experience no difficulty in making the transition from designing sophisticated stage sets to writing for young children. As he told Tania Osadca of *Newsday* in 1965: "In both cases I am putting on a production—and any production needs action, color, and something to stimulate the imagination." In a review of *I Saw a Ship A-Sailing; or, The Wonderful Games That Only Little Flower-Plant Children Can Play,* John Gruen of *Book World* writes: "All manner of enchantment . . . is to be found in [this book]," which "combines this artist's highly ethereal and romantic vision with an instinct for knowing which verses will elicit the best pictures." He continues, "[Montresor] brings a special fancifulness to

his illustrations. His imagery is dream-like, his colors of Venetian paintings and murals, and a tapestry-like quality lends his drawings their great sense of richness and depth. His approach to the world of Mother Goose is completely personal." Composer Gian-Carlo Menotti, with whom Montresor has collaborated on several productions, was quoted by *Show* magazine in 1962 as saying, "It comes almost as a shock to find an artist like Beni Montresor, who, although capable of applying his amazing versatility to almost any type of spectacle, never betrays his individuality as a painter."

BIOGRAPHICAL/CRITICAL SOURCES:

BOOKS

Colby, Jean Poindexter, *Writing, Illustrating, and Editing Children's Books,* Hastings House, 1967.

de Montreville, Doris, and Donna Hill, *Third Book of Junior Authors,* H. W. Wilson, 1972.

Hopkins, Lee Bennett, *Books Are by People,* Citation Press, 1969.

Kingman, Lee, and others, editors, *Newbery and Caldecott Medal Books: 1956-1965,* Horn Book, 1965.

Kingman, Lee, and others, compilers, *Illustrators of Children's Books: 1967-1976,* Horn Book, 1978.

Klemin, Diana, *The Art of Art for Children's Books,* Clarkson Potter, 1966.

Lanes, Selma G., *Down the Rabbit Hole,* Atheneum, 1971.

Something about the Author Autobiography Series, Volume 4, Gale, 1987.

PERIODICALS

Book Week, March 20, 1966.

Book World (children's issue), November 5, 1967.

Holiday, August, 1968.

Horn Book, October, 1962, August, 1965, April, 1966.

Library Journal, March 15, 1965.

Newsday, April 13, 1965.

Newsweek, March 2, 1981.

New York Times, September 4, 1966, April 15, 1969.

Opera News, February 8, 1964, March 23, 1968, December 11, 1976.

People, December 11, 1978.

Publishers Weekly, March 8, 1965.

Show, March, 1962.

Vogue, March 1, 1970.

Women's Wear Daily, November 28, 1967.*

*   *   *

MOODY, G.F.
   See HAMEL PEIFER, Kathleen

*   *   *

MOORE, Linda Perigo   1946-

PERSONAL: Born November 25, 1946, in Evansville, Ind.; daughter of John Myrl (a hospital administrator) and Loraine (Hudson) Perigo; married Stephen H. Moore (in sales management), August 12, 1967; children: J. Stuart. *Education:* Miami University, Oxford, Ohio, B.S., 1968; University of Louisville, M.Ed., 1973. *Politics:* "Cynicism." *Religion:* "Skeptic Moralism."

ADDRESSES: Home—4111 Wyndclyff Ct., Evansville, Ind. 47711. *Agent*—Amy Berkower, Writers House, Inc., 21 West 26th St., New York, N.Y. 10010.

CAREER: Writer. Department of Continuing Education, Louisville, Ky., instructor at St. Joseph Infirmary (now Audubon Hospital), 1969-70; Park-Du Valle Neighborhood Health Center, Louisville, 1971-74, began as assistant training director, became training director; Charlestown High School, Charlestown, Ind., counselor, 1974-75; Midtown Community Mental Health Center, Indianapolis, Ind., director of staff development, 1977-78; Indiana University, Indianapolis, member of associate faculty of speech department, 1980-81. Part-time instructor, Indiana University/Purdue University, and University of Southern Indiana.

WRITINGS:

Does This Mean My Kid's a Genius?, McGraw, 1981.
(With Mary Kay Ash) *Mary Kay on People Management*, Warner Books, 1984.
You're Smarter than You Think (Quality Paperback Book-of-the-Month Club selection), Holt, 1985.
(With Bart Conner) *Bart Conner's Winning the Gold*, Warner Books, 1985.
(With Ash) *Mary Kay*, 2nd edition, Harper, 1986.
(With Richard Simmons) *Richard Simmons' Reach for Fitness*, Warner Books, 1986.

Contributor to *Women's World*, *Glamour*, and *Writer's Digest*.

WORK IN PROGRESS: Tootie Tittlemouse and the Lights of Christmas, with Angie Sinclair; "Almost Ann," a syndicated advice column with Gary Provost and Linda Stasi.

SIDELIGHTS: In *Does This Mean My Kid's a Genius?*, Linda Perigo Moore examines what she calls our neglected minority: gifted children. Taken from extensive research and her own experiences as mother of a special child, the book supplies information on how to assess whether your child is gifted and what course to take once you know. It provides comprehensive information on intelligence tests, an expansive bibliography, and data on the physiological and psychological aspects of gifted children. Moore even divulges her own "Ten Commandments" for coping with special offspring.

In *Best Sellers* Alicia Dulac labeled Moore's book "high quality" and asserted that parents of all children will find valuable information within its pages of answers and suggestions. Stephanie Craig of the *Arizona Daily Star* agreed, stating that *Does This Mean My Kid's a Genius?* supplies imaginative alternatives for that portion of society that has had to go it alone for too long. "With an Erma Bombeck-style wit," writes Craig, "Moore takes us along on her arduous journey to find an appropriate educational system for her own child. Her insights and observations are well-founded and supported by evidence presented elsewhere in the book."

Linda Perigo Moore told *CA:* "I am the product of a deliriously placid childhood in Newburgh, Indiana. Newburgh is seven miles upstream from Evansville, the only town north of the Mason-Dixon line to have been occupied by the Confederacy, proud of a high school gymnasium that is bigger than the town library, and full of people who think that Kafka is some sort of ethnic bread.

"In high school I was the kind of child most parents wanted: class president, National Honor Society member, lead in the school play, etc., *ad nauseam*. I attended the first of four universities on academic scholarships and was asked to leave after dancing on a table in the student union.

"While growing up I felt cheated because I knew no ethnic roots—no pudgy Mediterranean grandmother, no boxes of cookies from relatives in 'an old country.' One side of my family came to Maryland before the Revolution, the other was spawned from a sailor who jumped Henry Hudson's ship.

"I realized early that I was a writer. A teacher flunked my fourth-grade poem for 'sounding too good to have been written by a kid.' I went through puberty being rejected by *Reader's Digest* (I didn't know anybody unforgettable) and got my first real encouragement during a college writing class (the professor stole my human interest piece and had it published under his own name).

"Like any respectable, educated young woman who was reared in the fifties and didn't want to be a nurse, I became a high school teacher, then counselor, then escapee. For several years I worked in hospitals in the area of staff development and training (maybe I sort of wanted to be a nurse). I became an adult when, after an administrative mix-up, I taught catheterization to a class of orderlies and didn't blush or laugh."

BIOGRAPHICAL/CRITICAL SOURCES:

PERIODICALS

Arizona Daily Star, January 17, 1982.
Best Sellers, January, 1982.
Evansville Courier and Press, February 28, 1982.

*   *   *

MORETON, John
See COHEN, Morton N(orton)

*   *   *

MORRESSY, John 1930-

PERSONAL: Born December 8, 1930, in Brooklyn, N.Y.; son of John Emmett and Jeanette (Geraghty) Morressy; married Barbara Turner, August 11, 1956. *Education:* St. John's University, Jamaica, N.Y., B.A., 1953; New York University, M.A., 1961.

ADDRESSES: Home—East Sullivan, N.H. *Office*—Department of English, Franklin Pierce College, Rindge, N.H. 03461. *Agent*—Curtis Brown Ltd., Ten Astor Place, New York, N.Y. 10003.

CAREER: Teacher, intermittently, 1956-63; St. John's University, Jamaica, N.Y., instructor in English, 1963-66; Monmouth College, West Long Branch, N.Y., assistant professor of English, 1966-67; Franklin Pierce College, Rindge, N.H., 1968—, began as associate professor, currently professor of English and writer in residence. *Military service:* U.S. Army, 1953-55.

MEMBER: Science Fiction Writers of America, Authors League of America, Authors Guild.

AWARDS, HONORS: Bread Loaf Writers' Conference fellowship, 1968; University of Colorado Writers' Conference fellowship, 1970; Balrog Award for best short fantasy, 1984.

WRITINGS:

NOVELS

The Blackboard Cavalier, Doubleday, 1966.
The Addison Tradition, Doubleday, 1968.
Starbrat, Walker & Co., 1972.

Nail Down the Stars, Walker & Co., 1973.
A Long Communion, Walker & Co., 1974.
Under a Calculating Star, Doubleday, 1975.
A Law for the Stars, Laser Books, 1976.
The Extraterritorial, Laser Books, 1977.
Frostworld and Dreamfire, Doubleday, 1977.
Ironbrand, Playboy Press, 1980.
Graymantle, Playboy Press, 1981.
Kingsbane, Playboy Press, 1982.
The Mansions of Space, Berkley Publishing, 1982.
The Time of the Annihilator, Ace Books, 1985.
A Voice for Princess, Ace Books, 1986.
A Questing of Kedrigern, Ace Books, 1987.

OTHER

The Humans of Ziax II (juvenile), Walker & Co., 1974.
The Windows of Forever (juvenile), Walker & Co., 1975.
Drought on Ziax II (juvenile), Walker & Co., 1978.
Other Stories, Northern New England Review Press, 1983.

Contributor to *Magazine of Fantasy and Science Fiction, Harper's, Esquire, Omni, Playboy,* and other magazines.

WORK IN PROGRESS: A collection of essays; a fantasy novel.

SIDELIGHTS: John Morressy told *CA:* "Perhaps because I've spent so much of my life in and around classrooms, learning plays an important part in all my books. My characters all learn something in the course of their books, though what they learn is not always what they hope, or expect, to learn. Life is like that, too. I try to write about what one must know, and how it is to be learned, and how taught.

"Most of my writing has been in fantasy and science fiction, because in these genres, instead of writing about neurosis, failure, anxiety, loneliness, despair, cruelty, sexual frustration, anomie, loss of identity, and the other wonders of contemporary life, I am free to speculate on the future of the human race and the creation of myths and heroes. I spend my time not among the whiners, but among seekers. It is old fashioned, I suppose, but I find it very rewarding.

"I do not believe that the novel is dead, although a great many people—too many of them writers—are trying to kill it. The novel has simply moved to a more interesting neighborhood. I have tried to move with it."

BIOGRAPHICAL/CRITICAL SOURCES:

PERIODICALS

Best Sellers, August 15, 1968.
Christian Science Monitor, August 29, 1968.
Fantasy Newsletter, September, 1980.
Newsday, October 30, 1977.
New York Times Book Review, July 28, 1968.
Times Literary Supplement, February 2, 1967.
Virginia Quarterly Review, winter, 1969.

*   *   *

MOSSE, George L(achmann)   1918-

PERSONAL: Born September 20, 1918, in Berlin, Germany; naturalized U.S. citizen; son of Hans (a publisher) and Felicia Lachmann-Mosse. *Education:* Attended Cambridge University, 1936-39; Haverford College, B.S., 1941; Harvard University, Ph.D., 1946.

ADDRESSES: Home—36 Glenway, Madison, Wis. 53222. *Office*—Department of History, University of Wisconsin—Madison, Madison, Wis. 53706.

CAREER: University of Iowa, Iowa City, 1945-55, began as instructor, became associate professor; University of Wisconsin—Madison, 1955—, began as associate professor, became professor of history, John C. Bascom Professor of History, 1965—. Visiting professor and fellow at universities in the United States, Europe, Africa, and Australia, including Koebner Professor of History at Hebrew University, Jerusalem, 1979—. Member of board of directors, Wiener Library, 1973—, and Leo Baeck Institute, 1978—; member of board of overseers, Tauber Center for Jewish Studies, Brandeis University, 1980—. Consultant, U.S. High Commission in Germany (U.S. Information Service), 1951, 1955.

MEMBER: American Society for Reformation Research (president, 1961-62), American Historical Association, American Society for Church History, American Association of University Professors (president, Iowa Conference, 1953-54), American Academy of Arts and Sciences.

AWARDS, HONORS: Huntington Library grant, 1953; Social Science Research Council grant, 1961; E. Harris Harbison Prize, Danforth Foundation, 1970; D.Litt., Carthage College, 1973; Aqui Storia Prize, 1975; Premio Prezzolihi (Florence), 1985; L.H.D., Hebrew Union College, 1987; Goethe-Medallie, Goethe Institut, 1988.

WRITINGS:

The Struggle for Sovereignty in England: From the Reign of Queen Elizabeth to the Petition of Right, Michigan State College Press, 1950, reprinted, Octagon, 1968.
The Reformation, Holt, 1953, 3rd revised edition, 1963.
The Holy Pretence: A Study of Christianity and Reason of State from William Perkins to John Winthrop, Basil Blackwell, 1957, Fertig, 1968.
(Editor with Hill, Cameron, and Petrovich) *Europe in Review: Readings and Sources since 1500*, Rand McNally, 1957, revised edition, 1964.
The Culture of Western Europe: The Nineteenth and Twentieth Centuries, Rand McNally, 1961, 3rd edition, Westview, 1988.
The Crisis of German Ideology: The Intellectual Origins of the Third Reich, Grosset, 1964, reprinted, Schocken, 1981.
(Compiler with Walter Ze'ev Laqueur) *1914: The Coming of the First World War*, Harper, 1966.
(With Laqueur) *The Left-Wing Intellectuals between the Wars, 1919-1939*, Gannon, 1966.
(Editor) *Nazi Culture: Intellectual, Cultural, and Social Life in the Third Reich*, Grosset, 1966, reprinted, Schocken, 1981.
(Editor and contributor) *International Fascism, 1920-1945*, Harper, 1966.
(Editor with Laqueur) *Literature and Politics in the Twentieth Century*, Harper, 1967.
(Editor with Laqueur) *The New History: Trends in Historical Research and Writing since World War Two*, Harper, 1967.
(Editor) *Education and Social Structure in the Twentieth Century*, Harper, 1967.
(With Helmut Georg Koenigsberger) *Europe in the Sixteenth Century*, Holt, 1968.
(Author of introduction) Max Nordau, *Degeneration*, Fertig, 1968.

Germans and Jews: The Right, the Left, and the Search for a "Third Force" in Pre-Nazi Germany, Fertig, 1970, reprinted, Wayne State University Press, 1987.

(Editor with Bela Vago) *Jews and Non-Jews in Eastern Europe, 1918-1945,* Wiley, 1974.

(Editor with Laqueur) *Historians in Politics,* Sage Publications, 1974.

(Editor) *Police Forces in History,* Sage Publications, 1974.

The Nationalization of the Masses: Political Symbolism and Mass Movements in Germany from the Napoleonic Wars through the Third Reich, Fertig, 1977.

Toward the Final Solution: A History of European Racism, Fertig, 1977.

Interviste Sul Nazismo, Laterza, 1977, translation published as *Nazism: A Historical and Comparative Analysis of National Socialism,* Transaction Books, 1978.

(Editor) *International Fascism: New Thoughts and New Approaches,* Sage Publications, 1979.

Masses and Man: Nationalist and Fascist Perceptions of Reality, Fertig, 1980.

Nationalism and Sexuality: Middle Class Morality and Sexual Norms in Modern Europe, Fertig, 1985.

German Jews beyond Judaism, Indiana University Press, 1985.

Contributor to numerous scholarly books on European history, culture, and politics; contributor to encyclopedias and yearbooks; contributor to numerous academic journals. Co-editor, *Journal of Contemporary History,* 1965—.

SIDELIGHTS: In his study *Nationalism and Sexuality: Middle Class Morality and Sexual Norms in Modern Europe,* historian George L. Mosse "compares the different European countries from the post of view of their notions of homosexuality and gender differences as functions of nationalism and examples of the morality of respectability," describes Robert Dawidoff in the *Los Angeles Times Book Review.* While the study focuses on sexual roles, "Nazism is Mosse's real subject as it has been in several of his books." The critic explains: "Here, [Mosse] simply broadens the definition of the victims of the Third Reich and the kinds of attitudes that energized their victimization." Dawidoff notes that Mosse's "thesis is powerful," and concludes that *Nationalism and Sexuality* "tries to guide our thinking about the human cost of the Third Reich in suggestive and significant ways."

Mosse's work has been translated into Polish, Italian, Spanish, and French.

BIOGRAPHICAL/CRITICAL SOURCES:

BOOKS

Drescher, Seymour and others, editors, *Political Symbolism in Modern Europe: Essays in Honor of George L. Mosse,* Transaction Books, 1982.

PERIODICALS

Commentary, October, 1970.

Los Angeles Times Book Review, May 19, 1985.
New York Times Book Review, July 12, 1970, February 8, 1981.
Times Literary Supplement, July 23, 1971, September 26, 1975, December 23, 1977.

*   *   *

MYERS, Katherine   1952-

PERSONAL: Born October 24, 1952, in Los Angeles, Calif.; daughter of Lindon N. (a machinist) and Louise (Wynant) Troseth; married Kelly L. Myers (a computer technician), October 10, 1973; children: Rachel, Tara, Matthew, Seth. *Education:* Attended public school in Washington. *Religion:* Church of Jesus Christ of Latter-day Saints.

ADDRESSES: Home—10255 Ralph Ct., Boise, Idaho 83709.

CAREER: Writer.

WRITINGS:

Dark Soldier (novel), Avon, 1983.
Winter Flame (novel), Avon, 1984.
Ribbons of Silver (novel), Avon, 1985.
Joy in the Morning (novel), Heritage Books, 1987.

SIDELIGHTS: Katherine Myers told *CA:* "I am the youngest in a family of eight children. My father's parents sailed from Norway to America, and my mother's great-grandmother crossed the plains as a pioneer settler. Having lived in all eleven western states as well as British Columbia while I was growing up, the west is a special place to me. I work part-time as a secretary, do volunteer costuming for the Idaho Shakespeare Festival, and am active in the things my children are involved with. My husband, Kelly, and I have built our home in Boise, Idaho. He is my best supporter and often takes care of the children or cooks dinner while I am locked away with the word processor. I am currently interested in writing for the L.D.S. market, and my last book, *Joy in the Morning,* is the story of pioneer ancestors based on the personal journal of my husband's great-great-grandfather, with the main two characters fictionalized.

"When I was a child my family often didn't have a television, and so, to entertain my sister and me, my mother read to us. By the time I was in fifth grade I was well acquainted with *Jane Eyre, Carson of Venus, The Good Earth, A Midsummer Night's Dream, Little Women, Gone with the Wind, David Copperfield,* and the Bible. Writing has been a great joy in my life, and although I will always try my hand at new creative ventures, this is my greatest pleasure. I don't write for money— I've gone beyond that desire. Instead, creating new works, stepping beyond the molds set by earlier works, and trying new ideas has proved to be my greatest reward. I will probably be ninety years old and in a wheelchair, pulling myself up to the desk to write."

N

NAVONE, John J(oseph) 1930-

PERSONAL: Surname is pronounced Na-*vo*-nay; born October 19, 1930, in Seattle, Wash.; son of James and Juliet (Micheli) Navone. *Education:* Gonzaga University, M.Phil., 1956; St. Mary's University, Halifax, Nova Scotia, Canada, S.T.M., 1963; Gregorian University, Th.D., 1965.

ADDRESSES: Home and office—Gregorian University, Piazza della Pilotta 4, Rome 00187, Italy.

CAREER: Entered Society of Jesus in 1949, ordained Roman Catholic priest, 1962; Seattle Preparatory School, Seattle, Wash., teacher, 1956-59; Gregorian University, Rome, Italy, 1967—, began as assistant professor, currently professor of theology. Annually teaches summer school, Seattle University.

WRITINGS:

History and Faith in the Thought of Alan Richardson, S.C.M. Press, 1966.
Personal Witness: A Biblical Spirituality, Sheed, 1967.
Themes of St. Luke, Gregorian University Press, 1970.
(Contributor) *Foundations of Theology*, Macmillan, 1972.
Everyman's Odyssey: Seven Plays Seen as Modern Myths about Man's Quest for Personal Integrity, Seattle University Press, 1974.
A Theology of Failure, Paulist Press, 1974.
Communicating Christ, St. Paul Publications, 1976.
Towards a Theology of Story, St. Paul Publications, 1977.
The Jesus Story: Our Life as Story in Christ, Liturgical Press, 1979.
(With Thomas Cooper) *Tellers of the Word*, Le Jacq Publishers, 1981.
Gospel Love: A Narrative Theology, Michael Glazier, 1984.
Triumph through Failure, St. Paul Publications (Australia), 1984.
Freedom and Transformation in Christ, Gregorian University Press, 1985.
The Story of the Passion, Gregorian University Press, 1985.
The Dynamic of the Question in Narrative Theology, Gregorian University Press, 1986.

Contributor to several periodicals in the United States and in Europe, including *La Civilta Cattolica*, a semi-official publication of the Vatican.

SIDELIGHTS: John J. Navone told *CA* that "an important motivating factor for writing is the need to prepare and improve or update lectures at the graduate level. Writing for the lecture and revising afterwards makes for both better lectures and better writing. Secondly, the discipline of writing is an excellent aid to clarifying and organizing and critically reflecting upon our thinking."

Navone is competent in Italian, French, German, Spanish, Latin, Portuguese, and Greek. Some of his works have been translated into Italian, French, Spanish, and Portuguese.

AVOCATIONAL INTERESTS: Drama, films, literature, music, art, European history, sociology, international relations, geopolitics, communications.

BIOGRAPHICAL/CRITICAL SOURCES:

PERIODICALS

The Weekly (Seattle), August 10, 1983.

* * *

NEEDLE, Jan 1943-

PERSONAL: Born February 8, 1943, in Holybourne, England; son of Bernard Lionel (an engineer) and Dorothy Mary (Brice) Needle. *Education:* Victoria University of Manchester, drama degree (with honors), 1971.

ADDRESSES: Home—Rye Top, Gellfield Ln., Uppermill, Oldham, Lancashire, England. *Agent*—Rochelle Stevens & Co., 15/17 Islington High St., London N1 1LQ, England.

CAREER: Portsmouth Evening News, Portsmouth, England, reporter, 1960-64; reporter and sub-editor for *Daily Herald and Sun*, 1964-68; free-lance writer, 1971—.

WRITINGS:

JUVENILE

Albeson and the Germans, Deutsch, 1977.
My Mate Shofiq, Deutsch, 1978.
Rottenteeth, (picture book), illustrations by Bentley, Deutsch, 1979.
The Size Spies, illustrations by Roy Bentley, Deutsch, 1980.
The Bee Rustlers, illustrations by Paul Wright, Collins, 1980.
A Sense of Shame and Other Stories, Deutsch, 1980.

Losers Weepers, illustrations by Jane Bottomley, Methuen, 1981.
Piggy in the Middle, Deutsch, 1982.
Another Fine Mess, Armada, 1982.
Going Out, Deutsch, 1983.
A Pitiful Place and Other Stories, Deutsch, 1984.
Tucker's Luck, Deutsch, 1984.
Great Days at Grange Hill, Deutsch, 1985.
Tucker in Control, Methuen, 1985.
Behind the Bike Sheds (also see below), Methuen, 1985.
A Game of Soldiers (based on the television series of the same title; also see below), Deutsch, 1985.
Wagstaffe the Wind-Up Boy, Deutsch, 1987.
Uncle in the Attic, Heinemann, 1987.
Skeleton at School, Heinemann, 1987.

OTHER

A Fine Boy for Killing (adult novel), Deutsch, 1979.
Wild Wood (adult novel), illustrations by William Rushton, Deutsch, 1981.
(With Peter Thompson) *Brecht* (criticism), University of Chicago Press, 1981.
(With others) *Rebels of Gas Street,* Collins, 1986.

Also author of television series "A Game of Soldiers," 1984, "Behind the Bike Sheds," 1985-86, "Truckers" (adult series), 1987-88, and "Soft Soap," a juvenile teleplay, 1987, and television series, 1988. Author of more than ten radio plays broadcast in England and New Zealand between 1971 and 1980.

WORK IN PROGRESS: Several children's novels; adult television series; two adult stage plays.

SIDELIGHTS: Jan Needle's juvenile and adult novels often deal with harsh and perplexing social issues. In *My Mate Shofiq,* an English boy befriends a Pakistani classmate who has attacked a local gang in order to protect his sisters. According to Gillian Cross in the *Times Literary Supplement,* Needle "shows how an exciting story can be written around the problems of racial integration." *Times Educational Supplement* contributor Leila Bragg calls *My Mate Shofiq* "a very thoughtful book, utterly absorbing, exiting and moving. No-one who has read it (not 'no child'-'no one') will ever be the same again." *Piggy in the Middle* also deals with violence and racial problems; the main character is a junior policewoman who faces her superior's indifference to a non-white's murder. As Marion Glastonbury in the *Times Educational Supplement* states, "the consequences of a racist killing for which no-one is formally charged, the harassment of the victim's family, the protests of race-relations officials, the cynical indifference of the Press, are compellingly described." But *New Statesman* critic Charles Fox complains of a "plethora of cliches and the fact that the prose needs to be read at a gallop." Jenny Woolf in *Punch,* however, approves that "the texture of [the policewoman's] life is shown raw and real," and sees *Piggy in the Middle* as "an extraordinarily perceptive account."

Needle once wrote *CA:* "I am not aware of when, or why, I started to write. It came naturally. I was first published when I was eight years old, in a small local newspaper, and I have never looked back.

"Although most of my books are published as children's stories, they are equally intended for adults. Many of them have problematical themes and explore difficult social problems. Even the comedy books are intended to amuse adults as well as children. I like each book to be different—and they do seem to defy critical categorization. I think I would be very bored to write the same kind of book over and over again."

AVOCATIONAL INTERESTS: Drama, European travel (especially France).

BIOGRAPHICAL/CRITICAL SOURCES:

PERIODICALS

New Statesman, March 13, 1981, December 3, 1982.
Punch, December 10, 1980, June 8, 1983.
Spectator, February 28, 1981.
Times Educational Supplement, March 26, 1982, January 21, 1983.
Times Literary Supplement, September 29, 1978, November 20, 1981.

*   *   *

NEELY, Bill   1930-

PERSONAL: Born August 18, 1930, in Jane Lew, W. Va.; son of Walter (a merchant) and Madge (Bush) Neely; children: Michael, Jodi, Walter III. *Education:* West Virginia Wesleyan College, A.B., 1952; West Virginia University, graduate study, 1952-53. *Politics:* Republican. *Religion:* Methodist.

ADDRESSES: Home and office—P.O. Box 500, Jane Lew, W. Va. 26378.

CAREER: Goodyear Tire & Rubber Co., Akron, Ohio, manager of racing public relations, 1961-66; Humble Oil Corp., Houston, Tex., public relations manager of central region, 1966-70; writer, 1970—.

MEMBER: Public Relations Society of America, Sigma Delta Chi.

WRITINGS:

Spirit of America, Regnery, 1971.
Grand National, Regnery, 1971.
A Closer Walk, Regnery, 1972.
Country Gentleman, Regnery, 1973.
Drag Racing, Regnery, 1974.
Stand on It, Little, Brown, 1974.
Cars to Remember, Regnery, 1975.
Playboy Book of Racing, Playboy Press, 1978.
Daytona U.S.A., Aztex, 1979.
Official Chili Cookbook, St. Martin's, 1980.
Roy Acuff's Nashville, Perigee, 1983.
A. J., Times Books, 1984.
Automobile Questions, Walker Press, 1984.
Cale, Times Books, 1986.
King Richard I, Macmillan, 1986.
Alone in the Crowd, Aztex, 1988.

Contributor to *Playboy* and *Sports Illustrated.*

WORK IN PROGRESS: A novel.

*   *   *

NEELY, Richard (Forlani)   1941-

PERSONAL: Born August 2, 1941; son of John Champ (a government executive) and Elinore (Forlani) Neely; married Carolyn Elaine Elmore, April 21, 1979; children: John Champ II. *Education:* Dartmouth College, A.B., 1964; Yale University, LL.B., 1967. *Politics:* Democrat. *Religion:* Episcopalian.

ADDRESSES: Home—Pinelea Country Club Rd., Fairmont, W.Va. 26554. *Office*—West Virginia Supreme Court of Appeals, 317 East State Capital, Charleston, W.Va. 25305. *Agent*—Marian Young, The Young Agency, 14 Maiden Lane, New York, N.Y. 10038.

CAREER: Admitted to the bar of West Virginia, 1967; private law practice, Fairmont, W.Va., 1969-73; Marion County Board of Public Health, Fairmont, chairman, 1971-72; West Virginia House of Delegates, Charleston, member, 1971-72; West Virginia Supreme Court of Appeals, Charleston, justice, 1973—, chief justice, 1980-81, 1985; University of Charleston, Charleston, professor of economics, 1979—. Frederick William Atherton Lecturer, Harvard University, 1982-83. Chairman of the board, Kane & Keyser Hardware Co., Belington, W.Va. *Military service:* U.S. Army, 1967-69; served in Vietnam; became captain; received Bronze Star and Vietnam Honor Medal First Class.

MEMBER: American Economic Association, American Legion, Veterans of Foreign Wars of the U.S.A., West Virginia Bar Association, Loyal Order of Moose, Phi Delta Phi, Phi Sigma Kappa.

WRITINGS:

How Courts Govern America, Yale University Press, 1981.
Why Courts Don't Work, McGraw, 1983.
The Divorce Decision: The Legal and Human Consequences of Ending a Marriage, McGraw, 1984.
Judicial Jeopardy, Addison Wesley, 1986.
The Product Liability Mess: How Business Can Be Rescued from State Court Politics, Free Press, 1988.

Contributor of articles to *Atlantic Monthly, New York Times,* and *Juris Doctor.*

SIDELIGHTS: "Nothing is as boring as a lawyer's brief, but few things are as fascinating as hearing an off-duty lawyer talking turkey about the way the legal system really works," comments Joseph Sobran in the *National Review.* "Richard Neely, a justice on West Virginia's Supreme Court of Appeals, writes little books that talk turkey." In *How Courts Govern America,* for example, Neely examines the country's judicial system and details problems in the legislative and executive branches of government that affect its performance. In Neely's opinion, American courts, armed with loose constitutional concepts like "equal protection" and "due process," protect citizens from inefficiencies inherent in the other two branches: the political expediency which precludes meaningful action on the part of the elected, and extreme regulation imposed by executive-controlled bureaucracies. "Aside from some casual assertions that judges are good at making economic policy because economics consists of 'scientific principles,' there is nothing silly in 'How Courts Govern America,'" states Martin Shapiro in the *New York Times Book Review.* "Indeed, it will serve the good purpose of exposing a wider audience to the notion that courts are and ought to be political actors." Similarly, *New York Review of Books* contributor Graham Hughes asserts that "there is nothing at all genteel about Richard Neely's bright, perceptive and informative book." In *How Courts Govern America,* concludes the critic, "Justice Neely offers the best analysis I have seen of the realities of cooperation and tension between courts, legislature, and executive administration."

Neely followed up *How Courts Govern America* with *Why Courts Don't Work,* a thorough assessment of the problems inherent in the judicial system. Neely is able to present such

a extensive study because, as the *Washington Post*'s Edwin M. Yoder, Jr., describes, "Judge Neely, though he is young among eminent American jurists, has direct knowledge of what he is talking about. He has seen firsthand how nearly every feature of our court system, good and bad, is the result of some living, breathing tradition or interest that cannot be 'reformed' without repercussions." Although *West Coast Review of Books* writer Sherman W. Smith finds the title "a little misleading . . . [for] the author does not decry the court system from a generic sense," the critic believes that the solutions which Neely presents "take into consideration the complex and varying views of the courts in the body politic, particularly as related to the most troublesome area—that of criminal justice." "Neely is intelligent, sensible, observant, learned and experienced," states Yoder, adding that "[Neely's] brief is compelling." The critic concludes that *Why Courts Don't Work* demonstrates that although "we may not be getting courts of the quality we think we deserve . . . we are, however, getting courts that suit our temperament, traditions, social priorities and, above all, our pocketbooks."

BIOGRAPHICAL/CRITICAL SOURCES:

PERIODICALS

Best Sellers, October, 1981.
Los Angeles Times, April 27, 1988.
National Review, October 30, 1981, April 19, 1985.
New York Review of Books, November 19, 1981.
New York Times Book Review, November 22, 1981, November 20, 1983.
Washington Post, December 19, 1983.
Washington Post Book World, January 17, 1982.
West Coast Review of Books, January, 1984.

*   *   *

NEFF, Donald (Lloyd) 1930-

PERSONAL: Born October 15, 1930, in York, Pa.; son of Harry William and Gertrude Marie (Kessler) Neff; children: Gregory Harry. *Education:* Attended Trinity College, San Antonio, Tex., 1949, York College, 1950-52, and New York University, 1952-53.

ADDRESSES: Home—2600 Upton St. N.W., Washington, D.C. 20008.

CAREER: York Dispatch, York, Pa., reporter, 1954-56; *Los Angeles Mirror-News,* Los Angeles, Calif., reporter, 1955-58; United Press International, New York City, reporter in Los Angeles, 1958-60; *Los Angeles Times,* Los Angeles, reporter, 1960-63, correspondent in Tokyo, Japan, 1963-64; *Time,* New York City, correspondent in Vietnam, 1965-66, contributing editor, 1967-68, Houston bureau chief, 1968-70, Los Angeles bureau chief, 1970-73, senior editor, 1973-75, Jerusalem bureau chief, 1975-78, New York bureau chief, 1978-79; *Washington Star,* Washington, D.C., news services editor, 1979-80; free-lance writer, 1980—. Notable assignments include coverage of the Vietnam War, the Apollo moon landing program, the Mariner Mars program, the U.S. presidential campaign of 1972, the Sinai interim agreement, 1976, Anwar Sadat's visit to Jerusalem, 1977, the Jonestown massacre, 1978, the Colombia cocaine connection, 1978, and the Three Mile Island near-meltdown, 1979.

MEMBER: Foreign Press Association (Israel chapter president, 1977, vice-president, 1978).

AWARDS, HONORS: Theta Sigma Phi Matrix award, 1962; California-Nevada AP Writing Contest award for best metropolitan spot news story, 1962; Overseas Press Club award for best magazine story of 1979, for ''The Colombia Connection''; American Book Award nomination for history, 1981, for *Warriors at Suez: Eisenhower Takes America into the Middle East.*

WRITINGS:

Warriors at Suez: Eisenhower Takes America into the Middle East, Linden Press, 1981.
Warriors for Jerusalem: The Six Days That Changed the Middle East, Linden Press, 1984.
Warriors against Israel, Amana Books, 1988.

Contributor of articles to various magazines.

SIDELIGHTS: A veteran journalist and formerly *Time*'s bureau chief in Jerusalem, Donald Neff has written a trilogy of books focusing on the Arab-Israeli conflicts of 1956, 1967, and 1973. His first, *Warriors at Suez: Eisenhower Takes America into the Middle East,* ''has an even greater significance [than a book of history], for it illuminates in ways still pertinent—the difficult problems of that troubled region,'' observes Richard J. Walton in the *Chicago Tribune Book World.* Detailing the Israeli, French, and British invasion of the Suez Canal and written ''in the style of the thriller it is, this story is as sobering as it is fascinating,'' continues the critic.

Christian Science Monitor contributor Robin Wright has similar praise for Neff's account of 1967's Six-Day War, *Warriors for Jerusalem: The Six Days That Changed the Middle East:* ''[Neff's] second volume is not simply a record of [the war] ... but a living, breathing drama that takes in the 'global scoreboard.''' Wright adds that the importance of *Warriors for Jerusalem* ''is the perspective Neff has woven into the narrative—his explanation about why this conflict set the stage for all that has happened since and how the subsequent impact has affected every corner of the globe.'' ''Though he presents no new evidence to change our view of events,'' comments Milton Viorst in the *New York Times Book Review,* ''[Neff] makes use of newly available documents and skillful personal interviews to enrich the text.''

Warriors against Israel, Neff's ''fascinating final volume,'' is comparably successful, as Archie Roosevelt remarks in the *Washington Post Book World:* ''It is not only a well-documented and authoritative account, but a riveting expose of how Henry Kissinger nudged the United States from its position as umpire in the contest to one of strong alliance with Israel.'' The critic concludes that he ''was impressed by the originality of Neff's presentation and surprised by his devastating conclusions, assembled from facts previously known to most of us only piecemeal. It is not only a good read, but essential background for serious students of developments in the Middle East today.''

BIOGRAPHICAL/CRITICAL SOURCES:

PERIODICALS

Chicago Tribune Book World, November 15, 1981.
Christian Science Monitor, April 11, 1984.
Los Angeles Times Book Review, July 29, 1984.
Maclean's, May 14, 1984.
New Republic, September 17, 1984.
New York Times Book Review, November 8, 1981, May 6, 1984.

Washington Post Book World, October 18, 1981, April 22, 1984, July 31, 1988.

* * *

NELSON, Benjamin N. 1911-1977

PERSONAL: Born February 11, 1911, in New York, N.Y.; died September 17, 1977, on a train in West Germany; son of Mark and Mary (Finesmith) Nelson; married Marie Alma Louise Poole Coleman, November 30, 1959. *Education:* City College (now of the City University of New York), B.A., 1931; Columbia University, M.A., 1933, Ph.D., 1944.

ADDRESSES: Home—29 Woodbine Ave., Stony Brook, N.Y. 11790.

CAREER: University of Chicago, Chicago, Ill., assistant professor of social science and history, 1945-48; University of Minneapolis, Minneapolis, Minn., co-chairman of department of social science and chairman of European heritage sequence of humanities program, 1948-56; Hofstra University, Hempstead, N.Y., professor of history and social science and chairman of department, 1956-59; State University of New York at Oyster Bay and Stony Brook, professor of sociology and anthropology, 1959-66, chairman of department, 1961-66; New School for Social Research, New York, N.Y., professor of sociology and history (graduate faculty), 1966-77. Permanent fellow in University Faculty Seminar; intern in contemporary civilization at Carnegie Institute, 1962; Alexander White Visiting Professor at University of Chicago, 1970; visiting professor at Columbia University, 1970-71; Philip Merlan Memorial Lecturer at Scripps College, 1973.

MEMBER: International Society for the Comparative Study of Civilization (president), International Sociological Association, American Academy of Arts and Sciences, American Anthropology Association, American Sociology Association, American History Association, Medieval Academy of America, American Philosophy Association, Society for Scientific Study of Religion, Society for the Arts, Religion, and Contemporary Cultures (director).

AWARDS, HONORS: Guggenheim fellow at Columbia University, 1944-45, 1949.

WRITINGS:

The Idea of Usury: From Tribal Brotherhood to Universal Otherhood, Princeton University Press, 1949, revised edition, University of Chicago Press, 1969.
(Editor with others) *Personality, Work, Community: An Introduction to Social Science,* Lippincott, 1957.
Freud and the Twentieth Century, Meridian Books, 1957, reprinted, P. Smith, 1974.
(Editor) *On Creativity and the Unconscious: Papers on the Psychology of Art, Literature, Love, Religion,* Harper, 1958.
(Editor with John Hine Mundy) *Essays in Medieval Life and Thoughts,* Biblo & Tannen, 1965.
(Contributor) Robert S. Cohen and Marx W. Wartofsky, editors, *Boston Studies in the Philosophy of Science,* Humanities Press, 1968.
(Contributor) *Beyond the Classics,* Harper, 1973.
Der Ursprug der Moderne: Vergleichende Studien zum Zivilisationsprozess, Suhrkamp (Frankfurt), 1977.
On the Roads to Modernity: Conscience, Science, and Civilizations, Selected Writings, edited by Toby E. Huff, Bowman & Littlefield, 1981.

Senior consultant editor of "Harper Torchbooks" series, 1967-77. General editor, "Civilizational Structures and Intercivilizational Encounters" series, Arno Press, 1976-77. Contributor of more than one hundred articles to professional journals and periodicals, including *American Sociological Review, Journal of Economic History, New York Times Book Review,* and *Journal for the Scientific Study of Religion, Sociological Analysis, and Social Research.* Member of editorial board, *Social Research,* 1966-71.

BIOGRAPHICAL/CRITICAL SOURCES:

BOOKS

Cohen, Robert S. and Marx W. Wartofsky, editors, *Methodology, Metaphysics, and the History of Science: In Memory of Benjamin Nelson,* D. Reidel, 1984.
Walter, E. V. and others, editors, *Civilizations East and West: A Memorial Volume for Benjamin Nelson,* Humanities Press, 1985.

OBITUARIES:

PERIODICALS

AB Bookman's Weekly, February 6, 1978.
New York Times, September 20, 1977.*

*   *   *

NELSON, Esther L.   1928-

PERSONAL: Born September 9, 1928, in New York, N.Y.; daughter of Rubin (a fabric cutter) and Freda (a nurse; maiden name, Seligman) Nelson; married Leon Sokolsky (an art teacher), November 18, 1949; children: Mara, Risa. *Education:* Brooklyn College (now Brooklyn College of the City University of New York), B.A., 1949; New York University, M.A., 1951; attended New School for Social Research and Bank Street College of Education.

ADDRESSES: Home—3605 Sedgwick Ave., Bronx, N.Y. 10463. *Office*—Dimension Five, P.O. Box 403, Kingsbridge Station, Bronx, N.Y. 10463.

CAREER: Knollwood School, Elmsford, N.Y., dance teacher, 1953-56; Scarsdale Dance Inc., Scarsdale, N.Y., dance teacher, 1953-70; Fieldston School, Riverdale, N.Y., dance teacher, 1958-63; Dimension Five (record company), Bronx, N.Y., partner, 1963—. Music and dance teacher, 1953-78. Lecturer at Brooklyn College of the City University of New York, Shippensburg College, and Millersville State College. Conductor of dance and music workshops for teachers. Performer on records for children. Member of Dance Library (Israel).

MEMBER: American Dance Guild, American Alliance for Health, Physical Education and Recreation (Dance Division).

AWARDS, HONORS: Nelson's record "Dance, Sing and Listen Again" was named one of the best children's recordings of 1979 by the American Library Association.

WRITINGS:

Dancing Games for Children of All Ages (Instructor Book Club selection), Sterling, 1973.
Movement Games for Children of All Ages (Instructor Book Club selection), Sterling, 1975.
Musical Games for Children of All Ages (Instructor Book Club selection), Sterling, 1976.

Singing and Dancing Games for the Very Young, Sterling, 1977.
Holiday Singing and Dancing Games, Sterling, 1980.
The Silly Songbook, Sterling, 1981.
The Funny Songbook, Sterling, 1984.
The Great Rounds Songbook, Sterling, 1985.
(Editor) *The Fun-to-Sing Songbook,* Sterling, 1986.

Author of children's records and cassettes with Bruce Haack. Contributor to *Dance Magazine* and *Early Childhood Day Care.*

WORK IN PROGRESS: Preschool Music and Dance (working title), for Instructor Books, and related cassette, for Dimension Five.

SIDELIGHTS: Esther L. Nelson wrote *CA:* "I have always loved and been involved with music and dance, and so it was natural for me to continue into adulthood and to get a masters degree in dance education. I thank my mother, Freda Nelson, for sharing her love of music with me (two of my books are dedicated to her). My branching into the fields of recordings and books was a natural progression, and both times came from parents of children in my dance classes.

"Dimension Five [owned with partner and composer Bruce Haack] now has a totally equipped sound studio where we record and produce our records and cassettes. We have sold more than 100,000 of our children's music and dance participation records and cassettes to schools, libraries, book clubs and stores and parents all over the country."

AVOCATIONAL INTERESTS: International travel, "singing and dancing with my granddaughter, to whom my newest book is dedicated."

*   *   *

NETHERCOT, Arthur H(obart)   1895-

PERSONAL: Born April 20, 1895, in Chicago, Ill.; son of Charles Walter and Anna Louise (Hobart) Nethercot; married Mary Josephine Macdougall, 1922 (deceased); married Gertrude M. von Bachelle, 1950; children: Arthur H., Jr., William Bradford. *Education:* Northwestern University, B.A., 1915, M.A., 1916; additional graduate study, Oxford University, 1919; University of Chicago, Ph.D., 1922.

CAREER: St. Alban's School for Boys, Knoxville, Ill., master, 1916-1917; Northwestern University, Evanston, Ill., 1919-1963, began as instructor, became professor of English, Franklyn Bliss Snyder Professor of English, 1961, Alumni Fund Lecturer, 1962. Fulbright lecturer, University of Cologne, 1965-66; visiting professor at several U.S. colleges and universities. *Military service:* U.S. Army, Ambulance Corps, 1917-18, Field Artillery, 1918-19; became second lieutenant.

MEMBER: Modern Language Association of America (secretary of drama group, 1942-43), Modern Humanities Research Association, American Association of University Professors (president of local chapter, 1948-49), Phi Beta Kappa (president of local chapter, 1940-41).

AWARDS, HONORS: Fulbright research fellow in India, 1956-57; Northwestern University Alumni Merit Award, 1960; Chicago Friends of Literature Award, 1964, for *The First Five Lives of Annie Besant* and *The Last Four Lives of Annie Besant.*

WRITINGS:

(Editor) *A Book of Long Stories*, Macmillan, 1927, reprinted, Arden Library, 1978.

Abraham Cowley: The Muse's Hannibal, Oxford University Press, 1931, revised edition, Russell, 1967.

(Co-editor) *Elizabethan and Stuart Plays*, Holt, 1934, revised edition published in two volumes, Volume 1: *Elizabethan Plays*, 1971, Volume 2: *Stuart Plays*, Irvington Books, 1971.

Sir William D'avenant: Poet Laureate and Playwright-Manager, University of Chicago Press, 1938, reprinted, Russell, 1967.

The Road to Tryermaine, University of Chicago Press, 1938, reprinted as *The Road to Tryermaine: A Study of the History, Background and Purposes of Coleridge's "Christabel,"* Greenwood Press, 1978.

Men and Supermen: The Shavian Portrait Gallery, Harvard University Press, 1954, 2nd edition, Ayer Co., 1966.

The First Five Lives of Annie Besant, University of Chicago Press, 1960.

The Last Four Lives of Annie Besant, University of Chicago Press, 1963.

Reputation of Abraham Cowley: Sixteen Sixty-Eighteen Hundred, Haskell, 1970.

Reputation of the Metaphysical Poets during the Age of Johnson and the Romantic Revival, Haskell, 1970.

Member of editorial board, *Shaw Review*, beginning 1959.

WORK IN PROGRESS: An autobiography, to be placed in the archives of Northwestern University.

AVOCATIONAL INTERESTS: Tennis, squash, bridge.*

*   *   *

NICHOLAS, William
See THIMMESCH, Nicholas Palen

*   *   *

NICKERSON, Jane Soames (Bon)   1900-1988
(Jane Soames)

PERSONAL: Born in 1900, in England; died January 10, 1988, in Long Island, N.Y.; married Hoffman Nickerson (a historian; deceased); children: William, Martinus; (stepchildren) Eugene H. Nickerson, Adam H. Nickerson. *Education:* B.A., Oxford University.

CAREER: London *Times*, correspondent in Paris, France; secretary to journalist Hilaire Belloc during the 1930s; writer.

WRITINGS:

(Under name Jane Soames) *The English Press: Newspapers and News*, preface by Hilaire Belloc, S. Nott, 1936, new and revised edition, Lindsay Drummond, 1938.

(Under name Jane Soames) *The Coast of Barbary*, J. Cape, 1938, published under name Jane Soames Nickerson as *A Short History of North Africa, from Pre-Roman Times to the Present: Libya, Tunisia, Algeria, Morocco*, Devin-Adair, 1961.

(Editor with Herbert van Thal) Belloc, *Belloc: A Biographical Anthology*, Knopf, 1970.

Homage to Malthus, introduction by Russell Kirk, Kennikat, 1975.

Translator of *The Origins of the First World War* (from the French), and of *The Political and Social Doctrine of Fascism* (from the Italian).*

*   *   *

NIMMO, Derek (Robert)   1933-

PERSONAL: Born September 19, 1933, in Liverpool, England; son of Harry and Marjorie (Sudbury-Hardy) Nimmo; married Patricia Sybil Anne Browne, April 9, 1955; children: Timothy, Amanda, Piers. *Education:* Attended school in Liverpool, England. *Politics:* Liberal. *Religion:* Church of England.

ADDRESSES: Home—110 Lexham Gardens, London W.8, England.

CAREER: Professional actor, 1955—, including roles in plays "Waltz of the Toreadors" and "Same Time Next Year," films "Casino Royale" and "A Talent for Loving," and television series "If It's Saturday Night It Must Be Nimmo," "Just a Nimmo," "Sorry I'm Single," "Life Begins at Forty," "Oh Brother," and "Hells Bells."

MEMBER: Garrick Club, Athenaeum Club.

AWARDS, HONORS: Award from Variety Club; silver medal from Royal Television Society.

WRITINGS:

(Editor and author of introduction) *Nimmo's Choice: A Collection of Cartoons*, Mowbray, 1974.

Derek Nimmo's Drinker's Companion, Hamlyn, 1979.

Shaken and Stirred, Hamlyn, 1982.

Oh Come on All Ye Faithful, Robson Books, 1986.

Not in Front of the Servants, Robson Books, 1987.

*   *   *

NOSANOW, Barbara Shissler   1931-
(Barbara Johnson Shissler)

PERSONAL: Born August 12, 1931, in Roanoke, Va.; daughter of Willis Morton (an electrical engineer) and Kathryn (Bradford) Johnson; married John Lewis Shissler, Jr. (deceased); married Lewis H. Nosanow (a doctor); children: (first marriage) John Lewis III, Ada Holland. *Education:* Smith College, A.B., 1951; Western Reserve University (now Case Western Reserve University), M.A., 1957.

ADDRESSES: Office—Educational Division, National Archives, Washington, D.C.

CAREER: Cleveland Museum of Art, Cleveland, Ohio, managing editor of *Journal of Aesthetics and Art Criticism*, 1957-62; Minneapolis Institute of Arts, Minneapolis, Minn., editor of publications and director of documents program, 1963-72; University of Minnesota Art Gallery, Minneapolis, director, 1972-76; National Archives, Washington, D.C., director of division of education, 1976—. Leader of several museum tours abroad.

WRITINGS:

(Under name Barbara Johnson Shissler) *Sports and Games in Art* (juvenile), Lerner, 1966.

(Under name Barbara Johnson Shissler) *The Worker in Art* (juvenile), Lerner, 1970.

(Under name Barbara Johnson Shissler) *The New Testament in Art* (juvenile), Lerner, 1970.

American Period Rooms at the Minneapolis Institute of Arts, Minneapolis Institute of Arts, 1970.

More Than Land Or Sky: Art from Appalachia, Smithsonian Institution Press, 1981.

Sawtooths and Other Ranges of Imagination: Contemporary Art from Idaho, Smithsonian Institution Press, 1983.

Contributor to *Catalogue of European Paintings in the Minneapolis Institute of Arts.**

                    *   *   *

NOTLEP, Robert
    See PELTON, Robert W(ayne)

O

O'BRIEN, E. G.
  See CLARKE, Arthur C(harles)

*   *   *

O'CONNOR, Karen 1938-
  (Karen O'Connor Sweeney)

PERSONAL: Resumed maiden name legally in 1979; born April 8, 1938, in Chicago, Ill.; daughter of Philip K. (a business broker) and Eva (Ennis) O'Connor; married John E. Sweeney, June 11, 1960 (divorced, November, 1979); married Charles R. Flowers (a real estate broker), April 9, 1983; children: (first marriage) Julie, James, Erin. *Education:* Clarke College, B.A., 1960.

ADDRESSES: Home and office—5050 La Jolla Blvd., No. 3B, San Diego, Calif. 92109.

CAREER: Elementary schoolteacher in North Hollywood, Calif., 1960-61; Los Angeles City Schools, Los Angeles, Calif., substitute teacher, 1963-66; tutor, 1972-76; writer, 1976—. Writing teacher at public schools in California, 1976-80, and for Institute of Children's Literature, 1982—; member of faculty at University of California at La Jolla, Riverside, Irvine, Davis, and Santa Cruz, 1981—. Former national language arts consultant for Glencoe Publishing.

MEMBER: American Society of Journalists and Authors (former chapter president), Society of Children's Book Writers, National Speakers Association.

AWARDS, HONORS: Screening certificate from Chicago International Film Festival, 1975, for "A Visit with 'Don Juan in Hell'"; nonfiction book award from California Press Women, 1980, for *Working with Horses: A Roundup of Careers,* and 1982, for *Maybe You Belong in a Zoo!: Zoo and Aquarium Careers;* Certificate of Merit from Bookbuilders West, 1981, for *In Christ Jesus;* in 1982 *Maybe You Belong in a Zoo!* was named a "notable children's trade book in the field of social studies" by the National Social Studies Teachers Association-Children's Book Council Joint Committee and an "outstanding science trade book for children" by the National Science Teachers Association-Children's Book Council Joint Committee; in 1983 *Sally Ride and the New Astronauts: Scientists in Space* and *Try These On for Size, Melody!* were each named an "outstanding science trade book for children" by the National Science Teachers Association-Children's Book Council Joint Committee.

WRITINGS:

Special Effects: A Guide for Super-Filmmakers (juvenile), F. Watts, 1980.
Working with Horses: A Roundup of Careers (juvenile), Dodd, 1980.
In Christ Jesus (juvenile), Benziger, 1981.
Maybe You Belong in a Zoo!: Zoo and Aquarium Careers (juvenile), Dodd, 1982.
Try These On for Size, Melody! (juvenile), Dodd, 1983.
Sally Ride and the New Astronauts: Scientists in Space (juvenile), F. Watts, 1983.
Contributions of Women: Literature (juvenile), Dillon, 1983.
Sharing the Kingdom: Animals and Their Rights (young adult), Dodd, 1984.
Let's Take a Walk on the Beach (juvenile), Child's World, 1986.
Let's Take a Walk in the City (juvenile), Child's World, 1986.
Waste, Trash, Litter, Garbage: A Universal Threat (juvenile), New Day Books, 1988.

UNDER NAME KAREN O'CONNOR SWEENEY

"A Visit with 'Don Juan in Hell'" (educational film), North American Film Co., 1975.
Everywoman's Guide to Family Finances, Major Books, 1976.
Improve Your Love Life, Major Books, 1976.
How to Make Money (juvenile), F. Watts, 1977.
"Gold: The First Metal" (educational film), North American Film Co., 1978.
I Am a Compleat Woman: An Adventure in Self-Discovery, Wilshire, 1978.
Entertaining (juvenile), F. Watts, 1978.
Illustrated Tennis Dictionary for Young People (juvenile), Harvey House, 1979.
Nature Runs Wild: True Disaster Stories (juvenile), F. Watts, 1979.

OTHER

Contributor to educational and religious textbooks. Work represented in anthologies, including *Metrovoices,* Glencoe Publishing, and *Strike Up the Band,* Scott, Foresman. Author of "Women Who Win" and "Everywoman's Guide to Money

Matters," columns in *Money-Making Opportunities.* Contributor of more than five hundred articles and stories to periodicals.

WORK IN PROGRESS: Writing and editing elementary language arts textbooks, publication by McGraw-Hill and Curriculum Concepts expected in 1988.

* * *

O'CONNOR, Philip F(rancis) 1932-

PERSONAL: Born December 3, 1932, in San Francisco, Calif.; son of John Joseph (an accountant) and Josephine (Browne) O'Connor; married Delores Doster, February 2, 1963 (divorced, 1978); children: Dondi, John, Christopher, Erin, Justin. *Education:* University of San Francisco, B.S., 1954; San Francisco State College (now University), M.A., 1961; University of Iowa, M.F.A., 1963.

ADDRESSES: Home—520 Lorraine Ave., Bowling Green, Ohio 43402. *Office*—Department of English, Bowling Green State University, Bowling Green, Ohio 43402.

CAREER: Clarkson College of Technology, Potsdam, N.Y., instructor, 1963-65, assistant professor of humanities, 1965-67; Bowling Green University, Bowling Green, Ohio, assistant professor, 1967-70, professor of English, 1970—, chairman of creative writing program, 1969-70 and 1985—. *Military service:* U.S. Army; became lieutenant.

AWARDS, HONORS: Iowa School of Letters Award in Short Fiction, 1971, for *Old Morals, Small Continents, Darker Times;* American Book Award nomination, 1980, for first novel, *Stealing Home;* McNaughton Award, 1988, for *Defending Civilization.*

WRITINGS:

Old Morals, Small Continents, Darker Times, University of Iowa Press, 1971.
A Season for Unnatural Causes: Stories, University of Illinois Press, 1975.
Stealing Home (novel; Book-of-the-Month Club alternate selection), Knopf, 1979.
Defending Civilization (novel), Weidenfeld & Nicolson, 1988.

WORK IN PROGRESS: Clowns, a novel, for Weidenfeld & Nicolson.

SIDELIGHTS: Stealing Home, Philip F. O'Connor's first novel, brought him a National Book Award nomination in 1980 and a number of favorable reviews. It is "a tender yet unsentimental examination of middle-class domestic life as seen through the unexpectedly revealing prism of Little League baseball," writes Jonathan Yardley in the *Washington Post Book World.* Protagonist Benjamin Dunne is losing his adolescent son's respect because he is average and not keeping up with the changing times. Dunne is also losing his wife to an impractical business scheme, and his daughter to mental illness. He finds a strategy to recoup only one of these losses by becoming the unlikely coach of his son's baseball team. Though his involvement wins him a higher place in his son's esteem, it also leads to an affair that tempts him to start a new life without his family. "O'Connor has clearly and accurately defined the malaise of contemporary life—loves taken for granted, emotions left unspoken, dreams and destinies left undefined," comments Michael J. Bandler in the *Chicago Tribune Book World.* Though Dunne may gain more than his share of sympathy next

to the unflattering portraits of women in the novel, says Bandler, in general the reviewer finds *Stealing Home* "an impressive, achingly credible glimpse of ordinary lives, extraordinarily told." Webster Schott, writing in the *New York Times Book Review,* also calls the book extraordinary because it "seriously examines difficult questions about human motive and need, and, failing to find clear answers, nevertheless proposes that we move on to the next set of unanswerable questions."

The creative writing professor's second novel *Defending Civilization,* "like *Stealing Home* . . . is a novel about the frailties of human character, and it is written with the same attention to nuance and subtlety that distinguished O'Connor's first book," Yardley observes; it is sometimes entertaining, but its subjects, he warns, "are anything except charming." Set in Britain just after the Korean War, the novel relates the inner conflicts of an idealistic lieutenant as he is drawn into deceptive schemes involving anti-aircraft weapons that his commanding officer knows are ineffective. The truth-loving Hanlon becomes the protege of Colonel Francis P. Shea, a sadistic trainer who respects no law but his own ambition. Shea arranges for an accomplice to blow up target planes to make it appear that he is a master at shooting the guns; then he places the defective weapons in American military bases. The guns will never be needed, he tells Hanlon, because air war with the Soviets is highly improbable. The super powers of the world would not threaten their security with such a war; the impoverished, powerless masses are the real enemy, he believes. Thus, says Carmine Di Biase in the *Columbus Dispatch,* Hanlon "is forced to revise his misconceived notion of the nobility of military service."

Hanlon had entered the military to regain self-respect after watching his friends die in Korea while he was safe in a university. Instead of war, Hanlon reports that he has seen "waste, corruption, hypocrisy, stupidity and lies . . . I'd done nothing about these evils. *My* scars weren't going to be badges of glory like my friends' but ugly emblems of guilt, invisible, unresolved and well-deserved." What follows from this realization, says Mike Kiley in *Tribune Books,* "is part psychodrama, part male bonding, part historic perspective (Vietnam on the horizon, the atomic bomb a new burden) and part suspense story. . . . [Hanlon] can keep quiet about some of Shea's underhanded tactics and be promoted along with Shea to a plum post, or he can stick to his convictions and be courtmartialed." Speaking to Fred Lutz of the Toledo *Blade,* O'Connor explains the title and the outcome: "Civilization is defended in one second, . . . the second when Hanlon decides not to play the game." Don Skiles of the *San Francisco Chronicle* relates, "In its conclusion, this funny, deceptively simple, insightful novel forces us to examine the full significance of the military mind-set, and what it may take to keep it in its place in our own day."

Generally pleased with reviews of *Defending Civilization,* O'Connor told *CA* that "the theme that is most important to me—the evolution of Hanlon's conscience—has been adequately appreciated by only a few reviewers." Anticipating a negative critical reception, his former literary agent and publisher were not enthusiastic about the publication of such a novel. However, inspired by the example of a British group protesting the presence of American cruise missiles at Greenham Common, the author was not willing to further postpone the completion of the novel he had been working on since 1961. Once he saw how to finish the novel, he made use of the issues he had been thinking about since his own tour of duty in England in the mid-1950s. According to many reviewers, *Defending Civilization* proves that a book with a serious subject need not be unpleasant to read. For example, Arthur Salm writes in the San Diego *Tribune*, ''The story . . . is smooth and compelling; the reading is effortless and irresistible. 'Defending Civilization' is like that rare movie that entertains you in the theater and then makes for good conversation over dinner.''

BIOGRAPHICAL/CRITICAL SOURCES:

BOOKS

O'Connor, Philip F., *Defending Civilization*, Weidenfeld & Nicolson, 1988.

PERIODICALS

Atlantic, June, 1979.
Black Warrior Review, Number 6, 1980.
Blade (Toledo, Ohio), August 14, 1988, August 31, 1988.
Chicago Tribune Book World, April 1, 1979.
Christian Science Monitor, April 9, 1979.
Columbus Dispatch, August 14, 1988.
Commonweal, May 11, 1979.
Critique: Studies in Modern Fiction, summer, 1983.
Nation, November 26, 1973.
National Review, November 9, 1979.
Newsweek, April 2, 1979.
New York Times, March 22, 1979.
New York Times Book Review, April 15, 1979, October 26, 1975.
Partisan Review, fall, 1972.
Publishers Weekly, February 5, 1979.
San Francisco Chronicle, August 28, 1988.
Tribune (San Diego, Calif.), August 5, 1988.
Tribune Books (Chicago), August 18, 1988.
Washington Post Book World, March 18, 1979, December 9, 1979, July 10, 1988.
West Coast Review of Books, May, 1979.

*   *   *

ONEAL, Elizabeth   1934-
   (Zibby Oneal)

PERSONAL: Born March 17, 1934, in Omaha, Neb.; daughter of James D. (a thoracic surgeon) and Mary Elizabeth (Dowling) Bisgard; married Robert Moore Oneal (a plastic surgeon), December 27, 1955; children: Elizabeth, Michael. *Education:* Attended Stanford University, 1952-55; University of Michigan, B.A., 1970. *Politics:* Democrat. *Religion:* Episcopalian.

ADDRESSES: Home—501 Onondaga St., Ann Arbor, Mich. 48104. *Agent*—Marilyn Marlow, Curtis Brown Ltd., 575 Madison Ave., New York, N.Y. 10022.

CAREER: University of Michigan, Ann Arbor, lecturer in English, 1976-85. Member of board of trustees, Greenhills School, 1975-79.

AWARDS, HONORS: Friends of American Writers Award, 1972, for *War Work*; Best Books of the Year list, *New York Times*, 1982, and Christopher Award, 1983, both for *A Formal Feeling*; *Horn Book* Honor Book, and *Boston Globe/Horn Book* Award, both 1986, both for *In Summer Light*; *The Language of Goldfish*, *A Formal Feeling*, and *In Summer Light* have all

been named to the American Library Association's Notable and Best Books for Young Adults Lists.

WRITINGS:

JUVENILES; UNDER NAME ZIBBY ONEAL

War Work, illustrated by George Porter, Viking, 1971.
The Improbable Adventures of Marvelous O'Hara Soapstone, illustrated by Paul Galdone, Viking, 1972.
Turtle and Snail, illustrated by Margot Tomes, Lippincott, 1979.
The Language of Goldfish (young adult novel), Viking, 1980.
A Formal Feeling (young adult novel), Viking, 1982.
Maude and Walter, illustrated by Maxie Chambliss, Lippincott, 1985.
In Summer Light (young adult novel), Viking, 1985.
Grandma Moses: Painter of Rural America (biography), Puffin, 1986.

SIDELIGHTS: Zibby Oneal's novels for young adults ''exhibit a depth and complexity rare in any kind of fiction,'' asserts Wendy Smith in *Publishers Weekly*. Her novels are characterized by teenagers coming into conflict not only with the people around them, but also with their own confusion and mixed emotions. *The Language of Goldfish*, Oneal's first novel, deals with Carrie Stokes, a daughter of wealthy parents whose struggle with puberty develops into a mental breakdown and a suicide attempt. Despite this weighty topic, *New York Times Book Review* contributor Joyce Milton feels ''it would be a mistake to include this novel in the wave of pop-sociological fiction about teen-age trauma,'' for several aspects of *The Language of Goldfish* are distinctive. Besides containing a believable situation, ''the book's technical strengths are many,'' comments Loralee MacPike in *Best Sellers*. ''The dialogue is good, its terseness reflecting the teenage milieu. The symbols . . . are there for the reader to find but are never forced. The characters are neither fiends nor angels, just real people doing their flawed best in a flawed world,'' elaborates the critic. Milton praises in particular Oneal's ability to evoke Carrie's situation with narrative technique: ''The people and events in Carrie's life are a bit flat and a bit hazy around the edges, which is entirely how she perceives them. In contrast, her inner turmoil—even during her dizzy spells when reality 'slips sideways'—is conveyed in language that is poetic and precise.'' But while Peter Blake admires Oneal's treatment of her subject, he comments in the *Times Literary Supplement* that Carrie's ''cure'' through psychoanalysis ''is a facile conclusion to an otherwise well-controlled book.'' MacPike, however, observes that the story ''offers reasonable hope, calm moments of joy, and the possibility of a future, without deviating from a serious appraisal of the problem's today's young people face.''

Oneal's second novel, *A Formal Feeling*, similarly demonstrates a teenager's efforts to deal with confusing feelings. Anne Cameron returns to her home for the holidays, a home strangely unfamiliar now that her mother is dead and her father remarried. Although stepfamilies are a standard topic for juvenile literature, *A Formal Feeling*'s Anne is not ''just one of those pretty, accomplished, hollow teen-agers who agonize over having been merely runner-up,'' remarks Georgess McHargue in the *New York Times Book Review*. This is due to the complexity of Oneal's portrait, for ''Anne, though reserved and difficult, is not self-pitying,'' states *Washington Post Book World* contributor Linda Barrett Osborne. ''She is so human and so in need of loving that she is sympathetic and engaging from the beginning, and the other characters balance her with a warmth that is genuine and free of sentimentality.'' The critic concludes by calling *A Formal Feeling* ''straightforward, absorbing, and perceptive, true to an adolescent's feelings about mothers and about grief.''

Oneal's ''literary resolution grows more polished and mature with each novel,'' maintains Michele Landsberg in the *New York Times Book Review*, assessing the author's third novel, *In Summer Light*, as ''her most ambitious and coherent work to date.'' Once again the protagonist is a young woman grappling with conflicting needs and emotions. Ill with mononucleosis, seventeen-year-old Kate Brewer has returned to her family's home, where she lives in the shadow of her famous artist father. Denying her need for her father's approval, Kate has suppressed her own talent and desire to create art. Part of the power of the book, writes Tim Wynne-Jones in the Toronto *Globe and Mail*, is Oneal's subtlety in presenting Kate's situation: ''We are not told that Kate is a frustrated artist, but from the start we see a sensibility that is careful to mark the difference between the color of nasturtiums and peaches simply because it matters,'' explains the critic. In addition, reviewers have noticed an artistic quality to Oneal's writing; *New Statesman* contributor Adele Geras comments that ''the prose, like a picture, is full of light and colour. . . . This book stays in the mind like the memory of a perfect summer day.'' ''Oneal uses an elegant dazzle of images to illuminate Kate's Oedipal conflict, while neatly side-stepping the boggy self-pity of so much adolescent fiction,'' observes Landsberg. The reviewer adds that ''best of all, [*In Summer Light*] keeps the action focused on Kate's inward movement toward freedom . . . through her own clear sight and growing emotional generosity.'' And Wynne-Jones concludes that it is to Oneal's credit that the character of Kate ''will be vital and vivid to readers long after the first-volume dust-jackets are torn and lost, and other artists on the covers of other editions have tried to put a likeness on what is essence: the fully realized fictional portrait.''

On her writing, Oneal commented to Smith: ''I feel a responsibility to make children understand that adolescence is a self-absorbed world—this may be why I always have islands in my books—but it's not a place you can stay forever. The movement away and out into the world, into concern for other people, has to happen; you aren't an adult until you make that move. Sure, you explore your feelings, because if you're hung up on your problems you're never going to be able to move on. So work that out, but then get out into the world.''

BIOGRAPHICAL/CRITICAL SOURCES:

BOOKS

Children's Literature Review, Volume 13, Gale, 1987.
Contemporary Literary Criticism, Volume 30, Gale, 1984.

PERIODICALS

Best Sellers, April, 1980.
Globe and Mail (Toronto), February 8, 1986.
New Statesman, October 10, 1986.
New York Times Book Review, April 27, 1980, November 14, 1982, November 24, 1985.
Publishers Weekly, February 21, 1986.
Times Literary Supplement, October 30, 1987.
Washington Post Book World, October 10, 1982.

—*Sketch by Diane Telgen*

ONEAL, Zibby
See ONEAL, Elizabeth

*   *   *

ORDE, Lewis   1943-

PERSONAL: Born January 23, 1943, in Reading, Berkshire, England; son of Coleman (a builder) and Berthe (Glinert) Orde. *Education:* Educated in London, England. *Politics:* ''A confusing mixture.''

ADDRESSES: Home and office—3088C Colony Rd., Durham, N.C. 27705. *Agent*—Harvey Klinger, 301 West 53rd St., New York, N.Y. 10019.

CAREER: Leicester Mercury, Leicester, England, reporter, 1967-68; *Men's Wear* (textile trade publication), London, England, reporter, 1968-70; United Trade Press, London, editor of clothing publications, 1970-75; Tip Top Tailors, Toronto, Ontario, communications manager and editor of house magazine, 1975-77; writer. Does volunteer work for the Arts Center of Carrboro, N.C. *Military service:* U.S. Army, 1964-67; became specialist fifth class.

MEMBER: Authors Guild, Authors League of America.

WRITINGS:

NOVELS

The Difficult Days Ahead, Paperjacks, 1977.
Rag Trade, St. Martin's, 1978.
(With Bill Michaels) *The Night They Stole Manhattan*, Putnam, 1980.
The Lion's Way, Arbor House, 1981.
Heritage, Arbor House, 1981.
Munich Ten, Arbor House, 1982.
Eagles, Arbor House, 1983.
The Tiger's Heart, Zebra Books, 1987.
The Proprietor's Daughter, Little, Brown, 1988.

SIDELIGHTS: Lewis Orde told *CA:* ''I like to take the summer off. No other job allows me to work just seven to eight months of the year. That's a terrible reason for being an author, but in my case it's the most truthful one. About twice a year I get the urge to look for a job, if only to have people to talk to. But I'm happy to say that I have not succumbed to that urge yet! It's also the only way I'm ever likely to strike it rich—much like buying a ticket on the Irish Sweepstakes, but you never know your luck.

''Basically I am a storyteller, capable of spinning a yarn. I'm certainly not a grammarian—but I believe that the ability to tell a story well, using credible characters, is more important than an extended formal education. My own education certainly was not extended; I left school at fifteen, much to the relief of my headmaster who wrote on one of my report cards, 'This boy is inclined to leave his brains on the soccer field or the cricket pitch, depending upon the season.' In retrospect, it was the only nice thing he said about me!''

AVOCATIONAL INTERESTS: Opera, sports, reading, people.

BIOGRAPHICAL/CRITICAL SOURCES:

PERIODICALS

New York Times Book Review, April 27, 1980.
Time, April 14, 1980.

OSMOND, Humphrey (Fortescue) 1917-

PERSONAL: Born July 1, 1917, in Surrey, England; son of George William Forber (a captain in the Royal Navy) and Dorothy (Gray) Osmond; married Amy Edith Roffey, November 12, 1947; children: Helen Lavinia, Euphemia Janet, Julian Fortescue. *Education:* Attended Haileybury and Imperial Service College; Guy's Hospital Medical School, University of London, M.R.C.S. and L.R.C.P., 1942; St. George's Hospital, London, D.P.M., 1949; Royal College of Physicians and Surgeons, Canada, certificate in psychiatry, 1952. *Politics:* "Labour Party supporter (England)." *Religion:* Anglican.

ADDRESSES: Office—Bureau of Research in Neurology and Psychiatry, New Jersey Neurological and Psychiatric Institute, Box 1000, Princeton, N.J. 08540.

CAREER: St. Georges Hospital, London, England, first assistant, 1948-51; Saskatchewan Hospital, Department of Psychiatry, Weyburn, clinical director, 1951-53, physician superintendent and director of research, 1953-61; New Jersey Neurological and Psychiatric Institute, Princeton, director of Bureau of Research in Neurology and Psychiatry, 1963—. Lecturer on schizophrenia at universities and hospitals in the United States and Canada. Member of board of directors, American Schizophrenia Foundation. Consultant to National Institute of Mental Health; consultant, especially on the socio-architecture of mental hospitals, to provincial governments of Saskatchewan and Ontario, and to states of Massachusetts, Pennsylvania, New York, and New Jersey. *Military service:* Royal Navy, 1942-47; became surgeon lieutenant.

MEMBER: Collegium Internationale Neuro-Psychopharmacologicum (founding member; fellow), World Academy of Arts and Sciences, American Psychiatric Association, Group for Advancement of Psychiatry, Canadian Medical Association, Canadian Psychiatric Association, British Medical Association, Royal Medico-Psychological Association, Saskatchewan Psychiatric Association (president, 1958), Royal College of Physicians of London.

WRITINGS:

(With Abram Hoffer) *The Chemical Basis of Clinical Psychiatry,* C. C Thomas, 1961.

(With Hoffer) *How to Live with Schizophrenia,* University Books, 1966, revised edition, Citadel Press, 1983.

(With Hoffer) *The Hallucinogens,* Academic Press, 1967.

(With Hoffer) *New Hope for Alcoholics,* University Books, 1968.

Medicine and Altered States (sound recording), Big Sur Recordings, 1968.

(Editor with Bernard Aaronson) *Psychedelics: The Uses and Implications of Hallucinogenic Drugs,* Anchor Books, 1970.

(Editor with Henri Yaker and Frances Cheek) *The Future of Time: Man's Temporal Environment,* Doubleday, 1971.

(With John A. Osmundsen and Jerome Agel) *Understanding Understanding,* Harper, 1973.

(With Miriam Siegler) *Models of Madness, Models of Medicine,* Macmillan, 1974.

(Editor with Hoffer and Harold Kelm) *Clinical and Other Uses of the Hoffer-Osmond Diagnostic Test,* R. E. Krieger, 1975.

(With Hoffer) *Megavitamin Therapy: In Reply to the American Psychiatric Association Task Force Report on Megavi-*

tamins and Orthomolecular Psychiatry, Canadian Schizophrenia Foundation, 1976.

(With Siegler) *Patienthood: The Art of Being a Responsible Patient,* Macmillan, 1979, published as *How to Cope with Illness: Dealing with Your Doctor, Your Relatives, and Yourself When You Are Ill,* 1981.

(With Agel) *Predicting the Past: Memos on the Enticing Universe of Possibility,* Macmillan, 1981.

Writer of one hundred papers on clinical psychiatry and allied subjects.

SIDELIGHTS: "While my central interest is the study of psychiatry with particular emphasis on schizophrenia," Humphrey Osmond once told *CA,* "this has led me to enquire into the umwelt or experiential world, first of mentally ill people and more recently of mentally well people. This interest was initiated from letters written between my old friend Aldous Huxley and myself, combined with my collaboration with Abram Hoffer. . . . Now engaged [with others] in developing a new human typology."*

*   *   *

OWENS, Robert Goronwy 1923-

PERSONAL: Born June 13, 1923, in West Haven, Conn.; son of Goronwy William and Irene (Brennan) Owens; married Barbara Perkins (a teacher), February 21, 1950; children: Shellie, Sydney. *Education:* University of Connecticut, B.A., 1945, Ph.D., 1955; Columbia University, M.A., 1950.

ADDRESSES: Office—Department of Educational Administration, Hofstra University, 1000 Fulton Ave., Hempstead, N.Y. 11550.

CAREER: Central School, Errol, N.H., teaching headmaster, 1945-47; principal of Broad Brook School, East Windsor, Conn., 1947-54, and of elementary schools in West Hartford, Conn., 1954-63; State University of New York at Buffalo, assistant professor of education, 1963-65; Brooklyn College of the City University of New York, Brooklyn, associate professor, 1965-69, professor of education, 1969—, associate professor of education administration, 1969-75, coordinator of Advanced Certificate Program in Educational Administration and Supervision. Consultant in secondary education to India Ministry of Education on Fulbright and U.S. State Department awards, 1960-61.

MEMBER: American Association of School Administrators, American Education Research Association, National Conference of Professors of Educational Administration, Phi Delta Kappa.

WRITINGS:

(Editor with others) *Summer School Programs in Transition,* Western New York School Study Council, State University of New York at Buffalo, 1965.

(With Lawrence T. Alexander, Stephen Lockwood, and Carl Steinhoff) *A Demonstration of the Use of Simulation in the Training of School Administrators,* Division of Teacher Education, City University of New York, 1967.

(With Steinhoff) *Organizational Climate in the More Effective Schools,* Division of Teacher Education, City University of New York, 1968.

A Regular Meeting of the Board, State University of New York at Albany, 1968.

Organizational Behavior in Schools, Prentice-Hall, 1970, 2nd edition published as *Organizational Behavior in Education,* Prentice-Hall, 1981, 3rd edition, 1987.

(With Steinhoff) *Administering Change in Schools,* Prentice-Hall, 1976.

(With B. Ashcroft) *Violence: A Guide for the Caring Professions,* Croom Helm, 1985.

Contributor of articles to *Overview, Connecticut Teacher, American School Board Journal, Journal of Educational Administration, Group and Organization Studies,* and other educational journals.

AVOCATIONAL INTERESTS: Sailing, skiing, horseback riding, cooking.*

P

PALMER, David (Walter) 1928-

PERSONAL: Born November 24, 1928, in Detroit, Mich.; son of Walter Samuel (a businessman) and Elizabeth Ruth (Besancon) Palmer; married Charlene Goldenberg (a poet and painter), June 16, 1951; children: Stephen David, Charna Ruth, Nicholas Alan, Renee Elizabeth. *Education:* Pasadena City College, A.A., 1949; University of California, Los Angeles, B.A., 1951, graduate study in English, 1951-52, M.L.S., 1961. *Politics:* Independent. *Religion:* Episcopalian.

*ADDRESSES: Home—*727 East St., Flint, Mich. 48503.

CAREER: Royal-Globe Insurance Group, Oakland, Calif., claims representative, 1956-59; University of California Press, Berkeley, public information writer, 1959-60; Humboldt State College (now California State University, Humboldt), Arcata, Calif., reference librarian, 1961-64; Rockford College, Rockford, Ill., library director, 1964-68; Baldwin-Wallace College, Berea, Ohio, library director, 1968-74; University of Michigan—Flint, library director, 1974—. Has given poetry readings at colleges and universities, Berkeley Town Hall Theatre, Chicago Art Institute, and on radio and television. *Military service:* U.S. Army, 1953-55.

MEMBER: American Library Association, Poetry Society of America, Riemenschneider Bach Institute.

WRITINGS:

Quickly, over the Wall (poetry and paintings), Wake-Brook, 1966.
(Contributor) *Peace or Perish: A Crisis Anthology,* Poets for Peace, 1983.
(Contributor) Bonnie Gordon, editor, *Songs from Unsung Worlds: Science in Poetry,* Birkhauser, 1985.

Also contributor to other anthologies, including *Dan River Anthology, 1984, Today's Poets: Chicago Tribune Sunday Magazine,* and *Poetry Today Supplement.* Contributor of poetry to magazines and journals, including *Beloit Poetry Journal, Contact, Dalhousie Review, Kayak, Phylon, Poet and Critic, Quixote,* and *San Francisco Review.* Regular reviewer, *Library Journal,* 1962-66; editor, *Beloit Poetry Journal,* 1964-67.

WORK IN PROGRESS: Midnight City Blues, a book of poetry.

AVOCATIONAL INTERESTS: Conversation, reading, music, painting, hiking, camping, tennis, swimming, sailing.

*   *   *

PALUMBO, Dennis J(ames) 1929-

PERSONAL: Born November 18, 1929, in Chicago, Ill.; son of Richard Anthony and Nora (Griffin) Palumbo; married Sachiko Onishi, April, 1954; children: Jean, Susan, Dennis E., Linda. *Education:* University of Chicago, M.A., 1958, Ph.D., 1960.

*ADDRESSES: Office—*School of Justice Studies, Arizona State University, Tempe, Ariz. 85287.

CAREER: Michigan State University, East Lansing, assistant professor of social science, 1960-61; University of Hawaii, Honolulu, assistant professor of political science, 1962-63; University of Pennsylvania, Philadelphia, associate professor of political science, 1963-66; Brooklyn College of the City University of New York, Brooklyn, professor of political science, 1966-76, director of graduate program in urban administration, 1971-74, director of undergraduate-graduate program of urban administration and information science, 1973-76; Indiana University, School of Public and Environmental Affairs, Indianapolis, professor of policy and administrative affairs, 1976-78, chairman of policy and administrative faculty, 1976-78; University of Kansas, Lawrence, director of Center for Public Affairs, 1977-83; Arizona State University, Tempe, director of Morrison Institute for Public Policy and professor of public affairs, 1983-86, School of Justice Studies, director of Ph.D. Program in Law and the Social Sciences, 1986-89, Regents' Professor of justice studies, 1988—.

Visiting professor, Columbia University, summer, 1971. Research associate, Council of State Governments, Chicago, Ill., 1959-60; associate researcher, Legislative Reference Bureau, Honolulu, Hawaii, 1962-63. Director, Research Center in Comparative Politics and Administration, Brooklyn College of the City University of New York. *Military service:* U.S. Air Force, Intelligence, 1950-54; became sergeant.

MEMBER: American Political Science Association, American Public Health Association, American Society of Public Administration, American Evaluation Association.

AWARDS, HONORS: I.D.A. Noyes scholarship, University of Chicago, 1959-60; U.S. Department of Health, Education, and Welfare, Public Health Service research grant, 1967-69; National Institute of Justice Research grant, 1981-84; National Highway Transportation and Safety Administration research grant, 1982-84.

WRITINGS:

Statistics in Political and Behavioral Science, with workbook, Appleton, 1969, 2nd edition, Columbia University Press, 1977.
American Politics, Appleton, 1973.
(Editor with George A. Taylor) *Urban Policy: A Guide to Information Sources,* Gale, 1979.
(With James P. Levine and Michael C. Musheno) *Criminal Justice: A Public Policy Approach,* Harcourt, 1980.
(Editor with Stephen B. Fawcett and Paula Wright) *Evaluating and Optimizing Public Policy,* Lexington Books, 1981.
(Editor with Marvin A. Harder) *Implementing Public Policy,* Lexington Books, 1981.
(Editor with Stuart Nagel) *Cross National Policy Studies Directory,* Policy Studies, 1984.
(With Levine and Musheno) *Criminal Justice in America: Law in Action,* Wiley, 1986.
(Editor) *The Politics of Program Evaluation,* Sage Publications, 1987.
Public Policy in America, Harcourt, 1988.

CONTRIBUTOR

Daniel Elazar, and others, editors, *Cooperation and Conflict,* F. E. Peacock, 1969.
Nagel, editor, *Policy Studies and Social Sciences,* Lexington Books, 1975.
Fred Greenstein and Nelson Polsby, editors, *Handbook of Political Science,* Addison-Wesley, 1976.
Nagel, editor, *Modeling in Criminal Justice,* Sage Publications, 1977.

Also contributor to *Policy Studies Review Annual,* edited by Ross Connor, 1986, and *Community Corrections: An Interactive Field Approach,* edited by David Duffee, 1989.

OTHER

Contributor to *Urban Affairs Quarterly, Public Administration Review, American Political Science Review, Commonweal, Intellect, Crime and Delinquency, American Journal of Politics, American Journal of Public Health, Policy Sciences, Evaluation Review, Evaluation & Program Planning, Social Sciences Quarterly,* and *Journal of Reasearch in Crime and Delinquency.*

WORK IN PROGRESS: An Introduction to Public Administration; Implementation and the Policy Making Process; Opening Up the Black Box.

SIDELIGHTS: Dennis J. Palumbo wrote *CA:* "I write because I enjoy it, because it is the best way to reach a large number of people, because I believe I have something important to say, and because I love words. But most important, writing enables me to see, almost as if I were an objective observer of myself, how I have improved over the years. Although much of my writing has been technical thus far, I expect to get better and believe my best years are yet to come. One can always look forward to doing the truly great work, even if it never happens."

PAREEK, Udai (Narain)   1925-

PERSONAL: Born January 21, 1925, in Jaipur, India; son of Vijailal and Gaindi Pareek; married Rama Sharma, May 13, 1945; children: Sushama, Surabhi, Anagat. *Education:* St. John's College, Agra, India, B.A., 1944; Teachers Training College, Ajmer, India, B.T., 1945; Calcutta University, M.A., 1950; Agra University, M.A., 1952; University of Delhi, Ph.D., 1956.

ADDRESSES: *Home*—1 Ganga Path, Suraj Nagar W., Jaipur 302006, India.

CAREER: Teachers Training School, Jaipur, India, teacher of psychology, 1945-48; Teachers Training College, Bikaner, India, lecturer in psychology, 1953-54; Delhi School of Social Work, Delhi, India, lecturer in psychology, 1954-55; National Institute of Basic Education, New Delhi, India, psychologist, 1956-62; Indian Agricultural Research Institute, New Delhi, psychologist, 1962-64; Small Industry Extension Training Institute, Hyderabad, India, director of extension education, 1964-66; University of North Carolina at Chapel Hill, visiting associate professor of psychology, 1966-68; National Institute of Health Adminstration and Education, New Delhi, professor of social sciences, 1968-70; University of Udaipur, Udaipur, India, director of School of Basic Sciences and Humanities and dean of faculty of social sciences, 1970-73; Indian Institute of Management, Ahmedabad, India, Larsen and Toubro Professor of Organisational Behaviour, 1973-85; Ministry of Health, Government of Indonesia, organization development advisor, 1985-88.

Member of governing board, Centre for Entrepreneurship Development, National Institute of Motivational and Institutional Development and Learning Systems, and Indian Institute of Health Management Research; member of advisory committee, Family Planning Foundation of India and Survey of Research in Psychology of the Indian Council of Social Science Research.

MEMBER: Psychometric Society, Society for the Psychological Study of Social Issues, Indian Psychological Association, American Psychological Association, American Sociological Association, National Training Laboratories (fellow), Madras Psychological Association, Andhra Pradesh Psychological Association (president, 1964-66), Indian Society of Applied Behavioural Science (president, 1987).

AWARDS, HONORS: Escorts Award, 1981, for *Designing and Managing Human Resource Systems.*

WRITINGS:

Developmental Patterns in Reaction to Frustration, Asia Publishing House (Bombay), 1964.
(With S. R. Mittal) *A Guide to the Literature of Research Methodology in Behavioural Sciences,* Behavioural Sciences Centre (Delhi), 1965.
(Editor) *Studies in Rural Leadership,* Behavioural Sciences Centre, 1966.
Behavioural Science Research in India: A Directory, 1925-1965, Acharan Sahkar, 1966.
A Guide to Indian Behavioural Science Periodicals, Behavioural Sciences Centre, 1966.
(With Rolf P. Lynton) *Training for Development,* Irwin, 1967.
(With S. R. Devi and Saul Rosenzweig) *Manual of the Indian Adaptation of the Adult Form of the Rosenzweig P. F. Study,* Roopa Psychological Corp., 1968.

(With Willis H. Griffin) *The Process of Planned Change in Education,* Somaiya, 1969.

Foreign Behavioural Research on India: A Directory of Research and Researchers, Acharan Sahkar, 1970.

(With T. V. Rao) *A Status Study on Population Research in India,* Volume 1, McGraw, 1974.

(With Rao) *Handbook of Psychological and Social Instruments,* Samashti, 1974.

(With Y. P. Singh and D. R. Arora) *Diffusion of an Interdiscipline,* Bookhive, 1974.

(With Rao and Ravi Matthai) *Institution Building in Education and Research: From Stagnation to Self-Renewal,* All India Management Association, 1977.

(With Rao) *Performance Appraisal and Review: Trainer's Manual, Operating Manual, and Skills Workbook,* Learning Systems, 1978.

(With Rao) *Developing Entrepreneurship,* Learning Systems, 1978.

Survey of Psychological Research in India, 1971-1976, Popular Prakashan, Part 1, 1980, Part 2, 1982.

(With Rao) *Designing and Managing Human Resource Systems,* Oxford University Press, 1981.

Beyond Management: Essays on the Processes of Institution Building, Oxford University Press, 1981.

(With Rao and D. M. Pestonjee) *Behavioural Processes in Organisations,* Oxford University Press, 1981.

(With Rao) *Handbook for Trainers in Educational Management,* UNESCO Regional Office for Education in Asia and the Pacific, 1981.

(With Rao) *Developing Motivation through Experiencing,* Oxford University Press, 1982.

(With Somnath Chattopadhyay) *Managing Organisational Change,* Oxford University Press, 1982.

Managing Conflict and Collaboration, Oxford University Press, 1982.

Education and Rural Development in Asia, Oxford University Press, 1982.

Role Stress Scales, Navin Publishers, 1982.

Role Pics: Coping with Role Stress, Navin Publishers, 1982.

Perilaku Organisasi (title means "Organizational Behaviour"), Pustak Binaman Pressindo (Jakarta, Indonesia), 1984.

(With Lynton) *Pelatihan dan Pengembangan Tenaga Kerja* (title means "Training and Manpower Development"), Pustak Binaman Pressindo, 1984.

Memahami Proses Perilaku Organisasi (title means "Teaching Organizational Behaviour"), Pustak Binaman Pressindo, 1985.

Medayagunakan Peran-Peran Keorganisasian (title means "Motivating Organizational Roles"), Pustak Binaman Pressindo, 1985.

Motivating Organizational Roles: Role Efficacy Approach, Rawat Publications (Jaipur, India), 1987.

Organizational Behaviour Processes, Rawat Publications, 1988.

CONTRIBUTOR

Dharni P. Sinha, editor, *Consultants and Consulting Styles,* Vision Books, 1979.

Harry C. Triandis and John W. Berry, editors, *Handbook of Cross-Cultural Psychology,* Volume 2, Allyn & Bacon, 1980.

R. S. Dwivedi, editor, *Manpower Management,* Prentice-Hall (India), 1980.

Dwivedi, editor, *Dynamics of Human Behaviour at Work,* Oxford University Press, 1981.

Pfeiffer and A. C. Ballew, editors, *Instrumentation Kit,* University Associates, 1988.

OTHER

Contributor to human resource and group facilitator annuals, edited by Pfeiffer. Editor of *Indian Psychological Abstracts* and *Manas.* Member of editorial board, *Psychologia, Managerial Psychology, Group and Organization Studies, Psychological Panorama,* and *New Trends in Education;* member of advisory group for *Theory and Models Kit* for University Associates.

SIDELIGHTS: Udai Pareek wrote *CA:* "My current work and writings are concerned with helping individuals, groups, and organizations to take charge of shaping their own destinies, and develop pro-social behavior. My main contribution has been to approach motivation from the point of view of hope (contrasted with fear), and the concept of 'extension motive'— an urge to be relevant to a larger group or cause, in a way extending oneself to others. I have been working on extension motive or need in organizations, so critical for developing countries."

*   *   *

PATERSON, Katherine (Womeldorf) 1932-

PERSONAL: Born October 31, 1932, in Qing Jiang, China; daughter of George Raymond (a clergyman) and Mary (Goetchius) Womeldorf; married John Barstow Paterson (a clergyman), July 14, 1962; children: Elizabeth Po Lin (adopted), John Barstow, Jr., David Lord, Mary Katherine (adopted). *Education:* King College, A.B., 1954; Presbyterian School of Christian Education, M.A., 1957; postgraduate study at Kobe School of Japanese Language, 1957-60; Union Theological Seminary, New York, N.Y., M.R.E., 1962. *Politics:* Democrat. *Religion:* Presbyterian Church in the United States.

ADDRESSES: Home—Vermont.

CAREER: Public school teacher in Lovettsville, Va., 1954-55; Presbyterian Church in the United States, Board of World Missions, Nashville, Tenn., missionary in Japan, 1957-62; Pennington School for Boys, Pennington, N.J., teacher of sacred studies and English, 1963-65; writer.

MEMBER: Authors Guild, PEN, Children's Book Guild of Washington.

AWARDS, HONORS: American Library Association (ALA) Notable Children's Book award, 1974, for *Of Nightingales That Weep;* ALA Notable Children's Book award, 1976, National Book Award for Children's Literature, 1977, runner-up for Edgar Allan Poe Award (juvenile division), Mystery Writers of America, 1977, and American Book Award nomination, children's fiction paperback, 1982, all for *The Master Puppeteer;* ALA Notable Children's Book award, 1977, John Newbery Medal, 1978, Lewis Carroll Shelf Award, 1978, and Division II runner-up, Michigan Young Reader's Award, 1980, all for *Bridge to Terabithia;* Lit.D., King College, 1978; ALA Notable Children's Book award, 1978, National Book Award for Children's Literature, 1979, Christopher Award (ages 9-12), 1979, Newbery Honor Book, 1979, CRABbery (Children Raving About Books) Honor Book, 1979, American Book Award nominee, children's paperback, 1980, William Allen White Children's Book Award, 1981, Garden State Children's Book Award, younger division, New Jersey Library Association, 1981, Georgia Children's Book Award, 1981, Iowa

Children's Choice Award, 1981, Massachusetts Children's Book Award (elementary), 1981, all for *The Great Gilly Hopkins;* U.S. nominee, Hans Christian Andersen Award, 1980; *New York Times* Outstanding Book List, 1980, Newbery Medal, 1981, CRABbery Honor Book, 1981, American Book Award nominee, children's hardcover, 1981, and children's paperback, 1982, all for *Jacob Have I Loved; The Crane Wife* was named to the *New York Times* Outstanding Books and Best Illustrated Books lists, both 1981; Parent's Choice Award, Parent's Choice Foundation, 1983, for *Rebels of the Heavenly Kingdom;* Irvin Kerlan Award, 1983, "in recognition of singular attainments in the creation of children's literature"; University of Southern Mississippi School of Library Service Silver Medallion, 1983, for outstanding contributions to the field of children's literature; nominee, Laura Ingalls Wilder Award, 1986; Regina Medal Award, Catholic Library Association, 1988, for demonstrating "the timeless standards and ideals for the writing of good literature for children."

WRITINGS:

JUVENILES

The Sign of the Chrysanthemum, Crowell Junior Books, 1973, reprinted, Trophy, 1988.
Of Nightingales That Weep, Crowell Junior Books, 1974.
The Master Puppeteer, Crowell Junior Books, 1976.
Bridge to Terabithia, Crowell Junior Books, 1977.
The Great Gilly Hopkins, Crowell Junior Books, 1978.
Angels and Other Strangers: Family Christmas Stories, Crowell Junior Books, 1979 (published in England as *Star of Night: Stories for Christmas,* Gollancz, 1980).
Jacob Have I Loved, Crowell Junior Books, 1980.
Rebels of the Heavenly Kingdom, Lodestar, 1983.
Come Sing, Jimmy Jo, Lodestar, 1985.
(With husband, John Paterson) *Consider the Lilies: Flowers of the Bible* (nonfiction), Crowell Junior Books, 1986.
Park's Quest, Lodestar, 1988.

TRANSLATOR

Sumiko Yagawa, *The Crane Wife,* Morrow, 1981.
Momoko Ishii, *Tongue-Cut Sparrow,* Lodestar, 1987.
Also translator of Hans Christian Andersen's *The Tongue Cut Sparrow,* for Lodestar.

OTHER

Who Am I? (curriculum unit), CLC Press, 1966.
To Make Men Free (curriculum unit; includes books, records, pamphlets, and filmstrip), John Knox, 1973.
Justice for All People, Friendship, 1973.
Gates of Excellence: On Reading and Writing Books for Children, Lodestar, 1981.

Contributor of articles and reviews to periodicals.

WORK IN PROGRESS: The Mandarin Ducks; The Spying Heart (tentative title); short pieces on reading and writing for children.

SIDELIGHTS: In much of her fiction for young adults, Katherine Paterson focuses on "the difficult but enlightening processes through which young people who are prematurely left to their own resources become acquainted with the compromises and obligations that are necessary to survival in the adult world," characterizes Jonathan Yardley in the *Washington Post Book World.* Critics remark on Paterson's honesty in presenting these kind of situations to a young audience, finding that her characters confront their problems without ever giving up

hope. But what reviewers think is even more remarkable is Paterson's ability to create realistic characters, believable settings, and thoroughly convincing dialogue. Although she develops a moral to some degree in her works, she does so without preaching. In a *Dictionary of Literary Biography* essay, M. Sarah Smedman comments on the author's skill: "The distinctive quality of Paterson's art is her colorful concision. Whether she is narrating or describing, her mode is understatement, her style pithy. She dramatizes, never exhorts, creating powerful scenes in which action subtly elicits and restrains emotional response. Gestures and dialogue are natural and real. Metaphors derive from the novel's setting and come alive through strong verbs and the often unnoticed but perfectly apt detail." Continues Smedman: "Paterson weaves plot strands and symbols seamlessly into tightly meshed stories in which each character, each episode, each image, each bit of dialogue helps to incarnate what the author is imagining." It is this ability to create an entire story that has endeared Paterson's writing to numerous readers and earned her two National Book Awards and Newbery Medals.

Paterson's background as a child in China and as a student in Japan has helped her create some of her memorable stories. Born in Qing Jiang, China, to missionary parents, Paterson often found herself an outsider in a foreign culture. When her family returned to the United States because of World War II, the author again felt a stranger because of her foreign experiences. As Smedman describes, "moving about between China and various locations in Virginia, North Carolina, and West Virginia, the young Paterson experienced a variety of cultures and almost continual change. Before she graduated . . . [from college] in 1954, she had attended thirteen schools." It was her sense of being an outsider, or a "weird little kid," as she has described herself, that led Paterson to writing. As she relates in her book *Gates of Excellence: On Reading and Writing Books for Children,* "the reader I want to change is that burdened child within myself. As I begin a book, I am in a way inviting her along to see if there might be some path through this wilderness that we might hack out together, some oasis in this desert where we might find refreshment, some sheltered spot where we might lay our burden down. This is done by means of a story—a story peopled by characters who are me but not simply me." This strong sense of being alien appears in Paterson's characters, making them people with whom her readers strongly identify.

Paterson's first three novels draw specifically on her knowledge of Japanese history and custom; *The Sign of the Chrysanthemum,* her first, takes place during the twelfth-century civil wars of Japan. In the midst of this chaos is Muna ("No Name"), a young orphan who embarks on a search for his samurai father and thus his identity and a place in society. Many critics comment on the aptness of setting that Paterson creates for this story: a *Kirkus Reviews* writer believes the story to be "suspended in delicate imagery" and "sustained by the carefully evoked setting." Even though one critic thinks some of the plot elements are melodramatic, most reviewers find them involving: "The story is exciting, moving, and unpredictable, and is presented with precision and economy of language," writes *Times Literary Supplement* contributor Graham Hammond. Similarly, Virginia Haviland notes in *Horn Book* that "the storytelling holds the reader by the quick pace of the lively episodes, the colorful details, and the superb development of three important characters." During the course of the novel, Muna comes to terms with his "namelessness" and forges an identity for himself, an ending many find honest.

As the *Kirkus Reviews* writer remarks, the story will please readers with "a realistic, stoical resolution which leaves some questions . . . open-ended."

Paterson returns to twelfth-century Japan for *Of Nightingales That Weep,* her second novel. The story follows a female character this time: Takiko is the young daughter of a samurai whose life is disrupted by her mother's remarriage. Displeased with her mother's new husband, Takiko decides to fend for herself among the royal court. Paterson makes optimum use of her setting; "again the exquisitely reconstructed backgrounds and episodes and the gradual character development will induce admirers of historical fiction to share Takiko's experience," remarks a *Kirkus Reviews* contributor. Marcus Crouch was originally daunted by this setting, finding it alien; however, he writes in the *Junior Bookshelf* that "once started, *Of Nightingales That Weep* turns out to be a hypnotically dominating book." Reflecting this opinion, Jennifer Farley Smith observes that the author's "feeling for the rawness and vitality of history makes the events of eight centuries ago seem hauntingly relevant, humanly near," she says in the *Christian Science Monitor.* Patricia Craig, however, writing in *Books and Bookmen,* does not think *Nightingales* is as effective as Paterson's earlier novel, for "it has something of the formality and simplicity of a retold folk tale. Its moral message is clear." But Smedman believes the story is subtle: "Takiko's gradual recognition and appreciation of Goro's veiled, steadfast love and her wholehearted response are rendered strong and unsentimental through the Japanese setting with its indigenous religious and social rituals, folklore and superstitions; through energizing contextual imagery; and through gentle irony—all integrally fused in the structure of the novel."

Paterson's setting jumps to the famine of late eighteenth-century Japan for her National Book Award-winning novel *The Master Puppeteer.* The Hanaza, a Japanese puppet theater, is the backdrop for a mystery involving a Robin Hood type bandit and Jiro, who becomes a puppeteer's apprentice in hopes of both feeding himself and winning honor. In creating the mystery, Paterson "has blended a literate mix of adventure and Japanese history with a subtle knowledge of young people," remarks Diana L. Spirt in *Introducing More Books: A Guide for the Middle Grades.* In following Jiro's development with his masters in the theater and his parents in the streets, the author demonstrates her ability to "exploit the tension between violence in the street and dreamlike confrontations of masked puppet operators," comments a *Kirkus Reviews* writer, thus making the book more "lively and immediate" than its predecessors.

In addition to her praise for the book's method, Spirt states that the work, although set in a distant time and place, presents the idea that "young people living in historical times and belonging to other cultures often faced problems and had feelings similar to those of today's youth." Smedman echoes this assessment, noting that "many of the social and political issues of eighteenth-century Japan are contemporary, world-wide problems as well: the conflict between the upper and lower classes, the rights of the poor, and the degree to which the young are bound to conform to the values of their parents." But instead of creating a dull fable, Paterson places these issues within a mystery involving enough to be nominated for a Mystery Writers of America Edgar Award. As Smedman asserts, "the tension between suspense and horror, attraction and revulsion, life inside the theater and out, stage plays and human history propels the narrative action and equilibrates the reader's response."

In her first Newbery Award-winner, *Bridge to Terabithia,* Paterson uses a more familiar, contemporary setting to tell the story of two "weird little kids" who become fast friends. The focus of the book is on the developing friendship between Jesse and Leslie, two outsiders from widely different backgrounds. The two children spend much of their time creating a fantasy world, Terabithia, where they can share their imaginings and ideas. Many critics praise Paterson for creating a realistic boy-girl friendship, something "so curiously unsung in literature," remarks Jill Paton Walsh in the *Christian Science Monitor.* According to Walsh, *Bridge to Terabithia* contains "a real marriage of minds between children whose imaginative gifts cut off from others and bind them together." Similarly, Mrs. Hildagarde Gray observes in *Best Sellers* that the book is "not a love story of physical encounter but a fusion of souls and minds," something she finds "rare" in current works.

The portrayal of this relationship works well because of the sharply drawn protagonists; "Jess is trapped in the middle without advantages, just the character young readers will most readily identify with," comments Richard Peck in the *Washington Post Book World.* His friend Leslie is the daughter of liberal middle-class parents who choose to live in a poor neighborhood; because of their lifestyle, Leslie has "committed the crime of being different, a point the young reader will grasp well before the adult reviewer," adds Peck. Jack Forman concurs, writing in *School Library Journal* that "Jess and Leslie are so effectively developed as characters that young readers might well feel that they were their classmates." In addition, the book contains strong background detail that reinforces the believability of the story. "We are shown those unspoken yet accurately observed customs that govern school conduct," says *Times Literary Supplement* contributor Julia Briggs. "Accurate and convincing in its details of everyday life, school playground tussles, poverty and work," observes Walsh, the novel "is never banal."

The novel develops into a more complex story when Leslie is killed while attempting to enter Terabithia during a storm and Jesse is left to reconcile himself to her death. Jesse's struggle to accept death reflects the author's own experiences; just as Paterson was recuperating from cancer, her son's best friend was killed by lightning. As one way to deal with her son's grief, Paterson began writing the story; however, as she relates in *Gates of Excellence,* when the story arrived at that point "I found I couldn't let my fictional child die. I wrote around the death. I even cleaned the kitchen—anything to prevent this death from taking place." Spurred by the remarks of a friend, Paterson realized that it was her own death she was afraid to face, and after coming to grips with that idea, she was able to continue with the novel.

Similarly, rather than focusing on the lost friendship, *Bridge to Terabithia* "centers on the importance of life continuing after tragedy," remarks Bernice E. Cullinan in *Literature and the Child.* "Rather than being destroyed by his friend's death, Jesse builds on the legacy Leslie leaves him and continues Terabithia, passing it on to his younger sister, May Belle." Jesse lets go of his grief for Leslie, yet holds on to the strength and imagination she taught him. The result, writes Cullinan, is a "well-crafted novel [that] is both gripping and memorable, its images evocative. . . . It celebrates the vision of imagination and touches children's hearts." "Typical of a Paterson novel," notes Smedman, "*Bridge to Terabithia* insightfully penetrates the thought and feelings of children and adults."

Concludes the critic: "The novel is wrought with the artistry characteristic of its author: the right word in the right place; the restraint of sentiment with wit; light ironic foreshadowing; the creation of a world through antithetical balance...; imagery engendered by the setting and woven seamlessly into the fabric of the novel."

Paterson sets a more comedic tone with her next novel, *The Great Gilly Hopkins,* even though the subject is a foster child abandoned by her mother. The novel was inspired by the author's own stint as a foster mother; as she relates in *Gates of Excellence,* Paterson realized that she had been "regarding two human beings as Kleenex, disposable," because of their temporary situation. This led her to imagine the character of Gilly Hopkins, a girl who fights against any sign of care or affection from her temporary family by lying, swearing, and making herself disagreeable to all who come too close. While one reviewer finds this makes the character unpleasant for too long, Natalie Babbitt remarks in the *Washington Post Book World* that even though "Gilly is a liar, a bully, a thief, ... because Paterson is interested in motivations rather than moralizing, the reader is free to grow very fond of her heroine— to sympathize, to understand, to identify with Gilly, and to laugh with her."

Babbitt also extends words of praise to the novel's other characters, commenting that "what Paterson has done is to combine a beautiful fairness with her affection for her creations, which makes them solidly three-dimensional." *New York Times Book Review* contributor Byrna J. Fireside also notes that the author "has a rare gift for creating unusual characters who are remarkably believable." Nevertheless, the critic feels that Paterson has overextended herself, "because too much is attempted in one book." Smedman differs, writing that the large cast of characters works to the book's advantage: "Gently, kindly, Paterson exposes stereotypical thinking and behavior of righteous but ineffectual social workers, school principals, teachers, and preachers, usually through estimable characters ... who, transcending the type, frustrate Gilly's prejudices." Like the author's previous works, *The Great Gilly Hopkins* avoids the predictable ending; while Gilly meets her mother and is taken home by her grandmother, she belatedly realizes that she does care about her foster family. "Without a hint of the prevailing maudlin realism," summarizes a *Kirkus Review* writer, "Paterson takes up a common 'problem' situation and makes it genuinely moving, frequently funny, and sparkling with memorable encounters." This effective treatment of her subject earned Paterson a second National Book Award.

Paterson's second Newbery Award-winner, *Jacob Have I Loved,* "is a provocative and powerful story of an adolescent's submergence by and victory over her bitter jealousy of her twin sister," describes Smedman. Gail Godwin asserts that "the attractiveness of this novel lies in its author's choice of setting [and] how she uses that setting to intensify the theme of sibling rivalry." Set on the Chesapeake island of Rass, the story is told through the eyes of Sara Louise "Wheeze" Bradshaw, "an ugly duckling of such endurance and rough charm that readers should take to her immediately," observes *Washington Post Book World* contributor Anne Tyler. Sure that she is unloved because her talented, fragile twin gets all the attention, Wheeze must struggle to overcome her low self-esteem. Although the novel is in the first person, "this is not a stereotypical good sister/bad sister story," notes Tyler. "It's convincingly complex, ambiguous." Paul Heins also finds the characterization to be effective; as he writes in *Horn Book,*

"the author has developed a story of great dramatic power, for Wheeze is always candid in recounting her emotional experiences and reactions. At the same time, the island characters come to life in skillful, terse dialogue."

It takes several years for Wheeze to discover her own self-worth and her value to others; consequently, the last sections of the novel are related from Wheeze's adult perspective. Some critics feel these sections detract from the novel's impact; Tyler finds that "there's a change of pace that's difficult to adjust to" while a *Kirkus Reviews* writer thinks the swift resolution "tends to flatten the tone and blur the shape of the novel." But Smedman, writing in *Children's Literature in Education,* believes that this brief recounting is entirely appropriate: "The subsequent and final two chapters do compress many events and much time in a very little space. However, they are essential to complete the webbing of the stories; and their swiftness and brevity are entirely in keeping with the nature of the events they record." The critic adds: "Louise realizes the nature and power of love, which comes to her ... instantaneously, with the concentrated force of a revelation."

Many reviewers observe an allusive element in *Jacob Have I Loved;* the title refers to the biblical story of the twins Jacob and Esau. Heins feels that "the Biblical allusions add immeasurably to the meaning of the story and illuminate the prolonged—often overwhelming—crisis in the protagonist's life." Smedman also remarks upon this level of the story, finding it adds deeper meaning even if the reader does not accept the Christian idea behind it: "Paterson's subtle art incorporates the third dimension inobtrusively, to be discovered and to enrich the story. For those who do not discover it, the story still works. Without violating the norms of realism, though perhaps stretching them to include a coincidence more possible than probable, it incorporates the wisdom of myth and fairy tales."

With *Rebels of the Heavenly Kingdom,* Paterson "has written a more accomplished work of fiction, and certainly a deeper and more resonant one, than most of the novels written these days for an adult readership," states Jonathan Yardley in the *Washington Post Book World.* Paterson returns to the historical novel form, setting the story in mid-nineteenth-century China. "Magnificent and momentous," notes Smedman in the *Dictionary of Literary Biography,* "this starkly realisitic adventure-romance rewards discriminating readers with the poignant stories of Wang Lee and Mei Lin, two young people caught in the devastation wrought by fanatic warlords whose religious ideals are shot through with political ambitions." More directly involved with historical events, the story follows the two's participation in the "Heavenly Kingdom," a religious, patriotic movement rebelling against the country's overlords.

Because the plot is closely tied to actual events, some reviewers think that the quality of the novel is compromised. Ruth M. McConnell, writing in the *School Library Journal,* comments that Paterson "does not adequately integrate the historical facts into the story," and adds that "often the characters are vehicles for the theme rather than individuals in their own right." *New York Times Book Review* contributor Hazel Rochman concurs, observing that "at times the plot ... seems manipulated to bring about Wang Lee's moral development; and too many characters are one-dimensional." In contrast to the criticisms that the characters appear distant, Walsh writes in the *Times Educational Supplement* that this separation is appropriate to the subjects of the novel: "If a certain strangeness in their manner of thinking distances us from [Paterson's] characters, . . . it is doubtless because she has accurately portrayed people who are indeed strange to us.''

As with her other novels, *Rebels of the Heavenly Kingdom* is also praised for its honesty in addition to its ability to entertain. "It is one of the many strengths of Paterson's fiction that . . . she always has her gaze set firmly on the realities of life," remarks Yardley. He adds that in her novel "she gives us a wholly believable 19th-century China, and she gives us an experience that is entirely true to the way life works." Walsh echoes this opinion, noting that although it relates a tale of adventure and romance, "the book has not lost the profound moral seriousness that distinguishes Katherine Paterson's contemporary writing, for all its rapid pace and plot."

In *Come Sing, Jimmy Jo,* Paterson "provides an engaging fantasy about what it might be like to become famous," describes Campbell Geeslin in the *New York Times Book Review.* Nevertheless, the novel "provides something more than entertainment," says Geeslin, for it follows the problems of young James as he becomes involved in his family's country music act. From a poor Appalachian family, James is thrust into a world where he becomes "Jimmy Jo," a world that further confuses his school and family life. Paterson again brings her flair for recreating language to this story; as Stephen Fraser remarks in the *Christian Science Monitor,* "what Katherine Paterson does so well is catch the cadence of the locale without sounding fake. There isn't a false note in her diction." Similarly, *Washington Post Book World* contributor Elizabeth Ward finds that "the remarkable thing about *Come Sing, Jimmy Jo* is the way Katherine Paterson is able to bring music to life through her prose, always a difficult thing for a writer to do convincingly." Adds Ward: "This is not just a story about country music. The whole book sings."

Even though they praise Paterson's recreation of the West Virginian atmosphere, some critics believe that the novel is not as realistic as her previous works. In the *Times Literary Supplement,* Neil Philip complains that "the story is in some ways rather trite, and not altogether convincing in its depiction of the working of the music business." Kristiana Gregory similarly remarks on the inconsistency of the book's conclusion: "The uplifting ending wraps everything into happily-ever-after, pleasant for sure, but not nearly as realistic as the rest of the book," the critic writes in the *Los Angeles Times Book Review.* In contrast, Fraser observes that "Paterson knows children, their fears and their joys. . . . This book is James's personal, inward journey, and it is deeply felt." And Ward thinks that *Come Sing, Jimmy Jo* reflects the quality of Paterson's other novels, for it "is full of what [Paterson] has called 'stronger themes,' the harsher aspects of human life which she feels children, too, need to read about." Concludes the critic: "At the same time it is as alive and hilarious as any book children are likely to read this year and in that, perhaps lies the 'stubborn seed of hope' she has promised always to plant for them."

"*Park's Quest,* her latest work, shows us Paterson at her best," comments Michele Landsberg in the *Washington Post Book World.* Park is the son of a pilot killed during the Vietnam War, and his "quest" to learn about his father is one he sees "as noble, and as important, as was the [Arthurian] knights' quest for the Holy Grail," describes *New York Times Book Review* contributor Alice McDermott. Park's mother, who refuses to discuss the child's father, agrees to send Park to visit his father's family in rural Virginia. In relating Park's unfa-

miliarity with his relatives, "Paterson is sharply observant and funny about the sheer awkwardness of daily life for the self-conscious prepubescent," notes Landsberg. Nevertheless, adds the critic, "she never makes the mistake of letting Park become narcissistically obsessed over trivia. Those small social agonies pale beside his wrenching curiosity about his father, his boyish triumphs, [and] his fear of [his] paralyzed grandfather." Similar to Paterson's other stories of personal searching, Park's "quest for knowledge about his father changes," relates McDermott, to something more realistic, a quest "for forgiveness."

Park's Quest also carries the mark of the author's other work in its believable portrayal of Park and his family. Observes Landsberg: "Character, in fact, is Paterson's great glory. Every word of dialogue falls as naturally as water, yet every word speaks volumes, revealing both adults and children as complex, interesting, ultimately lovable characters." And true to the Paterson tradition, *Park's Quest* deals with its protagonist's problems in a straightforward and honest manner. "No story of the Vietnam War, even one meant for children, can be made as simple and as noble as the war stories of old, or as the story of the quest for the Holy Grail," states McDermott. "Katherine Paterson clearly acknowledges this and in 'Park's Quest' she confronts the complexity, the ambiguity of the war and the emotions of those it involved with an honesty that young readers are sure to recognize and appreciate." Concludes the critic: "What is even more remarkable is that she has fashioned from this complexity a story for young adults that does not offer an antidote, or even a resolution . . . but that speaks instead of the opportunity for healing."

In writing about complex issues in her fiction, Paterson often concludes her stories in what seems to be an unsatisfactory, or "unhappy," manner. When *Language Arts* interviewer Linda T. Jones asked her the reason for her unconventional endings, Paterson responded: "The books ended the way I thought the books had to end. That's not satisfying to anybody, but it seems to me that if you're really 'in' a story then the story seems to have a life of its own. The story seems to have necessities and its own ending. When children ask me, as they often do, why Leslie Burke had to die [in *Bridge to Terabithia*], I honestly feel that I had no choice in the matter." The author continued: "If you try to change what is the inevitable ending of that story, you violate the story and the reader will recognize that."

Remaining true to a story is important for Paterson, especially because of the important role she thinks fiction can play in a reader's life. As she writes in *Gates of Excellence,* "fiction allows us to do something that nothing else quite does. It allows us to enter fully into the lives of other human beings. But, you may argue, these are not real people, they are fictitious—merely the figments of one writer's imaginations." However, Paterson notes, a character can be "more real to us than the people we live with every day, because we have been allowed to eavesdrop on her soul." Because readers can involve themselves in different experiences through books, Paterson thinks that "books, fiction, give us practice in life that we've never had to live through before, so when the time comes, we have in a sense been through that experience before," she remarked to Jones. "The book is there in the background to comfort us and assure us that we can go through with this. Books are great vehicles of hope for us and help and instruct us in all the good ways."

BIOGRAPHICAL/CRITICAL SOURCES:

BOOKS

Authors and Artists for Young Adults, Volume 1, Gale, 1989.
Children's Literature Review, Volume 7, Gale, 1984.
Contemporary Literary Criticism, Gale, Volume 12, 1980, Volume 30, 1984.
Cullinan, Bernice, with Mary K. Karrer and Arlene M. Pillar, *Literature and the Child,* Harcourt, 1981.
Dictionary of Literary Biography, Volume 52: *American Writers for Children since 1960: Fiction,* Gale, 1986.
Paterson, Katherine, *Gates of Excellence: On the Reading and Writing of Books for Children,* Elsevier/Nelson, 1981.
Peterson, Linda, and Marilyn Solt, *Newbery and Caldecott Medal and Honor Books: An Annotated Bibliography,* Twayne, 1982.
Spirt, Diana, *Introducing More Books: A Guide for the Middle Grades,* Bowker, 1978.

PERIODICALS

Best Sellers, February, 1978, January, 1981, August, 1985.
Books & Bookmen, December, 1975, March, 1977.
Children's Literature in Education, autumn, 1983.
Christian Science Monitor, November 6, 1974, May 3, 1978, January 21, 1981, October 7, 1983, September 6, 1985.
Horn Book, October, 1973, December, 1980.
Junior Bookshelf, August, 1977, August, 1981.
Kirkus Reviews, November 15, 1973, October 1, 1974, January 15, 1976, September 1, 1977, February 15, 1978, November 1, 1980, November 15, 1981, June 15, 1983, May 15, 1985, September 1, 1986.
Language Arts, February, 1981.
Los Angeles Times Book Review, November 23, 1986.
New York Times Book Review, November 13, 1977, April 30, 1978, December 2, 1979, December 21, 1980, July 17, 1983, May 16, 1985.
School Library Journal, November, 1977.
Signal, May, 1982.
Theory into Practice, autumn, 1982.
Times Educational Supplement, September 30, 1983.
Times Literary Supplement, September 19, 1975, December 10, 1976, September 29, 1978, December 14, 1979, November 20, 1981, August 16, 1985, May 9, 1986.
Washington Post Book World, November 13, 1977, May 14, 1978, November 9, 1980, November 8, 1981, June 12, 1983, May 12, 1985.

—*Sketch by Diane Telgen*

*   *   *

PATRICK, Maxine
See MAXWELL, Patricia

*   *   *

PAUCK, Wilhelm   1901-1981

PERSONAL: Born January 31, 1901, in Laasphe, Westphalia, Germany (now West Germany); came to United States in 1925; naturalized in 1937; died September 3, 1981, in Palo Alto, Calif.; son of Wilhelm (a physicist) and Maria (Hofmann) Pauck; married Olga C. Gumbel-Dietz, May 1, 1928 (died January 14, 1963); married Marion Hausner (a writer), November 21, 1964. *Education:* University of Berlin, Lic. Theology, 1925. *Politics:* Democrat. *Religion:* United Church of Christ.

ADDRESSES: Home—1742 Willow Rd., Apt. 404, Palo Alto, Calif. 94304. *Office*—Department of Religious Studies, Stanford University, Stanford, Calif. 94305.

CAREER: Chicago Theological Seminary, Chicago, Ill., instructor, 1926-28, assistant professor, 1928-31, professor of church history, 1931-39; University of Chicago, Chicago, Ill., professor of history, 1939-53; Union Theological Seminary, New York, N.Y., professor of church history, 1953-60, Charles A. Briggs Graduate Professor of Church History, 1960-67; Vanderbilt University, Nashville, Tenn., distinguished professor of church history, 1967-72; Stanford University, Stanford, Calif., visiting professor of religious studies and history, 1972-76.

MEMBER: American Academy of Arts and Sciences (fellow), American Society of Church History (president, 1936), American Theological Society (president, 1962-63).

AWARDS, HONORS: D.Th., University of Giessen, 1933; Litt.D., Upsala College, 1964, and Thiel College, 1967; D.D., Gustavus Adolphus College, 1967, and University of Edinburgh, 1968.

WRITINGS:

Das Reich Gottes auf Erden (title means "The Kingdom of God on Earth"), De Gruyter, 1928.
(Editor with Shirley Jackson Case) *A Bibliographical Guide to the History of Christianity,* University of Chicago Press, 1931, reprinted, University Microfilms (Ann Arbor, Mich.), 1967.
Karl Barth: Prophet of a New Christianity?, Harper, 1931.
(With H. Richard Niebuhr and Francis P. Miller) *The Church against the World,* Willett, Clark, 1935, reprinted, Library of Congress Microfilm Duplication Service, 1986.
The Heritage of the Reformation, Beacon Press, 1950, revised edition, Free Press, 1961.
(Editor and translator) *Luther: Lectures on Romans,* Westminster Press, 1961, reprinted, 1977.
(Editor with Miner Searle Bates) *Christianity throughout the World,* Scribner, 1964.
Harnack and Troeltsch: Two Historical Theologians, Oxford University Press, 1968.
(Compiler) *Melanchthon and Bucer,* Westminster, 1969.
(With wife, Marion Pauck) *Paul Tillich: His Life and Thought* (biography), Harper, Volume I: *Life,* 1976.
From Luther to Tillich: The Reformers and Their Heirs, edited by M. Pauck, Harper, 1985.
(Editor with James Luther Adams and Roger Lincoln Shinn) *The Thought of Paul Tillich,* Harper, 1985.

Also co-author of *Religion and Politics,* 1946, and *The Ministry in Historical Perspective,* 1956; author of *Luther and Melanchthon,* 1961. Contributor to theological and historical journals. Co-editor, *Church History,* 1939-53.

BIOGRAPHICAL/CRITICAL SOURCES:

BOOKS

Pelikan, Jaroslav, editor, *Interpreters of Luther: Essays in Honor of Wilhelm Pauck,* Fortress, 1968.

PERIODICALS

New Yorker, March 12, 1979.
New York Times, December 19, 1976.
Saturday Review, September 18, 1976.
Spectator, April 9, 1977.

OBITUARIES:

PERIODICALS

AB Bookman's Weekly, October 19, 1981.
New York Times, September 5-6, 1981.*

*   *   *

PEIFER, Kathleen Hamel
   See HAMEL PEIFER, Kathleen

*   *   *

PELTON, Robert W(ayne)   1934-
   (Tiffany Arthur, Kevin Martin, Robert W. Martin,
   Mark Milton, Robert Notlep, Devi Sonero)

PERSONAL: Born January 9, 1934, in Perry, N.Y.; son of
Daniel Mitchell (a detective) and Ruth Lois (Collister) Pelton;
divorced. *Education:* Attended Columbia University, 1953-
54, University of Hawaii, 1955-56, University of Southern
Mississippi, 1963-64, and Long Beach City College, 1966-
68.

ADDRESSES: Agent—Al Zuckerman, Writers House, Inc., 21
West 26th St., New York, N.Y. 10010.

CAREER: Litton Industries (engineering firm), Pascagoula,
Miss., marine engineer, 1957-63; Barnes & Reinecke (engineering firm), Chicago, Ill., architect, 1963-64; M. Rosenblatt
& Sons (marine consultants), San Francisco, Calif., marine
designer, 1964-67; Forster Design (marine consultants), Long
Beach, Calif., marine engineer, 1967-68; currently full-time
writer and lecturer. Consultant, Queen Mary Hotel-Museum
project, 1968. *Military service:* U.S. Navy, 1951-54; received
Silver Star, Bronze Star, and Purple Heart.

MEMBER: International Graphoanalysis Society, Toastmas-
ters International.

AWARDS, HONORS: Toastmaster of the Year Award, 1963,
1964.

WRITINGS:

(Under pseudonym Robert W. Martin) *Love Guide by Hand-
   writing Analysis,* Brandon House, 1968.
(Under pseudonym Robert Notlep) *The Autograph Collector:
   A New Guide,* Crown, 1969.
(Under pseudonym Tiffany Arthur) *Astrology in the Age of
   Aquarius,* Tower, 1970.
Beautiful Hair for Everyone, Workman Publishing, 1970.
What Your Handwriting Reveals, Hawthorn, 1970.
Complete Book of Voodoo, Putnam, 1972.
*One Hundred and One Things You Should Know about Mar-
   ijuana,* Western Islands, 1972.
Your Future—Your Fortune, Fawcett, 1973.
Voodoo Secrets—A through Z, A. S. Barnes, 1973.
Voodoo Charms and Talismans, Drake, 1973.
Lost Secrets of Astrology, Nash Publishing, 1973.
Handwriting and Drawings Reveal Your Child's Personality,
   Hawthorn, 1973.
Meatless Cooking the Natural Way, A. S. Barnes, 1974.
Natural Baking the Old-Fashioned Way, A. S. Barnes, 1974.
(With Karen Carden) *Snake Handlers: God Fearers? Or Fa-
   natics?,* Thomas Nelson, 1974.
Ancient Secrets of Fortunetelling, A. S. Barnes, 1976.
Compleat Booke of Ancient Astrological Secrets, A. S. Barnes,
   1976.

(With Keith Cottam) *Writer's Research Handbook,* A. S.
   Barnes, 1976.
Religious Revolving Puzzles, Standard Publishing, 1976.
Natural Cooking the Old-Fashioned Way, A. S. Barnes, 1976.
(With Merabe Hoke) *Bible Pinwheel Puzzles,* edited by J.
   Westers, Standard Publishing, 1976.
Bible Oddities, CSS Publishing, 1976.
(With Carden) *In My Name Shall They Cast Out Devils,* A. S.
   Barnes, 1976.
(With Carden) *The Persecuted Prophets,* A. S. Barnes, 1976.
Women of the Bible Quiz Book, CSS Publishing, 1977.
The Devil and Karen Kingston, Portals Press, 1977.
Confrontations with the Devil, A. S. Barnes, 1977.
(With G. M. Farley) *Satan Unmasked,* Portals Press, 1978.
Loony Laws: . . .You Didn't Know You Were Breaking, car-
   toons by Greg Jarnigan, Walker & Co., 1981.
(With Kristie Lynn) *How Sensuous Are You?: A Psychological
   Testing Guide to the Sensuality of Lovers,* Med-Psych
   Publications, 1981.
The Complete Book of Dream Interpretation, Arco, 1983.
*Infernal Revenue: A Jolly Peek at Some of the Scams That
   Waste Away Your Taxes,* Portals Press, 1984.

UNDER PSEUDONYM KEVIN MARTIN

How to Go to High School or College by Mail, Fell, 1969.
The Complete Gypsy Fortune-Teller, Putnam, 1970.
Telling Fortunes with Cards: A Guide to Party Fun, A. S.
   Barnes, 1970.
Compleat Booke of White Magic, A. S. Barnes, 1976.

UNDER PSEUDONYM MARK MILTON

Free for Teens, Ace Books, 1969.
Free for Housewives, Ace Books, 1970.
Handwriting Analysis, Tower, 1970.
Guide to Numerology, Tower, 1970.

UNDER PSEUDONYM DEVI SONERO

Phrenology: Secrets Revealed by Your Face and Head, Tower,
   1970.
Secrets of Hypnotism, Tower, 1970.

OTHER

Contributor to numerous magazines, including *Horoscope
Guide, Lookout, Law and Order, Police Times, Occult, American Astrology, Your Personal Astrology, Astrology Guide,
Medical Dimensions, Coronet, Today's Health in the Know,*
and *Modern Man.*

SIDELIGHTS: Robert W. Pelton once told *CA:* "I began writing while an architect on a part-time basis, for 3 years, then
quit the job to write full-time. I wrote and contracted 6 books
during that 3-year period, [and] have now written full-time for
[over] ten years.

"I write for days and weeks on end, then take a short trip, or
just quit and relax for a few days. . . . My advice to aspiring
writers: never quit. Simply be persistent and mass query publishers with your ideas for both books and articles. Keep your
material going out to editors and never take a rejection personally, or as an indication that your work is not good enough
to be put into print."

Pelton hopes that his "Karen Kingston book (case history of
a recent exorcism on a retarded child who was cured) will be
made into a movie." Many of his books have been translated
and are in print in over fifteen countries.

BIOGRAPHICAL/CRITICAL SOURCES:

PERIODICALS

Christian Science Monitor, December 6, 1973.*

*   *   *

PENN, David
See BALSIGER, David (Wayne)

*   *   *

PENNICK, Nigel Campbell   1946-

PERSONAL: Born October 1, 1946, in Guildford, England; son of Rupert Charles Campbell (a teacher) and Cynthia (Austin) Pennick; married Ann Elizabeth Trevelyan, September 8, 1973; children: Martin, Sean, Lindsey. *Education:* University of London, B.S., 1969. *Politics:* Libertarian.

ADDRESSES: Home—142 Pheasant Rise, Bar Hill, Cambridge CB3 8SD, England.

CAREER: Valuewear Ltd., London, England, invoice clerk, 1970; Natural Environment Research Council, Cambridge, England, microbiologist, 1970-85; writer and lecturer, 1985—. Biology researcher in Guelph, Ontario, Canada; Institute of Geomantic Research, founder and coordinator, 1975-81. Founder of magazine, *Symbol,* 1983. Organizer of conferences and symposia. Builder of labyrinths in England, North America, Austria, and Ireland. Exhibited paintings and constructions at Everyman Theatre, Liverpool, England, 1972.

MEMBER: Light Rail Transit Association.

WRITINGS:

Geomancy, Cokaygne, 1973.
The Mysteries of King's College Chapel, Cokaygne, 1974.
(With Robert Lord) *Terrestrial Zodiacs in Britain,* Institute of Geomantic Research, 1976.
(Contributor) Anthony Roberts, editor, *Glastonbury; Ancient Avalon; New Jerusalem,* Zodiac House, 1976.
The Ancient Science of Geomancy, Thames & Hudson, 1979.
Sacred Geometry, Turnstone, 1980, Harper, 1981.
The Subterranean Kingdom, Turnstone, 1981.
Hitler's Secret Sciences, Neville Spearman, 1981.
(Illustrator and author of foreword) Roberts, *A Synthonal Reappraisal of Geomancy,* Zodiac House, 1981.
Waterloo and City Railway, Electron Traction Publishers, 1982.
Trams in Cambridge, Electric Traction Publishers, 1983.
Early Tube Railways of London, Electric Traction Publishers, 1983.
Labyrinths: Their Geomancy and Symbolism, Runestaff, 1984.
Pagan Prophecy and Play, Runestaff, 1985.
The Cosmic Axis, Runestaff, 1985.
Das Kleine Handbuch der Angewandten Geomantie, Neue Erde Verlag, 1985.
Brett und Stein und Zauber, Neue Erde Verlag, 1986.
London's Early Tube Railways, Runestaff, 1987.
Earth Harmony, Century Hutchinson, 1987.
Lost Lands and Sunken Cities, Fortean Tomes, 1987.
Einst war uns die Erde Heilig, Felicitas-Hubner Verlag, 1987.
Games of the Gods, Century Hutchinson, 1988.
Bunkers under London, Valknut Productions, 1988.
(With Paul Devereux) *Lines on the Landscape,* Robert Hale, 1989.
Practical Magic in the Northern Tradition, Thorsons, 1989.

Runic Astrology, Thorsons, 1990.

Also author of *Caerdroia,* 1974, and *Tunnels under London,* 1980. Contributor to *Secret Britain,* 1986, and *The Atlas of Mysterious Places,* 1987. Author of "Hobbyhorse," a column in *Ley Hunter* magazine. Contributor of articles to scientific journals, and articles and reviews to over one hundred and twenty magazines and journals. Editor of *Arcana,* 1973, *Journal of Geomancy,* 1976-81, *Templar,* 1982-83, and *Walrus, Oracle of Albion,* and *Practical Geomancy.*

WORK IN PROGRESS: Organic Metaphysics.

SIDELIGHTS: Nigel Campbell Pennick once told *CA:* "My research has led me to believe that we have lost a fundamental science of living: geomancy—the harmonious placement of human constructions with regard to natural, psychic, and psychological factors—ignorance of which contributes to the illnesses and psychic woes of modern society. My research has recovered many techniques of this ancient knowledge from many worldwide traditions, and it is my intention to recover and reform these techniques and to apply them to modern houses and cities with regard to contemporary ways of living. In this way, hopefully we can regain our harmonious balance with the world, the cosmos, and each other. Hopefully my geomantic works will bring this to the notice of people who otherwise have no inkling of such possibilities. My future work will detail the moves necessary to regain harmony.

"I have been interested in the study of geomancy for about twenty years, having experienced various sacred places whose inherent harmony impressed me with the feeling that there was something more there than just a fortuitous combination of objects. I have researched geomancy in France, Ireland, Belgium, the Netherlands, Germany, and Canada. I have also been responsible for the recovery and subsequent publication of the manuscript of the Scottish geomant Ludovic MacLellan Mann.

"The possibility of the harmful uses of ancient energies, especially by certain authoritarian political groups, has been researched through, and many common tendencies have been detected. The Nazis' use of this was detailed in my book *Hitler's Secret Sciences.* Further research continues on similar structures elsewhere in Europe. I hope that by discovering these techniques and by making them public their harmful effects may be mitigated or abolished.

"The attrition of the sacred is the most fundamental part of the destructive side of modern civilization. Part of the task is to aid the reinstatement of the sacred in everyday life: but not just for sectarian causes—for the benefit of all."

*   *   *

PIERS, Robert
See ANTHONY, Piers

*   *   *

PINION, F(rancis) B(ertram)   1908-

PERSONAL: Born December 4, 1908, in Glinton, Peterborough, England; married Marjorie Fidler, August, 1935; children: Andrew, Catherine. *Education:* Cambridge University, B.A., 1930, M.A., 1936; Oxford University, diploma in education, 1944.

ADDRESSES: Home—65 Ranmoor Crescent, Sheffield S10 3GW, England.

CAREER: Headmaster of a grammar school in England, 1950-61; University of Sheffield, Sheffield, England, lecturer, 1961-68, senior lecturer, 1968-73, reader in English studies, 1973-74, sub-dean of Faculty of Arts, 1965-74. Visiting lecturer in English, University of Michigan, 1964-65. Lecturer at universities in the United States and Norway. Active in promoting work of the American Field Service in Yorkshire and East Midlands region, and former chairman of the committee for the selection of British students placed in America.

MEMBER: Victorian Studies Association of Western Canada, Thomas Hardy Society (honorary vice-president), D. H. Lawrence Society, George Eliot Fellowship (honorary vice-president).

AWARDS, HONORS: Litt.D. from Cambridge University, 1981; Mid-American State Universities Distinguished Foreign Scholar, 1981-82.

WRITINGS:

Educational Values in the Age of Technology, Pergamon, 1964.
(Author of critical commentary) Thomas Hardy, *The Mayor of Casterbridge*, Macmillan, 1966.
A Hardy Companion, Macmillan, 1968.
A Jane Austen Companion, Macmillan, 1973.
A Bronte Companion, Macmillan, 1975.
A Commentary on the Poems of Thomas Hardy, Macmillan, 1976.
Thomas Hardy: Art and Thought, Macmillan, 1977.
A D. H. Lawrence Companion, Macmillan, 1978.
A George Eliot Companion, Macmillan, 1981.
A Wordsworth Companion, Macmillan, 1983.
A Tennyson Companion, Macmillan, 1984.
A T. S. Eliot Companion, Macmillan, 1986.
A Wordsworth Chronology, Macmillan, 1988.
A Thomas Hardy Dictionary, Macmillan, 1989.

EDITOR

Robert Browning, *The Ring and the Book* (abridged edition), Macmillan, 1957.
A Selection of Shelley's Poetry, Macmillan, 1958.
Hardy, *Tess of the d'Urbervilles*, Macmillan, 1959.
A Wordsworth Selection, Macmillan, 1963.
Browning, *Men and Women*, Macmillan, 1963.
A Lamb Selection, Macmillan, 1965.
Browning, *Dramatis Personae*, Collins, 1969.
(With Evelyn Hardy) *One Rare Fair Woman*, Macmillan, 1972.
(And contributor) *Thomas Hardy and the Modern World*, Thomas Hardy Society, 1974.
Hardy, *The Mayor of Casterbridge*, Macmillan, 1975.
Hardy, *The Woodlanders*, Macmillan, 1975.
Hardy, *Two on a Tower*, Macmillan, 1975.
(And contributor) *Budmouth Essays on Thomas Hardy*, Thomas Hardy Society, 1976.
A George Eliot Miscellany, Thomas Hardy Society, 1982.
(With wife, Marjorie Pinion) *The Collected Sonnets of Charles (Tennyson) Turner*, Macmillan, 1988.

Also editor of additional selections of poetry for school use, published between 1941-64.

OTHER

Contributor to *Thomas Hardy Annual*, 1986. Also contributor to professional journals. Editor, *Thomas Hardy Society Review*, 1975-84.

WORK IN PROGRESS: A Tennyson Chronology; editing and compiling essays on Thomas Hardy.

*　　　*　　　*

PISMIRE, Osbert
　　See HIVNOR, Robert

*　　　*　　　*

PLAIDY, Jean
　　See HIBBERT, Eleanor Burford

*　　　*　　　*

PODENDORF, Illa (E.)　　1903(?)-1983

PERSONAL: Born c. 1903; died June 22, 1983, in Onawa, Iowa. *Education:* Drake University, B.S., 1934, University of Iowa, M.S., 1942.

ADDRESSES: Home—Onawa, Iowa.

CAREER: Educator and author. University of Chicago Laboratory School, Chicago, Ill., began as teacher, c. 1942, science department chairperson, 1954-68. Lectured extensively and conducted seminars on teaching science throughout the United States. Member of Commission on Science Education. Classroom materials consultant, Ideal School Supplies.

MEMBER: American Association for the Advancement of Science, National Science Teachers Association, Central Association of Science and Math Teachers, Council of Elementary Science Instructors, School Science and Mathematics Association (former board of directors member).

AWARDS, HONORS: Cited for distinguished service to science by National Society of Science Teachers, 1977.

WRITINGS:

(Editor) Margaret R. Friskey, *Johnny and the Monarch*, Children's Press, 1946.
(With Bertha Parker) *Animal World*, illustrations by Gregory Orloff, Row, Peterson, 1949.
(With Parker) *The Plant World*, illustrations by Louise Fulton, Row, Peterson, 1949.
(With Parker) *Domesticated Plants*, illustrations by Arnold W. Ryan, Row, Peterson, 1959.
101 Science Experiments, illustrations by Robert Borja, Children's Press, 1960.
Discovering Science on Your Own, illustrations by Borja, Children's Press, 1962.
Plant and Animal Ways, Standard Educational Corp., 1978.

"TRUE BOOK" SERIES

The True Book of Science Experiments, illustrations by Mary Salem, Children's Press, 1954.
. . . Pebbles and Shells, illustrations by Mary Gehr, Children's Press, 1954, published as *My Easy-to-Read True Book of Pebbles and Shells*, Grosset, 1960.
. . . Insects, illustrations by Chauncey Maltman, Children's Press, 1954, published as *Insects*, 1981.
. . . Trees, illustrations by Richard Gates, Children's Press, 1954, published as *My Easy-to-Read True Book of Trees*, Grosset, 1960, revised edition published as *Trees*, Children's Press, 1982.

. . . *Pets,* illustrations by Bill Armstrong, Children's Press, 1954, published as *My Easy-to-Read True Book of Pets,* Grosset, 1960, published as *Pets,* Children's Press, 1981.

. . . *Animal Babies,* illustrations by Pauline Adams, Children's Press, 1955, revised edition published as *Baby Animals,* 1981.

. . . *Seasons,* illustrations by Gehr, Children's Press, 1955, published as *Seasons,* 1981.

. . . *Sounds We Hear,* illustrations by Maltman, Children's Press, 1955.

. . . *Weeds and Wild Flowers,* illustrations by Gehr, Children's Press, 1955, published as *Weeds and Wild Flowers,* 1981.

. . . *Animals of the Sea and Shore,* illustrations by Maltman, Children's Press, 1956, revised edition, 1970, published as *My Easy-to-Read True Book of Animals of the Sea and Shore,* 1965, revised edition published as *Animals of Sea and Shore,* 1982.

. . . *More Science Experiments,* illustrations by Maltman, Children's Press, 1956.

. . . *Rocks and Minerals,* illustrations by George Rhoads, Children's Press, 1958, published as *My Easy-to-Read True Book of Rocks and Minerals,* Grosset, 1959, revised edition published as *Rocks and Minerals,* Children's Press, 1982.

. . . *Space,* illustrations by Borja, Children's Press, 1959, published as *My Easy-to-Read Book of Space,* Grosset, 1960, published as *Space,* Children's Press, 1982.

. . . *Jungles,* illustrations by Katherine Grace, Children's Press, 1959, published as *Jungles,* 1982.

. . . *Plant Experiments,* illustrations by Armstrong, Children's Press, 1960.

. . . *Animal Homes,* illustrations by John Hawkinson, Children's Press, 1960, published as *Animal Homes,* 1982.

. . . *Weather Experiments,* illustrations by Felix Palm, Children's Press, 1961.

. . . *Magnets and Electricity,* illustrations by Borja, Children's Press, 1961.

. . . *Spiders,* illustrations by Betsy Warren, Children's Press, 1963, revised edition published as *Spiders,* 1982.

. . . *Energy,* illustrations by George Wilde, Children's Press, 1963, revised edition, 1971, published as *Energy,* 1982.

Also directed the preparation of *The True Book Library of Science and Fascinating Facts,* a ten-volume edition of previously published titles in this series, 1961.

"STEPPING INTO SCIENCE" SERIES

Animals and More Animals, illustrations by Elizabeth Rice, Children's Press, 1970.

Toby on the Move, illustrations by Roger Herrington, Children's Press, 1970.

Food Is For Eating, illustrations by Margrit Fiddle, Children's Press, 1970.

Many Is How Many?, illustrations by Jack Haesly, Children's Press, 1970.

Things Are Made to Move, illustrations by Jane Ike, Children's Press, 1970.

Things Are Alike and Different, illustrations by Hawkinson, Children's Press, 1970.

Sounds All About, illustrations by Darrell Wiskur, Children's Press, 1970.

Shapes: Sides, Curves, and Corners, illustrations by Frank Rakoncay, Children's Press, 1970.

Predicting with Plants, illustrations by Tom Dunnington, Children's Press, 1971.

Shadows and More Shadows, illustrations by Wiskur, Children's Press, 1971.

Magnets, illustrations by Jim Temple, Children's Press, 1971.

Living Things Change, illustrations by Wiskur, Children's Press, 1971.

How Big Is a Stick?, illustrations by Richard Mlodock, Children's Press, 1971.

Every Day Is Earth Day, illustrations by Hawkinson, Children's Press, 1971.

Color, illustrations by Wayne Stuart, Children's Press, 1971.

Who, What, and When, illustrations by Sharon Elzaurdia, Children's Press, 1971.

Change and Time, illustrations by Frances Eckart, Children's Press, 1971.

Tools for Observing, illustrations by Donald Charles, Children's Press, 1971.

Touching for Telling, illustrations by Florence Frederick, Children's Press, 1971.

Things to Do with Water, illustrations by Larry Winborg, Children's Press, 1971.

OTHER

Also author of science education films for Coronet and Encyclopaedia Brittanica. Editor of elementary science section of the School Science and Mathematics Association journal.

SIDELIGHTS: Cited for distinguished service by the National Society of Science Teachers in 1977, Illa Podendorf pioneered the teaching of science during the 1930s and 1940s with her emphasis upon "hands-on science teaching in elementary schools," wrote Kenan Heise in the *Chicago Tribune.* As an educator for more than two decades, "she stressed creativity and problem-solving by students," added Heise. "Much of the classroom equipment she used was simply designed and was selected from materials available in the immediate environment." Following her retirement from teaching, Podendorf continued to promote her theories of science education through seminars and by authoring textbooks. She was also instrumental in the development of educational films and the creation of classroom materials.

OBITUARIES:

PERIODICALS

Chicago Tribune, June 26, 1983.*

*   *   *

POLANYI, Michael   1891-1976

PERSONAL: Born March 12, 1891, in Budapest, Hungary; emigrated to England, 1932; naturalized, 1939; died February 22, 1976, in Northampton, England; son of Michael (a civil engineer) and Cecile (Wohl) Polanyi; married Magdalene Elizabeth Kemeny (a chemical engineer), February, 1921; children: Michael George (died, 1975), John Charles. *Education:* University of Budapest, M. D., 1913, Ph. D., 1917; University of Berlin, D. Sc., 1919. *Politics:* Conservative. *Religion:* Church of England.

ADDRESSES: Home—22 Upland Park Rd., Oxford, England. *Office*—Merton College, Oxford, England.

CAREER: Lecturer in physical chemistry at Technical University, Karlsruhe, Germany; University of Berlin, Berlin, Germany, assistant professor, 1923; Kaiser Wilhelm Institute for Physical Chemistry, Berlin-Gahlem, department head, 1923; University of Manchester, Manchester, England, professor of physical chemistry, 1932-48, professor of social sciences, 1948-58, professor emeritus, 1958-76. Gifford Lecturer at University of Aberdeen, 1951-52; senior research fellow in philosophy, Merton College, Oxford University, 1958-61; senior fellow, Center for Advanced Studies, Wesleyan University, 1965-66. Visiting professor at University of Chicago, University of Virginia, University of California and Stanford University. Member of Centre de la Recherche Scientific in Paris; life member of Kaiser Wilhelm Gesellschaft and Max Planck Institute. *Military service:* Austro-Hungarian Army, medical officer.

MEMBER: American Academy of Arts and Sciences (honorary).

AWARDS, HONORS: Received honorary degrees from many universities and colleges, including University of Leeds, 1947, Princeton University, 1949, Notre Dame University, 1965, Wesleyan University, 1965, and University of Toronto, 1967; Lecomte du Nouy Award, 1959; Nuffield Gold Medal from Royal Society of Medicine, 1970.

WRITINGS:

Atomic Reactions, William & Norgate, 1932.
U. S. S. R. Economics, Manchester University Press, 1936.
The Rights and Duties of Science, Manchester School, 1939.
Contempt of Freedom: The Russian Experiment and After, Watts & Co., 1940.
Full Employment and Free Trade, Cambridge University Press, 1945.
Science, Faith, and Society, Oxford University Press, 1946.
Unemployment and Money (handbook for a film), Gaumont British, 1948.
The Logic of Liberty: Reflections and Rejoinders, University of Chicago Press, 1951, reprinted, 1981.
Beauty, Elegance, and Reality in Science, Butterworth & Co., 1957.
Personal Knowledge: Towards a Post-Critical Philosophy, University of Chicago Press, 1958.
The Study of Man, University of Chicago Press, 1959.
Beyond Nihilism, Cambridge University Press, 1960.
The Tacit Dimension, Doubleday, 1966, reprinted, Peter Smith, 1983.
Knowing and Being, University of Chicago Press, 1969.
Scientific Thought and Social Reality: Essays by Michael Polanyi, International University Press, 1974.
Meaning, University of Chicago Press, 1975.
Atomic Reactions, Gordon Press, 1980.

Author of film, "Full Employment and Money," Gaumont British, 1950. Contributor to scholarly and popular magazines in England, Germany, and United States, including *Nation, New Statesman,* and *Encounter.*

BIOGRAPHICAL/CRITICAL SOURCES:

BOOKS

Essays to Michael Polanyi on His Seventieth Birthday, Routledge & Kegan Paul, 1961.
Gelwick, Richard, *Michael Polanyi,* Oxford University Press, 1977.

PERIODICALS

Observer Review, August 17, 1969.
Times Literary Supplement, August 10, 1967, October 16, 1969.

OBITUARIES:

PERIODICALS

AB Bookman's Weekly, March 22, 1976.
New York Times, February 24, 1976.*

*   *   *

PONDER, Patricia
    See MAXWELL, Patricia

*   *   *

POPENOE, David   1932-

PERSONAL: Surname is pronounced *Pop*-en-oe; born October 1, 1932, in Los Angeles, Calif.; son of Paul (a family life specialist) and Betty (Stankovitch) Popenoe; married Katharine Sasse, July 18, 1959; children: Rebecca, Julia. *Education:* Antioch College, A.B., 1954; University of Pennsylvania, M.C.P., 1958, Ph.D., 1963. *Politics:* Democrat. *Religion:* Religious Society of Friends (Quaker).

ADDRESSES: Home—92 Moore St., Princeton, N.J. 08540. *Office*—Lucy Stone Hall, Rutgers University, New Brunswick, N.J. 08903.

CAREER: Philadelphia Redevelopment Authority, Philadelphia, Pa., program planner, 1956-58; Newark Central Planning Board, Newark, N.J., senior planner, 1958-59; Rutgers University, New Brunswick, N.J., assistant director of research and education, Urban Studies Center, 1961-64, director of academic affairs, Urban Studies Center, 1965-69, associate professor of urban planning at Livingston College, 1967-69, associate professor, 1969-77, professor of sociology at Douglass College, 1977—, chairman and graduate director of department of sociology, 1979-85, associate dean for social sciences, 1988—. Adjunct professor of public administration, New York University, 1964-65, 1967-68; lecturer in sociology, University of Pennsylvania, 1965-69; visiting professor, University of Stockholm, 1972-73, 1974, 1977, 1985, and National Swedish Building Research Institute, 1975; visiting scholar, Centre for Environmental Studies, London, 1978. *Military service:* U.S. Army, 1954-56.

MEMBER: International Sociological Association, American Sociological Association, American Institute of Certified Planners, American Association of University Professors, American Planning Association, Society for the Advancement of Scandinavian Studies.

AWARDS, HONORS: Research grants from National Institute of Mental Health, 1965, Rutgers Research Council, 1971, 1973-75, 1986, and National Swedish Building Research Institute, 1977; Rutgers Research Council faculty fellowship, 1972-73; Fulbright visiting lectureship, Israel, Greece, and Spain, 1973; Swedish Kennedy fellowship, 1975; Thord-Gray Memorial Fund grant from American Scandinavian Foundation, 1985-86 (declined); Senior Fulbright research scholarship, 1985-86; American Council of Learned Societies/Ford fellowship, 1985-86.

WRITINGS:

(Editor) *The Urban-Industrial Frontier: Essays on Social Trends and Institutional Goals in Modern Communities,* Rutgers University Press, 1969.
(Editor with Robert Gutman) *Neighborhood, City and Metropolis: An Integrated Reader in Urban Sociology,* Random House, 1970.

Sociology (introductory text), Prentice-Hall, 1971, 7th edition, 1988.

The Suburban Environment: Sweden and the United States, University of Chicago Press, 1977.

Private Pleasure, Public Plight: American Metropolitan Community Life in Comparative Perspective, Transaction Books, 1985.

(Editor with Willem van Vliet, Harvey Choldin, and William Michelson) *Housing and Neighborhoods: Theoretical and Empirical Contributions,* Greenwood Press, 1987.

Disturbing the Nest: Family Change and Decline in Modern Societies, Aldine de Gruyter, 1988.

CONTRIBUTOR

(With John E. Bebout) R. Blasingame and L. Grunt, editors, *Research on Library Services in Metropolitan Areas,* Rutgers Graduate School of Library Service, 1967.

B. P. Indik and F. K. Berrien, editors, *People, Groups and Organizations,* Teachers College, Columbia University Press, 1968.

Paul Meadows and Ephraim H. Mizruchi, editors, *Urbanism, Urbanization, and Change: Comparative Perspectives,* Addison-Wesley, 1969.

D. Glaser, editor, *Crime in the City,* Harper, 1970.

Marcia P. Effrat, editor, *The Community: Approaches and Applications,* Free Press, 1974.

V. Karn and C. Ungerson, editors, *The Consumer Experience in Housing,* Gower Press, 1980.

G. R. Wekerle and others, editors, *New Space for Women,* Westview, 1980.

Karn and Ungerson, editors, *The Consumer Experience in Housing,* Gower Publishing, 1980.

J. John Palen, editor, *City Scenes,* Little, Brown, 1981.

van Vliet and others, editors, *Housing Needs and Policy Approaches: International Perspectives,* Duke University Press, 1985.

H. Heclo and H. Madsen, editors, *Policy and Politics in Sweden,* Greenwood, 1987.

N. D. Glenn and M. T. Coleman, editors, *Family Relations: A Reader,* Dorsey Press, 1988.

E. Huttman and van Vliet, editors, *Handbook on Housing and the Built Environment in the United States,* Greenwood, 1988.

D. Chekki, editor, *Contemporary Community: Change and Challenge,* JAI Press, 1988.

Also contributor to R. Dunlap and Michelson, editors, *Handbook of Environmental Sociology,* forthcoming.

OTHER

Contributor of articles and reviews in the areas of sociology, urban studies, and social planning to professional journals. Editor with Gutman of a special issue of *American Behavioral Scientist* devoted to urban studies, February, 1963; editor of special issue of *Urban Education,* April, 1971.

*   *   *

PROUTY, Morton D(ennison), Jr. 1918-

PERSONAL: Born March 18, 1918, in Chicago, Ill.; son of Morton Dennison and Flora Harriett (Houghton) Prouty; married Elsie Shipman, November 4, 1945; children: Mrs. Catherine Horn, Mrs. Carol Ostberg. *Education:* University of Illinois, B.S., 1939; graduate study at Northwestern University, 1946-47. *Religion:* Presbyterian.

ADDRESSES: Home—413 Nottingham Rd., Florence, Ala. 35630.

CAREER: Arthur Anderson & Co., Chicago, Ill., staff accountant, 1939-41, 1945-49; Alabama-Tennessee Natural Gas Co., Florence, Ala., beginning in 1949, started as assistant treasurer, became corporate officer, then president, 1978-84; chairman, AlaTenn Resources, Inc., 1984—. Director, First National Bank of Florence. Ruling elder, First Presbyterian Church, Florence. *Military service:* U.S. Army, Anti-Aircraft Artillery, 1941-45, became major; received Bronze Star.

MEMBER: American Gas Association, Interstate Gas Association, American Institute of Certified Public Accountants, National Association of Accountants, American Accounting Association, Southern Gas Association, Alabama Society of Certified Public Accountants (associate member), Illinois Society of Certified Public Accountants, Rotary Club (Sheffield, Ala.).

WRITINGS:

Sparks on the Wind (poems), John Knox, 1961.
Footsteps on the Mountain (poems), Banner Press, 1969.
The Pharisee (narrative poem), Branden Press, 1975.
To a Young Mariner (poems), Nottingham Press, 1983.
The Heavens Are Telling (poems), Nottingham Press, 1986.
The Edge of Time (poems), Nottingham Press, 1988.

*   *   *

PUGH, Ralph B(ernard) 1910-1982

PERSONAL: Surname rhymes with "view"; born August 1, 1910, in Sutton, Surrey, England; died December 3, 1982; son of Bernard Carr (a journalist) and Mabel Elizabeth (Fitch) Pugh. *Education:* Queen's College, Oxford, B.A. (first class honors), 1932, M.A., 1937. *Religion:* Church of England.

ADDRESS: Home—67 Southwood Park, London N6 5SQ, England.

CAREER: Public Records Office, London, England, assistant keeper of public records, 1934-49; with Dominions Office, London, 1940-46; *Victoria History of the Counties of England,* London, editor, 1949-77; Oxford University, Oxford, England, lecturer in administrative history, 1952-59, supernumerary fellow, 1959-77; University of London, London, professor of English history, 1968-77, professor emeritus, 1977-82. Member, Institute for Advanced Study, Princeton, N.J., 1963-64 and 1969-70; Folger Shakespeare Library fellow, Washington, D.C., 1973; British Academy fellow of Newberry Library, Chicago, 1978.

MEMBER: British Records Association, Royal Historical Society, Society of Antiquaries of London (fellow), London Record Society, Wiltshire Archaeological and Natural History Society (president, 1950-51, 1953-55; vice-president, beginning 1955), Wiltshire Record Society (honorary editor, 1937-53; chairman, 1953-67; president, beginning 1967), Selden Society (vice-president, 1966-69), Records Club.

AWARDS, HONORS: D. Litt., London University, 1968.

WRITINGS:

(Editor) *Abstracts of Feet of Fines Relating to Wiltshire for the Reigns of Edward I and Edward II,* Wiltshire Record Society, 1939.

Calendar of Antrobus Deeds before 1625, Wiltshire Record Society, 1947.

(Editor and contributor to several volumes) *Victoria History of the Counties of England*, 52 volumes, Oxford University Press, 1949-77.

How to Write a Parish History, Allen & Unwin, 1954.

(Contributor) *Cambridge History of the British Empire*, Volume III, Cambridge University Press, 1959.

The Crown Estate: An Historical Essay (booklet), H.M.S.O., 1960.

The Records of the Colonial and Dominions Offices (Public Record Office handbooks), H.M.S.O., 1964.

Itinerant Justices in English History (Harte Memorial Lecture, 1965), University of Exeter, 1967.

Imprisonment in Medieval England, Cambridge University Press, 1968.

(Editor) *Court Rolls of the Wiltshire Manors of Adam de Stratton*, Wiltshire Record Society, 1970.

(Editor) *The Victoria History of the Counties of England: General Introduction*, Oxford University Press for Institute of Historical Research, 1970.

Some Reflections of a Medieval Criminologist, Oxford University Press, 1973.

(Editor) *Calendar of London Trailbaston Trials under Commissions of 1305 and 1306*, H.M.S.O., 1975.

(Editor) *Wiltshire Gaol Delivery and Trailbaston Trials, 1275-1306*, Wiltshire Record Society, 1978.

Also author of history of Old Wardour Castle included in a booklet published by H.M.S.O. Contributor to journals.

WORK IN PROGRESS: Further studies in medieval crime and on the management of Newgate prison in the seventeenth and eighteen centuries.

AVOCATIONAL INTERESTS: Sightseeing.

OBITUARIES:

PERIODICALS

Times (London), December 6, 1982.*

Q

QUAMMEN, David 1948-

PERSONAL: Born February 24, 1948, in Cincinnati, Ohio; son of W. A. and Mary (Egan) Quammen. *Education:* Yale University, B.A., 1970; Oxford University, B.Litt., 1973.

ADDRESSES: Home—Bozeman, Mont. *Agent*—Renee Wayne Golden, 9601 Wilshire Blvd., Suite 506, Beverly Hills, Calif. 90210.

CAREER: Writer.

AWARDS, HONORS: Rhodes scholar, 1970; National Magazine Award for essays and criticism, 1987; Guggenheim fellow, 1988.

WRITINGS:

To Walk the Line (novel), Knopf, 1970.
The Zolta Configuration (novel), Doubleday, 1983.
Natural Acts: A Sidelong View of Science and Nature, Nick Lyons, 1985.
The Soul of Viktor Tronko (novel), Doubleday, 1987.
Blood Line: Stories of Fathers and Sons, Graywolf, 1987.
The Flight of the Iguana: A Sidelong View of Science and Nature, Delacorte, 1988.

Author of monthly column, "Natural Acts," for *Outside*.

WORK IN PROGRESS: The Song of the Dodo, a nonfiction book concerning evolution and extinction on islands.

SIDELIGHTS: Although he writes a regular column on nature for *Outside* magazine, David Quammen is also a noted writer of fiction. His first novel was published when he was 22, and is based on his own experiences working in a Chicago ghetto. *To Walk the Line*, as Quammen described to *CA*, deals with "the birth, growth, and death of a friendship between a white ivy leaguer and a black militant, and is intended to map the gradual convergence of two radically different consciousnesses." *New York Times Book Review* contributor Martin Levin calls the doomed relationship between these two characters an "intriguing social paradox"; nevertheless, he believes the portrayal of these characters falls flat. In contrast, John Leonard observes in the *New York Times* that "what distinguishes Mr. Quammen's book is its humor, its lack of self-pity, the electric quality of its prose and a sense of the energy that flows between people, often to destructive effect." The result, concludes Leonard, "rings as true as a knife bounced off steel."

A drastic shift in topic and style marks Quammen's next novel, *The Zolta Configuration*, a political thriller involving the development of the first hydrogen bomb. Including facts and characters from the actual history of the bomb, the author "has put in a good deal of research on this book," comments T. J. Binyon in the *Times Literary Supplement*. Even though it "makes use of precise historical details...," notes Stanley Ellin in the *New York Times Book Review*, "never for an instant does it give off the musty whiff of scientific treatise. Mr. Quammen's portrayal of actual people involved in making the bomb brings each to life at a touch, so we have a profound emotional stake in them and in their experiences." The critic adds that Quammen "is so informed on [the history] and so adept in his presentation of it that the narrative never loses a beat in its drive to an ironic and wholly believable climax."

With his next novel, *The Soul of Viktor Tronko*, Quammen "has leaped to the head of the pack of American thriller writers," asserts *Tribune Books* contributor Alan Cheuse. The novel uses another historical idea for its premise, detailing the CIA's search for a possible Soviet "mole," or disinformation agent, within its midst. Although the idea is not new, "Quammen traverses this established terrain with skill, deftly interweaving plots, achingly conveying the ordeal of a 'hostile debriefing,'" comments *Time*'s William A. Henry III. *Washington Post* contributor Dennis Drabelle, however, finds the author's exposition somewhat confusing: "The novel proceeds via long conversation with retired agents, each of whom insists on depositing an arabesque of background and only then going on to answer [the investigator's] questions." This technique, writes Drabelle, "frequently leaves multiple skeins of narrative dangling." Nevertheless, the critic thinks *The Soul of Viktor Tronko* is a worthwhile book, for Quammen "writes posh prose" and "depicts violent action ... with a freshness that old hands might emulate. Finally," concludes Drabelle, "he solves the riddle of Dmitri [the 'mole'] deftly and surprisingly." William Hood echoes this praise, writing in the *New York Times Book Review* that the novel "is enhanced by [Quammen's] vivid prose, strong characters, and welcome wry humor. Readers will be well advised to pay strict attention—there are clues aplenty, but as in the real, upside-down, secret world of counterintelligence, there is a certain amount of dissembling; things aren't always what they seem."

Also a writer of short fiction, Quammen has collected some of his work in *Blood Line: Stories of Fathers and Sons;* the three novellas have invited comparisons with Nobel-winning authors Ernest Hemingway and William Faulkner. Explains *Tribune Books* contributor James Idema: "They're old-fashioned yarns, the kind that grab the reader, make him listen to the voices, hold him to the end and then linger in his consciousness. Perhaps even more remarkable is that fact that they are . . . unabashedly derivative." "In style, form and subject matter," elaborates Elaine Kendall of the *Los Angeles Times*, "[two of the] stories recall the Hemingway of 'In Our Time' and 'My Old Man.' Quammen's prose is not as stark and his imagery is more sensuous, but the bells toll loud and clear in homage." In a third novella, writes Kendall, "Quammen takes all the celebrated Faulkner mannerisms just one step further. The effect is eerie, as if Faulkner had bequeathed his locale, his characters and his structure to this contemporary Montana writer, with instructions to continue the work." Even though the stories in *Blood Line* are reminiscent of these authors, the work is "too compelling to dismiss" as imitation, comments Idema. "One is obliged to praise him for the faithfulness with which he has rendered" his stories in the styles of Hemingway and Faulkner. Concludes the critic: "These are at the same time first-rate stories and tours de force of literary assimilation."

While Quammen has garnered praise for his fiction, he is perhaps most noted for his essays on nature, collected in *Natural Acts: A Sidelong View of Science and Nature*. Quammen is not a professional scientist, as he remarks in the book's introduction, yet his work "is sound science since it raises substantive issues about why things are as they are—the nature of nature," states Bil Gilbert in the *Washington Post Book Review*. "*Natural Acts* is much superior to, in fact is not even in the genre of, earnest 'nature' books simply because Quammen is a man of scientific curiosity as well as a writer who does not need nor is inclined to substitute pious . . . cliches for real words or thoughts," adds Gilbert. *Christian Science Monitor* reviewer James Kaufmann concurs, writing that the author "typically recasts tired scientific phrasings or ideas in funky New Journalistic fashion."

As he does in his fiction, Quammen uses his writing skills to bring his observations of nature to life; *Commonweal* contributor Tom O'Brien remarks that the author "writes in a style at once incisive and graceful, with a sure sense of the ring of English sentences and the value of stunning images." Continues the critic: "Often his essays begin with an anecdote that quickly delivers the feel of nature, or a provocative one-liner that drags a reader into the center of an issue." And these issues need not be earth-shaking to be entertaining, notes *Chicago Tribune* columnist John Husar. "Quammen flames on and on through arcane yet relevant subjects. . . ," says Husar, "he breathes importance into the little-known nitty-gritty of biology. He describes wondrous places, people and situations that range from the vitality of rivers to the awesome mysteries of cold." In other words, asserts the critic, "this guy is a great, great outdoors writer."

The Flight of the Iguana, Quammen's second collection of natural history essays, "is even better" than his first, asserts Harry Middleton in the *New York Times Book Review*. Like *Natural Acts*, the essays in *The Flight of the Iguana* are "very funny and very offbeat" remarks the *Los Angeles Times*'s Lee Dembart; nevertheless, "part way through, the tone and focus shift. The articles become serious. . . ," adds Dembart, "and Quammen uses science as a way to reflect on other subjects, some political, some philosophical, some just wise ruminations on this and that." Although the author ranges over a variety of subjects, "he writes with effortless control over his material and a quiet passion about it," notes Dembart. Quammen's unorthodox style and personal approach, writes Middleton, results in "a prose loaded with ideas and emotion that is as thrilling and upsetting as a wild ride on a slightly unsettled roller coaster." "Quammen likes science for its own sake," states Dembart, "but he also likes it for the larger truths it suggests. He works the fringes of science and draws conclusions that are universal."

BIOGRAPHICAL/CRITICAL SOURCES:

PERIODICALS

Chicago Tribune, November 6, 1985.
Chicago Tribune Book World, June 16, 1985.
Christian Science Monitor, May 29, 1985.
Commonweal, June 5, 1987.
Los Angeles Times, March 3, 1988, June 24, 1988.
Los Angeles Times Book Review, July 31, 1983, September 21, 1986.
New York Times, November 13, 1970.
New York Times Book Review, November 15, 1970, July 3, 1983, April 21, 1985, September 14, 1986, July 12, 1987, June 26, 1988.
Time, August 17, 1987.
Times Literary Supplement, February 15, 1985.
Tribune Books, July 5, 1987, January 17, 1988.
Washington Post, August 4, 1987.
Washington Post Book Review, March 31, 1985, September 7, 1986, January 17, 1988.

—*Sketch by Diane Telgen*

R

RADDALL, Thomas Head   1903-

PERSONAL: Born November 13, 1903, in Hythe, Kent, England; brought to Canada, 1913; son of Thomas Head (an army officer) and Ellen (Gifford) Raddall; married Edith Freeman, June 9, 1927 (deceased); children: Thomas Head III, Frances. *Education:* Attended St. Leonard's School, Kent, England, and Chebucto School, Halifax, Nova Scotia, Canada.

ADDRESSES: Home—44 Park St., Liverpool, Nova Scotia, Canada B0T 1K0.

CAREER: Accountant for wood pulp and paper firms in Nova Scotia, 1923-38; full-time writer, 1938—. *Military service:* Canadian Merchant Marine, 1919-22; served as wireless operator on military transports. Canadian Army, 1942-43; 2nd (Reserve) Battalion, West Nova Scotia Regiment; became lieutenant.

MEMBER: Canadian Historical Society, Canadian Authors Association, Royal Society of Canada (fellow), Canadian Legion, Nova Scotia Historical Society.

AWARDS, HONORS: Governor-General's Award for best Canadian book of the year, fiction, 1944, for *The Pied Piper of Dipper Creek and Other Tales,* nonfiction, 1949, for *Halifax, Warden of the North,* and nonfiction, 1958, for *The Path of Destiny: Canada from the British Conquest to Home Rule, 1763-1850;* LL.D., Dalhousie University, 1949, St. Francis Xavier University, 1973; Boys' Clubs of America Junior Book Award, 1951; Lorne Pierce Medal, 1956; gold medal, Royal Society of Canada, 1956; D.Litt., St. Mary's University, 1969; Officer of the Order of Canada, 1970; D.C.L., King's College, 1972.

WRITINGS:

NOVELS

His Majesty's Yankees, Doubleday, 1942, reprinted, McClelland & Stewart, 1977, revised version for juveniles published as *Son of the Hawk,* Winston, 1950.

Roger Sudden, Doubleday, 1944, reprinted, McClelland & Stewart, 1972.

Pride's Fancy, Doubleday, 1946, reprinted, McClelland & Stewart, 1974.

The Nymph and the Lamp, Little, Brown, 1950, reprinted, McClelland & Stewart, 1973.

Tidefall, Little, Brown, 1953, published as *Give and Take,* Popular Library, 1954.

The Wings of Night, Doubleday, 1956.

The Governor's Lady, Doubleday, 1960, reprinted, McClelland & Stewart, 1979.

Hangman's Beach, Doubleday, 1966.

SHORT STORIES

The Pied Piper of Dipper Creek and Other Tales, Blackwood, 1939.

Tambour and Other Stories, McClelland & Stewart, 1945.

The Wedding Gift and Other Stories, McClelland & Stewart, 1947.

A Muster of Arms and Other Stories, McClelland & Stewart, 1954.

At the Tide's Turn and Other Stories, McClelland & Stewart, 1959.

The Dreamers, introduction by John Bell, Pottersfield Press, 1986.

HISTORY

(With C. H. L. Jones and T. W. Hayhurst) *The Saga of the "Rover,"* privately printed, 1931, revised edition published as *The Rover: The Story of a Canadian Privateer,* Macmillan, 1958.

(With Jones) *The Markland Sagas,* privately printed, 1934.

Ogomkegea: The Story of Liverpool, Nova Scotia, Liverpool Advance, 1934.

Canada's Deep Sea Fighters, Government of Nova Scotia, 1936, revised edition, 1937.

West Novas: A History of the West Nova Scotia Regiment, privately printed, 1947, Provincial, 1948.

Halifax, Warden of the North, McClelland & Stewart, 1948, reprinted, 1974, revised edition, Doubleday, 1965.

The Path of Destiny: Canada from the British Conquest to Home Rule 1763-1850, Doubleday, 1957.

Halifax and the World in 1809 and 1959, Halifax Insurance Co., 1959.

OTHER

(Author of foreword) Archibald MacMechan, *Tales of the Sea,* McClelland & Stewart, 1947.

(Author of foreword) Wallace R. MacAskill, *Lure of the Sea: Leaves from My Pictorial Log,* Eastern Photo Engravers, 1951.

Footsteps on Old Floors: True Tales of Mystery, Doubleday, 1968.

This Is Nova Scotia, Canada's Ocean Playground, Book Room, 1970.

A Pictorial Guide to Historic Nova Scotia: Featuring Louisbourg, Peggy's Cove and Sable Island, Book Room, 1970, revised edition, 1972.

(Author of foreword) Dudley Whitney, *The Lighthouse*, McClelland & Stewart, 1975.

In My Time: A Memoir, McClelland & Stewart, 1976.

The Mersey Story, Bowater-Mersey, 1979.

(Author of foreword) Bruce Armstrong, *Sable Island*, Doubleday, 1981.

Courage in the Storm (juvenile), illustrations by Are Gjesdal, Pottersfield Press, 1987.

Contributor of stories to *Sunday Leader*, *Maclean's*, *Sea Stories*, *War Stories*, *Blackwood's*, *Collier's*, *Saturday Evening Post*, *Adventure Magazine*, and other periodicals.

SIDELIGHTS: "As a novelist, short-story writer, and historian," Canadian writer Thomas Head Raddall "provides his readers with true information in entertaining and interesting works, and his books re-create life in Nova Scotia from the founding of Halifax in 1749 to the twentieth century," notes Allan Bevan in a *Dictionary of Literary Biography* essay. Both Raddall's fiction and history have won Governor-General's Awards, and his works contain the best of both fact and fiction, for his novels and stories are thoroughly and convincingly researched while his chronicles about Canada are told in an entertaining manner. "He is a great amateur scholar," comments *Saturday Night* contributor George Woodcock, "for nobody without an exceptional power to research and select facts intelligently could have written his historical novels, let alone his histories like *Halifax: Warden of the North*." But more than just "detailed historical settings," Raddall's fiction in particular includes "strong characters, almost all of whom share the ability to survive anything that their harsh province throws in their way. Their determination to surmount their difficulties is presented in almost heroic terms," observes Joanne Tompkins in *Books in Canada*. "Yet these heroes are ordinary folk with little sophistication or formal education. They are real people who are all the stronger for having succeeded on their own."

Raddall's first novel, *His Majesty's Yankees*, treats "events in Nova Scotia during the American Revolution with vividness and power," comment Joseph and Johanna Jones in *Canadian Fiction*. The novel recounts the involvement of Nova Scotia during the war, when the settlers in the northern colony sympathized and even fought for both sides, and were viewed with suspicion by both the British and Americans. "As Raddall was aware, his interpretation of Nova Scotia's role in the American Revolution was in conflict with the commonly accepted view which held that, whereas thirteen colonies had rebelled against Britain, Nova Scotia had remained completely loyal," asserts Alan R. Young in *Essays on Canadian Writers*. Raddall conducted extensive research for the work, visiting many of the key locations several times, a "technique that Raddall was to adopt whenever possible throughout his writing career," states Young. The result, writes Margaret Wallace in the *New York Times*, "adds up to a fine piece of story-telling." Although the critic finds a few "structural faults" in the novel, she maintains that "not since the unheralded appearance of Kenneth Roberts with 'Arundel' has any newcomer to the field of historical fiction shown such exciting potentialities." "What matters is that Raddall knows how to do intensive research and how to make the results palatable," remarks Anthony Boucher in the *New York Times Book Review*. As *Atlantic* contributor Wilson Follett explains, Raddall adds an "element of pure lyricism, omnipresent in the form of the Nova Scotian landscape . . . and some of [the passages] are so beautifully written that they will make many a reader homesick for a seaboard upon which he has never set foot."

MEDIA ADAPTATIONS: A radio version of *Roger Sudden*, adapted by Archibald MacMechan, was broadcast on the Canadian Broadcasting Company's "Tales of the Sea" in 1947.

BIOGRAPHICAL/CRITICAL SOURCES:

BOOKS

Barkhouse, Joyce, *A Name for Himself: A Biography of Thomas Head Raddall*, Irwin, 1986.

Cameron, Donald, *Conversations with Canadian Novelists*, Volume 2, Macmillan (Toronto), 1973.

Dictionary of Literary Biography, Volume 68: *Canadian Writers, 1920-59, First Series*, Gale, 1988.

Jones, Joseph and Johanna Jones, *Canadian Fiction*, Twayne, 1981.

Raddall, Thomas Head, *In My Time: A Memoir*, McClelland & Stewart, 1976.

Young, Alan R., *Thomas Head Raddall: A Bibliography*, Loyal Colonies Press, 1982.

PERIODICALS

Atlantic, January, 1943.
Books in Canada, June-July, 1987.
Essays on Canadian Writers, summer, 1985.
New York Times, November 15, 1942, March 18, 1945, September 22, 1957.
New York Times Book Review, February 25, 1968.
Saturday Night, November, 1976.
Saturday Review of Literature, April 14, 1945.

*   *   *

RANDHAWA, M(ohinder) S(ingh)   1909-1986

PERSONAL: Born February 2, 1909, in Zira, Ferozepore, India; died, March 3, 1986; son of Sher Singh and Shrimati Bachint (Kaur) Randhawa; married Shrimati Iqbal Kaur; children: S. S. (son), Asha (Mrs. R. Glassey), J. S. (son). *Education:* Forman Christian College, F.Sc. (medicine), 1926; Government College, Lahore, B.Sc. (with honors), 1929, M.Sc. (with honors), 1930; Punjab University, D.Sc., 1955. *Religion:* Sikh.

ADDRESSES: Home—Garden House, Garden Colony, Kharar, near Chandigarh, India. *Office*—Punjab Arts Council, Rose Garden, Sector 16, Chandigarh, India.

CAREER: Indian Civil Service, joined as assistant magistrate, 1934, served as magistrate in various parts of Uttar Pradesh, 1934-41; deputy commissioner, Rae Bareli, Uttar Pradesh, 1942-45; Indian Council of Agricultural Research, New Delhi, secretary, 1945-56; served as deputy commissioner, Delhi, India, 1946-48, and Ambala, Punjab, India, 1948-49; served as additional director-general and then director-general of rehabilitation, Jullundur, Punjab, 1949-51; commissioner of Ambala Division, Punjab, 1951-53; served as development commissioner, Punjab, 1953-55; worked for Indian Council of Agricultural Research, 1955-60; advisor, Natural Resources

Planning Commission, 1961-64; special secretary, Ministry of Food and Agriculture, 1964-66; chief commissioner, Chandigarh Union Territory, 1966-68; Punjab Agricultural University, Ludhiana, Punjab, vice-chancellor, 1968-76; Punjab Arts Council, Chandigarh, India, chairman, 1976-86. Chairman of advisory committee, Chandigarh Museum.

MEMBER: National Academy of Sciences (president), Northern India Science Association (president), Association of Vice-chancellors of Agricultural Universities in India, Phycological Society (India; past president), Lalit Kala Akademi (chairman), Punjabi Sahitya Akademi (president), All-India Fine Arts and Crafts Society (president).

AWARDS, HONORS: Robe of Honour, Punjab Government, 1968, for services to Punjabi literature; fellowship, Indian Standards Institution, 1968; Grant Gold Medal, Royal Agricultural-Horticultural Society of India, 1971; Padam Bhushan Award from President of India, 1972; Vidyawati Dharam Vira Award, Delhi Horticultural Society, 1978; Fellowship Award, Lalit Kala Akademi, 1982; Distinguished Punjabi Award, 3rd World Punjabi Conference (Bangkok), 1983. D.Sc., University of Udaipur, 1977, Punjabi University, 1978, and Ohio State University.

WRITINGS:

Zygnemaceae (monograph), Indian Council of Agricultural Research (New Delhi), 1934, reprinted, 1959.

The Art of E. H. Brewster and Achsah Brewster, Kitabistan (Allahabad, India), 1944.

(With others) *Developing Village India: Studies in Village Problems,* edited by U. N. Chatterjee, Indian Council of Agricultural Research, 1946, revised edition, Orient Longmans (Bombay), 1951.

Beautifying India, Rajkamal Publications (Delhi), 1950.

Out of the Ashes: Study of the Rehabilitation of Refugees in East Punjab, Public Relations Department (Punjab), 1954.

Kangra Valley Painting, Ministry of Information and Broadcasting (Delhi), 1954.

National Extension Service and Community Projects in Punjab, Community Projects Administration (Chandigarh), 1955.

The Krishna Legend in Pahari Painting, Lalit Kala Akademi (New Delhi), 1956.

Flowering Trees in India, Indian Council of Agricultural Research, 1957, 2nd edition published as *Beautiful Trees and Gardens,* 1961, abridged edition published as *Flowering Trees,* National Book Trust (New Delhi), 1965, Verry, 1969.

Agriculture and Animal Husbandry in India, Indian Council of Agricultural Research, 1958, revised edition, 1962.

Agricultural Research in India: Institutes and Organisations, Indian Council of Agricultural Research, 1958, 2nd revised edition, 1963.

Basohli Painting, Ministry of Information and Broadcasting, 1959.

(With others) *Farmers of India,* four volumes, Indian Council of Agricultural Research, 1959-68.

(With Prem Nath Hindi) *Punjab, Himachal Pradesh, Jammu and Kashmir,* Indian Council of Agricultural Research, 1959.

Kangra Paintings of the Bhagavata Purana, National Museum of India (New Delhi), 1960.

(With others) *Madras, Andhra Pradesh Mysore and Kerala,* Indian Council of Agricultural Research, 1961.

Beautifying Cities of India, Indian Council of Agricultural Research, 1961.

Kangra Paintings on Love, National Museum of India, 1962.

(Editor) *An Anthology of Great Thoughts,* Atma Ram (Delhi), 1962.

Kangra (in Punjabi), Nav Yuga Press (Delhi), 1963.

Kangra Paintings of the Gita Govinda, National Museum of India, 1963.

Natural Resources of India: A Brief Statement, Planning Commission, Government of India, 1963.

The Cult of Trees and Tree-Worship in Buddhist-Hindu Sculpture, All-India Fine Arts and Crafts Society, 1964.

Chamba Painting, Lalit Kala Akademi, 1967, International Publications Service, 1970.

(With Jagjit Singh, A. K. Dey, and Vishnu Mittre) *Evolution of Life,* Council of Scientific and Industrial Research (New Delhi), 1968.

(With John Kenneth Galbraith) *Indian Painting: The Scene, Themes and Legends,* Houghton, 1968.

(With Jaswant Singh Kanwar) *Micronutrient Research in Soil and Plants in India,* Indian Council of Agricultural Research, 1969.

Kangra Paintings of the Bihari Sat Sai, National Museum of India, 1970.

Kangra Ragamala Paintings, National Museum of India, 1970.

Kumaon Himalayas, Oxford Book Co. (New Delhi), 1970.

Beautiful Gardens, Indian Council of Agricultural Research, 1971.

Travels in the Western Himalayas in Search of Painting, Thompson Press (Delhi), 1974.

Gardens through the Ages, Macmillan, 1976.

Kishangarh Painting, Vakils Feffer & Simons (Bombay), 1980.

History of Agriculture in India, Indian Council of Agricultural Research, Volume 1, 1980, Volume 2, 1982, Volume 3, 1983, Volume 4, c. 1984.

(With S. D. Bhamhri) *Basohli Paintings of the Rasamanjari,* Abhinav, 1981.

Indian Miniature Painting, Roli Books, 1981.

Also author of *Indian Sculpture,* Vakils Feffer & Simons, of *Paintings of Baburnama,* Information Ministry Publications Division, and, with D. S. Randhawa, of *Guler Paintings,* Information Ministry Publications Division. Editor-in-chief, "Monographs on Algae" series, Indian Council of Agricultural Research, of *Roopa-Lekha* (journal of All-India Fine Arts and Crafts Society), and of *Everyday Science* (journal of Northern India Science Association).

SIDELIGHTS: M. S. Randhawa's *Indian Painting: The Scene, Themes and Legends,* produced with John Kenneth Galbraith, the former U.S. ambassador to India, was well received in the United States. "An unusually personal and engaging volume, obviously born of enthusiasm," according to Eliot Fremont-Smith in the *New York Times,* Randhawa and Galbraith's book displays thirty-five Indian paintings done between 1600 and 1820. Alan Pryce-Jones explains in *Book World* that Randhawa "has collected what observers—contemporary if possible—had to say about the court life and the social settings which inspire Indian painting; [Galbraith] has organized his findings into a continuous narrative. . . . The legends of the gods and the stories of court life which inspire so many of these pictures make excellent reading in themselves." Fremont-Smith concludes that *Indian Painting* "is extremely informative, delightful, enchanting in the proper meaning of that cosmeticized word, and it offers what will be for many a first, dazzling look at a robust and beautiful art."

BIOGRAPHICAL/CRITICAL SOURCES:

BOOKS

Presented to Dr. M. S. Randhawa on His Sixtieth Birthday by His Friends and Admirers: Essays on History, Literature, Art and Culture, Atma Ram, 1970.

PERIODICALS

Book World, October 13, 1968.
New Yorker, December 21, 1968.
New York Times, November 8, 1968.*

[Sketch reviewed by granddaughter, Karen Randhawa]

*   *   *

REA, Robert R(ight) 1922-

PERSONAL: Born October 2, 1922, in Wichita, Kan.; son of George Edgar and Fleda (Schollenberger) Rea; married Phyllis Edwards, February 14, 1945; children: Pamela. *Education:* Friends University, A.B., 1943; Indiana University, M.A., 1947; Ph.D., 1950.

ADDRESSES: Home—768 Cary Dr., Auburn, Ala. 36830. *Office*—Department of History, Auburn University, Auburn, Ala. 36849.

CAREER: Auburn University, Auburn, Ala., assistant professor, 1950-54, associate professor, 1955-61, professor of history, 1961—, research professor and alumni professor of history, 1965-73. Visiting professor of English history, Indiana University, 1954-55; visiting lecturer, University of Virginia, 1964-65. *Military service:* U.S. Naval Reserve, naval aviator, 1943-45.

MEMBER: Phi Alpha Theta.

AWARDS, HONORS: Southern Historical Association, Fellow of Folger Shakespeare Library.

WRITINGS:

The English Press in Politics, 1760-1774, University of Nebraska Press, 1963.
(With Taylor D. Littleton) *To Prove a Villain: The Case of King Richard III*, Macmillan, 1964.
(With Littleton) *The Spanish Armada*, American Book Co., 1964.
(With Milo B. Howard) *Memoire Justificatif of the Chevalier Montault de Monberaut: Indian Diplomacy in British West Florida, 1763-1765*, University of Alabama Press, 1965.
(Author of introduction and compiler of index) Philip Pittman, *The Present State of the European Settlements on the Mississippi: With a Geographical Description of that River Illustrated by Plans Draughts* (facsimile reproduction of 1770 edition), University of Florida Press (Gainesville), 1973.
Pensacola under the British (1763-1781), Fiesta of Five Flags (Pensacola, Fla.), c. 1974.
(Compiler and author of introductions with Howard) *The Minutes, Journals, and Acts of the General Assembly of British West Florida*, University of Alabama Press, 1979.
(Revisionist) John D. Ware, *George Gauld: Surveyor and Cartographer of the Gulf Coast*, University Presses of Florida (Gainesville), 1982.
(Author of introduction) James A. Servies, editor, *The Log of H.M.S. Mentor, 1780-1781: A New Account of the British Navy at Pensacola*, University Presses of Florida (Pensacola), 1982.

(Editor with William S. Coker) *Anglo-Spanish Confrontation on the Gulf Coast during the American Revolution*, Gulf Coast History and Humanities Conference (Pensacola), 1982.
(Editor and author of introduction with Wesley Phillips Newton; also contributor) *Wings of Gold: An Account of Naval Aviation Training in World War II; the Correspondence of Aviation Cadet/Ensign Robert R. Rea*, University of Alabama Press, 1987.
(Author of foreword) Richebourg G. McWilliams, *Fleur de Lys and Calumet*, University of Alabama Press, 1988.

WORK IN PROGRESS: Major Robert Farmar of Mobile.

AVOCATIONAL INTERESTS: Playing viola, both orchestral and chamber music; has coached fencing at Auburn University and University of Virginia.

*   *   *

REDDING, Robert Hull 1919-
(Max Beeton; Walt Denver, a house pseudonym)

PERSONAL: Born December 3, 1919, in Hilo, Hawaii; married Grace Feeny, July 14, 1956.

ADDRESSES: Home—1301 South 3rd, 18-D, Sequim, Wash. 98382.

CAREER: Resident of Alaska for forty-nine years, living in every geographical area except the Aleutians, and working in a wide variety of jobs; supply officer for the Alaska State Department of Public Works until 1977. *Military service:* U.S. Army Air Forces, 1942-46; became sergeant.

MEMBER: Pioneers of Alaska, Alaska-Yukon Pioneers.

AWARDS, HONORS: First prize for nonfiction, League of Alaska Writers, 1965; prizes in poetry, juvenile writing, and fiction, League of Alaska Writers, 1966.

WRITINGS:

The Partners (western novel), Doubleday, 1981.
Boeing, Planemaker to the World (nonfiction), Bison Books, 1983.
(Under house pseudonym Walt Denver) *Iron Heart* (Western novel), Zebra, 1985.
Suchatna (short stories), Clover Press, 1986.
Lock's Revenge (novel), Avalon, 1987.
Showdown at Lost Pass (novel), Avalon, 1988.
One Man's Homestead (adult nonfiction), Great Northwest Publishing Co., 1989.

Also author of "Chatanika Days," serialized in *Alaska Sportsman*, 1965-66.

JUVENILES

Aluk: An Alaskan Caribou, Doubleday, 1967.
Mara: An Alaskan Weasel, Doubleday, 1968.
North to the Wilderness: The Story of an Alaskan Boy (autobiographical), Doubleday, 1970.
The Young Eagles, Camprobber Publishers, 1977.
The Alaska Pipeline, Children's Press, 1980.
The Girl from Limbo, Fawcett, 1981.

Also author of children's books under pseudonym Max Beeton.

OTHER

Stories, articles, and poems have been published in youth magazines and adult periodicals.

BIOGRAPHICAL/CRITICAL SOURCES:

PERIODICALS

New York Times Book Review, June 25, 1967, November 3, 1968.

*   *   *

REEVES, Richard   1936-

PERSONAL: Born November 28, 1936, in New York, N.Y.; son of Furman W. (a judge) and Dorothy (Forshay) Reeves; married Carol A. Wiegand, June 1, 1959 (divorced, 1971); married Catherine E. O'Neill, July 28, 1979; children: (first marriage) Cynthia Ann, Jeffrey Richard. *Education:* Stevens Institute of Technology, M.E., 1960.

ADDRESSES: Agent—Lynn Nesbit, International Creative Management, 40 West 57th St., New York, N.Y. 10019.

CAREER: Ingersoll-Rand Co., Phillipsburg, N.J., engineer, 1960-61; *Phillipsburg Free Press*, Phillipsburg, editor, 1961-63; *Newark News*, Newark, N.J., reporter, 1963-65; *New York Herald Tribune*, New York City, reporter, 1965-66; *New York Times*, New York City, reporter, 1966-69, chief political correspondent, 1969-71; *New York*, New York City, editor, 1971-77; *Esquire*, New York City, national editor, 1977-79; syndicated columnist, 1979—; chief political correspondent, Public Broadcasting Service (PBS-TV), 1984—. Lecturer, Hunter College of the City University of New York, 1969-70, Columbia University, 1971-72. Host of NBC-TV series "Sunday," 1973-75; host of PBS-TV documentary, "American Journey," 1983. Consultant to Ford Foundation.

AWARDS, HONORS: Emmy Award, 1980, for documentary "Lights, Camera, Politics"; Christopher Book Award, 1983, for *American Journey*.

WRITINGS:

A Ford, Not a Lincoln, Harcourt, 1975.
Old Faces of 1976, Harper, 1976.
Convention, Harcourt, 1977.
Jet Lag: The Running Commentary of a Bicoastal Reporter, Andrews & McMeel, 1981.
American Journey: Traveling with Tocqueville in Search of Democracy in America (also see below), Simon & Schuster, 1982.
(With Malcolm Clarke) "American Journey" (documentary; based on his book of same title), Public Broadcasting Service (PBS-TV), 1983.
The Reagan Detour: Conservative Revolutionary, Simon & Schuster, 1985.
A Passage to Peshawar: Pakistan between the Hindu Kush and the Arabian Sea, Simon & Schuster, 1985.

Columnist for *Harper's*, 1971-72. Contributor of articles to magazines, including *New York Times Magazine*, *Harper's*, *Reader's Digest*, *New York*, *Playboy*, *Saturday Review*, *New Leader*, and *New Yorker*.

SIDELIGHTS: Veteran political reporter Richard Reeves has admitted to having "a bias in writing about politicians," as he writes in his first book, *A Ford, Not a Lincoln*. "I don't feel any great obligation to recount their many and varied personal virtues. That is what they, or the taxpayers, are paying for in the salaries and fees of press secretaries, media advisers, and advertising agencies," the journalist added. This resistance to sanitizing the faults of his subjects is reflected in his analysis of former President Gerald Ford, a report "concentrated on the President's first 100 days, but going considerably beyond to Gerald Ford's entire history," as Dorothy Rabinowitz describes it in *Saturday Review*. In the process of examining Ford's political career, Reeves hypothesizes that Ford's selection as vice-president and subsequent elevation to president was due to a political system which encourages mediocrity and the triumph of "the least objectionable alternative," as he defines it. In addition, Reeves "directs his most telling criticism at the icon of Gerald Ford, the man of candor," summarizes *Newsweek* contributor Paul D. Zimmerman. "He cites instances grand and petty in which he claims that Ford deceived the public, often out of . . . mendacious reflex." "Mr. Reeves builds his case not only on his 10-year experience in president-watching," writes Brad Knickerbocker in the *Christian Science Monitor*, "but on the candid observations of many of the President's own supporters and staff members, some quoted by name, others anonymous."

Reeves's direct, blunt tactics have disturbed some critics, who believe that they encourage bias and thus obscure the subject. "The author's approach to political writing is uncongenial although he is no more than a light muckraker," says *New Statesman* contributor Peter Jenkins. This investigative "fashion, all the rage in American journalism at the moment, has driven out understanding." Similarly, William F. Buckley, Jr., observes in the *New York Times Book Review* that "the candor-talk becomes particularly unpleasant as one comes reluctantly to the conclusion that Reeves is enjoying it for unwholesome reasons." Nevertheless, Buckley admits that "Reeves is among the two or three sprightliest political writers in America, and it is difficult for him to fail to be interesting." And Knickerbocker comments that *A Ford, Not a Lincoln* is "well-written, apparently well-researched, and its biases are up front (where they belong). It will make readers think, and that is its greatest value," concludes the critic. "Theories aside," notes Zimmerman, "Reeves's report is frightening and provocative in its demystification of a President whose hallmark is his openness."

For *Convention*, a report on the 1976 Democratic convention in New York City, the journalist used a comparable approach to his research by gathering information from widely varying sources, including diaries kept by delegates and interviews with both the famous and infamous. The result is that Reeves is able "to transmit the flavor of the convention—far better than a TV camera which, despite its fantastic capabilities, is still an impersonal instrument," remarks George E. Reedy in the *New York Times Book Review*. "This he does through a series of vignettes which recapture the things people really remember but usually do not record about such gatherings." Garry Willis finds this collection of anecdotes "a rich and gossipy book one reads with a guilty pleasure," he writes in the *New York Review of Books*. "[Reeves] replaces that old journalistic standby, the gabby cabdriver, with the pontificating hooker." *Washington Post Book World* contributor Haynes Johnson, however, believes that this "attempt to drag the sleazier side of New York's fleshpots and streetwalkers into the convention orbit" is distracting and ineffective. But what the author does, "and superbly," writes Johnson, "is to delineate that cast of political operators who descended, from all competing camps, on New York. He shows us the posturing, the pomposity, the arrogance, the overwhelming sense of exaggerated self-importance of scores of political hustlers."

Saturday Review contributor Robert Lekachman, however, thinks *Convention* "is more informative about New York and its media and unions than it is about Democratic politics.'' The critic believes that due to the lack of real controversy or suspense at the gathering, ''Reeves apparently decided to write an entertaining but trivial diary of minor happenings.'' ''Neither do you get from Reeves's book any sharp sense of [presidential nominee Jimmy] Carter and his key people,'' writes Johnson. ''But then,'' acknowledges the critic, ''that isn't his primary focus.'' John Leonard also sees a broad focus to the work, and criticizes the author for neglecting to search out any deeper meaning. ''What is missing from 'Convention' is Richard Reeves,'' the critic writes in the *New York Times*. ''One of our smartest political reporters and analysts, a man who fairly bristles with opinions, a porcupine among trained parrots and seals, has locked his generalizing impulse in a closet.'' *Newsweek* writer Peter S. Prescott expresses a similar opinion, noting that Reeves demonstrates ''no personal style or presence.'' Despite these supposed shortcomings, Reeves is still able to capture, ''with a high rate of success, the look and feel and smell of politics and all of its gaudy trappings,'' comments Johnson. ''The narrator's eye sweeps over the whole monumental cast,'' says James P. Potter in the *National Review*, ''and focuses on a score of the more colorful individuals in the crowd, providing a clear-sighted glimpse into this tinsel circus.''

Reeves turned from American politics to the American political system with *American Journey: Traveling with Tocqueville in Search of Democracy in America*. In collecting information for this book, Reeves decided to retrace the 1831 voyage of Alexis de Tocqueville, a Frenchman who wrote a survey of America and its people in *Democracy in America*. ''Following in the Master's pathway,'' describes Alden Whitman in the *Chicago Tribune Book World*, the author ''interviewed the present-day counterparts—and at least one direct descendant—of the businessmen, politicians, academics and others that Tocqueville spoke to.'' Because Reeves ''had the sense to write his own book,'' as *Los Angeles Times Book Review* contributor Michael Parfit explains, *American Journey* ''stands apart as a robust, detailed look at this nation's self-awareness, sharpened rather than overshadowed by Reeves' decision to take Tocqueville along.'' Reeves explained the role Tocqueville's work played in his study in an interview with *Christian Science Monitor* writer Maggie Lewis: ''He was important to me because his work and journals and the internal debates that were in the journals before he came to the conclusions gave me context in which to look at America that was separate from my own experience. It gave me a platform to try to see it from a distance.''

Although they acknowledge the originality of the author's retracing of Tocqueville's path, critics disagree on Reeves's degree of success in working with the classic text. While he calls much of *American Journey* ''fascinating, and chilling, reading,'' *New York Times Book Review* contributor Andrew Hacker faults the author for giving ''few signs of pondering what the basic message of 'Democracy in America' is, even though he intersperses quotations from it throughout his text.'' The critic is also disappointed that ''Reeves fails to relate his interviews to his predecessor's major themes.'' Similarly, Robert R. Harris believes that the author raises questions about his subject without providing answers; the critic states in the *Saturday Review* that ''while Reeves dutifully explores that complexity [of American democracy], he does not sort it out with much originality.'' But John Skow comments in *Time* that ''what Reeves does very well is throw important ideas, his own and Tocqueville's, into the air'' for the reader to explore. ''Reeves'

reporting and analysis compare well with Tocqueville's own, which is to say they are first rate.''

The broad scope of Reeves's study has also led to criticism; for example, Christopher Lehmann-Haupt of the *New York Times* finds that an average chapter of the book ''tries to cover so many disparate subjects that a reader usually feels as if he is trying breathlessly to catch up.'' ''For all his shrewd comment,'' observes Thomas R. Edwards in the *New York Review of Books*, the author's ''subjects remain the staples of popular journalism, and his tireless investigation of witnesses causes a problem of focus.'' But Jonathan Yardley, who calls Reeves ''a skillful reporter and a sophisticated student of political and social process,'' relates in the *Washington Post Book World* that he read *American Journey* ''with steadily increasing admiration for the care with which Reeves has brought together an enormous amount of seemingly discrete information, and for the intelligence with which he analyzes it.'' ''What obviously makes Reeves such a good reporter and his book such good reportage,'' details Whitman, ''is that he conveys his fascination with the United States in such crisp and lively writing. He has an ear for different voices and transmits them with flavor and economy.'' Parfit similarly notes that because of the book's anecdotal form, ''it offers more than just rhetorical conclusions.... Out of this story of encounters with individual Americans comes a view of a people, a view independent of and stronger than Reeves' sometimes understated analyses; people may be cynical and pessimistic ... but these same people remain devoted to the great hope of equality.'' This conclusion reflects the author's remark to Lewis that while he began this assignment with his usual cynical approach, ''I realized people are much more in control of their lives ... they're much more optimistic, and they were much more like each other and like the people Tocqueville saw.''

Reeves similarly uses a journey in writing *A Passage to Peshawar: Pakistan between the Hindu Kush and the Arabian Sea;* he traveled through the Asian country, recording his personal reactions to it and its people. The book ''is teeming with contrasts in landscape, incident and innuendo, all of which are tamed by the keen eye and vivid insights of the narrator,'' comments Peter Fuhrman in the *Christian Science Monitor*. ''In this case, it is Mr. Reeves who brings order to an otherwise chaotic profusion, or at the very least reduces it to an understandable progression of random occurrences.'' ''A good reporter, though, has to communicate more than personal adventures,'' asserts *New York Times Book Review* contributor Garrick Utley. ''The reader wants impressions distilled through a fine eye and a sensitive mind.'' Utley feels that Reeves succeeds in bringing Pakistan to his readers because his book ''is deliberately unambitious. It focuses on how a self-confessed American 'innocent abroad' faces up to his emotional reactions and biases when confronted with a way of life difficult for a Westerner to comprehend, let alone accept.''

A Passage to Peshawar relates these reactions to Pakistan through ''a series of interwoven essays that give us a feel for the dynamics of the place and especially for the region that is currently the focal point of American policy in the area—the wild Afghan border territory,'' describes *Washington Post* writer Richard Weintraub. ''In the process, he sets very basic points in sharp relief, cutting through some of the misconceptions that fog our understanding.'' Similar to his earlier works, the value of this volume ''rests largely with the author's ability to communicate, in language both precise and evocative, the tugs of modernity and tradition on the turbid soul of this populous nation,'' notes Fuhrman. ''Reeves, one of America's ablest political reporters, probes the many incongruities of Pakistan, questioning, examining, weighing with the conscience of a self-professed 'innocent abroad,' the traumas of the society lurching toward an uncertain destiny,'' adds the critic. Although Reeves has chosen a complex and sometimes cryptic subject for his book, Fuhrman feels that he ''succeeds masterfully.'' The critic concludes by calling *A Passage to Peshawar* ''a virtuoso performance by a first-rate journalist at the peak of his reportorial and interpretive powers.''

BIOGRAPHICAL/CRITICAL SOURCES:

BOOKS

Reeves, Richard, *A Ford, Not a Lincoln*, Harcourt, 1975.

PERIODICALS

Chicago Tribune, March 30, 1983.
Chicago Tribune Book World, August 22, 1982.
Christian Science Monitor, November 11, 1975, July 1, 1982, December 6, 1984.
Los Angeles Times, March 25, 1983.
Los Angeles Times Book Review, June 6, 1982.
.National Review, May 27, 1977.
New Republic, May 7, 1977, November 11, 1985.
New Statesman, March 5, 1976.
Newsweek, October 27, 1975, March 7, 1977, May 17, 1982.
New York Review of Books, October 16, 1975, April 28, 1977, July 15, 1982.
New York Times, March 8, 1977, June 2, 1982, March 27, 1983, March 30, 1983.
New York Times Book Review, October 26, 1975, March 20, 1977, June 13, 1982, December 9, 1984, November 10, 1985.
Saturday Review, October 18, 1975, March 19, 1977, May, 1982.
Time, November 10, 1975, May 31, 1982.
Washington Post, March 30, 1983, December 22, 1984, October 16, 1985.
Washington Post Book World, March 27, 1977, May 30, 1982.

—*Sketch by Diane Telgen*

*   *   *

REID, Desmond
See McNEILLY, Wilfred (Glassford)

*   *   *

REIN, Irving J.   1937-

PERSONAL: Surname rhymes with ''lane''; born September 16, 1937, in Chicago, Ill.; son of Sydney (a meat purveyor) and Ethel (Schreiber) Rein; married Lynn Miller (a university administrator), July 3, 1961; children: Perry, Lauren. *Education:* Attended Macalester College, 1955-56; University of Minnesota, B.A., 1959, B.S., 1960; Arizona State University, M.A., 1963; University of Pittsburgh, Ph.D., 1966. *Religion:* Jewish.

ADDRESSES: Home—1096 Cherry St., Winnetka, Ill. 60093. *Office*—Northwestern University, 1815 Chicago Ave., Evanston, Ill. 60208.

CAREER: Harvard University, Cambridge, Mass., instructor in speech, 1965-69; Northwestern University, Evanston, Ill., assistant professor of group communication and public address, 1969-72, associate professor, 1972-77, professor of communication studies, 1977—. Distinguished Visiting Professor, California State University, Los Angeles, 1972; Van Zelst Research Professor in Communication, 1983-84. Consultant on public and media communication presentations.

MEMBER: Speech Communication Association of America.

WRITINGS:

The Relevant Rhetoric, Free Press, 1969.
Rudy's Red Wagon: Communication Strategies in Contemporary Society, Scott, Foresman, 1972.
The Great American Communication Catalogue, Prentice-Hall, 1976.
The Public Speaking Book, Scott, Foresman, 1981.
(With Philip Kotler and Martin Stoller) *High Visibility: How Executives, Politicians, Entertainers, Athletes, and Other Professionals Create, Market and Achieve Successful Images*, Dodd, 1987.

Contributor to speech communication journals.

WORK IN PROGRESS: Place Wars, with Philip Kotler.

BIOGRAPHICAL/CRITICAL SOURCES:

PERIODICALS

Tribune Books (Chicago), June 15, 1987.

*   *   *

REYNOLDS, Jonathan   1942-

PERSONAL: Born February 13, 1942, in Fort Smith, Ark.; son of Donald W. (a publisher) and Edith (Remick) Reynolds; married Charlotte Kirk (a real estate agent), June 10, 1978; children: Frank, Edward. *Education:* Denison University, B.F.A., 1965; London Academy of Music and Dramatic Art, graduate study, 1965-69; also studied acting with Alvina Krause and William O. Brasmer.

ADDRESSES: Home—New York, N.Y. *Agent*—Flora Roberts, Inc., 157 West 57th St., New York, N.Y. 10019.

CAREER: Farm worker in Waitsfield, Vt., 1960; professional actor in New York, N.Y., and London, England, 1961-67; political organizer, 1968-69; writer, 1969—. Former talent coordinator and writer for ''The David Frost Show'' and ''The Dick Cavett Show.''

MEMBER: Dramatists Guild, Writers Guild, Screen Actors Guild, Actors' Equity Association.

AWARDS, HONORS: Rockefeller grant for playwriting, 1976.

WRITINGS:

PLAYS

Rubbers; and, Yanks 3 Detroit 0 Top of the Seventh (one-acts; first produced Off-Broadway at the American Place Theatre, May 30, 1975), Dramatists Play Service, 1976.
''Tunnel Fever, or The Sheep Is Out,'' first produced Off-Broadway at the American Place Theatre, May 10, 1979.
Geniuses (first produced Off-Broadway at Playwrights Horizons, May 13, 1982), Doubleday, 1982.
''Fighting International Fat,'' first produced Off-Broadway at Playwrights Horizons, June 5, 1985.

SCREENPLAYS

''Micki & Maude,'' Columbia Pictures, 1984.
''Leonard, Part 6,'' Columbia Pictures, 1987.

"Switching Channels," Tri-Star Pictures, 1988.

Also author of "Scramble Scramble," and "Nose Candy," both 1976.

SIDELIGHTS: Although Jonathan Reynolds has more recently taken to writing screenplays, including one for the well-received "Micki & Maude," he has gained more renown for his satiric plays "Rubbers," "Yanks 3 Detroit 0 Top of the Seventh," and "Geniuses." In creating these satires, "Reynolds seeks to challenge, even shock his audience by confronting and exposing the narcissism that underlies certain American institutions," observes Gaby Rodgers in the *New York Times.* Reynolds's method includes, as Rodgers relates, "characters [that] often talk in long monologues, and even as they perform outrageously hostile and antisocial acts, they reflect philosophically on the consequences."

In "Rubbers," these monologues are delivered in the course of a filibuster which takes place in the New York State Assembly. The filibuster is the reaction of a largely male assembly to a proposed bill permitting the public display of contraceptives. The resultant comedy, describes *Newsweek*'s Jack Kroll, kept him "laughing from start to finish." *New York Times* writer Clive Barnes elaborates, explaining that "the writing is not exactly witty but it has the loveliest feeling for the absurd about it." Barnes expresses some reservations, however: "the trouble is that the author never knows when he is going too far, so he is consistently more lively than lifelike." In contrast, John Simon of *New York* magazine thinks that "there is a great bulging middle that fairly explodes with satirical or merely demented laughter. Yet, even at their insanest," concludes Simon, "the jokes manage to zigzag to a target; to Reynolds's credit, very few laughs exist in a vacuum—unless it be the inside of a politician's skull."

"Yanks 3 Detroit 0 Top of the Seventh," detailing the comeback attempt of aging pitcher Duke Bronkowski, "is a Walter Mitty fantasy in reverse," notes Kroll. "Duke is a falling star who's about to be tossed back to the junk heap of ordinary humanity." The monologue in this instance is Duke's, one recited in hope of staving off a late inning collapse. Interrupted by his manager, other players, and a vision of his girlfriend, "[Duke's] soliloquy is full of sharp, funny lines, allusions to television coverage. . ., and verbal free swinging at any number of targets," catalogues Edith Oliver in the *New Yorker.* By following the pitcher's thoughts, "the play moves easily into fantasy and back again," comments Oliver. Barnes, however, faults the play for being "a sketch more than anything else. . . . [It is] overprolonged and yet—within the underlimitations of its length—well done," concedes the critic. Simon also calls the play overdrawn; "still," he concludes, "the author manages to wrest almost as many variations from his modest instrument as Bach could from an organ."

Reynolds's full-length play "Geniuses" has also been well-received. Describing the making of a multi-million dollar war movie, "Geniuses" is inspired by Reynolds's own experiences on the set of Francis Ford Coppola's film "Apocalypse Now." Although the parodying of Hollywood and filmmakers is not an original idea, Reynolds brings a new dimension to the situation by presenting his characters as smart people, asserts *New York Times* writer Walter Kerr. "Intelligence is [the new target]. The intelligence they actually posess, the intelligence that's being put to such unintelligent use, the intelligence that's being wasted just as all that money is being wasted," elaborates Kerr. "The fact that the people in 'Geniuses' tend to be smarties rather than simpletons opens up

satirical veins that haven't often been tapped in our theater." To *Washington Post* contributor David Richards, however, this approach is merely vicious: "While 'Geniuses' inspires a fair amount of laughter, the laughter is mean-spirited and without generosity," the critic comments. But Simon believes that this balance, this "equal measure [of] geniuses and maniacs, . . . is what makes them so amusing, endearing, scary, and related to us."

Overall, Simon characterizes the play as "a thoroughly funny farce about Hollywood away from home, when it tends to behave even worse. . . . Reynolds has wrought a highly civilized satire that stays almost consistently in high gear, even while its freewheeling ways manage to roll over and flatten everything." Other observers, however, have criticized the work as trivializing; Robert Brustein writes in the *New Republic* that "*Geniuses* never quite decides whether it wants to be social satire or commercial farce, the movie of *M*A*S*H** or its incarnation as a television series." *Nation* contributor Richard Gilman similarly accuses the play of "possessing the comic force of a TV sitcom," and containing nothing new. But a *Variety* reviewer finds the work "a fullblown surprise, a finely crafted piece of satirical yockery, with fully dimensioned characters, funny dialog, an intriguing plot and meaningful thematic underpinnings." Adds this critic: "Reynolds has a talent for daffy but accurate character jokes, and his darts are tipped with acid." And *New York Times* contributor Mel Gussow concludes that "much of the humor is bull's-eye parody, with the characters retaining a tinseled reality. . . . There is a comic genius afoot at Playwrights Horizons," adds Gussow, "and his name is Jonathan Reynolds."

BIOGRAPHICAL/CRITICAL SOURCES:

BOOKS

Contemporary Literary Criticism, Gale, Volume 6, 1976, Volume 38, 1986.

PERIODICALS

Los Angeles Times, December 20, 1984, March 28, 1985, April 2, 1985.
Nation, August 21, 1982.
New Republic, July 12, 1982.
Newsweek, June 16, 1975.
New York, June 16, 1975, May 31, 1982, June 17, 1985.
New Yorker, June 9, 1975, May 24, 1982, June 17, 1985.
New York Times, May 30, 1975, June 10, 1975, June 15, 1975, May 10, 1979, May 14, 1982, May 30, 1982, June 2, 1985, June 9, 1985.
Time, December 24, 1984.
Variety, May 26, 1982.
Village Voice, June 18, 1985.
Washington Post, April 1, 1983, December 21, 1984.*

—*Sketch by Diane Telgen*

*   *   *

RICHARD, James Robert
   See BOWEN, Robert Sydney

*   *   *

RICHARDS, Todd
   See SUTPHEN, Richard Charles

RICHARDSON, S(tanley) D(ennis)   1925-

PERSONAL: Born March 28, 1925, in Spalding, England; son of George Edward and Eunice (Mountford) Richardson; married Janet Jezzard (a medical doctor), September 13, 1957; children: Kaitrin, Martin. *Education:* Oxford University, M.A., 1950, B.Sc., 1952, D.Phil., 1955.

ADDRESSES: Home—Samways Acre, Motueka, New Zealand. *Office*—Samways Acre, High St. S., P.O. Box 47, Motueka, New Zealand.

CAREER: University of Aberdeen, Aberdeen, Scotland, lecturer, 1954-61; director of research, New Zealand Forest Service, 1961-66; University College of North Wales, Bangor, professor of forestry, 1966-74; independent consultant, 1974-75; affiliated with Asian Development Bank, 1975-80; affiliated with University of Technology, Papua, New Guinea, 1980-82; affiliated with New Zealand Forestry Council, 1982-85; independent adviser, 1985—. *Military service:* Royal Marines, 1942-46; became captain.

WRITINGS:

Forestry in Communist China, Johns Hopkins Press, 1966.
Manpower Planning in Forestry Development, [Rome], 1967.
The Role of Forest-Based Industries in the Economic and Social Development of West Irian, United Nations, 1968.
Forestry and Forest Industries, [Manila], 1978.
The Cotchell Report, Cotchell Pacific, 1987.

Contributor of more than one hundred articles to popular and professional journals.

WORK IN PROGRESS: Forestry in China—Revisited.

AVOCATIONAL INTERESTS: Food and its folklore.

* * *

RICO, Don(ato)   1917-1985

PERSONAL: Born September 26, 1917, in Rochester, N.Y.; died March 27, 1985, of cancer, in Hollywood, Calif.; son of Allesandro (a shoe worker) and Josephine (Bartholomay) Rico; married Michal Hart (an actress), September 28, 1962; children: Dianne, Donato III.

ADDRESSES: Home—1332 North Curson, Hollywood, Calif. 90046. *Agent*—Twentieth Century Artists Agency, 13273 Ventura Blvd., North Hollywood, Calif. 91604.

CAREER: Artist and writer; Marvel Comics Group, New York, N.Y., editor, 1939-57, and beginning 1977. Originator of "Blackout," "Gary Stark," and "Stevie Starlight" comic strips. Editor, Seven Arts Press. Instructor, University of California, Los Angeles, beginning 1973.

MEMBER: Dramatists Guild, Comic Arts Professional Society (co-founder and first president), Writers Guild of America.

WRITINGS:

NOVELS

Last of the Breed, Lancer Books, 1965.
Daisy Dilemma, Lancer Books, 1967.
Bed of Lesbos, Brandon House, 1968.
Lorelei, Belmont-Tower, 1969.
Passion Flower Puzzle, Lancer Books, 1969.
The House of Girls, New English Library, 1969.
Man from Pansy, Lancer Books, 1970.
Nightmare of the Eyes, Lancer Books, 1970.

The Golden Circle, Avon, 1975.

"CASEY GRANT CAPER" SERIES

The Ring-A-Ding Girl, Paperback Library, 1969.
The Swinging Virgin, Paperback Library, 1969.
So Sweet, So Deadly, Paperback Library, 1970.

OTHER

(With Walter E. Hurst) *How to Sell Your Song* (nonfiction), Seven Arts, 1961, reprinted, 1980.
(With Hurst) *How to Be a Music Publisher* (nonfiction), Seven Arts, 1979.
(Editor with Annette Kargodorian) *The Movie Industry Book: Part 2* (nonfiction), Seven Arts, 1982.

Author of sixty novels, both mysteries and westerns. Also author of scripts for "Adam 12" television series, produced by Universal Pictures, and for "Bloody Mary," produced by Translor. Illustrator of "Captain America," "Human Torch," "Captain Marvel," "Silver Streak," "Daredevil," "Johnny Jones," and "Golden Archer" comic strip series. Many of Rico's wood engravings are displayed at the Metropolitan Museum of Art in New York City and at the Library of Congress.

WORK IN PROGRESS: Stories for the "Captain America" comic strip series.

SIDELIGHTS: Don Rico once told *CA:* "I believe in truth and reflecting the life around me. I have always loved language and words and story-telling."

OBITUARIES:

PERIODICALS

Chicago Tribune, April 20, 1985.
Los Angeles Times, April 17, 1985.*

* * *

RIDING, Laura
See JACKSON, Laura (Riding)

* * *

RIVKIN, Allen (Erwin)   1903-

PERSONAL: Born November 20, 1903, in Hayward, Wis.; son of Samuel Richard (a merchant) and Rose (Rosenberg) Rivkin; married Laura Hornickel (a writer, under pseudonym Laura Kerr), November 8, 1952. *Education:* University of Minnesota, B.A., 1925. *Politics:* Democrat. *Religion:* Jewish.

ADDRESSES: Home—Los Angeles, Calif.

CAREER: Writer, 1925—. Has also worked as a newspaper man, publicity man, and advertising man. Television producer (produced the series "Troubleshooters," 1958-59); founder and president of Motion Picture Industry Council, 1951-52; liaison representative of American Bar Association, 1963-83; director of Jewish Film Advisory Committee, 1963-86; secretary of Writers-Producers Pension Fund, 1965-66; treasurer of Writers Guild Foundation, 1966—. Chairman of U.S. delegation to Cannes Film Festival, 1962; vice-president of Hollywood Guilds Festival Committee, 1962-63. National director of Democratic National Convention, 1960. Director of Hollywood for Roosevelt, 1936-44, Hollywood for Truman, 1948, Hollywood for Stevenson, 1952-56, and Hollywood for Kennedy, 1960. *Wartime service:* U.S. War Department, head motion picture officer in Special Services Division, 1942-44.

MEMBER: International Writers Guild (co-founder, 1963), Dramatists Guild, Academy of Motion Picture Arts and Sciences, Writers Guild of America (founder of West branch; vice-president, 1954; director of public relations, 1962-1983), Screen Writers Guild (founder; member of board of directors; president, 1960-62), West Side Riding and Asthma Club, Sigma Alpha Mu.

AWARDS, HONORS: American Academy of Motion Picture Arts and Sciences award nomination, Box Office Blue Ribbon award, and *Look* and *Photoplay* magazine awards, all 1948, all for "The Farmer's Daughter"; Books and Authors Seventh Annual Award, 1954, for "Timberjack"; Valentine Davies Award from Writers Guild of America, 1963, for community service; Morgan Cox Award from Writers Guild of America, 1972, for guild service.

WRITINGS:

(With Leonard Spigelgass) *I Wasn't Born Yesterday: An Anonymous Autobiography,* Macauley, 1935.
(With wife, Laura Kerr) *Hello, Hollywood: A Book about the Movies and the People Who Make Them,* Doubleday, 1962.
(Editor) *Who Wrote the Movie . . . And What Else Did He Write?,* Academy of Motion Picture Arts and Sciences, 1970.

SCREENPLAYS

"Radio Patrol," Universal, 1932.
"70,000 Witnesses," Paramount, 1932.
"Is My Face Red?" (also see below), RKO, 1932.
"Madison Square Garden," Paramount, 1932.
"The Devil Is Driving," Paramount, 1932.
"Headline Shooter," RKO, 1933.
"Picture Snatcher," Warner Bros., 1933.
"The Girl in 419," Paramount, 1933.
"Melody Cruise," RKO, 1933.
"Meet the Baron," Metro-Goldwyn-Mayer, 1934.
"Dancing Lady," Metro-Goldwyn-Mayer, 1934.
"Cheating Cheaters," Universal, 1934.
"Our Little Girl," Fox, 1935.
"Black Sheep," Fox, 1935.
"Bad Boy," Fox, 1935.
"Your Uncle Dudley," Fox, 1935.
"Champagne Charlie," Fox, 1936.
"Half Angel," Fox, 1936.
"Love under Fire," Fox, 1937.
"This Is My Affair," Fox, 1937.
"Straight, Place and Show," Twentieth Century-Fox, 1938.
"It Could Happen to You," Twentieth Century-Fox, 1939.
"Let Us Live," Columbia, 1939.
"Behind the News," RKO, 1940.
"Typhoon," Paramount, 1940.
"Dancing on a Dime," Paramount, 1941.
"Singapore Woman," Warner Bros., 1941.
"Highway West," Warner Bros., 1941.
"Joe Smith, American," Metro-Goldwyn-Mayer, 1942.
"Sunday Punch," Metro-Goldwyn-Mayer, 1942.
"The Kid Glove Killer," Metro-Goldwyn-Mayer, 1942.
"The Thrill of Brazil," Columbia, 1946.
"Till the End of Time," RKO, 1946.
"Dead Reckoning," Columbia, 1947.
"The Guilt of Janet Ames," Columbia, 1947.
"The Farmer's Daughter," RKO, 1947.
(With Kerr) "My Dream Is Yours," Warner Bros., 1948.
"Tension," Metro-Goldwyn-Mayer, 1949.

(With Kerr) "Grounds for Marriage," Metro-Goldwyn-Mayer, 1950.
"Gambling House," RKO, 1951.
"The Strip," Metro-Goldwyn-Mayer, 1951.
(With others) "It's a Big Country," Metro-Goldwyn-Mayer, 1952.
(With Kerr) "Battle Circus," Metro-Goldwyn-Mayer, 1954.
"Timberjack," Republic, 1954.
"Prisoner of War," Metro-Goldwyn-Mayer, 1954.
"The Eternal Sea," Republic, 1954.
"The Man from Texas," Republic, 1955.
(With Horace McCoy) "The Road to Denver," Republic, 1955.
"Girls on the Loose," Universal-International, 1957.
"Live Fast, Die Young," Universal-International, 1957.
"Big Operator," Metro-Goldwyn-Mayer, 1959.
(And co-producer) "Mister," Guggenheim, 1961.
"I Thought I'd Die Laughing," Leonard Field Productions, 1964.

OTHER

"Knock On Wood" (play), first produced on Broadway at Cort Theatre, May 28, 1935.

Also author of play, "Is My Face Red?", based on screenplay of the same title. Author of television scripts. Editor, *Writers Guild West Newsletter,* 1965-82, and *Writers Guild Directory.*

WORK IN PROGRESS: Hollywood Is No Laughing Matter.

SIDELIGHTS: Allen Rivkin, writer of more than twenty-seven film scripts and "clean-up man" on numerous other projects, was also an important Hollywood figure for his role as founder and active leader of the Screen Writers Guild for more than forty years. Political causes to which Rivkin subscribed are expressed in his writings for the screen, reports *Dictionary of Literary Biography* contributor Stephen O. Lesser, who adds "Rivkin's best films reflect an awareness of social issues." Rivkin's political sentiments were liberal, and he succeeded in winning the support of many Hollywood writers for the Democratic party for four decades, beginning in the 1930s. Of his many activities and successful campaigns fought on behalf of Guild members, Lesser concludes, "Few have helped the community of screenwriters in Hollywood as much as Allen Rivkin."

BIOGRAPHICAL/CRITICAL SOURCES:

BOOKS

Dictionary of Literary Biography, Volume 26: *American Screenwriters,* Gale, 1984.
Rivkin, Allen and Leonard Spigelgass, *I Wasn't Born Yesterday: An Anonymous Autobiography,* Macauley, 1935.

*   *   *

ROBBINS, Keith (Gilbert) 1940-

PERSONAL: Born April 9, 1940, in Bristol, England; son of Gilbert Henry John (a cashier) and Mary (Carpenter) Robbins; married Janet Thomson, August 24, 1963; children: Paul John Gilbert, Daniel Henry Keith, Lucy Helen, Adam Edward Ivo. *Education:* Magdalen College, Oxford, B.A., 1961; St. Antony's College, Oxford, D.Phil., 1964. *Politics:* Conservative. *Religion:* Baptist.

ADDRESSES: Home—15 Hamilton Dr., Glasgow G12 8DN, Scotland. *Office*—Department of Modern History, University of Glasgow, Glasgow G12 8QQ, Scotland.

CAREER: University of York, Heslington, York, England, lecturer in history, 1963-71; University College of North Wales, Bangor, professor of history, 1971-79; University of Glasgow, Glasgow, Scotland, professor of modern history, 1980—.

MEMBER: British Association of Contemporary Historians, Royal Historical Society (fellow), Ecclesiastical History Society (president, 1980-81), Historical Association (president, 1988—).

AWARDS, HONORS: Munich, 1938 was "highly commended" in Winston Churchill Prize competition, 1968; D.Litt., Glasgow, 1985.

WRITINGS:

Munich, 1938, Cassell, 1968.
Sir Edward Grey: A Biography of Lord Grey of Fallodon, Cassell, 1971.
(Contributor) Herbert van Thal, editor, *The Prime Ministers,* Volume 2: *From Lord John Russell to Edward Heath,* Allen & Unwin, 1975.
The Abolition of War: The Peace Movement in Britain, 1914-1919, University of Wales Press, 1976.
John Bright, Routledge & Kegan Paul, 1979.
The Eclipse of a Great Power: Modern Britain 1870-1975, Longman, 1983.
The First World War, Oxford University Press, 1984.
Nineteenth-Century Britain: Integration and Diversity, Oxford University Press, 1988.
Appeasement, Basil Blackwell, 1988.

Contributor to *International Affairs, Historical Journal, Journal of Ecclesiastical History, Slavonic and East European Review, Journal of Imperial and Commonwealth History,* and *Journal of Contemporary History.* Editor, *History,* 1977-86.

WORK IN PROGRESS: A bibliography of writings on British history since 1914.

BIOGRAPHICAL/CRITICAL SOURCES:

PERIODICALS

New Statesman, June 4, 1971.
Observer, May 26, 1968, June 6, 1971.
Statesman, June 14, 1968.
Times Literary Supplement, November 23, 1979, April 15, 1983.

*   *   *

ROBERTS, Leonard W(ard)   1912-1983

PERSONAL: Born January 12, 1912, in Osborne, Ky.; died April 29, 1983, in an automobile accident near Mare Creek, Ky.; son of Lewis Jackson (a minister) and Rhoda (a postmistress; maiden name, Osborn) Roberts; married Edith Reynolds (a teacher), June 18, 1939; children: Mrs. Sue Carolyn Adkins, Mrs. Margaret Biller, Mrs. Rita Kelley, Mrs. Lynneda Denny. *Education:* Berea College, A.B., 1939; University of Iowa, M.A., 1943; graduate study, Indiana University, summer, 1948; University of Kentucky, Ph.D., 1954. *Religion:* Christian.

ADDRESSES: Home—P.O. Box 266, Stanville, Ky. 41659. *Office*—Appalachian Studies Center, Pikeville College, Pikeville, Ky. 41501.

CAREER: Brevard College, Brevard, N.C., instructor in health education and music, 1940-42; University of North Carolina at Chapel Hill, teaching fellow, 1943-45; Berea College, Berea, Ky., instructor in English, 1945-50; Piedmont College, Demorest, Ga., professor of English, 1953-54; Union College, Barbourville, Ky., professor of English, head of department, and chairman of Division of Languages, all 1954-58; Morehead State University, Morehead, Ky., professor of English and chairman of department, 1958-61; West Virginia Wesleyan College, Buckhannon, professor of English and chairman of department, 1961-68; Pikeville College, Pikeville, Ky., professor of English, 1968-83, chairman of department, 1968-72. Folklore consultant. Consultant to Kentucky Arts Commission. Member of "Folklore in Schools" program, Mid-Appalachian Teachers, beginning 1976. *Military service:* U.S. Army, 1930-33.

MEMBER: Modern Language Association of America, National Council of Teachers of English, American Association of University Professors (secretary), American Folklore Society, National Folk Festival Association (vice-president, 1963-69, president, 1969-72), Kentucky Folklore Society, Tennessee Folklore Society, West Virginia Folklore Society, Pike County Historical Society (president), Preservation Council of Pike County, Big Sandy Valley Historical Society (secretary).

AWARDS, HONORS: Residence grants from University of Kentucky and West Virginia Wesleyan College.

WRITINGS:

(Compiler) *I Bought Me a Dog and Other Folktales from the Southern Mountains,* Council of Southern Mountaisn, 1954.
(Compiler) *South from Hell-fer-Sartin,* University of Kentucky Press, 1955.
(Compiler) *Nippy and the Yankee Doodle,* Council of Southern Mountains, 1958.
Up Cut Shin and Down Greasy, University of Kentucky Press, 1959, reprinted, 1988.
Folk Stories and Songs of the Couch Family, University of Kentucky Press, 1959.
(Contributor) Tristam P. Coffin, editor, *Our Living Traditions: An Introduction to American Folklore,* Basic Books, 1968.
Old Greasybeard: Tales from the Cumberland Gap, Folklore Associates, 1969.
Sang Branch Settlers: Folksongs and Tales of a Kentucky Mountain Family, University of Texas Press for American Folklore Society, 1974.
(Editor with Henry P. Scalf) G. Elliott Hatfield, *The Hatfields,* Big Sandy Valley Historical Society, 1974.
(Editor and author of foreword) Truda Williams McCoy, *The McCoys: Their Story as Told to the Author by Eye Witnesses and Descendants,* Preservation Council Press of the Preservation Council of Pike County (Kentucky), 1976.
(With C. Buell Agey) *In the Pine: Selected Kentucky Folksongs,* Pikeville College Press, 1978.
(Editor and annotator) Hobert McCoy and Orville McCoy, compilers, *Squirrel Huntin' Sam McCoy: His Memoir and Family Tree,* Pikeville College Press, 1979.

Also author of *20,000 Kentucky Superstitions.* Editor, *Laurel Review,* 1964-68, and *Twigs,* beginning 1969.

SIDELIGHTS: Folklorist Leonard W. Roberts once told *CA:* "Having grown up in Appalachia, I found myself drawn back to it from afar. Then I began to study the people, their history, ethnic origins, traditions, and way of life. This accounts for a great mass of folklore, traditions, [and] local history that I have in my archives and that I am endeavoring to put in order to publish as time permits."

In addition to his books on folklore, Roberts was active in the telling of folk tales and in folk singing and dancing. He performed and emceed at various folk festivals.*

[Death date provided by wife, Edith Roberts]

*   *   *

ROBSON, John M(ercel)   1927-

PERSONAL: Born May 26, 1927, in Toronto, Ontario, Canada; son of William R. M. and Christina (Sinclair) Robson; married Ann Provost Wilkinson (an associate professor of history), August 8, 1953; children: William, John, Ann Christine. *Education:* University of Toronto, B.A., 1951, M.A., 1953, Ph.D., 1956.

ADDRESSES: Home—28 McMaster Ave., Toronto, Ontario, Canada M4V 1A9. *Office*—Department of English, Victoria College, University of Toronto, 73 Queen's Park Crescent, Toronto, Ontario, Canada M5S 1K7.

CAREER: University of British Columbia, Vancouver, instructor in English, 1956-57; University of Alberta, Edmonton, assistant professor of English, 1957-58; University of Toronto, Victoria College, Toronto, Ontario, assistant professor, 1958-61, associate professor, 1961-66, professor of English, 1966—, principal of college, 1971-76. Chairman, Disraeli Project editorial committee, Queen's University, 1975.

MEMBER: Canadian Association of University Teachers, Association of Canadian University Teachers of English, British Studies Association, Victorian Studies Association, Research Society for Victorian Periodicals.

AWARDS, HONORS: Fellow of the Royal Society of Canada; fellowships from Humanities Research Council (Canada), Canada Council, and Guggenheim Foundation.

WRITINGS:

(Editor) Edmund Burke, *An Appeal from the New to the Old Whigs*, Bobbs-Merrill, 1961.
(Editor) *The Collected Works of John Stuart Mill*, University of Toronto Press, Volumes 2-3: *Principles of Political Economy*, 1965, Volumes 4-5: *Essays on Economics and Society*, 1967, Volume 10: *Essays on Ethics, Religion, and Society*, 1969, Volumes 7-8: *System of Logic: Ratiocinative and Inductive*, 1973, Volumes 12-13: *Essays on Politics and Society*, 1977, Volume 11: *Essays on Philosophy and the Classics*, 1978, Volume 9: *An Examination of Sir William Hamilton's Philosophy and of the Principal Philosophical Questions Discussed in His Writings*, 1979, Volume 1: *Autobiography and Literary Essays*, 1981, Volume 6: *Essays on England, Ireland, and the Empire*, 1982, Volume 21: *Essays on Equality, Law, and Education*, 1984, Volume 20: *Essays on French History and Historians*, 1985, (With wife, Ann Robson) Volumes 22-25: *Newspaper Writings*, 1987, Volumes 26-27: *Journals and Collected Speeches*, 1988.
(Editor) *John Stuart Mill: A Selection of His Works*, Macmillan, 1966.
(Editor) *Editing Nineteenth-Century Texts*, AMS Press, 1966.
The Improvement of Mankind: The Social and Political Thought of John Stuart Mill, University of Toronto Press, 1968.
The Hmnnn Retort, New Press, 1970.
(Editor and contributor) *Rhetoric: A Unified Approach to English Curricula*, Ontario Institute for Studies in Education, 1971.

Origin and Evolution of the Universe: Evidence for Design?, McGill-Queens University Press, 1987.

Author, with others, of *Word Games for Families that Are Still Speaking to One Another*, 1975. Contributor of chapters to books, and of reviews and articles to journals. Editor, *Mills News Letter*.

WORK IN PROGRESS: A study of nineteenth-century rhetoric; a book on questions.*

*   *   *

ROGERS, Alan   1933-

PERSONAL: Born February 25, 1933, in Wallington, Surrey, England; son of E. W. (a local preacher) and Edith (Cuthbert) Rogers; married Marjorie Dawe (a musician), August 1, 1958; children: Malcolm D., Katherine Hilary. *Education:* University of Nottingham, B.A., 1954, M.A., 1956, Certificate of Education, 1957, Ph.D., 1966. *Religion:* Church of England.

ADDRESSES: Office—School of Education, University of Reading, Reading, England.

CAREER: School teacher and part-time university teacher, 1957-59; University of Nottingham, Department of Adult Education, Nottingham, England, lecturer, 1959-65, senior lecturer, 1965-77, reader in history, 1977-79; New University of Ulster, Magee University College, Londonderry, Northern Ireland, professor of continuing education and director of Institute of Continuing Education, 1979-85; secretary-general of Commonwealth Association for the Education and Training of Adults, 1985—; University of Reading, Reading, England, visiting professor of adult education, 1985—. Member of Heritage Education Group.

MEMBER: Royal Historical Society (fellow), Society of Antiquaries (fellow), Royal Society of Arts (fellow).

WRITINGS:

(Editor) *The Making of Stamford*, Leicester University Press, 1965.
(Editor) *Stability and Change: Some Aspects of North and South Rauceby in the Nineteenth Century*, Department of Adult Education, University of Nottingham, 1969.
History of Lincolnshire, Darwin Finlayson, 1970, revised edition, Phillimore & Co., 1985.
Medieval Buildings of Stamford, Department of Adult Education, University of Nottingham, 1970.
This Was Their World: Approaches to Local History, B.B.C. Publications, 1972, 2nd edition published as *Approaches to Local History*, Longman, 1977.
(Editor) *Approaches to Nottingham's History*, Department of Adult Education, University of Nottingham, 1972.
(With John S. Hartley) *The Religious Foundations of Medieval Stamford*, Department of Adult Education, University of Nottingham, 1974.
(Editor with Trevor Rowley) *Landscapes and Documents*, Bedford Square Press for the Standing Conference for Local History, 1974.
(Editor) *Southwell Minster after the Civil Wars: A Study Paper*, Department of Adult Education, University of Nottingham, 1974.
(Editor) *The Spirit and the Form: Essays in Adult Education by and in Honour of Professor Harold Wiltshire*, Department of Adult Education, University of Nottingham, 1976.

(Editor) *Group Projects in Local History*, Dawson, 1977.

Knowledge and the People, Magee University College, New University of Ulster, 1981.

(Editor) *Coming into Line*, Centre for Local History, University of Nottingham, 1982.

(With Brian Groombridge and others) *The Universities and Continuing Education*, Institute of Continuing Education, Magee University College, New University of Ulster, 1982.

The Book of Stamford, Barracuda Books, 1983.

Teaching Adults, Open University Press, 1986.

Contributor to history journals. Editor, *Bulletin of Local History, East Midlands Region*, 1966-78.

WORK IN PROGRESS: A book on adult education and development.

SIDELIGHTS: Alan Rogers told *CA:* "I see my writing as an extension of my work in adult education—providing opportunities for anyone to learn what they want to learn, reaching out to new groups of people who are far away from me at the moment!"

*   *   *

ROGERS, Michael (A.) 1950-

PERSONAL: Born November 29, 1950, in Santa Monica, Calif.; son of Don Easterday (an engineer) and Mary (Gilbertson) Rogers; married Janet Hopson, October 23, 1976. *Education:* Stanford University, B.A., 1972.

ADDRESSES: Home—100 Alpine Terrace, Oakland, Calif. *Agent*—Gail Hochman, Brandt & Brandt, 1501 Broadway, New York, N.Y. 10036.

CAREER: Rolling Stone, New York, N.Y., contributing editor, 1973—; founding editor, *Outside* magazine, 1975-77; senior writer, *Newsweek*, 1983—.

MEMBER: Authors Guild, Authors League of America.

AWARDS, HONORS: American Association for the Advancement of Science—Westinghouse Award, 1974, for distinguished science writing; best feature article citation, Computer Press Association, 1987.

WRITINGS:

Mindfogger, Knopf, 1973.

Biohazard, Knopf, 1977.

Do Not Worry about the Bear (short stories), Knopf, 1979.

Silicon Valley, Simon & Schuster, 1982.

Forbidden Sequence, Bantam, 1988.

Books columnist, *Rolling Stone*, 1973-74. Contributor of short fiction to *Playboy*, *Esquire*, *Rolling Stone*, and *Gentleman's Quarterly*.

WORK IN PROGRESS: A novel to be set in California and Japan, for Bantam.

SIDELIGHTS: Michael Rogers told *CA:* "I write journalism to support my fiction habit. I enjoy journalism but fiction is the only form that makes me dance around the room when, once in a great while, I think I've done something very well."

AVOCATIONAL INTERESTS: Fly-fishing, skiing, travel.

BIOGRAPHICAL/CRITICAL SOURCES:

PERIODICALS

Chicago Tribune, March 11, 1979.

Nation, April 7, 1979.

Newsweek, June 14, 1982.

Washington Post Book World, April 12, 1979, June 22, 1982.

*   *   *

ROGO, D. Scott 1950-

PERSONAL: Born February 1, 1950, in Los Angeles, Calif.; son of Jack (an accountant) and Winifred (Jacobs) Rogo. *Education:* Attended University of Cincinnati, 1967-68; San Fernando Valley State College (now California State University, Northridge), B.A., 1971. *Politics:* Democrat.

ADDRESSES: Home—18132 Schoenborn St., Northridge, Calif. 91325.

CAREER: Parapsychologist and writer.

MEMBER: American Society for Psychical Research, Parapsychological Association.

WRITINGS:

NAD: A Study of Some Unusual Other-World Experiences, University Books, 1970.

A Psychic Study of the "Music of the Spheres," University Books, 1972.

Methods and Models for Education in Parapsychology, Parapsychology Foundation, 1973.

The Welcoming Silence, University Books, 1973, published as *Man Does Survive Death*, Citadel, 1977.

An Experience of Phantoms, Taplinger, 1974 (published in England as *Phantoms: Experiences and Investigations*, David & Charles, 1976).

Parapsychology: A Century of Inquiry, Taplinger, 1975.

In Search of the Unknown: The Odyssey of a Psychical Investigator, Taplinger, 1976.

Exploring Psychic Phenomena, Quest Books, 1976.

The Haunted Universe, New American Library, 1977.

Mind beyond the Body: The Mystery of ESP Projection, Viking, 1978.

Minds and Motion: The Riddle of Psychokinesis, Taplinger, 1978.

The Haunted House Handbook, Tempo, 1978.

The Poltergeist Experience, Viking, 1979.

(With Raymond Bayless) *Phone Calls from the Dead*, Prentice-Hall, 1979.

(With Jerome Clark) *Earth's Secret Inhabitants*, Tempo, 1979.

(With Ann Druffel) *The Tujunga Canyon Contacts*, Prentice-Hall, 1980.

UFO Abductions, New American Library, 1980.

Miracles, Dial, 1982.

ESP and Your Pet, Tempo, 1982.

Leaving the Body, Prentice-Hall, 1983.

Our Psychic Potentials, Prentice-Hall, 1984.

The Search for Yesterday, Prentice-Hall, 1985.

Life after Death, Aquarian Press, 1986.

On the Track of the Poltergeist, Prentice-Hall, 1986.

Mind over Matter, Aquarian Press, 1986.

Psychic Breakthroughs Today, Aquarian Press, 1987.

The Infinite Boundary, Dodd, 1987.

The Return from Silence, Aquarian Press, 1989.

Multiple Realities, Aquarian Press, 1990.

Contributor to parapsychology and paraphysics journals. Contributing editor, *Science of Mind;* consulting editor, *Fate.*

SIDELIGHTS: D. Scott Rogo's books have been translated into German, French, Spanish, Italian, Dutch, Danish, Finnish, Portuguese, Norwegian, and Japanese.

*   *   *

ROLFE, Lionel (Menuhin) 1942-

PERSONAL: Born October 21, 1942, in Medford, Ore.; son of Benjamin Lionel (a judge) and Yaltah (a pianist; maiden name, Menuhin) Rolfe; married Dianna Preston, 1964 (divorced, 1973); married Nigey Lennon (a writer), November 29, 1975; children: Heather, Haila. *Education:* Attended Los Angeles City College, 1960-62, and California State University, Los Angeles, 1963. *Politics:* "Left-wing Democrat." *Religion:* "Jewish-Atheist."

ADDRESSES: Home and office—952 Maltman Ave., Los Angeles, Calif. 90026.

CAREER: Free-lance writer. Associated with *Pismo Beach Times* in Pismo Beach, Calif., 1964; *East Whittier Review,* Whittier, Calif., editor and writer, 1965; *Turlock Daily Journal,* Turlock, Calif., editor and reporter, 1965-66; *Livermore Independent,* Livermore, Calif., editor and reporter, 1966; *Newhall Signal,* Newhall, Calif., reporter, 1968-70; *San Francisco Chronicle,* San Francisco, Calif., reporter, 1970; worked as editor of *Psychology Today* in Del Mar, Calif.; worked for television writer Art Ulene, 1975; *Grantsmanship Center News,* Los Angeles, assistant editor, 1977; *B'nai B'rith Messenger,* Los Angeles, editor, 1984-88.

AWARDS, HONORS: Award from Valley Press Club, 1967-68, for feature story on plight of migrant workers.

WRITINGS:

(With wife, Nigey Lennon) *Nature's Twelve Magic Healers: The Amazing Secrets of Cell Salts,* Parker Publishing, 1978.
The Menuhins: A Family Odyssey (nonfiction), Panjandrum, 1978.
Literary L.A., Chronicle Books, 1981.
(With Lennon) *The Heal Yourself Home Handbook of Unusual Remedies,* Parker Publishing, 1983.
(Contributor) *Unknown California* (anthology), Macmillan, 1985.
Last Train North (fiction), Panjandrum, 1987.
(With Lennon and Paul Greenstein) *Bread and Hyacinths,* Peregrine Smith, 1989.

Correspondent for *Israel Today.* Contributor of several hundred articles to periodicals, including *Newsweek.*

WORK IN PROGRESS: A biography; a history.

SIDELIGHTS: Lionel Rolfe told *CA:* "I have continued writing about literary figures for various Los Angeles and California newspapers and magazines. Usually, these pieces concentrate on writers in Los Angeles, but they are not necessarily so limited.

"The thread that has bound much of my work together has been California. *The Menuhins* was called by a number of different critics a 'Jewish *Roots.*' I traced my family back several centuries to write an odyssey that began in biblical times in ancient Jerusalem. Most of my research, however, concentrated on the beginnings of my family in the 1700s in Russia.

"My novel *Last Train North,* published in 1987 to mixed reviews, was a book about the '60s, and small town and underground newspapering in California. My wife Nigey Lennon, along with Paul Greenstein, has just finished a book called *Bread and Hyacinths,* to be published in 1989 by Peregrine Smith. The book is about Job Harriman, the socialist who almost became mayor of Los Angeles in 1911. It is also the story of what went wrong with Los Angeles, and indeed, the politics of a nation.

"Although I have always wanted to do fiction, at this point it seems as if most of my future projects will be historical nonfiction on California topics. For that reason, I consider myself a California journalist and author."

BIOGRAPHICAL/CRITICAL SOURCES:

PERIODICALS

Los Angeles Times Book Review, October 18, 1987.

*   *   *

RONEN, Dov 1933-

PERSONAL: Born September 30, 1933, in Bekescsaba, Hungary; immigrated to Israel, 1949; now naturalized U.S. citizen; son of Jacob and Lola Rubicsek; married Naomi Ross (a librarian), August 20, 1961; children: David, Mihal, Gili. *Education:* Hebrew University of Jerusalem, B.A., 1963; Indiana University, M.A., 1965, Ph.D., 1969.

ADDRESSES: Home—85 Griggs Rd., Brookline, Mass. 02146. *Office*—Center for International Affairs, Harvard University, 1737 Cambridge St., Cambridge, Mass. 02138.

CAREER: Purdue University, Lafayette, Ind., assistant professor of political science, 1969-71; Hebrew University of Jerusalem, Jerusalem, Israel, lecturer in political science and African studies, 1971-76; Harry S. Truman Research Institute, Africa Research Unit, Jerusalem, coordinator, 1973-76; Harvard University, Center for International Affairs, Cambridge, Mass., 1976—, began as research fellow, currently associate. Visiting associate professor, Brandeis University, 1978-80; Barnett Miller Visiting Professor, Wellesley College, spring, 1981.

MEMBER: International Political Science Association, American Political Science Association, African Studies Association.

WRITINGS:

Dahomey: Between Tradition and Modernity, Cornell University Press, 1975.
The Quest for Self-Determination, Yale University Press, 1979, Japanese edition, Tosui Shobo Press, 1988.
(Editor) *Democracy and Pluralism in Africa,* Lynne Rienner, 1986.
(Editor with Dennis L. Thompson) *Ethnicity, Politics and Development,* Lynne Rienner, 1986.

Contributor to *Encyclopedia Britannica.*

WORK IN PROGRESS: A book, *The Human Revolution.*

SIDELIGHTS: Dov Ronen told *CA:* "I am interested in human behavior. First I studied sociology, history, philosophy, and political science; later I came to African studies. After visiting in Nigeria in the midst of the civil war, I wanted to widen the scope. I asked myself: 'What brings people, any people, to fight for freedom? What brings others to try to repress this aspiration?' Some thoughts on these questions I provided in *The Quest for Self-Determination.*

"I am trying to understand human behavior in order to extrapolate from such an understanding [of] some recommendations for a better world, a world at peace. Such a world is attainable; if not for this, maybe the next generation."

*   *   *

ROSE, Florella
See CARLSON, Vada F.

*   *   *

ROSENSTONE, Robert A(llan)   1936-

PERSONAL: Born May 12, 1936, in Montreal, Quebec, Canada; son of Louis (a businessman) and Anne (Kramer) Rosenstone. *Education:* University of California, Los Angeles, B.A., 1957, Ph.D., 1965.

ADDRESSES: Office—California Institute of Technology, Pasadena, Calif. 91125.

CAREER: Los Angeles Examiner, Los Angeles, Calif., reporter and copy editor, 1960; *Los Angeles Times,* Los Angeles, public relations work, 1961-62; University of Oregon, Eugene, assistant professor of history, 1965-66; California Institute of Technology, Pasadena, professor of history, 1975—, executive officer of humanities, 1982-85. Summer professor, University of California, Los Angeles, 1966; visiting professor of American studies, Kyushu University, and Seinan Gakuin University, Fukuoka, Japan, 1974-75. Historical consultant for the feature film "Reds," 1981-82. Member, board of trustees, Beyond Baroque Literary/Arts Foundation, 1988—. *Military service:* California National Guard, 1961-67; active duty in U.S. Army, 1962.

MEMBER: PEN, American Historical Association, Organization of American Historians, Phi Beta Kappa.

AWARDS, HONORS: Old Dominion Fund grant, 1969-70; American Philosophical Society travel grant, 1970; Fulbright-Hays senior lecturer, 1974-75, in Fukuoka, Japan; Silver Medal from Commonwealth Club of California, 1975, for *Romantic Revolutionary: A Biography of John Reed;* National Endowment for the Humanities summer grant, 1977; National Endowment for the Humanities senior fellowships, 1981-82, 1989-90; East-West Center fellow in Honolulu, Hawaii, 1982; Fulbright-Hays research fellow in India, 1989-90.

WRITINGS:

(Editor) *Protest from the Right,* Glencoe Press, 1968.
Crusade of the Left: The Lincoln Battalion and the Spanish Civil War, Pegasus, 1970.
(Co-editor) *Seasons of Rebellion: Protest and Radicalism in Recent America,* Holt, 1972.
(Co-author) *Los cantos de la conmocion: Veinte anos de rock,* Tuquets (Barcelona), 1974.
Romantic Revolutionary: A Biography of John Reed, Knopf, 1975.
(Contributor) *Affairs of the Mind: The Salon in Europe and America from the Eighteenth to the Twentieth Century,* New Republic, 1980.
(Contributor) *Reform and Reformers in the PROGRESSIVE Era,* Greenwood Press, 1983.
(Writer of narration) "The Good Fight: The Lincoln Brigade and the Spanish Civil War" (feature-length documentary film), 1983.

Mirror in the Shrine: American Encounters with Meiji Japan, Harvard University Press, 1988.

Contributor to *Michigan Quarterly Review, Partisan Review, Ploughshares, New Republic, The Progressive,* and to historical journals. Co-editor, "Protest in the Sixties" issue of *Annals* of the American Academy of Political and Social Science, March, 1969.

WORK IN PROGRESS: History in Images/History in Words: The Challenge of the Visual Media to Our Idea of the Past.

SIDELIGHTS: Romantic Revolutionary: A Biography of John Reed has been translated into Italian, Spanish, French, Hungarian, and Norwegian.

BIOGRAPHICAL/CRITICAL SOURCES:

PERIODICALS

Los Angeles Times Book Review, October 16, 1988.
Nation, April 6, 1970.
New Republic, September 20, 1975.
New York Times Book Review, November 2, 1975, February 21, 1982.
Reviews in American History, June, 1976.

*   *   *

ROSNOW, Ralph L(eon)   1936-

PERSONAL: Born January 10, 1936, in Baltimore, Md.; son of Irvin (a merchant) and Rebecca (Faber) Rosnow; married Marion Medinger Quin. *Education:* University of Maryland, B.S., 1957; George Washington University, M.A., 1958; American University, Ph.D., 1962.

ADDRESSES: Home—177 Biddulph Rd., Radnor, Pa. 19087. *Office*—517 Weiss Hall, Temple University, Philadelphia, Pa. 19122.

CAREER: Boston University, Boston, Mass., assistant professor of communication research, 1963-67; Temple University, Philadelphia, Pa., associate professor, 1967-70, professor of psychology, 1970—, Thaddeus L. Bolton Professor of Psychology, 1982—, director of Social Psychology Division. Visiting professor at London School of Economics and Political Science, University of London, 1973, and Harvard University, spring, 1974. *Military service:* U.S. Army Reserve, Medical Specialist Corps, 1958-66; became first lieutenant.

MEMBER: American Association for the Advancement of Science (fellow), American Psychological Association (fellow), Society of Experimental Social Psychology, Eastern Psychological Association.

AWARDS, HONORS: Research grants or stipends from U.S. Public Health Service, Gerontology Division, 1964-65, National Institute of Mental Health, 1964-65 and 1965-66, National Science Foundation, 1966-67, 1967-68, 1969-71, and 1971-73, Harvard University, 1974, and Temple University, 1976, 1983, 1985, and 1987.

WRITINGS:

(Editor with Edward J. Robinson) *Experiments in Persuasion,* Academic Press, 1967.
(Editor with Robert Rosenthal and contributor) *Artifacts in Behavioral Research,* Academic Press, 1969.
(With J. A. Cheyne, Kenneth H. Craik, Benjamin Kleinmuntz, Rosenthal, and Kenneth H. Walters) *New Directions in Psychology IV,* Holt, 1970.

(Editor with Robert E. Lana) *Introduction to Contemporary Psychology*, Holt, 1972.

(Editor with Lana) *Readings in Contemporary Psychology*, Holt, 1972.

(With Rosenthal) *The Volunteer Subject*, Wiley Interscience, 1975.

(With Rosenthal) *Primer of Methods for the Behavioral Sciences*, Wiley, 1975.

(With G. A. Fine) *Rumor and Gossip: The Social Psychology of Hearsay*, Elsevier, 1976.

Paradigms in Transition: The Methodology of Social Inquiry, Oxford University Press, 1981.

(With Rosenthal) *Essentials of Behavioral Research: Methods and Data Analysis*, McGraw, 1984, 2nd edition, in press.

(With Rosenthal) *Understanding Behavioral Science: Research Methods for Research Consumers*, McGraw, 1984.

(With Rosenthal) *Contrast Analysis: Focused Comparisons in the Analysis of Variance*, Cambridge University Press, 1985.

(With Mimi Rosnow) *Writing Papers in Psychology*, Wadsworth, 1986.

(Editor with Marianthi Georgoudi) *Contextualism and Understanding in Behavioral Science: Implications for Research and Theory*, Praeger, 1986.

Editor of "Reconstruction of Society" series, Oxford University Press, 1975-77. Contributor to *Encyclopedia of Education*, 1971, and *International Encyclopedia of Psychiatry, Psychology, Psychoanalysis, and Neurology*; editorial advisor to *International Encyclopedia of Communications*. Consulting editor of *Encyclopedia of Communication, Sociometry, Journal of Personality and Social Psychology*, and *Journal of Mind and Behavior*. Referee for numerous journals.

WORK IN PROGRESS: With others, *Psychology: An Introduction*.

*   *   *

ROSS, Leah
See WEBB, Mary H(aydn)

*   *   *

ROWE, John (Seymour)   1936-

PERSONAL: Born March 20, 1936, in Sydney, Australia; son of Dudley Seymour (a lawyer) and Anne Ellen (Cullinaine) Rowe; married Marianne Hill, February 17, 1962; children: Luke, Jake. *Education:* Attended Royal Military College, Duntroon, Australia, 1954-57. *Politics:* Conservative. *Religion:* "Nil."

ADDRESSES: Home and office—118 Bower St., Manly, New South Wales 2095, Australia. *Agent*—Arnold Goodman, 500 West End Ave., New York, N.Y. 10024.

CAREER: Writer. Australian Army, career officer, 1954-68, leaving service as major.

MEMBER: Cabbage Tree Club, Palm Beach, Manly Surf Club.

WRITINGS:

Count Your Dead: A Novel of Vietnam, Angus & Robertson, 1968.

McCabe, P. M. (novel), Pan Books, 1972.

Chocolate Crucifix (novel), Wren Books, 1973.

Warlords (novel), Holt-Saunders, 1978.

The Aswan Solution (novel), Doubleday, 1979.

The Jewish Solution (novel), Holt-Saunders, 1980.

Long Live the King (novel), Stein & Day, 1984.

Vietnam: The Australian Experience, Time-Life Books, 1987.

WORK IN PROGRESS: A filmscript.

SIDELIGHTS: John Rowe once told *CA* that his Vietnam War experience, as a member of the Australian Army associated with the 73rd U.S. Airborne Brigade, "led to his first book *Count Your Dead*, his resignation from the army and a writing career as a novelist."

AVOCATIONAL INTERESTS: Wind surfing, skiing.

*   *   *

RUCHELMAN, Leonard I.   1933-

PERSONAL: Born June 28, 1933, in Brooklyn, N.Y.; son of Jacob (a businessman) and Sarah (Rosenblum) Ruchelman; married Diana G. Hoffberger, February 12, 1961; children: Lauren, Charles. *Education:* Brooklyn College (now of the City University of New York), B.A., 1954; Columbia University, Ph.D., 1965. *Religion:* Jewish.

ADDRESSES: Home—3019 Oakland Rd., Bethlehem, Pa. 18017. *Office*—Department of Government, Lehigh University, Bethlehem, Pa. 18015.

CAREER: West Virginia University, Morgantown, visiting assistant professor of political science, 1962-64; Alfred University, Alfred, N.Y., assistant professor, 1964-67, associate professor of political science, 1967-69, chairman of department, 1968-69; Lehigh University, Bethlehem, Pa., associate professor of government, 1969—, director of urban studies, 1972—. *Military service:* U.S. Army, 1954-56.

MEMBER: American Political Science Association, American Association of University Professors.

WRITINGS:

(Editor) *Big City Mayors: The Crisis in Urban Politics*, Indiana University Press, 1970.

Political Career: Recruitment through the Legislature, Fairleigh Dickinson University Press, 1970.

(Editor) *Who Rules the Police?*, New York University Press, 1973.

Police Politics: A Comparative Study of Three Cities, Ballinger, 1974.

(With Charles N. Brownstein) *Design of Municipal Services in Support of High Rise Office Buildings*, National Science Foundation, 1975.

The World Trade Center: Politics and Policies of Skyscraper Development, Syracuse University Press, 1977.

A Workbook in Program Design for Public Managers, State University of New York Press, 1985.

A Workbook in Redesigning Public Services, State University of New York Press, 1989.

Contributor of articles to *Midwest Journal of Political Science* and *Western Political Quarterly*.

SIDELIGHTS: Leonard I. Ruchelman once told *CA* that his interest "is in the area of urban leadership and executive leadership generally. Surprisingly, there is a dearth of scholarly material on these subjects and I am trying to fill the gap."*

RUNCIE, Robert (Alexander Kennedy)   1921-
(Robert A. K. Runcie)

PERSONAL: Born October 2, 1921, in Liverpool, England; son of Robert Dalziel (an electrical engineer) and Anne Runcie; married Angela Rosalind Turner (a professional pianist), September 5, 1957; children: James, Rebecca. *Education:* Brasenose College, Oxford, B.A. (with first class honors) and M.A., both 1948; studied at Westcott House, 1948-50.

ADDRESSES: Home—Lambeth Palace, London SE1 7JU, England.

CAREER: Ordained priest of Church of England, 1951; curate of Church of England in Gosforth, 1950-52; Westcott House (theology school), Cambridge, England, chaplain, 1953-54, vice-principal, 1954-56; Cambridge University, Cambridge, fellow, dean, and assistant tutor at Trinity Hall, 1956-60; vicar of Church of England in Cuddesdon, 1960-69; bishop of Church of England in St. Albans, 1970-80; Archbishop of Canterbury, 1980—. Principal of Cuddesdon Theological College, 1960-69; Teape Lecturer at St. Stephen's College, Delhi, India, 1962; select preacher at Cambridge University, 1957, 1975, and at Oxford University, 1959, 1973. Canon and prebendary of Lincoln, 1969; Anglican chairman of Anglican-Orthodox Joint Doctrinal Commission, 1973-80. Chairman of British Broadcasting Corp. (BBC) and Independent Broadcasting Authority Central Religious Advisory Committee, 1973-79. Freeman of the city of St. Albans, 1979, and of the city of London, 1981. *Military service:* British Army, Scots Guards, tank officer, 1941-45; served in Germany; received Military Cross.

MEMBER: Athenaeum Club.

AWARDS, HONORS: Honorary fellow of Trinity Hall, Cambridge, 1975, and of Brasenose College, Oxford, 1979; privy councillor, 1980; honorary bencher at Gray's Inn, 1980; D.D. from Oxford University, 1980, Cambridge University and University of the South, both 1981, and University of Durham, 1982; fellow of King's College, London, 1981; D.Litt. from University of Keele, 1981; D.C.L. from University of Kent at Canterbury, 1982; honorary degree from Berkeley Divinity School, 1986; Cross of the Order of the Holy Sepulchre, 1986.

WRITINGS:

(Editor) *Cathedral and City: St. Albans Ancient and Modern,* Humanities, 1977.
Windows onto God (collection of sermons), compiled by Eileen Mable, S.P.C.K., 1983.
(Under name Robert A. K. Runcie) *Seasons of the Spirit: The Archbishop of Canterbury at Home and Abroad,* excerpted by James B. Simpson, Eerdmans, 1983.
Faith Seeking Understanding: An Archbishop Looks at the Bible, S.L.G. Press, 1986.
(Compiler with Basil Hume) *Prayers for Peace: An Anthology of Readings and Prayers,* S.P.C.K., 1987.

SIDELIGHTS: In a London *Times* interview with Bernard Levin, Robert Runcie, Archbishop of Canterbury, explains his understanding of the decline in personal morality of the past twenty years or so: "I think . . . there are many reasons. I think the lack of neighbourliness in our society, and the more impersonal character of high technology and so on, means that the ways in which we communicate are less person-to-person. We are distanced very often from the results of our actions or our communications. I think also that we are a less reflective society, and can be desensitized by the amount of experience which we are asked to absorb by the mass media." Runcie further commented that when people exclude God from their lives "they become less human, and when people eliminate eternity they can't find contentment on earth, and when they leave out the heavenly city, they don't seem to be able to build a tolerable society on earth."

As Archbishop of Canterbury, Runcie officiated at the marriage of Prince Charles and Lady Diana Spencer in 1981; his homily on that occasion was quoted worldwide.

AVOCATIONAL INTERESTS: Keeping pedigreed Berkshire pigs.

BIOGRAPHICAL/CRITICAL SOURCES:

BOOKS

Duggan, Margaret, *Runcie: The Making of an Archbishop,* Hodder & Stoughton, 1984.

PERIODICALS

New York Times, September 8, 1979.
Time, August 10, 1981.
Times (London), March 30, 1987.
Times Literary Supplement, July 21, 1978, February 24, 1984.

*   *   *

RUNCIE, Robert A. K.
See RUNCIE, Robert (Alexander Kennedy)

*   *   *

RUSHER, William A(llen)   1923-

PERSONAL: Born July 19, 1923, in Chicago, Ill.; son of Evan Singleton and Verna Rae (Self) Rusher. *Education:* Princeton University, A. B., 1943; Harvard University, J. D., 1948. *Religion:* Anglican.

ADDRESSES: Home—30 East 37th St., New York, N. Y. 10016. *Office*—*National Review,* 150 East 35th St., New York, N. Y. 10016.

CAREER: Shearman & Sterling & Wright (law firm), New York City, associate, 1948-56; U. S. Senate, Washington, D.C., associate counsel to internal security subcommittee, 1956-57; *National Review,* New York City, publisher, director, and vice-president, 1957-88. Appeared on television program "The Advocates," Public Broadcasting System, 1970-73. Special counsel to finance committee of New York Senate, 1955; member of Advisory Task Force on Civil Disorders, 1972; member of National News Council, 1973-80; member of board of directors of Chinese Cultural Center, New York City; past vice-chairman of American Conservative Union. *Military service:* U. S. Army Air Forces, 1943-46; became captain.

MEMBER: American Bar Association, American African Affairs Association (co-chairman, 1965-75), University Club (New York), Metropolitan Club (Washington).

AWARDS, HONORS: D.Litt. from Nathaniel Hawthorne College, 1973; distinguished citizen award from School of Law, New York University, 1973.

WRITINGS:

Special Counsel, Arlington House, 1968.
(With Mark Hatfield and Arlie Schardt) *Amnesty?,* Sun River Press, 1973.
The Making of the New Majority Party, Sheed, 1975.

How to Win Arguments, Doubleday, 1981.
The Rise of the Right, Morrow, 1984.
A Short Course on South Africa, Communications Distribution, 1987.
(Contributor) *Crossing the Rubicon*, World Media Association, 1987.
The Coming Battle for the Media: Curbing the Power of the Media Elite, Morrow, 1988.

Author of syndicated column "The Conservative Advocate," Universal Press Syndicate, 1973-82, and NEA, 1982—.

SIDELIGHTS: Over the last three decades William A. Rusher has played an important role in the American conservative movement. As publisher of the nation's most influential conservative magazine, *National Review*, Rusher helped to bring the conservative message to a wide audience. In 1961, it was Rusher who with two friends, launched the committee that drafted Senator Barry Goldwater for the Republican Party nomination for president, a move which gave control of the Republican Party to its conservative wing and led in 1980 to the election of President Ronald Reagan. And in his books and syndicated column, Rusher has argued the conservative position on a host of controversial issues, including apartheid, economic policy, and the liberal bias of the national news media.

Rusher's *The Rise of the Right* traces the history of American conservatism since the 1950s and gives a firsthand account of how Rusher himself became a conservative activist and played a part in the movement's evolution. He credits three books for inspiring his political conversion: *The Road to Serfdom* by F. A. von Hayek, *Witness* by Whittaker Chambers, and *The Conservative Mind* by Russell Kirk. These books, Rusher claims, taught him the principles which are the foundation of his political beliefs. After leaving college with a degree in law, Rusher worked for several years with a Wall Street law firm before joining the Senate internal security subcommittee as associate counsel. The subcommittee was charged with investigating groups and individuals of all political persuasions who might constitute a threat to American security.

In 1957 Rusher joined William Buckley's *National Review*, a fledgling magazine founded in 1955 and at that time one of the nation's few journals of conservative opinion. Rusher sees the liberal opposition in uncompromising terms. As he explained when he became publisher, "the Liberal Establishment . . . shares Communism's materialist principles." In his role as publisher of the magazine, Rusher oversaw the business aspects of the magazine, and shared with Buckley the role of its spokesman. Nicknamed the WAR Department by the staff, Rusher's role was an important one. As William Buckley comments in the magazine's twentieth anniversary issue, "Bill Rusher is every bit as vital to *National Review* as I am."

Rusher was vital, too, in persuading Senator Barry Goldwater to run for president in 1964. In *The Rise of the Right*, Rusher recounts his efforts to get Goldwater nominated as the Republican Party's presidential candidate. "It was Mr. Rusher," Lewis H. Lapham writes in the *New York Times Book Review*, "who first conceived the idea of Senator Goldwater's candidacy, who organized the National Draft Goldwater Committee, set up the meetings in airport motels, who overcame the Senator's initial doubt and skepticism, who made possible the miracle." Though Goldwater went on to lose the election to President Lyndon Johnson, the nomination itself was an important victory for the nation's conservatives, who gained a strong voice in one of the two major political parties.

In the early 1970s Rusher was a regular on "The Advocates," a television program on which current political issues were discussed and debated by persons of opposing viewpoints. This experience led him in 1981 to write the book *How to Win Arguments*, a guide to holding one's own in a political debate. The book gives practical advice on how to best approach a debate, how to prepare an argument, and how to avoid putting oneself at a disadvantage. Although Dennis Drabelle of the *Washington Post* believes that the author "hints at more than he delivers" in *How to Win Arguments*, he finds that Rusher nonetheless "yields some trenchant political insights."

Rusher's political insights are also found in his syndicated newspaper column, "The Conservative Advocate." It is one of the most widely published political columns in the country today, appearing in over two hundred newspapers. The column exhibits what a writer for *Time* calls "a pungent wit" and "often veers from sharp attacks on liberalism into Panglossian mood pieces."

In 1988 Rusher turned his attention to liberal bias in the nation's media, publishing *The Coming Battle for the Media: Curbing the Power of the Media Elite*. Targeting the major news magazines, television networks, and daily newspapers, Rusher argues that these news organs constitute a "media elite" which is far to the left of the general public and whose coverage of the news is decidedly one-sided. Rusher cites a host of surveys showing that the politics of journalists is overwhelmingly liberal.

But Rusher is more concerned about the influence of politics on the coverage of the news. He gives examples where news stories were deliberately slanted to agree with the political perspective of the reporter involved. "It is hard to disagree with Rusher's view," Timothy Foote remarks in the *Washington Post Book World*, "that some good can come of doing what he does here, that is, jawboning the media about accuracy and fairness in reporting. There are surely too many single-source stories these days for comfort, too many stories anonymously leaked, and too many stories marked by breathtaking lack of balance or even the appearance of fairmindedness." Foote sees the media bias most evident in stories on "subjects like civil rights and education. There, heartfelt approval of the humane ends being sought blinds liberals to the failure of the means chosen." But David Shaw of the *New York Times Book Review* disagrees. "I am not so naive," Shaw writes, "as to suggest that no reporters or editors ever permit their liberal views to influence their stories; some of the examples offered by Mr. Rusher are singularly disturbing. . . . [But] it's wrongheaded to insist that bias is the rule, rather than the exception, in the better news organizations." Shaw allows, however, that Rusher's book contains "lawyerly arguments and [a] fine prose style."

BIOGRAPHICAL/CRITICAL SOURCES:

PERIODICALS

National Review, December 31, 1985, November 20, 1987, January 27, 1989.
New York Times, June 15, 1984.
New York Times Book Review, July 15, 1984, April 10, 1988.
Time, April 15, 1974.
Washington Post, August 4, 1981.
Washington Post Book World, May 16, 1988.

—*Sketch by Thomas Wiloch*

RUSSELL, Jeffrey Burton   1934-

PERSONAL: Born August 1, 1934, in Fresno, Calif.; son of Lewis Henry (a publishers' representative) and Ieda (Ogborn) Russell; married Diana Mansfield (a teacher of English), June 30, 1956; children: Jennifer, Mark, William, Penelope. *Education:* University of California, Berkeley, A.B., 1955, A.M., 1957; University of Liege, Belgium, graduate study, 1959-60; Emory University, Ph.D., 1960. *Politics:* Democrat. *Religion:* Catholic.

ADDRESSES: Office—Department of History, University of California, Santa Barbara, Calif. 93106. *Agent*—Gerard McCauley Agency, P.O. Box AE, Katonah, N.Y. 10536.

CAREER: University of New Mexico, Albuquerque, assistant professor of history, 1960-61; Harvard University, Cambridge, Mass., junior fellow, Society of Fellows, 1961-62; University of California, Riverside, assistant professor, 1962-65, associate professor, 1965-69, professor of medieval and religious history, 1969-75; University of Notre Dame, Notre Dame, Ind., Michael P. Grace Professor of Medieval Studies and director of Medieval Institute, 1975-79; University of California, Santa Barbara, professor of medieval and church history, 1979—.

MEMBER: American Historical Association, Mediaeval Academy of America, Medieval Association of the Pacific, American Society of Church History, Catholic Historical Association, Sierra Club, Phi Beta Kappa.

AWARDS, HONORS: Fulbright fellowship, 1959; Guggenheim fellowship, 1968; National Endowment for the Humanities senoir fellowship, 1972; grants in aid from American Council of Learned Societies and Social Science Research Council.

WRITINGS:

Dissent and Reform in the Early Middle Ages, University of Calfornia Press, 1965.
(Contributor) Lynn White, editor, *The Transformation of the Roman World,* University of California Press, 1966.
Medieval Civilization, Wiley, 1968.
A History of Medieval Christianity: Prophecy and Order, Crowell, 1968.
(Editor) *Religious Dissent in the Middle Ages,* Wiley, 1971.
Witchcraft in the Middle Ages, Cornell University Press, 1972.
The Devil: Perceptions of Evil from Antiquity to Primitive Christianity, Cornell University Press, 1977.
A History of Witchcraft: Sorcerers, Heretics and Pagans, Thames & Hudson, 1980.
(With Carl T. Berkhout) *Medieval Heresies: A Bibliography 1960-1979,* Pontifical Institute of Mediaeval Studies, 1981.
Satan: The Early Christian Tradition, Cornell University Press, 1981.
Lucifer: The Devil in the Middle Ages, Cornell University Press, 1984.
Mephistopheles: The Devil in the Modern World, Cornell University Press, 1986.
The Prince of Darkness: Radical Evil and the Power of Good in History, Cornell University Press, 1988.

Contributor to *Revue d'Histoire ecclesiastique, Medieval Studies, Church History, Speculum, American Historical Review, Catholic Historical Review,* and other journals of history.

WORK IN PROGRESS: Ruga in aevis.

SIDELIGHTS: Jeffrey Burton Russell once told *CA* that "using the history of evil as an example," he has explored "the ways in which concepts may be most fully understood and accurately defined in terms of their history and sociology." One of the results of Russell's efforts "to develop an historical method uniting philosophy and content analysis with traditional historical approaches," as he describes it, is his tetralogy which traces the history of the idea of the Devil in philosophy, literature, and theology from ancient to modern times. The series includes *The Devil: Perceptions of Evil from Antiquity to Primitive Christianity, Satan: The Early Christian Tradition, Lucifer: The Devil in the Middle Ages,* and *Mephistopheles: The Devil in the Modern World.*

In a review of *Mephistopheles, New York Times Book Review* contributor Robert Coles calls the tetralogy "impressive." He writes that "the author is not only a conscientious historian, . . . [he] is also an introspective essayist who acknowledges his own continuing struggle to understand the nature and source of evil." Russell, says D. J. Enright in the *Times Literary Supplement,* avoids the problem of choosing "between what might be deplored as insufficient documentation and the risk, or certainty, of boring, or maddening, the modern reader" by branching "out into a number of interesting and entertaining cognate topics."

While holding his readers' interest, the author pursues his main goal of exploring, as *New York Times Book Review* contributor D. J. R. Bruckner phrases it, "the devil in the mind." In other words, Russell explains how the idea of what the Devil is (and, by association, what God is) has evolved over time. Collectively, these books explain to "us a lot about the attention and passion we have given to that idea," concludes Coles. Russell's "books tell us much about what we were and what we are today—people who all along have been trying to make sense of the world and to stay around in it as a species, our devilish capacity for hate and slaughter notwithstanding."

AVOCATIONAL INTERESTS: Conservation and preservation of wilderness, numismatics, Baroque music, and British mystery stories.

BIOGRAPHICAL/CRITICAL SOURCES:

PERIODICALS

New York Times Book Review, April 28, 1985, March 8, 1987.
Times Literary Supplement, March 22, 1985.
Washington Post Book World, January 8, 1989.

*   *   *

RYKEN, Leland   1942-

PERSONAL: Born May 17, 1942, in New Sharon, Iowa; son of Frank (engaged in farming) and Eva (Bos) Ryken; married Mary Graham, August 22, 1964; children: Philip Graham, Margaret Lynn, Nancy Elizabeth. *Education:* Central College (now Central University of Iowa), B.A., 1964; University of Oregon, Ph.D., 1968. *Politics:* Republican. *Religion:* Presbyterian.

ADDRESSES: Home—1118 North Howard, Wheaton, Ill. 60187. *Office*—Department of English, Wheaton College, Wheaton, Ill. 60187.

CAREER: Wheaton College, Wheaton, Ill., professor of English, 1968—.

WRITINGS:

The Apocalyptic Vision in "Paradise Lost," Cornell University Press, 1970.

The Literature of the Bible, Zondervan, 1974.

(Contributor) Kenneth Gros Louis, editor, *Literary Interpretations of Biblical Narratives,* Abingdon, 1974.

Triumphs of the Imagination: Literature in Christian Perspective, Inter-Varsity Press, 1979.

The Christian Imagination: Essays on Literature and the Arts, Baker Book, 1981.

(Co-editor and contributor) *Milton and Scriptural Tradition: The Bible into Poetry,* University of Missouri Press, 1984.

(Editor) *The New Testament in Literary Criticism,* Ungar, 1984.

How to Read the Bible as Literature, Zondervan, 1984.

Windows to the World: Literature in Christian Perspective, Zondervan, 1985.

Culture in Christian Perspective: A Door to Understanding and Enjoying the Arts, Multnomah, 1986.

Worldly Saints: The Puritans as They Really Were, Zondervan, 1986.

Words of Delight: A Literary Introduction to the Bible, Baker Book, 1987.

Words of Life: A Literary Introduction to the New Testament, Baker Book, 1987.

Work and Leisure in Christian Perspective, Multnomah, 1987.

(Co-author) *Effective Bible Teaching,* Baker Book, 1988.

Contributor to scholarly journals.

WORK IN PROGRESS: Books on contemporary literary criticism in Christian perspective, the Bible in literature, and the Bible as literature.

S

SABINE, B(asil) E. V.   1914-

PERSONAL: Born February 14, 1914, in Manchester, England; son of John (a teacher) and Tony (a teacher; maiden name, O'Hara) Sabine; married Margaret Harrop (a teacher), January 4, 1943; children: Martin, Roger. *Education:* Oxford University, M.A., 1935. *Politics:* Radical. *Religion:* Church of England.

ADDRESSES: Home—Hazel Mount, Mottram, Hyde, Cheshire, England. *Office*—Brookes Hobson, 46/48 Long St., Middleton, Manchester, England.

CAREER: Tax inspector in England, 1938-53, senior inspector, 1953-79; Deloitte, Haskins, Sells (accountants), Manchester, England, taxation manager, 1979-88; tax inspector for Isle of Man, 1979—; affiliated with Brookes Hobson, Manchester, 1988—. Lecturer and broadcaster on taxation subjects.

MEMBER: International Fiscal Association, Institute of Taxation (fellow), Institute for Fiscal Studies, Economic Research Council.

AWARDS, HONORS: Order of the British Empire, 1984.

WRITINGS:

A History of Income Tax, Allen & Unwin, 1966.
British Budgets in Peace and War, 1932-1945, Allen & Unwin, 1970.
A Short History of Taxation, Butterworth & Co., 1980.
(Editor) *A Dictionary of Taxation,* Butterworth & Co., 1982.
Tax Appeals Handbook, Butterworth & Co., 1983.
Tolley's Focus on the Administration of Taxes: A Review of the Main Provisions of the Taxes Management Act, 1970, Tolley, 1983.
Time Limits for Tax Claims, Elections, and Reliefs, Butterworths, 1984.
Appeals before the Commissioners, Institute of Chartered Accountants, 1985.
"Economist" Pocket Taxpayer, Economist Publications, 1987.
(With Leslie Beckett) *Revenue Investigations Manual,* Butterworths, 1987.
Pocket Guide to Business Taxes, Economist Publications, 1988.

Contributor to tax journals.

SACKS, Oliver (Wolf)   1933-

PERSONAL: Born July 9, 1933, in London, England; immigrated to the United States in 1960; son of Samuel (a physician) and Elsie (a physician; maiden name, Landau) Sacks. *Education:* Queen's College, Oxford, B.A., 1954, M.A., B.M., and B.Ch., all 1958; attended University of California, Los Angeles, 1962-65.

ADDRESSES: Home and office—119 Horton St., Bronx, N.Y. 10464. *Agent*—International Creative Management, 40 West 57th St., New York, N.Y. 10019.

CAREER: Yeshiva University, Albert Einstein College of Medicine, Bronx, N.Y., 1965—, began as instructor, currently clinical professor of neurology; Beth Abraham Hospital, Bronx, staff neurologist, 1966—. Visiting professor, University of California, Santa Cruz, 1986. Consultant neurologist, Bronx State Hospital, 1966—, and at the Little Sisters of the Poor in New York City.

MEMBER: American Academy of Neurology (fellow).

AWARDS, HONORS: Hawthornden Prize, 1974, for *Awakenings;* Oskar Pfister Award, American Psychiatric Association, 1988; Guggenheim fellowship, 1989; Harold D. Vursell Memorial Award, American Academy and Institute of Arts and Letters, 1989.

WRITINGS:

Migraine: Evolution of a Common Disorder, University of California Press, 1970, revised and enlarged edition published as *Migraine: Understanding a Common Disorder,* 1985.
Awakenings, Duckworth, 1973, Doubleday, 1974, published with a new foreword by the author, Summit Books, 1987.
A Leg to Stand On, Summit Books, 1984.
The Man Who Mistook His Wife for a Hat, and Other Clinical Tales, Duckworth, 1985, Summit Books, 1986.
Seeing Voices: A Journey into the World of the Deaf, University of California Press, 1989.

Contributor to the *New York Review of Books* and to various other journals.

WORK IN PROGRESS: A study of visual memory and imagery in creative artists.

SIDELIGHTS: As a physician, professor and author of widely read books about his work in the field of neurology, Oliver Sacks has become a leading proponent of the rehumanization of the medical arts. Working day-to-day in the hospitals and nursing homes of the New York City area exploring organic disorders of the brain and their symptoms, Sacks resembles a general practitioner, "a medical man in the old-fashioned humanist tradition," in the words of *New York Times* reviewer Michiko Kakutani. "He sees medicine as part of the continuum of life." Sacks is unhurried by an overly ambitious schedule and, therefore, able to give time to patients, time for listening and discussing their conditions. He is also free of the technical bias characteristic of current medical practice, so he involves patients in developing their own treatments. "His outstanding quality is wonder," writes Douglas Hill in the Toronto *Globe and Mail,* "a constant amazed appreciation of how men and women afflicted with frustrating or terrifying handicaps can cope with them and even help themselves to master them."

Sacks's approach to his work is reflected in his writing. He avoids the technical language and biochemical analyses common in medical treatises. Instead, in journal articles and such books as *Migraine, Awakenings, A Leg to Stand On,* and *The Man Who Mistook His Wife for a Hat,* he uses a case history approach to write straightforward clinical biographies that go beyond medical analysis to capture the human side of illness. These human stories also chronicle Sacks's discovery of health as a complex interaction of mind, body, and lifestyle that requires a concerted effort on the part of patient and physician in order to arrive at an appropriate cure. As Walter Kendrick puts it in a *Voice Literary Supplement* article, "Sacks's aim in all his books has been to show that neuropsychologists are wrong when they confine themselves to dry tabulations of symptoms and dosages. Just as the subject ought to be the full human brain, not half of it, so the method should account for the human being—emotions, personal relationships, everything."

In his book *Migraine,* first published in 1970 and later updated and enlarged for publication in 1985, Sacks examines a condition known to mankind for thousands of years. As Sacks points out, though it is a common affliction, migraine is little understood, its cycles of agony and euphoria often different with each episode. Headache is but one of many symptoms that include convulsions, vomiting, depression, and hallucinations. Drawing upon his observation of the numerous patients he treated, Sacks focuses not on cures but on an explanation of the function migraine serves for its human sufferers. As Israel Rosenfield relates in the *New York Times Book Review,* Sacks maintains that the disorder "is part of the human repertory of passive reactions to danger. The complexity of human social activities often necessitates passivity—neuroses, psychosomatic reactions and the varieties of migraine—when the individual confronts essentially unsolvable problems."

Though useful to migraine sufferers for the answers it provides, Sacks's book has attracted a varied readership. Kakutani finds that "his commentary is so erudite, so gracefully written, that even those people fortunate enough to never have had a migraine in their lives should find it equally compelling." Rosenfield maintains that *Migraine* "should be read as much for its brilliant insights into the nature of our mental functioning as for its discussion of migraine."

Upon his arrival at Beth Abraham Hospital in the late 1960s, Sacks discovered a group of patients suffering from a range of debilitating symptoms, the worst of which was a "sleep" so deep the sufferer was beyond arousal. The patients, he learned, were survivors of a sleeping sickness epidemic that had occurred between 1916 and 1927. In his second book, *Awakenings,* Sacks tells of his attempts to help this group. Recognizing the similarities between the symptoms exhibited by his patients and those of sufferers of Parkinson's disease, Sacks decided to begin administering L-dopa, a drug proven effective in treating Parkinson's. L-dopa initially produced dramatic results; patients out of touch with the world for over four decades suddenly emerged from their sleep. However, Sacks discovered that the drug was not a miracle cure. Battling side-effects and the shock of waking a changed person in a changed world proved too much for some in the group. Some died; others withdrew into trance-like states. Others succeeded, however, but only by achieving a balance between the illness and the cure, the past and the present.

Sacks's portrayal of the complexities of this episode has earned him considerable praise from readers of *Awakenings.* "Well versed in poetry and metaphysics, [Sacks] writes from the great tradition of Sir Thomas Browne," writes *Newsweek* reviewer Peter S. Prescott. "probing through medicine and his own observations of fear, suffering and total disability toward an investigation of what it means not only to be, but to become a person." "Some would attribute this achievement to narrative skill, others to clinical insight," comments Gerald Weissman in the *Washington Post;* "I would rather call this feat of empathy a work of art."

A Leg to Stand On is a doctor's memoir of his experience as a patient. As Jerome Bruner explains in the *New York Review of Books,* Sacks's book "is about a horribly injured leg, his own, what he thought and learned while living through the terrors and raptures of recovering its function." In 1976 while mountaineering in Scandinavia, Sacks fell and twisted his left knee. Although surgery repaired the physical damage—torn ligaments and tendons—the leg remained immobile. Even worse, Sacks found he had lost his inner sense of the leg; it seemed to him detached and alien, not his own. His inability to recover disturbed him and the surgeon's dismissal of his concerns only heightened his anxiety.

"By describing his experience and its resolution," comments Vic Sussman in the *Washington Post Book World,* "Sacks shows how patients rapidly become isolated (even physician-patients) when medicine regards them as 'invalids, in-valid.'" This reflection on the doctor/patient relationship is what makes *A Leg to Stand On* more than a personal story. As Bruner notes, "It is also a book about the philosophical dilemma of neurology, about the philosophy of mind, about what it might take to create a 'neurology of the soul' while still hanging on to your scientific marbles." And, Sussman concludes, "Sacks' remarkable book raises issues of profound importance for everyone interested in health care and the humane application of science."

In his bestselling collection of case histories entitled *The Man Who Mistook His Wife for a Hat,* "Dr. Sacks tells some two dozen stories about people who are also patients, and who manifest strange and striking peculiarities of perception, emotion, language, thought, memory or action," observes John C. Marshall in the *New York Times Book Review.* "And he recounts these histories with the lucidity and power of a short-story writer." One of the case histories Sacks presents is that of an instructor of music who suffers from a visual disorder. While able to see the component parts of objects, he is unable to perceive the whole they compose. Leaving Sacks's office after a visit, this patient turns to grab his hat and instead grabs his wife's face. Another features two autistic twins unable to add or subtract but capable of determining the day of the week for any date past or present and of calculating twenty-digit prime numbers. "Blessed with deep reserves of compassion and a metaphysical turn of mind," comments Kakutani, "Dr. Sacks writes of these patients not as scientific curiosities but as individuals, whose dilemmas—moral and spiritual, as well as psychological—are made as completely real as those of characters in a novel."

Although it demonstrates the variety of abnormal conditions that can arise from damage to the brain, *The Man Who Mistook His Wife for a Hat* also touches larger themes. *Nation* contributor Brina Caplan is taken by the book's portrayal of "men and women [who] struggle individually with a common problem: how to reconcile being both a faulty mechanism and a thematic, complex and enduring self." As Walter Clemmons suggests in *Newsweek*, "Sacks's humane essays on these strange cases are deeply stirring, because each of them touches on our own fragile 'normal' identities and taken-for-granted abilities of memory, attention and concentration."

Commenting on his work and writing, Sacks once told an interviewer for *U.S. News and World Report*, "You get an idea of how much is given to us by nature when you see what happens if it's taken away and how the person—the human subject—survives its loss, sometimes in the most extraordinary and even creative ways." This creativity is what Sacks attempts to capture in his case histories and memoirs. *New York Times* reviewer Benedict Nightingale characterizes Sacks as "a most unusual man, as much a metaphysician as physician: passionate, inquiring, generous, imaginative and supremely literate, a sort of Isaac Bashevis Singer of the hospital ward."

Yet, Sacks's writing also serves his larger purpose. "What he's arguing for is a set of neglected values: empathetic, emotional, individual, storylike," notes Caplan. "To ignore those values, he suggests, means constructing a science of cold, rigid design." As Paul Baumann sums it up in a *Commonweal* article, "Sacks's larger ambition is to develop what he calls an 'existential neurology' or 'romantic science' that will shed the rigid computational paradigms of traditional neurology and open itself up to the dynamic 'powers' of the mind."

CA INTERVIEW

CA interviewed Oliver Sacks by telephone on July 25, 1987, at his home in the Bronx, New York.

CA: The practice of medicine obviously runs in your family—your mother, father, and three brothers have done it. Did you know early on that you'd be a doctor?

SACKS: I did and I didn't. On the one hand, it seemed to be fated, and I also wanted it. On the other hand, I wanted a lot else. My earlier thoughts were not on being a doctor, but first on being a physical scientist—possibly a chemist, later a biologist, then later a physiologist. I did in fact spend years in these, so I became a doctor a little belatedly and a little reluctantly. In a sense I was a naturalist first and I only came to individuals relatively late.

CA: Your fourth book, intriguingly titled The Man Who Mistook His Wife for a Hat, *has been quite a critical and popular*

success. Yet you told Daniel Goleman for the New York Times Book Review, *"I have no literary aspirations and don't regard myself as a writer." How did you come to be one?*

SACKS: First of all, I'm not sure what's meant by *writer*. I like pen and paper in hand. I've liked pen and paper in hand since I was six.

CA: And you take a great many notes on your patients, don't you?

SACKS: Yes. There's something about words, and the written word in particular, which is almost necessary for my own processes of thought. I regard myself as sort of a *describer*. I don't know consciously how much I want to move or educate or evoke. I do feel that, as a doctor, one is very privileged; one is entrusted with lives, with extraordinary stories of great scientific and human interest sometimes. It's one of the joys, also one of the responsibilities, and at times one of the afflictions of being a doctor that so many lives pass in front of one.

But I can't listen without hearing the way a story or case history is constructed. A patient tells you things, you ask questions, and you fit what you hear with other information so that gradually a story, a picture, comes out. It gets on paper, and it may get to a publisher. Though, needless to say, I've only published about a thousandth of what I've seen. And again, I think things don't remain at the level of pure observation, but they become objects for meditation. Everyone is interested, say, in the nature of memory. It's an eternal problem. And maybe one comes in as a clinician who sees people with special disturbances or maybe exaltations of memory. In some sense I think of myself as a reporter or transcriber or witness of what I see. I'm bearing witness. The idea of witness was originally a literary figure.

CA: There's a good example of your interest in words—their roots, original meanings, history. That's apparent in all your writing. Where did that come from? Has it always been with you?

SACKS: I think it has. Maybe it comes from being brought up in a house full of books, where reading aloud was still popular. But that's like asking me if I'm a breather. It seems to me that reading and writing are entirely natural and I've never known anything else. What I *do* find strange—and a bit frightening—are those people in medicine who are semi-literate and not at ease with words. I'm also bothered with the deterioration of language and thought which goes with it, which I think occurs in a lot of medical writing now. Medical writing was often natural and beautiful a half-century or quarter-century ago. Now it is filled with jargon—in an attempt to be precise, but in fact it backfires and is as imprecise as it is unbeautiful.

CA: Particularly interesting to me among the stories in The Man Who Mistook His Wife for a Hat *were the accounts of retardates who excelled in various specialized areas, such as Jose, "The Autist Artist." Have you done specialized work with retarded patients since writing the book?*

SACKS: No. I would like to go back and work with them again. I used to work with them from 1973 to 1975. Jose just happened to be someone I came in contact with fairly recently. In general I've been working more with elderly people with chronic diseases of one sort or another. I'm eager to go back and look at development in children, which would include retardates.

CA: Do you see trends toward improvement in the care and treatment of elderly people?

SACKS: Yes and no. That's to say, *yes* in a technical sense, *no* in a human sense, which I think is true of medicine generally. Though there are miracles all about us, I think human misery and human indignity are on the increase. But perhaps this will change. There are things like the hospice movement, which is a concerted attempt to get back to the human and moral depth of what is involved in terminal illness and dying. Not too many doctors and nurses can take this; hospices are not exactly popular with them. But I think one has to be worried at the relative lack of human dialogue in medicine. I think also the deterioration of writing which I spoke of partly goes with this lack of human dialogue in a time when everything tends to be technology. I have nothing against technology—I use plenty of it myself—but no one has put it better than Martin Buber when he said that "We must humanize technology before it dehumanizes us."

CA: In Awakenings, *the story of the survivors of sleeping sickness on whom you tried L-dopa, you wrote, "Given certain conditions, we* create *our own sickness. . . . And as we allow diseases, so we can collude with them." Do you think a large percentage of sickness is somehow invited and encouraged by the sufferers?*

SACKS: Mostly I think we don't take an active or responsible part in bringing disease on ourselves. I don't think anyone asks, for example, for cancer. But the tendency to undermine life with bad diet, stress, lack of exercise, and so forth, is in a way asking for some sort of trouble, cardiovascular or whatever. I think when I wrote those words the consideration was strongly in my mind with something like migraine, which was the subject of my first book. On the one hand, migraine is clearly an organic problem. There's a particular disposition; there's a strong genetic element. Given these genetic and constitutional elements, then, whether one gets a lot of migraine or not may depend quite a lot on the sort of life one leads, the part which migraine may come to play in one's life, and other such considerations. I think this, of course, would apply much less to chronic diseases without such an obviously psychosomatic component. But I am generally impressed by the fact that if one's spirits can somehow be directed towards life, one is less likely to become ill and more likely to recover quickly. The reverse is also true. The will to live and the will to die and the will to health and the will to sickness seem to be such palpable things.

CA: Awakenings *was dedicated to the memory of W. H. Auden, about whom you have also written elsewhere. How did he inspire your work particularly?*

SACKS: I met him towards the end of his life. Auden had a special relationship with doctors, which I think probably went back to the fact that his father was a doctor. For example, in his last book of poems, *Epistle to a Godson,* four of the poems are dedicated to doctors and are about medicine. The fourth of them is to me. Specifically, I discuss this at considerable length in a long foreword I've just written which will be attached to a hardback of *Awakenings* coming out this fall. Here I look back carefully on the influence of A. R. Luria and then Auden and then Leibnitz on *Awakenings.* Auden's father, George Auden, was a pioneer investigating sleeping sickness in England.

More generally, I think that Auden was very important in saying to me, Is the language of science adequate for conveying the human condition and what your patients go through, and can you combine the propositions and paradigms of science with something more human and more poetic? Because patients themselves tend to live in symbols and speak in symbols. I think the enlargement of language and of reference which lies between *Migraine* and *Awakenings* was considerably due to Auden's influence, and his emboldening me to a broader, deeper, richer language and approach. I'm not sure that I would have dared to do that alone. I may need various encouragers and emboldeners who become father figures for me—except I'm now becoming too old for father figures!

CA: Were you in any sense beyond the obvious one a collaborator with Harold Pinter on his play A Kind of Alaska, *based on* Awakenings?

SACKS: No, not at all. A messenger came one day and brought it. I had never met Pinter, and had no idea he was thinking about *Awakenings.* There was a fascinating letter with the manuscript of the play. He said he had read *Awakenings* when it came out, in 1973, was deeply moved, but then "forgot" it—the impression passed down into the depths of the psyche. Until, nine years later, *it* awakened, surfaced, came back transformed. He said that he had awoken one morning with the first words of the play—"Something is happening"—and the first image, of a woman, long-asleep, now awakening. Then the play wrote itself in days. A beautiful example of artistic incubation and emergence. I found reading the play uncanny; I felt Pinter had not only read my words with minute care, but all the thoughts and feelings I had had at the time. One friend said, "It's not like Pinter, it's just like the truth"—but then Pinter is just like the truth. You have to have art to get close to the truth.

CA: In A Leg to Stand On *you wrote about your own accident resulting from a fall while you were climbing a mountain, the seemingly strange complication with the leg, and your recovery. Music literally made the first step possible. Have you developed any further insight into how that worked?*

SACKS: I did write and think much more on it later. My thoughts are rather away from this now, but it is a major subject. At Mount Carmel Hospital (or Beth Abraham, to give it its proper name), where *Awakenings* is set, we have a good full-time music therapist. I work a lot with her. I acted as an advocate to persuade the state to fund a full-time music therapist. It didn't seem very probable that they would, but one could demonstrate to them so clearly how patients unable to walk or talk or function or get organized could be dramatically transformed by incorporating music into their therapy. Even the state was impressed. Now they pay for therapy, because they see it's not just a luxury but a necessity. It's possibly the most direct way of organizing activity in the brain on every level, from the motor to the highest level. But I'm not sure what happens, except it's clear that music works at a very elemental and primitive level, that it's universal, that children of twelve months can respond to music, that people who are severely demented and practically unconscious also respond to music. I almost find myself thinking that the organization of the nervous system—and of life, for that matter—has a musical quality in terms of rhythms and other things.

CA: The neuropsychologist Luria, whom you've just spoken of, urged you, in the matter of the leg, "Please publish your observations. It may do something to alter the 'veterinary' approach to peripheral disorders." Do you find that it has done so?

SACKS: The things which in a way please me most, although they often overwhelm me, are the letters I get. They overwhelm me because I get about 20,000 a year, and I sometimes feel that I have to answer them all, in my slow longhand and at length, and that this is about to take eight hours a day and exclude the rest of my life. But I certainly get from the letters—and also when I talk with people—at least a feeling that people are beginning to realize that a human element, as opposed to a veterinary or technological element, has to come back into medicine. And maybe I've put in my two cents' worth.

CA: The book about the accident and healing came eight years after the fact. Then just after you finished the writing, you slipped on ice and tore the quadriceps of the other leg. Is there a Freudian explanation for that second accident?

SACKS: I'm sure there is; a good analyst had specifically warned me against it several times. Whenever anything traumatic happens, there's a part of oneself which relives the trauma again and again. You see this in all sorts of other things, such as concentration camp survivors who keep dreaming of the barbed wire and the searchlights. I was also urged to write it so that I didn't do it again—as it were, to exorcise it. With my typical passion for compromise, I have a feeling I did both. No sooner had I completed the manuscript and said, That's that! than I had the second accident. It may have been a complete accident; who knows? But it certainly struck me as an irony that when the proofs came, actually I had *two* casts—one on my leg and one on my arm. I phoned up my publisher and told him about this. He wasn't too sympathetic. He said, "Oliver, you'd do anything for a footnote. No, you may *not* put it in the book."

I have thought that elsewhere I would like to write about it, because with the second accident I had none of the problems that I had in the first. I think there are various reasons for this: first, there was no nerve or joint injury; second, I was operated on within two hours rather than forty-eight hours; third and most importantly—and this is indeed a change in medical practice—I was stood up within hours of surgery instead of allowed to lie in bed for two weeks. They've found with people who have amputations that it is really necessary to fit them with a temporary artificial limb and almost have them stand down from the operating table, because body image starts to disappear within hours. I had the second operation done under spinal, and I found the non-feeling of spinal identical with the alienation feeling I described in my book. When I was in physiotherapy therapy afterwards for the second accident, the physiotherapist said to me, "You're one of the good quads." I said, "What do you mean, one of the good quads?" She said, "Well, you wouldn't believe it, but there are some bad quads who can't contract the muscle and in fact they feel that they don't even have the leg there." I thought, yes, I would believe it. I know a little bit about that! In general, I think that absolute immobilization for any length of time is increasingly realized to be very bad, not simply in terms of muscle atrophy, but in terms of literally forgetting how to move and losing the sense of body image.

CA: As a teacher, do you see students whose outlooks and performance bode well for future medical practice?

SACKS: Yes, I do. And I see those whose outlooks and performance bode ill. My hopes lie less with the very quick, bright students on the front row than with the ones who often don't say much but who think quietly in the back row. But I do see a very good generation coming up who in a way have recovered from some of the technical and also some of the commercial excitement of the '60s, the making-it-big attitude; and they've also seen some of the burnout which can happen to their colleagues, for whom the enjoyment has drained out of medicine, and are determined that this won't happen to them. I do feel a lesson has been learned, and on the whole I like the coming generation of students. I prefer seeing students rather than residents, because they are more open to suggestion at that point. They haven't been closed off.

CA: How do you feel about medical practice in Great Britain as compared to practice in the United States?

SACKS: I've spent half my life now over here, and though I don't know how competent I am to comment on that, I do think two things. First, I think the vanishing of the general practitioner here, in effect, is a very serious business. People don't have their own doctor—"my GP." One needs to have one's own doctor, one's own GP, as a start. This is different from having an internist or anything else. Your GP knows you as a person and stays in contact with you, even though he may refer you to all sorts of specialists and consultants. To some extent this was worst in the '60s and the early '70s. Medicine here had almost become a collection of specialists. Incidentally, I mentioned those poems of Auden's: several of them are dedicated to GPs of his own and precisely have to do with the passing of the GP and the specialists' taking over. But there's now something of a movement here back towards general practice. The GP is very important in England and Australia.

I think another thing, although I'm not a political creature and have never voted in my life (I may be culpably apolitical), is that people should not be penalized and bankrupted for grave illnesses which are not their own fault. I believe some sort of health service is almost a human right. I'm aware that the National Health Service in England has run into all sorts of problems. Whether these were avoidable or not, I don't know. The term *socialized medicine* has a terrible connotation here; I'm not even sure what's meant by socialized medicine. Incidentally, one of the reasons why I tend to the elderly and indigent patients myself is that they are covered by Medicare, and this forms for me something of a general practice rather like that I might do in England. I'm not very good at billing patients. I don't like doing that.

CA: You seem to be very happy in your medical practice, as in your writing. Is there anything you'd like to change, or anything new you'd like to try? You mentioned earlier you'd like to go back and work with children.

SACKS: Yes, there are lots of things I'd like to do, but that especially. As I said earlier, I've spent too much time at the geriatric end. I want to see children. I find myself offering to babysit for my friends, but I'm afraid they think I may stick pins into their babies, might treat them as neurological specimens! I have a strong need to see babies and children again. I haven't seen them for a while. That's partly a human thing, but it's also partly a neurological thing, a need to work with the developing organism, and not simply the deteriorating one. That would be much more fun.

MEDIA ADAPTATIONS: Harold Pinter's play, "A Kind of Alaska," is based on one of the case histories from *Awakenings*. An opera, based on the title case history of *The Man Who Mistook His Wife for a Hat,* was first produced under the same title in the fall of 1986 at the London Institute of Contemporary Art.

AVOCATIONAL INTERESTS: Bicycling, swimming, mountaineering.

BIOGRAPHICAL/CRITICAL SOURCES:

BOOKS

Sacks, Oliver, *A Leg to Stand On,* Summit Books, 1984.
Sacks, Oliver, *Awakenings,* published with a new foreword by the author, Summit Books, 1987.

PERIODICALS

Commonweal, March 28, 1986.
Globe and Mail (Toronto), February 21, 1987.
Los Angeles Times Book Review, March 23, 1986.
Nation, February 22, 1986.
Newsweek, July 15, 1974, August 20, 1984, December 30, 1985.
New York Review of Books, September 27, 1984, March 2, 1986, March 13, 1986, March 27, 1986.
New York Times, May 24, 1984, June 19, 1985, January 25, 1986.
New York Times Book Review, July 7, 1985, March 2, 1986.
People, March 17, 1986.
Times Literary Supplement, December 14, 1973, June 22, 1984, February 7, 1986.
U.S. News and World Report, July 14, 1986.
Voice Literary Supplement, February, 1986.
Washington Post, October 30, 1987.
Washington Post Book World, August 26, 1984, February 16, 1986.

—*Sketch by Bryan Ryan*

—*Interview by Jean W. Ross*

*   *   *

SAMKANGE, S. J. T.
See SAMKANGE, Stanlake (John Thompson)

*   *   *

SAMKANGE, Stanlake (John Thompson)   1922-1988
(S. J. T. Samkange)

PERSONAL: Born March 11, 1922, in Mariga, Rhodesia (now Zimbabwe); died March 6, 1988, of heart and lung ailments, in Harare, Zimbabwe; son of T. D. (a clergyman) and Grace C. Samkange; married Tommie Marie Anderson (a professor of psychology), February 6, 1958; children: Stanlake John Mudavanhie, Harry Mushore Anderson. *Education:* University College of Fort Hare, B.A., 1948; University of South Africa, B.A. (honors), 1951; Indiana University, M.Sc. in Ed., 1958, Ph.D., 1968. *Politics:* African Nationalist. *Religion:* Methodist.

CAREER: Political activist, businessman, educator, publisher, and author. Director of companies in Salisbury, Rhodesia (now Zimbabwe), 1958-65; honorary organizing secretary, Nyatsime College, Rhodesia; teacher of history at Northeastern University, Boston, Mass., for twelve years; political adviser to Bishop Abel Muzorewa of United African National Council,

Rhodesia, 1977-79; director of publishing house, Zimbabwe, beginning, 1979. Lecturer, Harvard University and Fisk University.

AWARDS, HONORS: Herskovits Award from African Studies Association, 1970, for *Origins of Rhodesia.*

WRITINGS:

The Chief's Daughter Who Would Not Laugh, Longmans, Green, 1964.
On Trial for My Country, Humanities, 1966.
Origins of Rhodesia, Praeger, 1968.
African Saga, Abindgon, 1971.
The Mourned One, Heinemann, 1975.
Year of the Uprising, Heinemann, 1978.
(With wife, Tommie Marie Samkange) *Hunhuism or Ubuntuism: A Zimbabwe Indigenous Political Philosophy,* Graham Publishing (Salisbury, Zimbabwe), 1980.
(Under name S. J. T. Samkange) *What Rhodes Really Said about Africans,* Harare Publishing House (Harare, Zimbabwe), 1982.
Christ's Skin Colour: Was He a White or Black Man?, Harare Publishing House, 1983.
(Under name S. J. T. Samkange) *The Origin of African Nationalism in Zimbabwe,* Harare Publishing House, 1985.
Among Them Yanks, Harare Publishing House, 1985.
(Under name S. J. T. Samkange) *On Trial for That U.D.I.: A Novel,* Harare Publishing House, 1986.

SIDELIGHTS: Stanlake Samkange was politically involved in the liberation of British-ruled Rhodesia for approximately three decades, until it became the independent republic of Zimbabwe in 1979. He worked for the African People's Union under Joshua Nkomo and also for the United African National Council as Bishop Abel Muzorewa's political adviser from 1977 to 1979. After Rhodesia's independence, Samkage opened Harare Publishing House in Zimbabwe.

BIOGRAPHICAL/CRITICAL SOURCES:

BOOKS

Zell, Hans M., and others, *A New Reader's Guide to African Literature,* Holmes & Meier, 1983.*

*   *   *

SANDERS, Noah
See BLOUNT, Roy (Alton), Jr.

*   *   *

SAXON, Peter
See McNEILLY, Wilfred (Glassford)

*   *   *

SCHILLER, A. Arthur   1902-1977

PERSONAL: Born September 7, 1902, in San Francisco, Calif.; died July 10, 1977; son of George Marcus (a public servant) and Bertha (Kohn) Schiller; married Irma H. Coblentz, August 22, 1926 (died, 1946); married Erna Kaske, January 23, 1947; children: (first marriage) Donald Coblentz, Jerome Paul. *Education:* University of California, Berkeley, A.B., 1924, M.A. and J.D., 1926; University of Munich, additional study, 1929; Columbia University, J.D., 1932. *Politics:* Democrat.

ADDRESSES: Home—145 East St., Oneonta, N.Y. 13820. *Office*—School of Law, Columbia University, New York, N.Y. 10027.

CAREER: Admitted to the Bar of California, 1926; Columbia University, New York, N.Y., lecturer, 1928-30, assistant professor, 1930-37, associate professor, 1937-49, professor of law, 1949-71, professor emeritus, 1971-77, director of African Law Center, 1956-71. Visiting professor at University of Indonesia, 1949, University of Graz, 1949, University of Erlangen, 1949, and University of Cape Town, 1968; exchange professor, Free University of Berlin, 1953. Fulbright lecturer, University of Aberdeen, 1957. Fellow, Social Science Research Council, 1929-30. Research assistant, New York State Law Revision Commission, 1935. U.S. observer, First International Congress of Africanists, Ghana, 1962; member, Council on Foreign Relations, Institute for Advanced Study, Princeton, N.J., 1973, Indonesian Academy of Arts and Sciences, and Riccobono Seminar on Roman Law. Consultant to U.S. Treasury Department Tax Division, 1938-40, and Institute for Pacific Relations, 1945, 1950; legal expert, United Nations Commission on Eritrea, 1951, 1952; adviser, Institute for International Legal Studies, University of Istanbul, 1955.

MEMBER: Societe International des Droits de l'Antiquite, International Association of Papryologists, African Law Association in America (founder and president, 1965-67), Ancient Civilization Group (co-founder, 1930), American Association of Papryologists, American Association of University Professors, American Society of Legal History (fellow), Oriental Club, Accademia Nazionale dei Lincei (foreign member).

AWARDS, HONORS: Social Science Research Council grant, University of Munich, 1929-30, University of Indonesia, 1949; Guggenheim fellow to Indonesia, 1949, Greece, Libya, and Italy, 1956, Italy, Switzerland, and England, 1963; Doctorr iuris honoris causa, University of Erlangen, 1950; Ford Foundation travel grants to Africa, 1959, 1963; Rockefeller Foundation fellow to Italy, Switzerland, and England, 1963.

WRITINGS:

(Author of introduction) *Ten Coptic Legal Texts*, Metropolitan Museum of Art, Volume 1, 1932, reprinted, 1973, Volume 2, 1932, reprinted, 1972.
Texts and Commentary for the Study of Roman Law, Law School, Columbia University, 1936.
Military Law and Defense Legislation, West Publishing, 1941, later edition published as *Military Law*, 4th edition, 1968.
(With Garrard Glenn) *The Army and the Law*, Columbia University Press, 1947.
(With Edwin R. Keedy) *Cases in the Law of Agency*, Bobbs-Merrill, 1948.
(Editor and author of introduction with E. A. Hoebel) Barends ter Haar, *Adat Law in Indonesia*, Institute for Pacific Relations, 1948, reprinted, AMS Press, 1977.
(With W. L. Westermann) *Apokrimata: Decisions of Septimius Severus on Legal Matters*, Columbia University Press, 1954.
The Formation of Federal Indonesia: 1945-1949, van Hoeve, 1955.
Foreign Law Classification in the Columbia University Law Library, Oceana, 1964.
Syllabus on African Law, Law School, Columbia University, 1967.
An American Experience in Roman Law: Writings from Publications in the United States, Vandenhoeck & Ruprecht, 1971.

Roman Law: Mechanisms of Development, Mouton, 1978.

Contributor of articles to American and foreign legal journals. Editor, *African Law Digest*, 1965-67, and *African Law Studies*, 1969.

WORK IN PROGRESS: Sententiae at Epistolae Hadriani; The Compilations of Customary Law in Northern Ethiopia.

SIDELIGHTS: A. Arthur Schiller traveled extensively and had a reading knowledge of Latin, Greek, Egyptian (Coptic), French, German, Italian, Spanish, Dutch, and Tigrinya (for his Ethiopic legal studies).

AVOCATIONAL INTERESTS: Woodworking.*

* * *

SCHLESINGER, Arthur M(eier), Jr. 1917-

PERSONAL: Name originally Arthur Bancroft Schlesinger; born October 15, 1917, in Columbus, Ohio; son of Arthur Meier (a professor of history) and Elizabeth (Bancroft) Schlesinger; married Marian Cannon (an author and artist), August 10, 1940 (divorced, 1970); married Alexandra Emmet, July 19, 1971; children: (first marriage) Stephen Cannon and Katharine Bancroft Kinderman (twins), Christina, Andrew Bancroft; (second marriage) Robert Emmet Kennedy. *Education:* Harvard University, A.B. (summa cum laude), 1938. *Politics:* Democrat. *Religion:* Unitarian.

ADDRESSES: Office—Graduate School and University Center, City University of New York, 33 West 42nd St., New York, N.Y. 10036-8099.

CAREER: Affiliated with Office of War Information, Washington, D.C., 1942-43, and with Office of Strategic Services, Washington, D.C., London, England, and Paris, France, 1943-45; free-lance writer, Washington, D.C., 1945-46; Harvard University, Cambridge, Mass., associate professor, 1946-54, professor of history, 1954-62; special assistant to President John F. Kennedy, 1961-63, and to President Lyndon B. Johnson, 1963-64; City University of New York, New York City, Albert Schweitzer Professor in the Humanities, 1966—. Chairman, Franklin Delano Roosevelt Four Freedoms Foundation, 1983—. Trustee of Robert F. Kennedy Memorial, Recorded Anthology of American Music, and Twentieth Century Fund. Advisor, Arthur and Elizabeth Schlesinger Library on the History of Women in America, and Library of America. Member, boards of Harry S Truman Library Institute, John Fitzgerald Kennedy Library, Ralph Bunche Institute, and Harriman Institute of Russian Studies. Member, Adlai Stevenson presidential campaign staff, 1952, 1956. Consultant, Economic Cooperation Administration, 1948, and Mutual Security Administration, 1951-52. *Military service:* U.S. Army, 1945; served in Europe.

MEMBER: American Historical Association, American Academy and Institute of Arts and Letters (president, 1981-84, chancellor of the Academy, 1985-88), Library of Congress Council of Scholars, Association for the Study of Afro-American Life and History, Organization of American Historians, Society for Historians of American Foreign Relations, Center for Inter-American Relations, Council on Foreign Relations, Americans for Democratic Action (national chairman, 1953-54), American Civil Liberties Union (member of national council), Massachusetts Historical Society, Colonial Society of Massachusetts, Phi Beta Kappa.

AWARDS, HONORS: Henry Fellow, Cambridge University, 1938-39; Harvard Fellow, 1939-42; Pulitzer Prize for history, 1946, for *The Age of Jackson,* and for biography, 1966, for *A Thousand Days: John F. Kennedy in the White House;* Guggenheim fellow, 1946; American Academy of Arts and Letters grant, 1946; Francis Parkman Prize, Society of American Historians, 1957, and Frederic Bancroft Prize, Columbia University, 1958, both for *The Age of Roosevelt, Volume 1: The Crisis of the Old Order;* National Book Award, 1966, for *A Thousand Days: John F. Kennedy in the White House,* and 1979, for *Robert Kennedy and His Times;* gold medal in history and biography, National Institute and American Academy of Arts and Letters, 1967; Ohio Governor's Award for history, 1973; Sidney Hillman Foundation Award, 1973, for *The Imperial Presidency;* Eugene V. Debs Award in education, 1974; Fregene Prize for literature, Italy, 1983. Honorary degrees from many schools and universities, including New School for Social Research, 1966, Utah State University, 1978, University of Louisville, 1978, Rutgers University, 1982, State University of New York at Albany, 1984, University of New Hampshire, 1985, University of Oxford (England), 1987, and Brandeis University, 1988.

WRITINGS:

Orestes A. Brownson: A Pilgrim's Progress (Catholic Book Club selection), Little, Brown, 1939, published as *A Pilgrim's Progress: Orestes A. Brownson,* 1966.
The Age of Jackson, Little, Brown, 1945, reprinted, 1968, abridged edition, New American Library, 1962.
The Vital Center: The Politics of Freedom, Houghton, 1949 (published in England as *The Politics of Freedom,* Heinemann, 1950).
(With Richard H. Rovere) *The General and the President and the Future of American Foreign Policy,* Farrar, Straus, 1951, revised edition published as *The MacArthur Controversy and American Foreign Policy,* 1965.
The Age of Roosevelt, Volume 1: The Crisis of the Old Order, 1919-1933 (Book-of-the-Month Club selection), Houghton, 1957, reprinted, 1988, Volume 2: *The Coming of the New Deal* (Book-of-the-Month Club selection), Houghton, 1959, reprinted, 1988, Volume 3: *The Politics of Upheaval* (Book-of-the-Month Club selection), Houghton, 1960, reprinted, 1988.
Kennedy or Nixon: Does It Make Any Difference?, Macmillan, 1960.
The Politics of Hope (essays), Houghton, 1963.
(With John M. Blum et al) *The National Experience,* Harcourt, 1963, 7th edition, 1989.
A Thousand Days: John F. Kennedy in the White House, Houghton, 1965, reprinted, Greenwich House, 1983.
The Bitter Heritage: Vietnam and American Democracy, 1941-1966, Houghton, 1967.
The Crisis of Confidence: Ideas, Power, and Violence in America, Houghton, 1969.
(With Lloyd C. Gardner and Hans J. Morgenthau) *The Origins of the Cold War,* Ginn-Blaisdell, 1970.
The Imperial Presidency (Book-of-the-Month Club selection), Houghton, 1973.
Robert Kennedy and His Times, Houghton, 1978.
The Cycles of American History, Houghton, 1986.

EDITOR

(With others) *Harvard Guide to American History,* Harvard University Press, 1954.
(With Quincy Howe) *Guide to Politics, 1954,* Dial, 1954.

(With Morton White) *Paths of American Thought,* Houghton, 1963.
Herbert Croly, *The Promise of American Life,* Belknap, 1967.
Edwin O'Connor, *The Best and the Last of Edwin O'Connor,* Little, Brown, 1970.
(With Fred L. Israel and William P. Hansen) *History of American Presidential Elections, 1789-1972,* four volumes, Chelsea House, 1971, supplemental volume, *1972-1984,* 1986.
The Coming to Power: Critical Presidential Elections in American History, Chelsea House, 1972.
The Dynamics of World Power: A Documentary History of United States Foreign Policy, 1945-1973, Chelsea House, 1973, Volume 1: *Western Europe,* Volume 2: *Eastern Europe and the Soviet Union,* Volume 3: *Latin America,* Volume 4: *Far East,* Volume 5: *United Nations, Middle East, Subsaharan Africa.*
History of U.S. Political Parties, Chelsea House, 1973, Volume 1: *1789-1860: From Factions to Parties,* Volume 2: *1860-1910: The Gilded Age of Politics,* Volume 3: *1910-1945: From Square Deal to New Deal,* Volume 4: *1945-1972: The Politics of Change.*
(With Roger Bruns) *Congress Investigates: A Documented History, 1792-1974,* five volumes, Chelsea House, 1975.
The American Statesmen, forty-five volumes, Chelsea House, 1982.
(With John S. Bowman) *The Almanac of American History,* Putnam, 1983.

OTHER

(Contributor) *Four Portraits and One Subject: Bernard De Voto,* Houghton, 1963.
(Author of foreword) Arthur M. Schlesinger, Sr., *Paths to the Present,* revised and enlarged edition, Houghton, 1964.
(Author of preface) Schlesinger, *The American as Reformer,* Harvard University Press, 1968.
(Author of introduction) Schlesinger, *The Birth of a Nation: A Portrait of the American People on the Eve of Independence,* Knopf, 1968.
(Author of introduction) Schlesinger, *Nothing Stands Still: Essays,* Belknap Press, 1969.

Also author of television screenplay, ''The Journey of Robert F. Kennedy.'' Author of pamphlets on political subjects. Author of introductions for ''World Leaders Past & Present'' series, 56 volumes, and ''Know Your Government'' series, for Chelsea House. Movie reviewer for *Show,* 1962-64, *Vogue,* 1966-72, and *Saturday Review,* 1977-80; member of jury, Cannes Film Festival, 1964. Contributor to magazines and to newspapers, including *Wall Street Journal.* Schlesinger's White House staff papers are collected in the John F. Kennedy Library in Boston, Mass.

SIDELIGHTS: ''Since World War II,'' reports Edwin A. Miles in the *Dictionary of Literary Biography,* ''Arthur Meier Schlesinger, Jr., has been perhaps the nation's most widely known and controversial historian.'' Twice awarded the Pulitzer Prize and the National Book Award, Schlesinger's oeuvre has gained widespread popularity as well as serious critical attention. He has also attracted attention through his political activism, especially his outspoken advocacy of a liberal position in the Democratic party. ''There is perhaps no single name more closely associated with the history, the biography, the political experience and the intellectual positions of liberalism's 'vital center,''' declares Benjamin R. Barber in *The*

New York Times Book Review, "than that of Mr. Schlesinger."

Schlesinger seemed destined for a remarkable career from an early age. His father, the senior Arthur M. Schlesinger, was a distinguished American historian who helped guide his son's career. The younger Schlesinger majored in history and literature at Harvard University, where he won the LeBaron Russell Briggs Prize for a freshman essay. His senior honors thesis, on the nineteenth-century American Catholic intellectual Orestes A. Brownson, was later published as *Orestes A. Brownson: A Pilgrim's Progress* and was acclaimed by many prominent authorities. The famous American historian Henry Steele Commager, for instance, declares in the *New York Times Book Review* that Schlesinger's study "not only rescues from undeserved oblivion a striking and authentic figure in our history, but announces a new and distinguished talent in the field of historical portraiture."

The impact of the Brownson biography brought Schlesinger material awards as well. He received fellowships to both Cambridge and Harvard Universities, and was invited to lecture on the period of President Andrew Jackson's administration by the Lowell Institute in Boston. The lectures Schlesinger delivered there in the fall of 1941 provided the groundwork for *The Age of Jackson,* a reevaluation of Andrew Jackson's presidency that "stands as a significant landmark in the writing of the nation's history," according to Miles. The volume captured the Pulitzer Prize for history in 1946 and provoked a controversy among historians that continues today.

In *The Age of Jackson* Schlesinger challenges the accepted interpretation of Jacksonian democracy as essentially a frontier phenomenon. Historians relying on Frederick Jackson Turner's "frontier thesis" see the political battles of Jackson's era as a sectional struggle between a firmly democratic West and the established powers of the East. Schlesinger argues that in fact Jacksonian democracy received much of its support from laborers living in Eastern states and suggests that it represented a clash of classes rather than of sections. He also maintains that Jackson's concept of democracy represented a significant change from Thomas Jefferson's ideal because of its willingness to use strong government to protect individuals from corporate interests, and draws parallels between Jacksonian politics and the philosophy of Franklin Roosevelt's New Deal programs.

In addition to the Pulitzer Prize, *The Age of Jackson* won Schlesinger a Guggenheim fellowship, sold more than 90,000 copies, and got its author an associate professorship in Harvard's history department—this for a twenty-eight-year-old who held only a bachelor's degree and had little teaching experience. Yet although many reviewers acclaim *The Age of Jackson* for its readability and thought-provoking analysis, others find Schlesinger's approach too partisan in its advocacy of Jacksonian principles. Allan Nevins, writing in the *New York Times,* calls the book "excessively hostile to Whig leaders and Whig ideas, the caustic treatment of Daniel Webster and Horace Greeley seeming especially unfair. It sometimes rides its thesis a bit too hard." "But," he adds "it is a remarkable piece of analytical history, full of vitality, rich in insights and new facts, and casting a broad shaft of illumination over one of the most interesting periods of our national life."

In the mid 1950s, Schlesinger began what many historians feel is his greatest contribution to the field: his multivolume *The Age of Roosevelt,* still in progress more than thirty years after its beginning. The three volumes that appeared between 1957

and 1960 were all Book-of-the-Month Club selections, and all "attest to his superb style, felicity of phrase, keen sense of drama, and successful blending of narrative and analytical history," says Miles. Yet although the first volume, *The Crisis of the Old Order, 1919-1933,* won prestigious awards from historical and scholastic institutions, it was not universally acclaimed. Norman MacKenzie, writing in the *New Statesman,* declares that it "lacked a cutting edge," and adds, "Mr. Schlesinger's appraisal is not only smooth; it is curiously isolated from the outside world." Many prominent reviewers and historians feel otherwise. "Probably no more thoughtful or surgical or compassionate study of the period in the United States has been written," asserts the *New Yorker;* and C. Vann Woodward maintains in the *Saturday Review* that the book "is a permanent enrichment of our historical literature."

Schlesinger sustained a presence in politics as well as in academics. Many of his works championed Democratic and liberal policies; *The Vital Center: The Politics of Freedom* reflects Schlesinger's anti-Communism, for instance, while *Nixon or Kennedy: Does It Make Any Difference?* urged voters to select the Democratic ticket in the 1960 election, and *The Politics of Hope* expressed his liberal philosophy and hopes for the Kennedy administration. In 1952 and 1956 he took leaves of absence from Harvard to support Adlai Stevenson's presidential campaigns as an advisor and speechwriter. After John F. Kennedy won his presidential bid in 1960, Schlesinger joined the administration as a special assistant to the President. Working with President Kennedy, Schlesinger helped formulate the "New Frontier" and, in foreign policy, the "Alliance for Progress." He also provided innovations, stimulated new ideas, and linked the scholastic, intellectual, and cultural communities with Kennedy's government.

The historian recalls his role in the Kennedy Administration in his book *A Thousand Days: John F. Kennedy in the White House,* which won Schlesinger his first National Book Award and his second Pulitzer Prize. "I felt I owed it," he says, "both to the memory of the President and to the historical profession to put it all down." The volume draws on notes Schlesinger had kept at Kennedy's request for the president's own memoirs, and caused much contention through its revelations about Kennedy's political circle, especially his frustration with Secretary of State Dean Rusk. John Roger Fredland, writing in *Saturday Review,* was one who found Schlesinger "unduly hard on Dean Rusk," calling his depiction of Kennedy's Secretary of State, the State Department as a whole, and the Foreign Service "both mischievous and unjust." But the book is not so much a history of the Kennedy administration as it is a description of its deliberations and decisions as Schlesinger remembers them. Some reviewers who expected a more scholarly treatment have been disappointed, but many others agree with Fredland in saying that "as a primary source . . . for future historians *A Thousand Days* deserves success and acclaim." James MacGregor Burns declares in the *New York Times Book Review* that "this is Arthur Schlesinger's best book. A great President has found—perhaps he deliberately chose—a great historian."

The late '60s and '70s proved disappointing politically for Schlesinger. He left the government soon after President Kennedy's assassination, disillusioned with Lyndon Johnson's administration. The historian criticized Johnson's Vietnam policy in *The Bitter Heritage: Vietnam and American Democracy, 1941-1966,* and backed Robert Kennedy's bid for the Democratic nomination in the 1968 election. Senator Robert Kennedy's murder in June of 1968 profoundly affected Schlesinger's ideology, according to Miles. In 1969 he produced *The Crisis of Confidence: Ideas, Power, and Violence in America,* a book that rejected the optimism of *The Politics of Hope,* published just six years earlier, and in 1973 he censured several presidents, including Johnson and Richard Nixon, for their misuse of presidential powers in *The Imperial Presidency.* Even the election of Democrat Jimmy Carter in 1976 did not lighten Schlesinger's gloom; he "called him the most conservative Democratic president since Grover Cleveland, and pronounced his administration the most incompetent since that of Warren G. Harding," declares Miles.

In 1978, perhaps as a reaction to the Carter presidency, Schlesinger published *Robert Kennedy and His Times,* an enormous project that won him his second National Book Award. The book reexamines the idealism of the Kennedy years in what Henry Fairlie, writing in the *New Republic,* calls "really a page-by-page revision of [*A Thousand Days*]." Yet there are marked differences between the two volumes: while *A Thousand Days* is a personal memoir, *Robert Kennedy* is a formal biography, and many reviewers found the later book more controversial than its predecessor. While succumbing to the fascination of the work, some commentators were disappointed in its uncritical portrait of Bobby Kennedy and believed that Schlesinger had created "something like a 916-page promotional pamphlet of exculpation and eulogy," as *New York Review of Books* contributor Marshall Frady puts it. "Schlesinger is, of course, scrupulously candid about the nature of the book in this regard," reports Eliot Fremont-Smith in the *Village Voice,* "but candor does not excuse everything. There's no question that he puts the most favorable light . . . on Kennedy's mistakes and flaws." However, he concludes, after "all this [is] said, I think *Robert Kennedy and His Times* is pretty good."

The election of Republican Ronald Reagan in 1980 further delayed Schlesinger's anticipation of a resurgent liberalism. *The Cycles of American History,* a collection of essays on history of American government published in 1986, "may be taken as the testament of a confirmed liberal forced to endure the age of Reagan," reports Barry Gewen in the *New Leader.* Yet the book is not a tirade against the Republican government, but rather a historical analysis of mechanisms that, Schlesinger believes, shape American history. He also suggests how these mechanisms may be used to shape tomorrow's America. In fourteen essays on subjects ranging from "The Future of the Vice Presidency" to "Affirmative Government and the American Economy," Schlesinger attempts "to measure America's behavior against America's aspirations," according to *Time* contributor Melvin Maddocks. John Kenneth Galbraith, writing for *Tribune Books,* calls the collection "a brilliant evocation of his view of the uses of history."

Misgivings about his political activism aside, professional historians value the contributions Schlesinger has made to their craft. Alan Brinkley, writing in the *New Republic,* states that, "despite the countless ways in which he has violated the conventions of his profession, he remains one of [the historical occupation's] most important voices." "It is not simply because he possesses a literary grace that few American scholars can match," he continues, "and not simply because the range of his interests and knowledge far exceeds that of most historians in this age of narrow specialization. It is because he possesses a rare ability to make history seem important, because he is willing to argue that the search for an understanding of the past is not simply an aesthetic exercise but a path to the understanding of our own time." "He is a reminder to profes-

sional historians," Brinkley concludes, " of the possibilities of reaching beyond their own ranks to the larger world in which they live."

CA INTERVIEW

CA interviewed Arthur Schlesinger, Jr., by telephone on March 16, 1988, at his office at the City University of New York in New York, New York.

CA: In a review of The Cycles of American History *for* New Leader, *Barry Gewen called you "our foremost example of the historian engage. . . ." Were you early on as interested in a public career as you were in an academic one?*

SCHLESINGER: I grew up in the 1930s, and I was a strong supporter of Franklin Roosevelt and the New Deal. Three years after I graduated from college came Pearl Harbor, and my generation went to war. Six years after graduation I was in the European Theater of Operations. So I was always involved. My father before me had a strong interest in politics, though he wasn't as much of an activist as I have been. I've always enjoyed politics; it's the most entertaining diversion in a democracy. And I guess I have always felt that, from the point of view of the historian, participation in events, although it generates problems, also bestows benefits.

CA: Because your scholarship and writing have centered largely on the twentieth century, and often on current events, obviously the public and private work are mutually enriching. Do you feel historians dealing with earlier periods can also gain perspective by working outside academia?

SCHLESINGER: As Edward Gibbon famously said in his autobiography, talking about his military service, "The captain of the Hampshire grenadiers . . . has not been useless to the historian of the Roman Empire." I think experience in the practicalities of life and the fortuities of decision is useful for the historian, whether he's writing about recent history or trying to reconstruct the remote past.

CA: You've credited both of your parents for inspiration as historians and political activists. Were there writers outside the field of history, strictly speaking, who served in some way as models? You often quote Emerson, Whitman, and many other writers.

SCHLESINGER: I believe that there have been a lot of wise men and women in the past who've written things that interest one or that help in making the choices one has to make in one's own life. I've learned a lot from them. Emerson, Tocqueville, William James, Reinhold Niebuhr—all very wise fellows.

CA: Your writing style has been called graceful, elegant, lively; and you began winning awards for it with a Pulitzer for The Age of Jackson, *published in 1945. Apart from the research, the knowledge of history, and the development of ideas, how did you acquire the writing skills that were evident so early in your work?*

SCHLESINGER: I learned a great deal when I was in college from a composition course I took with the writer and historian Bernard De Voto. He later became editor of the *Saturday Review* and he wrote "The Easy Chair" for *Harper's* for many years; he was a prolific writer and a very good historian. For some years at Harvard he gave an advanced course in composition. He was a merciless critic. You would write a paper for him, and it would come back with savage, insulting remarks. His general technique was to goad his students into an awareness of the falsity and excess in their writing, and the obscurity of thought that lies behind muddiness of expression. I learned a lot in that course, and I've been a great champion ever since of courses in English composition.

CA: I remember very well the eagerness with which people awaited and finally began to read A Thousand Days: John F. Kennedy in the White House, *and I recall the controversy that the book provoked. What I've always wondered about is the emotional difficulty that must have been involved for you in writing it so soon after Kennedy's death.*

SCHLESINGER: I suppose it was also a kind of emotional release, because one has a lot of pent-up feelings, memories, and it's helpful to set them all down.

CA: You began it so soon after Kennedy's death.

SCHLESINGER: Yes, I began it in the early spring of 1964.

CA: With the advantage of hindsight, is there anything you'd do differently in A Thousand Days *if you had the chance?*

SCHLESINGER: In fact, I did have the chance for second thoughts. In the subsequent book *Robert Kennedy and His Times* I was able to amplify and in some cases to correct, or at least fill out, the account of some of the things in *A Thousand Days.* When I wrote the book on Robert Kennedy, more information had come out about a number of things, I had learned more myself, and things that for various reasons I had felt I couldn't write in 1965 I was quite prepared to write in 1978. On things like the Cuban missile crisis, for example, or the counter-insurgency mania, or the assassination attempts on Fidel Castro, or the civil rights struggle, there are more details and fuller accounts in *Robert Kennedy and His Times* than in *A Thousand Days.*

CA: Do you think the Kennedys have gotten more than a usual share of bad press?

SCHLESINGER: It's a predictable thing. In the period fifteen to twenty years after a president dies, his reputation goes into eclipse. When I went to college in the 1930s, for example, the reputations of both Theodore Roosevelt, who died in 1919, and Woodrow Wilson, who died in 1924, were at a rather low ebb. Theodore Roosevelt was regarded as an adolescent braggart and Woodrow Wilson as a Presbyterian fanatic. Both their reputations have come back a great deal. When I wrote the first volume of *The Age of Roosevelt* in the 1950s, FDR's reputation was down. Of course now even the Republicans agree that he was an extraordinary president. I think JFK is in that same position now that FDR was in the '50s and Theodore Roosevelt and Woodrow Wilson were in the '30s. After a president has made a great impression, there comes a time of let-down and revisionism. People look back and say, ''What was so great about him?'' But I'm sure in the 1990s Kennedy's reputation will have a great revival.

CA: The Age of Roosevelt is your largest work and still growing. How did Franklin Delano Roosevelt capture your interest so fully as to become the subject of almost a life's work?

SCHLESINGER: I suppose it was growing up as I did in the 1930s. I came out of college in the Depression and I was in the war. At the time I was growing up, for many years Roosevelt was the only president we knew, because he was president much longer than anybody else. He was a very dominating and exciting figure when I was young.

In the early 1940s I was working on a book that eventually became *The Age of Jackson.* Working on that book, I read James Parton's famous biography of Jackson. Parton was a talented journalist who began his biography a few years after Jackson died. He interviewed all sorts of people who had known Jackson and in that way rescued for posterity comments and information that otherwise would have died with his sources. It seemed to me that it would be interesting to try to do the same kind of thing about Roosevelt, to talk to people who worked with him and were in the New Deal and get their testimony, as Parton had gotten the testimony of the people who had worked with Jackson. That was one of my original incentives for starting the biography.

CA: Did you envision it as such a large set of books from the start?

SCHLESINGER: I certainly envisaged it as a multi-volume work. Three volumes are out and I'm working on the fourth. The third volume was published in 1960, which was a hell of a long time ago. My scheme required me to deal in the fourth volume with foreign affairs of the 1930s, and at that point a lot of the papers were still classified and closed. In the years since, nearly everything through the Second World War has been declassified in both Britain and the United States, so I've completed my research at least up to Pearl Harbor.

CA: Do you ever get tired of Roosevelt during the writing?

SCHLESINGER: No. Certainly those days were a good deal better than these.

CA: Without meaning to imply that characterization and plot are wasted in the writing of biography and history, I wonder if you've ever been tempted to try your hand at fiction?

SCHLESINGER: I've been tempted, but I've never had time. I still hope to do it. If John Kenneth Galbraith and William F. Buckley, Jr., can write novels, I feel I can too!

CA: For The Cycles of American History, *you did extensive revisions on most of the essays that had been previously published. What prompted the revisions—changes in your thinking, a wish to incorporate events that occurred after the first writing, other factors?*

SCHLESINGER: Some of it was stylistic, some of it was updating and some of it was the incorporation of new materials, new thoughts, the development of ideas. And some of it was to eliminate repetition.

CA: Did you find that any of your ideas had changed?

SCHLESINGER: No, but in some cases ideas mature and develop. And in some cases I had carried ideas further in my own thoughts than I had when I wrote the original pieces.

CA: Your cyclical theory holds that the political climate swings with fairly predictable regularity between what you've called public purpose and private interest, with the Presidency reflecting the current mood. Would you comment on the current Presidential campaign from this point of view?

SCHLESINGER: I think a new phase in the cycle is impending. It's a little early, but the tide is beginning to turn. However, that change won't come full flood until the 1990s. Nineteen-eighty-eight is rather as if Kennedy were running against Nixon in 1958 rather than in 1960. I would expect the election in 1988 to be a squeaker. Its outcome probably will depend on the state of the economy. But whatever its outcome, Reaganism per se is finished, because Vice-President Bush is not a true-blue, bottled-in-bond Reaganite. Nor was Senator Dole, his chief opponent. Even within the Republican Party, the true-blue Reaganite contenders—Kemp, Robertson, Du Pont—did rather badly.

The nineties will be a much more liberal period. It seems that there is a discernible rhythm in our politics. We enter cycles where private interest seems the best way of dealing with our problems—conservative cycles. Then these phases run their natural course, and we enter periods where public purpose seems the best way of dealing with our problems. Its a thirty-year cycle. In that sense the Reagan 1980s are a replay of the Eisenhower 1950s, as the 1950s were a replay of the Harding and Coolidge and Hoover 1920s. In the same way we have at thirty-year intervals Theodore Roosevelt in 1901 and Franklin Roosevelt in '33 and John Kennedy in '61. If the rhythm holds, the nineties should be a time of innovation, idealism, and reform comparable to the Progressive period and the period of the New Deal and the period of the New Frontier and the Great Society.

There's no mystery about the thirty-year period. That's the span of a generation. Generations tend to be formed politically by the ideals that are dominant when they come of age politically: between the ages of sixteen and twenty-five. Thirty years later, when their turn in power comes, they tend to carry forward the ideals they imbibed when they were young.

CA: Do you think liberalism in this country has retained its intellectual underpinnings? Some writers feel otherwise.

SCHLESINGER: Of course it has. The conventional dismissal of liberalism blames liberals for everything that has gone wrong in this country for the last twenty years. In fact, we have not had a liberal administration in Washington since the Great Society vanished into the Vietnam quagmire in 1966. Nixon a liberal? Ford a liberal? Carter—the most conservative Democratic president since Grover Cleveland and almost as assiduous a critic of affirmative government as Reagan himself—a liberal? Reagan a liberal? We have not had liberal government in Washington for nearly a quarter of a century. The real question is whether, after twenty years of conservative government, conservatism retains any intellectual underpinnings.

The great distinction between conservatism and liberalism in contemporary America lies in the attitude toward government. The conservative regards government as the root of all evil. The liberal regards government as one of the means by which a free people meets its problems and promotes the general welfare. The Reagan experience is decisive refutation of the theory that, if we turn all our social and economic and human problems over to the deregulated marketplace, these problems will solve themselves. Very few of the troubles that assail American society today can be mitigated without affirmative government.

CA: Do you see the nature and function of the primaries changing in ways that may affect future Presidential campaigns?

SCHLESINGER: In its weird way the primary process has not worked badly. Through all this we've gotten to know the candidates pretty well. Six months ago they were a bunch of names. Now we know their faces, we know what they're like, we know their general direction of policy. The primary is also good for the candidates. It is not only a means of introducing the candidates to the country; it's a means of introducing the country to the candidates. Dukakis began by knowing mainly the Northeast, Simon the Middle West, Gore the South, and Dole Kansas. They've all had to go around the country and acquaint themselves much more than they had before with the great diversity of people and problems in the United States.

The great trouble with the primaries is that there are too many and that they go on too long. There's a fatigue factor; it's a grinding process. By the time the two survivors are ready for the general election, they're going to be exhausted men. Then after that one of them has four years of real responsibility as president. Woodrow Wilson said in 1908, talking about the way the whole process of presidential selection was developing, that it looked as if our future presidents would have to consist of "a race of wise and prudent athletes."

CA: History as a subject worthy of study took quite a beating in the 1960s and early seventies, as you and many other people have commented in print. What is the situation now for history on the university level?

SCHLESINGER: I think there has been some revival. Enrollment in history as a field of undergraduate concentration has increased. For graduate students, there's still a problem in the job market because many universities overhired faculty as they overbuilt plant in the 1960s, not realizing that the baby boom was coming to an end. But many people hired in the 1960s are now retiring, and I think the job market will improve.

I hope that these signs indicate a revival of interest in history, because I think history is to a nation the way memory is to an individual. Just as an individual deprived of memory becomes disoriented and doesn't know where he's going or what he's doing, so a nation that has forgotten its history may become disoriented. So I think history is very important.

CA: It's hard to understand why more students don't find history interesting. I wonder if that's partly due to the way it's sometimes taught on the lower levels.

SCHLESINGER: That may be a factor. Another factor may be that the speed of change means that history seems less related to students' lives and needs. The past becomes past much more quickly.

CA: As a teacher, what do you feel is the best thing you can give your students?

SCHLESINGER: It's been many years since I've taught undergraduates. I do my best to instill in my graduate students a sense of what history is about and the obligations and responsibilities of a historian. One thing I wish teachers would do is to teach students how to speak and write the English language. I think these true-false examinations, for example, are a great mistake. Often the only way people know what they think is when they are forced to write it down. There's not nearly enough writing in our schools in the lower grades.

CA: What do you consider the chief obligations and responsibilities of the historian to be?

SCHLESINGER: The aim of the historian is to reconstruct the past—and to do so according to its own pattern, not according to ours. All epochs, said Ranke, are equally close to God. But historians, try hard as they can to escape, remain prisoners of their own epoch and of their own experience. The historian's professional obligation is to do his best to transcend the present. He can never quite succeed. But he must resist the temptation to manipulate the past to suit the needs and prejudices of the present.

CA: What are your greatest concerns for the country?

SCHLESINGER: I think the greatest concern that everyone should have is the nuclear arms race. Beyond that, I feel there's always been, as was remarked by Tocqueville and others, an American obsession with the making of money. We go through these periodic times where private interest, private action, private enterprise seem to be the solution to everything. The ethos of greed dominates. The notion is that everyone making a fast buck for himself best promotes the general welfare. I think that can be carried a little far, and I think it has been carried a little far in these last years.

CA: The Age of Roosevelt goes on, and what else in your private or public work that you'd like to talk about?

SCHLESINGER: I'm now seventy years old, and I want to concentrate in the years that remain on writing some books.

CA: No temptation to get back into active politics?

SCHLESINGER: No. I very much hope that we'll get some good people in the White House and elsewhere, and I'll be glad to help, but, at the end of the day, I remain a historian and writer.

BIOGRAPHICAL/CRITICAL SOURCES:

BOOKS

Authors in the News, Volume 1, Gale, 1976.
Brandon, Henry, *Conversations with Henry Brandon,* Deutsch, 1966.
Cunliffe, Marcus, and Robin W. Winks, editors, *Pastmasters: Some Essays on American Historians,* Harper, 1969.
Dictionary of Literary Biography, Volume 17: *Twentieth-Century American Historians,* Gale, 1983.
Fitzgerald, Carol B., editor, *American History: A Bibliographic Review,* Volume 1, Meckler, 1985.
Garraty, John A., *Interpreting American History: Conversations with American Historians,* Macmillan, 1970.
Heller, Deane, and David Heller, *Kennedy Cabinet,* Monarch, 1961.
Ross, Mitchell S., *The Literary Politicians,* Doubleday, 1978.
Schlesinger, Arthur Meier, Sr., *In Retrospect: The History of a Historian,* Harcourt, 1963.

PERIODICALS

Akron Beacon Journal, December 30, 1973.
American Heritage, October, 1978.
American Historical Review, January, 1940, April, 1946, October, 1957, October, 1959, April, 1961.
Esquire, September 26, 1978.
Globe and Mail (Toronto), March 7, 1987.
Harper's, September, 1978.

Life, July 16, 1965.
Los Angeles Times, March 22, 1979.
Los Angeles Times Book Review, October 26, 1986.
Nation, July 22, 1939, October 20, 1945, March 23, 1957, January 31, 1959, November 12, 1960, August 6, 1977, August 20, 1977, September 30, 1978.
National Review, October 27, 1978.
New Leader, May 8, 1967, November 17, 1986.
New Republic, June 7, 1939, October 22, 1945, March 4, 1957, October 27, 1958, November 10, 1958, January 12, 1959, September 26, 1960, December 4, 1965, February 11, 1967, September 9, 1978, December 1, 1986.
New Statesman, August 17, 1957, May 26, 1961, November 10, 1978.
Newsweek, November 19, 1973, September 4, 1978, October 27, 1986.
New Yorker, September 15, 1945, March 16, 1957, September 10, 1960, December 11, 1965, December 10, 1973, November 17, 1986.
New York Herald Tribune Book Review, September 11, 1960.
New York Review of Books, January 6, 1966, February 23, 1967, December 13, 1973, October 12, 1978, November 6, 1986.
New York Times, April 23, 1939, September 16, 1945, March 3, 1957, January 4, 1959, November 24, 1965, January 16, 1967, October 31, 1985, November 13, 1986, April 14, 1988.
New York Times Book Review, January 4, 1959, April 7, 1963, November 28, 1965, April 9, 1967, June 4, 1967, June 22, 1969, November 18, 1973, January 7, 1979, November 16, 1986.
Playboy, May, 1966.
Saturday Review, March 2, 1957, December 4, 1965, February 4, 1967, September 18, 1971.
Time, March 11, 1957, January 19, 1959, December 17, 1965, November 26, 1973, September 4, 1978, December 1, 1986.
Times Literary Supplement, November 25, 1965, January 26, 1967, November 30, 1973, November 10, 1978, March 13, 1987.
Tribune Books (Chicago), November 2, 1986.
Village Voice, December 20, 1973, September 11, 1978.
Wall Street Journal, September 8, 1978.
Washington Post, February 18, 1970.
Washington Post Book World, December 14, 1986.

OTHER

Schlesinger, Arthur M., Jr., "A Conversation with Arthur M. Schlesinger, Jr." (recording), Center for Cassette Studies, 1975.

—*Sketch by Kenneth R. Shepherd*

—*Interview by Jean W. Ross*

*   *   *

SCHLESINGER, Stephen C(annon) 1942-

PERSONAL: Born August 17, 1942, in Boston, Mass.; son of Arthur Meier, Jr., (a professor of history and writer) and Marian (a painter; maiden name, Cannon) Schlesinger; married Judith Elster, 1984. *Education:* Harvard University, A.B. (cum laude), 1964, LL.B., J.D.; Cambridge University, certificate of one year study, 1965. *Politics:* Democrat. *Religion:* Unitarian.

ADDRESSES: Home—224 Riverside Dr., Apt. 7C, New York, N.Y. 10025. *Agent*—Mort Janklow, Janklow Associates, 598 Madison Ave., New York, N.Y. 10022.

CAREER: Urban Development Corporation, New York, N.Y., special assistant to chief executive officer, 1968-69; *The New Democrat*, New York, N.Y., editor and publisher, 1969-72; free-lance writer, 1973-74; *Time* Magazine, New York, N.Y., writer for "Press" and "National Affairs" section, 1974-78. Speech writer for Senator George McGovern, Democratic Presidential campaign, 1972; deputy director of issues for Senator Edward Kennedy, Democratic Presidential Campaign, 1980; special assistant to Governor Cuomo, New York State, 1983—. Teaching fellow in English, Harvard University, 1967-68; adjunct faculty member, New School for Social Research, 1976-77. Member of board of directors, Center for Democratic Policy.

AWARDS, HONORS: National Magazine Award nominee, 1978.

WRITINGS:

The New Reformers, Houghton, 1975.
(With Stephen Kinzer) *Bitter Fruit: The Untold Story of the American Coup in Guatemala*, Doubleday, 1982.

Contributor of articles to periodicals, including *Atlantic Monthly, Nation, Saturday Review,* and *Village Voice.*

SIDELIGHTS: Stephen C. Schlesinger and Stephen Kinzer's *Bitter Fruit: The Untold Story of the American Coup in Guatemala* examines the way in which collaboration between governments and big businesses can interfere in world politics. Using classified documents obtained by means of the Freedom of Information Act, the authors show how in 1954 the CIA and the Department of State conspired with the American-owned United Fruit Company to oust Guatemalan President Jacobo Arbenz Guzman, a democratically elected leader whose land reforms threatened the fruit company's interests. To justify its intervention the U.S. government took advantage of anti-communist hysteria, charging that Arbenz was communistically inclined.

Reviewers celebrate *Bitter Fruit* not only for its implied criticism of present U.S. policy in Latin America, but also for its well-documented investigation and its thriller-like atmosphere. Piero Gleijeses, reviewing the book for the *Washington Post Book World*, states that "the plot [the authors] uncover is full of cloak-and-dagger incidents—all well documented, with the CIA in the leading role—fully justifying the publisher's claim in its publicity material that the book will appeal not only to scholars and students of Latin America, but also to 'espionage fans.'" "Given current events," adds Jim Miller in *Newsweek*, "it also reads like a very timely warning of what can happen when America abuses its power."

BIOGRAPHICAL/CRITICAL SOURCES:

PERIODICALS

Chicago Tribune Book World, August 15, 1982.
Newsweek, March 29, 1982.
New York Times, March 7, 1982.
Times Literary Supplement, December 17, 1982.
Washington Post Book World, February 21, 1982.

*   *   *

SCHMIDT, Jerry A(rthur) 1945-

PERSONAL: Born May 9, 1945, in Jamestown, N.D.; son of Arthur (a vocational evaluator) and Marvel (Hust) Schmidt; married Karen Lambert (an elementary school teacher), May 31, 1967; children: Cory, Ryan. *Education:* Westmar College, B.A., 1967; Iliff School of Theology, M.Div., 1970; University of Nebraska, Ph.D., 1972.

ADDRESSES: Home—Lakewood, Colo.

CAREER: University of Denver, Denver, Colo., assistant professor of counselor education, 1972—; psychologist for Family Enrichment Foundation, Denver, 1975—.

MEMBER: American Psychological Association, Association for the Advancement of Behavior Therapy.

WRITINGS:

Help Yourself: A Guide to Self-Change, Research Press (Champaign, Ill.), 1976.
You Can Help Yourself, Harvest House Publishers (Eugene, Ore.), 1978, published as *New Beginnings: Gaining Control of Your Life*, 1982.
(With Raymond Brock) *The Emotions of a Man*, Harvest House Publishers, 1983.
Do You Hear What You're Thinking?, Victor Books, 1983.

Contributor to guidance journals.

WORK IN PROGRESS: Survival Skills for Secondary School Counselors; A Behavioral Counseling Workshop.

SIDELIGHTS: Jerry A. Schmidt comments: "My primary interest is preventive work in mental health. More specifically, giving laypersons practical interpersonal and intrapsychic skills, so that these life skills may be used throughout the life cycle. Anxiety management, rational self-talk, assertiveness, human potential and marriage and family life are my basic interests."

*   *   *

SCHOENBAUM, S(amuel) 1927-

PERSONAL: Born March 6, 1927, in New York, N.Y.; son of Abraham (a shopkeeper) and Sarah (Altschuler) Schoenbaum; married Marilyn Turk, June 10, 1946. *Education:* Brooklyn College (now of the City University of New York), B.A., 1947; Columbia University, M.A., 1949, Ph.D., 1953.

ADDRESSES: Home—613 Constitution Ave. N.E., Washington, D.C. 20002. *Office*—Department of English, University of Maryland, College Park, Md. 20742.

CAREER: Northwestern University, Evanston, Ill., 1953-71, began as instructor, became professor of English literature, Franklyn Bliss Snyder Professor, 1971-75; Queens College of the City University of New York, Flushing, N.Y., Distinguished Professor of English, 1975-76; University of Maryland, College Park, Distinguished Professor of Renaissance Literature, 1976—, director of Center for Renaissance and Baroque Studies. Member of Advisory Council of American Trust for the British Library. Trustee emeritus of Folger Shakespeare Library.

MEMBER: Shakespeare Association of America (member of board of trustees, 1976-79; president, 1980-81).

AWARDS, HONORS: Guggenheim fellowship, 1956-57, 1969-70; Huntington Library Grant, 1959 and 1967; Newberry Library Grant, 1968; award for nonfiction from Friends of Literature, 1970, for *Shakespeare's Lives;* named senior fellow of National Endowment for the Humanities, 1973-74.

WRITINGS:

Middleton's Tragedies: A Critical Study, Columbia University Press, 1955, reprinted, Gordian Press, 1970.

(Preparer) *The Bloody Banquet, 1639*, Oxford University Press for the Malone Society, 1961, reprinted, AMS Press, 1988.

(Editor of revised edition) Alfred Harbage, *Annals of English Drama, 975-1700: An Analytical Record of All Plays, Extant or Lost, Chronologically Arranged and Indexed by Authors, Titles, Dramatic Companies, Etc.*, University of Pennsylvania Press, 1964, with supplements published by Northwestern University Press, 1966 and 1970.

(Editor) *Renaissance Drama* (the annual report of the Modern Language Association Conference on Research Opportunities in Renaissance Drama), Northwestern University Press, Number 7, 1964, Number 8, 1965, Number 9, 1966.

As You Like It: An Outline-Guide to the Play, Barnes & Noble, 1965, adapted version by Barnes & Noble staff published as *William Shakespeare: As You Like It*, 1967.

Internal Evidence and Elizabethan Dramatic Authorship: An Essay in Literary History and Method, Northwestern University Press, 1966.

(Editor) *The Famous History of the Life of King Henry the Eighth*, New American Library, 1967.

(Editor) *Renaissance Drama*, New Series, Northwestern University Press, Volume 1: *Essays Principally on Masques and Entertainments*, 1968; Volume 2: *Essays Principally on Dramatic Theory and Form*, 1969; Volume 3: *Essays Principally on Drama in its Intellectual Context*, 1970; (with Alan Dessen) Volume 4: *Essays Principally on the Playhouse and Staging*, 1971; (with Dessen) Volume 5: *Essays Principally on Comedy*, 1972; (with Dessen) Volume 6: *Essays on Dramatic Antecedents*, 1973, Books on Demand, 1988; (with Joel H. Kaplan) Volume 7: *Drama and the Other Arts*, 1977.

Shakespeare's Lives, Oxford University Press, 1970.

(With Kenneth Muir) *A New Companion to Shakespeare Studies*, Cambridge University Press, 1971.

William Shakespeare: A Documentary Life, Oxford University Press (New York), 1975, abridged edition published as *William Shakespeare: A Compact Documentary Life*, 1977, revised edition, 1987.

William Shakespeare: The Globe and the World, Oxford University Press, 1979.

(Editor with C. Walter Hodges and Leonard Leone) *The Third Globe: Symposium for the Reconstruction of the Globe Playhouse*, Wayne State University Press, 1979.

William Shakespeare: Records and Images, Oxford University Press, 1981.

Shakespeare and Others, Folger Books, 1985.

(Editor with Stanley Wells and Gary Taylor) *William Shakespeare: The Complete Works*, Oxford University Press, 1987.

Macbeth Critical Essays, Garland Publishing, 1988.

Contributor to journals, including *Smithsonian, Times Literary Supplement, New York Review of Books, New York Times Book Review*, and *Washington Post Book World*. Member of executive board, *Shakespeare Quarterly*, 1977—, and *Studies in English Literature*, 1979—. Member of editorial committee, *Themes in Drama*, 1978, and *Hamlet Studies*, 1979.

WORK IN PROGRESS: William Shakespeare: A Critical Life, Oxford University Press.

SIDELIGHTS: S. Schoenbaum is one of the world's eminent twentieth-century Shakespeare scholars. *Times Literary Supplement*'s Stephen Orgel called Schoenbaums's *William Shakespeare: Records and Images* "a lucid, judicious and good-natured guide." He also noted that a companion volume, *William Shakespeare: A Documentary Life*, "is the place to go for anyone interested in the facts of Shakespeare's career." Schoenbaum's other writings include *Shakespeare's Lives*, an analytic and frequently humorous account of Shakespeare's other biographers and their work. A reviewer for the *New York Times* observes that it "will be a seminal book for most of us, for there are enough hints, suggestions and endorsements for future reading to last a lifetime."

Equally pleasant and informative, says Robert Giroux in the *Washington Post Book World*, is *Shakespeare and Others*, a collected of Schoenbaum's shorter prose representing twenty-five years of the distinguished professor's published comments. He introduces himself to readers as "a journal-wearied professional Shakespearian," but this condition does not prevent him "from writing with grace, wit and common sense," notes Giroux. "Schoenbaum's article of faith that 'scholarship and criticism should be fun for the practitioner' is amply demonstrated" in the book, Giroux concludes. Schoenbaum once told *CA*: "My aim has always been to appeal to as wide a non-specialist audience as possible, without compromising scholarly standards and without making complex issues seem any simpler than they are. I have lectured widely in nine countries, and written on film and cooking as well as on Shakespeare and Elizabethan matters."

AVOCATIONAL INTERESTS: Travel, theater, cinema, food, wines.

BIOGRAPHICAL/CRITICAL SOURCES:

BOOKS

Schoenbaum, S., *Shakespeare and Others*, Folger Books, 1985.

PERIODICALS

Atlantic, November, 1970, July, 1975, August, 1975.
Book World, October 8, 1978, November 11, 1979.
Los Angeles Times Book Review, March 15, 1987.
New York Times, December 24, 1970, May 20, 1975.
New York Times Book Review, April 13, 1975, June 1, 1975, May 22, 1977, November 25, 1979.
Observer Review, February 14, 1971.
Saturday Review, November 7, 1970.
Times Literary Supplement, January 22, 1971, April 18, 1975, May 12, 1978, May 23, 1980, May 23, 1982.
Washington Post Book World, May 17, 1981, November 24, 1985.

*   *   *

SCHUBERT, Dieter   1947-

PERSONAL: Born July 15, 1947, in Oschersleben, West Germany; son of Erich (a locksmith) and Elfriede (Boettcher) Schubert; married Ingrid Gabrys (an illustrator), November 5, 1976; children: Hannah. *Education:* Received degree from Muenster Academy of Design, 1975; graduate study at Duesseldorf Academy of Art, 1975-76, University of Muenster, 1975-77, and Gerrit Rietveld Academy (Amsterdam), 1977-80.

ADDRESSES: Home and office—Reigerweg 12, 1027 HC Amsterdam, Netherlands.

CAREER: Tengelmann Wholesale Trade, Hamm, West Germany, merchant, 1963-71; Academy of Restoration, Amsterdam, Netherlands, teacher, 1980—. Teacher at art expression workshop in Amsterdam, 1982—.

WRITINGS:

AUTHOR AND ILLUSTRATOR WITH WIFE, INGRID SCHUBERT-GABRYS; JUVENILES

There's a Crocodile under My Bed, Lemniscaat, 1980.
The Magic Bubble Trip, Lemniscaat, 1981, Kane Miller Book, 1985.
Who's a Sissy, Lemniscaat, 1983.
Funny Reading, Schroedelverlag, 1984.
Little Bigfeet, Lemniscaat, 1985.
Look at My Letter, Jacob Dijkstra, 1988.
The Monsterbook, Lemniscaat, 1989.

OTHER

(And illustrator) *Jack in the Boat*, Lemniscaat, 1982.
(And illustrator) *Where's My Monkey*, Lemniscaat, 1986.

Also author, with Schubert-Gabrys, of teleplays ''Look at Me'' and ''Who's Coming to My Little House?,'' both broadcast by Dutch School Television, 1982.

WORK IN PROGRESS: A book about Santa Claus/Father Christmas, with Schubert-Gabrys, for Lemniscaat.

SIDELIGHTS: Dieter Schubert told *CA:* ''While in Germany and Holland I studied painting, drawing, and 'free' graphics. During my study, I happened to get in touch with Piet Klaasse, a very famous illustrator in Holland, who at that time was a teacher at the Gerrit Rietveld Academy. At the start of my studies I had been preoccupied with illustrating stories for quite some time and, inspired by Piet Klaasse, I started to spend more time on illustration.

''Although I started illustrating adult literature (Kafka), I soon began illustrating for children. I later preferred illustrating for very small children because I find them very fascinating in their thoughts and adventures. What is more, by making up stories and illustrating them, one's own feelings from childhood come back again, and I take pleasure in that.

''My wife Ingrid (an illustrator as well) and I started to write and illustrate our own stories. In 1979 we contacted the publishing firm Lemniscaat who liked our first idea for a book. They made our first international contact at the Frankfurt Book Fair. In 1980 that first book, *There's a Crocodile under My Bed,* was translated into eleven languages and published in fourteen countries. In 1981 reprints appeared in three countries. Since then, a new book of ours has been published internationally each year.''

*   *   *

SCHUBERT-GABRYS, Ingrid   1953-

PERSONAL: Born March 29, 1953, in Essen, West Germany; daughter of Oswald (a landlord) and Maria (a landlady; maiden name, Smeets) Gabrys; married Dieter Schubert (an illustrator), November 5, 1976; children: Hannah. *Education:* Received degree from Muenster Academy of Design, 1976; graduate study at Duesseldorf Academy of Art, 1976-77, University of Muenster, 1976-77, and Gerrit Rietveld Academy (Amsterdam), 1977-80.

ADDRESSES: Home and office—Reigerweg 12, 1027 HC Amsterdam, Netherlands.

CAREER: Gabrys, Borken, West Germany, merchant, 1968-70; worked as a potter in Stadtlohn, West Germany, 1970-71; teacher in educational play-group for children in Muenster, West Germany, 1976-77; teacher at art expression workshop in Amsterdam, Netherlands, 1981—.

WRITINGS:

AUTHOR AND ILLUSTRATOR WITH HUSBAND, DIETER SCHUBERT; JUVENILES

There's a Crocodile under My Bed, Lemniscaat, 1980.
The Magic Bubble Trip, Lemniscaat, 1981, Kane Miller Book, 1985.
Who's a Sissy, Lemniscaat, 1983.
Funny Reading, Schroedelverlag, 1984.
Little Bigfeet, Lemniscaat, 1985.
Look at My Letter, Jacob Dijkstra, 1988.
The Monsterbook, Lemniscaat, 1989.

OTHER

Also author, with Schubert, of teleplays ''Look at Me'' and ''Who's Coming to My Little House?,'' both broadcast by Dutch School Television, 1982.

WORK IN PROGRESS: A book about Santa Claus/Father Christmas, with Schubert, for Lemniscaat.

SIDELIGHTS: Ingrid Schubert-Gabrys told *CA:* ''In 1978 my teacher at the Gerrit Rietveld Academy inspired and encouraged me to illustrate children's books. My first commission was for illustrating a children's book by author Roald Dahl. From that moment my interest in children's literature grew. My husband, Dieter Schubert, also an illustrator, and I started to write and illustrate our own stories. In 1979 we contacted the publisher Lemniscaat, and they liked our first idea for a book. That first story, *There's a Crocodile under My Bed*, was later translated into eleven languages and published in fourteen countries.''

*   *   *

SCHULLER, Gunther   1925-

PERSONAL: Born November 22, 1925, in New York, N.Y.; son of Arthur E. and Elsie (Bernartz) Schuller; married Marjorie Black, June 8, 1948; children: Edwin Gunther, George Alexander.

CAREER: Composer, conductor, and educator. Appeared as a boy soprano in the St. Thomas Church Choir at age twelve. New York Philharmonic Orchestra, New York City, played French horn under Arturo Toscanini, 1942; played French horn in Ballet Theatre Orchestra under Antal Dorati, 1943; Cincinnati Symphony Orchestra, Cincinnati, Ohio, principal French horn, 1943-45; Metropolitan Opera Orchestra, New York City, principal French horn, 1945-59; musical composer, 1959-67; New England Conservatory of Music, Boston, Mass., president, 1966-77, presented the conservatory's ''Ragtime Ensemble,'' 1972; Margun Music Inc. (a publishing firm), Newton Centre, Mass., founder and editor, 1975—.

Played French horn in the Miles Davis Monet, 1950. Teacher at Manhattan School of Music, 1950-63; music director of First International Jazz Festival, Washington, D.C., 1962;

Berkshire Music Center, acting head of composition department, 1963-65, head of department, 1965-69, artistic co-director of Tanglewood, 1969-72, artistic director, 1972-84; music director of Spokane Symphony, 1985-86; artistic director of Festival at Sandpoint, 1985—. Associate professor at Yale University, 1964-67. Organized and conducted "Twentieth Century Innovations," a concert series for Carnegie Hall Corporation, 1963-65. Host of "Changing Music," a series on WGBH-Television, 1973; broadcaster of "Contemporary Music in Evolution," a weekly series on WBAI-Radio. Has made guest appearances as conductor of numerous symphony orchestras in the United States, Canada, and Europe, including New York Philharmonic, British Broadcasting Corporation Symphony, Philharmonic Orchestra of London, French Radio Orchestra, Symphony Orchestra of Bavarian Radio, Berlin Philharmonic, and Tonhalle Orchestra of Zurich.

MEMBER: National Institute of Arts and Letters.

AWARDS, HONORS: National Institute of Arts and Letters award, 1960; Creative Arts Award, Brandeis University, 1960; Guggenheim grants, 1962, 1963; Darius Milhaud Award, 1964, for film score of Polish film "Yesterday in Fact"; D. Mus., Northeastern University, 1967, University of Illinois, 1968, Colby College, 1969, Williams College, 1975, Cleveland Institute of Music, 1977, New England Conservatory of Music, 1978, Rutgers University, 1980, and Manhattan School of Music, 1987; Deems Taylor Award, American Society of Composers, Authors, and Publishers, 1969, for *Early Jazz: Its Roots and Musical Development;* Alice M. Ditson Conducting Award, Columbia University, 1970; Rodgers and Hammerstein Award, 1971; Grammy Award for Chamber Music, National Academy of Recording Arts, 1973, for recording "Scott Joplin: The Red Back Book"; Friedheim Kennedy Center Award, 1988.

WRITINGS:

Horn Technique, Oxford University Press, 1962.
Early Jazz: Its Roots and Musical Development, Oxford University Press, 1968, reprinted, 1986.
(Editor) *Horn Passages in Symphonies of Franz Josef Haydn: A Compendium of All Difficult Exposed Excerpts from All of Haydn's Symphonies,* compiled by Thomas C. Haunton, Margun Music, 1980.
Musings: The Musical Worlds of Gunther Schuller, Oxford University Press, 1986.
(Editor with Martin Williams) *Big Band Jazz: From the Beginnings to the Fifties* (includes six albums or six cassettes), University of Illinois Press, 1986.
The Swing Era: The Development of Jazz, 1933-1945, Oxford University Press, 1988.

MUSICAL COMPOSITIONS

"Variants: A Jazz Ballet" (for jazz quartet and orchestra; choreographed by George Balanchine), first produced in New York, January 4, 1961.
"The Visitation" (opera in three acts; adaptation of Franz Kafka's novel *The Trial*), first produced in Hamburg, West Germany, by Hamburg State Opera, October, 1966.
"The Fisherman and His Wife" (children's opera in one act; adaptation of Grimm fairy tale; libretto by John Updike), first produced in Boston, Mass., May 7, 1970.

Also composer of music for jazz ensembles, including "Journey into Jazz," 1962, "Densities No. 1," 1963, chamber music, including "Movements," 1961, "Tre Invenzioni" 1972, and music for jazz and classical orchestras. Schuller's "Rag-

time Ensemble" at the New England Conservatory of Music has been recorded on "Scott Joplin: The Red Back Book," for Angel Records, and on "Rags to Jazz," for Golden Crest Records.

SIDELIGHTS: In her *New York Times Book Review* assessment of Gunther Schuller's *Musings: The Musical Worlds of Gunther Schuller,* Carol J. Oja speaks admiringly of this American composer and his crusading spirit: "Whether or not . . . Schuller was born to be a crusader, his life has been devoted to many causes, all working toward a common purpose—opening the ears and minds of Americans to the music of their time and land. By definition, it seems, an American composer has to be a fighter. But few have struggled on so many fronts so ceaselessly; Mr. Schuller not only promotes his own music and that of composer colleagues but embraces jazz with open arms and subscribes to what he terms 'a global view of music.'" In support of Oja's claims, in the 1950s Schuller popularized a new musical movement called "third stream" as a means of overcoming stereotypes. This movement blends the rhythms and improvisation of jazz with the more traditional techniques of Western music. It was during this time that Schuller worked closely with John Lewis of the Modern Jazz Quartet. Then, in 1972 Schuller played an integral role in the revival of ragtime when he formed the Ragtime Ensemble at the New England Conservatory of Music. More recently Schuller founded Margun Music publishing company, whose motto is "all musics are created equal." In accord with Schuller's earlier endeavors, Margun Music is "devoted to category busting," notes Oja.

A significant part of Schuller's reaching out to the "ears and minds of Americans" has come by way of his book *Early Jazz: Its Roots and Musical Development.* According to *New York Times Book Review* critic Frank Conroy, "here, at last, is the definitive work" on jazz: "'Early Jazz' is written in the best intellectual tradition. It is clear, thorough, objective, sophisticated and original. A remarkable book by any standard, it is unparalleled in the literature of jazz." *Early Jazz* focuses on the African origins of jazz and wends its way into 1930s America. A *Yale Review* contributor, who also finds the work definitive, expresses that "Schuller's treatment of the giants of early jazz . . . is magisterial in its careful attention to detail and its comprehensive grasp of the evidence. . . . At the same time, . . . Schuller is careful to give due attention to lesser luminaries." And finally, Oja describes *Early Jazz* as a "thrilling analysis," which comes as no surprise from one who considers Schuller "a powerful presence in American musical life—one of the most challenging consciences of our time."

BIOGRAPHICAL/CRITICAL SOURCES:

BOOKS

Berger, Melvin, *Guide to Chamber Music,* Dodd, 1985.
Ewen, David, *American Composers: A Biographical Dictionary,* Putnam, 1982.

PERIODICALS

Down Beat, February, 1986.
New York Times Book Review, May 12, 1968, February 16, 1986.
Saturday Review, July 13, 1968.
Times Literary Supplement, November 28, 1968.
Yale Review, spring, 1969.
Washington Post Book World, February 26, 1989.

SCHULTE, Elaine L(ouise) 1934-
(Elaine L. Young)

PERSONAL: Born November 18, 1934, in Indiana; daughter of Dietrich and Louise (Matthew) Young; married Frank L. Schulte (a business executive and photographer), October 1, 1955; children: Gregory L., Richard M. *Education:* Purdue University, B.S., 1956. *Religion:* Presbyterian.

ADDRESSES: Home—P.O. Box 746, Rancho Sante Fe, Calif. 92067.

CAREER: J. Walter Thompson (advertising agency), Los Angeles, Calif., member of staff, 1956-57; writer, 1957—. Lecturer at conferences, colleges, schools, and libraries throughout the U.S. Lecturer at community colleges in California.

MEMBER: National League of Pen Women, Alpha Chi Omega.

AWARDS, HONORS: Distinguished Alumna Award from Purdue University, 1986.

WRITINGS:

Zack and the Magic Factory (juvenile novel), Thomas Nelson, 1976.
Whither the Wind Bloweth (young adult novel), Avon, 1982.
On the Wings of Love (adult novel), Zondervan, 1983.
Westward, My Love (adult historical novel), Zondervan, 1986.
Dreams of Gold (adult historical novel), Zondervan, 1986.
Echoes of Love (adult contemporary novel), Zondervan, 1986.
Song of Joy (adult contemporary novel), Zondervan, 1987.

Also author of four juvenile novels for the "Ginger" series, Cook, 1989; also author of three adult historical novels for the "California Pioneer" series, Cook, 1989. Contributor of articles, stories, and poems to national and foreign magazines.

WORK IN PROGRESS: Three more historical novels for the "California Pioneer" series, which covers the period from 1845 to 1900.

SIDELIGHTS: Elaine L. Schulte told *CA:* "It seems that God has given me the desires of my heart to write historicals for adults and contemporary problem novels for children."

Schulte lived in Belgium for three years and traveled extensively throughout Europe and Africa. Many of her travel articles have been syndicated to major U.S. newspapers.

AVOCATIONAL INTERESTS: Archaeology (has explored sites in Egypt, Turkey, Greece, Israel, Italy, France, Mexico, and the U.S. Southwest) and history (has researched California sites for information on "everything from the covered wagon trail. . . to the early settlements in the state's gold rush country").

MEDIA ADAPTATIONS: "Zack and the Magic Factory" was adapted from Schulte's novel of the same title, and aired on ABC-TV in 1981.

*   *   *

SCHULTZ, Mort(on) J(oel) 1930-

PERSONAL: Born October 13, 1930, in New York, N.Y.; son of William J. and Dorothy (Meyers) Schultz; married Janice Peck, June 15, 1952; children: Howard, Steven. *Education:* Rutgers University, B.Letters, 1952, M.A., 1962.

ADDRESSES: Home and office—19 Bedford Rd., Somerset, N.J. 08873.

CAREER: U.S. Department of the Army, Edison, N.J., civilian magazine editor, 1954-58; Lockheed Electronics Co., Plainsfield, N.J., public relations representative, 1958-63; freelance writer, 1963—. *Military service:* U.S. Army, Infantry, 1952-54; became first lieutenant.

MEMBER: American Society of Journalists and Authors, National Association of Home and Workshop Writers, Society of Automotive Engineers.

WRITINGS:

Photographic Reproduction, McGraw, 1963.
The Teacher and Overhead Projection, Prentice-Hall, 1965.
Teaching Ideas That Make Teaching Fun, Parker & Son, 1969.
Practical Handbook of Painting and Wallpapering, Fawcett, 1969.
How to Fix It, McGraw, 1971.
A Thousand One Questions and Answers about Your Car, McGraw, 1973.
Popular Mechanics Complete Car Repair Manual, Hearst Books, 1975.
Popular Mechanics Complete Appliance Repair Manual, Hearst Books, 1975.
McGraw-Hill Illustrated Auto Repair Course, McGraw, 1978.
Wiring, Creative Homeowner Press, 1980.
Crown's Diesel Engine Repair Manual, Crown, 1984.
Your Ford, Consumer Reports Books, 1988.
How to Install Dealer Options In Your Own Car, Grolier, 1988.

Contributor of articles to periodicals, including *Better Homes and Gardens, Motor, Homeowner, Popular Mechanics, Family Circle, Reader's Digest, Popular Science, Family Handyman, Medical Economics,* and *Information Week*.

*   *   *

SCHWARTZ, Arthur Nathaniel 1922-

PERSONAL: Born June 14, 1922, in Chicago, Ill.; son of Isadore (a clergyman) and Faye (Garfinkle) Schwartz; married Cherie Louise Snyder, 1981 (divorced); married Patty Lee Murphy, 1987; children: (prior marriages) Andrew Christopher, David Paul, Brian Jeremy, Cynthia Osborne, Jonathan Matthew. *Education:* Concordia Seminary, St. Louis, Mo., B.A., 1944; additional study at University of Houston, 1950-51, and Eastern Washington State College (now University), 1957; Washington University, Ph.D., 1962.

ADDRESSES: Home—1840-53 South Marengo, Alhambra, Calif. 91803. *Office*—Leonard Davis School of Gerontology, University of Southern California, Los Angeles, Calif. 90007.

CAREER: Veterans Administration Hospital, American Lake, Tacoma, Wash., staff clinical psychologist, 1962-65; Veterans Administration Center, Los Angeles, Calif., chief of clinical psychology section, 1965-72, clinical researcher on aging, 1967-72; University of Southern California, Los Angeles, lecturer on aging, 1970—, adjunct professor of psychology, 1973-79, assistant clinical professor of preventive and family medicine at School of Medicine and lecturer at Leonard Davis School of Gerontology, 1982—, director of long term care education, 1972—, director of adult counseling training program, 1973-79, geriatric coordinator for residency training program, School of Medicine; California Lutheran Homes, Alhambra, director of training and research, 1981.

Elementary school teacher in Seymour, Ind., 1942-43. Instructor at University of Puget Sound, 1962-64, Pacific Lutheran University, 1963-65, and University of California, Los Angeles, 1967-70; associate professor at California State University, Los Angeles, 1969-73; member of faculty at California School of Professional Psychology, 1970-72; professor of clinical geropsychology and director of gerontology program, Caribbean Center for Advanced Studies, Puerto Rico, 1979-80. Private practice in clinical psychology in Tacoma, Wash. Therapist and director of gerontological training programs at Peterson-Guedel Family Center, 1969—. President of Gero/Sci Associates. Chairman of Los Angeles County Affiliated Committee on Aging, 1969-71; member of board of directors of Los Angeles County Psychology Center, 1971—; member of state of California and White House Conference on Aging, 1971; member of board of examiners of Nursing Home Administrators of California, 1972-77. Consultant to Ethel Percy Andrus Gerontology Center, University of Southern California, 1968—.

MEMBER: American Psychological Association, Gerontological Society (fellow).

AWARDS, HONORS: Received outstanding service award from U.S. Veterans Administration, 1971; National Institute of Mental Health fellowship, 1972; Better Life Award for Education from California Association of Mental Health Facilitites, 1979; meritorious service award from California Association of Homes for the Aging, 1980; Jessie L. Terry Community Service Award; outstanding science award for education and training and Mayor's Award from city of San Juan, Puerto Rico, 1980; research award for contributions from American College of Health Care Administrators, 1987.

WRITINGS:

(Editor with I. N. Mensh) *Professional Obligations and Approaches to the Aged,* C. C Thomas, 1964, revised edition, 1973.
(Contributor) P. Woodruff and J. Birren, editors, *Aging: Scientific Perspectives and Social Issues,* Van Nostrand, 1975.
Survival Handbook for Children with Aging Parents, Follett, 1977.
(With J. Peterson) *Introduction to Gerontology,* Holt, 1979.
(Contributor) P. Ragan, editor, *Aging Parents,* University of Southern California Press, 1979.
(Contributor) S. S. Sargent, editor, *Nontraditional Therapy and Counseling with the Aged,* Springer Publishing, 1980.
Aging and Life: Introduction to Gerontology, Holt, 1984.

Contributor to over thirty research articles to *Geriatrics, Concern, Journal of Gerontology, Journal of Projective Techniques,* and *Personality Assessment,* and other journals.

WORK IN PROGRESS: A research report on nursing home staffs and families.

SIDELIGHTS: Arthur Nathaniel Schwartz told *CA:* "Generally speaking, I write about aging (gerontology) because I am uncomfortable—sometimes incensed—about the appalling attitudes of American society toward the old—negative attitudes that are in many instances subtly reinforced by professional helpers and researchers in the field. Writing about aging is, for me, the kind of arduous exercise, like early morning running or wood-chopping, found to relieve tension. It helps maintain intellectual 'tone' and often makes me sleep better, and pushes me to stay on the cutting edge of my field of interest."

SEARLS, Hank
See SEARLS, Henry Hunt, Jr.

*   *   *

SEARLS, Henry Hunt, Jr.   1922-
(Hank Searls)

PERSONAL: Born August 10, 1922, in San Francisco, Calif.; son of Henry Hunt Searls; married Berna Ann Cooper; children: Courtney, Henry, Peter. *Education:* Attended University of California at Berkeley, 1940; U.S. Naval Academy, B.S., 1944.

ADDRESSES: Agent—Scott Meredith Literary Agency, Inc., 845 Third Ave., New York, N.Y. 10022.

CAREER: U.S. Navy, 1941-54, became lieutenant commander; Hughes Aircraft, Culver City, Calif., writer, 1955-56; Douglas Aircraft, Santa Monica, Calif., writer, 1956-57; Warner Brothers, Burbank, Calif., writer, 1959; free-lance writer, 1959—.

MEMBER: Authors League of America, Writers Guild of America (West).

WRITINGS:

UNDER NAME HANK SEARLS

The Big X (novel), Harper, 1959.
The Crowded Sky (novel), edited by Natalie Rosenstein, Harper, 1960, reprinted, Berkley Publishing, 1988.
Astronaut (novel), Pocket Books, 1962.
Pilgrim Project (novel), McGraw, 1964.
The Hero Ship (novel), World Publishing, 1969.
The Lost Prince: Young Joe, the Forgotten Kennedy (nonfiction), World Publishing, 1969.
Pentagon (novel), Geis, 1971.
Overboard (novel), Norton, 1977.
Jaws 2 (screenplay novelization), Bantam, 1978.
Firewind (novel), Doubleday, 1981.
Sounding (novel), Ballantine, 1982.
Blood Song (novel), Villard Books, 1984.
Jaws: The Revenge (screenplay novelization), Berkley Publishing, 1987.
Kataki: A Novel of Revenge, McGraw, 1987.
The Adventures of Mike Blair (anthology), Mysterious Press, 1988.

AVOCATIONAL INTERESTS: Sailing, skiing, skin diving, flying.

*   *   *

SEGAL, David R(obert)   1941-

PERSONAL: Born June 22, 1941, in New York, N.Y.; son of Harry (a civil servant) and Daisy Rose (an educator; maiden name, Gold) Segal; married Mady Wechsler (a professor), December 25, 1966; children: Eden Heather. *Education:* Harpur College of the State University of New York (now State University of New York at Binghamton), B.A.(cum laude), 1962; University of Chicago, M.A., 1963; Ph.D., 1967.

ADDRESSES: Home—9007 Gettysburg Lane, College Park Woods, Md. 20740. *Office*—Department of Sociology, University of Maryland, College Park, Md. 20742.

CAREER: University of Michigan, Ann Arbor, assistant professor, 1966-71, associate professor of sociology, 1971-75, acting director of Center for Research on Social Organization; University of Maryland, College Park, professor of sociology, government, and politics, 1975—. Visiting member of faculty at U.S. Army War College, 1973-75; visiting professor at U.S. Military Academy at West Point, 1988-89; guest lecturer at colleges and universities in the United States and Canada. Fellow at Center for Social Organization Studies, 1965-66; guest scholar at Brookings Institution, 1981-83; visiting scientist at Battelle Human Affairs Research Center, 1981—; guest scientist at Walter Reed Army Institute of Research, 1982—. Civilian chief of social processes technical area at U.S. Army Research Institute for the Behavioral and Social Sciences, 1973-75. Member of manpower, personnel, and training panel of Naval Research Advisory Committee, 1979-81; member of editorial board of National Defense University Press, 1981-83. Project director for Twentieth Century Fund, 1982-88; member of advisory panel of Advanced Technology, Inc., 1982; consultant to Booz-Allen & Hamilton, Andrulis Research Corp., and General Research Corp. Staff consultant to the National Security and International Affairs Division, U.S. General Accounting Office, 1988—.

MEMBER: International Sociological Association (member of executive council of research committee on armed forces and conflict resolution, 1982-86; vice-president, 1986—), International Studies Association, American Sociological Association (member of council of the section on peace and war), American Association for Public Opinion Research, American Society for Public Administration, Military Operations Research Society (chairman of working group of human resource management, 1976), Inter-University Seminar on the Armed Forces and Society (member of executive council, 1974-82; associate chairman, 1982-88; member of board of director, 1987—).

AWARDS, HONORS: Horace H. Rackham fellow at University of Michigan, 1968; Ruth M. Sinclair Memorial Honors Program Award, 1970; James K. Pollock visiting research scholar at DATUM and University of Bonn, 1971; U.S. Department of the Army, commendation, 1975, certificate of achievement, 1976; Mid-Career Award from American Society for Public Administration, 1984.

WRITINGS:

Society and Politics, Scott, Foresman, 1974.
(Editor with Nancy Goldman, and contributor) *The Social Psychology of Military Service,* Sage Publication, 1976.
(With Jerald G. Bachman and John D. Blair) *The All-Volunteer Force: A Study of Ideology in the Military,* University of Michigan Press, 1977.
(Editor with H. Wallace Sinaiko, and contributor) *Life in the Rank and File,* Pergamon, 1986.
Recruiting for Uncle Sam, University Press of Kansas, 1989.

Associate editor of "Sage Research Progress on War, Revolution, and Peacekeeping" series, Sage Publications, 1979-82. Contributor to over twenty-eight books. Also contributor of over one hundred articles and reviews to political science and sociology journals. Associate editor of *American Sociologist,* 1973-75, *Sociological Focus,* 1973-79, *Journal of Political and Military Sociology,* 1974-77, 1981-83, and *Western Sociological Review,* 1977-81; guest editor of *Youth and Society,* 1978. *Armed Forces and Society,* associate editor, 1980-82, editor, 1982-88.

WORK IN PROGRESS: A book on the multinational force and observers in the Sinai.

SIDELIGHTS: David R. Segal told *CA:* "My major field of interest in graduate school was political sociology, and this interest led to the publication of my first book. One could not study politics in the 1960s, however, without recognizing the central importance of the military as an instrument of policy. Social scientists at the time were avoiding studies of the military, afraid, I suspect, of being tainted by coming too close to the unclean. I felt the military was too important to go unstudied, and it was unlikely to go away, so I spent some time looking at it. When the era of the all-volunteer force dawned, it was clear to me that it was one of the largest scale social experiments ever attempted and it too was worthy of study. The military has transformed the basic relationship between the citizen and the state in America in ways that we are only beginning to understand."

*   *   *

SEIDLER, Grzegorz Leopold   1913-

PERSONAL: Born September 18, 1913, in Stanislawow, Poland; son of Teodor (a lawyer) and Eugenia (Dawidowicz) Seidler; married Alina Bogusz (an editor), March 1, 1969. *Education:* Jagiellonian University, Doctorate, 1938; additional study at University of Vienna and Oxford University.

ADDRESSES: Home—7 AM, 17 Lublin, Poland. *Office*—Faculty of Law, Maria Curie-Sklodowska University, Plac Marii Curie-Sklodowskiej 5, 20-031 Lublin, Poland.

CAREER: Jagiellonian University, Krakow, Poland, lecturer in history of philosophy, 1945-50; Maria Curie-Sklodowska University, Lublin, Poland, chair of philosophy of law, 1950—, rector, 1959-69. Visiting professor at Christian-Albrechts-University, Kiel, West Germany, 1980-81; visiting fellow at Cambridge University, 1981-82. Director of Polish Cultural Institute, London, England, 1969-71. Member of Polish Parliament, 1985—.

AWARDS, HONORS: Banner of Labour first class, and Commander's Cross with star of Order of Polonia Restituta (both state decorations); honorary doctorate, Maria Curie-Sklodowska University and Academy of Economics, Krakow; named professeur honoraire a la faculte, Europeenne des Sciences du Fonciev.

WRITINGS:

Technika prac parlamentarnych, privately printed, 1938.
O istocie wladzy panstwowej, Ksiegarnia Powszechna (Krakow), 1946.
Ewolucja problemow budzetowych w polskim prawie konstytucyjnym, Ksiaznica (Krakow), 1946.
Rozwazania nad norma ustrojowa, Ksiaznica, 1947.
Wladza ustawodawcza i wykonawcza, Swiat i Wiedza (Krakow), 1948.
Teoria panstwa i prawa, Panstwowe Wydawinictwo Naukowe (Krakow), 1951.
Wspolczesne kierunki w nauce prawa, Panstwowe Wydawnictwo Naukowe, 1951.
Mysl polityczna Starozytnosci, Wydawnictwo Literackie (Krakow), 1955, 3rd edition, 1961.
Doktryny prawne imperializmu, Panstwowe Wydawnictwo Naukowe, 1957, 4th edition, Wydawnictwo Literackie, 1979.
Soziale Ideen in Byzanz, Akademie-Verlag (Berlin), 1960.
Mysl polityczna Sredniowiecza, Wydawnictwo Literackie, 1961.
The Emergence of the Eastern World, Oxford University Press, 1968.

Przedmarksowska mysl polityczna, Wydawnictwo Literackie, 1974.

(Contributor) Roman Schnur, editor, *Staatsraeson: Studien zur Geschichte politischen Begriffs,* Duncker & Humblot (Berlin), 1975.

Z zagadnien filozofii prawa, Wydawnictwo Literackie, 1978, 2nd edition, 1984.

Two Essays in Political Theory, University of Pittsburgh, 1979.

W nurcie Oswiecenia, Wydawnictwo Literackie, 1984.

In Search of Dominant Idea, Wydawnictwo Polonia, 1984.

Rechtssystem und Gesellschaft, Verlag Peter Lang, 1985.

Zwei Konzeptionen der Buerokratie, Universitat Innsbruck, 1987.

The World Order, Wydawnictwo Polonia, 1988.

Contributor to *Slavic Review, Studies on Voltaire and the Eighteenth Century,* and journals in Poland and Germany. Editor-in-chief of *Annales Universitatis Mariae Curie-Sklodowska,* 1955—.

WORK IN PROGRESS: Research on main ideas in European culture, including allegories and symbols as factors shaping consciousness.

SIDELIGHTS: Grzegorz Leopold Seidler told *CA:* "My studies aim at achieving a broad synthesis, so that the history of political thought would become fairly coherent and focused on principal evolutionary tendencies. In my opinion studies in the history of political thought of necessity lead to a comparison of our own value system and our ideas with those of the past. Only a past that is united with the present is significant in the shaping of human consciousness, which is always being formed in the present. Dangers faced by present-day world (nuclear war, pollution demographic explosion, international debt) require viewing our contemporary problems in world context."

*   *   *

SEIMER, Stanley J(ames) 1918-

PERSONAL: Born December 28, 1918, in Elgin, Ill.; son of Amil Ernest and Maude (Wilcox) Seimer; married 1942; children: Kathie, Elizabeth, Priscilla. *Education:* Northwestern University, B.S., 1940, M.B.A., 1942; Harvard University, D.C.S., 1956. *Religion:* Presbyterian.

ADDRESSES: Home—3890 Griffin Rd., Syracuse, N.Y. 13215. *Office*—Organization and Management Department, Syracuse University, 116 College Place, Syracuse, N.Y. 13210.

CAREER: Brust Tool Manufacturing Co., Chicago, Ill., tool and die maker, 1940-44; Chicago Bridge and Iron Co., Chicago, industrial engineer in ship building division, 1944; Boston University, Boston, Mass., instructor in product management, 1947-48; Northwestern University, Evanston, Ill., assistant professor, 1948-55; Syracuse University, Syracuse, N.Y., associate professor, 1955-67, professor of organization and management, 1967—. Visiting professor, Cornell University; conductor of special programs on organization and management at various schools. Consultant to corporations, associations, and other organizations. *Military service:* U.S. Naval Reserve, 1944-46; became lieutenant, junior grade.

MEMBER: American Management Association, Academy of Management (member of research and publications committee), Society for Advancement of Management, American Economics Association, University Club (Syracuse).

WRITINGS:

Suggestion Plans in American Industry, Syracuse University Press, 1959.

Casebook in Industrial Management, Irwin, 1961.

Suggestion Systems: Industrial Engineering Handbook, McGraw, 1970.

Integrated Materials Management in the United States, privately printed, 1972.

Elements of Supervision, Grid Publishing (Columbus, Ohio), 1973.

Casebook in Operations Management, Grid Publishing, 1979.

WORK IN PROGRESS: Management Theory and Practice (tentative title).

AVOCATIONAL INTERESTS: Tennis, hiking, woodworking.*

*   *   *

SEUFERT, Karl Rolf   1923-

PERSONAL: Born December 1, 1923, in Frankfurt am Main, Germany (now West Germany); married Christine Hoelzer, July 13, 1952; children: Elizabeth, Rudolf. *Education:* Roman Catholic.

ADDRESSES: Home—12 Hallgartener Platz, 6227 Oestrich-Winkel 3, Rheingau, Hessen, West Germany.

CAREER: Teacher of German, history, and geography in German schools, 1945-87; served as director of studies at Kriftel Junior High School.

MEMBER: German Writers Union.

AWARDS, HONORS: Friedrich Gerstaecker Award (best historical adventure book published in Germany), 1962, for *Die Karawane der weissen Maenner;* Junior Book Award, Boys' Clubs of America, 1964, for *Caravan in Peril* (translation of *Die Karawane der weissen Maenner*); Deutscher Jugendbuch Preis, 1969 and 1972; Kurt-Luettgen-Sachbuch Preis for nonfiction, 1972; Leserattenpreis, Zweites Deutsches Fernsehen, 1981, for *Pfad der Traenen;* five books cited by German Junior Book Awards on its annual list of "best books."

WRITINGS:

Die Karawane der weissen Maenner, Herder (Freiburg, West Germany), 1961, translation by Stella Humphries published as *Caravan in Peril,* Pantheon, 1963.

Die Tuerme von Mekka: Der abenteuerliche Weg des Richard Francis Burton nach Medina und Mekka (novel; main title means "The Towers of Mecca"), Herder, 1963, 3rd edition, 1966.

Die vergessenen Buddhas: Erzaehlungen aus China (stories about China before Mao Tse-tung; main title means "The Forgotten Buddhas"), Herder, 1965.

Das Jahr in der Steppe: Die abenteuerlichen Erlebnisse des Chinesen Fang im Lande der Mongolen (novel; main title means "The Year in the Prairie"), Herder, 1967.

Und morgen nach Nimrud: Austen Henry Layard auf der Suche nach den verschollenen Palaesten Assurs, Arena-Verlag (Wuerzburg, West Germany), 1967.

Abenteuer Afrika: Forscher, Reisende, Abenteurer, Herder, 1971.

Einmal China und zurueck (stories about Red China), Signal-Verlag (Baden-Baden, West Germany), 1971.

Huegel der Goetter und Koenige (history of Henry Austen Layard's discovery of the Old Orient; title means "Hill of Gods and Kings"), Arena-Verlag, 1971.

Ihr Ritt nach Lhasa: Die abenteuerlichen Reise von Evariste Huc und Joseph Gabet ins geheimnisvolle Land Tibet, Arena-Verlag, 1972.

Die Schaetze von Copan: John Lloyd Stephens entdeckt die Hochkultur des Mayas im Dschungel Mittelamerikas, Arena-Verlag, 1972.

Dreitausend Jahre Afrika: Geschichte der Entdeckungen und Erforschungen Afrikas, Signal-Verlag, 1973.

Durch den schwarzen Kontinent; von Mungo Park bis Henri Lhote: Abenteuer und Schicksale bekannter Afrikaforscher, Arena-Verlag, 1973.

Pfad der Traenen (novel; title means "Path of Tears"), Arena-Verlag, 1980.

Gegen den Wind nach Westen: Thomas T. Cooper auf der Suche nach einem Handelsweg von China nach Indien (novel), Loewe-Verlag (Bayreuth, West Germany), 1981.

Und morgen woanders (short stories), Arena-Verlag, 1981.

Das Raetsel der grossen Steine: Archaeologische Entdeckungen, Arena-Verlag, 1983.

. . . ist ein feins Laendlein: Eine Kulturgeschichte des Rheingaus von den Aufaengen bis zur Gegenwart (title means "'. . . It Is a Quaint Jewel Country: A History from Its Beginning to the Present Day'"), Walther-Verlag, 1983.

Unter den Huegeln das Gold (novel; title means "Under the Hills the Gold"), Loewe-Verlag, 1986.

Das Zeichen von Lambareue (novel; title means "The Sign of Lambareue"), Loewe-Verlag, 1987.

Sie kamen von Mitternacht (novel), Herder, 1988.

Also author, for Arena-Verlag, of *Die Strasse der wilden Abenteuer* (title means "Street of Wild Adventure"), *Die Abenteuer sind noch nicht zu Ende* (title means "Adventures Are Not Over"), *Vorstoss zum Reich der Mitte* (title means "March to China"), and *Unterwegs auf vielen Strassen* (short stories; title means "On My Way in Many Streets").

*   *   *

SHACKLETON, C. C.
See ALDISS, Brian W(ilson)

*   *   *

SHERMAN, Charlotte A.
See SHERMAN, Jory (Tecumseh)

*   *   *

SHERMAN, Jory (Tecumseh)   1932-
(Frank Anvic, Cort Martin, Hank Mitchum, Charlotte A. Sherman, Wilma Tarrant; Walt Denver, a house pseudonym)

PERSONAL: Born October 20, 1932, in St. Paul, Minn.; son of Keith Edward (a franchise consultant) and Mercedes (a stenographer; maiden name, Sheplee) Sherman; married Remy Montes Roxas, June 10, 1951 (deceased); married Felicia, August 15, 1958 (divorced December, 1967); married Charlotte Balcom (a writer), March 2, 1968; children: Francis Antonio, Jory Vittorio, Forrest Redmond, Gina Felice, Misty April, Marcus Tecumseh; (stepchildren) Gerald LeRoy Wilhite, David Dean Wilhite, Janet Lynn Wilhite. *Education:* Attended San Francisco State College (now University) and University of Minnesota. *Politics:* Democrat.

ADDRESSES: Home—P.O. Box 1069, Branson, Mo. 65616.

CAREER: Denver Dry Goods, Denver, Colo., advertising copywriter, 1949-50; American President Lines, San Francisco, Calif., computer programmer, 1953-54; Great Plays Co., Lethbridge, Alberta, actor, 1954-55; *San Francisco Examiner,* San Francisco, editor, 1960-61; American Art Enterprise, North Hollywood, Calif., magazine editor, 1961-65; free-lance editor, 1965-67; newspaper columnist, 1965—. San Bernardino County press chairperson for Gerald Brown; press chairperson for John Tunney and Jesse Unruh. Teacher of creative writing for adults at Southwest Missouri State University and elsewhere. President, MicroDramas Co., Rialto, Calif., 1969-71. Editor, Academy Press, Chatsworth, Calif., 1971-72. *Military service:* U.S. Navy, 1950-53.

MEMBER: Writers Guild of America, Authors League of America, Authors Guild, Western Writers of America, Ozark Writers League (co-founder), Missouri Writers Guild, Twin Counties Press Club (member of board of directors, 1966-70), Desert-Mountain Press Club, Baja California Writers Association.

AWARDS, HONORS: Best Newspaper Column Award, 1970, Best Radio Station Public Service Program Award, 1970 and 1971, all from Twin Counties Press Club; Best Newspaper Column Award, 1985, Best Novel Award, 1985, Best Magazine Article Award, 1985, Best Major Work Award, 1987, for *Song of the Cheyenne,* all from Missouri Writers Guild.

WRITINGS:

So Many Rooms, Galley Sail Publications, 1960.

My Face in Wax, Windfall Press, 1965.

Lust on Canvas, Anchor Publications, 1965.

The October Scarf, Challenge Books, 1966.

The Sculptor, Private Edition Books, 1966.

The Fires of Autumn, All Star Books, 1967.

Nightsong, All Star Books, 1968.

Blood Jungle, Triumph News, 1968.

(Under pseudonym Cort Martin) *The Star,* Dominion, 1968.

(Under pseudonym Cort Martin) *Quest,* Powell Publications, 1969.

(Under pseudonym Cort Martin) *The Edge of Passion,* Saber Books, 1969.

The Love Rain, Tecumseh Press, 1971.

(Under pseudonym Frank Anvic) *The All Girl Crew,* Barclay, 1973.

(Under pseudonym Frank Anvic) *The Hard Riders,* Barclay, 1973.

There Are Ways of Making Love to You, Tecumseh Press, 1974.

(Under pseudonym Frank Anvic) *We Have Your Daughter,* Brandon Books, 1974.

(Under pseudonym Frank Anvic) *Bride of Satan,* Brandon Books, 1974.

Gun for Hire, Major Books, 1975.

(Under pseudonym Charlotte A. Sherman) *The Shuttered Room,* Major Books, 1975.

Ride Hard, Ride Fast, Major Books, 1976.

(Under pseudonym Wilma Tarrant) *Her Strange Needs,* Carlyle Communications, 1976.

(Under pseudonym Wilma Tarrant) *Trying out Tricia,* Carlyle Communications, 1976.

Buzzard Bait, Major Books, 1977.

Satan's Seed, Pinnacle Books, 1978.

Chill, Pinnacle Books, 1978.

The Bamboo Demons, Pinnacle Books, 1979.

Hellfire Trail, Leisure Books, 1979.

The Reincarnation of Jenny James, Carlyle Books, 1979.
The Fugitive Gun, Leisure Books, 1980.
Vegas Vampire, Pinnacle Books, 1980.
The Phoenix Man, Pinnacle Books, 1980.
House of Scorpions, Pinnacle Books, 1980.
Shadows, Pinnacle Books, 1980.
Dawn of Revenge, Zebra Books, 1980.
Mexican Showdown, Zebra Books, 1980.
Death's Head Trail, Zebra Books, 1980.
Blood Justice, Zebra Books, 1980.
Winter Hell, Zebra Books, 1980.
Bukowski: Friendship, Fame, and Bestial Myth, Blue Horse
    Publications, 1981.
Duel in Purgatory, Zebra Books, 1981.
Law of the Rope, Zebra Books, 1981.
Apache Arrows, Zebra Books, 1981.
Boothill Bounty, Zebra Books, 1981.
Hard Bullets, Zebra Books, 1981.
Trial by Sixgun, Zebra Books, 1981.
(Under pseudonym Cort Martin) *First Blood,* Zebra Books,
    1981.
My Heart Is in the Ozarks, First Ozark Press, 1982.
The Widow Maker, Zebra Books, 1982.
Arizona Hardcase, Zebra Books, 1982.
The Buff Runners, Zebra Books, 1982.
Gunman's Curse, Pinnacle Books, 1983.
Dry-gulched, Zebra Books, 1983.
Wyoming Wanton, Zebra Books, 1983.
Tucson Twosome, Zebra Books, 1983.
Blood Warriors, Zebra Books, 1983.
(Under house pseudonym Walt Denver) *Pistolero,* Zebra Books,
    1983.
(Under pseudonym Hank Mitchum) *Stagecoach Station 8: Fort
    Yuma,* Bantam, 1983.
Death Valley, Zebra Books, 1984.
Red Tomahawk, Zebra Books, 1984.
Blood Trail South, Zebra Books, 1984.
Song of the Cheyenne, Doubleday, 1987.
Winter of the Wolf, Walker & Co., 1987.
Horne's Law, Walker & Co., 1988.

Also creator and producer of "Hellrider" series, Pinnacle Books, 1985, "Killsquad" series, Avon, 1986, "Remington" series, Avon, 1986, "Powell's Army" series, Zebra Books, 1986, "Brazo" series, Zebra Books, 1986, "Dateline" series, Paperjacks, 1987, and "Rivers West" series, Bantam, 1987-88. Author of columns, "View on Living," *Grand Terrace Living,* 1966-67, "Ensenada at Bay," *Ensenada Hello,* 1966-67, "The New Notebook," *San Bernardino Independent,* 1970-71, "Baja Notebook," *Fiesta,* 1972-75, "Bear with Me," *Big Bear News,* 1972-75, and a column in *San Bernardino Mountain Highlander,* 1975-76. Author of two series of educational tapes for radio, "Youth and Drugs" and "Youth and Alcohol," distributed by Classroom World Productions. Contributor of poetry to literary journals. West Coast editor, *Outsider;* advisory editor, *Black Cat Review.*

WORK IN PROGRESS: The Buckskinner, a mountain man trilogy for Tor Books; *The Way of the Eagle,* a novel on the Mescalero Apache, and *Red Storm,* a sequel to *The Way of the Eagle,* both for Doubleday.

SIDELIGHTS: Jory Sherman told *CA:* "Now that I no longer write series novels, I have more time to devote to longer works. Writing these gives me a great deal of satisfaction. I am trying to break the mold of the Western novel, take it in new directions, demonstrate that the novel of the American West is our

native art form and should no longer be relegated to the low end of the market in bookstores.

"I recently taught a course at Southwest Missouri State University on creating the novel and this helped solidify my ideas on writing. It seems to me, at fifty-five, that the writing has gotten easier, but no less challenging. I find myself delving deeper into each scene, trying to see more vividly into the hearts of my characters."

AVOCATIONAL INTERESTS: Black powder guns, hunting, fishing, canoeing, computer programming, local and western history.

BIOGRAPHICAL/CRITICAL SOURCES:

PERIODICALS

Listen, April, 1971.

*   *   *

SHI, David Emory   1951-

PERSONAL: Born August 19, 1951, in Atlanta, Ga.; son of Joseph E. B. (a professor) and Evelyn (Frye) Shi; married Susan Thomson (a principal), June 22, 1974; children: Jason, Jessica. *Education:* Furman University, B.A. (magna cum laude), 1973; University of Virginia, M.A., 1975, Ph.D., 1976.

ADDRESSES: Home—526 Pine Rd., Davidson, N.C. 28036. *Office*—Department of History, Davidson College, Davidson, N.C. 28036. *Agent*—Gerard McCauley Agency, Inc., P.O. Box AE, Katonah, N.Y. 10536.

CAREER: Davidson College, Davidson, N.C., instructor, 1976-77, assistant professor, 1977-87, Frontis W. Johnston Professor of History and chairman of department, 1987—. *Military service:* U.S. Army Reserve, 1973-83.

MEMBER: American Historical Association, American Studies Organization, Organization of American Historians, Southern Historical Association, Historical Society of North Carolina, Phi Beta Kappa.

AWARDS, HONORS: National Endowment for the Humanities fellow, 1982-83; National Humanities Center fellow, 1983; Huntington Library fellow, 1986-87; ODK Outstanding Teacher Award.

WRITINGS:

Matthew Josephson, Bourgeois Bohemian, Yale University
    Press, 1981.
*The Simple Life: Plain Living and High Thinking in American
    Culture,* Oxford University Press, 1985.
(Compiler and author of introduction) *In Search of the Simple
    Life: American Voices, Past and Present,* Peregrine Smith,
    1986.
(With George B. Tindall) *America: A Narrative History,* brief
    2nd edition, Norton, 1988.
*The Age of Realism: American Thought and Culture, 1855-
    1920,* Oxford University Press, in press.

Contributor to history journals, literary magazines, and newspapers, including *American Heritage, South Atlantic Quarterly, Southern Review, Virginia Quarterly Review, Philadelphia Inquirer, Washington Post,* and *Atlanta Constitution.*

SIDELIGHTS: "My research has been eclectic, ranging across American intellectual and cultural history," David Emory Shi told *CA.* "Most of it has been tied together by a value-oriented approach, examining ways in which individuals or groups have struggled to develop and maintain a particular philosophy of living or artistic perspective.'' In *The Simple Life: Plain Living and High Thinking in American Culture,* for example, Shi explores the enduring American fascination with the ideal of the ''simple life.'' ''Beginning with the Puritans and ending with the Reagan presidency, David E. Shi documents three centuries of conflict between our cherished image as 'spiritual commonwealth and republic of virtue' and the distracting actuality of America as 'cornucopia of economic opportunities and consumer delights,''' describes *Los Angeles Times Book Review* critic Elaine Kendall. ''Uncovering irreconcilable differences at every stage of the way, 'The Simple Life' becomes a festival of irony.'' While *New York Times Book Review* contributor Israel Rosenfield faults the author for failing to analyze the inherent contradictions and frequent insincerity of the idea of the ''simple life,'' he admits that ''Mr. Shi's study is interesting for the light it sheds on America's moral development.'' As Jackson Lears similarly concludes in the *Nation,* ''[Shi] does a masterful job of bringing [his sources] together in a balanced, sensitive and comprehensive account of this major theme in American cultural history.''

BIOGRAPHICAL/CRITICAL SOURCES:

PERIODICALS

Los Angeles Times Book Review, February 24, 1985.
Nation, May 30, 1981, March 9, 1985.
New York Times Book Review, May 10, 1981, January 20, 1985.
Times Literary Supplement, June 26, 1981.

*   *   *

SHISSLER, Barbara Johnson
See NOSANOW, Barbara Shissler

*   *   *

SIMMONS, D(avid) R(oy) 1930-

PERSONAL: Born September 6, 1930, in Auckland, New Zealand; son of Wilfred Henshall and Mabel Clair (Bedingfield) Simmons; married Winifred Mary Harwood, August 16, 1955; children: Christopher, Nigel. *Education:* Auckland Teachers College, Teachers Certificate, 1950; Sorbonne, University of Paris, Dip. des Etudes de Civil. France., 1953; University of Rennes, Dip. des Etudes Celt., 1954; University of Auckland, B.A., 1962, M.A., 1965.

ADDRESSES: Home and office—12 Minto Rd., Remuera, Auckland, New Zealand.

CAREER: Teacher at primary school in New Zealand, 1950-51; Otago Museum, Dunedin, New Zealand, assistant keeper, 1962-68, keeper in anthropology, 1968; Auckland Institute and Museum. Auckland, New Zealand, ethnologist, 1968-85, assistant director, 1978-85.

MEMBER: Royal Society of New Zealand, New Zealand Archaeological Association (past member of council), Polynesian Society (past member of council), Art Galleries and Museums Association (past member of council).

AWARDS, HONORS: Elsdon Best Memorial Medal from Polynesian Society, 1980, for *The Great New Zealand Myth: A Study of the Origin and Migration Traditions of the Maori;* awarded M.B.E., 1985.

WRITINGS:

Little Papanui and Otago Prehistory, Otago Museum Trust Board, 1967.
(Editor) Father C. Servant, *Habits and Customs of the New Zealanders, 1838-42,* A. H. & A. W. Reed, 1972.
(Editor) John Duncan Henry Buchanan, *The Maori History and Place Names of Hawkes Bay,* A. H. & A. W. Reed, 1973.
The Great New Zealand Myth: A Study of the Origin and Migration Traditions of the Maori, A. H. & A. W. Reed, 1976.
(With Brian Brake and James McNeish) *Art of the Pacific,* Oxford University Press, 1979.
Catalogue of Maori Artifacts in the Museums of Canada and the United States of America, Auckland Institute and Museum, 1982.
Whakairo: Maori Tribal Art, Oxford University Press, 1984.
(Contributor) *Te Maori,* Abrams, 1984.
(Contributor) *Ta Moko: The Art of Maori Tattoo,* Reed-Methuen, 1986.
(Contributor) *Maori Auckland,* Bush Press, 1986.
Catalogue of Maori Artifacts in European Museums, Auckland Institute and Museum, 1988.

WORK IN PROGRESS: Catalogue of Maori Artifacts in United Kingdom Museums, Auckland Institute and Museum.

SIDELIGHTS: D. R. Simmons told *CA:* ''Celtic languages and literature are the wellspring from which medieval literature comes. To understand the Celtic background, I learned Breton. I retain a love of medieval and Celtic literature.

''Here in New Zealand my family has always been associated with things Maori. The mental landscape expressed in the language is also expressed in the art at many different levels. As a museum ethnologist it was my task to make available the heritage of the past and present for those who wish to find inspiration, whether it be for a new meeting house or in designing an industrial form.

''Now that I have retired from the museum my writing still seeks to inspire people with the beauty of the past, so that they may live fuller lives and so that the past is part of the future.''

*   *   *

SIRE, James W(alter) 1933-

PERSONAL: Born October 17, 1933, in Inman, Neb.; son of Walter Guy and Elsie (Mulford) Sire; married Marjorie Ruth Wanner (a laboratory technician), June 14, 1955; children: Carol, Eugene, Richard, Anne. *Education:* University of Nebraska, B.A., 1955; Washington State University, M.A., 1958; University of Missouri—Columbia, Ph.D., 1964. *Religion:* Christian.

ADDRESSES: Office—Inter-Varsity Press, 5206 Main, Downers Grove, Ill. 60515.

CAREER: University of Missouri—Columbia, instructor in English, 1958-64; Nebraska Wesleyan University, Lincoln, assistant professor, 1964-66, associate professor of English, 1966-68; Inter-Varsity Press, Downers Grove, Ill., editor, 1968—. Part-time associate professor at Northern Illinois University, 1969-70, and Trinity College, Deerfield, Ill., 1971-75; visiting summer professor at University of Nebraska, 1966, University of Missouri, 1967, Regent College, 1977, and New

College, Berkeley, 1983-84. *Military service:* U.S. Army, Ordnance, 1955-57; became first lieutenant.

MEMBER: Conference on Christianity and Literature, Milton Society, American Scientific Affiliation.

WRITINGS:

(With Robert Beum) *Papers on Literature: Models and Methods,* Holt, 1970.
Program for a New Man, Inter-Varsity Press, 1973.
Jeremiah, Meet the Twentieth Century, Inter-Varsity Press, 1975.
The Universe Next Door, Inter-Varsity Press, 1976, 2nd edition, 1988.
How to Read Slowly, Harold Shaw, 1978.
Scripture Twisting, Inter-Varsity Press, 1980.
Beginning with God, Inter-Varsity Press, 1981.
Meeting Jesus, Harold Shaw, 1988.
Shirley MacLaine and the New Age Movement, Inter-Varsity Press, 1988.

SIDELIGHTS: James W. Sire told *CA:* "Though I have written since 1976 a number of books, articles, and reviews, *The Universe Next Door* remains my own favorite and, apparently, a favorite among readers. While the book concentrates on outlining seven basic worldviews, including Christian theism, naturalism, pantheism, and the new consciousness, it does so from a uniquely Christian perspective. I have been pleased to see that over a hundred colleges and universities, both state and private, have used this book as a text in a wide variety of courses from philosophy and religion, on the one hand, to English and history on the other. I left the university teaching world over ten years ago, but am pleased to see that my books have continued to keep me on campus. I have also been pleased that the Christian perspective in these books has been getting a hearing even on secular campuses."

He adds, "I now travel widely in the U.S., Canada, and England, lecturing on the Christian faith, primarily on university campuses."

*   *   *

SKELTON, Robin 1925-
(Georges Zuk)

PERSONAL: Born October 12, 1925, in Easington, East Yorkshire, England; son of Frederick William (a schoolmaster) and Eliza (Robins) Skelton; married Margaret Lambert, 1953 (divorced, 1957); married Sylvia Mary Jarrett, February 4, 1957; children: (second marriage) Nicholas John, Alison Jane, Eleanor Brigid. *Education:* Attended Christ's College, Cambridge, 1943-44; University of Leeds, B.A. (first class honors), 1950, M.A., 1951.

ADDRESSES: Home—1255 Victoria Ave., Victoria, British Columbia, Canada. *Office*—Department of Creative Writing, University of Victoria, Victoria, British Columbia, Canada V8W 2Y2.

CAREER: University of Manchester, Manchester, England, assistant lecturer, 1951-54, lecturer in English, 1954-63; University of Victoria, Victoria, British Columbia, associate professor, 1963-66, professor of English, 1966—, director of creative writing program, 1967-73, founding chairman of department of creative writing, 1973-76. Northern Universities Joint Matriculation Board, examiner, 1954-58, chairman of examiners in English O Level, 1958-60; centennial lecturer,

University of Massachusetts, 1962-63; visiting professor, University of Michigan, 1967; lecturer, Eastern Washington State Creative Writing Summer School, 1972. Managing director, Lotus Press, 1950-51; founder and director, Pharos Press, 1972—; editor in chief, Sono Nis Press, 1976-83. Founder member, Peterloo Group (artists and poets), 1957-60; founding secretary, Manchester Institute of Contemporary Arts, 1960-62; member of board of directors, Art Gallery of Greater Victoria, 1968-69, 1970-73. Collage-maker, with individual shows in Victoria, 1966, 1968, and 1980. Has appeared on broadcasts for BBC-Radio and other radio and television stations, and given numerous readings and lectures. *Military service:* Royal Air Force, 1944-47; served in India; became sergeant.

MEMBER: Royal Society of Literature (fellow), Writers' Union of Canada (first vice-chairman, 1981, chairman, 1982-83), PEN.

WRITINGS:

POETRY

Patmos and Other Poems, Routledge & Kegan Paul, 1955.
Third Day Lucky, Oxford University Press, 1958.
Begging the Dialect: Poems and Ballads, Oxford University Press, 1960.
Two Ballads of the Muse, Rampant Lions Press, 1960.
The Dark Window, Oxford University Press, 1962.
A Valedictory Poem, privately printed, 1963.
An Irish Gathering, Dolmen Press, 1964.
A Ballad of Billy Barker, privately printed, 1965.
Inscriptions, privately printed, 1967.
Because of This and Other Poems, Manchester Institute of Contemporary Arts, 1968.
The Hold of Our Hands: Eight Letters to Sylvia, privately printed, 1968.
Selected Poems, 1947-67, McClelland & Stewart, 1968.
Answers, Enitharmon Press, 1969.
(Under pseudonym Georges Zuk) *Selected Verse,* Kayak, 1969.
An Irish Album, Dolmen Press, 1969.
A Different Mountain, Kayak, 1971.
The Hunting Dark, McClelland & Stewart, 1971.
A Private Speech: Messages 1962-1970, Sono Nis Press, 1971.
Remembering Synge: A Poem in Homage for the Centenary of His Birth, 16 April 1971, Dolmen Press, 1971.
A Christmas Poem, privately printed, 1972.
Hypothesis, Dreadnaught Press, 1972.
Musebook, Pharos Press, 1972.
Three for Herself, Sceptre Press, 1972.
Country Songs, Sceptre Press, 1973.
The Hermit Shell, privately printed, 1974.
Timelight, McClelland & Stewart, 1974.
Fifty Syllables for a Fiftieth Birthday, privately printed, 1975.
(Under pseudonym Georges Zuk) *The Underwear of the Unicorn,* Oolichan Books, 1975.
Callsigns, Sono Nis Press, 1976.
Because of Love, McClelland & Stewart, 1977.
Three Poems, Sceptre Press, 1977.
Landmarks, Sono Nis Press, 1979.
Collected Shorter Poems, 1947-1977, Sono Nis Press, 1981.
Limits, Porcupine's Quill, 1981.
De Nihilo, Aloysius Press, 1982.
Zuk, Porcupine's Quill, 1982.
Wordsong, Sono Nis Press, 1983.
Collected Longer Poems, 1947-1977, Sono Nis Press, 1985.
Distances, Porcupine's Quill, 1985.
Openings, Sono Nis Press, 1988.

FICTION

The Man Who Sang in His Sleep (short stories), Porcupine's Quill, 1984.
The Parrot Who Could (short stories), Sono Nis Press, 1987.
Telling the Tale (short stories), Porcupine's Quill, 1987.
Fires of the Kindred (novel), Press Porcepic, 1987.

PLAYS

"The Author," first produced in Victoria, B.C., 1968.
The Paper Cage, Oolichan Press, 1982.

NONFICTION

John Ruskin: The Final Years, Manchester University Press, 1955.
The Poetic Pattern, University of California Press, 1956.
Painters Talking: Michael Snow and Tony Connor Interviewed, Peterloo Group, 1957.
Cavalier Poets, Longmans, Green, 1960.
Teach Yourself Poetry, English Universities Press, 1963, Dover, 1965.
J. M. Synge and His World, Viking, 1971.
Paintings, Graphics, and Sculpture from the Collection of Robin and Sylvia Skelton, privately printed, 1971.
The Practice of Poetry, Barnes & Noble, 1971.
The Writings of J. M. Synge, Bobbs-Merrill, 1971.
J. M. Synge, Bucknell University Press, 1972.
The Limners, Pharos Press, 1972.
The Poet's Calling, Barnes & Noble, 1975.
Poetic Truth, Barnes & Noble, 1978.
Explorations within a Landscape: New Porcelain by Robin Hopper, Robin Hopper, 1978.
Spellcraft: A Manual of Verbal Magic, McClelland & Stewart, 1978.
Herbert Siebner: A Monograph, Sono Nis Press, 1979.
They Call It the Cariboo, Sono Nis Press, 1980.
House of Dreams: Collages, Porcupine's Quill, 1983.
Talismanic Magic, Samuel Weiser, 1985.
Memoirs of a Literary Blockhead (autobiography), Macmillan, 1988.
The Practice of Witchcraft Today, R. Hale, 1988.
Portrait of My Father (memoir), Sono Nis Press, 1989.

EDITOR

Leeds University Poetry 1949, Lotus Press, 1950.
(With D. Metcalfe) *The Acadine Poets, Series I-III*, Lotus Press, 1950.
J. M. Synge, *Translations*, Dolmen Press, 1961.
Synge, *The Collected Poems of J. M. Synge*, Oxford University Press, 1962.
Synge, *Four Plays and "The Aran Islands,"* Oxford University Press, 1962.
Edward Thomas, *Selected Poems*, Hutchinson, 1962.
Six Irish Poets: Austin Clarke, Richard Kell, Thomas Kinsella, John Montague, Richard Murphy, Richard Weber, Oxford University Press, 1962.
Viewpoint: An Anthology of Poetry, Hutchinson, 1962.
(Series editor) *The Collected Works of John Millington Synge*, Volume 1: *The Poems*, Volume 2: *The Prose*, edited by Alan Price, Volume 3: *The Plays, Book 1*, edited by Ann Saddlemyer, Volume 4: *The Plays, Book 2*, edited by Saddlemyer, Oxford University Press, 1962, reprinted, Catholic University Press, 1982.
Five Poets of the Pacific Northwest: Kenneth O. Hanson, Richard Hugo, Carolyn Kizer, William Stafford, and David Wagner, Oxford University Press, 1964.

Poets of the Thirties, Penguin, 1964.
David Gascoyne, *Collected Poems*, Oxford University Press/Deutsch, 1965.
(With David R. Clark) *Irish Renaissance: A Gathering of Essays, Letters, and Memoirs from the "Massachusetts Review,"* Dolmen Press, 1965.
Selected Poems of Byron, Heinemann, 1965, Barnes & Noble, 1966.
(With Saddlemyer) *The World of W. B. Yeats: Essays in Perspective*, Oxford University Press, 1965, University of Washington Press, 1967.
Poetry of the Forties, Penguin, 1968.
Introductions from an Island: A Selection of Student Writing, University of Victoria, annual editions, 1969, 1971, 1973, 1974, 1977.
Synge, *Riders to the Sea*, Dolmen Press, 1969.
(With Alan Clodd) Gascoyne, *Collected Verse Translations*, Oxford University Press, 1970.
Herbert Read: A Memorial Symposium, Methuen, 1970.
The Collected Plays of Jack B. Yeats, Bobbs-Merrill, 1971.
Synge, *Some Sonnets from "Laura in Death" after the Italian of Francesco Petrarch* (bilingual edition), Dolmen Press, 1971.
Thirteen Irish Writers on Ireland, David Godine, 1973.
(With William David Thomas) *A Gathering in Celebration of the 80th Birthday of Robert Graves*, University of Victoria, 1975.
Six Poets of British Columbia, Sono Nis Press, 1980.
Ezra Pound, *From Syria: The Worksheets, Proofs, and Text*, Copper Canyon Press, 1981.

TRANSLATOR

(And editor) *Two Hundred Poems from "The Greek Anthology,"* McClelland & Stewart, 1971, University of Washington Press, 1972.
(And editor) *George Faludy: Twelve Sonnets*, Pharos Press, 1983.
(With others, and editor) *Selected Poems of George Faludy, 1933-80*, University of Georgia Press, 1985.
(And editor) *George Faludy: Corpses, Brats, and Cricket Music* (bilingual edition), William Hoffer, 1986.
Federico Garcia Lorca, *Selected Poems and Ballads*, Guernica Editions, 1990.

OTHER

Contributor of poems, articles, and reviews to periodicals, including *Observer, Times Literary Supplement, Manchester Guardian, Critical Quarterly, Massachusetts Review, Poetry, Canadian Literature, London Magazine, Poetry Northwest, Listener, New Statesman,* and *Quarterly Review of Literature.* Drama critic, *Union News,* 1950; poetry reviewer, *Books,* 1957; poetry reviewer, 1957-58, and drama reviewer, 1958-60, *Manchester Guardian;* poetry reviewer, *Critical Quarterly,* 1960; art reviewer, Victoria *Daily Times,* 1964-66; mystery book columnist, *Toronto Star,* 1988—. Editor, *The Gryphon,* 1949-50; co-founder and editor, 1967-71, and sole editor, 1972-83, *Malahat Review.*

Almost all of Skelton's manuscripts, worksheets, proofs, literary correspondence, and unpublished works, as well as a collection of published work, are contained in the Robin Skelton Collection in the Rare Book room of the MacPherson Library at the University of Victoria.

SIDELIGHTS: Among the many publications to his credit, Robin Skelton has over two dozen poetry collections, several critical studies on writers as well as the art of poetry, two plays, three story collections, a social history, and a novel. In addition, Skelton has turned his talents to editing works by other writers, and helped establish and edit the prestigious literary magazine *Malahat Review.* In an interview with Martin Townsend in the *Quill & Quire,* the Canadian author gives three reasons for his "wanton productivity": "I'm compulsive—what else? I feel slightly ill if I'm not writing something—I've got printer's ink in my blood, I think. Also, I'm never satisfied with pigeonholing myself. I find myself frequently daring myself to do something I don't think I can do." Skelton added that for him, writing is the best way to explore something: "If I want to find something out I have to write about it. If I want to read a foreign poet badly, I usually have to attempt translations, which I might or might not publish. My attitude, really, is that if there's a book you want to read and nobody seems to have produced it, produce it yourself."

Skelton has held this self-reliant attitude throughout his career. As a Codes and Cyphers Sergeant for the Royal Air Force, Skelton wrote and produced scripts for All India Radio; while still a student at Leeds University, Skelton edited the University magazine and bought the Lotus Press, a small literary publisher. After graduation the poet joined the staff of Manchester University, and published a volume of poetry as well as several critical studies. Nevertheless, Skelton felt his own work was being stifled, for as he recalls in *Contemporary Authors Autobiography Series,* "my poetry was ignored by most of my colleagues (one of them always left the staff lounge whenever it was mentioned) and I was never invited to meet visiting poets (who sometimes asked after me), or to give readings." It was not until Skelton emigrated to British Columbia, Canada, in 1963, that his poetry began improving: "The escape from English gentility," Skelton recalls in *Quill & Quire,* "was, stylistically, most important. I had to reinvent my language."

Perhaps owing to his varied background and independent outlook, Skelton's poetry is characterized as self-conscious although this self-consciousness manifests itself in an array of forms. Keith Garebian, in a *Dictionary of Literary Biography* essay, calls Skelton "a meditative poet [who] expands his technical freedom while reflecting on profound subjects that often refuse to be fixed in a single form and phrase." Just as his desire for variety has expressed itself in diverse literary forms, Skelton's poetry experiments with many different poetic configurations, this same "technical freedom." "Skelton is a craftsman whose work shows that he has not merely studied but *absorbed* the major traditions of poetry in English, and can write with gracefully assured precision in a variety of tones and rhythmic forms," notes David Jackel in *Canadian Forum.*

In a review of *The Collected Shorter Poems, 1947-1977,* however, a *Choice* writer comments that while Skelton's work traverses many different themes and forms, "nearly all of the poems trace the development of a single personality. . . . The tone is wry, witty, self-mocking, conversational but clearly directed toward statement." "Skelton is a thoroughly self-conscious poet," states D. P. Thomas in the *Fiddlehead,* "capable of standing aside and quizzing his own directions." Nevertheless, Skelton's work is not didactic or overly philosophical; he "is less a philosopher, in most of the commoner sense of the term, than a spokesman for predicaments," comments Thomas. The poet himself echoes this assessment in a *Waves* interview with Dorothy Stott: "In a way, I don't think about what my poems say; my poems are doing the thinking for me. I don't know if that makes sense but the poems tell me, the poems talk to me, I don't necessarily talk through my poems. A lot of the opinions that come out of the poems are not necessarily my own personal opinions and this is something that people don't usually realize. I explain it by saying that a poem is not an affidavit." Although criticism of the author's poetry covers numerous aspects, "in fact all attempts to characterize Skelton's writing centre on confirming his extreme skill and craftsmanship," writes Louise McKinney in the *Quill & Quire.* The critic summarizes: "From the sonorous, internal rhymes of his beautifully baroque early work to the pared-away intensity of the late, Skelton's skill has made him a leading Canadian poet."

After almost thirty years of focusing his creative writing on poetry, Skelton began publishing collections of short stories. "In the stories, I can tell jokes that I can't tell in poetry, and I can point out social oddities, and I can speculate along the lines of 'what if something bizarre happened. . . ,'" the author remarked to Townsend. "There's a whole part of my thinking, feeling, and sense of humour that doesn't get into the verse." *The Man Who Sang in His Sleep,* Skelton's first collection, "contains 10 stories which are sometimes charming, occasionally darker (funny in a Hitchcock sort of way) and always entertaining," remarks Antanas Sileika in the Toronto *Globe and Mail.* Although Skelton is giving voice to a different side of his creativity, these stories contain the same sense of identity found in much of his poetry. Sileika notes that "the voice used in these stories is invariably engaging, the kind that encourages eavesdropping if one overheard it in a bar," while Townsend observes in a review of *The Parrot Who Could* that "the tales nearly always appear richly humorous through their endearingly comical first-person perspective." T. F. Rigelhof similarly praises the stories in *Telling the Tale:* "Skelton casually but craftily honors the conventions that are traditional to [the supernatural] genre," the critic notes in the Toronto *Globe and Mail.* "His narrators speak directly to the reader and frequently seem to be doing little more than passing along stories that they have heard." "Skelton's narrative voice is a rich medium that is a pleasure in itself," remarks Townsend. "Though a few of the story endings may be predictable from the first page and some of the punch lines weak, many among these tales can be read over and over again with pleasure because each paragraph succeeds in its own right with wit and grace."

Despite his varied and vast body of work, Skelton told Townsend that "I find it hard to write fiction and poetry at the same time. At the moment I seem to be emphasizing the writing of fiction, but I know perfectly well that if I tell you now that I am going to concentrate on fiction from now on, I would probably write a poem before the week is out!" When asked about his literary future, Skelton responded that he has at least two books, one fiction and one nonfiction, in the works. The prolific author concluded: "I can't say what's going to happen after that, I'm really not sure. I've got several things I'm interested in doing. At the moment I think it is possible I'll continue writing fiction. But I've been writing so hard these last two or three years that I'm not really contemplating any enormous new task until at least the spring of next year!" Skelton also has his teaching, editing, and exhibiting of collages and stone carving from which to choose; any selection is bound to benefit from his expertise, for as Rigelhof comments, "Skelton, in his more than 20 years in [Canada], has done much to raise standards in numerous areas of our literary life."

AVOCATIONAL INTERESTS: Book collecting, art collecting, making collages, stone carving, philately.

BIOGRAPHICAL/CRITICAL SOURCES:

BOOKS

Authors in the News, Gale, 1975.
Contemporary Authors Autobiography Series, Volume 5, Gale, 1987.
Dictionary of Literary Biography, Gale, Volume 27: *Poets of Great Britain and Ireland,* 1984, Volume 53: *Canadian Writers since 1960, First Series,* 1986.
Turner, Barbara E., editor, *Skelton at Sixty,* Porcupine's Quill, 1987.

PERIODICALS

Books and Bookmen, June, 1971.
Canadian Forum, August, 1977.
Choice, September, 1981, July, 1986.
Fiddlehead, March, 1969.
Globe and Mail (Toronto), September 1, 1984, August 8, 1987, September 5, 1987, April 9, 1988.
Nation, August 30, 1971.
New Statesman, April 30, 1971, August 22, 1975.
Quill & Quire, December, 1975, March, 1986, July, 1987, January, 1988.
Saturday Review, May 1, 1971.
Times Literary Supplement, September 11, 1981.
Waves, Number 1, 1983.

—*Sketch by Diane Telgen*

*   *   *

SMILEY, Virginia Kester   1923-

PERSONAL: Born February 21, 1923, in Rochester, N.Y.; daughter of Harold P. and Isabell (Fleming) Kester; married Robert P. Smiley (a gravure engraver), September 8, 1945; children: Suzanne, Kimberly. *Education:* Attended public schools in Rochester, N.Y. *Politics:* Republican. *Religion:* Protestant.

ADDRESSES: Home—669 Webster Rd., Webster, N.Y. 14580.

CAREER: Writer. Worked in Rochester, N.Y., as a telephone operator, 1941-42, secretary at a hospital, 1942-43, and in the offices of Hickok Manufacturing Co., 1943-44, and Birdseye-Snyder Co., 1944-45.

MEMBER: Mystery Writers of America, Romance Writers of America, Society of Children's Book Writers, Genessee Valley Writers (former secretary).

WRITINGS:

Little Boy Navaho (juvenile), Abelard, 1954.
The Buzzing Bees (juvenile), Abelard, 1956.
Swirling Sands, Dodd, 1958.
Nurse Kate's Mercy Flight, Ace Books, 1968.
A Haven for Jenny, Bouregy, 1970.
High Country Nurse, Bouregy, 1970.
A Horse for Matthew Allen, Ginn, 1972.
Under Purple Skies, Bouregy, 1972.
Guest at Gladehaven, Dell, 1972.
Mansion of Mystery, Dell, 1973.
Nurse for Morgan Acres, Bouregy, 1973.
Cove of Fear, Bouregy, 1974.
Nurse for the Civic Center, Bouregy, 1974.

Libby Williams, Nurse Practitioner, Bouregy, 1975.
Liza Hunt, Pediatric Nurse, Bouregy, 1976.
Nurse Delia's Choice, Bouregy, 1977.
Nurse Karen's Summer of Fear, Bouregy, 1979.
Love Rides the Rapids (young adult), Bouregy, 1980.
Sugarbush Nurse (young adult), Bouregy, 1981.
Starburst, Berkley Publishing, 1982.
Love in the Wings (young adult), Bantam, 1987.
Blue Ribbon Romance (young adult), Bantam, 1989.

Also author of *Sugarbush Spring* and *Tender Betrayal.* Contributor of short stories to juvenile and young adult magazines.

WORK IN PROGRESS: Annie Riley, the Fresh Air Kid and *Cappy Wilson Meets the Shadow* for middle-grade readers; *Star Boarder* for young adults.

SIDELIGHTS: Virginia Kester Smiley once told *CA:* "I write 'light' nurse romances and 'light' mystery and suspense romances because I believe there is a need for this type of book—something to pick up and read easily in an evening, in a bus, on a plane, etc. I think with so many serious adult type novels being published there is a need for romances. I do an occasional juvenile because I enjoy writing for the young. Whenever I find a fan letter from a child in my mailbox, the hours I spend glued to the typewriter are worthwhile. The trend in books has changed in [recent] years, with the sensual books very much 'in.' They are 'escape' reading with a huge following. *Starburst* was my first attempt at this type."

Smiley more recently added: "I'm doing young adult novels, and also books for the eight- to twelve-year-olds, and I love it. I look forward to facing the computer every day."

*   *   *

SMITH, C. Ray   1929-

PERSONAL: Born March 3, 1929, in Birmingham, Ala.; son of Calvin Ray and Sara Amanda (Kelly) Smith; married Leslie Armstrong, December 17, 1971 (divorced, 1978); children: Sinclair Scott. *Education:* Kenyon College, B.A., 1951; Yale University, M.A., 1958.

ADDRESSES: Home—P.O. Box 32, Lenhartsville, Pa. 19534. *Office*—210 East 36th St., New York, N.Y. 10016.

CAREER: Interior Design, New York City, assistant editor, 1958-60; *Progressive Architecture,* Stamford, Conn., senior editor, 1961-70; *Theatre Crafts,* New York City, editor, 1969-74; *Interiors,* New York City, editor, 1974-77; Parsons School of Design, New York City, teacher of design history, 1977—; Fashion Institute of Technology, New York City, teacher of design history, 1985—. *Military service:* U.S. Army, 1952-54; served in Europe.

MEMBER: American Institute of Architects (fellow), U.S. Institute for Theatre Technology (fellow), Society of Architectural Historians, Architectural League of New York.

WRITINGS:

The American Endless Weekend, American Institute of Architects, 1972.
Supermannerism: New Attitudes in Post-Modern Architecture, Dutton, 1977.
AIGA Graphic Design, U.S.A.: I, Watson-Guptill, 1980.
(With Marian Page) *The Wood Chair in America,* Estelle Brickel, 1982.
(With Allen Tate) *Interior Design in the Twentieth Century,* Harper, 1986.

Interior Design in Twentieth-Century America: A History, Harper, 1987.

EDITOR

Jo Mielziner, *The Shapes of Our Theatre,* C. N. Potter, 1970.
The Theatre Crafts Book of Costume, Rodale Press, 1973.
The Theatre Crafts Book of Makeup, Masks, and Wigs, Rodale Press, 1974.
John Margolies, *The End of the Road,* Penguin, 1981.

OTHER

Contributor to *Encyclopedia of Contemporary Architects, Academic American Encyclopedia,* and *Britannica Encyclopedia of American Art.* Contributor to magazines and newspapers, including *New York, Avenue,* and *New York Times Magazine.* Editor, *Oculus,* 1981—.

SIDELIGHTS: C. Ray Smith wrote to *CA:* "My work is descriptive, attempting to conjure up a verbal picture and guide to the photographs and plans of the works discussed and illustrated. I am dedicated to telling, foremost, what the designer's intentions have been; my reasoning is that criticism of the applied arts must know the programmatic needs of the client/users in order to form accurate critiques of the final products and, in addition where architecture is concerned, discussion with the designers is essential to an understanding of what is invisible behind or within the walls—air conditioning and structural systems, particularly.

"Mannerism has been perhaps the leading direction of architecture in [the United States], in Europe, and in Japan since around 1960. It corresponds to the architectural mannerism of sixteenth-and seventeenth-century Italy and England. In the 1960s in the United States, as *Supermannerism: New Attitudes in Post-Modern Architecture* describes, this overall mannerism approach was accompanied by a pop art overtone that made it correspondent with popular culture—therefore 'supermannerism' or 'superman-nerism.'"

AVOCATIONAL INTERESTS: Theatre, music, travel.

* * *

SMITH, George O(liver) 1911-1981
(Wesley Long)

PERSONAL: Born April 9, 1911, in Chicago, Ill.; died May 27, 1981, in Rumford, N.J.; son of Henry Robert (a factory superintendent) and Mary Jane (Twigg) Smith; married Helen Kunzler, December 5, 1936 (divorced, 1948); married Dona Louise Stewart Campbell, 1949 (died, 1974); children: (first marriage) Diane Helen Smith Conroy, George Oliver, Jr.; (second marriage) Douglas Stewart. *Education:* Attended University of Chicago, 1929-30. *Religion:* "Hedonist."

ADDRESSES: Home—47 Waterman Ave., Rumford, N.J. 07760. *Agent*—Lurton Blassingame, Blassingame, McCauley & Ward, 432 Park Ave. S., New York, N.Y. 10016.

CAREER: In radio service and repair business in Chicago, Ill., 1932-35; radio engineer for General Household, 1935-38, Wells-Gardiner, 1938-40, Philco, 1940-42, 1946-51, and Crosley, 1942-44; Emerson Radio, New York, manager in components engineering, 1951-57; International Telephone & Telegraph, senior technical information analyst in defense communications, 1959-74; writer, 1974-81. *Wartime service:* National Defense Research Council, Washington, D.C., editorial engineer for Office of Scientific Research and Development, 1944-45.

AWARDS, HONORS: Naval Ordnance Development Award, 1945; citation from Office of Scientific Research and Development, National Defense Research Council, 1945; First Fandom Award, World Science Fiction Convention, 1980, for contributions to the genre of science fiction.

WRITINGS:

SCIENCE FICTION NOVELS

Pattern for Conquest: An Interplanetary Adventure, Gnome Press, 1949.
Nomad, Prime Press, 1950.
Operation Interstellar, Century, 1950.
Hellflower, Abelard Press, 1953.
Highways in Hiding, Gnome Press, 1956, abridged edition published as *The Space Plague,* Avon, 1957.
Troubled Star, Avalon, 1957.
Fire in the Heavens, Avalon, 1958.
The Path of Unreason, Gnome Press, 1958.
Lost in Space, Avalon, 1959.
The Fourth "R," Ballantine, 1959, published as *The Brain Machine,* Lancer Books, 1968, new edition edited by Lester Del Rey, Garland Publishing, 1975.

SHORT STORY COLLECTIONS

Venus Equilateral (includes "QRM—Interplanetary"), Prime Press, 1947, new edition edited by Lester Del Rey, Garland Publishing, 1975, revised and enlarged edition published as *The Complete Venus Equilateral,* Ballantine, 1976.
The Worlds of George O., Bantam, 1982.

OTHER

Mathematics: The Language of Science (juvenile nonfiction), Putnam, 1961.
Scientist's Nightmares (juvenile nonfiction), Putnam, 1972.

Also contributor, under pseudonym Wesley Long, of short stories in "Plutonian Lens" science-fiction series to *Astounding Science Fiction.* Reviewer, *Space Science Fiction.*

SIDELIGHTS: George O. Smith's career is reflected in his fiction. For many years he worked as an electrical engineer, and he was involved in radar research during World War II. The technology of his fictional solar system is extrapolated from his own experience in these fields. As *Dictionary of Literary Biography* contributor Bruce Herzberg reports, "Smith kept the future world of his fiction within the bounds of available scientific knowledge. He explains, often in great detail, how scientific speculation is transformed by engineering skill into material reality." "Like [Arthur C.] Clarke, Isaac Asimov, and other professional scientists who write extrapolative science fiction," Herzberg concludes, "Smith shows that physics and technology provide problems for conquest and a field for heroic imagination as satisfyingly dangerous and immediate as attacks of bug-eyed monsters."

Smith is perhaps best known for his short stories published in John W. Campbell's *Astounding Science Fiction* in the 1940s. The first of them, "QRM—Interplanetary," appeared in November, 1942, and caused such a sensation that Campbell featured Smith's next story on the magazine's cover. These stories, collected in 1947 under the title *Venus Equilateral,* are set in a space station circling the sun in the same orbit as Venus, serving as a communications link between Mars, Venus and the Earth. They "rely on realistic and calculable difficulties that must be overcome by scientific imagination (rather than imaginary science) and feasible hardware," and they "established Smith's reputation as a writer of extrapolative science fiction based on the best current technical knowledge," declares Herzberg. According to Lawrence I. Charters in the *Science Fiction and Fantasy Book Review,* the stories reflect "Smith's technical background, and both book and author are representative of Campbell's belief in the engineer/scientist as problem solver."

While Smith's work remains popular with science fiction readers, most critics agree that his writing has its failings. Algis Budrys, writing in the *Magazine of Fantasy and Science Fiction,* characterizes "QRM—Interplanetary" as "surely one of the least expertly plotted stories of 1942, and one of the most lecturesome and least tech-development stories [Smith] ever wrote." Nonetheless, he concludes, Smith's fiction has value because its heroes displayed a confidence in their ability to manipulate the universe. "What Smith was superb at was not at depicting what it's like to do engineering, and it's not at all central to his effectiveness that his idealized protagonists were engineers," says Budrys. "They could have been cabbage-throwers, as long as they displayed the same unquestioning comradeship, the same unencumbered sense that they had the handle on the universe, and the same validated ability to grab that handle and twist. . . . When you read the stories, you are them."

BIOGRAPHICAL/CRITICAL SOURCES:

BOOKS

Dictionary of Literary Biography, Volume 8: *Twentieth-Century American Science Fiction Writers,* Gale, 1981.
Smith, George O., *The Worlds of George O.,* Bantam, 1982.

PERIODICALS

Analog, March, 1977.
Horn Book, April, 1973.
Magazine of Fantasy and Science Fiction, March, 1981.
New York Times Book Review, May 21, 1961.
Science Fiction and Fantasy Book Review, October, 1982.
Science Fiction Review, November, 1982.

OBITUARIES:

PERIODICALS

AB Bookman's Weekly, July 27, 1981.
New York Times, June 4, 1981.*

*   *   *

SMITH, Paul B(rainerd)   1921-

PERSONAL: Born June 1, 1921, in Toronto, Ontario, Canada; son of Oswald Jeffrey (a minister) and Daisy (Billings) Smith; married Mary Anita Lawson, June 8, 1946; children: Oswald Glen, Jennifer Jann, Andrea Jill. *Education:* Attended Bob Jones University, 1939-41, and University of British Columbia, 1941-42; McMaster University, B.A., 1945; University of Toronto, graduate study, 1945-46.

ADDRESSES: Office—Peoples Church, 374 Sheppard Ave. E., Willowdale, Ontario, Canada.

CAREER: Peoples Church, Toronto, Ontario, associate pastor, 1952-58, minister, 1959—. Evangelistic crusader in Canada, Great Britain, the United States, Australia, the West Indies, Canal Zone, India, New Zealand, the Orient, South Africa, and Scandinavia; speaker at conferences on world missions and at Bible conferences in the United States and Canada.

Founder of Oswald J. Smith Elementary School and Paul B. Smith Academy, 1971.

WRITINGS:

Candid Conclusions, Marshall, Morgan & Scott, 1947.
Church Aflame, Marshall, Morgan & Scott, 1953.
After Midnight, Marshall, Morgan & Scott, 1956.
Naked Truth, Marshall, Morgan & Scott, 1957.
Eastward to Moscow, Peoples Press Printing Society, 1959.
World Conquest, Marshall, Morgan & Scott, 1960.
The Question of South Africa, Peoples Press Printing Society, 1961.
Daily Gospel: 365 One-Minute Daily Devotions, Zondervan, 1963, new edition, G. R. Welch, 1981.
Headline Pulpit, Marshall, Morgan & Scott, 1964.
Perilous Times, Attic Press, 1967.
Other Gospels, Marshall, Morgan & Scott, 1970.
The Church on the Brink, Tyndale, 1977.
The Senders: World Missions Conferences and Faith Promise Offerings, G. R. Welch, 1979.
Jesus, by John, G. R. Welch, 1980.
Jesus, by Matthew, G. R. Welch, 1981.
Revelation, G. R. Welch, 1986.
Jesus, by Mark, G. R. Welch, 1987.
Spiritual Growth, G. R. Welch, 1988.

SIDELIGHTS: Since Paul B. Smith became minister of Peoples Church, the congregation has had to build six new buildings, and Sunday School attendance has quadrupled. Smith's Sunday morning worship services are televised to 150,000 viewers.

*   *   *

SNOW, C(harles) P(ercy)   1905-1980

PERSONAL: Born October 15, 1905, in Leicester, England; died of a perforated ulcer, July 1, 1980, in London, England; son of William Edward (an organist and shoe factory clerk) and Ada Sophia (Robinson) Snow; married Pamela Hansford Johnson (a novelist and critic), July 14, 1950 (died June 18, 1981); children: Philip Charles Hansford. *Education:* University College, Leicester, B.Sc. (London; first class honours in chemistry), 1927, M.Sc. (London; physics), 1928; Christ's College, Cambridge, Ph.D. (physics), 1930.

ADDRESSES: Home—85 Eaton Ter., London S.W. 1, England. *Agent*—Curtis Brown Ltd., 575 Madison Ave., New York, N.Y. 10022.

CAREER: Cambridge University, Christ's College, Cambridge, England, fellow, 1930-50, tutor, 1935-45; English Electric Co. Ltd., London, physicist and director of scientific personnel, 1944-47, director, 1947-64; British Civil Service, London, England, commissioner, 1945-60; British Ministry of Technology, London, parliamentary under-secretary, 1964-66. Writer, 1932-80. Director, Educational Film Centre Ltd., 1961-64; member of board of directors, London bureau, University of Chicago Press; member, Arts Council, 1971-80. Rede Lecturer, Cambridge University, 1959; Godkin Lecturer, Harvard University, 1960; Regent's Professor of English, University of California, Berkeley, 1960. Rector, St. Andrews University, 1962-64; fellow, Morse College, Yale University, 1962. Member of Royal College of Malta Commission, 1956-60. *Wartime service:* British Ministry of Labour, director of technical personnel, 1942-45.

MEMBER: Royal Society of Literature (fellow), American Academy of Arts and Sciences—National Institute of Arts and Letters (honorary member), Society for European Culture, British Migraine Association (president, 1965), Library Association (president, 1961), H. G. Wells Society (vice-president, 1964); Savile Club, Athenaeum Club, and Marylebone Cricket Club (all London); Century Club (New York).

AWARDS, HONORS: Commander, Order of the British Empire, 1943, for services to the Ministry of Labour; British Annual of Literature medal, 1949, for *Time of Hope;* James Tait Black Memorial Prize, Edinburgh University, 1955, for *The Masters* and *The New Men;* knighted, 1957; created life peer Baron Snow of Leicester, 1964; Diamond Jubilee medal, Catholic University of America, 1964; Centennial Corporation award, Albert Einstein Medical Center, 1965; resolution of esteem, Congressional Committee on Science and Aeronautics, 1966; Centennial Engineering medal, Pennsylvania Military College, 1966; Cambridge University, extraordinary fellow of Churchill College and honorary fellow of Christ's College, both 1966; honorary fellow, Hatfield Polytechnic College, and York University, Toronto, both 1967; award for creative leadership in education, School of Education, New York University, 1969; International Dimitrov Prize, Bulgaria, 1980. Recipient of honorary doctorates and other academic awards from American, Canadian, English, Scottish, and Soviet universities, colleges, and academies, including LL.D. from University of Leicester, 1959, University of Liverpool, 1960, St. Andrews University, 1962, Brooklyn Polytechnic Institute, 1962, University of Bridgeport, 1966, York University, Toronto, 1967, Loyola University, 1970, Newfoundland University, 1973, and Hull University, 1980, D.Litt. from Dartmouth College, 1960, Bard College, 1962, Temple University, 1963, Syracuse University, 1963, University of Pittsburgh, 1964, Ithaca College, 1967, Westminster College, 1968, Western Ontario University, 1971, University of Cincinnati, 1976, New York University, 1976, Widener University, 1978, and Union College, 1979, D.H.L. from Kenyon College, 1961, Washington University, 1963, University of Michigan, 1963, Hebrew Union College, 1968, Alfred University, 1969, University of Akron, 1969, University of Louisville, 1976, and Pace University, 1977, Doctor of Philological Sciences from Rostov State University, 1963, and D.Sc. from Pennsylvania Military College, 1966.

WRITINGS:

NOVELS

Death under Sail (mystery), Doubleday, 1932, reprinted, Scribner, 1981, revised edition, Heinemann, 1959.
New Lives for Old (science fiction; published anonymously), Gollancz, 1933.
The Search, Gollancz, 1934, Bobbs-Merrill, 1935, reprinted, Penguin, 1965, revised edition, Macmillan (London), 1959.
The Malcontents, Scribner, 1972.
In Their Wisdom, Scribner, 1974.
A Coat of Varnish (mystery), Scribner, 1979.

Also author of unpublished novels, *Youth Searching,* and *The Devoted.*

"STRANGERS AND BROTHERS" CYCLE; NOVELS

Strangers and Brothers, Faber, 1940, Scribner, 1960, reprinted, Scribner, 1985, published as *George Passant* (also see below), Penguin, 1973.
The Light and the Dark (also see below), Faber, 1947, Macmillan, 1948, reprinted, Penguin, 1979.

Time of Hope (also see below), Faber, 1949, Macmillan, 1950, reprinted, Penguin, 1978.
The Masters (British Book Society selection; also see below), Macmillan, 1951, reprinted, Scribner, 1979.
The New Men (also see below), Macmillan (London), 1954, Scribner, 1955.
Homecoming, Scribner, 1956 (published in England as *Homecomings* [also see below], Macmillan, 1956, reprinted, Penguin, 1979).
The Conscience of the Rich (also see below), Scribner, 1958, reprinted, Penguin, 1979.
The Affair (British Book Society and Book-of-the-Month Club selection; also see below), Scribner, 1960, reprinted, Penguin, 1979.
Corridors of Power (also see below), Scribner, 1964.
The Sleep of Reason (Book-of-the-Month Club selection; also see below), Macmillan (London), 1968, Scribner, 1969.
Last Things (Book-of-the-Month Club selection; also see below), Scribner, 1970.
Strangers and Brothers: Omnibus Edition, Volume 1: *Time of Hope, George Passant, The Conscience of the Rich, The Light and the Dark,* Volume 2: *The Masters, The New Men, Homecomings, The Affair,* Volume 3: *Corridors of Power, The Sleep of Reason, Last Things,* Scribner, 1972.

ESSAYS, ADDRESSES, AND LECTURES

The Two Cultures and the Scientific Revolution (Rede Lecture), Cambridge University Press, 1959, expanded edition published as *The Two Cultures: And a Second Look* (also see below), 1963, New American Library, 1964.
The Moral Un-Neutrality of Science (also see below), [Philadelphia], 1961.
Science and Government (Godkin Lectures; also see below), Harvard University Press, 1961.
Recent Thoughts on the Two Cultures, Birkbeck College, University of London, 1961.
A Postscript to "Science and Government," Harvard University Press, 1962.
On Magnanimity (Rector's Address), St. Andrews University, 1962.
The State of Siege (John Findlay Greene Foundation Lectures; also see below), Scribner, 1969.
Kinds of Excellence (Kenneth Aldred Spencer Lecture), University of Kansas Libraries, 1970.
Public Affairs (lectures; includes "The Two Cultures: And a Second Look," "The Moral Un-Neutrality of Science," "Science and Government," "The State of Siege," and "The Case of Leavis and the Serious Case"), Scribner, 1971.

Also contributor to *Essays and Studies* of the English Association, 1961.

CRITICISM

Richard Aldington: An Appreciation, Heinemann, 1938.
The English Realistic Novel, Modern Language Teachers' Association of Sweden, 1957.
Variety of Men (biographies and reminiscences), Scribner, 1967.
Trollope: His Life and Art, Scribner, 1975 (published in England as *Trollope,* Macmillan, 1975).
The Realists: Eight Portraits, Scribner, 1978 (published in England as *The Realists: Portraits of Eight Novelists— Stendhal, Balzac, Dickens, Dostoevsky, Tolstoy, Galdos, Henry James, Proust,* Macmillan, 1978).
The Physicists: A Generation That Changed the World (history), Little, Brown, 1981.

PLAYS

"The Ends of the Earth," televised by British Broadcasting Corp., 1949, produced on stage as "Views over the Park," in Hammersmith at Lyric Theatre, 1950.
(With wife, Pamela Hansford Johnson) *The Supper Dance*, Evans Brothers, 1951.
(With Johnson) *Family Party*, Evans Brothers, 1951.
(With Johnson) *Spare the Rod*, Evans Brothers, 1951.
(With Johnson) *To Murder Mrs. Mortimer*, Evans Brothers, 1951.
(With Johnson) *Her Best Foot Forward*, Evans Brothers, 1951.
(With Johnson) *The Pigeon with the Silver Foot: A Legend of Venice* (one-act), Evans Brothers, 1951.
"The Young and Antient Men: A Chronicle of the Pilgrim Fathers," BBC-TV, 1952.
(Adapter with Johnson, and author of introduction) Georgi Dzhagarov, *The Public Prosecutor* (produced in London at Hampstead Theatre Club, 1967), translated from the Bulgarian by Marguerite Alexieva, University of Washington, 1969.

Also author of unproduced play, "Nights Ahead," and, with William Gerhardi, of play "The Fool of the Family."

CONTRIBUTOR

Arthur Bryant, editor, *Imaginary Biographies*, Allen & Unwin, 1936.
Alister Kershaw and Frederic-Jacques Temple, *Richard Aldington: An Intimate Portrait*, Southern Illinois University Press, 1966.
Maurice Goldsmith, *The Science of Society*, Penguin, 1966.
B. S. Benedikz, editor, *On the Novel: A Present for Walter Allen on His 60th Birthday from His Friends and Colleagues*, Dent, 1971.
Dora B. Weiner and William R. Keylor, editors, *From Parnassus: Essays in Honor of Jacques Barzun*, Harper, 1976.

OTHER

(Editor with Johnson) *Winter's Tales 7: Stories from Modern Russia*, St. Martin's, 1961, published as *Stories from Modern Russia*, 1962.
(Author of introduction) Arnold A. Rogow, *The Jew in a Gentile World*, Macmillan, 1961.
(Author of preface) Jessica Brett Young, *Francis Brett Young: A Biography*, Heinemann, 1962.
(Author of introduction) Charles Reznikoff, *By the Waters of Manhattan: Selected Verse*, New Directions, 1962.
C. P. Snow: A Spectrum—Science, Criticism, Fiction (selections from novels, speeches, and articles), edited by Stanley Weintraub, Scribner, 1963.
(Author of preface) Ronald Millar, *The Affair, The New Men and The Masters* (three plays based on Snow's novels of the same titles), Macmillan (London), 1964.
(Author of introduction) John Holloway, *A London Childhood*, Routledge & Kegan Paul, 1966, Scribner, 1967.
(Author of foreword) G. H. Hardy, *A Mathematician's Apology*, Cambridge University Press, 1967.
(Author of introduction) Sir Arthur Conan Doyle, *The Case-Book of Sherlock Holmes*, Murray & Cape, 1974.
"The Role of Personality in Science" (sound recording; read by the author), J. Norton Publishers, 1974.
"The Two Cultures of C. P. Snow: A Contemporary English Intellectual Discusses Science and the State of Man" (sound recording), Center for Cassette Studies, 1975.

Also contributor of many scientific papers, primarily on infra-red investigation of molecular structures, to *Proceedings of the Royal Society*, 1928-29, 1930-32, and 1935. Contributor of weekly articles on Cambridge cricket to *The Cricketer*, summers, 1937-39. Editor, "Cambridge Library of Modern Science" series, beginning 1931. Contributor to periodicals, including *New Statesman, Nation, Look, Sunday Times, Financial Times*, and *Science*. Editor, *Discovery*, 1938-40.

WORK IN PROGRESS: A second series of *Variety of Men* (biographies and reminiscences).

SIDELIGHTS: C. P. Snow was "an attentive observer of life in three disparate worlds—the world of science, the world of literature, and the world of government and administration—and to some extent a participant in all of them," according to Arthur C. Turner in the *New York Times Book Review*. Alan Gardner in *Saturday Review* further characterized him as possessing "the intellect of a professor; the confidence of a soothsayer; the erudition of a top-flight statesman; the devil-may-care approach of a warm-blooded novelist; and the hardsell technique of a successful businessman." "In truth," Gardner concluded, he was "all these things." Trained as a scientist, Snow achieved success as an administrator and novelist, and became "a household word in many places and [had] a celebrity achieved by few writers after Shaw and Hemingway," stated *New Yorker* contributor George Steiner. "All of his life," announced a reporter for the *National Observer*, "[was] spent combining and understanding the interactions of science, art, and government, and he [became] an accepted master in all three disciplines."

Snow began his career as a scientist through necessity rather than by choice. The second of four sons born to parents of low income, Snow's education was limited to what he could afford. In order to attend college at all he required financial aid, and at that time the only assistance available to students from his background was in the sciences. So, in 1925, he enrolled in the newly created department of physics and chemistry at Leicester University College. As his brother Philip Snow stated in his *Stranger and Brother: A Portrait of C. P. Snow*, "It would not have been possible to do this from the school's Arts side to which, he told me, he would have otherwise transferred as early as he could."

Although Snow proved to be a first-rate student of theory, professors soon realized that in handling laboratory equipment he was less than adept. Nonetheless, he won another scholarship to Cambridge University, based on his performance at Leicester. Soon after he received his Ph.D. he was elected a fellow of Christ's College, "which meant that he might hope to find a permanent place at the University: among scientists he was beginning to be spoken of . . . as a bright young man," wrote William Cooper in his study *C. P. Snow*. In 1933, however, "a piece of research that went wrong through oversight" helped convince Snow that his true vocation lay elsewhere, stated Cooper. Philip Snow further suggested that his brother's awkwardness in the laboratory "was the real reason for his abandoning scientific research, especially as some of his technical predictions turned out to be false."

Instead, Snow turned his energies to writing and there, as Turner declared, the "young Cambridge scientist of the 1930's found his true metier." In 1932, Snow published a murder mystery, *Death under Sail*, which met with some popular success. He then produced an anonymous science-fiction story and a mainstream novel, *The Search*. Of the latter Philip Snow remarked, "It reflected some of his agony over his scientific failure, the main character abandoning science to write a book on the political state of Europe.'' Snow's work met with enough critical success to convince him fully that his future lay in literature. ''From then on,'' stated Cooper, ''he did no more research. However, he continued to teach science in the university, and was appointed to a college Tutorship in 1934.''

Snow's horizons expanded during the 1940s. At the onset of the Second World War, he left Cambridge for government service. He was approached by a branch of the Royal Society to assist in recruiting other scientists for Britain's war effort, a function later assumed by the Ministry of Labour. During the war, Cooper stated, Snow's ''chief role was to exercise personal judgement on how individual scientists might best be employed, in research, in government research establishments or industry, or as technical officers in the Armed Forces; and to plan how the number of scientists and engineers in the country might be increased.'' Snow continued in this line of work as a commissioner for scientific appointments in the civil service after the war. From 1945 until 1960, said Cooper, he ''participated in all the major appointments of scientists to the government service; and he acted as an essential point of reference in questions of official policy relating to scientific manpower and technological education.'' For his services in these areas, a knighthood was conferred upon him in 1957. In 1964 he was awarded a life peerage to enable him to serve the government in the House of Lords as parliamentary secretary to the newly formed Ministry of Technology. ''The route [Snow's] career took was not especially devious,'' stated Russell Davies in the *New York Review of Books,* ''but on the other hand it was longer and steeper than such ascents are likely to be again, now that society is no longer surprised to discover brains among the poor.''

The circumstances of Snow's education and his unique career as an administrator, a scientist and a writer gave him an original perspective on the relationship of science and literature. He saw that people interested in literature and people engaged in scientific pursuits were unable to talk to one another. The disparity between the two groups was so great that he began referring to them as ''The Two Cultures.'' Philip Snow indicated that this phrase, coined by his brother, and ''likely to be used for a good many years yet, was a product of his upbringing; it was partly the result of the range of his early reading, partly of the lack of educational opportunity at a crucial stage which forced him towards science.'' Snow articulated his views on these subjects in the Cambridge University Rede lecture of 1959, which he called *The Two Cultures and the Scientific Revolution.*

In *The Two Cultures and the Scientific Revolution* Snow highlighted two weaknesses in modern thought which he saw as ultimately disastrous for Western civilization. Snow's first thesis suggested that scientists and other educated people can no longer communicate effectively with each other; scientists tend to regard literature as unproductive, while literary thinkers see science as incomprehensible. According to Cooper, Snow felt that this condition ''is in any case intellectually and socially undesirable,'' and ''in the case of a country in the particular situation that [Great Britain] is in, it could in a short time be catastrophic.'' Why? Because what Snow labelled the ''scientific revolution''—the industrial application of electronics, the peaceful use of atomic energy, and the expansion of robotics and automation—will change the world to an even greater extent than did the industrial revolution of the nineteenth century. Snow argued, said Cooper, that this lack of communication between scientists and non-scientists would lead to di-

saster; he stated that ''the splintering of a culture into an increasing number of fragments, between which communication becomes less and less possible, inevitably leads to attrition and decay.'' A way to change this situation, Snow suggested, is through educational reforms which stress sciences and mathematics in the elementary levels and the humanities in the higher grades.

Snow's second thesis, according to Cooper, was that this lack of communication between scientists and others ''obscures the existence of the major gap in the world today, namely that between the countries which are technologically advanced and the rest—major because it is a more deep-seated cause of possible world conflict than any other.'' Snow saw the contrast between the poverty of the undeveloped Third World nations and the wealth of the Western powers as a threat to world peace. He believed that ''the prime social task of the advanced countries, for the sake of their own continued peaceful existence if no one else's, is to reduce the gap. This can only be done by helping the less advanced countries to industrialize as rapidly as possible,'' declared Cooper. In order for Western civilization to survive, Snow suggested, the entire world must be advanced to their level. ''It is technically possible to carry out the scientific revolution in India, Africa, South-east Asia, Latin America, the Middle East, within fifty years,'' Snow stated in his lecture. ''There is no excuse for western man not to know this. And not to know that this is the one way out through the three menaces which stand in our way—H-bomb war, over-population, the gap between the rich and the poor. This is one of the situations where the worst crime is innocence.'' Snow concluded, ''We have very little time. So little that I dare not guess at it.''

Snow's theses were recognized as important by many critics and inspired a variety of interpretations. For instance, John Wren-Lewis pointed out in the *New Statesman* that although Snow's message was ''assumed to have been a warning about the danger of lack of communication between 'humanities' and 'sciences,''' Snow was really more concerned ''with a much larger issue than this: indeed, the whole point of his lecture was to argue that the failures of communication that beset our academic life are merely symptoms of a much more fundamental division in western society which extends back through the Victorian era and beyond. . . .'' Wren-Lewis declared that Snow's ''message was that our civilisation has to come to terms not only with the actual discoveries and applications of science, but, much more important, with the cultural revolution that made the advances of science and technology over the past three centuries possible.'' ''In other words,'' he concluded, ''we have to come to terms with the experimental spirit, which is not at all the same thing as 'doing more science' or even 'knowing more science.'''

Snow's own career demonstrated that the two cultures need not be mutually exclusive. Robert Gorham Davis asserted in his study *C. P. Snow,* ''A scientist by training, a writer by vocation, Snow offers himself as a unique living bridge between the two cultures. But his capacities and experience extend further than this.'' Davis pointed out that Snow was an executive as well as a scientist and author, and that a knowledge of science was at least as necessary to people in that occupation as to people with a literary background. ''If we are to speak of 'cultures' in the plural,'' he said, ''there is no need to be limited to two. Administrators in the universities, in business, and government belong neither to science nor the arts, and may be considered a culture of their own. 'One of the most bizarre features of any industrial society in our time,'

Snow wrote in *Science and Government,* 'is that the cardinal choices have to be made by a handful of men . . . who cannot have a first-hand knowledge of what these choices depend upon or what their results may be.' Nonscientific administrators now decide how science is to be organized and used.'' Snow's unique position enabled him to act as a sort of arbiter; Davis declared, ''By bringing together two kinds of imagination which he had himself experienced, [Snow] could enable scientists and literary men to appreciate each other, and the lay public to appreciate both.''

Reaction to Snow's theses varied. It impressed a variety of people ranging from then-Senator John F. Kennedy to Bertrand Russell to the Russian ambassador to Britain. What Charles Snow had to say, Philip Snow declared, ''had long been obvious to thinking people but nothing was being done about it. . . . His honest account of the lack of communication between scientists and non-scientists on everyday and more critically important levels aroused the deepest feelings of anxiety. Many found the truth unpalatable, and books and articles—from the highly commendatory to unwarrantably vituperative—came pouring out.'' Philip Snow quotes Kennedy as calling *The Two Cultures and the Scientific Revolution* ''one of the most provocative discussions that I have ever read of this intellectual dilemma which at the same time is of profound consequence to our public policy.'' The greatest assault came from F. R. Leavis, whose vitriolic attack was published in the *Spectator* in 1962. Leavis's onslaught, which included personal slights on Snow's character, ''seemed to do Snow little professional harm at first, but it has had some destructive effects in later years,'' said Davies. ''For one thing, Leavis was abominably rude to Snow, who accepted this with a kind of stolid disgust,'' Davies continued, ''and the result has been that ever since, many British critics and less-than-critics have been able to disparage Snow freely, happy in the knowledge that he has suffered worse.'' Snow finally responded to Leavis's criticisms in an article in the *Times Literary Supplement* in 1970.

Critics recognized that the theses stated in *The Two Cultures and the Scientific Revolution* reintroduced themes found in Snow's novels and reflected his career as an administrator as well. As Davis put it, ''Not since Disraeli has a popular, political-minded novelist been so intimately involved with the actual exercise of power. Not since H. G. Wells has a popular, social-minded novelist known so much at first hand about science. For nearly twenty years before 1958, Snow had been in an ideal position to carry out in his fiction the program defined in 'The Two Cultures.''' Davis concluded that Snow ''could dramatize for his readers the struggle toward those social goods which he condemned the major writers of his century for betraying,'' especially in works such as *The Sleep of Reason, The Masters,* and *Corridors of Power.*

Snow addressed this struggle, along with other questions, in what is generally regarded as his greatest work, the eleven books that make up the cycle called *Strangers and Brothers.* In these novels, declared Douglas Hill of the Toronto *Globe and Mail,* the author examined ''the world of public affairs, the academic, scientific and political arenas judged as moral testing grounds.'' Snow first conceived of a sequence of interrelated novels early in 1935. Philip Snow remarked, ''It was to take him five years to plan the sequence in general and to produce, as his next book after *The Search* in 1934, the first of the *Strangers and Brothers* series, initially entitled *Strangers and Brothers* [published in 1940] and later changed

to *George Passant.* This was to be followed by *The Conscience of the Rich, The Masters,* and *Time of Hope.*''

Snow's program was interrupted by the war, and later volumes in the sequence were delayed because of his work for the government. However, he kept the idea alive, and by the war's end had a firm idea of what the sequence should be. Philip Snow quoted from a note written by his brother in 1945: ''Each of the novels [in the *Strangers and Brothers* sequence] will be intelligible if read separately, but the series is planned as one integral work of art and I should like it so considered and so judged. The work has two explicit intentions—first to carry out an investigation into human nature . . . through a wide variety of characters, major and minor, second, to depict a number of social backgrounds in England in the period 1920-50 from the dispossessed to Cabinet Ministers. For each major character, the narrator is occupied with the questions: How much of his fate is due to the accident of his class and time? and how much to the essence of his nature which is unaffected by class and time?'' ''All the social backgrounds are authentic,'' Snow concluded. ''I have lived in most of them myself; and the one or two I have not lived in I know at very close second-hand.''

Readers familiar with Snow's life and career detected many elements from the author's experiences in his novels. Philip Snow pointed out that Snow based many of his characters on people he had known. Many readers identified Lewis Eliot, the narrator of the entire sequence, with Snow himself; one reason for this was because Eliot was born in 1905, the same year as Snow. *Dictionary of Literary Biography* contributor David Shusterman commented, ''Though dissimilarities exist between the author and his narrator—the main one being that Lewis Eliot is a lawyer—there are some striking similarities. The chief of these is that the narrator becomes a member of the Labour party and lives securely, for the most part, within the establishment.'' In one case, at least, fiction anticipated life. In the novel *Corridors of Power* Eliot was chosen by defense minister Roger Quaife as his closest political associate; the year the book was published, Snow himself joined Harold Wilson's government. However, some critics have questioned how closely Snow and Eliot should be identified. ''Though it may be unwise to assert that Eliot's reactions throughout the sequence are Snow's, nevertheless many readers of the sequence have made this assertion,'' declared Shusterman. ''Certainly there is not much evidence, except of the most superficial kind, that the two are very different.''

The character of Lewis Eliot is one of the factors that ties these novels together. According to Cooper, the structure of the sequence is basically simple; the accounts trace ''the life-story of the narrator, Lewis Eliot, in terms of alternation between what Snow himself [called] 'direct experience' and 'observed experience.''' In some of the novels, the actions of the narrator Lewis Eliot himself were emphasized; this was what Snow called ''direct experience.'' In other books, Eliot functioned as an interested third party, observing the actions of the featured characters and commenting on them. This was what Snow called ''observed experience.'' Cooper continued, ''The design of the sequence is continuously cyclical. With *Time of Hope* Lewis Eliot first of all tells his own story over a certain period of time and then, in the next five novels, the stories of some of his friends during more or less the same period. . . . With *Homecomings* Lewis begins a second similar cycle over a later period. And *Last Things,* again a novel of 'direct experience,' draws the whole work together.''

Alfred Kazin in his book *Contemporaries* characterized the novels in this sequence as "remarkably intelligent," and called them the product of long and hard thought. "The action," said Davis, "consists largely of talk among small groups of people. This talk is directed toward practical or emotional ends; rarely are literary, scientific, or political ideas developed for their own sake. In Snow's novels people seldom write letters, and they telephone chiefly to arrange face-to-face meetings. At these meetings something unexpected is usually revealed—often reluctantly, hesitantly, as a result of close questioning—which makes it necessary to plan at once a meeting with somebody else." He explained, "The novels consist of a series of short dramatic chapters, each marking a stage in the careful step-by-step development of some issue or affair."

One of the components which made Snow's novels effective, claimed Cooper, was his prose style. He stated that "the major point about Snow's style is that it has been developed firstly to give *absolute conviction on the plane of immediate fact*, though it has been developed so flexibly that it can also be used for both narrative and analytical purposes." "It has a compelling tone which arises not only, or even mainly, from knowledge, but from the author's total involvement in what he is doing," concluded Cooper. "To read it is to believe it." G. S. Fraser, a contributor to *The Politics of Twentieth-Century Novelists,* defined Snow's efforts as "a sort of puritan prose; he does not convey the oddly self-enjoying quality of human life half as much in his novels as he does in some of his prose memoirs. He writes, I think, good puritan, or perhaps good early Royal Society, prose: a naked, plain, and natural style." "In effect," concluded Rubin Rabinovitz in *The Reaction against Experiment in the English Novel, 1950-1960,* "this means that Snow has eschewed all devices such as allusion, symbolism, the stream of consciousness, complex uses of time (there are rarely even any flashbacks in his books); little attention is given to the sounds of words or the rhythm of sentences; rarely are there any vivid passages or striking metaphors; and there is no conscious use of allegory or myth. Instead the prose is straightforward and never difficult to understand—'readable,' as Snow puts it."

Other reviewers felt differently; Bernard Bergonzi, writing in *The Situation of the Novel,* declared that "Snow's linguistic resources are still inadequate to meet his emotional demands." Julian Symons in his *Critical Occasions* found an "alkaline flatness" in Snow's writing, but asserted, "The style is that of a lucid and uncommonly honest recorder, rather than of an artist." Stanley Weintraub, writing in *MOSAIC IV/3,* declared, "The administrative, often scientific, prose, precise, flat and unemotional, with its figures of speech more often from chemistry or anthropology or medicine than from aesthetics, seems Snow's personal bridging of the 'Two Cultures.'"

Some critics viewed Snow's style as old-fashioned, but recognized that this was not necessarily a defect in his work. Symons commented that Snow "ignores half a century of experimental writing." He continued, "Mr. Snow is not imperceptive of the revolution in the novel's technique connected with the names of James Joyce, Wyndham Lewis, Joyce Cary and many others; he ignores them deliberately in pursuit of an aesthetic which has never been openly formulated, but is perhaps his own version of realism—a realism that looks back to Trollope rather than to the symbolic naturalism of Zola . . ." Davis also compared Snow's work to that of Anthony Trollope. "Trollope's Barsetshire novels," he concluded, "[have]

many of the same ingredients as the 'Strangers and Brothers' series, dramatized in the same way. Complex institutions—governmental and clerical—are staffed by the worldly, the selfish, the conscientious, the refractory, battling for principles, place, and power." Davies saw similarities between Snow's work and that of seventeenth-century French novelist Jean-Louis Balzac. "It was Balzac's mock-modest claim that society was doing the storytelling, and that his own function was merely 'secretarial,'" the critic explained.

Part of the reason Snow's novels differ from most modern literary works is that they are intended to be didactic rather than artistic. Kazin suggested that Snow was reactionary in the form his novels took because his interest was not in the book itself, but in the questions and ideas raised by it: "Snow, in opposing his work to the formal esthetic of [Virginia] Woolf and Joyce, has also saved himself from artistic risks and demands in which he is not interested." Peter Fison, writing in *Twentieth Century,* declared, "[To] blame Snow's style for lacking virtues which are not only irrelevant but would be completely out of place in the character of his work is . . . inadequate." Frederick R. Karl stated in *The Politics of Conscience: The Novels of C. P. Snow,* "In short, Snow is that phenomenon among twentieth-century novelists: a serious moralist concerned with integrity, duty, principles, and ideals. . . . His novelistic world is not distorted or exaggerated; his work rests not on artistic re-creation but on faithful reproduction, careful arrangement, and common-sensical development of character and situation." In short, Karl maintained, "Snow has attempted in his modest way to bring fiction back to a concern with commonplace human matters without making the novel either journalistic, naturalistic, or prophetic."

On one level, Snow's novels concern people faced with old questions in the new world of the twentieth century. *Strangers and Brothers* is, as Robert K. Morris described it in *Continuance and Change: The British Novel Sequence,* the "most sustained attempt at codifying fictionally the dilemmas and directions of our age." "Specifically, Snow asks," stated Karl, "what is man like in the twentieth century? how does a good man live in a world of temptations? how can ambition be reconciled with conscience? what is daily life like in an age in which all things are uncertain except one's feelings?" But Snow also used the sequence to describe the placement and use or abuse of power in twentieth-century society. His depiction of the workings of power politics, stated Fraser, deal "with centrally important questions of 'pure' politics, in the sense that I have defined that: the relationships between knowledge and power (or knowledge and charisma), between expedience and justice, between one's affection for a certain person, say, and one's perception that another person, for whom one has little affection, is the better man for a certain job." Snow's novels, he declared, "are at least unique in modern fiction in giving us a dry but accurate notion of how we are ruled and some quite deep insights into the consciences of our rulers."

On another level, *Strangers and Brothers* is about relations between people. Cooper declared, "In content [the cycle] is essentially a personal story—the story of a man's life, through which is revealed his psychological and his moral structure—yet by extension and implication it is an enquiry into the psychological and moral structure of a large fraction of the society of our times." Philip Snow cited a letter C. P. Snow wrote to Mrs. Maryke Lanius in 1961, reading in part: "The phrase *Strangers and Brothers* is supposed to represent the fact that in part of our lives each person is alone (each of us lives in isolation and in such parts of the individual life we are all strangers) and in part of our lives, including social activities, we can and should feel for each other like brothers.'' Snow continued, ''Socially I am optimistic and I believe that men are able to grapple with their social history. That is, the brothers side of the overall theme contains a completely definite hope. But some aspects of the individual life do not carry the same feeling. Have you ever seen anyone you love die of disseminated sclerosis? This is the strangers part of the thing. I don't believe we subtract from our social optimism if we see the individual tragedies with clear eyes. On the contrary, I believe we strengthen ourselves for those tasks which are within our power.''

Snow's tasks were for the most part finished by 1970. He left government service in 1966 and returned to writing full-time, completing the *Strangers and Brothers* sequence with *Last Things*. Between lectures and addresses he continued to attend debates in the House of Lords, and completed three novels and several works of nonfiction. As the sixties and seventies progressed, however, his optimism began to fade. ''The Vietnam war, antagonism between Russia and America, the unsettled state of the Third World were all causes for concern,'' declared Philip Snow, and attacks of what, at the time, was believed to be migratory arthritis also contributed to his depression. Snow's health worsened and he died in 1980 of a massive hemorrhage precipitated by a perforated gastric ulcer. His last book, *The Physicists,* a series of biographical sketches, was published posthumously.

In spite of Snow's tendency toward pessimism in his later years, stated Karl, ''It is possible to see Snow's entire career as a way of bringing people closer together, not of course through the vulgar way of the evangelist or the popular humanitarian, but through demonstrating man's common aims.'' This is evident in Snow's novels and in his lectures, Kazin claimed; the author, he said, ''is simply pursuing the same theme: that the similarities among men are sufficiently great to warrant their rapprochement.'' In this reconciliation of brother with brother, Cooper declared, one can still see a strain of optimism. ''The split in the culture [alarmed] him; and the gap between the rich advanced nations and the poverty-stricken backward ones [troubled] him both practically and morally,'' Cooper asserted. ''But both gaps can be reduced by men of goodwill if they set themselves out to do it. There is no reason why the human *social* condition should be tragic. It can be affected by human action. There *is* hope for the future.''

MEDIA ADAPTATIONS: Sir Ronald Millar adapted several of Snow's novels as plays, including *The Affair,* a three-act play produced in London at the Strand Theatre in 1961-62, and published by Scribner in 1962; it also opened in Boston at the Henry Miller Theater on September 6, 1982. ''The New Men'' was first produced in Brighton at the Theatre Royal in 1962, but later that year it moved to London, where it was produced at the Strand Theatre. *The Masters: A Play* was first produced in London at the Savoy Theatre on May 29, 1963, and published by Samuel French in 1964. These three were also published by Macmillan of London in one volume under the title *The Affair, The New Men and The Masters* in 1964. Other Millar versions include *The Case in Question: A Play,* an adaptation of *In Their Wisdom,* produced at the Theatre Royal in Haymarket in 1975, and published by Samuel French in the same year, and *A Coat of Varnish: A Play in Two Acts,* produced at the Theatre Royal in Haymarket in 1982, and pub-

lished by Samuel French in 1983. Arthur and Violet Ketels adapted ''Time of Hope'' to the stage; it was produced in Philadelphia in 1963.

BIOGRAPHICAL/CRITICAL SOURCES:

BOOKS

Allen, Walter, *The Modern Novel,* Dutton, 1965.
Allsop, Kenneth, *The Angry Decade,* P. Owen, 1958.
Atkins, John, *Six Novelists Look at Society,* Calder, 1977.
Bergonzi, Bernard, *The Situation of the Novel,* University of Pittsburgh Press, 1970.
Boytinck, Paul, *C. P. Snow: A Reference Guide,* G. K. Hall, 1980.
Bradbury, Malcolm, *Possibilities: Essays on the State of the Novel,* Oxford University Press, 1973.
Burgess, Anthony, *The Novel Now: A Guide to Contemporary Fiction,* Norton, 1967.
Contemporary Literary Criticism, Gale, Volume 1, 1973, Volume 4, 1975, Volume 6, 1976, Volume 9, 1978, Volume 13, 1980, Volume 19, 1981.
Cooper, William (pseudonym of Harry Summerfield Hoff), *C. P. Snow,* Longmans, Green, 1959.
Davis, Robert Gorham, *C. P. Snow,* Columbia University Press, 1965.
Dictionary of Literary Biography, Gale, Volume 15: *British Novelists, 1930-1959,* 1983, Volume 77: *British Mystery Writers, 1920-1939,* 1989.
Enright, D. J., *Conspirators and Poets,* Dufour, 1966.
Fuller, Edmund, *Books with Men behind Them,* Random House, 1959.
Greacen, Robert, *The World of C. P. Snow,* London House & Maxwell, 1963.
Halperin, John, *C. P. Snow: An Oral Biography; Together with a Conversation with Lady Snow (Pamela Hansford Johnson),* St. Martin's, 1983.
Johnson, Pamela Hansford, *Important to Me: Personalia,* Macmillan, 1974, Scribner, 1975.
Karl, Frederick R., *A Reader's Guide to the Contemporary English Novel,* Farrar, Straus, 1962.
Karl, Frederick R., *C. P. Snow: The Politics of Conscience,* Southern Illinois University Press, 1963.
Kazin, Alfred, *Contemporaries,* Little, 1962.
Leavis, F. R., *The Two Cultures: The Significance of C. P. Snow,* Random House, 1963.
Morris, Robert K., *Continuance and Change: The Contemporary British Novel Sequence,* Southern Illinois University Press, 1972.
Newquist, Roy, *Counterpoint,* Simon & Schuster, 1964.
Panichas, George, editor, *The Politics of Twentieth-Century Novelists,* Hawthorne, 1971.
Rabinovitz, Robin, *The Reaction against Experiment in the English Novel, 1958-1960,* Columbia University Press, 1967.
Ramanthan, Suguna, *The Novels of C. P. Snow,* Macmillan (London), 1978.
Raymond, John, editor, *The Baldwin Age,* Eyre & Spottiswoode, 1960.
Schusterman, David, *C. P. Snow,* Twayne, 1975.
Snow, C. P., *The Two Cultures and the Scientific Revolution,* Cambridge University Press, 1959.
Snow, Philip, *Stranger and Brother: A Portrait of C. P. Snow,* Macmillan, 1982, Scribner, 1983.
Symons, Julian, *Critical Occasions,* Hamish Hamilton, 1966.
Thale, Jerome, *C. P. Snow,* Oliver & Boyd, 1964.

Wain, John, *Essays on Literature and Ideas,* St. Martin's 1963.

Weintraub, Stanley, editor, *C. P. Snow: A Spectrum—Science, Criticism, Fiction,* Scribner, 1963.

PERIODICALS

American Scholar, summer, 1965.

Atlantic, February, 1955, April, 1958, June, 1960, November, 1964, February, 1969, September, 1970, June, 1972, December, 1974, January, 1980.

Best Sellers, September 15, 1964, May 1, 1967, January 15, 1969, June 15, 1969, September 15, 1970.

Books and Bookmen, March, 1965, January, 1969, February, 1969, December, 1970, November, 1971, December, 1971, August, 1972, January, 1973, May, 1973, March, 1975, April, 1979, November, 1979.

Chicago Tribune Book World, November 11, 1979, September 20, 1981.

Choice, April, 1970, February, 1985.

Christian Science Monitor, January 13, 1955, October 11, 1956, February 27, 1958, May 12, 1960, September 29, 1960, September 17, 1964, May 4, 1967, January 16, 1969, August 27, 1970.

Commonweal, December 21, 1951, February 4, 1955, June 27, 1958, February 12, 1960, May 13, 1960, October 2, 1964.

Critical Quarterly, winter, 1973.

Detroit News, May 30, 1972.

Economist, November 21, 1970.

Encounter, January, 1965.

Esquire, March, 1969.

Globe and Mail (Toronto), March 31, 1984.

Guardian, April 14, 1960.

Harper's Magazine, February, 1969.

Library Journal, May 15, 1969, July, 1970.

Life, April 7, 1961, May 5, 1967, January 17, 1969.

Listener, October 31, 1968, October 10, 1974, September 13, 1979.

London Magazine, January, 1969.

Los Angeles Times, October 18, 1981.

Los Angeles Times Book Review, June 28, 1987.

MOSAIC IV/3, spring, 1971.

Nation, December 8, 1956, March 15, 1958, June 25, 1960, July 17, 1967, December 9, 1968, April 28, 1969, May 29, 1972.

National Observer, November 18, 1968, January 13, 1969.

National Review, October 6, 1964, May 22, 1967, February 25, 1969, June 8, 1979, June 13, 1980.

New Leader, August 28, 1967.

New Republic, February 23, 1948, October 8, 1956, June 2, 1958, April 11, 1960, May 30, 1960, April 13, 1963, November 28, 1964, May 27, 1967, February 1, 1969, November 27, 1971, October 25, 1975, December 16, 1978.

New Statesman, October 6, 1956, March 29, 1958, June 6, 1959, April 16, 1960, March 6, 1964, November 6, 1964, May 26, 1967, November 1, 1968, September 19, 1969, October 30, 1970, October 29, 1971, July 7, 1972, October 18, 1974, November 3, 1978, September 14, 1979, October 10, 1980.

New Statesman and Nation, December 6, 1947, August 4, 1951, May 1, 1954, September 6, 1956, September 22, 1956.

Newsweek, September 14, 1964, April 24, 1967, August 17, 1970.

New Yorker, November 3, 1956, May 10, 1958, May 28, 1960, December 16, 1961, November 7, 1964, May 27, 1967, July 12, 1969, May 13, 1972, January 13, 1975, November 20, 1978, November 26, 1979.

New York Herald Tribune Book Review, February 22, 1948, July 16, 1950, October 28, 1951, January 9, 1955, October 7, 1956, February 23, 1958, March 2, 1958, May 8, 1960, October 2, 1960.

New York Review of Books, November 5, 1964, August 3, 1967, March 11, 1971, September 21, 1972, February 21, 1980, December 17, 1981.

New York Times, February 29, 1948, July 16, 1950, December 16, 1951, January 9, 1955, October 7, 1956, February 23, 1958, February 11, 1969, April 26, 1972, May 7, 1972, October 30, 1972, October 17, 1979.

New York Times Book Review, January 3, 1960, May 8, 1960, September 25, 1960, September 13, 1964, April 23, 1967, January 19, 1969, August 23, 1970, December 6, 1970, December 26, 1971, May 7, 1972, October 27, 1974, December 2, 1979, March 22, 1981, July 12, 1981, December 27, 1981.

Partisan Review, Volume 30, 1963.

Prairie Schooner, fall, 1972.

Publishers Weekly, November 30, 1959, April 14, 1969.

Punch, May 24, 1967, October 11, 1967, October 30, 1968.

Reporter, October 8, 1964.

San Francisco Chronicle, February 22, 1948, May 9, 1960, October 13, 1960.

Saturday Review, November 3, 1951, January 8, 1955, October 13, 1956, February 22, 1958, May 7, 1960, October 1, 1960, March 4, 1961, March 4, 1964, September 12, 1964, October 23, 1965, November 26, 1966, December 17, 1966, April 1, 1967, May 27, 1967, January 11, 1969, August 22, 1970, December 25, 1971, May 27, 1972, June 17, 1972, January 11, 1975, January 6, 1979.

Saturday Review and World, April 6, 1974.

Saturday Review of Literature, March 27, 1948, July 15, 1950.

Saturday Review of the Arts, June 17, 1972.

Scientific American, June, 1964.

South Atlantic Quarterly, summer, 1965, autumn, 1973.

Southern Review, spring, 1973.

Spectator, May 14, 1954, September 14, 1956, April 11, 1958, August 7, 1959, April 15, 1960, March 9, 1962, June 16, 1967, November 15, 1968, November 7, 1970, July 8, 1972, December 5, 1981.

Time, October 8, 1956, May 16, 1960, April 20, 1962, September 18, 1964, January 3, 1969, January 10, 1969, August 24, 1970, June 12, 1972, November 25, 1974, October 12, 1981.

Times Educational Supplement, August 22, 1980, March 26, 1982.

Times Literary Supplement, November 8, 1947, July 20, 1951, May 7, 1954, September 7, 1956, March 28, 1958, August 15, 1958, April 15, 1960, November 5, 1964, May 18, 1967, October 31, 1968, July 3, 1969, July 9, 1970, October 23, 1970, November 19, 1971, June 30, 1972, December 25, 1972, October 11, 1974.

Twentieth Century, March, 1960, June, 1960.

Village Voice Literary Supplement, March, 1982.

Vogue, March 1, 1961.

Washington Post, November 24, 1971, December 6, 1978.

Washington Post Book World, January 5, 1969, August 23, 1970, May 7, 1972, September 17, 1972, November 19, 1978, November 18, 1979, March 15, 1981, October 4, 1981, September 26, 1982, July 12, 1987.

Wilson Library Bulletin, January, 1954, January, 1961.
Yale Review, spring, 1955, June, 1960, spring, 1969.

OBITUARIES:

PERIODICALS

AB Bookman's Weekly, August 11, 1980.
Bookseller, July 17, 1980.
Chicago Tribune, July 3, 1980.
Daily Telegraph (London), July 2, 1980, July 3, 1980, July 7, 1980, July 12, 1980, July 31, 1980, September 15, 1980, September 26, 1980.
Financial Times (London), July 12, 1980.
Guardian, July 2, 1980.
Newsweek, July 14, 1980.
New York Times, July 2, 1980.
Observer, July 6, 1980, September 15, 1980.
Publishers Weekly, July 25, 1980.
Saturday Review, August, 1980.
Sunday Times (London), July 6, 1980.
Time, July 14, 1980.
Times (London), July 2, 1980, July 11, 1980, September 15, 1980, September 26, 1980.
Times Educational Supplement, July 11, 1980.
Washington Post, July 3, 1980.

—*Sketch by Kenneth R. Shepherd*

[Sketch reviewed by brother, Philip Snow]

*   *   *

SNOW, Philip (Albert) 1915-

PERSONAL: Born August 7, 1915, in Leicester, England; son of William Edward (an organist and shoe factory clerk) and Ada Sophia (Robinson) Snow; married Mary Anne Harris, May 2, 1940; children: Stefanie Dale Vivien Vuikamba (Mrs. Peter Edward Waine). *Education:* Christ's College, Cambridge, B.A., 1937, M.A. (with honours), 1940.

ADDRESSES: Home—Gables, Station Rd., Angmering, Sussex BN16 4HY, England.

CAREER: Government of Fiji and Western Pacific, provincial commissioner, magistrate, and Assistant Colonial Secretary, 1938-52; Justice of the Peace, Warwickshire, England, 1952-75, West Sussex, 1976—. Bursar, Rugby School, 1952-76; examiner on Pacific Subjects, Oxford and Cambridge Universities, 1955—. Founder, Fiji Cricket Association, 1946, vice-patron, 1952—; captain, Fiji Cricket Team, New Zealand First-Class Tour, 1948; permanent representative, Fiji on International Cricket Conference, 1965—. Member, First World Cup Committee, 1971-75; chairman, Associate Member Countries, 1982—. Leader of expedition to Vanua Levu, Fiji, to investigate rock carvings, 1949. Literary executor and executor of Lord C. P. Snow. *Wartime service:* Aide de camp to Governor and Commander in Chief, Fiji, 1939; civil defense officer, Lautoka, Fiji, 1942-44; Fiji Government liaison officer to U.S. and New Zealand forces, 1942-44.

MEMBER: National Independent Schools Bursars' Association of Great Britain, Northern Ireland, and Commonwealth (vice-chairman, 1959-61; chairman, 1961-64), Royal Anthropological Institute (fellow), Royal Society of Arts (fellow), Marylebone Cricket Club (London), Hawks Club (Cambridge), Mastermind Club (London).

AWARDS, HONORS: Foreign Specialist award, U.S. Government, 1964, for *Visits to Schools and Universities in U.S.A.*

and Canada; Member, Order of the British Empire, 1979, on recommendation of Government of Fiji; National Award for third best history/biography, Arts Council of Great Britain, 1979, for *The People from the Horizon: An Illustrated History of the Europeans among the South Sea Islanders;* Officer, Order of the British Empire, 1985; special honorary life membership, Marylebone Cricket Club, for services to international cricket.

WRITINGS:

Civil Defense Services, Fiji Government Printer, 1942.
(Editor) *Fiji Civil Service Journal,* Fiji Government Printer, 1945.
Cricket in the Fiji Islands, Whitcombe & Tombs, 1949.
Rock Carvings in Fiji, Fiji Society, 1953.
(Contributor) *Cricket Heroes,* Phoenix Books, 1959.
(With D. M. Sherwood and F. J. Walesby) *Visits to Schools and Universities in U.S.A. and Canada,* Public Schools Bursars' Association of U.K. and Commonwealth, 1964.
(Contributor) E. W. Swanton and Michael Melford, editors, *The World of Cricket,* M. Joseph, 1966.
(Editor, author of introduction, and contributor) *Best Stories of the South Seas,* Faber, 1967.
A Bibliography of Fiji, Tonga, and Rotuma, University of Miami Press, 1969.
(Author of introduction) George Palmer, *Kidnapping in the South Seas* (Colonial History series), Dawsons of Pall Mall, 1972.
(Author of introduction) B. C. Seeman, *Viti* (Colonial History series), Dawsons of Pall Mall, 1972.
(With daughter, Stefanie Waine) *The People from the Horizon: An Illustrated History of the Europeans among the South Sea Islanders,* Phaidon, 1979.
(Contributor) Swanton and John Woodcock, editors, *Barclays World of Cricket,* Collins, 1980, 2nd revised edition, edited by Swanton, Woodcock, and George Plumptre, 1986.
Stranger and Brother: A Portrait of C. P. Snow, Macmillan, 1982, Scribner, 1983.

Also author of *Bula,* 1959, and, with J. S. Woodhouse, of *Visit of Her Majesty the Queen and H.R.H. Prince Philip to Rugby School on the Occasion of the Quatercentenary Year,* 1967; also editor, with G. K. Roth, of *Fijian Customs,* 1944. Contributor to reference works, including *The Far East and Australasia, Wisden Cricketers' Almanack,* and *Dictionary of National Biography.* Contributor of articles on the Pacific to the *Times* (London), *Daily Telegraph, American Anthropologist, Journal of Polynesian Society, Discovery, Journal de la societe des oceanistes, Sunday Times, Times Literary Supplement, Fiji Museum Journal, Journal of the Royal Anthropological Institute,* and *Journal of the Royal Geographical Society.*

WORK IN PROGRESS: Items on Pacific history; an autobiography.

SIDELIGHTS: Philip Snow, younger brother of the late Right Honorable Lord C. P. Snow of Leicester, was for a time a Colonial Administrator in Fiji. One result of this was his *Bibliography of Fiji, Tonga and Rotuma,* a "compilation which [is] not merely valuable but essential to any workers in the Pacific area or students of its history," according to a *Times Literary Supplement* reviewer. Another was a series of letters from C. P. Snow which Philip Snow cites in his biography *Stranger and Brother: A Portrait of C. P. Snow,* written during the second World War and in the period immediately following it.

"The definitive biography [of C. P. Snow] has yet to be written; it will be a monumental task for somebody, and must be some way off," Philip Snow states in the foreword to his biography. "In the meantime, without attempting any sort of analysis of his work—though I have identified many of the characters in the *Strangers and Brothers* series—" he continues, "I have set out to paint an informal picture of a man who has been the main influence in my life." Reviewers echo the the author's assessment; for instance, Victoria Glendinning, a reviewer for the *Listener,* asserts that the book "is neither a formal or a critical biography, and the personality of the painter is not excluded from the work." Edward M. White, writing in the *Los Angeles Times Book Review,* states, "This is not a critical work or one which will add much to one's appreciation of the novels," but declares, "this loving and pleasant tribute offers the guilty pleasures of personality to those who would enjoy the man as well as the books." *Washington Post Book World* contributor Edward M. Yoder, Jr., appraises *Stranger and Brother* as "a useful guide to a major accomplishment in old-fashioned storytelling, and to the remarkable man who achieved it."

Philip Snow is proficient in the Hindi and Fijian languages. He posseses what is probably the best private collection on Pacific literature in the United Kingdom, and the best collection in the world of the works of Lord Snow and Pamela Hansford Johnson.

AVOCATIONAL INTERESTS: South Sea islands.

BIOGRAPHICAL/CRITICAL SOURCES:

BOOKS

Johnson, Pamela Hansford, *Important to Me: Personalia,* Macmillan, 1974, Scribner, 1975.
Knox-Mawer, June, *Tales from Paradise,* B.B.C. Ariel, 1986.
Snow, Philip, *Stranger and Brother: A Portrait of C. P. Snow,* Macmillan, 1982, Scribner, 1983.
Swanton, E. W., *Follow On,* Collins, 1977.

PERIODICALS

Atlantic, April, 1983.
Best Sellers, May, 1983.
British Book News, May, 1980, March, 1983.
Choice, May, 1970.
Daily Mail (London), October 7, 1982.
Daily Telegraph (London), January 28, 1952, December 12, 1953, June 23, 1958, February 10, 1966, March 5, 1970, March 2, 1973, March 9, 1973, December 2, 1976, November 27, 1979, November 18, 1982, October 27, 1983, January 5, 1984, March 26, 1984.
History Today, April, 1980.
Listener, October 28, 1982.
London Review of Books, November 18, 1982.
Los Angeles Times Book Review, April 17, 1983.
National Review, March 18, 1983.
New Statesman, November 5, 1982.
Observer, October 24, 1982.
Spectator, October 16, 1982, December 18, 1982.
Times (London), June 10, 1954, July 6, 1960, February 18, 1967, July 11, 1968, July 21, 1971, July 11, 1973, July 27, 1977, March 9, 1981, October 27, 1983, April 12, 1984, August 17, 1987, August 19, 1987.
Times Literary Supplement, August 26, 1950, June 23, 1957, August 15, 1968, June 18, 1970, January 7, 1983.
Washington Post Book World, May 7, 1983.

SOAMES, Jane
  See NICKERSON, Jane Soames (Bon)

*   *   *

SOLENSTEN, John M(artin)   1929-

PERSONAL: Born September 16, 1929, in Madelia, Minn.; son of Martin Christian and Agnes Lucille Solensten; children: Peter John, Peggy Ann. *Education:* Gustavus Adolphus College, B.A., 1951; Bowling Green State University, Ph.D., 1968. *Religion:* Lutheran.

ADDRESSES: Office—Department of English, Concordia College, St. Paul, Minn. 55104. *Agent*—John A. Ware, John A. Ware Literary Agency, 392 Central Park W., New York, N.Y. 10025.

CAREER: Eberhardt Co., Minneapolis, Minn., broker and banker, 1953-55; high school teacher in South Dakota and Minnesota, 1955-62; Wartburg College, Waverly, Iowa, instructor in English, 1962-64; Wittenberg University, Springfield, Ohio, assistant professor of English, 1964-68; Mankato State University, Mankato, Minn., associate professor of English, 1968-74; Concordia College, St. Paul, Minn., professor of English, 1974—. Gives writing workshops at local high schools and at Huron College, Mankato State University, and Bemidji State College. *Military service:* U.S. Army, 1951-53; served as American liaison to Turkish Armed Forces Command in Korea.

MEMBER: National Council of Teachers of English, Associated Writing Programs, Popular Culture Association, Norwegian-American Historical Association.

AWARDS, HONORS: Award from Native American Playwriting Contest, Tulsa, Okla., 1981, for "Good Thunder"; award from Minnesota Voices Project, 1981, for *The Heron Dancer;* award from Associated Writing Programs, 1982, for *Good Thunder.*

WRITINGS:

The Heron Dancer (stories), New Rivers Press, 1981.
Good Thunder (novel), State University of New York Press, 1983.
There Lies a Fair Land (anthology of Norwegian-American writing), New Rivers Press, 1986.
Mowing the Cemetery (stories), Lone Butte Press, 1988.

PLAYS

"Watonwan" (three-act), first produced January 17, 1978.
"Good Thunder" (three-act), first produced in Tulsa, Okla., at Tulsa Performing Arts Centre, February 17, 1982.
"Bonhoeffer," first produced in Duluth, Minn., at Duluth Community Theatre, 1986.

OTHER

Contributor of plays, poems, and stories to periodicals, including *Fiction International, Iowa Review, Western American Literature, Carleton Miscellany, Journal of Popular Culture, Plainswoman,* and *Northland Review.*

SIDELIGHTS: John M. Solensten told *CA:* "Writing while teaching full-time creates plenty of stress, but also keeps up important interaction with other writers.

"I am not a native American. My interest in native Americans is based on personal friendships developed in the army, while teaching in South Dakota, and in working with the Native American Cultural Center in Minneapolis. My own heritage is Icelandic-Norwegian Lutheran. Often there is a quiet, deep tension between this heritage and Norse/Native American mythologies. I cherish 'survivors'—those who have come through various kinds of victimization to some new faith in themselves.

"Although I am a college teacher working in an academic setting I have been at various times a lumberjack, a mortgage broker, a public relations writer, a mechanic, and a farmhand. I think this experience keeps the 'common touch,' the awareness of how things work in everyday life, clear in my writing."

BIOGRAPHICAL/CRITICAL SOURCES:

PERIODICALS

New York Times Book Review, July 24, 1983.

* * *

SOLOMON, Joan   1930-

PERSONAL: Born November 26, 1930, in Johannesburg, South Africa; daughter of Philip (a printer) and Rose (a seamstress; maiden name, Isaacs) Mendelsohn; married Louis Solomon (a surgeon), July 1, 1951; children: Caryn, Ryan, Joyce. *Education:* University of Witwatersrand, B.A. (with first-class honors), 1949; University of Cape Town, B.Ed., 1950, B.F.A., 1987.

ADDRESSES: Home—Bristol, England. *Office*—Open University, London, England.

CAREER: Worked as an English teacher in Johannesburg, South Africa, 1951-52; employed as a child welfare social worker in Cape Town, South Africa, 1952-53; Baragwanath Hospital, Johannesburg, social worker, 1953-54; owner of advertising art studio in Upington, South Africa, 1954-57; free-lance tutor in London, England, 1958-62; University of Witwatersrand, Johannesburg, lecturer in English, 1963-76; taught English as a foreign language in London, 1978-81; Open University, London, lecturer in English, 1981—. Taught creative writing to groups of black students in Soweto, South Africa.

WRITINGS:

JUVENILES

Kate's Party, Hamish Hamilton, 1978.
Spud Comes to Play, Hamish Hamilton, 1978.
Berron's Tooth, Hamish Hamilton, 1978.
A Day by the Sea, Hamish Hamilton, 1978.
Shabnam's Day Out, Hamish Hamilton, 1980.
Gifts and Almonds, Hamish Hamilton, 1980.
Wedding Day, Hamish Hamilton, 1981.
A Present for Mum, Hamish Hamilton, 1981.
Sweet Tooth Sunil, Hamish Hamilton, 1983.
Chopsticks and Chips, Hamish Hamilton, 1987.
Spiky Sunday, Hamish Hamilton, 1987.
Everybody's Hair, A. & C. Black, 1988.

OTHER

Also author of *Joyce's Day, Joyce Visits Granny, Joyce at the Circus, Sipho's Trumpet, Joyce's ABC, Bobbi's New Year,* and *News for Dad;* also author of eight books in the "Science in a Social Context" series, Association for Science Educa-

tion, 1983. Contributor of articles and photographs to periodicals.

WORK IN PROGRESS: Children's books; research on minority communities; research on racism, sexism, and classism in children's literature.

SIDELIGHTS: Joan Solomon told *CA:* "I love working with children. I listen to them, I look at them, I photograph them and thank them for the privilege of taking me into their world."

* * *

SOMMERFELD, Ray(nard) M(atthias)   1933-

PERSONAL: Born August 10, 1933, in Sibley, Iowa; son of Ernest Robert (a minister) and Lillian (a nurse; maiden name, Matthias) Sommerfeld; married Barbara Ann Spear, June 9, 1956; children: Andrea Joan, Kristin Elaine. *Education:* Attended University of Miami, Coral Gables, Fla., 1952; University of Iowa, B.S.C., 1956; M.A., 1957, Ph.D., 1963. *Politics:* Independent. *Religion:* Lutheran.

ADDRESSES: Home—5100 R.R. 620 N., Austin, Tex. 78732. *Office*—Graduate School of Business, University of Texas, Austin, Tex. 78712.

CAREER: University of Texas at Austin, assistant professor, 1963-66, associate professor, 1966-68, professor, 1968-72, Arthur Young Professor of Accounting, 1973-76; Arthur Young & Co. (certified public accountants), Reston, Va., director of tax education, 1976-78; University of Texas at Austin, John Arch White Professor, 1978-83, Glenn A. Welsh Professor, 1983-84, James Bayless/Rauscher Pierce Refsnes Professor, 1984—. *Military service:* U.S. Air Force, 1957-60. U.S. Air Force Reserve, 1960-65; became captain.

MEMBER: American Institute of Certified Public Accountants, American Accounting Association (vice president, 1982-84, president-elect, 1985-86, president, 1986-87), American Taxation Association (president, 1975-76), National Tax Association, Texas Society of Certified Public Accountants (member of board of directors, 1967-69).

WRITINGS:

Tax Reform and the Alliance for Progress, University of Texas Press, 1965.
(With Hershel M. Anderson and Horace R. Brock) *An Introduction to Taxation,* Harcourt, 1969, revised edition published as *An Introduction to Taxation, 1989,* 1988.
The Dow Jones-Irwin Guide to Tax Planning, Dow Jones-Irwin, 1974, revised edition, 1978.
Federal Taxes and Management Decisions, Irwin, 1974, 1989-90 edition, 1989.
(With G. Fred Streuling) *Tax Research Techniques,* American Institute of Certified Public Accountants, 1976, 2nd edition, 1981.
(With Anderson) *An Introduction to Taxation: Advanced Topics,* 2nd edition, Harcourt, 1982.
(With others) *HBJ Federal Tax Course,* Harcourt, 1984, revised edition published as *HBJ Federal Tax Course 1987,* 1987.
Essentials of Taxation, with reference guide, Addison-Wesley, 1989.

Contributor to journals. Member of editorial advisory board, *Tax Adviser,* 1974-76, *Accounting Review,* 1975-81, and *Accounting Horizons,* 1986-88. Editor of series in taxation, Prentice-Hall, 1980—.

SIDELIGHTS: Ray M. Sommerfeld once commented: "Most of my books have grown from my dissatisfaction with otherwise available educational materials. I specialize in federal taxation."

* * *

SONERO, Devi
See PELTON, Robert W(ayne)

* * *

SPADA, James 1950-

PERSONAL: Born January 23, 1950, in Staten Island, N.Y.; son of Joseph Vincent and Mary (Ruberto) Spada. *Education:* Attended Wagner College, 1968-71, Hunter College of the City University of New York, 1972-75, and California State University, 1979-80. *Politics:* Liberal Democrat. *Religion:* "Discarded."

ADDRESSES: Home—Los Angeles, Calif. *Office—Barbra Quarterly,* 7985 Santa Monica Blvd., Los Angeles, Calif. 90046. *Agent*—Kathy Robbins, 866 Second Ave., New York, N.Y. 10017.

CAREER: Writer and publisher. New York State Council on the Arts, New York City, office assistant, 1966 and 1969; Wagner College Library, Staten Island, N.Y., assistant librarian in periodicals department, 1969-70; editor and publisher, *EMK: The Edward M. Kennedy Quarterly,* 1969-72; U.S. Senate, Washington, D.C., intern to Senator Edward M. Kennedy, 1970; *In the Know,* New York City, managing editor, 1975, editor, 1975-76; *Barbra Quarterly,* Los Angeles, Calif., editor and publisher, 1980-83.

MEMBER: Authors Guild, Authors League of America, American Civil Liberties Union.

WRITINGS:

Barbra: The First Decade—The Films and Career of Barbra Streisand, Citadel, 1974.
The Films of Robert Redford, Citadel, 1977.
The Spada Report, New American Library, 1979.
(With Christopher Nickens) *Streisand: The Woman and the Legend,* Doubleday, 1981, updated paperback edition, 1983.
(With George Zeno) *Monroe: Her Life in Pictures,* Doubleday, 1982.
(With Karen Swenson) *Judy and Liza,* Doubleday, 1983.
Hepburn: Her Life in Pictures, Doubleday, 1984.
The Divine Bette Midler, Macmillan, 1984.
Fonda: Her Life in Pictures, Doubleday, 1985.
Shirley and Warren, Macmillan, 1985.
Grace: The Secret Lives of a Princess—An Intimate Biography of Grace Kelly, Doubleday, 1987.

WORK IN PROGRESS: A biography of Peter Lawford for Bantam; *Legend,* a fictional biography of a movie star; a screenplay with Christopher Nickens.

SIDELIGHTS: Celebrity biographer James Spada had published several pictorial profiles of Hollywood luminaries—stars such as Barbra Streisand, Marilyn Monroe, Katherine Hepburn, Robert Redford, and Jane Fonda—and was working on one of the late Grace Kelly, Princess of Monaco, when, as he tells *CA,* he stumbled upon "a remarkable story that hadn't been told before." Kelly, an Oscar-winning actress of the

1950s—cinema's "ice-princess"—became a top audience-draw with her stunning looks, subtle English accent, and controlled, mannered demeanor. In 1956, at the height of her career, the Philadelphia-born Kelly made world headlines when she abandoned Hollywood to become real-life royalty: the wife of Prince Rainier of Monaco, ruler of the tiny Mediterranean principality nestled on the coast of southeastern France. There she lived as Princess Grace of Monaco—raising three children—until her sudden death in 1982 from injuries received in an automobile accident.

While conducting interviews for his book on Grace Kelly, and in reviewing some of her early personal correspondence, Spada, however, discovered a woman much different than the one suggested by her public persona. As he candidly remarks to Michael Kilian of the *Chicago Tribune,* Spada came upon two important revelations about Grace Kelly: "The first . . . was how the most sexually active woman in Hollywood was able to come across as the most chaste. The second was that Prince Rainier actually believed that she was a virgin." Spada's original picture-book project expanded into a full-length narrative text, 1987's *Grace: The Secret Lives of a Princess—An Intimate Biography of Grace Kelly,* which, as Yvonne Cox notes in *Maclean's,* "portrays a beautiful young actress whose cool, white-gloved exterior concealed a smouldering sexuality and a compulsion to bed her leading men."

In the biography, which he contends to Kilian is "not a hatchet job," Spada shows how in her early career, young Grace rebelled against the mores of both her wealthy authoritarian family and strict Catholic upbringing, and conducted sexual affairs with a number of Hollywood's leading men, including William Holden, Gary Cooper, Ray Milland, and Bing Crosby. Spada's account does much to describe Grace's actions in light of the influences of her family—the prominent Kellys of Philadelphia. In particular, Grace's father Jack—Irish immigrant, ex-Olympic rowing champion, and self-made millionaire—emerges, according to Ellin Stein in the *New York Times Book Review,* "as a bigoted domestic tyrant" whose lack of faith in Grace was a large factor in the young actress's attraction to married older men. One account tells of how the elder Kelly, upon hearing of Grace's Best Actress Oscar for "The Country Girl," expressed astonishment at such an accomplishment coming from his meekest daughter—and not from his favorite, Peggy. Other family insights surface in the story of how Grace's mother threatened to campaign against her own son, John—a promising mayoral candidate—because he once dated a transsexual. Some reviewers find the tales of the Kelly family one of the book's more intriguing features. "Although it can, and no doubt will, be read simply as a now-it-can-be-told report on the life and loves of America's favorite movie star-turned-princess," writes Bruce Cook in the *Washington Post Book World,* "nevertheless, it is far more interesting considered as a history of the Kelly family of Philadelphia told from the point-of-view of its most prominent (though by no means most powerful) member."

Outside of her family woes, Grace's marriage to Prince Rainier was also less than ideal, according to Spada. "More of a business merger than a fairy-tale romance," remarks Piers Brendon in the *Observer,* the Kelly family paid a two million dollar dowry for their daughter's entrance into high society. Prince Rainier on the other hand, notes Cook, "thought that an American movie star on the throne would almost certainly increase tourism in the five-mile square principality (it did, tremendously); he needed an heir; and, when it came right down to it, he—and Monaco—could use the money [Grace's] rich father could provide.'' Regarding Grace's motivations in the marriage, Cook concurs with Spada's contention that guilt played a major role. Grace's ''Catholic upbringing left her guilty about her sexual dalliances,'' writes Spada, ''and angry at her family for continually objecting to her attempts to legitimize herself in their eyes through marriage.''

Reception of *Grace: The Secret Lives of a Princess* has been mixed. Some reviewers comment that disclosures of Kelly's sexual exploits are not all that astonishing. ''People who want to find out if Grace Kelly was a sensuous woman need only see *To Catch a Thief*,'' writes a critic for *Time*, while Cox comments that Spada's account ''simply adds a light sexual frosting to her already well-documented life.'' Heather Neill in the *Listener*, acknowledging that ''Spada presents us with a sympathetic portrait of his heroine,'' adds that his ''book hovers between voyeurism and hagiography.'' Other reviewers, however, have found the biography more than just an expose of a revered screen idol. ''Indeed, the truly interesting new light the book sheds on Grace Kelly is not that her love life was more active than previously suspected,'' comments Stein, ''but that she suffered a very modern conflict over her real-life role.'' Spada himself remarks to Kilian that he wanted to ''put aside [Kelly's] 'one-dimensional' image and reveal her as the vital human being she was. She was very complex, very troubled, very passionate and very intelligent.'' The *Times Literary Supplement*'s Victoria Glendinning lauds the biographer's achievement: ''In exposing for the first time Grace Kelly's promiscuity, James Spada claims justifiably to be revealing a more interesting person than the legend allows.''

Although primarily known for his celebrity biographies, Spada is branching out into other areas of writing: He comments to *CA*: ''I hope that my recent writings have greatly improved on my earlier efforts. Writing is a vocation I find rewarding, educational, rending, draining, fulfilling, frustrating, and lovely. My writings will continue to grow as I do. Although I have enjoyed much success with celebrity biographies, I hope to be as well known as a novelist.... My first novel, *Legend*, will be a fictional biography of a legendary female movie star.''

CA INTERVIEW

CA interviewed James Spada by telephone on August 15, 1988, at his home in Los Angeles, California.

CA: The subjects of your celebrity biographies are all movie people, though most of them are interesting for other reasons as well. Did you come to doing biography through a special love for films?

SPADA: Yes. I've always been a movie fan; when I was thirteen, I was president of a Marilyn Monroe fan club. I've always been fascinated by the larger-than-life glamour of these people, and have found certain ones extremely interesting in terms of their early struggles for success and their later struggles, in spite of ridicule, to change their careers, do more serious work. I'm intrigued by people who have succeeded against the odds.

CA: You worked as a press aide to Senator Edward M. Kennedy and published, from 1969 to 1972, EMK: The Edward M. Kennedy Quarterly. *Did your work with Kennedy sharpen some of the skills that became useful in doing the biographies?*

SPADA: Yes. There's a certain rhetorical style that you use in writing political material that's very different from the style you use when you're writing about movies. It was helpful to me to practice that succinct style and the flair for drama that you use in political writing.

CA: You're best known for your 1987 book on Grace Kelly, but let's go back to the beginning of your star biographies. Barbra Streisand was the subject of your first book, published in 1974, and a 1981 book, Streisand: The Woman and the Legend. *What did you find especially compelling about Streisand?*

SPADA: She was the first movie star after Marilyn Monroe that I became fascinated by. I've known other people who've gone from Marilyn to Barbra in terms of a special interest. You wouldn't think they would have anything in common; they're very different women. But what they do have in common is a tremendous charisma. When I watch Barbra Streisand on the screen, I can't take my eyes off her. I think she's a wonderful actress, and she has a tremendous beauty, despite the fact that she's not classically beautiful. She's a very strong-willed person; she knows what she wants, and she's a perfectionist. Her persona is compelling, and so is her struggle against the odds. Most of us as teenagers think that if we're not the most popular in the class, or the best-looking, we're going to have a much more difficult time succeeding. Barbra Streisand is an example of how you can be a misfit, totally unconventional, and still succeed tremendously. I think that's one of the reasons—not just for me, but for everyone else—that she's so popular.

CA: Do you go into any biography with a sort of philosophy about what you owe the subject and the reader?

SPADA: I don't think I owe the subject anything except to tell the truth. And I owe the reader the same thing. Especially with the Grace Kelly book, there were a lot of people who said, Why dredge all this up? Why tell us that she wasn't as chaste as we thought she was? My answer was that, as a biographer, I did not expect to find that out, but I did; would they expect me then to keep that from the reader? I think whatever you find out, you need to reveal. If there is more of an obligation to the subject, it's to present the information at least objectively and perhaps even compassionately. I came to understand Grace Kelly. To learn that she was somewhat promiscuous because she never got the love she needed from her father made me very sympathetic to her; and that made her a very sympathetic character for the reader. I'm very pleased that people who've read the book tell me they came away from it liking Grace more, and understanding her better. I have found that most of the criticism of the book is from people who haven't read it.

The main reason I think people read celebrity biographies is to find out how people became celebrities: what made them succeed, they wonder, and do I possibly have what they had? Could I do it? I have an obligation to readers to let them understand what it was about a person that made him or her succeed. One thing I found that struck me is that every single one of my subjects had struggles. None of them had it easy in the beginning. They all faced rejection and ridicule, and they all persevered. I'm sure it's been said many times, but stick-to-itiveness is probably the main ingredient in success.

CA: Shirley MacLaine had terrible failures before she made any really successful movies, as you show in your book on MacLaine and her brother, Warren Beatty.

SPADA: They all did, even someone like Streisand, whom you think of as an overnight success. Her first album won Album of the Year; her first television show won an Emmy; her first Broadway appearance, in "I Can Get It for You Wholesale," was a huge success. Her first starring role on Broadway, in "Funny Girl," was phenomenal. But you don't know about all the times she went around to casting directors and wasn't even allowed to read, and how hard she had to struggle just to get a recording contract. People said that she was great but she wouldn't sell records; she'd just have a small clique of fans. It's amazing, the myopia of people who are in some kind of position of power to make or break stars. It's astounding that anybody who's original *ever* gets a chance, because producers don't like new and different: they want another Bruce Springsteen. If you're too different, it's very difficult to be heard.

CA: With the "Life in Pictures" books, do you go out looking for the pictures first to be sure you can find enough of them and clear permissions and use fees?

SPADA: It works both ways. You know the subject's life in outline form. For instance, when I did my book on Jane Fonda, I certainly wanted to have enough pictures of her with Roger Vadim, who was one of her husbands. So I searched them out. But if I found a picture of her with a boyfriend I didn't know she'd had, I then had to do some research and find some print clippings about that relationship so that I could do captions for the picture.

CA: Do you have favorites among the subjects you've met with personally for your books?

SPADA: Frankly, the only subject of mine whom I interviewed for the book was Robert Redford. There are degrees of cooperation. With Redford I got complete cooperation and interviewed him. On my second Streisand book, I did not get to interview Barbra, but I interviewed many of her associates and friends. For Katharine Hepburn I received no cooperation at all. It's a situation of taking what you can get. It was very interesting to meet Robert Redford. He's a fascinating man, very bright and very committed, but also somewhat difficult. It took me nine months to get an interview, which lasted about five minutes. Then it took another three months to get with him again, and this time he gave me several hours. It was frustrating, but rewarding in the long run.

CA: Many of the surprises you got about Grace Kelly came from her early love Don Richardson. Was it when you began talking with him that you realized you had the makings of a big book?

SPADA: Absolutely. The book began as a pictorial tribute. It was going to be somewhat like my second Streisand book, lots of pictures with a text. I worried about what I could write about that would be fresh, because there had been two biographies in 1984, but I decided that I would do the best job I could and try to get as much new information as possible. I came across Don Richardson's name in one of the previous biographies, where he was given about two paragraphs. I thought, This guy's got to be more interesting than that. He was one of her acting teachers at the American Academy of Dramatic Arts. I thought he would at least tell me what she was like as a student and why he thinks she was such a successful actress.

So I wrote to him, and he called me up, and at the end of a two-hour conversation my hair was standing on end. He painted a completely different picture of Grace Kelly than I ever imagined. When I hung up the phone I was excited because I knew this was hot stuff, if I may use the expression—not just the sexual relations, but the fact that this was a totally different woman from what I expected, and I had already written a third of the manuscript.

I wondered, How reliable is Richardson? He seemed like a good source: he's a professor at UCLA, and he had letters from Grace over the years, which he showed me. I believed him in my gut. But I also had to confirm what he told me. So I started to call back those people whom I had not asked the right questions of before. Also, coincidentally, after waiting about six months, I got interviews with Grace's sisters—one in particular, Lizanne, who confirmed almost all the things that Don Richardson told me that she had an opportunity to know about. Once that happened, I realized that I had stumbled upon a remarkable story that hadn't been told before, and I sent a three-page single-spaced memo to Paul Bresnick, my editor at Doubleday. He agreed that it had become a different kind of book, and its format was changed into the straight biography that it was published as, my first in that genre.

I was thrilled. As much as I had enjoyed doing the picture books, I realized that, if a full-fledged biography is an "A" book, they were "B" books. They didn't highlight me as a writer, and they also didn't offer the reader that much that was new. Whereas I knew that this book on Grace Kelly was going to be the definitive biography, and it was going to be a serious writing job. I had begun to worry that I was turning into a picture editor rather than a writer, so this was very exciting.

CA: Beyond its revelations about Grace's earlier life, your book showed that she didn't have such a happy life with her prince either. Was that as much a revelation to you, in researching the book, as her assortment of early lovers?

SPADA: Yes, it was. I believed the fairy tale, as everyone else did, that she had lived happily ever after. That, on its face, should have been seen as a fairy tale, because no one lives happily ever after. But she should have lived more happily than she did. What happened to Grace was that she went from the frying pan into the fire. She married a man very much like her father, and she recreated the situation she had with her own family, which was that her father was the center of the universe. She said it was very difficult for her to adjust, because when she was in Hollywood her career was the most important thing; when she got to Monaco, it was her husband who became the most important thing—to an extraordinary degree. He was the country, and Grace didn't have anyone she knew there. Her mother-in-law didn't like her; her sister-in-law didn't like her; the people of Monaco didn't think she was very bright because she didn't speak French, and she was an American and an actress. She had a very tough time. It's a rather sad story—Grace tried very hard to be happy and didn't succeed. I hope that she serves as something of a lesson to people that there are no princes on white horses. There are no magic formulas. Marrying a prince or winning the lottery is not going to make you happy; you have to find happiness within yourself.

CA: With books like the ones on Redford, MacLaine and Beatty, Hepburn, and Fonda, you've done a lot of research on the films and how they were made. Is that kind of research an enjoyable part of the work for you?

SPADA: Sure, because I love movies. When I did the Robert Redford book, since it was authorized, I was able to get screenings from the various studios of all of his movies. A girlfriend and I went to a huge theater, and the two of us sat in a middle row all by ourselves and saw five Robert Redford movies one afternoon! They were uncut; they were beautiful prints. It was very nice. And it's fun to discover movies you never saw before. Maybe they're not the best movies in the world, but they all have elements you enjoy—and maybe they're long-lost gems. That's one of the nicest parts of what I do.

CA: What's been your biggest research headache in all of your books?

SPADA: Getting people to agree to talk to me. That was certainly true with *Grace,* and it's difficult with most of the subjects. People are unwilling to give you an interview unless the subject approves, assuming the subject is alive. That's why it was very helpful for me to have Barbra Streisand's approval; she told all her friends it was okay to talk to me. When the subject is dead, like Grace Kelly, it's a little easier. But I found that there was a great deal of protection around Grace. People want to keep her image the way it was. It wasn't until Don Richardson talked to me and I was able to ask the right questions that I got people to start opening up to me.

But generally, it's very difficult. Often your letters are ignored, and you've got to follow up. On the other hand, ultimate success can give you a nice sense of accomplishment. I was turned down by Jimmy Stewart twice for an interview for the Grace Kelly book. Then I wrote to Cary Grant, who immediately said yes, and I did the interview. So I wrote to Jimmy Stewart again, saying, ''Dear Mr. Stewart: I've just finished interviewing Cary Grant, and the section of my book on 'To Catch a Thief' is going to be rich with anecdotes now. The section on 'Rear Window' rather suffers by comparison. Won't you reconsider?'' And he did. Once you get a big star like Grant, you can kind of shame his contemporaries into giving you an interview.

CA: Biographers have had a hard time lately. I think of Kitty Kelley, who was taken to court by Frank Sinatra before she ever wrote her book about him, and of Ian Hamilton, who wasn't allowed to quote directly from J. D. Salinger's letters for his biography. Do you worry about being hauled into court; is it a factor in anything you decide to write now?

SPADA: Yes. But all it does is make me more diligent than I already was about making sure everything's true. As we learned from Sinatra's ill-advised move against Kitty Kelley and the case of Ian Hamilton, the only things you can stop a book over are libel or copyright infringement. I'm not going to risk printing something unless I am absolutely certain that it's true and I can prove it. There are several things I did not use in the Grace Kelly book that I'm sure are true, but because I couldn't get anyone on record to say that they were true, and I couldn't otherwise prove them, I didn't use them. Also, I had all of the letters that Grace sent to Don Richardson. But the crackerjack Doubleday legal department advised me that there'd been a new Supreme Court ruling that letters are not the property of the person who receives them, but of the person who sent them. Thus, the literary rights to the letters Grace sent to Don Richardson had become the property of Prince

Rainier, and unless I paraphrased rather than quoted them, I could leave myself open to legal action. So, with a broken heart, I paraphrased her letters. They were very rich and idiosyncratic and full of interesting observations, and they had to be watered down in the book.

This is too bad, because it cheats the reader. I don't understand why Salinger did what he did. If someone's going to write a biography of me, I want it to be as good a biography as it can be, and to reflect me as well as it can. The book is always going to be written, with or without the help of the subject; it's just not going to be as good without. Some would say that the letters are the property of Salinger—why should someone else be allowed to use them at will and make money off his life? And what if Salinger wanted to keep them for his own book? But the letters were in libraries; it's not as if Salinger had kept them private for possible use in his autobiography. He'll probably never write one.

CA: You told Contemporary Authors *several years ago, ''Although I have enjoyed much success with celebrity biographies, I hope to be best known as a novelist.'' Is that still an ambition? Is there a novel in the works?*

SPADA: Yes. But it's difficult for anyone in any field to break new ground. It's been quite easy for me to get a new contract for a celebrity biography and extremely difficult to get a novel contract, simply because I was viewed as just a celebrity biographer. But the fact that the Grace Kelly book was a bestseller rather changed that. I'm in a much stronger position now as an author, and I've written five chapters of a novel which is a fictional biography of a famous Hollywood movie star. It's a way of bridging the gap: a novel about Hollywood by a man who has written about the real Hollywood.

CA: What else would you like to do in your work that you haven't gotten around to yet?

SPADA: At the moment I'm finishing up a screenplay with a Christopher Nickens, a fellow biographer; we're doing revisions. We're quite excited about this. My agent likes it very much, so we're keeping our fingers crossed. Being a movie fan and a writer, I felt it was logical to write a movie. It's not something I'd want to do full-time, but I would love to have a movie produced from something I wrote, either the script or the original story. And the screenplay is quite a departure for both of us—it's a supernatural thriller.

And I'm working on another new book right now for Bantam—a biography of Peter Lawford. Like Grace Kelly's life, Lawford's encompasses much more than just Hollywood. It includes Washington and Las Vegas and the Rat Pack and Marilyn Monroe. There were a lot of things going on in Lawford's life that had nothing to do with movies. That's interesting to me because my interests are wider than just Hollywood. But once I finish the Lawford book, my inclination is either to go into novels full-time or to do something else in nonfiction—like a family biography or a crime story. I think I've done enough celebrity biographies for now; I would like to expand. That doesn't mean I'll never do another celebrity biography, but I would like to explore the waters in other areas.

CA: You seem to be very happy as a writer.

SPADA: I am. I feel very good at the moment about my career and my work. I enjoy the detective work that my biographies require now. It's very rewarding, when you've spent months trying to track someone down or find a piece or information and then finally find it. And I love the creative process of fiction, whether it's a novel or a screenplay. I enjoy writing more than ever, and to have been really successful, to be a bona-fide best-selling author, after fourteen years of trying was tremendously rewarding to me—like a fantasy come true. I'm at a very good place in my life and career right now.

AVOCATIONAL INTERESTS: Physical education, sports, drawing, painting, music, photography, antiques, cooking, collecting (books, prints, records, magazines, photos, quilts).

BIOGRAPHICAL/CRITICAL SOURCES:

BOOKS

Spada, James, *Grace: The Secret Lives of a Princess—An Intimate Biography of Grace Kelly*, Doubleday, 1987.

PERIODICALS

Chicago Tribune, May 3, 1987.
Listener, July 16, 1987.
Maclean's, July 27, 1987.
Newsweek, April 27, 1987.
New York Times Book Review, November 4, 1984, July 19, 1987.
Observer, June 28, 1987.
People, July 6, 1987.
Time, April 27, 1987.
Times Literary Supplement, July 24, 1987.
Washington Post Book World, June 21, 1987.

—*Sketch by Michael E. Mueller*

—*Interview by Jean W. Ross*

*   *   *

SPILLANE, Frank Morrison   1918- (Mickey Spillane)

PERSONAL: Born March 9, 1918, in Brooklyn, N.Y.; son of John Joseph (an bartender) and Catherine Anne Spillane; married Mary Ann Pearce, 1945 (divorced); married Sherri Malinou, November, 1965 (divorced); married Jane Rodgers Johnson, October, 1983; children: (first marriage) Kathy, Mark, Mike, Carolyn; (third marriage; stepdaughters) Britt, Lisa. *Education:* Attended Kansas State College (now University). *Religion:* Converted to Jehovah's Witnesses in 1952.

ADDRESSES: Home—Murrells Inlet, Myrtle Beach, S.C.; and 225 East 57th St., New York, N.Y. 10022.

CAREER: Writer of mystery and detective novels, short stories, books for children, comic books, and scripts for television and films. Spillane with producer Robert Fellows formed an independent film company in Nashville, Tenn., called Spillane-Fellows Productions, which filmed features and television productions, 1969. Creator of television series, "Mike Hammer," 1984-87. Actor; has appeared in over 110 commercials for Miller Lite Beer. *Military service:* U.S. Army Air Forces; taught cadets and flew fighter missions during World War II; became captain.

AWARDS, HONORS: Junior Literary Guild Award, l979, for *The Day the Sea Rolled Back*.

WRITINGS—Under name Mickey Spillane:

MYSTERY NOVELS

I, the Jury (also see below), Dutton, 1947, reprinted, New American Library, 1973.
Vengeance Is Mine! (also see below), Dutton, 1950.
My Gun Is Quick (also see below), Dutton, 1950, reprinted, Signet, 1988.
The Big Kill (also see below), Dutton, 1951, reprinted, New English Library, 1984.
One Lonely Night, Dutton, 1951, reprinted, New English Library, 1987.
The Long Wait, Dutton, 1951, reprinted, New American Library, 1972.
Kiss Me, Deadly (also see below), Dutton, 1952.
The Deep, Dutton, 196l.
The Girl Hunters (also see below), Dutton, 1962.
Day of the Guns, Dutton, 1964, reprinted, New American Library, 1981.
The Snake, Dutton, 1964.
Bloody Sunrise, Dutton, 1965.
The Death Dealers, Dutton, 1965, reprinted, New American Library, 1981.
The Twisted Thing, Dutton, 1966, published as *For Whom the Gods Would Destroy*, New American Library, 1971.
The By-Pass Control, Dutton, 1967.
The Delta Factor, Dutton, 1967.
Body Lovers, New American Library, 1967.
Killer Mine, New American Library, 1968.
Me, Hood!, New American Library, 1969.
Survival: Zero, Dutton, 1970.
Tough Guys, New American Library, 1970.
The Erection Set, Dutton, 1972.
The Last Cop Out, New American Library, 1973.
The Flier, Corgi, 1973.
Mickey Spillane: Five Complete Mike Hammer Novels (contains *I, the Jury, Vengeance Is Mine!, My Gun Is Quick, The Big Kill*, and *Kiss Me, Deadly*), Avenel Books, 1987.
The Killing Man, Dutton, 1989.

Also author of *Return of the Hood*.

OTHER

"The Girl Hunters"(screenplay; based on Spillane's novel of the same title and starring Spillane in role of Mike Hammer), Colorama Features, 1963.
The Day the Sea Rolled Back (children's book), Windmill Books, 1979.
The Ship That Never Was (children's book), Bantam, 1982.
Tomorrow I Die (short stories), Mysterious Press, 1984.

Also author of *The Shrinking Island*. Creator and writer of comic books. Author of several television and movie screenplays. Contributor of short stories to magazines.

SIDELIGHTS: Mickey Spillane started his writing career in the early 1940s scripting comic books for Funnies, Inc. Spillane made the switch from comic books to novels in 1946 when, needing $1,000 to buy a parcel of land, he decided the easiest and quickest way to earn the money was to write a novel. Three weeks later, he sent the finished manuscript of *I, the Jury* to Dutton. Although the editorial committee questioned its good taste and literary merit, they felt the book would sell. *I, the Jury* did indeed sell—well over eight million copies have been sold to date. In addition to buying the property, Spillane was able to construct a house on the site as well. This book would be the start of a long and prolific career that would make Spillane famous, wealthy, and a personality in his own right.

Spillane described himself to Margaret Kirk in the *Chicago Tribune* in this manner: "I'm a money writer, I write when I need money. And I'm not writing for the critics. I'm writing for the public. An author would never do that. They write one book, they think they're set. I'll tell you when you're a good writer. When you're successful. I'd write like Thomas Wolfe if I thought it would sell."

Not only did *I, the Jury* introduce Spillane to the book buying public, but it also gave birth to the character, Mike Hammer, a 6-foot, 190-pound, rough and tough private investigator. Spillane's next several novels recorded the action-packed adventures of Hammer as he drank, fought, and killed his way through solving mystery after mystery. While Hammer is not featured in all of Spillane's mysteries, he is undoubtedly the most popular of Spillane's leading men. Art Harris describes Hammer in the the *Washington Post:* "There was no one like Hammer. Sam Spade was tame. Never before had a private eye spilled blood on such a vast scale. He shot quick, punched hard, fought off beautiful women and always got the bad guys. Mobsters got it. Commies got it. And if a woman deserved it, well, she got it, too."

Spillane's audience has been very loyal to his Hammer character and his other mystery novels. During his more than forty year career, over 180 million copies of his books have been sold in over sixteen languages. Seven of his books are still listed among the top fifteen all-time fiction best sellers published in the last fifty years. "I'm the most translated writer in the world, behind Lenin, Tolstoy, Gorki, and Jules Verne," Spillane said to Harris. "And they're all dead." Spillane went on to declare: "I have no fans. You know what I got? Customers. And customers are your friends."

Although his first eight novels sold very well most reviewers dismissed his work, calling it mindless as well as much too violent and too sexual. For example, a critic for the *Saturday Review* describes *I, the Jury* as the prototype for future Spillane novels with its—"lurid action, lurid characters, lurid plot, lurid finish." And Newgate Callendar explains in the *New York Times Book Review* that "the usual Spillane mix [is a mix of] sex, sadism, assorted fun and games with gun and fist."

"Spillane is like eating takeout fried chicken: so much fun to consume, but you can feel those lowlife grease-induced zits rising before you've finished the first drumstick," notes Sally Eckhoff in the *Voice Literary Supplement*. "*My Gun Is Quick* is just the book to have with you on a Hamptons weekend or a stint at an exclusive art colony where everybody else is reading Huysmans. Guaranteed they leave you alone. But don't try to slide into *Me, Hood* unless you want to permanently transform yourself into a snarling closet crimebuster. Any more of those seamed stockings, pawnshops, and stereotypical Irish gumshoes, and you'll be screaming for a Bergman movie to break your trance." In his 1951 review of *The Big Kill, New York Times* writer Anthony Boucher comments: "As rife with sexuality and sadism as any of his novels, based on a complete misunderstanding of law and on the wildest coincidence in detective fiction, it still can boast the absence of the hypocritical 'crusading' sentiments of Mike Hammer. For that reason, and for some slight ingenuity in its denouement, it may rank as the best Spillane—which is the faintest praise this department has ever bestowed."

In 1952, Spillane began a nine year break from writing mystery novels. Some people have attributed this hiatus to his religious conversion to the sect of Jehovah's Witnesses, while others feel that Spillane earned enough money from his writings and by selling the film rights to several of his books to live comfortably, enjoying life in his new beach home on Murrells Inlet located in Myrtle Beach, S.C. Although he stopped writing mysteries, Spillane wrote short stories for magazines and scripts for television and films. He also appeared on a number of television programs often performing in parodies of his tough detective characters.

Spillane reappeared on the publishing scene in 1961 with his murder mystery *The Deep* and in the following year Mike Hammer returned to fight crime in *The Girl Hunter*. The public was ecstatic—buying copies of the novel as soon as they were placed on the shelf. Reviewers seemed to soften their criticism somewhat at Hammer's return. For example, Boucher writes in his review of *The Girl Hunter* that "Spillane's rough tough Mike Hammer has been away for so long . . . that it's possible for even an old enemy of his, like me, to view him afresh and recognize that he does possess a certain genuine vigor and conviction lacking in his imitators."

Many of Spillane's later books also were somewhat praised by critics. For example, a reviewer for the *Times Literary Supplement* remarks: "Nasty as much of it is, [*The Deep*] has a genuine narrative grip; and there is a certain sociological conscience at work in the presentation of the street which has bred so much crime and an unusual perception in the portrait of an old Irish patrol officer." And Callendar comments in the *New York Times Book Review* that "editorials were written condemning [Spillane's novels], and preachers took to the pulpit. But things have changed, and one reads Spillane's . . . *The Erection Set* with almost a feeling of sentimental *deju vu*. The sex, sadism and assorted violence remain. Basically, what the Spillane books are about is the all-conquering hero myth. We all like to escape into a fantasy world to identify with the figure who is all-knowing, all-powerful, infinitely virile, sending off auras of threat in solar pulsations."

In 1979 Spillane's publisher dared him to write a children's book. A number of editors at the company felt he could never change his style of writing in order to appeal or be acceptable to a much younger, more impressionable audience. Not one to back down from a challenge, Spillane produced *The Day the Sea Rolled Back* and three years later, *The Ship that Never Was*. In general, reviewers have praised the books for their suspense and clean-cut high adventure. For example, a critic for the *Washington Post Book World* notes: "Yes, Mickey Spillane has written a kids' book, and quite an entertaining one too. As you might expect there's plenty of suspense, but violence is held in the wings; Spillane has trimmed his sails a bit for the young set."

In 1984 Spillane shared these thoughts with the *Washington Post:* "I'm 66. . . . If you're a singer, you lose your voice. A baseball player loses his arm. A writer gets more knowledge, and if he's good, the older he gets, the better he writes. They can't kill me. I still got potential."

MEDIA ADAPTATIONS: I, the Jury was filmed in 1953, *The Long Wait* in 1954, *Kiss Me, Deadly* in 1955, and *My Gun Is Quick* in 1957, all by United Artists; *The Delta Factor* was filmed in 1970 by Colorama Features; a remake of "I, the Jury" was filmed in 1981 by Twentieth Century-Fox. "Mickey Spillane's Mike Hammer," a television series based on Spillane's mystery novels and his character, Mike Hammer, was produced by Revue Productions, distributed by MCA-TV Lid., and premiered in 1958; another television series based on Spillane's writings, "Mike Hammer," starring Stacey Keach, was produced and broadcasted from 1984-87.

BIOGRAPHICAL/CRITICAL SOURCES:

BOOKS

Contemporary Literary Criticism, Gale, Volume 3, 1975, Volume 13, 1980.

PERIODICALS

Books and Bookmen, September, 1967, June, 1969.
Chicago Tribune, April 18, 1986.
Chicago Tribune Magazine, April 8, 1984.
Christian Century, January 29, 1969.
Detroit Free Press, June 11, 1967, March 23, 1969.
Detroit News, September 14, 1967.
New York Times, November 11, 1951, October 26, 1952.
New York Times Book Review, October 14, 1962, February 27, 1966, August 13, 1967, February 27, 1972, May 20, 1973.
People, July 28, 1986.
Publishers Weekly, May 15, 1967.
Saturday Review, May 29, 1965, September 27, 1970, March 25, 1972, April 7, 1973.
Times Literary Supplement, November 10, 1961, September 19, 1980.
Voice Literary Supplement, July, 1988.
Washington Post, October 24, 1984.
Washington Post Book World, May 10, 1981.
Writer's Digest, September, 1976.*

—*Sketch by Margaret Mazurkiewicz*

*   *   *

SPILLANE, Mickey
    See SPILLANE, Frank Morrison

*   *   *

SPIRES, Elizabeth   1952-

PERSONAL: Born May 28, 1952, in Lancaster, Ohio; daughter of Richard C. (in grounds maintenance) and Sue (a real estate broker; maiden name, Wagner) Spires; married Madison Smartt Bell (a novelist), June 15, 1985. *Education:* Vassar College, B.A., 1974; Johns Hopkins University, M.A., 1979.

ADDRESSES: Office—Department of English, Goucher College, Towson, Md. 21204.

CAREER: Charles E. Merrill Publishing Co., Columbus, Ohio, assistant editor, 1976-77; free-lance writer, 1977-81; Washington College, Chestertown, Md., visiting assistant professor of English, 1981; Loyola College, Baltimore, Md., adjunct assistant professor of English, 1981-82; Johns Hopkins University, visiting assistant professor in writing seminars, 1984-85, 1988-89; Goncher College, Towson, Md., writer in residence, 1985-86, 1988-90.

AWARDS, HONORS: W. K. Rose fellowship, Vassar College, 1976; National Endowment for the Arts fellowship, 1981; Pushcart Prize, Pushcart Press, 1981, for "Blame"; Ingram Merrill Foundation award, 1981; Amy Lowell Travelling Poetry scholarship, 1986-87.

WRITINGS:

Boardwalk (poems), Bits Press, 1980.
Globe (poems), Wesleyan University Press, 1981.
The Falling Star (juvenile), C. E. Merrill, 1981.
Count with Me (juvenile), C. E. Merrill, 1981.
The Wheels Go Round (juvenile), C. E. Merrill, 1981.
Simon's Adventure (juvenile), Antioch Publishing Co., 1982.
Things That Go Fast (juvenile), Antioch Publishing Co., 1982.
Swan's Island (poems), Holt, 1985.
Annonciade (poems), Viking, 1989.

Contributor of poems to anthologies, including *Best American Poems, 1989,* and to periodicals, including *New Yorker, Mademoiselle, Poetry, American Poetry Review, Yale Review, Partisan Review, New Criterion,* and *Paris Review.*

WORK IN PROGRESS: The Shape-Shifter, a book of poems.

SIDELIGHTS: Elizabeth Spires writes: "I think by the time I was twelve, I knew I would be a writer, though at the time I thought I would write short stories, not poetry (I was under the influence of Flannery O'Connor at the time). . . . I'm an Anglophile by nature, particularly interested in English literature and literary landmarks. I certainly feel that living in England has given me a different perspective on the U.S. and allowed me to see it in a 'fresher' way. Being outside my native country has pushed me toward thinking more about global problems, such as the ever-present threat of war, and about cultural differences and idiosyncrasies. Besides writing about London, I find myself lately interested in writing about childhood experiences related to growing up Catholic. I've also been thinking a lot about the future, what life ten or twenty or thirty years from now will be like, both for myself as an individual, and for society as a whole.

"My poetry has been influenced by my close reading, and love, of the poetry of John Donne, Elizabeth Bishop, Robert Lowell, John Berryman, W. D. Snodgrass, C. K. Williams, and Robert Frost. That's not an exhaustive list at all, though. When I finish my new book, *The Shape-Shifter,* I hope to perhaps try my hand at something quite different, perhaps a juvenile novel which veers away from the 'realistic' towards something concerned with magic, the motif of transformation in everyday life."

BIOGRAPHICAL/CRITICAL SOURCES:

PERIODICALS

Baltimore Evening Sun, October 9, 1981.
Boston Review, April, 1989.
Missouri Review, Volume 9, number 3, 1986.
New York Times Book Review, March 14, 1982, June 1, 1986.
Vassar Quarterly, summer, 1987.
Washington Post Book World, February 21, 1982.

*   *   *

STACK, Edward M(acGregor)   1919-

PERSONAL: Born November 7, 1919, in Warren, Pa.; son of Alvan Huey (an engineer) and Jean Elizabeth (MacGregor) Stack. *Education:* Princeton University, A.B., 1941, A.M., 1949, Ph.D., 1950.

ADDRESSES: Home—3925 Arrow Dr., Raleigh, N.C. 27612.

CAREER: Louisiana State University, Baton Rouge, visiting assistant professor of Romance languages, 1950-51; University of Virginia, Charlottesville, instructor in Romance languages, 1951-52; University of Texas at Austin, assistant professor of Romance languages, 1952-57; Whittier College, Whittier, Calif., professor of Romance languages and chairman of department, 1957-60; Villanova University, Villanova, Pa., professor, 1960; Electronic Teaching Labs, Washington, D.C., consultant and producer, 1960-63; North Carolina State University, Raleigh, professor of foreign languages and literatures, 1963-88, professor emeritus, 1988—. Lecturer, George Washington University, 1961. Specialist, U.S. Department of State, 1963; chairman, State of North Carolina Language Laboratories Committee, 1964—. *Military service:* U.S. Army, Field Artillery, 1942-47; received Army Commendation Medal. U.S. Air Force Reserve; captain.

MEMBER: American Association of Teachers of French, American Association of University Professors, Modern Language Association of America.

WRITINGS:

(Editor and translator) Francois duc de La Rochefoucauld, *Selected Maxims and Reflections,* Nonpareil Press, 1956.
Reading French in the Arts and Sciences, Houghton, 1957, 4th edition, 1987.
Elementary Oral and Written French, Oxford University Press, 1959.
The Language Laboratory and Modern Language Teaching, Oxford University Press, 1960, 3rd edition, 1971.
French Handbook and Guide, American Book Co., 1960, revised edition, 1966.
Le Pont Neuf: A Structural Review, Prentice-Hall, 1966, 3rd edition, 1978.

Also author of about 200 programmed language tapes in French, Spanish, German, and Russian. Some of Stack's books have appeared in foreign language editions, including German, Italian, Japanese, and Finnish.

WORK IN PROGRESS: A 4th edition of *Le Pont Neuf.*

AVOCATIONAL INTERESTS: Printing, classical music.

*   *   *

STANFORD, Don
    See STANFORD, Donald E(lwin)

*   *   *

STANFORD, Donald E(lwin)   1913-
    (Don Stanford)

PERSONAL: Born February 7, 1913, in Amherst, Mass.; son of Ernest Elwood (a professor) and Alice (Carroll) Stanford; married Edna Goodwin, July, 1937 (divorced, 1946); married Maryanna Peterson, August 14, 1953; children: (first marriage) Don David. *Education:* Stanford University, B.A., 1933, Ph.D., 1953; Harvard University, M.A., 1934.

ADDRESSES: Home—776 Delgado Dr., Baton Rouge, La. 70808. *Office*—Department of English, Louisiana State University, Baton Rouge, La. 70803.

CAREER: Colorado State College (now University), Fort Collins, instructor in English, 1935-37; Dartmouth College, Hanover, N.H., instructor in English, 1937-41; University of Nebraska, Lincoln, instructor in English, 1941-42; Louisiana State University, Baton Rouge, instructor, 1949-50, assistant pro-

fessor of English, 1953-54, associate professor, 1954-62, professor, 1962-69, Alumni Professor of English, 1979-83, Alumni Professor Emeritus, 1983—; *Southern Review,* Louisiana State University, Baton Rouge, La., editor, 1963-83, editor emeritus, 1983—, consulting editor, 1987—. Visiting associate professor, Duke University, 1961-62; visiting professor, Texas A & M University, 1984. Member of advisory board, *Hopkins Quarterly,* 1981—.

MEMBER: Modern Language Association of America, PEN, Melville Society, Hopkins Society (member of board of scholars), South-Atlantic Modern Language Association, South-Central Modern Language Association, Phi Kappa Phi, Phi Beta Kappa.

AWARDS, HONORS: Guggenheim fellowship, 1959-60; National Endowment for the Humanities award, 1972, 1978; Louisiana State University Foundation distinguished faculty fellowship, 1973-74; Research Master award, 1982.

WRITINGS:

(Under name Don Stanford) *New England Earth* (poems), Colt Press, 1941.
(Under name Don Stanford) *The Traveler* (poems), Cummington Press, 1955.
(Editor and author of introduction) *The Poems of Edward Taylor,* Yale University Press, 1960, 2nd abridged edition with new introduction, Yale University Press, 1963, reprinted, University of North Carolina Press, 1989.
(Editor) *Edward Taylor's Metrical History of Christianity,* Microphoto, 1962.
(Editor) *Nine Essays in Modern Literature,* Louisiana State Press, 1965.
Edward Taylor, University of Minnesota Press, 1965.
(Contributor) Everett Emerson, editor, *Chapters in Early American Literature,* University of Wisconsin Press, 1972.
(Editor) *Selected Poems of Robert Bridges,* Carcanet Press, 1974.
(Editor) *Selected Poems of S. Foster Damon,* Cummington Press, 1974.
In the Classic Mode: The Achievement of Robert Bridges, University of Delaware Press, 1978.
(Editor) *The Selected Letters of Robert Bridges,* two volumes, University of Delaware Press, 1983.
Revolution and Convention in Modern Poetry: Studies in Ezra Pound, T. S. Eliot, Wallace Stevens, Edwin Arlington Robinson, and Yvor Winters, University of Delaware Press, 1983.
(Editor) *Dictionary of Literary Biography,* Gale, Volume 19: *British Poets, 1880-1914,* 1983, Volume 20: *British Poets, 1914-1945,* 1983.
(Editor) *Poems of John Masefield,* Carcanet Press, 1984.
(Editor) *Letters of John Masefield to Margaret Bridges,* Carcanet Press, 1984.
The Cartesian Lawnmower and Other Poems, Robert Barth, 1984.

Editor, Louisiana State University "Humanities" series, 1962-67. Contributor to *Shakespeare Quarterly, Journal of Modern Literature, Philological Quarterly, Hudson Review, Early American Literature, Tulane Studies in English,* and other periodicals.

WORK IN PROGRESS: Robert Bridges and His Circle.

AVOCATIONAL INTERESTS: Foreign travel.

STEARNS, Peter N. 1936-

PERSONAL: Born March 3, 1936, in London, England; son of Raymond Phineas (a teacher) and Elizabeth (Scott) Stearns; children: Duncan Scott, Deborah Clark, Clio Elizabeth, Cordelia Raymond. *Education:* Harvard University, A.B., 1957, A.M., 1959, Ph.D., 1963.

ADDRESSES: Home—509 South Linden Ave., Pittsburgh, Pa. 15208. *Office*—Department of History, Carnegie-Mellon University, Schenley Park, Pittsburgh, Pa. 15213.

CAREER: University of Chicago, Chicago, Ill., instructor, 1962-63, assistant professor, 1963-66, associate professor of history, 1966-68; Rutgers University, New Brunswick, N.J., professor of history, 1968-74, chairman of department, 1969-74; Carnegie-Mellon University, Pittsburgh, Pa., Heinz Professor of History, 1974—, head of department, 1986—.

MEMBER: American Historical Association, Society for French Historical Studies, Social Science History Association, Phi Beta Kappa.

AWARDS, HONORS: Koren Prize, Society for French Historical Studies, 1966, for article in *American Historical Review;* Newcomen Prize, Newcomen Society, 1966, for article in *Business History Review;* Guggenheim fellowship, 1973-74.

WRITINGS:

European Society in Upheaval, Macmillan, 1967, revised edition, 1975.
Priest and Revolutionary, Harper, 1967.
(Editor) *A Century for Debate,* Dodd, 1969.
Modern Europe, 1789-1914, Scott, Foresman, 1969.
Workers and Protest, Peacock, 1971.
Revolutionary Syndicalism and French Labor, Rutgers University Press, 1971.
(Editor) *Impact of Industrialization,* Prentice-Hall, 1972.
European Experience since 1815, Harcourt, 1973.
(Editor with Stanley Chodorow) *The Other Side of Civilization: Readings in Everyday Life,* Volume 1: *The Ancient World to the Reformation,* Volume 2: *The Sixteenth Century to the Present,* Harcourt, 1973, 3rd edition, 1985.
The Revolutionary Tide in Europe, Norton, 1974 (published in England as *The Revolutions of 1848,* Weidenfeld & Nicolson, 1974).
(Editor with Daniel Walkowitz) *Workers in the Industrial Revolution: Recent Studies of Labor in the United States and Europe,* Transaction Books, 1974.
Lives of Labor: Work in a Maturing Industrial Society, Holmes & Meier, 1975.
Old Age in European Society: The Case of France, Holmes & Meier, 1976.
The Face of Europe, Forum Press, 1977.
(Editor and author of introduction) *The Rise of the Modern Woman,* Forum Press, 1978.
Paths to Authority: The Middle Class and the Industrial Labor Force in France, 1820-1848, University of Illinois Press, 1978.
Be a Man!: Males in Modern Society, Holmes & Meier, 1979.
Old Age in Preindustrial Society, Holmes & Meier, 1982.
(Editor) Ethel Spencer, *The Spencers of Amberson Avenue,* University of Pittsburgh Press, 1983.
(With Linda W. Rosenzweig) *Themes in Modern Social History,* Carnegie-Mellon University Press, 1985.
(Editor with David van Tassel) *Old Age in Bureaucratic Society: The Elderly, the Experts, and the State in American Society,* Greenwood Press, 1986.

(With Carol Stearns) *Anger: The Struggle for Emotional Control in American History,* University of Chicago Press, 1986.
Makers of Modern Europe, Ginn, 1986.
World History: Patterns of Change and Continuity, Harper, 1987.
(Editor with others) *Documents in World History,* Volume 1: *The Great Traditions—From Ancient Times to 1500,* Volume 2: *The Modern Centuries—From 1500 to the Present,* Harper, 1987.
(Editor) *Emotion and Social Change,* Holmes & Meier, 1988.
Life and Society in the West: The Modern Centuries, Harcourt, 1988.
World History, Addison-Wesley, 1988.
(Editor) *Expanding the Past, a Reader in Social History: Essays from the Journal of Social History,* New York University Press, 1988.
"Demon in the Breast": The Evolution of American Jealousy, New York University Press, 1989.

Contributor to history journals. General editor with Rosenzweig, *Project on Social History Curriculum,* six volumes, 1982; editor and managing editor, *Journal of Social History.*

WORK IN PROGRESS: A history of emotion and gender in Western society.

*   *   *

STEELMAN, Robert J(ames) 1914-

PERSONAL: Born March 7, 1914, in Columbus, Ohio; son of Charles William and Nell (Blair) Steelman; married Janet Eyler, August 23, 1941; children: Karen (Mrs. Gene Berson), Michael. *Education:* Ohio State University, B.S., 1938. *Politics:* "Unaffiliated." *Religion:* Presbyterian.

ADDRESSES: Home and office—875 Amiford Dr., San Diego, Calif. 92107. *Agent*—Richard Curtis Associates, 164 East 64th St., New York, N.Y. 10021.

CAREER: U.S. Army, Signal Corps, civilian electronics engineer, 1939-46; U.S. Navy, civilian electronics engineer, 1946-69; writer.

WRITINGS:

Stages South, Ace Books, 1956.
Apache Wells, Ballantine, 1959.
Winter of the Sioux, Ballantine, 1959.
Call of the Arctic (Arctic adventure novel), Coward, 1960.
Ambush at Three Rivers, Ballantine, 1964.
Dakota Territory, Ballantine, 1974.
Cheyenne Vengeance, Doubleday, 1974.
The Fox Dancer, Doubleday, 1975.
Sun Boy, Doubleday, 1975.
Portrait of a Sioux, Doubleday, 1976.
Lord Apache, Doubleday, 1977.
The Galvanized Reb, Doubleday, 1977.
Surgeon to the Sioux, Doubleday, 1979.
White Medicine Man, Ace Books, 1979.
The Great Yellowstone Steamboat Race, Doubleday, 1980.
The Man They Hanged, Doubleday, 1980.
The Prairie Baroness, Doubleday, 1981.
The Santee Massacre, Dell, 1982.
Border Riders, Leisure Books, 1983.
Royal Charlie, Charter Books, 1983.
The Holdout, Walker & Co., 1984.
Blood and Dust, New American Library, 1987.

Contributor to men's adventure and western magazines, including *Ranch Romances*.

WORK IN PROGRESS: Continuing research on the frontier West.

SIDELIGHTS: "My writing is largely of the Old West," Robert J. Steelman told *CA.* "I try hard to make my books authoritative and true to the times. Perhaps my principal aim is to do what I can to elevate the 'western' to some literary significance, rather than see it condemned to a second-rate genre status."

BIOGRAPHICAL/CRITICAL SOURCES:

PERIODICALS

Roundup, July, 1957.

* * *

STEINEM, Gloria 1934-

PERSONAL: Born March 25, 1934, in Toledo, Ohio; daughter of Leo and Ruth (Nuneviller) Steinem. *Education:* Smith College, B.A. (magna cum laude), 1956; University of Delhi and University of Calcutta, India, graduate study, 1957-58.

ADDRESSES: Office—Ms. Foundation for Education and Communication, Inc., One Times Square, 10th Floor, New York, N.Y. 10036.

CAREER: Editor, writer, lecturer. Independent Research Service, Cambridge, Mass., and New York City, director, 1959-60; *Glamour* magazine, New York City, contributing editor, 1962-69; *New York* magazine, New York City, co-founder and contributing editor, 1968-72; *Ms.* magazine, New York City, co-founder and editor, 1972-87, columnist, 1980-87, consulting editor, 1987. Contributing correspondent to NBC's "Today" show. Active in civil rights and peace campaigns, including those of United Farm Workers, Vietnam War Tax Protest, and Committee for the Legal Defense of Angela Davis; active in political campaigns of Adlai Stevenson, Robert Kennedy, Eugene McCarthy, Shirley Chisholm, and George McGovern. Editorial consultant to Conde Nast Publications, 1962-69, Curtis Publishing, 1964-65, Random House Publishing, 1988—, and McCall Publishing.

MEMBER: PEN, National Press Club, Society of Magazine Writers, Authors Guild, Authors League of America, American Federation of Television and Radio Artists, National Organization for Women, Women's Action Alliance (co-founder; chairperson, 1970—), National Women's Political Caucus (founding member; member of national advisory committee, 1971—), Ms. Foundation for Women (co-founder; member of board, 1972—), Coalition of Labor Union Women (founding member, 1974), Voters for Choice (co-founder), Phi Beta Kappa.

AWARDS, HONORS: Chester Bowles Asian fellow in India, 1957-58; Penney-Missouri journalism award, 1970, for *New York* article "After Black Power, Women's Liberation"; Ohio Governor's journalism award, 1972; named Woman of the Year, *McCall's* magazine, 1972; Doctorate of Human Justice from Simmons College, 1973; Bill of Rights award, American Civil Liberties Union of Southern California, 1975; Woodrow Wilson International Center for Scholars fellow, 1977; Ceres Medal from United Nations; Front Page Award; Clarion Award; nine citations from *World Almanac* as one of the twenty-five most influential women in America.

WRITINGS:

The Thousand Indias, Government of India, 1957.
The Beach Book, Viking, 1963.
(Contributor) Peter Manso, editor, *Running against the Machine,* Doubleday, 1969.
(With G. Chester) *Wonder Woman,* Holt, 1972.
(Author of introductory note) Marlo Thomas and others, *Free to Be . . . You and Me,* McGraw, 1974.
Outrageous Acts and Everyday Rebellions, Holt, 1983.
Marilyn: Norma Jeane, Holt, 1986.
Bedside Book of Self-Esteem, Little, Brown, 1989.

Writer for television, including series "That Was the Week that Was," NBC, 1964-65. Author of films and political campaign material. Former author of column, "The City Politic," in *New York.* Contributor to periodicals, including *Esquire, Ms., Show, Vogue, Life,* and *Cosmopolitan.* Editorial consultant, *Seventeen,* 1969-70, and *Show.*

WORK IN PROGRESS: A book about the women in America's most rich and powerful families, for Simon & Schuster.

SIDELIGHTS: Gloria Steinem is recognized as one of the foremost organizers of the modern women's movement. Her grandmother, Pauline Steinem, was the president of a turn-of-the-century women's suffrage group and was a representative to the 1908 International Council of Women, but Gloria was not substantially influenced by her while growing up in Toledo, Ohio. Her parents divorced when she was young, and at the age of ten Gloria was left alone to care for herself and her mentally ill mother. She left home when she was seventeen to attend Smith College on a scholarship. Like most women in that era, she was engaged by her senior year; however, Steinem broke her engagement to continue her political science studies in India. She adjusted quickly to life there, adopting native dress and ways. Because English served as the common language, she was "able to really talk, and tell jokes, and understand political arguments," she told Miriam Berkley in *Publishers Weekly.* Steinem was also able to get involved, freelancing for Indian newspapers and seeking out the company of Indian social activists. As a member of a group called the Radical Humanists, she traveled to southern India at the time of the terrible caste riots there, working as a member of a peacemaking team. Her experiences in India gave her a deep sympathy for the underclasses, as well as an enduring love of that country.

When the time came for her to return to the United States, Steinem did so filled with an "enormous sense of urgency about the contrast between wealth and poverty," she stated in her interview with Berkley. But because she "rarely met people who had shared this experience," it became "like a dream. It had no relation to my real, everyday life. . . . I couldn't write about it." Instead, she established a successful free-lance career writing articles about celebrities, fashions, and tropical vacations, while devoting her spare time to work for the civil rights movement. Berkley describes Steinem's life in the early 1960s as "schizophrenically split between career and conscience." "I was . . . divided up into pieces as a person," the author told Elisabeth Bumiller in the *Washington Post.* "I was working on one thing, and caring about another, which I think is the way a lot of us have to live our lives. I'm lucky it came together."

Steinem's best-known article from her early career is "I Was a Playboy Bunny." Assigned to cover the 1963 opening of the New York City Playboy Club for *Show* magazine, she went undercover to work as a "Bunny," or waitress, for two weeks. The resulting article is an "excellent, ironic, illuminating bit of reporting," says Angela Carter in the *Washington Post Book Review*. Steinem was instructed by the "Bunny Mother" in techniques for stuffing her bodice and bending over to serve drinks; she was cautioned against sneezing, which would split the seams of a Bunny costume; she was presented with a copy of the "Bunny Bible," the lengthy code of conduct for Playboy waitresses; and she was informed that all new Bunnies were required to have a pelvic examination performed by the club's specially-appointed doctor. "I Was a Playboy Bunny" is "hysterically funny," according to Ann Marie Lapinski in the *Chicago Tribune*, but it is also full of feminist consciousness as some of [Steinem's] later reportage," believes Carter, who comments, "If it is implicit rather than explicit, it is no less powerful for that." Of her experiences in the club, Steinem remarked to *Los Angeles Times* interviewer Elenita Ravicz, "Being a Bunny was more humiliating than I thought it would be. True, it was never the kind of job I would have considered under ordinary circumstances, but I expected it to be more glamorous and better paid than it was. . . . Customers there seemed to be there because they could be treated as superiors. . . . There is a real power difference when one group is semi-nude and the other is fully-clothed."

By the mid-sixties, Steinem was getting more substantial writing assignments and earning respect for her pieces on political figures. In 1968 she and Clay Felker founded *New York* magazine; Steinem supplied the monthly column "The City Politic" and articles such as "Ho Chi Minh in New York." She was still seen as something of a trendy celebrity by many in the male-dominated world of journalism, however. Bumiller quotes a 1969 *Time* article describing Steinem as "one of the best dates to take to a New York party these days. . . . Writers, politicians, editors, publishers and tuned-in businessmen are all intensely curious about her. Gloria is not only a successful free-lance writer and contributing editor of New York magazine; she is also a trim, undeniably female, blonde-streaked brunette. . . . She does something for her soft suits and clinging dresses, has legs worthy of her miniskirts, and a brain that keeps conversation lively without getting tricky." But her popularity was about to wane because of her interest in controversial women's issues.

Her colleagues' reactions to a 1969 article she wrote about a New York abortion hearing shocked Steinem. She told Ravicz, "I went to that hearing and listened to women stand up and talk about how dangerous and difficult it was for them to get an illegal abortion. . . . They had tears running down their faces as they talked, many of them for the first time, about how they'd had to risk permanent injury and even give sexual favors to their abortionists. I wrote an article about the hearing and my male colleagues, really nice men I got along well with, took me aside one by one and said, 'don't get involved with these crazy women. You've taken so much trouble to establish your reputation as a serious journalist, don't throw it all away.' That was when I realized men valued me only to the extent I imitated them."

Instead of abandoning the subject, Steinem followed up her coverage of the abortion hearing with an extensively researched article on reproductive and other feminist issues. Her article "After Black Power, Women's Liberation" won her the Penney-Missouri journalism award, but it also "unleashed a storm of negative reactions . . . from male colleagues. The response from the publishing establishment, and its reluctance to publish other work on the subject, opened her eyes. She

began to pursue not only writing but also speaking engagements and became an active part of the women's movement she had once only observed," relates Berkley. Steinem came to believe that a magazine controlled by women was necessary if a truly open forum on women's issues was to exist. Accordingly, she and others began working toward that goal. Clay Felker offered to subsidize a sample issue and to include a thirty-page excerpt of the new publication in *New York* magazine; Steinem and the rest of the staff worked without pay, and produced the first issue of *Ms.* in January of 1972. "We called it the spring issue," Steinem recalled to Berkley. "We were really afraid that if it didn't sell it would embarrass the women's movement. So we called it Spring so that it could lie there on the newsstands for a long time." Such worries were unfounded, for the entire 300,000-copy run of *Ms.* sold out in eight days.

Steinem was suddenly the editor of a very successful monthly magazine. She was somewhat ambivalent about the position: "I backed into [starting *Ms.*]," she admitted to Beth Austin in an interview for the *Chicago Tribune*. "I felt very strongly there should be a feminist magazine. But I didn't want to start it myself. I wanted to be a free-lance writer. I'd never had a job, never worked in an office, never worked with a group before. It just happened, through a series of events that included my having worked for *New York* magazine." Steinem believed that she would turn the editorship of *Ms.* over to someone else as soon as the magazine was squarely on its feet. "I said, 'I'm going to do this two years, that's it.' I kept on saying that until . . . I'd already been doing it for almost seven years. Then I took a fellowship at the Woodrow Wilson Center, which is part of the Smithsonian Institution in Washington. So I was away from the office for the first time for substantial periods of time. . . . I just missed it terribly. And I suddenly realized that, where I thought I'd been delaying life, there *was* life."

As a spokesperson for the women's movement, Steinem has been criticized as subversive and strident by some and as overly tolerant and conservative by others. An overview of her opinions and her development as a feminist is provided by her 1983 publication *Outrageous Acts and Everyday Rebellions*. It is a collection representing twenty years of her writing on a variety of subjects, including politics, pornography, her mother, and Marilyn Monroe. Carter criticizes the book, complaining that Steinem presents only "the acceptable face of feminism" and that she is "straightjacketed by her own ideology." But Diane Johnson offers a more favorable appraisal in the *New York Times Book Review:* "Reading Miss Steinem's essays . . . one is struck by their intelligence, restraint and common sense, as well as by the energetic and involved life they reflect. . . . This is a consciousness-raising book. . . . Her views, like her writing itself, are characterized by engaging qualities of unpretensious clarity and forceful expression." Douglas Hill concurs in the Toronto *Globe and Mail:* "Honesty, fairness and consistency gleam in these pages. And Steinem writes superbly. . . . It's her special strength to write as cleanly and affectingly about her mother's mental illness as about the practice of genital mutilation endured by 75 million women worldwide or the inadequacies of William Styron's fiction." *Detroit News* reviewer Fiona Lowther concludes, "Make no mistake: Whether you disagree with or espouse wholly or in part what Steinem stands for—or what you think she stands for—she is a worthy observer and reporter of the contemporary scene."

Steinem's next book grew from the essay in *Outrageous Acts* concerning Marilyn Monroe, the actress who became internationally famous for her "sex goddess" image in the 1950s and died by her own hand in 1962. When photojournalist George Barris decided to publish a series of photographs taken of Monroe shortly before her death, Steinem was asked to contribute the text. While researching *Marilyn: Norma Jeane,* she became aware that although over forty books had already been published about the late film star, only a few were written by women. Most of the biographies focused on the scandalous aspects of Monroe's death and personal relationships, or reinforced her image as the ultimate pin-up. Steinem explained to *Washington Post* interviewer Chip Brown, "I tried to take away the fantasy of Marilyn and replace it with reality.... The book doesn't have a thesis so much as an emphasis—an emphasis on Norma Jeane, on the private, real, internal person. I hadn't read a book about Marilyn that made me feel I knew her. My purpose was to try to get to know or to portray the real person inside the public image." Commenting on the ironic fact that Monroe derived little pleasure from her physical relationships, Steinem suggested to Brown, "It's hard for men to admit that a sex goddess didn't enjoy sex.... It's part of the desire to believe she was murdered—the same cultural impulse that says if she's a sex goddess she had to have enjoyed sex doesn't want to believe she killed herself, doesn't want to accept her unhappiness.... This country is media-sick. People who are seen in the media are considered to be more real, or different, or special or magic.... I tried to make Marilyn real."

"Steinem's 'Marilyn' is a sort of feminist rebuttal to Norman Mailer's conquer-and-transcend biography of the same name," offers Brown. "His book is an extravagant concerto for the 'Stradivarius of sex.' Monroe is the supreme object.... Steinem's approach is not so mystical.... And while at times her writing is wheat germ to Mailer's caviar, she makes some sensible arguments.... She draws Monroe as a prisoner of childhood, compulsively using sex to get 'childlike warmth and nurturing'.... [She] stresses the limited choices women had then—and underscores Monroe's struggle for independence, her desire to be taken seriously." London *Times* reviewer Fiona MacCarthy finds fault with Steinem's "passionate involvement with the helpless child in Marilyn," believing that it is an example of "the new phenomenon of women letting women off too lightly.... Her sentimental vision of the real Marilyn entrapped in the sex-goddess body sometimes makes one wonder where is now the Gloria Steinem who worked on the campaign trail in the 1960s both as a reporter and an aide to George McGovern. Has she lost all astuteness?" But Diana Trilling argues that *Marilyn: Norma Jeane* is "thoughtful and absorbing." Her *New York Times Book Review* evaluation calls the biography "a quiet book; it has none of the sensationalism that has colored other purportedly serious books about the film star, Norman Mailer's in particular.... In writing about Marilyn Monroe, Gloria Steinem for the most part admirably avoids the ideological excess that we have come to associate with the women's movement—Monroe emerges from her book a far more dimensional figure than she would have been if she had been presented as simply the victim of a male-dominated society."

"One aspect of writing about a woman like Marilyn is that you feel you're exploiting her all over again," Steinem disclosed to George James in the *New York Times Book Review.* That feeling led her to donate all her earnings from *Marilyn: Norma Jeane* to the establishment of the Marilyn Monroe Children's Fund. Under the auspices of Ms. Foundation for Women, which sponsors feminist causes, the Marilyn Monroe Children's Fund finances a variety of children's welfare projects. Steinem continues to work energetically for social change through her writing, fund-raising and speaking engagements. Bumiller asked the feminist leader about the state of the women's movement today: "She says it's not dead or even sick, but has instead spread out from the middle class to be integrated into issues like unemployment and the gender gap. Feminism, she says, has brought America closer to the democracy it ought to be, and has found words like sexual harrassment for events that '10 years ago were called life.' She sees four enormous goals ahead: 'reproductive freedom, democratic families, a depoliticized culture and work redefined.... Remember. We are talking about overthrowing, or humanizing—pick your verb, depending on how patient you feel—the sex and race caste systems. Now that is a big job.''

MEDIA ADAPTATIONS: "I Was a Playboy Bunny" was produced by Joan Marks as an ABC television movie, "A Bunny's Tale," starring Kirstie Alley, and first broadcast February 25, 1985.

BIOGRAPHICAL/CRITICAL SOURCES:

PERIODICALS

Chicago Tribune, October 2, 1983, January 11, 1987.
Detroit News, August 28, 1983.
Esquire, June, 1984.
Globe and Mail (Toronto), February 8, 1986.
Los Angeles Times, December 11, 1984, December 10, 1986, May 6, 1987.
New York Times, April 4, 1987, May 10, 1988.
New York Times Book Review, September 4, 1983, December 21, 1986.
People, June 11, 1984, February 25, 1985.
Publishers Weekly, August 12, 1983.
Times (London), February 19, 1987.
Washington Post, October 12, 1983, December 7, 1986.
Washington Post Book World, October 9, 1983.

—*Sketch by Joan Goldsworthy*

*   *   *

STEISS, Alan Walter 1937-

PERSONAL: Born February 15, 1937, in Woodbury, N.J.; son of Walter and Martha (Schroeder) Steiss; married Patricia McClintock, June 13, 1959; children: Carol Jean, Darren Christopher, Todd Alan. *Education:* Bucknell University, A.B., 1959; University of Wisconsin, M.A., 1966, Ph.D, 1969.

ADDRESSES: Home—4820 Greenway Ct., Ann Arbor, Mich. 48103. *Office*—Division of Research Development and Administration, University of Michigan, Ann Arbor, Mich. 48109.

CAREER: State of New Jersey, Division of State and Regional Planning, Trenton, assistant planner, 1960-61, senior planner, 1961-62, principal planner, 1962-63, supervising planner, 1963-64, section chief, 1964-65; Virginia Polytechnic Institute and State University, Blacksburg, assistant professor, 1967-69, associate professor, 1969-72, professor, 1972-88, assistant director, 1968-69, director of Center for Urban and Regional Studies, 1969-70, chairman of Division of Environmental and Urban Systems, 1969-75, associate dean, 1974-78, acting dean for research in Office of the Provost, 1978-83, director of sponsored programs, 1982-88, associate provost for research, 1983-88; University of Michigan, Ann Arbor, professor of urban planning and director of Division of Research Development and Administration, 1988—. Lecturer at numerous universities. Member of firm, Planning Science Organization, 1967-73, and Anthony J. Catanese & Associates, 1973; principal investigator, National Training and Development Service Urban Management Curriculum Development Project, 1976-78. Chairman of the Montgomery County (Va.) Public Service Authority, 1979-83. Consultant to numerous state and industrial groups; also consultant to various localities in Virginia on loss in net tax revenues through annexation, 1985-86.

MEMBER: American Institute of Planners (chairman of committee on programs for programs for planning students, 1960-64), Association of Collegiate Schools of Planning (member of executive committee, 1970-71; secretary, 1971-72), American Association of University Professors, National Urban Coalition, Urban America, Inc., Psi Chi, Lambda Alpha, Lambda Chi Alpha, Tau Delta Rho.

AWARDS, HONORS: Named one of the outstanding young men in America by U.S. Junior Chamber of Commerce, 1970; named outstanding educator of America, 1972; Teaching Excellence Award, 1975.

WRITINGS:

(With James Collins and George McKnight) *The Setting for Regional Planning in New Jersey,* New Jersey Department of Conservation of Economic Development, 1961.

(With Collins) *An Open Space Plan for New Jersey,* New Jersey Department of Conservation and Economic Development, 1963.

(With Harold F. Wise, Henry Fagin, and Edward Schten) *Planning Administration,* Wisconsin Department of Resource Development, 1966.

A Framework for Planning in State Government, Council of State Governments, 1968.

(Contributor) James T. Murray, editor, *Dynamic Factors in Transportation,* Duke University Press, 1970.

(Contributor) *Handbook for Regional Research and Regional Planning,* Akademie fur Raumforschung and Landesplanung, 1970.

(With Anthony J. Catanese) *Systemic Planning: Theory and Application,* Heath, 1970.

(With Charles Burchard and F. D. Regetz) *A Public Service Option for Architectural Curricula,* Association of Collegiate Schools of Architecture, 1971.

Public Budgeting and Management, Heath, 1972.

Urban Systems Dynamics, Heath, 1974.

Models for the Analysis and Planning of Urban Systems, Heath, 1974.

Administracion y Presupuestos Publicos, Editorial Diana, 1974.

(With John Dickey, Michael Harvey, and Bruce Phelps) *Dynamic Change and the Urban Ghetto,* Heath, 1975.

Local Government Finance: Capital Facilities Planning and Debt Administration, Heath, 1975.

Performance/Program Budgeting, NTDS, 1978.

Performance Administration, Heath, 1980.

Management Control in Government, Heath, 1982.

(With Herbert and Killough) *Governmental Accounting and Control,* Heath, 1984.

Strategic Management and Organizational Decision Making, Heath, 1985.

(With Herbert and Killough) *Accounting and Control for Governmental and Other Nonbusiness Organizations,* McGraw, 1987.

Financial Management in Public Organizations, Heath, 1988.

Also author of other research reports on land use and urban planning. Contributor of more than fifty articles to planning and urban affairs journals in the United States and Europe.

WORK IN PROGRESS: Strategic Planning in Public Organizations.

SIDELIGHTS: Alan Walter Steiss told *CA:* "My colleagues ask me how I find time to teach, hold down a full-time administrative post, and still find time to write a book every year or so. I tell them I teach because I enjoy the challenge of young minds who question rather than accept dogma. I work as an administrator because it affords me an opportunity to put into practice that which I teach (and to again from such experience new insights to take back to the classroom—what some call 'war stories'). And I write books because the discipline of putting one's thoughts down in this extended format represents a culmination of the other two activities."

*   *   *

STEPHENS, W(illiam) P(eter) 1934-

PERSONAL: Born May 16, 1934, in Penzance, Cornwall, England; son of Alfred Cyril William Joseph and Jennie Eudora (Trewavas) Stephens. *Education:* Attended Cambridge University, 1952-57, University of Lund, 1957-58, University of Strasbourg, 1965-67, and University of Muenster, 1966-67; Cambridge University, M.A., 1961, B.D., 1971; University of Strasbourg, Docteur es sciences religieuses, 1967.

ADDRESSES: Office—Faculty of Divinity, King's College, Old Aberdeen AB9 2UB, Scotland.

CAREER: Hartley Victoria College, Manchester, England, assistant tutor in New Testament, 1958-61, Ranmoor Chair of Church History, 1971-73; University of Nottingham, Nottingham, England, Methodist chaplain, 1961-65; minister of Methodist church in Shirley, Croydon, England, 1967-71; Wesley College, Bristol, England, Randles Chair of Historical and Systematic Theology, 1973-80; The Queen's College, Birmingham, England, research fellow, 1980-81, lecturer in church history, 1981-86; University of Aberdeen, Aberdeen, Scotland, professor of church history, 1986—, dean of faculty of divinity, 1987—. Fernley Hartley Lecturer, 1972; James A. Gray Lecturer at Duke University, 1976. Chairman of Shirley Group of Churches, 1969-70, Croydon Anti-Apartheid Group, 1970-72, Withington World Development Movement, 1972-73, and British Council of Churches Advisory Committees on Western Europe, 1974-85, and East-West Relations, 1975-86. Member of Bristol City Council, 1976-83.

MEMBER: World Methodist Council and Lutheran World Federation International Commission, Society for Study of Theology (secretary, 1963-76), Conference of European Churches (member of advisory committee, 1974—), British Roman Catholic-Methodist Commission.

WRITINGS:

The Holy Spirit in the Theology of Martin Buber, Cambridge University Press, 1970.

Faith and Love (sermons), Epworth, 1971.

The Holy Spirit, edited by Dow Kirkpatrick, Tidings, 1974.

Christmas Conferring, Epworth, 1978.

Our Churches, Catholic Truth Society, 1978.

Methodism in Europe, [Cincinnati], 1982.

The Theology of Huldrych Zwingli, Oxford University Press, 1986.

John Wesley: Contemporary Perspectives, edited by John Stacey, Epworth, 1988.

Also author of articles on theological and pastoral issues and on churches in Eastern and Western Europe.

WORK IN PROGRESS: The Theology of Heinrich Bullinger.

SIDELIGHTS: W. P. Stephens once told *CA:* "My writing on the reformation is primarily for scholars and students. My other works are intended for a wider audience, frequently interpreting . . . a theology or a tradition which [is not the reader's] own."

Stephens is competent in French, German, Swedish, Latin, and Greek.

*   *   *

STERLING, Dorothy   1913-

PERSONAL: Born November 23, 1913, in New York, N.Y.; daughter of Joseph (a lawyer) and Elsie (Darmstadter) Dannenberg; married Philip Sterling (a writer), May 14, 1937; children: Peter, Anne. *Education:* Attended Wellesley College; Barnard College, B.A., 1934. *Politics:* Independent.

ADDRESSES: Home and office—Box 755, South Wellfleet, Mass. 02667.

CAREER: Architectural Forum, New York City, secretary, 1936-41; *Life,* New York City, researcher, 1941-49; free-lance writer. Consulting editor, Firebird Books, Scholastic Book Services; editorial consultant on black history, Beacon Press.

MEMBER: Authors Guild, Authors League of America, National Association for the Advancement of Colored People.

AWARDS, HONORS: Nancy Bloch Award for children's book which best fosters intercultural understanding, 1958, for *Captain of the Planter: The Story of Robert Smalls,* and 1959, for *Mary Jane;* Carter G. Woodson Award, National Council for the Social Studies, 1977, for *The Trouble They Seen: Black People Tell the Story of Reconstruction.*

WRITINGS:

FICTION FOR CHILDREN

Sophie and Her Puppies (Junior Literary Guild selection), photographs by Myron Ehrenberg, Doubleday, 1951.
The Cub Scout Mystery, illustrated by Paul Galdone, Doubleday, 1952.
Billy Goes Exploring (Junior Literary Guild selection), photographs by Ehrenberg, Doubleday, 1953.
The Brownie Scout Mystery, illustrated by Reisie Lonette, Doubleday, 1955.
The Silver Spoon Mystery (Junior Literary Guild selection), illustrated by Grace Paull, Doubleday, 1958.
Secret of the Old Post-Box, illustrated by Paull, Doubleday, 1960.
Ellen's Blue Jays, illustrated by Winifred Lubell, Doubleday, 1961.

NONFICTION FOR CHILDREN

Trees and Their Story (Junior Literary Guild selection), photographs by Ehrenberg, Doubleday, 1953.
Insects and the Homes They Build, photographs by Ehrenberg, Doubleday, 1954.
(With husband, Philip Sterling) *Polio Pioneers: The Story of the Fight against Polio,* photographs by Ehrenberg, Doubleday, 1955.

The Story of Mosses, Ferns, and Mushrooms, photographs by Ehrenberg, Doubleday, 1955.
Wall Street: The Story of the Stock Exchange, photographs by Ehrenberg, Doubleday, 1955.
The Story of Caves (Junior Literary Guild selection), illustrated by Lubell, Doubleday, 1956.
Creatures of the Night, illustrated by Lubell, Doubleday, 1960.
Caterpillars, illustrated by Lubell, Doubleday, 1961.
Forever Free: The Story of the Emancipation Proclamation, illustrated by Ernest Crichlow, Doubleday, 1963.
Spring Is Here!, illustrated by Lubell, Doubleday, 1964.
Fall Is Here!, illustrated by Lubell, Natural History Press, 1966.
It Started in Montgomery: A Picture History of the Civil Rights Movement, Scholastic Book Services, 1972.

NONFICTION FOR YOUNG ADULTS

United Nations, N.Y., photographs by Ehrenberg, Doubleday, 1953, revised edition published as *United Nations,* 1961.
Freedom Train: The Story of Harriet Tubman, illustrated by Crichlow, Doubleday, 1954.
Captain of the Planter: The Story of Robert Smalls, illustrated by Crichlow, Doubleday, 1958.
Lucretia Mott: Gentle Warrior, Doubleday, 1964.
(With Benjamin Quarles) *Lift Every Voice: The Lives of Booker T. Washington, W. E. B. Du Bois, Mary Church Terrell, and James Weldon Johnson,* illustrated by Crichlow, Doubleday, 1965.
The Outer Lands: A Natural History Guide to Cape Cod, Martha's Vineyard, Nantucket, Block Island, and Long Island, illustrated by Lubell, Natural History Press, 1967, revised edition, Norton, 1978.
Tear down the Walls!: A History of the American Civil Rights Movement, Doubleday, 1968.
The Making of an Afro-American: Martin Robison Delany, 1812-1885, Doubleday, 1971.
Black Foremothers: Three Lives, illustrated by Judith Eloise Hooper, Feminist Press, 1979, 2nd edition, 1988.

EDITOR

I Have Seen War: Twenty-five Stories from World War II, Hill & Wang, 1960.
Speak out in Thunder Tones: Letters and Other Writings by Black Northerners, 1787-1865, Doubleday, 1973.
The Trouble They Seen: Black People Tell the Story of Reconstruction, Doubleday, 1976.
We Are Your Sisters: Black Women in the Nineteenth Century, Norton, 1984.
Turning the World Upside Down: Proceedings of the Anti-Slavery Convention of American Women Held in the City of New York, May 9-12, 1837, Feminist Press, 1987.

OTHER

(With Donald Gross) *Tender Warriors* (adult nonfiction), photographs by Ehrenberg, Hill & Wang, 1958.
Mary Jane (young adult novel), illustrated by Crichlow, Doubleday, 1959.
(Contributor) *Notable American Women,* Harvard University Press, 1980.
(Contributor) *Dictionary of American Negro Biography,* Norton, 1982.

Editorial consultant, Perspective Books's series of biographies of notable black men and women, Doubleday. Contributor of nature articles to *Book of Knowledge.*

WORK IN PROGRESS: Biography of abolitionist-feminist Abby Kelley (1811-1887), for Norton.

SIDELIGHTS: Dorothy Sterling's first published works consist of fiction and nonfiction stories for young readers. Her fiction stories are commonly mysteries, whereas nonfiction titles of the time reveal Sterling's interest in science and nature: *Trees and Their Story, Insects and the Homes They Build,* and *The Story of Caves.* Although she had written a handful of books in the early 1950s, it was not until the completion of her biography *Freedom Train: The Story of Harriet Tubman* that Sterling finally viewed herself as a writer. In *Something about the Author Autobiography Series,* Sterling remarks: "I decided to write a biography of a woman, a heroic figure who would say to girls, 'You are as strong and capable as boys'. . . . I went to the Schomburg Collection in New York, a major research center for black history, and for the first time learned about the crusade to end slavery and its black and white supporters. I was excited, but also bewildered and angry. Why had I never heard of Harriet Tubman or Sojourner Truth?" The author adds, "I had found a subject about which I cared deeply. At the age of forty, I had finally become a writer."

One of Sterling's most touching works about the black fight for equality in America is *Mary Jane,* a novel about a twelve-year-old girl who must face the ordeal of being among the first black children to integrate a large Southern junior high school in the 1950s. As Sterling recounts in her *Something about the Author* autobiographical entry, "ordinarily, I am a slow writer, completing a page or two a day, but I wrote *Mary Jane* at top speed, with my legs so tightly wrapped around my typewriter table that they ached at the end of the day. . . . [*Mary Jane*] was boycotted in the South and in some northern cities when it was first issued, but by the 1960s, after sit-ins and freedom rides had focused national attention on segregation, it became a best-seller and was reprinted in nine foreign countries." M. S. Libby of the *New York Herald Tribune Book Review* calls *Mary Jane* "a fine book" in which Sterling presents "many sides of a tangled unhappy situation . . . in a wise and fair-minded way." Zena Sutherland, writing in the *Bulletin of the Center for Children's Books,* notes that "the author has carefully avoided either an unrealistic complete capitulation on the part of [Mary Jane's] fellow citizens or a dramatic event that makes the girl a heroine." The result, says the critic, is a book in which "the people and events have a powerful emotional impact on the reader." A *Times Literary Supplement* critic, remarking that *Mary Jane*'s appeal goes beyond the twelve-year-olds for whom it was written, concludes that even though Sterling's moral is "too blatant to be concealed, . . . she has coated the pill so skillfully that it is sweet to the taste."

Reviewers have also had almost nothing but praise for Sterling's various nonfiction works on black America. Her biographies of Harriet Tubman, Robert Smalls, and Martin Robison Delany are noted not only for their careful documentation and sparing use of imagined dialogue, but for their drama and poignancy as well. Toni Morrison, for example, writes in the *New York Times Book Review* that Sterling's *The Making of an Afro-American: Martin Robison Delany* gives readers "a substantial portrait along with good narrative. . . . [His life is] expertly handled minus pathos or propaganda. Miss Sterling gives us what good biographies ought to give: an exhaustive, untampered with, skillful re-telling of a life of consequence." In a *Negro Digest* review of *Tear down the Walls!: A History of the American Civil Rights Movement,* Nikki Giovanni states that Sterling's presentation is "one of the more understanding

ones for youngsters. . . . She tells our story with such compassion and understanding that it is difficult to believe she is non-Black."

With the appearance of *Black Foremothers: Three Lives* and *We Are Your Sisters: Black Women in the Nineteenth Century,* Sterling has shifted her focus to the black female plight in America. In terms of Sterling's role as editor of *We Are Your Sisters,* Sam Cornish explains in the *Christian Science Monitor* that "by juxtaposing letters, notes, and childhood memories of slaves and free women, this comprehensive anthology goes a long way toward telling the story of the black woman in the 19th century. The images are poignant: milk placed in a wooden bowl on the floor; children eating from oyster shells; . . . the awful consequences when a hungry slave would be caught stealing a sugar cube." The critic concludes by observing: "Wrought with an honesty that transcends mere trendiness, Sterling's book somehow becomes more than the sum of the documents, by both known and anonymous women, from which it draws." *Philadelphia Inquirer* reviewer Houston A. Baker, Jr., likewise praises Sterling's text for providing "the everyday lives of black women in captivating outline. . . . The collection is methodically edited, adept in its presentation of central figures, scholarly in its apparatus, and wonderfully helpful in its detailed bibliography and index."

BIOGRAPHICAL/CRITICAL SOURCES:

BOOKS

Arbuthnot, May Hill and Zena Sutherland, *Children and Books,* 4th edition, Scott, Foresman, 1972.
Children's Literature Review, Volume 1, Gale, 1976.
Something about the Author Autobiography Series, Volume 2, Gale, 1986.

PERIODICALS

Best Sellers, March 15, 1963, October 1, 1968, June 15, 1971.
Bulletin of the Center for Children's Books, May, 1959.
Chicago Sunday Tribune, April 13, 1958.
Christian Science Monitor, May 14, 1959, June 26, 1984.
Nation, February 13, 1954.
Negro Digest, January, 1969.
New York Herald Tribune Book Review, February 21, 1954, May 11, 1958, May 10, 1959.
New York Times, January 24, 1954.
New York Times Book Review, May 19, 1963, January 31, 1965, May 5, 1968, May 2, 1971, April 29, 1984.
Philadelphia Inquirer, September 9, 1984.
Saturday Review, April 17, 1954, January 19, 1963.
Times Literary Supplement, May 29, 1959.

*   *   *

STERLING, Robert R. 1931-

PERSONAL: Born May 16, 1931, in Bugtussle, Okla.; son of Riley Paul (a farmer) and Lillian (Newman) Sterling; married Margery Stoskopf, May 2, 1954; children: Robert, Kimberly. *Education:* University of Denver, B.S., 1956, M.B.A., 1958; University of Florida, Ph.D., 1964. *Religion:* Quaker.

ADDRESSES: Office—Department of Business/Accounting, University of Utah, Salt Lake City, Utah, 84117.

CAREER: Harpur College (now State University of New York at Binghamton), assistant professor of social science, 1963-66; Yale University, New Haven, Conn., science faculty fellow, 1966-67; University of Kansas, Lawrence, began as associate professor, became professor of business administration, 1967-70, Arthur Young Distinguished Professor, 1970-74; director of research, American Accounting Association, 1972-74; Rice University, Houston, Tex., Jesse Jones Distinguished Professor, 1974-80, dean of Graduate School of Administration, 1976-80; University of Alberta, Edmonton, Winspear Distinguished Professor, 1980-81; senior fellow, Financial Accounting Standards Board, 1981-83; University of Utah, Salt Lake City, Garff Distinguished Professor of Business, 1983—. Bicentennial Distinguished International Lecturer in Europe, 1976; Hoover Distinguished International Lecturer in Australia, 1979. Publisher and editor, Scholars Book Co. Member of board of directors, National Bureau of Economic Research, United Way, and Trust Corp. International.

MEMBER: International Association for Research on Income and Wealth, Accounting Researchers International Association (fellow; president, 1974-80), American Accounting Association (vice-president, 1975-76), Accountants for Public Interest (director), National Association of Accountants (director), American Association of University Professors, Southwest Accounting Association (president), Houston Philosophical Society (director).

AWARDS, HONORS: Gold Medal for best research published in English, American Institute of Certified Public Accountants, 1968, 1974; National Science Foundation faculty fellow.

WRITINGS:

Theory of the Measurement of Enterprise Income, University Press of Kansas, 1969.
(Editor with William F. Bentz) *Accounting in Perspective: Contributions to Accounting Thought by Other Disciplines,* South-Western, 1971.
(Editor) *Asset Valuation and Income Determination: A Consideration of the Alternatives,* Scholars Book Co., 1971.
(Editor) *Research Methodology in Accounting,* Scholars Book Co., 1972.
(Editor) *Institutional Issues in Public Accounting,* Scholars Book Co., 1974.
(With A. L. Thomas) *Accounting for a Simplified Firm Owning Depreciable Assets: Seventeen Essays and a Synthesis Based on a Common Case,* Scholars Book Co., 1979.
Toward a Science of Accounting, Scholars Book Co., 1979.
(Editor with Kenneth W. Lemke) *Maintenance of Capital: Financial vs. Physical,* Scholars Book Co., 1982.

Also author of *An Essay on Recognition,* 1985. Author of papers on accounting and research methodology. Editor, "Accounting Classics Series"; member of editorial board, *Abacus;* member of editorial board and book review editor, *Accounting Review.**

*   *   *

STERN, Gerald   1925-

PERSONAL: Born February 22, 1925, in Pittsburgh, Pa.; son of Harry and Ida (Barach) Stern; married Patricia Miller, September 12, 1952 (divorced); children: Rachael, David. *Education:* University of Pittsburgh, B.A., 1947; Columbia University, M.A., 1949, post-graduate study, 1950-52; post-graduate study at University of Paris, 1949-50.

ADDRESSES: Home—650 South Governor, Iowa City, Iowa 52240. *Office*—Creative Writing Program, Department of English, University of Iowa, Iowa City, Iowa 52242.

CAREER: Lake Grove School, Lake Grove, N.Y., English teacher and principal, 1951-53; Victoria Drive Secondary School, Glasgow, Scotland, English teacher, 1953-54; Temple University, Philadelphia, Pa., instructor in English, 1956-63; Indiana University of Pennsylvania, Indiana, Pa., associate professor of English, 1963-67; Somerset County College, Somerville, N.J., professor of English, 1968-82; University of Iowa, Iowa City, professor of English, 1982—. Lecturer, Douglas College, spring, 1968; visiting poet, Sarah Lawrence College, spring, 1978, University of Pittsburgh, fall, 1978. Visiting professor, Columbia University, 1980, Bucknell University, spring, 1988; Fanny Hurst professorship, Washington University, 1985. Chairman of creative writing, University of Alabama, Tuscaloosa, 1984. Stern conducts poetry workshops and gives readings at colleges, universities, theaters, and art centers. Consultant in literature to Pennsylvania Council on the Arts. *Military service:* U.S. Army Air Corps, 1946-47.

MEMBER: Modern Language Association, PEN, Poetry Society of America, National Council of Teachers of English, Associated Writing Programs (Norfolk, Va.; member of board of directors), New Jersey Arts Council, New Jersey Poets & Writers.

AWARDS, HONORS: National Endowment for the Arts grant to be a master poet for Pennsylvania, 1973-75, creative writing grants, 1976, 1981, and 1987; Lamont Poetry Selection, 1977, and nomination for National Book Critics Circle Award, 1978, both for *Lucky Life;* creative writing grant, State of Pennsylvania, 1979; Guggenheim fellowship, 1980; Governor's Award for Excellence in the Arts, State of Pennsylvania, 1980; Bess Hokin Award, *Poetry,* 1980; Bernard F. Connor's Award, *Paris Review,* 1981; *American Poetry Review* award, 1982; Melville Caine Award, Poetry Society of America, 1982, for *The Red Coal;* Jerome J. Shestack Poetry Prize, *American Poetry Review,* 1984.

WRITINGS:

POEMS

Pineys, Rutgers University Press, 1971.
The Naming of Beasts, Cummington Press, 1972.
Rejoicings: Selected Poems 1966-72, Fiddlehead Poetry Books, 1973.
Lucky Life, Houghton, 1977.
The Red Coal, Houghton, 1981.
Paradise Poems, Random House, 1984.
Lovesick, Harper, 1987.
Selected Essays, Harper, 1988.
New and Selected Poems, Harper, 1989.

OTHER

Author of "Father Guzman," a long poem published in *Paris Review,* spring, 1982. Contributor to anthologies; contributor to poetry journals and popular magazines, including *New Yorker, Nation, Paris Review, Poetry Now, American Poetry Review,* and *Poetry.*

SIDELIGHTS: Gerald Stern writes: "If I had to explain my art I would talk about it in terms of staking out a place that no one else wanted, because it was not noticed, because it was abandoned or overlooked. I am talking about something of immense importance—and not just to me—but most others would not see it that way; they would see something else. On a most literal level, I am talking about weeds, and waste places and lovely pockets, and in my poems I mean it on a literal as well as on a psychological and symbolic level. That is, I am writing about actual places and ascribing value to them; but of course, I am thinking also of what those places stand for, and might stand for, in the reader's or listener's mind if I awakened his lost places. In one sense there is a battle—or at least a dialogue—going on between light and dark, present and past, city and country, civilization and savagery, power and lack of it, and I would seem to favor the latter. But I don't write from a philosophical point of view; and furthermore I am seized by the contradictions, and I have irony; but most of all I have affection for both sides, if I may call them sides, and I move towards reconciliation and forgiveness. I am moved a lot by Jewish mysticism and Chasidism and by the historic idea of the Jew—from a poetic and mythic point of view. A lot of my poems have as a setting nature, or the garden, but I am in no sense of the word a nature poet; I am equally at home in the city and the country and go where my spirit takes me, whether it be upper Broadway or the Delaware River.''

New York Times Book Review critic Vernon Shetley writes that ''Stern's poems lay bare his emotions while revealing almost nothing about their origins.'' They achieve their effects, the reviewer continues, ''through accumulations of rhetorical weight or sudden flashes of disjunctive memory.'' His poems, too, reveal ''his refusal to look beyond the self,'' says Shetley. It is a preoccupation which has caused some critics such as *Chicago Tribune Book World* critic L. M. Rosenberg to compare his tone to Walt Whitman's, though Stern's reference to the self is of a personal nature, and not the universal self of Whitman's work. There is also a strong interest in Stern for the process of memory. ''For Gerald Stern,'' notes David Wojahn in *Poetry East,* ''nothing possesses us as wholly as the past.'' This is the general theme of his poetry collections, *The Red Coal* and *Paradise Poems,* which also focus on ''the purpose of the poet, suffering, death, redemption, and the definition of paradise,'' according to *Literary Review* contributor Jane Sommerville. In addition to these books, the poet's earlier collections, such as *Lucky Life* and *Rejoicings: Selected Poems 1966-72,* are all written with Stern's characteristically ''exuberant style,'' as Sommerville calls it. His book *Lovesick,* however, also seems ''to express a stronger note of finality, than those in earlier collections,'' remarks a *Publishers Weekly* reviewer.

Leonard Michaels, in a *New York Times Book Review* article, finds Stern's poetry to be ''very subtle at times and often marvelous,'' and further contends that he is ''a very brilliant moving poet.'' *Harper's* critic Hayden Carruth is also appreciative of Stern's work. He writes: ''It is extremely difficult to bring off the kind of poem Stern writes, doomsday among the tricycles and kittens. Most poets who try end up with trite magazine verse, predictabilities of faded irony. But Stern succeeds. His low-voiced, prosy syntax gives us direct statements, simple and true, moving almost monotonously toward the hysterical outbreak of silence, the twisted smile. But he draws back; he doesn't push to that catastrophe—not quite. Instead he resumes, again and again, poem after poem. . . .''

BIOGRAPHICAL/CRITICAL SOURCES:

BOOKS

Contemporary Literary Criticism, Volume 40, Gale, 1986.
Somerville, Jane, *Gerald Stern: The Speaker as Meaning,* Wayne State University Press, 1988.

PERIODICALS

Chicago Tribune Book World, September 13, 1981.

Dallas Times Herald Books, July 29, 1984.
Georgia Review, spring, 1978, winter, 1981.
Harper's, June, 1978.
Literary Review, fall, 1984.
New York Times, October 9, 1977.
New York Times Book Review, May 10, 1981.
Poetry, August, 1982.
Poetry East, fall, 1981, fall, 1988.
Publishers Weekly, June 6, 1987.

*   *   *

STERN, Nancy (B.) 1944-

PERSONAL: Born July 15, 1944, in New York, N.Y.; daughter of Murray and Selma (Karp) Fortgang; married Robert A. Stern; children: Lori, Melanie. *Education:* Barnard College, A.B., 1965; New York University, M.S., 1968; State University of New York at Stony Brook, Ph.D., 1977.

ADDRESSES: Office—Department of Business Computer Information Systems, Hofstra University, 1000 Fulton Ave., Hempstead, N.Y. 11550.

CAREER: Hofstra University, Hempstead, N.Y., assistant professor, 1977-78, associate professor, 1978-83, professor of business computer information systems, 1983—. Advisory editor for John Wiley & Sons.

MEMBER: Association for Computing Machinery, History of Science Society, Society for the History of Technology.

WRITINGS:

Flowcharting: A Tool for Understanding Computer Logic, Wiley, 1975.
(With husband, Robert A. Stern) *Structured COBOL Programming,* Wiley, 1980, 5th edition, 1988.
From ENIAC to UNIVAC: An Appraisal of the Eckert-Mauchy Computers, Digital Press, 1981.
(With R. A. Stern) *An Introduction to Computers and Information Processing,* Wiley, 1982, 2nd edition, 1985.
(With R. A. Stern) *Computers in Society,* Prentice-Hall, 1983.
(With others) *RPG II and RPG III Programming,* Wiley, 1984.
(With others) *Assembler Language Programming for IBM and IBM Compatible Computers,* Wiley, 1986.
(With R. A. Stern) *A Users Guide to Microcomputers,* Wiley, 1986.
(With R. A. Stern) *Structured COBOL by Design,* Wiley, 1988.
Turbo Basic Programming, Wiley, 1989.
Quick BASIC Programming, Wiley, 1989.

Also author of articles on the history of computing. Assistant editor in chief, *Annals of the History of Computing.*

WORK IN PROGRESS: A history of computing.

*   *   *

STEVENSON, David 1942-

PERSONAL: Born April 30, 1942, in Largs, Ayrshire, Scotland; son of Alan Carruth and Sheila (Steven) Stevenson; married Wendy B. McLeod; children: Ian McLeod, Neil Alan. *Education:* Trinity College, Dublin, B.A., 1966; University of Glasgow, Ph.D., 1970.

ADDRESSES: Office—Department of History, University of Aberdeen, Aberdeen AB9 2UB, Scotland.

CAREER: University of Aberdeen, Aberdeen, Scotland, lecturer, 1970-78, senior lecturer in history, 1978-84, reader in

Scottish history and director of the Centre for Scottish Studies, 1984—.

MEMBER: Royal Historical Society (fellow), Scottish History Society (honorary secretary, 1976-84).

AWARDS, HONORS: Hume Brown Senior Prize, 1974, for *The Scottish Revolution, 1637-1644: The Triumph of the Covenanters.*

WRITINGS:

The Scottish Revolution, 1637-1644: The Triumph of the Covenanters, David & Charles, 1973.
Revolution and Counter-Revolution in Scotland: 1644-1651, Royal Historical Society, 1977.
Alasdair MacColla and the Highland Problem in the Seventeenth Century, John Donald, 1980.
Scottish Covenanters and Irish Confederates, Ulster Historical Foundation, 1981.
The Government of Scotland under the Covenanters, Scottish Historical Society, 1982.
(Editor) *From Lairds to Louns: Country and Burgh Life in Aberdeen, 1600-1800,* Aberdeen University Press, 1986.
(With wife, Wendy B. Stevenson) *Scottish Texts and Calendars: An Analytical Guide to Serial Publications,* Longwood, 1987.
The Origins of Freemasonry: Scotland's Century, 1590-1710, Cambridge University Press, 1988.
The First Freemasons: Scotland's Early Lodges and Their Members, Pergamon, 1988.
The First World War and International Politics, Oxford University Press, 1989.

SIDELIGHTS: David Stevenson's first book, *The Scottish Revolution, 1637-1644: The Triumph of the Covenanters,* covers the political history of Scotland in the years immediately before the Scottish Covenant became involved in the English civil war. It ends with the Scottish troops marching across the English border to aid Parliament in opposition to King Charles I of England. Where *The Scottish Revolution* ends, its sequel, *Revolution and Counter-Revolution in Scotland,* begins. In the second book, the historian records the low points in Scottish and English history and the defeats and failures that led to the eventual conquest of Scotland by Cromwell in the second half of the English civil war.

In Edward Playfair's review of *The Scottish Revolution* and *Revolution and Counter-Revolution in Scotland* for the *Times Literary Supplement,* he lauds Stevenson's attempt to write "pure political history, with only so much of personalities, battles and religion as is needed to make the events clear." An earlier *Times Literary Supplement* article calls *The Scottish Revolution* "an absorbing and excellent book" and a "very full account of the rise of the Covenanters." Concerning *Revolution and Counter-Revolution* Playfair concludes, "this is a remarkably interesting, well-analysed and well-written history."

BIOGRAPHICAL/CRITICAL SOURCES:

PERIODICALS

Times (London), July 6, 1980.
Times Educational Supplement, December 4, 1981.
Times Literary Supplement, March 8, 1974, September 8, 1978.

STOETZER, O(tto) Carlos (Enrique) 1921-

PERSONAL: Born June 28, 1921, in Buenos Aires, Argentina; came to United States in 1950; son of Carlos G. (a banker) and Francisca (Hoech) Stoetzer; married Rona Geib, October 29, 1955; children: Anthony, Erik. *Education:* University of Perugia, certificate, 1942; University of Debreczen, certificate, 1943; University of Freiburg, Dr.jur., 1945; attended Academy of International Law, 1947; Georgetown University, Ph.D., 1961. *Politics:* Independent. *Religion:* Roman Catholic.

ADDRESSES: Home—1 Rocky Brook Rd., Wilton, Conn. 06897. *Office*—Department of History, Fordham University, Bronx, N.Y. 10458.

CAREER: Worked for the French and British military governments and Allied Military Headquarters in Germany after World War II, as a correspondent in Argentina, and as an interpreter. Pan American Union, Organization of American States (OAS), Washington, D.C., assistant in cultural department, 1950-51, assistant in philatelic division, 1951-53, assistant in travel division, 1953-56, secretary in the Office of the General Assembly, Meeting of Consultation and Permanent Council of the OAS, 1955-61, acting secretary of the Inter-American Institute of Agricultural Sciences, 1958-61; Manhattanville College, Purchase, N.Y., associate professor, 1961-63; Institute for Latin American Studies, Hamburg, Germany, chief of history and law division, 1963-64; Manhattanville College, Purchase, associate professor of political science, 1964-66; Fordham University, Bronx, N.Y., associate professor, 1966-79, professor of history, 1980—. Honorary professor at Universidad del Salvador, Buenos Aires, 1982. Alliance Francaise du Comte de Fairfield, vice-president, 1970-71, president, 1971-72; honorary vice-president of Argentine graduate scholarship committee, University of Bridgeport, 1972-77.

MEMBER: Society for Iberian and Latin American Thought (vice-president, 1976-77; president, 1977-79), Latin American Studies Association, Argentine Association of American Studies, Conference on Latin American History.

AWARDS, HONORS: Knight Commander of Order of Isabella the Catholic, Spanish government, 1959.

WRITINGS:

Panamerika: Idee und Wirklichkeit—Die Organisation der Amerikanischen Staaten (title means "Pan America: Theory and Reality—The Organization of American States"), Uebersee Verlag, 1964, revised edition published as *The Organization of American States: An Introduction,* Praeger, 1965.
(Contributor) Friedrich Wehner, editor, *Ibero-Amerika: Ein Handbuch,* Uebersee Verlag, 5th edition, 1964.
El pensamiento politico en la America espanola durante el periodo de la emancipacion, 1789-1825: Las bases hispanicas y las corrientes europeas (main title means "Political Thought in Spanish America During the Period of Emancipation, 1789-1825"), two volumes, Instituto de Estudios Politicos (Madrid), 1966.
(Author of preface) Martin J. Bane, *The Popes and Western Africa: An Outline to Mission History, 1460s-1960s,* Alba House, 1968.
(Contributor) Friedrich Wehner, editor, *Idee und Wirklichkeit in Iberoamerika: Beitraege zur Politik und Geistesgeschichte* (title means "Theory and Reality in Latin America: Studies in the Field of Politics and Intellectual History"), Hoffman & Campe (Hamburg), 1969.

Grundlagen des Spanischamerikanischen Verfassungsdenkens
   (title means "Foundation of Spanish American Consti-
   tutional Thought"), Verfassung & Recht, 1969.
*Benjamin Constant and the Doctrinaire Liberal Influence in
   Latin America*, Verfassung & Recht, 1978.
The Scholastic Roots of the Spanish-American Revolution,
   Fordham University Press, 1979.
(Contributor) Warren F. Kuehl, editor, *Biographical Dictio-
   nary of Internationalists*, Greenwood Press, 1983.

Contributor of articles to *International Philosophical Quarterly* and *Inter-American Review of Bibliography/Revista In-
teramericana de Bibliografia*, and to Latin American studies
journals in the United States and abroad.

*WORK IN PROGRESS: The Krausean Impact in the Hispanic
World*, for Fordham University Press.

SIDELIGHTS: O. Carlos Stoetzer once told *CA:* "Having been
tossed around in my life from one end of the Atlantic to another (Southern Cone, Europe, United States), I developed an
early interest in the interaction of the different Western cultures and civilizations, especially that of the Hispanic peoples.
This also led to a fairly long association with the Organization
of American States and made me aware of the significance of
inter-American relations. Over the past three decades I have
become increasingly interested in the flow of ideas from the
Old World to Latin America and have worked since the 1950s
on my main subject: the complex picture of political thought
and ideology during the period of independence of Latin
America. I am especially interested in the controversial concept of whether the Spanish-American Revolution was an echo
of the American and French Revolutions and thus linked to
the foreign impact of the Enlightenment, or whether, as I have
tried to show, it was a purely Spanish family affair and thus
intimately connected with Scholastic philosophy, especially
the Late Scholastic version of Spain's Golden Century.

"Finally, in my writings I try to awaken an interest in the
Hispanic world and especially a deeper understanding of its
culture, thought, and history, so that both North Americans
and non-Hispanic Europeans realize that the Hispanic world
is a full member of the Western world and wishes to be treated
as such."

Stoetzer speaks and reads German, Spanish, English, French,
and Italian, and reads Portuguese and Dutch.

*   *   *

STRAUB, Peter (Francis)   1943-

PERSONAL: Born March 2, 1943, in Milwaukee, Wis.; son
of Gordon Anthony and Elvena (Nilsestuen) Straub; married
Susan Bitker (a counselor), August 22, 1966; children: Benjamin Bitker, Emma Sydney Valli. *Education:* University of
Wisconsin—Madison, B.A., 1965; Columbia University, M.A.,
1966; attended University College, Dublin, 1969-72. *Politics:*
"Mainstream undecided."

ADDRESSES: Home—P.O. Box 395, Greens Farms, Conn.
06436. *Office*—53 West 85th St., New York, N.Y. 10024.

CAREER: University School, Milwaukee, Wis., English teacher,
1966-69; writer, 1969—.

MEMBER: International PEN, Authors Guild, Authors League
of America, Writers Action Group.

AWARDS, HONORS: "Best Novel" nomination, World Fantasy Awards, 1981, for *Shadowland;* British Fantasy Award
and August Derleth Award, both 1983, for *Floating Dragon*.

WRITINGS:

Ishmael (poetry), Turret Books, 1972, Underwood/Miller, 1973.
Open Air (poetry), Irish University Press, 1972.
Marriages (novel), Coward, 1973.
Julia (also see below; novel), Coward, 1975, reprinted in En-
   gland as *Full Circle*, Corgi, 1977.
If You Could See Me Now (also see below; novel), Coward,
   1977.
Ghost Story (novel), Coward, 1979.
Shadowland (novel), Coward, 1980.
The General's Wife (story), D. M. Grant, 1982.
Floating Dragon (novel), Putnam, 1983.
Leeson Park and Belsize Square: Poems 1970-1975, Under-
   wood/Miller, 1983.
(With Stephen King) *The Talisman* (novel), Viking, 1984.
Wild Animals: Three Novels (contains *Julia, If You Could See
   Me Now*, and *Under Venus;* also see below), Putnam,
   1984.
Blue Rose (novella), Underwood/Miller, 1985.
Under Venus, Berkley, 1985.
Koko (novel), Dutton, 1988.
Mystery (novel), Dutton, 1989.

Straub's novels appear in a number of foreign languages.

SIDELIGHTS: One of the most popular practitioners of horror
and suspense fiction—more than ten million copies of his novels have been sold—American writer Peter Straub is the author
of such well-known titles as *Ghost Story, Shadowland, Floating Dragon, The Talisman* (with Stephen King), and *Koko*.
Straub employs an array of ghastly elements—hauntings,
vengeful agents of murder, gruesome deaths, fantastical happenings—and is especially good at, as *Maclean's* Barbara
Matthews notes, "stark cold horror—the kind worshippers of
the genre love to spirit away and read quickly, inhaling fright
and holding it in their lungs until it becomes brittle enough to
shatter if so much as a telephone rings." More than spine-
tingling thrillers, however, Straub's novels are also imaginative explorations into the realistic, often personal, roots of the
unreal. Patricia L. Skarda writes in *Dictionary of Literary Biography Yearbook* that Straub's "best work . . . focuses on
private experiences on the margin where nature and superna-
ture meet, where reality converges with dream, where writing
leaves off and the imagination takes over." Straub commented
to Joseph Barbato in *Publishers Weekly* on the effects he wishes
to elicit: "I want readers to feel as if they've left the real
world behind just a little bit, but are still buoyed up and con-
fident, as if dreaming. I want them left standing in midair with
a lot of peculiar visions in their heads."

Straub decided to become a novelist—though not a horror novelist—in the early 1970s, after abandoning an academic career
in English. A former high school teacher who left the United
States for Dublin's University College, Straub was at work on
a doctorate when he became disenchanted. "The plan was to
get a Ph.D. and come back to get a better job," he told Joseph
McLellan in the *Washington Post*. "Then, in Ireland, I suddenly realized what the trouble really was: I had always thought
of myself as a novelist although I had not written a novel. I
could feel fiction growing inside me, characters and situations
forming themselves in my mind as I walked down the street."
Already a published poet, Straub began work in 1972 on his
first novel, *Marriages*, about the extramarital affair of an

American businessman in Europe. Published a year later, *Marriages* received favorable reviews. Ronald Bryden in the *Listener* called it "the other side of the Jamesian tradition: an American chronicle of the quest for European richness, complexity and depth," while a *Times Literary Supplement* critic characterized Straub as a "poetic novelist," adding, "it may be this skill which enables him to place so securely the sense of gesture, and the texture of atmosphere, which characterizes *Marriages*."

Straub was at work on a second novel, *Under Venus,* when financial reasons prompted a change to his writing efforts. "'Marriages' had not done very well," he told Barbato, ". . . just about the time that publishers were beginning to cut back on midlist—and bottom-list—authors. And I was one of those guys coming along with more of the same. It unnerved me. I knew I could never hold a real job—that I'd be an impossible employee anywhere. I had to save my life by writing a book that could get published." Furthermore, despite numerous revisions, *Under Venus* failed to attract a publisher (later it appeared in the three-novel collection *Wild Animals*). Straub's agent stepped in and suggested he try writing a Gothic. "I found that I had a natural bent toward this kind of thing," he told Barbato. "Later, I had to deal with that, because I had never seen myself as that type of writer. I dealt with it by trying to see just how much I could do with that peculiar stock of imagery and leaden conventions that you're given as a horror novelist."

Straub's horror debut occurred in 1975 with *Julia,* the harrowing tale of an American woman in England haunted by the torturous ghost of a murdered child—and the emerging knowledge of responsibility in the death of her own daughter (the victim of an emergency tracheotomy). While some reviewers noted inconsistent plotting and characterization, many acknowledged Straub's flair for the gothic. "In the last resort, *Julia* . . . succeeds in the brutal business of delivering supernatural thrills," wrote Michael Mason in the *Times Literary Supplement;* Straub "has thought of a nasty kind of haunting, and he presses it upon the reader to a satisfying point of discomfort." Valentine Cunningham in *New Statesman* called the book "an extraordinarily gripping and tantalising read. . . . Every dubious solution and ambivalent pattern is possible, for almost anything becomes believable under the novelist's stunningly gothic manipulations."

After *Julia,* Straub wrote *If You Could See Me Now,* a tale set in the midwestern United States about the vengeful spirit of a murdered girl who returns to inflict horrors upon the community where she died. Critics particularly praised the novel's narrative timing, structure, and the authenticity of local settings. "Straub is good at slick manipulation of pace," wrote Jonathan Keates in *New Statesman,* "punctuating the story with chunks of police statement . . . , and he has an equally nifty way with rustic grotesques." Keates called the book "crisp, classy buggaboo . . . full of neatly managed understatements and chillingly calculated surprises." Peter Ackroyd in *Spectator* singled out the book's "filmic" qualities: "*If You Could See Me Now* makes great play, for example, with contrasts of speech and silence, of crowd scenes and empty landscapes, and of the ways in which a written 'close-up' can be employed to suggest deep 'emotion.' Some of the book's scenes, in fact, can only be understood in visual terms."

Following these ventures, Straub embarked upon the novel that would become his breakthrough, the 1979 bestselling *Ghost Story*. Drawing upon various horror story motifs and conventions, *Ghost Story* is the tale of a rural New England community terrorized when a young woman, killed years earlier, returns to exact retribution from four elderly townsmen (The Chowder Society) responsible for her death. The Chowder Society's members, who regularly meet to exchange ghost stories, become involved in a frantic race to save themselves and the town from the gruesome revenge of the "shapeshifter" Eva Galli. "What's interesting about 'Ghost Story' is that Mr. Straub . . . seems to have decided to write a summarizing American tale of the supernatural, and to throw into it every scrap of horror-cliche and campfire trash that he can muster," commented Christopher Lehmann-Haupt in the *New York Times*. "Still, because Mr. Straub is so good at writing eerie set-pieces and because the very complexity of his story keeps it baffling to the end, I look back on the time spent reading 'Ghost Story' as on an interval distorted by fever."

Straub's aim in *Ghost Story,* as Jennifer Dunning quotes the author in the *New York Times,* was to "take the genre and pull it upstairs a little bit. . . . Not exactly transcend the genre, but make a little more of the material than has been made of it in the recent past." *Ghost Story* draws from early masters in the field, including Nathaniel Hawthorne, Henry James, Edgar Allen Poe, and Sheridan Le Fanu. Some reviewers objected to the novel's overt deference to these influences. "Although Straub's 'affection' for the proven devices of his betters is estimable, many of these allusions seem rather pedantic and pointless," wrote Jack Sullivan in the *Washington Post Book World*. Douglas Hill commented in *Maclean's* that "at times the book stumbles over its structure: all the epigraphs and cute chapter titles are merely pretentious." "There was a certain amount of audacity in the overt references to the great writers," Straub admitted to Thomas Lask in the *New York Times,* "but today the form is debased, and it is a messianic thing to me to elevate it and make it honorable." A number of reviewers were, however, impressed with Straub's creation. Gene Lyons in the *New York Times Book Review* called *Ghost Story* "a quite sophisticated literary entertainment," while Valerie Lloyd remarked in *Newsweek* that "with considerable technical skill, Peter Straub has constructed an extravagant entertainment which, though flawed, achieves in its second half some awesome effects." She concluded: "It is, I think, the best thing of its kind since Shirley Jackson's 'The Haunting of Hill House.'"

Straub moved back to the United States after the success of *Ghost Story* and embarked upon a period which produced some of his best known and bestselling titles. His next novel *Shadowland,* however, received mixed reviews and, according to Skarda, "confused an audience expecting ghoulish ghosts." The story of two boys who become involved in a world of magic where anything happens, *Shadowland*'s "prophecy and telepathy, use and misuse of sleights of hand and mind convert a strange Arizona prep school and a Vermont home into a platonic inversion where every shadow seems substance." Lehmann-Haupt noted that in *Shadowland* Straub "appears to be taking the classic elements of the Grimms' fairy tale as far as they can go." Some critics remarked that the fantastical events in the novel appeared too much at random, thereby diminishing the suspense. "*Shadowland* ultimately has neither the gnomic simplicity of the fairy-tale nor the eery sense of a grossly interrupted reality, which [Straub] caught more successfully in *Ghost Story*," commented Thomas Sutcliffe in the *Times Literary Supplement*.

Straub's 1983 bestselling novel, *Floating Dragon,* seemed to meet the expectations generated by *Ghost Story*. In a sweeping story of a malevolent spirit which periodically visits an affluent Connecticut suburb with death and destruction, Straub creates "a compendium of horrors designed to punish the shallow housewives, adulterers, corporate tycoons, and even the children in a commuter community," notes Skarda. "*Floating Dragon,* beneath its remarkable repertoire of horrific details, is a simple moral tale of the confrontation between good and evil," wrote Alan Bold in the *Times Literary Supplement.* "Nevertheless, it represents a new level of sophistication in the Gothic novel. Straub plays games with the structure, rapidly switching from third-person to first-person narrative, and teases the reader with biblical symbols and red herrings. The novel is sustained with great skill as the battle between good and evil is impressively, if agonizingly, stretched over the disturbingly supernatural plot." Alan Ryan commented in the *Washington Post Book World:* "If *Floating Dragon* is sometimes baffling, flawed in some structural elements, and perhaps a little too long for its own good, it is at the same time both ruthlessly contemporary and steeped in tradition, gruesomely chilling, and told with a narrative strength and a lively colloquial style that readers should welcome."

In his next novel, Straub teamed up with friend and fellow horror writer Stephen King—via word processors connected by telephone—to produce the 1984-85 blockbuster *The Talisman.* Drawing upon both writers' immense popularity, the book was an instant bestseller; critics, however, felt that it was a bit overstocked with mad capers and special effects. The fantasy/adventure story of a boy who goes in search of a magic object to cure his dying mother, *The Talisman* outlines a power struggle between good and evil in a strange world. "There's a dizzying amount of flipping in this book," noted Peter Gorner in the *Chicago Tribune,* "and often the point is elusive." Lehmann-Haupt wrote that *The Talisman* "suffers from a surfeit of monstrosity. It takes forever to develop its smallest plot complications. It telegraphs its clues with the subtlety of falling telephone poles. It stoops to outrageous sentimentality over its boy hero. . . . It repeats and repeats unto silliness." These elements, however, are also part of the book's appeal, according to Frank Herbert in the *Washington Post Book World:* "*The Talisman* is exactly what it sets out to be—a fine variation on suspense and horror filled with many surprises, a ground King and Straub have plowed before with great success, together and individually. Together, they demonstrate once more that they are the Minnesota Fats of the novel-into-film. When they say six ball in the side pocket, that's where the six ball goes."

Straub's 1988 bestseller, *Koko,* is a notable departure from his past supernatural novels. A psychological suspense thriller, *Koko* is the story of four Vietnam War veterans who travel to the Far East to track down a former platoon member they believe has become a deranged killer. Straub remarked to *Bestsellers 89* on his change of direction: "By the time I began *Koko,* I had pretty much done everything I could think to do with supernatural fiction. . . . Whether I knew it or not, I was saying goodbye to imagery and situations involving hallucination versus reality with which I had been involved for years. . . . What I wanted to do next was to work with the set of feelings that lay behind horror—to move in closer to the world, to work more strictly within the realistic tradition." Straub's venture has been well-received. A reviewer for *Publishers Weekly* called *Koko* "a dizzying spin through those eerie psychic badlands where nightmare and insanity seem to fuse with reality." Emily Tennyson added in the *Detroit Free Press:* "Like the war that Straub seeks to analyze and explain,

'Koko' wrenches the spirits of those who took part and were taken apart by Vietnam. Much more than a tale of escape and murder, 'Koko' is an examination of fear in the human soul." While *Koko* affirms Straub's ability to create terror, it is also a positive sign of a new scope to his fiction. Lucius Shepard remarks in the *Washington Post Book World:* "Judged as a thriller, *Koko* deserves to be compared with the best of the genre, to novels such as *Gorky Park* and *The Honorable Schoolboy.* . . . *Koko* is vastly entertaining, often brilliantly written, full of finely realized moments and miniatures of characterization. . . . What all this most hearteningly signals is that Peter Straub is aspiring toward a writerly range which may cause his future novels to face more discriminating judgments yet."

MEDIA ADAPTATIONS: Julia was adapted for the 1981 Peter Fetterman film, "The Haunting of Julia" (entitled "Full Circle" in England); *Ghost Story* was adapted for the 1981 Universal Pictures film of the same title. *Floating Dragon* was adapted for cassette by Listen for Pleasure Cassettes in 1987; *Koko* was adapted for cassette by Simon & Schuster Audioworks in 1989.

AVOCATIONAL INTERESTS: Jazz, opera.

BIOGRAPHICAL/CRITICAL SOURCES:

BOOKS

Bestsellers 89, Issue 1, Gale, 1989.
Contemporary Literary Criticism, Volume 28, Gale, 1984.
Dictionary of Literary Biography Yearbook: 1984, Gale, 1985.

PERIODICALS

Chicago Tribune, May 16, 1979, December 16, 1981, November 8, 1984.
Detroit Free Press, November 13, 1988.
Listener, March 15, 1973.
Maclean's, May 21, 1979, January 12, 1981, March 14, 1983.
New Statesman, February 27, 1976, June 24, 1977.
Newsweek, March 26, 1979, December 24, 1984.
New York Times, April 3, 1979, April 27, 1979, May 20, 1979, October 24, 1980, December 16, 1981, January 26, 1983, November 8, 1984.
New York Times Book Review, April 8, 1979, March 6, 1983.
People, January 28, 1985.
Publishers Weekly, January 28, 1983, May 11, 1984, August 12, 1988.
Spectator, July 9, 1977.
Times Literary Supplement, March 23, 1973, February 27, 1976, April 17, 1981, March 11, 1983.
Washington Post, October 31, 1980, February 6, 1981, February 16, 1981, November 27, 1984.
Washington Post Book World, April 8, 1979, October 14, 1984, August 21, 1988.

—*Sketch by Michael E. Mueller*

*   *   *

STRAUSS, Walter L(eopold)   1922-1988

PERSONAL: Born April 23, 1922, in Nuremberg, Germany (now West Germany); came to the United States in 1936, naturalized in 1943; died January 14, 1988, of a heart attack, in Manhattan, New York; son of Justin (a toy manufacturer and mathematician) and Adolfine (Lowenthal) Strauss; married Lore Seidenberger (a modern dancer), June 25, 1950; children: Claudia Dardig, Thomas, Michael, Daniel. *Educa-*

tion: Pratt Institute of Technology (now Pratt Institute), degree in chemical engineering, 1942; attended University of Minnesota, 1943, and University of Wyoming, 1944; New School for Social Research, M.A., 1972.

ADDRESSES: Home—P.O. Box 325, Marlborough Rd., Scarborough, N.Y. 10510. *Office*—42 Memorial Plaza, Pleasantville, N.Y. 10570.

CAREER: Publisher, editor, author. Unichem Industries, New York City, president, 1953-70; Topspot Corporation, New York City, president, 1970-73; Abaris Books, Inc., New York City, founder, president, and general editor, beginning 1973. Visiting professor at State University of New York at Binghamton, 1979-80, and Cooper Union for the Advancement of Science and Art, beginning 1981. Member of Briarcliff Manor government committee, 1975-78. *Wartime service:* U.S. Army, Office of Strategic Services, 1943-45; became second lieutenant; received Silver Star.

MEMBER: College Art Association of America, Verein fuer Kunstwissenschaft.

WRITINGS:

The Human Figure: Albrecht Duerer's Dresden Sketchbook, Dover, 1972.
Albrecht Duerer's Complete Engravings, Woodcuts, and Dry-Points, Dover, 1972.
The Chiaroscuro Woodcuts of the German and Netherlandish Masters of the Sixteenth Century, New York Graphic Society, 1973 (published in England as *Chiaroscuro: The Clair-Obscur Woodcuts by the German and Netherlandish Masters of the Sixteenth and Seventeenth Centuries,* Thames & Hudson, 1973).
The German Single-Leaf Woodcut, 1500-1550, four volumes, Hacker, 1974.
(Editor and author of commentary) *The Book of Hours of the Emperor Maximilian I,* Abaris, 1974.
The Complete Drawings of Albrecht Duerer, six volumes, Abaris, 1975.
The German Single-Leaf Woodcut, 1550-1600—A Pictorial Catalogue, three volumes, Abaris, 1975.
(Editor) *Tribute to Wolfgang Stechow,* Pratt Graphics Center, 1976.
Hendrick Goltzius: Master Engraver, two volumes, Abaris, 1977.
The Intaglio Prints of Albrecht Duerer and Their Preparatory Drawings, Kennedy Galleries, 1977.
The Iconography of Astrology, Dover, 1977.
(With Dorothy Alexander) *The German Single-Leaf Woodcut: 1600-1700—A Pictorial Catalogue,* two volumes, Abaris, 1977.
(Translator and author of commentary) Albrecht Duerer, *The Painter's Manual: A Manual of Measurement of Lines, Areas, and Solids by Means of Compass and Ruler,* Abaris, 1978.
(Compiler with Marjon van der Meulen) *The Rembrandt Documents,* Abaris, 1979.
(Translator and editor) Werner Sumowski, *Drawings of the Rembrandt School,* Abaris, 1979.
(Editor) *Albrecht Duerer: Woodcuts and Woodblocks,* Abaris, 1979.
(With Carol Bronze) *The Japanese Woodcut Illustrations,* Abaris, 1979.
(Translator with Nancy M. Gordon) *Albrecht Duerer: Drawings, Prints, Paintings,* Abaris, 1982.

(Contributor) *Essays in Northern European Art Presented to Egbert Haverkamp-Begemann,* Doornspijk, 1983.

Also contributor to *Thayer's Life of Beethoven,* edited by Elliot Forbes, Princeton University Press. General editor of the "Illustrated Bartsch" book series, Abaris, 1977-88. Contributor of articles and reviews to art journals, including *Master Drawings, Art Bulletin, Print Review, Art Journal,* and *Gazette des Beaux-Arts.* Past editor of *Print Review.*

SIDELIGHTS: Walter L. Strauss wrote to *CA:* "My main interest is in the history of art and in its philosophical foundation."

Strauss was fluent in German, French, Russian, Spanish, and Japanese.

AVOCATIONAL INTERESTS: Travel (Central Europe, Japan, the Persian Gulf).

OBITUARIES:

PERIODICALS

New York Times, January 19, 1988.

[Sketch reviewed by son Daniel Strauss]

*   *   *

STREETEN, Paul Patrick   1917-

PERSONAL: Born July 18, 1917, in Vienna, Austria; married Ann Higgins, June 9, 1951; children: Patricia Doria, Judith Andrea; stepchildren: Jay D. Palmer. *Education:* University of Aberdeen, M.A., 1940; Balliol College, Oxford, B.A. (with first class honors), 1947, M.A., 1952; attended Nuffield College, Oxford, 1947-48.

ADDRESSES: Home—2000 Commonwealth Ave., Apt. 1104, Boston, Mass. 02135. *Office*—World Development Institute, Boston University, 264 Bay State Rd., Boston, Mass. 02215.

CAREER: Oxford University, Oxford, England, fellow of Balliol College, 1948-66 and 1968-78, university lecturer and associate of Institute of Economics and Statistics, 1960-64, director of Institute of Commonwealth Studies and warden of Queen Elizabeth House, 1968-78; Ministry of Overseas Development, London, England, deputy director-general of economic planning staff, 1964-66; University of Sussex, Institute of Development Studies, Stanmer, Brighton, England, professor of economics, acting director, and fellow, 1966-68, member and vice-chairman of governing body; currently director, World Development Institute, Boston University, Boston, Mass. Visiting professor, Stanford University, 1956; visiting professor, University of Buenos Aires, 1963; visiting lecturer, Economic Development Institute of the World Bank. Research fellow, Johns Hopkins University, 1955-56; fellow, Center for Advanced Studies, Wesleyan University, 1962. Member of council, Walloon Institute of Economic Development; member of provisional council, University of Mauritius, 1965; UNESCO, member of United Kingdom National Commission, 1966, and vice-chairman of Advisory Committee on Social Sciences; member of the board, Commonwealth Development Corp., 1967-72; member of council, Dominion Students Trust, London; member of Africa Publications Trust. Member of Royal Commission of Environmental Pollution, 1974-76. Special advisor to the World Bank, 1976-80. Member of the board of trustees, Foundation for International Studies, University of Malta; member of advisory committee, Arab Planning Institute, Kuwait. *Military service:* British Army and Royal Marine

Commandos, Hampshire Regiment, 1941-43; became sergeant; wounded in Sicily.

MEMBER: Society for International Development (president of United Kingdom chapter), Royal Economic Society, American Economic Association, United Oxford and Cambridge Club.

AWARDS, HONORS: Rockefeller fellow in United States, 1950-51; LL.D., University of Aberdeen, 1980; honorary fellow, Institute of Development Studies, University of Sussex; honorary fellow, Balliol College, Oxford.

WRITINGS:

Economic Integration: Aspects and Problems, Sijthoff, 1961, 2nd edition, 1963.

EDITOR

(And translator) Gunnar Myrdal, *The Political Element in the Development of Economic Theory,* Routledge & Kegan Paul, 1953.
(And reviser and contributor) *The Great Economists,* Eyre & Spottiswoode, 1955.
(And author of foreword) Myrdal, *Value in Social Theory,* Routledge & Kegan Paul, 1958.
(With M. Lipton) *The Crisis of Indian Planning,* Oxford University Press, 1968.
Unfashionable Economics: Essays in Honor of Lord Balogh, Weidenfeld & Nicolson, 1970.
(With Hugh Corbet) *Commonwealth Policy in a Global Context,* Cass, 1971.
(With Diane Elson) *Diversification and Development: The Case of Coffee,* Praeger, 1971.
Aid to Africa, Praeger, 1972.
The Frontiers of Development Studies, Macmillan, 1972.
Trade Strategies for Development, Macmillan, 1973.
The Limits of Development Research, Pergamon, 1974.
Foreign Investment, Transnationals and the Developing Countries, Macmillan, 1977.
Development Perspectives, Macmillan, 1981.
First Things First, Oxford University Press, 1981.
(With Richard Jolly) *Recent Issues in World Development,* Pergamon, 1982.
What Price Food? Agricultural Policies in Developing Countries, Macmillan, 1987.
Beyond Adjustment: The Asian Experience, International Monetary Fund, 1988.

CONTRIBUTOR

Vollbeschaeftigung, Bund Verlag (Cologne), 1950.
K. Kurihara, editor, *Post-Keynesian Economics,* Allen & Unwin, 1954.
Studi in memoria di Benevenuto Griziotti, Editore A. Guiffre, 1959.
Theorie et politique de l'expansion regionale, Librairie Encyclopedique (Brussels), 1961.
G. D. N. Worswick and P. H. Ady, editors, *The British Economy in the Nineteen-Fifties,* Clarendon Press, 1962.
von Beckerath and Giersch, editors, *Probleme der normativen Oekonomik und der wirtschaftspolitischen Beratung,* [Berlin], 1963.
Bergedorfer Protokolle: Economic Aid—A Way to Growth or Decline?, Decker Verlag, 1964.
P. D. Henderson, editor, *Economic Growth in Great Britain,* Weidenfeld & Nicolson, 1966.

Kurt Martin and John Knapp, editors, *The Teaching of Development Economics,* Cass, 1967.
Hans K. Schneider, editor, *Grundsatzprobleme wirtschaftspolitischer Beratung,* Duncker & Humblot (Berlin), 1968.
(Member of international team of six assistants) Myrdal, *Asian Drama: An Inquiry into the Poverty of Nations,* three volumes, Twentieth Century Fund, 1968.
Klaus Hufner and Jens Naumann, editors, *Economics of Education in Transition,* Ernst Klett Verlag (Stuttgart), 1969.
SEANZA Lectures, Central Bank of Ceylon, 1969.
A. N. Agarwala and S. P. Singh, editors, *Accelerating Investment in Developing Countries,* Oxford University Press, 1969.
John Harry Dunning, editor, *The Multinational Enterprise,* Praeger, 1972.
Dunning, editor, *Economic Analysis and the Multinational Enterprise,* Allen & Unwin, 1974.
Gerald M. Meier and Dudley Seers, editors, *Pioneers in Development,* Oxford University Press, 1985.

OTHER

Also mission leader for *Basic Needs in Danger,* 1983. Editor of *World Development* and Oxford University Institute of Economics and Statistics *Bulletin,* 1961-64. Contributor to *UNESCO Dictionary of Political and Social Terms* and *Collier's Encyclopedia;* contributor of about 100 articles to journals in England, Germany, France, Belgium, Italy, Canada, and India. Former secretary and member of editorial board, "Oxford Economic Papers."

WORK IN PROGRESS: Research on global issues and on private overseas investment, aid, basic needs, and food pricing policies.

BIOGRAPHICAL/CRITICAL SOURCES:

BOOKS

Lall, Sanjaya and Frances Stewart, *Theory and Reality in Development: Essays in Honour of Paul Streeten,* Macmillan, 1986.

*   *   *

STROTHER, Elsie (Frances Warmoth Weitzel) 1912-

PERSONAL: Born June 15, 1912, in New York, N.Y.; daughter of Frank S. (a sugar planter) and Phyllis S. (Aitken) Warmoth; married first husband George J. Weitzel, March 22, 1935 (died, 1959); married second husband Dean C. Strother (a general in the U.S. Air Force), December 29, 1964; children: (first marriage) Carroll (Mrs. G. L. B. Rivers), Sallie (Mrs. Jamie Gough). *Education:* Attended New York School of Design, Grand Central Fine Arts School, and St. James Ecole in Paris, France.

ADDRESSES: Home—8 Polo Dr., Colorado Springs, Colo. 80906.

CAREER: Art teacher in private schools in Aiken, S.C., 1950-59, and in Charleston, S.C., 1959-62. Painter, especially of animals.

MEMBER: National League of American Pen Women (vice-president of local branch).

WRITINGS:

FOR YOUNG ADULTS

The Royal Cheetah and the Untouchables, Westminster, 1974.

Rendezvous at Live Oaks, Avalon, 1975.
Island of Terror, Avalon, 1976.
Follow through to Love, Avalon, 1977.
A Kiss to Remember, Avalon, 1980.
Safari into Danger, Elgen, 1981.
A Time for Deceit, Avalon, 1981.
That Special Kiss, Avalon, 1982.
Love's Sweet Treasure, Avalon, 1983.
Counterfeit Kisses, Avalon, 1984.
Flash Flood, Perfection Forum 6, 1984.
A Glowing Treasure, Avalon, 1985.
Cries in the Night, Avalon, 1985.
A Fearful Heart, Avalon, 1987.

OTHER

Author of column "The Children's Nook," in *Aiken Standard and Review*, beginning 1951. Contributor of stories and articles to children's magazines.

WORK IN PROGRESS: Murder in Primary Colors, an adult novel; a historical novel set in Haiti in 1800.

SIDELIGHTS: Elsie Strother told *CA* that she was "brought up in the West Indies with education acquired through governesses, tutors, and voluminous reading. I have traveled and lived all over the world and have painted and written about most of it."

AVOCATIONAL INTERESTS: Golf, music.

*   *   *

STRYK, Lucien   1924-

PERSONAL: Born April 7, 1924; married; children: two. *Education:* Indiana University, B.A., 1948; Sorbonne, University of Paris, M.F.S., 1950; University of Maryland, M.F.S., 1950; graduate study at University of London, 1950-51; University of Iowa, M.F.A., 1956.

ADDRESSES: Home—342 Delcy Dr., DeKalb, Ill. 60115. *Office*—Department of English, Northern Illinois University, DeKalb, Ill. 60115.

CAREER: Free-lance writer in England, 1952-54; Northern Illinois University, DeKalb, 1958—, began as assistant professor, currently professor of English. Has given readings of his poetry on radio and at more than 350 colleges and universities throughout the United States and Great Britain. Visiting lecturer in Japan at Niigata University, 1956-58, and Yamaguchi University, 1962-63. *Military service:* U.S. Army, 1943-45.

MEMBER: Asia Society, Modern Language Association.

AWARDS, HONORS: Grove Press fellowship, 1960; Asia Society grant, Yale University, 1961; Fulbright grant for travel to Iran, 1961-62; Ford Foundation fellowship, University of Chicago, 1963; first prize (shared with John Berryman and Hayden Carruth) in *Chicago Daily News* New "Chicago" Poem Competition, 1963; Swallow Press new poetry series award, 1965; Excellence in Teaching Award, Northern Illinois University, 1967; Isaac Rosenbaum Poetry Award, 1968; National Translation Center grant, 1969; Society of Midland Authors Poetry Award, 1973 and 1978; Robert F. Fergusson Memorial Award, Friends of Literature, 1974; winner, All Nations Poetry Contest, 1974; National Endowment for the Arts poetry fellowship, 1975-76; Islands and Continents Translation Award, 1978; Illinois Arts Council Poetry on the Buses Contest, 1978;

Illinois Arts Council Literary Award, 1979, 1983, artist's grant, 1983; Governor's Award for the Arts (Illinois), 1980; Rockefeller Foundation fellowship, 1983; Illinois Poet Laureate Award, 1987.

WRITINGS:

Taproot (poetry), Fantasy Press (Oxford, England), 1953.
The Trespasser (poetry), Fantasy Press, 1956.
Notes for a Guidebook (poetry), Swallow Press, 1965.
The Pit and Other Poems, Swallow Press, 1969.
Awakening (poetry), Swallow Press, 1973.
Selected Poems, Swallow Press, 1976.
The Duckpond (poetry), Omphalos Press (London), 1978.
Zen Poems, Embers Handpress (Cambridge, England), 1980.
Encounter with Zen: Writings on Poetry and Zen, Swallow Press, 1981, published as *Encounter with Zen: Writing on Poetry and Zen*, Ohio University Press, 1982.
Cherries, Ampersand Press (Bristol, R.I.), 1983.
Bird of Time: Haiku of Basho, Flatlands Press, 1983.
Willows (poems), Embers Handpress, 1983.
Collected Poems, 1953-1983, Swallow Press, 1984.
Traveler, My Name: Haiku of Basho, Embers Handpress, 1984.
Bells of Lombardy, Northern Illinois University Press, 1986.

EDITOR

(And translator with Takashi Ikemoto) *Zen: Poems, Prayers, Sermons, Anecdotes, Interviews*, Doubleday-Anchor, 1965, reprinted with a new introduction, Swallow Press, 1981.
Heartland: Poets of the Midwest, Northern Illinois University Press, Volume 1, 1967, Volume 2, 1975.
(And author of introduction and commentary) *World of the Buddha: A Reader*, Doubleday, 1968, published as *World of the Buddha: An Introduction to Buddhist Literature*, Grove, 1982.
(And translator with Ikemoto) *Afterimages: Zen Poems of Shinkichi Takahashi*, Swallow Press, 1970.
(And translator with Ikemoto, and author of introduction) *The Penguin Book of Zen Poetry*, Penguin, 1977.
Prairie Voices: A Collection of Illinois Poets, Spoon River Poetry Press, 1980.

CONTRIBUTOR

Japanese Image, Orient-West, 1965.
David Ray, editor, *From the Hungarian Revolution*, Cornell University Press, 1966.
W. W. West, editor, *On Writing, by Writers*, Ginn, 1966.
Developing Writing Skills, Prentice-Hall, 1966.
Stained the Water Clear, Reed College, 1967.
E. Earle Stibitz, editor, *Illinois Poets: A Selection*, Southern Illinois University Press, 1968.
A Book of Sonnets, Twayne, 1969.
Southern Poetry Review Anthology, North Carolina University Press, 1969.
Thomas Lask, editor, *New York Times Book of Verse*, Macmillan, 1970.
A. Poulin, Jr., editor, *Contemporary American Poetry*, 4th edition, Houghton, 1985.
Stephen Berg, editor, *Singular Voices*, Avon, 1985.

TRANSLATOR

(With Ikemoto) *Twelve Death Poems of the Chinese Zen Masters*, Hellcoal Press, 1973.
(With Ikemoto and Taigan Takayama) *Zen Poems of China and Japan: The Crane's Bill*, Doubleday-Anchor, 1973.

Three Zen Poems, after Shinkichi Takahashi, Sceptre Press, 1976.
Haiku of the Japanese Masters, Rook Press, 1977.
The Duckweed Way: Haiku of Issa, Rook Press, 1977.
On Love and Barley: Haiku of Basho, Penguin, 1985.
Triumph of the Sparrow: Zen Poems of Shinkichi Takahashi, University of Illinois Press, 1986.

OTHER

Zen Poems (sound recording), Folkways Records, 1980.
Selected Poems (sound recording), Folkways Records, 1983.

Contributor to periodicals, including *Georgia Review, American Poetry Review, Encounter, Nation, Poetry, Saturday Review, Listener, London Magazine, New Statesman*, and *Twentieth Century*.

A collection of Stryk's manuscripts is housed in Mugar Memorial Library, Boston University, Boston, Massachusetts.

WORK IN PROGRESS: A volume of poetry.

SIDELIGHTS: Lucien Stryk told *CA:* "I have become strongly interested and rather actively involved in public poetry readings, feel that they are rarely done well, and hope that with training it may be possible to make an art of poetry reading. As an exponent of Zen Buddhism, I am of course interested in reaching as many as possible so as to make them aware of its liberating possibilities. Travel has been enormously important to my life, and I hope that it will continue to be—especially in the Far East."

Although he acknowledges the effect of Zen on his poetry, Stryk says in *Modern Poetry Studies* that the label "Zen poet" "tends to define me too closely. I've never called myself a Zen poet and I certainly don't think of myself as being a Zen poet, and when I've had occasion I've made disclaimers concerning that. I think of myself as a Midwestern American poet who has, of course, been very deeply affected by Zen; so much of my life has been devoted to the study of Zen and its literature that . . . my writing is unquestionably affected by it. But I have by and large let others make their own judgments about that."

According to Dennis Lynch and Gay Davidson in the same journal, Stryk's work "shows the truth of the Japanese Proverb, 'The more Zen poetry has, the better poetry is.'" Joseph Parisi writes of Stryk's *Awakening in Poetry:* "Everywhere the benevolent influence of [Stryk's] Zen masters touches the clean, spare lines shaped with the elegance of an Oriental scroll painting . . . . The very compression and understatement of Styk's style serves to heighten experience: we ache for these people. A more flamboyant technique could easily turn these situations into melodrama; . . . [instead], method and material join in a sympathy as authentic as it is rare."

Stryk's poetry has been translated into Japanese, Chinese, French, Spanish, Swedish, and Italian.

BIOGRAPHICAL/CRITICAL SOURCES:

BOOKS

Heyen, William, editor, *American Poets in 1976*, Bobbs-Merrill, 1976.
West, W. W., editor, *On Writing, by Writers*, Ginn, 1966.

PERIODICALS

American Poetry Review, Volume 6, number 4, 1977.
Chicago Review, June, 1967, number 88, 1973.

Loblolly, number 2, 1985.
Modern Poetry Studies, Volume 10, number 1, 1980.
Poetry, October, 1970, September, 1971.

*   *   *

STUART, Ian
See MacLEAN, Alistair (Stuart)

*   *   *

SULEIMAN, Susan Rubin

PERSONAL: Born in Budapest, Hungary; came to the United States in 1950, naturalized in 1956; daughter of Michael N. (a rabbi) and Lillian (Stern) Rubin; married Ezra N. Suleiman (a professor of politics), February 27, 1966 (divorced); children: Michael, Daniel. *Education:* Barnard College, B.A. (magna cum laude), 1960; University of Paris, Certificat de l'Institut Phonetique, 1961; Harvard University, M.A., 1964, Ph.D., 1969.

ADDRESSES: Home—70 Horace Rd., Belmont, Mass., 02178. *Office*—Department of Romance Languages and Literatures, Harvard University, Cambridge, Mass. 02138.

CAREER: Columbia University, New York, N.Y., instructor, 1966-68, assistant professor of French, 1969-76, director of study program at Reid Hall, Paris, France, 1973; Occidental College, Los Angeles, Calif., assistant professor, 1976-81, associate professor of French, 1981, director of study in France, 1978-79, 1981, coordinator of Interdisciplinary Colloquium on Women and Society, 1979-80; Harvard University, Cambridge, Mass., associate professor of Romance languages and literatures, 1981-83, John L. Loeb Associate Professor of Humanities, 1983-84, professor of Romance languages and comparative literatures, 1984—.

MEMBER: Modern Language Association of America, American Comparative Literature Association (member of advisory board), American Association of Teachers of French, Phi Beta Kappa.

AWARDS, HONORS: Woodrow Wilson fellow, 1961-62; traveling fellow of Harvard University, 1965-66; National Endowment for the Humanities grant, 1977, fellowship, 1980; American Council of Learned Societies grant, 1977-78; Guggenheim fellowships, 1983-84 (declined), 1987-88; Rockefeller Foundation humanities fellowship, 1984.

WRITINGS:

(Editor and author of preface) Paul Nizan, *Pour une nouvelle culture* (title means "Toward a New Culture"), Grasset, 1971.
(Translator) Guillaume Apollinaire, *Apollinaire on Art: Essays and Reviews, 1902-1918*, edited by Leroy C. Breunig, Viking, 1972, reprinted, Da Capo, 1988.
(Translator) Saul Friedlander, *History and Psychoanalysis*, Holmes & Meier, 1978.
(Editor with Inge Crosman, and contributor) *The Reader in the Text: Essays on Audience and Interpretation*, Princeton University Press, 1980.
Authoritarian Fictions: The Ideological Novel as a Literary Genre, Columbia University Press, 1983.
(Contributor) Brian Thompson and Carl Viggiani, editors, *Witnessing Andre Malraux: Visions and Revisions*, Wesleyan University Press, 1983.

(Contributor) Shirley Garner, Claire Kahane, and Madelon Sprengnether, editors, *The (M)Other Tongue: Essays in Feminist Psychoanalytic Interpretation,* Cornell University Press, 1985.

(Editor and contributor) *The Female Body in Western Culture: Contemporary Perspectives,* Harvard University Press, 1986.

(Contributor) Douwe Fokkema and Hans Bertens, editors, *Approaching Postmodernism,* John Benjamins, 1986.

(Contributor) Nancy K. Miller, editor, *The Poetics of Gender,* Columbia University Press, 1986.

(Contributor) Norman L. Kleeblatt, editor, *The Dreyfus Affair: Art, Truth, and Justice,* University of California Press, 1987.

(Contributor) Shlomith Rimmon-Kenan, editor, *Discourse in Psychoanalysis and Literature,* Methuen, 1987.

(Contributor) Clayton Koelb and Susan Noakes, editors, *The Comparative Perspective on Literature: Approaches to Theory and Practice,* Cornell University Press, 1988.

Also author of *Women and the Avant-Garde: From Surrealism to Postmodernism,* 1989. Contributor of more than thirty articles, translations, and reviews to language and literature journals. Member of editorial boards of *French Review* and *Style;* member of advisory board of *Camera Obscura: A Journal of Feminism and Film Theory.*

WORK IN PROGRESS: Research on problems of avant-garde writing, women's writing, fiction and ideology.

SIDELIGHTS: Susan Rubin Suleiman told *CA:* "The role of the translator in the contemporary literary world is very important, although too rarely recognized. Without competent and dedicated translators there would be no wide-scale cross-cultural communication. Imagine having to learn Russian to read Dostoevsky, Japanese to read Mishima, Spanish to read Borges, Fuentes, Garcia Marquez. All of this is obvious—yet it is a universal fact that translators are (save for a few notable exceptions) underpaid and unappreciated. Reviewers of a book rarely mention the translator, and publishers rarely put the translator's name on the cover. This may explain why there are so few full-time literary translators. I myself, like some of my colleagues, translate only occasionally, either because I'm interested in a specific book or because people I can't refuse ask me to do a translation for them. As an occasional occupation, I find translation a highly pleasurable activity: it offers plenty of challenges, but it's still so much easier than writing your own book.

"My own interest in women's writing and feminist theory has evolved gradually over the past ten years. When I first started publishing I was chiefly influenced by the French structuralists, and what most interested me was: *how* do literary works produce certain effects, including the effect of meaning? Today, I am interested not only in that question (I have no intention of renouncing my former allegiances), but also in broader questions relating to the cultural and ideological implications of literary works. Concurrently, I have become more and more involved, both personally and professionally, in questions relating to women.

"I see this kind of evolution among many of my women friends and colleagues. For women of my generation, who went to college in the late 1950s and early 1960s, feminism was not a 'given' from the start: it was something that one *came to,* sooner or later. There were no women's studies programs, no female professors, and above all, there was no body of feminist criticism when I went to graduate school. Today, it is no exaggeration to say that some of the most exciting, most vibrantly new work in literary studies is the work of feminist critics. One does not have to write exclusively about women in order to do feminist criticism. What matters are the questions one asks, not the particular writers or works one is dealing with. And the exciting thing is that many of the questions that seem most interesting today could not even have been formulated, much less explored, twenty years ago.''

BIOGRAPHICAL/CRITICAL SOURCES:

PERIODICALS

Times Literary Supplement, January 20, 1984.

*   *   *

SUTPHEN, Dick
   See SUTPHEN, Richard Charles

*   *   *

SUTPHEN, Richard Charles   1937-
   (Dick Sutphen; Todd Richards, a pseudonym)

PERSONAL: Surname pronounced Sut-fen; born April 3, 1937, in Omaha, Neb.; son of Earle Charles (a salesman) and Jennie E. (a secretary; maiden name, Roberts) Sutphen; married second wife, Judith Ann, July 5, 1969 (divorced); married Trenna Laraine (divorced); married Nancy Tara, March 2, 1984; children: (from first three marriages) Scott, Todd, Steven, Jessi, Travis; (from fourth marriage) Hunter, Cheyenne. *Education:* Attended Art Center School, Los Angeles, Calif., 1956-57. *Politics:* Democrat. *Religion:* "Metaphysics."

ADDRESSES: P.O. Box 38, Malibu, Calif. 90265.

CAREER: Art director for advertising firms in Omaha, Neb., 1955, 1958-59; *Better Homes and Gardens,* Des Moines, Iowa, designer, 1959-60; Knox Reeves Advertising, Minneapolis, Minn., art director, 1964-65; Dick Sutphen Studio, Inc., Minneapolis, and Scottsdale, Ariz., operator of advertising design and illustration services and publisher of books for the advertising market, 1965-76; Sutphen Corp./Valley of the Sun Publishing, Malibu, Calif., owner, 1976—. Conductor of Sutphen Seminars, 1976—. Designer of contemporary (studio) cards for Hallmark, and creator of a line of Arizona-oriented studio cards and framed prints; producer of more than 300 hypnosis and self-help cassette tape programs and a line of 28 video cassettes. Publisher of *Master of Life* (a "New Age" quarterly periodical/catalogue).

WRITINGS:

(Under pseudonym Todd Richards) *Your Voice Makes My Knees Tickle!* (verse), Valley of the Sun, 1972.

UNDER NAME DICK SUTPHEN

(Editor) *Old Engravings and Illustrations,* two volumes, Dick Sutphen Studios, 1965.

(Editor) *Uncensored Situations,* Dick Sutphen Studios, 1966.

(Editor) *The Wildest Old Engravings and Illustrations,* Dick Sutphen Studios, 1966.

(Editor) *Designy Devices,* Dick Sutphen Studios, 1967.

Antiques, Filigree and Rococo, Dick Sutphen Studios, 1967.

The Mad Old Ads, McGraw, 1967.

Studio Cards, Famous American Studios, 1968.

The Encyclopedia of Small Spot Engravings, Valley of the Sun, 1969.

Sometimes the Words of Love Have No Words, Valley of the Sun, 1969.

A Deep Breath of Yesterday, Valley of the Sun, 1970.

I Love to Have You Touch Me, Valley of the Sun, 1971.

Sex, Liquor, Tobacco, and Candy Are Bad for You, Valley of the Sun, 1972.

Know Thy Higher Self, Valley of the Sun, 1972.

Burying Pompeii, Valley of the Sun, 1973.

Open Hand Love (poems), Valley of the Sun, 1975.

You Were Born to Be Together, Simon & Schuster, 1976.

The Pen and Ink and Cross Hatch Styles of the Early Illustrators, Art Direction Book, 1976.

Attention-Getting Old Engravings, Art Direction Book, 1976.

Past Life Hypnotic Regression Course, Valley of the Sun, 1977.

The Dick Sutphen Assertiveness Training Course, Valley of the Sun, 1978.

Past Lives, Future Loves, Simon & Schuster, 1978.

Unseen Influences, Simon & Schuster, 1980.

(With Trenna Sutphen) *The Master of Life Manual,* Valley of the Sun, 1980.

(With T. Sutphen) *Bushido SST Graduate Manual,* Valley of the Sun, 1981.

(With Lauren Leigh Taylor) *Past-Life Therapy in Action,* Valley of the Sun, 1983.

Rattlesnake Karma, Valley of the Sun, 1984.

Poet: 1970-1985, Valley of the Sun, 1985.

Enlightenment Transcripts, Valley of the Sun, 1986.

Sedona: Psychic Energy Vortexes, Valley of the Sun, 1986.

Lighting the Light Within, Valley of the Sun, 1987.

Predestined Love, Simon & Schuster, 1988.

WORK IN PROGRESS: Finding Your Answers Within for Simon & Schuster.

AVOCATIONAL INTERESTS: Zen, Eastern philosophy, martial arts, running, tennis.

BIOGRAPHICAL/CRITICAL SOURCES:

BOOKS

Weisman, Alan, *We, Immortals,* Pocket Books, 1979.

PERIODICALS

American Artist, June, 1967.

*   *   *

SWEENEY, Karen O'Connor
    See O'CONNOR, Karen

*   *   *

SWIGART, Rob   1941-

PERSONAL: Surname is pronounced with a long "i"; born January 7, 1941, in Chicago, Ill; son of Eugene (a businessman) and Ruth (an actress and theatrical producer; maiden name, Robison) Swigart; married Jane Bugas (a writer), March 26, 1969; children: Saramanda Nell, Tess Miranda. *Education:* Princeton University, B.A., 1962; State University of New York at Buffalo, Ph.D., 1972. *Politics:* "Buddhist." *Religion:* Zen.

ADDRESSES: Home—255 Cerrito Ave., Redwood City, Calif. 94061. *Office*—Department of English, San Jose State University, San Jose, Calif. 95114. *Agent*—Ellen Levine Literary Agency, Inc., 432 Park Ave. S., Suite 1205, New York, N.Y. 10016.

CAREER: Cincinnati Enquirer, Cincinnati, Ohio, reporter, 1963; Harper & Row Publishers, Inc., New York, N.Y., salesman, 1965-69; San Jose State University, San Jose, Calif., assistant professor of English, 1972—. Owner, producer, cameraman, editor, and sound recordist for Marley & Swigart Films, 1973—. *Military service:* U.S. Army, 1964-65. U.S. Army Reserve, 1965-70.

MEMBER: Authors Guild, Authors League of America, American Association for the Advancement of Science, Science Fiction Writers of America, Mystery Writers of America, Planetary Society, California Academy of Sciences.

WRITINGS:

Still Lives (poems), No Dead Lines, 1976.

Little America (also see below; novel), Houghton, 1977.

A.K.A.: A Cosmic Fable (novel), Houghton, 1978.

The Time Trip (novel), Houghton, 1979.

The Book of Revelations (novel), Dutton, 1981.

(Contributor and translator) *Women Poets of the World,* Macmillan, 1983.

Vector, Bluejay/St. Martin's, 1986.

Portal (novel), Activision, 1986.

Toxin, St. Martin's, 1989.

Author of documentary filmscripts "Inishmaan: Beyond the Pale," "Firstborn," and "Little America" (based on his novel of the same title), and documentary videotape "The Clean-Room Environment"; also author of technical articles on computers and other topics for Apple Computer, Inc., and other firms. Contributor of articles and poems to periodicals, including *Poetry, Atlantic Monthly, New York Quarterly, Choice, Poetry Northwest,* and *Antaeus.*

WORK IN PROGRESS: Three books, *The White Pig, Down Time* (short stories), and *Lovelocks.*

SIDELIGHTS: To read the novels of Rob Swigart is to enter the realm of the fantastic, faddish, and mythological. Steven Kosek, writing in the *Chicago Tribune Book World,* remarks that Swigart's novels "are best described as weird word-cartoons in the style of Kurt Vonnegut and Tom Robbins. They fall into that small genre, a cosmic fable." Dealing with such subjects as time travel and reincarnation, Swigart's works have explored both man's technological future and his ancient past. Describing his approach to fiction, Swigart told *CA:* "I am . . . concerned with the ethics of science and the nature of vision and how it can be created or recreated."

In reviews of Swigart's work, critics have commented on both his concern with themes of time, technology, and the cosmos, and on his style. Discussing *The Book of Revelations* in the *Los Angeles Times,* Robert Gish calls Swigart's use of current, popular issues and ideas "more than just allusive, trendy talk by another post-contemporary author. . . . Swigart's novel pays plenty of attention to the futuristic 'fads' of our moment—concerns incipient in the 1980s as good bets to change from science fiction to science" in the future. These elements include UFOs, aphrodisiacs, computers, and communication with animals. Offering a somewhat different assessment of Swigart's use of "futuristic fads," Kosek refers to the same novel as "an anachronistic cartoon whose subject is terribly out of fashion."

A similar divergence of opinion exists concerning Swigart's style, with mixed reviews regarding the influence of Kurt Vonnegut on Swigart's prose. Kosek feels that *The Book of Revelations* "lacks some important quality of narration. . . . Swigart has managed to mimic the bits and pieces of Vonnegut and Robbins, but has altogether missed the spirit of their novels." Conversely, Jerome Klinkowitz states in a *Chicago Tribune Book World* review that "Rob Swigart cut his teeth on Kurt Vonnegut, and the lessons of *Slaughter House Five* have been well learned in [*The Time Trip*]. . . . It presents a nice smooth narrative line with no real complications." And Gish, who labels Swigart a "worker in the vineyards of Vonnegut," declares that "for fanciful description and believable make-believe, Swigart's *Book* proves there's still hope . . . for . . . the resurrection of the novel as a literary form."

AVOCATIONAL INTERESTS: Aikido (black belt, 1982), cello, flying (pilot).

BIOGRAPHICAL/CRITICAL SOURCES:

PERIODICALS

Chicago Tribune Book World, April 22, 1979, November 1, 1981.
Los Angeles Times, September 25, 1981.
New York Times Book Review, November 1, 1981.

*   *   *

SWINBURNE, Richard 1934-

PERSONAL: Born December 26, 1934, in Smethwick, England; son of William Henry (a college professor) and Gladys (Parker) Swinburne; married Monica Holmstrom, August 4, 1960; children: Juliet Caroline, Nicola Margaret. *Education:* Exeter College, Oxford, B.A., 1957; St. John's College, Oxford, B.Phil., 1959, M.A., 1961. *Religion:* Church of England.

ADDRESSES: Office—Oriel College, University of Oxford, OX1 4EW, England.

CAREER: University of Leeds, Leeds, England, Leverhulme research fellow in history and philosophy of science, 1961-63; University of Hull, Hull, England, lecturer, 1963-69, senior lecturer in philosophy, 1969-72; University of Keele, Keele, England, professor of philosophy, 1972-84; University of Oxford, Oxford, England, Nolloth Professor of the Philosophy of the Christian Religion, 1985—. Visiting associate professor of philosophy, University of Maryland, 1969-70; Wilde Lecturer in Natural and Comparative Religion, University of Oxford, 1975-78; Gifford Lecturer, University of Aberdeen, 1983-84.

MEMBER: British Society for Philosphy of Science, Philosophy of Science Association, Royal Institute of Philosophy, Aristotelian Society.

WRITINGS:

Space and Time, St. Martin's, 1968, 2nd edition, 1981.
The Concept of Miracle, St. Martin's, 1970.
An Introduction to Confirmation Theory, Methuen, 1973.
(Editor) *The Justification of Induction,* Oxford University Press, 1974.
The Coherence of Theism, Oxford University Press, 1977.
The Existence of God, Oxford University Press, 1979.
Faith and Reason, Oxford University Press, 1981.
(Editor) *Space, Time, and Causality,* Reidel, 1983.
(With Sydney Shoemaker) *Personal Identity,* Blackwell, 1984.
The Evolution of the Soul, Oxford University Press, 1986.

Contributor to professional journals.

SIDELIGHTS: In connection with his dual interest in the philosophy of science and religion, Richard Swinburne writes: "I believe that detailed philosophical examination of large claims of science or theology can elucidate the meaning of those claims and the ways in which they are to be established or refuted. *Space and Time* puts modern theories of physics under the philosophical microscope. An *Introduction to Confirmation Theory* analyzes what in science and elsewhere is evidence for what. *The Coherence of Theism, The Existence of God,* and *Faith and Reason* form a trilogy on the philosophy of religion. *The Coherence of Theism* examines the meaning of the claim that there is a God; *The Existence of God* examines the evidence for and against that claim and concludes that probably there is a God; *Faith and Reason* examines the relation of reasoned arguments to religious faith. *The Evolution of the Soul,* of which my contribution to *Personal Identity* was a first installment, examines the differences between humans and the primeval matter out of which they have evolved, and claims that these differences are to be explained by humans having souls."

BIOGRAPHICAL/CRITICAL SOURCES:

PERIODICALS

Times Literary Supplement, August 14, 1969, April 2, 1971, October 19, 1973, January 25, 1980, May 28, 1982, February 15, 1985, December 11, 1987.

*   *   *

SWINGLEHURST, Edmund 1917-

PERSONAL: Born March 14, 1917, in Chile; son of Edward (a banker) and Lydia Jones; married Janice Anderson; children: (previous marriage) Julian, Mark, Elissa; (present marriage) Nicholas. *Education:* Attended school in Devon, England. *Politics:* None. *Religion:* Christian.

ADDRESSES: Office—Thomas Cook, 45 Berkeley St., London W1A1, England.

CAREER: Headmaster of school in Chile, 1939-44; Grant Advertising, Buenos Aires, Argentina, account executive, 1944-46; E. R. Squibb, Buenos Aires, publicity manager, 1947-50; artist in Paris, France, 1950-53; Thomas Cook, London, England, group manager of public relations, 1953-82, consultant, 1982—.

MEMBER: Anglo-Chilean Society, Canning House.

WRITINGS:

(Self-illustrated) *How! The Whole Truth about the Wild West* (humor), Parrish, 1957.
(Editor) *French Lovers Are Lovely* (cartoons), Arco, 1957.
(Self-illustrated) *All Abroad!* (travel humor), Parrish, 1958.
(With Willy Trebich) *The Broken Swastika,* Cooper, 1971.
The Romantic Journey: The Story of Thomas Cook and Victorian Travel, Pica, 1973.
(With wife, Janice Anderson) *The Victorian and Edwardian Seaside,* Hamlyn, 1978.
Wonders of the World, Hamlyn, 1978.
French Phrase Book, Hamlyn, 1979.
German Phrase Book, Hamlyn, 1979.
Italian Phrase Book, Hamlyn, 1979.
Spanish Phrase Book, Hamlyn, 1979.
Guide to the Channel Islands, Hamlyn, 1979.

England, WHS Distributors, 1980.
Greek Phrase Book, Hamlyn, 1981.
Portuguese Phrase Book, Hamlyn, 1981.
Scottish Walks and Legends, Granada, 1981.
Outdoor and Activity Holidays in Britain (Wish You Were Here Guide), Magnum Books, 1981.
Cook's Tours, Blandford Press, 1981.
Beautiful Britain, W. H. Smith & Son, 1983.
The Midi, Weidenfeld & Nicolson, 1986.
Britain: Land of Contrasts, Marks & Spencer, 1986.
Italy, Batsford, 1987.
Venice Guide, Collins, 1987.

Also author of *Paris, Rome, Florence, Hong Kong, Los Angeles*, and *San Francisco*, published by Hamlyn, and, with J. Anderson, of *Ephemera of Travel and Transport*, 1981.

SIDELIGHTS: Some of Edmund Swinglehurst's books have been published in French, German, Italian, Spanish, Greek, and Portuguese.

AVOCATIONAL INTERESTS: Travel, art.

*   *   *

SYMMES, Robert Edward
   See DUNCAN, Robert (Edward)

T

TABRAH, Ruth Milander 1921-

PERSONAL: Born February 28, 1921, in Buffalo, N.Y.; daughter of Henry and Ruth H. (Flock) Milander; married Frank L. Tabrah (a physician), May 8, 1943 (divorced August, 1971); children: Joseph Garner, Thomas. *Education:* University of Buffalo, B.A., 1941; University of Washington, Seattle, graduate study, 1944-45. *Politics:* Democrat. *Religion:* Buddhist.

ADDRESSES: Home—876 Curtis St., Apt. 3905, Honolulu, Hawaii 96813-5134.

CAREER: Writer, editor, and free-lance photojournalist; editor, Buddhist Study Center Press, 1980—; ordained Shin Buddhist priest in Kyoto, Japan, 1983. Hawaii School Advisory Council, elected member, 1962-66, chairman, 1964-66; Hawaii State Board of Education, Honolulu, elected member, 1966-68; National Association of State Boards of Education, vice-president of Western Division, 1968-72, director-at-large, 1971. Co-host of weekly series on Hawaii public television, "Hawaii Now." Consultant to U.S. Office of Education, 1969-72, and The Consulting Organization, 1972—.

MEMBER: PEN, Authors League of America, League of Women Voters, American Association of University Women, Phi Beta Kappa.

AWARDS, HONORS: Distinguished Woman in Education Award, American Association of University Women, 1970.

WRITINGS:

Pulaski Place, Harper, 1950.
The Voices of Others, Putnam, 1959, published as *Town for Scandal*, Pocket Books, 1960.
Hawaiian Heart, Follett, 1964.
Hawaii Nei, Follett, 1967.
The Red Shark, Follett, 1970.
Buddhism: A Modern Way of Life and Thought, Jodo (Honolulu), 1970.
The Old Man and the Astronauts: A Melanesian Tale, Island Heritage, 1975.
Lanai, Island Heritage, 1975.
Living Shin Buddhism, Press Pacifica, 1979.
Hawaii: A Bicentennial History, Norton, 1980.
Maui: The Romantic Island, K.C. Publications, 1985.

Emily's Hawaii, Press Pacifica, 1986.
(Translator) *Shoshinge*, Buddhist Study Center Press, 1986.
Hawaii's Incredible Anna, Press Pacifica, 1987.
The Golden Children of Hawaii, Island Heritage, 1987.
Kavai: The Unconquerable Island, K.C. Publications, 1988.
Ajata Satru: The Story That Tells Us Who We Are, Buddhist Study Center Press, 1988.

Also author of *Ni'ihau: The Last Hawaiian Island*, 1987.

EDITOR OF "FOLKTALES" SERIES; PUBLISHED BY ISLAND HERITAGE

George Suyeoka, *Momotaro*, 1972.
Guy Buffet and Pam Buffet, *Adventures of Kama Pua'a*, 1972.
G. Buffet and P. Buffet, *Pua Pua Lena Lena and the Magic Kiha-Pu: An Adaptation from the Hawaiian Legends*, 1972.
G. Buffet and P. Buffet, *Kahala: Where the Rainbow Ends*, 1973.
Shan Mui, *The Seven Magic Orders*, 1973.
Robert B. Goodman and Robert A. Spicer, *Urashima Taro*, 1973.
Goodman and Spicer, *The Magic Brush*, 1974.
Issunboshi, 1974.
Philipo Springer, *Makaha: The Legend of the Broken Promise*, 1974.

OTHER

Contributor to periodicals.

WORK IN PROGRESS: A novel plus nonfiction book on Shinran-Shonin, the thirteenth-century Japanese Buddhist leader; a translation of Shinran's thirteenth-century *Kyo-Gyo-Shin-Sho*.

SIDELIGHTS: Ruth Milander Tabrah told *CA* she is "a writer who was born wanting to do exactly what I've spent my life doing—putting into words what it means to be fully human, exciting readers by opening new windows in their minds, telling what I see and feel and think with honesty and without shame."

Tabrah speaks French and German as well as some Japanese and Spanish. She has travelled extensively while researching her books.

AVOCATIONAL INTERESTS: Painting, skin diving.

TAEUBER, Conrad   1906-

PERSONAL: Surname is pronounced *Toy*-ber; born June 15, 1906, in Hosmer, S.D.; son of Richard E. (a minister) and Emmy (Mussgang) Taeuber; married Irene Barnes (a demographer), June 26, 1929 (died, 1974); married Dorothy Harris, September 10, 1979; children: (first marriage) Richard Conrad, Karl Ernst. *Education:* University of Minnesota, A.B., 1927, M.A., 1929, Ph.D., 1931; University of Heidelberg, graduate study, 1929-30; University of Wisconsin, graduate study, 1930-31.

ADDRESSES: Home—4222 Sheridan St., Hyattsville, Md. 20782. *Office*—Kennedy Institute Center for Population Research, Georgetown University, Washington, D.C. 20057.

CAREER: Mount Holyoke College, South Hadley, Mass., assistant professor, 1931-33; Federal Emergency Relief Administration, Washington, D.C., associate economic analyst, 1934-35; Bureau of Agricultural Economics, Washington, D.C., agricultural economist, 1935-40, senior social scientist, 1940-42, principal social scientist and acting head of division of farm population and rural welfare, 1942-43, head agricultural economist, 1943-46; Food and Agriculture Organization of United Nations, Washington, D.C., chairman of statistics branch, 1946-51; U.S. Bureau of the Census, Washington, D.C., associate director, 1951-73; Georgetown University, Kennedy Institute, Washington, D.C., associate director and Joseph F. Kennedy Sr. Professor of Demography, 1973—.

MEMBER: International Statistical Institute, American Statistical Association, American Sociological Association, Population Association of America (past president), Inter-American Statistical Institute (president, 1967-73), American Association for the Advancement of Science, Sociological Research Association, Rural Sociological Society, Cosmos Club (Washington).

AWARDS, HONORS: Award from University of Minnesota, 1951; Exceptional Service Award, Department of Commerce, 1963.

WRITINGS:

(With Charles E. Lively) *Rural Migration in the United States,* U.S. Government Printing Office, 1939, reprinted, Da Capo, 1971.
(With first wife, Irene Taeuber) *The Changing Population of the United States,* Wiley, 1958.
(With I. Taeuber) *The People of the United States in the Twentieth Century,* U.S. Government Printing Office, 1971.
(With Paul N. Ylvisaker) *Density: Five Perspectives,* Urban Land Institute, 1972.
Population and Food Supply (sound recording), Jeffrey Norton, 1974.
(Editor with Richard D. Lambert) *America in the Seventies: Some Social Indicators,* American Academy of Political and Social Science, 1978.
(Editor with Lambert) *America Enters the Eighties: Some Social Indicators,* American Academy of Political and Social Science, 1981.*

*   *   *

TAEUBER, Karl E(rnst)   1936-

PERSONAL: Surname is pronounced *Toy*-ber; born March 31, 1936, in Washington, D.C.; son of Conrad (a sociologist) and Irene (a demographer; maiden name, Barnes) Taeuber; married

Alma Ficks (a sociologist) March 17, 1960; children: Shawn Eric, Stacy Robin, Wendy Kim. *Education:* Yale University, B.A., 1955; Harvard University, M.A., 1957, Ph.D., 1959; University of Chicago, graduate study, 1958-59.

ADDRESSES: Home—1911 Vilas Ave., Madison, Wis. 53711. *Office*—Department of Sociology, University of Wisconsin, Madison, Wis. 53706.

CAREER: University of Chicago, Chicago, Ill., assistant professor of sociology and research associate of Population and Training Center, 1961-63; University of California, Berkeley, research associate in demography, 1963-64; University of Wisconsin—Madison, 1964—, began as assistant professor, currently professor of sociology, chairman of sociology department, 1970-73, Institute for Research on Poverty, fellow, 1966—, assistant director, 1978-80, director of Center for Demography and Ecology, 1980-85. Social scientist, RAND Corp., 1969-70. Member of board of directors, Social Science Research Council, 1970-75. Member, Madison School District Integration Monitoring Committee, 1984-88. *Military service:* U.S. Public Health Service Commissioned Corps, assistant scientist at National Cancer Institute, with rank of lieutenant, 1959-61.

MEMBER: Population Association of America (director, 1966-69), American Sociological Association.

WRITINGS:

(With wife, Alma F. Taeuber) *Negroes in Cities,* Aldine, 1965.
(With Leonard Chiazze, Jr., and William Haenszel) *Migration in the United States,* U.S. Government Printing Office, 1966.
Demographic Trends Affecting the Future Labor Force, Institute for Research of Poverty, University of Wisconsin—Madison, 1977.
(Editor with James A. Sweet and Larry L. Bumpass) *Social Demography,* Academic Press, 1978.

*   *   *

TALMON, Shemaryahu   1920-

PERSONAL: Surname is pronounced Tal-*mon;* born May 28, 1920, in Poland; son of Litmann and Hella (Ell) Zelmanowicz; married Yonina Garber (a professor), November 17, 1948 (deceased); married Penina Moraq (a lecturer), March 18, 1969; children: (first marriage) Efrath, Tamar; (second marriage) Nogah, Tammy. *Education:* Hebrew University of Jerusalem, M.A., 1945, Ph.D., 1955. *Religion:* Jewish.

ADDRESSES: Home—5 Smuts St., Jerusalem, Israel. *Office*—Department of Bible Studies, Hebrew University, Jerusalem, Israel.

CAREER: University of Leeds, Leeds, England, lecturer in Semitic studies, 1950-51; University of Tel-Aviv, Tel-Aviv, Israel, lecturer in Bible studies, 1953-55; Hebrew University of Jerusalem, Jerusalem, Israel, instructor, 1955-57, lecturer in Bible studies, 1958-61; Brandeis University, Waltham, Mass., professor of Near Eastern studies, 1961-63; Hebrew University of Jerusalem, senior lecturer, 1963-66, associate professor, 1966-74, Magnes Professor of Bible Studies, 1974—, rector of University College, Haifa, 1968-69, dean of faculty of humanities, 1975-78, fellow, Institute for Advanced Studies, 1983-84. Rector, Hochschule fuer Juedische Studien, Heidelberg,

West Germany, 1981—. Visiting professor, Harvard University, 1970-71, University of California, Berkeley, 1978-79, and Theologische Fakultaet Luzern, 1980-81; Foster Visiting Professor of Bible Studies, Brandeis University, 1971-72. Fellow, National Humanities Center, Research Triangle Park, N.C., 1987-88. *Military service:* Israeli Defence Army, Infantry, 1948-49; became captain.

MEMBER: World Association of Jewish Studies, Israel Exploration Society, Israel Historical Society, Israel Society of Bible Research, Society of Old Testament Study (Great Britain), Society of Biblical Literature (United States), American Oriental Society, American Schools of Oriental Research.

WRITINGS:

(Editor) *Selections from the Pentateuch in the Samaritan Version,* Hebrew University, 1957.

(Editor with M. Avi-Yonah and A. Malamat) *Views of the Bible World* (in English and Hebrew), International Publishers, Volume 2, 1959, Volume 3, 1960.

(Editor) *Textus: Annual of the Hebrew University Bible Project,* Magnes Press of Hebrew University, Volume 4, 1964, Volume 5, 1966, Volume 6, 1967, Volume 7, 1969, Volume 8, 1973, Volume 9, 1981, Volume 10, 1982.

Darkhe hasipur ba-Mikra (on the Bible in literature), Akademon, Hebrew University, 1965.

(Editor) *Toldot nosah ha-Mikra bamehkar he-hadish* (readings on the history of Biblical text in recent literature; chiefly in English), Akademon, Hebrew University, 1966.

(Author of introduction) Roman-Francois Butin, *The Ten Nequdoth of the Torah,* Ktav Publishing, 1969.

The Old Testament Test: The Cambridge History of the Bible, Volume 1, edited by P. R. Akroyd and C. F. Evans, Cambridge University Press, 1970.

(Editor with F. M. Cross) *Qumran and the History of the Biblical Text,* Harvard University Press, 1975.

(Editor with Gregor Siefer) *Religion und Politik in der Gesellschaft des 20. Jahrhunderts: Ein Symposion mit israelischen und deutschen Wissenschaftlern,* B. Keil, 1978.

(Editor with K. Yaron and J. Emanuel) *Kaan we'ahshav: Iyunim behaguto hahevratit wehadatit shel M. Buber,* Hamerkaz 'al shem Martin Buber (Jerusalem), 1982.

(Editor with A. Falaturi and W. Strolz) *Zukunftshoffnung und Heilserwartung in den monotheistischen Religionen,* Herder (Freiburg), 1983.

(Editor with U. Luz, M. Klopfenstein, and E. Tov) *Die Mitte der Schrift?,* Lang (New York City), 1986.

Gesellschaft und Literatur in der Hebraeischen Bibel: Gesammelte Aufsaetze, Neukirchener, 1986.

King, Cult, and Calendar in Ancient Israel: Collected Studies, Magnes Press (Jerusalem), 1986, W. S. Heinman, 1987.

(Contributor) R. Alter and F. Kermode, editors, *Literary Guide to the Bible,* Harvard University Press, 1987.

Also contributor to *Encyclopaedia Biblica, Hebrew Bible Dictionary, Enciclopedia de la Biblica, Interpreter's Dictionary of the Bible,* and *Theologisches Woerterbuch zum Alten Testament.* Contributor of more than one hundred articles and numerous reviews to journals in Israel, United States, England, Netherlands, Italy, Spain, and Germany.

WORK IN PROGRESS: The Covenanters from the Judean Desert, a sociological analysis; *The Biblical Narrative,* an introduction to biblical prose literature; a critical edition of the Book of Jeremiah; a commentary on the Books of Ezra and Nehemiah; biblical motifs and conceptual thought.

TANNER, William
See AMIS, Kingsley (William)

*   *   *

TANSELLE, G(eorge) Thomas   1934-

PERSONAL: Surname is pronounced *Tan*-sell; born January 29, 1934, in Lebanon, Ind.; son of K. Edwin and Madge R. (Miller) Tanselle. *Education:* Yale University, B.A. (magna cum laude), 1955; Northwestern University, M.A., 1956, Ph.D., 1959.

ADDRESSES: Office—John Simon Guggenheim Memorial Foundation, 90 Park Ave., New York, N.Y. 10016.

CAREER: Chicago City Junior College, Chicago, Ill., instructor in English, 1958-60; University of Wisconsin—Madison, instructor, 1960-61, assistant professor, 1961-63, associate professor, 1963-68, professor of English, 1968-78; John Simon Guggenheim Memorial Foundation, New York, N.Y., vice-president, 1978—.

Adjunct professor of English and comparative literature, Columbia University, 1980—; member of faculty, Summer Rare Book School, Columbia University School of Library Service, 1984-87. Board of directors, Literary Classics of the United States, Inc., 1979—. Member of Planning Institute of Commission on English, Ann Arbor, summer, 1961, executive committee, Center for Editions of American Authors, 1970-73, Soviet-American symposium on editing, Indiana University, 1976, executive committee, Center for Scholarly Editions, 1976—, and North American Committee for 18th-century short title catalog, 1978—. Member of advisory committees and advisory boards of various organizations, including Center for Books, and Library of Congress, 1978—. Speaker before many literary organizations and at numerous conferences.

MEMBER: Modern Language Association of America, Modern Humanities Research Association, National Council of Teachers of English, Society for Textual Scholarship (president, 1981-83), Renaissance Society of America, American Society for Eighteenth-Century Studies, Society for Bibliography of Natural History, American Printing History Association (member of board of trustees, New York Chapter, 1979-85), Printing Historical Society, Private Libraries Association, Manuscript Society (member of board of directors, 1974-79), Melville Society (president, 1982—), Typophiles, Guild Book Workers, American Antiquarian Society (council member, 1974—), Bibliographical Society of America (member of council, 1970; president, 1984-88), Fellows Morgan Library, Bibliographical Society (London), Edinburgh Bibliographical Society, Oxford Bibliographical Society, Cambridge Bibliographical Society, Bibliographical Society of the University of Virginia, Wisconsin Academy of Sciences, Arts, and Letters, Indiana Research Libraries Association, Book Club of California, Yale Club, Century Club, Grolier Club (secretary, 1982-86, president, 1986), Caxton Club, Phi Beta Kappa.

AWARDS, HONORS: Kiekhofer Teaching Award, University of Wisconsin, 1963; Guggenheim fellowship, 1969-70; Jenkins Prize for Bibliography, Union College, 1973; American Council of Learned Societies fellowship, 1973-74; National Endowment for the Humanities fellowship, 1977-78; English-Speaking Union "Books-Across-the-Sea Ambassador of Honor" book awards for *Herman Melville: Typee, Omoo, Mardi,* 1983, and *Herman Melville: Redburn, White-Jacket, Moby-Dick,* 1984; Laureate Award, American Printing History Association, 1987, ''for distinguished contribution to the study of the history of publishing and printing.''

WRITINGS:

Royall Tyler, Harvard University Press, 1967.
(Co-editor) *The Writings of Herman Melville,* Northwestern University Press and Newberry Library, 1968—.
A Guide to the Study of the United States Imprints, Belknap, 1971.
A Checklist of Editions of Moby Dick, Northwestern University Press and Newberry Library, 1976.
Selected Studies in Bibliography, University of Press of Virginia, 1979.
(Editor) *Herman Melville: Typee, Ommo, Mardi,* Library of America, 1982.
(Editor) *Herman Melville: Redburn, White-Jacket, Moby-Dick,* Library of America, 1983.
Textual Criticism since Greg: A Chronicle, 1950-1985, University Press of Virginia, 1988.
A Rationale of Textual Criticism, University of Pennsylvania Press, 1989.

Contributor to books and scholarly journals, including *Studies in Bibliography,* 1964—, *Book Collector, Library, Shakespeare Quarterly, Gutenberg Jahrbuch, Modern Language Review, American Literature,* and *PMLA.* Member of editorial board, *Contemporary Literature,* 1962—, *Abstracts of English Studies,* 1964-78, *Papers of the Bibliographical Society of America,* 1968—, *Resources for American Literary Study,* 1971—, *Analytical and Enumerative Bibliography,* 1977—, *Review,* 1978—, *American Literature,* 1979-82, and *Literary Research,* 1986—. Member of advisory board of *Burton's Anatomy of Melancholy,* 1978—, and *Publishing and Printing History, A Guide to Manuscript Resources in the U.S.,* 1980—.

*   *   *

TARRANT, Wilma
   See SHERMAN, Jory (Tecumseh)

*   *   *

TATE, Ellalice
   See HIBBERT, Eleanor Burford

*   *   *

TAYLOR, Andrew (John Robert)   1951-
   (John Robert Taylor)

PERSONAL: Born October 14, 1951, in Stevenage, England; son of Arthur John (a teacher and minister) and Hilda (a physiotherapist; maiden name, Haines) Taylor; married Caroline Silverwood (a librarian), September 8, 1979. *Education:* Emmanuel College, Cambridge, B.A. (with honors), 1973, M.A., 1976; University of London, M.A. (library and information studies), 1979. *Politics:* None.

ADDRESSES: Home and office—The Carriage House, 13 Lords Hill, Coleford, Gloucestershire GL16 8BG, England.

CAREER: Borough of Brent, London, England, librarian, 1976-78, 1979-81; free-lance writer and subeditor for London area publishers, 1981—.

AWARDS, HONORS: John Creasey Memorial Award, Crime Writers Association, 1982, and Edgar nomination, Mystery Writers of America, both for *Caroline Minuscule;* Gold Dag-ger nomination, Crime Writers Association, 1985, for *Our Fathers' Lies.*

WRITINGS:

CRIME NOVELS AND THRILLERS

Caroline Minuscule, Gollancz, 1982, Dodd, 1983.
Waiting for the End of the World, Dodd, 1984.
Our Fathers' Lies, Dodd, 1985.
An Old School Tie (Book-of-the-Month Club alternate selection), Dodd, 1986.
Freelance Death, Gollancz, 1987, Dodd, 1988.
The Second Midnight, Dodd, 1987.
Blacklist, Collins, 1988.
(Under name John Robert Taylor) *Hairline Cracks* (young adult), Armada, 1988.
(Under name John Robert Taylor) *The Private Nose* (juvenile), Walker, 1989.

WORK IN PROGRESS: Two linked thrillers for young teenagers, the first with the working title of *Snapshot;* two adventure thrillers for Collins, the first with the working title of *Toyshop.*

SIDELIGHTS: Andrew Taylor wrote *CA:* ''The urges to read and write fiction are rather like Internal Revenue Service demands: mysterious, but you ignore them at your peril. For a long time I was one of those writers who never get around to writing anything. One lunchtime, on a grey February day in 1980, I suddenly realized that a lifetime of undemanding and unsatisfying jobs stretched before me; if I didn't start writing now, I never would. There and then I pushed aside the sandwich crumbs and scribbled the first few pages of what eventually became *Caroline Minuscule.* Long before I'd finished the first draft, I knew I was hooked. The square peg had found the square hole. Before the book was accepted by a publisher, I chucked in my safe, sensible job and became precariously self-employed.

''My first four books were crime novels; I chose the genre because I knew and liked it. Recently I've started writing adventure thrillers, which are intended for a wider market, and fiction for children of various ages. An element of crime or mystery is common to most of the books I have written. A recurring theme is the way in which the past exerts a continuing influence on the present. I see myself primarily as a storyteller, and my medium is the written word. There is only one valuable piece of advice I can give to aspiring writers: write.''

BIOGRAPHICAL/CRITICAL SOURCES:

PERIODICALS

Times (London), August 5, 1982.
New York Times Book Review, October 23, 1983, January 26, 1986.

*   *   *

TAYLOR, John Robert
   See TAYLOR, Andrew (John Robert)

*   *   *

TAYLOR, Samuel (Woolley)   1907-

PERSONAL: Born February 5, 1907, in Provo, Utah; son of John Whitaker and Janet Maria (Woolley) Taylor; married

Elizabeth Gay Dimick; children: Sara Taylor Weston. *Education:* Attended Brigham Young University. *Religion:* Church of Jesus Christ of Latter-day Saints (Mormon).

ADDRESSES: Home—1954 Stockbridge Ave., Redwood City, Calif. 94061.

CAREER: Writer, 1932—. Has worked in carding, spinning, and weaving departments of woolen mills. *Military service:* U.S. Army Air Forces, chief of public relations magazine section, 1943-45; served in European theater; became second lieutenant; received Legion of Merit, Bronze Star, and three battle stars.

MEMBER: Authors League of America (San Francisco chairman, 1948), Writers Guild of America, California Writers Club.

WRITINGS:

(With Eric Friedheim) *Fighters Up* (nonfiction), McRae, 1945.
The Man with My Face (novel), A. A. Wyn, 1948.
Heaven Knows Why (novel; originally published in *Collier's* as "The Mysterious Way"), A. A. Wyn, 1948, reprinted, Millenial, 1979.
Family Kingdom (biography), McGraw, 1951, reprinted, Western Epics, 1974.
The Grinning Gismo (novel), A. A. Wyn, 1951.
"The Square Needle" (play), first produced in Hollywood in 1951.
I Have Six Wives (biography), Greenberg, 1956.
Line Haul (history), Filmer Publishing, 1959.
"The Absent-Minded Professor" (screenplay), Walt Disney, 1964.
Uranium Fever (history), Macmillan, 1970.
Nightfall at Nauvoo (history), Macmillan, 1971.
The Kingdom or Nothing: The Life of John Taylor, Militant Mormon, Macmillan, 1976.
Rocky Mountain Empire (history), Macmillan, 1978.
(With Raymond W. Taylor) *The John Taylor Papers: Records of the Last Utah Pioneer* (biography), two volumes, Pioneer Press, 1984.

Also author of screenplay "Bait," 1954. Ghost writer for the annual *Report of the Commanding General of the United States Strategic Air Forces in Europe to the Secretary of War*, 1944-45. Contributor of numerous stories and articles to popular magazines, including *Saturday Evening Post, Liberty, Collier's, American, Esquire, Reader's Digest,* and *Family Circle.*

WORK IN PROGRESS: Two biographies, *The 201 File* and *The Two-Step Ladder.*

SIDELIGHTS: Samuel Taylor once told *CA:* "I have been a professional writer since college days, which is longer than I like to remember. My only non-writing work since then was a period of two weeks during the early days of World War II, when I directed the building of a submarine net to save San Francisco from enemy attack. I have published an uncounted number of articles and fiction stories in national magazines. My work ranges from short-shorts to serials and one-shot book-lengths. During my misspent youth I ground out pulp-paper stories—detectives, westerns, sports, adventure (even a confession). My book, *Family Kingdom*, was the story of my father's family of six wives and three dozen kids. It was published in part by *Holiday* and the U.S. State Department distributed this magazine excerpt throughout the world. A considerable amount of my work has been based on the Mormon culture. Seven of my published books mined this lode, as well

as the two-volume *The John Taylor Papers: Records of the Last Utah Pioneer.*"

The grandfather of Samuel Taylor, John Taylor, was the successor to Brigham Young and an important leader during and after the Mormon migration to the Great Basin. In *The Kingdom or Nothing: The Life of John Taylor, Militant Mormon,* the author describes these early years of Mormon history through his grandfather's eyes. *Washington Post Book World* contributor Fawn M. Brodie feels that this approach "gives [Taylor] the liberty to create scenes that are often poignant and moving, but it deprives him of historical perspective and judgmental summing up." Overall, however, Brodie esteems this book to be a "massive and powerful life story that deserves . . . to reach a wide non-Mormon audience."

MEDIA ADAPTATIONS: A screenplay adaptation was made of *The Man with My Face* in 1951; *Heaven Knows Why* has been purchased for a movie production.

BIOGRAPHICAL/CRITICAL SOURCES:

PERIODICALS

Washington Post Book World, June 13, 1976.

*   *   *

THEMERSON, Stefan   1910-

PERSONAL: Born January 5, 1910, in Poland; married Franciszka Weinles (an artist). *Education:* Educated in Warsaw, Poland.

ADDRESSES: Home—28 Warrington Crescent, London W9, England.

CAREER: Writer. *Military service:* Polish Army, 1940-44; served in France and England.

AWARDS, HONORS: Polish Order of Merit, 1976.

WRITINGS:

Dno Nieba (poems; title means "On the Bottom of the Sky"), [London], 1943.
Croquis dans les tenebres (poems; title means "Sketches in Darkness"), Hachette, 1944.
The Lay Scripture (prose poem), Froshaug, 1947.
Jankel Adler (essay), Gaberbocchus, 1948.
Bayamus (novel), Editions Poetry London, 1949, revised edition, Gaberbocchus, 1965.
Adventures of Peddy Bottom (juvenile), Editions Poetry London, 1951, revised edition, Gaberbocchus, 1954.
Wooff Wooff; or, Who Killed Richard Wagner? (fiction), Gaberbocchus, 1951, revised edition, 1967.
Professor Mmaa's Lecture (novel), Gaberbocchus, 1953, reprinted, Overlook Press, 1976.
"Factor T" and *"Semantic Sonata"* (essays), Gaberbocchus, 1956, revised edition, 1972.
Kurt Schwitters in England (essay), Gaberbocchus, 1958.
Cardinal Polatuo (novel), Gaberbocchus, 1961.
Semantic Divertissements (humor), Gaberbocchus, 1962.
(Contributor) I. J. Good, editor, *The Scientist Speculates*, Heinemann, 1962.
Tom Harris (novel), Gaberbocchus, 1967, Knopf, 1968.
Appolinaire's Lyrical Ideograms, Gaberbocchus, 1968.
St. Francis and the Wolf of Gubbio (opera), Gaberbocchus, 1972.
Special Branch (essay), Gaberbocchus, 1972.

Logic Labels and Flesh (philosophical essays), Gaberbocchus, 1974.

On Semantic Poetry, Gaberbocchus, 1975.

General Piesc; or, The Case of the Forgotten Mission (fiction), Gaberbocchus, 1976.

The Chair of Decency (the 1981 Johan Huizinga Lecture), Atheaneum (Amsterdam), 1982.

The Urge to Create Visions (avant-garde film and photography), De Harmonie-Gaberbocchus, 1983.

The Mystery of the Sardine (novel), Faber (London), 1986, Farrar, Straus (New York), 1986.

(Contributor) Wim Tigges, editor, *Explorations in the Field of Nonsense*, DQR Studies in Literature 3, Rodopi (Amsterdam), 1987.

Hobson's Island (novel), Faber, 1988.

OTHER

Author of children's books in Polish, 1930-37. Also filmmaker with wife, Franciszka Themerson, of avant-garde films, "Apteka," 1931, "Europa," 1932, "Moment Musical," 1933, "Zwarcie," 1935, "The Adventures of a Good Citizen," 1937, "Calling Mr. Smith," 1943, and "The Eye and the Ear," 1944.

SIDELIGHTS: Stefan Themerson's children's books in Polish represent only one facet of his artistic capabilities. In the last fifty years, reports Hugh Hebert in the *Guardian*, Themerson has been an "avant-garde film maker and photographer, typographer, literary critic, publisher, cultural philosopher, and the kind of novelist of whom reviewers say as each book comes out, why isn't he better known?" Because of his eclectic background, critics expect his novels to transcend the ordinary, writes Albert Goldman in the *New York Times Book Review*. Commenting on the 1967 novel *Tom Harris*, Goldman reports, "These expectations are at least partially fulfilled. *Tom Harris* is an epistemological . . . story that poses the question whether any man can truly be known by any other man."

Written as a mystery, arranged in two parts, and told by an unnamed narrator, *Tom Harris* spoofs several conventions of the novel form, according to critics who differ widely in their estimations of its success. While *Punch* reviewer Martin Shuttleworth dismisses the book as "incoherent, incompetent, and rather dim," and the *Atlantic*'s Phoebe Adams laments that after a "promising beginning, the book drifts into philosophizing about life," other reviewers cite *Tom Harris*'s redeeming qualities. In his *Books and Bookmen* review, for instance, David Spiller notes the book's close "concern with fundamental human problems; the effects of class, intelligence and physical characteristics upon individuals and society; and notably, an obsession with reality and unreality." And, writing in *Best Sellers*, James A. Phillips allows that Themerson asks some "tricky" questions. "I doubt if this book will gain a wide following, but I, for one, am curious enough to want to see Themerson's next novel," Phillips concludes.

Themerson's next novel, *The Mystery of the Sardine*, combines philosophical concerns with humor and suspense. "What an extraordinary writer Stefan Themerson is," remarks Lynton Lesserday in a *Punch* review. Compared to the "great, enormous doorstops" presented by similar novelists, this mystery is a lean book "absolutely jam-packed with ideas." The plot essentially involves terrorists, but Themerson makes the novel a "comedy of erudition" by providing side trips into the ironies of mathematics, philosophy, and political thought, Lesserday maintains. Victoria Glendinning of the London *Times* compares reading *The Mystery of the Sardine* to "playing chess with someone who is better at it than you are." However, readers are as likely to be provoked to laughter as to serious thinking, states Hebert, who likens the book to a product of "the Monty Python team. Except that they wouldn't do it with half the elegance or a quarter of the learning Themerson brings to it."

Critics generally praise *The Mystery of the Sardine*, though some appreciate its bizarre elements more than others. Sardines play a minor role in the story, which includes a twelve-year-old genius who disproves Euclid's geometry, and a bomb delivered by a large poodle. "The novel has its attractions as well as its frustrations," notes Neville Shack in the *Times Literary Supplement*. "There is a capacity to surprise, both in its transitions and its rum *non sequiturs*. . . . Overall, the licence to be far-fetched ensures a gusto and makes light of everything, even when it exasperates." *New York Times Book Review* contributor Will Blythe, on the other hand, calls it a "supremely entertaining" thriller "that makes mincemeat of plausibility, flaunts its red herrings, defies its genre. . . . Death and philosophy, however, have rarely been so much fun."

Themerson, the son of a doctor who wrote fiction, was born and educated in Poland. In 1938, he and his wife, a painter and his partner in filmmaking, moved to France. After the fall of France during the Second World War they escaped, at different times, to England, where they still reside. Themerson's books have been published in Polish, Italian, French, German, Swedish, and Dutch.

BIOGRAPHICAL/CRITICAL SOURCES:

PERIODICALS

Atlantic, May, 1968.
Best Sellers, April 15, 1968.
Books and Bookmen, August, 1967.
Globe and Mail (Toronto), October 18, 1986.
Guardian, February 7, 1987.
New York Times Book Review, May 26, 1968, December 28, 1986.
Punch, May 31, 1967, February 5, 1986.
Times (London), February 2, 1986.
Times Literary Supplement, June 15, 1967, February 21, 1986.

*　　*　　*

THIELE, Colin (Milton) 1920-

PERSONAL: Surname is pronounced Tee-lee; born November 16, 1920, in Eudunda, South Australia; son of Carl Wilhelm (a farmer) and Anna (Wittwer) Thiele; married Rhonda Gill (a teacher and artist), March 17, 1945; children: Janne Louise (Mrs. Jeffrey Minge), Sandra Gwenyth (Mrs. Ron Paterson). *Education:* University of Adelaide, B.A., 1941, Diploma of Education, 1947; Adelaide Teachers College, Diploma of Teaching, 1942.

ADDRESSES: Home—24 Woodhouse Crescent, Wattle Park, South Australia 5066, Australia.

CAREER: South Australian Education Department, English teacher and senior master at high school in Port Lincoln, 1946-55, senior master at high school in Brighton, 1956; Wattle Park Teachers College, Wattle Park, South Australia, lecturer, 1957-61, senior lecturer in English, 1962-63, vice-principal, 1964, principal, 1965-73; director, Murray Park College of Advanced Education, 1973; Wattle Park Teachers Centre, Wattle Park, principal, 1973-80. Common Wealth Literary Fund lecturer on Australian literature; speaker at conferences on literature and education in Australia and the United States. *Military service:* Royal Australian Air Force, 1942-45.

MEMBER: Australian College of Education (fellow), Australian Society of Authors (council member, 1965—; president, 1987—), English Teachers Association (president, 1957), South Australian Fellowship of Writers (president, 1961).

AWARDS, HONORS: W. J. Miles Poetry Prize, 1944, for *Progress to Denial;* Commonwealth Jubilee Literary Competitions, first prize in radio play section, for "Edge of Ice," and first prize in radio feature section, both 1951; South Australian winner in World Short Story Quest, 1952; Fulbright scholar in United States and Canada, 1959-60; Grace Leven Poetry Prize, 1961, for *Man in a Landscape;* Common Wealth Literary Fund fellowship, 1967-68; *Blue Fin* was placed on the Honours List, Hans Anderson Award, 1972; Visual Arts Board award, 1975, for *Magpie Island;* Austrian State Prize for Children's Books, 1979, for *The SKNUKS,* and 1986, for *Pinquo;* Book of the Year Award, Children's Book Council of Australia, 1982, for *The Valley Between;* Mystery Writers of America citation for *The Fire in the Stone;* numerous commendations in Australian Children's Book Council awards.

WRITINGS:

Progress to Denial (poems), Jindyworobak, 1945.
Splinters and Shards (poems), Jindyworobak, 1945.
The Golden Lightning (poems), Jindyworobak, 1951.
(Editor) *Jindyworobak Anthology* (verse), Jindyworobak, 1953.
Man in a Landscape (poems), Rigby, 1960.
(Editor with Ian Mudie) *Australian Poets Speak,* Rigby, 1961.
(Editor) *Favourite Australian Stories,* Rigby, 1963.
(Editor, and author of commentary and notes) *Handbook to Favourite Australian Stories,* Rigby, 1964.
In Charcoal and Conte (poems), Rigby, 1966.
Heysen of Hahndorf (biography), Rigby, 1968, Tri-Ocean, 1969.
Barossa Valley Sketchbook, illustrations by Jeanette McLeod, Tri-Ocean, 1968.
Labourers in the Vineyard (novel), Rigby, 1970.
Selected Verse (1940-1970), Rigby, 1970.
Coorong, photographs by Mike McKelvey, Rigby, 1972.
Range without Man: The North Flinders, Rigby, 1974.
The Little Desert, photographs by Jocelyn Burt, Rigby, 1975.
Grains of Mustard Seed, South Australia Education Department, 1975.
Heysen's Early Hahndorf, Rigby, 1976.
The Bight, photographs by McKelvey, Rigby, 1976.
Lincoln's Place, illustrations by Robert Ingpen, Rigby, 1978.
Maneater Man, Rigby, 1979.
The Seed's Inheritance, Lutheran Publishing House, 1986.
South Australia Revisited, illustrations by Charlotte Balfour, Rigby, 1986.
Something to Crow About, illustrations by Rex Milstead, Commonwealth Books, 1986.
Coorong, illustrations by Barbara Leslie, Wakefield Press, 1986.
A Welcome to Water, photographs by David Simpson and Ted James, Wakefield Press, 1986.
Ranger's Territory, Angus & Robertson, 1987.

CHILDREN'S BOOKS AND SCHOOL TEXTS

The State of Our State, Rigby, 1952.
(Editor and annotator) *Looking at Poetry,* Longmans, Green, 1960.
The Sun on the Stubble (children's novel), Rigby, 1961.

Gloop the Gloomy Bunyip (children's story in verse; also see below), illustrations by John Bailey, Jacaranda, 1962.
(Editor with Greg Branson) *One-Act Plays for Secondary Schools,* Rigby, Books 1-2, 1962, one-volume edition of Books 1-2, 1963, Book 3, 1964, revised edition of Book 1 published as *Setting the Stage,* 1969, revised edition of Book 2 published as *The Living Stage,* 1970.
Storm Boy, illustrations by Bailey, Rigby, 1963, Rand McNally, 1966, new edition with illustrations by Ingpen, Rigby, 1974, film edition with photographs by David Kynoch, Rigby, 1976, original edition reprinted by Harper, 1978.
(Editor with Branson) *Beginners, Please* (anthology), 1964.
February Dragon (children's novel), Rigby, 1965, Harper, 1976.
The Rim of the Morning (short stories), Rigby, 1966.
Mrs. Munch and Puffing Billy, illustrations by Nyorie Bungey, Rigby, 1967, Tri-Ocean, 1968.
Yellow-Jacket Jock, illustrations by Clifton Pugh, F. W. Cheshire, 1969.
Blue Fin (children's novel), illustrations by Roger Haldane, Rigby, 1969, Harper, 1974.
Flash Flood, illustrations by Jean Elder, Rigby, 1970.
Flip Flop and Tiger Snake, illustrations by Elder, Rigby, 1970.
Gloop the Bunyip (children's story in verse; contains material from *Gloop the Gloomy Bunyip*), illustrations by Helen Sallis, Rigby, 1970.
(Editor with Branson) *Plays for Young Players* (for primary schools), Rigby, 1970.
The Fire in the Stone, Rigby, 1973, Harper, 1974, film edition, Puffin Books, 1983.
Albatross Two, Rigby, 1974, published as *Fight against Albatross Two,* Harper, 1976.
Uncle Gustav's Ghosts, Rigby, 1974.
Magpie Island, illustrations by Haldane, Rigby, 1974, Puffin Books, 1981.
The Hammerhead Light, Rigby, 1976, Harper, 1977.
Storm Boy Picture Book, photographs by Kynoch, Rigby, 1976.
The Shadow on the Hills, Rigby, 1977, Harper, 1978.
The SKNUKS, illustrations by Mary Milton, Rigby, 1977.
River Murray Mary, illustrations by Ingpen, Rigby, 1979.
Ballander Boy, photographs by David Simpson, Rigby, 1979.
Chadwick's Chimney, illustrations by Ingpen, Methuen, 1980.
The Best of Colin Thiele, Rigby, 1980.
Tanya and Trixie, photographs by Simpson, Rigby, 1980.
Thiele Tales, Rigby, 1980.
The Valley Between, Rigby, 1981.
Little Tom Little, photographs by Simpson, Rigby, 1981.
Songs for My Thongs, Rigby, 1982.
The Undercover Secret, Rigby, 1982.
Pinquo, Rigby, 1983.
Coorong Captive, Rigby, 1985.
Seashores and Shadows, Walter McVitty Books, 1985, published as *Shadow Shark,* Harper, 1988.
Farmer Schulz's Ducks, Walter McVitty Books, 1986.
Shatterbelt, Walter McVitty Books, 1987.
Klontare, Weldon, 1988.
The Ab-Diver, Horwitz, Grahame, 1988.
Jodie's Journey, Walter McVitty Books, 1988.
The March of Mother Duck, Walter McVitty Books, in press.

THE "PITCH, POTCH AND PATCH" STORIES SERIES

Patch Comes Home, Reading Rigby, 1982.
Potch Goes Down the Drain, Reading Rigby, 1984.
Pitch the Pony, Reading Rigby, 1984.

PLAYS

"Burke and Wills" (verse; first performed at Adelaide Radio Drama Festival, 1949), published in full in *On the Air*, edited by P. R. Smith, Angus & Robertson, 1959.
"Edge of Ice" (verse), first performed on radio, 1952.
"The Shark Fishers" (prose), first performed, 1954.
"Edward John Eyre" (verse), first performed at Adelaide Radio Drama Festival, 1962.

Author of other verse plays for radio, and radio and television features, documentaries, children's serials, and schools broadcast programs.

OTHER

National book reviewer for Australian Broadcasting Commission. Thiele's poetry and short stories have appeared in many anthologies and journals; also contributor of articles and reviews to periodicals.

WORK IN PROGRESS: A collection of poems for children, for Omnibus Books.

SIDELIGHTS: Colin Thiele once told *CA:* "One of the tasks of the writer is indeed to 'hold the mirror up to Nature,' to reveal humanity to humanity, to comment on the variousness of the human condition. And although society and the environment in which people live have changed beyond recognition, and will continue to do so, human beings are still human beings. They still show human strengths and human weaknesses—kindness, cruelty, love, malice, wisdom, stupidity, and all the rest. They still suffer loneliness and rejection, still respond to love and compassion, still rise to heights of altruism and nobility, still stoop to depths of pettiness, perfidy, and meanness. In exploring these themes, it doesn't much matter whether the writer uses settings in Sleepy Hollow or at the Crossroads of the World—wherever they are. The universal verities of life can be revealed anywhere because they reside in the hearts of human beings, not in facades of city streets or ephemeral houses. It is to reflect these convictions that I hold up my particular mirror—unpolished and inadequate as it may be."

Thiele's children's books have been translated into numerous languages, including German, Russian, French, Italian, Chinese, Japanese, Afrikaans, Swedish, Finnish, Greek, Danish, Dutch, and Czechoslovakian.

MEDIA ADAPTATIONS: Storm Boy and *Blue Fin* were made into feature films by the South Australian Film Corp. in 1976 and 1978, respectively; *The Fire in the Stone* was made into a television feature by the South Australian Film Corp. in 1983.

BIOGRAPHICAL/CRITICAL SOURCES:

BOOKS

Contemporary Literary Criticism, Volume 17, Gale, 1981.
McVitty, Walter, *Innocence and Experience*, Nelson, 1981.
Something about the Author Autobiography Series, Gale, Volume 2, 1986.

PERIODICALS

Australian Book Review, Children's Supplement, 1964, 1967, 1969.
Books and Bookmen, July, 1968.
Bulletin of the Center for Children's Books, Volume 20, November, 1966.
Childhood Education, December, 1966, April, 1967.

Kirkus Reviews, January 1, 1966.
New York Times Book Review, May 1, 1966, February 23, 1975.
Young Readers Review, September, 1966.

*   *   *

THIMMESCH, Nicholas Palen 1927-1985
(Nick Thimmesch; William Nicholas, joint pseudonym)

PERSONAL: Surname is pronounced Tim-esh; born November 13, 1927, in Dubuque, Iowa; died July 11, 1985 of liver cancer in Chevy Chase, Md., son of Leo Nicholas (a salesman) and Victoria Maria (a teacher; maiden name Glatzmaier) Thimmesch; married Susan Plum, April 18, 1953 (divorced, 1975); children: Nicholas, Elizabeth, Martha, Peter, Michael. *Education:* Iowa State University, B.A., 1950, and graduate study. *Politics:* Independent. *Religion:* Roman Catholic.

ADDRESSES: Home—6301 Broadbranch Rd., Chevy Chase, Md. 20815. *Office*—1150 17th St. N.W., Washington, D.C. 29936.

CAREER: Reporter for the *Davenport* (Iowa) *Times*, 1950-52, and *Des Moines Register*, 1952-55; *Time*, New York City, 1955-67, began as correspondent based in Detroit, New York City, and Washington, D.C., became chief of New York bureau; *Newsday*, Garden City, Long Island, N.Y., chief of Washington bureau, 1967-69; syndicated columnist based in Washington, D.C., 1969-85. Resident journalist, American Enterprise Institute for Public Policy Research, 1981-85. Instructor of communication skills, State University of Iowa, 1953-55. Fellow, Institute of Politics, John F. Kennedy School of Government, Harvard University, 1980-81. Commentator for CBS-TV and CBS-radio, and for Cable News Network, 1981; regularly appeared on NBC's "Meet the Press" and CBS's "Face the Nation." Member of national advisory council, St. John's University, Minn. Boxing judge in Michigan. *Military service:* U.S. Merchant Marine.

MEMBER: H. L. Mencken Society.

WRITINGS:

(With William O. Johnson under joint pseudonym William Nicholas) *The Bobby Kennedy Nobody Knows*, Fawcett, 1967.

ALL UNDER NAME NICK THIMMESCH

(With Johnson) *Robert Kennedy at Forty*, Norton, 1965.
The Condition of Republicanism, Norton, 1968.
(Editor) *Aliteracy: People Who Can Read But Won't*, American Enterprise Institute for Public Policy Research, 1984.

Also editor of "A Liberal Media Elite?," papers from a conference sponsored by American Enterprise Institute for Public Policy Research. Contributor to journals, including *Sports Illustrated*, *New York Times Magazine*, *Esquire*, *Life*, *Cosmopolitan*, and *McCalls*. Contributing editor, *New York* magazine, 1976-78.

OBITUARIES:

PERIODICALS

Chicago Tribune, July 13, 1985.
Los Angeles Times, July 12, 1985.
National Review, August 9, 1985.
New York Times, July 13, 1985.

Washington Post, July 12, 1985.
Washington Times, July 12, 1985.*

*   *   *

THIMMESCH, Nick
   See THIMMESCH, Nicholas Palen

*   *   *

THORP, Willard Long   1899-

PERSONAL: Born May 24, 1899, in Oswego, New York; son of Charles Nicholas (a minister) and Susan Gertrude (Long) Thorp; married Clarice G. Brows (a lawyer), August 21, 1947; children: (previous marriage) Barbara Gerhard, Robin Frazier. *Education:* Amherst College (now), A.B., 1920, University of Michigan, A.M., 1921; Columbia University, Ph.D., 1924. *Religion:* Congregationalist.

ADDRESSES: Home—9 Harkness Rd., Pelham, Mass. 01002.

CAREER: University of Michigan, Ann Arbor, instructor in economics, 1920-21; Amherst College, Amherst, Mass., instructor, 1921-22, professor of economics, 1926-34; Dun & Bradstreet, Inc., New York, N.Y., economist and editor of *Dun's Review,* 1935-40; U.S. Government, Washington, D.C., deputy assistant secretary of state for economic affairs, 1945-46, assistant secretary of state, 1946-52; Amherst College, professor of economics and director of Merrill Center for Economics, 1952-65, acting president, 1957; Organization for Economic Cooperation and Development, chairman of Development Assistance Committee, 1963-68. Distinguished visiting professor, University of Florida, 1971. Staff member, National Bureau of Economic Research, 1923-33, 1956—; chief statistician, New York State Board of Housing, 1925-26; director, U.S. Bureau of Foreign and Domestic Commerce, 1933-34; director of Consumer Affairs Division, National Emergency Council, 1934; chairman of advisory council, National Recovery Act, 1934-35; economic advisor to Secretary of Commerce, 1939-40; trustee, Associated Gas-Electric Corp., 1940-46, Amherst College, 1942-48, 1949-55, and 1956-61, and Brandeis University, 1956-62; member, United States delegation to Paris Peace Conference, 1946; U.S. Representative to United Nations Economic and Social Council, 1947-50; alternate representative, United Nations General Assembly, 1947-48; Chief of United Nations Economic Survey Mission to Cyprus, 1960; member of Board of Governors of President's Special Mission to Bolivia, 1961; member of Commission on Rapid Social Change, World Council of Churches. Member of board of governors, American National Red Cross, 1949-52. *Military service:* U.S. Army, 1918, World War I; became second lieutenant.

MEMBER: American Economic Association (vice president, 1935), American Statistical Association (president, 1947), Social Science Research Council, American Academy of Arts and Sciences (fellow), American Association of University Professors (member of executive council, 1957-60), Council on Foreign Relations, Century Club, Phi Beta Kappa, Chi Phi, Delta Sigma Rho.

AWARDS, HONORS: LL.D. from Marietta College, 1935, Amherst College, Albright College, 1950, University of Massachusetts, 1960, and University of Michigan, 1960; Congregational-Christian Social Action Churchmanship Award, 1950; Distinguished Achievement Medal, Claremont Graduate School, 1984.

WRITINGS:

The Integration of Industrial Operation, U.S. Government Printing Office, 1924.
Business Annals, National Bureau of Economic Research, 1926, reprinted, 1983.
Economic Institutions, Macmillan, 1928.
(With Willard Hotchkiss and D. T. Farnham) *Mergers, Consolidations and Affiliations,* American Management Association, 1929.
(With others) *Controlled and Competitive Enterprise,* American Management Association, 1937.
(Editor) *Economic Problems in a Changing World,* Farrar & Rhinehart, 1939.
Questions Based on Economic Problems, Farrar & Rhinehart, 1939.
The Structure of Industry, U.S. Government Printing Office, 1941.
Elements in European Recovery, U.S. Government Printing Office, 1948.
Aspects of International Petroleum Policy, U.S. Department of State, 1950.
Trade, Aid, or What?, Johns Hopkins Press, 1954.
The Formulation of Foreign Economic Policy, U.S. Government Printing Office, 1957.
(With Richard Quandt) *The New Inflation,* McGraw, 1959.
Cyprus, United Nations, 1961.
(Editor) *The American Assembly: The United Nations and the Far East,* second edition, Prentice-Hall, 1962.
The Reality of Foreign Aid, Praeger, 1971.

Also author of *Development Assistance Efforts and Policies,* annuals published by Organization for Economic Cooperation and Development, 1963-67.

*   *   *

TILLARD, Jean-M(arie) Roger   1927-

PERSONAL: Born September 2, 1927, in St. Pierre, France; came to Canada, 1959; son of Ferdinand and Madeleine (Ferron) Tillard. *Education:* Universite Angelicum, Rome, T.Ph.D., 1953; Universite le Saulchoir, Paris, Ph.D., 1958; Magisterium in Sacred Divinity, Rome, 1963. *Religion:* Roman Catholic.

ADDRESSES: Office—Faculte de Theologie, 96 Empress, Ottawa, Ontario, Canada K1R 7G3.

CAREER: Entered Roman Catholic Order of Preachers (Dominican), 1950; ordained priest, 1957; Dominican Faculte de Theologie, Ottawa, Ontario, assistant professor, 1959-60, associate professor, 1960-64, professor of divinity, 1964—. Visiting professor at University of Brussels, 1969—, Oxford University, and Universities of Fribourg, Quebec, Nottingham, and Geneva. Consultant to Vatican Secretariate for Christian Unity, 1968—; consultor of Vatican Secretariate for ecumenism.

MEMBER: International Commission of Theology, International Roman Catholic and Anglican Joint Commission, International Roman Catholic and Orthodox Commission, Faith and Order (vice-president).

AWARDS, HONORS: Ph.D. in Divinity, Trinity College, Toronto, 1980; Ph.D. in Theology, St. Michael's University, 1983.

WRITINGS:

L'Eucharistie Paque de l'Eglise, Cerf (Paris), 1964, translation by Dennis L. Wienk published as *The Eucharist: Pasch of God's People,* Alba House, 1967.

Le sacrement, evenement du salut, La Pensee Catholique (Brussels), 1964.

En alliance avec Dieu, Desclee de Brouwer (Paris), 1964.

(Editor with Yves Marie Joseph Congar) *Adaptation et renovation de la vie religieuse,* Cerf, 1967.

The Mystery of Religious Life (essays), edited by R. F. Smith, B. Herder, 1967.

Le Salut, mystere de pauvrete, Cerf, 1968.

Le religieux au coeur de l'Eglise, Cerf, 1969.

Religieux, aujourd'hui, Lumen Vitae (Brussels), 1969.

(With Jean Zizioulas and Jean-Jacques von Allmen) *L'Eucharistie,* Mame (Paris), 1971.

Religieux, un chemin d'evangile, 2nd edition, Lumen Vitae, 1975, translation by Olga Prendergast published as *A Gospel Path: The Religious Life,* 1975.

Devant Dieu et pour le monde: Le projet des religieux, Cerf, 1975.

(With others) *Foi populaire, foi savante: Actes du Ve. Colloque du Centre d'etudes d'histoire des religions populaires tenu au College dominican de theologie,* Cerf, 1976.

Il y a charisme et charisme: La vie religieuse, Lumen Vitae, 1977, translation by Prendergast published as *There Are Charisms and Charisms: The Religious Life,* 1977.

Appel du Christ, appels du monde: Les religieux relisent leur appel, Cerf, 1978.

L'eveque de Rome, Cerf, 1982, translation published as *The Bishop of Rome,* Michael Glazier, 1983.

Dilemmas of Modern Religious Life, Michael Glazier, 1984.

Eglise d'eglises: L'ecclesiologie de communion, Cerf, 1987.

Contributor to *Nouvelle Revue Theologique, La Maison Dieu, One in Christ,* and *La Vie Spirituelle.*

*   *   *

TOBIAS, Ronald B(enjamin)   1948-

PERSONAL: Born October 25, 1948, in Newark, N.J.; son of Irving R. (an attorney) and Elise (Jorish) Bean; married Valerie Jonsson, June 5, 1982. *Education:* Kansas State University, B.A., 1969; Bowling Green State University, M.F.A., 1971.

ADDRESSES: Home—8003 Pinon Place, Bozeman, Mont. 59717. *Office*—Department of Film and Television, Montana State University, Bozeman, Mont. 59717. *Agent*—George R. Walden, 170 East 77th St., New York, N.Y. 10021.

CAREER: Bowling Green State University, Bowling Green, Ohio, instructor in writing and literature, 1971-74; Virginia Commonwealth University, Richmond, instructor in writing and literature, 1975-78; University of Texas at Dallas, associate professor of writing and translation and writer in residence, 1978-88; Montana State University, Bozeman, professor of cinematography, 1988—.

MEMBER: Associated Writing Programs, American Literary Translators Association.

WRITINGS:

(Contributor) *Itinerary* (anthology), Bowling Green State University Press, 1977.

They Shoot to Kill: A Psychological Survey of Criminal Sniping, Paladin Press, 1981.

(Contributor) *Contemporary Writing from the Continents* (anthology), Ohio University Press, 1981.

(With Diego C. and Nancy Asencio) *Our Man Is Inside: Outmaneuvering the Terrorists,* Little, Brown, 1983.

(With D. Asencio) *Terror in the Embassy,* Editorial Norma (Bogota), 1984.

Kings and Desperate Men, Beyond Baroque Press, 1985.

Strategy in Fiction and Film, Writers Digest Books, 1989.

Contributor of articles, fiction, poetry, translations, and reviews to periodicals, including *Penthouse, Descant, Chelsea, Field & Stream, Boston Globe,* and *Maine Times.*

BIOGRAPHICAL/CRITICAL SOURCES:

PERIODICALS

Dallas Morning News, October 17, 1980, April 1, 1981.
Detroit Free Press, May 14, 1981.
Los Angeles Herald Examiner, May 29, 1983.
Newsweek, May 2, 1983.
Philadelphia Enquirer, May 2, 1983.
San Francisco Chronicle, April 3, 1983.
Washington Post, April 3, 1983.
Washington Post Book World, February 13, 1983.

*   *   *

TODD, Janet M(argaret)   1942-

PERSONAL: Born September 10, 1942, in Wales; daughter of George and Elizabeth (Jones) Dakin; married Aaron R. Todd (a professor of mathematics), December 21, 1966; children: Julian, Clara. *Education:* Cambridge University, B.A., 1964; University of Leeds, diploma, 1968; University of Florida, Ph.D., 1971.

ADDRESSES: Office—Sidney Sussex College, Cambridge CB2 3HU, England.

CAREER: School teacher in Cape Coast, Ghana, 1964-65; University College of Cape Coast, Cape Coast, Ghana, lecturer in English, 1965-66; English teacher in Bawku, Ghana, 1966-67; University of Puerto Rico, Mayaguez, assistant professor of English, 1972-74; Rutgers University, Douglass College, New Brunswick, N.J., assistant professor, 1974-78, associate professor, 1978-81, professor of English, 1981-83; Sidney Sussex College, Cambridge, England, fellow in English, 1983—. Visiting professor, University of Southampton, 1982-83, and Jawarharlal Nehru University, New Delhi, and University of Rajasthan, 1988.

MEMBER: Modern Language Association of America, Women's Caucus of Modern Languages, American Society of Eighteenth Century Studies, Jane Austen Society.

AWARDS, HONORS: ACLS Award, 1978-79; Guggenheim fellowship, 1981-82.

WRITINGS:

In Adam's Garden: A Study of John Clare's Pre-Asylum Poetry, University of Florida Press, 1973.

Mary Wollstonecraft: An Annotated Bibliography, Garland Publishing, 1976.

(Editor) *A Wollstonecraft Anthology,* Indiana University Press, 1977.

Women's Friendship in Literature, Columbia University Press, 1980.

(Editor) *Gender and Literary Voice,* Holmes & Meier, 1980.

(Editor) *Jane Austen: New Perspectives*, Holmes & Meier, 1983.

(Co-author) *English Congregational Hymns in the Eighteenth Century*, University of Kentucky Press, 1983.

(Editor) *A Dictionary of British and American Women Writers 1660-1800*, Methuen, 1986.

Feminist Literary History, Polity Press and Routledge, 1988.

The Sign of Angellica: Women, Writing and Fiction, 1660-1800, Virago, 1989.

SIDELIGHTS: Much of Janet M. Todd's scholarly writing concerns literature by and about women. About her *Feminist Literary History*, for example, Barbara Hardy writes in the *Times Literary Supplement:* "Janet Todd's lucid, common-sensical and tolerant study of feminism is markedly attentive to history, in a defence of the American socio-historical tradition, and in her own emphasis on historicism." Finding that the book "takes in more than its central subject," Todd adds: "Admirable, too, is her political reminder of that feminism which lies outside the theory and practice of literary criticism."

Todd told *CA:* "I am concerned with bringing women writers into the mainstream of English literary history and of reevaluating established literature according to a feminist perspective. I am especially interested in the late eighteenth and early nineteenth century because so many of our cultural attitudes were then being formed."

BIOGRAPHICAL/CRITICAL SOURCES:

PERIODICALS

Times Literary Supplement, June 20, 1980, July 26, 1985, February 27, 1987, June 3-9, 1988.

*   *   *

TOPAZ, Jacqueline
   See HYMAN, Jackie (Diamond)

*   *   *

TOPOLSKI, Daniel   1945-

PERSONAL: Born June 4, 1945, in London, England; son of Feliks (an artist) and Marion (an actress; maiden name, Everall) Topolski. *Education:* New College, Oxford, B.A., 1967, diploma in social anthropology, 1968.

ADDRESSES: Home—69 Randolph Ave., London W 9, England. *Agent*—Blake Friedmann, 42 Bloomsbury St., London WC1B 3QJ, England.

CAREER: British Broadcasting Corp., London, England, assistant producer in current affairs and arts, 1969-72, conducted research expedition to Iran, 1973; free-lance journalist, 1973—. Rower and coach of British team for World Rowing Championship, 1969—; coach of Oxford University's rowing crew for Boat Race on the Thames, 1973-87; national rowing coach and coordinator of Great Britain's Women's Olympic Rowing Team, 1979-80.

MEMBER: Royal Geographical Society (fellow), London Rowing Club, Leander Rowing Club.

AWARDS, HONORS: Churchill fellow of Winston Churchill Memorial Trust, 1980.

WRITINGS:

PHOTOGRAPHER

Muzungu: One Man's Africa, Arlington Books, 1976.

(Editor) *The Francis Chichester Guide to London*, Francis Chichester, 1977.

Travels with My Father: A South American Journey, Elm Tree, 1983.

Boat Race: The Oxford Revival, Collins, 1985.

(Contributor) *Book of the Best*, Faber, 1987.

True Blue, Doubleday, 1989.

OTHER

Rowing reporter for *London Standard*. Contributor of articles and photographs to periodicals and newspapers, including *You*, *New Society*, *Sports*, *Radio Times*, *Daily Mail*, and *London Telegraph*.

SIDELIGHTS: Daniel Topolski is best known as a world-class oarsman and senior coach for the Oxford University Boat Crew from 1973 to 1987. He told *CA* that he started coaching the team "at a time when they were suffering a long string of defeats. Since 1974 they have lost their annual race but twice (as of 1988—I finished last year after a record sequence of ten wins in a row) and it was this revival that prompted Collins to ask me to write a personal, behind-the-scenes account of those years. After 25 competitive years and a World Gold medal, I continue to row myself partly for my own satisfaction, fitness, and pleasure and partly to keep myself in touch with what I am asking my rowers to do."

Topolski's book *Boat Race: The Oxford Revival* is an account of the author's experiences as the Oxford coach. "With some flair as a writer," comments Ian Thomson in a *Times Literary Supplement* article about *Boat Race*, "he explains how success resulted from obsession, how deep a psychological change came over Oxford rowing when he was invited to put the finishing touches to successive Oxford crews and how he set to work to develop elitism in oarsmanship." Thomson concludes: "A few incidents are reported and remarks made that are unworthy of British rowing; but, those apart, this book is factually detailed and eminently readable." London *Times* contributor Alan Gibson writes that *Boat Race* "is partisan, as [Topolski's] very title declares, but it is vigorously and entertainingly written."

Topolski has also written several books concerning his travels throughout the world, about which he told *CA:* "When I write about my journeys I combine my visual information, in the old-fashioned travelers' way, with commentary on geography, anthropology, sociology, and the human and political scene. The purpose is to provide an overall view of the people I meet and the places I see en route. My travelling has taken me to China, South East Asia, East and central Africa, India, Japan, the Middle East, the Himalayas, all of South America and North America, and East and West Europe. Each day of traveling is a highlight, since I travel close to the ground so to speak, on local transport and living away from the hotel circuits. It is this side of life that is reflected in the books I write, a very personal reaction to the daily habits of the people I see and meet, as well as my own efforts to cope with what is going on around me, socially, visually, politically, physically."

AVOCATIONAL INTERESTS: Theatre, film, world affairs, travel, rowing, marathon running, and sports in general.

BIOGRAPHICAL/CRITICAL SOURCES:

PERIODICALS

Financial Weekly, March 27, 1980.
London Telegraph, April 1, 1980.
New Yorker, April 7, 1980.
Times (London), March 27, 1983, April 4, 1985.
Times Literary Supplement, November 15, 1985.

*   *   *

TORDAY, Ursula 1888-
(Paula Allardyce, Charity Blackstock, Lee Blackstock, Charlotte Keppel)

PERSONAL: Born in 1888 in London, England; daughter of Emil (an anthropologist) and Caia (Macdonell) Torday. *Education:* Attended London School of Economics; Oxford University, B.A., 1935. *Politics:* "Left."

ADDRESSES: Home—23 Montagu Mansions, London W1H 1LD, England. *Agent*—John Johnson, Clerkenwell House, 45-47 Clerkenwell Green, London EC1R 0HT, England.

CAREER: Novelist. Worked as a secretary; assisted in the placement of Jewish refugee children, 1947-54.

WRITINGS:

(Under pseudonym Charity Blackstock) *Miss Fenny,* Hodder & Stoughton, 1957, (paperback edition), Nordon, 1978, published under pseudonym Lee Blackstock as *The Woman in the Woods,* Doubleday, 1958.

UNDER PSEUDONYM PAULA ALLARDYCE

After the Lady, Ward, Lock, 1954.
The Doctor's Daughter, Ward, Lock, 1955, reprinted, Severn House, 1975.
Game of Hazard, Ward, Lock, 1955.
Adam and Evelina, Ward, Lock, 1956, reprinted, Severn House, 1975.
The Man of Wrath, Ward, Lock, 1956.
The Lady and the Pirate, Ward, Lock, 1957.
Southarn Folly, Ward, Lock, 1957, reprinted, Severn House, 1975.
Beloved Enemy, Ward, Lock, 1957, reprinted, Severn House, 1976.
My Dear Miss Emma, Ward, Lock, 1958, reprinted, Playboy Press, 1980.
A Marriage Has Been Arranged, Ward, Lock, 1959, reprinted, Severn House, 1976.
Johnny Danger, Ward, Lock, 1960, published as *Rebel Lover,* Playboy Press, 1979.
The Gentle Highwayman, Ward, Lock, 1961.
Witches' Sabbath, Hodder & Stoughton, 1961, Macmillan, 1962.
Adam's Rib, Hodder & Stoughton, 1963, published as *Legacy of Pride,* Dell, 1975.
The Respectable Miss Parkington-Smith, Hodder & Stoughton, 1964, published as *Paradise Row,* Dell, 1976.
Octavia; or, The Trials of a Romantic Novelist, Hodder & Stoughton, 1965.
The Moonlighters, Hodder & Stoughton, 1967.
Six Passengers for the Sweet Bird, Hodder & Stoughton, 1967.
Waiting at the Church, Hodder & Stoughton, 1968, published as *Emily,* Dell, 1976.
The Ghost of Archie Gilroy, Hodder & Stoughton, 1970, published as *Shadowed Love,* Dell, 1977.

Miss Jonas's Boy, Hodder & Stoughton, 1972.
The Gentle Sex, Hodder & Stoughton, 1974, published as *The Carradine Affair,* Playboy Press, 1976.
Miss Philadelphia Smith, Coward, McCann, 1977.
The Rogue's Lady, Playboy Press, 1978.
Haunting Me, St. Martin's, 1979.
The Vixen's Revenge, Playboy Press, 1980.

UNDER PSEUDONYM CHARITY BLACKSTOCK

Dewey Death (also see below), Heinemann, 1956.
The Foggy, Foggy Dew (also see below), Hodder & Stoughton, 1958.
Dewey Death, and the Foggy, Foggy Dew (introduction by Anthony Boucher), House & Maxwell, 1959.
The Bitter Conquest, Hodder & Stoughton, 1959.
The Briar Patch, Hodder & Stoughton, 1960.
The Exorcism, Hodder & Stoughton, 1961, published as *A House Possessed,* Lippincott, 1962, reprinted, Queens House, 1978.
The Gallant, Hodder & Stoughton, 1962, reprinted, Remploy, 1977.
Mr. Christopoulos, Hodder & Stoughton, 1963.
The English Wife, Coward, McCann, 1964 (published in England as *The Factor's Wife,* Hodder & Stoughton, 1964).
Monkey on a Chain, Coward, McCann, 1965 (published in England as *When the Sun Goes Down,* Hodder & Stoughton, 1965).
The Children (nonfiction), Little, Brown, 1966 (published in England as *Wednesday's Children,* Hutchinson, 1967).
The Knock at Midnight, Hodder & Stoughton, 1966, Coward, McCann, 1967.
The Widow, Coward, McCann, 1967 (published in England as *Party in Dolly Creek,* Hodder & Stoughton, 1967).
The Lemmings, Coward, McCann, 1969 (published in England as *The Melon in the Cornfield,* Hodder & Stoughton, 1969).
The Daughter, Coward, McCann, 1970.
The Encounter, Coward, McCann, 1971.
The Jungle, Coward, McCann, 1972.
The Lonely Strangers, Coward, McCann, 1972.
People in Glass Houses, Coward, McCann, 1975.
Ghost Town, Coward, McCann, 1976.
The Shirt Front, Coward, McCann, 1977 (published in England as *I Met Murder on the Way,* Hodder & Stoughton, 1977).
Miss Charley, Hodder & Stoughton, 1979.
With Fondest Thoughts, Hodder & Stoughton, 1980.
Dream Towers, Hodder & Stoughton, 1981.

UNDER PSEUDONYM LEE BLACKSTOCK

All Men Are Murderers, Doubleday, 1958 (published in England as *The Shadow of Murder,* Hodder & Stoughton, 1959).

UNDER PSEUDONYM CHARLOTTE KEPPEL

Madam, You Must Die, Hodder & Stoughton, 1974.
When I Say Goodbye, I'm Clary Brown, Hodder & Stoughton, 1977.
The Villains: A Haunting Tale of the Marshes, Piatkus, 1980, St. Martin's, 1981.
I Could Be Good to You, St. Martin's, 1980.
The Ghosts of Fontenoy, Piatkus, 1981.

SIDELIGHTS: Ursula Torday once told *CA:* "I have always done rather wild and crazy things, usually without any premeditation. I suppose the craziest was interviewing the King and Queen of Thailand: I daresay they were as startled as I was.

"I also interviewed the late President Makarios, with his private gunmen standing against the wall in case my hand strayed to my handbag. Later, when less mobile, I did a lot of cruising, which I always enjoy in a lazy and sybaritic manner: I used to adore the Caribbean but now it has become too touristy for me.

"My main thing, however, was working for seven years with Jewish children from the concentration camps. I am a goy but have become the best assimilated Jew in existence. After the war I was roped into a scheme run by the Rothschilds for bringing these children over from the homes in France and Belgium to stay for a while with Jewish families here. No one in his senses would think of placing damaged and neurotic young people with ordinary middle-class housewives. It was rather like my interviewing; I simply charged in, knowing nothing about anything and armed with precious little but chutzpah and determination—certainly not money, for we were always broke. We never had a disaster and afterwards I worked in the homes themselves. It was a long time ago and my 'children' are now nearly fifty. I wrote a nonfiction book on this, *The Children*, and have used the theme for several novels."

AVOCATIONAL INTERESTS: Travelling.

*   *   *

TOWNSEND, Peter (Wooldridge)   1914-

PERSONAL: Born November 22, 1914, in Rangoon, Burma; son of Edward Copleston (a lieutenant colonel, Indian Army, and a member of Burma Legislative Council) and Gladys (Hatt-Cook) Townsend; married Rosemary Pawle, 1941 (divorced, 1952); married Marie-Luce Jamagne, 1959; children: (first marriage) Giles, Hugo; (second marriage) Marie-Isabelle, Marie-Francoise, Pierre. *Education:* Attended Haileybury College and Royal Air Force College. *Religion:* Church of England.

ADDRESSES: Home—La Mare aux Oiseaux, 78610 Saint Leger-en-Yvelines, France.

CAREER: Royal Air Force, 1935-56, pilot in fighter squadron, 1935-36, pilot in torpedo squadron, Singapore, 1936-37, commander of fighter squadron during Battle of Britain, 1939-41, equerry to King George VI, 1944-52, deputy master of the Royal household, 1950, equerry to Queen Elizabeth II, 1952-53, air attache in Brussels, Belgium, 1953-56, retired as group captain (colonel), 1956; full-time author and journalist, 1956—.

AWARDS, HONORS: Military—Distinguished Service Order, 1941; Distinguished Flying Cross and bar; mentioned in dispatches. Civilian—Commander of Royal Victorian Order, 1947; Officer of Legion of Honor (France); Officer of Order of Orange Nassau (Netherlands); Chevalier of Order of Dannebrog.

WRITINGS:

Earth, My Friend (autobiographical travelogue), Hodder & Stoughton, 1959, Coward, 1960.
Un Duel d'aigles: R.A.F. contre Luftwaffe, Laffont, 1969, published as *Duel of Eagles,* Simon & Schuster, 1970.
The Last Emperor: Decline and Fall of the British Empire, Weidenfeld & Nicolson, 1975, published as *The Last Emperor: An Intimate Account of George VI and the Fall of His Empire,* Simon & Schuster, 1976.
Time and Chance: An Autobiography, Collins, 1978.
The Smallest Pawns in the Game, Granada, 1980.

The Girl in the White Ship, Collins, 1981, Holt, 1983.
The Postman of Nagasaki, Collins, 1984.
Duel in the Dark, Harrap, 1986, published as *The Odds against Us,* Morrow, 1987.

Contributor of articles to newspapers and magazines.

SIDELIGHTS: Peter Townsend's first book, *Earth, My Friend,* resulted from a global tour which covered 57,000 miles and took almost two years to complete. Since then Townsend has written of the global experiences of war, covering both his own adventure as a pilot in World War II as well as its side effects, ranging from displacement, boat people, nuclear trauma, and the torture of children. in *Duel of Eagles,* Townsend "refights the Battle of Britain both as participant and historian, mixing anecdote and analysis in a narrative that is taut and thrilling on some pages," comments Allen R. Dodd, Jr., in *Saturday Review.* Townsend brings a fresh perspective to his account, for not only does he use his own memories as a squadron leader, but also those of the German pilots he fought, including some who were both on the giving and receiving ends of gunfire exchanges with Townsend. Calling the book "diligently researched and modestly related," *New York Times Book Review* contributor Len Deighton observes that Townsend's "talks with German aircrews give his book a vibrancy that most history lacks." A *Times Literary Supplement* writer offers a similar opinion: "By blending the English and German perspectives and faithfully researching all the available sources, the author has produced an unusually intimate story of the greatest air battle in history as well as accounting for the factors that determined its outcome." But Townsend uses analyses of the events of the Battle of Britain as well, including accounts of the decisions by the British and German commanders. While Dodd remarks that "the analytical view is always a product of hindsight," he notes that Townsend's inclusion of personal portraits are essential to this view: "Without these glimpses, without knowing what people thought they were fighting for, one cannot arrive at an accurate judgment of the results. In this respect *Duel of Eagles* has an authenticity that makes it a valuable addition to the literature [of the Battle of Britain]."

Townsend similarly seeks out first-hand accounts for his book *The Smallest Pawns in the Game,* a book which documents the centuries-long practice of brutalizing children during wartime. The author first uses examples from ancient history and progresses to postwar stories of children in Africa, South America, the Mideast, and the Far East, among other places. "It was a terribly tough assignment," Townsend told Susan Heller Anderson in the *New York Times.* "At times I was so moved I couldn't continue. But then I got more professional, more blase." This attitude is reflected in his approach, for "wisely, Townsend for the most part lets [the] facts, and, wherever possible, the victims, speak for themselves," states *Times Literary Supplement* contributor Nesta Roberts. Nevertheless, Townsend "does not allow you to escape into the unreal world of TV war," remarks Jean C. Young in the *Washington Post.* "He vividly describes the atrocities of war, focusing on what it can do to children." As Townsend related to Anderson, "everywhere I was impressed by the children's dignity, their longing for revenge, sometimes their forgiveness."

The plight of Vietnam's boat people also made an impression upon the author, for in *The Girl in the White Ship* Townsend focuses on the story of Hue Hue, the only survivor of a boatload of fifty Vietnamese who died en route to Malaysia. Again, "the author's style is purely functional, spare and unadorned," writes the *Los Angeles Times*'s Elaine Kendall. This plain style gives the story a greater power, asserts Kendall, for the author "leans on human similarities until all strangeness melts; the distance between us vanishes, and this South Vietnamese family becomes as familiar and understandable as the neighbors across the street." Bringing the stories of these kind of victims is Townsend's goal; Anderson reports him as saying, "One or two people have told me they couldn't read [*The Smallest Pawns*]. In a way that's who the book is for." The author added that these books "aren't political analysis. They are a record. Doing them has been very moving and extremely humbling. It filled me with admiration for these children. I am their witness."

BIOGRAPHICAL/CRITICAL SOURCES:

PERIODICALS

Los Angeles Times, February 10, 1983.
New York Times, August 24, 1980.
New York Times Book Review, January 31, 1971, December 19, 1980.
Saturday Review, March 13, 1971.
Spectator, February 18, 1978.
Times Literary Supplement, October 23, 1970, March 10, 1978, December 19, 1980.
Washington Post, September 27, 1980.
Washington Post Book World, March 1, 1987.

*　　*　　*

TREAHEARNE, Elizabeth
See MAXWELL, Patricia

*　　*　　*

TRIPP, Miles (Barton) 1923-
(John Michael Brett, Michael Brett)

PERSONAL: Born May 5, 1923, in Ganwick Corner, near Barnet, England; son of Cecil Lewis and Brena Mary (Yells) Tripp. *Education:* Attended county school in Hertfordshire.

CAREER: Free-lance writer.

MEMBER: Society of Authors (England), Crime Writers Association (England; chairman, 1968-69).

WRITINGS:

Faith Is a Windsock, P. Davies, 1952.
The Image of Man, Darwen Finlayson, 1955.
A Glass of Red Wine, Macdonald and Co., 1960.
Kilo Forty, Macmillan, 1963, Holt, 1964.
(Under pseudonym Michael Brett) *Diecast*, Fawcett, 1963, published under pseudonym John Michael Brett, Pan Books, 1966.
The Skin Dealer, Holt, 1964.
(Under psuedonym Michael Brett) *A Plague of Dragons*, Arthur Barker, 1965, published under pseudonym John Michael Brett, Pan Books, 1966.
A Quartet of Three, Macmillan, 1965.
The Chicken (also see below), Macmillan, 1966.
(Under pseudonym John Michael Brett) *A Cargo of Spent Evil*, Arthur Barker, 1966.
The Fifth Point of the Compass, Macmillan, 1967.
One Is One, Macmillan, 1968.
The Chicken [and] *Zilla*, Pan Books, 1968.

Malice and the Maternal Instinct, Macmillan, 1969.
The Eighth Passenger, Heinemann, 1969.
A Man without Friends (also see below), Macmillan, 1970.
Five Minutes with a Stranger, Macmillan, 1971.
The Claws of God, Macmillan, 1972.
Obsession, Macmillan, 1973.
Woman at Risk, Macmillan, 1974.
A Woman in Bed, Macmillan, 1976.
The Once a Year Man, Macmillan, 1977.
The Wife-Smuggler, Macmillan, 1978.
Cruel Victim, Macmillan, 1979.
High Heels, Macmillan, 1980.
Going Solo, Macmillan, 1981.
One Lover Too Many, Macmillan, 1983.
A Charmed Death, Macmillan, 1984.
Some Predators Are Male, Macmillan, 1985.
Death of a Man-Tamer, Macmillan, 1987.
The Frightened Wife, Macmillan, 1987.

Also author of television adaptation "A Man without Friends," based on his novel, broadcast in England, 1972.

*　　*　　*

TROBISCH, Ingrid (Hult) 1926-

PERSONAL: Born February 17, 1926, in Moshi, Tanzania; daughter of Ralph Daniel (a Lutheran minister and missionary) and Gertrude (a teacher; maiden name, Jacobson) Hult; married Walter Trobisch (a writer and counselor), June 2, 1952 (died October, 1979); children: Katrine Trobisch Stewart, Daniel, David, Stephen, Ruth. *Education:* Augustana College, Rock Island, Ill., B.A., 1947; Sorbonne, University of Paris, M.A., 1951. *Religion:* Lutheran.

ADDRESSES: Home—2840 Natural Bridge, Springfield, Mo. 65804.

CAREER: Missionary and teacher in Cameroun, 1953-63; teacher of courses on marriage in Third World countries, 1963-69; marriage and family counselor in St. Georgen, Austria, and lecturer in Australia, Indonesia, New Guinea, Africa, and the United States, 1969—.

WRITINGS:

On Our Way Rejoicing, Harper, 1964, reprinted, Tyndale, 1986.
(With Jean Banyolak) *Better Is Thy Love Than Wine*, Inter-Varsity Press, 1972.
The Joy of Being a Woman, Harper, 1975.
(With husband, Walter Trobisch) *My Beautiful Feeling* (also see below), Inter-Varsity Press, 1977.
(With Elizabeth Roetzer) *An Experience of Love*, Fleming H. Revell, 1981.
(With Roetzer) *Bright Legacy—Ten Women*, Servant Press, 1983.
Learning to Walk Alone: Personal Reflections on a Time of Grief, Servant Books, 1985.
(With W. Trobisch) *The Misunderstood Man: Why Men Suffer and What Can Be Done about It*, Inter-Varsity Press, 1983, published as *All a Man Can Be and What a Woman Should Know* (also see below), 1986.
(Editor) *My Journey Homeward* (collection of late husband W. Trobisch's letters), Servant Books, 1986.
(Contributor of introduction and biography) *The Complete Works of Walter Trobisch: Answers about Love, Sex, Self-Esteem, and Personal Growth* (includes *I Loved a Girl, Love Is A Feeling to Be Learned, Living with Unfulfilled De-*

sires, My Beautiful Feeling, My Parents Are Impossible, I Married You, My Wife Made Me a Polygamist, A Baby Just Now?, All a Man Can Be, Love Yourself, Spiritual Dryness and *Martin Luther's Quiet Time*), Inter-Varsity Press, 1987.

The Hidden Strength: Rooted in the Security of God's Love, Here's Life Publishers, 1988.

SIDELIGHTS: Ingrid Trobisch once told *CA:* "My books have been written to supplement those of my husband, one of which, *I Loved a Girl,* has been translated into seventy languages. All my books have been translated into the major European languages. We both [have sought] to bring a positive message on marriage and family life in today's world."

More recently, she added, "My professional life, as a Family Life counselor and author, has been strongly intertwined with that of my late husband, Walter Trobisch. I have done the translation of his German and French manuscripts into English and after his early death, have completed some of his unfinished manuscripts, namely *The Misunderstood Man* [later edition published as *All A Man Can Be*]. I also compiled the book *My Journey Homeward,* taken from his letters. An important collection of all of Walter Trobisch's books was published in 1987 by Inter-Varsity Press. I wrote the opening chapter, the biography of Walter Trobisch, for this collection. All of our books have been published in the major European languages as well as several African languages. We have written for readers all over the world."

*   *   *

TRUSSLER, Simon   1942-

PERSONAL: Born June 11, 1942, in Tenterden, Kent, England; son of John and Joan (Ovenden) Trussler; married Glenda Leeming (a lecturer), August 23, 1966 (divorced, 1983); married Laverne Anderson, August 29, 1984; children: (first marriage) two; (second marriage) one. *Education:* University College, London, B.A., 1963, M.A., 1966. *Politics:* Radical.

ADDRESSES: Home—Great Robhurst, Woodchurch, Ashford, Kent, England. *Office*—Goldsmiths College, University of London, Lewisham Way, New Cross, London SE14 6NW, England.

CAREER: Lecturer in English at Hammersmith College of Art, London, England, 1963-65, and Enfield College of Technology, London, 1965-67; London drama critic, *Drama Review,* 1963-70; *Tribune,* London, drama critic, 1965-73; Tufts University, London Programme, London, lecturer in drama, 1973-81; University of London, Goldsmiths College, London, senior lecturer in drama, 1986—. Lecturer in drama, Oxford University Delegacy for Extra-Mural Studies. Visiting professor of drama, University of California, Santa Barbara, 1983; visiting lecturer in drama, University of Kent, 1984-86. Founding member of Board of Management, British Theatre Institute, 1975; associate director, British Centre of the International Theatre Institute, 1979.

WRITINGS:

(Editor with Charles Marowitz) *Theatre at Work,* Methuen, 1967, Hill & Wang, 1968.
(Editor) *New English Dramatists XIII,* Penguin, 1968.
(Editor) *Burlesque Plays of the Eighteenth Century,* Oxford University Press, 1969.

(Author of an introduction and notes) William Duncan Taylor, compiler, *Eighteenth Century Comedy,* Oxford University Press, 1969.
The Plays of John Osborne: An Assessment, Gollancz, 1969.
(With Glenda Leeming) *The Plays of Arnold Wesker: An Assessment,* Gollancz, 1972.
John Arden, Columbia University Press, 1973.
The Plays of Harold Pinter: An Assessment, Gollancz, 1973.
A Classification for the Performing Arts, British Theatre Institute, 1974.
Edward Bond, Longman, 1976.
Theatre Checklist: David Edgar, TQ Publications, 1979.
(Compiler) *Royal Shakespeare Company* (annual), Royal Shakespeare Company, 1979—.
(Editor) *New Theatre Voices of the Seventies,* Eyre Methuen, 1981.
(Editor) *Twentieth-Century Drama,* Macmillan, 1982.
(Commissioning editor) *Oxford Companion to the Theatre,* 4th edition, Oxford University Press, 1983.
Shakespearean Concepts, Methuen, 1989.

Contributor of commentaries to four volumes in the "Methuen Student Editions" series, Methuen, 1983-87, and to eleven volumes in the "Swan Theatre Plays" series, Methuen, 1986-88. Editor of "Writer-Files" series, Methuen, 1985. Contributor to periodicals, including *Plays and Players, Times, Teacher, London Magazine, Flourish,* and *Listener.* Founding editor, *Prompt,* 1962, *Theatre Quarterly,* 1971, and *Theatre International,* 1981. Editor of *Encore,* 1965, *Theatrefacts,* 1974, and *New Theatre Quarterly,* 1985—.

WORK IN PROGRESS: Editing the complete edition of the theatrical writings of Kenneth Tynan.

*   *   *

TULLY, John (Kimberley)   1923-

PERSONAL: Born July 7, 1923, in Sutton Coldfield, England; son of John (an actor) and Ruby (an actress; maiden name, Kimberley) Tully; married Margaret Else; children: Richard, David, Katharine, Diana. *Education:* Attended schools in North Wales.

ADDRESSES: Home—209 Jersey Rd., Isleworth, Middlesex TW7 4RE, England.

CAREER: Began writing for newspapers, later turned to film, television, and books. *Military service:* Royal Air Force, 1940-45; became flight sergeant.

MEMBER: Writers Guild of Great Britain (vice-chairman, 1976-77; joint chairman, 1977-78).

WRITINGS:

Woman Alive (play), Evans Brothers, 1958.
The Crocodile (juvenile; also see below), BBC Publications, 1972.
The Raven and the Cross (juvenile; also see below), BBC Publications, 1974.
The Glass Knife (juvenile), Methuen, 1974.
The White Cat (juvenile), Methuen, 1975.
"The Man from Nowhere" (film script), Children's Film Foundation, 1976.
"One Hour to Zero" (film script), Children's Film Foundation, 1976.
Johnny Goodlooks (juvenile), Methuen, 1977.
Inspector Holt and the Fur Van, Collins English Library, 1977.

Inspector Holt Gets His Man, Collins English Library, 1977.
Johnny and the Yank (juvenile), Methuen, 1978.
Muhammad Ali: King of the Ring, Collins English Library, 1978.
Where Is Bill Ojo?, Collins English Library, 1978.
The Bridge, Collins English Library, 1979.
Cats in the Dark, Collins English Library, 1980.
Inspector Holt and the Chinese Necklace, Collins English Library, 1984.
Natfact 7 (young adult), Methuen, 1984.
Slade (novel), Methuen, 1985.
The Man with Three Fingers, Collins English Library, 1987.

"STARPOL" SERIES; JUVENILES

Hunter 5, Ginn, Books 1-4, 1984, Books 5-8, 1985.
Hunter 3, Books 1-6, Ginn, 1987.
Hunter 4, Books 1-6, Ginn, 1988.

OTHER

Author of television serials, including "The Viaduct," 1972, "Thursday's Child," 1973, "Tom's Midnight Garden," 1974, "Kizzy," 1976, "The Phoenix and the Carpet," 1977, "Countdown," "Maths Counts," and "Mathspy"; also author of documentary films for Shell Oil Co., British Gas Council, Midland Bank, Mobil Oil Corp., Amoco Oil Co., British Electricity Council, British Central Electricity Generating Board, British Aerospace, and Services Sound & Vision Corp. Writer of television plays, including "The Crocodile," "The Raven and the Cross," "The King of Argos," "A Choice of Friends," "The Jo-Jo Tree," and "The Silver Fish." Also contributor to television series, including "Going to Work," "Exploring Science," and "Merry-Go-Round."

WORK IN PROGRESS: A novel, *Wilf's War.*

SIDELIGHTS: John Tully told *CA:* "The BBC commissioned me to dramatise a children's novel. Broadcasting dates were fixed. The studio facilities were lined up. All that was lacking was a suitable book to dramatise. There are many good novels written for children but few fit the precise demands of time, budget, scope, and aims of a particular TV series. Everyone in the department was reading books furiously, to no avail. At last the producer, in desperation, suggested to me, 'Why don't you write an original television play, and then write the novel to go with it?' I snapped up the idea and wrote *The Crocodile.* While the play was in production I started writing the book, with a traumatic realisation that if children were being advised to read it, this had better be good! Not just a 'book of the film,' but something worth reading in its own right. I hope I succeeded. By the time I completed a second, similar exercise, *The Raven and the Cross,* I had caught the book-writing bug. What tales I could tell if I were not restricted by the mechanics of television! So why not write a book for its own sake, with no holds barred? The result was *The Glass Knife.*

"Drama was and is, I suppose, my first love because I was brought up in the theatre, both sides of the family being up to their hairlines in grease paint. My grandmother was writing popular melodramas and touring them around England before I was born. My childhood memories are of plays, revues, variety bills, and backstreet digs.

"I have written for a number of adult TV series as well as many children's programmes and I have learned a curious fact, that popular 'adult' material is often the most 'childish.' It's the kids who want to know the truth about the world in terms

more thoughtful and sincere." Tully's books have been published in Germany, Sweden, Demark, South Africa, Holland, and France.

*   *   *

TURNER, Frederick C(lair)   1938-

PERSONAL: Born October 3, 1938, in Cambridge, Mass.; son of Clair Elsmere (a college professor) and Naomi (Cocke) Turner; married Caroline Tingey Craven, August 27, 1960; children: Frederick C. II, Elizabeth Wingate, Caroline Truxtun. *Education:* Harvard University, A.B. (magna cum laude), 1961; Fletcher School of Law and Diplomacy, M.A., 1962, M.A.L.D., 1963, Ph.D., 1965. *Politics:* Democrat. *Religion:* Unitarian Universalist.

ADDRESSES: Home—30 Timber Dr., Storrs, Conn. 06268. *Office*—Department of Political Science, University of Connecticut, Storrs, Conn. 06268.

CAREER: Harvard University, Cambridge, Mass., assistant to director of Latin American studies, 1963-64; University of Connecticut, Storrs, assistant professor, 1965-68, associate professor, 1968-70, professor of political science, 1970—. Latin American representative, Roper Public Opinion Research Center, 1972—. Visiting lecturer in political science, Yale University, 1967-69.

MEMBER: International Political Science Association, American Political Science Association, Latin American Studies Association, American Association of University Professors, Center for Inter-American Relations, New England Council on Latin American Studies.

AWARDS, HONORS: First place in distinguished faculty awards program, University of Connecticut, 1968; University of Connecticut Alumni Association award for faculty excellence in teaching, 1969; National Endowment for the Humanities grant, 1972-73; National Science Foundation grant, 1972-76.

WRITINGS:

The Dynamic of Mexican Nationalism, University of North Carolina Press, 1968, revised edition published in Spanish as *La dinamica del nacionalismo mexicano,* translation by Guillermo Gaya Nicolau, Editorial Grijalbo, 1971.
Catholicism and Political Development in Latin America, University of North Carolina Press, 1971.
Responsible Parenthood: The Politics of Mexico's New Population Policies (monograph), American Enterprise Institute for Public Policy Research, 1974.
Politics, Propaganda, and Cinema, University of Connecticut Cooperative Corp., 1982.
(Editor with Jose E. Miguens) *Juan Peron and the Reshaping of Argentina,* University of Pittsburgh Press, 1983.

Contributor to anthologies on Latin American politics; contributor to professional journals.

AVOCATIONAL INTERESTS: English literature, especially the novels of D. H. Lawrence.*

*   *   *

TYLER, Ron(nie) C(urtis)   1941-

PERSONAL: Born December 29, 1941, in Temple, Tex.; son of Jasper J. and Melba Curtis (James) Tyler; married Paula Eyrich, August 24, 1974. *Education:* Temple Junior College, A.A., 1962; Abilene Christian College (now University),

B.S.E., 1964; Texas Christian University, M.A., 1966, Ph.D., 1968.

ADDRESSES: Home—3102 Hemphill Park, Austin, Tex. 78705. *Office*—Texas State Historical Association, 2/306 Richardson Hall, University Station, Austin, Tex. 78712.

CAREER: Austin College, Sherman, Tex., instructor, 1967-68, assistant professor of history, 1968-69; Amon Carter Museum of Western Art, Fort Worth, curator of history, 1969-82, director of publications, 1974-82, assistant director for history and publications, 1982-84, assistant director for collections and programs, 1984-86; Texas Christian University, Fort Worth, Tex., adjutant professor of history, 1971-72; University of Texas at Austin, professor of history, 1986—, director of Texas State Historical Association and Center for Studies in Texas History, 1986—. Chair, visiting committee for deparment of history, Abilene Christian University, 1985—; chair, committee to implement the research and educational agreement between the states of Texas and Coahuila and the University of Texas at Austin and the Universidad de Coahuila by President Cunningham, University of Texas at Austin, 1988—; chair, acquisitions advisory committee for the capitol, Texas State Preservation Board, 1988.

MEMBER: American Association of State and Local History, American Antiquarian Society, American Philosophical Association, Conference on Latin American History, Western History Association, Southwestern Council on Latin American Studies, Texas Christian University (fellow), Texas State Historical Association (fellow; president; vice-president; council member), Texas Institute of Letters, Texas Folklore Society, Texas Association of Museums (chair of publications committee; council member), Tarrant County Historical Society (president, 1975-77; vice-president; member of the board), Austin Historical Center, Book Club of Texas, Phi Beta Kappa.

AWARDS, HONORS: American Philosophical Society grant, 1970-71; H. Bailey Carroll Award, Texas State Historical Association, 1973, for best article in *Southwestern Historical Quarterly;* Coral Horton Tullis Memorial Prize, Texas State Historical Association, 1975, for *The Big Bend: A History of the Last Texas Frontier.*

WRITINGS:

Joseph Wade Hampton, Editor and Individualist, Texas Western Press, 1969.
Vision, Destiny—War!: Manifest Destiny and the Mexican War, Steck, 1970.
(Editor with Lawrence R. Murphy) *The Slave Narratives of Texas,* Encino Press, 1971.
(Contributor) Francis Edward Abernethy, editor, *Observations and Reflections on Texas Folklore,* Encino Press, 1972.
(With Leonard Sanders) *How Fort Worth Became the Texas-most City,* Texas Christian University Press, 1973.

Santiago Vidaurri and the Confederacy, Texas State Historical Association, 1973.
The Mexican War: A Lithographic Record, Texas State Historical Association, 1973.
(Contributor) *American Printmaking before 1876: Fact, Fiction, and Fantasy,* Library of Congress, 1975.
The Cowboy, Ridge Press, 1975.
The Big Bend: The Last Texas Frontier, National Park Service, 1975.
The Image of America in Caricature and Cartoon, Amon Carter Museum, 1975, revised edition, 1976.
The Rodeo Photographs of John Addison Stryker, Encino Press, 1977.
(Picture editor) *Texas: The Land and Its People,* Hendrick-Long, 2nd edition, 1978, 3rd edition, 1986.
(Contributor) *Encyclopedia of Southern History,* Louisiana State University Press, 1979.
(Editor) *Posada's Mexico,* Library of Congress, 1979.
(With Gary Winogrand) *Stock Photographs: The Fort Worth Fat Stock Show and Rodeo,* University of Texas Press, 1980.
(Author of introduction) Mary Austin Holley, *Texas,* Overland Press, 1981.
(Editor) *Alfred Jacob Miller: Artist on the Oregon Trail,* Amon Carter Museum, 1982.
Visions of America: Pioneer Artists in a New Land (Book-of-the-Month Club alternate selection), Thames & Hudson, 1983.
(Author of introduction) *Pecos to Rio Grande: Interpretations of Far West Texas by Eighteen Artists,* Texas A & M University Press, 1983.
(Editor) *Prints of the American West: Papers Presented at the Ninth Annual North American Print Conference,* Amon Carter Museum, 1983.
(Editor with wife Paula Eyrich Tyler) *Texas Museums: A Guidebook,* University of Texas Press, 1983.
(Contributor) Linda Ayres and others, editors, *American Paintings: Selections from the Amon Carter Museum,* Oxmoor House, 1986.
(Contributor) *America: Art and the West,* American-Australian Foundation for the Arts/International Cultural Corporation of Australia Ltd., 1986.
(Editor with others, and contributor) *American Frontier Life: Early Western Painting and Prints,* Abbeville Press, 1987.
Views of Texas: The Watercolors of Sarah Ann Hardinge, 1852-1856, Amon Carter Museum, 1988.
(Contributor) *The May Family Collection of American Paintings,* Huntsville Museum of Art, 1988.

Contributor to history journals, including *Americas, American History Illustrated, Southwestern Historical Quarterly, The American West, Journal of Negro History, Southwestern Latin Americanist, Chronicles of Oklahoma,* and *Arizona and the West.* Editor of *Southwestern Historical Quarterly,* 1986—.

U

ULLMAN, Montague 1916-

PERSONAL: Born September 9, 1916, in New York, N.Y.; son of William and Nettie (Eisler) Ullman; married Janet Simon, January 26, 1941; children: Susan, William, Lucy. *Education:* College of the City of New York (now City College of the City University of New York), B.S., 1934; New York University, M.D., 1938.

ADDRESSES: *Home and office*—55 Orlando Ave., Ardsley, N.Y. 10502.

CAREER: Licensed to practice medicine in New York, 1941; certified by American Board of Psychiatry and Neurology, 1945; private psychoanalytic practice, 1946-66; State University of New York, Downstate Medical Center, Brooklyn, associate professor, 1961-63, professor of psychiatry, 1963-76; Maimonides Medical Center, Brooklyn, N.Y., director of department of psychiatry, 1967-73; Albert Einstein College of Medicine, 1976-86, clinical professor of psychiatry, 1976-86, clinical professor emeritus, 1986—. Member of faculty, Westchester Center for the Study of Psychoanalysis and Psychotherapy, 1976-87. Consultant in mental hygiene and psychiatry, Skidmore College, 1957-71; supervising consultant, Gothenberg Institute for Psychodynamic Psychotherapy (Sweden), 1974—. *Military service:* U.S. Army, 1942-45; became captain.

MEMBER: Society of Medical Psychoanalysts (president, 1957-58), American Psychiatric Association (life fellow), American Society for Psychical Research (president, 1971-80), Parapsychological Association (president, 1966), Alpha Omega Alpha, Sigma Xi.

AWARDS, HONORS: Parapsychological Award from Parapsychology Foundation, 1968, Mid S. Weiss Award, American Society for Psychical Research, 1989.

WRITINGS:

Behavioral Changes in Patients Following Strokes, C. C Thomas, 1962.
(Editor with Robert Cavanna) *Proceedings of the International Conference on Hypnosis, Drugs, Dreams and Psi* (held at Le Piol, France, 1967), Garrett Press, 1968.
(With Gertrude Stokes) *A Giant Step*, Faculty Press, 1969.
(With Stanley Krippner) *Dream Studies and Telepathy*, Parapsychology Foundation, 1970.

(Editor with others) *Handbook of Parapsychology*, Van Nostrand Reinhold, 1977.
(Consulting editor) *Handbook of Dreams*, Van Nostrand Reinhold, 1979.
(With Krippner and Alan Vaughan) *Dream Telepathy*, Macmillan, 1979.
(With Nan Zimmerman) *Working with Dreams: Expand, Heal and Transform Your Life through Your Dreams*, J. P. Tarcher, 1979.
(Editor with Benjamin Wolman) *Handbook of States of Consciousness*, Van Nostrand Reinhold, 1986.
(With Claire Limmer) *Variety of Dream Experiences*, Continuum, 1987.

SIDELIGHTS: Montague Ullman told *CA:* "An early interest in psychical research developed during undergraduate days surfaced again during my years of psychoanalytic practice. This came to fruition when, after leaving practice and joining the Maimonides Medical Center on a full time basis, the Dream Laboratory was established in 1962. This was the first Dream Laboratory in the country devoted to experimental studies on dream telepathy." His present concern is to help bring people back into an active and helpful relationship with their own dream life. He currently divides his time between the United States and Sweden teaching dream work.

AVOCATIONAL INTERESTS: Tennis.

*   *   *

ULLRICH, Helen D(enning) 1922-

PERSONAL: Born November 28, 1922, in Berkeley, Calif.; daughter of Stephen L. (an executive) and Margaret L. (Woll) Denning; married Robert L. Ullrich (a consultant), September 22, 1962; children: Louise. *Education:* University of California, Berkeley, B.S., 1944; Columbia University, M.A., 1954.

ADDRESSES: *Home*—1116 Miller Ave., Berkeley, Calif. 94708. *Office*—Nutrition Communications Associates, 1116 Miller Ave., Berkeley, Calif. 94708.

CAREER: University of California Extension Service, Berkeley, nutrition specialist, 1956-63; nutrition consultant in Berkeley, 1963-67; University of California, Berkeley, nutrition specialist, 1968-79; Society for Nutrition Education, Oakland, Calif., executive director, 1973-82; Nutrition Communications Associates, Berkeley, owner/principal, 1983—.

MEMBER: American Association for the Advancement of Science, American Dietetic Association, Society for Nutrition Education (founding member).

WRITINGS:

(Contributor) Jack Hayes, editor, *Food for Us All: 1969 Yearbook of Agriculture,* U.S. Government Printing Office, 1969.

(Contributor) Jean Mayer, editor, *U.S. Nutrition Policies in the Seventies,* W. H. Freeman, 1973.

(Contributor) D. S. McLaren, editor, *Nutrition in the Community,* Wiley, 1976.

Health Maintenance through Food and Nutrition, Gale, 1981.

(Contributor) H. E. Mitzel, editor, *Encyclopedia of Educational Research,* 5th edition, McGraw, 1982.

(Contributor) G. M. Briggs and J. Weininger, editors, *Nutrition Update,* Volume III, Wiley, 1985.

(Co-author) *Children and Weight: A Changing Perspective,* Nutrition Communications Associates, 1985, revised edition, 1988.

Editor of *Journal of Nutrition Education,* 1968-79.

SIDELIGHTS: Helen D. Ullrich told *CA:* "After working in consumer education with a utility company and a food pro-

cessor, I spent two years in Hawaii in research on the nutrient content of foods indigenous to the area. From there I went into the field of nutrition education as a nutrition specialist with a state university, presenting programs and training for both the lay public and staff assigned to provide sound nutritional information for the public. After several years, I joined the University of California's Extension Service, again as a nutrition specialist.

"During the years of working with professionals who deal with the public, either in industry or with an educational institution, I realized the need for a specialized journal and, eventually, an organization devoted to all phases of nutrition education. My work in the founding of the *Journal of Nutrition* and the Society for Nutrition Education advanced that goal. After leaving the Society for Nutrition Education, I started my own consulting company. I continue to help the professional to be more effective in carrying out nutrition education, and I am still concerned that there be effective programs for communicating sound nutritional information to the people and programs to assess that people have the means to purchase adequate food. I am especially concerned that nutrition education programs—and appropriate food assistance programs—be continued and expanded for schoolchildren and their parents. Food habits are formed early in life, yet our educational process continues throughout life."

V

van der VAT, Dan(iel Francis Jeroen) 1939-

PERSONAL: Born October 28, 1939, in Alkmaar, Netherlands; son of Daniel G. (a writer) and Kathleen (Devanney) van der Vat; married Christine Mary Ellis (a teacher), 1962; children: Karen, Sara. *Education:* University of Durham, B.A. (with honors), 1960. *Politics:* "No party, no dogma." *Religion:* None.

ADDRESSES: Home—8 Aquarius, Eel Pie Island, Twickenham TW1 3EA, England. *Office—Guardian,* 119 Farringdon Rd., London EC1R 3ER, England. *Agent*—Curtis Brown Ltd., 162-168 Regent St., London W1R 5TA, England.

CAREER: Journal, Newcastle upon Tyne, England, journalist, 1960-63; *Daily Mail,* London, England, reporter, 1963-65; *Sunday Times,* London, reporter, 1965-67; *Times,* London, foreign correspondent, 1967-81; *Guardian,* London, chief foreign leader writer, 1982—.

MEMBER: National Union of Journalists, Society of Authors, Nautical Research Society, Navy Records Society, Campaign for Nuclear Disarmament, Eel Pie Island Association.

WRITINGS:

The Grand Scuttle: The Sinking of the German Fleet at Scapa Flow in 1919, Hodder & Stoughton, 1982, Naval Institute Press, 1985.
The Last Corsair: The Story of the Emden, Hodder & Stoughton, 1983, published as *Gentlemen of War: The Amazing Story of Captain Karl von Mueller and the S.M.S. Emden,* Morrow, 1984.
The Ship That Changed the World, Hodder & Stoughton, 1985.
The Atlantic Campaign: An Epic History of World War II's Struggle at Sea, Harper, 1988.

Writer for television and radio. Contributor to journals.

WORK IN PROGRESS: Various projects.

SIDELIGHTS: Dan van der Vat told *CA* that his "involvement in naval history is the result of a chapter of accidents." After a reporting assignment in the Orkney Islands fell through, van der Vat began exploring the area "and came across a little museum in the town of Stromness which had a special display on the subject of the scuttling of the German fleet after the first World War." His imagination captured by the incident, van der Vat went to research the subject; he found, however, that "the greatest act of material destruction in all naval or military history did not have a single entire book devoted to it. That is how it began." While researching his account of the demolition of the German fleet, *The Grand Scuttle: The Sinking of the German Fleet at Scapa Flow in 1919,* the author came across the remarkable account of the German light cruiser *Emden,* which led to the writing of *The Last Corsair: The Story of the Emden.*

"*The Ship That Changed the World,*" continues van der Vat, "is the first book to use German and French as well as British sources in telling how Germany's naval Mediterranean Division brought Turkey into the war and thus cut off Russia in 1914. For my latest book I have turned to the Second World War with a new look at the struggle over the submarines and convoys in *The Atlantic Campaign: An Epic History of World War II's Struggle at Sea.* As ever, my approach is that of a reporter with the chance to give a considered version of an event with all the records available. I have always been in the business of writing stories."

BIOGRAPHICAL/CRITICAL SOURCES:

PERIODICALS

Daily Telegraph, June 24, 1982.
Economist, August 14, 1982.
Guardian, September 23, 1982.
Times (London), June 24, 1982.
Times Literary Supplement, September 24, 1982, December 30, 1983.
Washington Post, June 25, 1984.

*   *   *

VANDERWOOD, Paul J(oseph) 1929-

PERSONAL: Born June 3, 1929, in Brooklyn, New York; son of Joseph and Mildred (Horstman) Vanderwood. *Education:* Bethany College, Bethany, W.Va., B.A., 1950; New York University, graduate study, 1953-54; Memphis State University, M.A., 1957; University of Texas at Austin, Ph.D., 1970.

ADDRESSES: Home—8705 Jefferson Ave., San Diego, Calif. 92041. *Office*—Department of History, San Diego State University, San Diego, Calif. 92182.

CAREER: Memphis Press-Scimitar, Memphis, Tenn., reporter, 1954-63; Peace Corps evaluator, 1963; San Diego State University, San Diego, Calif., 1969—, began as assistant professor, currently professor of history. Member of Conference on Latin American History, American Film Institute, and of Pacific Coast and Rocky Mountain Councils of Latin American Studies. *Military service:* U.S. Army, 1951-63; became lieutenant.

MEMBER: Border Studies Association.

AWARDS, HONORS: National Association of State and Local History award, 1971; Hubert B. Herring Award, Pacific Coast Council of Latin American Studies, 1976, 1981; exceptional service merit awards, San Diego State University, 1984, 1987.

WRITINGS:

Night Riders of Reelfoot Lake, Memphis State University Press, 1969.
Disorder and Progress: Bandits, Police, and Mexican Development, University of Nebraska Press, 1981.
Los Rurales Mexicanos, Fondo de Cultura Economica, 1982.
(Editor and author of introduction) *Juarez* (screenplay), University of Wisconsin Press, 1983.
Border Fury: A Postcard Record of Mexico's Revolution and U.S. War Preparedness, 1910-1917, University of New Mexico Press, 1988.

Contributor of articles and reviews to newspapers and scholarly journals.

WORK IN PROGRESS: A book on a world perspective of the millennial movement at Tamochic, Mexico, in 1891; a book on border photographer Robert Runyon; a book on Mexican heroes in American film.

BIOGRAPHICAL/CRITICAL SOURCES:

PERIODICALS

American Historical Review, December, 1970, April, 1982.
Hispanic American Historical Review, November, 1982.
Journal of American History, September, 1970.
Latin American Research Review, December, 1988.

*   *   *

Van LEEUWEN, Jean   1937-

PERSONAL: Surname is pronounced Van *Loo*-en; born December 26, 1937, in Glen Ridge, N.J.; daughter of Cornelius (a clergyman) and Dorothy (Charlton) Van Leeuwen; married Bruce David Gavril (a digital computer systems designer), July 7, 1968; children: David Andrew, Elizabeth Eva. *Education:* Syracuse University, B.A., 1959.

ADDRESSES: Home—7 Colony Row, Chappaqua, N.Y. 10514.

CAREER: Random House, Inc., New York City, 1963-68, began as assistant editor, became associate editor of juvenile books; Viking Press, Inc., New York City, associate editor of juvenile books, 1968-70; Dial Press, New York City, senior editor of juvenile books, 1971-73; currently full-time writer.

AWARDS, HONORS: William Allen White Award, 1978, and 1978-79 North Carolina Children's Book Award, both for *The Great Christmas Kidnapping Caper; Seems Like This Road Goes on Forever* was named one of the best books of 1979, American Library Association (ALA), Young Adult Services Division; Massachusetts Honor Book Award, 1981, for *The Great Cheese Conspiracy; More Tales of Oliver Pig, Amanda Pig and Her Big Brother Oliver*, and *Tales of Amanda Pig* have all been named as ALA Notable Books.

WRITINGS:

JUVENILES

(Editor) *A Time of Growing*, Random House, 1967.
Timothy's Flower, Random House, 1967.
One Day in Summer, Random House, 1969.
The Great Cheese Conspiracy, Random House, 1969.
I Was a Ninety-Eight Pound Duckling, Dial, 1972, reprinted, Bantam, 1987.
Too Hot for Ice Cream, Dial, 1974.
The Great Christmas Kidnapping Caper, Dial, 1975.
Seems Like This Road Goes on Forever, Dial, 1979.
Tales of Oliver Pig, Dial, 1979.
More Tales of Oliver Pig, Dial, 1981.
The Great Rescue Operation, Dial, 1982.
Amanda Pig and Her Big Brother Oliver, Dial, 1982.
Benjy and the Power of Zingies, Dial, 1982.
Tales of Amanda Pig, Dial, 1983.
Benjy in Business, Dial, 1983.
More Tales of Amanda Pig, Dial, 1985.
Benjy the Football Hero, Dial, 1985.
Oliver, Amanda, and Grandmother Pig, Dial, 1987.
Oliver and Amanda's Christmas, Dial, 1989.
Dear Mom: You Are Ruining My Life, Dial, 1989.

SIDELIGHTS: About Jean Van Leeuwen's "Read-It-Yourself" series involving sister and brother Amanda and Oliver Pig, *New York Times Book Review* contributor Mary Gordon writes: "One of the great values of these books is their ability to dramatize the ridiculous and trivial and sickeningly frequent fights that siblings endure every day of their lives, and yet suggest the siblings' essential fondness for one another, their dependency, their mutual good will." The critic concludes by remarking that "at their best, and there are no real failures, the Oliver and Amanda stories can provide the early reader, and those who are press ganged into reading to him or her, with pleasant, solid, buoying experiences of the commodity all too rare in real life: the happy family."

Van Leeuwen told *CA:* "Trying to find some common denominator in my writing, I guess I would say that more and more I am trying to do two things—to use humor to put across something serious that I want to say, and to recreate certain remembered turning points in my own life in terms that will be meaningful to readers of today. My only comment about my way of working is that it is slow—achingly, frustratingly, agonizingly slow."

AVOCATIONAL INTERESTS: Photography, reading, gardening, music.

BIOGRAPHICAL/CRITICAL SOURCES:

PERIODICALS

New York Times Book Review, November 5, 1967, November 10, 1985, January 19, 1986, January 10, 1988.

Van SLYKE, Helen (Lenore)   1919-1979
(Sharon Ashton)

PERSONAL: Born July 9, 1919, in Washington, D.C.; died July 3, 1979, of an embolism following surgery, in New York, N.Y.; daughter of Frederick H. and Lenore (Siegel) Vogt; married William Woodward Van Slyke, August 9, 1946 (divorced January, 1952).

ADDRESSES: Home and office—350 East 57th St., New York, N.Y.; also maintained residence in Key Largo, Fla.

CAREER: Washington Evening Star, Washington, D.C., fashion editor, 1938-43; *Glamour,* New York City, beauty editor, 1945-55, promotion director, 1955-60; Henri Bendel (department store), New York City, promotion and advertising director, 1960-61; Norman, Craig & Kummel (advertising agency), New York City, vice-president and creative director, 1961-63; House of Fragrance, New York City, president, 1963-68; Helena Rubenstein, New York City, vice-president of creative activities, 1968-72; full-time writer and lecturer. Volunteer worker, Lighthouse for the Blind.

MEMBER: Fashion Group (served as president), Advertising Women of New York Friends of New York Public Library.

AWARDS, HONORS: Today's Woman award, Cerebral Palsy Foundation, 1977.

WRITINGS:

CONTEMPORARY ROMANCES

The Rich and the Righteous, Doubleday, 1971.
All Visitors Must Be Announced, Doubleday, 1972, paperback edition published as *The Best People,* Warner Books, 1982.
The Heart Listens, Doubleday, 1973.
The Mixed Blessing, Doubleday, 1975.
The Best Place to Be, Doubleday, 1976.
Always Is Not Forever, Doubleday, 1977.
Sisters and Strangers, Doubleday, 1978.
A Necessary Woman, Doubleday, 1979.
No Love Lost, Lippincott, 1980.
(With James Elward) *Public Smiles, Private Tears,* Harper, 1982.

OTHER

(Under pseudonym Sharon Ashton) *The Santa Ana Wind* (mystery novel), Doubleday, 1974, reprinted (under name Helen Van Slyke), Popular Library, 1981, reprinted (under both name Helen Van Slyke and pseudonym Sharon Ashton), Warner Books, 1982.

Contributor to *Harpers Bazaar, Saturday Evening Post, Vogue,* and *Writer.*

SIDELIGHTS: The contemporary romance novels of bestselling author Helen Van Slyke sold over six million copies in her lifetime. A successful New York City fashion, advertising, and cosmetics executive, who at age eighteen was the youngest editor of a major U.S. newspaper, Van Slyke began writing novels later in life, targeting her books to the concerns of modern women. Although Van Slyke's female protagonists are frequently of society's upper classes, their struggles with the often conflicting demands of personal ambition and societal expectations won Van Slyke a popular following among female readers. Joseph McClellan in the *Washington Post Book World* commented on Van Slyke's achievements: "If [her] books are used as escapist literature, it is a higher form of escapism that the gothic brooding, plantation passion and pirate abductions that are staples in this trade. In comparison, Van Slyke wrote about reality—contemporary reality—and she wrote with honesty, almost with the approach of a sociologist."

Van Slyke once commented to *CA:* "I left my executive post in business at age 50-plus to pursue a new career as a novelist. Looking back now, I wonder how I dared such a gamble, and how fortunate I am that it paid off so well in satisfaction and earning! I write long, absorbing novels directed primarily at a woman's audience, though I do have a few male readers. My forte is taking a contemporary theme (widowhood, mother-daughter relationships, inter-racial marriage, etc.) and building around it. By trade and inclination, I'm a story teller and the key to the success of more than five million copies sold is, I think, that I have fulfilled a need for the sentimental but realistic novel with characters readers remember and with whom they can identify."

Van Slyke added: "I work six days a week, five hours a day. Writing a book takes seven to eight months. 'Promotion' at publication time—travel, appearances, speeches, etc.—consume another two months. Which leaves me relaxation and 'thinking time' of about two months a year. I write to entertain, to please and as a rewarding career, not only financially but in terms of the satisfaction which comes with reader and reviewer response."

Van Slyke's novels have been translated into fourteen foreign languages.

AVOCATIONAL INTERESTS: Reading, decorating, travel.

MEDIA ADAPTATIONS: Van Slyke's novel *The Best Place to Be* was adapted by Ross Hunter into a television mini-series and broadcast by NBC-TV in May, 1976.

BIOGRAPHICAL/CRITICAL SOURCES:

PERIODICALS

Detroit News, May 6, 1980.
New York Times, January 19, 1979.
New York Times Book Review, June 8, 1980.
Washington Post Book World, April 17, 1982.
Writer's Digest, February, 1980.

OBITUARIES:

PERIODICALS

Chicago Tribune, July 6, 1979.
New York Times, July 5, 1979.
Publishers Weekly, July 16, 1979.
Washington Post, July 5, 1979.*

*   *   *

Van VOGT, A(lfred) E(lton)   1912-

PERSONAL: Born April 26, 1912, near Winnipeg, Manitoba, Canada; son of Henry (an attorney) and Agnes (Buhr) Van Vogt; married Edna Mayne Hull, May 9, 1939 (died January 20, 1975); married Lydia I. Brayman (a linguist and superior court interpreter), October 6, 1979. *Education:* Attended schools in Manitoba; also studied at University of Ottawa and University of California. *Religion:* Rationalist.

ADDRESSES: c/o Simon & Schuster, 1230 Avenue of the Americas, New York, N.Y. 10020.

CAREER: Professional writer, 1932—, chiefly of science fiction. Census clerk, Ottawa, Ontario, Canada, 1931-32; western representative of trade papers, Maclean Publishing Co., Toronto, Ontario, 1935-39. First managing director of Hubbard Dianetic Research Foundation of California, Los Angeles, 1950-53; co-owner, Hubbard Dianetic Center, Los Angeles, 1953-61. Founder, 200 Language Club, 1974. *Wartime service:* Served in Department of National Defense, Ottawa, 1939-41.

MEMBER: International Society for General Semantics, International Dianetic Society (president, 1958—), Authors Guild, Authors League of America, Science Fiction Writers of America, California Association of Dianetic Auditors (president, 1959-82).

AWARDS, HONORS: Guest of honor at 4th World Science Fiction Convention, 1946, European Science Fiction Convention, 1978, and Metz Festival, France, 1985; Manuscripters Literature award, 1948; Ann Radcliffe Award, Count Dracula Society, 1968; award from Academy of Science Fiction, Fantasy, and Horror Films, 1979; Jules Verne Award, 1983; honorary B.A., Golden Gate College.

WRITINGS:

SCIENCE FICTION NOVELS

Slan (originally serialized in *Astounding Science Fiction,* September-December, 1940; also see below), Arkham, 1946, revised edition, Simon & Schuster, 1951, reprinted, Berkley, 1982.
The Book of Ptath (originally serialized in *Unknown,* 1943; also see below), Fantasy Press, 1947, published as *Two Hundred Million A.D.,* Paperback Library, 1964, published as *Ptath,* Zebra Books, 1976.
The Voyage of the Space Beagle (based on material, including "Black Destroyer," serialized in *Astounding Science Fiction,* 1939-43, and in *Other Worlds,* 1950; also see below), Simon & Schuster, 1950, reprinted, Pocket Books, 1981, published as *Mission: Interplanetary,* New American Library, 1952.
The House That Stood Still, Greenberg, 1950, reprinted, Pocket Books, 1980, published as *The Mating Cry,* Beacon, 1960 (published in England as *The Undercover Aliens,* Panther, 1976).
The Mixed Men (originally serialized in *Astounding Science Fiction,* 1943-45), Gnome Press, 1952, published as *Mission to the Stars,* Berkley, 1955, reprinted, Pocket Books, 1980.
The Universe Maker (originally serialized in *Startling Stories,* 1949, under title "The Shadow Man"; also see below), Ace Books, 1953, reprinted, Pocket Books, 1982.
(With wife, E. Mayne Hull) *Planets for Sale* (originally serialized in *Astounding Science Fiction,* 1943-46; also see below), Fell, 1954.
The Mind Cage, Simon & Schuster, 1957, reprinted, Pocket Books, 1981.
Siege of the Unseen (originally serialized in *Astounding Science Fiction,* 1946, under title "The Chronicler"; bound with *The World Swappers* by John Brunner; also see below), Ace Books, 1959.
The War against the Rull (partially based on material serialized in *Astounding Science Fiction,* 1940-50), Simon & Schuster, 1959, reprinted, Pocket Books, 1982.

(With Hull) *The Winged Man* (originally serialized in *Astounding Science Fiction,* 1944), Doubleday, 1966.
The Silkie, Ace Books, 1969.
Quest for the Future (based on material originally serialized in *Astounding Science Fiction,* 1943-46), Ace Books, 1970.
Children of Tomorrow, Ace Books, 1970.
The Battle of Forever, Ace Books, 1971.
The Darkness on Diamondia, Ace Books, 1972.
Future Glitter, Ace Books, 1973 (published in England as *Tyranopolis,* Sphere, 1977).
The Secret Galactics, Prentice-Hall, 1974, published as *Earth Factor X,* DAW Books, 1976.
The Man with a Thousand Names, DAW Books, 1974.
Supermind (based on material originally serialized in *If,* 1968, under title "The Proxy Intelligence"; also see below), DAW Books, 1977.
The Anarchistic Colossus, Ace Books, 1977.
Renaissance, Pocket Books, 1979.
The Cosmic Encounter, Doubleday, 1980.
Computerworld, DAW Books, 1983, published as *Computer Eye,* Morrison, Raven-Hill, 1985.

"WEAPON SHOP" SERIES; SCIENCE FICTION NOVELS

The Weapon Makers (originally serialized in *Astounding Science Fiction,* 1943), Hadley, 1947, revised edition, Greenberg, 1952, reprinted, Pocket Books, 1979, published as *One against Eternity,* Ace Books, 1955.
The Weapon Shops of Isher (based on material serialized in *Astounding Science Fiction,* 1941-42, and in *Thrilling Wonder Stories,* 1949), Greenberg, 1951, reprinted, Pocket Books, 1981, bound with *Gateway to Elsewhere* by W. P. Jenkins, Ace Books, 1954.

"GOSSEYN" SERIES; SCIENCE FICTION NOVELS

The World of A (originally serialized in *Astounding Science Fiction,* 1945; also see below), Simon & Schuster, 1948, published as *The World of Null-A,* Ace Books, 1953, revised edition, Berkley, 1970, reprinted, 1982.
The Pawns of Null-A (originally serialized in *Astounding Science Fiction,* 1948-49, under title "The Players of A"), Ace Books, 1956, published as *The Players of Null-A,* Berkley, 1966, reprinted, 1982.
Null-A Three, DAW Books, 1985.

"CLANE LINN" SERIES; SCIENCE FICTION NOVELS

Empire of the Atom (partially based on material serialized in *Astounding Science Fiction,* 1946-47), Shasta Publishers, 1957.
The Wizard of Linn (originally serialized in *Astounding Science Fiction,* 1950), Ace Books, 1962.

SHORT STORIES AND NOVELLAS

(With Hull) *Out of the Unknown,* Fantasy Publishing (Los Angeles), 1948, expanded edition, Powell, 1969 (published in England as *The Sea Thing and Other Stories,* Sidgwick & Jackson, 1970).
Masters of Time (includes "Masters of Time" [originally serialized in *Astounding Science Fiction,* 1942, under title "Recruiting Station"; also see below] and "The Changeling" [originally serialized in *Astounding Science Fiction,* 1944; also see below]), Fantasy Press, 1950, reprinted, McFadden-Bartell, 1967.
Away and Beyond, Pellegrini & Cudahy, 1952.

Destination: Universe!, with an introduction by the author, Pellegrini & Cudahy, 1952.

Earth's Last Fortress (originally published as "Masters of Time"; bound with *Lost in Space* by George O. Smith; also see below), Ace Books, 1960.

The Beast (revised and enlarged version of "The Changeling"; also see below), Doubleday, 1963 (published in England as *The Moonbeast*, Panther, 1969).

The Twisted Man, (includes material serialized in *Astounding Science Fiction*, 1947, *Super Science Stories*, 1950, and *If*, 1963; bound with *One of Our Planets Is Missing* by Calvin M. Knox), Ace Books, 1964, published as *Rogue Ship*, Doubleday, 1965.

Monsters, edited and with an introduction by Forrest J. Ackerman, Paperback Library, 1965, published as *Science Fiction Monsters*, 1967, published as *The Blal*, Zebra Books, 1976.

The Far-Out Worlds of A. E. Van Vogt, Ace Books, 1968, enlarged edition published as *The Worlds of A. E. Van Vogt*, 1974.

More Than Superhuman, Dell, 1971.

The Proxy Intelligence and Other Mind Benders (also see below), Paperback Library, 1971.

M-33 in Andromeda, Paperback Library, 1971.

The Book of Van Vogt, DAW Books, 1972, published as *Lost: Fifty Suns*, 1979.

The Best of A. E. Van Vogt, edited by Angus Wells, Sidgwick & Jackson, 1974.

The Gryb, Zebra Books, 1976.

The Best of A. E. Van Vogt, Pocket Books, 1976.

Pendulum, DAW Books, 1978.

OMNIBUS VOLUMES

Triad (includes *The Voyage of the Space Beagle*, *Slan*, and *The World of A*), Simon & Schuster, 1959.

A Van Vogt Omnibus, Sidgwick & Jackson, Volume 1: *Planets for Sale*, *The Beast*, [and] *The Book of Ptath*, 1967, Volume 2: *The Mind Cage*, *The Winged Man*, [and] *Slan*, 1971.

Two Science Fiction Novels: Three Eyes of Evil and Earth's Last Fortress (*Three Eyes of Evil* originally published as *Siege of the Unseen*), Sidgwick & Jackson, 1973.

The Universe Maker and The Proxy Intelligence, Sidgwick & Jackson, 1976.

OTHER

(Contributor) Lloyd Arthur Esbach, editor, *Of Worlds Beyond*, Fantasy Press, 1947.

(With Charles E. Cooke) *The Hypnotism Handbook* (nonfiction), Borden, 1956.

The Violent Man (novel), Farrar, Straus, 1962.

(Author of introduction) William F. Nolan, editor, *The Pseudo-People*, Sherbourne Press, 1965 (published in England as *Almost Human*, Souvenir Press, 1966).

The Money Personality, Parker, 1973, published as *Unlock Your Money Personality*, Morrison, Raven-Hill, 1983.

Reflections of A. E. Van Vogt: The Autobiography of a Science Fiction Giant, with a Complete Bibliography, Fictioneer Books, 1975.

(Contributor) Brian Ash, editor, *Visual Encyclopedia of Science Fiction*, Harmony, 1977.

(Contributor) Rex Malik, editor, *Future Imperfect*, Pinter, 1980.

(Contributor) Martin H. Greenberg, editor, *Fantastic Lives*, Southern Illinois University Press, 1981.

Professional Writer (cassette), J. Norton Publishers, 1984.

Also author of *The Search for Certainty*, 1970, and of play, "The Invalid's Wife." Contributor to periodicals, including *Astounding Science Fiction, Locus, Science Fiction Writers of America Bulletin*, and *Foundation 3*.

SIDELIGHTS: "Along with Robert Heinlein and Isaac Asimov, A. E. Van Vogt must be counted one of the three major SF writers of the Forties," declare Alexei and Cory Panshin of the *Magazine of Fantasy and Science Fiction*. Together they formed the nucleus of a group of writers linked with John W. Campbell, editor of *Astounding Science Fiction*. Their work marked the beginning of what is known as the Golden Age of Science Fiction. Within a year and a half of the publication of Van Vogt's first story, "Black Destroyer," in 1939, records *Dictionary of Literary Biography* contributor Arthur Jean Cox, he "had become an important figure in science fiction, the only writer at that time approximating the stature of Robert A. Heinlein; and, after Heinlein had left for World War II, Van Vogt easily and happily dominated *Astounding Science Fiction*, the most important science-fiction magazine of its day, for some years." Sam Moskowitz reports in *Seekers of Tomorrow: Masters of Modern Science Fiction* that a 1947 poll of science fiction readers "saw Van Vogt edge out such formidable competitors as A. Merritt, H. P. Lovecraft, Robert A. Heinlein, and Henry Kuttner as science fiction's most popular author."

In his stories Van Vogt originated and explored ideas and themes that have since become mainstays of science fiction. As a reviewer for the *Washington Post Book World* states, he "gave permanent form to some of science fiction's most cherished dreams." "From the first," says Donald A. Wolheim in *The Universe Makers*, "his stories have concerned themselves with extraordinary powers, with new concepts in science or in mental gymnastics, and he constantly seems to strive to create new systems of thought and mental order which will permit the creation of supermen."

Slan, for instance, is the story of a young mutant who can read minds, among other powers, fleeing persecution by the society that killed his parents. Although other writers had previously used the superman motif in science fiction stories, declares Moskowitz, "Van Vogt seems to have been the first science-fiction author with the courage to explore the sociological implications of the superhuman race living in and among humans." *Slan* "is still, after forty years, widely regarded as a classic, and continues the mainstay of [Van Vogt's] fame," says Cox. "By any standard," Moskowitz concludes, "it was a milestone in science fiction." Other Van Vogt masterpieces include *The Weapon Shops of Isher* and *The Weapon Makers*, "both grand galactic adventures, omnipotence fantasies laden with dark resonances from incompletely defined elements of mystery," as Charles Platt describes them in *Dream Makers: The Uncommon People Who Write Science Fiction*.

Also famous is Van Vogt's "Null-A" sequence, which relates the adventures of Gilbert Gosseyn, "a developing superman with the ability to transport himself or anything else instantaneously almost anywhere in the galaxy," as Gene DeWeese describes him in the *Science Fiction Review*. Gosseyn "used that power and others to unravel great mysteries and battle great enemies, both seen and unseen. The action was nonstop, and the solution to each mystery only revealed another, more complex mystery," continues DeWeese. But action and mystery were not the focus of the stories; instead, Van Vogt used the science fiction genre to "impress upon the reader something of the [non-Aristotelian] doctrines of . . . the general semantics movement," concludes Cox.

This fascination with a system of thought—in this case, general semantics—is characteristic of Van Vogt's writing. General semantics studies the ways in which the meanings of words and other symbols affect human behavior. The system tries to explain the thought process that goes on in a person's mind when a word is spoken or heard. This system allows Gosseyn "to logically and accurately analyze [his] situation without letting [his] emotions get in the way," according to DeWeese. Van Vogt plots his books using another, dream-related, system, says Platt, that fills "his science-fiction adventures with fantastic images, symbolic figures, a constant sense of discovery and revelation, and a sense of free, flying motion." The author is also an exponent of the Gallishaw method—a technique of writing "in 800-word scenes, the action in each developing through five carefully delineated steps," explains Cox. Van Vogt exhibits as well a "keen interest in such salient concepts as hypnotism, telepathy, semantics, 'similarization,' and Dianetics," declares Jeffrey M. Elliot in *Science Fiction Voices #2*.

Many critics find Van Vogt's recent work not as good as that which he did for *Astounding* in the 1940s. "Van Vogt thinks they have not properly understood what it is he is trying to do now," declares Cox. The author himself explains to Elliot, "For years, until the 1960s, I consciously wrote pulp-style sentences. They have a certain lush poetry in them. In the late 1960s, I began to concentrate on content and even allowed my protagonist to be neurotic, also. However, these current stories don't seem to win the same approval as when I followed the earlier system." DeWeese, for example, writing about the third volume of Gosseyn's adventures, states, "*Null-A Three* is very close to being a parody of the first two books." Various stylistic oddities tend to detract from the story line, DeWeese continues; he adds, "In the early books, the narrative was so exciting that most readers never noticed such things, but this time there's so little action that they are impossible to overlook." Other critics, however, have enjoyed Van Vogt's current fiction. Gerald Jonas, writing in the *New York Times Book Review* about *Cosmic Encounter*, says, "It is not easy to summarize an A. E. Van Vogt novel, nor to say exactly why one likes it. I liked 'Cosmic Encounter.'"

Despite the diversity of opinion that surrounds Van Vogt's recent efforts, most critics agree with Elliot that "there are few science fiction writers alive today who can boast the singular achievements of A. E. Van Vogt, a long-time talent in the field, who has spent his lifetime giving meaning and import to the shape of things to come." His work taken as a whole, says Cox, shows strengths that outweigh his weaknesses: "The convergence of [the author's] unpredictable restless inventiveness with the violence of feeling with which he charges his characters constitutes a large part of that archetypal power often noted by his admirers; the rest derives from his habit of turning his face ever outward to the Universe, of measuring everything by the Infinite and considering all human matters *sub specie aeternitatis*. He reaches out eagerly to grasp the Cosmos."

BIOGRAPHICAL/CRITICAL SOURCES:

BOOKS

Contemporary Literary Criticism, Volume 1, Gale, 1973.
Dictionary of Literary Biography, Volume 8: *Twentieth-Century American Science Fiction Writers*, Gale, 1981.
Elliot, Jeffrey M., *Science Fiction Voices #2*, Borgo Press, 1979.

Knight, Damon, *In Search of Wonder*, Advent Press, 1956.
Magill, Frank N., editor, *Survey of Science Fiction Literature*, Volume 5, Salem Press, 1979.
Magill, Frank N., editor, *Survey of Modern Fantasy Literature, Volume 1*, Salem Press, 1983.
Moskowitz, Sam, *Seekers of Tomorrow: Masters of Modern Science Fiction*, Hyperion Press, 1966.
Platt, Charles, *Dream Makers: The Uncommon People Who Write Science Fiction*, Berkley, 1980.
Searles, Baird, Martin Last, Beth Meacham, and Michael Franklin, *A Reader's Guide to Science Fiction*, Avon Books, 1979.
Van Vogt, A. E., *Reflections of A. E. Van Vogt: The Autobiography of a Science Fiction Giant, with a Complete Bibliography*, Fictioneer Books, 1975.
Wolheim, Donald A., *The Universe Makers*, Harper, 1971.

PERIODICALS

Algol, spring, 1977.
Amazing Science Fiction, March, 1982.
Analog Science Fact/Science Fiction, July, 1978, December, 1979, February, 1986.
Fantasy Review, September, 1985.
Foundation, March, 1973.
Future, January, 1979.
Magazine of Fantasy and Science Fiction, July, 1976.
New York Herald Tribune Book Review, February 9, 1947, March 21, 1948, August 19, 1951, June 1, 1952, October 26, 1952.
New York Times, June 11, 1950, December 17, 1950, August 5, 1951, August 10, 1952, October 12, 1952, March 17, 1957.
New York Times Book Review, April 14, 1974, October 3, 1976, July 31, 1977, May 11, 1980.
Science Fiction Chronicle, November, 1980.
Science Fiction Review, November, 1977, November, 1985.
Times Literary Supplement, April 4, 1968, April 9, 1970, November 9, 1973, March 15, 1974, August 8, 1975.
Washington Post Book World, March 22, 1981, July 26, 1981, September 29, 1985.

—*Sketch by Kenneth R. Shepherd*

*   *   *

VARA, Madeleine
See JACKSON, Laura (Riding)

*   *   *

VATIKIOTIS, P(anayiotis) J(erasimos)   1928-

PERSONAL: Born February 5, 1928, in Jerusalem, Palestine (now Israel); son of Jerassimos Y. (a civil servant) and Paraskevi (Meimarachi) Vatikiotis; married Patricia Mumford, March 22, 1956; children: Michael, Helen, Daphne. *Education:* American University in Cairo, B.A., 1948; Louisiana State University, M.A., 1951; Johns Hopkins University, Ph.D., 1954.

ADDRESSES: Office—Department of Economic and Political Studies, School of Oriental and African Studies, University of London, London WC1E 7HP, England.

CAREER: American University in Cairo, Cairo, Egypt, instructor in social sciences, 1948-49; Johns Hopkins University, School of Advanced International Studies, Washington, D.C., instructor in Arabic, 1952-53; Indiana University at Bloomington, 1953-65, began as instructor, became professor of government; University of London, School of Oriental and African Studies, London, England, lecturer, 1964-65, professor of politics, 1965—, chairman of Centre for Middle Eastern Studies, 1966-69. *Military service:* U.S. Army, 1954-56.

AWARDS, HONORS: Guggenheim fellow, 1961-62.

WRITINGS:

The Fatimid Theory of State, Orientalia Publications (Pakistan), 1957, reissued, Institute of Islamic Culture (Pakistan), 1981.
The Egyptian Army in Politics, Indiana University Press, 1961.
Politics and the Military in Jordon: A Study of the Arab Legion, 1921-57, Praeger, 1967.
(Editor) *Egypt since the Revolution,* Praeger, 1968.
The Modern History of Egypt, Praeger, 1969, 2nd edition published as *The History of Egypt from Mohammed Ali to Sadat,* Johns Hopkins Press, 1980, 3rd edition, 1985.
Conflict in the Middle East, Allen & Unwin, 1971.
Revolution in the Middle East and Other Case Studies, Rowman & Littlefield, 1972.
Greece: A Political Essay, Sage Publications, 1975.
Nasser and His Generation, St. Martin's, 1978.
Arab and Regional Politics in the Middle East, St. Martin's, 1984.
Islam and the State, Croom Helm, 1987.

CONTRIBUTOR

P. W. Thayer, editor, *Tensions in the Middle East,* Johns Hopkins Press, 1958.
Roy Macridis, editor, *Foreign Policy in World Politics,* 2nd revised edition (Vatikiotis was not associated with earlier edition), Prentice-Hall, 1962.
Jesse Harris Proctor, editor, *Islam and International Relations,* Praeger, 1965.
Peter Holt, *Political and Social Change in Modern Egypt,* Oxford University Press, 1968.
Paul Hammond and Sidney Alexander, editors, *Political Dynamics in the Middle East,* Elsevier (Netherlands), 1972.
Alvin Cottrell and James Theberge, editors, *The Western Mediterranean: Its Political, Economic, and Strategic Importance,* Praeger, 1973.
Ivo Lederer and Wayne Vucinich, editors, *The Soviet Union and the Middle East: Post World War II Era,* Hoover Institution, 1974.
Abraham L. Udovitch, editor, *The Middle East: Oil, Conflict and Hope,* Lexington Books, 1976.
G. Wise and C. Issawi, editors, *Middle Eastern Perspectives: The Next Twenty Years,* Darwin Press, 1981.
A. S. Cudsi and Ali E. Hillal Dessouki, editors, *Islam and Power,* St. Martin's, 1981.
Gabriel Warburg, editor, *Islam, Nationalism and Radicalism in Egypt and the Sudan,* Praeger, 1983.
Annual Survey of Jewish Affairs, Associated University Presses, 1983.
Benjamin Netanyahn, editor, *Terrorism: How the West Can Win,* Farrar, Strauss, 1986.
Milton J. Esman and Hamar Rabinovitch, editors, *Ethnicity, Pluralism and the State in the Middle East,* Cornell University Press, 1988.

WORK IN PROGRESS: *John Metaxas of Greece, 1936-41.*

SIDELIGHTS: P. J. Vatikiotis told *CA:* "I prefer writing essays to books, partly because I am too skeptical to seek final solutions. Another kind of writing I attempt in my spare time is short sketches on life amid Middle East foreign communities. These may be published someday under the title, 'The Not So Magic East.'" Vatikiotis speaks Greek, Arabic (three dialects fluently), French, and some Italian.

*   *   *

VIRGINES, George E. 1920-

PERSONAL: Born February 11, 1920, in Chicago, Ill.; son of Nickolas (a chef) and Mary (Drogush) Virgines; married Loraine Dunlap, February 11, 1941; children: Valerie Virgines Judge, Linda Virgines Neiman. *Education:* Attended technical high school in Chicago, Ill.

ADDRESSES: Home and office—P. O. Box 13761, Albuquerque, N.M. 87192.

CAREER: Worked as chauffer, florist, baker, salesman, handyman, and truck driver prior to 1942; Super Electric Construction Co., Chicago, Ill., 1945-60 and 1969-80, held various positions, including truck driver and machinery operator; full-time writer and consultant, 1960-69. Toured country for many years as a fancy gun handling expert and exhibition shooter with the Roving Gunslingers Western Variety and Wild West Show. Deputy sheriff in Lincoln, N.M., 1962-69, and DuPage County, Ill., 1967-69. Speaker on western lore. Consultant to Franklin Mint. *Military service:* U.S. Army, 1942-45; served in Africa and Italy; became staff sergeant; received two battle stars.

MEMBER: United States Marshal Foundation, Westerners (deputy marshal of Chicago Posse, 1965-73; sheriff of Chicago corral, 1973-75).

AWARDS, HONORS: Awarded honorary commissions as law officer from several states, including Illinois, Alabama, Oregon, Texas, and South Dakota, and from Arizona Rangers and Texas Rangers; recipient of presentation gun from the Colt Firearms Co. and handcrafted silver replica of the Arizona Rangers' badge from A. A. White Co., for work on the Arizona Rangers Commemorative Gun; also recipient of presentations from the Westerners and several fast draw clubs and associations.

WRITINGS:

Saga of the Colt Six-Shooter and the Famous Men Who Used It, Fell, 1969.
Famous Guns and Gunners, Pine Mountain Press, 1980.
Police Relics, Collector Books, 1982.
Western Legends and Lore, Pine Mountain Press, 1984.
Badges and Law and Order, Cochran Publishing, 1987.

Also author of booklet *History of the Arizona Rangers* for Colt Firearms Co., 1972; contributor of chapters to books on firearms. Contributor of over one hundred articles on western lore, lawmen, outlaws, firearms, badges, and police relics to *Guns, Gunworld, Frontier Times, True West, Relics, Rarities, New Mexico Magazine, Western Horseman, Real West,* and other publications.

WORK IN PROGRESS: *Police Collectibles: Pictorial Guide.*

SIDELIGHTS: George E. Virgines told *CA:* "Being a student and collector of our Western frontier history has made this subject very appealing both to read and research. The other compelling reason for my writing is that too many times I could not find enough information in books on the subjects that I was interested in. So this is one reason to propel me into becoming a writer. Lucky for me there was a market for me to reach that gave a purpose to write on the various subjects that interest collectors and readers of western lore, firearms, police history, and collectibles.

"My advice to aspiring writers of non-fiction is to study, read, and research every facet of their subject before attempting to write on anything. Check your facts, forward, backward, believe nobody, and double check again.

"In regards to the contemporary literary scene there seems to be a real lack of knowledgeable reviewers on many nonfiction historical books or collector type books."

W

WAGSTAFF, (John) Malcolm 1940-

PERSONAL: Born May 16, 1940, in Congleton, England; son of Arthur Ronald (a watchmaker and jeweler) and Alice (a secretary; maiden name, Taylor) Wagstaff; married Patricia Ann Thompson (a teacher), September 11, 1962; children: Robert Joseph, Daniel John. *Education:* University of Liverpool, B.A., 1962; graduate study at University of Athens, 1962-63; University of Southampton, Ph.D., 1975.

ADDRESSES: Office—Department of Geography, University of Southampton, Southampton, Hampshire, England. *Agent*—Frances Kelly, 9 King Edward Mansions, 629 Fulham Rd., London S.W.1, England.

CAREER: University of Durham, Durham, England, Centre of Middle Eastern and Islamic Studies, research assistant, 1963-66; University of Southampton, Southampton, Hampshire, England, lecturer, 1966-80, senior lecturer, 1980—.

MEMBER: Royal Geographical Society, Institute of British Geography, British Society for Middle Eastern Studies, British Institute of Archaeology at Ankara (council member, 1977-86).

AWARDS, HONORS: NATO fellowship, 1966-68.

WRITINGS:

(With Gerald H. Blake and Peter Beaumont) *The Middle East,* Wiley, 1976, 2nd edition, Fulton, 1988.
(Editor with Colin Renfrew) *An Island Polity: The Archaeology of Exploitation in Melos,* Cambridge University Press, 1982.
The Development of Rural Settlements, Avebury, 1982.
The Evolution of Middle Eastern Landscapes: An Outline to A.D. 1840, Croom Helm, 1985.
(Editor) *Landscape and Culture: Geographical and Archaeological Perspectives,* Blackwell, 1987.

Contributor of articles and reviews to professional journals, including *Balkan Studies, Geographical Review, Journal of Hellenic Studies,* and *Anatolian Studies.*

WORK IN PROGRESS: Research on the Peloponnese in the eighteenth century and on Lt. Col. William Martin Leake.

SIDELIGHTS: In *An Island Polity: The Archaeology of Exploitation in Melos,* Malcolm Wagstaff and co-editor Colin Renfrew record the findings of an expedition of archaeologists studying the nature of change. In a *Times Literary Supplement* review, A. M. Snodgrass described the book as "an admirable presentation of the findings of the expedition's fieldwork." Snodgrass also praised each of the editors, noting that "Malcolm Wagstaff's contributions throughout are conspicuous for their industry, learning and level-headedness."

Wagstaff told *CA:* "Scholars have the duty to communicate the result of their investigations to the public who supports them, and I write partly to fulfill that obligation and partly because writing helps to clarify my own thinking. I find writing both exciting and demanding."

BIOGRAPHICAL/CRITICAL SOURCES:

PERIODICALS

Times Literary Supplement, July 2, 1982.

* * *

WALKER, C(larence) Eugene 1939-

PERSONAL: Born January 8, 1939, in Monongahela, Pa.; son of Lewis G. (an auditor) and Olga Theresa (Brioli) Walker; married Lois E. Strom (a research assistant), February 28, 1964 (divorced, 1980); children: Chad Eugene, Kyle Lewis, Cass Emanuel. *Education:* Geneva College, B.S. (summa cum laude), 1960; Purdue University, M.S., 1963, Ph.D., 1965. *Politics:* Democrat. *Religion:* Methodist.

ADDRESSES: Home—1133 North Bank Side Circle, Edmond, Okla. 73034. *Office*—Department of Psychiatry and Behavioral Sciences, University of Oklahoma Health Science Center, P.O. Box 26901, Oklahoma City, Okla. 73190.

CAREER: Licensed psychologist in state of Oklahoma. Veterans Administration Neuropsychiatric Hospital, Marion, Ind., psychology trainee, 1961-62; Veterans Administration Regional Office, Mental Hygiene Clinic, Indianapolis, Ind., psychology trainee, 1962-63; West Tenth Street Veterans Administration Hospital, Indianapolis, psychology trainee, 1963, intern in clinical psychology, 1963-64; Westmont College, Santa Barbara, Calif., assistant professor of psychology, 1964-68, chairman of Division of Education and Psychology, 1966-68, director of Institutional Research, 1967-68; private practice of clinical psychology in Santa Barbara, 1965-68; Camarillo State

Hospital, Camarillo, Calif., staff psychologist, 1965-68; Baylor University, Waco, Tex., assistant professor, 1968-70, associate professor of psychology, 1970-74; private practice of clinical psychology in Waco, 1970-74; Oklahoma Children's Memorial Hospital, Oklahoma City, Okla., director of Outpatient Pediatric Psychology Clinic, 1974-79, associate chief of Mental Health Services, 1980—; University of Oklahoma, College of Medicine, Oklahoma City, associate professor, 1974-79, professor of psychology, 1980—, chief of Pediatric Psychology Service, 1974-80, director of Pediatric Psychology Training, 1977—.

Has presented numerous scientific papers and reports at psychological symposiums and conventions. Member of student appeals board, College of Medicine, University of Oklahoma, 1979-80. Member of several governance committees at Oklahoma Children's Memorial Hospital, 1977—. Consultant to several hospitals, educational programs, and institutions in California, Texas, and Oklahoma.

MEMBER: American Psychological Association (fellow; chairman of Newsletter Editors Committee), Association for the Advancement of Psychology, American Association for the Advancement of Science, Society of Pediatric Psychology (former president), American Society of Clinical Hypnosis, American Scientific Affiliation (fellow), Corresponding Committee of Fifty (former chairman), Southwestern Psychological Association (former secretary-treasurer and former president), Oklahoma Psychological Association (former president), Central Texas Psychological Association (former president), Sigma Xi.

WRITINGS:

Learn to Relax, Prentice-Hall, 1975.
(With Allen G. Hedberg) *An Introduction to Behavior Therapy*, Behavioral Advances, 1975.
(With Hedberg, Paul Clement, and Logan Wright) *Clinical Procedures of Behavior Therapy*, Prentice-Hall, 1981.
(With B. L. Bonner and L. Milling) *Physical and Sexual Abuse of Children*, Pergamon, in press.

EDITOR

(And contributor) *Research Symposium #2*, California Department of Mental Hygiene, 1968.
(With Hedberg, Wright, and Donald K. Freedheim) *A Newsletter Editor's Handbook*, Division of State Psychological Association Affairs, American Psychological Association, 1974.
(With Hedberg and Larry E. Beutler) *Careers in Clinical Psychology: Is There a Place for Me?* (booklet), Section II, Division of Clinical Psychology, American Psychological Association, 1977.
Clinical Practice of Psychology, Pergamon, 1981.
(With M. C. Roberts) *Handbook of Clinical Child Psychology*, Wiley, 1983.
Handbook of Clinical Psychology, Dow Jones-Irwin, 1983.
(With A. Zeiner and D. Bendell) *Health Psychology: Treatment and Research Issues*, Plenum, 1985.
Clinical Psychology: Historical and Research Foundations, Plenum, in press.
(With Bonner and Milling) *Handbook of Pediatric Psychology*, Society of Pediatric Psychology, in press.

CONTRIBUTOR

O. H. Herron, editor, *New Dimensions in Student Personnel Administration*, International Textbook Co., 1970.

G. R. Collins, editor, *Our Society in Turmoil*, Creation House, 1970.
Paul J. Woods, editor, *Source Book on the Teaching of Psychology*, Scholar's Press, 1973.
Phyllis McGrab, editor, *Psychological Management of Pediatric Problems*, University Park Press, 1978.
Wright, editor, *Encyclopedia of Pediatric Psychology*, University Park Press, 1979.
John McNamara, editor, *Behavioral Approaches to Medicine: Application and Analysis*, Plenum, 1980.
T. Ollendick and M. Hersen, editors, *Handbook of Child Psychopathology*, Plenum, 1981.
D. M. Doleys, R. L. Meredith, and A. R. Ciminero, editors, *Behavioral Psychology in Medicine: Assessment and Treatment Strategies*, Plenum, 1981.
J. H. Humphrey, editor, *Stress in Childhood*, AMS Press, 1984.
D. J. Keyser and R. C. Sweetland, editors, *Test Critiques*, Test Corporation of America, Volume 1, 1985, Volume 5, 1986.
P. Keller and L. Ritt, editors, *Innovations in Clinical Practice*, Professional Resource Exchange (Sarasota, Fla.), Volume 4, 1985, Volume 6, in press.
P. Karoly, editor, *Handbook of Health Psychology Assessment*, Wiley, in press.

OTHER

Also author of "The Sex Form," a test for assessing sexual functioning and adjustment. Author of audio tapes produced by Self Control Systems, *Creative Parenting: Helping Children Learn to Be Happy Adults*, 1980, and *Stress Management* and *Effective Communications between Parents and Teenagers*, both 1981. Contributor of articles to psychology journals, including *Journal of Consulting and Clinical Psychology*, *Archives of Sexual Behavior*, *Journal of Child and Adolescent Psychotherapy*, *Behavior Therapist*, *Clinical Psychologist*, and *Psychological Reports*. Contributing editor of *Journal of the American Scientific Affiliation*, 1966-68, and *Professional Psychology*, 1969-76; book review editor of *Clinical Psychologist*, 1968-69, *Journal of Clinical Child Psychology*, 1975—, *Journal of Pediatric Psychology*, 1975—, and *American Psychologist*, 1980—.

WORK IN PROGRESS: A Fear Survey for Children: Preliminary Data and Factor Analysis, with C. Elliott.

*   *   *

WALKER, David   1950-

PERSONAL: Born November 11, 1950, in Aberdeen, Scotland; son of John (a steelworker) and Irene (a teacher; maiden name, Connor) Walker; married Karen Irving (a social worker). *Education:* University of Sussex, M.A., 1972; St. Catharine's College, Cambridge, M.A., 1975.

ADDRESSES: Home—6 Midhurst Ave., London N10 3EN, England. *Agent*—Michael Sissons, A. D. Peters & Co. Ltd., 10 Buckingham St., London WC2N 6BU, England.

CAREER: Times Newspapers Ltd., London, England, journalist, 1973-77; *Economist*, London, journalist, 1979-81; *London Times*, London, journalist, 1981-86; *London Daily Telegraph*, journalist, 1986-87; *London Daily News*, London, journalist, 1987; London *Times*, London, journalist, 1987—. Presenter of "Analysis" program, BBC-Radio Four. Robert T. McKenzie fellow, London School of Economics, 1987-88.

AWARDS, HONORS: Harkness fellowship, Harkness Foundation Commonwealth Fund, 1977-79.

WRITINGS:

(With Jeremy Tunstall) *Media Made in California,* Oxford University Press, 1981.
(Contributor) *Yearbook of Social Policy,* Routledge & Kegan Paul, 1981.
Municipal Empire: The Town Halls and Their Beneficiaries, Temple Smith, 1983.
(With Michael Cockerell and Peter Hennessy) *Sources Close to the Prime Minister: Inside the Hidden World of the News Manipulators,* Macmillan, 1984.

Contributor to magazines.

SIDELIGHTS: David Walker told *CA:* "A problem for a journalist writing a book is expanding the usual short deadlines over a long period and writing at length instéad of at breadth. But once the new rhythm is learned, books take on a weightiness which journalism lacks."

*   *   *

WALKER, Edward Joseph 1934-
(Ted Walker)

PERSONAL: Born November 28, 1934, in Lancing, England; son of Edward Joseph (a carpenter) and Winifred (Schofield) Walker; married first wife Lorna Benfell, August 11, 1956 (died, April 1, 1987); married second wife Audrey Joan Hicks, July 8, 1988; children: (first marriage) Edward, Susan, Margaret, William. *Education:* St. John's College, Cambridge, B.A. (with honors), 1956. *Politics:* "Leftish." *Religion:* "Apprehensive agnostic."

ADDRESSES: Home—Argyll House, The Square, Eastergate, Chichester, West Sussex, England.

CAREER: Poet. High School for Boys, Chichester, Sussex, schoolmaster and teacher of French and Spanish, 1953-67; full-time author and broadcaster, 1967-71; New England College, Arundel, Sussex, poet in residence and professor of creative writing, 1971—.

MEMBER: Society of Authors, Royal Society of Literature (fellow).

AWARDS, HONORS: Eric Gregory award, Society of Authors, 1964; Cholmondeley Award for Poets, Society of Authors, 1966, for *The Solitaries;* Alice Hunt Bartlett Prize, Poetry Society, 1967, for *The Solitaries;* Major Arts Council of Great Britain award, 1978; J. R. Ackerley Prize, English Centre of International PEN, 1982, for *The High Path.*

WRITINGS:

UNDER NAME TED WALKER

Those Other Growths (poems), Northern House, 1964.
Fox on a Barn Door (poems), J. Cape, 1965, Braziller, 1966.
The Solitaries (poems), Braziller, 1967.
The Night Bathers (poems), J. Cape, 1970.
Gloves to the Hangman (poems), J. Cape, 1973.
Burning the Ivy (poems), J. Cape, 1979.
The Lion's Cavalcade (poems), J. Cape, 1980.
The High Path (autobiography), Routledge & Kegan Paul, 1982.

You've Never Heard Me Sing (short stories), Heinemann, 1985.
Hands at a Live Fire (poems), Secker & Warburg, 1987.
In Spain (nonfiction), Secker & Warburg, 1987.

Contributor of poems and short stories to *New Yorker;* contributor of short stories to other periodicals. Founding editor, with John Cotton, *Priapus.*

SIDELIGHTS: A British writer, editor, radio and television dramatist, and translator, Ted Walker is best known for his carefully crafted poems, many of which follow the tradition of English nature poetry. In his precise observation of animals, fish, and birds, Walker detects a natural harmony that is missing in civilized life. He describes his works as "in the main a poetry of fear and loss which looks for the beauty that remains among the ruins of lost faith, lost innocence and lost animal strength," according to the *Library Journal.*

"His best poems are the ones in which he dramatizes segments of being that have been crushed or suppressed by the conditions of civilized life, 'wants kept caged on roofs/ of the mind's tenements,'" writes Laurence Lieberman in the *Yale Review.* "In weaker poems, the shifts from description to message— statement of human analogy—are abrupt and unaccountable, and jar in the reader's ear. In the best poems, these two movements are carried on simultaneously, joined and jointed, seamlessly, in the poem's drama."

Though Walker turned to prose for his autobiography *The High Path,* this work exhibits many of the qualities of his poems. There is the same respect for language—reflecting what *Times Literary Supplement* reviewer Edward Blishen calls "the poet's habit of not allowing words to report for duty half-asleep." Blishen commends Walker's powers of observation and his ability to make "sense of the brimming nonsense of a life," adding that the poet's father "had a term for anything beautifully done: *umpity poo.* There seems no better term for *The High Path.*"

Since the appearance of his autobiography, Walker has published more prose than poetry. He has written a book about his travels in Spain and a collection of short stories entitled *You've Never Heard Me Sing. In Spain* is a "labor of love," says Xan Fielding in the *Times Literary Supplement,* in which Walker tells how he submersed himself in Spanish culture, living in the country's small villages as a typical rural Spaniard would. *You've Never Heard Me Sing* is a collection of his previously-published stories from the *New Yorker* and other magazines. *Times Literary Supplement* reviewer Tim Dooley calls this work a "very satisfying, quietly moving book." The "growing recognition of [Walker's] achievement as a prose writer," Dooley asserts, "will be strengthened by the publication of this collection of his short fiction."

BIOGRAPHICAL/CRITICAL SOURCES:

BOOKS

Contemporary Literary Criticism, Volume 13, Gale, 1980.
Walker, Ted, *The High Path,* Routledge & Kegan Paul, 1982.

PERIODICALS

Books and Bookmen, May, 1967.
Kenyon Review, January, 1967.
Library Journal, July, 1966.
New Statesman, May 12, 1967.
New York Times Book Review, November 20, 1966.
Observer, March 26, 1967.
Poetry, March, 1967, May, 1967.

Times Literary Supplement, June 18, 1970, June 8, 1973, January 14, 1983, November 15, 1985, November 17, 1987, May 20, 1988.
Yale Review, winter, 1968.

*　　*　　*

WALKER, Ted
See WALKER, Edward Joseph

*　　*　　*

WALLACE, Barbara Brooks

PERSONAL: Born in Soochow, China; daughter of Otis Frank (a businessman) and Nicia E. Brooks; married James Wallace, Jr. (in U.S. Air Force), February 27, 1954; children: James. *Education:* Attended schools in Hankow, Tientsin, and Shanghai, China, in Baguio, Philippines, and in Claremont, Calif.; attended Pomona College, 1940-41; University of California, Los Angeles, B.A., 1945. *Religion:* Episcopalian.

ADDRESSES: Home—2708 George Mason Pl., Alexandria, Va. 22305. *Agent*—Johnson & Thompson, 28th and O St., Washington, D.C.

CAREER: Writer.

MEMBER: National League of American Pen Women, Children's Book Guild of Washington, D.C., Alpha Phi.

AWARDS, HONORS: Juvenile book award, National League of American Pen Women, 1970, for *Claudia,* and 1974, for *The Secret Summer of L.E.B.;* William Allen White Children's Book Award, 1983, for *Peppermints in the Parlor.*

WRITINGS:

JUVENILES

Claudia, Follett, 1969.
Andrew the Big Deal, Follett, 1971.
The Trouble with Miss Switch, Abingdon, 1971.
Victoria, Follett, 1972.
Can Do, Missy Charlie, Follett, 1974.
The Secret Summer of L.E.B., Follett, 1974.
Julia and the Third Bad Thing, Follett, 1975.
Palmer Patch, Follett, 1976.
Hawkins, Abingdon, 1977.
Peppermints in the Parlor, Atheneum, 1980.
The Contest Kid Strikes Again, Abingdon, 1980.
Hawkins and the Soccer Solution, Abingdon, 1981.
Miss Switch to the Rescue, Abingdon, 1981.
Hello, Claudia!, Modern Curriculum Press, 1982.
Claudia and Duffy, Modern Curriculum Press, 1982.
The Barrel in the Basement, Atheneum, 1985.
Argyle, Abingdon, 1987.
The Interesting Thing That Happened at Perfect Acres, Inc., Atheneum, 1988.

WORK IN PROGRESS: A Victorian melodrama for young readers.

*　　*　　*

WALSH, P(atrick) G(erard)　1923-

PERSONAL: Born August 16, 1923, in Accrington, Lancashire, England; son of Peter and Joanna (Fitzpatrick) Walsh; married Eileen Quin, July 18, 1953; children: Anthony, Patricia, Stephen, John, David. *Education:* Attended Preston Catholic College, 1934-42; University of Liverpool, B.A., 1949, M.A., 1951; University College, Dublin, Ph.D., 1957. *Religion:* Roman Catholic.

ADDRESSES: Home—17 Broom Rd., Glasgow G43 2TP, Scotland. *Office*—Department of Humanity, University of Glasgow, Glasgow G12 8QQ, Scotland.

CAREER: University College, Dublin, Ireland, lecturer in classics, 1952-59; University of Edinburgh, Edinburgh, Scotland, lecturer, 1959-66, reader in humanity, 1967-71, professor of Medieval Latin, 1971-72; University of Glasgow, Glasgow, Scotland, professor of humanity, 1972—. Visiting professor, University of Toronto, 1966-67, and Yale University, 1970-71. *Military service:* British Army, Intelligence Corps, 1943-46.

WRITINGS:

Livy: His Historical Aims and Methods, Cambridge University Press, 1961.
(Translator) Paulinus of Nola, *Letters,* two volumes, Paulist/Newman, 1966-67.
(Translator with Anthony Ross) St. Thomas Aquinas, *Courage,* Eyre & Spottiswoode, 1966.
The Roman Novel, Cambridge University Press, 1970.
Courtly Love in the Carmina Burana, Edinburgh University Press, 1972.
Livy, Oxford Univeristy Press, 1974.
(Editor) *Livy, Book XXI,* University Tutorial Press, 1974.
(Translator) O. Quasten, editor, *Poems of Paulinus of Nola,* Paulist/Newman, 1975.
(Editor) *Thirty Poems from the Carmina Burana,* University of Reading, 1976.
(Editor and translator) *Andreas Capellanus on Love,* Duckworth, 1982.
(Editor) Livy, *Ab urbe condita libri XXVI-XXVII,* Teubner, 1982.
(Editor with P. Sharratt) *George Buchanan Tragedies,* Scottish Academic Press, 1984.

Contributor to classical journals.

WORK IN PROGRESS: Translations of Cassiodorus' *Commentary on the Psalms.*

BIOGRAPHICAL/CRITICAL SOURCES:

PERIODICALS

Times Literary Supplement, March 18, 1983.*

*　　*　　*

WARD, Benedicta　1933-

PERSONAL: Born February 4, 1933, in Durham, England; daughter of Oswald Alleyn (a minister) and Florence Susannah (Linnet) Ward. *Education:* University of Manchester, B.A. (with honors), 1955; St. Anne's College, Oxford, D.Phil., 1977.

ADDRESSES: Home—Convent of the Incarnation, Fairacres, Oxford, England.

CAREER: Member of a contemplative enclosed order of women religious in the Church of England. Lecturer in England and the United States. Tutor in medieval history, Centre for Medieval and Renaissance Studies; member of the theology faculty of Oxford University.

WRITINGS:

Prayers and Meditations of St. Anselm, Penguin, 1973.
The Sayings of the Desert Fathers, Mowbrays, 1975.
The Wisdom of the Desert Fathers, SLG Press, 1975.
(Editor and contributor) *The Influence of St. Bernard,* SLG Press, 1976.
Lives of the Desert Fathers, Mowbrays, 1978.
Miracles and the Medieval Mind, Scolar Press, 1981.
Harlots of the Desert, Mowbrays, 1988.
The Desert of the Heart, DLT, 1988.

CONTRIBUTOR

M. Basil Pennington, editor, *Contemplative Community,* Cistercian Publication, 1972.
Pennington, editor, *Bernard of Clairvaux,* Cistercian Publications, 1973.
Pennington, editor, *One Yet Two,* Cistercian Publications, 1976.
G. Bonner, editor, *Famulus Christi,* Cistercian Publications, 1976.
Dictionary of Spirituality, Society for Promoting Christian Knowledge, 1983.
Study of Spirituality, Oxford University Press, 1984.
The Translator's Art, Penguin, 1987.
P. Toon, editor, *Guidelines for Spirituality,* Penguin, 1987.

WORK IN PROGRESS: Translating William of Malmesbury's *Gesta Pontificum,* for Oxford University Press; translating *Exordium Magnum Cistercian,* for Cistercian Publications; two other books.

*   *   *

WATERTON, Betty (Marie)   1923-

PERSONAL: Born August 31, 1923, in Oshawa, Ontario, Canada; daughter of Eric Williams and Mary Irene (Hewson) Wrightmeyer; married Claude Waterton (a Royal Canadian Air Force pilot), April 7, 1942; children: Eric, Julia, Karen (Mrs. James Alexander Maxwell). *Education:* Attended Vancouver School of Art. *Religion:* Fundamentalist.

ADDRESSES: Home—10135 Tsaykum Rd., R. R. 1, Sidney, British Columbia, Canada V8L 3R9.

CAREER: Vancouver Sun, Vancouver, British Columbia, retoucher, 1957; free-lance caricaturist during the early 1960s; KVOS-TV, Vancouver, animator during the mid-1960s; adult education teacher of art, School District 63, Sidney, British Columbia.

MEMBER: Canadian Society of Children's Authors, Illustrators, and Performers.

AWARDS, HONORS: Authors Literature Prize from Canadian Society of Children's Authors, 1979; Canadian Library Association, Amelia Frances Howard-Gibbon Medal and runner-up for Children's Book of the Year Award, both 1979, both for *A Salmon for Simon.*

WRITINGS:

A Salmon for Simon (juvenile), illustrations by Ann Blades, Douglas & McIntyre, 1978, McElderry Book, 1979.
Pettranella (juvenile), illustrations by Blades, Vanguard Press, 1981.
Mustard (juvenile), Scholastic-TAB Publications, 1983.
The Cat of Quinty, Thomas Nelson, 1984.
The White Moose, Ginn, 1984.
Orff, 27 Dragons (and a Snarkel!), Annick Press, 1984.

Quincy Rumpel, Douglas & McIntyre, 1984.
Starring Quincy Rumpel, Douglas & McIntyre, 1986.
Quincy Rumpel, P.I., Douglas & McIntyre, 1988.
Noodles, illustrations by Joanne Fitzgerald, Douglas & McIntyre, 1989.

SIDELIGHTS: Betty Waterton told *CA:* "A seventh-generation Canadian, I have lived most of my life on the West Coast. My father had been from time to time an unpublished writer of short stories. I was an early versifier and once earned a dollar for a poem published in the *Vancouver Sun.* After this triumph I disappeared from the literary scene until somewhere in midlife, when I began to write for children."

*   *   *

WAYNE, David
See BALSIGER, David (Wayne)

*   *   *

WAYS, C. R.
See BLOUNT, Roy (Alton), Jr.

*   *   *

WEBB, Mary H(aydn)   1938-
(Leah Ross)

PERSONAL: Born August 13, 1938, in Cleveland, Ohio; daughter of Hiram Collins (a writer, editor, and teacher) and Rachel (a librarian; maiden name, Norris) Haydn; married S. David Webb, September 1, 1958 (divorced, 1967); children: Alexander Matthew. *Education:* Attended Cornell University, 1956-58; University of California, Berkeley, A.B. (with honors), 1960; University of Florida, M.A., 1967. *Politics:* Independent. *Religion:* Independent.

ADDRESSES: Home and office—2439 Jefferson Ave., Apt. B, Berkeley, Calif. 94703.

CAREER: University of California, Berkeley, reader in Department of English, 1960-64; Santa Fe Junior College, Gainesville, Fla., instructor in liberal arts, 1966-67; Merritt College, Oakland, Calif., instructor in English, 1967-68; reading teacher in public school in Alachua, Fla., 1968-69; Micanopy Group Companies, Alachua, research assistant, 1969-70; Division of Family Services, Gainesville, social worker and community development specialist, 1970-72; Neighborhood Youth Corps, Gainesville, counselor, 1973; University of Florida Press, Gainesville, copy editor, 1973-74; University of Florida, Personalized Learning Center, Gainesville, secretary and supervisor, 1974; Lees' Pre-School Center, Alachua, director, 1974-75; Black Repertory Group, Berkeley, theater arts technician, 1975-76; Los Medanos College, Pittsburg, Calif., language arts instructor, 1976-86; Berkeley Adult School, Berkeley, English instructor, 1977—; VISTA College, Berkeley, English instructor, 1979—; also teacher at Diablo Valley College and at Rossmoor, a senior community, and conductor of private workshops. Co-founder, Muntu Books, 1985. Lecturer; organizer, teacher, and director for Modern Dance Program of Center Dance Group, Alachua, 1965-67, 1968-72; has worked with children as governess and as organizer of summer vacation trips; member of several community programs for low-income families.

MEMBER: National Writers Union, Film Arts Foundation, Peralta Federal Teachers Union, Phi Beta Kappa.

WRITINGS:

(Under pseudonym Leah Ross) *Dark Roads* (novel), Harcourt, 1975.

The God-Hustlers (novel; also see below), Muntu Books, 1985.

''The God-Hustlers'' (play; adapted from her novel), first produced at the Laney Theater in Oakland, Calif., on May 31, 1987.

Also author of unproduced play, ''Artaud and His Double''; author of screenplay adaptations of *Dark Roads* and *The God-Hustlers,* and of comedy screenplay, ''Beating the Odds.''

WORK IN PROGRESS: A novel, as yet untitled, ''based on a hitchhiking trip through Europe and Africa that I took with my then 10-year-old son in 1972-73.''

SIDELIGHTS: Mary H. Webb told *CA:* ''I believe that everyone is creative and that as Isaac Singer said, 'everyone has a story to tell.' That is what I teach in my Creative Writing classes. So, in my own work, I try to tell my story, to carve out the arena of my real and imagined experiences so that other people can touch the world that I perceive.

''I consider myself to be a visionary writer because I write about the possibilities I see for human life as well as about its terrors; the human dilemma, i.e. being human on this planet at this time, is what all serious writers are writing about. I believe in the possibility of a change of consciousness in the world and that that change will come about through art, politics, psychology and spirituality.

''I write about the cultural edge, about that line people from different cultures cross when they become truly involved with each other and learn how to communicate at very deep levels. My writing is multi-cultural and committed to the idea that we live on one planet and must learn to live there with peace and love if we are to survive.''

Dramatic readings of Webb's work, including *The God-Hustlers,* have been given at several bookstores and theaters around California.

*   *   *

WEBB, Rodman B.   1941-

PERSONAL: Born April 18, 1941, in New York, N.Y. *Education:* Boston University, B.S., 1964; University of Hawaii, M.A., 1967; Rutgers University, Ed.D., 1974.

ADDRESSES: Home—17 Southwest 23rd Dr., Gainesville, Fla. 32607. *Office*—Norman Hall, University of Florida, Gainesville, Fla. 32611.

CAREER: Crossley S-D Surveys, New York, N.Y., marketing research associate, 1962-65; English teacher in Honolulu, Hawaii, 1967-69; University of Florida, Gainesville, associate professor, 1971-86, professor of education, 1986—.

MEMBER: American Educational Research Association, American Education Studies Association, John Dewey Society, Southeastern Philosophy of Education Society.

WRITINGS:

The Presence of the Past: John Dewey and Alfred Schutz on the Genesis and Organization of Experience, University Presses of Florida, 1976.

Schooling and Society, Macmillan, 1981, 2nd edition with Robert R. Sherman, 1989.

(With Patricia T. Ashton) *Making a Difference,* Longman, 1986.

(Editor with Sherman) *Qualitative Research in Education,* Falmer Press, 1989.

Contributor to education journals. Founding editor with Sherman of *International Journal of Qualitative Studies in Education,* 1988.

*   *   *

WEISS, Ann E(dwards)   1943-

PERSONAL: Born March 21, 1943, in Newton, Mass.; daughter of Donald Loring (a teacher) and Dorothy (a teacher; maiden name, Poole) Charlton; married Malcolm E. Weiss (a writer), January 31, 1966; children: Margot Elizabeth, Rebecca Bates. *Education:* Brown University, A.B., 1965.

ADDRESSES: Home—R.D. 1, Box 415, North Whitefield, Me. 04353. *Agent*—Marilyn Marlow, Curtis Brown, Ltd., 575 Madison Ave., New York, N.Y. 10022.

CAREER: Scholastic Magazines, Inc., New York, N.Y., writer and assistant editor, 1965-69, associate editor, 1969-72; freelance writer, 1972—.

AWARDS, HONORS: Christopher Award, 1974, for *Save the Mustangs,* and 1984, for *The Nuclear Arms Race: Can We Survive It?; Save the Mustangs, The School on Madison Avenue, God and Government,* and *The Supreme Court* were named notable children's trade books by the National Council for the Social Studies Children's Book Council for 1974, 1978, 1982, and 1988, respectively; Outstanding Science Trade Book for Children Award, National Science Teachers Association Children's Book Council, 1976, for *The Vitamin Puzzle,* and 1981, for *The Nuclear Question.*

WRITINGS:

JUVENILES

Five Roads to the White House, Messner, 1970.

We Will Be Heard: Dissent in the United States, Messner, 1972.

Save the Mustangs: How a Federal Law Is Passed, Messner, 1974.

(With husband, Malcolm E. Weiss) *The Vitamin Puzzle,* Messner, 1976.

The American Presidency, Messner, 1976.

The American Congress, Messner, 1977.

News or Not?, Dutton, 1977.

Polls and Surveys: A Look at Public Opinion Research, F. Watts, 1979.

The School on Madison Avenue: Advertising and What It Teaches (Junior Literary Guild selection), Dutton, 1979.

What's That You Said?, Harcourt, 1980.

Party Politics, Party Problems, Harper, 1980.

The Nuclear Question, Harcourt, 1981.

Tune In, Tune Out: Broadcasting Regulation in the United States, Houghton, 1981.

God and Government: The Separation of Church and State, Houghton, 1982.

The Nuclear Arms Race: Can We Survive It?, Houghton, 1983.

Over-the-Counter Drugs, F. Watts, 1984.

Biofeedback: Fact or Fad?, F. Watts, 1984.

Bioethics: Dilemmas in Modern Medicine, Enslow Publishers, 1985.

Good Neighbors? The U.S. and Latin America, Houghton, 1985.

Seers and Scientists: Can the Future Be Predicted?, Harcourt, 1986.
The Supreme Court, Enslow Publishers, 1987.
U.S. Prisons: A System in Trouble, Enslow Publishers, 1988.
Lies, Deception, and Truth, Houghton, 1988.

WORK IN PROGRESS: A book on welfare; a book on the public's right-to-know.

* * *

WELLS, Henry W(illis)   1895-1978

PERSONAL: Born in 1895 in Sewanee, Tenn.; died March 22, 1978, in Bronx, N.Y.; married Katharine Alleb Powell. *Education:* Amherst College, graduated, 1917; Columbia University, Ph.D., 1924.

ADDRESSES: Home—777 Kappock St., Bronx, N.Y.

CAREER: Writer. Member of graduate department of Columbia University for forty years, worked as professor of English and comparative literature; secretary of American Society for Theater Research and U.S. Institute for Theater Technology; director of Committee for Refugee Education.

WRITINGS:

The Realm of Literature, Columbia University Press, 1927, Kennikat, 1964.
The Judgement of Literature, Norton, 1928.
Elizabethan and Jacobean Playwrights, Columbia University Press, 1939, Greenwood Press, 1975.
New Poets from Old: A Study in Literary Genetics, Columbia University Press, 1940, Russell & Russell, 1964.
Poetic Imagery Illustrated from Elizabethan Literature, Columbia University Press, 1942.
The American Way of Poetry, Columbia University Press, 1943.
Edwin J. Pratt: The Man and His Poetry, Ryerson Press, 1947.
Introduction to Emily Dickinson, Hendricks House, 1947.
Where Poetry Stands Now, Ryerson Press, 1948.
(Editor) *One Thousand and One Poems of Mankind: Memorable Short Poems from the World's Chief Literatures*, Tupper & Love, 1953.
Poet and Psychiatrist: Merrill Moore, M.D.; A Critical Portrait with an Appraisal of Two Hundred of His Poems, Twayne, 1955.
(Adapter into modern English) William Langland, *The Vison of Piers Plowman*, Sheed & Ward, 1959, Greenwood Press, 1968.
The Classical Drama of India: Studies in Its Values for the Literature and Theatre of the World, Asia Publishing House, 1963.
Introduction to Wallace Stevens, Indiana University Press, 1963.
(Editor) *Six Sanskrit Plays, in English Translation*, Asia Publishing House, 1964.
(Translator) *Ancient Poetry from China, Japan, and India*, University of South Carolina Press, 1968.
(Editor with Roger Sherman Loomis, and translator) *Representative Medieval and Tudor Plays*, Books for Libraries Press, 1970.
(Translator and adapter into English verse) *Classical Triptych: Sakuntala, The Little Clay Cart and Nagananda; New Renderings into English Verse*, University of Mysore, 1970.
(Editor with Arthur Christy) *World Literature*, Books for Libraries Press, 1971.
Traditional Chinese Humor: A Study in Art and Literature, Indiana University Press, 1971.

(Editor) Po Chue-i, *Translations from Po Chue-i's Collected Works*, translated by Howard S. Levy, Paragon, 1971.
(Translator with Ch'eng Hsi) *An Album of Wang Wei*, Lingch'so-hsuean (Hong Kong), 1974.
(Translator) Saka Shibutsu, *Diary of a Pilgrim to Ise*, Chinese Materials Center (San Francisco), 1977.
(With H. H. Anniah Gowda) *Style and Structure in Shakespeare*, Vikas Publishing (New Delhi), 1979.
On Spanish Paintings in the Hispanic Museum, New York (booklet), Rhinoceros Press, 1981.

Contributor to journals in India, Taiwan, and Japan.

SIDELIGHTS: Although most of Henry W. Wells's writings are concerned with English literature and drama, he also wrote several articles on Sanskrit drama and the drama of China, India, and Japan. Wells devoted a series of articles to the similarities between Chinese poets and those from England and America.

OBITUARIES:

PERIODICALS

New York Times, March 24, 1978.*

* * *

WETHERBEE, Winthrop (III)   1938-

PERSONAL: Born July 10, 1938, in Boston, Mass.; son of Winthrop, Jr. (a physician) and Carolyn (Hall) Wetherbee; married Andrea Kempf, March 26, 1962; children: Peter, Jonathan. *Education:* Harvard University, B.A., 1960; University of Leeds, M.A., 1962; University of California, Berkeley, Ph.D., 1967.

ADDRESSES: Home—604 Highland Rd., Ithaca, N.Y. 14850. *Office*—Department of English, Cornell University, Ithaca, N.Y. 14853.

CAREER: Cornell University, Ithaca, N.Y., assistant professor, 1967-72, associate professor, 1972-74, professor of English, 1974-80; University of Chicago, Chicago, Ill., professor of English, 1980-85; Cornell University, professor of classics and English, 1985—.

MEMBER: Mediaeval Academy of America.

AWARDS, HONORS: American Council of Learned Societies fellowship, 1970-71; Guggenheim fellowship, 1974-75; National Endowment for the Humanities fellowship, 1987.

WRITINGS:

Platonism and Poetry in the Twelfth Century, Princeton University Press, 1972.
The Cosmographia of Bernardus Silvestris, Columbia University Press, 1973.
Chaucer and the Poets: An Essay on "Troilus and Criseyde," Cornell University Press, 1984.
Chaucer's Canterbury Tales, Cambridge University Press, 1989.

WORK IN PROGRESS: Study of the poetry of John Gower.

* * *

WHARTON, Joanna
See HAMEL PEIFER, Kathleen

WHIGHAM, Peter (George)   1925-1987

PERSONAL: Born March 6, 1925, in Oxford, England; came to the United States in 1965; died August 6, 1987, from injuries sustained in an automobile accident; son of Robert George Murray (a chartered accountant) and Ellen Rose (Carr) Whigham; married Jean Scratton (a teacher), December 27, 1953; married second wife, Priscilla Minn (a social worker), August 16, 1969; children: (first marriage) Charlotte, Robert Guy, Frances. *Education:* "Self-educated." *Politics:* "Anarcho-Syndicalist (Ghandian)." *Religion:* Pantheist.

ADDRESSES: Home—Hayward, Calif.

CAREER: Successively a gardener in the Wye Valley of England, a schoolmaster, an actor in provincial repertory, a reporter for a newspaper in mid-Wales, a schoolmaster again, and a free-lance scriptwriter and broadcaster for British Broadcasting Corp., including broadcaster and adviser for "Ezra Pound's Provence"; writer and translator in Italy during the early 1960s; lecturer in verse composition at University of California, Santa Barbara, 1966-68; lecturer in comparative literature at University of California, Berkeley, beginning 1969.

AWARDS, HONORS: The Blue-Winged Bee: Love Poems of the VIth Dalai Lama was honored by the Poetry Book Society in 1969.

WRITINGS:

POETRY

(Editor with Denis Goacher) Ezra Pound, *Women of Trachis,* Spearman, 1956.
(With Goacher) *Clear Lake Comes from Enjoyment,* Neville Spearman, 1959.
(With Goacher) *The Marriage Rite,* Ditchling Press, 1960.
(Author of introduction) William Carlos Williams, *Asphodel, that Greeny Flower,* Poets' and Painters' Press (London), 1963.
The Ingathering of Love (also see below), Unicorn Press (Santa Barbara), 1967.
The Blue-Winged Bee: Love Poems of the VIth Dalai Lama [and] *The Ingathering of Love* (Poetry Book Society choice in England), Anvil Press Poetry, 1969.
ASTAPOVO; or, What We Are to Do, Anvil Press Poetry, 1970.
The Fletcher Song Book (poems set to music by Preston Wood), Anvil Press Poetry, 1970.
The Crystal Mountain, Anvil Press Poetry, 1970.
Langue d'oeil, Press of the Pegacycle Lady, 1971.
(Editor) *The Music of the Troubadours,* translated by Timothy Wardell, Ross-Erikson, 1980.
Things Common, Properly: Selected Poems, 1942-1982, edited by Peter Jay, Black Swan Books, 1984.

TRANSLATOR

(With Mary de Rachewiltz) Umberto Mastroianni, *The Detail and the Design* (poems), Edizione Segnacolo, 1963.
Boris de Rachewiltz, *Black Eros* (anthropological study), Lyle Stuart, 1964.
de Rachewiltz, *Introduction to African Art,* New American Library, 1965.
The Poems of Catullus, Penguin, 1966, 2nd edition with "some forced deletions restored," 1969, bilingual edition, University of California Press, 1969.
(With Peter Jay) *The Poems of Meleager,* University of California Press, 1975.

Letter to Juvenal: 101 Epigrams from Martial, Anvil Press Poetry, 1985.

OTHER

Scripts for British Broadcasting Corp. Third Programme include "Cathay," "On Democracy," and "William Carlos Williams." Contributor of poetry to numerous anthologies, including *23 Modern Poets, Penguin Book of Love Poems,* and *Twenty Times in One Place.* "Dialogues," a long continuing work, began appearing in *Spectrum* (English department journal at University of California, Santa Barbara) in 1967.

SIDELIGHTS: "All that I am interested in," Peter Whigham once told *CA,* "centers round my work or is directed towards it. I do not, strictly speaking, find any 'separation' in my pursuits."

BIOGRAPHICAL/CRITICAL SOURCES:

PERIODICALS

Poetry, May, 1971.
Times Literary Supplement, August 14, 1969.

OBITUARIES:

PERIODICALS

Los Angeles Times, August 29, 1987.
New York Times, October 1, 1987.*

*　　*　　*

WHITAKER, C(leophaus) S(ylvester), Jr.   1935-

PERSONAL: Born February 21, 1935, in Pittsburgh, Pa.; son of Cleophaus Sylvester (a mortician) and Edith (McColes) Whitaker; married Jeanne Theis, August 18, 1956 (divorced, 1964); children: Mark Theis, Paul McColes. *Education:* Swarthmore College, B.A. (with high honors), 1956; Princeton University, M.A., 1958, Ph.D., 1964.

ADDRESSES: Home—8 Orchard Rd., Piscataway, N.J. 08854. *Office*—Rutgers University, New Brunswick, N.J. 08903.

CAREER: Princeton University, Princeton, N.J., instructor, 1960-61, lecturer in politics, 1961-62; University of California, Los Angeles, assistant professor, 1962-68, associate professor, 1968-69, professor-designate of politics, 1969, associate dean of student and academic affairs in Graduate Division, 1964-67; Princeton University, professor of politics and public affairs, 1969-74, chairman of Afro-American studies program, 1969-70; Brooklyn College of the City University of New York, Brooklyn, N.Y., Martin Luther King Distinguished Professor, 1974-78; Rutgers University, New Brunswick, N.J., professor of political science and Africana studies, 1978—, director of international programs, 1983—. Fulbright professor in Liberia, 1981-82, 1982-83. Member of advisory board of Zenith Books.

MEMBER: American Political Science Association, International Studies Association, African Studies Association (member of board of directors, 1984-87).

AWARDS, HONORS: Social Science Research Council fellow in England and Nigeria, 1958-60; Ford Foundation award, 1980-82.

WRITINGS:

(Contributor) J. S. Coleman and Carl G. Rosberg, editors, *Political Parties and National Integration in Tropical Africa,* University of California Press, 1964.

(Contributor) Gwendolen M. Carter, editor, *National Unity and Regionalism in Eight African States*, Cornell University Press, 1966.

The Politics of Tradition: Continuity and Change in Northern Nigeria, 1945-1965, Princeton University Press, 1970.

(Editor) *Perspectives on the Second Republic in Nigeria*, Crossroads Press, 1981.

Contributor to political affairs journals.

WORK IN PROGRESS: Political Change in an African Kingdom; Kano City Women.

BIOGRAPHICAL/CRITICAL SOURCES:

BOOKS

Weisbord, Marvin, *Some Form of Peace*, Viking, 1968.

*   *   *

WILBUR, C. Keith   1923-

PERSONAL: Born June 21, 1923, in Providence, R.I.; son of Clifford Keith (a chemist) and Ruth (Williams) Wilbur; married Ruth Elizabeth Asker, June 29, 1946; children: David Williams, Carol Ann, Bruce Alan, Jody Elizabeth. *Education:* Bates College, B.S., 1948; University of Vermont, M.D., 1952. *Religion:* Congregational (Church of Christ).

ADDRESSES: Home and office—397 Prospect St., Northampton, Mass. 01060.

CAREER: Salem Hospital, Salem, Mass., intern and resident, 1952-53; family practice of medicine in Northampton, Mass., 1953—. Staff member at Cooley Dickinson Hospital and Smith College infirmary. Chairman, Northampton Historical Fair, 1969, and Northampton Historical Commission. Member, Northampton Bicentennial Committee. *Military service:* U.S. Navy, 1942-46; commanded submarine chaser; became lieutenant junior grade.

MEMBER: American Academy of Family Practice (fellow), National Tree Farmers Association, National Wood Carvers Association, Company of Military Historians (fellow), Massachusetts Medical Society, Massachusetts Archaeological Society, Sixth Massachusetts Continentals, Hampshire County Medical Society, Northampton Historical Society, Old Deerfield Pocumtuck Society, College Club (Bates College).

AWARDS, HONORS: Heritage Foundation Award, 1963, for pageant "Rebels and Redcoats."

WRITINGS:

Picture Book of the Continental Soldier, Stackpole, 1969.
Picture Book of the Revolution's Privateers, Stackpole, 1973.
Medical Crisis in Washington's Army, Bristol Pharmaceutical Co., 1976.
The New England Indians, Globe Pequot, 1978.
Revolutionary Medicine, 1700-1800, Globe Pequot, 1980.
New England Indian Handicrafts, Globe Pequot, 1982.
(With wife, Ruth E. Wilbur) *Bid Us God Speed: The History of the Edwards Church, Northampton, Massachusetts, 1833-1983*, Phoenix Publishing, 1983.
Pirates and Patriots of the Revolution, Globe Pequot, 1984.
Tall Ships of the World, Globe Pequot, 1986.
Medical Antiques, Schiffer, 1987.
Land of the Nonotucks, Northampton Historical Society, 1987.
Early Explorers of North America, Globe Pequot, in press.

Also author of historical pageant "Rebels and Redcoats."

SIDELIGHTS: C. Keith Wilbur told *CA:* "My boyhood introduction to early American history was unforgettable. It was by the shore of Narragansett Bay that I'd picked up another flat stone to scale across the water. It came as something of a shock to realize that I was holding an arrowhead in my hand chipped to perfection—and I'd very nearly sent it skipping! Untouched for centuries, I had a find that was worth pondering over and treasuring.

"Once into Indian lore, I made my own headdress, then a wigwam, and a full-sized dugout canoe. Yet the surface of history was only scratched, for the books in the library were filled with exciting narratives of exploration and colonization of these Indian lands. It seems even possible that Old World prehistoric peoples had visited America well before the Viking exploits! The story of America is heady stuff—Jamestown and Plymouth, the French and Indian wars, our independence from King George's heavy hand, the clipper ships probing the seven seas, and so on. No fiction here, just the real adventures by real people who shaped America's destiny.

"Indeed I am fascinated by our early American heritage. It belongs to and is part of all of us. My writings and pen and ink sketches are a way of sharing what I have experienced and learned with our readers."

*   *   *

WILDEN, Anthony   1935-

PERSONAL: Born December 14, 1935, in London, England; son of Frank Clover (a watchmaker) and Lilian (Ballard) Wilden; married Patricia Rosalie Anderson, 1956, (divorced, 1971); children: Mark Andrew, Christopher Paul. *Education:* Attended University of Victoria, Victoria, British Columbia, 1960-61, 1963-65; Johns Hopkins University, Ph.D., 1968.

ADDRESSES: Home—6211 Sumas St., Burnaby, British Columbia, Canada V5B 2T7. *Office*—Department of Communication, Simon Fraser University, Burnaby, British Columbia, Canada V5A 1S6.

CAREER: Farmworker, factory worker, timber cruiser, stockcar driver, free-lance photographer, autoelectric mechanic, used-car salesman, and correspondence school instructor, 1952-61; teacher of classics and French, Shawnigan Lake School, British Columbia, 1962-65; Johns Hopkins University, Baltimore, Md., teaching assistant, 1965-67; University of California at San Diego, assistant professor of literature, 1968-74 (on leave, 1971-74); visiting professor at Faculty de Droit et des Sciences Economiques, Universite du Benin, Lome, Togo, 1971, and Center for the Study of Mass Communication, Ecole Pratique des Hautes Etudes, Sorbonne, University of Paris, 1971-72; Michigan State University, East Lansing, National Science Foundation Ecosystems Project, research associate in department of electrical engineering and systems science, 1973-74; Simon Fraser University, Burnaby, British Columbia, professor of communication, 1974—. Visiting professor at Fairhaven College, 1976, and University of British Columbia, 1977. Lecturer and consultant in a number of fields, including film theory, structuralism, cybernetics, psychiatry, anthropological theory, water control projects, urban ecosystems, resource conservation, and communications and social relations.

MEMBER: Semiotic Society of America.

WRITINGS:

(With Jacques Lacan) *The Language of the Self,* Johns Hopkins University Press, 1968, revised edition, 1976, reprinted as *Speech and Language in Psychoanalysis,* 1981.

System and Structure: Essays in Communication and Exchange, Tavistock Publications, 1972, 3rd edition, Boreal Express, 1983.

(Contributor) D. E. Washburn and D. R. Smith, editors, *Coping with Increasing Complexity,* Gordon & Breach, 1974.

(Contributor) K. Riegel, editor, *Structure and Transformation,* Wiley, 1975.

(Contributor with Tim Wilson) Carlos Sluzki and Donald Ransom, editors, *Double Bind: The Foundation of the Communicational Approach to the Family,* Grune & Stratton, 1976.

Le Canada imaginaire, Comeditex, 1979, translation published as *The Imaginary Canadian,* Pulp Press, 1980.

(Contributor) M. Maruyama and A. Harkins, editors, *Cultures of the Future,* Mouton, 1980.

(Contributor) Kathleen Woodward, editor, *The Myths of Information: Technology and Post-Industrial Culture,* Routledge & Kegan Paul, 1980.

(With Rhonda) *Women in Production: The Chorus Line 1932-1980* (videotape montage), 5th edition, Simon Fraser University, 1982.

(With R. Hammer) *Busby Berkeley and the Mechanical Bride: From Flying Down to Rio to The Lullaby of Broadway 1933-35* (videotape montage), Simon Fraser University, 1984.

(Contributor) Paul Bouissac, Michael Herzfeld, and Roland Posner, editors, *Iconicity: Festschrift for Thomas A. Sebeok,* Stauffenberg Verlag, 1986.

The Rules Are No Game: The Strategy of Communication, Routledge & Kegan Paul, 1986.

Man and Woman, War and Peace: The Strategist's Companion, Routledge & Kegan Paul, 1986.

(With R. Hammer) *Really Men: Men on Men* (videotape montage), 2nd edition, Simon Fraser University/Vancouver Institute for Policy Studies, 1988.

(Contributor) K. Krippendorff, editor, *Communication and Control in Society,* Gordon & Breach, in press.

Contributor of articles to other books ands to *Enciclopedia Einaudi.* Contributor to *Semiotica, Modern Language Notes, Contemporary Psychoanalysis, Communications, Psychology Today,* and other periodicals.

WORK IN PROGRESS: Marx, Freud, and Ideology: The Perspective of Context Theory; left and right brain coding and communication; montage; ecology, economics, and long range survival; critical analysis of the media; visual literacy; popular culture; strategy and tactics; guerrilla strategy; the twentieth-century war.

SIDELIGHTS: Anthony Wilden's *System and Structure: Essays in Communication and Exchange* approaches communicational theory and practice from a metadisciplinary perspective. The book employs and criticizes concepts drawn from such diverse fields as psychoanalysis, exchange theory, psychology, philosophy, linguistics, cybernetics, biology, anthropology, systems ecology, and semiotics. Wilden is especially critical of social and scientific discourse which are ethnocentric, logocentric, and phallocentric, which he considers symptoms of pathological communication.

Bob Scholte calls *System and Structure* "exceptional in scope, importance, and degree of complexity. . . . The integrative theme

of Wilden's wide-ranging argument is the problem of knowledge—specifically, the genesis, structure, function, and critique of scientific discourse." Carlos Sluzki and Donald Ransom, editors of *Double Bind: The Foundation of the Communicational Approach to the Family,* believe that *System and Structure* provides "a contribution to our 'knowledge about knowledge' at an abstract level, as well as supplying ammunition in the struggle with the concrete reality that information is power and that scientific discourse is a hidden weapon in the arsenal of social control." According to Gary Lee Stonum, *System and Structure* is "the first full-scale attempt to join the methods and assumptions of the Parisian *sciences humaines* with those of cybernetics and general systems theory. Wilden's subject is an immensely ambitious one, human communication in and between systems—social systems, person, psychic systems, and also texts and systems of discourse."

Wilden's writing has been translated into French, Spanish, Danish, and Italian.

AVOCATIONAL INTERESTS: Change; flying (Wilden has a private aviator's license).

BIOGRAPHICAL/CRITICAL SOURCES:

BOOKS

Carlos Sluzki and Donald Ransom, editors, *Double Bind: The Foundation of the Communicational Approach to the Family,* Grune & Stratton, 1976.

PERIODICALS

American Anthropologist, March, 1976.
American Political Science Review, September, 1976.
Australian Journal of Psychology, December, 1974.
Co-Evolution Quarterly, summer, 1974.
Contemporary Psychology, July, 1974.
Diacritics, fall, 1974.
Educational Resources Information Center, June, 1974.
Erasmus, April, 1973.
Journal of Industrial Relations, March, 1974.
Modern Language Notes, October, 1976.
New Society, October, 1972.
Prisma, September, 1973.
Psychology Today, June, 1973.
Telos, winter, 1974-75.
Times Literary Supplement, December 8, 1972.
Village Voice, January 19, 1988.

*   *   *

WILLIAMS, Eric (Ernest)   1911-1983

PERSONAL: Born July 13, 1911, in London, England; died December 24, 1983, in Porto Cheli, Greece; son of Ernest and Mary Elizabeth (Beardmore) Williams; married Joan Mary Roberts, 1940; married Sibyl Grain, MBE, April 1, 1948. *Education:* Attended Christ's College, London, England.

ADDRESSES: Home—"Wherever he and his wife happen to be"; c/o Union Bank of Switzerland, Bubenbergplatz 3, Bern, Switzerland.

CAREER: Lewis's Ltd., London, England, interior architect, 1932-40, book buyer, 1946-49; scriptwriter, London Films, London, England, 1949, and Wessex Film Productions Ltd., 1949-50; self-employed writer and journalist, 1949. *Military service:* Royal Air Force, 1939-45; became squadron leader; awarded Military Cross for successful escape from a German prison camp in 1943.

WRITINGS:

Goon in the Block, J. Cape, 1945.
The Wooden Horse, Collins, 1949, Harper, 1950, reprinted, Collins, 1979.
The Tunnel, Collins, 1951, Coward, 1952, revised edition for young readers, Collins, 1959, reprinted, Penguin, 1985, original edition reissued as *The Tunnel Escape,* Berkley, 1963.
(Editor) *The Escapers: A Chronicle of Escape in Many Wars, with Eighteen First-Hand Accounts,* Eyre & Spottiswoode, 1953, reprinted, Remploy, 1979, published as *The Book of Famous Escapes: A Chronicle of Escape in Many Wars, with Eighteen First-Hand Accounts,* Norton, 1954.
Complete and Free: A Modern Idyll, Eyre & Spottiswoode, 1957.
Dragoman Pass: An Adventure in the Balkans, Coward, 1959, reprinted, Remploy, 1979.
(Editor and author of introduction) *Great Escape Stories,* Weidenfeld & Nicolson, 1958, McBride, 1959, published as *The Will to Be Free: Great Escape Stories,* Thomas Nelson, 1971.
The Borders of Barbarism, Heinemann, 1961, Coward, 1962, reprinted, Remploy, 1979.
(Editor and author of introduction) *More Escapers in War and Peace, with Eighteen First-Hand Accounts,* Collins, 1968, published as *More Escapes,* Remploy, 1979.
People: English in Action, Edward Arnold, 1970.
Great Air Battles, Pan, 1971.

Contributor to film script, "The Wooden Horse," produced by Korda in 1951. Contributor to *Sunday Express* (London).

SIDELIGHTS: Books by British writer Eric Ernest Williams have autobiographical elements. *The Wooden Horse,* the bestseller that secured his writing career with more than two million copies sold in twenty-five editions, is the story of his clever escape from Stalag-Luft III, a German prison camp. Every day, prisoners were allowed to exercise by vaulting over a hollow wooden horse, which concealed a man who spent his days digging a secret tunnel under the prison camp wall. When the tunnel was finished, Williams and a companion escaped, procured false identification documents, and made their way to Sweden. Williams was awarded the Military Cross for the successful escape.

Dragoman Pass: An Adventure in the Balkans and *The Borders of Barbarism* are based on an overland expedition he made through Hungary, Rumania, Bulgaria, and Yugoslavia. He spent 1962 in Denmark supervising the building of his motorsailer yacht, then sailed for the Mediterranean, whose coasts and islands he explored. In 1962, Williams and his second wife settled in Porto Cheli, Greece, where he lived until his death in 1983.

BIOGRAPHICAL/CRITICAL SOURCES:

PERIODICALS

Observer, July 3, 1977.
Times Literary Supplement, March 28, 1968.
Yale Review, June, 1968.

OBITUARIES:

PERIODICALS

Chicago Tribune, January 2, 1984.
Times (London), January 2, 1984.
Washington Post, January 2, 1984.*

WILLIAMSON, Porter B(eyers)   1916-

PERSONAL: Born April 12, 1916, in Burket, Ind.; son of Ernest B. and Minnie M. (Mollenhour) Williamson; married Jennie M. Goshert (a registered nurse); children: Gary Beyers. *Education:* Indiana University, LL.B., 1939, B.S., 1945, J.D., 1950.

ADDRESSES: Office—University Station, Box 40457, Tucson, Ariz. 85717.

CAREER: Worked in general practice of law, 1945-50; Bendix Aviation, South Bend, Ind., director of controlled materials program, 1950-57, member of executive staff, 1957-67; Douglas Aircraft, Missile and Space Division, Huntington Beach, Calif., member of executive staff, 1967-73; University of Arizona, Tucson, lecturer, 1973. Prosecuting attorney for Indiana's 54th Judicial Circuit. Lecturer at Arizona State University; guest on television and radio programs. *Military service:* U.S. Army Air Forces, member of special and general staff of General George S. Patton, 1941-45; became major.

WRITINGS:

Arizona Real Estate Laws, MSC, Inc., 1969.
Arizona Zoning and Subdivision Laws, MSC, Inc., 1970.
Arizona Property and Tax Laws, MSC, Inc., 1973.
I Remember General Patton's Principles, MSC, Inc., 1979, published as *Patton's Principles: A Handbook for Managers Who Mean It!,* Simon & Schuster, 1982.
General Patton's Principles: For Life and Leadership, MSC, Inc., 1988.

Also author of "These Rights Are Yours," a column published in the *Indianapolis Star,* 1956-62.

WORK IN PROGRESS: A novel, *Strength from Weakness;* two movie scripts, "General Patton's Revenge" and "The Publishing Racket."

SIDELIGHTS: Porter B. Williamson wrote *CA* with this advice for new authors: "Never send a manuscript to a corporation! Send it to an individual by exact name—after a telephone call to the corporation. Put a limit on time for acceptance!"

*   *   *

WILLIS, Charles
   See CLARKE, Arthur C(harles)

*   *   *

WILTON, Elizabeth   1937-

PERSONAL: Born July 27, 1937, in Adelaide, Australia; daughter of J. Raymond (a professor of mathematics) and Winifred (a Young Women's Christian Association worker; maiden name, Welbourn) Wilton; married Charles F. Stevenson (a teacher), December 26, 1970; children: Daniel Charles, Richard Wilton, Catherine Elizabeth. *Education:* Attended Adelaide Teachers College and South Australia College of Advanced Education. *Politics:* Australian Labor Party. *Religion:* Society of Friends (Quakers).

ADDRESSES: Home—4 Tindara Ave., Windsor Gardens, South Australia 5087.

CAREER: Education Department, Adelaide, Australia, senior assistant, 1956-64; Crippled Children's Association, Adelaide, teacher of children with cerebral palsy, 1965-67; Education Department, Adelaide, head teacher in special education and guidance, 1968-70; teacher of severely intellectually disabled children, 1980-85, teacher of special class in primary school, 1985-88. Teacher with local adult illiteracy program.

MEMBER: Australian Society of Authors.

WRITINGS:

FOR CHILDREN

A Ridiculous Idea, Angus & Robertson, 1967, reprinted, Friendly Press (Waterford), 1987.
Riverboat Family (Junior Literary Guild selection), Angus & Robertson, 1967, Farrar, Straus, 1969.
The Twins and the 'Tortle,' Rigby, Ltd., 1968.
The Twins and the Christmas Tree, Rigby, Ltd., 1968.
The Little Sea-Dragon, Rigby, Ltd., 1968.
Prettyfoot, Rigby, Ltd., 1968.
The Foolish Fairy, Rigby, Ltd., 1968.
The Unknown Land, Rigby, Ltd., 1969.
Adventure, Ahoy!, Rigby, Ltd., 1969.
Land of His Dreams, Rigby, Ltd., 1969.
A Remarkable Obstacle, Rigby, Ltd., 1969.
On the Banks of the Yavva, Rigby, Ltd., 1969.
Red Ribbons and Mr. Anders, Angus & Robertson, 1970.
Riverview Kids, Angus & Robertson, 1971.

WORK IN PROGRESS: To Everything a Season; a historical novel of Western Victoria, and the gold rushes set in the Grampians Mountains in Victoria; *On A Shooting Star,* the story of a German-Jewish boy who migrated to Australia in 1939 and of his father—a prisoner on the *Dunera.*

SIDELIGHTS: Elizabeth Wilton once told *CA:* "I write because I have to—I cannot help it. I feel it particularly important to collect the stories that old people have to tell of their early days in this country—before those stories are lost forever. I try to emphasise attitudes toward peace, and the integrity of creation. I am interested in history, literature, children, and education."

AVOCATIONAL INTERESTS: Listening to music, watching ballet, bush-walking, gardening, Esperanto.

*   *   *

WING, J(ohn) K(enneth)   1923-

PERSONAL: Born October 22, 1923. *Education:* Received M.D. and Ph.D. from University of London.

ADDRESSES: Office—Medical Research Council Social Psychiatry Unit, Institute of Psychiatry, De Crespigny Park, London SE5 8AF, England.

CAREER: Medical Research Council, Social Psychiatry Unit, London, England, director, 1965—; Institute of Psychiatry, Denmark Hill, England, and London School of Hygiene, London, England, professor of social psychiatry, 1970—. Consultant psychiatrist, Maudsley Hospital, London, England. *Military service:* Royal Naval Volunteer Reserve, 1941-45; became lieutenant.

WRITINGS:

(With G. W. Brown, M. Bone, and B. Dalison) *Schizophrenia and Social Care,* Oxford University Press, 1966.
(Editor) *Early Childhood Autism,* Pergamon, 1966.
(Editor with E. H. Hare) *Psychiatric Epidemiology,* Oxford University Press, 1970.

(Editor with R. Bransby) *Psychiatric Case Registers,* H.M.S.O., 1970.
(With Brown) *Institutionalism and Schizophrenia,* Cambridge University Press, 1970.
(With A. M. Hailey) *Evaluating a Community Psychiatric Service,* Oxford University Press, 1972.
(With J. E. Cooper and N. Sartorius) *Measurement and Classification of Psychiatric Symptoms: An Instructional Manual for the PSE and Catego Program,* Cambridge University Press, 1974.
Reasoning about Madness, Oxford University Press, 1978.
(Editor) *Schizophrenia: Toward a New Synthesis,* Academic Press, 1978.
(With J. Leach) *Helping Destitute Men,* Tavistock, 1979.
(Editor with R. Olsen) *Community Care for the Mentally Disabled,* Oxford University Press, 1979.
(Editor with P. Kielholz and W. M. Zinn) *Rehabilitation of Patients with Schizophrenia and with Depression,* Hans Huber (Bern), 1981.
(Editor with Paul Bebbington and Lee N. Robins) *What Is a Case? The Problem of Definition in Psychiatric Community Surveys,* McIntyre (London), 1981.
(Editor with Brenda Morris) *Handbook of Psychiatric Rehabilitation Practice,* Oxford University Press, 1981.
(Editor) *Long-term Community Care: Experience in a London Borough,* Cambridge University Press, 1982.
(Editor with wife, Lorna Wing) *Psychoses of Uncertain Aetiology,* Cambridge University Press, 1982.

WORK IN PROGRESS: Investigation of social factors in causation and treatment of psychiatric disorders.

*   *   *

WISMER, Donald (Richard)   1946-

PERSONAL: Surname is pronounced *Whiz*-mer; born December 27, 1946, in Chicago, Ill.; son of Donald Minor (a contract administrator) and Katherine (Brandstrader) Wismer; married Leah Rubel, December 17, 1976; children: Sarah Miriam, Asher Zvi, Akiva Meir. *Education:* Indiana University, B.A., 1968, M.A., 1973; Southern Connecticut State College, M.S., 1977.

ADDRESSES: Home—P.O. Box 207, Kents Hill, Me. 04349. *Office*—Maine State Library, State House Station 64, Augusta, Me. 04333. *Agent*—James Allen, P.O. Box 278, 535 East Harford St., Milford, Penn. 18337.

CAREER: Indiana University, Bloomington, library assistant, 1967-73; Harvard University, Cambridge, Mass., stack supervisor at Widener Library, 1974-76; Bigelow Laboratory for Ocean Sciences, West Boothbay Harbor, Me., librarian, 1977; Maine State Library, Augusta, circulation coordinator, 1977-81, Automated Data Services coordinator, 1981-84, Reference and Information Services Division director, 1984—. Trustee, Cary Memorial Library, Wayne, Me.

MEMBER: Science Fiction Writers of America, American Library Association, Maine Library Association (president of Special Library Group, 1979-80; member of executive board).

WRITINGS:

The Islamic Jesus: An Annotated Bibliography of Sources in English and French, Garland Publishing, 1977.
Starluck (science fiction novel), Doubleday, 1982.
Warrior Planet (science fiction novel), Baen, 1987.
Planet of the Dead (science fiction novel), Baen, 1988.

Also contributor to anthologies. Contributor to library science journals. Editor of *Downeast Libraries,* 1981-83.

WORK IN PROGRESS: A Roll of Stars, a science fiction novel.

SIDELIGHTS: Donald Wismer told *CA:* "Almost all librarians want to be authors, too, but few take that giant step. The hardest part of writing fiction is sitting down at the word processor and doing it. I've been telling high school classes that two things are essential: first, do it; second, become expert at something, develop a saleable skill. That way, you can always survive if you fail at writing, and few succeed.

"I could write for years about writing style. I believe in simple sentences, linked by adverbs in such a way that the reader is carried bodily from one paragraph to another. Verbosity is sometimes indicated, but rarely. Each genre has its own tradition.

"Write what you like to read, and write what you know. My novels are science fiction, set on worlds not our own, hundreds or thousands of years in the future, but I know the genre from having read science fiction greedily for many years.

"I set the first sixty pages of *Starluck* to paper sometime in 1974. I wrote a sixty-page chase scene on the theory that grabbing the reader's interest is the best way to begin a story. I still think so. I tend to believe that a writer should simply start writing and see where the book leads. Once a framework of ideas is in place (setting, characters, and their backgrounds), a story will proceed logically forward, and the plot will twist and turn according to the premises already set forth in earlier pages.

"I propose to write rollicking good stories that the reader can't put down. They will be science fiction because that's the genre that most excites me, the one I read most, and incidentally the one in which individual titles tend to stay in print. And I also want to inspire, not to any particular religion, but to a vision toward perfection of life. My protagonists in the near future will always tend toward physical exercise, good diet, and the view that life will end, that it's a temporary and valuable thing, something that can be directed by an effort of will and consequent action. I want my readers to think about that. I want them to distinguish between largely passive activities, such as watching television or listening to music, and active ones, such as learning, doing, and achieving. I want them to take charge of themselves, if only in the long run. Luckily, that sort of attitude makes for good storytelling, and that's what I aim to do."

*   *   *

WITT, Hubert 1935-

PERSONAL: Born June 20, 1935, in Breslau, Germany (now Wroclaw, Poland); son of August (a railroad employee) and Berta (Werner) Witt; married Sina Heins, March 5, 1960 (died, 1984); married, wife's name Sabine, March 25, 1988; children: (first marriage) Ines, Jan; (second marriage) Raban. *Education:* Attended University of Leipzig, 1953-57.

ADDRESSES: Home—Fechnerstrasse 5, 7022 Leipzig, German Democratic Republic. *Office*—Institute for Literature, Leipzig, German Democratic Republic.

CAREER: Editor, writer, and translator. Reclam Verlag, Leipzig, German Democratic Republic, manuscript reader of German philology, philosophy, and twentieth-century literature,

1959-75, 1978-85; Institute for Literature, Leipzig, university teacher, 1986—.

MEMBER: Schriftstellerverband der Deutschen Demokratischen Republik.

WRITINGS:

EDITOR

Erinnerungen an Brecht (anthology), Reclam, 1964, revised edition, 1966, translation of revised edition by John Peet published as *Brecht as They Knew Him,* International Book Publishers, 1974.
(And translator from the Yiddish) *Der Fiedler vom Getto* (poetry from Poland), Reclam, 1966, abridged edition published as *Meine juedischen Augen,* Claassen, 1969.
(And translator) Oswald von Wolkenstein, *Um dieser welter Lust* (poetry), Insel, 1968.
Bertolt Brecht, *Von der Freundlichkeit der Welt* (poetry), Insel, 1971.
(With Annie Voigtlaender) *Denkzettel* (anthology of political lyrics from West Germany and West Berlin), Roederberg, 1974.
Thinking It Over (short stories from the German Democratic Republic), Seven Seas Publishers, 1977.
(And translator from the Yiddish) Mendele Mojcher Sforim, *Fischke der Lahme* (novel), Reclam and Hanser, 1978.
Heinrich Boell, *Mein trauriges Gesicht: Humoresken und Satiren,* Reclam, 1979.
Brecht, *Der Staedtebauer* (short stories), Insel, 1979.
(And translator) Walther von der Vogelweide, *Frau Welt, ich hab von dir getrunken* (poetry), Ruetten & Loening, 1979.
(And translator from the Yiddish) Rajzel Zychlinski, *Vogelbrot* (poetry), Insel, 1981.
(And translator from the Yiddish) Itzik Manager, *Poesiealbum* (poetry), Verlag Neues Leben, 1984.
Stephan-Hermlin: Texte/Materialien/Bilder, Reclam, 1985.
Die nicht erloschenen Woerter (anthology of West German poetry from 1945), Volk und Welt, 1986.

OTHER

(Translator) Langston Hughes, editor, *Gedichte aus Afrika* (poetry), Reclam, 1972.

Translator with others for Reclam of the poetry of Carl Michael Bellman, 1965—, Ossip Mandelstam, 1975, Jannis Ritsos, 1979, and Louis Aragon, 1986. Also author of afterwords to books by Bertolt Brecht, Johann Peter Hebel, Joseph Roth, Stephan Hermlin, Guenter Kunert, and Arno Schmidt.

WORK IN PROGRESS: Editing and translating the medieval lyrics of Neidhart von Reuenthal, *Der Ackermann und der Tod* by Johann von Saaz, the novel *Stempenju* by Scholem Alejchen; an anthology of minnesinger poetry.

*   *   *

WITTEN, Ian H(ugh) 1947-

PERSONAL: Born March 4, 1947, in England; son of Raymond Charles (an architect) and Grace May (Giles) Witten; married Pamela Wendy (an educator), 1971; children: Anna Siobhan, Nicola Cathy, Scott Robert. *Education:* Gonville and Caius College, Cambridge, B.A. (with first class honors), 1969, M.A., 1973; University of Calgary, M.Sc., 1970; University of Essex, Ph.D., 1976.

ADDRESSES: Office—Department of Computer Science, University of Calgary, 2500 University Dr. N.W., Calgary, Alberta, Canada T2N 1N4.

CAREER: University of Essex, Essex, England, lecturer, 1970-79, senior lecturer in electrical engineering science, 1979-80; University of Calgary, Calgary, Alberta, professor of computer science, 1980—, and head of department, 1982-85. Visiting professor at University of Calgary, 1977, and Technical University of Graz, 1985. Lecturer for Plessey Electronics Systems Ltd., 1979, and Texas Instruments, 1980. Public speaker; guest on television and radio programs; consultant to Bell-Northern Research, City Computer Systems, Monotype International, Cadre Information Systems, and First Byte.

MEMBER: Canadian Information Processing Society, Institute of Electrical Engineers (England; chartered engineer), Association for Computing Machinery.

AWARDS, HONORS: Commonwealth scholar at University of Calgary, 1969-70; Erskine fellow at University of Canterbury, 1977, 1986; grants from Science Research Council, 1979, Monotype International, 1979, British Government Communications Headquarters, 1979-81, and Canadian National Sciences and Engineering Research Council, 1981—.

WRITINGS:

The Representation and Storage of Information, Open University Press, 1975.
Operating Systems, Open University Press, 1975.
(Contributor) G. J. Klir, editor, *Applied General Systems Research,* Plenum, 1977.
Introduction to Microprocessors, Open University Press, 1979.
Communicating with Microcomputers, Academic Press, 1980.
Software Design, Open University Press, 1980.
Principles of Computer Speech, Academic Press, 1982.
Talking with Computers, Prentice-Hall, 1986.
(With T. C. Bell and J. G. Cleary) *Text Compression,* Prentice-Hall, in press.

Contributor of over 100 articles to technical and computer journals. Member of editorial board of *Encyclopedia of Computer Science and Engineering, International Journal of Man-Machine Studies,* and *Journal of Experimental and Theoretical Artificial Intelligence.*

SIDELIGHTS: Ian H. Witten wrote *CA* that the goal of his current research is "to develop interfaces for computers which exploit information about a user's past behaviour to expedite his interaction in the future. The work represents the continuation of a long-term research effort in man-computer interaction with special emphasis on low-cost personal computer systems of the future. It covers a spectrum from 'artificial intelligence' applications through language design and organization of distributed systems to methods of digital signal processing.

"Recently I have worked on adaptive text compression (using information about past text to encode upcoming characters), machine learning (seeking ways to summarize, re-structure, and generalize past experience), and user modeling (characterizing user behavior). Current work includes investigation of more powerful techniques for modeling discrete sequential data (such as user behavior), function induction and programming by example (i.e., explicit generalization of functions or programs from past input), support of temporal commitment (encouraging the user to transcend temporal monotonicity and explicitly manipulate the time domain himself), and plan rec-

ognition (so that the user's intentions can be inferred from his behavior).

"My work on speech synthesis naturally brought me into contact with speech analysis in the form of digital processing of signals. My separate interests in adaptive systems and speech converge in the area of identification of time series. I have applied linear techniques to unusual problems, such as the identification of curves used in handwriting.

"Other research areas include a serious project on positional play in chess, which has excited considerable interest, Chinese-language computer systems; semiotics and computers, and text processing. An interesting accomplishment was the development of a hand-controlled speech toy which was an enormous success, attracting over seventy requests for circuit cards by would-be constructors, including one from the Libyan Government, which wished to use it as a technology exhibit in a science fair! The device has been used since its invention by a developmental psychologist as a stimulus for autistic children."

*   *   *

WITTREICH, Joseph Anthony, Jr. 1939-

PERSONAL: Surname is pronounced *Wit*-trick; born July 23, 1939, in Cleveland, Ohio; son of Joseph Anthony (a supervisor) and Mamie (Pucel) Wittreich. *Education:* University of Louisville, B.A., 1961, M.A., 1962; Western Reserve University (now Case Western Reserve University), Ph.D., 1966.

ADDRESSES: Office—Ph.D. Program, English, The Graduate Center, City University of New York, 33 West 42nd St., New York, N.Y. 10036.

CAREER: University of Wisconsin—Madison, assistant professor, 1966-70, associate professor, 1970-74, professor of English, 1974-76; University of Maryland, College Park, professor of English, 1977-87; City University of New York, New York, N.Y., Graduate Center, distinguished professor of English, 1988—. Guest lecturer at California State University, Los Angeles, summer, 1970, and fall, 1972.

MEMBER: Modern Language Association of America, Milton Society of America (member of executive committee), Renaissance Society.

AWARDS, HONORS: American Philosophical Society fellow, 1967; Henry E. Huntington fellow, 1968, 1976; Folger fellow, 1971, 1974; National Endowment for the Humanities fellow, 1974, 1976, 1986; Newberry Library fellow, 1974; Wisconsin Institute for Research in the Humanities fellow, 1975; Guggenheim fellow, 1979.

WRITINGS:

(Author of introduction) William Hayley, *Life of Milton,* facsimile edition, Scholars' Facsimiles & Reprints, 1970.
(Contributor) John T. Shawcross and Michael Lieb, editors, *Achievements of the Left Hand: Essays on John Milton's Prose Work,* University of Massachusetts Press, 1974.
Angel of Apocalypse: Blake's Idea of Milton, University of Wisconsin Press, 1975.
(Contributor) Shawcross and others, editors, *Milton Encyclopedia,* Bucknell University Press, 1976.
(Contributor) Balachandra Raja, editor, *Homage to Milton,* University of Georgia Press, 1976.
Visionary Poetics: Milton's Tradition and His Legacy, Huntington Library, 1979.

"Image of That Horror": History, Prophecy, and Apocalypse in "King Lear," Huntington Library, 1984.
Interpreting "Simon Agnostes," Princeton University Press, 1986.
Feminist Milton, Cornell University Press, 1987.

EDITOR

(And author of introduction and notes) *The Romantics on Milton: Formal Essays and Critical Asides,* Press of Case Western Reserve University, 1970.

(And author of introduction) *Early Lives of William Blake,* Scholars' Facsimiles & Reprints, 1970.

(And author of introduction and notes) *Nineteenth-Century Accounts of William Blake,* Scholars' Facsimiles & Reprints, 1970.

Richard Meadowcourt, *Milton's "Paradise Regained": Two Eighteenth-Century Critiques,* facsimile edition, Scholars' Facsimiles & Reprints, 1971.

Calm of Mind: Tercentenary Essays on "Paradise Regained" and "Samson Agnostes," Press of Case Western Reserve University, 1971.

(With Stuart Curran and contributor) *Blake's Sublime Allegory: Essays on "The Four Zoas," "Milton," and "Jerusalem,"* University of Wisconsin Press, 1973.

(With Eric Rothstein) *Literary Monographs,* University of Wisconsin Press, Volume 6: *Medieval and Renaissance Literature,* 1975, Volume 7: *Thackery, Hawthorne, Melville, and Dreiser,* 1975, Volume 8: *Mid-Nineteenth-Century Writers: Eliot, De Quincy, Emerson,* 1976.

(And contributor) *Milton and the Line of Vision,* University of Wisconsin Press, 1975.

(With Richard Ide and contributor) *Composite Orders: The Genres of Milton's Last Poems,* University of Pittsburgh Press, 1983.

(With C. A. Patrides and contributor) *The Apocalypse in English Renaissance Thought and Literature,* Cornell University Press, 1984.

OTHER

Contributor of numerous articles, essays, and reviews to periodicals, including *PMLA, Blake Studies, Studies in Philology, English Language Notes, Milton Quarterly, Milton Studies, Bucknell Review, Keats-Shelley Journal, Huntington Library Quarterly, Genre, Renaissance Quarterly, Seventeenth-Century News, Blake Newsletter,* and *Journal of English and Germanic Philology. Blake Studies,* member of editorial advisory board, 1968-78, guest editor, 1972; member of editorial advisory board, *Literary Monographs,* 1971-75, *Genre,* 1973—, and *Milton and the Romantics.*

WORK IN PROGRESS: Milton: Revolutionary Artist.

BIOGRAPHICAL/CRITICAL SOURCES:

PERIODICALS

Times Literary Supplement, August 16, 1985, February 5, 1988.

*   *   *

WOLCOTT, Leonard Thompson

PERSONAL: Born in Buenos Aires, Argentina; son of Maynard (an agriculturist) and Edna (Thompson) Wolcott; married Carolyn Muller, September 31, 1951; children: Joy (Mrs. Bruce Vaughan). *Education:* Asbury College, B.A.; Hartford Seminary Foundation, M.A.; Drew University, D.Phil.

ADDRESSES: Home—3372 Mimosa Dr., Nashville, Tenn. 37211.

CAREER: Minister, United Methodist Church; field worker for United Methodist Church in India, 1945-50, 1963, 1974; Scaritt College for Christian Workers, Nashville, Tenn., Mabel K. Howell Professor of Church and World Mission, 1953-80; affiliated with Institut Superieur de Theologie, Mulungwishi, Zaire, 1980-81; writer. Lecturer at universities and colleges in India, and lecturer throughout America. Member of staff of Centro de Estudios Teologicos, Quito, Ecuador, 1970-71. Ford Foundation Southern Regional Scholar in Indian Studies. Consultant at Sat Tal Ashram, India, 1974.

MEMBER: Association of Professors of Missions (secretary-treasurer, 1960-62), American Association of University Professors, American Oriental Society, Society of Biblical Literature, American Society of Missiology, North American Academy of Ecumenists, Midwest Fellowship of Professors of Missions (president, 1973-74).

AWARDS, HONORS: Green and Tipple Fellowships from Drew University, 1943, 1944; grant from Dr. William's Trust (British) for research.

WRITINGS:

Twelve Modern Disciples, Upper Room, 1964.
Meditations on Ephesians, Abingdon, 1965.
(With wife, Carolyn Wolcott) *Religions Around the World,* Abingdon, 1967.
La Iglesia en El Mundo, Centro de Estudios Teologicos, 1972.
(With C. Wolcott) *Through the Moongate,* Friendship Press, 1978.
New Testament Odyssey, Kerr, 1979.
Introduction a l'etude du Nouveau Testament et son message, C.P.D.I., 1983.
(With C. Wolcott) *Wilderness Rider,* Abingdon, 1984.
(With C. Wolcott) *We Go Forward,* Discipleship Resources, 1984.
(Contributor) *Cokesbury Basic Bible Commentary,* Graded Press, 1988.
Missionary Pioneers, Graded Press, 1988.

Author of poetry; also author of study-guide books and curriculum materials for church school. Regular columnist, *Indian Witness* (Lucknow). Contributor to *Journal of Asian Studies,* and to *International Review of Mission,* and other church magazines.

SIDELIGHTS: Leonard Thompson Wolcott told *CA:* "A delight in the artistry of words came to me from my grandfather whom I never saw. An editor, book reviewer, aspiring journalist, he died at age 29, but left a library of literary classics which I read when I was a boy. And it came to me from my mother who never tired of writing poetry, short stories, and novels.

"My own writing started with poetry published in my teen years in magazines and anthologies. Rhythm and sound combinations are what interest me in poetry. These and atmosphere. My first full-length—a play—was accepted by a drama publisher when I was a university student. It was a play of college students, war, and peace. Afterwards I took time away from my writing by living in the drama of the world, among a variety of cultures, in many environments, speaking in different languages, even writing in three of them besides English.

"Most of my writing has been by assignment: curricula for church school, articles for church magazines, exegetical studies, book reviews, biographies, studies in Bible, in world religions, in ideological movements. The assignments continue. The most difficult (and exclusive) medium to break into, and the least remunerative, is that of scholarly journalism. I have enjoyed contributing to these journals, too.

"At last I am free from a teaching profession, free to write what I please. It will take another hundred years to do all I have in mind!

"Life is inexhaustible in its variety of wonders and beauties, of magic and meanings, of joys even through tears, and of possibilities even despite cruelties. Writing (like acting and painting) is for me the most satisfying way creatively to respond to this life. So I must write, whether for money or not, whether for readers or not (but both are welcomed)!

"For the arts and for literature this is a Hellenistic type of age: an age that has inherited the products, but has lacked the creativity, of an earlier classic period. Much of today's literature, therefore, tends to be arty, smarty, using a limited vocabulary of thought, repeating a stylized jargon. Nevertheless, out of the welter of modern mass communication occasional writers are appearing who are uniquely themselves, who escape the cliches, who climb out of the rut of existential dreariness, and who do not need the props of shock and ribaldry. There are writers who observe all of life closely and react to it sensitively. They have something to say. May they be read by many for long."

Wolcott spent a sabbatical in 1963 researching in rural and industrial India. Wolcott has lived at other periods in England, Germany, and Zaire, and has travelled widely in Europe, Asia, Africa, and South America. He is competent in Hindi, French, German, and Spanish.

AVOCATIONAL INTERESTS: Folk dancing, bird study, drama, violin, Sanskrit, and Greek.

*   *   *

WOLFE, Alvin William   1928-

PERSONAL: Born March 1, 1928, in Schuyler, Neb.; son of Walter W. and Olga (Herbrich) Wolfe; married Barbara Bikle, 1952; children: Charlotte, Dennison, Eleanor. *Education:* University of Nebraska, A.B., 1950; Northwestern University, Ph.D., 1957.

ADDRESSES: Home—17920 Burnside Rd., Lutz, Fla. 33549. *Office*—Department of Anthropology, University of South Florida, Tampa, Fla. 33620.

CAREER: Beloit College, Beloit, Wis., instructor, 1954-55; Middlebury College, Middlebury, Vt., instructor, 1955-57; Lafayette College, Easton, Pa., assistant professor, 1957-61; Washington University, St. Louis, Mo., assistant professor, 1961-64, associate professor of anthropology, 1964-68; University of Wisconsin—Milwaukee, professor of anthropology, 1968-74; University of South Florida, Tampa, professor of anthropology, 1974—. *Military service:* U.S. Army, 1945-47.

MEMBER: American Anthropological Association, American Association for the Advancement of Science, American Sociological Association, American Association of University

Professors, American Folklore Society, Society for Applied Anthropology (president, 1978), Society for Urban Anthropology (president, 1986), Phi Beta Kappa.

WRITINGS:

In the Ngombe Tradition: Continuity and Change in the Congo, Northwestern University Press, 1961.
Internship Training in Applied Anthropology: A Five-Year Review (monograph), Center for Applied Anthropology, 1981.
Papers on Network Models, Center for Applied Anthropology, University of South Florida, 1988.

Also contributor to anthropology journals. Editor, *City & Society.*

WORK IN PROGRESS: Network Models in the Social Sciences.

*   *   *

WOOD, James E(dward), Jr.   1922-

PERSONAL: Born July 29, 1922, in Portsmouth, Va.; son of James Edward and Elsie Elizabeth (Bryant) Wood; married Alma Leacy McKenzie, August 12, 1943; children: James Edward III. *Education:* Carson-Newman College, B.A., 1943; Southern Baptist Theological Seminary, B.D., 1947, Th.M., 1948, Ph.D., 1957; Columbia University, M.A., 1949; Yale University, Chinese certificate; Naganuma School of Japanese Studies, Tokyo, diploma; attended University of Tennessee, 1943-44, and Oxford University, 1983. *Politics:* Democrat.

ADDRESSES: Home—3306 Lake Heights, Waco, Tex. 76708. *Office*—BU Box 7308, Baylor University, Waco, Tex. 76798.

CAREER: Baptist clergyman and educator, 1942—. Pastor in Baptist churches in Tennessee and Kentucky, 1942-48; Seinan Gakuin University, Fukuoka, Japan, professor of religion and literature, 1950-55; Baylor University, Waco, Tex., assistant professor, 1955-57, associate professor, 1957-59, professor of history of religions and director of J. M. Dawson Institute of Church and State Studies, 1959-73, Simon and Ethel Bunn Professor of Church-State Studies, 1980—, chairman of church-state studies, 1962-73, 1980—, chairman of Far Eastern educational exchange program committee, 1969-72. Visiting lecturer, Ashland Theological Seminary, 1971; visiting professor, Southern Baptist Theological Seminary, 1974, Oklahoma Baptist University, 1977, and North American Baptist Theological Seminary, 1974, 1979. Executive director, Baptist Joint Committee on Public Affairs, 1972-80; member of several commissions for Baptist World Alliance, including Commission of Religious Liberty and Human Rights, 1965-75, Commission of Freedom, Justice, and Peace, 1975-80, and Commission of Human Rights, 1980-85. Participant in numerous interfaith organizations; has lectured and presented papers at numerous professional meetings. Editor in chief, Markham Press, Baylor University, 1970-72. Consultant, World Council of Churches, 1963-65; advisor, First Freedom, 1981—.

MEMBER: American Academy of Religion, American Society of Church History, National Council on Religion and Public Education (president), National Council of Churches (member of religious liberty committee, 1979-81), Public Education and Religious Liberty (member of executive committee), American Society of International Law, American Civil Liberties Union (president of Waco chapter, 1969-72), American Association of University Professors, Texas Civil Liberties Union (member of board, 1969-72), Council of Washington Representatives on the United Nations (member of executive committee; chairman, 1978-80), Phi Eta Sigma, Pi Kappa Delta, Alpha Psi Omega, Rotary International.

AWARDS, HONORS: Distinguished alumnus award, Carson-Newman College, 1974; Religious Liberty Award, Alliance for the Preservation of Religious Liberty, 1980; Henrietta Szold Award, Hadassah (Texas region), 1981; award for distinguished service in human rights, Waco Conference of Christians and Jews, 1986.

WRITINGS:

A History of American Literature: An Anthology, Kenkyusha (Japan), 1952.

(With E. Bruce Thompson and Robert T. Miller) *Church and State in Scripture, History, and Constitutional Law,* Baylor University Press, 1958.

(Editor and contributor) *Church and State,* Scottish Rite, 1960, reprint published in two volumes, Greenwood Press, 1989-90.

(Editor and contributor) Joseph Martin Dawson, *A Thousand Months to Remember: An Autobiography,* Baylor University Press, 1964.

(Contributor) *We Hold These Truths,* Americans United, 1964.

The Problem of Nationalism in Church-State Relationships, Herald Press, 1969.

(Editor and contributor) *Jewish-Christian Relations in Today's World,* Baylor University Press, 1971.

(Editor and Contributor) *Religion and Public Education,* Baylor University Press, 1972.

(Editor and contributor) *Baptists and the American Experience,* Judson Press, 1976.

Nationhood and the Kingdom, Broadman Press, 1977.

(Contributor) *Taxation and the Free Exercise of Religion,* Baptist Joint Committee, 1978.

(Editor and contributor) *Religion and Politics,* Baylor University Press, 1983.

(Editor and contributor) *Religion and the State: Essays in Honor of Leo Pfeffer,* Baylor University Press, 1985.

Secular Humanism and the Public Schools, National Council of Churches, 1986.

(Contributor) *Out of Darkness into the Light,* Baptist World Alliance, 1986.

(Editor and contributor) *Ecumenical Perspectives on Church and State: Catholic, Protestant, and Jewish,* Baylor University Press, 1988.

Readings on Church and State, Baylor University Press, 1989.

Contributor to over sixteen books. Also contributor to *Encyclopedia of Modern Christian Missions, Encyclopedia of Southern Baptists,* and *Dictionary of Theology,* 1983. Contributor of more that one hundred articles and reviews to professional journals. *Journal of Church and State,* founder and editor, 1959-73, 1980—, member of editorial board, 1973-80; editor, *Report from the Capital,* 1975-80; member of editorial board, *National Council on Religion and Public Education Bulletin,* 1982—; member of board of advisors, *Religious Freedom Reporter,* 1982—.

Y

YEAZELL, Ruth Bernard 1947-

PERSONAL: Born April 4, 1947, in New York, N.Y.; daughter of Walter and Annabelle (Reich) Bernard; married Stephen C. Yeazell, August 14, 1969 (marriage ended, 1980). *Education:* Swarthmore College, B.A. (with honors), 1967; Yale University, M.Phil., 1970, Ph.D., 1971.

ADDRESSES: Office—Department of English, 2225 Rolfe Hall, University of California, 405 Hilgard Ave., Los Angeles, Calif. 90024.

CAREER: Boston University, Boston, Mass., assistant professor of English, 1971-75; University of California, Los Angeles, assistant professor, 1975-77, associate professor, 1977-80, professor of English, 1980—.

MEMBER: Modern Language Association of America (member of executive council, 1985-88), Phi Beta Kappa.

AWARDS, HONORS: Woodrow Wilson fellow, 1967-68; Guggenheim fellow, 1979-80; National Endowment for the Humanities fellow, 1988.

WRITINGS:

Language and Knowledge in the Late Novels of Henry James, University of Chicago Press, 1976.
(Editor) *The Death and Letters of Alice James: Selected Correspondences,* University of California Press, 1981.
(Editor) *Sex, Politics, and Science in the Nineteenth Century Novel,* John Hopkins University Press, 1986.

Associate editor, *Nineteenth-Century Fiction,* 1977-80; member of advisory board, *Publications of the Modern Language Association,* 1980-84.

WORK IN PROGRESS: "A book on the idea of female modesty and its implications for fiction in eighteenth- and nineteenth-century England."

SIDELIGHTS: In *The Death and Letters of Alice James,* editor Ruth Bernard Yeazell has collected some of the writings from the last years of the brilliant but repressed younger sister of noted writer Henry and famed psychologist William James. "Yeazell's discriminating selection of Alice James's often witty and sad letters was chosen for their 'inherent appeal and for the representativeness, to help the reader sense the range of [Alice James's] concerns and the shape of her mortal career,'"

notes Diane Johnson in the *New York Times Book Review.* While the James children were all encouraged to develop their intellectual talents, Alice, perhaps because of her gender, felt herself held back in many ways; from an early age she experienced numerous "nervous" conditions that kept her an invalid until her death from cancer. Nevertheless, observes Johnson, "Yeazell in her introduction to Alice James's letters . . . avoids the temptation to make of the talented and wasted Alice either a heroine or a victim. . . . Working with one thread, the theme of death," continues the critic, the editor "illumines in detail a preoccupation with death that seems, from a perspective more strictly psychological, to have controlled Alice's life." Despite Alice James's physical and emotional problems, however, her writings demonstrate her considerable literary gifts; *Yale Review* contributor Patricia Meyer Spacks writes that Yeazell "calls attention to the fictionalizing process in Alice James's correspondence, exemplified in several letters where she imaginatively converts herself to a corpse and triumphs over her mortality by using the fantasized cadaver as an argumentative counter." "Ably edited by Yeazell," claims R. J. Kelly in *Library Journal,* these letters "offer a fascinating glimpse of a remarkable woman and of one of America's most distinguished families." Katherine Winton Evans concurs; calling *The Death and Letters of Alice James* a "well-edited and intelligently annotated collection," she comments in the *Washington Post Book World* that the book will "shed light on the curious Victorian phenomenon of nervous prostration and give a vivid picture of a self-imprisoned 19th-century woman."

BIOGRAPHICAL/CRITICAL SOURCES:

PERIODICALS

Library Journal, November 1, 1980.
Los Angeles Times Book Review, January 4, 1981.
New Republic, December 20, 1980.
New York Times Book Review, December 14, 1980.
Times Literary Supplement, May 20, 1977.
Washington Post Book World, November 30, 1980.
Yale Review, summer, 1981.

*   *   *

YOOLL, Andrew M(ichael) Graham
See GRAHAM-YOOLL, Andrew M(ichael)

YOUNG, Elaine L.
    See SCHULTE, Elaine L(ouise)

*   *   *

YOUNG, Hugo (John Smelter)   1938-

PERSONAL: Born October 13, 1938, in Sheffield, England; son of Gerard Francis (an industrialist) and Diana (Murray) Young; married Helen Mason, 1966; children: Cecilia, Dominic, Emily, Victoria. *Education:* Attended Ampleforth College; Balliol College, Oxford, M.A. in Law (honors), 1961.

ADDRESSES: Home—22 Christchurch Hill, London NW3, England. *Office—The Guardian,* 119 Farrington Rd., London EC1, England. *Agent*—Anne McDermid, Curtis Brown Ltd., 162 Regent St., London W1, England.

CAREER: Yorkshire Post, Leeds, England, leader writer, 1961-63; Commonwealth Fund, Harkness fellow at Princeton University, Princeton, N.J., 1963-64; congressional fellow with U.S. Congress, Washington, D.C., 1964-65; *Sunday Times,* London, England, member of editorial staff, 1965, chief leader writer, 1966-77, political editor, 1973-84, political columnist, 1977-84, joint deputy editor, 1981-84; *The Guardian,* London, political columnist, 1984—; director, *The Tablet,* 1985—. Writer and presenter of BBC Radio programs "No, Minister," 1981, "But, Chancellor," 1983, and "The Thatcher Phenomenon," 1985.

AWARDS, HONORS: Columnist of the Year, British Press Awards, 1980, 1983, 1985; What the Papers Say Award, Granada TV, 1985.

WRITINGS:

(With Lewis Chester and Stephen Fay) *The Zinoviev Letter,* Heinemann, 1967, Lippincott, 1968.
(With Bryan Silcock and Peter Dunn) *Journey to Tranquility: The History of Man's Assault on the Moon,* J. Cape, 1969, Doubleday, 1970.
The Crossman Affair, Hamish Hamilton, 1976.
(With Anne Sloman) *No, Minister: An Inquiry into the Civil Service,* British Broadcasting Corp., 1982.
(With Sloman) *But, Chancellor: An Inquiry into the Treasury,* British Broadcasting Corp., 1984.
(With Sloman) *The Thatcher Phenomenon,* British Broadcasting Corp., 1986.
One of Us: A Biography of Margaret Thatcher, Macmillan, 1989.

SIDELIGHTS: Veteran political columnist and reporter Hugo Young has conducted several investigations into the nature and quality of British public service with several British Broadcasting Corp. radio programs. For these programs, Young conducted interviews with the people who make Britain's policy in a number of areas, including ministers, ex-ministers and a number of other high civil service officials. "It was good listening and the collected broadcasts [in *No, Minister: An Inquiry into the Civil Service*], topped and tailed with new material from the presenter Hugo Young and the producer Anne Sloman, make good reading," claims an *Economist* reviewer. The critic adds that *No, Minister* "is an ideal, up-to-date source book for the reader wishing to judge for himself or herself just how great an influence that great Victorian invention—a career civil service, recruited on the basis of merit rather than patronage or political affiliation—exercises in a testing period of government." Similarly, *But, Chancellor: An Inquiry into the Treasury* "is the enhanced transcript of Hugo Young's interviews with and about Britain's economic policy-makers," describes Sarah Hogg in the London *Times.* This transcript "is, in its way, a unique document," continues the critic. "Well packaged by the most perceptive of journalists, it is a series of discussions with the elite of mandarin country . . . [and] a rare drawing back of the curtain of Civil Service anonymity."

Times Literary Supplement contributor Burke Trend, however, believes Young's books present "conventional" views and "[fail] to attempt to examine [their subjects] in greater depth or to expose some of the implications, and possible consequences, of a more radical approach to the problem of open government." But Hogg notes that Young himself points out the limitations of these interviews; the critic comments that "it is not by any means an overwhelming disadvantage: the relentless projection of [his subject's] ethos is in itself revealing." And comparable to Young's other civil service inquiries, *The Thatcher Phenomenon,* which asks civil officials their opinions of British Prime Minister Margaret Thatcher, "is a considerable achievement," states an *Economist* critic. "Those interviewed spoke more freely than might have been expected, and even the most assiduous Thatcher-watcher will find new things in its pages."

BIOGRAPHICAL/CRITICAL SOURCES:

PERIODICALS

Economist, July 10, 1982, March 17, 1984, April 19, 1986.
Observer Review, November 23, 1969.
Spectator, March 10, 1984, March 8, 1986.
Time, July 13, 1970.
Times (London), March 8, 1984.
Times Literary Supplement, May 4, 1984, September 12, 1986.

Z

ZALD, Mayer N(athan) 1931-

PERSONAL: Born June 17, 1931, in Detroit, Mich.; son of Harold and Ann (Levitt) Zald; married Joan Kadri (a social worker), June 15, 1958; children: Ann Karen, David Harold, Harold S. J. *Education:* Attended Wayne State University, 1949-51; University of Michigan, B.A., 1953, Ph.D., 1961; University of Hawaii, M.A., 1955.

ADDRESSES: Home—2110 Vinewood, Ann Arbor, Mich. 48104. *Office*—Department of Sociology, University of Michigan, Ann Arbor, Mich. 48109.

CAREER: University of Chicago, Chicago, Ill., instructor, 1960-61, assistant professor of sociology and psychology, 1961-64; Vanderbilt University, Nashville, Tenn., associate professor, 1964-68, professor of sociology, 1968-77, chairman of department, 1971-75; University of Michigan, Ann Arbor, professor of sociology and social work, 1977—, chairman of department, 1981-86. Member of executive committee, Center for Community Studies, Nashville, 1966-69; member of committee of examiners in sociology for Graduate Record Examination, 1972-74; member of behavioral science panel, National Institute of Mental Health, 1973-76; member of sociology panel, National Science Foundation, 1980-81. External reviewer for the sociology departments of several universities. Consultant on race relations and the corporation, Illinois Bell Telephone Co., 1962. *Military service:* U.S. Army, 1955-56.

MEMBER: American Sociological Association (member of council, 1981-83; vice-president, 1986-87), Sociological Research Association, Society for the Scientific Study of Social Problems, American Association of University Professors, American Civil Liberties Union, Law and Society Association, Southern Sociological Society (chairman, 1968-69; member of executive committee, 1977-78).

AWARDS, HONORS: Elizabeth McCormick Memorial Foundation predoctoral research fellowship, 1959-60; Career Development Award grants, National Institute of Mental Health, 1967-72.

WRITINGS:

(Editor and contributor) *Social Welfare Institutions: A Sociological Reader,* Wiley, 1965, (editor with George T. Martin) new edition, Columbia University Press, 1981.
(Editor) *Organizing for Community Welfare,* Quadrangle, 1967.

Organizational Change: The Political Economy of the YMCA, University of Chicago Press, 1970.
(Editor) *Power in Organizations,* Vanderbilt University Press, 1970.
Occupations and Organizations in American Life: The Organization-Dominated Man?, Markham, 1971.
(Author of foreword) Robert Mayer, *Social Planning and Social Change,* Prentice-Hall, 1972.
(With Gary L. Wamsley) *The Political Economy of Public Organizations,* Heath, 1973.
(With John Ehnes) *Handbook of Organizational Statistics,* Department of Sociology, Vanderbilt University, 1975.
(Editor with William Rushing) *Organizations and Beyond: Selected Essays of James D. Thompson,* Heath, 1976.
(With James A. Lowenthal and Michael Berger) *Administrative Regulations: A Sociological Perspective,* Center for Research on Social Organization, University of Michigan, 1979.
(Editor with John D. McCarthy) *Dynamics of Social Movements: Resource Mobilization, Social Control and Outcomes,* Winthrop, 1979.
(Author of foreword) Lawrence Root, *Fringe Benefits: Social Insurance in the Steel Industry,* Sage Publications, 1982.
(With McCarthy) *Social Movements in an Organizational Society: Collected Essays,* Transaction Books, 1986.
(Editor with Gerald Suttles) *The Challenge of Social Control: Citizenship and Institution Building in Modern Society, Essays in Honor of Morris Janowitz,* Ablex Publishing, 1986.

CONTRIBUTOR

L. Hazelrigg, editor, *Prisons and Society,* Doubleday, 1968.
Fremont Lynden, G. Shipman, and M. Kroll, editors, *Policies, Decisions, and Organizations,* Appleton-Century-Crofts, 1969.
Michael Aiken and Paul E. Mott, editors, *The Structure of Community Power: Readings,* Random House, 1970.
F. Cox, John Erlich, Jack Rothman, and J. Tropman, editors, *Strategies of Community Organizations,* F. E. Peacock, 1970.
Charles Bonjean and Louis Zurcher, editors, *Planned Social Intervention: An Inter-Disciplinary Anthology,* Chandler Publishing Co., 1970.
Sandor Halebsky, editor, *The Sociology of the City,* Scribner, 1972.

Richard English and Yeheskel Hasenfeld, editors, *Human Services Organizations,* University of Michigan Press, 1974.
M. D. Pugh and Joseph B. Perry, editors, *Collective Behavior: A Source Book,* West Publishing, 1979.
Louis Kriesberg, editor, *Research in Social Movements,* Volume 3: *Conflict and Change,* JAI Press, 1980.
R. Westrum and K. Samaga, editors, *Complex Organization: Growth, Struggle and Change,* Prentice-Hall, 1984.

Also contributor to numerous anthologies and textbooks in the sociology of organizations and institutions.

OTHER

Contributor of articles and reviews to *American Journal of Sociology, American Sociological Review, Annual Review of Sociology, Human Relations, Contemporary Sociology, Pacific Sociological Review, Review of Religious Research, Social Forces, Crime and Delinquency, Social Problems, Social Service Review, Sociology of Education, Urban Affairs Quarterly,* and *Accounting, Organizations and Society.*

Consulting editor, Elsevier Scientific Publications, 1980-81; member of editorial boards, ''Research in Political Sociology'' series, JAI Press, 1983—, and ''Social Justice'' series, Plenum Press, 1985—. *American Journal of Sociology,* member of editorial board, 1960-74, associate editor, 1962-63; member of editorial boards of *Social Problems,* 1965-68, *Journal of Health and Human Behavior,* 1967-70, and *Journal of Voluntary Action Research,* 1972—; advisory editor of *Social Forces,* 1974—, and *Administration and Society,* 1976—; associate editor, *American Sociological Review,* 1979-82.

WORK IN PROGRESS: Research on social control of institutions.

AVOCATIONAL INTERESTS: Tennis, reading, bird-watching, music.

*   *   *

ZELERMYER, William   1914-

PERSONAL: Born January 7, 1914, in Chelsea, Mass.; son of Louis and Eva Dora (Solomon) Zelermyer; married Herma Zetterbaum, June 30, 1940 (died, 1969); married Betty Cheplin Wolkin, May 16, 1971; children: (first marriage) Benjamin, Milton. *Education:* Williams College, A.B., 1935; Harvard University, J.D., 1939.

ADDRESSES: Home—23394 Barlake Dr., Boca Raton, Fla. 33433.

CAREER: Curtiss-Wright Corp., Buffalo, N.Y., administrative assistant, 1941-45; private law practice in Buffalo, 1945-46; Rider College, Trenton, N.J., assistant professor of business law, 1946-48; Syracuse University, Syracuse, N.Y., assistant professor, 1948-52, associate professor, 1952-59, professor of law and public policy, beginning 1959, chairman of department, 1963-79.

MEMBER: American Bar Association, American Association of University Professors, American Business Law Association (secretary-treasurer, 1957-58; vice-president, 1958-59; president, 1959-60), Beta Gamma Sigma.

WRITINGS:

Invasion of Privacy, Syracuse University Press, 1959.
Legal Reasoning, Prentice-Hall, 1960.
The Process of Legal Reasoning, Prentice-Hall, 1963.

Introduction to Business Law: A Conceptual Approach, Macmillan, 1964, 2nd edition, 1971.
Changing Aspects of Business Law, Heath, 1966.
Business Law, Heath, 1967.
The Legal System in Operation: A Case Study from the Procedural Beginning to the Judicial Conclusion, West Publishing, 1977.

Contributor to professional journals. Co-editor, American Business Law Association *Bulletin;* member of advisory board, *American Business Law Journal.*

AVOCATIONAL INTERESTS: Music.

*   *   *

ZUCKERMAN, Solly   1904-

PERSONAL: Created Baron of Burnham Thorpe (life peer), 1971; born May 30, 1904, in Cape Town, South Africa; son of Moses (a merchant) and Rebecca (Glaser) Zuckerman; married Joan Rufus Isaacs, 1939; children: Paul, Stella. *Education:* University of Cape Town, B.Sc., 1923, M.A., 1925; University of London, D.Sc., 1932, M.D., 1946.

ADDRESSES: Office—University of East Anglia, Norwich NR4 7TJ, England.

CAREER: University of Cape Town, Cape Town, South Africa, demonstrator in anatomy, 1923-25; University of London, University College, London, England, demonstrator in anatomy, 1928-32; Yale University, New Haven, Conn., research associate, 1933-34; Oxford University, Oxford, England, university lecturer and demonstrator in human anatomy, 1934-45; University of Birmingham, Birmingham, England, Sands Cox Professor of Anatomy, 1943-68, professor emeritus, 1968—; University of East Anglia, Norwich, England, professor emeritus at large, 1969—; British Industrial Biological Research Association, president, 1974—. Fellow Commoner, Christ Church, Cambridge; research anatomist to Zoological Society of London, 1928-32. Hunterian Professor, Royal College of Surgeons, 1937; Gregnog Lecturer, University of Wales, 1956; Mason Lecturer, University of Birmingham, 1957; Lees Knowles Lecturer, Cambridge University, 1965; Romanes Lecturer, Oxford University, 1975; Rhodes Lecturer, University of South Africa, 1975. Fellow of University College, London, 1955—; visitor, Bedford College, 1968-85.

Member, Ministry of Works Scientific Committee, 1945-47, Committee on Future Science Policy, 1946-48, Ordnance Board, 1947-69, Fuel and Power Scientific Advisory Committee, 1948-55; deputy chairman, Advisory Council on Scientific Policy, 1948-64; member, British Agricultural Research Council, 1949-59; chairman of British Committee on Scientific Manpower, 1950-64, Natural Resources Committee, 1951-64, and Defence Research Policy Committee, 1960-64; chief scientific advisor to British Secretary of State for Defense, 1960-66, and to Her Majesty's Government, 1966-71; chairman, Central Advisory Committee for Science and Technology, 1965-70; member of Royal Commission on Environmental Pollution, 1970-74; president of Parliamentary and Scientific Committee, 1973-76; member of advisory committee on medical research, World Health Organization, 1973-77; member of general advisory council, British Broadcasting Corp., 1957-62, and NATO Science Committee, 1957-66; trustee, British Museum, 1967-77. *Military service:* Royal Air Force, scientific adviser to combined operations, 1942-46, honorary group captain, 1943-

46; Supreme Headquarters, Allied Expeditionary Force, chief adviser on air planning, 1943-46.

MEMBER: Royal College of Physicians (fellow), Royal College of Surgeons (honorary fellow), Royal Society (fellow), Zoological Society of London (honorary secretary, 1955-77, honorary fellow, 1984), Fauna Preservation Society (president), Association of Learned and Professional Society Publishers (president, 1973-77), Anatomical Society, Physiological Society, Society for Endocrinology, American Philosophical Society, American Academy of Arts and Sciences (honorary member), Academia das Ciencias de Lisboa (honorary member), Beefsteak Club, Brook's Club.

AWARDS, HONORS: Union research scholar, 1925; Rockefeller research fellow, 1933-34; Beit Memorial research fellow, 1934-37; William Julius Mickle fellow, 1935; Companion of the Bath, 1946; knighted, 1956; Knight Commander of the Bath, 1964; Order of Merit, 1968; Zoological Society of London gold medal, 1971; received Medal of Freedom with silver palm (United States); Chevalier de la Legion d'Honneur (France); Companion d'Honneur (France); honorary degrees from University of Bordeaux, 1961, University of Sussex, 1963, University of Jacksonville, 1964, University of Bradford, 1966, University of Birmingham, 1970, University of Hull and Columbia University, both 1977, University of East Anglia and St. Andrews University, both 1980, and University of Reading, 1984.

WRITINGS:

The Social Life of Monkeys and Apes, Harcourt, 1932, 2nd edition, 1981.

Functional Affinities of Man, Monkeys, and Apes: A Study of the Bearings of Physiology and Behavior on the Taxonomy and Phylogeny of Lemurs, Monkeys, Apes, and Man, Harcourt, 1933.

(Author of foreword and postscript) Harrison Scott Brown, *The Next Hundred Years,* Weidenfeld & Nicolson, 1957.

(Author of introductory reading guide) *Biology: A Course of Selected Readings by Authorities,* International University Society, 1958, published as *Classics in Biology: A Course of Selected Readings by Authorities,* Philosophical Library, 1960.

Land Ownership and Resources, Department of Estate Management, Cambridge University, 1960.

A New System of Anatomy, Oxford University Press, 1961, 2nd edition, 1981.

(With Alva R. Myrdal and Lester B. Pearson) *The Control of Proliferation: Three Views,* Institute of Strategic Studies, 1966.

Scientists and War: The Impact of Science on Military and Civil Affairs, Hamish Hamilton, 1966, Harper, 1967.

(Contributor) Ashley Montague, editor, *Man and Aggression,* Oxford University Press, 1968.

Beyond the Ivory Tower: The Frontiers of Public and Private Science, Weidenfeld & Nicolson, 1970, Taplinger, 1971.

Cancer Research: A Report by Lord Zuckerman, H.M.S.O., 1972.

Food Quality and Safety: A Century of Progress, H.M.S.O., 1976.

The Zoological Society of London, 1826-1976 and Beyond, Academic Press, 1976.

From Apes to Warlords: The Autobiography (1904-1946) of Solly Zuckerman, Hamish Hamilton, 1978.

Look Forward to the Electronic Future, Abell House, 1980.

Perspectives in Primate Biology, Academic Press, 1981.

Nuclear Illusion and Reality, Viking, 1982.

Star Wars in a Nuclear World, Kimber, 1986.

PUBLISHED LECTURES

The Image of Technology, Oxford University Press, 1967.

Attitudes to Enquiry and Understanding, Middlesex Hospital Medical School, 1968.

Medicine and Tomorrow's Community, University of Glasgow, 1969.

Technology and Society: A Challenge to Private Enterprise, International Chamber of Commerce (Paris), 1971.

(Contributor) *Experienta Supplementum 17,* Birkhauser Verlag (Stuttgart), 1972.

Doctors and Patients, Royal Society of Medicine, 1974.

Advice and Responsibility, Oxford University Press, 1975.

EDITOR

(With Peter Eckstein) *The Thyroid Gland: Proceedings of a Symposium Held Jointly by the Society for Endocrinology and the Endocrinological Section of the Royal Society of Medicine,* [London], 1953.

(With Eckstein) *The Technique and Significance of Oestrogen Determinations,* Cambridge University Press, 1955.

The Ovary, two volumes, Academic Press, 1962, 2nd edition, 1977.

The Concepts of Human Evolution: The Proceedings of a Symposium Organized by the Anatomical Society of Great Britain and Ireland and the Zoological Society of London, Academic Press, 1973.

Great Zoos of the World: Their Origins and Significance, Westview Press, 1980.

Also editor of *Science and War,* 1940.

OTHER

Contributor of numerous articles to scientific journals.

WORK IN PROGRESS: Monkeys, Men and Missiles, second volume of autobiography; further works on the nuclear arms race.

SIDELIGHTS: In 1971 Solly Zuckerman was created Baron Zuckerman, Baron of Burnham Thorpe in recognition of his thirty years of service as an advisor to the government of Great Britain. Zuckerman, an anatomist and expert on primate behavior, became a civilian scientific and strategic advisor during World War II and continued to offer the government his recommendations on scientific and defense issues until the early 1970s. Over the years Zuckerman's influence spread from the specific issue of nuclear arms to general matters of public policy, including health, technology, and environmental matters. *Los Angeles Times Book Review* contributor Jack Miles notes that the tone of Zuckerman's advice ''always has been practical and ad hoc. It has not been his way to play the prophet or the visionary, rallying others round with anguished eloquence, but rather to be the technical expert, pointing out without flinching the practical consequences of different policies.'' A list of Zuckerman's writings reflects his eclectic background. Works such as *The Social Life of Monkeys and Apes* and *Perspectives in Primate Biology* explore his observations as a zoologist, *A New System of Anatomy* and *The Ovary* are the results of more than fifty years' work as a professor of anatomy, and *Beyond the Ivory Tower: The Frontiers of Public and Private Science, Nuclear Illusion and Reality,* and *Star Wars in a Nuclear World* contain his thoughts on the political ramifications of modern technology. According to a *Times Literary Supplement* reviewer, Zuckerman ''has helped to steer [England] through several complete turns of the arms race spiral: from high explosives and bombers to hydrogen bombs, missiles, satellites, and nerve gas, and to such civil advances in science and technology as transistors, computers, lasers, and molecular biology. He is still there, guiding us towards the era of data banks, genetic engineering, and biological warfare.''

John Ziman contends in the *Times Literary Supplement* that Zuckerman ''himself is almost a stereotype—the poor boy from the colonies who wins his way meritocratically to the very top.'' Zuckerman was born in Cape Town, South Africa, in 1904, and he grew up there, fascinated by the troops of baboons he could observe practically without leaving home. An excellent student, he attended the University of Cape Town on scholarship, earning a B.A. with distinction in 1923 and an M.A. in anatomy in 1925. For seven years thereafter, he worked on multiple doctorates at the University of London, also serving as a university demonstrator in human anatomy and a research anatomist for the Zoological Society of London. Zuckerman used his observations of living primates, from both South Africa and the London Zoo, to complete *The Social Life of Monkeys and Apes,* published in 1932. The work was addressed to scholars, but it also found a general readership; a *Nation* reviewer praised the ''the happiness and phraseology and a sense of humor that make his finished work, though carefully thought through and closely argued, an exciting narrative.'' Zuckerman then turned to primate biology; his 1933 title *Functional Affinities of Man, Monkeys, and Apes* led to a reconsideration of human reproductive cycles and, indirectly, to the development of the birth control pill. Zuckerman was engaged in further work on the physiology of reproductive systems when the Second World War erupted.

''It does not seem a logical progression from ape anatomist to wartime bombing policy-maker, but in a strange way it was,'' writes Anthony Holden in the *Spectator*. Indeed, at the British government's request, Zuckerman began to study the effects of bomb blasts on human victims. This grisly study produced a humane conclusion—Zuckerman demonstrated that area bombing of civilian populations held far less military advantage than aerial destruction of the transport links by which troops and supplies were moved. He persuaded the top military commanders to adopt his position and then formed the tactical bombing plans that hampered German rail transport prior to the Normandy Invasion. After the war Zuckerman returned to civilian life as Sands Cox Professor of Anatomy at the University of Birmingham, a position he held for twenty-two years. He continued to serve on numerous government committees and councils, however, eventually becoming scientific advisor to the British Secretary of Defense in 1960. On May 24, 1966, Prime Minister Harold Wilson named him chief scientific advisor to Her Majesty's Government. The high-profile position sent Zuckerman throughout Europe and the United States for discussions on the development, testing, and deployment of nuclear weapons. In 1971 he retired and was awarded the life-time peerage, as well as several international decorations, for his services to his country.

Lord Zuckerman was one of the first scientists to propose that, ''when both sides possess them, nuclear weapons have no military application,'' according to Paul Ableman in the *Spectator*. Ableman adds that in Zuckerman's view nuclear weapons ''are not war-winning weapons because wars having any

rational aim cannot be fought with them.'' Zuckerman continues to be concerned that technology has outrun the ability of politicians to control and direct it; he is particularly critical of the Strategic Defense Initiative and of any suggestion that an aggressor country might win a war that sparked a limited nuclear exchange. ''Zuckerman does not endorse unilateral disarmament, nor naivete in approaching negotiations with the Soviet Union,'' writes *New Republic* contributor Charles S. Maier, ''but he does argue that the West will not improve its security by building more nuclear weapons.'' In *Nuclear Illusion and Reality* and *Star Wars in a Nuclear World* Zuckerman suggests that scientists should be actively involved in the policy-making that results from their sophisticated technology. Miles concludes that it is ''impressive to see this 80-year-old veteran of wars hot and cold taking his place alongside old . . . colleagues in diplomacy. . . . Like them, he intends to issue a warning. But like them, he wants the result to be, in the formulation of another brilliant military man, 'not fear in the ordinary sense, but rather a growing exasperation over the rigidity and traditionalism which prevent the formulation of adequate plans to remove so obvious a man-made risk.'''

From Apes to Warlords: The Autobiography (1904-1964) of Solly Zuckerman recounts the scientist's youth, education, and early involvement in government affairs. In the *New York Times Book Review*, Michael Howard notes that the book reveals ''a man whose abilities gained him a position of great influence within the British military establishment during World War II, whence he could observe the making of policy at the highest level and reach some important conclusions about the contributions that scientists can make to strategy and, more important, those they cannot.'' Howard concludes that the volume's value ''not only to the historian but also to the strategic analyst is therefore very great indeed. . . . If more scientists possessed [Zuckerman's] rare blend of toughness and humility, fewer billions of dollars would have been squandered on useless research projects over the last 30 years.''

BIOGRAPHICAL/CRITICAL SOURCES:

BOOKS

Zuckerman, Solly, *From Apes to Warlords: The Autobiography (1904-1964) of Solly Zuckerman,* Hamish Hamilton, 1978.

PERIODICALS

Guardian, April 7, 1967, April 12, 1971.
Los Angeles Times Book Review, April 25, 1982.
Nation, August 24, 1932.
New Republic, July 5, 1982.
New York Times Book Review, July 18, 1982, April 23, 1987.
Spectator, February 4, 1978, June 13, 1981, February 20, 1982.
Times (London), January 28, 1982.
Times Literary Supplement, February 1, 1968, January 8, 1971, March 8, 1978, April 16, 1982, March 13, 1987.

—*Sketch by Anne Janette Johnson*

*   *   *

**ZUK, Georges
See SKELTON, Robin**